The McGraw-Hill Literature Series

Focus
Perception
Insights
Encounters

American Literature:
A Chronological Approach

English Literature:
A Chronological Approach

American Literature:
A Thematic Approach

British and Western Literature:
A Thematic Approach

G. Robert Carlsen
General Editor

ENGLISH LITERATURE
A Chronological Approach

G. Robert Carlsen • Ruth Christoffer Carlsen

TREASURY EDITION

WEBSTER DIVISION, McGRAW-HILL BOOK COMPANY
New York, St. Louis, San Francisco, Dallas, Atlanta

Cover Art:

SALISBURY CATHEDRAL FROM THE BISHOP'S GARDEN
John Constable
Metropolitan Museum of Art, New York City
Bequest of Mary Stillman Harkness

Editorial Direction: John Rothermich
Editors: Carroll Moulton and Kenneth Pitchford
Editing and Styling: Sue McCormick
Design Supervision: Valerie Greco
Production: Salvador Gonzales

Photo Editor: Alan Forman
Photo Research: Sheila Corr
Text and Cover Design: Blaise Zito Associates, Inc.
Cover Concept: Alan Forman

This book was set in Baskerville with Avant Garde Gothic by Black Dot.
The color separation was done by Black Dot.

Library of Congress Cataloging in Publication Data
Carlsen, G. Robert, 1917–
English literature, a chronological approach.

  (The McGraw-Hill literature series)
  Includes index.
  Summary: A text-book survey of English literature
from Anglo-Saxon times to the present, for use by senior
high school students.
  1. English literature. [1. English literature—
Collections] I. Title. II. Series.
PR1109.C28 1985   820'.9   83-24807
ISBN 0-07-009845-X

Old English Literature 650–1100

Medieval Literature 1100–1500

Renaissance Literature 1500–1660

Neo-Classical Literature   1660–1798

The Romantic Period 1798—1837

Victorian Literature 1837–1901

Modern Literature   1901–

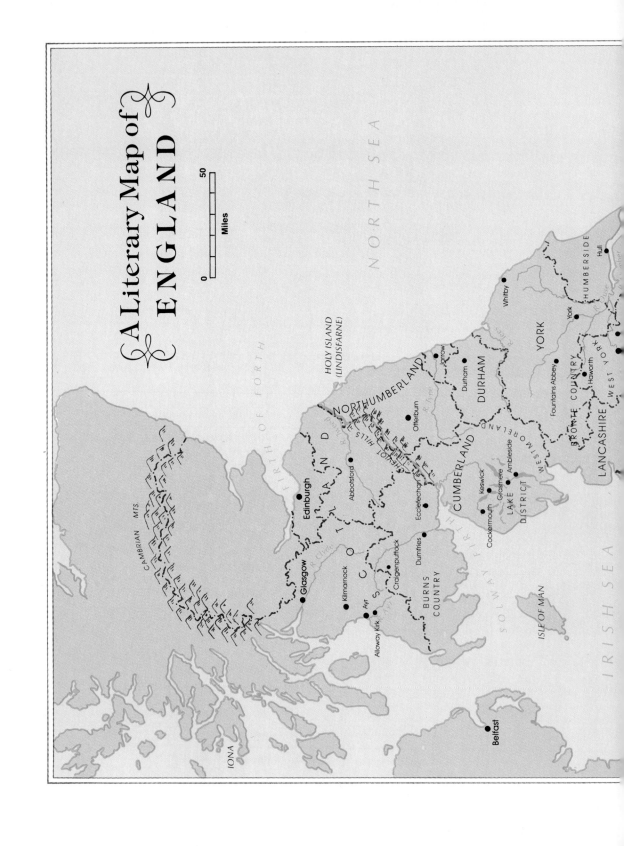

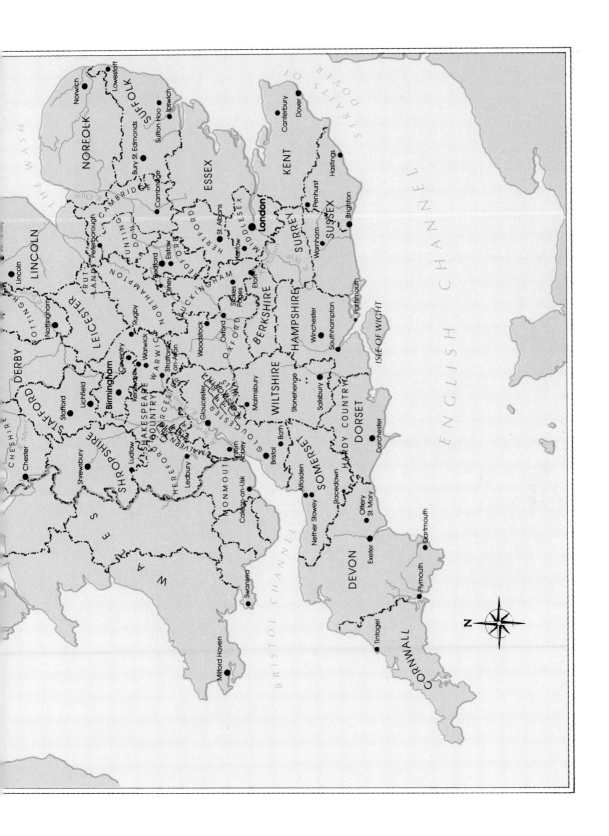

OPENING OF ST. MATTHEW'S GOSPEL, Book of Kells, The Board of Trinity College, Dublin

Old English Literature

English literature is usually divided into three periods: Old English (c. 650–1100), Middle English (c. 1100–1500), and modern (since 1500). As one approaches Old English literature, it is useful to know how well developed Old English already was—and how it developed toward the next stage in becoming the energetic and versatile language we call our everyday English. For thousands of years, an enterprising people had lived in England before the first Old English was written down. We call these earliest people "Iberian," meaning that we think *Iberians* they may have come from Spain, but also, eventually, from further east along the Mediterranean—Crete, Phoenicia, or Egypt. Whoever they were, they built Stonehenge and standing stone circles like it, an engineering feat that still remains mysterious (like the building of the Egyptian pyramids in roughly the same time span).

SUCCESSIVE LAYERS OF INVASION

From about 2000 B.C. onward until the end of the 11th century A.D., the history of Britain—and its language—is one of successive layers of invasion. These invasions were not like those on the continent, however, in which most early traces of the preceding cultures were obliterated. Because England was an island and small roving bands rather than massive migrations were more practical, each new invasion gradually added to the existing admixture of tongues rather than replacing them. We might call these successive additions to the language "contributions," except that the wars, the raids, the ravages, the burned libraries, the sacked towns were no polite series of lawn parties. Where the language was concerned, it was as though a set of inscriptions on a stone was corrosively scarred and hacked across by one sword blade after another, until an entirely different pattern of meaning became visible.

The long tenure of the Iberians was decisively disturbed by the Celts—with a multitude of tribal names—and their priestly class, the *Celts* Druids. Shortly, two main Ibero-Celtic tongues emerged—Goidelic becoming the Gaelic of Ireland, Brythonic becoming the Welsh of Wales and the Breton of Brittany. Then the Romans came, first in 55 B.C. *Romans* under Julius Caesar, then in 43 A.D. under Claudius. Hadrian's Wall in the North of England (completed in 123 A.D.) secured intermittent pe-

1

Teutonic Invasions

riods of peace—until the urgent Roman withdrawal from the island in 407 A.D. was required to defend a crumbling empire at home. Predictably, this was followed in the fifth century by relentless Teutonic (German) invasions of Britain from the north, east, and south (the west being alternately befriended and threatened by the Irish). These invasions did not cease until six centuries later with the Norman Conquest, in 1066.

King Arthur

Danes

At first the Romano-Celts successfully resisted the Anglo-Saxons in the west of the island. We now know as a hard, irrefutable historical fact that a real, flesh-and-blood King Arthur *did* reign (c. 475–515) and for a few decades held back the irreversible tide. But Angles, Saxon, Jute, and later Dane and Viking carried the day. By 450 A.D., the island's Ibero - Celtic - Romano - Saxo - Jutish Anglian speech was called, simply, English. Later would come the word England (from *Englaland*).

OLD ENGLISH SOCIETY

Below: **CROSS OF THE SCRIPTURES**
Clonmacnoise, Bord Failte, Ireland

The Angles and Saxons, like other Germanic peoples, were large, light-complexioned, fair-haired people extremely fond of eating, drinking, gambling, boasting, and fighting. They were also courageous, loyal, generous, hospitable, prudent, and highly moral. These first three virtues were essential in binding together the groups of well-born warriors *(athelings)* who pledged their unwavering service to a king or a chieftain, who in turn provided them with food, arms, and gifts. The king was elected by a council or *witan* (the wise men) composed of the chief nobles and higher churchmen. *Earldorman* (elderman) was the only title of nobility—which became *earl* in the eleventh century. The *thane,* usually a person of wealth and position but owing allegiance to a king or earl, came below the nobility. Then came the *geneat* (companion) owning his land but owing allegiance to thane, earl, or king. Below the companion were various types of peasants, owing rents or services to those who owned the land they farmed. Finally there were the *theows* (serfs) and the *thralls* (slaves), frequently prisoners of war, who performed menial tasks on the land or in the houses of the well-to-do.

CHRISTIANITY AND THE BEGINNING OF ENGLISH PROSE

Christianity came to England from two directions—from the north and from the south. In the north it originated from the Celtic Christianity of Ireland, first brought to the "Emerald Isle" by St. Patrick in 432. In the century that followed, Ireland became a center of Christianity and learning. In 563 the Irish monks established a mission at Iona (see map) and began Christianizing the north under the leadership of St. Aidan. In the south Augustine and a group of forty monks landed in Kent in 597 and soon were preaching in the rest of England.

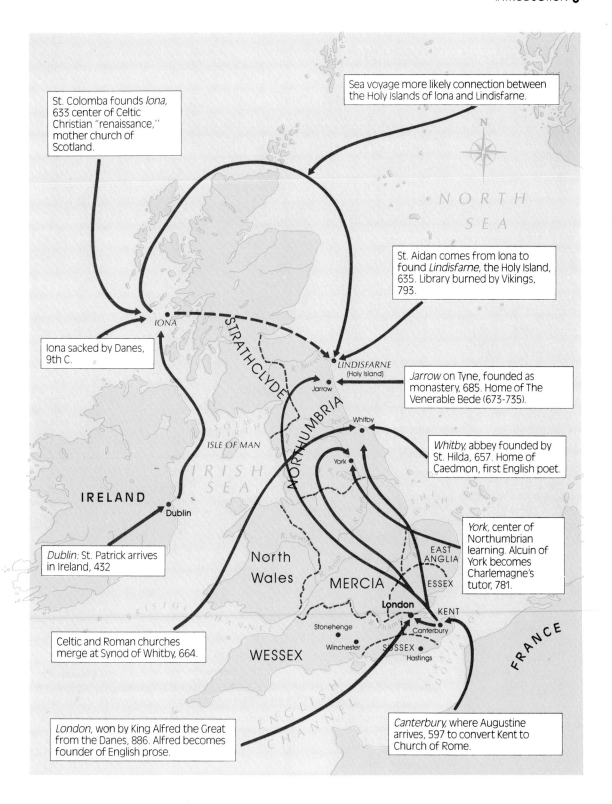

St. Colomba founds *Iona,* 633 center of Celtic Christian "renaissance," mother church of Scotland.

Sea voyage more likely connection between the Holy Islands of Iona and Lindisfarne.

St. Aidan comes from Iona to found *Lindisfarne,* the Holy Island, 635. Library burned by Vikings, 793.

Iona sacked by Danes, 9th C.

Jarrow on Tyne, founded as monastery, 685. Home of The Venerable Bede (673-735).

Whitby, abbey founded by St. Hilda, 657. Home of Caedmon, first English poet.

York, center of Northumbrian learning. Alcuin of York becomes Charlemagne's tutor, 781.

Dublin: St. Patrick arrives in Ireland, 432

Celtic and Roman churches merge at Synod of Whitby, 664.

London, won by King Alfred the Great from the Danes, 886. Alfred becomes founder of English prose.

Canterbury, where Augustine arrives, 597 to convert Kent to Church of Rome.

IONA

STRATHCLYDE

LINDISFARNE (Holy Island)

Jarrow

NORTHUMBRIA

Whitby

York

IRELAND

Dublin

ISLE OF MAN

IRISH SEA

NORTH SEA

North Wales

MERCIA

EAST ANGLIA

ESSEX

London

KENT

Stonehenge

Canterbury

Winchester

SUSSEX

WESSEX

Hastings

FRANCE

ENGLISH CHANNEL

BRISTOL CHANNEL

A portion of Hadrian's Wall as it appears today in Northumberland.

Monasteries

In the seventh century the Benedictines began establishing monasteries, mainly in Northumbria. Many of these monasteries became great centers of learning (see map). It was in the scriptoria, or writing rooms, of these monasteries that English first began to be written. Most of the writing was about scripture or theology and was in Latin because native tongues, as elsewhere in Europe, were not considered proper for learned writing, a prejudice that was to continue well into the seventeenth century.

DETAIL FROM THE LINDISFARNE GOSPELS
The British Library, London

Bede

The most outstanding writer of Anglo-Latin prose was Bede (see page 14), who lived most of his life in the monastery at Jarrow (see map). A prolific writer, the foremost scholar of his time in Europe, regarded by all of Western Europe until the Reformation as the greatest ecclesiastical authority, Bede wrote *The Ecclesiastical History of the English People*, his most important work for us today. While telling the history of the Church in England from Roman times in excellent Latin, Bede also recounts much secular history in charming ancedotes. Bede

(673–735) and his successors, most notably Alcuin of York, the personal tutor of Charlemagne (742–814), King of the Franks, made England the most cultivated nation of Western Europe until the island was devastated by the Norsemen and its monasteries destroyed shortly after Bede's death.

Alfred the Great   It is to Alfred the Great (849–899), born more than a hundred years after Bede's death, that we owe the beginnings of native prose and probably also the preservation of early English poetry. After defeating the Danes decisively in 878, Alfred rebuilt his kingdom, reestablished just law, and set out to restore England to the leadership in learning it had in the seventh and eighth centuries. One snippet of Bede in Old English (since lost) makes clear that a new idea was occurring to him toward the end of his life. He had begun to translate the Gospel of St. John—not into Latin—but into the native language, English. This revolutionary idea became the ruling passion of King Alfred's life—namely, to pick up where Bede had broken off and create a durable body of Old English prose written by himself and his scholars. What he produced was a sort of "great books" set of translations from Europe's classics, including Bede's English history. It is probably to Alfred, too, that we owe the beginnings of the most important prose work in Old English, the *Anglo-Saxon Chronicles*. These chronicles, or annals, *Anglo-Saxon* cover the history of England from Caesar to 1154. Thus, while Bede is *Chronicles* truly the father of English history and of literature, King Alfred is rightfully considered the father of English prose.

OLD ENGLISH POETRY

While prose was largely historical, poetry was the imaginative vehicle for Old English writers in a number of literary genres, or types. Chief among these was the epic, a long poem on a serious theme which narrated the adventures of a hero. One of the most remarkable works in *Beowulf* English literature is also one of the earliest, the epic of *Beowulf* (see page 30), a poem of over 3,000 lines which celebrates the life and death of the hero who is the title character. Told and retold by the Germanic invaders of England, the poem was probably written down in its present form about the year 800, although the origins of the story seem to be several centuries earlier. The poem presents warrior heroes, perilous journeys, and fantastic monsters; the theme, simply stated, is the eternal struggle of good against evil.

Lyrics   Shorter forms of poetry also flourished. The lyric, a brief poem that usually reveals some intense, highly personal emotion, is one of the oldest forms of poetry. In this period, lyrics were often elegiac in tone: they lamented the passing of an earlier, more joyful time, as in "The Wanderer" (see page 21). But lyrics could also be cheerful and humorous, as in the intellectual puzzles called riddles (see page 24)—short poems which skillfully exploited personification, metaphor, and puns. Occasionally a lyric comes down to us which crystallizes the writer's

WHITBY ABBEY, North Yorkshire
British Tourist Authority

religious faith, as in the song (or hymn) of Caedmon. From a slightly later period, we have lyrics on a broad variety of nonreligious (secular) subjects: love songs, lullabies, and short poems which celebrate the landscape and the coming of spring.

Stylistic devices

Although all the selections printed here are given in translation, we can still notice some of the particular stylistic devices associated with Old English poetry. The poetry is constructed in half-line units, usually joined by alliteration. Alliteration could come either with consonants,

Caedmon's Hymn

as in the third line of Caedmon's Hymn, "*weorc Wuldor-Faeder swa he wundra gehwaes,*" or with vowels alliterating with each other, as in the fourth line, "*ece Drihten or onstealde*" (this device is now distinguished by the term assonance). The language is usually simple, but heightened by imagery; some images are as deliberately complex as those we find in the Riddles, while others are more direct, particularly the repeated references to the emblems of battle and the qualities of nature. Occasionally we find metaphors called "kennings," in which a natural object is described by combining two other descriptions: in line 9 of *Beowulf*, the "sea" is, in Old English, "the whale-road."

Oral tradition

Perhaps the most obvious feature of Old English poetry is its use of repetition and variation, deriving from the oral background of many of the poets and the poems. The poet, or "scop" (which means the shaper, or maker), originally sang the poems, perhaps accompanied by a harp or lyre. Thus a stock of traditional phrases would be needed that would be subtly varied according to the demands of alliteration and of the subject. The repetition adds a sense of formality to the poetry, no matter what the subject, while the variation shows us the poet's skills. Throughout the range of Old English literature, whether we are looking at the prose histories and sermons or the poems concerned with battles, saints' lives, meditations, and proverbs, we sense the vitality of the writers, although, with few exceptions, we do not know their names. The literature may be anonymous, but it is nonetheless striking and memorable.

AN INTRODUCTION TO OLD ENGLISH

Old English writers are accused of being unrelievedly gloomy, melancholy, and grim. Yet one of the most famous prose passages in Old English is far from morose. In its few sentences, the startling simplicity of its diction creates a scene that is moving and memorable. It appears in the Old English translation of Bede's *Ecclesiastical History*, Book II, Chapter 13, concerning the conversion of Northumbria. Think of a typical castle of that time—not as a majestic edifice, but as a rude collection of stones enclosing a central hall where the main (and sometimes only) fire burned in the middle of the room without benefit of fireplace or chimney: the smoke rose through a hole in the ceiling. Windows, of course, had no glass and so were open to the elements. (These are probably the "doors" referred to here, since the doors themselves could

In 563 Irish monks established a mission at Iona. From here they sent missionaries into what is now Scotland and Northern England. The present buildings date from the sixteenth century.

IONA ABBEY, Strathclyde
British Tourist Authority

be shut.) In winter, this cold, dark castle had only one comparatively comfortable—or even habitable—place to gather: the circle formed by the open fire in the great hall. Such is the setting of this pagan parable.

The passage itself occurs in the midst of a discussion at the Court of Northumbria (in northern England) concerning the true meaning of

Ninth-century penny bearing the head of King Alfred.

life. Others have spoken. Then comes the wise counselor's turn. His words are possibly as good an introduction to the depth and quality of Old English as any other single example. The whole passage is as brief as the moment he describes.

> One of the king's wise counselors, getting permission to speak before the king and his earls, took his turn to say: "It seems to me, dear king, that man's life on earth is but a moment, one filled with uncertainty, as when you sit feasting with your earls and thanes by a bright fire here in your warm hall during the rain and snow and hail of wintertime—when all of a sudden a sparrow flies into the hall from outside, darts in one door, then out the other. For one brief eyeblink, the sparrow too feels the warmth of the fire, but then must fly swiftly back into the wintry night outside. Man's life is like that one short moment. What comes before and what comes after we cannot know."*

*Based on the Old English translation of Bede's *Ecclesiastical History of the English,* Book II, Chapter 13, "The Conversion of Northumbria," in *Sweet's Anglo-Saxon Primer,* rev. Norman Davis, Oxford, 1953, pp. 90–91.

ROMAN ERA 55 B.C.-407 A.D.

EVENTS BEFORE 100 A.D.

2500 B.C. "Iberian" people build Stonehenge.

1200-600 B.C. Celtic settlers arrive.

55 B.C. Julius Caesar invades Britain.

43 A.D. Emperor Claudius oversees conquest of Caractacus.

61 A.D. Queen Boudicca (Boadicea) leads revolt, seizing Londinium.

78 A.D. Roman General Agricola begins indecisive conquest of the north.

Teutonic influx begins, 410; invasions recur till 1066

Romans withdraw from Britain, 407

Ambrosius Aurelanius, c.460-c.475

Vortigern rules c.425-c.459

Jute kings, Hengist and Horsa land, c.428

Villa-style in towns: Lincoln, York, 300-350

Hadrian's Wall, 123 A.D.

Septimius Severus quells the north, 208

100 **200** **300** **400**

St. Patrick and Christianity reach Ireland, 432

DIALECTS OF OLD ENGLISH

NORTHUMBRIAN

MERCIAN

Severn R.

Thames R.

WEST SAXON

KENTISH

King Arthur

St. Augustine

Old English

POST ROMAN
ERA 407-520

KENTISH
PRIMACY
520-593

NORTHUMBRIAN
PRIMACY 593-626

MERCIAN PRIMACY
626-802

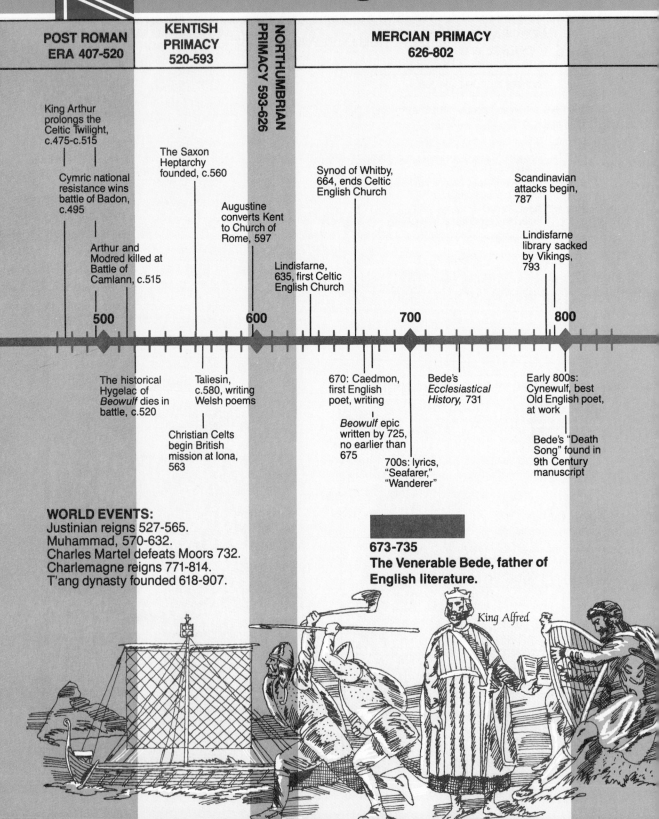

King Arthur
prolongs the
Celtic Twilight,
c.475-c.515

Cymric national
resistance wins
battle of Badon,
c.495

The Saxon
Heptarchy
founded, c.560

Synod of Whitby,
664, ends Celtic
English Church

Scandinavian
attacks begin,
787

Augustine
converts Kent
to Church of
Rome, 597

Lindisfarne
library sacked
by Vikings,
793

Arthur and
Modred killed at
Battle of
Camlann, c.515

Lindisfarne,
635, first Celtic
English Church

500   **600**   **700**   **800**

The historical
Hygelac of
Beowulf dies in
battle, c.520

Taliesin,
c.580, writing
Welsh poems

670: Caedmon,
first English
poet, writing

Bede's
*Ecclesiastical
History,* 731

Early 800s:
Cynewulf, best
Old English poet,
at work

Beowulf epic
written by 725,
no earlier than
675

Bede's "Death
Song" found in
9th Century
manuscript

Christian Celts
begin British
mission at Iona,
563

700s: lyrics,
"Seafarer,"
"Wanderer"

WORLD EVENTS:
Justinian reigns 527-565.
Muhammad, 570-632.
Charles Martel defeats Moors 732.
Charlemagne reigns 771-814.
T'ang dynasty founded 618-907.

673-735

**The Venerable Bede, father of
English literature.**

King Alfred

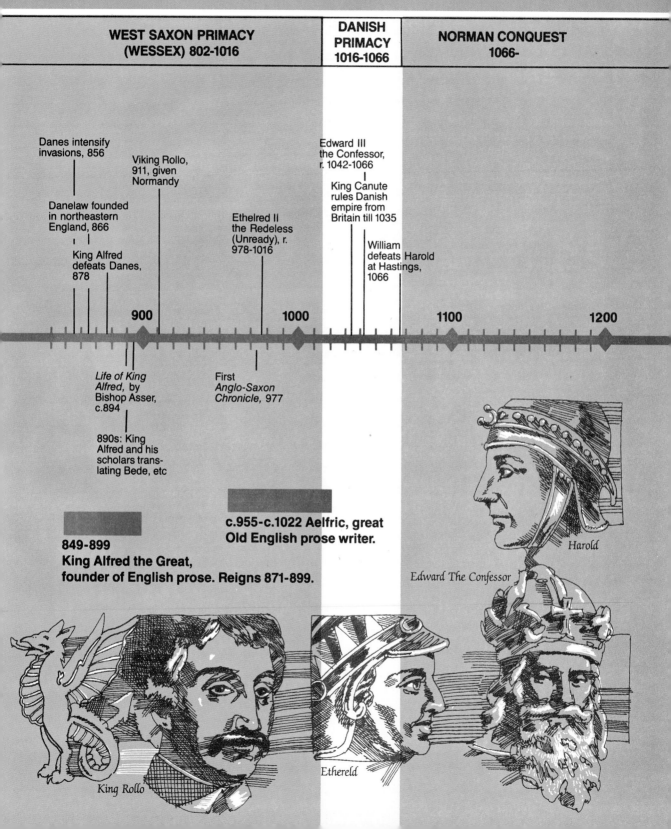

| WEST SAXON PRIMACY (WESSEX) 802-1016 | DANISH PRIMACY 1016-1066 | NORMAN CONQUEST 1066- |

Danes intensify invasions, 856

Viking Rollo, 911, given Normandy

Danelaw founded in northeastern England, 866

King Alfred defeats Danes, 878

Ethelred II the Redeless (Unready), r. 978-1016

Edward III the Confessor, r. 1042-1066

King Canute rules Danish empire from Britain till 1035

William defeats Harold at Hastings, 1066

900   **1000**   **1100**   **1200**

Life of King Alfred, by Bishop Asser, c.894

First *Anglo-Saxon Chronicle,* 977

890s: King Alfred and his scholars translating Bede, etc

c.955-c.1022 Aelfric, great Old English prose writer.

849-899
King Alfred the Great, founder of English prose. Reigns 871-899.

Harold

Edward The Confessor

King Rollo

Ethereld

Bede

673–735

The Venerable Bede was "discovered" when still a boy by the founder of two neighboring monasteries in Northumbria. Clearly a lad of unusual intelligence, he was entered in the monastic school at Jarrow on the river Tyne when he was seven years old. He ended up living at Jarrow for the remaining fifty-five years of his life. His earliest teachers were not wrong to think he showed signs of being extraordinarily gifted. In his day, he became the most learned man in all of Europe. His forty books were circulated widely in medieval lands and were considered the last word on their subjects for centuries—grammars, literary criticism, scientific treatises, Biblical commentaries, and saints' lives. The golden age he created almost single-handedly made Jarrow a center for learning unrivaled anywhere on the continent. He is considered not only "the teacher of all the Middle Ages," but also the most important English historian of all time. Even more important, he can truthfully be called the father of English literature, even though all but a few lines of his enormous output was in Latin.

First of all, without him, we would know little beyond the findings of archaeologists about Britain's history between the Roman withdrawal and the Norman Conquest. Second, he wrote in a period of relative calm between the first Teutonic onslaughts of the fifth century and the Viking and Danish onslaughts of the late eighth century. This breathing space gave time for such a scholar as Bede to preserve the irreplaceable manuscripts of Old English writers, some of which escaped the widespread burning of libraries in the time immediately following his death. So it is in part because of his lifelong industry that we can say today that Old English literature is the earliest, largest, and finest surviving body of writing in all of post-Roman Europe.

Bede would not have thought this anything to make a fuss about. Unlike other European scholars of the time, Bede was insatiably curious, not merely about ancient or early church history,

but more particularly about the history of his own nation. This attitude of viewing the English as a nation was original with him and is one reason why our language is called "English" (Angle-ish) after the Anglian settlers of Northumbria, rather than "Saxon," as the Celts contemptuously referred to the speech of all these invaders.

Bede's most famous and enduring work vividly reveals his stubborn Northumbrian streak—an unappeasable loyalty to the land of his birth and a love for its people. Its Latin title is variously translated *A Ecclesiastical History of the English People* or *A History of the English Church and People* (731 A.D.). First he briefly collates several Latin historians to sketch in the Roman conquest and occupation. Then, with the arrival of Augustine at what is now Canterbury in 597 (sent by Pope Gregory I to preach Christianity in England), he goes on to tell the story of his country with infectious relish and intriguing detail, stopping arbitrarily at 731, four years before his death. Without him, it would be hard to understand why so many early centers of English learning were at first located in the Anglian north. Fortunately, he explains the southward spread through Britain of the Celtic Christian "renaissance;" this branch of missionary Christianity sprang from the zeal of St. Patrick (c. 373–c. 463 A.D.) in Ireland more than a century and a half before Augustine reached Canterbury. When the two forms of Christianity met (at the Synod of Whitby in 664), they resolved their differences. Then these two "renaissances" merged and sent missionaries to the benighted continent to spread learning among the ignorant peoples there.

Bede and his *Ecclesiastical History* have remained famous over the centuries and two passages have been referred to and quoted continually. The first, included in the Introduction, compares human life to a storm-battered sparrow that flutters near a castle fire for one "eyeblink" before disappearing again into the winter night from where it came. The

This early scribe from an illuminated manuscript is thought to be Venerable Bede.

from the **LIFE OF ST. COTHBERT**
The British Library

second is the passage that follows, telling the story of the miraculous "invention" of Old English Christian poetry by the illiterate cowherd, Caedmon of Whitby. Nine lines of "Caedmon's Hymn" appear in the midst of Bede's Latin historical prose. These lines are now thought to be all we can say for sure that Caedmon wrote, though much else was once attributed to him. The fragment shows the Old English style of alliteration and a form of metaphor called "kenning," both of which will be discussed in relation to the most powerful Old English lyric poem, "The Wanderer."

"I have labored honestly to transmit whatever I could ascertain from common report for the instruction of posterity"—thus writes Bede in the prefatory letter he attached to his

major work, *A History of the English Church and People* (731 A.D.). He was, perhaps, a bit modest in saying that he was working "from common report," since the preface also makes clear Bede's enormous amount of research, both in documents and in interviews with a number of monks, about the early history of England and of the Church in England.

The following selection is one of the most famous passages, describing as it does the life and work of Caedmon, a monk who felt that he could never compose poetry but who was, on a particular occasion, given a vision which inspired him. The subject is that of divine inspiration, but the plain style and the homely details which make this passage so memorable come from Bede.

from A HISTORY OF THE ENGLISH CHURCH AND PEOPLE

Translated by Leo Sherley-Price

Chapter 24: *A brother of the monastery is found to possess God's gift of poetry* [680 A.D.]

In this monastery of Streanaeshalch[1] lived a brother singularly gifted by God's grace. So skilful was he in composing religious and devotional songs that, when any passage of Scripture was explained to him by interpreters, he could quickly turn it into delightful and moving poetry in his own English tongue. These verses of his have stirred the hearts of many folk to despise the world and aspire to heavenly things. Others after him tried to compose religious poems in English, but none could compare with him; for he did not acquire the art of poetry from men or through any human teacher but received it as a free gift from God. For this reason he could never compose any frivolous or profane verses; but only such as had a religious theme fell fittingly from his devout lips. He had followed a secular occupation until well advanced in years without ever learning anything about poetry. Indeed it sometimes happened at a feast that all the guests in turn would be invited to sing and entertain the company; then, when he saw the harp coming his way, he would get up from table and go home.

On one such occasion he had left the house in which the entertainment was being held and went out to the stable, where it was his duty that night to look after the beasts. There when the time came he settled down to sleep. Suddenly in a dream he saw a man standing beside him who called him by name. 'Caedmon,' he said, 'sing me a song.' 'I don't know how to sing,' he replied. 'It is because I cannot sing that I left the feast and came here.' The man who addressed him then said: 'But you shall sing to me.' 'What should I sing about?' he replied. 'Sing about the Creation of all things,' the other answered. And Caedmon immediately began to sing verses in praise of God the Creator that he had never heard before, and their theme ran thus:
Now we should praise   our Protector in
        heaven,
the almighty Maker   and his mind-
        designs,
the work of our wondrous Father,   since
        he first wrought miracles,
endless Ruler,   of ageless order.
His earliest work   for earthborn men
heaved up heaven's roof,   oh holiest
        Creator;
then in middle-earth,[2]   mankind's
        Protector
and endless Ruler,   added at last
this world where we live,   oh wonderful
        Lord.[3]
This is the general sense, but not the actual words that Caedmon sang in his dream; for verses, however masterly, cannot be translated literally from one language into another without losing much of their beauty and dignity. When Caedmon awoke, he remembered everything that he had sung in his dream,

1. **Streanaeshalch,** more commonly known as Whitby.
2. **middle-earth,** the earth on which we live. It is in the "middle" because it is between the hall of the gods and the underworld, or (in Christian terms) between heaven and hell.
3. **Now . . . Lord.** A modern English, alliterative version of all nine lines of "Caedmon's Hymn" has been supplied here by the editors.

and soon added more verses in the same style to a song truly worthy of God.

Early in the morning he went to his superior the reeve,[4] and told him about this gift that he had received. The reeve took him before the abbess,[5] who ordered him to give an account of his dream and repeat the verses in the presence of many learned men, so that a decision might be reached by common consent as to their quality and origin. All of them agreed that Caedmon's gift had been given him by our Lord. And they explained to him a passage of scriptural history or doctrine and asked him to render it into verse if he could. He promised to do this, and returned next morning with excellent verses as they had ordered him. The abbess was delighted that God had given such grace to the man, and advised him to abandon secular life and adopt the monastic state.[6] And when she had admitted him into the Community as a brother, she ordered him to be instructed in the events of sacred history. So Caedmon stored up in his memory all that he learned, and like one of the clean animals chewing the cud, turned it into such melodious verse that his delightful renderings turned his instructors into auditors. He sang of the creation of the world, the origin of the human race, and the whole story of Genesis. He sang of Israel's exodus from Egypt, the entry into the Promised Land, and many other events of scriptural history. He sang of the Lord's Incarnation, Passion, Resurrection, and Ascension into heaven, the coming of the Holy Spirit, and the teaching of the Apostles. He also made many poems on the terrors of the Last Judgement, the horrible pains of Hell, and the joys of the Kingdom of Heaven. In addition to these, he composed several others on the blessings and judgements of God, by which he sought to turn his hearers from delight in wickedness and to inspire them to love and do good. For Caedmon was a deeply religious man, who humbly submitted to regular discipline and hotly rebuked all who tried to follow another course. And so he crowned his life with a happy end.

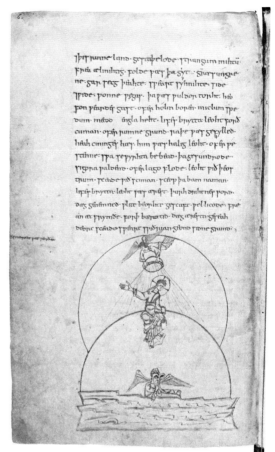

THE CREATION
from the so-called Caedmon Ms.
Bodleian Library, Oxford
Ms. Janius X P. 6

4. **reeve,** a manager who oversees the affairs of an estate for its owner; here, the supervisor or custodian of the abbey.

5. **abbess,** a woman who heads an abbey; in this case, St. Hilda (614–680), who in 657 founded Whitby Abbey, a double house for nuns and monks, and governed it wisely for twenty-two years. It was under her rule that Caedmon (d. 680) came to live there. The chapter in Bede preceding the one on Caedmon tells the story of her life.

6. **monastic state.** Until this time, Caedmon had been a lay brother at the abbey, working as a cowherd. To indicate her belief in his miraculous gifts, St. Hilda invited him to become a monk, which required that he take special vows and join the abbey choir.

Nū wē sculan herian   heofonrīces Weard,

Now we should praise   the Guardian of the heavenly kingdom,

Metodes mihte   and his mōdgeþonc,

God's might   and his wisdom,

weorc Wuldorfæder;   swā hē wundra gehwæs,

the works of the Father of glory;   how all wonders he,

ēce Dryhten,   ord onstealde.

eternal Lord,   established from the first.

Hē ærest gesceōp   eorðan bearnum

Hè first created   for the children of earth

heofon tō hrōfe,   hālig Scyppend;

heaven as a roof,   holy Creator;

ðā middangeard,   moncynnes Weard,

then in middle-earth,   mankind's Guardian,

ēce Dryhten,   æfter tēode

eternal Lord,   afterwards made

fīrum foldan,   Frēa ælmihtig.

the earth for men,   God almighty.

Above, "Caedmon's Hymn" in Old English with a modern
poetic translation line for line.

FOR UNDERSTANDING

1. Look at the first paragraph of Bede's account of Caedmon. Why is the time scheme in this paragraph out of order? Can you think of a common form of writing today in which stories are not told chronologically? Would the story be more interesting and the miracle more startling if we didn't know the outcome at the beginning?

2. There are two passages in the story that contain references to domestic animals. What are they? How does the first passage strengthen the impact of the second? How is one of these related to the story of Christianity? Does this affect the flavor of the Caedmon story?

FOR INTERPRETATION

After most of the selections in this anthology, there will be a section like this one, in which the emphasis will be on sifting through the implications of a piece of writing. Sometimes you will be asked to think more deeply about a piece you've just read, to see it from several different angles, to explain its effect on you or on readers in general. You will be looking for ideas or insights that may lie below the surface of a mere factual account of the piece. You may be asked to use evidence provided in the notes to make a case for seeing a particular work in one of several possible ways. To look at writing in such ways is "to interpret" literature. When this is done systematically, it is called "literary criticism."

Locating Bede and Caedmon in Time and Place

Whitby, the abbey home of Caedmon and St. Hilda, lay about fifty miles directly across the sea from Jarrow, about half again as far by the coast route. Having made Whitby famous, both Caedmon and St. Hilda died in 680. This was the year when Bede first gained attention at Jarrow as a lad of seven, Jarrow having been founded only a few years before. It wasn't until a half century later that Bede would write down this account of Caedmon's miraculous gift of poetry. By then, Jarrow had eclipsed Whitby in fame, to become one of the most renowned centers of learning in all of Europe.

How might any of these facts have affected Bede's telling of Caedmon's story?

Bede as Historian

Bede scrupulously researched his subjects and interviewed eyewitnesses to events that occurred within living memory. Many of his methods were innovative and point the way to modern historical research. Yet his work unskeptically includes accounts of miracles and other supernatural events. Most historians now feel that it is not difficult to sort out hard fact from this aspect of Bede. The case of Caedmon's miracle seems less clear-cut, however, and opinion is divided. On the one hand, it rings true, is credible, and has an air of authenticity about it. On the other, scholars have whittled away at a mass of material once attributed to Caedmon until only the nine lines of the hymn are left as being unquestionably his. Much of the rest appears to have been composed later than Bede's story, as if by scribes eager to contribute to Caedmon's fame. This doesn't necessarily mean that a body of Caedmon's work didn't once exist, since many documents accumulated in Northumbria, principally at Whitby, Jarrow, Lindisfarne, and York, went up in smoke during the Danish occupation.

What kind of case would you build to argue in favor of the story's credibility? Which details or facts would you cite? How would you argue the opposite point of view? Which elements are most effective here?

Which case, on the whole, seems most convincing to you?

Introduction to THE WANDERER

"The Wanderer" is a remarkable Old English lyric poem because of the depth of feeling it expresses. It wells over with grief, sometimes (ironically) at those very moments when the poet explicitly warns us against speaking of our sufferings to each other. Aside from the powerful emotions it contains, the poem may be the most perfect in form of all Old English lyrics, because it shows the fewest signs of accidental mutilation or of deliberate tamperings by later copyists. Its companion piece, "The Seafarer," is similar in tone. But it is flawed by alteration, accidental or intentional, which makes it more obscure and less focused in impact.

We do not know when this pair of poems was written or by whom. Both are in the *Exeter Book,* a collection containing Old English poetry. It was given to Exeter Cathedral, where it still exists, by a Wessex bishop, Leofric, who was Chancellor to King Edward the Confessor (died 1066 A.D.). The shrewdest guess we can make about the original dates for these poems is, roughly, the 700s. Both poems are dramatic monologues spoken by specific characters—in each case, a sailor who may or may not directly represent the author. In "The Seafarer," the hard life at sea is praised in preference to easy living on land. Many see in it elements of Christian allegory.

Not so with "The Wanderer." Here, the life of a sailor is also presented as grueling—but for a different reason, one that makes all the difference in giving the poem its unique emotional force. The sailor in this poem begins in despair, looking out over the desolate sea, aimlessly wayfaring from place to place in perpetual exile. (The title might most accurately be given in modern English as "The Exile.") For he was not always a sailor, however wise the griefs of harsh seafaring may have made him. Once he was an earl, a thane, a soldier pledged in fealty to his feudal liege-lord who in return for the earl's sworn loyalty gave him a gift (usually a ring or a goblet) as a pledge of the lord's duty to protect his solemnly sworn vassal.

This exchange of pledges took the form of a lavish public ritual that was renewed annually—after which there was merriment and feasting in the lord's great hall among the lord and his vassals, as well as the songs of minstrels celebrating the clan's great history.

Today we all too often fall prey to the vague notion that feudalism was some form of abject slavery that flourished in what we wrongly call The Dark Ages. But the gift-giving ceremony and feasting among liege and vassals had nothing in it of the brutal slavery of the Roman Empire and even of pre-Emancipation America. Slavery did exist in feudal times, of course, but as this poem and *Beowulf* clearly show, it was not a part of the liege-vassal relationship, which the exiled sailor here remembers with heartbroken joy. His lord is now dead, the feasts are over, the times are filled with danger, death, destruction, and evil.

This situation is intensely expressive of a Britain during the period of its greatest upheavals; first the Celtic conquest, then the Anglo-Saxon conquest, then the Viking raids and the Danish occupation. Bede's monastery sacked. Iona ravaged. Not a single monk or nun left in all Northumbria who could read or write. The abbey of Whitby stripped of its valuables. And often the Geats or Angles or Frisians who came to Britain had left (or were driven from) their homelands because of burned-out castles, scattered tribes, slaughtered kinsmen. If we think for a moment of people in our own century similarly displaced by the currents of war—the European refugees of World War II, the exiles from Southeast Asia and Central America—the poem's moment moves closer to us in time.

It is easier, then, to see the sailor as he is, torn between recalling a happier life, now vanished forever, and mourning his present state: solitary, friendless, homeless, driven without hope from place to place in search of some remnant of his people. "Mutability"—the inevitability of loss and change—is a major set-theme of England's Renaissance, expressed with such a freshness there that one might think the sixteenth century first discovered it. Yet never did a poem exploit the theme so effectively as does "The Wanderer." Another traditional theme appears here, the "Ubi sunt" motif of medieval Latin lyrics, the two Latin words beginning any variation on the question, "Where are those who lived before?" The eloquent expression given to this theme in "The Wanderer" shows the poet to be an elegant and knowledgeable writer, highly skilled in his craft.

The poet's excellence can be most clearly seen in the masterful use of the Old English alliterative measure. An easy way to understand this measure is to think of four important words you want to emphasize, surrounded by other words that connect them into sentences. The *scop* (poet) lets the *gleeman* (harper) know when to pluck the harp as the poem is chanted because he emphasizes the four most important words in each line, two or three of which start with the same sound. The first or second of the four words (or both) must always alliterate with the third word. And the fourth word must—with an effect either of surprise or of finality—present a new sound.

So imagine a harper plucking chords four times under each line the *scop* chants as the fire flickers and we become a circle of flame-lit figures settling down to listen with half-closed eyes. Little by little, we begin to look out with the grieving sailor across an empty and icy sea, recalling a happier time long since past.

The Wanderer

Translated by Kenneth Pitchford

Often the wayfarer   waits for the grace
of the Almighty's mercy,   though he mournfully be
cast on the ceaseless   coursing of waters
to furrow oar-fingers   through frosty seas,
riding unreckoned   the ways of his fate.   5
And the world-strider says,   well knowing the cost
of the ravages wreaked   on his ruined kin:

"Often I stand alone   at each new dawning,
wracked with woes   that none awake now
can hear, griefs deeper   than I dare utter   10
or speak of openly.   I certainly know
an earl is noble   who never reveals
what is bound fast   within his breast,
hiding that stronghold   however he will.
Nor may the failing heart   fetter its fortune,   15
nor the maimed mind   master its clamor
—so say the fame-thirsty   who frequently seal
foreboding spirits   in their breast-coffers.

"Such is *my* fate,   and mine the bound soul,
often heartbroken,   my homeland lost to me,   20
far from my kinfolk,   fettered in spirit,

my gold-giving friend[1]   long ago gone,
rank-wrapped in earth,   I having since
wandered winter-minded   over wave-bindings,
to glimpse again the hall   of a giver of rings[2]   25
whom I seek far and near,   if only to find
someone in the mead-hall   who might recognize me,
left without friends,   befriended at last,
received with rejoicing.   They would realize then
how slippery   sorrow can be as a friend   30
for him who has lacked   his one loving protector.

"The way of exile awaits him,   not windings of gold,
mind and flesh frozen,   not fertile as earth.
He recalls trusted friends   and their treasure-giving,
and how he was feasted   in his first youth   35
by his good gold-lord.[3]   Gone are those joys.

"All this he thinks   who must thirst for
the long-lost speeches   of loving friends,
when sorrow and sleep   sew up together
the wits of the wayfarer   and will him to see   40
at least in his brain   how he embraces
and kisses his kind lord   and lays on his knee
hands and head   as he once had done
in days long gone   beside the giftstool.[4]
"But his eyes fly open too soon,   friendless man,   45
seeing before him   only furrow-dark waves,
brimfowls[5] bathing   on broad-spread feathers,
sees snow and spume   and hailstones mingled.
Then he feels his heart's   heaviest wounds,
sorely lacking his sweet ones.   Sorrow returns.   50

"Then kinsmen remembered   careen through his mind.
He greets them with gladness   and gleefully scans
these soulmates of heroes.   They swim away, lost,
their floating forms   speaking familiar advice
the mind can no longer recall.   Care returns   55

---

1. **gold-giving friend,** liege-lord to whom one has
sworn loyalty as a vassal. In return, the vassal is given a
token, such as a gold ring, to stand for their mutual
commitment and interdependence.
2. **giver of rings.** See first footnote, above.
3. **good gold-lord.** See first footnote, above.
4. **how he embraces . . . giftstool.** This is a description
of the ritual in which the vassal swears fealty and pays
homage to his feudal lord.
5. **brimfowls,** seabirds.

The remains of Tintagel Castle, Tintagel, on the rugged coast of Cornwall, thought to be the site of the historic Arthur's castle.

for him who still must   send one more time
his aching spirit   over icebound waves.

"And as I wander   the whole world over,
why is this mind   of mine still undarkened
when it lingers upon   the life of earls[6]   60
and sees how swiftly   their halls are forsaken
by courageous comrades?   Even the common world
each succeeding day   dwindles and falls.

"Consider no man wise   who cannot reckon
many winters in the world.   The wise man is patient,   65
neither hot-blooded   nor hasty in speech,
neither weak-seeming   nor rash in battle,
drawn neither to fear nor to folly   nor fond of belongings,
never bold in boasting   before the doing.
He chooses caution   before claiming too soon   70
what the brave spirit   may become in action
when the heart's sinews   have learned to hold fast.

"And the wise man foresees   how futile wealth is
when all the world's riches   yield only wasteland,
now scattered   throughout the scarred fields,   75
now weltered by winds   where walls stand
frost-fractured,   felled the dwellings,
ruined the winehall,   the rulers laid low,
delight undreamt of,   daring knights fallen,
some rash by the wall,   some dragged off by war,   80
forced to far paths,   some by the falcon plucked up
across the wide sea,   one by the gray wolf
driven to his death,   one drawn-faced
earl hidden beneath   an earthen cave.
Thus the Creator of men   chastised the world   85
till those living in castles   ceased their merriment
and this whole ageless effort   of giants stood idle.

"So he who thinks wisely   and well on this ruin,
and has thought deeply   through this dark life,
must fully and freely   in all faith consider   90
these slaughterous shambles   and say these words:
'Where has the horse gone, where the human,   where the heroic
    treasure-giver?
Where have the hearty feasts gone?   Where the high-spirited
    halls?

6. **earls,** heroes, nobles.

Each gilded cup!   Each girded warrior!
Each proud prince!   And all those precious times gone   95
dark under nightshade   as if they never had been.
Now in the place of those   pleasant companions there stands
a wall wonderfully high,   one worked with serpentine shapes,[7]
and the strength of ash spears   to steal away earls,
weapons wanton to bleed   with their glorious fate.'   100

"And on these rocky slopes   still the storms batter,
snow storms,   the earth snowbound
in woe-stricken winter.   And the stark winds
deepen and dim while   down from the north come
hard bursts of hail,   a heavy blight upon men.   105
All is uneasy   in earthly realms.
Fate changes the fortunes   of all folk under heaven.
Here chattel[8] is fleeting,   here comrades are fleeting,
here man is fleeting,   here maid is fleeting,
this whole firm-set earth   faltering empty."   110

So spoke the wise man at heart   and sat, still deep in his
     thoughts.
Good is he who stays true to his faith.   He must not tell too
     quickly
what gnaws at his heart   before knowing the remedy
and proudly performing it.   Good is the prayer for honor
and fortune from our Father in heaven,   who alone stands   115
     fast for us all.

7. **wall . . . shapes.** No commentator seems willing to
say for sure just what this wall might represent. It could
be the carved face of a tomb or cenotaph (monument
honoring someone dead). If so, why is it "wonderfully
high"? It could be the outer wall of a fort from which the
ash spears in the next line could be thrown. Or it could
be the wall between life and death, carved with snakelike
runes, to which pagan Teutonic myth and poetry sometimes allude.
8. **chattel,** property, possessions.

FOR UNDERSTANDING

1. Find examples of the "mutability" and "ubi
sunt" motifs mentioned in the introduction to
"The Wanderer." How are these two themes interrelated? In what order do they appear in the
poem? What is the effect of this?
2. Why doesn't the wanderer just decide to settle
down somewhere and start a new life—instead of
hopelessly searching for his old life? What is he
looking for?

FOR INTERPRETATION

1. Find the references to the Deity in the poem;
are these pagan or Christian in tone? Or could
they be either or both? This is a question to keep in

mind as you read the *Beowulf* selection that follows.

2. Look at the second-to-last sentence in the poem. Some see in it a reference to suicide as the only way out of the wanderer's dilemma. Try to defend—or refute—this interpretation.

While pagan religions sometimes tolerated suicide as a last resort, Christianity has always opposed it. The very last sentence of the poem is the most Christian in tone of any passage in the poem. Doesn't this rule out a suicide/pagan interpretation for the second-to-last sentence? Or could both the pagan and Christian tones coexist side by side in the poem as an intentional religious tension? If so, how would this reflect the times in which the poem may have been written?

3. What kind of images from the world of nature does the poem present? How do they reflect the mood of the wanderer?

FOR APPRECIATION

After many of the selections in this book, a For Appreciation section will focus upon particular literary devices or techniques—or upon elements of literary style. An understanding of these aspects of writing will help you not only to appreciate the specific work under discussion, but also increase your appreciation for literature in general.

Kennings.

This is a device common in Old English poetry. It also occurs, although less frequently, in Middle English poetry. A kenning is a long-winded or fanciful metaphor made up of strung-together adjectives and nouns that stand for a thing without directly naming it. We've already seen Caedmon's kennings for God in his "Hymn." We'll meet the kenning again in the *Beowulf* selection. A well-known kenning is the one for Beowulf's boat, "the foamy-necked floater." In the same poem, the sea is often referred to as "the whale-acre" or "the swan's riding." In a poetry with few similes, these indirect descriptive phrases come with an effect of wit and beauty and have an impact that mingles playfulness with emotional power.

Find some examples of kennings in "The Wanderer."

Homilies.

Of all the forms of writing the Middle Ages indulged in at greatest length, the one that can easily become the most boring is homiletic writing. A homily can be a single sermon that is based on a Biblical text. Or it can be a passage in any work that gives stern and solemn advice on how to live life and is most concerned with morals and conduct. When the latter is involved, the homily can be made up of a string of maxims or adages that seem self-evident, to say the least. A famous, often-quoted homiletic passage occurs in Shakespeare's *Hamlet* ("To thine own self be true"). People who admiringly quote these words of advice usually don't remember that Shakespeare put them in the mouth of a doddering old fool, Polonius.

Find the homiletic passages in "The Wanderer." Some have argued that these must be later additions to a poem that is otherwise restricted to a very concrete and dramatic situation in which a solitary figure speaks to us of his grief. Do you agree or disagree with this view of these passages? Base your answer only on how well you feel these passages work in the poem before you.

You might find yourself disagreeing with a particular adage in a homily and yet enjoying the poem as a whole. Young people, for example, might find it tiresome to hear that only an older person can have wisdom. Beyond agreement or disagreement, what dramatic purpose might such a passage serve?

LANGUAGE AND VOCABULARY

With the help of a dictionary define the words *stoicism* and *irony*. (Where the word *stoicism* is concerned, set aside its reference to a school of Greco-Roman philosophy and focus on how it applies to a certain attitude toward life in general.)

With the definition of these words before you, try to answer this question: Is the stoicism in this poem "genuine" or is it "ironic"?

Most people think irony can only be used as a put-down: "Well, that was smart of you, wasn't it?" How might irony function differently here—so as to heighten the emotional impact of the grief expressed in the poem?

COMPOSITION

One of the easiest ways to get the hang of the alliterative line of Old English is to make up some yourself. Pick the name of a friend of yours in the class. Put it together with three other important words and as many interconnecting words as you need. Of the four important words, two or three should start with the same sound. All vowel sounds that start important words are viewed as alliterating with each other. There are only three kinds of patterns. Here's an example of each (with the four important words in big type):

GARY, the AMAZING   GUITAR-playing
    WHIZ
ENERGETIC LAURA, the   LIMBER
    GYMNAST
DAVID sometimes DRIVES me   to DIS-
    TRACTION with his GIGGLING.

Notice that the lines can be sentences or only phrases. Notice that it is always the first or second word—or both—that alliterate with the third. It's also important that the fourth important word *doesn't* alliterate with the others. Now try some, using the names of your friends. Remember to say something nice about them.

A.F. Kersting

An old Saxon Church, Bradford-on-Avon, Wiltshire.

Riddles

Nowhere is the Old English poet's delight in metaphor and simile more apparent than in the short poems known as "riddles" which have survived in the collection called the Exeter Book. This manuscript, preserved in the library of Exeter Cathedral, is the largest collection of Old English poetry. It contains primarily religious and meditative poems, but it also has a series of maxims and ninety-five riddles. Each riddle is an extended metaphor (or conceit) in which the elements serve as clues to solving the puzzle.

14

I was a warrior's weapon once.
Now striplings have woven silver wires,
And gold, around me. I've been kissed by soldiers,
And I've called a field of laughing comrades
To war and death. I've crossed borders   5
On galloping steeds, and crossed the shining
Water, riding a ship. I've been filled
To the depth of my heart by girls with glittering
Bracelets, and I've lain along the bare
Cold planks, headless, plucked and worn.   10
They've hung me high on a wall, bright
With jewels and beautiful, and left me to watch
Their warriors drinking. Mounted troops
Have carried me out and opened my breast
To the swelling wind of some soldier's lips.   15
My voice has invited princes to feasts
Of wine, and has sung in the night to save
What savage thieves have stolen, driving them
Off into darkness. Ask my name.

29

I saw a silvery creature scurrying
Home, as lovely and light as heaven
Itself, running with stolen treasure
Between its horns. It hoped, by deceit
And daring and art, to set an arbor   5
There in that soaring castle. Then,
A shining creature, known to everyone
On earth, climbed the mountains and cliffs,
Rescued his prize, and drove the wily
Impostor back to darkness. It fled   10
To the west, swearing revenge. The morning
Dust scattered away, dew
Fell, and the night was gone. And no one
Knew where the soft-footed thief had vanished.

FOR UNDERSTANDING

1. Riddle #14 offers a series of short "scenes," each one of which defines the speaker/object. What different kinds of scenes are mentioned? What different moods are created?

2. In Riddle #14 the speaker/object lists these details in an order which may seem random. Can you suggest any pattern for the order in which the details appear?

3. What words in Riddle #29 are especially helpful for solving the riddle?

4. Riddle #29 is spoken by an observer, rather than by the object itself, as in Riddle #14. Why is this choice appropriate for this particular riddle?

Introduction to BEOWULF

The epic poem *Beowulf* (bā⁺əwŭlf) is the oldest surviving epic in any modern European language. The poem refers to historical events that we can date as early as 516 or 520. It gives us semi-historical glimpses of slightly later Scandinavian feuds—between Swedes and Geats and Frisians and Danes. It echoes or parallels other European epics from the *Nibelungenlied* (c. 1200 A.D.) to various Scandinavian and Icelandic sagas, and its monster-battles are remarkably similar to those in over 200 European folktales that can be grouped under the collective title, "The Bear's Son." ("Beowulf" means "bear.") Three of its most poetic passages show the decisive influence of Virgil's *Aeneid*, a classical text supposedly unknown to people of these "dark ages." It also reflects the oral tradition of folk epic, as opposed to written literary epics that come later, such as those by Spenser and Milton.

It must have lived solely in spoken or chanted form during the Scandinavian migrations to Britain, brought by Geatish or Frisian Angles to Northumbria. There, in the eighth century of Bede's day, it found its all-but-final shape as a formal composition. But the Christian values that enter the poem at this point blend harmoniously into the whole story of pagan valor. And the poem is genuinely *English* in spirit, showing us scenes of life as it was lived, not in sixth century Scandinavia, but in seventh or eighth century England.

All this certainly makes the poem interesting to scholars concerned with the history of this period. More importantly the poem lives as literature. It speaks eloquently to us across the gulf of centuries—though it reaches most people today solely through translation or retelling. The reason is simple: the poem contains an exciting story narrated with all the spellbinding tricks of a first-rate spinner of yarns. In other folk or tribal epics, great importance is placed upon genealogies (So-and-So begat So-and-So who begat So-and-So, etc.) and on detailed accounts of feuds with neighboring tribes. All this is necessary to preserving the history and identity of a tribe. The one sure device, like a memory time capsule, for storing these things, both before and after the invention of writing, was the epic poem.

In *Beowulf,* however, a remarkable thing has happened. All this material is placed in a secondary position—recalled between the major actions during the celebration feast or sung as a lay by a minstrel after a successful battle. This leaves the major outline of the epic stark and undiminished in force: Beowulf the untried youth and Beowulf the honored old king facing the three great battles of his life. It's easy to see this story as an allegory: initiation into adulthood, the testing of one's courage as an adult, and the honorable conquest *of* and *by* one's own death. But the account of these three adventures is told so concretely, with such detail, and with such a rousing sense of adventure and sympathy that it can hold any audience if told in a language they can understand. With the monster-battles placed firmly at the center of the drama—a true novelty in the conception of an epic—the overall tone, except for the end, is celebratory and affirmative. Even the last episode is moving in its quiet solemnity. Only the human feuds that preoccupy so many other epics, told as digressions here, contain the time's darker "complexities of blood and mire"—tale after tale filled with ominous tragedies of treachery and cataclysm.

Beowulf as a character clearly represents a heroic ideal. In him, the pagan "Wyrd," or destiny, is subtly harmonized with the Christian concept of God's will or providence. We are perhaps a little surprised at how honestly he expresses the thirst for fame that fuels his exploits. But such a drive isn't uncommon today, though we usually see it acted out now in the fields of entertainment or politics rather than in the military. Otherwise, all his virtues are still easily admired: he is courageous, honest, generous, and loyal. He does experience fear (in the fight with Grendel's mother) and sadness (at his premonition of evil times ahead). But he risks his life for the good of his people in fighting the

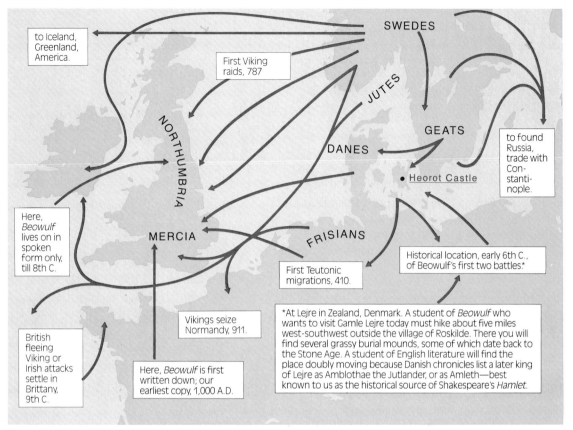

to Iceland, Greenland, America.

First Viking raids, 787

SWEDES

JUTES

NORTHUMBRIA

GEATS

to found Russia, trade with Constantinople.

DANES

• Heorot Castle

Here, *Beowulf* lives on in spoken form only, till 8th C.

MERCIA

FRISIANS

Historical location, early 6th C., of Beowulf's first two battles.*

First Teutonic migrations, 410.

Vikings seize Normandy, 911.

British fleeing Viking or Irish attacks settle in Brittany, 9th C.

Here, *Beowulf* is first written down; our earliest copy, 1,000 A.D.

*At Lejre in Zealand, Denmark. A student of *Beowulf* who wants to visit Gamle Lejre today must hike about five miles west-southwest outside the village of Roskilde. There you will find several grassy burial mounds, some of which date back to the Stone Age. A student of English literature will find the place doubly moving because Danish chronicles list a later king of Lejre as Amblothae the Jutlander, or as Amleth—best known to us as the historical source of Shakespeare's *Hamlet*.

fire-dragon. He is a model for the hero of any time, to be compared with the Greek Hercules, the Roman Aeneas, the French Roland, the Spanish Cid, the German Siegfried, the Celtic Arthur. For none of these astonishingly strong and brave men does life have any unanswered questions or doubts—such as would rack Shakespeare's Macbeth or Hamlet at the uncertain end of an otherwise optimistic age.

The symbolic role of Beowulf as a fighter of monsters and dragons is as old as time. It had already acquired its central importance to all mythologies when history began. The ancient Babylonian epic in which Gilgamesh kills the she-monster Tiamat is clearly a retelling of myths told and retold before writing existed. From Gilgamesh to Britain's patron saint, St. George the Dragon-Killer, many anthropologists now suspect that all such stories commemorate in some way the passing of female political power (the dragon or sea-monster or snake) to a patriarchy. This is only one reason why the fight

with Grendel's mother may be the most engrossing of the three episodes in this epic. It is the spookiest, the most suspenseful, the most emotion-packed, the most awesome in detail. (For example, it takes armor-clad Beowulf a full day to sink to the bottom of the she-troll's lake and reach her dry lair beneath the water.)

Beowulf's three battles appear below. They account for about a third of the whole poem. (His fifty years of rule as king take up a half line in the original—between the second and third battles!) The translation here tries to catch the feeling of the alliterative measure that makes the poem a joy to speak or hear spoken, especially with some stringed instrument, like a guitar, plucking chords now and then under the four most significant words in each line. As the poem opens, the Danish king, Hrothgar the Scylding, has built a grand hall, Heorot, where people have feasted happily until the start of Grendel's twelve-year reign of terror—and the arrival of Beowulf to put an end to that terror forever.

BEOWULF Translated by Michael Alexander

I—Grendel and the Coming of Beowulf

Listen, we know how Scyld¹ founded the Danish dynasty and how his descendant, King Hrothgar, son of Healfdene,² built the great hall of Heorot³ for feasting and gift-giving.

So the company of men led a careless life,
all was well with them: until One began
to encompass evil, an enemy from hell.
Grendel they called this cruel spirit,
the fell⁴ and fen⁵ his fastness⁶ was,
the march⁷ his haunt. This unhappy being
had long lived in the land of monsters
since the Creator cast them out
as kindred of Cain. For that killing of Abel⁸
the eternal Lord took vengeance.
There was no joy of that feud: far from mankind
God drove him out for his deed of shame!
From Cain came down all kinds misbegotten
—ogres and elves and evil shades—
as also the Giants,⁹ who joined in long
wars with God. He gave them their reward.

With the coming of night came Grendel also,
sought the great house and how the Ring-Danes¹⁰
held their hall when the horn had gone round.
He found in Heorot the force of nobles
slept after supper, sorrow forgotten,
the condition of men. Maddening with rage,
he struck quickly, creature of evil:
grim and greedy, he grasped on their pallets
thirty warriors, and away he was out of there,
thrilled with his catch: he carried off homeward,
his glut of slaughter, sought his own halls.

As the day broke, with the dawn's light
Grendel's outrage was openly to be seen:

1. **Scyld** (shild).
2. **Healfdene** (hā′ alf den nə).
3. **Heorot** (hā′ ô rot).
4. **fell,** wasteland, moor, or barren hill.
5. **fen,** marsh or bog.
6. **fastness,** stronghold.
7. **march,** frontier.
8. **Cain . . . Abel.** In *Genesis* 4, God cursed Cain for killing his brother Abel. In medieval legend, a race of monsters are the descendants of Cain.
9. **ogres . . . Giants,** in Teutonic mythology, orders of beings between the animal and the human. Giants are also mentioned in *Genesis* 6. The punishment of rebellious giants by God appears as a theme in a number of pagan mythologies.
10. **Ring-Danes,** Hrothgar's people, variously called Bright-, Ring-, and Spear-Danes, as well as North-, South-, East-, and West-Danes, or Scyldings. Similarly, Geats are variously referred to as Weather-, Storm-, War-, or Sea-Geats, as well as kinsmen of Hygelac, or Hrethlings (descendants of Hrethel), etc.

From BEOWULF, trans. Michael Alexander (Penguin Classics, 1973).

OSBERG SHIP, Carved prow
University Museum of Antiquities, Oslo

night's table-laughter turned to morning's
lamentation. Lord Hrothgar
sat silent then, the strong man mourned,
glorious king, he grieved for his thanes[11]
as they read the traces of a terrible foe,
a cursed fiend. That was too cruel a feud,
too long, too hard!
              Nor did he let them rest
but the next night brought new horrors,
did more murder, manslaughter and outrage
and shrank not from it: he was too set on these things.

*For twelve winters, Grendel preyed on Heorot castle. News of the terror spread
to the Geats,[12] who lived in a kingdom between Sweden and Denmark. Young
Beowulf,[13] the son of Edgetheow,[14] lived there. He was also grandson of King
Hrethel and nephew of the present Geat king, Hygelac.*

30

35

11. **thanes,** warrior comrades
of an Old English king. Such men
ranked above ceorls (churls, free-
men) but below earls (nobles).

12. **Geats** (gā′ ats).
13. **Beowulf** (bā′ ə wŭlf).
14. **Edgetheow** (ej′ thā ō).

This was heard of at his home by one of Hygelac's followers,   40
a good man among the Geats, Grendel's raidings;
he was for main strength of all men foremost
that trod the earth at that time of day;
build and blood matched.

                  He bade a seaworthy
wave-cutter[15] be fitted out for him; the warrior king   45
he would seek, he said, over swan's riding,[16]
that lord of great name, needing men.
The wiser sought to dissuade him from voyaging
hardly or not at all, though they held him dear;
they whetted his quest-thirst, watched omens.   50
The prince had already picked his men
from the folk's flower, the fiercest among them
that might be found. With fourteen men
he sought sound-wood; sea-wise Beowulf
led them right down to the land's edge.   55

Time running on, she rode the waves now,
hard in by headland. Harnessed warriors
stepped on her stem; setting tide churned
sea with sand, soldiers carried
bright mail-coats to the mast's foot,   60
war-gear well-wrought; willingly they shoved her out,
thorough-braced craft, on the craved voyage.

Away she went over a wavy ocean,
boat like a bird, breaking seas,
wind-whetted, white-throated,   65
till the curved prow had ploughed so far
—the sun standing right on the second day—
that they might see land loom on the skyline,
then the shimmer of cliffs, sheer fells behind,
reaching capes.
            The crossing was at an end;   70
closed the wake. Weather-Geats
stood on strand, stepped briskly up;
a rope going ashore, ring-mail clashed,
battle-girdings. God they thanked
for the smooth going over the salt-trails.   75

15. **seaworthy wave-cutter,** an often-quoted kenning for *ship*. Kennings are discussed in the study notes of "The Wanderer."
16. **swan's riding,** a kenning for *the ocean*.

A guard challenged them. When Beowulf explained they had come in peace, King Hrothgar's herald led them to the castle. Finally, Beowulf met Hrothgar and offered to fight Grendel single-handedly—since he had the strength of thirty men in his grip. Hrothgar accepted his offer gratefully and invited the Geats to a banquet.

During the feasting that followed, Queen Wealhtheow[17] gave thanks to
God that Beowulf had come. Beowulf swore to her that he would conquer
Grendel or die.

17. **Wealhtheow** (wä′ äl thä ō).

II—The Battle with Grendel

Then at last Heorot heard once more
words of courage, the carousing of a people
singing their victories; till the son of Healfdene
desired at length to leave the feast,
be away to his night's rest; aware of the monster   5
brooding his attack on the tall-gabled hall
from the time they had seen the sun's lightness
to the time when darkness drowns everything
and under its shadow-cover shapes do glide
dark beneath the clouds. The company came to its feet.   10

Then did the heroes, Hrothgar and Beowulf,
salute each other; success he wished him,
control of the wine-hall, and with this word left him:
'Never since I took up targe[18] and sword   18. **targe,** shield.
have I at any instance to any man beside,   15
thus handed over Heorot, as I here do to you.
Have and hold now the house of the Danes!
Bend your mind and your body to this task
and wake against the foe! There'll be no want of liberality
if you come out alive from this ordeal of courage.'   20

Then Hrothgar departed, the Protector of the Danes
passed from the hall at the head of his troop.
The war-leader sought Wealhtheow his queen,
the companion of his bed.
                    Thus did the King of Glory,
to oppose this Grendel, appoint a hall-guard   25
—so the tale went abroad—who took on a special
task at the court—to cope with the monster.
The Geat prince placed all his trust
in his mighty strength, his Maker's favour.

He now uncased himself of his coat of mail,   30
unhelmed his head, handed his attendant
his embellished sword, best of weapons,
and bade him take care of these trappings of war.
Beowulf then made a boasting speech,
the Geat man, before mounting his bed: 35
'I fancy my fighting-strength, my performance in combat,

at least as greatly as Grendel does his;
and therefore I shall not cut short his life
with a slashing sword—too simple a business.
He has not the art to answer me in kind,   40
hew at my shield, shrewd though he be
at his nasty catches. No, we'll at night play
without any weapons—if unweaponed he dare
to face me in fight. The Father in His wisdom
shall apportion the honours then, the All-holy Lord,   45
to whichever side shall seem to Him fit.'

Then the hero lay down, leant his head
on the bolster there; about him many
brave sea-warriors bowed to their hall-rest.
Not one of them thought he would thence be departing   50
ever to set eyes on his own country,
the home that nourished him, or its noble people;
for they had heard how many men of the Danes
death had dragged from that drinking-hall.
But God was to grant to the Geat people   55
the clue to war-success in the web of fate—
His help and support; so that they all did
overcome the foe—through the force of one
unweaponed man. The Almighty Lord
has ruled the affairs of the race of men   60
thus from the beginning.
                        Gliding through the shadows came
the walker in the night; the warriors slept
whose task was to hold the horned building,
all except one. It was well-known to men
that the demon could not drag them to the shades   65
without God's willing it; yet the one man kept
unblinking watch. He awaited, heart swelling
with anger against his foe, the ordeal of battle.
Down off the moorlands' misting fells came
Grendel stalking; God's brand was on him.   70
The spoiler meant to snatch away
from the high hall some of human race.
He came on under the clouds, clearly saw at last
the gold-hall of men, the mead-drinking place
nailed with gold plates. That was not the first visit   75
he had paid to the hall of Hrothgar the Dane:
he never before and never after
harder luck nor hall-guards found.

Walking to the hall came this warlike creature
condemned to agony. The door gave way,   80

**FIGHT WITH A SEVEN
HEADED DRAGON**
British Library, London

toughened with iron, at the touch of those hands.
Rage-inflamed, wreckage-bent, he ripped open
the jaws of the hall. Hastening on,
the foe then stepped onto the unstained floor,
angrily advanced: out of his eyes stood   85
an unlovely light like that of fire.
He saw then in the hall a host of young soldiers,
a company of kinsmen caught away in sleep,
a whole warrior-band. In his heart he laughed then,
horrible monster, his hopes swelling   90
to a gluttonous meal. He meant to wrench
the life from each body that lay in the place
before night was done. It was not to be;
he was no longer to feast on the flesh of mankind
after that night.   Narrowly the powerful   95
kinsman of Hygelac kept watch how the ravager
set to work with his sudden catches;
nor did the monster mean to hang back.
As a first step he set his hands on
a sleeping soldier, savagely tore at him,   100
gnashed at his bone-joints, bolted huge gobbets,
sucked at his veins, and had soon eaten
all of the dead man, even down to his
hands and feet.   Forward he stepped,
stretched out his hands to seize the warrior   105
calmly at rest there, reached out for him with his
unfriendly fingers: but the faster man
forestalling, sat up, sent back his arm.
The upholder of evils at once knew
he had not met, on middle earth's   110
extremest acres, with any man
of harder hand-grip: his heart panicked.
He was quit of the place no more quickly for that.

Eager to be away, he ailed for his darkness
and the company of devils; the dealings he had there   115
were like nothing he had come across in his lifetime.
Then Hygelac's brave kinsman called to mind
that evening's utterance, upright he stood,
fastened his hold till fingers were bursting.
The monster strained away: the man stepped closer.   120
The monster's desire was for darkness between them,
direction regardless, to get out and run
for his fen-bordered lair; he felt his grip's strength

crushed by his enemy. It was an ill journey
the rough marauder had made to Heorot.   125

The crash in the banqueting-hall came to the Danes,
the men of the guard that remained in the building,
with the taste of death. The deepening rage
of the claimants to Heorot caused it to resound.
It was indeed wonderful that the wine-supper-hall   130
withstood the wrestling pair, that the world's palace
fell not to the ground. But it was girt firmly,
both inside and out, by iron braces
of skilled manufacture. Many a figured
gold-worked wine-bench, as we heard it,   135
started from the floor at the struggles of that pair.
The men of the Danes had not imagined that
any of mankind by what method soever
might undo that intricate, antlered hall,
sunder it by strength—unless it were swallowed up in   140
the embraces of fire.
                    Fear entered into
the listening North Danes, as that noise rose up again
strange and strident. It shrilled terror
to the ears that heard it through the hall's side-wall,
the grisly plaint of God's enemy,   145
his song of ill-success, the sobs of the damned one
bewailing his pain. He was pinioned there
by the man of all mankind living
in this world's estate the strongest of his hands.

Not for anything would the earls' guardian   150
let his deadly guest go living:
he did not count his continued existence
of the least use to anyone. The earls ran
to defend the person of their famous prince;
they drew their ancestral swords to bring   155
what aid they could to their captain, Beowulf.
They were ignorant of this, when they entered the fight,
boldly-intentioned battle-friends,
to hew at Grendel, hunt his life
on every side—that no sword on earth,   160
not the truest steel, could touch their assailant;
for by a spell he had dispossessed all
blades of their bite on him.
                    A bitter parting
from life was that day destined for him;

the eldritch[19] spirit was sent off on his
far faring into the fiends' domain.

It was then that this monster, who, moved by spite
against human kind, had caused so much harm
—so feuding with God—found at last
that flesh and bone were to fail him in the end;
for Hygelac's great-hearted kinsman
had him by the hand; and hateful to each
was the breath of the other.
                              A breach in the giant
flesh-frame showed then, shoulder-muscles
sprang apart, there was a snapping of tendons,
bone-locks burst. To Beowulf the glory
of this fight was granted; Grendel's lot
to flee the slopes fen-ward with flagging heart,
to a den where he knew there could be no relief,
no refuge for a life at its very last stage,
whose surrender-day had dawned. The Danish hopes
in this fatal fight had found their answer.

He had cleansed Heorot. He who had come from afar,
deep-minded, strong-hearted, had saved the hall
from persecution. He was pleased with his night's work,
the deed he had done. Before the Danish people
the Geat captain had made good his boast,
had taken away all their unhappiness,
the evil menace under which they had lived,
enduring it by dire constraint,
no slight affliction. As a signal to all
the hero hung up the hand, the arm
and torn-off shoulder, the entire limb,
Grendel's whole grip, below the gable of the roof.

There was, as I heard it,[20] at hall next morning
a great gathering in the gift-hall yard
to see the wonder. Along the wide highroads
the chiefs of the clans came from near and far
to see the foe's footprints. It may fairly be said
that his parting from life aroused no pity in any
who tracked the spoor-blood of his blind flight
for the monster's mere-pool;[21] with mood flagging
and strength crushed, he had staggered onwards;
each step evidenced his ebbing life's blood.

The tarn[22] was troubled; a terrible wave-thrash
brimmed it, bubbling; black-mingled,

165

170

175

180

185

190

195

200

205

19. **eldritch,** ghastly, alien; literally, elvish (inhuman, monstrous).

20. **as I heard it.** The occasional use of the first person reminds us that a bard is chanting this aloud to the accompaniment of a harp.

21. **mere-pool,** lake. The Old English *mere* is still occasionally used in its original sense, referring to a lake, pond, or marsh.

22. **tarn,** lake.

the warm wound-blood welled upwards.
He had dived to his doom, he had died miserably;
here in his fen-lair he had laid aside
his heathen soul. Hell welcomed it.   210

When the Geats returned from the lake where Grendel died, Hrothgar
congratulated Beowulf and told him he would be treated like a son from now
on. A great banquet was held at which the king gave Beowulf costly presents.
Then the people all went to bed, unafraid for once, though the warriors still
laid their armor at their heads as they had done for years.

III—The Battle with Grendel's Mother

Then they sank into sleep. A savage penalty
one paid for his night's rest! It was no new thing for that
    people
since Grendel had settled in the gold-giving hall,
working his evil, until the end came,
death for his misdeeds. It was declared then to men,   5
and received by every ear, that for all this time
a survivor had been living, an avenger for their foe
and his grim life's-leaving: Grendel's Mother herself,
a monstrous ogress, was ailing for her loss.
She had been doomed to dwell in the dread waters,   10
in the chilling currents, because of that blow
whereby Cain became the killer of his brother,
his own father's son. He stole away, branded,
marked for his murder, from all that men delight in,
to inhabit the wastelands.
               Hosts of the ill ones   15
sprang from his begetting; as Grendel, that hateful
accursed outcast, who encountered at Heorot
a watchful man, waiting for the fight.
The grim one fastened his grip upon him there,
but he remembered his mighty strength,   20
the gift that the Lord had so largely bestowed on him,
and, putting his faith in the favour of the Almighty
and His aid and comfort, he overcame the foe,
put down the hell-fiend. How humbling was that flight
when the miserable outcast crept to his dying-place!   25
Thus mankind's enemy. But his Mother now purposed
to set out at last—savage in her grief—
on that wrath-bearing visit of vengeance for her son.

She came down to Heorot, where the heroes of the Danes
slept about the hall. A sudden change   30
was that for the men there when the Mother of Grendel
found her way in among them—though the fury of her
    onslaught
was less frightful than his; as the force of a woman,
her onset in a fight, is less feared by men,
where the bound blade, beaten out by hammers,   35
cuts, with its sharp edges shining with blood,
through the boars that bristle above the foes' helmets!

Many a hard sword was snatched up in the hall
from its rack above the benches; the broad shield was raised,
held in the hand firm; helmet and corselet[23]   40   23. **corselet,** body armor or
lay there unheeded when the horror was on them.   breastplate.
She was all eager to be out of the place
now that she was discovered, and escape with her life.
She caught a man quickly, clutched him to herself,
one of the athelings,[24] and was away to the fen.   45   24. **athelings,** heroes or nobles.
This was the hero that Hrothgar loved better
than any on earth among his retinue,
destroyed thus as he slept; he was a strong warrior,
noted in battle. (Beowulf was not there:
separate lodging had been assigned that night,   50
after the treasure-giving, to the Geat champion.)
Heorot was in uproar; the hand had gone with her,
blood-stained, familiar.

Hrothgar called Beowulf to his chamber and mourned the death of his best
friend, Ashhere.[25] The king said that Grendel's mother was even more powerful   25. **Ashhere** (ash′ her ə).
than her son. Grief-stricken by her son's death, she would now continue to
ravage them in revenge for his death. Hrothgar pleaded for Beowulf's help,
which Beowulf offered immediately. A troop then went out with Beowulf to
search the wild, uninhabitable lake-country for the she-monster's lair.

Going on ahead with a handful of the
keener men to reconnoitre,   55
Beowulf suddenly saw where some ash-trees
hung above a hoary rock
—a cheerless wood! And the water beneath it
was turbid with blood; bitter distress
was to be endured by the Danes who were there,   60
a grief for the earls, for every thane
of the Friends of the Scyldings,[26] when they found there   26. **Scyldings** (shild′ ingz).
the head of Ashhere by the edge of the cliff.

ST. GEORGE AND THE DRAGON
British Library, London

The men beheld the blood on the water,
its warm upwellings. The war-horn sang   65
an eager battle-cry. The band of foot-soldiers,
sitting by the water, could see multitudes
of strange sea-drakes swerving through the depths,
and water-snakes lay on the ledges of the cliffs,
such serpents and wild beasts as will sally out   70
in middle morning to make havoc
in the seas where ships sail.
                          Slithering away
at the bright phrases of the battle-horn,
they were swollen with anger. An arrow from the
bow of Beowulf broke the life's thread   75
of one wave-thrasher; wedged in his throat
the iron dart; with difficulty then
did he swim through the deep, until death took him.
They struck him as he swam, and straightaway,
with their boar-spears barbed and tanged;   80
gaffed[27] and battered, he was brought to the cliff-top,
strange lurker of the waves. They looked with wonder
at their grisly guest!
                  The Geat put on
the armour of a hero, unanxious for his life:
the manufacture of the mailed shirt,   85
figured and vast, that must venture in the deep,
made it such a bulwark to his bone-framed chest
that the savage attack of an incensed enemy
could do no harm to the heart within it.

*A Danish earl lent Beowulf a mighty sword, Hrunting. Beowulf reminded
Hrothgar of his vow to treat him as a son. If he came to harm, his gifts should
remain with the Geats and his friends should be protected. For with Hrunting,
Beowulf concluded, he meant to conquer or die!*

After these words the Weather-Geat prince   90
dived into the Mere—he did not care
to wait for an answer—and the waves closed over
the daring man. It was a day's space almost
before he could glimpse ground at the bottom.

The grim and greedy guardian of the flood,   95
keeping her hungry hundred-season watch,
discovered at once that one from above,
a human, had sounded the home of the monsters.
She felt for the man and fastened upon him
her terrible hooks; but no harm came thereby   100
to the hale body within—the harness so ringed him

27. **gaffed,** struck at with a pole tipped by a sharp iron hook.

that she could not drive her dire fingers
through the mesh of the mail-shirt masking his limbs.

When she came to the bottom she bore him to her lair,   105
the mere-wolf, pinioning the mail-clad prince.
Not all his courage could enable him
to draw his sword; but swarming through the water,
throngs of sea-beasts threw themselves upon him
with ripping tusks to tear his battle-coat,
tormenting monsters. Then the man found   110
that he was in some enemy hall
where there was no water to weigh upon him
and the power of the flood could not pluck him away,
sheltered by its roof: a shining light he saw,
a bright fire blazing clearly.   115

It was then that he saw the size of this water-hag,
damned thing of the deep. He dashed out his weapon,
not stinting the stroke, and with such strength and violence
that the circled sword screamed on her head
a strident battle-song. But the stranger saw   120
his battle-flame refuse to bite
or hurt her at all; the edge failed
its lord in his need. It had lived through many
hand-to-hand conflicts, and carved through the helmets
of fated men. This was the first time   125
that this rare treasure had betrayed its name.[28]
Determined still, intent on fame,
the nephew of Hygelac renewed his courage.
Furious, the warrior flung it to the ground,
spiral-patterned, precious in its clasps,   130
stiff and steel-edged; his own strength would suffice him,
the might of his hands. A man must act so
when he means in a fight to frame himself
a long-lasting glory; it is not life he thinks of.

The Geat prince went for Grendel's mother,   135
seized her by the shoulder—he was not sorry to be
    fighting—
his mortal foe, and with mounting anger
the man hard in battle hurled her to the ground.
She promptly repaid this present of his
as her ruthless hands reached out for him;   140
and the strongest of fighting-men stumbled in his
    weariness,
the firmest of foot-warriors fell to the earth.

28. **name,** literally, its "good name," its reputation for glory. The sword's actual name may be related to an Old Norse word meaning *thruster*. In Old English poetry, swords not only have names, they have personalities.

She was down on this guest of hers and had drawn her
    knife,
broad, burnished of edge; for her boy was to be avenged,
her only son. Overspreading his back,   145
the shirt of mail shielded his life then,
barred the entry to edge and point.
Edgetheow's son would have ended his venture
deep under ground there, the Geat fighter,
had not the battle-shirt then brought him aid,   150
his war-shirt of steel. And the wise Lord,
the holy God, gave out the victory;
the Ruler of the Heavens rightly settled it
as soon as the Geat regained his feet.

He saw among the armour there the sword to bring him
    victory,   155
a Giant-sword from former days: formidable were its
    edges,
a warrior's admiration. This wonder of its kind
was yet so enormous that no other man
would be equal to bearing it in battle-play
—it was a Giant's forge that had fashioned it so well.   160
The Scylding champion, shaking with war-rage,
caught it by its rich hilt, and, careless of his life,
brandished its circles, and brought it down in fury
to take her full and fairly across the neck,
breaking the bones; the blade sheared   165
through the death-doomed flesh. She fell to the ground;
the sword was gory; he was glad at the deed.

Light glowed out and illumined the chamber
with a clearness such as the candle of heaven
sheds in the sky. He scoured the dwelling   170
in single-minded anger, the servant of Hygelac;
with his weapon high, and, holding to it firmly,
he stalked by the wall. Nor was the steel useless yet
to that man of battle, for he meant soon enough
to settle with Grendel for those stealthy raids   175
—there had been many of them—he had made on the
    West-Danes;
far more often than on that first occasion
when he had killed Hrothgar's hearth-companions,
slew them as they slept, and in their sleep ate up
of the folk of Denmark fifteen good men,   180
carrying off another of them
in foul robbery. The fierce champion
now settled this up with him: he saw where Grendel

lay at rest, limp from the fight;
his life had wasted through the wound he had got   185
in the battle at Heorot. The body gaped open
as it now suffered the stroke after death
from the hard-swung sword; he had severed the neck.

And above, the wise men who watched with Hrothgar
the depths of the pool descried soon enough   190
blood rising in the broken water
and marbling the surface. Seasoned warriors,
grey-headed, experienced, they spoke together,
said it seemed unlikely that they would see once more
the prince returning triumphant to seek out   195
their famous master. Many were persuaded
the she-wolf of the deep had done away with him.
The ninth hour had come; the keen-hearted Scyldings
abandoned the cliff-head; the kindly gold-giver
turned his face homeward. But the foreigners sat on,   200
staring at the pool with sickness at heart,
hoping they would look again on their beloved captain,
believing they would not.
                              The blood it had shed
made the sword dwindle into deadly icicles;
the war-tool wasted away. It was wonderful indeed   205
how it melted away entirely, as the ice does in the spring
when the Father unfastens the frost's grip,
unwinds the water's rope—He who watches over
the times and the seasons; He is the true God.

The Geat champion did not choose to take   210
any treasures from that hall, from the heaps he saw there,
other than that richly ornamented hilt,
and the head of Grendel. The engraved blade
had melted and burnt away: the blood was too hot,
the fiend that had died there too deadly by far.   215
The survivor of his enemies' onslaught in battle
now set to swimming, and struck up through the water;
both the deep reaches and the rough wave-swirl
were thoroughly cleansed, now the creature from the
      otherworld
drew breath no longer in this brief world's space.   220

Then the seamen's Helm came swimming up
strongly to land, delighting in his sea-trove,
those mighty burdens that he bore along with him.
They went to meet him, a manly company,
thanking God, glad of their lord,   225

seeing him safe and sound once more.
Quickly the champion's corselet and helmet
were loosened from him. The lake's waters,
sullied with blood, slept beneath the sky.

Then they turned away from there and retraced their steps,   **230**
pacing the familiar paths back again
as bold as kings, carefree at heart.
The carrying of the head from the cliff by the Mere
was no easy task for any of them,
brave as they were. They bore it up,   **235**
four of them, on a spear, and transported back
Grendel's head to the gold-giving hall.[29]
Warrior-like they went, and it was not long
before they came, the fourteen bold Geats,
marching to the hall, and, among the company   **240**
walking across the land, their lord the tallest.
The earl of those thanes then entered boldly
—a man who had dared deeds and was adorned with their
    glory,
a man of prowess—to present himself to Hrothgar.
Then was the head of Grendel, held up by its locks,   **245**
manhandled in where men were drinking;
it was an ugly thing for the earls and their queen,
an awesome sight; they eyed it well.

29. **gold-giving hall.** During a public ritual in his hall, the lord gives a gold token to each of those who pledge loyalty to him. This Old English emphasis on gift-giving, feasting, and celebrating in the mead-hall of the lord is discussed in the notes for "The Wanderer."

Then Beowulf told Hrothgar of his battle with Grendel's mother, and Hrothgar thanked Beowulf. The people feasted and slept. On the next morning, there was more gift-giving and speeches of farewell. Hrothgar praised Beowulf for bringing peace between the Geats and the Danes. Beowulf and his companions set sail.

IV—The Battle with the Fire-Dragon

When he got home, Beowulf told both the king and queen the story of his adventures in Denmark. When he finished his story, he was much praised and admired.

When King Hygelac died, his son became king. After a time, he too died and Beowulf finally became king. He reigned peaceably for fifty years.[30] Then a fire-dragon who guarded a treasure-hoard rose up to torment the nation, consuming the whole countryside with flames. Beowulf had new weapons made, for he was determined to fight the dragon, again single-handedly. With twelve attendants he went to search for the dragon's cave. At last, Beowulf turned to his men before the barrow[31] of the treasure-hoard. All was ready for the battle with the dragon.

30. **fifty years.** This figure is considered to represent a suitably large round number, with no intention of being definite or literal about the length of Beowulf's reign.
31. **barrow,** a mound of earth or stones built over a grave or treasure-hoard or dragon-lair.

SIGURD KILLS THE DRAGON FAFNIR
Detail of the Portal of Hylstad Church, Norway
C.M. Dixon/University Historical Museum, Oslo

Beowulf made speech, spoke a last time
a word of boasting: 'Battles in plenty
I ventured in youth; and I shall venture this feud
and again achieve glory, the guardian of my people,
old though I am, if this evil destroyer   5
dares to come out of his earthen hall.'

Then he addressed each of the men there
on this last occasion, courageous helm-bearers,
cherished companions: 'I would choose not to take
any weapon to this worm, if I well knew   10
of some other fashion fitting to my boast
of grappling with this monster, as with Grendel before.
But as I must expect here the hot war-breath
of venom and fire, for this reason I have
my board[32] and corselet. From the keeper of the barrow   15
I shall not flee one foot; but further than that
shall be worked out at the wall as Weird[33] shall decide for us,
every man's master. My mood is strong;
I forgo further words against the winged fighter.

    Men in armour! Your mail-shirts protect you: 20
await on the barrow the one of us two
who shall be better able to bear his wounds
after this onslaught. This affair is not for you,
nor is it measured to any man but myself alone
to match strength with this monstrous being,   25
attempt this deed. By daring will I
win this gold; war otherwise
shall take your king, terrible life's-bane!'

The strong champion stood up beside his shield,
brave beneath helmet, he bore his mail-shirt   30
to the rocky cliff's foot, confident in his strength,
a single man; such is not the coward's way!
Then did the survivor of a score of conflicts,
the battle-clashes of encountering armies,
excelling in manhood, see in the wall   35
a stone archway, and out of the barrow broke
a stream surging through it, a stream of fire
with waves of deadly flame; the dragon's breath
meant he could not venture into the vault near the hoard
for any time at all without being burnt.   40

Passion filled the prince of the Geats:
he allowed a cry to utter from his breast,
roared from his stout heart: as the horn clear in battle

32. **board,** shield.
33. **Weird,** the pagan Wyrd (fate, destiny) or—in Christian terms—God's providence or will.

his voice re-echoed through the vault of grey stone.
The hoard-guard recognized a human voice,   45
and there was no more time for talk of friendship:
hatred stirred. Straightaway
the breath of the dragon billowed from the rock
in a hissing gust; the ground boomed.

He swung up his shield, overshadowed by the mound,   50
the lord of the Geats against this grisly stranger.
The temper of the twisted tangle-thing was fired
to close now in battle. The brave warrior-king
shook out his sword so sharp of edge,
an ancient heirloom. Each of the pair,   55
intending destruction, felt terror at the other:
intransigent beside his towering shield
the lord of friends, while the fleetness of the serpent
wound itself together; he waited in his armour.
It came flowing forward, flaming and coiling,   60
rushing on its fate.
                 For the famous prince
the protection lent to his life and person
by the shield was shorter than he had shaped it to be.
He must now dispute this space of time,
the first in his life when fate had not assigned him   65
the glory of the battle. The Geat chieftain
raised his hand, and reached down such a stroke
with his huge ancestral sword on the horribly-patterned
    snake
that, meeting the bone, its bright edge turned
and it bit less strongly than its sorely-straitened lord   70
required of it then. The keeper of the barrow
after this stroke grew savage in mood,
spat death-fire; the sparks of their battle
blazed into the distance.
                 He boasted of no triumphs then,
the gold-friend of the Geats, for his good old sword   75
bared in the battle, his blade, had failed him,
as such iron should not do.
                 That was no easy adventure,
when the celebrated son of Edgetheow
had to pass from that place on earth
and against his will take up his dwelling   80
in another place; as every man must give up
the days that are lent him.
                 It was not long again
to the next meeting of those merciless ones.
The barrow-guard took heart: his breast heaved

with fresh out-breath: fire enclosed   85
the former folk-king; he felt bitter pain.

The band of picked companions did not come
to stand about him, as battle-usage asks,
offspring of athelings; they escaped to the wood,
saved their lives.   Sorrow filled   90
the breast of one man. The bonds of kinship
nothing may remove for a man who thinks rightly.
This was Wiglaf, Weoxstan's[34] son,
well-loved shieldsman, a Scylding prince
of the stock of Alfhere;[35] he could see his lord   95
tormented by the heat through his mask of battle.

34. **Weoxstan** (wā′ ō stan, or wāy′ ōk stan).
35. **Alfhere** (alf′ hèr ə).

Wiglaf recalled Beowulf's generosity to his own family. Weoxstan's very armor,
now his own, had been won for bravery and loyalty in old battles.

                 For the youthful warrior
this was the first occasion when he was called on to stand
at his dear lord's shoulder in the shock of battle.
His courage did not crumble, nor did his kinsman's
      heirloom   100
weaken at the war-play: as the worm found out
when they had got to grips with one another.

Wiglaf then spoke many words that were fitting,
addressed his companions; dark was his mood.
'I remember the time, as we were taking mead   105
in the banqueting hall, when we bound ourselves
to the gracious lord who granted us arms,
that we would make return for these trappings of war,
these helms and hard swords, if an hour such as this
should ever chance for him. He chose us himself   110
out of all his host for this adventure here,
expecting action; he armed me with you
because he accounted us keen under helmet,
men able with the spear—even though our lord
intended to take on this task of courage   115
as his own share, as shepherd of the people,
and champion of mankind in the achieving of glory
and deeds of daring.   That day has now come
when he stands in need of the strength of good fighters,
our lord and liege. Let us go to him,   120
help our leader for as long as it requires,
the fearsome fire-blast. I had far rather

that the flame should enfold my flesh-frame there
alongside my gold-giver—as God knows of me.
To bear our shields back to our homes   125
would seem unfitting to me, unless first we have been able
to kill the foe and defend the life
of the prince of the Weather-Geats. I well know
that former deeds deserve not that, alone
of the flower of the Geats, he should feel the pain,   130
sink in the struggle; sword and helmet,
corselet and mail-shirt, shall be our common gear.'

He strode through the blood-smoke, bore his war-helmet
to the aid of his lord, uttered few words:
'Beloved Beowulf, bear all things well!   135
You gave it out long ago in your youth
that, living, you would not allow your glory
ever to abate. Bold-tempered chieftain,
famed for your deeds, you must defend your life now
with all your strength. I shall help you.'   140

When these words had been spoken, the worm came on
        wrathful,
attacked a second time, terrible visitant,
sought out his foes in a surge of flame,
the hated men.
              Mail-shirt did not serve
the young spear-man; and shield was withered   145
back to the boss[36] by the billow of fire;
but when the blazing had burnt up his own,
the youngster stepped smartly to take
the cover of his kinsman's. Then did that kingly warrior
remember his deeds again and dealt out a sword-blow   150
with his full strength: it struck into the head
with annihilating weight. But Nailing[37] snapped,
failed in the battle, Beowulf's sword
of ancient grey steel. It was not granted to him
that an iron edge could ever lend him   155
help in a battle; his hand was too strong.
I have heard that any sword, however hardened by wounds,
that he bore into battle, his blow would overtax
—any weapon whatever; it was the worse for him.

A third time the terrible fire-drake   160
remembered the feud. The foe of the people
rushed in on the champion when a chance offered:
seething with warspite, he seized his whole neck
between bitter fangs: blood covered him,

36. **boss,** the central knob or stud on the face of a shield. It can be used offensively in thrusting.

37. **Nailing.** The meaning of this sword's name is clear: *nailer.*

Beowulf's life-blood, let in streams.   165
Then I heard how the earl alongside the king
in the hour of need made known the valour,
boldness and strength that were bred in him.
His hand burned as he helped his kinsman,
but the brave soldier in his splendid armour   170
ignored the head and hit the attacker
somewhat below it, so that the sword went in,
flashing-hilted; and the fire began
to slacken in consequence.
                          The king once more
took command of his wits, caught up a stabbing-knife   175
of the keenest battle-sharpness, that he carried in his harness:
and the Geats' Helm[38] struck through the serpents' body.

So daring drove out life: they had downed their foe
by common action, the atheling pair,
and had made an end of him. So in the hour of need   180
a warrior must live. For the lord this was
the last victory in the list of his deeds
and works in the world. The wound that the earth-drake
had first succeeded in inflicting on him
began to burn and swell; he swiftly felt   185
the bane beginning to boil in his chest,
the poison within him. The prince walked across
to the side of the barrow, considering deeply;
he sat down on a ledge, looked at the giant-work,
saw how the age-old earth-hall contained   190
stone arches anchored on pillars.
Then that excellent thane with his own hands washed
his battle-bloodied prince, bathed with water
the famous leader, his friend and lord,
sated with fighting; he unfastened his helmet.   195

Beowulf spoke; he spoke through the pain
of his fatal wound. He well knew
that he had come to the end of his allotted days,
his earthly happiness; all the number
of his days had disappeared: death was very near.   200
'I would now wish to give my garments in battle
to my own son, if any such
after-inheritor, an heir of my body,
had been granted to me. I have guarded this people
for half a century; not a single ruler   205
of all the nations neighbouring about
has dared to affront me with his friends in war,
or threaten terrors. What the times had in store for me

38. **Geats' Helm,** a kenning
that depicts Beowulf as the helmet (protector) of his people.

I awaited in my homeland; I held my own well,
sought no secret feud, swore very rarely[39]   210
a wrongful oath. In all of these things,
sick with my life's wound, I may still rejoice:
for when my life shall leave my body
the Ruler of Men may not charge me
with the slaughter of kinsmen.
                    Quickly go now,   215
beloved Wiglaf, and look upon the hoard
under the grey stone, now the serpent lies dead,
sleeps rawly wounded, bereft of his treasure.
Make haste, that I may gaze upon that golden inheritance,
that ancient wealth; that my eyes may behold   220
the clear skilful jewels: more calmly then may I
on the treasure's account take my departure
of life and of the lordship I have long held.'

39. **very rarely,** a typical Old English understatement meaning *never.*

V—The Death and Funeral of Beowulf

Wiglaf entered the vault as Beowulf requested and saw the priceless treasures there. He carried off a gleaming banner and an armload of goblets and dishes.

The envoy made haste in his eagerness to return,
urged on by his prizes. He was pressed by anxiety
as to whether he would find his fearless man,
the lord of the Geats, alive in the open
where he had left him, lacking in strength.   5
Carrying the treasures, he came upon his prince,
the famous king, covered in blood
and at his life's end; again he began
to sprinkle him with water, until this word's point
broke through the breast-hoard.
                    The battle-king spoke,   10
an aged man in sorrow; he eyed the gold.
'I wish to put in words my thanks
to the King of Glory, the Giver of All,
the Lord of Eternity, for these treasures that I see,
that I should have been able to acquire for my people   15
before my death-day an endowment such as this.
My life's full portion I have paid out now
for this hoard of treasure; you must attend to the people's
needs henceforward; no further may I stay.
Bid men of battle build me a tomb   20
fair after fire, on the foreland by the sea

that shall stand as a reminder of me to my people,
towering high above Hronesness[40]
so that ocean travellers shall afterwards name it
Beowulf's barrow, bending in the distance   25
their masted ships through the mists upon the sea.'

He unclasped the golden collar from his neck,
staunch-hearted prince, and passed it to the thane,
with the gold-plated helmet, harness and arm-ring;
he bade the young spear-man use them well: 30
'You are the last man left of our kindred,
the house of the Waymundings! Weird has lured
each of my family to his fated end,
each earl through his valour; I must follow them.'

This was the aged man's uttermost word   35
from the thoughts of his breast; he embraced the pyre's
seething surges;[41] soul left its case,
going its way to the glory of the righteous.

How wretchedly it went with the warrior then,
the younger soldier, when he saw on the ground   40
his best-beloved at his life's end
suffering miserably! The slayer lay also
bereft of life, beaten down in ruin,
terrible earth-drake. He was unable any longer
to rule the ring-hoard, the writhing serpent,   45
since the hammer's legacy, hard and battle-scarred,
the iron edges, had utterly destroyed him;
the far-flier lay felled along the ground
beside his store-house, still from his wounds.
He did not mount the midnight air,   50
gliding and coiling, glorying in his hoard,
flaunting his aspect; he fell to the earth
at the powerful hand of that prince in war.
Not one of the men of might in that land,
however daring in deeds of every kind,   55
had ever succeeded, from all I have heard,
in braving the venomous breath of that foe
or putting rude hands on the rings in that hall
if his fortune was to find the defender of the barrow
waiting and on his guard. The gaining of the hoard   60
of beautiful treasure was Beowulf's death;
so it was that each of them attained the end
of his life's lease.

40. **Hronesness,** a great hill or headland on the coast of Geatland.

41. **he embraced . . . surges.** He makes a gesture, accepting the burning pyre which, shortly, will consume his body after he dies.

SUTTON HOO HELMET
Trustees of The British Museum, London

It was not long then
till they budged from the wood, the battle-shirkers,
ten of them together, those traitors and weaklings   65
who had not dared deploy their spears
in their own lord's extreme need.
They bore their shields ashamedly,
their armour of war, to where the old man lay.
They regarded Wiglaf. Wearily he sat,   70
a foot-soldier, at the shoulder of his lord,
trying to wake him with water; but without success.
For all his desiring it, he was unable to hold
his battle-leader's life in this world
or affect anything of the All-Wielder's;   75
for every man's action was under the sway
of God's judgement, just as it is now.

There was a rough and a ready answer
on the young man's lips for those who had lost their nerve;
Wiglaf spoke, Weoxstan's offspring,   80
looked at them unlovingly, and with little joy at heart:
'A man who would speak the truth may say with justice
that a lord of men who allowed you those treasures,
who bestowed on you the trappings that you stand there in
—as, at the ale-bench, he would often give   85
to those who sat in hall both helmet and mail-shirt
as a lord to his thanes, and things of the most worth
that he was able to find anywhere in the world
—that he had quite thrown away and wasted cruelly
all that battle-harness when the battle came upon him.   90
The king of our people had no cause to boast
of his companions of the guard. Yet God vouchsafed him,
the Master of Victories, that he should avenge himself
when courage was wanted, by his weapon single-handed.
I was little equipped to act as body-guard   95
for him in the battle, but, above my own strength,
I began all the same to support my kinsman.
Our deadly enemy grew ever the weaker—
when I had struck him with my sword—less strongly welled
the fire from his head. Too few supporters   100
flocked to our prince when affliction came.
Now there shall cease for your race the receiving of treasure,
the bestowal of swords, all satisfaction of ownership,
all comfort of home. Your kinsmen every one,
shall become wanderers without land-rights   105
as soon as athelings over the world
shall hear the report of how you fled,

a deed of ill fame. Death is better
for any earl than an existence of disgrace!'

Wiglaf sent a messenger back to Beowulf's castle with the news of the death.
Mourners went to where Wiglaf still guarded the body. Wiglaf lamented
Beowulf before them and then ordered that wood be brought to kindle the
funeral pyre of their great warrior-chief.

Then in his wisdom Weoxstan's son   110
called out from the company of the king's own thanes
seven men in all, who excelled among them,
and, himself the eighth warrior, entered in beneath
that unfriendly roof. The front-stepping man
bore in his hand a blazing torch.   115

When the men perceived a piece of the hoard
that remained unguarded, mouldering there
on the floor of the chamber, they did not choose by lot
who should remove it; undemurring,
as quickly as they could, they carried outside   120
the precious treasures; and they pushed the dragon,
the worm, over the cliff, let the waves take him
and the flood engulf the guardian of the treasures.
The untold profusion of twisted gold
was loaded onto a wagon, and the warrior prince   125
borne hoary-headed to Hronesness.

The Geat race then reared up for him
a funeral pyre. It was not a petty mound,
but shining mail-coats and shields of war
and helmets hung upon it, as he had desired.   130
Then the heroes, lamenting, laid out in the middle
their great chief, their cherished lord.
On top of the mound the men then kindled
the biggest of funeral-fires. Black wood-smoke
arose from the blaze, and the roaring of flames   135
mingled with weeping. The winds lay still
as the heat at the fire's heart consumed
the house of bone. And in heavy mood
they uttered their sorrow at the slaughter of their lord.

A woman of the Geats in grief sang out   140
the lament for his death. Loudly she sang,
her hair bound up, the burden of her fear
that evil days were destined her
—troops cut down, terror of armies,
bondage, humiliation. Heaven swallowed the smoke.   145

Then the Storm-Geat nation constructed for him
a stronghold on the headland, so high and broad
that seafarers might see it from afar.
The beacon to that battle-reckless man
they made in ten days. What remained from the fire   150
they cast a wall around, of workmanship
as fine as their wisest men could frame for it.
They placed in the tomb both the torques and the jewels,
all the magnificence that the men had earlier
taken from the hoard in hostile mood.   155
They left the earls' wealth in the earth's keeping,
the gold in the dirt. It dwells there yet,
of no more use to men than in ages before.

Then the warriors rode around the barrow,
twelve of them in all, athelings' sons.   160
They recited a dirge to declare their grief,
spoke of the man, mourned their King.
They praised his manhood and the prowess of his hands,
they raised his name; it is right a man
should be lavish in honoring his lord and friend,   165
should love him in his heart when the leading-forth
from the house of flesh befalls him at last.

This was the manner of the mourning of the men of the
        Geats,
sharers in the feast, at the fall of their lord:
they said that he was of all the world's kings   170
the gentlest of men, and the most gracious,
the kindest to his people, the keenest for fame.

FOR UNDERSTANDING

1. Of the three battles that appear in their entirety here, Beowulf's fight with Grendel is different from the other two in one important respect–his choice of weapons. Explain what this difference is and describe the weapons he uses in each of the three battles.
2. What is Beowulf's primary motivation in all three fights?
3. Of the three supernatural enemies that Beowulf fights, one is depicted as having an emotion other than fear or hatred. Which is it, and what is the emotion?
4. At the edge of the pool into which Beowulf sinks to confront Grendel's mother, two groups of people watch for the result. What are the two groups and how does their behavior differ? To which group do the "wise men" and "seasoned warriors" belong?
5. Look at the fire-dragon episode, starting with the failure of Beowulf's shield to protect him. Make a list of the items in the sequence of failures or betrayals that lead to his death.
6. Beowulf's superhuman grip gives him victory in the battle with Grendel. How does it function in the fight with the fire-dragon?
7. After Beowulf's death, Wiglaf curses the deserters. At Beowulf's funeral a woman sings a lament. What do the curse and the lament have in common?
8. Weird, or fate, is mentioned twice in this selection. Find these two passages and compare them.

FOR INTERPRETATION

1. Assume that the poet has made a deliberate decision about how much detail to give us in the descriptions of Grendel and Grendel's mother. What do we know about how they look? What don't we know?

Argue that the omissions are particularly well chosen in heightening the impact the monsters have on our imagination.

2. There is a good deal of gory detail in all three battles. Which has the most, which the least? Can you see any reason for these differences?

3. Small, seemingly irrelevant details can sometimes make a whole passage come vividly alive. In the climax of the battle with Grendel, the poet says, "hateful to each was the breath of the other." Why is this detail more riveting than a description of eyes rolling or teeth gnashing?

4. Is there any point to the water monsters that the poet introduces before Beowulf jumps into the lake beneath which Grendel's mother lurks?

5. When Grendel's mother first invades Heorot, the poet makes a peculiar male chauvinist remark that she is less frightening than Grendel because of her gender. Do later events tend to bear out this statement or not?

6. In the fire-dragon battle, a memorable passage occurs just after Beowulf receives his mortal wound. Turn to these lines again (187–191) and read them closely. After being wounded, what concrete things does Beowulf do before speaking? How do the specific things he does or sees contribute to the power of this moment? What he sees, particularly, seems to have no relationship to what comes just before or after. Could you argue that this fact is part of the effectiveness of the passage? What else makes this moment "come alive"?

7. In Wiglaf's bitter speech to the deserters after Beowulf's death, how does he resemble the solitary figure in "The Wanderer"? If Wiglaf's curse comes true, how will the deserters share the fate of "The Wanderer"?

8. Beowulf's death and funeral introduce an emotion new to the poem: grief for the fallen and beloved protector of his people. The poem takes on a simple but dignified solemnity quite different in tone from the blood-and-thunder of the three battles. A number of elements contribute to this new tone—such as Beowulf's description of his own tomb, or the woman's lament. Find others that strike you as important in creating the mood with which the poem concludes.

9. No pity or compassion is shown by the poet or any of the characters toward the suffering and death of the three supernatural enemies. They are "glad" that these evil beings are dead. At first, we may claim that we are unused to seeing the death—even of an enemy—presented in such a merciless light. But in many popular science fiction movies, "aliens" are regarded in the same way. Can you find other examples of this attitude in our own time?

FOR APPRECIATION

Simile.

The simile is the simplest form of imagery in poetry other than literal description. It can always be recognized easily because it uses "like" or "as" in comparing one thing to another. Old English poetry is notable for the almost complete absence of simile. The poetry is rich in other kinds of imagery, however, such as the kenning.

This makes the one best-known simile in all of Old English doubly interesting, for it is unusual–in fact, downright strange–in other ways as well. The lines containing the simile occur in the second battle, after hot monster-blood has melted away the blade of the sword Beowulf has used:

> The blood it had shed
> made the sword dwindle into deadly icicles;
> the war-tool wasted away. It was wonderful
> indeed
> how it melted away entirely, as the ice does
> in spring
> when the Father unfastens the frost's grip,
> unwinds the water's rope–He who watches
> over
> the times and the seasons; He is the true
> God.

The simile itself starts with *as*: "as the ice does . . ." But notice the progression here. First the sword has become icicles, this after melting from the hot blood. Then we get the simile comparing the melting to the spring thaw. And before we can ask how this relates to the "icicles," we are carried away into two beautiful lines describing spring: "unfastens the frost's grip, unwinds the water's rope." Then we get a line and a half praising God in a homiletic manner. The conclusion, "true God," could make one wonder about pagan/Christian tensions again (false versus true). Then we are back with Beowulf in the monster's hall.

The distance we travel in these lines is considerable, and we come out with much still to understand and explain. It's not too hard to explain the icicles: the blade melted in the hot blood, but once removed, it "froze" again. This, perhaps, is the key to these perennially puzzling lines, since the spring thaw is also notorious for successions of meltings and freezings–frost's grip and water's rope. And the same God who watches over this see-sawing process has also watched over Beowulf, even when the sword melted on him. Thus, the supernatural powers of the monsters are, indeed, false gods, while this one is "the true God."

Does this explication account for the simile–or only for its details, while sapping it of its freshness and force? Can you arrive at a different explanation or approach? Many are possible.

The Epic Hero and His "Rites of Passage."

The translator of the *Beowulf* selection, Michael Alexander, argues that Beowulf is a true epic because it shares with other epics four essential qualities: 1. Inclusiveness of scope 2. Objectivity of treatment 3. Unity of consciousness 4. Significance of action.

It is inclusive because it explains the whole cosmos. It is objective in that it is fair in its reporting, even to an important extent where the monsters are concerned. It has unity in that it reflects how a whole culture–that of England in the sixth or seventh century–regarded life. Its action has significance in that the battles reflect the ongoing human struggle between good and evil.

The epic hero is also a figure with certain predictable qualities, all of which Beowulf reflects. Some of these are discussed in the introduction. Modern anthropology also suggests that all heroes can be seen as going through the same series of tests or "rites of passage." On most lists of such tests are those things which most people have rituals for–the vital moments marking an important stage in life: birth, initiation, marriage, kingship, and death. It is possible to see Beowulf's

three battles in this light. The first would be his initiation into manhood (even though he has fought and killed other monsters before this). The second, that follows immediately, would be the first test of his manhood, preparing him for kingship (which follows when he gets home). The last would be death as a rite of passage, which the king makes to redeem his people from guilt or destruction. If this has any validity, the last rite must be seen as extremely paradoxical in that following Beowulf's death, his people, the Geats, experience what amounts to complete genocide, including a total loss of their language, history, customs, and homeland. Except for this English poem, we would not even know they existed. Allegorical interpretations of Beowulf abound, all more or less in disfavor now. Perhaps you will see other ways of looking at this blood-and-thunder, dragon-slaying adventure tale. No one interpretation can account for it completely; that is one of the reasons for its inexhaustible fascination for us.

COMPOSITION

Kennings are now out of fashion in modern poetry. But it's fun to make up some. What you do is take an ordinary everyday object and make a many-hyphenated cluster of adjectives and nouns that stand for it without naming it directly. For example:

My quiet-humming highway-glider (of a car)
The string-and-synthesizer amped-up sound-bangers (of a rock group)
A muscle-lifted lightning-mover (of a leaping dancer)
Our book-bound fact-frying brain factory (of a school)

Actually, American Indian tribal poetry often has phrases that are startlingly like the kennings of Old English. Try making up some of your own. The idea is to heap on the words that really express the activity or thing or person without being too obvious at first glance. The kenning will then become funny or witty or moving once the reader or listener connects it with what it describes.

COMPOSITION WORKSHOP

THE RESEARCH PAPER

The research paper requires that you become acquainted with a subject that you know little about and asks you to report your findings in a fixed and precise way. Research papers require time and effort but the personal rewards you will reap are great: you will become something of a minor expert on the subject you have chosen.

There are two types of research paper —the *expository* type and the *argumentative* type. The expository research paper seeks only to provide the reader with information. An example would be a paper detailing the increasingly visible role of women in American politics. The argumentative research paper, on the other hand, attempts to arrive at a conclusion based on the facts revealed. An example of this type would be a paper that asserts, or "argues," that the quality of life in the United States has improved since more women have come to assume high political office.

Regardless of which type of research paper you intend to write, you will want to follow a systematic step-by-step plan that begins with selecting a topic and gathering information (the so-called "raw data") and ends with the writing of a final draft. Such a plan is outlined in the Composition Workshop sections of *English Literature: A Chronological Approach.*

GETTING STARTED

Your first consideration ought to be selecting a topic that interests you. Is there some subject you have been meaning to explore but have never found the time to read up on, such as the occult or the Black experience in this and other countries? If so, this may be you big chance. Just be sure that the topic you choose can be investigated in more than one source.

Be aware also that some topics take more time than others to develop fully. In most cases, you will have from four to eight weeks to gather information for the report and to prepare its various drafts. Common sense should tell you that certain topics are therefore too broad for such a limited

time span. If you had two years of preparation time, it is conceivable that you could develop a topic as broad as "The Middle Ages in England." But with only a month or two of preparation time available, you would be far better off with a narrower topic, such as "The Wandering Minstrel in Medieval England."

A third point to keep in mind is that potential topics are all around us. They are implied in almost everything our experience touches, and, hence, no "lead" should be ruled out. If you are interested in reporting on some facet of modern medicine, try to arrange to speak briefly with your family doctor.

Remember, finally, that a research paper is the end-product of a search for the truth. Experts sometimes disagree on various points, and you will find yourself having to weigh one view against another. Above all, you will have to approach your subject with an open mind and report your findings as accurately as possible, no matter how disquieting or contrary to your expectations they may prove to be.

ASSIGNMENT

Since this is a literature course, your teacher may wish to limit the range of your selection to literary topics. A logical starting point for ideas, then, would be this book. Perhaps your reading from Bede's *The Ecclesiastical History of the English People* and of the introductory materials that accompany it have caused you to wonder about the role of the Church in the daily lives of the people. Possibly your reading of the sections of *Beowulf* have aroused your curiosity about monsters and dragons in the Middle Ages.

As you read and study the units that follow this one, keep an eye out for topics that engage your interest or curiosity. Keep a list of them in a notebook and try to add to it often. When you have accumulated a half dozen topics, submit a list of them to your teacher, underlining those topics which you feel hold the most promise.

This courting scene is from one of the "Devonshire Hunt" tapestries, which date from the 1430s.

COURTING SCENE from FALCONRY
Victoria and Albert Museum

Medieval Literature

THE NORMAN CONQUEST

For people who have gone to school in English-speaking countries, the date 1066 is almost as familiar as 1492. The whole period of English language and literature that we call Medieval, or Middle, English, a span of four and a quarter centuries, lies between the Battle of Hastings and the discovery of America. Our selections come only from the last hundred years of this span, but there's a recent revival of interest in the whole period, and it would be wrong to assume that only in its last hundred years did memorable writing occur. In fact, some of the lyrics and ballads presented here may have existed for quite a long time before they first attained written form and became popular in the 1400s.

What exactly happened in 1066? The date itself, of course, pertains to the Norman Conquest of England, led by the Duke of Normandy, who became the first English Norman king, William I, called the Conqueror. His small tactical invading host met the massed forces of the last Saxon king, Harold, on Senlac Hill just outside the Sussex port village of Hastings on the morning of October 14, 1066. The English had just won a brilliant and decisive victory against a large-scale Danish invasion in the north of England but were exhausted by their break-neck rush southwards to stem this second invasion. William was badly outnumbered, but before the day was over, Harold, the English king, lay dead among a mass of dead and dying English, and William's army, with far fewer casualties, had clearly won a great victory. *William the Conqueror*

Harold

Who were these Normans? "Norman" means "northman," indicating that these people were another branch of those Scandinavian peoples whose attacks on Europe and Britain can be arbitrarily dated as "beginning" in 787—to continue unchecked for centuries. Often they plundered and raided; sometimes they settled. Collectively, whether as Danes, Vikings, Swedes, or Normans, they controlled the entire northern regions of the world, reaching in one direction past Iceland and Greenland to America itself and in the other direction penetrating to the heart of the vast Asian steppes where they founded Russia and traded briskly with Constantinople and merchants of the silk route from China. Among all the Scandinavians, the Normans were particu- *The Normans*

Sir Goeffrey Luttrell attended by his wife and daughter-in-law. Note the splendor of the feudal lord dressed for battle.

Luttrell Psalter, English,
East Anglian, c. 1340
The British Library, London

larly aggressive. They bit off southern Italy and Sicily to found the Norman Kingdom of Sicily (or "the Two Sicilies"). At one time they contended for control of the Latin Kingdom of Jerusalem during Crusading times.

In 911, William's ancestor had acquired Normandy from the French. The Normans who settled there learned a kind of French and pledged lip-service fealty to the weak or decrepit French monarchy, but at the same time intermarried with Alfred's royal line in England.

Edward the Confessor
Harold's predecessor, Edward the Confessor, was a reflection of this intermingling: he was a Francophile who had already introduced French at his English court. Technically, William could argue that he had a right to the English throne. When Edward died earlier in 1066, William made his bid for power.

LIFE AND LANGUAGE AFTER HASTINGS

The Majority of People
For 90 percent of the people living in England there was no change at all after Hastings, except a change in masters. Most of those people were serfs, who might even have been unaware that anything particularly happened on October 14. A smaller group consisted of monastic clusters of monks or nuns. When left undisturbed, they continued their scriptural work, turning out an unbroken succession of Latin writings still without peer in the rest of Europe, even though Bede's golden age

The Great Hall, Penhurst Place, Kent. The 60-foot high roof of chestnut beams was begun in 1339 and added to a century later. Philip Sidney (page 190) was born here.

Photo: A.F. Kersting

was long since past. Unlike the Danes before him, William burnt no libraries and sacked no centers of learning.

The Nobility

For the remaining 10 percent of the English, the change was indeed significant. These were the English nobility, whom William evicted from their lands and castles and completely replaced with his own handpicked Norman nobility. Norman French became the official court tongue spoken by William's exclusive and elite nobility. But Latin remained the spoken and written language of the church, and English remained the spoken language of most of the people. Written English also continued to be produced, including some early medieval masterpieces that show almost no influence of the Norman French used in court.

Influx of French Words

The great influx of French words into English did not occur until much later, when King John (of Magna Carta fame) lost most of his continental lands, including Normandy, in a battle with the French king in 1204. Following this, English began to be spoken even by those who had used Norman French exclusively before, thus explaining why, only after this date and not before, so many French words entered the language.

Normans "Anglified"

But if the Normans, by chance, altered English for the better, they themselves lost their separate identity as they were absorbed and "anglified," just as earlier invading forces had been assimilated and "britannified" whenever they settled on the island rather than merely plundering it. William and his followers found England a promising and progressive nation with advanced governmental structures, which William preserved and improved upon with his typical Norman flair for administrative detail. An example of this was the Domesday Book of 1086, the first census ever taken in any thorough way, at least in medieval Europe. Of course, the purpose was to permit him to tax the English more efficiently, since the Normans were there for profit, not out of loyalty to the country or its people. But because of this census, they also administered the tax more fairly. And the country prospered.

THE TWELFTH-CENTURY "RENAISSANCE"

The Arthurian Legends

One sign of the increasing prosperity of England was its participation in what is now known to historians as the "Little Twelfth-Century Renaissance." Though the actual Renaissance of Michelangelo and Shakespeare did not begin until the fifteenth century, this early period of vibrant intellectual activity was more than just a "false dawn." Europe's first university (Bologna, late eleventh century) set an example for the later founding of the universities of Paris and Oxford, which became centers of the "little renaissance." There were two other major developments during the twelfth century. Writing in Latin,

Medieval craftsmen at work. The twelfth and thirteenth centuries were the great ages of cathedral building in England and Europe.

from The Book of St. Albans
illustrated by Matthew Paris (1200–1259)
The Board of Trinity College, Dublin

Geoffrey of Monmouth, a Welsh clergyman educated at Oxford, became the first writer to set down the legend of King Arthur in a form that made it available to all of Europe. This material, the subject of Arthurian romance, seized the imagination of writers in every language and became extremely popular in song and story with audiences of every description. Geoffrey was steeped in Welsh and Breton oral remnants of the historical Arthur's story, combining these freely with material drawn from Bede, other Latin writings, and his own imagination. Geoffrey's version was considerably augmented by later writers and by the waxing and waning of fads and fashions concerning specific characters and themes in the whole living body of Arthurian legend. A writer named Wace paraphrased Geoffrey's material in Norman-French poetry, and Layamon translated and further augmented Wace's version in English verse.

Geoffrey of Monmouth

Wace and Layamon

The embroidered Arthurian saga, however, first developed its widest influence in French audiences both on the continent and in the Norman court. It only stands to reason that neither Angles nor Saxons in their own literature would wish to celebrate Arthur, their last and mightiest Celtic enemy; in fact, they *continued* fighting Celts into the eleventh century—in Cornwall, in Wales, in Scotland. With the Normans, Arthur presented no difficulty as a subject; on the contrary, they *also* had defeated the English, as Arthur had, though their conquest was permanent, not a temporary "twilight" as Arthur's had been. This seemingly small difference in detail, however, gives to Arthurian romance at the outset its dimension of tragic heroism, one that triumphs over insurmountable odds—but only for a suspended timeless moment in which "there once was Camelot."

Tragic Heroism

This new tragic temperament is fundamentally different from the stoic acceptance of death in Old English, even given its tragic overtones in "The Wanderer" and *Beowulf*. By the time Arthurian legend had made its way back into English—principally with Sir Thomas Malory's masterpiece, *Le Morte Darthur*—it was developing side by side with the beginning of English drama as represented here by the Wakefield Master (page 136). In the next period, English drama would exploit this tragic temperament in the work of Marlowe and Shakespeare, a temperament quite different from the classic Greek tragedy of ancient times, but one that would coalesce in a definitive vision of the human predicament that is still a significant facet of how we see the world today.

Sir Thomas Malory

Wakefield Master

Effigy of Sir Thomas Ardeone and his wife Matilda at St. Peter's Church, Elford, Staffordshire.

Photo: the late F.H. Crossley
Carron M.H. Ridgway
Conway Library
Courtauld Institute of Art

Durham Cathedral combines Gothic splendor and Norman solidarity.
The first church, built in 995, was later replaced by the cathedral. In
1020 the church became the final burial place of Venerable Bede.

Photo: J. Bethell Photography
St. Albans

The strength and beauty of Norman and Gothic architecture still combine in the ruins of the Castle Acre Priory Church in Norfolk. The lower arches date from 1090; the upper arches were added in the fifteenth century.

J. Bethell Photography

The Romance and Courtly Love

Chivalry

The second important occurrence in the little twelfth-century renaissance was the rise of "courtly love," or chivalry. This doctrine immediately attached itself to Arthurian romance, making it (until the coming of Malory) a vehicle for the dissemination of this attitude throughout medieval society. We can still feel its force in the way we commonly use the word "romance"—not to describe a tale of heroic adventure, but to refer to a love affair. Until the introduction of the concept of courtly love by Eleanor of Aquitaine, women were primarily classifiable as human property which could be made use of by men at will—for pleasure, for their unpaid labor, for begetting male heirs, and for sealing peace treaties (as in *Beowulf*) by exchanging them in marriage with former enemies.

Eleanor of Aquitaine

While a woman "owned" in any of these ways by a powerful man was safe from other men, she had no say in most of these matters, and the idea of her being valued as a specific person didn't often occur to anyone (except a few poets, like the anonymous Old English writer of "The Wife's Lament"). Eleanor (twice married herself for her property, first by the French king, then by the English king) and her daughter, Marie of Champagne, wrote a book called *The Art of Courtly Love,* using Andreas Capellanus (Andrew the chaplain) as their mouthpiece. He later disowned the book, but the ideas in it swept like wildfire throughout Europe and were immediately embodied in the most popular stories of that time, Arthurian legends. The code of courtly love concedes that marriage is mostly a matter of political negotiations between men and thus extremely unlikely to involve "love," a word that

The Art of Courtly Love

Cottages dating from the Middle Ages,
Lavenham, Suffolk.

Photo: Brian Boyd, British Tourist Authority

for the first time in the twelfth century took on meanings we take for granted now. Consequently, Eleanor said, women had a right to love and be loved by any respectful man under the strict rules and regulations she and her daughter laid down. These did not include adultery, but short of that, there was a way to go about solving almost any other difficulty that lay in the path of true love.

The traveling singers called troubadours, a significant proportion of whom were women poets, took up these themes with gusto. Thus a separate story, the tragic tale of Tristan and Iseult, was hauled into the mainstream of Arthurian romance, though it did not belong there to begin with. Eleanor, it should be pointed out, was a serious reformer and astute political strategist who at one point challenged her English husband, Henry II, in a rebellion aimed at seizing the crown from him. England, unlike France, had no bar to the direct and sole rule by a female sovereign—and already had seen several. Eleanor lost her battle and was imprisoned for sixteen years, but survived to rule England in place of her much-absent son, King Richard I, the Lion-Hearted, and later smoothed the way to the throne for another son, ill-famed King John. Full-scale studies now are emphasizing how important she was as a historical influence upon both French and English literature.

Troubadours

Henry II

Richard, the Lion-Hearted

A PLAGUE AND TWO WARS

The twelfth-century renaissance was prevented from blossoming by the single greatest catastrophe that ever occurred in the history of Europe: the Great Plague of 1348. In two years the plague swept across

The Great Plague

both the continent and Britain, leaving in its wake one third to one half of all the people dead. Whole villages and towns were deserted. No one was unaffected. Literature and learning suffered a century-long setback. The full-blown Renaissance of the fifteenth century could occur only after Europe had recovered from what must have felt to them much as a nuclear holocaust would feel to us now.

Later, in the lives of Chaucer, Malory, and the Wakefield Master, two long-term situations remained chronically unresolved and prevented England from regaining the ground it had lost during the plague. First was the Hundred Years War in which England tried—and failed—to reclaim its French possessions. The war mostly preoccupied the nobility, but it kept them from such peaceful pursuits as patronizing poets and giving support to cultural development at home. Second, there was the War of the Roses (first given this title by Sir Walter Scott in the nineteenth century), which drew the attention of the nobility away from their failure in France to a seemingly interminable quarrel about the royal succession that resulted in a smoldering civil war in England. Chaucer was patronized by Richard II, the last Plantagenet before the bloody quarrel began. Malory, however, was directly involved—and switched to the wrong side at the wrong time, which partially explains why he spent much of his last twenty years of life unpardoned in jail where, after two swashbuckling escape attempts, he wrote his singular masterpiece, *Le Morte Darthur*.

Hundred Years War

War of the Roses

The Peasants

All during the medieval period, the peasants themselves had been gradually gaining in self-awareness, spurred by unsettled times. The Normans at first imposed a much stricter form of feudalism on the people than they had been used to under their Alfredian monarchs. Tied by fuedalism to the land, most of the people were impoverished serfs with few rights beyond the land-tie and fewer hopes for a brighter future. The Magna Carta of 1215 forced the King to grant the barons more privileges, and brought the formation of the first parliament in 1265. Still, the common folk pitched in; they furnished the labor and were sometimes the artistic focal point for the building of the great English Cathedrals—among them, Durham completed in 1133, Canterbury in 1175, Salisbury in 1258, York Minster (nave) in 1291. Popular ballads and lyrics, sung in the fields and the alehouses, were the literary creations of these restricted people.

The Magna Carta

Great Cathedrals

This tight control might have gone on even longer were it not for the plague. In reading "The Pardoner's Tale," included here, you will see how this catastrophe influenced Chaucer's treatment of a traditionally scary tale. The immediate result of the startling depopulation that occurred—a toll levied by death impartially on all classes alike—was a shortage of readily available manual labor, the traditional task of the serf. Because of this, people became increasingly aware that society could not run smoothly without their cooperation. In those times, political concerns were often expressed in religious terms. Thus the

An illuminated manuscript showing knights at dinner in the "great hall," from the Bodleian Library, Oxford.

Lollard movement began its long underground life as a radical religious doctrine, founded by John Wyclif, to surface only in the Puritan revolution of the seventeenth century. More immediately, a number of disruptive peasant revolts occurred, the most famous being those led by Wat Tyler in 1381 and by Jack Cade in 1450. These revolts were always put down swiftly and brutally, but they frightened the nobility and, with the growth of towns and cities, a certain relaxation of attitudes toward the common folk became necessary. This is strikingly evident in Chaucer where the concerns of the people are given as much importance as those of the ruling classes. They were especially a sympathetic source for Chaucer's own rich vein of bawdy and irreverent earthiness which coexisted paradoxically alongside his gifts as a master of psychological portraiture. His "verse novel" *Troilus and Criseyde,* for example, has psychological subtleties that Victorian novelists like George Eliot (page 643) and Henry James (page 886) might have envied.

John Wyclif

Wat Tyler and Jack Cade

MIDDLE ENGLISH LITERATURE: THE LAST HUNDRED YEARS

Drama, the Art of the People

Cycles of Plays

More directly, popular art—the art of the people—found expression in cycles of plays performed annually on Corpus Christi day (late May or early June) in England's farming towns, mostly in the north and the midlands. These plays began as part of the church service celebrating and retelling the Christian story, but they soon moved out of the church proper and became richly interwoven with the daily concerns of the people. They were as often focused on the common life of their own time as on the familiar religious stories that still framed them. A typical cycle was made up of short plays with only a few characters, each taking about a half hour to act, each based on a different element of the Christian story, from the creation of the world, through Christ's birth, his crucifixion, his resurrection, and concluding with the Last Judgment. Each play was put on by a different guild in the town, often written by its brightest member; guilds were a rudimentary form of trade union that was part of the general arousal of populist consciousness. Each play was mounted on a big, enclosed rectangular box on wheels—a vehicle called a "pageant." This pageant, with curtains or doors that opened on one of its long sides, took its place in the sequence of other plays in the cycle, visiting one town square after another, always in succession, so that anyone sitting in one square for much of the day could see the whole story performed, or they could move on and see favorite plays or players again and again throughout the long festival day of Corpus Christi. The Wakefield Master, who wrote *The Second Shepherds' Play,* included here in its entirety, is the first English dramatist who comes down to us as a distinct personality standing behind a body of dramatic work, even though his name remains unknown. The writer is, at any rate, a genuine embodiment of all these developments in the consciousness of the people, including the deadpan mixture of secular mischief and comedy with religious high seriousness.

The Guilds

"Pageants"

The Second Shepherd's Play

Chaucer

The Canterbury Tales

The master of variety is Geoffrey Chaucer (page 82), who produced a work that both defines and reflects the medieval world. In *The Canterbury Tales,* Chaucer gives us the two dominant forces of his world and his literature: the sacred and the secular. It is surely no accident that the pilgrims are journeying to Canterbury, to the shrine of the martyred St. Thomas à Becket; their journey is thus, at least superficially, spiritual in nature. And it is equally important that the pilgrims reflect a wide span of society with members from the nobility, the religious orders, and the working classes (here ranging from upper-middle to definitely lower class). Similarly, the tales told by the pilgrims

A medieval tithe barn in Abbotsbury, Dorset. The word tithe *means a* tenth part. *A tenth part of the produce of a piece of land was paid annually to support the Church. Tithes were stored in such barns.*

Photo: Adam Woolfitt
British Tourist Agency

form almost an encyclopedia of Middle English literature: verse romances, saints' lives, bawdy stories, sermons, historical tragedies, satires—and a running narrative that creates the story of the tellers as well as the tales themselves.

Encyclopedia of Middle English Literature

The Canterbury Tales also display the characteristic medieval approach to realistic detail. Chaucer seems to delight in such detail for its own sake, telling us what the pilgrims were wearing and whether there was a wart on someone's nose. But the details also function symbolically, in that they reveal internal qualities. We saw a similar use of external detail in Old English descriptions of weather, but medieval literature carries the double value of such realistic description even further. Anything, and everything, may be said to be both real and symbolic, demonstrating both what we can see and what we cannot.

Realistic Detail

Symbolic Detail

Malory

Sir Thomas Malory (page 124) was a different kind of embodiment of the Middle English sensibility. A robust personality in a waning age, he seems misplaced in time. He switched loyalties during the War of the Roses to the House of Lancaster just when the tide had turned toward the House of York. Though of a lower class than Chaucer, he combines some of Chaucer's universality of taste with some of the populist qualities in the Wakefield Master. Malory's long imprisonment after

A Robust Personality

Le Morte Darthur   the war resulted in his one work, *Le Morte Darthur.* Cobbling together a multitude of French and English sources, he condenses whole, long-winded sidetracks into a single sentence, brings together other widely separated elements, and makes them cohere. In short, his rearrangement and virtual reinvention of the whole body of Arthurian legend in accordance with his own personal taste put a definitive stamp on this material. It is to Malory that all later versions are ultimately indebted,

Camelot   including the musical *Camelot.*

Times had changed since Eleanor of Aquitaine. Malory reflects this by treating the aspect of courtly love with less reverence and more occasional skepticism. He also tends to emphasize the element of sheer action in his yarns. But he can call up a genuine eloquence sufficient to embody the tragic flaw in the glorious Arthurian twilight—an expression (some think) of his nostalgia for a less unsettled world before the House of Plantagenet was sundered into the Houses of York and Lancaster.

THE VIEW FROM STRATFORD

Continuity   Despite every devastation and disruption during the Middle Ages, a remarkable continuity becomes apparent, stretching from Bede's time to Malory's—and beyond. For example, a midlands boy growing up in Stratford in the sixteenth century would have had plenty of chances to imbibe the midlands' penchant for public entertainments. Stratford was well known for its fairs to which players, acrobats, jugglers, and minstrels swarmed. And touring companies of actors could hardly fill Stratford's demand for drama—they came increasingly, more each year, bringing plays not far removed from the Wakefield Master in subject or approach. In *The Repentance of Mary Magdalene,* for example, a comedy character called Vice had ample scope for tomfoolery before being punished at the play's close. Also available in prosperous towns like Stratford would have been Malory's book, widely distributed in

William Caxton   successive editions following the one by William Caxton, England's first printer. Consider how broad a range of feeling and experience already existed in the writing this midlands boy would have access to. And when he arrived in London of the 1580s or early 1590s, he was already forming in his own mind a version of this amalgam of courtly love, tragic vision, and earthiness that we now call Shakespearian. How could this writer, intent mainly on achieving a huge popular success and with no thought of preserving the plays which earned him that success—how could such a writer, combining coarseness and elegance like some impossible elixir of oil and water, come to be thought of in time by so many as the greatest writer who ever lived? This unit not only offers us a literature great in its own right, but also promises to give us more than a few clues to answering such a question.

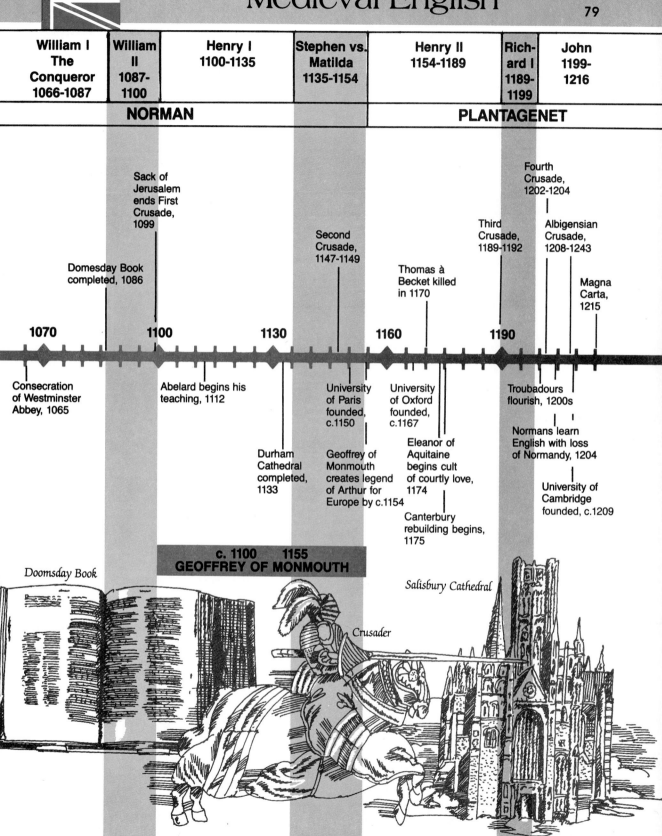

William I The Conqueror 1066-1087	William II 1087-1100	Henry I 1100-1135	Stephen vs. Matilda 1135-1154	Henry II 1154-1189	Richard I 1189-1199	John 1199-1216
NORMAN				**PLANTAGENET**		

Sack of Jerusalem ends First Crusade, 1099

Domesday Book completed, 1086

Second Crusade, 1147-1149

Thomas à Becket killed in 1170

Third Crusade, 1189-1192

Fourth Crusade, 1202-1204

Albigensian Crusade, 1208-1243

Magna Carta, 1215

1070   **1100**   **1130**   **1160**   **1190**

Consecration of Westminster Abbey, 1065

Abelard begins his teaching, 1112

University of Paris founded, c.1150

University of Oxford founded, c.1167

Troubadours flourish, 1200s

Durham Cathedral completed, 1133

Geoffrey of Monmouth creates legend of Arthur for Europe by c.1154

Eleanor of Aquitaine begins cult of courtly love, 1174

Normans learn English with loss of Normandy, 1204

Canterbury rebuilding begins, 1175

University of Cambridge founded, c.1209

c. 1100   1155
GEOFFREY OF MONMOUTH

Doomsday Book

Crusader

Salisbury Cathedral

Medieval English

Henry III 1216-1272	Edward I 1272-1307	Edward II 1307-1327	Edward III 1327-1377

PLANTAGENET

Fifth Crusade, 1218-1221

Seventh Crusade, 1248-1254

St. Francis dies 1226

Expulsion of Jews from England, 1290

Jacques de Molay burned, 1314

Genghis Khan dies 1227

First Parliament, 1265

Marco Polo's last journey ends. 1295

Great Plague starts in Europe, 1348; one-third of all people die

Sixth Crusade, 1228-1229

Eighth Crusade, 1270-1271

1220 **1250** **1280** **1310** **1340**

Sonnet form invented in Sicily, c.1221

Salisbury Cathedral completed, 1258

Dante's *Divine Comedy* set in 1300

Petrarch crowned poet laureate by Roman senate, Easter 1341

Aquinas stops work on his *Summa,* 1273

Langland begins *Piers Plowman,* c. 1362

Ghenghis Khan

c. 1332 WILLIAM LANGLA

c. 1340

Alighieri

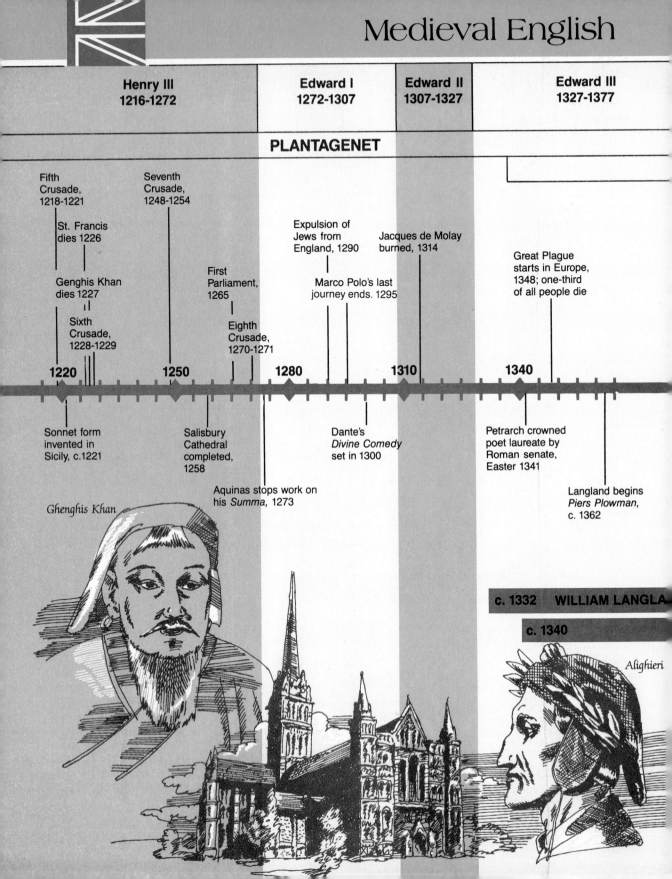

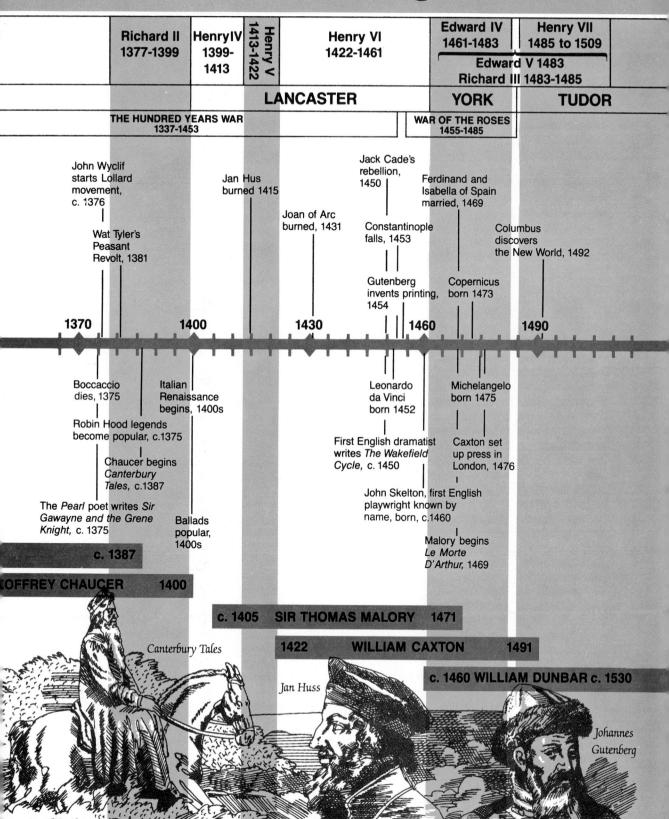

Richard II 1377-1399	Henry IV 1399-1413	Henry V 1413-1422	Henry VI 1422-1461	Edward IV 1461-1483	Henry VII 1485 to 1509
				Edward V 1483 Richard III 1483-1485	

LANCASTER — **YORK** — **TUDOR**

THE HUNDRED YEARS WAR 1337-1453

WAR OF THE ROSES 1455-1485

John Wyclif starts Lollard movement, c. 1376

Jan Hus burned 1415

Jack Cade's rebellion, 1450

Ferdinand and Isabella of Spain married, 1469

Wat Tyler's Peasant Revolt, 1381

Joan of Arc burned, 1431

Constantinople falls, 1453

Columbus discovers the New World, 1492

Gutenberg invents printing, 1454

Copernicus born 1473

1370   **1400**   **1430**   **1460**   **1490**

Boccaccio dies, 1375

Italian Renaissance begins, 1400s

Leonardo da Vinci born 1452

Michelangelo born 1475

Robin Hood legends become popular, c.1375

First English dramatist writes *The Wakefield Cycle,* c. 1450

Caxton set up press in London, 1476

Chaucer begins *Canterbury Tales,* c.1387

John Skelton, first English playwright known by name, born, c.1460

The *Pearl* poet writes *Sir Gawayne and the Grene Knight,* c. 1375

Ballads popular, 1400s

Malory begins *Le Morte D'Arthur,* 1469

c. 1387

OFFREY CHAUCER   1400

c. 1405   SIR THOMAS MALORY   1471

1422   WILLIAM CAXTON   1491

c. 1460 WILLIAM DUNBAR c. 1530

Canterbury Tales

Jan Huss

Johannes Gutenberg

Geoffrey Chaucer

1340?–1400

In the fourteenth century, Geoffrey Chaucer, the dominant literary figure in England, almost single-handedly brought to England the high literary culture of the early European renaissance. This man, said John Dryden, another famous English poet, was a "perpetual fountain of good sense . . . He must have been a man of a most wonderful comprehensive nature, because, as it has been truly observed of him, he has taken into the compass of his *Canterbury Tales* the various manners and humours (as we now call them) of the whole English nation, in his age. Not a single character escaped him. All his pilgrims are severally distinguished from each other. The matter and manner of their tales and of their telling are so suited to their different educations, humours and callings, that each of them would be improper in any other mouth. Even the grave and serious characters are distinguished by their several sorts of gravity . . . Some of his persons are vicious, and some virtuous, some are unlearned, or (as Chaucer calls them) lewd, and some are learned . . . 'Tis sufficient to say, according to the proverb, that here is God's plenty. We have our forefathers and great-granddames all before us, as they were in Chaucer's days: their general characters are still remaining in mankind, for mankind is ever the same, and nothing lost out of Nature, though everything is altered."

Geoffrey Chaucer was the son of a prominent bourgeois wine merchant, whose apparent success at his trade gave him contacts with the royal court. As was common in the Middle Ages, Chaucer's father placed the boy at about thirteen as a page in a great household, that of the Countess of Ulster. Here his tasks and training gave him an education in manners and provided him an opportunity to observe court life and society at first hand.

In 1360, Chaucer was captured in France during one of those endless campaigns that the English kings were then conducting. He was ransomed by King Edward III for about $1,200. Sometime during the period from 1360 to 1367,

Geoffrey Chaucer, The British Library, London

Chaucer joined the household of the king, and during those years he seems to have served the king as a trusted messenger and a minor diplomat.

From 1367 to 1386, the poet apparently prospered greatly. He was frequently sent to the continent "on the King's secret affairs." In 1372, he was sent to Genoa, Italy, to negotiate trade agreements, the first of several trips to Italy. On these, he undoubtedly became acquainted with the works of Boccaccio, Petrarch, and Dante, the three greatest Italian writers of the century preceding the Renaissance.

In 1374, Chaucer was made Controller of Customs and Subsidy on Wools, Skins and Hides for the Port of London. In this job, he had an opportunity to meet many different kinds of people: ship captains, business leaders,

A medieval walled city (labelled Constantinople) drawn as an English city with battlemented walls, church, shops, and houses.

Luttrell Psalter, English
East Anglian, c. 1340
The British Library, London

dockhands, sailors. In 1382, he also became Controller of Customs of Wines, a trade about which he must have learned a good deal from his father.

In 1386, Chaucer moved from his residence in Aldgate, London, to a new home in the County of Kent. He represented Kent in the Parliament of 1386. Early in the reign of young King Richard II, he was appointed clerk of the King's Works, where he was responsible for construction and repairs affecting royal residences, parks, walls, and bridges. Since he had to pay laborers before the Treasury paid him, he had to keep dunning the Treasury for funds already paid out of his own pocket. In 1390, he was twice robbed and once beaten up because he was known to carry large sums. After nearly two years of this, Chaucer must have requested and received a new job as deputy forester of one of the King's forests. During these years and probably till his death, Chaucer was continually in financial difficulties, but it is a tribute to his diplomacy that he kept in the good graces of three succeeding monarchs in a troublesome time. He died on October 25, 1400.

Of Chaucer's personal life we know little, except what he reveals in his poems. Presumably, he led the life of a family man. His wife, Phillipa, appears in one of his poems, *The House of Fame,* as a woman whose tone of voice and manner in walking the poet compares

unfavorably with that of an eagle. Chaucer also pictures himself in his poems as a round, jolly man, innocent but eager to learn. He once described what must have been his routine after balancing his customs accounts:

> For when your labor all is done
> And your accounts are all set true
> In place of rest or something new
> Home to your house you go alone
> And just as dumb as any stone
> You sit to read another book
> Until you wear that glassy look,
> And thus live a hermit's life
> Although your abstinence is slight.

Chaucer wrote many poems, but the two works for which he holds his place as one of the wisest and most broadly talented of English poets are *The Canterbury Tales* (of which two parts are reprinted here: the "Prologue" and part of the "Pardoner's Tale") and *Troilus and Criseyde,* one of the finest long narrative love poems in the English language.

Chaucer's life helps us to explain some of the qualities of his work. His strong, practical bent of mind is not surprising in a man whose business experience required him to be talented at detecting smugglers. His naïve innocence, which is the character he gives himself in his poems, is obviously a literary pose, a mask he uses to allow his readers to make their own evaluations of the people and situations he presents. This mask may also have been the protective disguise of the diplomat and the poet who had to live and deal with arrogant kings, shrewd merchants, and sophisticated diplomats. His knowledge and insight into the characters of many different kinds of people were essential qualities for those who would succeed in the world of business, diplomacy, and, for that matter, any world.

The values of studying Chaucer's poetry are the values of studying humankind. The English poet Blake summed up his favorite poet: "Chaucer's characters live age after age. Every age is a Canterbury Pilgrimage; we all pass on, each sustaining one of these characters, nor can a child be born, who is not one of these characters of Chaucer."

CHAUCER'S LANGUAGE

Nations and languages, like people, have moments of creative power, when they declare their genius. Geoffrey Chaucer was lucky enough to have lived at such a moment in the history of England. The Norman Conquest of 1066 was long past, and the English people had developed a language and a culture that combined much of what was best in their Anglo-Saxon ancestors and their Norman rulers. By 1340, which is approximately the year of Chaucer's birth, the English language had become a tongue which derived its strength from a Germanic grammar and its grace from the sweet-sounding and wide-ranging words it borrowed from French. The English language had become a rich and musical tongue for a poet who had to read poetry aloud.

Chaucer's poetry was fresh and lively and close to the spoken language of his time. Chaucer wrote in the dialect of the city of London, and his popularity was, in fact, one of the reasons that this dialect became the ancestor of modern standard British English (and thus of modern standard American English). Dryden, who had lost the secret of reading Chaucer's English, once said he had the "rude sweetness of a Scotch tune." Actually his language and his rhythm are quite smooth, once one knows the secret of reading Middle English (English of the period 1066–1500).

In the poetry below, you can examine the opening lines of the "Prologue" in the original Middle English. Though it looks like a foreign language, its proper pronunciation sounds like a more familiar, but quaint and primitive, version of English, which it is. The best way to learn to speak Chaucer's English with accuracy is to hear and imitate an experienced reader of Middle English. For this your class may wish to listen to the passages from *The Canterbury Tales* read in Middle English recorded on one of the fine recordings available.

Here are the first eighteen lines of the "Prologue" to *The Canterbury Tales* in Chaucer's English. Compare them with the translation on page 87.

Whan that Aprille with his shoures soote
The droghte of Marche hath percéd to the
    roote,
And bathed every veyne in swich licour,
Of which vertu engendred is the flour;
Whan Zephirus eek with his swete breeth
Inspiréd hath in every holt and heeth
The tendre croppes, and the yonge sonne
Hath in the Ram his halfe cours y-ronne,
And smale fowles maken melodye,
That slepen al the night with open yë,
(So priketh hem nature in hir corages),
Than longen folk to goon on pilgrimages
(And palmers for to seken straunge strondes)
To ferne halwes, couthe in sondry londes;
And specially, from every shires ende
Of Engelond, to Caunterbury they wende,
The holy blisful martir for to seke,
That hem hath holpen, whan that they were
    seke.

THE PROLOGUE

When Chaucer set out to write what is now his most famous work, *The Canterbury Tales,* he wished to present a dramatic sequence of stories in prose and verse. He conceived of a group of travelers on a pilgrimage. To pass the time, each of his pilgrims was to tell two tales going to and two tales coming back from the shrine of Thomas à Becket at Canterbury. While he never even completed this framework with more than one tale for each of his pilgrims, he left a sufficient fragment to give us a good idea of his

John Lydgate, monk of Bury St. Edmonds, leaving Canterbury with the Canterbury Pilgrims. A 16th century Flemish miniature from his book Troy Book & Story of Thebes.

talents and to assure himself of a permanent place in English literature.

Chaucer's device of framing his tales within a pilgrimage gives him opportunity for dramatic action and for the development of character through the portraits of the pilgrims in the "Prologue" as well as through the story which each pilgrim chooses to tell.

The "General Prologue" which introduces *The Canterbury Tales* is a portrait gallery of English society from the lowest class up to the Knight. Only royalty—the top of the social ladder—is omitted. Unlike a modern playwright, who merely lists a cast of characters, Chaucer introduces them to us in detail. As you read the prologue, note the ways Chaucer has varied his

portraits, arranging them in ways that suggest contrasts. Some move from top to toe, some highlight the character's past experience, some point out their most characteristic habits and actions. He enlivens and complicates our reaction to each character by including his own apparently simple-minded evaluations of each one.

While most of the characters are types, Chaucer gives them an appearance of hard reality by recording them in detail: their clothing, their features, their scruples, their opinions, their characters. This seemingly infinite series of details is actually a tight-knit pattern that sums up a human personality. In order to read the prologue well, you must weigh the

A woodcut from Caxton's second edition of The Canterbury Tales
(1484) showing the pilgrims at supper at the Tabard Inn.

The British Library, London

meaning of every detail and assess the combined effect of all details.

Perhaps the most important character in the prologue is the poet himself, who in the court of medieval England used to read his poems aloud. In the prologue, Chaucer gives a parody of himself. The character, Chaucer, is a plump, bumbling man, eager to please, and generally uncritical. This fictional substitute has a fatal overconfidence in his own ability to see things as they are. Thus, Chaucer the poet often uses Chaucer the guide to put over a joke on the reader. It is his way of asking the reader to look behind appearances. He tells us: Don't accept the world at face value, and don't accept the judgment of others; *evaluate everything for yourself.*

No wonder Chaucer was such a successful diplomat: He has given us his vision of reality, of the world around us, and he has made us think it is our own.

In the Middle Ages, pilgrimages were a popular form of entertainment and devotion—a combined religious and social outing. Every spring, as the roads of England became passable once more, pilgrims descended in throngs upon the shrine of England's famous Archbishop and martyr, Thomas à Becket. As we meet the Canterbury pilgrims, there are some thirty or so gathered one evening in the Tabard Inn, run by a genial host, Harry Bailly, in Southwark (su′thèrk) in the suburbs of London. They are preparing for their journey on horseback next morning to the shrine of St. Thomas, some 55 miles to the southeast. After Thomas à Becket was brutally murdered by the followers of King Henry II in 1170, his blood, preserved in vials, was thought to work miracles in healing the sick, thus making his shrine a popular one from the fourteenth century to our own day. T. S. Eliot wrote his famous verse play *Murder in the Cathedral* (1935) to commemorate the Archbishop's martyrdom.

THE CANTERBURY TALES
Translated by Neville Coghill

Prologue

When in April the sweet showers fall
And pierce the drought of March to the
    root, and all
The veins are bathed in liquor of such
    power
As brings about the engendering of the
    flower,
When also Zephyrus[1] with his sweet breath   5
Exhales an air in every grove and heath
Upon the tender shoots, and the young
    sun
His half-course in the sign of the *Ram*[2]
    has run,
And the small fowl are making melody
That sleep away the night with open eye   10
(So nature pricks them and their heart
    engages)
Then people long to go on pilgrimages
And palmers[3] long to seek the stranger
    strands
Of far-off saints, hallowed in sundry lands,
And specially, from every shire's end   15
In England, down to Canterbury they
    wend
To seek the holy blissful martyr, quick
To give his help to them when they were
    sick.
    It happened in that season that one day
In Southwark, at *The Tabard,* as I lay   20
Ready to go on pilgrimage and start
For Canterbury, most devout at heart,
At night there came into that hostelry[4]
Some nine and twenty in a company
Of sundry folk happening then to fall   25

In fellowship, and they were pilgrims all
That towards Canterbury meant to ride.
The rooms and stables of the inn were
    wide;
They made us easy, all was of the best.
And, briefly, when the sun had gone to
    rest,   30
I'd spoken to them all upon the trip
And was soon one with them in fellowship,
Pledged to rise early and to take the way
To Canterbury, as you heard me say.
    But none the less, while I have time
    and space,   35
Before my story takes a further pace,
It seems a reasonable thing to say
What their condition was, the full array
Of each of them, as it appeared to me
According to profession and degree,   40
And what apparel they were riding in;
And at a Knight I therefore will begin.

The Knight

There was a *Knight,* a most distinguished
    man,
Who from the day on which he first began
To ride abroad had followed chivalry,   45
Truth, honour, generousness and cour-
    tesy.
He had done nobly in his sovereign's war
And ridden into battle, no man more,
As well in Christian as in heathen places,
And ever honoured for his noble graces.   50

1. **Zephyrus** (zef′ ər əs), the west wind.
2. **the Ram,** a zodiac sign often called Aries. During April the sun passes through the first part of this constellation.
3. **palmers,** travelers bearing crossed palm leaves to proclaim their religious pilgrimages.
4. **hostelry** (hos′ təl rē), inn. The Tabard Inn existed in Chaucer's time. The inn sign was a tabard, or knight's tunic, with emblazoned arms.

From Chaucer: THE CANTERBURY TALES, trans. Nevill Coghill (Penguin Classics, Revised edition 1977) pp. 19-42, 262-276. Copyright 1951 by Nevill Coghill; Copyright © Nevill Coghill, 1958, 1960, 1975, 1977. Reprinted by permission of Penguin Books Ltd.

When we took Alexandria,[5] he was
    there.
He often sat at table in the chair
Of honour, above all nations, when in
    Prussia.
In Lithuania he had ridden, and Russia,
No Christian man so often, of his rank.[6]   55
When, in Granada, Algeciras sank
Under assault, he had been there, and in
North Africa, raiding Benamarin;
In Anatolia he had been as well
And fought when Ayas and Attalia fell,[7]   60
For all along the Mediterranean coast
He had embarked with many a noble host.
In fifteen mortal battles he had been
And jousted for our faith at Tramissene[8]
Thrice in the lists, and always killed his
    man.   65
This same distinguished knight had led
    the van
Once with the Bey of Balat,[9] doing work
For him against another heathen Turk;
He was of sovereign value in all eyes.
And though so much distinguished, he
    was wise   70
And in his bearing modest as a maid.
He never yet a boorish thing had said
In all his life to any, come what might;
He was a true, a perfect gentle-knight.[10]

Speaking of his equipment, he pos-
    sessed   75
Fine horses, but he was not gaily dressed.
He wore a fustian tunic[11] stained and dark
With smudges where his armour had left
    mark;
Just home from service, he had joined
    our ranks
To do his pilgrimage and render thanks.   80

The Squire

He had his son with him, a fine young
    Squire,
A lover and cadet, a lad of fire
With locks as curly as if they had been
    pressed.
He was some twenty years of age, I guessed.

In stature he was of a moderate length,   85
With wonderful agility and strength.
He'd seen some service with the cavalry
In Flanders and Artois and Picardy[12]
And had done valiantly in little space
Of time, in hope to win his lady's grace.   90
He was embroidered like a meadow bright
And full of freshest flowers, red and white.
Singing he was, or fluting all the day;
He was as fresh as is the month of May.
Short was his gown, the sleeves were long
    and wide;   95
He knew the way to sit a horse and ride.
He could make songs and poems and re-
    cite,
Knew how to joust and dance, to draw
    and write.
He loved so hotly that till dawn grew pale
He slept as little as a nightingale.   100
Courteous he was, lowly and serviceable,
And carved to serve his father at the table.

The Yeoman

There was a *Yeoman*[13] with him at his
    side,
No other servant; so he chose to ride.

---

5. **Alexandria** in Egypt was captured by Christian forces in 1365.

6. Chaucer's knight had taken part in many "religious" wars—perhaps too many to be actual fact. Teutonic knights fought Slavic forces in the Baltic areas, Prussia and Lithuania, and in Russia.

7. **Algeciras** (äl′ jə sēr′ räs) was captured from the Moors in **Granada** (grə nä′ dä) in southern Spain in 1344. **Benamarin** was a Moorish kingdom in northwest Africa. **Anatolia** (a′ nə tō′ lē ə), a part of Turkey in Asia Minor. **Ayas** (ä′ yäs), near Antioch, a port in southwest Turkey, won from the Turks in 1367. **Attalia** (ä tä′ lē ə), scene of a Turkish defeat in 1361.

8. **jousted** (joust′ əd) **at Tramissene.** Single combats between picked champions are common in medieval literature.

9. **Bey of Balat** (ba′ lät), a Turkish chieftain.

10. **gentle-knight,** proper knight, a member of the gentry.

11. **fustian** (fus′ chən) **tunic,** a cotton and linen over-blouse, usually belted.

12. **Flanders, Artois** (är′ toiz; modern French, är′ twä), **Picardy,** sections of France.

13. **yeoman** (yō′ mən), from the class below the gentry household.

This Yeoman wore a coat and hood of
  green, 105
And peacock-feathered arrows, bright
  and keen
And neatly sheathed, hung at his belt the
  while
—For he could dress his gear in yeoman
  style,
His arrows never drooped their feathers
  low—
And in his hand he bore a mighty bow. 110
His head was like a nut, his face was brown.
He knew the whole of woodcraft up and
  down.
A saucy brace[14] was on his arm to ward
It from the bow-string, and a shield and
  sword
Hung at one side, and at the other slipped 115
A jaunty dirk, spear-sharp and well-
  equipped.
A medal of St Christopher[15] he wore
Of shining silver on his breast, and bore
A hunting-horn, well slung and bur-
  nished clean,
That dangled from a baldrick[16] of bright
  green. 120
He was a proper forester I guess.

The Prioress

There also was a *Nun,* a Prioress.
Her way of smiling very simple and coy.
Her greatest oath was only "By St Loy!"
And she was known as Madam Eglantyne.[17] 125
And well she sang a service, with a fine
Intoning through her nose, as was most
  seemly,
And she spoke daintily in French, ex-
  tremely,
After the school of Stratford-atte-Bowe;[18]
French in the Paris style she did not
  know. 130
At meat her manners were well taught
  withal;
No morsel from her lips did she let fall.
Nor dipped her fingers in the sauce too
  deep;
But she could carry a morsel up and keep

The smallest drop from falling on her
  breast. 135
For courtliness she had a special zest,
And she would wipe her upper lip so
  clean
That not a trace of grease was to be seen
Upon the cup when she had drunk; to eat,
She reached a hand sedately for the
  meat. 140
She certainly was very entertaining,
Pleasant and friendly in her ways, and
  straining
To counterfeit a courtly kind of grace,
A stately bearing fitting to her place,
And to seem dignified in all her dealings. 145
As for her sympathies and tender feel-
  ings,
She was so charitably solicitous
She used to weep if she but saw a mouse
Caught in a trap, if it were dead or bleeding
And she had little dogs she would be
  feeding 150
With roasted flesh, or milk, or fine white
  bread.
And bitterly she wept if one were dead
Or someone took a stick and made it
  smart;

14. **a saucy brace,** a fancy leather wristguard for arch-
ers.
15. **St Christopher.** Possession of this medal was believed to protect travelers. The legend tells of Christopher who ferried people across a river on his shoulders.
One day he carried a strangely heavy child. The child
was Jesus and the saint was blessed by the contact.
  Note translator's English punctuation: no period
following St.
16. **baldrick** (bäl′ drik), a shoulder cord or band.
17. **St Loy** (loi) or **Eligius** (ə li′ je əs), a seventh-
century French goldsmith who became a renowned
church figure. Both the man and his name were suitably
elegant for the lady Prioress. Coming from a prosperous
family, the Prioress was the director—Mother Superior
—of her Priory, or convent. As such she was under oath
not to leave the convent. **Eglantyne** (eg′ lən tīn), the
name means "sweetbriar;" it is a name often given to
ladies in medieval romances.
18. **Stratford-atte-Bowe,** refers to Bow, an area in East
London but at that time about two miles outside London.
The Prioress speaks French with the accent of an English
finishing school rather than in the Parisian French
manner.

She was all sentiment and tender heart.
Her veil was gathered in a seemly way,   155
Her nose was elegant, her eyes glass-
    grey;
Her mouth was very small, but soft and
    red,
Her forehead, certainly, was fair of
    spread,
Almost a span across the brows, I own;
She was indeed by no means under-
    grown.   160
Her cloak, I noticed, had a graceful
    charm.
She wore a coral trinket on her arm,
A set of beads, the gaudies[19] tricked in
    green,
Whence hung a golden brooch of bright-
    est sheen
On which there first was graven a
    crowned A,   165
And lower, *Amor vincit omnia.*[20]
    Another *Nun,* the chaplain at her cell,
Was riding with her, and *three Priests* as
    well.

The Monk

    A *Monk* there was, one of the finest sort
Who rode the country;[21] hunting was his
    sport.   170
A manly man, to be an Abbot able;
Many a dainty horse he had in stable.
His bridle, when he rode, a man might
    hear
Jingling in a whistling wind as clear,
Aye, and as loud as does the chapel bell   175
Where my lord Monk was Prior of the
    cell.
The Rule of good St Benet or St Maur[22]
As old and strict he tended to ignore;
He let go by the things of yesterday
And took the modern world's more spa-
    cious way.   180
He did not rate that text at a plucked hen
Which says that hunters are not holy men
And that a monk uncloistered is a mere
Fish out of water, flapping on the pier,
That is to say a monk out of his cloister.   185

That was a text he held not worth an oys-
    ter;
And I agreed and said his views were
    sound;
Was he to study till his head went round
Poring over books in cloisters? Must he
    toil
As Austin[23] bade and till the very soil?   190
Was he to leave the world upon the shelf?
Let Austin have his labour to himself.
    This Monk was therefore a good man
    to horse;
Greyhounds he had, as swift as birds, to
    course.
Hunting a hare or riding at a fence   195
Was all his fun, he spared for no expense.
I saw his sleeves were garnished at the
    hand
With fine grey fur, the finest in the land,
And on his hood, to fasten it at his chin
He had a wrought-gold cunningly fash-
    ioned pin;   200
Into a lover's knot it seemed to pass.
His head was bald and shone like looking
    glass;
So did his face, as if it had been greased.
He was a fat and personable priest;
His prominent eyeballs never seemed to
    settle.   205
They glittered like the flames beneath a
    kettle;

---

19. **gaudies,** the prayer-counting beads of a rosary.
20. **Amor vincit omnia,** love conquers all.
21. **rode the country.** The monk was an "out-rider," in charge of the estates of the monastary and, as such, less confined than other monks.
22. **Rule of good St Benet . . .** St Benedict originated the Benedictine order in Italy in the sixth century. His disciple, St Maurus, brought the order to France. Members of this order take vows of poverty and obedience. They are to remain cloistered, apart from the world, and devoted to scholarship and prayer. This reference identifies the monk's own order as well as its ancient rules and duties—among them edicts against hunting—which he took so lightly.
23. **Austin.** St Augustine of the fifth century was credited with the rule that all members of religious orders who are able should do manual work. The monk's argument that follows is, How will the world be served (the clergy had many official posts) if all the capable religious isolate themselves from it?

The Wife of Bath

The Parson

The Miller

Supple his boots, his horse in fine condi-
    tion.
He was a prelate fit for exhibition,
He was not pale like a tormented soul.
He liked a fat swan best, and roasted
    whole.   210
His palfrey was as brown as is a berry.

The Friar

   There was a *Friar,* a wanton one and
       merry,
A Limiter,[24] a very festive fellow.
In all Four Orders[25] there was none so
    mellow
So glib with gallant phrase and well-
    turned speech.   215
He'd fixed up many a marriage, giving
    each
Of his young women what he could af-
    ford her.
He was a noble pillar to his Order.
Highly beloved and intimate was he
With County folk within his boundary,   220
And city dames of honour and posses-
    sions;
For he was qualified to hear confessions,
Or so he said, with more than priestly
    scope;

He had a special license from the Pope.
Sweetly he heard his penitents at shrift   225
With pleasant absolution, for a gift.
He was an easy man in penance-giving
Where he could hope to make a decent
    living;
It's a sure sign whenever gifts are given
To a poor Order that a man's well
    shriven,   230
And should he give enough he knew in
    verity
The penitent repented in sincerity.
For many a fellow is so hard of heart
He cannot weep, for all his inward smart.
Therefore instead of weeping and of
    prayer   235
One should give silver for a poor Friar's
    care.
He kept his tippet[26] stuffed with pins for
    curls,

---

24. **Limiter,** a friar given the right to beg for alms within a limited district.
25. **all Four Orders.** The four main religious orders of mendicant friars, under vows of poverty, chastity, and obedience are: Franciscan, Dominican, Carmelite, and Augustinian. These orders lived in the secular field (not in monastic solitude) by begging alms, preaching, and hearing confessions.
26. **tippet** (tip′ it), a hanging end of a sleeve or hood.

And pocket-knives, to give to pretty girls.
And certainly his voice was gay and sturdy,
For he sang well and played the hurdy-
    gurdy.   240
At sing-songs he was champion of the
    hour.[27]
His neck was whiter than a lily-flower
But strong enough to butt a bruiser
    down.
He knew the taverns well in every town
And every innkeeper and barmaid too   245
Better than lepers, beggars and that
    crew,
For in so eminent a man as he
It was not fitting with the dignity
Of his position, dealing with a scum
Of wretched lepers; nothing good can
    come   250
Of commerce with such slum-and-gutter
    dwellers,
But only with the rich and victual-sellers.
But anywhere a profit might accrue
Courteous he was and lowly of service
    too.
Natural gifts like his were hard to match.   255
He was the finest beggar of his batch,
And, for his begging-district, paid a rent;
His brethren did no poaching where he
    went.
For though a widow mightn't have a
    shoe,
So pleasant was his holy how-d'ye-do   260
He got his farthing from her just the
    same
Before he left, and so his income came
To more than he laid out. And how he
    romped,
Just like a puppy! He was ever prompt
To arbitrate disputes on settling days[28]   265
(For a small fee) in many helpful ways,
Not then appearing as your cloistered
    scholar
With threadbare habit hardly worth a
    dollar,
But much more like a Doctor or a Pope.
Of double-worsted was the semi-cope   270
Upon his shoulders, and the swelling fold

About him, like a bell about its mould
When it is casting, rounded out his dress.
He lisped a little out of wantonness[29]
To make his English sweet upon his
    tongue.   275
When he had played his harp, or having
    sung,
His eyes would twinkle in his head as
    bright
As any star upon a frosty night.
This worthy's name was Hubert, it ap-
    peared.

The Merchant

    There was a *Merchant* with a forking
        beard   280
And motley[30] dress; high on his horse he
    sat,
Upon his head a Flemish beaver hat
And on his feet daintily buckled boots.
He told of his opinions and pursuits
In solemn tones, he harped on his in-
    crease   285
Of capital; there should be sea-police[31]
(He thought) upon the Harwich-Holland
    ranges;[32]
He was expert at dabbling in exchanges.[33]
This estimable Merchant so had set
His wits to work, none knew he was in
    debt,   290

27. He was best among the group for ballad singing.
28. **settling days,** days set aside to settle disputes out of court.
29. **wantonness** meant gaiety but it also carried the modern sense of decadence. Both the affected lisp and the white neck were commonly used symbols of depravity.
30. **motley** was multicolored or figured cloth. The various guilds had distinctive fabrics for their clothing, and this reference may suggest the membership of the merchant in a guild of those who exported wools and skins.
31. **sea-police.** Piracy was a constant threat to sea trade. To guard the seas, the king hired private ships paid for by taxes on merchandise.
32. **Harwich-Holland** (här' ij) **ranges.** This originally referred to the old English port of Orwell, and the range is the sea between it and the Dutch coast.
33. The suggestion is that the merchant carried on speculative money exchange.

He was so stately in administration,
In loans and bargains and negotiation.
He was an excellent fellow all the same;
To tell the truth I do not know his
 name.[34]

The Oxford Student

 An *Oxford Cleric,* still a student though, **295**
One who had taken logic long ago,[35]
Was there; his horse was thinner than a
 rake,
And he was not too fat, I undertake
But had a hollow look, a sober stare;
The thread upon his overcoat was bare. **300**
He had found no preferment in the
 church
And he was too unworldly to make search
For secular employment. By his bed
He preferred having twenty books in red
And black, of Aristotle's philosophy, **305**
Than costly clothes, fiddle or psaltery.[36]
Though a philosopher, as I have told,
He had not found the stone for making
 gold.[37]
Whatever money from his friends he
 took[38]
He spent on learning or another book **310**
And prayed for them most earnestly, re-
 turning
Thanks to them thus for paying for his
 learning.
His only care was study, and indeed
He never spoke a word more than was
 need,
Formal at that, respectful in the extreme, **315**
Short, to the point, and lofty in this
 theme.
A tone of moral virtue filled his speech
And he would gladly learn, and gladly
 teach.

The Lawyer

 A *Serjeant at the Law* who paid his calls,
Wary and wise, for clients at St Paul's[39] **320**
There also was, of noted excellence.
Discreet he was, a man to reverence,

Or so he seemed, his sayings were so wise.
He often had been Justice of Assize[40]
By letters patent, and in full commis-
 sion.[41] **325**
His fame and learning and his high posi-
 tion
Had won him many a robe and many a
 fee.
There was no such conveyancer as he;
All was fee-simple to his strong diges-
 tion,[42]
Not one conveyance could be called in
 question; **330**
Though there was nowhere one so busy
 as he,

34. This may indicate contempt for the merchant class or, since many figures were drawn from life, it may be a barrier to possible identification.
35. **taken logic long ago.** According to the medieval university course of study, this would indicate that the cleric (used here to apply to a student preparing for the Church) had completed a bachelor's degree and was engaged in advanced study.
36. **twenty books . . . psaltery.** The number of books is merely suggestive of a library unusually large and expensive in those times. Such a collection might have cost more than three fine houses, obviously leaving the student unable to afford such luxuries as a psaltery (sôl′ tər ē), a zitherlike instrument.
37. **making gold,** a play on "philosopher," which also meant "alchemist"—the medieval chemist who attempted to turn base metal into gold.
38. Giving alms to a student was considered a reverent act. Students were often supported by such patronage.
39. **Serjeant at the Law** is a lawyer of long experience and high estate appointed to serve the king. **. . . at St Paul's.** The reference is disputed, but the porch of St Paul's Cathedral in London seems to have been a meeting place for lawyers and their clients.
40. **Assize** (ə sīz′), justices for the periodic circuit courts were assigned by the king from among the elite group of sergeants at law.
41. **letters patent** (pat′ nt) **and . . . commission,** a public appointment as judge in an open letter from the king. The latter is a direct letter giving the judge wide power to hear all sorts of cases.
42. **conveyancer** (kən vā′ ən sər), one who prepares deeds for transfer of property. The reference also suggests that the lawyer was a buyer of land in his own name rather than merely an agent. At this time many in the legal profession were becoming members of the landed class through new wealth and their ability to break old inherited land titles. **Fee simple** means *with clear title* and refers to the ability to arrange for the removal of inherited land claims, thus causing wide resentment of lawyers by the old gentry.

He was less busy than he seemed to be.
He knew of every judgment, case and
    crime
Recorded, ever since King William's time.[43]
He could dictate defences or draft deeds;   **335**
No one could pinch a comma from his
    screeds,[44]
And he knew every statute off by rote.
He wore a homely parti-coloured coat[45]
Girt with a silken belt of pin-stripe stuff;
Of his appearance I have said enough.   **340**

The Franklin

    There was a *Franklin*[46] with him, it ap-
    peared;
White as a daisy-petal was his beard.
A sanguine man, high-coloured and be-
    nign,[47]
He loved a morning sop of cake in wine.
He lived for pleasure and had always
    done,   **345**
For he was Epicurus' very son,[48]
In whose opinion sensual delight
Was the one true felicity in sight.
As noted as St Julian was for bounty[49]
He made his household free to all the
    County.   **350**
His bread, his ale were finest of the fine
And no one had a better stock of wine.
His house was never short of bake-meat
    pies
Of fish and flesh, and these in such sup-
    plies
It positively snowed with meat and drink   **355**
And all the dainties that a man could
    think.
According to the seasons of the year
Changes of dish were ordered to appear.
He kept fat partridges in coops, beyond,
Many a bream[50] and pike were in his pond.   **360**
Woe to the cook unless the sauce was hot
And sharp, or if he wasn't on the spot!
And in his hall a table stood arrayed
And ready all day long, with places laid.
As Justice at the Sessions[51] none stood
    higher;   **365**

He often had been Member for the
    Shire.[52]
A dagger and a little purse of silk
Hung at his girdle, white as morning
    milk.
As Sheriff he checked audit, every en-
    try.[53]
He was a model among landed gentry.   **370**

The Five Tradesmen

    A *Haberdasher*, a *Dyer*, a *Carpenter*,
A *Weaver* and a *Carpet-maker* were
Among our ranks, all in the livery
Of one impressive guild-fraternity.[54]
They were so trim and fresh their gear
    would pass   **375**
For new. Their knives were not tricked
    out with brass
But wrought with purest silver, which
    avouches
A like display on girdles and on pouches.
Each seemed a worthy burgess, fit to
    grace
A guild-hall with a seat upon the dais.[55]   **380**
Their wisdom would have justified a plan

43. Some scholars suggest this is an exaggeration, since available records did not go back to the time of William the Conqueror (1066–1087).
44. **screeds.** His writing was above reproach.
45. **homely parti-coloured coat,** a plain striped coat.
46. **Franklin,** traveling companion to the lawyer; he was a wealthy landowner, a country gentleman of rank but not of noble birth.
47. **sanguine . . . benign.** He has a cheerful disposition and is ruddy in appearance.
48. **Epicurus** (ep′ ə kyūr′ əs), Greek philosopher, 342?–270 B.C., associated with luxurious living.
49. **St Julian,** the legendary patron of hospitality.
50. **bream,** carp.
51. **Sessions,** sittings of the Justice of the Peace, a lower court than the assize of the knight's authority.
52. **Member . . . ,** member of Parliament for his county.
53. The Franklin was also a county auditor.
54. All of these men had separate trades and distinctive dress, so their common costume suggests a unifying social or religious organization.
55. **upon the dais.** These were citizens prominent enough for the raised seats of honor in the guild hall.

The Manciple

The Knight

The Prioress

To make each one of them an alderman;[56]
They had the capital and revenue,
Besides their wives declared it was their
    due.
And if they did not think so, then they
    ought;   385
To be called *"Madam"* is a glorious
    thought,
And so is going to church and being seen
Having your mantle carried like a queen.

The Cook

    They had a *Cook* with them who stood
    alone
For boiling chicken with a marrow-bone,   390
Sharp flavouring-powder and a spice for
    savour.
He could distinguish London ale by fla-
    vour,
And he could roast and seethe and broil
    and fry,
Make good thick soup and bake a tasty
    pie.
But what a pity—so it seemed to me,   395
That he should have an ulcer on his knee.
As for blancmange, he made it with the
    best.

The Ship's Captain

    There was a *Skipper* hailing from far
    west;
He came from Dartmouth, so I under-
    stood.
He rode a farmer's horse as best he
    could,   400
In a woollen gown that reached his knee.
A dagger on a lanyard[57] falling free
Hung from his neck under his arm and
    down.
The summer heat had tanned his colour
    brown,
And certainly he was an excellent fellow.   405
Many a draught of vintage, red and yel-
    low,
He'd drawn at Bordeaux, while the trad-
    er snored.[58]
The nicer rules of conscience he ignored.
If, when he fought, the enemy vessel
    sank,

56. **an alderman** had to have a certain amount of
property. These men were sufficiently wealthy.
57. **lanyard** (lan′ yərd),   a cord around the neck.
58. **Bordeaux** (bôr dō′),   a seaport in southern France.
The suggestion is that he'd stolen the wine.

He sent his prisoners home; they walked
   the plank.   410
As for his skill in reckoning his tides,
Currents and many another risk besides,
Moons, harbours, pilots, he had such dis-
   patch
That none from Hull to Carthage[59] was
   his match.
Hardy he was, prudent in undertaking;   415
His beard in many a tempest had its shak-
   ing,
And he knew all the havens as they were
From Gottland to the Cape of Finis-
   terre,[60]
And every creek in Brittany and Spain;
The barge he owned was called *The Mau-
delayne*.   420

The Doctor

   A *Doctor* too emerged as we proceeded;
No one alive could talk as well as he did
On points of medicine and of surgery,
For, being grounded in astronomy,
He watched his patient closely for the
   hours   425
When, by his horoscope, he knew the
   powers
Of favourable planets, then ascendent,
Worked on the images for his depen-
   dent.[61]
The cause of every malady you'd got
He knew, and whether dry, cold, moist or
   hot;[62]   430
He knew their seat, their humour and
   condition.
He was a perfect practising physician.
These causes being known for what they
   were,
He gave the man his medicine then and
   there.
All his apothecaries in a tribe[63]   435
Were ready with the drugs he would pre-
   scribe,
And each made money from the other's
   guile;
They had been friendly for a goodish
   while.

He was well-versed in Aesculapius[64] too
And what Hippocrates and Rufus knew   440
And Dioscorides, now dead and gone,
Galen and Rhazes, Hali, Serapion,
Averroes, Avicenna, Constantine,
Scotch Bernard, John of Gaddesden, Gil-
   bertine.
In his own diet he observed some mea-
   sure;   445
There were no superfluities for pleasure,
Only digestives, nutritives and such.
He did not read the Bible very much.
In blood-red garments, slashed with
   bluish grey
And lined with taffeta, he rode his way;   450
Yet he was rather close as to expenses
And kept the gold he won in pestilences.
Gold stimulates the heart, or so we're told.
He therefore had a special love of gold.

The Wife of Bath

   A worthy *woman* from beside *Bath* city   455
Was with us, somewhat deaf, which was a
   pity.
In making cloth she showed so great a
   bent
She bettered those of Ypres and of
   Ghent.[65]
In all the parish not a dame dared stir
Towards the altar steps in front of her,   460
And if indeed they did, so wrath was she
As to be quite put out of charity.[66]

---

59. **Hull to Carthage,** seaports from England to Spain
(Carthagena).
60. **Gottland, Finisterre** (fin′ i ster′), from Sweden to
Brittany.
61. The medical ideas are from astrology rather than
astronomy.
62. **. . . hot.** The balance of the "humours" in the body
was thought to be the key to health and disease.
63. This is an old jibe implying a moneymaking alliance
between doctors and druggists.
64. The doctor was familiar with all the current medical
authorities from the Greeks, real and legendary, through
the Arabs to contemporary Europeans and the English.
65. **Ypres** (ē′ prə), **Ghent** (gent), Flemish cities renowned for weaving.
66. The good wife was angry if any offerings were made
in church before she brought up her gifts of lacework.

Her kerchiefs were of finely woven
    ground;
I dared have sworn they weighed a good
    ten pound,
The ones she wore on Sunday, on her
    head.   465
Her hose were of the finest scarlet red
And gartered tight; her shoes were soft
    and new.
Bold was her face, handsome, and red in
    hue.
A worthy woman all her life, what's more
She'd had five husbands, all at the church
    door,[67]   470
Apart from other company in youth;
No need just now to speak of that, for-
    sooth.
And she had thrice been to Jerusalem,
Seen many strange rivers and passed
    over them;
She'd been to Rome and also to Bou-
    logne,   475
St James of Compostella and Cologne,[68]
And she was skilled in wandering by the
    way.
She had gap-teeth, set widely, truth to
    say.
Easily on an ambling horse she sat
Well wimpled up,[69] and on her head a hat   480
As broad as is a buckler or a shield;
She had a flowing mantle that concealed
Large hips, her heels spurred sharply
    under that.
In company she liked to laugh and chat
And knew the remedies for love's mis-
    chances,   485
An art in which she knew the oldest
    dances.

The Parson

    A holy-minded man of good renown
There was, and poor, the *Parson* to a
    town,
Yet he was rich in holy thought and work.
He also was a learned man, a clerk,[70]   490
Who truly knew Christ's gospel and
    would preach it

Devoutly to parishioners, and teach it.
Benign and wonderfully diligent,
And patient when adversity was sent
(For so he proved in great adversity)   495
He hated cursing to extort a fee,[71]
Nay rather he preferred beyond a doubt
Giving to poor parishioners round about
Both from church offerings and his prop-
    erty;
He could in little find sufficiency.   500
Wide was his parish, with houses far
    asunder,
Yet he neglected not in rain or thunder,
In sickness or in grief, to pay a call
On the remotest, whether great or small,
Upon his feet, and in his hand a stave.[72]   505
This noble example to his sheep he gave,
That first he wrought, and afterwards he
    taught;
And it was from the Gospel he had caught
Those words, and he would add this fig-
    ure too,
That if gold rust, what then will iron do?   510
For if a priest be foul in whom we trust
No wonder that a common man should
    rust;
And shame it is to see—let priests take
    stock—
A filthy shepherd and a snowy flock.
The true example that a priest should
    give   515
Is one of cleanness, how the sheep should
    live.
He did not set his benefice to hire[73]

67. **church door,** where many medieval weddings were performed. This establishes that all five marriages were legitimate and recognized by the church as such.
68. **. . . Cologne.** She had been on pilgrimages to many shrines.
69. **wimpled,** veiled with a loose covering similar to a hood around the head and under the chin.
70. **clerk,** scholar.
71. It was an accepted custom to excommunicate or to refuse church comforts to parishioners who did not pay their church dues. Instead, the parson offered charity to his poor followers from his own funds.
72. **stave,** a walking stick.
73. It was a common abuse that clergy of the parson's rank would leave their rural posts for more comfortable city dwellings and hire substitutes.

And leave his sheep encumbered in the
    mire
Or run to London to earn easy bread
By singing masses for the wealthy dead,   520
Or find some Brotherhood and get en-
    rolled.
He stayed at home and watched over his
    fold
So that no wolf should make the sheep
    miscarry.
He was a shepherd and no mercenary.
Holy and virtuous he was, but then   525
Never contemptuous of sinful men,
Never disdainful, never too proud or fine,
But was discreet in teaching and benign.
His business was to show a fair behavior
And draw men thus to Heaven and their
    Saviour,   530
Unless indeed a man were obstinate;
And such, whether of high or low estate,
He put to sharp rebuke to say the least.
I think there never was a better priest.
He sought no pomp or glory in his deal-
    ings,   535
No scrupulosity had spiced his feelings.
Christ and His Twelve Apostles and their
    lore
He taught, but followed it himself before.

The Plowman

   There was a *Plowman* with him there,
    his brother.
Many a load of dung one time or other   540
He must have carted through the morn-
    ing dew.
He was an honest worker, good and true,
Living in peace and perfect charity,
And, as the gospel bade him, so did he,
Loving God best with all his heart and
    mind   545
And then his neighbour as himself, re-
    pined
At no misfortune, slacked for no content,
For steadily about his work he went
To thrash his corn, to dig or to manure

Or make a ditch; and he would help the
    poor   550
For love of Christ and never take a penny
If he could help it, and, as prompt as any,
He paid his tithes[74] in full when they were
    due
On what he owned, and on his earnings
    too.
He wore a tabard smock and rode a
    mare.[75]   555
   There was a *Reeve,* also a *Miller,* there,
A College *Manciple* from the Inns of Court,
A papal *Pardoner* and, in close consort,
A Church-Court *Summoner,* riding at a
    trot,[76]
And finally myself—that was the lot.   560

The Miller

   The *Miller* was a chap of sixteen stone,[77]
A great stout fellow big in brawn and
    bone.
He did well out of them, for he could go
And win the ram at any wrestling show.
Broad, knotty and short-shouldered, he
    would boast   565
He could heave any door off hinge and
    post,
Or take a run and break it with his head.
His beard, like any sow or fox, was red
And broad as well, as though it were a
    spade;
And, at its very tip, his nose displayed   570
A wart on which there stood a tuft of hair
Red as the bristles in an old sow's ear.
His nostrils were as black as they were
    wide.

74. This plowman is exceptional, an idealized and rather well-to-do worker. Having "tithes" to pay indicates some property.
75. **tabard smock,** a loose belted smock. A **mare** was an unfashionable mount.
76. **Reeve,** the supervisor of an English manor house. **Manciple** (man′ sə pəl), a steward and food buyer. **Pardoner,** a seller of clerical pardons for sins. **Summoner,** a minor officer of the clerical courts who summoned people to answer to charges.
77. **sixteen stone,** 224 pounds. The stone is a British unit equal to 14 pounds.

| The Reeve | The Merchant | The Clerk |

He had a sword and buckler at his side,
His mighty mouth was like a furnace
    door.   575
A wrangler and buffoon, he had a store
Of tavern stories, filthy in the main.
His was a master-hand at stealing grain.
He felt it with his thumb and thus he knew
Its quality and took three times his due—   580
A thumb of gold, by God, to gauge an
    oat![78]
He wore a hood of blue and a white coat.
He liked to play his bagpipes up and
    down
And that was how he brought us out of
    town.

The Manciple

    The *Manciple* came from the Inner
    Temple,[79]   585
All caterers might follow his example
In buying victuals; he was never rash
Whether he bought on credit or paid
    cash.
He used to watch the market most pre-
    cisely
And got in first, and so he did quite
    nicely.   590

Now isn't it a marvel of God's grace
That an illiterate fellow can outpace
The wisdom of a heap of learned men?
His masters—he had more than thirty
    then—
All versed in the abstrusest legal knowl-
    edge,   595
Could have produced a dozen from their
    College
Fit to be stewards in land and rents and
    game
To any Peer in England you could name,
And show him how to live on what he had
Debt-free (unless of course the Peer were
    mad)[80]   600
Or be as frugal as he might desire,
And make them fit to help about the Shire
In any legal case there was to try;
And yet this Manciple could wipe their
    eye.[81]

---

78. Millers were proverbially dishonest, and here Chaucer plays on an old saying "An honest miller has a golden
thumb." The Miller's thumb is gold from his profits.
79. **the Inner Temple.** The Manciple worked for one
of the London Inns of Court, or legal colleges.
80. Some members of the lawyer's society managed large
estates.
81. **wipe their eye,** defraud them.

The Reeve

The *Reeve* was old and choleric[82] and
    thin;   605
His beard was shaven closely to the skin,
His shorn hair came abruptly to a stop[83]
Above his ears, and he was docked on top
Just like a priest in front; his legs were
    lean,
Like sticks they were, no calf was to be
    seen.   610
He kept his bins and garners[84] very trim;
No auditor could gain a point on him.
And he could judge by watching drought
    and rain
The yield he might expect from seed and
    grain.
His master's sheep, his animals and hens,   615
Pigs, horses, dairies, stores and cattle-
    pens
Were wholly trusted to his government.
And he was under contract to present
The accounts, right from his master's
    earliest years.
No one had ever caught him in arrears.   620
No bailiff, serf or herdsman dared to
    kick,
He knew their dodges, knew their every
    trick;
Feared like the plague he was, by those
    beneath.
He had a lovely dwelling on a heath,
Shadowed in green by trees above the
    sward.   625
A better hand at bargains than his lord,
He had grown rich and had a store of
    treasure
Well tucked away, yet out it came to
    pleasure
His lord with subtle loans or gifts of
    goods,[85]
To earn his thanks and even coats and
    hoods.   630
When young he'd learnt a useful trade
    and still
He was a carpenter of first-rate skill.
The stallion-cob he rode at a slow trot
Was dapple-grey and bore the name of
    Scot.
He wore an overcoat of bluish shade   635
And rather long; he had a rusty blade
Slung at his side. He came, as I heard tell,
From Norfolk, near a place called Baldes-
    well.
His coat was tucked under his belt and
    splayed.
He rode the hindmost of our cavalcade.[86]   640

The Summoner

There was a *Summoner* with us at that
    Inn,
His face on fire, like a cherubin,[87]
For he had carbuncles. His eyes were nar-
    row,
He was as hot and lecherous as a sparrow.
Black, scabby brows he had, and a thin
    beard.   645
Children were afraid when he appeared.
No quicksilver, lead ointments, tartar
    creams,
No brimstone, no boracic, so it seems,
Could make a salve that had the power to
    bite,
Clean up or cure his whelks of knobby
    white   650
Or purge the pimples sitting on his
    cheeks.
Garlic he loved, and onions too, and
    leeks,
And drinking strong wine till all was hazy.
Then he would shout and jabber as if
    crazy,
And wouldn't speak a word except in
    Latin   655

---

82. **choleric,** a complexion indicating a sharp and irritable disposition.
83. The shorn hair was a sign that the Reeve was a serf, here, undoubtedly chief of the manor's peasants.
84. **garner,** granary.
85. The treasures that he loaned for thanks had been taken from the lord in the first place.
86. In his place at the rear of the procession, the Reeve was farthest from his traditional enemy, the Miller.
87. Red as the face of a cherub in medieval painting.

The Summoner

The Monk

The Franklin

When he was drunk, such tags as he was
    pat in;[88]
He only had a few, say two or three,
That he had mugged up out of some de-
    cree;
No wonder, for he heard them every day.
And, as you know, a man can teach a jay   660
To call out "Walter" better than the
    Pope.[89]
But had you tried to test his wits and grope
For more, you'd have found nothing in
    the bag.
Then *"Questio quid juris"* was his tag.[90]
He was a noble varlet and a kind one,   665
You'd meet none better if you went to
    find one . . .

The Pardoner

    He and a gentle *Pardoner* rode together,
A bird from Charing Cross[91] of the same
    feather,
Just back from visiting the Court of
    Rome.
He loudly sang *"Come hither, love, come
    home!"*   670
The Summoner sang deep seconds to this
    song,

No trumpet ever sounded half so strong.
This Pardoner had hair as yellow as wax,
Hanging down smoothly like a hank of
    flax.
In driblets fell his locks behind his head   675
Down to his shoulders which they over-
    spread;
Thinly they fell, like rat-tails, one by one.
He wore no hood upon his head, for fun;
The hood inside his wallet had been
    stowed,
He aimed at riding in the latest mode;   680
But for a little cap his head was bare
And he had bulging eye-balls, like a hare.
He'd sewed a holy relic on his cap;
His wallet lay before him on his lap,
Brimful of pardons come from Rome all
    hot.   685
He had the same small voice a goat has got.

88. He knew a few terms from familiar decrees.
89. The jay was trained to say "Walter," much as a parrot
is taught "Polly."
90. This Latin phrase means "The question is what legal
point is involved."
91. **Charing Cross,** a place outside London near a
familiar religious organization. More pardoners claimed
to belong to it than was actually the case.

His chin no beard had harboured, nor
    would harbour,
Smoother than ever chin was left by
    barber. . . .
There was no pardoner of equal grace,
For in his trunk he had a pillow-case   690
Which he asserted was Our Lady's veil.
He said he had a gobbet[92] of the sail
Saint Peter had the time when he made
    bold
To walk the waves, till Jesu Christ took
    hold.
He had a cross of metal set with stones   695
And, in a glass, a rubble of pigs' bones.
And with these relics, any time he found
Some poor up-country parson to astound,
In one short day, in money down, he drew
More than the parson in a month or two,   700
And by his flatteries and prevarication
Make monkeys of the priest and congre-
    gation.
But still to do him justice first and last
In church he was a noble ecclesiast.
How well he read a lesson or told a story!   705
But best of all he sang an Offertory,[93]
For well he knew that when that song was
    sung
He'd have to preach and tune his
    honey-tongue
And (well he could) win silver from the
    crowd.
That's why he sang so merrily and loud.   710

   Now I have told you shortly, in a clause,
The rank, the array, the number and the
    cause
Of our assembly in this company
In Southwark, at that high-class hostelry
Known as *The Tabard,* close beside *The
    Bell.*[94]   715
And now the time has come for me to tell
How we behaved that evening; I'll begin
After we had alighted at the Inn,
Then I'll report our journey, stage by
    stage,
All the remainder of our pilgrimage.   720
But first I beg of you, in courtesy,

Not to condemn me as unmannerly
If I speak plainly and with no concealings
And give account of all their words and
    dealings,
Using their very phrases as they fell.   725
For certainly, as you all know so well,
He who repeats a tale after a man
Is bound to say, as nearly as he can,
Each single word, if he remembers it,
However rudely spoken or unfit,   730
Or else the tale he tells will be untrue,
The things pretended and the phrases
    new.
He may not flinch although it were his
    brother,
He may as well say one word as another.
And Christ Himself spoke broad in Holy
    Writ,   735
Yet there is no scurrility in it,
And Plato says, for those with power to
    read,
"The word should be as cousin to the
    deed."
Further I beg you to forgive it me
If I neglect the order and degree   740
And what is due to rank in what I've
    planned.
I'm short of wit as you will understand.

Harry Bailly, the Host

   Our *Host* gave us great welcome; every-
    one
Was given a place and supper was begun.
He served the finest victuals you could
    think,   745
The wine was strong and we were glad to
    drink.
A very striking man our Host withal,

---

92. **gobbet,** piece.
93. **offertory,** psalms sung or chanted during the ritual presentation of the bread and wine for communion or during the collection after the sermon. Here the sermon came between offertory and offering.
94. **The Bell,** another inn; unlike The Tabard, it cannot be historically identified.

The Shipman

The Pardoner

The Friar

And fit to be a marshal in a hall.
His eyes were bright, his girth a little
    wide;
There is no finer burgess in Cheap-
    side.[95]   750
Bold in his speech, yet wise and full of
    tact,
There was no manly attribute he lacked,
What's more he was a merry-hearted man.
After our meal he jokingly began
To talk of sport, and, among other things   755
After we'd settled up our reckonings,
He said as follows: "Truly, gentlemen,
You're very welcome and I can't think
    when
—Upon my word I'm telling you no lie—
I've seen a gathering here that looked so
    spry,   760
No, not this year, as in this tavern now.
I'd think you up some fun if I knew how.
And, as it happens, a thought has just oc-
    curred
To please you, costing nothing, on my
    word.
You're off to Canterbury—well, God
    speed!   765
Blessed St Thomas answer to your need!

And I don't doubt, before the journey's
    done
You mean to while the time in tales and
    fun.
Indeed, there's little pleasure for your
    bones
Riding along and all as dumb as stones.   770
So let me then propose for your enjoy-
    ment,
Just as I said, a suitable employment.
And if my notion suits and you agree
And promise to submit yourselves to me
Playing your parts exactly as I say   775
Tomorrow as you ride along the way,
Then by my father's soul (and he is dead)
If you don't like it you can have my head!
Hold up your hands, and not another
    word."
    Well, our consent of course was not de-
    ferred,   780
It seemed not worth a serious debate;
We all agreed to it at any rate
And bade him issue what commands he
    would.

95. **Cheapside,** a major street in London.

"My lords," he said, "now listen for your
    good,
And please don't treat my notion with
    disdain.   785
This is the point. I'll make it short and
    plain.
Each one of you shall help to make things
    slip
By telling two stories on the outward trip
To Canterbury, that's what I intend,
And, on the homeward way to journey's
    end   790
Another two, tales from the days of old;
And then the man whose story is best told,
That is to say who gives the fullest mea-
    sure
Of good morality and general pleasure,
He shall be given a supper, paid by all,   795
Here in this tavern, in this very hall,
When we come back again from Canter-
    bury.
And in the hope to keep you bright and
    merry
I'll go along with you myself and ride
All at my own expense and serve as
    guide.   800
I'll be the judge, and those who won't obey
Shall pay for what we spend upon the
    way.
Now if you all agree to what you've heard
Tell me at once without another word,
And I will make arrangements early for
    it."   805
   Of course we all agreed, in fact we
    swore it
Delightedly, and made entreaty too
That he should act as he proposed to do,
Become our Governor in short, and be
Judge of our tales and general referee,   810
And set the supper at a certain price.
We promised to be ruled by his advice
Come high, come low; unanimously thus
We set him up in judgement over us.
More wine was fetched, the business
    being done;   815
We drank it off and up went everyone
To bed without a moment of delay.

FOR INTERPRETATION

The following questions and propositions require you to shape opinions, to assess arguments, and to draw valid conclusions. Be sure you can cite evidence to support your conclusions from your reading of the "Prologue."
1. Chaucer the poet does not admire the monk as completely as does Chaucer the pilgrim.
2. From his portraits of the religious figures on the pilgrimage, we can be sure that Chaucer admired the Church of his time wholeheartedly.
3. One of the most famous poems of the twentieth century, T. S. Eliot's *The Waste Land*, opens also with a passage about April and spring:

> April is the cruellest month, breeding
> Lilacs out of the dead land, mixing
> Memory and desire, stirring
> Dull roots with spring rain. . . .

Contrast this with the opening of the "Prologue." What are the implications of each as to the attitudes of the twentieth century and the attitudes of the fourteenth toward nature, spring, and love?
4. Generally, Chaucer portrays characters from the top of the social and moral scale to the bottom. If you were assembling a group of people from modern life, what people would you choose as modern equivalents for each of the pilgrims?

FOR APPRECIATION

Characterization and Contrast

The trained eye not only observes details with accuracy but also sees the inner meaning that details suggest. Chaucer's genius rested very largely on his ability to discover and record our complex human nature with precision and humor. Though one would never guess it on first reading, Chaucer's descriptions of people rely heavily on his knowledge of human character as described in medieval books on rhetoric, medicine, and astrology. In order to fully appreciate Chaucer's portrait sketches, it is helpful to see what attributes these medieval psychologists emphasized in their catalog of human characteristics:

Name.
Nature—place of origin, family, age, sex, bodily

appearance: a special medieval study relating complexion to disposition indicating whether bright or dull, affable or rude, and all the qualities of mind and body bestowed by nature.

Manner of Life—occupation or trade, and the character of a person's home life.

Fortune—rich or poor, success or failure, and social rank.

Habit—characteristic habit or action, and some special knowledge or bodily skill achieved through training or practice.

Feeling—any fleeting passion: joy, fear, etc.

Interests—subjects of special importance to a person, hobbies and enthusiasms.

Purposes—plans or ambitions.

Achievements—deeds accomplished in which the person takes pride.

Accidents—current and past happenings.

Conversation.

Moral Nature—individual moral sensibilities or chief moral weaknesses.

These attributes, combined with a knowledge of medieval medicine and astrology, provided the basis of Chaucer's analysis of human character. It is astounding that he can record so much about a person so casually and yet so completely.

1. Chaucer varies the attributes he selects for his characters, making one typical and general and another individual and specific, as he chooses. To fully appreciate his portrayal of human character, write an analysis of at least one of the pairs of characters listed below. Use the list of attributes to guide you. Decide what is the total impression of a character Chaucer wishes to give. Notice how he uses different combinations of these attributes to achieve the desired impression. On this basis, compare or contrast his rich thumbnail portraits of the following pilgrims:

a. The Knight and the Squire (accomplishments, rank, ages, clothing, feeling, habit)

b. The Nun and the Monk (conversation, feeling, manner of life, interests, moral nature vs. interests, achievements)

c. The Oxford Cleric and the Franklin (purposes and manner of life)

d. The Haberdasher, Dyer, Carpenter, Weaver, and Carpet-maker and the Wife of Bath (This will compare Chaucer's only group portrait with his most individual one.)

e. The Friar and the Parson (These are both religious portraits but opposite in nature.)

f. The Reeve and the Pardoner (These two lower-class portraits are much alike.)

2. Which pilgrims are presented without satire or irony in their portraits?

THE PARDONER'S PROLOGUE AND TALE

The Pardoner prefaces his tale with a "confessional" statement in which he brags of his skill as a preacher and then says that he will show them just how good he is by giving them his standard sermon. The portion of "The Pardoner's Tale" printed below is the central anecdote of that sermon, and would have been called an exemplum *(Latin, meaning "example") by the medieval preacher. The story exemplifies his favorite text: "Avarice is the root of evil." Actually, the origins of this story are lost in antiquity; a haunting venture into the supernatural, the plot is one whose universal appeal has made it popular in different versions from China to modern Germany. Dealing with the ultimate mysteries of life and death, its power comes from its simplicity. The prevailing sense of death at the beginning of the story is reminiscent of the Black Death, or plague, which killed one third to one half of all people living in Europe during the 1340s. But the story is also compelling because of its teller, a man who confesses his own desire for money and then tells a story showing how such avarice leads to death. Even more perplexing is the aftermath to the story, a surprising moment in which the Pardoner seems to forget who his audience really is.*

The Pardoner's Prologue

But let me briefly make my purpose
    plain
I preach for nothing but for greed of gain
And use the same old text, as bold as
    brass,
Radix malorum est cupiditas.[1]
And thus I preach against the very vice   5
I make my living out of—avarice.
And yet however guilty of that sin
Myself, with others I have power to win
Them from it, I can bring them to repent
But that is not my principal intent.   10
Covetousness is both the root and stuff
Of all I preach. That ought to be enough.
    Well, then I give examples thick and fast
From bygone times, old stories from the
    past

A yokel mind loves stories from of old,   15
Being the kind it can repeat and hold.
What! Do you think, as long as I can preach
And get their silver for the things I teach,
That I will live in poverty, from choice?
No! Let me preach and beg from kirk to
    kirk[2]   20
And never do an honest job of work,
No, nor make baskets, like St Paul, to gain
A livelihood. I do not preach in vain.
There's no apostle I would counterfeit;
I mean to have money, wool and cheese
    and wheat   25
Though it were given me by the poorest
    lad
Or poorest village widow, though she had
A string of starving children, all agape.[3]
No! Let me drink the liquor of the grape

---

1. **Radix malorum est cupiditas,** (Latin). Avarice is the root of evil.
2. **kirk,** church (a Scots form of the word).
3. **agape,** staring.

"The Pardoner's Tale," tr. Neville Coghill. Reprinted by permission of Penguin Books, Ltd.

Woodcut of the Pardoner from Caxton's second edition of The Canterbury Tales.

The British Library, London

And keep a jolly wench in every town! 30
But listen, gentlemen; to bring things
   down
To a conclusion, would you like a tale?
Now as I've drunk a draught of corn-ripe
   ale,
By God it stands to reason I can strike

On some good story that you all will like. 35
For though I am a wholly vicious man
Don't think I can't tell moral tales. I can!
Here's one I often preach when out for
   winning.
Now please be quiet. Here is the begin-
   ning.

The Pardoner's Tale

   It's of three rioters I have to tell,
Who long before the morning service bell
Were sitting in a tavern for a drink.
And as they sat, they heard the hand-bell
   clink
Before a coffin going to the grave; 5
One of them called the little tavern-knave

And said "Go and find out at once—look
   spry!
Whose corpse is in that coffin passing by;
And see you get the name correctly too."
"Sir," said the boy, "no need, I promise
   you; 10
Two hours before you came here I was
   told.

He was a friend of yours in days of old,
And suddenly, last night, the man was
 slain,
Upon his bench, face up, dead drunk
 again.
There came a privy[1] thief, they call him
 Death, 15
Who kills us all round here, and in a breath
He speared him through the heart, he
 never stirred.
And then Death went his way without a
 word.
He's killed a thousand in the present
 plague,
And, sir, it doesn't do to be too vague 20
If you should meet him; you had best be
 wary.
Be on your guard with such an adversary,
Be primed to meet him everywhere you
 go,
That's what my mother said. It's all I
 know."
 The publican[2] joined in with, "By St
 Mary. 25
What the child says is right; you'd best be
 wary,
This very year he killed, in a large village
A mile away, man, woman, serf at tillage,
Page in the household, children—all
 there were.
Yes, I imagine that he lives round there. 30
It's well to be prepared in these alarms,
He might do you dishonour." "Huh,
 God's arms!"
The rioter said, "Is he so fierce to meet?
I'll search for him, by Jesus, street by street.
God's blessed bones! I'll register a vow! 35
Here, chaps! The three of us together
 now,
Hold up your hands, like me, and we'll be
 brothers
In this affair, and each defend the others,
And we will kill this traitor Death, I say!
Away with him as he has made away 40
With all our friends. God's dignity! To-
 night!"
 They made their bargain, swore with
 appetite,

These three, to live and die for one another
As brother-born might swear to his born
 brother.
And up they started in their drunken
 rage 45
And made towards this village which the
 page
And publican had spoken of before.
Many and grisly were the oaths they swore,
Tearing Christ's blessed body to a shred;[3]
"If we can only catch him, Death is dead!" 50
 When they had gone not fully half a
 mile,
Just as they were about to cross a stile,
They came upon a very poor old man
Who humbly greeted them and thus
 began,
"God look to you my lords, and give you
 quiet!" 55
To which the proudest of these men of riot
Gave back the answer, "What, old fool?
 Give place!
Why are you all wrapped up except your
 face?
Why live so long? Isn't it time to die?"
 The old, old fellow looked him in the
 eye[4] 60
And said, "Because I never yet have
 found,
Though I have walked to India, search-
 ing round
Village and city on my pilgrimage,
One who would change his youth to have
 my age.
And so my age is mine and must be still 65
Upon me, for such time as God may will.
 "Not even Death, alas, will take my life;
So, like a wretched prisoner at strife
Within himself, I walk alone and wait
About the earth, which is my mother's
 gate, 70

1. **privy** (priv′ ē), secretive, stealthy.
2. **publican** (pub′ lə kən), innkeeper.
3. **to a shred.** They swore by various parts of Christ's body.
4. Note that this figure has symbolic meaning.

Knock-knocking with my staff from night
    to noon
And crying, 'Mother, open to me soon!
Look at me, Mother, won't you let me in?
See how I wither, flesh and blood and skin!
Alas! When will these bones be laid to
    rest?   75
Mother, I would exchange—for that
    were best—
The wardrobe in my chamber, standing
    there
So long, for yours! Aye, for a shirt of hair
To wrap me in!' She has refused her grace,
Whence comes the pallor of my withered
    face.   80
  "But it dishonoured you when you began
To speak so roughly, sir, to an old man,
Unless he had injured you in word or deed.
It says in holy writ, as you may read,
'Thou shalt rise up before the hoary head   85
And honour it.' And therefore be it said
'Do no more harm to an old man than
    you,
Being now young, would have another
    do
When you are old'—if you should live till
    then.
And so may God be with you, gentlemen,   90
For I must go whither I have to go."
  "By God," the gambler said, "you
    shan't do so,
You don't get off so easy, by St John!
I heard you mention, just a moment gone,
A certain traitor Death who singles out   95
And kills the fine young fellows here-
    about.
And you're his spy, by God! You wait a
    bit.
Say where he is or you shall pay for it,
By God and by the Holy Sacrament!
I say you've joined together by consent   100
To kill us younger folk, you thieving
    swine!"
  "Well, sirs," he said, "if it be your design
To find out Death, turn up this crooked
    way
Towards that grove. I left him there
    to-day

Under a tree, and there you'll find him
    waiting.   105
He isn't one to hide for all your prating.
You see that oak? He won't be far to find.
And God protect you that redeemed
    mankind,
Aye, and amend you!" Thus that ancient
    man.
  At once the three young rioters began   110
To run, and reached the tree, and there
    they found
A pile of golden florins on the ground,
New-coined, eight bushels of them as
    they thought.
No longer was it Death those fellows
    sought.
For they were all so thrilled to see the
    sight,   115
The florins were so beautiful and bright,
That down they sat beside the precious
    pile.
The wickedest spoke first after a while.
"Brothers," he said, "you listen to what I
    say.
I'm pretty sharp although I joke away.   120
It's clear that Fortune has bestowed this
    treasure
To let us live in jollity and pleasure.
Light come, light go! We'll spend it as we
    ought.
God's precious dignity! Who would have
    thought
This morning was to be our lucky day?   125
  "If one could only get the gold away,
Back to my house, or else to yours,
    perhaps—
For as you know, the gold is ours, chaps—
We'd all be at the top of fortune, hey?
But certainly it can't be done by day.   130
People would call us robbers—a strong
    gang,
So our own property would make us hang.
No, we must bring this treasure back by
    night
Some prudent way, and keep it out of sight.
And so as a solution I propose   135
We draw for lots and see the way it goes.
The one who draws the longest, lucky man,

Shall run to town as quickly as he can
To fetch us bread and wine—but keep
    things dark—
While two remain in hiding here to mark   140
Our heap of treasure. If there's no delay,
When night comes down we'll carry it
    away,
All three of us, wherever we have
    planned."
    He gathered lots and hid them in his
    hand
Bidding them draw for where the luck
    should fall.   145
It fell upon the youngest of them all,
And off he ran at once towards the town.
    As soon as he had gone the first sat down
And thus began a parley with the other:
"You know that you can trust me as a
    brother;   150
Now let me tell you where your profit
    lies;
You know our friend has gone to get
    supplies
And here's a lot of gold that is to be
Divided equally amongst us three.
Nevertheless, if I could shape things thus   155
So that we shared it out—the two of us—
Wouldn't you take it as a friendly turn?"
    "But how?" the other said. "He knows
    the fact
That all the gold was left with me and you;
What can we tell him? What are we to do?"   160
    "Is it a bargain," said the first, "or no?
For I can tell you in a word or so
What's to be done to bring the thing
    about."
"Trust me," the other said, "you needn't
    doubt
My word. I won't betray you, I'll be true."   165
    "Well," said his friend, "you see that
    we are two,
And two are twice as powerful as one.
Now look; when he comes back, get up in
    fun
To have a wrestle; then, as you attack,

I'll up and put my dagger through his
    back   170
While you and he are struggling, as in
    game;
Then draw your dagger too and do the
    same.
Then all this money will be ours to spend,
Divided equally of course, dear friend.
Then we can gratify our lusts and fill   175
The day with dicing at our own sweet will."
Thus these two miscreants agreed to slay
The third and youngest, as you heard me
    say.
    The youngest, as he ran towards the
    town,
Kept turning over, rolling up and down   180
Within his heart the beauty of those bright
New florins, saying, "Lord, to think I might
Have all that treasure to myself alone!
Could there be anyone beneath the throne
Of God so happy as I then should be?"   185
    And so the Fiend, our common enemy,
Was given power to put it in his thought
That there was always poison to be bought,
And that with poison he could kill his
    friends.
To men in such a state the Devil sends   190
Thoughts of this kind, and has a full per-
    mission
To lure them on to sorrow and perdition;
For this young man was utterly content
To kill them both and never to repent.
    And on he ran, he had no thought to
    tarry,   195
Came to the town, found an apothecary
And said, "Sell me some poison if you will,
I have a lot of rats I want to kill
And there's a polecat⁵ too about my yard
That takes my chickens and it hits me
    hard;   200
But I'll get even, as is only right,
With vermin that destroy a man by
    night."

5. **polecat,** a European carnivorous animal like a ferret, not the American skunk.

The chemist answered, "I've a prepa-
    ration
Which you shall have, and by my soul's
    salvation
If any living creature eat or drink   205
A mouthful, ere he has the time to think,
Though he took less than makes a grain
    of wheat,
You'll see him fall down dying at your
    feet;
Yes, die he must, and in so short a while
You'd hardly have the time to walk a
    mile,   210
The poison is so strong, you understand."
  This cursed fellow grabbed into his
    hand
The box of poison and away he ran
Into a neighbouring street, and found a
    man

Who lent him three large bottles. He
    withdrew   215
And deftly poured the poison into two.
He kept the third one clean, as well he
    might,
For his own drink, meaning to work all
    night
Stacking the gold and carrying it away.
And when this rioter, this devil's clay,   220
Had filled his bottles up with wine, all
    three,
Back to rejoin his comrades sauntered he.
  Why make a sermon of it? Why waste
    breath?
Exactly in the way they'd planned his death
They fell on him and slew him, two to
    one.   225
Then said the first of them when this was
    done,

"Now for a drink. Sit down and let's be
    merry.
For later on there'll be the corpse to bury."
And, as it happened, reaching for a sup,
He took a bottle full of poison up   230
And drank; and his companion, nothing
    loth,
Drank from it also, and they perished
    both.

    •   •   •   •   •

    Dearly beloved, God forgive your sin
And keep you from the vice of avarice!
My holy pardon frees you all of this,   235
Provided that you make the right
    approaches,
That is with sterling, rings, or silver
    brooches.
Bow down your heads under this holy
    bull![6]
Come on, you women, offer up your wool!
I'll write your name into my ledger; so!   240
Into the bliss of Heaven you shall go.
For I'll absolve you by my holy power,
You that make offering, clean as at the
    hour
When you were born. . . . That, sirs, is
    how I preach
And Jesu Christ, soul's healer, aye, the
    leech[7]   245
Of every soul, grant pardon and relieve
    you
Of sin, for that is best, I won't deceive you.
    One thing I should have mentioned in
    my tale,
Dear people. I've some relics in my bale
And pardons too, as full and fine, I hope,   250
As any in England, given me by the Pope.
If there be one among you that is willing
To have my absolution for a shilling
Devoutly given, come! and do not harden
Your hearts but kneel in humbleness for
    pardon   255
Or else, receive my pardon as we go.
You can renew it every town or so
Always provided that you still renew

Each time, and in good money, what is due.
It is an honour to you to have found   260
A pardoner with his credentials sound
Who can absolvė you as you ply the spur
In any accident that may occur.
For instance—we are all at Fortune's
    beck—
Your horse may throw you down and
    break your neck.   265
What a security it is to all
To have me here among you and at call
With pardon for the lowly and the great
When soul leaves body for the future state!
And I advise our Host here to begin,   270
The most enveloped of you all in sin.
Come forward, Host, you shall be first to
    pay.
And kiss my holy relics right away.

6. **holy bull,** decree from the Pope.
7. **leech,** physician.

FOR UNDERSTANDING

Be prepared to defend or to refute any of the propositions below. Check the story, if you are not sure of your grounds.
1. The portrait of the Pardoner in the "Prologue" doesn't suit a person who could tell such a sensitive tale as this.
2. The details given about the old man in the story clearly indicate that he is Death.
3. The Pardoner's intention in telling this story is to cheat the pilgrims.

FOR APPRECIATION

A Short Story in Verse

Chaucer's remarkable gifts as a storyteller are particularly visible in his control of a story's pace, in his mastery of dialogue, in his patterning of the right details to create a mood. Chaucer quickly and picturesquely establishes the chilly setting of his tale in the predawn tavern scene with the three rioters. He is acutely sensitive, as one forced to read his poems to a live audience must be, to the necessity for a fast-moving tale. As John Dryden remarked of Chaucer's narrative skill: "As he knew what to say, so he knows also when to leave off—a continence which is practiced by few writers." Find examples of this restraint in the story.

The Short Story, Dialogue, Details

Note that the whole story takes only 232 lines. Two thirds of these are dialogue. The third which is not dialogue generally introduces some conversation. Thus, Chaucer sets his mood, develops his characters, and advances his plot almost totally by dialogue. Yet he is able to give distinctive characters to the tavern-knave, the old man, the publican, and each of the three rioters.

By his patterning of details, Chaucer manages to keep a sense of doom hanging heavy over his tale. Reread the story to see how the following factors contribute to this: the plague; the predawn setting; the clinking bell; the simple and restrained utterances of the boy and the old man; the bravado and the dramatic ironies of the rioter's speech that suggest so forcefully that from within the rioters shall come the flame which will devour them.

1. The characters in this story have ironic speeches. Cite several instances where they are saying far more than they think they are.

2. Explain how the simple, natural dialogue increases the terror of the supernatural forces that are effortlessly achieving their end.

3. How can Chaucer's power to give meaning to details be seen in the youngest rioter's excuse to the apothecary when asking for poison?

LANGUAGE AND VOCABULARY

A. Determine the meaning of these italicized words from the context of Chaucer's "Prologue."

  1. the *engendering* of the flower (line 4);

2. their heart *engages* (line 11);

3. into that *hostelry* (line 23);

4. that dangled from a *baldric* of bright green (line 120);

5. so charitably *solicitous* she used to weep (lines 197–198);

6. he knew in *verity* (line 231);

7. a profit might *accrue* (line 253);

8. too unworldly to make search for *secular* employment (line 303).

After examining the expressions, look up the italicized words to verify your guesses.

B. From period to period, words shift in their meanings; that is, they undergo *semantic* change. The original work of Chaucer would demonstrate this fact very clearly, but even the translation you have uses words with meanings no longer common, such as these from the "Prologue":

    bathed in *liquor* of such power;
    to seek the stranger *strands;*
    had followed *chivalry;*
    a perfect *gentle-knight;*
    a lover and *cadet;*
    embroidered like a meadow bright;
    a *saucy* brace;
    a *proper* forester I guess;
    to *counterfeit* a courtly kind of grace.

Use your dictionary to be sure that you know what meanings are intended in this selection. (Some dictionaries give older meanings first, but many put them after the current meanings.) Especially in reading older literature, make it a habit to notice when words have changed their meanings.

On the other hand, the translator has tried to use words that suggest in modern English what was originally intended in Chaucer's language.

C. The Knight is said to be "modest as a maid." The Squire is "embroidered like a meadow bright" and "fresh as is the month of May."

What other similes do you find in the "Prologue"?

Middle English Lyrics

Poetry and music have always been closely intertwined. In Old English poetry, a harper strummed a stringed instrument as accompaniment to a poem that was spoken aloud. In Middle English, long poems like those of Chaucer are no longer recited to a musical background, but short poems become even more closely associated with music—they actually become words to a song. When the sung words tell a story, the poem is called a ballad; when the words convey intense emotion encompassed in a single moment of time, the poem is called a lyric—the same word we still use for the text of a popular song or show tune. Many Middle English lyrics are anonymous, although sometimes we also have the melodies to which they were sung.

It seems clear that a new lyricism in Middle English can be traced back directly to the twelfth century, even though the earliest manuscripts for most of these lyrics date from the thirteenth century onwards. When Eleanor of Aquitaine became queen of England in 1152, she brought with her the influence of the Provençal troubadours and, as patron of a number of poets, encouraged this popular art form to take root in England. Her grandfather, William IX of Poitiers, was the first troubadour poet in Europe, bringing back new Near-Eastern varieties of song and lyric from his stay in Palestine after the First Crusade. In France, troubadours were called *trouvères,* in Germany *minnesingers,* and in England minstrels—but whatever they were called they caused a popular upsurge in songs and lyrics of all kinds. In England, these included drinking songs, songs to the Virgin Mary, songs welcoming spring, and songs about death. "Now Go'th Sun Under Wood" dates, in manuscript, from the early thirteenth century, "I Sing of a Maiden" and "Western Wind" from the early fifteenth century, and "The Corpus Christi Carol" from the early sixteenth century. These poems all foreshadow the flowering of lyrical poetry in the Renaissance.

Now Go'th Sun Under Wood

Now goth[1] sonne under wode[2]—
Me reweth,[3] Marie, thy faire rode.[4]
Now goth sonne under tree—
Me reweth, Marie, thy sone and thee.

1. **goth,** goeth.
2. **wode,** wood.
3. **me reweth,** literally, it is rueful to me; therefore, I pity.
4. **rode,** face.

Detail: Hunting Scene, Devonshire Tapestry
Victoria and Albert Museum
Crown copyright

I Sing of a Maiden

I sing of a maiden
    That is makeless:[1]
King of alle kinges
    To[2] her son she ches.[3]

He came also[4] stille   5
    Where his mother was
As dew in Aprille
    That falleth on the grass.

He came also stille
    To his mother's bower[5]   10
As dew in Aprille
    That falleth on the flower.

He came also stille
    Where his mother lay
As dew in Aprille   15
    That falleth on the spray.

Mother and maiden
    Was never none but she—
Well may such a lady
    Godes mother be.   20

1. **makeless.** There are two meanings here: mateless and matchless.
2. **to,** for.
3. **ches,** chose.
4. **also,** as.
5. **bower,** room, and, figuratively, womb.

The Corpus Christi[1] Carol

    Lully lullay, lully, lullay
    The falcon hath born my make[2] away.

He bore him up, he bore him down,
He bore him into an orchard brown.

In that orchard there was a hall   5
That was hanged with purple and pall.[3]

And in that hall there was a bed,
It was hanged with gold so red.

And in that bed there lieth a knight,
His woundes bleeding day and night.   10

By that bed's side there kneeleth a may[4]
And she weepeth both night and day.

And by that bed's side there standeth a stone,
Corpus Christi written thereon.

1. **Corpus Christi,** the body of Christ.
2. **make,** mate.
3. **purple and pall,** rich purple cloth.
4. **may,** maiden.

Western Wind

Western wind, when will thou blow,
The small rain down can rain?
Christ, if my love were in my arms
And I in my bed again!

FOR UNDERSTANDING

Now Go'th Sun Under Wood

1. Some editions give this poem the title "Sunset on Calvary." Why doesn't the speaker just refer to that moment? What details create that reference?
2. This poem is made up of two couplets that are similar, but not exactly the same. What is the emotional force of the repeated words? What is the emotional force of the different words?

I Sing of a Maiden

1. What are the details in the poem which imply that the maiden is really the Virgin Mary? Why is that revelation kept for the last line?
2. The second, third, and fourth stanzas are very much alike, with only a slight variation in the metaphor. What is the emotional effect of those three stanzas?

The Corpus Christi Carol

1. The poem begins with a refrain that we are intended to hear after each of the stanzas. What effect does the refrain create?
2. What is the actual situation implied in the poem? What details might suggest a religious significance in that situation?
3. What is the emotional force of: "an orchard brown," "purple and pall," "gold so red"?
4. One might describe this poem in cinematic terms: The camera (speaker's voice) moves closer and closer to the scene, focusing first on the setting, then on the characters, and finally on the stone and its inscription. What is the effect of this progression?

Western Wind

1. What do we know about the speaker of this poem? Why is the speaker talking about the weather?
2. What kind of language is characteristic of the poem? What word doesn't seem characteristic—and why is it used?
3. One way that the poem works is through an implicit but unstated contrast. Look for this contrast between the first two lines and the last two.

INTERPRETATION AND APPRECIATION

A Closer Look at "Western Wind"

To look at one of these short poems in some detail may give an idea of how packed with meaning a lyric can be. "Western Wind" is surely the simplest if not the shortest poem here. It is direct and forceful in expression, uses the easiest vocabulary imaginable (only two words are more than a syllable long), and comes across to most readers with an undeniably powerful impact. Yet in its simplicity and directness a good many elements are combined to achieve the poem's effect—its images, its rhythms, its creation of an imaginary person who might be speaking these words, the exact order in which we learn the details the poem contains, even the pauses.

Many readers point out at once that part of the poem's effect is its surprising violation of common-sense expectations at certain points. For one thing, a question addressed to the wind in the first two lines is followed, not by an answer, but by an exclamation—an outcry—in the last two lines, addressed either as a prayer or an oath to the

Christian Deity. For another, the word "small" rings on most ears as a strange choice; the word indisputably has an emotional effect that is part of the poem's strength, but it's hard to say just how this effect works. In the last two lines, the details seem to come in the wrong order (from a logical or commonsense point of view), but this feels eerily *right* in context. Finally, the rhythm of the poem is a common lyrical alternation of four-beat lines and three-beat lines, but both four-beat lines (the first and third) start with strong accents, and in the third this is followed by a disruption of the so-far regular rhythms of the poem ("if my love").

How can these details be related to the emotional impact of the poetry, which most readers will agree is only intensified by these very things? Before we can answer this question, we must establish what we can say about the poem to start with. First of all, we do not know the gender of the speaker or where the loved one is, only that the latter is absent and sorely missed. Second, we can suspect that it is the speaker of the lines who is away from home, since otherwise the narrator wouldn't need to wish that he or she could be in "my bed again." Otherwise we know nothing about the setting; we do not even know if the outcry of longing is for an absent spouse, because the embrace and the bed are kept separate as wishes—the first may in fact never have occurred before.

The address to the western wind makes one feel that an outdoor setting is likely. Some readers infer the setting to be a becalmed ship whose passengers have run short of water. Others infer a coastal setting, looking eastward across the sea (eastward to home?), in a landscape parched by drought. Are there enough details to decide in favor of either setting? At any rate, the word "small" adds a number of possibilities to our accruing sense of the poem's richness. The west-ern wind (particularly on the west coast of a landmass) brings a rain that is heavy and steady when it is composed of small raindrops rather than the large drops of a brief thunderstorm. The thirst expressed by the second line (whether of the people on a ship, or of the crops in a parched landscape) is for a long, fulfilled slaking by a fine rain. Considering this, "small" here comes para-doxically to mean almost the opposite of what it first seems to mean.

Then the regular rhythms of the first two lines are suddenly disrupted by what we think will be an answer, but is instead an outcry, in the form either of a prayer or a profanity, followed by disturbed rhythms in what remains ("if my love" and "in my bed"). The effect is to show up the vague wish for different weather in the first two lines with the real urgency the speaker feels in the last two. But what would be the difference if the last two lines went "Christ, if I lay in my own bed,/ With my love in my arms again!" Many have agreed that the whole power of the poem would be destroyed by this shift of order. But why? Do we not think of *where* we want to lie before we think of who would be there with us? With the order as it is in the poem, the effect is surely to emphasize the intensity of the longing for the beloved as more important than where the embrace would occur. Perhaps you will see other reasons for preferring the order as given in the poem. You may in fact see other possible settings or speakers for the poem than cited here. If so, explain your views to the class. (One inter-pretation is that the speaker is necessarily someone left at home by a lover who has gone away. Is this possible?) One of the beauties of poems as power-ful as "Western Wind" is that they often allow a multitude of interpretations—even conflicting ones—without losing their ability to move us and intrigue our imaginations.

Middle English Ballads

We do not know the authors of the popular ballads (or folk ballads), nor can we be sure when during the Middle Ages the ballads were composed. They seem to grow out of the same oral tradition of storytelling that is described in *Beowulf*, but even that theory will not tell us who the storytellers were. Nor can we be sure where they lived, although the many dialect words suggest Scotland or northern England as a location. Moreover, as collectors of ballads began searching for material, they found different versions of the same ballad; this diversity may imply revision of the "original" ballad by people living in different places or at different times. Although ballads were probably composed from the twelfth century on, interest in them was slight until the eighteenth century. Then writers began to praise them as simple but natural, and scholars interested in England's literary past began to hunt for native English material. Thus, Bishop Percy published *Reliques of English Poetry*

in 1765, and Sir Walter Scott, the novelist, published *Minstrelsy of the Scottish Border* in 1803. The influence of such scholarship can be seen when we remember that Wordsworth and Coleridge published a joint collection in 1798 called *Lyrical Ballads*. The major collection of ballads came almost a hundred years later, with the work of F.J. Child, who collected five volumes of ballads between 1882 and 1898. Thus "Sir Patrick Spens" may be cited as Child, no. 58, because that is how it is listed in *The English and Scottish Ballads*.

The basic form consists of a four-line stanza (quatrain) with four strong beats in lines 1 and 3 and three strong beats in lines 2 and 4. Lines 2 and 4 normally rhyme; there is often a refrain, or frequent repetition of words and phrases. The simplicity of form joins with the ballad's usually stark or tragic content to produce haunting poetry, evocative through what it leaves out as well as what it describes.

The incident recounted in this poem is grounded in history. In 1281, the King of Scotland forced Sir Patrick Spens to sail a ship bearing the King's daughter, Princess Margaret, to her husband, the King of Norway. On the return voyage, Sir Patrick and the Scots lords who accompanied the Princess were drowned.

Sir Patrick Spens

The king sits in Dumferline town,
  Drinking the blude-reid[1] wine:
"O whar will I get a guid sailor
  To sail this ship of mine?"

Up and spak an eldern knicht,[2]   5
  Sat at the king's richt knee:
"Sir Patrick Spens is the best sailor
  That sails upon the sea."

1. **blude-reid,** blood-red.
2. **eldern knicht,** old knight.

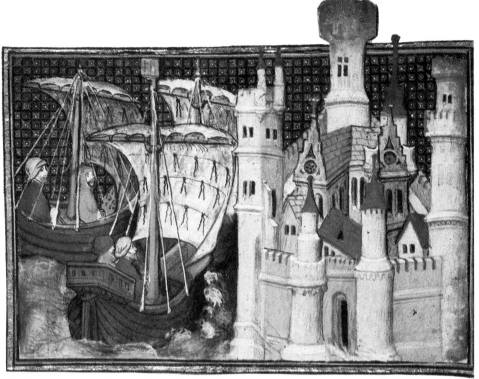

Salisbury arrives at Conway Castle by ship, from
Histoire du Richard II.

The king has written a braid³ letter
    And signed it wi' his hand,   10
And sent it to Sir Patrick Spens,
    Was walking on the sand.

The first line that Sir Patrick read,
    A loud lauch⁴ lauched he;
The next line that Sir Patrick read,   15
    The tear blinded his ee.

"O wha is this has done this deed,
    This ill deed done to me,
To send me out this time o' the year,
    To sail upon the sea?   20

"Make haste, make haste, my mirry men all,
    Our guid ship sails the morn."
"O say na sae,⁵ my master dear,
    For I fear a deadly storm.

"Late late yestre'en I saw the new moon   25
    Wi' the auld moon in her arm,⁶
And I fear, I fear, my dear master,
    That we will come to harm."

O our Scots nobles were richt laith⁷
    To weet⁸ their cork-heeled shoon,⁹   30
But lang owre a' the play were played
    Their hats they swam aboon.¹⁰

---

3. **braid,** broad, plainspoken.
4. **lauch,** laugh.
5. **na sae,** not so.
6. **yestre'en . . . auld moon in her arm,** yesterday
evening. The illusion of an old moon within the new one
was thought to be an omen of a great storm.
7. **richt laith,** right (very) loath.
8. **weet,** wet.
9. **shoon,** shoes.
10. **owre,** before; **a' the play,** all the play before the
business ended; **aboon,** above.

O lang, lang may their ladies sit,
　　Wi' their fans into their hand,
Or e'er they see Sir Patrick Spens
　　Come sailing to the land.

O lang, lang may the ladies stand,
　　Wi' their gold kembs[11] in their hair,
Waiting for their ain[12] dear lords,
　　For they'll see thame na mair.[13]

Half o'er,[14] half o'er to Aberdour
　　It's fifty fadom[15] deep,
35　And there lies guid Sir Patrick Spens,
　　Wi' the Scots lords at his feet.

11. **kembs,** combs.
12. **ain,** own.
13. **thame na mair,** them no more.
14. **half o'er,** over (half way).
40　15. **fadom,** fathom.

Edward

"Why does your brand sae drap wi' bluid,[1]
　　Edward, Edward?
Why does your brand sae drap wi' bluid,
　　And why sae sad gang ye, O?"
"O I ha'e killed my hawk sae guid,　　　　　　　5
　　Mither, mither,[2]
O I ha'e killed my hawk sae guid,
　　And I had nae mair but he, O."

"Your hawkes bluid was never sae reid,[3]
　　Edward, Edward.　　　　　　　　　　　　10
Your hawkes bluid was never sae reid,
　　My dear son I tell thee, O."
"O I ha'e killed my reid-roan steed,
　　Mither, mither,
O I ha'e killed my reid-roan steed,　　　　　　15
　　That erst[4] was sae fair and free, O."

"Your steed was auld and ye ha'e gat mair,[5]
　　Edward, Edward.
Your steed was auld and ye ha'e gat mair:
　　Some other dule ye dree,[6] O."　　　　　　20
"O I ha'e killed my fader[7] dear,
　　Mither, mither,

1. **brand sae drap wi' bluid,** sword so drip with blood.
2. **mither,** mother.
3. **reid,** red.
4. **erst,** used to be.

5. **ye ha'e gat mair.** You have more horses.
6. **dule ye dree.** Some other sorrow you suffer.
7. **fader,** father.

"O I ha'e killed my fader dear,
　　Alas and wae[8] is me, O!"

"And whatten penance wul ye dree[9] for that,　　**25**
　　Edward, Edward?
And whatten penance wul ye dree for that,
　　My dear son, now tell me, O?"
"I'll set my feet in yonder boat,
　　Mither, mither,　　**30**
I'll set my feet in yonder boat,
　　And I'll fare over the sea, O."

"And what wul ye do wi' your towers and your ha',[10]
　　Edward, Edward?
And what wul ye do wi' your towers and your ha',　　**35**
　　That were sae fair to see, O?"
"I'll let thame stand til they down fa',
　　Mither, mither,
I'll let thame stand till they down fa',
　　For here never mair maun I be, O."　　**40**

"And what wul ye leave to your bairns[11] and your wife,
　　Edward, Edward?
And what wul ye leave to your bairns and your wife,
　　Whan ye gang over the sea, O?"
"The warldes room late them beg thrae life,[12]　　**45**
　　Mither, mither,
The warldes room late them beg thrae life,
　　For thame never mair wul I see, O."

"And what wul ye leave to your ain mither dear,
　　Edward, Edward?　　**50**
And what wul ye leave to your ain mither dear,
　　My dear son, now tell me, O?"
"The curse of hell frae me sal[13] ye bear,
　　Mither, mither,
The curse of hell frae me sal ye bear,　　**55**
　　Sic counseils[14] ye gave to me, O."

8. **wae,** woe.
9. **whatten . . . wul ye dree.** What penance will you suffer?
10. **ha',** hall, castle.
11. **bairns,** children.

12. **warldes . . . thrae life.** Let them beg throughout the whole world for life.
13. **frae me sal,** from me shall.
14. **sic counseils,** such advice.

From the seventeenth century to the present, "Barbara Allan" has continued to be the most popular single ballad of all, counting versions in Scotland, England, and America. In 1666, English diarist Samuel Pepys tells of singing it with delight. In 1635, a Scots version, "Bar'bry Ellen," was brought to Salem in New England by one Ralph Ellwood. English versions also came to the New World early and stayed late, not only in New England, but in the Kentucky mountains, in Mississippi, in Georgia, and in Nebraska. Ninety-eight different versions have been collected by folklorists from Virginia alone. In our century, it became the central song in a Broadway musical, Dark of the Moon, *as well as a pop tune on the Hit Parade in the 1950s. The perennial fascination of the work lies as much in the poetry as in the song's haunting melody.*

Barbara Allan

It was in and about the Martinmas[1] time,
    When the green leaves were a-fallin',
That Sir John Graeme in the West Country
    Fell in love with Barbara Allan.

He sent his man down through the town   5
    To the place where she was dwellin',
"O haste and come to my master dear,
    'Gin[2] ye be Barbara Allan."

O slowly, slowly rase[3] she up,
    To the place where he was lyin',   10
And when she drew the curtain by:
    "Young man, I think you're dyin'."

"O it's I'm sick, and very, very sick,
    And 'tis a'[4] for Barbara Allan."
"O the better for me ye sal[5] never be,   15
    Though your heart's blood were a-spillin'.

"O dinna ye mind,[6] young man," said she,
    "When ye the cups were fillin',
That ye made the healths gae[7] round and round,
    And slighted Barbara Allan?"   20

He turned his face unto the wall,
    And death with him was dealin':
"Adieu, adieu, my dear friends all,
    And be kind to Barbara Allan."

And slowly, slowly, rase she him up,   25
    And slowly, slowly left him;
And sighing said she could not stay,
    Since death of life had reft[8] him.

She had not gane a mile but twa,[9]
    When she heard the dead-bell knellin',   30
And every jow[10] that the dead-bell ga'ed[11]
    It cried, "Woe to Barbara Allan!"

"O mother, mother, make my bed,
    O make it soft and narrow:
Since my love died for me today,   35
    I'll die for him tomorrow."

1. **Martinmas,** November 11, St. Martin's Day, commemorating St. Martin of Tours.
2. **'Gin,** if.
3. **rase,** rose.
4. **a',** all.
5. **sal,** shall.
6. **dinna ye mind.** Don't you remember.
7. **gae,** go.
8. **reft,** deprived.
9. **twa,** two.
10. **jow,** stroke.
11. **ga'ed,** made (literally, go'ed, past tense of "go").

FOR UNDERSTANDING

Sir Patrick Spens

1. How does the picture of the king, told in the first two lines, show his attitude toward the job he is assigning? What is the significance of the fact that the king does not seem to know the best sailor in his kingdom? Who suggests the name of Sir Patrick to the king? Why is it significant that he "sat at the king's right knee"?

2. The fourth stanza has a vivid contrast between the first two lines and the last two. How has Sir Patrick's attitude changed in the last two lines?

3. Is Sir Patrick really asking a question in the fifth stanza, or is he simply raging against an unjust fate?

4. Why doesn't the narrator describe the storm? How do the images in the eighth stanza convey the scene and the emotional effect of the drowning?

5. Where do the narrator's sympathies lie?

6. Is the basic conflict between the king and Sir Patrick or between Sir Patrick and the elder knight? Is it between a simple man of action and a group of politicians or between duty and common sense? Or is it between each of these pairs?

7. Ballads often represent the voice of the common people protesting against the social order in which they live. If you look at this ballad from this point of view, what is it saying?

Edward

1. Dialogue makes up the whole poem. Who are the two speakers?

2. What is Edward's rank in society? What lines in the song supply this information?

3. Is the mother really seeking information? Or does she know the answer all along?

4. Why does Edward try to avoid telling the truth to his mother?

5. The poem represents an intense moment of conflict between mother and son, but not the whole story that led to this moment. Can you reconstruct the essential story from hints given in the poem? What kind of woman is the mother? What do you suppose were her motives?

Barbara Allan

1. What does the poem suggest about the social classes to which the main characters belong? Why is the class distinction important in the poem?

2. How does the poem evoke our sympathy for Sir John? How does it evoke sympathy for Barbara Allan?

3. "Martinmas" (line 1) refers to a festival in honor of St. Martin, who is best known for his generosity; the incident when he shared his cloak with a beggar, and then had a vision in which the beggar turned out to be Christ, is a frequently pictured moment. As a church festival, Martinmas had taken the place of an older pagan festival; the saint therefore also acquired an association with drinking parties and was considered the patron of reformed drunkards. Moreover, Martinmas implied to the English what "Indian summer" does to Americans–a short return of mild weather in the middle of the autumn. How are these associations with Martinmas relevant to the poem?

Sir Thomas Malory
William Caxton

1405–1471
1422–1491

There is much confusion as to the identity of Sir Thomas Malory, but the most likely person seems to be the individual born in the early 1400s in Newbold Revel, Warwickshire, to John Malory, a respectable small landholder. Seemingly well educated, since he could read both French and Latin, Malory probably inherited the family estate when his father died in 1443 or 1444, and he was knighted sometime after this. In 1445 he served a term in Parliament, but a few years later his life underwent a startling change. He was charged with attempted murder, stealing cattle, attacking an abbey, and stealing money. By January of 1452, he was in prison in London, where he waited more than eight years for a trial that never came.

But it was not in Malory's nature to wait patiently, and he used sword and dagger, bribery, and political influence to get outside the prison walls. Unfortunately, his freedom only lasted for short periods. There is evidence that indicates he fought in the War of the Roses, but not always on the same side. King Edward

"How Arthur took and wedded Guinevere" from the frontispiece to the third book of Malory's Morte Darthur, *printed by Wynkyn de Worde in 1529.*

The British Library, London

Miniature from "Poems of Charles, Duke of Orleans" (c. 1500), showing the Tower of London in the foreground and London Bridge with medieval houses in background.

The British Library, London

One of the earliest representations of a printing press, a detail of the title page of De Rerum Natura *by Lucetius showing the first mark of Badius Ascensius (Paris 1514).*

Roberey New Photographics, Ltd.
© St. Bride Printing Library

evidently felt bitter enough towards Malory to twice deny him amnesty when others were pardoned under a general order.

Malory was imprisoned much of the time at Newgate prison, close to the house of the Grey Friars, who were reputed to have a splendid library. Perhaps he was permitted access to their manuscripts. Certainly he was well aware of how the world of knights and chivalry was giving way to hired mercenaries and power grabs. To escape this reality, he may have immersed himself in the Arthurian legends. At this time, these were either in Latin or French. Perhaps he saw a need for translation so that the English people could once again know the glory of their past. Malory, still in prison, finished his manuscript in 1470. Presumably, when he died in 1471, he was still there. When his estate was examined, it was discovered that he had died penniless, for the oftentimes rash Malory had prudently made all his property over to his wife.

It was fortunate for Malory that William Caxton, a successful English businessman, was a contemporary of his. At the command of his patroness, Margaret of Burgundy, Caxton translated a collection of stories about Troy into English. Unable to supply the demand for copies by using scribes, Caxton went to Cologne, where he studied the new art of printing. Returning to Bruges, he first published his own book in 1475. The next year he took his press to London, and in 1478 he published Chaucer's *Canterbury Tales*, brought out a second edition in 1484, and followed this with Malory's *Le Morte Darthur* in 1485.

Though Caxton probably did not believe Malory's tales to be historically accurate, he encouraged the reader in his preface to lay aside skepticism, though he adds, "ye are at your liberty to accept or reject the truth of Malory's narrative." Shrewd businessman that he was, he praised the example set forth by the acts of chivalry in the stories, showing the "gentle and virtuous deeds that some knights performed." Then he warned the reader that acts of "cowardice, murder, hate and sin" occurred in the book as well. He seemed to sense that such a warning could only increase reader interest.

Jousting outside the walls of Camelot, from the Chronicles of Hainault.

© Bibliotheque Royale Albert ler
Bruxelles

from LE MORTE DARTHUR

People have always had a need for heroes fighting against great odds for right and justice. Generally such glorious characters are placed in some period of the distant past. So it is not surprising that the highly imaginative people of the Middle Ages chose King Arthur as the person around whom to build a massive body of legends, just as Robin Hood became the hero for a later time and the lawmen of our Old West intrigue today's Americans.

It is an accepted fact that there was a British king named Arthur living in the sixth century who repelled an invasion of the Anglo Saxons. But it was not until much later that the legends began to flourish. Chivalry was invented; Merlin the magician, the round table, and a roster of individual knights were created; and Camelot rose in all its beauty. But there never was a time when knights adventured through the countryside to right some wrong, which most often meant rescuing a young lady in distress. Nor was there a magician with charms and potions nor a landscape like that which surrounded Camelot.

Malory used as the source for his book "certain French books" about King Arthur and his life. For a time, the French kept these legends alive when they had gone underground in England. Far more than a translator, Malory produced one of the great pieces of English prose by his innate sense for the dramatic incident, by rearranging, expanding, or condensing his materials to suit his own purposes, by using natural-sounding dialogue, by giving a base of reality to what is basically a fanciful tale, *and by his casual understatement in tense moments that forces the reader to use his or her imagination.*

Malory intended the collection of eight stories to be titled, The Book of King Arthur and his Knights of the Round Table, *but Caxton, perhaps reasoning that a shorter title would be more dramatic and make the collection appear as one story, changed it to* Le Morte Darthur *(death of Arthur), which is actually the last of the tales in the collection and the one from which the selection you will read is drawn.*

The story begins after Arthur, urged on by his nephew, Gawain, had taken his knights to France, where he had half-heartedly besieged the castle of Lancelot to punish him for his involvement with Queen Guinevere. Warned that his illegitimate son, Mordred, was leading a revolt against him at home, Arthur and his army had sailed back to England, where Mordred's forces attacked them as they were landing. Gawain was killed, but before he died, sent for Lancelot to come to Arthur's aid. The selection picks up the story at this point.

The Death of King Arthur

Then was it told the king that Sir Mordred had picked a new field upon Barham Down.[1] And so upon the morn King Arthur rode thither to him, and there was a great battle betwixt them, and much people were slain on both parties. But at the last King Arthur's party stood best, and Sir Mordred and his party fled unto Canterbury.

And there the king had all the downs searched for his knights that were slain and interred them; and salved them with soft salves that full sore were wounded. Then much people drew unto King Arthur, and then they said that Sir Mordred warred upon King Arthur with wrong.

And anon King Arthur drew him with his host down by the seaside westward, toward Salisbury. And there was a day assigned betwixt King Arthur and Sir Mordred, that they should meet upon a down beside Salisbury, and not far from the seaside. And this day was assigned on Monday after Trinity Sunday, whereof King Arthur was passing glad that he might be avenged upon Sir Mordred.

Then Sir Mordred araised much people about London, for they of Kent, Sussex and Surrey, Essex, Suffolk and Norfolk held the most party with Sir Mordred. And many a full noble knight drew unto him and also to the king; but they that loved Sir Lancelot drew unto Sir Mordred.

So upon Trinity Sunday at night King Arthur dreamed a wonderful dream, and in his dream him seemed that he saw upon a platform a chair, and the chair was fast to a wheel, and thereupon sat King Arthur in the richest cloth of gold that might be made. And the king thought there was under him, far from him, an hideous deep black water, and therein was all manner of serpents and worms and wild beasts, foul and horrible. And suddenly the king thought that the wheel turned up-so-down, and he fell among the serpents, and every beast took him by a limb. And then the king cried as he lay in his bed, 'Help! help!'

And then knights, squires and yeomen awaked the king, and then he was so amazed that he wist not where he was. And then so he stayed awake until it was nigh day, and then he fell on slumbering again, not sleeping nor thoroughly waking. So the king seemed verily that there came Sir Gawain unto him with a number of fair ladies with him. So when King Arthur saw him he said,

'Welcome, my sister's son, I thought ye had been dead. And now I see thee on live,

---

1. **Barham Down,** "Barcon Downe" in Malory. Now a village near Canterbury.

*The battle between Arthur and Mordred, from the
fifteenth century* St. Alban's Chronicle.

much am I beholden unto Almighty Jesu. Ah, fair nephew, what been these ladies that hither be come with you?'

'Sir,' said Sir Gawain, 'all these be ladies for whom I have foughten for, when I was man living. And all these are those that I did battle for in righteous quarrels, and God hath given them that grace at their great prayer, because I did battle for them for their right, that they should bring me hither unto you. Thus much hath given me leave God for to warn you of your death: for an ye fight as to-morn with Sir Mordred, as ye both have assigned, doubt ye not ye shall be slain, and the most party of your people on both parties. And for the great grace and goodness that Almighty Jesu hath unto you, and for pity of you and many more other good men there shall be slain, God hath sent me to you of His especial grace to give you warning that in no wise ye do battle as to-morn, but that ye take a treaty for a month from today. And proffer you largely, so that to-morn ye put in a delay. For within a month shall come Sir Lancelot with all his noble knights, and rescue you worshipfully, and slay Sir Mordred and all that ever will hold with him.'

Then Sir Gawain and all the ladies vanished, and anon the king called upon his knights, squires, and yeomen, and charged them mightly to fetch his noble lords and wise bishops unto him. And when they were come the king told them of his dream: that Sir Gawain had told him and warned him that an he fought on the morn he should be slain. Then the king commanded Sir Lucan the Butler[2] and his brother Sir Bedivere the Bold, with two bishops with them, and charged them in any wise to take a treaty for a month from that day with Sir Mordred:

'And spare not, proffer him lands and goods as much as you think reasonable.'

So then they departed and came to Sir Mordred where he had a grim host of an hundred thousand. And there they entreated Sir Mordred long time, and at the last Sir Mordred was agreed for to have Cornwall and Kent during King Arthur's life; and after that all England, after the days of King Arthur. Then were they condescended that King Arthur and Sir Mordred should meet betwixt both their hosts, and every each of them should bring fourteen persons. And so they came with this word unto Arthur. Then said he,

'I am glad that this is done,' and so he went into the field.

And when King Arthur should depart he warned all his host that an they see any sword drawn, 'look ye come on fiercely and slay that traitor, Sir Mordred, for I in no wise trust him.' In like wise Sir Mordred warned his host that 'an ye see any manner of sword drawn look that ye come on fiercely and so slay all that ever before you standeth, for in no wise I will not trust for this treaty.' And in the same wise said Sir Mordred unto his host: 'for I know well my father will be avenged upon me.'

And so they met as their pointment was, and were agreed and accorded thoroughly. And wine was fetched, and they drank together. Right so came out an adder of a little heathbush, and it stang a knight in the foot. And so when the knight felt him so stung, he looked down and saw the adder; and anon he drew his sword to slay the adder, and thought none other harm. And when the host on both parties saw that sword drawn, then they blew large and small trumpets, and horns, and shouted grimly, and so both hosts dressed themselves against the other. And King Arthur took his horse and said, 'Alas, this unhappy day!' And so rode to his party, and Sir Mordred in like wise.

And never since was there seen a more dolefuller battle in no Christian land, for there was but rushing and riding, and strik-

---

2. **Butler,** once a high title, designating the noble in charge of the king's wine.

"How Sir Mordred presumed and took on him to be King of England," Frontispiece to the 21st Book of Malory's Le Morte Darthur *(1529).*
The British Library, London

ing, and many a grim word was there spoken of either to other, and many a deadly stroke. But ever King Arthur rode throughout the battle of Sir Mordred many times and did full nobly, as a noble king should do, and at all times he fainted never. And Sir Mordred did his devour that day and put himself in great peril.

And thus they fought all the long day, and never stinted till the noble knights were laid to the cold earth. And ever they fought still till it was near night, and by then was there an hundred thousand laid dead upon the earth. Then was King Arthur wild with wroth out of measure, when he saw his people so slain from him.

And so he looked about him and could see no more of all his host, and good knights left no more alive but two knights: the one was Sir Lucan de Butler and his brother, Sir Bedivere; and yet they were full sore wounded.

'Jesu mercy!' said the king, 'where are all my noble knights become? Alas, that ever I should see this doleful day! For now,' said King Arthur, 'I am come to mine end. But would to God,' said he, 'that I wist now where were that traitor Sir Mordred that hath caused all this mischief.'

Then King Arthur looked about and was ware where stood Sir Mordred leaning upon his sword among a great heap of dead men.

'Now, give me my spear,' said King Arthur unto Sir Lucan, 'for yonder I have espied the traitor that all this woe hath wrought.'

'Sir, let him be,' said Sir Lucan, 'for he is unhappy. And if ye pass this unhappy day ye shall be right well revenged. And, good lord, remember ye of your night's dream and what the spirit of Sir Gawain told you to-night, and yet God of His great goodness hath preserved you hitherto. And for God's sake, my lord, leave off this, for, blessed be God, ye have won the field: for yet we been here three on live, and with Sir Mordred is not one of live. And therefore if ye leave off now, this wicked day of Destiny is past!'

'Now befall me death, befall me life,' said the king, 'now I see him yonder alone, he shall never escape mine hands! For at a better avail shall I never have him.'

'God speed you well!' said Sir Bedivere.

Then the king gat his spear in both his

hands, and ran toward Sir Mordred, crying and saying,

'Traitor, now is thy death-day come!'

And when Sir Mordred saw King Arthur he ran until him with his sword drawn in his hand, and there King Arthur smote Sir Mordred under the shield with a thrust of his spear throughout the body more than a fathom. And when Sir Mordred felt that he had his death wound he thrust himself with the might that he had up to the hilt of King Arthur's spear, and right so he smote his father, King Arthur, with his sword holding in both his hands, upon the side of the head, that the sword pierced the helmet and the casing of the brain. And therewith Mordred dashed down stark dead to the earth.

And noble King Arthur fell in a swough to the earth, and there he swooned oftentimes, and Sir Lucan and Sir Bedivere oftentimes heaved him up. And so weakly betwixt them they led him to a little chapel not far from the sea, and when the king was there, him thought him reasonably eased.

Then heard they people cry in the field.

'Now go thou, Sir Lucan,' said the king, 'and find out for me what betokens that noise in the field.'

So Sir Lucan departed, for he was grievously wounded in many places; and so as he rode he saw and harkened by the moonlight how that pillagers and robbers were come into the field to pillage and to rob many a full noble knight of brooches and bracelets and of many a good ring and many a rich jewel. And who that were not dead all out, there they slew them for their harness and their riches.

When Sir Lucan understood his work he came to the king as soon as he might, and told him all what he had heard and seen.

'Therefore by my counsel,' said Sir Lucan, 'it is best that we bring you to some town.'

'I would it were so,' said the king, 'but I may not stand, my head works so . . . Ah, Sir Lancelot!' said King Arthur, 'this day have I sore missed thee! And alas, that ever I was against thee! For now have I my death, whereof Sir Gawain me warned in my dream.'

Then Sir Lucan took up the king the one side and Sir Bedivere the other side, and in the lifting up the king swooned, and in the lifting Sir Lucan fell in a swoon, that part of his guts fell out of his body; and therewith the noble knight's heart burst. And when the king awoke he beheld Sir Lucan, how he lay foaming at the mouth and part of his guts lay at his feet.

'Alas,' said the king, 'this is to me a full heavy sight, to see this noble duke so die for my sake, for he would have helped me that had more need of help than I! Alas, that he would not complain him, for his heart was so set to help me. Now Jesu have mercy upon his soul!'

Then Sir Bedivere wept for the death of his brother.

'Now leave this mourning and weeping, gentle knight,' said the king, 'for all this will not avail me. For wit thou well an I might live myself, the death of Sir Lucan would grieve me evermore. But my time passeth on fast,' said the king. 'Therefore,' said King Arthur unto Sir Bedivere, 'take thou here Excalibur, my good sword, and go with it to yonder water's side; and when thou comest there, I charge thee throw my sword in that water, and come again and tell me what thou seest there.'

'My lord,' said Sir Bedivere, 'your commandment shall be done, and quickly bring you word again.'

So Sir Bedivere departed. And by the way he beheld that noble sword, and the hilt and hand-guard was all precious stones. And then he said to himself, 'If I throw this rich sword in the water, thereof shall never come good, but harm and loss.' And then Sir Bedivere hid Excalibur under a tree, and so soon

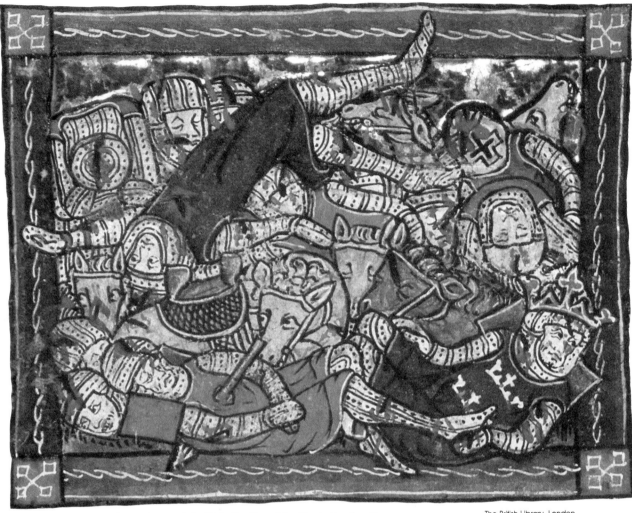

Arthur wounded, from "Quest of the Holy Grail and Le Morte Darthur."

as he might he came again unto the king and said he had been at the water and thrown the sword into the water.

'What saw thou there?' said the king.

'Sir,' he said, 'I saw nothing but waves and winds.'

'That is untruly said of thee,' said the king. 'And therefore go thou quickly again, and do my commandment as thou art to me loved and dear: spare not but throw it in.'

Then Sir Bedivere returned again and took the sword in his hand; and yet him thought sin and shame to throw away that noble sword. And so again he hid the sword and returned again and told the king that he had been at the water and done his commandment.

'What sawest thou there?' said the king.

'Sir,' he said, 'I saw nothing but waters wap and waves wan.[3]

3. **wap . . . wan,** waters lap and waves dark.

'Ah, traitor unto me and untrue,' said King Arthur, 'now hast thou betrayed me twice! Who would think that thou who has been to me so loved and dear, and also named so noble a knight, that thou would betray me for the riches of this sword? But now go again quickly; for thy long tarrying putteth me in great jeopardy of my life, for I have taken cold. And but if thou do now as I bid thee, if ever I may see thee, I shall slay thee with mine own hands, for thou wouldest for my rich sword see me dead.'

Then Sir Bedivere departed and went to the sword and quickly took it up, and so he went unto the water's side. And there he bound the girdle about the hilt, and threw the sword as far into the water as he might. And there came an arm and an hand above the water, and took it and clutched it, and shook it thrice and brandished, and then vanished with the sword into the water.

So Sir Bedivere came again to the king and told him what he saw.

'Alas!' said the king, 'help me hence, for I dread me I have tarried over long.'

Then Sir Bedivere took the king upon his back and so went with him to the water's side. And when they were there, even fast by the bank floated a little barge with many fair ladies in it, and among them all was a queen, and all they had black hoods. And all they wept and shrieked when they saw King Arthur.

'Now put me into that barge,' said the king.

And so he did softly, and there received him three ladies with great mourning. And so they set him down, and in one of their laps King Arthur laid his head. And then the queen said,

'Ah, my dear brother! Why have you tarried so long from me? Alas, this wound on your head hath caught overmuch cold!'

And anon they rowed away from the land, and Sir Bedivere beheld all those ladies go from him. Then Sir Bedivere cried and said,

'Ah, my lord Arthur, what shall become of me, now ye go from me and leave me here alone among mine enemies?'

'Comfort thyself,' said the king, 'and do as well as thou mayst, for in me is no trust for to trust in. For I must into the vale of Avalon to heal me of my grievous wound. And if thou hear nevermore of me, pray for my soul!'

But ever the queen and ladies wept and shrieked, that it was pity to hear. And as soon as Sir Bedivere had lost sight of the barge he wept and wailed, and so took the forest and went all that night.

And in the morning he was ware, betwixt two bare woods, of a chapel and an hermitage. Then was Sir Bedivere glad, and thither he went, and when he came into the chapel he saw where lay an hermit grovelling on all fours, close thereby a tomb was new dug. When the hermit saw Sir Bedivere he knew him well, for he was but little tofore Bishop of Canterbury, that Sir Mordred put to flight.

'Sir,' said Sir Bedivere, 'what man is there here interred that you pray so fast for?'

'Fair son,' said the hermit, 'I wot not verily but by guessing. But this same night, at midnight, here came a number of ladies and brought here a dead corpse and prayed me to inter him. And here they offered an hundred tapers, and gave me a thousand gold coins.'

'Alas,' said Sir Bedivere, 'that was my lord King Arthur, which lieth here buried in this chapel.'

Then Sir Bedivere swooned, and when he awoke he prayed the hermit that he might abide with him still, there to live with fasting and prayers:

'For from hence will I never go,' said Sir Bedivere, 'by my will, but all the days of my life here to pray for my lord Arthur.'

'Sir, ye are welcome to me,' said the hermit, 'for I know you better than ye think that I do: for ye are Sir Bedivere the Bold, and the full noble duke Sir Lucan de Butler was your brother.'

Then Sir Bedivere told the hermit all as

you have heard tofore, and so he stayed with the hermit that was beforehand Bishop of Canterbury. And there Sir Bedivere put upon him poor clothes, and served the hermit full lowly in fasting and in prayers.

Thus of Arthur I find no more written in books that been authorised, neither more of the very certainty of his death heard I nor read, but thus was he led away in a ship wherein were three queens; that one was King Arthur's sister, Queen Morgan le Fay, the other was the Queen of North Galis, and the third was the Queen of the Waste Lands.

Now more of the death of King Arthur could I never find, but that these ladies brought him to his grave, and such one was interred there which the hermit bare witness that was once Bishop of Canterbury. But yet the hermit knew not in certain that he was verily the body of King Arthur; for this tale Sir Bedivere, a knight of the Table Round, made it to be written.

Yet some men say in many parts of England that King Arthur is not dead, but carried by the will of our Lord Jesu into another place; and men say that he shall come again, and he shall win the Holy Cross. Yet I will not say that it shall be so, but rather I would say: here in this world he changed his life.[4] And many men say that there is written upon the tomb this:

HIC IACET ARTHURUS REX
QUONDAM REXQUE FUTURUS[5]

4. **changed his life,** changed his form of life.
5. **HIC . . . FUTURUS.** Here Lies Arthur, Once and Future King.

FOR UNDERSTANDING

Malory created in his book a complete society, describing how it grew, flowered, and decayed. In this piece you read, you could see not only the death of a great hero, but of his followers and the Round Table. With chivalry dead, peace and justice in the world died as well.

1. At the meeting between Mordred and Arthur, what incident breaks the truce?
2. At the end of the battle, how many are left alive on Arthur's side? How many on Mordred's?
3. What happens in the fight between Arthur and Mordred?
4. What is Sir Lucan's report of the field after the battle?
5. What does Sir Bedivere report he has seen at the lake each of the times he is charged with throwing Excalibur into the water?
6. What happens when Bedivere takes Arthur to the lake?
7. What does Sir Bedivere find when he stumbles upon the chapel with its hermit?

FOR INTERPRETATION

Discuss the following statements, using examples from the selection you have just read to support your opinion.
1. This story demonstrates that knights, too, were very human, with both good and bad traits.
2. Beowulf and Arthur are two superheroes who have few characteristics in common.
3. Evil triumphs in this legend.
4. Arthur's story lives on, for there is something in human nature that yearns after the good, the beautiful, the unobtainable perfection that Camelot represents.

FOR APPRECIATION

Find an example of each of the following techniques in *Le Morte Darthur*.
1. Dialogue.
2. Dramatic incidents.
3. Realistic actions and reactions.
4. Tense moments where readers have to use their own imagination to fill out the action.

COMPOSITION

Take the death of a modern-day hero—John F. Kennedy, Bobby Kennedy, Martin Luther King, John Lennon, or one of your own choice. Use your imagination to create dialogue, vivid words, and action that will make the scene come alive.

Introduction to the Second Shepherds' Play

The Middle English mystery plays are also known as "Corpus Christi plays" since they were usually performed on the Feast of Corpus Christi (celebrating the Eucharist) in June. And unlike the earlier liturgical drama, these plays ranged over the events of the entire Bible, not just the events in the life of Jesus. Thus we find plays dealing with events such as the Creation, the murder of Abel, the "sacrifice" of Isaac by Abraham, and the building of the Ark, as well as plays centering on the Nativity and the events surrounding Easter. Four different cycles of such plays still exist, as do town records which give us vital information about the staging of these plays. In some cases, we can even see the connection between the trade guild and the play it sponsored; the York *Crucifixion,* for example, was presented by the Pinners, the makers of nails.

We do not know the names of any of the authors of the almost 150 mystery plays which exist in the different cycles, but five plays by one writer stand out, by virtue of their imaginative plotting, their vividly realistic characterization, and their complex verse form. This playwright is known as "the Wakefield Master" since the plays for that particular cycle were performed at Wakefield, Yorkshire. The writer seems to have had a special gift for comedy, judging from this play and from another play about the building of the Ark, which featured a henpecked Noah who has several fights with his wife, physical and verbal. In *The Second Shepherds' Play,* the playwright takes the short account in the Bible of an angel appearing to shepherds at night and expands that moment by first writing about the three shepherds themselves. Each one is different, with a different complaint—and each complaint is expressed in realistic details ranging from taxes to the problems of marriage to the weather. A fourth shepherd, Mak, is also a thief who tries to solve some of his immediate

problems (no food, no money, and a hungry wife and children) by stealing one of the sheep. Stealing a sheep and hiding it in a baby's cradle may seem irrelevant to the occasion until we get to the end of the play. Then, with the shepherds, we meet the true infant in the cradle. By blending the comic with the sacred, the realistic with the spiritual, the Wakefield Master is making clear the spiritual impact of the Christmas story.

To tell this two-level story, the playwright used a particularly intricate rhyme scheme. The basic form is a nine-line stanza and a complicated rhyme scheme (aaaabcccb) that includes a midline, or internal, rhyme in the first four lines of each stanza. The translator has reproduced many of these rhymes. The changing rhythms of the stanza, from four strong beats in the first four lines, to one in the fifth, to three in the sixth, seventh, and eighth, and two in the ninth, show the technical mastery of the playwright and also create variety for the actor and the audience.

The original staging of this play was probably quite simple. Two basic sets are needed—Mak's cottage and the stable; the first could easily be on one side of the stage, and the second on the other, with the field of the shepherds in between. The script of the play, in Middle English, includes only a few stage directions; the modern English version which follows has more, to make the action clearer. The action of the play is continuous, moving swiftly from field to cottage to field to stable; however, there are four main units of action which structure the play. In the first, the three shepherds talk about their problems but turn to singing together. Then, Mak steals a sheep while the others are sleeping and takes it to his cottage where his wife Gill plans to hide it in the cradle. Next, the shepherds discover that they have lost a sheep and immediately go to Mak's cottage,

*A medieval manor farm, a miniature from the Frontispiece
to the* Georgics *by Virgil (Flemish, late 15th century).*

where they accidentally discover the truth. And in the play's closing action, an angel appears to the shepherds and they visit the stable, where they give gifts to the Christ-child.

Even though *The Second Shepherds' Play,* as well as the master's four other plays, must necessarily accept the religious frame within which all five are written, the playwright went further here than most of the writers of the time in focusing directly upon the discontents of the people. As E. K. Chambers has said, "There is no tenderness about him, and no impulse to devotion. He is a realist, even more than his contemporary of York, a satirist with a hard outlook upon a hard age, in which wrong triumphs over right, but he is saved by an abundant sense of humour." There is even a mention in one play of the Lollards, the socially radical religious rebellion led by John Wyclif. This movement continued to prosper among the peasants, often underground, until it could surface openly as part of the Protestant upheavals of the seventeenth century. Neither heresy nor social discontent, of course, is ever overtly endorsed, although such concerns do sometimes seem to be foremost in the writer's mind, as if he were sure of the audience interest these references would have. Yet when a religious climax occurs, pulling the context back into traditional shape, the Wakefield Master shows the eloquence of his gift for the sheerly lyrical, too, thus achieving a balance between the very strong opposing forces inherent in the work itself.

THE SECOND SHEPHERDS' PLAY

MODERNIZED VERSION BY ANTHONY CAPUTI

CHARACTERS

FIRST SHEPHERD, COLL

SECOND SHEPHERD, GIB

THIRD SHEPHERD, DAW

MAK

GILL, *his wife*

ANGEL

MARY

[Enter the FIRST SHEPHERD.*]*

FIRST SHEPHERD: Lord, but it's cold,
  and I'm wretchedly wrapped.
  My hands nearly numb, so long have
  I napped.
  My legs creak and fold, my fingers   5
  are chapped;

By permission of Anthony Caputi.

It is not as I would, for I am all
  lapped
        In sorrow.
In storms and tempest,   10
Now in the east, now in the west,
Woe is him has never rest
        Midday nor morrow!

But we poor shepherds that walk on
  the moor.   15
We're like, in faith, to be put out of
  door;
No wonder, as it stands, if we be
  poor,
For the tilth of our lands lies fallow as   20
  a floor,
      As ye ken.
We are so lamed,
So taxed and shamed,

We are made hand-tamed   25
    By these gentlery-men.

Thus they rob us of rest. Our Lady
    them harry!
These men that are lord-fast, they
    make the plough tarry.   30
Some say it's for the best; but we find
    it contrary.
Thus are tenants oppressed, in point
    to miscarry,
        In life.   35
Thus hold they us under;
Thus they bring us in blunder.
It were a great wonder
        If ever we should thrive.

'Gainst a man with painted sleeves, or   40
    a brooch, now-a-days,
Woe to him that shall grieve, or one
    word gainsay!
No man dare him reprove, what
    mastery he has.   45
Yet no man believes one word that he
    says,
        No letter.
He can make purveyance,
With boast and arrogance;
And all is for maintenance   50
        Of men that are greater.

There shall come a swain as proud as
    a po,[1]
He must borrow my wain,[2] and my   55
    plough also,
That I am full fain to grant ere he go.
Thus live we in pain, anger, and woe
        By night and day.
Whatever he has willed   60
Must at once be fulfilled.
I were better be killed
        Than once say him nay.

It does me good, as I walk round
    alone,   65
Of this world for to talk in manner of
    groan.

To my sheep will I stalk, now as I
    moan;
There abide on a ridge, or sit on a   70
    stone,
        Full soon.
For I know, pardie,[3]
True men if they be,
I'll get more company   75
        Ere it be noon. *(Moves aside)*

[Enter the SECOND SHEPHERD.*]*

SECOND SHEPHERD: Ben'c'te[4] and
    Dominus! What may this bemean?
Why fares this world thus; the like
    has seldom been.   80
Lord, the weather is spiteful, and the
    winds bitter keen,
And the frosts so hideous, they water
    my een.[5]
        No lie.   85
Now in dry, now in wet,
Now in snow, now in sleet,
My shoes freeze to my feet,
        And all is awry.

But as far as I ken, wherever I go,   90
We poor wedded men endure much
    woe,
Crushed again and again, it falls oft
    so.
And Silly Capel, our hen, both to and   95
    fro
        She cackles;
But begin she to croak,
To groan or to choke,
For our cock it's no joke,   100
        For he's in the shackles.

These men that are wed have never
    their will.

---

1. **po,** peacock.
2. **wain,** wagon.
3. **pardie,** pardieu: by God; indeed.
4. **Ben'c'te,** Benedicte.
5. **een,** eyes.

When they're full hard bestead,[6] they
   sigh and keep still.   **105**
God knows they are led full hard and
   full ill;
In bower nor in bed say they aught
   until
       Ebb tide.   **110**
My part have I found,
And my lesson is sound:
Woe to him that is bound,
      For he must abide.

But now late in our lives—a marvel to **115**
   me,
That I think my heart rives such
   wonders to see,
What destiny drives that it should so
   be—   **120**
Some men will have two wives, and
   some men three
      In store.
He has woe that has any;
But so far ken I,   **125**
He has moe[7] that has many,
      For he feels sore.

But young men a'wooing, before
   you've been caught,
Be well ware of wedding, and keep **130**
   in your thought,
To moan, "Had I known," is a thing
   that serves naught.
Mickle[8] mourning has wedding to
   home often brought,   **135**
      And griefs,
With many a sharp shower;
You may catch in an hour
What shall seem full sour
      As long as you live.   **140**

For as ever read I epistle[9] I've one as
   my dear,
As sharp as a thistle, as rough as a
   brere;[10]
She is browed like a bristle, with a **145**
   sour lenten cheer;

Had she once wet her whistle, she
   could sing full clear
      Her paternoster.
She's as great as a whale;   **150**
She has a gallon of gall;
By him that died for us all
      I would I'd run till I'd lost her.

FIRST SHEPHERD: Gib, look over the
   row! Full deafly, ye stand.   **155**
SECOND SHEPHERD: Yea, the devil
   in your maw—ye blow on your hand.
Saw ye anywhere Daw?
FIRST SHEPHERD: Yea, on a lea-land
I heard him blow. He comes here at **160**
   hand,
      Not far.
Stand still.
SECOND SHEPHERD: Why?
FIRST SHEPHERD: I think he comes **165**
   by.
SECOND SHEPHERD: He'll trick us
   with a lie
      Unless we beware.

[Enter the THIRD SHEPHERD, *a boy.]*

THIRD SHEPHERD: Christ's cross me **170**
   speed, and Saint Nicholas!
Thereof had I need; and it's worse
   than it was.
Whoso can take heed and let the
   world pass;   **175**
It's rank as a weed and brittle as glass,
      And slides.
      This world fared never so,
With marvels more and moe,
      Now in weal, now in woe, **180**
      Everything writhes.

Never since Noah's flood were such
   floods seen,

6. **bestead,** situated.
7. **moe,** more.
8. **mickle,** much.
9. **epistle,** in the New Testament.
10. **brere,** briar.

Winds and rains so rude, and storms
   so keen; 185
Some stammered, some stood in
   doubt, as I ween.
Now God turn all to good! I say as I
   mean,
      Hereunder. 190
These floods so they drown,
Both in fields and in town,
And bear all down,
      They make you wonder.

We that walk in the nights our cattle 195
   to keep,
We see queer sights when other men
   sleep.
Yet methinks my heart lightens; I see
   my pals peep. 200
They are two tall wights! Now I'll give
   my sheep
      A turn.
O full ill am I bent,
As I walk on this land. 205
I may lightly repent,
      If my toes I spurn.

(to the other two) Ah, sir, God you save,
   and master mine!
A drink would I have, and somewhat 210
   to dine.
FIRST SHEPHERD: Christ's curse, my
   knave, thou'rt a lazy swine!
SECOND SHEPHERD: The boy likes
   to rave! Let him stand there and 215
   whine
      Till we've made it.
Ill thrift on thy pate!
Though the fellow came late,
Yet is he in state 220
      To dine—if he had it.

THIRD SHEPHERD: Such servants as
   I, that sweat and swink,[11]
Eat our bread full dry, that's what I
   think. 225
We're oft wet and weary when master
   men wink,[12]

Yet come full late both dinners and
   drink.
      But neatly 230
Both our dame and our sire,
When we've run in the mire,
Can nip at our hire,
      And pay us full lately.

But hear a truth, master, for you the 235
   fare make:
I shall do, hereafter, work as I take;
I shall do a little, sir, and between
   times play.
For I've never had suppers that 240
   heavily weigh
      In fields.
And why should I bray?
I can still run away.
What sells cheap, men say, 245
      Never yields.

FIRST SHEPHERD: Thou are an ill
   lad, to ride a-wooing
With a man that had but little of
   spending. 250
SECOND SHEPHERD: Peace, boy! I
   bade; no more jangling,
Or I shall make thee afraid, by the
   Heaven's King,
      With thy frauds. 255
Where are the sheep, boy; lorn?
THIRD SHEPHERD: Sir, this same day
   at morn
I them left in the corn,
      When they rang lauds.[13] 260

They have pasture good; they cannot
   go wrong.
FIRST SHEPHERD: That's right. Oh,
   by the rood, these nights are long!
Yet I would, ere we go, let's have us a 265
   song.

11. **swink,** toil.
12. **wink,** doze.
13. **lauds,** the early morning service.

SECOND SHEPHERD: So I thought as
    I stood, to cheer us along.
THIRD SHEPHERD: I grant.
FIRST SHEPHERD: The tenor I'll try.   270
SECOND SHEPHERD: And I the
    treble so high.
THIRD SHEPHERD: Then the middle
    am I.
      Let's see how ye chant. *(They*   275
sing.)

[Enter MAK *with a cloak over his smock.]*

MAK: Now, Lord, of names seven, that
    made the moon so pale,
And more stars than I can name; Thy
    good will fails;
I am so in a whirl that my jogged   280
    brain ails
Now would God I were in heaven—
    where no child wails—
      Heaven so still.
FIRST SHEPHERD: Who is it that   285
    pipes so poor?
MAK: God knows what I endure,
Here a'walking on the moor,
    And not my will!

SECOND SHEPHERD: From where do   290
    ye come, Mak?
      What news do ye bring?
THIRD SHEPHERD: Is he come?
    Then everyone take heed to his
    things.   295

[Takes the cloak from MAK.*]*

MAK: What! I am a yeoman (hear me
    you) of the king,
Make way for me, the Lord's tidings I
    bring,
      And such.   300
Fie on you! Go hence!
This is no pretence.
I must have reverence.
      And much!

FIRST SHEPHERD: Why make ye so   305
    quaint, Mak? It's no good to try.

SECOND SHEPHERD: Why play ye
    the saint, Mak? We know that you lie.
THIRD SHEPHERD: We know you
    can feint, Mak, and give the devil the   310
    lie.
MAK: I'll make such complaint, 'lack,[14]
    I'll make you all fry.
      At a word.
    And tell what ye doth.   315
FIRST SHEPHERD: But, Mak, is that
    truth?
    Go gild that green tooth
      With a turd.

SECOND SHEPHERD: Mak, the devil's   320
    in your eye! A stroke would I lend
    you.
THIRD SHEPHERD: Mak, know ye
    not me? By God, I could 'tend you.
MAK: God keep you all three! Perhaps   325
    I can mend you.
    You're a fair company.
FIRST SHEPHERD: Can ye so bend
    you?
SECOND SHEPHERD: Rascal jape![15]   330
    Thus late, as thou goes,
    What will men suppose?
    Sure thou hast an ill nose
      For stealing of sheep.

MAK: And I am true as steel, all men   335
    say,
But a sickness I feel that takes my
    health away;
My belly's not well, not at all well
    today.   340
THIRD SHEPHERD: "Seldom lies the
    devil dead by the way."
MAK: Therefore
Full sore am I and ill;
And I'll lie stone still   345
If I've eat even a quill
      This month and more.

14. **'lack,** alack; an expression of surprise or dismay.
15. **jape,** fool.

Shepherds watching their flock, an illustration from Queen Mary's Psalter *(English, early 14th century).*

The British Library, London

FIRST SHEPHERD: How fares thy
    wife? By my hood, tell me true.
MAK: Lies sprawling by the fire, but   350
    that's nothing new;
    And a house full of brood. She drinks
      well, too;
    Come ill or good that she'll always do
        But so.   355
    Eats as fast as she can;
    And each year gives a man
    A hungry bairn[16] to scan,
        And some years two.

    And were I more gracious and richer   360
      by far,
    I were eaten still out of house and of
      barn.
    And just look at her close, if ye come
      near;   365
    There is none that knows what 'tis to
      fear
        Than ken I.
    Will ye see what I proffer—
    I'll give all in my coffer
    And masses I'll offer   370
        To bid her goodbye.

SECOND SHEPHERD: I am so long
    wakéd, like none in this shire,
    I would sleep if I takéd less for my   375
      hire.
THIRD SHEPHERD: I am cold and
    near naked, and would have a fire.
FIRST SHEPHERD: I am weary,
    for-rakéd,[17] and run in the mire.   380
      Stay awake, you!
SECOND SHEPHERD: Nay, I'll lie
    down by,
    I must sleep must I.
THIRD SHEPHERD: I've as good need   385
    to put by
      As any of you.

    But, Mak, come hither! Between us
    must you be.
MAK: You're sure you don't want to   390
    talk privately?
      Indeed?
    From my top to my toe,
    Manus tuas commendo,

16. **bairn,** child.
17. **for-rakéd,** exhausted.

Pontio Pilato,[18]   395
    Christ's cross me speed!

[Then he rises, the shepherds being asleep, and says]

Now were time for a man that wants
  for gold
To stealthily enter into a fold,
And nimbly to work then, yet be not   400
  too bold,
For he might pay for the bargain, if it
  were told,
    At the ending.
Now were time for to spell—   405
But he needs good counsel
That fain would fare well,
    And has little spending.

But about you a circle as round as a
  moon,   410
Till I've done what I will, till it be
  noon,
Ye must lie stone still till I have done.
And I shall say thereto of words a
  few.   415
    On height.
Over your heads my hands I lift;
Your eyes go out and senses drift
Until I make a better shift
    If it be right.   420

Lord, how they sleep hard! That may
  ye all hear.
I never was a shepherd, but now will
  I learn.
If the flock be scared, when I shall   425
  creep near.
How! Draw hitherward! Now mends
  our cheer
    From sorrow.
A fat sheep, I dare say;   430
A good fleece, dare I lay!
Pay back when I may,
    But this will I borrow.

[MAK crosses the stage to his house.]

How, Gill, are thou in? Get us some
  light.   435

WIFE: Who makes such din this time of
  the night?
I am set for to spin; no hope that I
  might
Rise a penny to win. I curse them on   440
  height.
    So sore
A housewife thus fares,
She always has cares
And all for nothing bears   445
    All these chores.

MAK: Good wife, open the latch! Seest
  thou not what I bring?
WIFE: I'll let thee draw the catch. Ah,
  come in my sweeting!   450
MAK: Yea, thou dost not reek of my
  long standing.
WIFE: By thy bare neck for this you're
  like to swing.
MAK: Go away: 455
I'm good for something yet.
For in a pinch can I get
More than they that swink and sweat
    All the long day.

Thus it fell to my lot, Gill, I had such   460
  grace.
WIFE: It were a foul blot to be hanged
  for the case.
MAK: But I have escaped, Gill, a far
  narrower place.   465
WIFE: Yet so long goes the pot to the
  water, men say,
    At last
Comes it home broken.
MAK: Well know I the token,   470
  But let it never be spoken;
    But come and help fast.

I would he were slain; I want to eat.
This twelvemonth have I not ta'en of
  one sheep's meat.   475
WIFE: Should they come ere he's slain,
  and hear the sheep bleat—

---

18. **Manus . . . Pilato.** "Thy hands I commend to Pontius Pilate."

MAK: Then might I be ta'en! That puts
    me in a heat!
        Go bar   480
  The gate door.
WIFE: Yes, Mak,
  For if they come at thy back—
MAK: Then might I pay for the pack!
  May the devil us warn.   485

WIFE: A good trick have I spied, since
    thou ken none.
  Here shall we him hide till they be
    gone—
  In my cradle abide. Let me alone,   490
  And I shall lie beside in childbed, and
    groan.
MAK: Thou hast said;
  And I'll say thou was light[19]
  Of a male child this night.   495
WIFE: It's luck I was born bright,
    And cleverly bred.

For shrewdness this trick can't be
  surpassed;
Yet a woman's advice always helps at   500
  the last!
Before they 'gin to spy, hurry thou
  fast.
MAK: Unless I come ere they rise,
    they'll blow a loud blast!   505
        I'll go sleep.

[MAK *returns to the shepherds and resumes his place.*]

Yet sleeps all this company;
And I shall go stalk privily,
As it had never been me
    That carried their sheep.   510

FIRST SHEPHERD: *Resurrex a*
  mortuis![20] Take hold of my hand.
Judas carnas dominus![21] I can not well
  stand;
My foot sleeps, by Jesus; and I'm dry   515
  as sand.
I thought we had laid us near English
  land.

SECOND SHEPHERD: Ah, yea!
I slept so well, I feel   520
As fresh as an eel,
As light on my heel
    As leaf on a tree.

THIRD SHEPHERD: Lord bless us all!
  My body's all a-quake!   525
My heart jumps from my skin, sure
  and that's no fake.
Who makes all this din? So my head
  aches.
I'll teach him something. Hark,   530
  fellows, awake!
    We were four.
See ye aught of Mak now?
FIRST SHEPHERD: We were up ere
  thou.   535
SECOND SHEPHERD: Man, I give
  God a vow,
    That he went nowhere.

THIRD SHEPHERD: I dreamed he
  was lapped in a gray wolf's skin.   540
FIRST SHEPHERD: So many are
  wrapped now—namely, within.
THIRD SHEPHERD: When we had so
  long napped, methought he did begin
A fat sheep to trap; but he made no   545
  din.
SECOND SHEPHERD: Be still!
Thy dream makes thee brood;
It's but fancy, by the rood.
FIRST SHEPHERD: Now God turn all   550
  to good,
    If it be his will!

SECOND SHEPHERD: Rise, Mak! For
  shame! Thou liest right long.
MAK: Now Christ's holy name be us   555
  among!
    What is this? By Saint James, I may
    not move along!
    I think I be the same. Ah! my neck

---

19. **light,** delivered.
20. and 21. **Resurrex a mortuis!, Judas . . . dominus!**
These exclamations are in mock Latin.

has lain wrong
    Enough! *(They help* MAK *up.)* 560
Mickle thanks! Since yestere'en,
Now, by Saint Stephen,
I was flayed with a dream
    That my heart did cuff. 565

I thought Gill began to croak and
    labor full sad,
Indeed at the first cock had borne a
    young lad
To increase our flock. Guess whether 570
    I'm glad;
I am now more in hock than ever I
    had.
        Ah, my head!
A house full of bairns! 575
'Devil knock out their brains!
For father is the pains,
    And little bread!

I must go home, by your leave, to
    Gill, as I thought. 580
I pray you look in my sleeve that I
    steal naught;
I am loath you to grieve or from you
    take aught.
THIRD SHEPHERD: Go forth; ill 585
    might thou live! Now would I we
    sought,
        This morn,
That we had all our store.
FIRST SHEPHERD: But I will go 590
    before;
Let us meet.
SECOND SHEPHERD: Where?
THIRD SHEPHERD: At the crooked
    thorn. 595

[MAK *crosses to his cottage.*]

MAK: Undo this door, here! How long
    shall I stand?
WIFE: Who makes such a stir! Go walk
    in quicksand!
MAK: Ah, Gill, what cheer? It is I, 600
    Mak, your husband.
WIFE: Then may we see here the devil
    in a band,
        Sir Guile.

Lo, he comes with a knot 605
At the back of his crop.[22]
I'll soon to my cot
    For a very long while.

MAK: Will ye hear what she makes to
    get her a gloze?[23] 610
She does naught but plays, and
    wiggles her toes.
WIFE: Why, who wanders? Who wakes?
    Who comes?
        Who goes? 615
Who brews? Who bakes? What makes
    me this hose?
        And then,
It's a pity to behold,
Now in hot, now in cold, 620
Full of woe is the household
    That wants a woman.

But what end has thou made with
    the shepherds, Mak?
MAK: The last word that they said, 625
    when I turned my back,
They would look that they had their
    sheep, count the pack.
I'm sure they'll not be glad to find
    one they lack, 630
        Pardie.
But howsoever it goes,
They will surely suppose,
From me the trouble 'rose,
        And cry out upon me. 635
But thou must do as thou hight.[24]

WIFE: Of course I will.
I shall swaddle him right; you trust in
    your Gill.
If it were a worse plight, yet could I 640
    help still.
I will lie down straight. Come, cover
    me.
MAK: I will.
WIFE: Behind! 645
It may be a narrow squeak.

22. **knot . . . crop,** an allusion to hanging.
23. **gloze,** an excuse.
24. **hight,** promised.

MAK: Yes, if too close they peak,
Or if the sheep should speak!
WIFE: 'Tis then time to whine.

Hearken when they call; for they will   650
come anon.²⁵
Come and make ready all, and sing
on thine own;
Sing lullaby thou shall, for I must
groan   655
And cry out by the wall on Mary and
John,
For sore.
Sing a lullaby, fast.
Like thou sang at our last;   660
If I play a false cast,
Trust me no more!

[The SHEPHERDS *meet at the crooked
hawthorn.]*

THIRD SHEPHERD: Ah, Coll, good
morn! Why sleep thou not?
FIRST SHEPHERD: Alas, that ever I   665
was born! We have a foul blot.
A fat lamb have we lorn.²⁶
THIRD SHEPHERD: Marry, God
forbid!
SECOND SHEPHERD: Who should do   670
us that scorne?
That were a foul spot.
FIRST SHEPHERD: Some shrew.
I have sought with my dogs
All Horbury Bogs,   675
And with fifteen hogs
Found I but one ewe.

THIRD SHEPHERD: Now trust me if
ye will; by Saint Thomas of Kent,
Either Mak or Gill was at that assent.   680
FIRST SHEPHERD: Peace, man, be
still! I saw when he went.
Thou slanders him ill. Thou ought to
repent.
Good speed.
SECOND SHEPHERD: Now if ever I lie,   685
If I should even here die,
I would say it were he
That did that same deed.

THIRD SHEPHERD: Go we thither, I   690
rede,²⁷ at a running trot.
I shall never eat bread till the truth
I've got.
FIRST SHEPHERD: Nor drink, in my
heed, until we solve this plot.   695
SECOND SHEPHERD: Till we know
all, indeed, I will rest no jot,
My brother!
One thing I will plight:
Till I see him in sight   700
Shall I never sleep one night
Where I do another.

[At MAK'S *house they hear* GILL *groan and*
MAK *sing a lullaby.]*

THIRD SHEPHERD: Will ye hear how
they hack? Our sir likes to croon.
FIRST SHEPHERD: Heard I never   705
one crack so clear out of tune!
Call on him.
SECOND SHEPHERD: Mak! Undo
your door soon.
MAK: Who is that spake as it were   710
high noon
On loft?
Who is that, I say?
THIRD SHEPHERD: Good fellows,
were it day.   715
MAK: As far as ye may,
Good, speak soft,

Over a sick woman's head that is ill at
ease;
I had rather be dead e'er she had any   720
dis-ease.
WIFE: Go to another place! I may not
well wheeze.
Each foot that ye tread goes to make
me sneeze,   725
So "he-e-e-e'."

25. **anon,** soon.
26. **lorn,** lost.
27. **rede,** advise.

FIRST SHEPHERD: Tell us, Mak, if ye
   may,
How fare ye, I say?
MAK: But are ye in town today?   730
   Now how fare ye?

Ye have run in the mire, and are all
   wet yet.
I shall make you a fire, if ye will sit.
A nurse would I hire, and never   735
   doubt it.
But at my present hire—well, I hope
   for a bit
     In season.
I've more bairns than ye knew,   740
And sure the saying is true,
"We must drink as we brew,"
     And that's but reason.

I would ye dined ere ye go. Methinks
   that ye sweat.   745
SECOND SHEPHERD: Nay, that
   mends not our mood, neither drink
   nor meat.
MAK: Why, what ails you sir?
THIRD SHEPHERD: Yea, our sheep   750
   that we get
Are stolen as they go. Our loss is not
   sweet.
MAK: Sirs, drink!
   Had I been there,   755
   Someone had paid full dear.
FIRST SHEPHERD: Some men think
   that ye were;
And that makes us think.

SECOND SHEPHERD: Mak, some men   760
   say that it should be ye.
THIRD SHEPHERD: Either ye or your
   spouse; who else could it be?
MAK: Now, if ye suspect us, either Gill
   or me,   765
   Come and rip our house, and then ye
   may see
     Who had her.
If I any sheep got
Any cow or stott[28]—   770
And Gill, my wife, rose not
    Since here she laid her.

As I am true and leal,[29] to God here I
   pray.
That this be the first meal that I shall   775
   eat this day.
FIRST SHEPHERD: Mak, as I have
   weal,[30] have a care, I say:
"He learned timely to steal that could
   not say nay."   780
WIFE: I swelt![31]
   Out, thieves from my home!
   Ye come to rob us, ye drones!
MAK: Hear ye not how she groans?
   Your heart should melt.   785

WIFE: Out, thieves, from my bairn! Get
   out of the door!
MAK: Knew ye what she had borne,
   your hearts would be sore.
Ye do wrong, I you warn, that thus   790
   come before
To a woman that has borne. But I say
   no more.
WIFE: Ah, my middle!
   I pray to God so mild,   795
   If ever I you beguiled,
   Let me eat this child
     That lies in this cradle.

MAK: Peace, woman, for God's pain
   and cry not so!   800
Thou shalt hurt thy brain, and make
   me full of woe.
SECOND SHEPHERD: I think our
   sheep be slain. Think you not so?
THIRD SHEPHERD: All work we in   805
   vain; as well may we go.
     But, drat it,
I can find no flesh,
Hard nor nesh,[32]
Salt nor fresh,   810
     But two empty platters.

28. **stott,** bullock.
29. **leal,** loyal.
30. **weal,** riches.
31. **swelt,** faint.
32. **nesh,** tender.

Many of the play cycles are still being performed. Here modern players are performing a mystery play showing shepherds.

York Department of Tourism

There's no cattle but this, neither
    tame nor wild,
None, as have I bliss, that smells as he
    smelled.   815
WIFE: No, so God me bless, and give
    me joy of my child!
FIRST SHEPHERD: We have marked
    amiss; I hold us beguiled.
SECOND SHEPHERD: Sir, done.   820
    Sir, Our Lady him save!
    Is your child a knave?
MAK: Any lord might him crave,
        This child as his son.

When he wakens, he skips, that a joy   825
    is to see.
THIRD SHEPHERD: In good time be
    his steps, and happy they be!
Who were his godfathers, tell now to
    me?   830

MAK: So fair fall their lips!
FIRST SHEPHERD: Hark now, a lie!
MAK: So God them thank,
    Parkin and Gibbon Waller, I say,
    And gentle John Horn, in good faith,   835
    He gave all the array
        And promised a great shank.

SECOND SHEPHERD: Mak, friends
    will we be, for we are all one.
MAK: We! Now I hold for me, from   840
    you help get I none.
    Farewell, all three! All glad were ye
    gone!

[The SHEPHERDS *go out.]*

THIRD SHEPHERD: Fair words may
    there be, but love there is none   845
        This year.
FIRST SHEPHERD: Gave ye the child
    anything?

SECOND SHEPHERD: I trow,[33] not
    one farthing!   850
THIRD SHEPHERD: Fast back will I
    fling;
Abide ye me here.

[The SHEPHERDS *re-enter the house.]*

Mak, take it to no grief, if I come to
    thy bairn.   855
MAK: Nay, thou does me mischief, and
    foul has thou fared.
THIRD SHEPHERD: The child will
    not grieve, that little day-star.
Mak, with your leave, let me give your 860
    bairn
        But sixpence.
MAK: Nay, go 'way; he sleeps.
THIRD SHEPHERD: Methinks he
    peeps.   865
MAK: When he wakens he weeps!
    I pray you, go hence!

THIRD SHEPHERD: Give me leave
    him to kiss, and lift up the clout.[34]
What the devil is this? What a   870
    monstrous snout!
FIRST SHEPHERD: He is marked
    amiss. Let's not wait about.
SECOND SHEPHERD: "Ill spun
    cloth," iwis, "aye comes foul out." 875
        Aye, so!
He is like to our sheep!
THIRD SHEPHERD: How, Gib, may I
    peep?
FIRST SHEPHERD: I trow, nature will 880
    creep
        Where it may not go!

SECOND SHEPHERD: This was a
    quaint fraud, and a far cast!
It should be noised abroad.   885
THIRD SHEPHERD: Yea, sirs, and
    classed.
Let's burn this bawd, and bind her
    fast.
Everyone will applaud to hang her at 890
    last,
        So shall thou.

Will ye see how they swaddle
His four feet in the middle?
Saw I never in cradle   895
    A horned lad ere now.

MAK: Peace, peace, I ask. You'll give
    the child a scare.
For I am his father, and yon woman
    him bare.   900
FIRST SHEPHERD: After what devil
    shall he be called?
        "Mak?" Lo, Mak's heir!
SECOND SHEPHERD: Let be all that.
    Now God give him care, 905
        I say.
WIFE: A pretty child is he
To sit on a woman's knee;
A dilly-downe, pardie,
    To make a father gay. 910

THIRD SHEPHERD: I know him by
    the ear-mark; that's a good token.
MAK: I tell you, sirs, hark! His nose
    was broken;
Later told me a clerk that he was 915
    forespoken.[35]
FIRST SHEPHERD: Liar! You deserve
    to have your noddle broken!
        Get a weapon.
WIFE: He was taken by an elf, 920
    I saw it myself;
When the clock struck twelve
    He was misshapen.

SECOND SHEPHERD: Ye two are well
    made to lie in the same bed. 925
THIRD SHEPHERD: Since they
    maintain their theft, let's see them
    both dead.
MAK: If I do wrong again, cut off my
    head!   930
        I'm at your will.

---

33. **trow,** assert as true; admit.
34. **clout,** cloth.
35. **forespoken,** bewitched.

FIRST SHEPHERD: Sirs, take this
  plan, instead,
     For this trespass:
We'll neither curse nor fight,   935
Quarrel nor chide,
But seize him tight
     And cast him in canvas.

[They toss MAK *in a sheet and go back to the fields.]*

FIRST SHEPHERD: Lord, but I am
  sore; I feel about to burst.   940
In faith, I may no more; therefore
  will I rest.
SECOND SHEPHERD: As a sheep of
  seven score he weighed in my fist.
Now to sleep anywhere methinks were   945
  the best.
THIRD SHEPHERD: Now I pray you,
Let's lie down on this green.
FIRST SHEPHERD: Oh, these thieves
  are so keen.   950
THIRD SHEPHERD: Let's forget what
  has been,
     So I say you. *(They sleep.)*

[An ANGEL *sings "Gloria in excelsis"; then let him say]*

ANGEL: Rise, herd-men kind! For now
  is he born   955
That shall take from the fiend what
  Adam had lorn:
That devil to shame this night is he
  born;
God is made your friend now at this   960
  morn.
     He behests
To Bethlehem go ye,
Where lies the Free;[36]
In a manger he'll be   965
     Between two beasts.

FIRST SHEPHERD: This was a sweet
  voice as any I've heard.
A wonder enough to make a man
  scared.   970
SECOND SHEPHERD: To speak of
  God's son from on high he dared.

All the wood on the moor with
  lightning glared,
     Everywhere.   975
THIRD SHEPHERD: He said the babe
  lay
In Bethlehem today.
FIRST SHEPHERD: That star points
  the way.   980
     Let us seek him there.

SECOND SHEPHERD: Say, what was
  his song? Heard ye not how he
  cracked it,
  Three briefs to a long?[37]   985
THIRD SHEPHERD: Yea, marry, he
  hacked it;
Was no crotchet[38] wrong, nor nothing
  that lacked it.
FIRST SHEPHERD: For to sing us   990
  among, right as he knacked it,[39]
     I can.
SECOND SHEPHERD: Let's see how
  ye croon.
  Can ye bark at the moon?   995
THIRD SHEPHERD: Hold your
  tongues, have done!
FIRST SHEPHERD: Hark after, then!

SECOND SHEPHERD: To Bethlehem
  he bade that we should go;   1000
  I am full afeared that we have been
  too slow.
THIRD SHEPHERD: Be merry and
  not sad; for sure this we know,
This news means joy to us men below,   1005
     Of no joy.
FIRST SHEPHERD: Therefore thither
  hie we,
Be we wet and weary,
To that child and that lady.   1010
     We must see this boy.

SECOND SHEPHERD: We find by the
  prophecy—let be your din!

---

36. **the Free,** The Divine One.
37. **Three . . . long,** musical notes.
38. **crotchet,** a quarter note.
39. **knacked it,** did it cleverly.

Of David and Isaiah and others of
    their kin,   1015
They prophesied by clergy that in a
    virgin
Should he light and lie, to slacken our
    sin
        And slake it,   1020
Our Race from woe.
For Isaiah said so:
"Ecce virgo
    Concipiet"[40] a child that is
    naked.   1025

THIRD SHEPHERD: Full glad may we
    be that this is that day
Him lovely to see, who rules for aye.
Lord, happy I'd be if I could say
That I knelt on my knee so that I   1030
    might pray
        To that child.
But the angel said,
He was poorly arrayed,
And in a manger laid,   1035
        Both humble and mild.

FIRST SHEPHERD: Patriarchs and
    prophets of old were torn
With yearning to see this child that is
    born.   1040
They are gone full clean, and their
    trouble they've lorn.
But we shall see him, I ween,[41] ere it
    be morn,
        To token.   1045
When I see him and feel,
Then know I full well
It is true as steel
        That prophets have spoken:

To so poor as we are that he would   1050
    appear,
To find us and tell us by his
    messenger!
SECOND SHEPHERD: Go we now, let
    us fare, for the place is near.   1055
THIRD SHEPHERD: I am ready,

prepared; let us go with good cheer
    To that bright
Lord, if thy will be—
We are simple all three—   1060
Grant us some kind of glee
    To comfort thy wight.[42] *(They
    enter the stable.)*

FIRST SHEPHERD: Hail, comely and
    clean! Hail, young child!   1065
Hail, Maker, as I mean, born of
    maiden so mild!
Thou has cursed, I ween, the devil so
    wild;
The false guiler of men, now goes he   1070
    beguiled.
        Lo, he merry is!
Look, he laughs, the sweeting!
Well, to this meeting
I bring as my greeting   1075
        A bob of cherries!

SECOND SHEPHERD: Hail, sovereign
    Savior, our ransom thou hast
    bought!
Hail, noble child and flower, that all   1080
    things has wrought!
Hail, full of favor, that made all of
    naught!
Hail! I kneel and I cower. A bird
    have I brought   1085
        To my bairn.
Hail, little tiny mop!
Of our creed thou art crop.
I would drink of thy cup,
        Little day-star.   1090

THIRD SHEPHERD: Hail, darling
    dear, thou art God indeed!
I pray thee be near when that I have
    need.

---

40. **Ecce . . . Concipiet.** "Behold, a virgin shall conceive." See *Isaiah* 7:14; *Luke* 1:31; and *Matthew* 1:23.
41. **I ween.** I imagine.
42. **wight,** man.

Hail! Sweet is thy cheer! My heart
would bleed
To see thee lie here in so poor
a weed,
    With no pennies.
I would give thee my all,
Though I bring but a ball;
Have and play thee withal,
    And go to the tennis.

MARY: The Father of Heaven, God
omnipotent,
That set all in seven days, his Son has
sent.
My name he has blessed with peace
ere he went.
I conceived him through grace as God
had meant;
    And now he's born.
I shall pray him so
To keep you all from woe!
Tell this wherever ye go,
    And mind this morn.

FIRST SHEPHERD: Farewell, lady, so
fair to behold,
With thy child on thy knee!
SECOND SHEPHERD: Still he lies full
cold.
Lord, how favored I be. Now we go
forth, behold.
THIRD SHEPHERD: Forsooth, already
this seems a thing told
    Full oft.
FIRST SHEPHERD: What grace we
have found!
SECOND SHEPHERD: Spread the
tidings around!
THIRD SHEPHERD: To sing are we
bound:
Let take aloft! *(They sing.)*

(line numbers: 1095, 1100, 1105, 1110, 1115, 1120, 1125, 1130)

FOR UNDERSTANDING

1. What differences do you find in the three shepherds, Coll, Gib, and Daw?

2. What qualities in Mak enable him to fool the
shepherds?
3. In what ways is Gill an appropriate mate for
Mak?
4. The shepherds leave Mak's cottage without discovering the truth and then return; why do they
come back?
5. How fitting is Mak's punishment?

FOR INTERPRETATION

1. Imagine that you are directing a production of
this play. First you need to cast the characters: how
old would each one be, what physical features
might you look for, what intellectual level needs to
be conveyed? Are there other distinctions you
want to establish? Use the lines of the play for
suggestions. Then consider the problem of interpretation. What character(s) are we most sympathetic to? How would you try to create sympathy
for them?
2. Although this play is over 500 years old, it is still
performed today, both by professional and amateur actors. What are the qualities of the play
which might appeal to a modern audience?

FOR APPRECIATION

The Double Plot
The most striking feature of this play is the use of
a double plot—two stories which may seem at first
to be very different and yet which turn out to have
significant connections. The double plot is a favorite structure in later English drama; the comedies
of Shakespeare usually have at least two plots
running simultaneously and sometimes three or
four. The double plot in *The Second Shepherds' Play*
may be the first appearance of such a structure in
English drama.
1. Look for verbal echoes between the first three
scenes and the last one.
2. What similarities of situation can you find between the main action of the play and the last
scene?
3. What are the effects of the resemblances you
have found?

COMPOSITION WORKSHOP

COMPILING A SOURCE LIST

Once you and your teacher have agreed upon the topic you will pursue, your next step is to assemble a list of sources that you intend to use in your research. The place where this is done is the library. You may start with your school library, but, depending on the scope of your topic, a trip to the public library might be necessary as well.

The reference section is where most of your preliminary research will take place. Just as a professional writer would never plunge headlong into an unfamiliar subject area, you will want to ease into your new topic by consulting a general encyclopedia. This will provide you with an overview of your topic, and if you use a well-researched encyclopedia, such as the *Encyclopaedia Britannica*, you derive an added benefit. A bibliography—or list of books—accompanies many of the articles. After you have completed this phase of your research and feel reasonably well-acquainted with the new material, you may proceed to the specialized reference books that apply to your topic. There will probably be several of these that supply needed information. Two that are particularly useful for topics on British literature are the *Cambridge History of English Literature* and the *Cambridge Bibliography of English Literature*. The latter is a usable listing of important books about British authors and their works.

The library's card catalog will be your next stop. Here, you will find books listed three ways—according to subject, to author, and to title. Since you are dealing with a literary topic, you will want to keep in mind that books about your author will appear under the author's name in the *subject* catalog. Thus, if you are researching some aspect of *The Canterbury Tales*, you will want to look in the subject catalog under both the headings "Canterbury Tales" and "Chaucer." Appeal to the author catalog will tell you only that copies of *The Canterbury Tales* exist in the library.

If your topic is one that is still under active study and investigation, the *Readers' Guide to Periodical Literature* might be worth a check. This invaluable research tool lists titles of articles from about 110 magazines and journals, each indexed by author and by subject. Supplements to the *Readers' Guide* are published monthly and are eventually bound into volumes covering a two-year period.

GETTING THE FACTS DOWN

Professional writers and researchers have developed a system for recording sources that has proved useful to countless students. It calls for the use of 3 × 5-inch cards, one for each source that you cite. This affords you the flexibility of grouping titles in any fashion that seems convenient at a given point in your research. It also provides you with a ready reference for the final bibliography that will come at the end of your finished paper. It is wise to make out a bibliography card for any source that seems promising. If you later discover that a source provides no information, the card can be easily eliminated.

The information that goes on each card is as follows. For each book, note:
- the author's full name
- the complete title of the book (including subtitle, if any)
- the publisher, the city and year of publication
- the name (if any) of an editor or translator

For a magazine article, note the author, title, issue date and number of the magazine, and page number on which the article appears. There is no hard and fast rule as to how the information is to be recorded on the cards, but if you utilize the following format, paying particular attention to punctuation, the task of putting together your final bibliography will be greatly simplified.

1. *Standard entry for a book:*
Yeats, William Butler. The King of the Great Clock Tower. London: Cuala Press, 1934.

2. *Book with a subtitle:*
Bullough, Geoffrey. Mirror of Minds: Changing Psychological Beliefs in English Poetry. Toronto: University of Toronto Press, 1962.

3. *Book with several authors:*
Eliot, T. S., and Aldous Huxley. Three Critical Essays on Modern English Poetry. London: Folcroft, 1973.

4. *Book compiled from different sources by editor:*

Baugh, A., ed. <u>Chaucer's Major Poetry</u>. New York: Appleton-Century-Crofts, 1963.

5. *Work with several volumes:*

Harrison, G. B. <u>Major British Writers</u>. 2 vols. New York: Harcourt, Brace & Jovanovich, 1959.

6. *Book newly edited by other than author:*

Dickens, Charles. <u>Hard Times</u>. Ed. Robert Donald Spector. New York: Bantam Books, 1964.

7. *Standard entry for an article:*

Donno, E. S. "Old Mouse-eaten Records: History in Sidney's <u>Apology</u>." <u>Studies in Philology</u> 72 (1975): 275-98.

8. *Encyclopedia article:*

"Francis Bacon." <u>Encyclopaedia Britannica</u>. 1949 ed.

9. *Unsigned newpaper article:*

"A Shakespeare Festival." <u>Oakdale Register</u> 6 March 1979: c4.

10. *Article in a collection:*

Ornstein, Robert. "The Mystery of Hamlet." <u>Hamlet: Enter Critic</u>. Ed. Claire Sacks and Edgar Whan. New York: Appleton-Century-Crofts, 1963.

Be sure to include on your bibliography cards (but not in your final bibliography) the library call number for books you have obtained from a library. It is also a good idea to number each of the cards in the upper right-hand corner. This will save you the trouble, later on when you are taking notes, of copying down the full citation each time you quote a source.

It is important to keep in mind that the initial research plan and initial search are preliminary. Later, as you take the time to study more deeply the identified sources, you will come to recognize which sources are most vital to your area of research. You will find references to these sources, moreover, in the bibliographies of the books you begin with. Hence, the research process is a cumulative one.

ASSIGNMENT

Begin research on your topic by consulting general and specialized sources in the reference section of the library. Examine the bibliographies that are generally provided in these references for books and articles that might make promising sources. Equipped with a pack of 3 × 5-inch bibliography cards, head next for the card catalog. Isolate as many sources as you can for further investigation and study. Be sure to leave no stone unturned when considering possible headings in the subject catalog. Make a bibliography card for each source you identify, and submit your completed pack to your teacher for approval.

YOUTH
Nicholas Hilliard

Renaissance Literature

1500–1660

During the fifteenth century when the Italian Renaissance began, it affected all fields of human endeavor—literature, the arts, the sciences, religion, and politics. At the heart of the Renaissance was a wish to think through once again the answers to fundamental questions about human nature. The fifteenth century in Italy was a time of prosperity and expansion that displayed a new mood of confidence in human resources and in human reason, a mood that often tended to undermine established authority. There was an emphasis on reviving ancient learning through the study of Latin and Greek, a mark of the Renaissance as it spread throughout the rest of Europe during the sixteenth century.

THE EARLY RENAISSANCE IN ENGLAND

In England, the first Tudor monarch, Henry VII, in the last decade and a half of the fifteenth century was mostly concerned with healing the wounds of political dissension and economic depression after the War of the Roses (see Timeline). There was no massive explosion of change and growth such as could be seen elsewhere. Under Henry VIII (1509–1547), the next Tudor, the country did begin to prosper once more and the Protestant Reformation finally appeared in the emergence of the Anglican Church, headed by Henry, and in the growth of a more radical sect, the Puritans. *Henry VII*

Henry VIII

Reformation

In Henry's reign, only slight stirrings of Renaissance activities can be seen: Sir Thomas More, a Tudor statesman whom Henry beheaded for his disobedience, emphasized classical learning; Hans Holbein, a German painter, settled in England and painted or sketched a succession of English faces with a radiant Renaissance clarity; music began to be written in new continental styles. Erasmus, a scholar of the new humanism, began to lecture at Cambridge in 1509. Humanism emphasized human reason and common sense as a guide to solving society's problems. Sir Thomas Wyatt (page 175) and Henry Howard, Earl of Surrey, began writing the first poetry in modern English sometime in *Thomas More*

Wyatt and Surrey

157

Little Moreton Hall in Cheshire is a moated half timbered manor house dating from the 15th century and completed in the 16th century.

British Tourist Authority

the late 1520s. Their poems did not see print until 1557 when they were published in *Tottel's Miscellany* fifteen years after Wyatt's death, twenty years after Surrey's beheading.

Sonnets   Wyatt wrote the first sonnets in modern English, a form he adapted for English from Petrarch, Italy's great sonneteer during the four-

Blank verse   teenth century. And Surrey "invented" blank verse for modern English, getting the five beats flowing again in a language that had undergone much change since the time when Chaucer, more than a century before, had solved a similar problem for Middle English. All these stirrings, however, would also have to be regarded as less than decisive were it not for the fact that about twenty years into the reign of

Elizabeth I   the last Tudor, Elizabeth I (1558–1603), the English Renaissance comes as vividly alive as the Italian had been—but in this case in a poetry unrivaled before in any language.

Sidney and Spenser   Sir Philip Sidney (page 190) and Edmund Spenser (page 181) not only took up the example of Wyatt and Surrey, they also went further

Bermondsey is now central London but was still a village in the late 16th century. Note the Tower of London in the background. Here the painter vividly captures the life and the spirit of Tudor England at the end of the century.

Marriage Feast at Bermondsey
Joris Hofnagel (1590)
Courtesy of the Marquess of Salisbury

in typically Renaissance directions than any poets before them had ventured. *The Faerie Queene* of Spenser is the first attempt to write an epic in English that would be modeled along classical lines. And Sidney's sonnet sequence, *Astrophel and Stella,* though influenced by Petrarch and by Wyatt, is one of the few great sonnet sequences in English. The visionary and allegorical world that Spenser creates in his long, unfinished epic is a far cry from our first but very unclassical epic, *Beowulf.* The world Spenser paints does not reflect a hard-bitten stoic resignation. It is alive and glowing, flooded with color and detail—a crowded Renaissance tapestry that expresses certain optimism even though the epic's hero must predictably survive many grim and

The Faerie Queene

Pastoral verse awesome perils in his mystical quest. In his other poems, Spenser introduces another classical standard, that of pastoral verse, and gives us shepherds and country folk singing and dancing among themselves, not according to Renaissance realism but in accordance with how these figures behave in classical pastoral poetry.

THE HIGH RENAISSANCE—ELIZABETHAN DRAMA

It is in the drama that the English Renaissance attains greatness and finds its own individual voice and vision. This drama was both *Iconoclastic* iconoclastic *and* popular. It was a drama acted out in the open sun, at *and popular* first in an inn yard or marketplace, one that spoke to an audience that came from all walks of life, nobles and commoners, men and women alike. The largest group watching and listening, in fact, were those people who had paid only a penny for the show—and they had to stand for hours on the ground in front of the raised stage waiting under an open sky for the play to start and then unfold before them. These "penny groundlings" were the discriminating ear into which the new English language uttered its first dramatic masterpieces in long speeches of bright images and vivid rhetoric. The penny groundling, though usually not from the higher classes, had a fine ear for words. Thus from the first, groundlings applauded or booed the poetry as much as the sheep's blood the actors spilled across the boards in scenes of violent action.

Unlike classical theater, violence in Elizabethan drama took place *Classical rules* right before the audience's eyes rather than offstage. Other classical *Abandoned* rules also were abandoned. Most plays did not occur on one day in one place only—or in any other way "obey the unities." Instead, they moved through time and geography freely, much as a movie camera is free to move around in the movies of our own time. In the case of Elizabethan theater, however, there were no sets to help the audience create the *Language and* scene—only the rich language and the watcher's own imagination were *Imagination* used to do that. And that would be more than enough. As the prologue to Shakespeare's *Henry V* says

> Can this cockpit hold
> The vasty fields of France? Or may we cram
> Within this wooden O the very casques
> That did affright the air at Agincourt? . . .
> Think, when we talk of horses, that you see them
> Printing their proud hoofs i' th' receiving earth.
> For 'tis your thoughts that now must deck our kings,
> Carry them here and there, jumping o'er times,
> Turning the accomplishment of many years
> Into an hour-glass. . . .

The Children of Charles I
Sir Peter Lely
Petworth House, West Sussex
Photo: The National Trust

CHRISTOPHER MARLOWE

The last public celebration of miracle plays in England was at Coventry in 1580. At that time, James Burbage's first theater had already been open four years in London and there had been, even earlier, a few attempts at both tragedy and comedy in Surrey's blank verse. Extended verse in English tended to spread and take on a measure then known as "the fourteener." These seven-beat lines (of fourteen syllables) were too long for a single breath and broke up naturally into hymn-tune units of four and three. This made for a singsong quality. Against this leaden traditional line, Surrey's five-beat line of blank verse (or unrhymed iambic pentameter) had one great advantage. It could take off and soar with a sudden lift of eloquence or rhetorical bombast.

Tamburlaine

In 1587 this is precisely what happened when the Lord Admiral's Men, a relatively new acting company, presented their brilliant and famous leading actor, Edward Alleyn, in a new play called *Tamburlaine* by Marlowe. Never had the English theater-going public heard such a powerful use of blank verse. It seemed to sing and fly outspread above the atrocities that peppered the play's action with a deadly realism. The popular audience of the day, no less than ours, wanted its blood and thunder. After all, the theaters had to compete for attention with such bloodcurdling real life entertainments as bearbaiting and public executions. The former often took place in pits right next to the theater.

In *Tamburlaine* alone, a captive is transported in a cage and used as the hero's footstool. Another captive is chained on a wall and shot at by enemy troops. (In one performance shots went astray, killing a pregnant woman in the audience—only causing more people to mob the next performance.) At another point the hero, whip in hand, makes his entrance riding a chariot pulled by two conquered kings with bits in their mouths. As he whips them he cries, "Holla, ye pampered jades of Asia!/What, can ye draw but twenty miles a day?" These lines became the rage of London (and were quoted in an early play of Shakespeare). There was something more to the play than its mere string of atrocities. There was its language. Many of the lines of verse were complete in themselves, ending with a heavy pause or period (thus, "end-stopped"). The effect was to make a mighty banging of the five accents, all closed within a single breath, that came to be known as Christopher Marlowe's "mighty line."

Marlowe's "mighty line"

Marlowe's Popularity

Here was an instrument the English dramatist had never possessed before in such a highly developed form, one open to all sorts of subtle tinkering to suit dramatic changes of mood or pace. For seven more years, the poetry-intoxicated public swarmed to listen as Marlowe gave them the most popular plays England had ever seen performed anywhere. It did not matter that literary people, such as Sidney's sister, the Countess of Pembroke—a sophisticated and accomplished poet herself—looked down their long noses at this popular rabble and their cheap entertainments. Their call for a return to classical standards and offstage catastrophes fell on verse-drugged ears. It was certainly ignored by the university-educated classicists who wrote for the popular theater, like Marlowe. It mattered as little to playwrights less well-educated than he, such as Will Shakespeare, an actor who had recently begun to write history plays in the early 1590s before a new

This splendid staircase in Hatfield House (Hertfordshire) speaks eloquently of the English craftsmanship as well as the prosperity, power, and life-style of the wealthy Elizabethans.

British Tourist Authority

outbreak of plague closed the London theaters for two years starting in 1592.

WILLIAM SHAKESPEARE

Marlowe's Influence

In seven years, Marlowe had written seven plays. In half that time, Shakespeare had already written something like a half dozen. Three of these were history plays so heavily influenced by Marlowe that some later scholars would insist that Marlowe must have written them. Both men were twenty-nine at the height of the plague in 1593 when Marlowe was struck down and killed in a tavern brawl. After the plague, Shakespeare joined a new acting company, the Lord Chamberlain's Men, and continued writing plays at the same rate—nearly two a year—for the next twenty years. His leading actor was often the great tragic actor Richard Burbage, who also co-managed the theater upon his father's death. When Shakespeare stopped writing in 1613, he had written, we think, thirty-seven plays, the most astonishing body of dramatic verse ever produced by a single writer. Taken as a whole, the quality of his output varies, the less successful plays appearing early and, with a few exceptions, toward the end of his career. The high points pop up throughout the twenty years, although they begin to appear with more frequency past the ten-year midpoint and perhaps reach an all-time high with the last tragedies *(King Lear* 1605, *Macbeth* 1606, *Antony and Cleopatra* 1607) and with the final comedy, *The Tempest,* about 1611.

Nearly two plays a year

Shakespeare leaves Marlowe behind

In developing as a playwright, Shakespeare leaves behind Marlowe's "mighty line" with its strong but simple end-stopped music. His increasingly serpentine lines begin and end with less and less correlation to the conclusion of sentences. Dramatically, the early plays are relatively bright-colored affairs. As he matures, the shadows deepen—in middle tragedies like *Romeo and Juliet* (1595), in problem-comedies like *Measure for Measure* (1604), and in the more somber mood of later tragedies, beginning noticeably with *Hamlet* (1601). Then at the very end of his writing career, in a string of comedies now called "romances," both the light and the dark have mellowed, to culminate in the resonant magic of *The Tempest*. In his last play, *Henry VIII* (1613), he returned to a history play like those he wrote early in his career.

Shakespeare's Non-dramatic verse

Shakespeare also published two long narrative poems, *Venus and Adonis* (1593) and *The Rape of Lucrece* (1594), as well as a famous sequence of sonnets (1609). You will have the opportunity to study some of the sonnets later (page 206). The narrative works alone would have assured any other poet a measure of fame as an important minor Elizabethan poet, and the sonnet sequence unquestionably contains flashes of greatness.

The Sun Inn, Saffron Walden, Essex shows ordinary Elizabethan housing. The parageting (raised plasterwork) is dated 1676 and is on medieval timber-framed houses.

J. Bethell Photography

THE RENAISSANCE IN THE SEVENTEENTH CENTURY

Cavaliers and Metaphysicals

The Elizabethan World-view is Replaced

For two decades an Elizabethan world-view had coalesced which, in its trembling perfection, held the promise of utterly new recognitions that might be made as easily as discovering new worlds that lie beyond all known maps. Then the queen herself, the greatest Renaissance monarch in all of Europe, closed her eyes in 1603—and that world-view also blinked closed, to be replaced by the decadence of the court of James I and some last royal splendors before the Puritans joined to raze it to the ground in the reign of Charles I, putting an end to that king's life. One thing Marlowe and Shakespeare and Jonson all had in common as writers for the theater, though each was of differing religious persuasions: they all saw the rise of the Puritans as a dangerously oversolemn, life-threatening absolutism. And well they might; after all, the Puritans first began attacking the theater before the three playwrights had written a line. The Puritans would succeed in shutting down all the playhouses in 1642. The English theater, when it opened again in 1660, would never recapture the sense of wonder these writers had embodied in their verse.

Ben Jonson

Ben Jonson, ten years younger than his friend Shakespeare, was also a dramatist though a classically educated one who was made uneasy by Shakespeare's popular appeal. Oddly enough, Jonson's influence in the Stuart age (see Timeline) was to be primarily as a lyric rather than as a dramatic poet. His low-key short poems with their spare, trim language would set the tone for those who called them-

"the sons of Ben"

selves "the sons of Ben." These poets would appear in both schools that dominated lyric poetry before the Puritan revolution, the Cavaliers and the Metaphysicals. The Cavalier poets are represented here by their best writer, Robert Herrick (page 314). The tone of voice is always light and soft, the music song-like, the subject matter recalling the medieval cult of "courtly love," for these poems were often written as elaborate compliments to a lovely lady. They were called Cavaliers because they were often royalist in sympathy, attended upon the king in court, and generally valued a life of fashionable and showy elegance. Despite the pitfalls on all sides of this artificial pose, the best side of these values can be seen in Herrick—his quick sympathy and warm humor being pleas for tolerance as well as complaisance.

The Metaphysicals never called themselves by this word. It was first used as a description of them by Dr. Samuel Johnson in the eighteenth century. They themselves thought of their work in no such clear light.

John Donne

John Donne (page 304), the leading metaphysical poet, wrote some of the greatest love poems in English during his wild and reckless youth as a Catholic in danger of the martyrdom his own brother did not escape. Still, after a midlife in which his large family constantly fought off poverty, he at last betrayed his own motto, "Better dead than

Traveling players with entertainment in progress from Moyses Waler's
"Album Amicorum" (c. 1610).

The British Library, London

altered." He did this meekly enough by converting to the Anglican
faith so that he could rise in the Church of England to the eminence of
his last years as Dean of St. Paul's Cathedral in London. In this role, his
wild and fiery sermons castigated his jam-packed audiences for the
sinfulness of their fleshly lusts and ambitions. He bewitched flocks of
fashionable women in the 1620s to sob and suffer through his sermons.
He had similarly bewitched the readers of his early love lyrics, which he
now of course abjured, though they floated in wider manuscript
circulation than ever, a thing he could fortunately do nothing about. At
the same time, he can be said to have been one of the most effective
forces in delaying the Puritan revolution with his vigorous preaching.
There could be no movement against wit and elegance—or the
theater—while he lived.

Dean of St. Paul's

Both Donne's love lyrics and religious poetry share much in
common. The metaphysical passion is for connecting opposites—the
commonplace with the rare, the body with the spirit, the intellectual

Connecting opposites

with the passionate. To attain their goal, the metaphysical poets often used a violent metaphor or conceit in which "the most heterogeneous ideas are yoked by violence together," as Dr. Johnson observed. The best-known metaphysical conceit comes from Catholic poet Richard Crashaw. In addressing the naked and bloody body of Christ on the cross, he sees that the blood is, in fact, a kind of clothing:

Richard Crashaw

> Thee with thy self they have too richly clad,
> Opening the purple wardrobe in thy side.

Compare with this the few lines from a lyric that are among the most celebrated of passages in all of Elizabethan verse. They come from Thomas Nashe's "In Plague Time":

> Beauty is but a flower
> Which wrinkles will devour;
> Brightness falls from the air,
> Queens have died young and fair,
> Dust hath closed Helen's eye.
> I am sick, I must die,
>   Lord, have mercy on us!

What a different world these two passages reflect, the somber meditation and the eloquent lyric. Their different intensities, linking thought and feeling, would soon give way to a more detached and rationally "scientific" sensibility in English verse in the Neoclassical age (page 355) to follow.

George Herbert

The Anglican minister George Herbert (page 316) wrote strictly religious verse, and while he shows the same tendency as Donne toward complicated imagery and agitated states of mind, he is like the "sons of Ben" in the simplicity of his diction, his homespun vocabulary, and the directness of his speaking voice. His best work presents psychological portraits of the paradoxes and passions by which faith is tempered.

Andrew Marvell

Andrew Marvell (page 321) is quite a departure from both Donne and Herbert—and poles apart from Crashaw. His metaphysical bent is toward straightforward images that capture intellectual contradictions inherent in the beliefs to which people cling. His poems are filled with an elegance that categorizes him as another Cavalier, but he was a Puritan from first to last, and lashed out at the decadence of the Restoration court. Katherine Philips (page 327) was not a Puritan, but

Katherine Philips

she was a metaphysical poet with a direct and pointed style like Marvell's. She was by no means the first woman poet in English, but she may be the first extremely good one. Called "the matchless Orinda" by fellow metaphysical poet Abraham Cowley and devoted to the best of the late metaphysicals, Henry Vaughan, she was a royalist intellectual who founded a classical school for girls and who wrote emotionally powerful verse about love and friendship.

From medieval times through the Renaissance the art of the weaver flourished. This country scene, from the late 16th century, is linen canvas embroidered with silk.

Detail of Bradford Table Carpet
Victoria and Albert Museum
Crown Copyright

JOHN MILTON

John Milton's (page 329) early poems show him to be a competent metaphysical apprentice, though like the younger Marvell, he was also a Puritan—and also an uncompromising one. Like Marvell and unlike other Puritans, he loved the theater. Again, like Marvell, he was a learned classicist consciously using classical models for his pastoral verse, for his one masque (a courtly entertainment), his epic poems, and his one tragedy. In midlife, he set poetry aside and became an ardent pamphleteer for the Puritan cause. These prose works have been preserved and show a great mind wrestling with such radical ideas as divorce, free speech, and the people's right to execute a tyrant. His masterpiece is the greatest epic in English, *Paradise Lost* (1667). Early in his life he set himself the task of gaining enough experience and knowledge to contribute to English the epic that Spenser never quite managed to complete. He was first drawn to the medieval imagery of knighthood and chivalry, which decided him upon retelling the Arthu-

Paradise Lost

rian legend in epic form. It wasn't until after the Puritan revolution had been won that he returned to achieve the epic he seemed uniquely equipped to write. But instead of Arthur's passing, he tells the dramatic story of the fall of Adam and Eve to Satan's blandishments in the Garden of Eden. His narrative is accomplished in magnificent poetry studded with classical allusions and in a blank verse that moves farther beyond Shakespeare's toward the reverberating rhythm often called the great Miltonic "organ tone."

RENAISSANCE PROSE

John Bunyan

If Marvell and Milton both to some degree present us with a contradiction in combining their dazzling imagery with their plain-spun Puritan political sympathies, John Bunyan (page 340) presents us with no such tension. He is plain-spun all through and almost free from contradictions of any kind. He is Puritan pure and simple, and as such is the last great religious allegorist in English, weaving a sparse and efficient prose style that is as unadorned as a Puritan bonnet set in place for use but not for show. The warmth and sincerity that Bunyan generates

Pilgrim's Progress

from the readily grasped allegory in *Pilgrim's Progress* are remarkable for their dramatic immediacy. Jailed by royalists for his fervent preaching, he wrote his masterpiece there. The intense spirituality and the direct style both help to explain why American pioneers classically carried three books across the American continent: the *King James Bible,* Milton's *Paradise Lost,* and Bunyan's *Pilgrim's Progress.*

Francis Bacon

Sir Francis Bacon's (page 193) principal achievement is perhaps the scientific and philosophical work that led to the creation of the Royal Society in 1660, though he died long before in 1626. Yet he belongs to literature as well, if only for those short prose works he wrote that allow one to credit him with being the first writer of the familiar essay in English. These brief pieces are opinionated and pithy, but are also usually thought-provoking. The prose is one of almost classical purity, tinged with humorous examples that keep the moralizing brief and

King James Bible

down-to-earth. Flanked by Bacon and Bunyan on both sides, the *King James Bible* epitomizes seventeenth-century prose at its best. A simple, elevated style is achieved and maintained throughout in this only masterpiece ever created by committee. The personal voices of the various authors are all drawn into the seamless perfection of the whole. It can still move us more than a modern version of the same text, even though the later is more accessible to us. Too many quotations and songs and hymns and sayings come straight out of the King James version ever to make it seem remote from us. And there is an elegance about the diction that is at once elevated and straightforward in its approach. By such great prose writers as Bacon, Bunyan, and the translators of the *King James Bible,* a solid base is laid for further growth in English prose.

Fashionable dress among ladies and gentlemen of Henry VIII's court was meant to emphasize wealth and importance of the wearers. Long trains of expensive material, deep sleeves, and exaggerated shoulders all helped towards the desired effect. Costume sketches by Holbein.

The Age of The

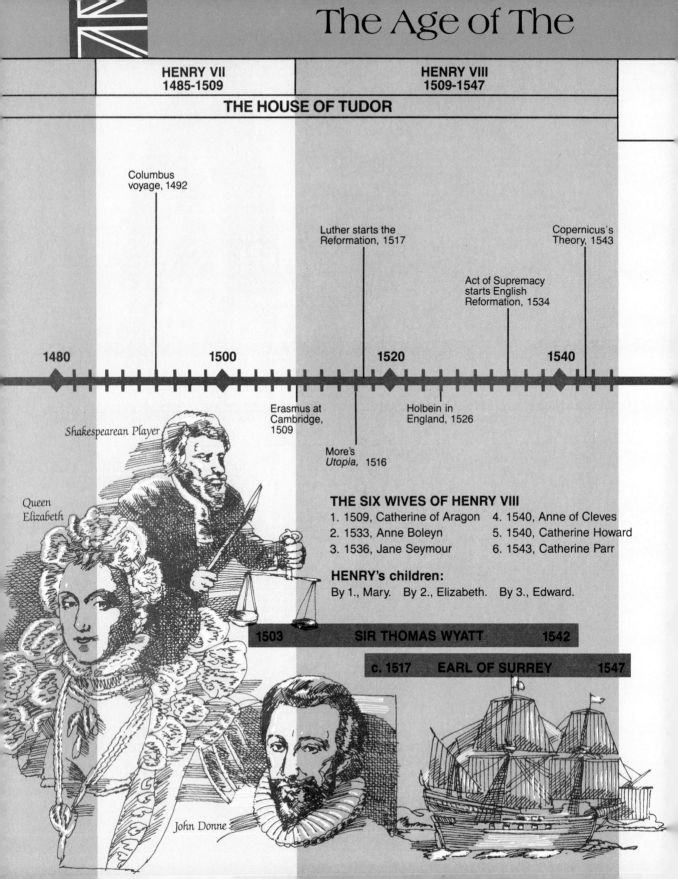

HENRY VII 1485-1509	HENRY VIII 1509-1547

THE HOUSE OF TUDOR

Columbus voyage, 1492

Luther starts the Reformation, 1517

Copernicus's Theory, 1543

Act of Supremacy starts English Reformation, 1534

1480   **1500**   **1520**   **1540**

Erasmus at Cambridge, 1509

Holbein in England, 1526

More's *Utopia,* 1516

Shakespearean Player

Queen Elizabeth

THE SIX WIVES OF HENRY VIII
1. 1509, Catherine of Aragon
2. 1533, Anne Boleyn
3. 1536, Jane Seymour
4. 1540, Anne of Cleves
5. 1540, Catherine Howard
6. 1543, Catherine Parr

HENRY's children:
By 1., Mary.   By 2., Elizabeth.   By 3., Edward.

1503   **SIR THOMAS WYATT**   1542

c. 1517   **EARL OF SURREY**   1547

John Donne

English Renaissance

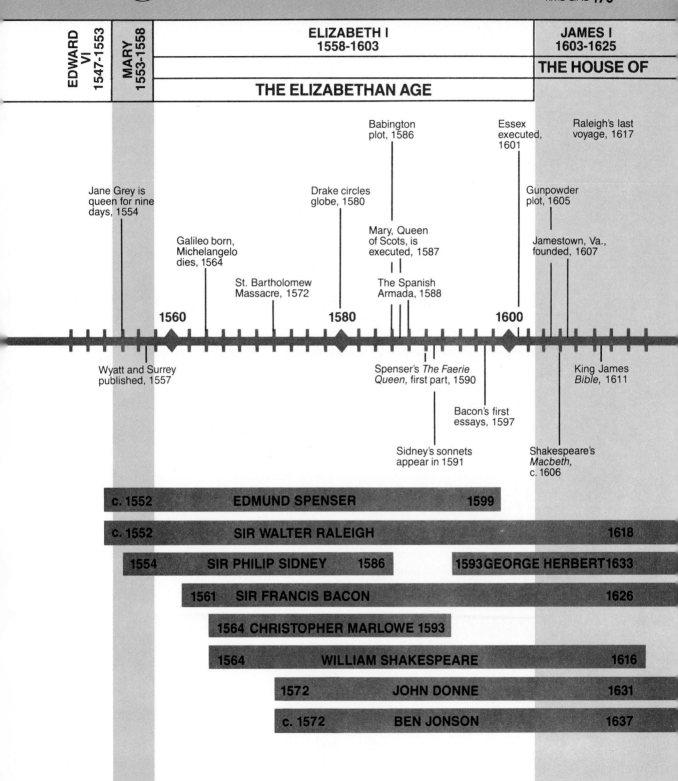

EDWARD VI 1547-1553	MARY 1553-1558	ELIZABETH I 1558-1603	JAMES I 1603-1625
			THE HOUSE OF
		THE ELIZABETHAN AGE	

Babington plot, 1586

Essex executed, 1601

Raleigh's last voyage, 1617

Jane Grey is queen for nine days, 1554

Drake circles globe, 1580

Gunpowder plot, 1605

Galileo born, Michelangelo dies, 1564

Mary, Queen of Scots, is executed, 1587

Jamestown, Va., founded, 1607

St. Bartholomew Massacre, 1572

The Spanish Armada, 1588

1560

1580

1600

Wyatt and Surrey published, 1557

Spenser's *The Faerie Queen,* first part, 1590

King James *Bible,* 1611

Bacon's first essays, 1597

Sidney's sonnets appear in 1591

Shakespeare's *Macbeth,* c. 1606

| c. 1552 | EDMUND SPENSER | 1599 |

| c. 1552 | SIR WALTER RALEIGH | 1618 |

| 1554 | SIR PHILIP SIDNEY | 1586 | 1593 GEORGE HERBERT 1633 |

| 1561 | SIR FRANCIS BACON | 1626 |

| 1564 CHRISTOPHER MARLOWE 1593 |

| 1564 | WILLIAM SHAKESPEARE | 1616 |

| 1572 | JOHN DONNE | 1631 |

| c. 1572 | BEN JONSON | 1637 |

The Age of The English Renaissance

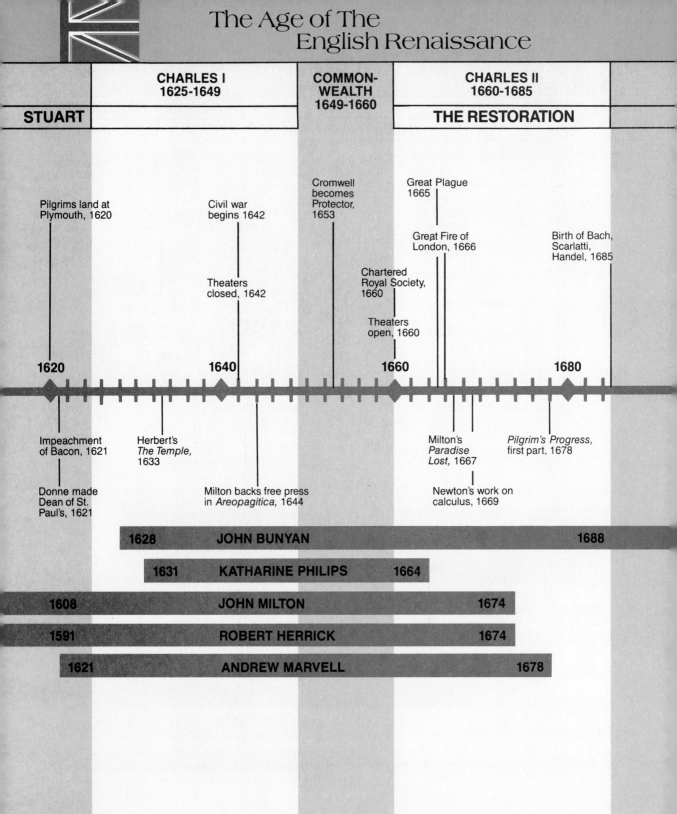

STUART

CHARLES I 1625-1649	COMMON-WEALTH 1649-1660	CHARLES II 1660-1685
		THE RESTORATION

Pilgrims land at Plymouth, 1620

Civil war begins 1642

Cromwell becomes Protector, 1653

Great Plague 1665

Great Fire of London, 1666

Birth of Bach, Scarlatti, Handel, 1685

Theaters closed, 1642

Chartered Royal Society, 1660

Theaters open, 1660

1620

1640

1660

1680

Impeachment of Bacon, 1621

Herbert's *The Temple*, 1633

Milton's *Paradise Lost,* 1667

Pilgrim's Progress, first part, 1678

Donne made Dean of St. Paul's, 1621

Milton backs free press in *Areopagitica,* 1644

Newton's work on calculus, 1669

1628   **JOHN BUNYAN**   1688

1631   **KATHARINE PHILIPS**   1664

1608   **JOHN MILTON**   1674

1591   **ROBERT HERRICK**   1674

1621   **ANDREW MARVELL**   1678

Sir Thomas Wyatt 1503–1542

In the first half of the fifteenth century, during the reign of Henry VIII, two writers stand out to foreshadow the glories of a Renaissance poetry that was later to flourish in England. With the age of Chaucer irreplaceably past and the English language irrevocably altered in the intervening century of foreign and domestic upheaval, it was for Sir Thomas Wyatt the Elder and his younger friend and disciple Henry Howard, Earl of Surrey, to reinvent English poetry in the new "modern" language—as if for the first time. The Italian Renaissance was already well past full flower and Wyatt, while fulfilling his role as diplomat statesman, saw something of its waning firsthand on his mission to Italy in 1527. He was himself the epitome of the Renaissance courtier—soldier, statesman, horseman—and a poet and humanist as well. He met Italian writers like Ariosto and Machiavelli, but even more important, he brought back a determination to create in English the kind of poem the great Italian poet Petrarch had written, a fourteen-line rhymed form called a sonnet.

So it happened that the first sonnets appeared in English—first written by Wyatt, later by Surrey, and toward the end of the century by a multitude of English poets including Shakespeare. Wyatt used one of Petrarch's own rhyme schemes for twenty-five of the thirty sonnets he wrote. In addition to these sonnets in the Italian, or Petrarchan, form, Wyatt wrote five sonnets in a modified form which was also used by Surrey in his fifteen sonnets—a variety we now call the English or Shakespearian sonnet. But if Wyatt thus gave English one of its great poetic forms, Surrey gave English poetry an equally valuable tool—blank verse, unrhymed five-beat lines. When Surrey's translation of the fourth book of Virgil's *Aeneid* was printed posthumously, this historic first example of blank verse in English was referred to on the title page as "a straunge metre." It may have seemed strange in 1554, but from that beginning comes the inexhaustible uses that such writers as

SIR THOMAS WYATT Hans Holbein
Copyright reserved. Reproduced by Gracious permission of Her Majesty Queen Elizabeth II

Shakespeare, Milton, and Wordsworth have made of this meter. The work of both Wyatt and Surrey became widely available only in 1557, long after their deaths, in the first modern anthology of English poetry, *Tottel's Miscellany* (that day's word for *anthology* being *miscellany)*. It had a profound effect on every Elizabethan poet from Spenser to Shakespeare.

On the whole, Wyatt's work is more personal than Surrey's and follows less the Italian convention of the abject, submissive lover. Wyatt's meter is also much less smooth than Surrey's, which occasionally tends toward the singsong. Because of this, Tottel rewrote some of Wyatt's roughest passages. Critics ever since, in studying Wyatt's originals, have been at a loss to explain the strange *un*-iambic lilt that Wyatt's original rhythms can have. Some say it results from ignorance or ineptness on Wyatt's part. Others say it shows that the language was still in a state of drastic change and shifting stress. A few even say that the rugged meter actually dramatizes Wyatt's emotional tone.

As humanist statesmen, both poets were at different times accused of treason, a charge which resulted in Surrey's execution at the age of thirty. In Wyatt's case, the charges (which were twice raised and twice dismissed) probably stemmed from his having been in love with Anne Boleyn, some eight years before Henry VIII married her. Most readers take the following sonnet, "Whoso List to Hunt," as a direct reference to his love for Anne. A sequel to this love affair occurred when Wyatt's son, loyal in his own day to Anne's daughter, the Princess Elizabeth, fomented a rebellion on Elizabeth's behalf during the persecutions carried out by her Catholic sister Queen Mary. Unlike his father, Sir Thomas Wyatt the Younger was executed for his loyalty to the daughter who as queen was to give a name to the Elizabethan Age. It is probably no accident that not long after the son's death, despite Mary's certain

Henry Howard, Earl of Surrey Hans Holbein

distaste, *Tottel's Miscellany* appeared to honor the father and thus assure him his place as the first significant poet in modern English.

Whoso List to Hunt

Whoso list[1] to hunt, I know where is an hind,[2]
But as for me, alas, I may no more.
The vain travail hath wearied me so sore,
I am of them that farthest cometh behind.
Yet may I by no means my wearied mind   5
Draw from the deer, but as she fleeth afore
Fainting I follow. I leave off therefore
Since in a net I seek to hold the wind.
Who list her hunt, I put him out of doubt,
As well as I may spend his time in vain.   10
And graven with diamonds in letters plain
There is written her fair neck round about:
'*Noli me tangere* for Caesar's I am,[3]
And wild for to hold though I seem tame.'

1. **list,** wishes, desires.
2. **hind,** deer.
3. *Noli* . . . **I am.** The Latin phrase means "Do not touch me." These are the words of the resurrected Jesus to Mary Magdalene outside the tomb (Vulgate, John XX,

17). Renaissance commentators claimed that Caesar inscribed the words, "Do not touch me, for I am Caesar's," on the collars of his free-roaming deer to protect them from hunters.

FOR UNDERSTANDING

A Prose Paraphrase

Sometimes writing a prose paraphrase can help in understanding a poem. Here, for example, is a paraphrase of Wyatt's poem:

If someone is interested in hunting, I know where a deer can be found. I'm so exhausted by chasing her that I can't hunt anymore. In fact, I have fallen behind others who are still hunting her. Still, there's no way I can keep my tired mind from thinking about her, because I still follow her in a daze as she escapes before me. I must stop this, since it's as useless as trying to hold back the wind by stretching a net against it. As far as anyone else who wants to hunt her, I can tell him he needn't wonder about his chances—it will be as much a waste of his time as it has been of mine. This is because around her beautiful neck she wears letters engraved with diamonds, which spell out these words: "Don't touch me, for I belong to the king, and I am as dangerous as a wild beast to embrace, even though I seem gentle and domesticated."

1. Does this do justice to the literal meaning of the poem? If so, why does the prose version seem so dull and obvious when set beside the poem? If you had only this prose paraphrase, would it be possible to imagine what the original poem was like—or how good or bad it might be? What does a prose paraphrase necessarily leave out? Is the literal prose meaning of a poem more important than its other elements?

2. Since Wyatt has been said to be uneven rhythmically, did you find any lines of the poem less graceful or flowing than they might have been?

FOR APPRECIATION

The Sonnet

One of the favorite forms of Renaissance poets throughout Europe was the sonnet. Some background may be helpful to appreciate this sonnet and the others that follow.

The sonnet was invented in Sicily during the first half of the thirteenth century. This makes it one of the oldest forms to emerge in European poetry after the fall of Rome. In English, the sonnet is a rhymed poem in fourteen lines of iambic pentameter. The rhyme scheme usually follows one of two major patterns or forms.

The Italian (or Petrarchan) Form

This version developed earliest and reached its definition in the work of the fourteenth-century sonneteer Petrarch. The first eight lines of Wyatt's Italian sonnet are rhymed *abbaabba*. The last six lines usually rhyme *cdecde* or *cdcdcd*—or in any other arrangement of two or three sounds that avoids rhyming the last two lines. Wyatt modifies the Italian pattern here by ending with two rhymed lines: *cddcee*. In any case, the Italian sonnet has four or five rhyme sounds at most.

Looking again at the Wyatt sonnet, you will find that the first eight lines make a self-contained unit having only two rhyme sounds. This unit is called the *octave*. The last six lines, permitting more variation, are called the *sestet*. With the sonnet thus divided into two groups of eight and six lines, the Italian form has been compared to a wave hitting the shore of consciousness (the octave) and then receding (the sestet). The moment when the wave begins receding after the eighth line is called the *volta* or turning point. Most sonnets in the Italian form have such a turning point. Here, in Wyatt's adaptation of Petrarch, he uses an unusual volta in the ninth line. He returns to the assertion of the sonnet's opening, but then for the first time presents startling proof of that assertion (that chasing the deer is useless). The rest of the sestet is taken up with this proof—the vivid image of the diamond necklace that seems to spell out the message of the last two lines.

The English (or Shakespearian) form of the sonnet will be discussed in the study notes following Sidney's poems.

Sir Walter Raleigh   1552–1618

No poet of Sir Walter Raleigh's considerable skills ever lived so varied and turbulent a life or left so many different marks upon history. As a soldier, he distinguished himself in the Netherlands and in Ireland. As a sea warrior, he displayed himself at his most reckless and daring in the victories against the Spanish in Cadiz, the Azores, and the New World. As an explorer and colonizer, he founded Virginia (thereby introducing tobacco and potatoes into Great Britain) and twice challenged Spain's claim to Guiana, the last time in 1617 leading directly to his execution. As a thinker, he is credited with creating a society of skeptics known as the School of Night, which included Marlowe, George Chapman, and some dabblers in natural science. As a scientist himself, he set up a laboratory and did chemical research during his last fifteen-year imprisonment in the Tower. As a historian during the same period, he also wrote his *History of the World,* a significant contribution to English prose. As a courtier, he "came from the mud of obscure campaigns to the most brilliant court of Europe, a plain captain, and for ten years that court held no more brilliant figure than his."

During those ten years from 1582 to 1592, Raleigh ambitiously wielded political power as Queen Elizabeth's favorite—and wrote accomplished poetry about his love for the queen, poetry that won the admiration of such poets as Spenser himself. At their meeting at Spenser's Irish home in 1589, Raleigh read to his amazed host from his own epic poem, *The Ocean's Love to Cynthia,* of which only the eleventh and part of the twelfth book have survived. In this fragment, the dejected Raleigh speaks of his life as a seafaring adventurer when he tried "To seek new worlds for gold, for praise, for glory," only to be recalled in disgrace by Elizabeth. Seldom has a poet written so movingly of personal conflicts that strode so broad a stage of historical fact. Of all those poets from Shakespeare to Donne who made little or no effort to print or otherwise preserve their verse, Raleigh is the extreme example. Only a remnant of his work survives, but even that

Sir Walter Raleigh
Nicholas Hilliard
National Portrait Gallery, London

portion shows him to be more akin to Shakespeare and Donne than his own more untroubled contemporaries born earlier in the sixteenth century. His bittersweet and even sardonic lyrics have a powerful melancholy that strikes a surprisingly personal note when set beside the perfect but more impersonal lyric typical of Elizabethan verse.

In the following poem, Raleigh has recast an old ballad to express a characteristically bittersweet attitude toward romantic love. Walsingham Abbey in Norfolk was one of the great shrines and centers of pilgrimage in medieval England. The ballad consists of a dialogue between a pilgrim returning from Walsingham and an old man. Starting with the old man, the first seven stanzas are spoken alternately by these two; the last four stanzas are spoken by the pilgrim alone.

Walsinghame

"As you came from the holy land
  of Walsinghame,
Met you not with my true love
  by the way as you came?"

"How shall I know your true love,   5
  that have met many one
As I went to the holy land,
  that have come, that have gone?"

"She is neither white nor brown,
  but as the heavens fair: 10

There is none hath a form so divine
  in the earth or the air."

"Such an one did I meet, good sir,
  such an angelic face.
Who like a queen, like a nymph, did appear
  by her gait, by her grace."

"She hath left me here all alone,
  all alone as unknown,
Who sometimes did lead me with herself,
  and me loved as her own."   20

Queen Elizabeth Dancing with Robert Dudley, Earl of Leicester (c. 1580)

Reproduced by permission of Viscount De L'Isle, V.C., Kg, from his collection at Penhurst Place, Kent

"What's the cause that she leaves you alone
    and a new way doth take,
Who loved you once as her own
    and her joy did you make?"

"I have loved her all my youth,   25
    but now, old, as you see;
Love likes not the falling fruit
    from the withered tree."

"Know that love is a careless child
    and forgets promise past;   30
He is blind, he is deaf when he list
    and in faith never fast.

"His desire is a dureless* content
    and a trustless joy;
He is won with a world of despair   35
    and is lost with a toy.

"Of womenkind such indeed is the love,
    (or the word 'love' abused)
Under which many childish desires
    and conceits are excused.   40

"But Love is a durable fire
    in the mind ever burning—
Never sick, never old, never dead,
    from itself never turning."

---

* **dureless,** unenduring.

UNDERSTANDING AND INTERPRETATION

1. Be sure you know which of the two speakers is speaking each stanza. Then search for clues that might tell anything more about the speakers. How do we know that one speaker is an old man? What do we know about the pilgrim? Is that character young or old? Male or female?

2. In the last long speech of the poem, two different sorts of love are referred to. Only the second of these is capitalized. The first is referred to as "he" because the classical god of love was Cupid. How do these two loves differ? If the first love is Cupid, what might the second refer to?

3. Readers frequently find the first two exchanges unbelievable. When the pilgrim asks the old man how his true love might be recognized, the old man's description could still apply to a great many beautiful women. In spite of this, the pilgrim recognizes the old man's true love from the description and says that he has seen her. Is there any way of looking at this exchange that makes it more believable?

4. A great many of Raleigh's poems are specifically about his bitterness at Queen Elizabeth for abandoning him and replacing him with a new favorite, the Earl of Essex. When this occurred, Raleigh was forty years old. It is true that Queen Elizabeth was neither white nor brown, but had red hair with a ruddy complexion. If this is the person the old man is describing, she would certainly be recognizable to the pilgrim. The latter, in fact, says that the true love *did* appear "like a queen." On the basis of these details, would you argue for or against identifying the true love with Queen Elizabeth? Does it make any difference to an appreciation of the poem?

Edmund Spenser   1552–1599

It was not surprising for an English Renaissance poet to be of royal blood, like Surrey, or to come from a historically important family of means, like Sidney—or even to become a major historical figure in his own right, like Raleigh. What was surprising was that Edmund Spenser, a writer of humble birth and means, should universally come to be regarded both by his public and by other poets of his day as "the prince of poets in his time." That distinction has stayed with Spenser ever since, with grateful admissions of indebtedness expressed by such later poets as Milton, Keats, and T. S. Eliot. Like no other poet, Spenser at once pays homage to Chaucer with his use of archaic diction and to continental trends with his extensive experiments in different verse forms. The most important of these is the nine-line stanza he invented for use in his epic, *The Faerie Queene*. From the first his stanzaic and metrical experiments made him the leading figure in the Areopagus—a group of poets, including Sidney, who were attempting to import classical standards into English poetry.

Spenser first got his taste for verse at a school for poor students in London, taught by the brilliant humanist Richard Mulcaster. Later Spenser worked his way through Cambridge University on a scholarship and worked thereafter as secretary to prominent men in Elizabethan society. After 1580, when he became secretary to the Lord Deputy of Ireland, he spent the rest of his life in that country. In 1589, Raleigh visited Spenser in Ireland and enthusiastically heard Spenser read from his newly begun epic. As a result, Spenser dedicated the first three books of *The Faerie Queene* to Raleigh when they were published in 1590. After they appeared, Spenser's position as first poet of England was never in dispute. In addition to the epic poem, Spenser also wrote an important sonnet sequence, *Amoretti,* based on his (reciprocated) love for Elizabeth Boyle. When he took her as his second wife in 1594, he celebrated their wedding with the extraordinary marriage poem, *Epithalamion.* Here, the

Edmund Spenser
Benjamin Wilson
Reproduced by permission of the Master
and Fellows of Pembroke College, Cambridge

bridegroom is himself the poet who thus could combine the personal and the ceremonial in twenty-four stanzas, one for each hour of this most important day in his life.

Spenser's major work was the long narrative epic which he called *The Faerie Queene* and which was written, of course, to honor Queen Elizabeth herself. It is an extremely complex piece, showing us the poet's skill with narrative, with vivid description, and with variation of emotional effect. Moreover, it stands as one of the major allegorical poems in English. Although he only completed six of them, Spenser originally planned to write twelve books (the standard number for epics). In each book, he planned to treat one of the twelve moral virtues specified by Aristotle. Each book centers around a knight who represents one of these virtues. All the narrative exists on at least two planes at once. Thus each book is simultaneously a story and an allegory—an adventure that represents a spiritual experience. The hero of the first book is the Red Cross Knight, a "tall clownish young man." He has been deceived into deserting his true love, Una (whose name means "one"—and who represents Truth), and into following a woman who calls herself Fidessa (or "faithfulness") but who is really named Duessa (which means "two"). Duessa leads him to the House of Pride, ruled over by Lucifera, the goddess of Pride. Her name clearly connects her to Lucifer, or Satan; so the Red Cross Knight is now staying at Satan's court. The procession of the Seven Deadly Sins shows Spenser's art at its finest. The description of the sins is superb; each of them passes by, each with its particular mode of dressing, each riding on its special animal. If the language of this passage seems especially old-fashioned, it is because Spenser deliberately chose archaic words to give his epic the flavor of a fairy tale from bygone days.

from The Faerie Queene

BOOK I, CANTO IV

17
So forth she[1] comes and to her coach does climb,
Adorned all with gold and garlands gay,
That seemed as fresh as Flora in her prime
And strove to match in royal rich array
Great Juno's golden chair, the which they say   5
The gods stand gazing on when she does ride
To Jove's high house through heaven's brass-paved way,
Drawn of fair peacocks, that excel in pride
And, full of Argus' eyes,[2] their tails dispreaden[3] wide.

18
But this was drawn of six unequal[4] beasts,   10
On which her six sage counselors did ride,
Taught to obey their bestial behests,
With like conditions to their kinds[5] applied.
Of which the first, that all the rest did guide,
Was sluggish Idleness, the nurse of sin.   15
Upon a slothful ass he chose to ride,
Arrayed in habit black and amis[6] thin,
Like to an holy monk, the service to begin.

1. **she,** Lucifera, the goddess of Pride; the most important of all the deadly sins.
2. **Argus' eyes.** Argus was the thousand-eyed monster whose eyes Juno stole for her special bird, the peacock.
3. **dispreaden** (dis prəd′ ən), spread, in an archaic form. Spenser deliberately uses the older forms to give a fairy-tale quality to the poem.
4. **unequal,** different.
5. **kinds,** natures.
6. **amis,** hood.

A woodcut of St. George and the Dragon, from the first edition of The Faerie Queene.

19

And in his hand his portess[7] still he bare,
That much was worn but therein little read;
For of devotion he had little care,
Still drowned in sleep and most of his days dead.
Scarce could he once uphold his heavy head
To looken whether it were night or day.
May seem[8] the wain[9] was very evil led
When such an one had guiding of the way,
That knew not whether right he went or else astray.

20

25

7. **portess,** breviary; a book of prayers, hymns, etc.

8. **may seem,** it may seem.
9. **wain** (wān), cart.

20

From worldly cares himself he did esloin[10]
And greatly shunnéd manly exercise;
From every work he challengéd essoin,[11]   **30**
For contemplation sake. Yet otherwise
His life he led in lawless riotize,[12]
By which he grew to grievous malady;
For in his lustless[13] limbs, through evil guise,[14]
A shaking fever reigned continually.   **35**
Such one was Idleness, first of this company.

21

And by his side rode loathsome Gluttony,
Deforméd creature, on a filthy swine;
His belly was up-blown with luxury,
And eke[15] with fatness swollen were his eyne,[16]   **40**
And like a crane his neck was long and fine,[17]
With which he swallowed up excessive feast,
For want whereof poor people oft did pine.[18]
And all the way, most like a brutish beast,
He spewéd up his gorge, that[19] all did him detest.   **45**

22

In green vine leaves he was right fitly clad,
For other clothes he could not wear for heat;
And on his head an ivy garland had,
From under which fast trickled down the sweat.
Still as he rode, he somewhat[20] still did eat,   **50**
And in his hand did bear a boozing can,
Of which he supped so oft that on his seat
His drunken corse he scarce upholden can,
In shape and life more like a monster than a man.

23

Unfit he was for any worldly thing,
And eke unable once[21] to stir or go,   **55**
Not meet[22] to be of counsel to a king,
Whose mind in meat and drink was drownéd so
That from his friend he seldom knew his foe.
Full of diseases was his carcass blue,[23]   **60**

10. **esloin,** withdraw.
11. **challenged essoin** (ə
oin'), claimed exemption.
12. **riotize,** riotousness.
13. **lustless,** feeble.
14. **guise,** behavior.
15. **eke,** also.
16. **eyne,** eyes.

17. **fine,** thin.
18. **pine,** starve.
19. **that,** so that.
20. **somewhat,** something.
21. **once,** at all.
22. **meet,** fit.
23. **blue,** livid.

And a dry[24] dropsy through his flesh did flow,
Which by misdiet daily greater grew.
Such one was Gluttony, the second of that crew.

24
And next to him rode lustful Lechery
Upon a bearded goat whose rugged hair   65
And whally[25] eyes (the sign of jealousy)
Was like the person self[26] whom he did bear;
Who rough and black and filthy did appear,
Unseemly man to please fair lady's eye.
Yet he of ladies oft was lovéd dear,   70
When fairer faces were bid standen by.
O who does know the bent of women's fantasy?

25
In a green gown he clothéd was full fair,
Which underneath did hide his filthiness;
And in his hand a burning heart he bare,   75
Full of vain follies and newfangledness.[27]
For he was false and fraught[28] with fickleness,
And learnéd had to love with secret looks,
And well could[29] dance, and sing with ruefulness,
And fortunes tell, and read in loving[30] books,   80
And thousand other ways to bait his fleshly hooks.

26
Inconstant man, that lovéd all he saw
And lusted after all that he did love;
Ne[31] would his looser life be tied to law,
But joyed weak women's hearts to tempt and prove[32]   85
If from their loyal loves he might them move.
Which lewdness filled him with reproachful pain
Of that foul evil,[33] which all men reprove,
That rots the marrow and consumes the brain,
Such one was Lechery, the third of all this train.   90

27
And greedy Avarice by him did ride
Upon a camel loaden all with gold;
Two iron coffers hung on either side,

24. **dry,** thirst-producing.
25. **whally,** greenish.
26. **person self,** the very person.
27. **newfangledness,** novelties.
28. **fraught,** loaded.

29. **could,** knew how to.
30. **loving,** probably means *erotic* here.
31. **ne,** not.
32. **prove,** try.
33. **foul evil,** syphilis.

With precious metal full as they might hold;
And in his lap an heap of coin he told;[34]   95
For of his wicked pelf[35] his god he made,
And unto hell himself for money sold.
Accurséd usury was all his trade.
And right and wrong alike in equal balance weighed.

28
His life was nigh unto death's door y'placed,[36]   100
And threadbare coat and cobbled shoes he ware,
Ne scarce good morsel all his life did taste;
But both from back and belly still did spare
To fill his bag and richess to compare.[37]
Yet child ne kinsman living had he none   105
To leave them to; but thorough[38] daily care
To get and nightly fear to lose his own,
He led a wretched life, unto himself, unknown.[39]

29
Most wretched wight,[40] whom nothing might suffice,
Whose greedy lust did lack in greatest store,[41]   110
Whose need had end, but no end covetise,[42]
Whose wealth was want,[43] whose plenty made him poor,
Who had enough, yet wishéd ever more—
A vile disease. And eke in foot and hand
A grievous gout tormented him full sore,   115
That well he could not touch, nor go,[44] nor stand.
Such one was Avarice, the fourth of this fair band.

30
And next to him malicious Envy rode
Upon a ravenous wolf, and still did chaw
Between his cankered[45] teeth a venomous toad,   120
That all the poison ran about his chaw.[46]
But inwardly he chawéd his own maw[47]
At neighbors' wealth, that made him ever sad;
For death it was when any good he saw,
And wept that cause of weeping none he had;   125
But when he heard of harm, he waxéd wondrous glad.

---

34. **told,** counted.
35. **pelf** (pelf), wealth.
36. **y'placed,** an archaic form of placed.
37. **compare,** acquire.
38. **thorough,** through.
39. **unknown,** friendless.
40. **wight** (wīt), person.

41. **store,** plenty.
42. **covetise,** covetousness.
43. **want,** poverty.
44. **go,** walk.
45. **cankered,** corroded.
46. **chaw,** jaw.
47. **maw,** guts.

31

All in a kirtle[48] of discolored say[49]
He clothed was, y'painted full of eyes;
And in his bosom secretly there lay
An hateful snake, the which his tail upties   **130**
In many folds and mortal sting implies.[50]
Still as he rode, he gnashed his teeth to see
Those heaps of gold with gripple[51] Covetise,
And grudgéd[52] at the great felicity
Of proud Lucifera and his own company.   **135**

32

He hated all good words and virtuous deeds,
And him no less that any like did use;[53]
And who with gracious bread the hungry feeds,
His alms for want of faith he doth accuse;
So every good to bad he doth abuse.[54]   **140**
And eke the verse of famous poets' wit
He does backbite, and spiteful poison spews
From leprous moúth on all that ever writ.
Such one vile Envy was, that fifth in row did sit.

33

And him beside rides fierce revenging Wrath   **145**
Upon a lion loath[55] for to be led;
And in his hand a burning brand[56] he hath,
The which he brandisheth about his head.
His eyes did hurl forth sparkles fiery red,
And staréd stern on all that him beheld,   **150**
As ashes pale of hue and seeming dead;
And on his dagger still his hand he held,
Trembling through hasty rage when choler[57] in him
      swelled.

34

His ruffian[58] raiment all was stained with blood,
Which he had spilt, and all to rags y'rent,   **155**
Through unadviséd rashness woxen wood;[59]

48. **kirtle** (kér' tl), jacket.
49. **discolored say,** multicolored wool.
50. **implies,** covers up.
51. **gripple,** grasping.
52. **grudged,** grumbled.
53. **use,** practice.
54. **abuse,** its regular meaning, plus the
root meaning of *twist.*

55. **loath,** unwilling.
56. **brand,** sword.
57. **choler** (kol' ər), anger.
58. **ruffian,** disordered.
59. **woxen wood,** grown mad.

For of his hands he had no government,
Ne cared for blood in his avengement.
But when the furious fit was overpassed,
His cruel facts[60] he often would repent;   160
Yet willful man, he never would forecast[61]
How many mischiefs should ensue his heedless haste.

35
Full many mischiefs follow cruel Wrath;
Abhorréd bloodshed and tumultuous strife,
Unmanly murder and unthrifty scath,[62]   165
Bitter despite, with rancor's rusty knife,
And fretting grief, the enemy of life.
All these, and many evils mo,[63] haunt ire,
The swelling spleen[64] and frenzy raging rife,
The shaking palsy and Saint Francis' fire.[65]   170
Such one was Wrath, the last of this ungodly tire.[66]

36
And after all, upon the wagon beam[67]
Rode Satan, with a smarting whip in hand,
With which he forward lashed the lazy team
So oft as Sloth still in the mire did stand.   175
Huge routs[68] of people did about them band,
Shouting for joy; and still before their way
A foggy mist had covered all the land;
And underneath their feet all scattered lay
Dead skulls and bones of men whose life had gone astray.

60. **facts,** deeds.
61. **forecast,** foretell.
62. **scath,** damage.
63. **mo,** more.
64. **spleen,** temper; also the bodily organ in which anger was thought to be created.
65. **Saint Francis' fire,** erysipelas, a skin disease characterized by shiny red inflammation.
66. **tire,** procession.
67. **beam,** shaft.
68. **routs** (routs), crowds.

FOR UNDERSTANDING

1. There is a distinct organization that governs the poem. Each sin is described within three stanzas wherein the details (what animal is ridden, what clothes are worn) fit the sin described. But are there any important differences? Which sins have different details associated with them?

2. Why are the sins described in this particular order? Would the effect be different if, for example, Wrath came first and Idleness last?

FOR INTERPRETATION

1. Spenser uses the traditional Seven Deadly Sins for his procession. He presents them by means of the device used in medieval drama, personification, in which each abstract qualilty becomes a concrete and specific person. If Spenser were writing today, would he use the same sins, or are there others that seem more central now? What are the actions and thoughts that we consider sinful?

2. Look at stanza 17 and stanza 36, which form the beginning and end of this excerpt. What creates the different emotional effect of these stanzas? How is that difference related to meaning?

FOR APPRECIATION

The Spenserian Stanza

The Faerie Queene is written in a special stanza form called the Spenserian stanza. It was specifically invented by Spenser for use in his epic. Critics generally agree that it "stands out as one of the most remarkably original metrical innovations in the history of English verse." By examining the stanzas from *The Faerie Queene* presented here, you can see that they contain nine iambic lines rhymed *ababbcbcc.* The first eight lines are in iambic pentameter, but the ninth has an extra beat and thus is called an iambic hexameter or alexandrine. You will notice that the *b* rhymes outnumber the other rhymes and dominate the center of the stanza, into which the opening and closing rhymes are interwoven. In addition, the alexandrine at the end makes the couplet less abrupt and gives a long drawn-out, suspended feeling to the end of each stanza. Many later poets used the Spenserian stanza in important works, including Byron, Shelley, and Keats.

COMPOSITION

After getting the hang of the Spenserian stanza from this passage, you might try writing something in this stanza yourself. You'll find that the last line with its six beats is a bit tricky. You might want to use an allegorical framework as Spenser has. Or you might simply want to describe a place or a person or to create an extended metaphor.

Sir Philip Sidney   1554–1586

Among all the Elizabethan poets, the "fair-haired boy" is surely Sir Philip Sidney. Of an influential family, he acquired a fine classical education and moved effortlessly to the center stage of English society. The nephew of Queen Elizabeth's lifelong favorite, the Earl of Leicester, he was adored by both Elizabeth and Leicester—as if he were their adopted child. Surprisingly, he remained unspoiled by these attentions and was not even particularly ambitious, unlike his friends Raleigh and Spenser, both from less brilliant backgrounds than his.

Sidney's three major accomplishments as a writer all show mastery of a different sort. His moving essay, *The Defense of Poesy,* makes large claims for the ennobling powers of the imagination in general and for poetry in particular. It is one of the first extended pieces of literary criticism in modern English. His prose romance, *Arcadia,* has a convoluted plot full of mistaken identities, disguises, unrequited love, and supernatural beings. It was written to honor his sister, the Countess of Pembroke, herself a poet of considerable skill and, especially, a patroness of the arts who shared her brother's zeal to import classical standards into English verse and drama. This elegant and courtly book by a Protestant and undoubted royalist was carried—as a symbol for all to see—by Charles I on his walk to the scaffold in 1649.

Of all his writing, however, it is his great sonnet sequence *Astrophel and Stella* ("Star-Lover and Star"), that has always been most admired. Though Sidney bemoans the cruelty of his beloved according to the Petrarchan conventions of courtly love, he also chafes against their artificiality at times, as Shakespeare was to do. In Sidney's case, the beloved can be identified as Penelope Devereux, the beautiful sister of Elizabeth's last favorite, the Earl of Essex. Sidney and Penelope met when she was only thirteen and he soon became a serious suitor for her hand, urged on by her dying father's wish. Family fortunes, however, ruled otherwise. In 1581 Penelope married Lord Rich and in 1583

Sir Philip Sidney
Unknown Artist
Reproduced by courtesy of the Marquess of Bath, Longleat House, Warminster, Wiltshire, England

Sidney married Frances, daughter of Sir Francis Walsingham, one of Elizabeth's powerful counselors. Sidney's sequence was probably written between the two dates, for it has several noticeable puns on the word *rich* and some uncomplimentary references to Stella's jealous husband.

In his sonnets, Sidney sometimes expresses a fierce impulsiveness that also flashed out in his life as part of the individualism inherent in the role of courtier. When he was thirty-two years old, he dashed impetuously onto an insignificant battlefield in the Netherlands, doffing his two cuisses (thigh armor) to match his partly garbed commander. While fainting of thirst after receiving a mortal thigh wound, he offered water meant for him to a stricken pikeman, saying, "Thy necessity is yet greater than mine." The distraught queen gave him a state funeral in London at St. Paul's Cathedral. The outpouring of mourners on that day in 1586 occurred one week after the execution of Mary Queen of Scots and expressed the nation's solidarity in face of an expected Spanish invasion, which came as the Armada and was resoundingly defeated in 1588.

Of the two sonnets from *Astrophel and Stella* here, the first is about writing poetry and, fittingly enough, begins the sequence. The second is Sidney's lovely invocation to the moon which slyly and effortlessly encloses a self-effacing lover's complaint, both accomplished as though writing these lines involved no more skill than the several breaths required to say them aloud.

from **Astrophel and Stella**

Sonnet 1

Loving in truth, and fain[1] in verse my love to show,
That she (dear she) might take some pleasure of my pain:
Pleasure might cause her read, reading might make her know,
Knowledge might pity win, and pity grace obtain.
I sought fit words to paint the blackest face of woe,   5
Studying inventions fine, her wits to entertain:
Oft turning others' leaves, to see if thence would flow
Some fresh and fruitful showers upon my sun-burn'd brain.
But words came halting forth, wanting Invention's stay,[2]
Invention, Nature's child, fled step-dame Study's blows,   10
And other's feet[3] still[4] seem'd but strangers in my way.
Thus great with child to speak, and helpless in my throes,
Biting my truand[5] pen, beating myself for spite,
Fool, said my Muse[6] to me, look in thy heart and write.

1. **fain,** wishing, desiring.
2. **stay,** support.
3. **feet,** also, poetic feet or measure.
4. **still,** always.
5. **truand,** truant, idle.
6. **Muse.** A long tradition has led poets to call their source of inspiration their "muse." This usually refers, as a personification, to the mental quality of inspiration itself, but it can sometimes refer to the real person who may have inspired a particular poem.

Sonnet 31

With how sad steps, Oh Moon, thou climb'st the skies,
How silently, and with how wan a face!
What, may it be that even in heav'nly place
That busy archer[1] his sharp arrows tries?
Sure, if that long-with-love-acquainted eyes   5
Can judge of love, thou feel'st a lover's case;
I read it in thy looks: thy languished grace,
To me that feel the like, thy state descries[2]
Then even of fellowship, Oh Moon, tell me,
Is constant love deemed there but want of wit?   10
Are beauties there as proud as here they be?
Do they above love to be loved, and yet
Those lovers scorn whom that love doth possess?
Do they call virtue there ungratefulness?

1. **busy archer,** Cupid.
2. **descries,** perceives.

FOR UNDERSTANDING

1. The statement being made in the first sonnet could be outlined under four headings. State the headings and show how the lines for each develop the point being made.

2. Both sonnets use personification as a device. The personifications of lines 9–10 in the first sonnet are a bit hard to follow at first. Invention is personified as someone who should help the limping words of the poet. But since Invention, Sidney says, is the simple and untrained child of Nature, it flees from the blows that Study gives it.

The personification of the moon in the second sonnet is much easier to follow. What details in the poem help to personify the moon?

3. In the last six lines of the second sonnet, the turning point (beginning with "Then") involves a change of tone from the first eight lines. Describe this change of tone and its effect.

FOR APPRECIATION

The Shakespearian Sonnet

Wyatt's sonnet (p. 176), is an Italian (or Petrarchan) sonnet. The other main kind of sonnet is represented by Sidney's first poem here, the English (or Shakespearian) sonnet. In this case, the poem is not organized by the rhymes into a group of eight lines (the octave) followed by a group of six lines (the sestet) with a turning point (volta) occurring between the two parts. Instead, the looser rhyme scheme makes a natural division into four parts—three groups of four lines (quatrains) followed by two lines (couplet). This English innovation came about mainly because English is a rhyme-poor language and cannot sustain fourteen lines with only three or four rhyme sounds.

The four-part division of the English sonnet, which Wyatt and Surrey first experimented with, makes possible the presentation of three examples of something, followed by the couplet as a clincher. But the English sonnet can also be organized in groups of eight and six, with or without a volta between the two parts. In fact, the English form permits a great many different ways to go about expressing the single idea a good sonnet usually contains.

Sidney's first sonnet has an added feature. Instead of pentameter lines, he has made this sonnet of six-beat lines, giving us fourteen hexameter lines, or alexandrines. This is the standard line-length of the sonnet in French, but it is extremely difficult to bring off in English, which Sidney succeeds in doing here.

Sidney's second sonnet is another example of the Italian form, with a volta beginning in the ninth line. The sestet is rhymed differently from Wyatt's Italian sonnet, but it also ends in a couplet, like Wyatt's.

Francis Bacon   1561–1626

As a well-educated young man of good background, Francis Bacon took up the practice of law in 1582 and became a member of Parliament in 1584. His views emphasizing the need for conciliation between the queen and Parliament earned him the disfavor of the queen. He found preferment, however, through the queen's favorite, the Earl of Essex, who became Bacon's patron and friend. When the earl's conflict with the queen flared into open rebellion, Bacon might have fallen with Essex as others did. Instead, he offered to prosecute the earl for treason, but only in the faint hope of saving his patron's life, Bacon said. His political fortunes improved significantly under James I to the point where, as Lord Chancellor, he ruled England while the king was touring Scotland. In 1621, public scandal again arose when Bacon confessed to charges of bribery and judicial corruption. Stripped of his offices and forcibly retired, he devoted the last years of his life to literary and scientific writing.

Bacon's triple legacy—to political history, to literature, and to science—reminds one of a figure like Ben Franklin, except that Franklin's political career was certainly more exemplary than Bacon's. Their direct and pithy prose are comparable, however, and their scientific cast of mind reflects the growth of empiricism with its emphasis on direct observation, controlled research, and rejection of all presuppositions. In these areas, of course, Bacon is the admitted pioneer. The French writer Montaigne was Bacon's only model for creating the familiar essay for the first time in English. Bacon's typical essay of this sort is brief and full of terse directives for the conduct of life. Some of these have become famous as everyday sayings or aphorisms, such as: "Some books are to be tasted, others to be swallowed, and some few to be chewed and digested."

His greatest influence and importance lies in his learned work on scientific thought and research, much of it written in Latin. He set empirical standards for scientific experimentation in *The Advancement of Learning*

Sir Francis Bacon
Unknown Artist
National Portrait Gallery, London

and *Novum Organum* (New Instrument). In *The New Atlantis* he envisioned a government-funded center for scientific work that was realized by the founding of the Royal Society in 1660. Riding in his carriage on a wintry road in 1626, he suddenly conceived of the idea of using snow as a refrigerant. He bought a chicken and buried it in the snow, but while waiting to observe the preservative effects of this procedure, he caught the chill from which he died.

Of Studies

Studies serve for delight, for ornament, and for ability. Their chief use for delight is in privateness and retiring; for ornament, is in discourse; and for ability, is in the judgment and disposition of business. For expert men can execute, and perhaps judge of particulars, one by one; but the general counsels, and the plots and marshaling of affairs, come best from those that are learned. To spend too much time in studies is sloth; to use them too much for ornament, is affectation; to make judgment wholly by their rules, is the humor of a scholar. They perfect nature, and are perfected by experience: for natural abilities are like natural plants, that need pruning, by study; and studies themselves do give forth directions too much at large, except they be bounded in by experience. Crafty men contemn[1] studies, simple men admire them, and wise men use them; for they teach not their own use; but that is a wisdom without them, and above them, won by observation. Read not to contradict and confute; nor to believe and take for granted; nor to find talk and discourse; but to weigh and consider. Some books are to be tasted, others to be swallowed, and some few to be chewed and digested; that is, some books are to be read only in parts; others to be read, but not curiously[2]; and some few to be read wholly, and with diligence and attention. Some books also may be read by deputy, and extracts made of them by others; but that would be only in the less important arguments, and the meaner sort of books; else distilled books are like common distilled waters, flashy things. Reading maketh a full man; conference a ready man; and writing an exact man. And therefore, if a man write little, he had need have a great memory; if he confer little, he had need have a present wit: and if he read little, he had need have much cunning, to seem to know that he doth not. Histories make men wise; poets witty; the mathematics subtile; natural philosophy deep; moral grave; logic and rhetoric able to contend. *Abeunt studia in mores.*[3] Nay, there is no stond[4] or impediment in the wit but may be wrought out by fit studies; like as diseases of the body may have appropriate exercises. Bowling is good for the stone and reins[5]; shooting for the lungs and breast; gentle walking for the stomach; riding for the head; and the like. So if a man's wit be wandering, let him study the mathematics; for in demonstrations, if his wit be called away never so little, he must begin again. If his wit be not apt to distinguish or find differences, let him study the Schoolmen; for they are *cumini sectores*[6]. If he be not apt to beat over matters, and to call up one thing to prove and illustrate another, let him study the lawyers' cases. So every defect of the mind may have a special receipt.

Of Parents and Children

The joys of parents are secret; and so are their griefs and fears. They cannot utter the one; nor they will not utter the other. Children sweeten labors; but they make misfortunes more bitter. They increase the cares of life; but they mitigate the remembrance of death. The perpetuity by generation is common to beasts; but memory, merit, and noble works are proper to men. And surely a man shall see the noblest works and foundations have proceeded from childless men; which have sought to express the images of their minds, where those of their bodies have failed. So the care of posterity is most in them that have no posterity. They that are the first raisers of their houses are most indulgent towards their children; beholding them as the continuance not only of their kind but of

1. **contemn,** despise.
2. **curiously,** earnestly, with curiosity.
3. *Abeunt . . . mores.* Latin, "Zeal develops into habit."
4. **stond,** difficult.
5. **reins,** kidneys.
6. *cumini sectores,* Latin, hair splitters.

Hans Eworth and Family
Unknown Artist
Reproduced by courtesy of the Marquess of Bath
Longleat House Warminster, Wiltshire, England

their work; and so both children and creatures.

The difference in affection of parents towards their several children is many times unequal; and sometimes unworthy; especially in the mother; as Solomon saith, *A wise son rejoiceth the father, but an ungracious son shames the mother.*[1] A man shall see, where there is a house full of children, one or two of the eldest respected, and the youngest made wantons; but in the midst some that are as it were forgotten, who many times nevertheless prove the best. The illiberality of parents in allowance towards their children is an harmful error; makes them base; acquaints them with shifts; makes them sort[2] with mean company; and makes them surfeit more when they come to plenty. And therefore the proof is best, when men keep their authority towards their children, but not their purse. Men have a foolish manner (both parents and schoolmasters and servants) in creating and breeding an emulation between brothers during childhood, which many times sorteth to discord when they are men, and disturbeth families. The Italians make little difference between children and nephews or near kinsfolks; but so they be of the lump, they care

1. *A wise son . . . the mother.* From *Proverbs*, X, 1.
2. **sort,** associate.

not though they pass not through their own body. And, to say truth, in nature it is much a like matter; insomuch that we see a nephew sometimes resembleth an uncle or a kinsman more than his own parent; as the blood happens. Let parents choose betimes the vocations and courses they mean their children should take; for then they are most flexible; and let them not too much apply themselves to the disposition of their children, as thinking they will take best to that which they have most mind to. It is true, that if the affection or aptness of the children be extraordinary, then it is good not to cross it; but generally the precept is good, *optimum elige, suave et facile illud faciet consuetudo.*[3] Younger brothers are commonly fortunate, but seldom or never where the elder are disinherited.

3. *Optimum . . . consuetudo.* A precept of the Pythagoreans: "Choose the best; habit will make it pleasant and easy."

FOR UNDERSTANDING

Of Studies
Notice that Bacon never uses the first or second personal pronouns. He never addresses the reader as *you* and, in general, never recognizes that there are two sexes. His writing consists of a number of pronouncements as if what he is saying are undebatable truths.
1. What in general seems to be the heart of his perceptions about studies?
2. In which of Bacon's categories of reading would you place these essays: to be tasted; to be swallowed; to be chewed and digested?

Of Parents and Children
Bacon did not marry until he was forty-five years old. This may have colored his writings about marriage and families. Let's just suppose this essay, formal as it is, is basically autobiographical.

What then were some of the things that happened to Bacon in his own family as he was growing up?

FOR INTERPRETATION

Of Studies
The school curriculum today is quite different from what it was in Bacon's time. He contends that certain subjects will help an individual in a particular way. Reflect on the subjects you are now taking in school. Try to pin down what each is supposed to do for you. For example, Bacon says that "histories make men wise."

Of Parents and Children
This essay was written almost 400 years ago. Do you see in the families of today some of the same problems and relationships that apparently Bacon had in mind when he wrote this essay?

FOR APPRECIATION

Of Studies
One of the most noticeable elements in this essay is Bacon's use of parallel structure. In the first sentence he says studies serve; *for* delight; *for* ornament; *for* ability.

What are the parallel structures in the second sentence?

What are the parallel structures in the famous quotation about books?

When there are many instances of parallelism such as in this essay, what is the effect on the writing?

Of Parents and Children
"Of Studies" extensively uses the rhetorical device of parallel structure. "Of Parents and Children" uses another device, the balanced sentence. Here the two parts are balanced one against the other like a teeter-totter. Most often the two parts seem to contradict one another. The first five sentences of this essay are all balanced sentences. Try writing one of your own.

Christopher Marlowe 1564–1593

This portrait is thought to be of Christopher Marlowe.

Courtesy of the Master, Fellows, and Scholars of Corpus Christi College, Cambridge

Two months before the birth of Shakespeare, Christopher Marlowe was born into the humble family of a Canterbury shoemaker. By the time Marlowe perished in a tavern brawl twenty-nine years later, he had written seven plays and originated fundamental changes in Elizabethan drama unequaled by any other writer of his day. At the same age Shakespeare had created apprentice work that by itself would have left him with scarcely a mention in the history of the period. Because of Marlowe's enormous popularity, Shakespeare took Marlowe's blank-verse plays as a major point of departure in his own development—as can be seen by his many echoes of Marlowe, the only contemporary Shakespeare acknowledges in this way.

Marlowe got his classical education at Cambridge on scholarship (B.A., 1584), but in 1587 his M.A. was delayed because of the young student's frequent absences. Surprisingly, the

Queen's Privy Council intervened on his behalf, referring to his employment "in matters touching his country's benefit." At the same time that he was serving the crown as a secret political agent or spy, he was an alleged member of Raleigh's School of Night, a group of iconoclastic thinkers and scientists. At his death, in fact, Marlowe was slated for questioning by authorities about testimony of playwright Thomas Kyd, Marlowe's former roommate, that Marlowe openly espoused "heretical religious and lewd moral principles." As if all these dark matters were not enough for one postgraduate student, Marlowe achieved his first tumultuous dramatic success in 1587 with his play *Tamburlaine*. It marked the public debut of "Marlowe's mighty line," the instrument by which the great drama of the English Renaissance was to be realized.

While blank verse had been attempted since the Earl of Surrey introduced it, it was Marlowe's gift to grasp the potential values of this measure and to wield it as a vigorous and eloquent means for captivating his sun-drenched audience as they stood encircled within the newly built English theaters. But Marlowe had to clear away two obstacles even to get a hearing for his blank verse. One was the miserable doggerel in which popular theater was written—rhymed lines of fourteen jigging syllables (called *fourteeners*) stuffed by their unlearned authors ("mother-wits") with ludicrous imagery. Marlowe inserted a short prologue into *Tamburlaine* to declare his contempt for these plays:

> From jigging veins of rhyming mother-wits
> And such conceits as clownage keeps in pay,
> We'll lead you to the stately tent of war. . . .

The other obstacle was the idea that the classical hexameter could become the chief poetic tool of English drama. Sidney's sister and the poets in Sidney's group of classicists were particularly adamant about this. Marlowe's choice of measure cut clean to the heart of the question in lines of five sonorous but athletic stresses carefully matched to the breath patterns of English speech.

Following *Tamburlaine* and its equally successful sequel, each new play of Marlowe generated the kind of excitement we associate today only with popular music or the movies. His plays also caught the temper of those times, since each featured a character who is exalted and then destroyed by some extreme but illusory self-transcendence, some Renaissance "overreaching" of the human condition. Shakespeare's *Richard III* is clearly a study of exuberant villainy only one remove from *Tamburlaine*. Even as late a play as Shakespeare's *Macbeth* can be seen in part as a final consideration of the "overreacher."

The two set speeches here are from *The Tragical History of Dr. Faustus*, both spoken by the title character. In selling his soul to the devil, Faustus gains youth and special supernatural powers. Thus, the first speech occurs after he orders his demon to summon up the soul of Helen for him. Marlowe gives Faustus these famous lines to speak on first looking at Helen's immortal beauty. The second speech is the desperate monologue of belated repentance that Faustus utters as his life closes and hell yawns wide for his soul. As fine as anything Shakespeare wrote, these lines, particularly, have chilled generations of readers and playgoers with their eerie realism, their powerfully imagined psychology, their remarkably taut-strung verse. This scene—and the whole play—was not only to influence Shakespeare but a succession of writers that includes Milton, Blake, Goethe, Thomas Mann, and many others.

Why, then, after such successes, did a tavern brawl end Marlowe's life among the rough-and-tumble political agents he had once worked with? Some have plausibly suggested that Marlowe, his future in the theater assured, was trying to cut himself free of the secret service—to "come in from the cold"—but that his erstwhile companions simply did not trust him or what he might say during the upcoming investigation into his well-known religious and moral heterodoxies. Whatever the reason, Marlowe had set Elizabethan drama on its course—and there was a master, scarcely tried as yet, to pick up where Marlowe left off. "Therefore when flint and iron wear away/Verse is immortal and shall ne'er decay."

To the Apparition of Helen

FAUST. Was this the face that launched a thousand ships
   And burnt the topless[1] towers of Ilium?[2]
   Sweet Helen, make me immortal with a kiss.
   [*Kisses her.*]
   Her lips sucks forth my soul—see where it flies!
   Come, Helen, come, give me my soul again.   5
   Here will I dwell, for heaven is in these lips
   And all is dross that is not Helena.
   I will be Paris, and for love of thee
   Instead of Troy shall Wittenberg[3] be sacked,
   And I will combat with weak Menelaus   10
   And wear thy colors on my pluméd crest;
   Yea, I will wound Achilles in the heel
   And then return to Helen for a kiss.
   O thou art fairer than the evening air
   Clad in the beauty of a thousand stars!   15
   Brighter art thou than flaming Jupiter
   When he appeared to hapless Semele,[4]
   More lovely than the monarch of the sky
   In wanton Arethusa's azur'd arms;[5]
   And none but thou shalt be my paramour!   20

1. **topless,** unseeably high.
2. **Ilium.** The Trojan War occurred after Paris of Troy (or Ilium) stole the beautiful Helen from her Greek husband Menelaus. The Greeks besieged Troy, then sacked and burned it. In the siege Paris gave the Greek hero Achilles a mortal wound in his heel, the one place where Achilles was vulnerable to injury.
3. **Wittenberg,** the small German university town where Dr. Faustus is traditionally said to have lived and taught.
4. **Semele,** a Theban woman loved by the god Jupiter. When she demanded to see him in all the grandeur of his divinity, the flame and lightning of the god destroyed her.
5. **Arethusa's azur'd arms.** In Greek mythology, the nymph of the fountain Arethusa was never the paramour of Jupiter, monarch of the sky, unless Marlowe means that the blue sky of Jupiter is reflected in the fountain's "azur'd arms."

The Damnation of Faustus

[*The clock strikes eleven.*]

FAUST. Ah, Faustus,
Now hast thou but one bare hour to live
And then thou must be damned perpetually!
Stand still, you ever-moving spheres of heaven,
That time may cease and midnight never come;　　　　5
Fair Nature's eye, rise, rise again, and make
Perpetual day; or let this hour be but
A year, a month, a week, a natural day,
That Faustus may repent and save his soul!
O lente lente currite noctis equi.[1]　　　　10
The stars move still, time runs, the clock will strike,
The devil will come, and Faustus must be damned.
O, I'll leap up to my God! Who pulls me down?
See, see, where Christ's blood streams in the firmament!—
One drop would save my soul—half a drop! ah, my Christ!　　　　15
Rend not my heart for naming of my Christ;
Yet will I call on him—O, spare me, Lucifer!
Where is it now? 'Tis gone; and see where God
Stretcheth out his arm and bends his ireful brows.
Mountains and hills, come, come and fall on me　　　　20
And hide me from the heavy wrath of God,
No, no—
Then will I headlong run into the earth:
Earth, gape! O no, it will not harbor me.
You stars that reigned at my nativity,　　　　25
Whose influence hath allotted death and hell,
Now draw up Faustus like a foggy mist
Into the entrails of yon laboring clouds
That when they vomit forth into the air,
My limbs may issue from their smoky mouths,　　　　30
So that my soul may but ascend to heaven.
[*The watch strikes.*]
Ah, half the hour is past; 'twill all be past anon.
O God,
If thou wilt not have mercy on my soul,
Yet for Christ's sake whose blood hath ransomed me　　　　35
Impose some end to my incessant pain:
Let Faustus live in hell a thousand years,

---

1. *O lente . . . equi.* Latin, "Run slowly, slowly, O steeds of the night," after a line from Ovid's *Amores.*

A hundred thousand, and at last be saved!
O, no end is limited to damnéd souls!
Why wert thou not a creature wanting soul?   40
Or why is this immortal that thou hast?
Ah, Pythagoras' *metempsychosis*[2]—were that true,
This soul should fly from me, and I be changed
Unto some brutish beast. All beasts are happy,
For when they die   45
Their souls are soon dissolved in elements,
But mine must live still[3] to be plagued in hell.
Cursed be the parents that engendered me!
No, Faustus, curse thyself, curse Lucifer
That hath deprived thee of the joys of heaven.   50
[*The clock strikes twelve.*]
It strikes, it strikes! Now, body, turn to air
Or Lucifer will bear thee quick[4] to hell!
[*Thunder and lightning.*]
O soul, be changed to little water drops
And fall into the ocean, ne'er be found.
My God, my God, look not so fierce on me!   55
[*Enter* DEVILS.]
Adders and serpents, let me breathe awhile!
Ugly hell, gape not—come not, Lucifer—
I'll burn my books—ah, Mephistophilis!
[*Exeunt* DEVILS *with Faustus.*]

2. **metempsychosis,** the Pythagorean doctrine of the transmigration of souls.
3. **still,** always.
4. **quick,** alive.

UNDERSTANDING AND APPRECIATION

1. Both of these speeches have been widely admired for their intensity of feeling. Both speeches, despite their extreme difference in mood, move by a kind of erratic or impulsive flitting from one thought to another—as though the lines attempt to suggest the psychology of a feverish mind.

Try to trace the trajectory of thought that occurs to Faustus as he looks at Helen.

2. The second speech is remarkable for its terror and pathos. One of the chief techniques Marlowe uses to achieve these emotional effects is a drastic stretching of the normal iambic pentameter of the lines. Two strong beats often take the place of one iambic pulsation (as in "See, see . . ." beginning line 14). Yet one can still usually feel the five strong pulsations in each line. This is an example that helps to explain why many poets who write in English prefer to speak of five-beat lines rather than iambic pentameter lines. The latter really describes something possible in Greek or Latin but neither possible nor desirable in English.

Try following the rhythms of this speech. Where do they seem to depart most from normal blank verse? How would you read some of the most agitated lines aloud?

William Shakespeare   1564–1616

With the exception of Chaucer, we know more about the facts of William Shakespeare's life than almost any major writer in English who preceded him. Still, considering that Shakespeare is universally regarded as the greatest writer in the English language, the mere biographical facts tell us disappointingly little about who this man was, what he believed, how he experienced the joys and sorrows of life, or how he went about writing his astonishing body of lyric, narrative, and dramatic poetry. This lack of information has come to be seen as a blessing in disguise, however, since it compels us to draw from the works themselves whatever can be said on these subjects. Tradition is probably correct in giving Shakespeare's birthday as April 23, 1564, called St. George's Day in honor of England's patron saint. On the same day in 1616, his fifty-second birthday, Shakespeare died in Stratford-upon-Avon, Warwickshire, the midlands town of his birth, where he had retired in 1610 as an honored and respected gentleman after two decades spent in London becoming a successful professional actor, producer, and playwright.

He left behind two published narrative poems (1593 and 1594) that he had carefully overseen through the press, a sequence of 154 sonnets printed in 1609, evidently without his authorization, and about thirty-seven plays, none of which he had taken the trouble to publish, even though some had appeared during his lifetime in more or less mangled, sometimes "pirated" versions. The narrative poems, of which he seemed proudest, would alone have earned him a place in literary history as a minor poet influenced by the classical school of Spenser and Sidney. Considering the sonnet sequence as well, he might be seen today as an important, perhaps major, poet touched at moments by greatness. Ironically enough, then, it is only because of the work he made no effort to preserve for posterity, the plays he wrote to be acted in the popular open theaters of his day, that he has come to be viewed as the greatest

William Shakespeare
Unknown Artist
National Portrait Gallery, London

writer in English, if not the world. Fortunately for us, seven years after Shakespeare's death, two of Shakespeare's fellow actors who had been shareholders with him in the company he wrote for, published thirty-six of his plays in an edition now known as the Shakespeare *First Folio* of 1623. This folio and the *King James Bible* of 1611 are widely regarded as being the two greatest books in the history of the English language. Without the folio, we would have no way of knowing that some of Shakespeare's plays—including *Macbeth*—had ever existed. In some cases we are still not sure, in fact, of exactly what Shakespeare did or did not write—but the once-controversial idea that someone other than Shakespeare wrote his work is now thought to be, on substantial grounds, not worth serious reconsideration. Aside from the work itself, there are something over 200 documents from Shakespeare's time that attest to his existence as an Elizabethan and as a poet and a playwright.

The relative obscurity of Shakespeare's life when compared to a later writer like John Donne and the almost haphazard survival of his greatest plays are worth emphasizing. Later ages including our own have tended to put a spotlight on all things pertaining to Shakespeare, contrary to how people in his own age viewed him. To them, he was a hardworking middle-class professional who gained wealth and honor in a trade considered slightly disreputable by many and condemned as outright wicked by the growing number of Puritans who called for the closing down of the theaters. Some few, like the poet Ben Jonson—his rival, antagonist, and friend—saw his remarkable greatness for what it was; most people in his day, quite possibly including himself, did not. Like him, they confidently believed Ben Jonson to be the greater writer, if only because he more consistently observed classical standards in his work.

What, then, gives Shakespeare this unwavering reputation for greatness in age after age? First of all, there is the intense sympathy that his work conveys for people of every type and class, from the most exalted monarch to the humblest gravedigger or porter. No one, even a villain, is presented without compassion—without some understanding from deep inside that character as to how it feels to be that very person living precisely under those conditions in exactly that way. Second, there is a warmth of humor that suffuses the comedies and comes out even in the histories and tragedies, an affectionate chuckling *with* the character over all-too-human foibles that may be extreme in some but are potentially shared by all. Marlowe's fierce eloquence has nothing of this quality, and Jonson's comedic spirit all too often shades off into cruelty and contempt for the characters being satirized. Third, there is a communicable zest for the heroic, whether seen in daring exploits, courageous speculation, or the ardors of what we would now call romantic love. This zest can be expressed as exhilaration through elevated language, as zeal and boldness in facing the unknown, or as passions that are variously

earthy, sensuous, or idealistic. Fourth, this overarching tolerance for diverse and wide-ranging expressions of human nature has the strength—at Shakespeare's greatest—to witness a tragic vision unique to Shakespeare's writing. No theory of tragedy, ancient or modern, is sufficient to diagram the workings of this dramatic power. Last, there is an ultimate vision of wholeness in all of Shakespeare's poetry, a recognition of the healing power of the imagination, its profound health, the always-possible reconciliation of extremes that eventually comes about at whatever cost. This essential "goodness" in Shakespeare can be palpably felt in the performance of almost any of his plays. It swells like a sunflower at the heart of his comedies. It exists as a hope, a pinprick spark of light in the severest tragedy—like a bright flaw surrounded by its own unreflective diamond-hearted darkness.

Growing up in the socially prominent family of a Stratford glover and alderman, Shakespeare was likely to have gone to the local free grammar school, receiving an education which literally consisted exclusively of studying Latin grammar by rote. But unlike nearly all the other sixteenth-century writers represented here, he did not go on to attend a university, possibly because of a turn for the worse in his father's financial fortunes. Instead, by eighteen, he had married Anne Hathaway, a woman eight years his senior who was from a comfortably landed family, possibly of Puritan leanings. Six months later their first child Susanna was born, and two years later their twins, Judith and Hamnet. The latter, Shakespeare's only son, died at the age of eleven in 1596. Between the birth of the twins in 1585 and the first reference to Shakespeare as a London actor in 1592, there occurs the so-called seven "Lost Years," during which he has been imagined—without foundation in fact—as teaching school, or becoming a sailor, soldier, scrivener, or lawyer. In any case, by 1592 Shakespeare was already working in companies of players, a profession that to most Londoners also included bearbaiters, bullbaiters, acrobats, jugglers, as well as roustabouts, rogues, and cutpurses.

Shakespeare's career thereafter can be oversimplified by seeing the plays as falling roughly into four periods over the next two decades, produced at a fairly consistent rate of nearly two a year. (1) The early histories of the 1590s. (2) The romantic comedies around the turn of the century. (3) The great tragedies of the early 1600s. (4) The romances of the 1610s. The early blood and thunder of the histories gives way to a warmth of typically Elizabethan humor unlike Jonson's harsher satires. Then the great tragedies of the third period—*Hamlet*, *Othello*, *King Lear*, and *Macbeth*—show humanity through the darkening glass of malcontent world-weariness, not unlike the grimmer mood of other playwrights in the reign of James I, most notably John Webster and Thomas Middleton. The romances of the last period, however, suggest the possibilities for a transcendence of human suffering through contrition, expiation, and reconciliation —qualities that might have healed the dissensions that after Shakespeare's death were to open society to the years of strife and civil war between Puritan and Royalist.

There is a range of quality in Shakespeare's work, of course—it is not *all* magnificent; despite the glorious poetry, the reputed ease of composition, the wide vein of invention, the Bard was mortal and was known to nod at times. The range extends across extremes, from the purely atrocious, like the early tragedy *Titus Andronicus*, to the relatively uninspired and mediocre, like the late history *Henry VIII*, to the sublime humor of comedies like *Twelfth Night*—to the incalculable greatness of mature tragedies like *Macbeth* or visionary romances like *The Tempest*.

This progression has suggested to many that the late work must have corresponded to a personal embittering of Shakespeare's otherwise unclouded disposition. But the reasons ascribed do not even begin to peer into the creative process where his tragic vision took form. Disappointment at a bleak marriage could well have expressed itself before. The loss of his only son, paradoxically, did not seem to affect the sunny comedies following that event. The decline of the Elizabethan world view following the execution of Essex cannot adequately explain the late thoroughgoing confrontation with the powers of darkness, much less their absolution in the last work. Despite the decadence of James's court, the era in which the tragedies were

written was one of unparalleled peace and prosperity. And the intolerant absolutism of the Puritans with their censorious attitude toward the "cakes and ale" of life was already held up for scorn and ridicule in the early comedies. The fact is that no one will ever be able to find a formula that "explains away" his work, no matter what facts they muster. As Jonson said, "He was not for an age, but for all time!"

Shakespeare's Sonnets

Following the publication of Sidney's sonnet sequence in 1591, a sudden vogue of sonneteering struck England. During the high tide of this fashion, no less than fifteen English sequences were printed. Just before the waning in 1598, an Elizabethan writer referred to Shakespeare's "sugar'd sonnets" being circulated in manuscript among his friends. All this would tend to place the writing of Shakespeare's sequence between 1592 and 1598. It is strange, therefore, that this sequence did not see print until 1609, a time when sonnets were thought to be as out-of-date as yesterday's newspaper. It is certain that copy for the printing was surreptitiously acquired and that the edition was produced without the poet's authorization. It is also possible that not long after its appearance, the book was suppressed by someone powerful enough to halt its further sale. A second edition did not appear until 1640, as compared to nearly eight and twelve editions each of Shakespeare's two narrative poems in roughly the same period. If we add to this puzzling situation the unusually high quality of the poetry in most of this sequence, we have the makings of a literary enigma that has fascinated readers and scholars from the seventeenth century onwards.

The sequence is unique among its peers in that the poems are addressed not to one beloved but to two, one a fair youth, the other a dark lady of exceptional musical gifts. A rough plot for the sequence clearly emerges despite some possible disorganization in the printed version, our only source. The first seventeen sonnets advise the fair youth to marry and beget offspring, but in the remainder of the 126 sonnets addressed to him, a deeper, more personal note of affectionate friendship is sounded. A rival poet gives the poet of the sequence bouts of jealousy, but it is the woman

Dagger Scene from Macbeth
Thomas Beach (c. 1785)
The Garrick Club
Photo: E.T. Archive, Ltd., London

J.P. Kemble as Macbeth and Mrs. Siddons (see page 430) as Lady Macbeth.

with whom he is in love who causes him the most grief, for she pursues and wins the love of his best friend. The last twenty-six sonnets are written directly to this woman, the dark lady. The poet's anger at his betrayal by this woman and his best friend is something to behold. But the poet's love for the dark lady is also unmistakable.

Naturally, some people become fixated on who the historical figures behind these characters might be. Most recent speculation tends to support the idea that the fair youth was the Earl of Southampton, Shakespeare's patron and a crony of the Earl of Essex. This leads to identifying the rival poet as Marlowe. One critic has even identified the dark lady rather ingeniously as an Italian musician at Elizabeth's court who was also an accomplished poet and early feminist, Emilia Bassano Lanier. A 1611 edition of her poems, newly rescued from obscurity, contains an attack on men that might have been prompted by the publication in 1609 of Shakespeare's uncomplimentary references to the dark lady in his sequence.

Though definitive identifications will forever elude us—and are ultimately of no great significance—some of this can be intriguing fun so long as it does not distract us from the magnificence of the sonnets themselves. With their brief outcries of joy, anger, despair, or jealousy, they stand free of all historical controversy if only because Shakespeare has done what Sidney's muse asked of him: "Fool, said my muse to me, look in thy heart and write."

Sonnet 29

When in disgrace with Fortune and men's eyes,
I all alone beweep my outcast state,
And trouble deaf heaven with my bootless[1] cries,
And look upon myself and curse my fate,
Wishing me like to one more rich in hope,   5
Featured like him, like him with friends possessed,
Desiring this man's art, and that man's scope,
With what I most enjoy contented least;
Yet in these thoughts myself almost despising,
Haply[2] I think on thee, and then my state,   10
Like to the lark at break of day arising
From sullen earth, sings hymns at heaven's gate;
For thy sweet love rememb'red such wealth brings,
That then I scorn to change my state with kings.

1. **bootless,** useless.
2. **haply,** perhaps.

Sonnet 64

When I have seen by Time's fell[1] hand defaced
The rich, proud cost of outworn buried age,
When sometime[2] lofty towers I see down-rased
And brass eternal slave to mortal rage;[3]
When I have seen the hungry ocean gain   5
Advantage on the kingdom of the shore,
And the firm soil win of the wat'ry main,
Increasing store with loss and loss with store;[4]
When I have seen such interchange of state,
Or state itself confounded to decay,   10
Ruin hath taught me thus to ruminate,
That Time will come and take my love away.
This thought is as a death, which cannot choose
But weep to have that which it fears to lose.

1. **fell,** deadly, merciless.
2. **sometime,** formerly.
3. **brass eternal . . . mortal rage.** Brass designed to last forever subject to destructive violence. This refers to the destruction of brass memorial tablets by human vandalism.
4. **Increasing . . . loss with store.** Adding to the ocean's store by the land's loss of soil and adding to the ocean's loss by the land's encroaching soil.

Sonnet 65

Since brass, nor stone, nor earth, nor boundless sea,
But sad mortality o'ersways[1] their power,
How with this rage shall beauty hold a plea,
Whose action is no stronger than a flower?
Oh, how shall summer's honey breath hold out   5
Against the wrackful[2] siege of batt'ring days,
When rocks impregnable are not so stout,
Nor gates of steel so strong but Time decays?
Oh, fearful meditation: where, alack,
Shall Time's best jewel from Time's chest[3] lie hid?   10
Or what strong hand can hold his swift foot back,
Or who his spoil of beauty can forbid?
Oh, none, unless this miracle have might,
That in black ink my love may still shine bright.

1. **o'ersways,** overmasters.
2. **wrackful,** destructive.
3. **chest,** strongbox, coffin.

Sonnet 73

That time of year thou mayst in me behold
When yellow leaves, or none, or few, do hang
Upon those boughs which shake against the cold,
Bare ruined choirs[1] where late the sweet birds sang.
In me thou seest the twilight of such day   5
As after sunset fadeth in the west,
Which by and by black night doth take away,
Death's second self, that seals up all in rest.
In me thou seest the glowing of such fire
That on the ashes of his youth doth lie,   10
As the deathbed whereon it must expire,
Consumed with that which it was nourished by.[2]
This thou perceiv'st, which makes thy love more strong,
To love that well which thou must leave ere long.

1. **choirs,** the part of the church or chapel where the
service was sung, usually by the church chorus.
2. **Consumed . . . nourished by.** That is, the air, which
keeps the fire going but also allows the fire to burn itself
out.

Sonnet 116

Let me not to the marriage of true minds
Admit impediments. Love is not love
Which alters when it alteration finds,
Or bends with the remover to remove:
Oh, no! it is an ever-fixèd mark,   5
That looks on tempests and is never shaken;
It is the star to every wandering bark,
Whose worth's unknown, although his height be taken.
Love's not Time's fool, though rosy lips and cheeks
Within his bending sickle's compass come;   10
Love alters not with his brief hours and weeks,
But bears it out even to the edge of doom.
If this be error and upon me proved,*
I never writ, nor no man ever loved.

* **upon me proved,**   demonstrated by my example.

Sonnet 129

The expense of spirit in a waste of shame
Is lust in action; and, till action, lust
Is perjured, murd'rous, bloody, full of blame,
Savage, extreme, rude, cruel, not to trust;
Enjoyed no sooner but despisèd straight;   5
Past reason hunted and, no sooner had,
Past reason hated as a swallowed bait,
On purpose laid to make the taker mad:
Mad in pursuit, and in possession so;
Had, having, and in quest to have, extreme;   10
A bliss in proof[1] and, proved,[2] a very woe;
Before, a joy proposed; behind, a dream.
All this the world well knows; yet none knows well
To shun the heaven that leads men to this hell.

1. **in proof,**   when tasted.
2. **proved,**   thoroughly tested.

Sonnet 130

My mistress' eyes are nothing like the sun;
Coral is far more red than her lips' red;
If snow be white, why then her breasts are dun;[1]
If hairs be wires, black wires grow on her head.
I have seen roses damask'd,[2] red and white,   5
But no such roses see I in her cheeks;
And in some perfumes is there more delight
Than in the breath that from my mistress reeks.
I love to hear her speak, yet well I know
That music hath a far more pleasing sound;   10
I grant I never saw a goddess go;
My mistress, when she walks, treads on the ground.
And yet, by heaven, I think my love as rare
As any she belied with false compare.

1. **dun,** dull grayish brown.
2. **damask'd** (dam′ ə skd), decorated with varied colors.

INTERPRETATION AND APPRECIATION

The Shakespearian Sonnet

The English, or Shakespearian, sonnet was initially a response to the lack of rich rhyme resources in English when compared to other European languages. Thus the English sonnet has three quatrains (each with two separate rhymes of its own, placed in alternation for easier rhyming: a b a b, c d c d, e f e f) and a final rhymed couplet. Shakespeare, however, takes up this four-part division and in his 154 sonnets exploits their deployment in an amazing number of different ways. The selections here show this. Take sonnet 29. If you divide this sonnet into its three quatrains and couplet, you will see that Shakespeare has written it as though it were in the Italian form. The first two quatrains are really one continuous statement—an eight-line group exactly like the Italian octave. Look at the opening of the third quatrain; the ninth line begins with the word, "Yet. . . ." It becomes clear that this quatrain and the final couplet make a six line answer to the first eight, just like an Italian sestet—and it begins with a clearly marked volta or turning point. None of the other sonnets here, however, follows this Italian pattern; all have different organizations, and not one of them has a volta.

Sonnet 29

1. Do you think the details of unhappiness in the first eight lines are causes of the poet's sorrow or results of it?
2. The poet needs to convince us that his mood has changed in the last six lines. How does he do this through language, imagery, and sentence structure?

Sonnets 64 and 65

Look at the next two selections; they are an example of a "sonnet pair," which Shakespeare often uses in his sequence. In this case, the first sonnet raises a fear which it doesn't try to answer. Then the next sonnet, after summarizing the one before, asks three questions, one in each quatrain, on the way to giving an answer in the couplet.
1. In sonnet 64, mentally circle the word "when" wherever it opens a line. Use this clue as a guide to the organization of this sonnet, different from those we've discussed before. The tenth line

seems, in a reading aloud, especially profound. It's also the first time we have reached the main clause in a very long sentence. What does this line mean? Consider all the punning possibilities for the word "state."

2. Explain how these opening words give an overarching rhetorical shape and rhythmic sweep to the whole of sonnet 65: Since/Oh/Oh/Oh.

Sonnet 73

Divide the poem into its three quatrains and couplet. Each of the three quatrains is a long metaphor (or "conceit") explaining how the poet feels. In the first quatrain, he compares himself to a time of year. In the second, the comparison is to a time of day. In the third, the metaphor refers to a phase in the burning down of a fire (which can be encompassed by an hour). The progression, then, is season, day, hour. The couplet finally explains these comparisons: they will make his lover more loving, since they must leave each other before long.

1. Explain the exact season, time of day, stage in the burning of a fire that is involved in the three quatrains. Why were these chosen and not others?

2. Would the theme of the poem be improved if the quatrains were reversed: fire, day, season? Why or why not?

3. In the second line, try to visualize what he says about the leaves. First there are yellow leaves (do you see a great many of them?). Then there are none—so completely wipe them out of your mental picture. Then there are a few, after all—so put just a few back from your first mental picture. What is the point of this progression? Why doesn't he say "yellow leaves, or few, or none"? Wouldn't that be more orderly or more logical?

Sonnet 116

The structure that carries the meaning and the emotions along in this sonnet can be seen by watching for repetitions of the word "love" or the pronoun "it" referring back to "love." Try writing a prose paraphrase of this sonnet.

Sonnets 129 and 130

Sonnets 129 and 130 are like 64 and 65 in being right next to each other, but they are as remote from each other thematically as the previous pair are close.

1. Sonnet 129 has been chosen by more than one critic as the single greatest sonnet ever written in English. Yet look at it. It is not concrete: it is just one long list of unpleasant words, mostly adjectives. Try arguing that this sonnet is, in fact, skillful in the strategy it employs and that it has a music unlike any of the other sonnets here.

2. Sonnet 130 is an example of the anti-Petrarchan attitude at its most extreme and best. The standard Petrarchan-influenced sonnet speaks of teeth like jewels, eyes like dark pools, breath like perfume, etc. Shakespeare's approach may seem uncomplimentary to the woman he loves, but is it?

COMPOSITION

Write a sonnet of your own. Before you start, try to foresee what the whole shape of your poem will be like. Will you use the eight/six split? Will you choose three examples and a couplet that unites them? Will you keep asking a question that is only answered in the last two lines? Many people think that poems are sufficiently good if they are "sincere." Sincerity in poetry, however, can sometimes be captured best by carefully planning how you will create the effects you want the reader to be moved by. (Of course, it should all *seem* simple once you've done it!)

AN INTRODUCTION TO **MACBETH**

The Theater of Shakespeare's Day

Because later times put Shakespeare on a pedestal, we often lose sight of the actual conditions under which his plays were written. The Elizabethan theater was an exciting arena to work in, but it was hardly exalted or highly esteemed. This may be a major reason for Shakespeare's determination to become a gentleman, to have a coat of arms, to own valuable property in his home town, and to be considered a solid and respectable citizen when he retired to live among those he had grown up with. But while Shakespeare had become more urbane in outlook, Stratford had become more Puritan in sentiment, so his neighbors would have been more impressed by the wealth he had accrued than by his former profession.

The flowering of Elizabethan drama, ironically, had its humble beginnings in the mystery cycles of medieval times that were performed during religious festivals in farming communities like Stratford that were scattered throughout England. As the more worldly morality play, such as *Everyman,* emerged, the religious connections were gradually severed. Soon touring companies of players were visiting small towns like Stratford, presenting decidedly lowbrow farce laced with slapstick. Until the close of the theaters by the Puritans in 1642, English drama was never to lose this connection with the common folk, without whose approval no amount of aristocratic patronage could have kept alive such a sprawling admixture of contradictions and impurities. Thus, before the 1570s the early theater was mostly dispersed and regional. With the growth in magnificence of Elizabeth's court the increasingly sophisticated Londoner became impatient to see more diverse fare than the provincial touring companies had to offer. This was one reason why London rapidly became the focal point of the new theater. The increasing audience soon made it impractical to continue performing plays solely in open courtyards in inns, hemmed in by limited access and frequent interruptions from deliveries and the comings and goings of carriages.

A further difficulty lay in the tendency—if not downright eagerness—of London authorities to allow as few plays as possible to be performed within the city limits. Though the queen herself doted on the players and throughout her reign attended special performances at court of the most popular plays, including Shakespeare's, she could not completely overrule the anti-theatrical sentiment of the various Lord Aldermen of London. The answer to all these limitations came when James Burbage ingeniously leased property just outside the city limits and in 1576 built there the first structure in England devoted exclusively to the performance of plays. He called this building *The Theatre* and people of all ages and classes started flocking to it from the first. A last difficulty in the way of the swiftly developing commercial drama was an ordinance of 1572 that required such vagabonds as jugglers, tinkers, pedlars, and players to be whipped home unless they were employed by a peer of the realm. Undaunted, Burbage applied to the Earl of Leicester, not for money, but for patronage in the form of the licensed protection of a peer when his proposed company was performing or on tour. Thus Leicester's Men was formed, which became the pattern for all succeeding companies.

In less than ten years there were five theaters functioning, all in "liberties," that is, in areas outside of or within London that were not under the jurisdiction of the city government. With more players at work and with more playhouses for them to work in, the appearance of a new generation of playwrights was inevitable. At first it was the "University Wits" who tried their hand. Sometimes they were overclassical in approach or otherwise lacked the common touch but most of them learned fast. These included John Lyly and George Peele from Oxford and a more successful Cambridge group that included Thomas Nashe, Robert Greene, and Christopher Marlowe. After much shuffling of writers and players, two important companies formed. The earliest of these was the Lord Admiral's Men, in which the great tragic actor Edward Alleyn first acted Marlowe's brilliant ranting roles. Later came the Lord Chamberlain's Men, in which Burbage's son Richard performed the leading tragic roles and began appearing in the plays of a relatively unknown young actor with no university background, Will Shakespeare. As Richard Burbage gained in stature as an actor, Shakespeare grew in depth and subtlety as a playwright, creating plays precisely tailored to Burbage's capacities and also frankly designed to win the same mass audience that had swarmed to the Marlowe/Alleyn collaborations. Shakespeare also took note of another popular playwright who lacked a university background like himself. This was Thomas Kyd whose plays, *The Spanish Tragedy* and a since-lost early version of *Hamlet,* provided English with its first bloody revenge tragedies, a genre that Shakespeare was later to perfect with his own *Hamlet.*

After the Lord Chamberlain's Men became securely established, Shakespeare had no need to look elsewhere for his dramatic needs than to his own imagination and among his own players. A company shareholder along with other actors, he remained with these associates for the rest of his dra-

matic career. All were soberly businesslike in their pursuit of success and it was only a matter of time before the company writer became the most successful popular playwright of the era. Later, the group made one more major change for the better. Following old James Burbage's death in 1597, they planned and then in 1599 erected the first playhouse owned by the actors who performed in it. A landmark in theatrical history and in Shakespeare's life, the Globe Theatre was built in a "liberty" just south of the Thames River, on Bankside in Southwark, where it was rebuilt after a fire in 1611 and then continued to stand until the Puritans tore it down in 1644. People were already coming over the river to visit the bearbaiting pit next door when the Globe first opened to perform the bloody tragedy *Julius Caesar.* Strategically located in what was rapidly becoming a new entertainment district, the sumptuous new theater no doubt contributed to the play's success. Southwark had changed a great deal since it first appeared in English literature as the tiny suburb on the outskirts of London where Chaucer's Canterbury pilgrims met in the Tabard Inn on the eve of their pilgrimage. The Globe continued to prosper in this new location; within days of the coronation of James I in 1603, the company found itself with a new patron and a new name. From then on, it was called the King's Men, the premier acting company in the land during the greatest theatrical era the world may ever have known.

The total number of plays estimated to have been written in this period is set at better than 5,000—of which 623 printed plays have survived. What plays have been irrevocably lost without so much as a mention we will never know. It is staggering to think that, except for the *First Folio,* a number of Shakespeare's greatest plays would have been among them. Even as the Elizabethan drama turned from its first blush of feverish invention and optimism and faded into the more

The Globe

eere bayting h

The Globe Theater shown in a detail from a 1647 print by Weneeslavs Hollar.

Hamlyn Group Picture Library

somber tones of the Jacobean drama, England was changing as well. The tide of Puritanism was rising throughout the land and the unusual conditions for this reckless, ebullient theatrical age, with its equal portions of tolerance and daring, at last drew closed. Long before the empty shell of the Globe was utterly destroyed even as a landmark to what had been, the drama had fizzled out into decadence and irrelevance. The arena for imaginative writing was shifting to the new metaphysical poetry of Royalists like John Donne and George Herbert—and Puritans like Andrew Marvell and the early John Milton.

What has continued to live, however, is Shakespeare's plays themselves, in new stage productions through age after age. Most re-

cently in our day we have found that his work accommodates itself with surprising ease to the new media of film and television. Above all, the great Shakespearian roles—such as Hamlet, Cleopatra, Lear, Falstaff, and Lady Macbeth—have for more than three centuries been the ultimate challenge to actors and actresses. His characters emerge on the stage or from the printed page as complicated individuals. Comedy and tragedy stand side by side, even as we find them in life. A grim, tense scene is followed by a lively, amusing one; a moment of quiet and poetry may be succeeded by the noise of a full-scale battle. All of this is set forth in magnificent, forceful poetry—a flow of language which fits the action of each moment as a good lyric fits the music of a song.

The Elizabethan Stage

Macbeth contains twenty-eight separate scenes. Most of these scenes take only ten minutes or so to perform; many take less. Action shuttles rapidly back and forth between indoors and out; from one castle to another; from battlefields to witches' caves. The fast pace of a Shakespearean play depended in part upon the kind of stage on which it was performed.

The theater building itself was a kind of enclosed courtyard open to the skies (Shakespeare in *Henry V* calls it "this wooden O"). The stage was a simple platform jutting out into the audience. At the rear were doors for exits and entrances, and there may also have been a small curtained alcove in which "interior" scenes could be played. There was probably a balcony above the stage, from which kings could address armies, and from which Juliet could look down upon Romeo. The basic materials of this theater were imagination and language: there was no elaborate scenery as we know it today—no trees, no houses or buildings, no rooms filled with furniture. Because there was no need to shift the sets, the scenes followed each other in a rapid continuous action like that of a movie. Often, at the start of a scene, Shakespeare has a character speak lines that tell the audience the time of day and year, the place of action, and who the speaker is. If lines such as these disturb the modern reader, it must be remembered that these plays are first meant to be seen, not read. The reader's responsibility is to make the action come alive, as in a theater.

In writing *Macbeth,* Shakespeare made use of some common beliefs of his age. First, Shakespeare's audience accepted the concept of the Divine Right of Kings, namely that a ruler's power came directly from God. Therefore, anyone who killed a king (as Macbeth kills Duncan) was, in effect, at war with God. Second, ghosts and witches were accepted as real by the audience of that day and represented as such on the stage. Consequently, we must imaginatively accept them as real ourselves, since they exist dramatically both for us and for the characters in the play.

One difficult question concerning *Macbeth* could not be answered until the play was first performed. How would King James I, the patron of Shakespeare's company, react to the play? Not long before, James had ascended to the throne of England, but he was still king of Scotland as well. When Shakespeare's company produced another play that was directly about James, the king had not objected, but members of his council had thought that it was wrong to portray the monarch on the stage and presumably the play was abandoned. In the case of *Macbeth,* the bloody-minded title character assassinates a supposed ancestor of James named Banquo. This raises a subject that might well make any monarch uneasy. The play tries to smooth away this possible objection by having the witches predict that the "treble sceptres" of royalty would one day be carried by Banquo's descendants. But the figures of the witches themselves introduce another possible source of consternation for the king, since both in his book on demonology and in his life, he was most concerned to expose fraudulent or hysterical charges of witchcraft directed against innocent people. Of course, like most people in his day, he did not question for one moment the idea that real witches did, in fact, exist. In modifying the story of Macbeth as it appears in Holinshed's *Chronicles,* Shakespeare may have further tried to mitigate any royal objection to *Macbeth,* since Holinshed has the usurper reigning unpunished for years while in Shakespeare the reign lasts only a brief time.

The play's interest, in any case, transcends the particular historical background which produced it. *Macbeth* is, after all, one of Shakespeare's greatest tragedies. It is the story of a man who, finding himself faced with a moment of choice, lets the dark forces of his nature predominate. He weighs the choice carefully, considers the alternatives, and deliberately chooses the course he knows

John Henderson as Macbeth
after George Romney
The Garrick Club,
Photo: E.T. Archive, Ltd.

to be evil. From that moment on, he seems unable to turn back. The good within him no longer has power to control events. He heads step by step into a total disintegration of mind and spirit. He loses everything he finds valuable in the world, murdering with increasing wildness. The play begins with Macbeth at the height of success and honor and follows him down the long dark path to despair.

Shakespeare complicates the seemingly simple story of crime and punishment by making us understand Macbeth's motives, and by suggesting, at moments, that other forces are swaying his decisions—the prophecies of the witches, the encouragement and the challenges of his wife, the tempting ease of the first murder. Thus the play focuses not only on Macbeth's mistaken choice, but on the moral responsibility he carries for making it.

Generations of playgoers have felt horror and fear in watching the story of Macbeth; but they have also been moved to pity because of the anguish in Macbeth's soul. Shakespeare makes us look at ourselves and ponder the potential for good and evil.

Where will that moment come in our own lives when a choice may push us in a new direction? Will we be able to control our fate better than did Macbeth? Will we recognize the turning point of our lives?

The Tragedy of MACBETH

CHARACTERS

DUNCAN, *king of Scotland*

MALCOLM
DONALBAIN *his sons*

MACBETH
BANQUO *generals of the king's army*

MACDUFF
LENNOX
ROSS
MENTEITH *noblemen of Scotland*
ANGUS
CAITHNESS

FLEANCE, *son to Banquo*
SIWARD, *Earl of Northumberland, general of the English forces*

YOUNG SIWARD, *his son*
SEYTON, *an officer attending on Macbeth*
BOY, *son to Macduff*
AN ENGLISH DOCTOR
A SCOTCH DOCTOR
A SARGEANT
A PORTER
AN OLD MAN
THREE MURDERERS
LADY MACBETH
LADY MACDUFF
GENTLEWOMAN *attending on Lady Macbeth*
HECATE
THREE WITCHES
APPARITIONS
LORDS, GENTLEMEN, OFFICERS, SOLDIERS, ATTENDANTS, AND MESSENGERS

Act I
Scene 1

Scotland. A desert place.

Thunder and lightning. Enter THREE WITCHES.

FIRST WITCH. When shall we three meet again
  In thunder, lightning, or in rain?
SECOND WITCH. When the hurlyburly's[1] done,
  When the battle's lost and won.
THIRD WITCH. That will be ere the set of sun.
FIRST WITCH. Where the place?
SECOND WITCH.   Upon the heath.
THIRD WITCH. There to meet with Macbeth.
FIRST WITCH. I come, Graymalkin![2]
SECOND WITCH. Paddock[3] calls.
THIRD WITCH.   Anon!

5

1. **hurlyburly,** uproar, as of battle.

2. **Graymalkin** (grā′ mal′ kin), usually an old cat, figuratively an untidy old woman. The demons of the witches were thought to take the forms of cats, toads, etc.
3. **Paddock** (pad′ ək), a toad or frog, animals used in conjuring witchcraft.

ALL. Fair is foul, and foul is fair.
　Hover through the fog and filthy air.

　[*Exeunt.*[4]]

4. **Exeunt,** the plural form of exit meaning "they leave."

Scene 2

A camp near Forres.

Alarum within. Enter King DUNCAN, MALCOLM, DONALBAIN, LENNOX, *with Attendants, meeting a bleeding* SERGEANT.

KING. What bloody man is that? He can report,
　As seemeth by his plight, of the revolt
　The newest state.
MALCOLM.　　　　This is the sergeant
　Who like a good and hardy soldier fought
　Gainst my captivity. Hail, brave friend!　　　　　　5
　Say to the King the knowledge of the broil[5]
　As thou didst leave it.
SERGEANT.　　　　　Doubtful it stood,
　As two spent swimmers that do cling together
　And choke their art.[6] The merciless Macdonwald—
　Worthy to be a rebel, for to that　　　　　　10
　The multiplying villainies of nature
　Do swarm upon him—from the western isles
　Of kerns and gallowglasses[7] is supplied;
　And fortune, on his damnèd quarrel smiling,[8]
　Showed like a rebel's whore. But all's too weak;　　15
　For brave Macbeth,—well he deserves that name,—
　Disdaining fortune, with his brandished steel,
　Which smoked with bloody execution,
　Like valor's minion, carved out his passage
　Till he faced the slave;[9]　　　　　　20
　Which ne'er shook hands nor bade farewell to him
　Till he unseamed him from the nave to the chaps[10]
　And fixed his head upon our battlements.
KING. O valiant cousin! worthy gentleman!
SERGEANT. As whence the sun 'gins his reflection　　25
　Shipwracking storms and direful thunders break,
　So from that spring whence comfort seemed to come
　Discomfort swells. Mark, King of Scotland, mark:
　No sooner justice had, with valor armed,
　Compelled these skipping kerns to trust their heels　30
　But the Norweyan lord, surveying vantage,[11]

5. **broil,** battle.

6. **choke their art,** prevent themselves from swimming.

7. **kerns** (kərns) **and gallow-glasses** (gal' ō glas' əs). Both terms mean Irish or Scottish foot soldiers. The latter were more heavily armed.
8. **fortune . . . smiling,** success personified. The quarrel is Macdonwald's contention or cause.

9. **slave,** merely a term of abuse: low character, villain. The hand shaking refers to the formalities of dueling.
10. **unseamed . . . to the chaps,** cut apart from navel to jaws.

11. **Norweyan . . . surveying vantage,** Norwegian seeing his advantage.

With furbished arms and new supplies of men,
Began a fresh assault.
KING.   Dismayed not this
  Our captains, Macbeth and Banquo?
SERGEANT.   Yes,
  As sparrows eagles, or the hare the lion.   35
  If I say sooth, I must report they were
  As cannons overcharged with double cracks;[12] so they
  Doubly redoubled strokes upon the foe.
  Except they meant to bathe in reeking wounds,
  Or memorize another Golgotha,[13]   40
  I cannot tell—
  But I am faint; my gashes cry for help.
KING. So well thy words become thee as thy wounds;
  They smack of honor both. Go get him surgeons.

  [*Exit* SERGEANT, *attended.*]

  [*Enter* ROSS.]
  Who comes here?
MALCOM.   The worthy thane[14] of Ross.   45
LENNOX. What a haste looks through his eyes! So should
    he look
  That seems to speak things strange.
ROSS.   God save the King!
KING. Whence cam'st thou, worthy thane?
ROSS.   From Fife, great King,
  Where the Norweyan banners flout the sky
  And fan our people cold.   50
  Norway himself, with terrible numbers,
  Assisted by that most disloyal traitor
  The thane of Cawdor, began a dismal conflict,
  Till that Bellona's bridegroom, lapped in proof,[15]
  Confronted him with self-comparisons,   55
  Point against point, rebellious arm 'gainst arm,
  Curbing his lavish[16] spirit; and to conclude,
  The victory fell on us.
KING.   Great happiness!
ROSS.   That now
  Sweno, the Norways' king, craves composition;[17]
  Nor would we deign him burial of his men
  Till he disbursèd, at Saint Colme's Inch,[18]   60
  Ten thousand dollars to our general use.
KING. No more that thane of Cawdor shall deceive
  Our bosom interest.[19] Go pronounce his present death
  And with his former title greet Macbeth.   65
ROSS. I'll see it done.

12. **double cracks,** double charges.

13. **memorize another Golgotha** (gol′ gǝ thǝ), kill so many as to make a place of killing as renowned as was Golgotha in Jerusalem when Christ was crucified.

14. **thane,** a Scots nobleman, as a baron.

15. **Bellona's** (bǝ lō′ nǝz) **bridegroom . . . .** The reference is to Macbeth whose great skill in battle makes him seem like the bridegroom of the Roman war goddess . . . **lapped in proof,** dressed for battle.
16. **lavish,** great, rebellious, defiant.
17. **craves composition,** seeks an armistice.
18. **Saint Colme's Inch,** an island, now Inchcolm in the Firth of Forth off Edinburgh. Dollars, of course, were not the coinage of Macbeth's time. This is an anachronism.
19. **bosom interest.** Cawdor cannot interfere again in the king's vital concerns.

"What are these,
So withered, and so wild in their attire,
That look not like the inhabitants o' the earth . . . ?"

ROYAL SHAKESPEARE THEATRE, 1962
Stratford-Upon-Avon
Photo: Holte Photographers Ltd.

KING. What he hath lost, noble Macbeth hath won.

[*Exeunt.*]

Scene 3

A heath near Forres.

Thunder. Enter the THREE WITCHES.

FIRST WITCH. Where hast thou been, sister?
SECOND WITCH. Killing swine.
THIRD WITCH. Sister, where thou?
FIRST WITCH. A sailor's wife had chestnuts in her lap,
  And munched and munched and munched. "Give me,"
    quoth I.   5

"Aroint thee, witch!" the rump-fed ronyon[20] cries.
Her husband's to Aleppo[21] gone, master o' the *Tiger;*
But in a sieve I'll thither sail,
And, like a rat without a tail,
I'll do, I'll do, and I'll do.   10
SECOND WITCH. I'll give thee a wind.
FIRST WITCH. Thou'rt kind.
THIRD WITCH. And I another.
FIRST WITCH. I myself have all the other;
And the very ports they blow,[22]   15
All the quarters that they know
I' the shipman's card.[23]
I will drain him dry as hay.
Sleep shall neither night nor day
Hang upon his penthouse lid;[24]   20
He shall live a man forbid.
Weary se'nnights,[25] nine times nine,
Shall he dwindle, peak,[26] and pine;
Though his bark cannot be lost,
Yet it shall be tempest-tossed.   25
Look what I have.
SECOND WITCH. Show me, show me.
FIRST WITCH. Here I have a pilot's thumb,[27]
Wrecked as homeward he did come.

[*Drum within.*]

THIRD WITCH. A drum, a drum!   30
Macbeth doth come.
ALL. The weird sisters, hand in hand,
Posters[28] of the sea and land,
Thus do go about, about:
Thrice to thine, and thrice to mine,   35
And thrice again, to make up nine.
Peace! The charm's wound up.

[*Enter* MACBETH *and* BANQUO.]

MACBETH. So foul and fair a day I have not seen.
BANQUO. How far is't called to Forres? What are these,
So withered, and so wild in their attire,   40
That look not like the inhabitants o' the earth,
And yet are on't? Live you? or are you aught
That man may question? You seem to understand me,
By each at once her choppy finger laying
Upon her skinny lips. You should be women,   45
And yet your beards forbid me to interpret
That you are so.

20. **Aroint . . . ronyon.** Get away . . . fat and seedy creature.
21. **Aleppo** (a lep′ ō), a Syrian city.

22. **very ports.** This may be read **various points** or to blow out of all harbors. Witches traditionally could control the four winds and here she means to keep the *Tiger* tossing and out of port.
23. **card,** compass.
24. **penthouse lid,** upper lid, the roof of the eye.
25. **se'nnights,** seven-night periods, weeks.
26. **peak,** become peaked.

27. **pilot's thumb.** According to witchcraft parts of bodies used in black magic were especially powerful if they came from one who had suffered a violent death.

28. **posters,** those who post about, travelers.

MACBETH. Speak, if you can. What are you?

FIRST WITCH. All hail, Macbeth! Hail to thee, thane of
Glamis!

SECOND WITCH. All hail, Macbeth! Hail to thee, thane of
Cawdor!

THIRD WITCH. All hail, Macbeth, that shalt be King
hereafter!   50

BANQUO. Good sir, why do you start and seem to fear
Things that do sound so fair? I' the name of truth,
Are ye fantastical,[29] or that indeed
Which outwardly ye show? My noble partner
You greet with present grace and great prediction   55
Of noble having and of royal hope,
That he seems rapt withal: to me you speak not.
If you can look into the seeds of time,
And say which grain will grow and which will not,
Speak then to me, who neither beg nor fear   60
Your favors nor your hate.

FIRST WITCH. Hail!

SECOND WITCH. Hail!

THIRD WITCH. Hail!

FIRST WITCH. Lesser than Macbeth, and greater,   65

SECOND WITCH. Not so happy, yet much happier.

THIRD WITCH. Thou shalt get[30] kings, though thou be
none.
So all hail, Macbeth and Banquo!

FIRST WITCH. Banquo and Macbeth, all hail!

MACBETH. Stay, you imperfect speakers, tell me more!   70
By Sinel's death[31] I know I am thane of Glamis,
But how of Cawdor?[32] The thane of Cawdor lives,
A prosperous gentleman; and to be King
Stands not within the prospect of belief,
No more than to be Cawdor. Say from whence   75
You owe this strange intelligence, or why
Upon this blasted heath you stop our way
With such prophetic greeting? Speak, I charge you.

[WITCHES *vanish.*]

BANQUO. The earth hath bubbles, as the water has,
And these are of them. Whither are they vanished?   80

MACBETH. Into the air, and what seemed corporal
melted
As breath into the wind. Would they had stayed!

BANQUO. Were such things here as we do speak about?
Or have we eaten on the insane root[33]
That takes the reason prisoner?   85

29. **Are ye fantastical?** Banquo asks the witches if they are creatures of the imagination or as real as they seem.

30. **get,** beget. Banquo was the legendary ancestor of the royal Stuarts.
31. **Sinel's death.** Sinel was Macbeth's father.
32. **Cawdor?** Macbeth had not learned about Cawdor's treason. The history here is complicated, and the play seems to have condensed three different campaigns.

33. **insane root,** a legendary root which could cause insanity when eaten. Hemlock is one possibility.

MACBETH. Your children shall be kings.
BANQUO.   You shall be King.
MACBETH. And thane of Cawdor too. Went it not so?
BANQUO. To the selfsame tune and words. Who's here?

[*Enter* ROSS *and* ANGUS.]

ROSS. The King hath happily received, Macbeth,
 The news of thy success; and when he reads   90
 Thy personal venture in the rebels' fight,
 His wonders and his praises do contend
 Which should be thine or his. Silenced with that,
 In viewing o'er the rest o' the selfsame day,
 He finds thee in the stout Norweyan ranks,   95
 Nothing afeard of what thyself didst make,
 Strange images of death. As thick as hail
 Came post with post,[34] and every one did bear
 Thy praises in his kingdom's great defense
 And poured them down before him.
ANGUS.   We are sent   100
 To give thee from our royal master thanks;
 Only to herald thee into his sight,
 Not pay thee.
ROSS. And for an earnest[35] of a greater honor,
 He bade me, from him, call thee thane of Cawdor;   105
 In which addition,[36] hail, most worthy thane!
 For it is thine.
BANQUO.   What, can the devil speak true?
MACBETH. The thane of Cawdor lives. Why do you dress
   me
 In borrowed robes?
ANGUS.   Who was the thane lives yet;
 But under heavy judgment bears that life   110
 Which he deserves to lose. Whether he was combined
 With those of Norway, or did line the rebel
 With hidden help and vantage, or that with both
 He labored in his country's wreck, I know not;
 But treasons capital, confessed and proved,   115
 Have overthrown him.
MACBETH.   (*Aside*) Glamis, and thane of Cawdor!
 The greatest is behind.[37] (*To* ROSS *and* ANGUS) Thanks
   for your pains.
 (*Aside to* BANQUO) Do you not hope your children shall
   be kings,
 When those that gave the thane of Cawdor to me
 Promised no less to them?
BANQUO.   That, trusted home,[38]   120

34. **post with post,** report after report.

35. **earnest,** a token as a pledge.

36. **in which addition,** with which new rank.

37. **behind,** still to come.

38. **trusted home,** taken seriously; Banquo jests.

Might yet enkindle you unto the crown,
Besides the thane of Cawdor. But 'tis strange;
And oftentimes, to win us to our harm,
The instruments of darkness tell us truths,
Win us with honest trifles, to betray's   125
In deepest consequence.
Cousins, a word, I pray you. *(To* ROSS *and* ANGUS, *who*
    approach.)
MACBETH.   *(Aside)* Two truths are told,
As happy prologues to the swelling act
Of the imperial theme.[39]—I thank you, gentlemen.—
(Aside) This supernatural soliciting   130
Cannot be ill; cannot be good. If ill,
Why hath it given me earnest of success,
Commencing in a truth? I am thane of Cawdor.
If good, why do I yield to that suggestion
Whose horrid image doth unfix my hair,   135
And make my seated heart knock at my ribs,
Against the use of nature?[40] Present fears
Are less than horrible imaginings.
My thought, whose murder yet is but fantastical,
Shakes so my single state of man that function   140
Is smothered in surmise, and nothing is
But what is not.[41]
BANQUO.   Look, how our partner's rapt.
MACBETH. *(Aside)* If chance will have me King, why,
    chance may crown me,
Without my stir.[42]
BANQUO.   New honors come upon him,
Like our strange garments, cleave not to their mold   145
But with the aid of use.[43]
MACBETH.   *(Aside)* Come what come may,
Time and the hour runs through the roughest day.
BANQUO. Worthy Macbeth, we stay upon your leisure.[44]
MACBETH. Give me your favor.[45] My dull brain was
    wrought
With things forgotten. Kind gentlemen, your pains   150
Are registered where every day I turn
The leaf to read them. Let us toward the King.
(To BANQUO*)* Think upon what hath chanced; and,
    at more time,
The interim having weighed it, let us speak
Our free hearts each to other.
BANQUO.   *(To* MACBETH*)* Very gladly.   155
MACBETH. Till then, enough. Come, friends.

[*Exeunt.*]

---

39. **imperial theme,** the prophecy that Macbeth will be king.

40. **against the use of nature,** unnaturally. Macbeth does not ordinarily feel fear, but imagining the murder of Duncan stands his hair on end.

41. **but what is not.** The ideas occurring to Macbeth are so wild that he feels paralyzed by them. His imaginings seem more real than the world about him.

42. **without my stir,** without my efforts.

43. **aid of use.** Macbeth's new honors like new clothes are still sitting stiffly on him rather than being comfortably adjusted.

44. **upon your leisure.** We are waiting for you.

45. **favor.** Pardon me. Macbeth excuses himself for being preoccupied with forgotten business.

Scene 4

Forres. A room in the Palace.

Flourish. Enter King DUNCAN, MALCOLM, DONALBAIN, LENNOX, *and Attendants.*

KING. Is execution done on Cawdor? Are not
Those in commission yet returned?

MALCOLM.   My liege,
They are not yet come back. But I have spoke
With one that saw him die who did report
That very frankly he confessed his treasons,   5
Implored your Highness' pardon and set forth
A deep repentance. Nothing in his life
Became him like the leaving it. He died
As one that had been studied in his death,
To throw away the dearest thing he owed   10
As 'twere a careless trifle.

KING.   There's no art
To find the mind's construction in the face.[46]
He was a gentleman on whom I built
An absolute trust.

[*Enter* MACBETH, BANQUO, ROSS, *and* ANGUS.]

                              O worthiest cousin,
The sin of my ingratitude even now   15
Was heavy on me! Thou art so far before,[47]
That swiftest wing of recompense is slow
To overtake thee. Would thou hadst less deserved,
That the proportion both of thanks and payment
Might have been mine! Only I have left to say,   20
More is thy due than more than all can pay.

MACBETH. The service and the loyalty I owe,
In doing it, pays itself. Your Highness' part
Is to receive our duties; and our duties
Are to your throne and state, children and servants,   25
Which do but what they should, by doing everything
Safe toward your love and honor.

KING.   Welcome hither.
I have begun to plant thee and will labor
To make thee full of growing. Noble Banquo,
That hast no less deserved, nor must be known   30
No less to have done so, let me infold thee
And hold thee to my heart.

BANQUO.   There if I grow,
The harvest is your own.

---

46. **face.** No one is able to read a person's purpose or character in his or her face.

47. **before.** Macbeth's services are so far ahead of Duncan's rewards that he cannot thank him adequately.

KING. My plenteous joys,
Wanton in fullness, seek to hide themselves
In drops of sorrow.[48] Sons, kinsmen, thanes,
And you whose places are the nearest, know
We[49] will establish our estate upon
Our eldest, Malcolm, whom we name hereafter
The Prince of Cumberland;[50] which honor must
Not unaccompanied invest him only,
But signs of nobleness, like stars, shall shine
On all deservers. From hence to Inverness,[51]
And bind us further to you.

MACBETH. The rest is labor, which is not used for you.
I'll be myself the harbinger, and make joyful
The hearing of my wife with your approach;
So, humbly take my leave.

KING. My worthy Cawdor!

MACBETH. *(Aside)* The Prince of Cumberland! That is a
step
On which I must fall down, or else o'erleap,
For in my way it lies. Stars, hide your fires;
Let not light see my black and deep desires.
The eye wink at the hand; yet let that be,
Which the eye fears, when it is done, to see.

[*Exit.*]

KING. True, worthy Banquo: he is full so valiant,
And in his commendations I am fed;
It is a banquet to me. Let's after him,
Whose care is gone before to bid us welcome.
It is a peerless kinsman.

[*Flourish. Exeunt.*]

Scene 5

Inverness. MACBETH'S *Castle.*

Enter MACBETH'S *Wife, alone, reading a letter.*

LADY MACBETH. "They met me in the day of success; and I
have learned by the perfectest report they have more
in them than mortal knowledge. When I burned in
desire to question them further, they made themselves
air, into which they vanished. Whiles I stood rapt in
the wonder of it, came missives from the King, who
all-hailed me 'thane of Cawdor,' by which title, before,

35

40

45

50

55

5

48. **drops of sorrow,** tears of
joy. Here **wanton** means "per-
verse."
49. **we.** Duncan uses the royal
plural for himself.
50. Duncan thus establishes his
son as his heir. At this period in
Scottish history, the line of succession was rarely father to son.
But the Scottish lords are
pledged to support the royal
claim of the Prince of Cumberland. According to some early
accounts, Macbeth had a legitimate claim to the throne. By this
announcement Duncan rules out
the possibility that Macbeth could
succeed "without stir." Duncan
concludes that his followers shall
also benefit from this move.
51. **to Inverness,** Macbeth's
castle where Duncan will be further indebted as a guest.

these weird sisters saluted me, and referred me to the
coming on of time with 'Hail, King that shalt be!' This
have I thought good to deliver thee, my dearest
partner of greatness, that thou mightst not lose the   10
dues of rejoicing by being ignorant of what greatness
is promised thee. Lay it to thy heart, and farewell."

Glamis thou art, and Cawdor, and shalt be
What thou art promised. Yet do I fear thy nature;   15
It is too full o' the milk of human kindness
To catch the nearest way.[52] Thou wouldst be great;
Art not without ambition, but without
The illness should attend it. What thou wouldst highly,
That wouldst thou holily;[53] wouldst not play false,   20
And yet wouldst wrongly win. Thou'ldst have, great
  Glamis,
That which cries "Thus thou must do," if thou have it;
And that which rather thou dost fear to do
Than wishest should be undone. Hie thee hither,
That I may pour my spirits in thine ear   25
And chastise with the valor of my tongue
All that impedes thee from the golden round[54]
Which fate and metaphysic aid[55] doth seem
To have thee crowned withal.

[*Enter* MESSENGER.]

                    What is your tidings?
MESSENGER. The King comes here tonight.
LADY MACBETH. Thou'rt mad to say it!   30
Is not thy master with him? who, were't so,
Would have informed for preparation.[56]
MESSENGER. So please you, it is true. Our thane is
  coming.
One of my fellows had the speed of him,[57]
Who, almost dead for breath, had scarcely more   35
Than would make up his message.
LADY MACBETH.   Give him tending;
He brings great news.

[*Exit* MESSENGER.]

                    The raven himself is hoarse[58]
That croaks the fatal entrance of Duncan
Under my battlements. Come, you spirits[59]
That tend on mortal thoughts, unsex me here,
And fill me, from the crown to the toe, top-full   40
Of direst cruelty! Make thick my blood;[60]
Stop up the access and passage to remorse,

52. **The nearest way.** Murder
is the quickest way to the throne,
but Lady Macbeth thinks her
husband has too gentle a disposition for it.
53. **holily.** Lady Macbeth feels
that Macbeth prefers to behave as
a saint while she feels that ambition and saintliness are not compatible.

54. **golden round,** crown.
55. **. . . aid,** supernatural help
—the witches' prophecy.

56. Duncan's visit at this time
seems incredible, like fate playing
into her hands. Lady Macbeth
suggests that if the visit were to
be as announced, she would have
had notice from Macbeth.
57. **had the speed of him,** went
faster than he did.

58. **raven . . . hoarse.** The wild
bird seems unusually excited.
Birds of ill-omen occur repeatedly in this play.
59. **spirits.** Lady Macbeth asks
to join forces with evil spirits that
seem to be propelling the action
and understand murderous designs.
60. **thick my blood.** This would
give her a melancholy fierceness.

That no compunctious visitings of nature[61]
Shake my fell purpose, nor keep peace between[62]   45
The effect and it! Come to my woman's breasts
And take my milk for gall, you murdering ministers,
Wherever in your sightless substances
You wait on nature's mischief! Come, thick night,   50
And pall thee in the dunnest smoke of hell,[63]
That my keen knife see not the wound it makes,
Nor heaven peep through the blanket of the dark
To cry "Hold, hold!"

[*Enter* MACBETH.]

                    Great Glamis! worthy Cawdor!
Greater than both, by the all-hail hereafter!
Thy letters have transported me beyond   55
This ignorant present, and I feel now
The future in the instant.[64]
MACBETH.   My dearest love,
Duncan comes here tonight.
LADY MACBETH.   And when goes hence?
MACBETH. Tomorrow, as he purposes.
LADY MACBETH.   O, never
Shall sun that morrow see!   60
Your face, my thane, is as a book where men
May read strange matters. To beguile the time,
Look like the time;[65] bear welcome in your eye,
Your hand, your tongue; look like the innocent flower,
But be the serpent under't. He that's coming   65
Must be provided for; and you shall put
This night's great business into my dispatch,[66]
Which shall to all our nights and days to come
Give solely sovereign sway and masterdom.
MACBETH. We will speak further.
LADY MACBETH.   Only look up clear.   70
To alter favor ever is to fear.
Leave all the rest to me.

[*Exeunt.*]

Scene 6

Inverness. Before MACBETH'S *Castle.*

Hautboys[67] *and torches. Enter King* DUNCAN, MALCOLM,
DONALBAIN, BANQUO, LENNOX, MACDUFF, ROSS, ANGUS,
and Attendants.

KING. This castle hath a pleasant seat.[68] The air

---

61. That no natural compassion deflect her plan.
62. Peace would indicate an interference between her plan and the action.

63. **and pall thee,** make for yourself a thick cover.

64. **instant,** at present.

65. **look like the time,** act as you would normally at this time.

66. **into my dispatch,** into my hands; leave it to me.

67. **Hautboys** (hō′ boiz), instruments related to oboes, played in the King's honor.

68. **seat,** site.

Nimbly and sweetly recommends itself
Unto our gentle senses.
BANQUO.   This guest of summer,
The temple-haunting martlet,[69] does approve
By his loved mansionry that the heaven's breath
Smells wooingly here. No jutty, frieze,
Buttress, nor coign of vantage,[70] but this bird
Hath made his pendent bed and procreant cradle.
Where they most breed and haunt, I have observed
The air is delicate.

[*Enter* LADY MACBETH.]

KING.   See, see, our honored hostess!
The love that follows us sometime is our trouble,
Which still we thank as love. Herein I teach you
How you shall bid God 'ield[71] us for your pains
And thank us for your trouble.
LADY MACBETH.   All our service
In every point twice done, and then done double,
Were poor and single business to contend
Against those honors deep and broad wherewith
Your Majesty loads our house. For those of old,
And the late dignities heaped up to them,
We rest your hermits.[72]
KING.   Where's the thane of Cawdor?
We coursed[73] him at the heels and had a purpose
To be his purveyor;[74] but he rides well,
And his great love, sharp as his spur, hath holp[75] him
To his home before us. Fair and noble hostess,
We are your guest tonight.
LADY MACBETH.   Your servants ever
Have theirs, themselves, and what is theirs, in
   compt,
To make their audit at your Highness' pleasure,
Still to return your own.[76]
KING.   Give me your hand;
Conduct me to mine host. We love him highly
And shall continue our graces towards him.
By your leave, hostess.

[*Exeunt.*]

Scene 7

Inverness. Inside MACBETH'S *Castle.*

Hautboys. Torches. Enter a Sewer[77] and other Servants with

5

10

15

20

25

30

---

69. The fact that the martlet, the European swallow, stays near this mansion shows that it is as pleasant as a temple.
70. On every projection of the building, overhang, or advantageous angle this bird has built its hanging nest.

71. **bid God 'ield,** yield, repay us.

72. **dignities . . . hermits,** for the recent titles; we will gratefully pray for you as do those humble servants, "hermits," poor people committed to a life of prayer.
73. **coursed,** chased.
74. **purveyor,** to precede him and announce him.
75. **holp,** helped.

76. **theirs . . . return your own.** This is a hostess's courtesy: "My house is yours." It reminds the king that all nobles hold their possessions and servants by his permission and that Macbeth and his lady stand ready to repay him at any time.

77. **sewer,** a butler who serves meals.

dishes and table service. They cross over the stage. Then enter
MACBETH.

MACBETH. If it were done when 'tis done, then 'twere
    well
It were done quickly. If the assassination
Could trammel up the consequence,[78] and catch,
With his surcease, success; that but this blow
Might be the be-all and the end-all here,
But here, upon this bank and shoal of time,
We'd jump the life to come.[79] But in these cases
We still have judgment here, that we but teach
Bloody instructions, which, being taught, return
To plague the inventor. This even-handed justice
Commends the ingredients of our poisoned chalice
To our own lips. He's here in double trust:[80]
First, as I am his kinsman and his subject,
Strong both against the deed; then, as his host,
Who should against his murderer shut the door,
Not bear the knife myself. Besides, this Duncan
Hath borne his faculties so meek,[81] hath been
So clear in his great office, that his virtues
Will plead like angels, trumpet-tongued, against
The deep damnation of his taking-off;
And pity, like a naked new-born babe,
Striding the blast, or heaven's cherubim, horsed
Upon the sightless couriers of the air,
Shall blow the horrid deed in every eye,
That tears shall drown the wind.[82] I have no spur
To prick the sides of my intent, but only
Vaulting ambition, which o'erleaps itself
And falls on the other.[83]

[*Enter* LADY MACBETH.]

                How now! What news?
LADY MACBETH. He has almost supped. Why have you
    left the chamber?
MACBETH. Hath he asked for me?
LADY MACBETH.   Know you not he has?
MACBETH. We will proceed no further in this business.
    He hath honored me of late, and I have bought
    Golden opinions from all sorts of people,
    Which would be worn now in their newest gloss,[84]
    Not cast aside so soon.
LADY MACBETH.   Was the hope drunk
    Wherein you dressed yourself? Hath it slept since?
    And wakes it now, to look so green[85] and pale

5

10

15

20

25

30

35

---

78. **trammel up the consequence,** hold or prevent the evil results—punishment, damnation, the likelihood of being murdered in his own turn. Macbeth rehearses the reasons against the murder.

79. **life to come.** Macbeth feels that for the gamble in this lifetime he'd be risking eternity, as well as teaching others how to murder him in his turn.

80. **double trust.** Macbeth weighs his responsibilities as a protector of the king.

81. **faculties so meek.** Duncan is gentle and Macbeth realizes that the king's virtues make his murder especially gross.

82. **drown the wind.** Tears falling like heavy rain will halt the storm winds.

83. **other,** side. His ambition is like a too-eager rider who leaps over the horse rather than onto it. Macbeth feels without a spur such as hate for Duncan, his ambition to leap onto the throne will only cause others to seek to topple him.

84. **newest gloss.** Macbeth would not throw away his growing reputation.

85. **... green,** sallow, sickly. Lady Macbeth mocks Macbeth's clothing of "golden opinions" as being less than his "drunken" hope for royal robes. She continues to berate him as unreliable and cowardly.

At what it did so freely? From this time
Such I account thy love. Art thou afeard
To be the same in thine own act and valor   **40**
As thou art in desire? Wouldst thou have that
Which thou esteem'st the ornament of life,
And live a coward in thine own esteem,
Letting "I dare not" wait upon "I would,"
Like the poor cat i' the adage?[86]

MACBETH.   Prithee peace!   **45**
I dare do all that may become a man.
Who dares do more is none.

LADY MACBETH.   What beast was't then
That made you break this enterprise to me?[87]
When you durst do it, then you were a man;
And to be more than what you were, you would   **50**
Be so much more the man. Nor time nor place
Did then adhere,[88] and yet you would make both.
They have made themselves, and that their fitness
    now
Does unmake you. I have given suck, and know
How tender 'tis to love the babe that milks me.   **55**
I would, while it was smiling in my face,
Have plucked my nipple from his boneless gums,
And dashed the brains out, had I so sworn as you
Have done to this.

MACBETH.   If we should fail?

LADY MACBETH.   We fail!
But screw your courage to the sticking-place,[89]   **60**
And we'll not fail. When Duncan is asleep—
Whereto the rather[90] shall his day's hard journey
Soundly invite him—his two chamberlains
Will I with wine and wassail[91] so convince
That memory, the warder of the brain,
Shall be a fume, and the receipt of reason   **65**
A limbeck only.[92] When in swinish sleep
Their drenched natures lie as in a death,
What cannot you and I perform upon
The unguarded Duncan? what not put upon   **70**
His spongy officers, who shall bear the guilt
Of our great quell?[93]

MACBETH.   Bring forth men-children only;
For thy undaunted mettle should compose
Nothing but males. Will it not be received,[94]
When we have marked with blood those sleepy two   **75**
Of his own chamber and used their very daggers,
That they have done't?

86. cat i' the adage. The proverb is an old one that says in effect: If the cat would catch fish it must wet its feet.

87. beast . . . to me. Macbeth has stated that he is as brave as anyone and implied that only a wild beast could do more. Lady Macbeth picks up his expression to taunt him: it was a beast, then, who told me of the plan to kill Duncan.

88. then adhere. When Macbeth wrote his letter giving rise to her hope the circumstances were not at hand as they are now.

89. sticking-place. The metaphor is of a crossbow which was screwed tight to fit the bowstring before it could be shot.

90. whereto the rather, to which very readily. (Duncan is tired from travel.)

91. wassail (wos' əl), technically, a spiced ale.

92. limbeck (lim' bek'), the cap of a still into which fumes rise. The metaphor is that a drunken person is like a still full of alcoholic fumes instead of consciousness.

93. quell, killing, murder.

94. received, accepted, believed.

"If it were done when 'tis done, then 'twere well
It were done quickly."

Royal Shakespeare Theatre, 1967
Stratford-Upon-Avon
Photo: Holte Photographers Ltd.

LADY MACBETH.　　　　Who dares receive it other,
　As we shall make our griefs and clamor roar
　Upon his death?
MACBETH.　　　　I am settled and bend up
　Each corporal agent[95] to this terrible feat.
　Away, and mock the time with fairest show;
　False face must hide what the false heart doth know.

　[*Exeunt.*]

80　95. **each corporal agent,** each bodily part and faculty. That he "bend up" to the feat refers back to the metaphor of the crossbow.

FOR UNDERSTANDING

Temptation in a Prophecy

1. What are we told about Macbeth's life and character up to the time the play begins? What opinion do others have of him?

2. Look carefully at the witches' original prophecy to Macbeth and Banquo. Do the witches indicate that they have any power to turn their predictions into reality?

   a. If you were in Macbeth's and Banquo's positions, what meaning would you draw from the witches' prophecies?

   b. What is the difference in Macbeth's and Banquo's reactions to the witches?

3. How does Shakespeare contrast Macbeth's character with that of Lady Macbeth in Scenes 5 and 7? What arguments does Lady Macbeth use to force Macbeth to a decision?

FOR INTERPRETATION

1. What choices does Macbeth make during this act?

2. How is the Macbeth we see at the end of this act different from the Macbeth we saw and heard about at the outset of the play?

FOR APPRECIATION

Figures of Speech

Shakespeare uses many similes and metaphors. The valor of Macbeth and Banquo is described in a simile: the Norwegians dismayed them as (no more than) sparrows dismay eagles.

Many metaphors and similes are easy to interpret. Now and then, a line may contain not only a simile or metaphor but also an archaic or obsolete word. Then, even the learned may have to pause to weigh the meaning of the line.

When we are told that Macbeth "Like valor's minion, carved out his passage," we must understand that *valor* is a personification, that *minion* means favorite or darling, and that *carved out* involves a metaphor.

Be prepared to explain the following lines.

1. I must report they were/As cannons overcharged with double cracks. . . .

2. Where the Norweyan banners flout the sky/And fan our people cold.

3. Sleep shall neither night nor day/Hang upon his penthouse lid. . . .

LANGUAGE AND VOCABULARY

1. The "Prologue to the Canterbury Tales" and "The Pardoner's Tale" were translations of Chaucer's Middle English into Modern English—the version you read was not the original one; but *Macbeth* is given almost as Shakespeare wrote it over three hundred and fifty years ago. (The only important exception is the appearance of place indications at the head of each scene throughout the play. All such indications are modern additions.)

In the older selections from English literature there are special difficulties about using the method of context clues to find the meanings of words. But perhaps you can guess the meanings of the italicized words in the following context from Act I.

   a. . . . With *furbished* arms and new supplies of men. . . .

   b. . . . With hidden help and *vantage*. . . .

   c. . . . the fatal entrance of Duncan/Under my *battlements*.

2. One great problem in reading older literature comes from the way words change their meanings —undergo semantic change. Thus, today the word *cousin* means a son or daughter of an aunt or uncle but in Shakespeare's day it was used for almost any relative. The following words, from Act I of *Macbeth*, show semantic change; find out what they meant in Shakespeare's usage:

   Scene 2: *broil, quarrel, slave, survey, memorize, dismal, lavish, composition, present;*

   Scene 3: *poster, fantastical, post, earnest, addition, line, soliciting.*

The footnotes and the glossary of this book will help, but you will also need a large (unabridged) dictionary that gives more complete information. In selecting the meanings to interpret Shakespeare, you may have to guess about the one that fits best.

3. Look up these words and notice what status or usage label (obs. or archaic) the dictionary uses to describe them: *kern, gallowglass, minion, withal, coign.*

4. Shakespeare's English was not pronounced exactly as modern English is pronounced. It takes years of intense study to understand the principles underlying Shakespearean pronunciation, and even then one finds puzzling situations. In a general way, however, many of the words were pronounced with greater mouth opening than we would use today. Thus most words spelled with *ea*—like *heat* and *mean*—were pronounced with what we call a long a (ā) sound. *Weak* sounded like modern English *wake*, not like modern English *week*. In the first lines of Act I, *heath, weak,* and *unseamed* would all have been pronounced with the ā sound. Try reading several lines of *Macbeth* aloud pronouncing *ea* words with the ā sound.

Act II

Scene 1

Inverness. Court of MACBETH'S *Castle.*

Enter BANQUO, *and* FLEANCE *bearing a torch before him.*

BANQUO. How goes the night, boy?
FLEANCE. The moon is down; I have not heard the clock.
BANQUO. And she goes down at twelve.
FLEANCE.   I take't, 'tis later, sir.
BANQUO. Hold, take my sword. There's husbandry[1] in
   heaven;
Their candles are all out. Take thee that too.
A heavy summons[2] lies like lead upon me,
And yet I would not sleep. Merciful powers,
Restrain in me the cursèd thoughts that nature
Gives way to in repose!

[Enter MACBETH, *and a Servant with a torch.]*

                 Give me my sword.
Who's there?
MACBETH. A friend.
BANQUO. What, sir, not yet at rest? The King's abed.
He hath been in unusual pleasure, and
Sent forth great largess to your offices.[3]
This diamond he greets your wife withal
By the name of most kind hostess, and shut up[4]
In measureless content.
MACBETH.   Being unprepared,
Our will became the servant to defect,
Which else should free have wrought.[5]
BANQUO.   All's well.
I dreamt last night of the three weird sisters.
To you they have showed some truth.

1. **husbandry,** thrift.

5

2. **summons,** to sleep, drowsiness.

10

15

3. **great largess to your offices,** gifts and rewards for the servants of Macbeth's household; **offices** were the areas of work—the kitchen, etc.
4. **shut up,** concluded with great contentment.

5. Macbeth says he would have lodged the king more suitably if he'd had notice to prepare.

20

MACBETH.   I think not of them.
Yet, when we can entreat an hour to serve,
We would spend it in some words upon that business,
If you would grant the time.
BANQUO.   At your kind'st leisure.
MACBETH. If you shall cleave to my consent, when 'tis,   25
It shall make honor for you.
BANQUO.   So I lose none
In seeking to augment it, but still keep
My bosom franchised and allegiance clear,[6]
I shall be counseled.
MACBETH.   Good repose the while!
BANQUO. Thanks, sir. The like to you!   30

[*Exeunt* BANQUO *and* FLEANCE.]

MACBETH. Go bid thy mistress, when my drink is ready,
She strike upon the bell. Get thee to bed.

[*Exit Servant.*]

Is this a dagger which I see before me,
The handle toward my hand? Come, let me clutch
      thee.
I have thee not, and yet I see thee still.   35
Art thou not, fatal vision, sensible
To feeling as to sight?[7] or art thou but
A dagger of the mind, a false creation,
Proceeding from the heat-oppressèd brain?
I see thee yet, in form as palpable   40
As this which now I draw.
Thou marshal'st me the way that I was going,
And such an instrument I was to use.
Mine eyes are made the fools o' the other senses,
Or else worth all the rest. I see thee still;   45
And on thy blade and dudgeon gouts[8] of blood,
Which was not so before. There's no such thing.
It is the bloody business which informs
Thus to mine eyes. Now o'er the one half-world
Nature seems dead, and wicked dreams abuse   50
The curtained sleep. Witchcraft celebrates
Pale Hecate's offerings;[9] and withered murder,
Alarumed by his sentinel, the wolf,
Whose howl's his watch,[10] thus with his stealthy pace,
With Tarquin's ravishing strides,[11] towards his design   55
Moves like a ghost. Thou sure and firm-set earth,
Hear not my steps, which way they walk, for fear
Thy very stones prate of my whereabout

6. **franchised . . . clear,** above reproach, stainless. Banquo would be glad for further honor if he can get it honorably.

7. **sensible to feeling as to sight,** tangible, can the dagger be felt?

8. **dudgeon** (duj' ən), handle; **gouts** (gouts), great drops.

9. **Hecate** (hek' ət), a classical goddess of witchcraft and magic. Witches were still thought to make sacrifices to the devil.
10. **his watch.** The howl of the wolf is the time signal for murder.
11. **strides.** Murder moves on like an infamous Roman king.

And take the present horror from the time
Which now suits with it. Whiles I threat, he lives;   60
Words to the heat of deeds too cold breath gives.

[*A bell rings.*]

I go, and it is done. The bell invites me.
Hear it not, Duncan, for it is a knell
That summons thee to heaven, or to hell.

[*Exit.*]

Scene 2

The same.
Enter LADY MACBETH.

LADY MACBETH. That which hath made them drunk hath
    made me bold;
  What hath quenched them hath given me fire. Hark!
    Peace!
  It was the owl that shrieked, the fatal bellman[12]
  Which gives the stern'st good-night. He is about it.
  The doors are open, and the surfeited grooms
  Do mock their charge with snores. I have drugged
    their possets,[13]
  That death and nature do contend about them
  Whether they live or die.
MACBETH.   *(Within)* Who's there? What, ho?
LADY MACBETH. Alack, I am afraid they have awaked,
  And 'tis not done. The attempt, and not the deed,   10
  Confounds us. Hark! I laid their daggers ready;
  He could not miss 'em. Had he not resembled
  My father as he slept, I had done't.

[*Enter* MACBETH.]

                My husband!
MACBETH. I have done the deed. Didst thou not hear a
  noise?
LADY MACBETH. I heard the owl scream and the crickets
  cry.   15
  Did you not speak?
MACBETH.   When?
LADY MACBETH.   Now.
MACBETH.   As I descended?
LADY MACBETH. Ay.

12. **fatal bellman,** one who, according to ancient London custom, rang the bell for prisoners the night before their execution.   5

13. **possets** (pos′ its), hot wine drinks customarily taken before going to bed.

MACBETH. Hark!
Who lies i' the second chamber?

LADY MACBETH. Donalbain.

MACBETH. *(Looking on his hands.)* This is a sorry sight. 20

LADY MACBETH. A foolish thought, to say a sorry sight.

MACBETH. There's one did laugh in's sleep, and one
      cried "Murder!"
That they did wake each other. I stood and heard
      them.
But they did say their prayers, and addressed them
Again to sleep.

LADY MACBETH. There are two lodged together.[14] 25

MACBETH. One cried "God bless us!" and "Amen" the
      other,
As they had seen me with these hangman's hands.
List'ning their fears,[15] I could not say "Amen,"
When they did say "God bless us!"

LADY MACBETH. Consider it not so deeply. 30

MACBETH. But wherefore could not I pronounce
      "Amen"?
I had most need of blessing, and "Amen"
Stuck in my throat.

LADY MACBETH. These deeds must not be thought
After these ways; so, it will make us mad.

MACBETH. Methought I heard a voice cry "Sleep no
      more! 35
Macbeth does murder sleep"—the innocent sleep,
Sleep that knits up the raveled sleave[16] of care,
The death of each day's life, sore labor's bath,
Balm of hurt minds, great nature's second course,[17]
Chief nourisher in life's feast—

LADY MACBETH. What do you mean? 40

MACBETH. Still it cried "Sleep no more!" to all the house;
"Glamis hath murdered sleep, and therefore Cawdor
Shall sleep no more; Macbeth shall sleep no more!"

LADY MACBETH. Who was it that thus cried? Why, worthy
      thane,
You do unbend your noble strength to think 45
So brainsickly of things. Go get some water
And wash this filthy witness from your hand.
Why did you bring these daggers from the place?
They must lie there. Go carry them and smear
The sleepy grooms with blood.

MACBETH. I'll go no more. 50
I am afraid to think what I have done;
Look on't again I dare not.

LADY MACBETH. Infirm of purpose!

14. **together.** Lady Macbeth confirms that Donalbain had had to share a room with another guest.

15. **As they had seen ... list'ning their fears,** as if they had seen Macbeth listening to their fearful exclamations.

16. **raveled sleave,** tangled floss.

17. **second course.** Sleep is the second and heavier course in life's feast.

"Infirm of purpose!
Give me the daggers. The sleeping and the dead
Are but as pictures."

Royal Shakespeare Theatre, 1962
Stratford-Upon-Avon
Photo: Holte Photographers Ltd.

Give me the daggers. The sleeping and the dead
Are but as pictures. 'Tis the eye of childhood
That fears a painted devil. If he do bleed,   55
I'll gild the faces of the grooms withal,
For it must seem their guilt.

[*Exit. Knocking within.*]

MACBETH.   Whence is that knocking?
How is't with me, when every noise appalls me?
What hands are here? Ha! they pluck out mine eyes!
Will all great Neptune's ocean wash this blood   60
Clean from my hand? No. This my hand will rather
The multitudinous seas incarnadine,[18]
Making the green one red.

18. **incarnadine** (in kär′ nə dən; also, dīn, dēn′),   color red.

[*Reenter* LADY MACBETH.]

LADY MACBETH. My hands are of your color, but I shame
To wear a heart so white. (*Knocking within.*) I hear a
knocking   65
At the south entry. Retire we to our chamber;
A little water clears us of this deed.
How easy is it then! Your constancy
Hath left you unattended. (*Knocking within.*) Hark!
more knocking.
Get on your nightgown, lest occasion call us   70
And show us to be watchers. Be not lost
So poorly in your thoughts.
MACBETH. To know my deed, 'twere best not know
myself.
                                    (*Knocking within.*)
Wake Duncan with thy knocking! I would thou
couldst!

[*Exeunt.*]

Scene 3

The same.
Enter a PORTER. *Knocking within.*

PORTER. Here's a knocking indeed! If a man were porter
of hell gate, he should have old[19] turning the key.
(*Knocking within.*) Knock, knock, knock! Who's there, i'
the name of Beelzebub? Here's a farmer that hanged
himself on the expectation of plenty. Come in time!   5
Have napkins enow about you; here you'll sweat

19. **have old,**   have a lot to do; **old** is a term of emphasis.

for't.[20] *(Knocking within.)* Knock, knock! Who's there, in the other devil's name? Faith, here's an equivocator,[21] that could swear in both the scales against either scale; who committed treason enough for God's sake, yet could not equivocate to heaven. O, come in, equivocator! *(Knocking within.)* Knock, knock, knock! Who's there? Faith, here's an English tailor come hither for stealing out of a French hose. Come in, tailor. Here you may roast your goose.[22] *(Knocking within.)* Knock, knock! Never at quiet! What are you? But this place is too cold for hell. I'll devil-porter it no further. I had thought to have let in some of all professions that go the primrose way to the everlasting bonfire. *(Knocking within.)* Anon, anon! *(Opens the gate.)* I pray you remember the porter.[23]

[*Enter* MACDUFF *and* LENNOX.]

MACDUFF. Was it so late, friend, ere you went to bed,
That you do lie so late?

PORTER. Faith, sir, we were carousing till the second
cock;[24] and drink, sir, is a great provoker.

MACDUFF. I believe drink gave thee the lie last night.

PORTER. That it did, sir, i' the very throat on me; but I
requited him for his lie; and, I think, being too
strong for him, though he took up my legs
sometime, yet I made a shift to cast him.

MACDUFF. Is thy master stirring?

[*Enter* MACBETH.]

Our knocking has awaked him; here he comes.

LENNOX. Good morrow, noble sir.

MACBETH.   Good morrow, both.

MACDUFF. Is the King stirring, worthy thane?

MACBETH.   Not yet.

MACDUFF. He did command me to call timely on him.
I have almost slipped the hour.

MACBETH.   I'll bring you to him.

MACDUFF. I know this is a joyful trouble to you;
But yet 'tis one.

MACBETH. The labor we delight in physics pain.[25]
This is the door.

MACDUFF.   I'll make so bold to call,
For 'tis my limited service.

[*Exit.*]

LENNOX. Goes the King hence today?

MACBETH.   He does; he did appoint so.

20. **sweat for't.** Ironically, the porter is playing at being a porter at hell's gate letting in familiar types of sinners. The farmer committed suicide at the thought of a break in wheat prices. Food speculation was a traditional subject for condemnation.

21. **The other devil's name . . . equivocator** (i kwiv′ ə kāt′ ər). The porter can only remember the name **Beelzebub;** Mephistopheles, etc., escape his muddled brain. The **equivocator** was Shakespeare's gibe at those who held that religious reservations justified disloyalty to the English crown.

22. **roast your goose.** This is a pun on the fact that a tailor's iron was called a tailor's goose. The tailor is damned for imitating tight French styles and stealing ends of fabrics.

23. **remember the porter**—with a tip.

24. **second cock.** The first cock cried at midnight, the second at three A.M.

25. **physics pain,** cures.

LENNOX. The night has been unruly. Where we lay,
  Our chimneys were blown down; and, as they say,
  Lamentings heard i' the air, strange screams of death, 45
  And prophesying with accents terrible,
  Of dire combustion and confused events
  New hatched to the woeful time. The obscure bird[26]
  Clamored the livelong night. Some say the earth
  Was feverous and did shake.
MACBETH.   'Twas a rough night. 50
LENNOX. My young remembrance cannot parallel
  A fellow to it.

  [*Reenter* MACDUFF.]

MACDUFF. O horror, horror, horror! Tongue nor heart
  Cannot conceive nor name thee!
MACBETH AND LENNOX.   What's the matter?
MACDUFF. Confusion now hath made his masterpiece! 55
  Most sacrilegious murder hath broke ope
  The Lord's anointed temple and stole thence
  The life o'the building![27]
MACBETH.   What is't you say? the life?
LENNOX. Mean you his Majesty?
MACDUFF. Approach the chamber, and destroy your sight 60
  With a new Gorgon.[28] Do not bid me speak.
  See, and then speak yourselves.

  [*Exeunt* MACBETH *and* LENNOX.]

                         Awake, awake!
  Ring the alarum bell. Murder and treason!
  Banquo and Donalbain! Malcolm! awake!
  Shake off this downy sleep, death's counterfeit,[29] 65
  And look on death itself! Up, up, and see
  The great doom's image! Malcolm! Banquo!
  As from your graves rise up and walk like sprites,[30]
  To countenance this horror! Ring the bell!

  [*Bell rings.*]
  [*Enter* LADY MACBETH.]

LADY MACBETH. What's the business, 70
  That such a hideous trumpet calls to parley
  The sleepers of the house? Speak, speak!
MACDUFF.   O gentle lady,
  'Tis not for you to hear what I can speak.
  The repetition, in a woman's ear,
  Would murder as it fell.

  [*Enter* BANQUO.]

26. **the obscure bird,** the bird of darkness, the owl.

27. **o' the building.** The body was the temple of the soul and the king was the Lord's anointed.

28. **Gorgon** (gôr′gən), one of the hideous sisters in Greek mythology whose looks turned one to stone.

29. **counterfeit,** sleep imita· death.

30. **sprites,** ghosts.

                    O Banquo, Banquo,   75
Our royal master's murdered!
LADY MACBETH.   Woe, alas!
What, in our house?
BANQUO.   Too cruel anywhere.
Dear Duff, I prithee contradict thyself
And say it is not so.

[*Reenter* MACBETH, LENNOX, *and* ROSS.]

MACBETH. Had I but died an hour before this chance,   80
  I had lived a blessèd time; for from this instant
  There's nothing serious in mortality;[31]
  All is but toys; renown and grace is dead;
  The wine of life is drawn, and the mere lees[32]
  Is left this vault to brag of.   85

[*Enter* MALCOLM *and* DONALBAIN.]

DONALBAIN. What is amiss?
MACBETH.   You are, and do not know't.
  The spring, the head, the fountain of your blood
  Is stopped; the very source of it is stopped.
MACDUFF. Your royal father's murdered.
MALCOLM.   O, by whom?
LENNOX. Those of his chamber, as it seemed, had done't.   90
  Their hands and faces were all badged[33] with blood;
  So were their daggers, which unwiped we found
  Upon their pillows.
  They stared, and were distracted; no man's life
  Was to be trusted with them.   95
MACBETH. O, yet I do repent me of my fury,
  That I did kill them.
MACDUFF.   Wherefore did you so?
MACBETH. Who can be wise, amazed, temp'rate, and
    furious,
  Loyal and neutral, in a moment? No man.
  The expedition of my violent love   100
  Outran the pauser, reason. Here lay Duncan,
  His silver skin laced with his golden blood,
  And his gashed stabs looked like a breach in nature
  For ruin's wasteful entrance; there, the murderers,
  Steeped in the colors of their trade, their daggers   105
  Unmannerly breeched with gore. Who could refrain
  That had a heart to love, and in that heart
  Courage to make's love known?
LADY MACBETH.   Help me hence, ho!

[*Faints.*]

---

31. **in mortality.** There is nothing worthwhile in life.

32. **lees.** The metaphor is of a wine cellar (vault) from which Duncan, the good wine, has been removed leaving only sediment, dregs.

33. **badged,** marked as if with a crest.

MACDUFF. Look to the lady.

MALCOLM.   *(Aside to* DONALBAIN*)* Why do
    we hold our tongues,
That most may claim this argument for ours?   110

DONALBAIN. *(Aside to* MALCOLM*)* What should be spoken
    here, where our fate,
Hid in an auger-hole,[34] may rush, and seize us?
Let's away;
Our tears are not yet brewed.

MALCOLM. *(Aside to* DONALBAIN*)*
                  Nor our strong sorrow
Upon the foot of motion.[35]

BANQUO.   Look to the lady.   115

[LADY MACBETH *is carried out.*]

And when we have our naked frailties hid,[36]
That suffer in exposure, let us meet,
And question this most bloody piece of work,
To know it further. Fears and scruples shake us.
In the great hand of God I stand, and thence   120
Against the undivulged pretense I fight
Of treasonous malice.[37]

MACDUFF.   And so do I.

ALL.   So all.

MACBETH. Let's briefly put on manly readiness
And meet i' the hall together.

ALL.   Well contented.

[*Exeunt all but* MALCOLM *and* DONALBAIN.]

MALCOLM. What will you do? Let's not consort with
    them.   125
To show an unfelt sorrow is an office
Which the false man does easy. I'll to England.

DONALBAIN. To Ireland I. Our separated fortune
Shall keep us both the safer. Where we are,
There's daggers in men's smiles; the near in blood,[38]   130
The nearer bloody.

MALCOLM.   This murderous shaft that's shot
Hath not yet lighted,[39] and our safest way
Is to avoid the aim. Therefore to horse;
And let us not be dainty of leave-taking,
But shift away. There's warrant in that theft   135
Which steals itself when there's no mercy left.

[*Exeunt.*]

34. **auger-hole.** Donalbain, as a royal heir, is fearful for his own safety; he says that danger may lurk in any place. Witches were believed capable of hiding even in small drilled holes.

35. **foot of motion.** Our grief has not yet begun to show or act.

36. **. . . hid.** Banquo reminds the others that they're still in night clothes.

37. **treasonous malice.** Banquo senses but can't define the motive for such treason.

38. **near in blood.** The royal heirs are most in danger.

39. **not yet lighted.** There's more murder to come.

Scene 4

Outside MACBETH'S *Castle.*
Enter ROSS *with an* OLD MAN.

OLD MAN. Threescore and ten I can remember well;
Within the volume of which time I have seen
Hours dreadful and things strange; but this sore night
Hath trifled former knowings.[40]

ROSS.   Ah, good father,   5
Thou seest the heavens, as troubled with man's act,
Threaten his bloody stage. By the clock 'tis day,
And yet dark night strangles the traveling lamp.[41]
Is't night's predominance, or the day's shame,
That darkness does the face of earth entomb,
When living light should kiss it?

OLD MAN.   'Tis unnatural,   10
Even like the deed that's done. On Tuesday last
A falcon, tow'ring in her pride of place,
Was by a mousing owl hawked at and killed.[42]

ROSS. And Duncan's horses—a thing most strange and
    certain—
Beauteous and swift, the minions of their race,   15
Turned wild in nature, broke their stalls, flung out,
Contending 'gainst obedience, as they would make
War with mankind.

OLD MAN.   'Tis said they eat each other.

ROSS. They did so, to the amazement of mine eyes
That looked upon't.

[*Enter* MACDUFF.]

                  Here comes the good Macduff.   20
How goes the world, sir, now?

MACDUFF.   Why, see you not?

ROSS. Is't known who did this more than bloody deed?

MACDUFF. Those that Macbeth hath slain.

ROSS.   Alas, the day!
What good could they pretend?[43]

MACDUFF.   They were suborned.[44]
Malcolm and Donalbain, the King's two sons,
Are stol'n away and fled, which puts upon them   25
Suspicion of the deed.

ROSS.   'Gainst nature still!
Thriftless ambition, that will ravin up[45]
Thine own life's means! Then 'tis most like
The sovereignty will fall upon Macbeth.   30

40. trifled former knowings, has made unimportant everything I knew before.

41. traveling lamp, the sun.

42. falcon . . . killed. It is another indication of how "time is out of joint" that a mere owl should kill a hunting falcon instead of its usual prey of mice.

43. pretend? How could they put forth a reasonable excuse?
44. suborned, bribed; Macduff suggests that they had been paid to do the murder.

45. ravin (rav′ ən), eat up.

MACDUFF. He is already named, and gone to Scone[46]
  To be invested.

ROSS.   Where is Duncan's body?

MACDUFF. Carried to Colmekill,[47]
  The sacred storehouse of his predecessors
  And guardian of their bones.

ROSS.   Will you to Scone?   35

MACDUFF. No, cousin, I'll to Fife.[48]

ROSS.   Well, I will thither.

MACDUFF. Well, may you see things well done there.
    Adieu,
  Lest our old robes sit easier than our new![49]

ROSS. Farewell, father.

OLD MAN. God's benison go with you, and with those   40
  That would make good of bad, and friends of foes!

[*Exeunt.*]

46. **Scone,** the legendary coronation place for Scottish kings.

47. **Colmekill,** the island where ancient Scottish kings were buried.

48. **Fife,** Macduff's home.

49. Macduff hopes Macbeth's coming rule will not be threatening to the other nobles.

FOR UNDERSTANDING

A King Is Killed

1. How does Macbeth's conscience react before and during the murder? And Lady Macbeth's conscience? After the murder how does each of them react?

2. Why does Lady Macbeth faint?

3. What evidence is there that Banquo, Macduff, and others do not trust Macbeth?

4. Why do Duncan's sons flee rather than remain to inherit the crown?

FOR INTERPRETATION

1. The first twenty lines of Scene 4 do not really give us any plot information. What use do they serve?

2. If you were staging a production of *Macbeth,* would you have the dagger that Macbeth sees in Scene 1 visible to the audience? Explain your answer.

FOR APPRECIATION

Characterization by Use of Detail

In Act II, Scene 2, note that Shakespeare uses an abundance contrasted by a lack of specific detail to emphasize the difference between the highly imaginative Macbeth and his matter-of-fact wife.

Beginning with Macbeth's line, "One cried, 'God bless us!'" count the specific statements that reveal Macbeth's horror at the sight of his bloodstained hands. Consider his four successive speeches.

In contrast, what one command does his wife give concerning those same hands?

Act III

Scene 1

Forres. The Palace.[1]
Enter BANQUO.

BANQUO. Thou hast it now: King, Cawdor, Glamis, all,
As the weird women promised; and I fear
Thou play'dst most foully for't. Yet it was said
It should not stand in thy posterity,
But that myself should be the root and father   5
Of many kings. If there come truth from them—
As upon thee, Macbeth, their speeches shine[2]—
Why, by the verities on thee made good,
May they not be my oracles as well
And set me up in hope? But, hush, no more!   10

[*Trumpets sound a fanfare. Enter* MACBETH, *as King;* LADY
MACBETH, *as Queen;* LENNOX, ROSS, *Lords and
Attendants.*]

MACBETH. Here's our chief guest.
LADY MACBETH.   If he had been forgotten,
It had been as a gap in our great feast,
And all-thing unbecoming.[3]
MACBETH. Tonight we hold a solemn supper, sir,
And I'll request your presence.[4]
BANQUO.   Let your Highness   15
Command upon me,[5] to the which my duties
Are with a most indissoluble tie
For ever knit.
MACBETH.   Ride you this afternoon?
BANQUO. Ay, my good lord.
MACBETH. We should have else desired your good
    advice,   20
Which still hath been both grave and prosperous,
In this day's council; but we'll take tomorrow.
Is't far you ride?
BANQUO. As far, my lord, as will fill up the time
'Twixt this and supper. Go not my horse the better,   25
I must become a borrower of the night[6]
For a dark hour or twain.
MACBETH.   Fail not our feast.
BANQUO. My lord, I will not.
MACBETH. We hear our bloody cousins are bestowed
In England and in Ireland, not confessing   30
Their cruel parricide,[7] filling their hearers

1. Some months later. Suspicions are mounting about Macbeth.

2. **speeches shine.** The witches' prophecies are glowingly fulfilled.

3. **all-thing,** altogether.

4. **solemn supper . . . ,** formal banquet. **I'll,** Macbeth uses **I** rather than the royal we as a gesture of special friendship.
5. **Command upon me.** Banquo replies formally, "Your request is my command."

6. **. . . borrower of the night.** Unless my horse is faster than expected, I'll be riding in the dark for several hours.
7. **cousins . . . parricide.** Malcolm and Donalbain are in England, denying the murder of their father and with "strange invention" accusing Macbeth.

With strange invention. But of that tomorrow,
When therewithal we shall have cause of state
Craving us jointly.[8] Hie you to horse. Adieu,
Till you return at night. Goes Fleance with you?
BANQUO. Ay, my good lord. Our time does call upon's.
MACBETH. I wish your horses swift and sure of foot,
And so I do commend you to their backs.
Farewell.

[*Exit* BANQUO.]

Let every man be master of his time
Till seven at night. To make society
The sweeter welcome, we will keep ourself
Till supper time alone; while then, God be with you!

[*Exeunt all but* MACBETH *and an* ATTENDANT.]

Sirrah, a word with you. Attend those men
Our pleasure?
ATTENDANT. They are, my lord, without the palace gate.
MACBETH. Bring them before us.

[*Exit* ATTENDANT.]

            To be thus is nothing,
But to be safely thus.[9] Our fears in Banquo
Stick deep, and in his royalty of nature
Reigns that which would be feared. 'Tis much he
   dares,
And, to that dauntless temper of his mind
He hath a wisdom that doth guide his valor
To act in safety. There is none but he
Whose being I do fear; and under him
My genius is rebuked, as it is said
Mark Antony's was by Caesar.[10] He chid the sisters
When first they put the name of King upon me,
And bade them speak to him. Then, prophet-like,
They hailed him father to a line of kings.
Upon my head they placed a fruitless crown
And put a barren scepter in my gripe,[11]
Thence to be wrenched with an unlineal hand,[12]
No son of mine succeeding. If't be so,
For Banquo's issue have I filed[13] my mind;
For them the gracious Duncan have I murdered;
Put rancors in the vessel of my peace[14]
Only for them, and mine eternal jewel[15]
Given to the common enemy of man,
To make them kings, the seed of Banquo kings!

35

40

45

50

55

60

65

8. **cause of state craving us jointly,** serious matter requiring our mutual attention.

9. **safely thus.** It is pointless to be king unless the throne is safe.

10. **genius is rebuked . . . by Caesar.** Banquo's fortune puts to shame Macbeth's guardian spirits just as Anthony was forewarned by a fortune-teller (according to Plutarch) that he would be overwhelmed by Caesar.
11. **gripe** (grīp), grip.
12. **unlineal hand,** out of direct line of hereditary descent.
13. **filed,** defiled.

14. **rancors in . . . peace,** poisoned his easy conscience.
15. **mine eternal jewel,** my soul—Macbeth has sold out to the devil only to benefit Banquo's heirs.

Rather than so, come, Fate, into the list[16]
And champion me to the utterance! Who's there?

[*Reenter* ATTENDANT, *with two* MURDERERS.]

Now go to the door and stay there till we call.

[*Exit* ATTENDANT.]

Was it not yesterday we spoke together?
MURDERERS. It was, so please your Highness.
MACBETH.   Well then, now
    Have you considered of my speeches? Know
    That it was he, in the times past, which held you
    So under fortune,[17] which you thought had been
    Our innocent self. This I made good to you
    In our last conference, passed in probation with you,
    How you were borne in hand, how crossed, the
      instruments,
    Who wrought with them, and all things else that
      might
    To half a soul and to a notion crazed
    Say "Thus did Banquo."
FIRST MURDERER.   You made it known to us.
MACBETH. I did so; and went further, which is now
    Our point of second meeting. Did you find
    Your patience so predominant in your nature
    That you can let this go? Are you so gospeled[18]
    To pray for this good man and for his issue,
    Whose heavy hand hath bowed you to the grave
    And beggared yours for ever?
FIRST MURDERER.   We are men, my liege.
MACBETH. Ay, in the catalogue ye go for men,
    As hounds and greyhounds, mongrels, spaniels, curs,
    Shoughs, water-rugs and demi-wolves are clept[19]
    All by the name of dogs. The valued file[20]
    Distinguishes the swift, the slow, the subtle,
    The housekeeper, the hunter, every one
    According to the gift which bounteous nature
    Hath in him closed, whereby he does receive
    Particular addition, from the bill
    That writes them all alike; and so of men.
    Now, if you have a station in the file,
    Not i' the worst rank of manhood, say't;
    And I will put that business in your bosoms
    Whose execution takes your enemy off,
    Grapples you to the heart and love of us,
    Who wear our health but sickly in his life,
    Which in his death were perfect.

70

75

80

85

90

95

100

105

16. **list,** tournament ground.

17. Macbeth has recruited for murderers Scottish gentlemen in dire straits who before had held Macbeth responsible for their troubles. He has convinced them that Banquo was the source of their grievances and so set up the murder to look like a grudge killing.

18. **gospeled,** so taught.

19. **shoughs** (shəfs), lapdogs; **water-rugs,** water spaniels; **clept** (klept), called.
20. **file,** top group, first class.

SECOND MURDERER.   I am one, my liege,
  Whom the vile blows and buffets of the world
  Have so incensed that I am reckless what
  I do to spite the world.
FIRST MURDERER.   And I another,   110
  So weary with disasters, tugged with fortune,
  That I would set my life on any chance,
  To mend it or be rid on't.
MACBETH.   Both of you
  Know Banquo was your enemy.
MURDERERS.   True, my lord.
MACBETH. So is he mine; and in such bloody distance   115
  That every minute of his being thrusts
  Against my near'st of life; and though I could
  With barefaced power sweep him from my sight
  And bid my will avouch it,[21] yet I must not,
  For certain friends that are both his and mine,   120
  Whose loves I may not drop, but wail his fall
  Who I myself struck down. And thence it is
  That I to your assistance do make love,
  Masking the business from the common eye
  For sundry weighty reasons.
SECOND MURDERER.   We shall, my lord,   125
  Perform what you command us.
FIRST MURDERER.   Though our lives—
MACBETH. Your spirits shine through you. Within this
   hour at most
  I will advise you where to plant yourselves,
  Acquaint you with the perfect spy o' the time,[22]
  The moment on't; for't must be done tonight,   130
  And something from the palace; always thought
  That I require a clearness; and with him—
  To leave no rubs nor botches in the work—
  Fleance his son, that keeps him company,
  Whose absence is no less material to me   135
  Than is his father's, must embrace the fate
  Of that dark hour. Resolve yourselves apart;
  I'll come to you anon.
MURDERERS.   We are resolved, my lord.
MACBETH. I'll call upon you straight. Abide within.

[*Exeunt* MURDERERS.]

  It is concluded. Banquo, thy soul's flight,   140
  If it find heaven, must find it out tonight.

[*Exit.*]

21. **. . . avouch it.** Macbeth admits that he could authorize Banquo's death by his kingly rights.

22. **spy o' the time,** information about the perfect moment for the murder.

Scene 2

The Palace.
Enter LADY MACBETH *and a* SERVANT.

LADY MACBETH. Is Banquo' gone from court?
SERVANT. Ay, madam, but returns again tonight.
LADY MACBETH. Say to the King, I would attend his
leisure
For a few words.
SERVANT. Madam, I will.

[*Exit.*]

LADY MACBETH. Naught's had, all's spent,
Where our desire is got without content. 5
'Tis safer to be that which we destroy
Than by destruction dwell in doubtful joy.[23]

[*Enter* MACBETH.]

How now, my lord? Why do you keep alone,
Of sorriest fancies your companions making,
Using those thoughts which should indeed have died 10
With them they think on? Things without all remedy
Should be without regard; what's done is done.
MACBETH. We have scotched[24] the snake, not killed it.
She'll close[25] and be herself, whilst our poor malice
Remains in danger of her former tooth. 15
But let the frame of things disjoint,[26] both the worlds
suffer,
Ere we will eat our meal in fear, and sleep
In the affliction of these terrible dreams
That shake us nightly. Better be with the dead,
Whom we, to gain our peace, have sent to peace, 20
Than on the torture of the mind to lie
In restless ecstasy. Duncan is in his grave;
After life's fitful fever he sleeps well.
Treason has done his worst: nor steel nor poison,
Malice domestic, foreign levy,[27] nothing, 25
Can touch him further.
LADY MACBETH. Come on;
Gentle my lord, sleek o'er your rugged looks;
Be bright and jovial among your guests tonight.
MACBETH. So shall I, love; and so, I pray, be you.
Let your remembrance apply to Banquo; 30
Present him eminence[28] both with eye and tongue:
Unsafe the while, that we

23. **doubtful joy.** Lady Macbeth shares Macbeth's worry about Banquo.

24. **scotched,** injured.
25. **close.** The snake (the threat) may become whole again.
26. **frame of things disjoint.** Heaven and hell may come apart and both perish before Macbeth will live with this fear.

27. **levy** (le′vē), an invading army.

28. **eminence,** praise Banquo.

Must lave our honors in these flattering streams,
And make our faces vizards[29] to our hearts,
Disguising what they are.

LADY MACBETH. You must leave this.

MACBETH. O, full of scorpions is my mind, dear wife!
Thou know'st that Banquo, and his Fleance, lives.

LADY MACBETH. But in them Nature's copy's not
eterne.[30]

MACBETH. There's comfort yet; they are assailable;
Then be thou jocund. Ere the bat hath flown
His cloistered flight, ere to black Hecate's summons
The shard-borne beetle[31] with his drowsy hums
Hath run night's yawning peal, there shall be done
A deed of dreadful note.

LADY MACBETH. What's to be done?

MACBETH. Be innocent of the knowledge, dearest chuck,
Till thou applaud the deed. Come, seeling night,[32]
Scarf up the tender eye of pitiful day,
And with thy bloody and invisible hand
Cancel and tear to pieces that great bond
Which keeps me pale! Light thickens, and the crow
Makes wing to the rooky wood.[33]
Good things of day begin to droop and drowse,
Whiles night's black agents to their preys do rouse.
Thou marvell'st at my words; but hold thee still:
Things bad begun make strong themselves by ill.
So prithee go with me.

[*Exeunt.*]

29. vizard (viz' ərd), the shield of a medieval helmet, masking the face. 35

30. eterne (i tern'), eternal, immortal; a human being's lease from nature is not a permanent one. 40

31. shard-borne, borne aloft on scaly wings.

32. seel (sēl), to close the eyes; to blind. This entire metaphor comes from the hooding of falcons to tame them before training. 45

33. rooky wood, the forest filled with rooks (crows). 50

55

Scene 3

A park near the Palace.
Enter three MURDERERS.

FIRST MURDERER. But who did bid thee join with us?

THIRD MURDERER. Macbeth.

SECOND MURDERER. He needs not our mistrust, since he
delivers
Our offices,[34] and what we have to do,
To the direction just.

FIRST MURDERER. Then stand with us.
The west yet glimmers with some streaks of day.
Now spurs the lated traveler apace
To gain the timely inn,[35] and near approaches
The subject of our watch.

34. offices, duties, instructions.

5

35. lated traveler . . . timely inn. The evening traveler hurries to reach the inn before it is too dark.

THIRD MURDERER.   Hark! I hear horses.

BANQUO. *(Within)* Give us a light there, ho!

SECOND MURDERER.   Then 'tis he. The rest

That are within the note of expectation   10

Already are i' the court.

FIRST MURDERER.   His horses go about.

THIRD MURDERER. Almost a mile; but he does usually—

So all men do—from hence to the palace gate

Make it their walk.[36]

SECOND MURDERER.   A light, a light!

[*Enter* BANQUO, *and* FLEANCE *with a torch.*]

THIRD MURDERER.   'Tis he.

FIRST MURDERER. Stand to't.   15

BANQUO. It will be rain tonight.

FIRST MURDERER.   Let it come down!

[*They set upon* BANQUO.]

BANQUO. O treachery! Fly, good Fleance, fly, fly, fly!

Thou mayst revenge. O slave!

[*Dies.* FLEANCE *escapes.*]

THIRD MURDERER. Who did strike out the light?

FIRST MURDERER.   Was't not the way?

THIRD MURDERER. There's but one down; the son is fled.

SECOND MURDERER.   We have lost   20

Best half of our affair.

FIRST MURDERER. Well, let's away, and say how much is

done.

[*Exeunt.*]

36. Banquo and Fleance, as is customary, dismount some distance from the palace and walk the last stretch alone. Their servants take the horses to stable them. This, of course, makes the attack easier.

Scene 4

Hall in the Palace.
A banquet prepared. Enter MACBETH, LADY MACBETH,
ROSS, LENNOX, LORDS *and Attendants.*

MACBETH. You know your own degrees,[37] sit down. At
first

And last the hearty welcome.

LORDS.   Thanks to your Majesty.

MACBETH. Ourself will mingle with society

And play the humble host.

Our hostess keeps her state,[38] but in best time   5

We will require her welcome.

37. **own degrees,** relative ranks that determine protocol in seating at the table.

38. **her state.** Macbeth chooses to leave his royal seat and sit with his guests; Lady Macbeth stays on the raised throne.

LADY MACBETH. Pronounce it for me, sir, to all our
    friends,
For my heart speaks they are welcome.

[*Enter* FIRST MURDERER *to the door.*]

MACBETH. See, they encounter thee with their hearts'
    thanks.
Both sides are even: here I'll sit i' the midst.   10
Be large in mirth; anon we'll drink a measure
The table round. (*Approaching* MURDERER *at door*)
    There's blood upon thy face.
MURDERER. 'Tis Banquo's then.
MACBETH. 'Tis better thee without than he within.
Is he dispatched?   15
MURDERER. My lord, his throat is cut. That I did for
    him.
MACBETH. Thou art the best o' the cutthroats! Yet he's
    good
That did the like for Fleance. If thou didst it,
Thou art the nonpareil.
MURDERER.   Most royal sir,
    Fleance is 'scaped.   20
MACBETH. (*Aside*) Then comes my fit again. I had else
    been perfect,
Whole as the marble, founded as the rock,
As broad and general as the casing air.[39]
But now I am cabined, cribbed, confined, bound in
To saucy doubts and fears.—But Banquo's safe?   25
MURDERER. Ay, my good lord. Safe in a ditch he bides,
With twenty trenchèd gashes on his head,
The least a death to nature.
MACBETH.   Thanks for that!
(*Aside*) There the grown serpent lies; the worm that's
    fled
Hath nature that in time will venom breed,[40]   30
No teeth for the present. Get thee gone. Tomorrow
We'll hear ourselves again.

[*Exit* MURDERER.]

LADY MACBETH.   My royal lord,
You do not give the cheer. The feast is sold
That is not often vouched,[41] while 'tis a-making,   35
'Tis given with welcome. To feed were best at home.
From thence, the sauce to meat is ceremony;
Meeting were bare without it.

39. **rock . . . casing air,** as solid as a rock and as free as the surrounding air.

40. **venom breed.** Macbeth refers to Banquo's offspring escaping.

41. **vouched** (voucht), without the host's constant attention, welcome, and cheer, a dinner is as one bought in an inn.

[*The* GHOST OF BANQUO *enters, and sits in* MACBETH'S *place.*]

MACBETH.   Sweet remembrancer!
Now good digestion wait on appetite,
And health on both!
LENNOX.   May't please your Highness sit.
MACBETH. Here had we now our country's honor roofed,   40
Were the graced person of our Banquo present;
Who may I rather challenge for unkindness
Than pity for mischance!
ROSS.   His absence, sir,
Lays blame upon his promise. Please't your Highness
To grace us with your royal company?   45
MACBETH. The table's full.
LENNOX.   Here is a place reserved, sir.
MACBETH. Where?
LENNOX. Here, my good lord. What is't that moves your
Highness?
MACBETH. Which of you have done this?
LORDS.   What, my good lord?
MACBETH. Thou canst not say I did it. Never shake   50
Thy gory locks at me.
ROSS. Gentlemen, rise. His Highness is not well.
LADY MACBETH. Sit, worthy friends. My lord is often
thus,[42]
And hath been from his youth. Pray you keep seat.
The fit is momentary; upon a thought   55
He will again be well. If much you note him,
You shall offend him and extend his passion.
Feed, and regard him not.—Are you a man?
MACBETH. Ay, and a bold one, that dare look on that
Which might appall the devil.
LADY MACBETH.   O proper stuff!   60
This is the very painting of your fear;
This is the air-drawn dagger which, you said,
Led you to Duncan. O, these flaws and starts,
Imposters to true fear, would well become
A woman's story at a winter's fire,   65
Authorized by her grandam.[43] Shame itself!
Why do you make such faces? When all's done,
You look but on a stool.
MACBETH. Prithee, see there! behold! look! lo! how say
you?
Why, what care I? If thou canst nod, speak too.   70
If charnel-houses and our graves must send

42. **often thus.** Macbeth was subject to fits of hallucinations.

43. **. . . grandam,** "old wives tales."

Those that we bury back, our monuments
Shall be the maws of kites.[44]

[*Exit* GHOST.]

LADY MACBETH.   What, quite unmanned in folly?
MACBETH. If I stand here, I saw him.
LADY MACBETH.   Fie, for shame!
MACBETH. Blood hath been shed ere now, i' the olden
  time,   75
Ere humane statute purged the gentle weal;[45]
Ay, and since too, murders have been performed
Too terrible for the ear. The time has been,
That, when the brains were out, the man would die,
And there an end! But now they rise again,   80
With twenty mortal murders on their crowns,
And push us from our stools. This is more strange
Than such a murder is.
LADY MACBETH.   My worthy lord,
Your noble friends do lack you.
MACBETH.   I do forget.[46]
Do not muse at me, my most worthy friends.   85
I have a strange infirmity, which is nothing
To those that know me. Come, love and health to all!
Then I'll sit down. Give me some wine, fill full.

[GHOST *reenters.*]

I drink to the general joy o' the whole table,
And to our dear friend Banquo, whom we miss;   90
Would he were here! To all, and him, we thirst,
And all to all.
LORDS.   Our duties, and the pledge.
MACBETH. Avaunt! and quit my sight! let the earth hide
  thee!
Thy bones are marrowless, thy blood is cold;
Thou hast no speculation[47] in those eyes   95
Which thou dost glare with.
LADY MACBETH.   Think of this, good peers,
But as a thing of custom. 'Tis no other;
Only it spoils the pleasure of the time.
MACBETH. What man dare, I dare.
Approach thou like the rugged Russian bear,   100
The armed rhinoceros, or the Hyrcan[48] tiger;
Take any shape but that, and my firm nerves
Shall never tremble. Or be alive again
And dare me to the desert with thy sword.
If trembling I inhabit then,[49] protest me   105

44. **charnel-houses** (chär′ nl),
burial places for ancient bones;
maws of kites, stomachs of car-
rion birds—if the dead return
we'd do better to leave their bodies to birds of prey than to put up
monuments.

45. **the gentle weal,** before
laws against murder made the
savage state gentle, civilized.

46. Macbeth remembers his
guests.

47. **speculation,** power of sight.

48. **Hyrcan** (hər′ kən), from an
ancient Asian country near the
Caspian Sea.

49. **inhabit then,** prove (myself) a weakling.

The baby of a girl. Hence, horrible shadow!
Unreal mock'ry, hence!

[*Exit* GHOST.]

                        Why, so; being gone,
I am a man again. Pray you, sit still.

LADY MACBETH. You have displaced the mirth, broke
   the good meeting
With most admired disorder.

MACBETH.   Can such things be,   110
And overcome us like a summer's cloud,
Without our special wonder? You make me strange
Even to the disposition that I owe,[50]
When now I think you can behold such sights,
And keep the natural ruby of your cheeks,   115
When mine is blanched with fear.

ROSS.   What sights, my lord?

LADY MACBETH. I pray you speak not. He grows worse
   and worse;
Question enrages him. At once, good night.
Stand not upon the order of your going,[51]
But go at once.

LENNOX.   Good night, and better health   120
Attend his Majesty!

LADY MACBETH.   A kind good night to all!

[*Exeunt all but* MACBETH *and* LADY MACBETH.]

MACBETH. It will have blood, they say; blood will have
   blood.
Stones have been known to move and trees to speak;
Augures and understood relations have
By maggot-pies and choughs and rooks brought forth[52]   125
The secret'st man of blood. What is the night?

LADY MACBETH. Almost at odds with morning, which is
   which.

MACBETH. How say'st thou, that Macduff denies his
   person[53]
At our great bidding?

LADY MACBETH.   Did you send to him, sir?

MACBETH. I hear it by the way, but I will send.   130
There's not a one of them but in his house
I keep a servant fee'd.[54] I will tomorrow,
And betimes I will, to the weird sisters.
More shall they speak; for now I am bent to know,
By the worst means, the worst. For mine own good   135
All causes shall give way. I am in blood

50. **disposition that I owe.** Macbeth is bewildered by this change in his brave nature.

51. **order of your going.** Do not wait upon the order of rank for leaving. Ordinarily the highest noble would leave first.

52. **augures** (ô′gyərz). Auguries, predictions of soothsayers have revealed murders by means of birds—magpies and crows.

53. Macduff refuses Macbeth's calls.

54. **fee'd,** paid by Macbeth as a spy.

Stepped in so far that, should I wade no more,
Returning were as tedious as go o'er.
Strange things I have in head, that will to hand,
Which must be acted ere they may be scanned.[55]
LADY MACBETH. You lack the season of all natures, sleep.
MACBETH. Come, we'll to sleep. My strange and self-abuse
Is the initiate fear that wants hard use.
We are yet but young in deed.

[*Exeunt.*]

140

55. **scanned.** Macbeth considers strange things that must be acted on before they are carefully thought out.

Scene 5

A heath.
Thunder. The THREE WITCHES *enter, meeting* HECATE.

FIRST WITCH. Why, how now, Hecate? You look angerly.
HECATE. Have I not reason, beldams[56] as you are,
Saucy and overbold? How did you dare
To trade and traffic with Macbeth
In riddles and affairs of death;
And I, the mistress of your charms,
The close contriver of all harms,
Was never called to bear my part,
Or show the glory of our art?
And, which is worse, all you have done
Hath been but for a wayward son,
Spiteful and wrathful, who, as others do,
Loves for his own ends, not for you.
But make amends now. Get you gone,
And at the pit of Acheron[57]
Meet me i' the morning. Thither he
Will come to know his destiny.
Your vessels and your spells provide,
Your charms and everything beside.
I am for the air; this night I'll spend
Unto a dismal and a fatal end.
Great business must be wrought ere noon.
Upon the corner of the moon
There hangs a vaporous drop profound.[58]
I'll catch it ere it comes to ground;
And that distilled by magic sleights,
Shall raise such artificial sprites
As by the strength of their illusion
Shall draw him on to his confusion.

5

10

15

20

25

56. **beldams** (bel′ dəmz), old hags.

57. **Acheron** (ak′ ə ron′), river leading to the classical underworld of the dead, Hades; **the pit** probably refers to a Scottish cavern.

58. **drop profound.** According to an ancient magic the moon gave off drops of venom under certain enchantments.

He shall spurn fate, scorn death, and bear   30
His hopes 'bove wisdom, grace, and fear;
And you all know security
Is mortals' chiefest enemy.

[*Music and a song within: "Come away, come away," etc.*]

Hark! I am called; my little spirit, see,
Sits in a foggy cloud, and stays for me.   35

[*Exit.*]

FIRST WITCH. Come, let's make haste. She'll soon be back
   again.

[*Exeunt.*]

Scene 6

Forres. The Palace.
Enter LENNOX *and another* LORD.

LENNOX. My former speeches have but hit your
      thoughts,
   Which can interpret farther. Only I say
   Things have been strangely borne. The gracious
      Duncan
   Was pitied of Macbeth; marry, he was dead.⁵⁹
   And the right-valiant Banquo walked too late;   5
   Whom, you may say, if't please you, Fleance killed,
   For Fleance fled. Men must not walk too late.
   Who cannot want the thought⁶⁰ how monstrous
   It was for Malcolm and for Donalbain
   To kill their gracious father? Damnèd fact!   10
   How it did grieve Macbeth! Did he not straight,
   In pious rage, the two delinquents tear,
   That were the slaves of drink and thralls of sleep?
   Was not that nobly done? Ay, and wisely too;
   For 'twould have angered any heart alive   15
   To hear the men deny't. So that, I say,
   He has borne all things well; and I do think
   That, had he Duncan's sons under his key—
   As, an't please heaven, he shall not—they should find
   What 'twere to kill a father; so should Fleance.   20
   But, peace! for from broad words,⁶¹ and 'cause he
      failed
   His presence at the tyrant's feast, I hear
   Macduff lives in disgrace. Sir, can you tell

59. **. . . was dead.** Macbeth pitied Duncan after he was dead.

60. **Who cannot want the thought.** Who could keep from thinking?

61. **broad words,** outspoken statements against Macbeth.

Where he bestows himself?

LORD. The son of Duncan,
From whom this tyrant holds[62] the due of birth,   25   62. **holds,** withholds.
Lives in the English court, and is received
Of the most pious Edward with such grace
That the malevolence of fortune nothing
Takes from his high respect. Thither Macduff
Is gone to pray the holy king, upon his aid   30
To wake Northumberland and warlike Siward;[63]   63. **Siward,** the earl of North-
That by the help of these—with Him above   umberland.
To ratify the work—we may again
Give to our tables meat, sleep to our nights,
Free from our feasts and banquets bloody knives,   35
Do faithful homage and receive free honors—
All which we pine for now. And this report
Hath so exasperate the King that he
Prepares for some attempt of war.

LENNOX. Sent he to Macduff?

LORD. He did; and with an absolute "Sir, not I!"   40
The cloudy[64] messenger turns me his back,   64. **cloudy,** gloomy.
And hums, as who should say, "You'll rue the time
That clogs me with this answer."[65]   65. The messenger mutters as if
                                                               protesting having to carry the
LENNOX. And that well might   unwelcome news.
Advise him to a caution to hold what distance
His wisdom can provide. Some holy angel   45
Fly to the court of England and unfold
His message ere he come, that a swift blessing
May soon return to this our suffering country
Under a hand accursed!

LORD. I'll send my prayers with him.

[*Exeunt.*]

FOR UNDERSTANDING

Mounting Consequences

1. What is the difference between Macbeth's behavior in the murder of Duncan and his behavior in the murder of Banquo? What changes in the character of Macbeth does this show?
2. What signs are there that Macbeth's conscience is troubling him?
3. How has the relationship of Macbeth and Lady Macbeth changed?
4. What unforeseen consequences have followed the choices Macbeth has made?
5. What signs are there that Macbeth's character and personality are beginning to crumble?

FOR INTERPRETATION

1. Act III, like Act II, ends with a scene that is partly informational and partly choric. What purpose do you see in Lennox's opening speech?
2. The metaphoric quality of Shakespeare's poetry in Acts II and III has been widely admired. With each of the following examples, explain the literal meaning of the passage, then describe its dramatic purpose or function within the scene where it occurs.
a. Sleep that knits up the raveled sleave of care. . . .
b. The wine of life is drawn. . . .
c. There's daggers in men's smiles. . . .

d. We have scotched the snake, not killed it.
e. Scarf up the tender eye of pitiful day. . . .
f. . . . wicked dreams abuse/The curtained sleep.
g. . . . destroy your sight/With a new Gorgon.

LANGUAGE AND VOCABULARY

1. Find the following phrases and clauses in Acts II and III of *Macbeth* and unlock them by means of context clues.
a. . . . the *surfeited* grooms/Do mock their charge with snores.
b. This my hand will rather/The *multitudinous* seas incarnadine. . . .
c. Those that Macbeth hath slain. . . . They were *suborned.*
d. God's *benison* go with you. . . .
e. Upon my head they placed a fruitless crown/And put a barren *scepter* in my gripe. . . .
f. . . . Then be thou *jocund.*
g. If thou didst it,/Thou art the *nonpareil.*
2. What did the following italicized words mean in Shakespeare's day?

my bosom *franchised*

sensible to feeling as to sight
do mock their *charge*
the night has been *unruly*
of dire *combustion*

3. In Macbeth's soliloquy, Act II, Scene 1, beginning "Is this a dagger that I see before me?" the obsolete Middle English word, *dudgeon,* is of semantic interest.

Originally dudgeon was the name of the kind of wood which woodturners and cutlers used for the haft (handle) of a dagger. In time, the haft itself was called the dudgeon. It is thus that Shakespeare uses it: "on thy blade and dudgeon gouts (drops) of blood."

Is the above movement an example of the broadening or the narrowing of the meaning of a word?
4. In reconstructing the pronunciation of the English of Shakespeare's day, scholars have concluded that words like *bake* and *take,* now pronounced with ā, were then pronounced *back* and *tack,* with a sustained short a (ă) sound.

In keeping with the above semantic trend, how did Elizabethans pronounce the following: fade, made, hate, rate?

Act IV
Scene 1

A cavern. In the middle, a boiling cauldron.
Thunder. Enter the THREE WITCHES.

FIRST WITCH. Thrice the brinded cat[1] hath mewed.
SECOND WITCH. Thrice, and once the hedge-pig whined.
THIRD WITCH. Harpier[2] cries, " 'Tis time, 'tis time."
FIRST WITCH. Round about the cauldron go;
In the poisoned entrails throw.
Toad, that under cold stone
Days and nights has thirty-one
Swelter'd venom sleeping got,
Boil thou first i' the charmèd pot.
ALL. Double, double, toil and trouble;
Fire burn and cauldron bubble.
SECOND WITCH. Fillet of a fenny snake,
In the cauldron boil and bake;

1. **brinded cat** (brind' əd), streaked, another of the animals like Graymalkin who are associates of the witches.

5

2. **Harpier** (här' pē ər), another of the witches' demons.

10

Eye of newt and toe of frog,
Wool of bat and tongue of dog,   15
Adder's fork and blind-worm's sting,
Lizard's leg and howlet's wing
For a charm of powerful trouble,
Like a hell-broth boil and bubble.
ALL. Double, double, toil and trouble;   20
Fire burn, and cauldron bubble.
THIRD WITCH. Scale of dragon, tooth of wolf,
Witches' mummy, maw and gulf
Of the ravined salt-sea shark,
Root of hemlock digged i' the dark,   25
Liver of blaspheming Jew,
Gall of goat and slips of yew
Slivered in the moon's eclipse,
Nose of Turk and Tartar's lips,
Finger of birth-strangled babe   30
Ditch-delivered by a drab,
Make the gruel thick and slab.
Add thereto a tiger's chaudron,[3]
For the ingredients of our cauldron.
ALL. Double, double, toil and trouble;   35
Fire burn and cauldron bubble.
SECOND WITCH. Cool it with a baboon's blood,
Then the charm is firm and good.

[*Enter* HECATE.]

HECATE. O, well done! I commend your pains,
And every one shall share i' the gains.   40
And now about the cauldron sing,
Like elves and fairies in a ring,
Enchanting all that you put in.

[*Music and a song "Black spirit," etc.* HECATE *retires.*]

SECOND WITCH. By the pricking of my thumbs,
Something wicked this way comes.   45
        Open locks,
        Whoever knocks!

[*Enter* MACBETH.]

MACBETH. How now, you secret, black, and midnight
    hags!
What is't you do?
ALL.   A deed without a name.
MACBETH. I conjure you, by that which you profess,   50
Howe'er you come to know it, answer me.
Though you untie the winds and let them fight

3. **chaudron** (chôd′ rən),
entrails.

Against the churches; though the yesty waves
Confound and swallow navigation up;
Though bladed corn be lodged and trees blown down; 55
Though castles topple on their warders' heads;
Though palaces and pyramids do slope
Their heads to their foundations; though the treasure
Of nature's germens⁴ tumble all together,
Even till destruction sicken; answer me 60
To what I ask you.

FIRST WITCH.   Speak.

SECOND WITCH.   Demand.

THIRD WITCH.   We'll answer.

FIRST WITCH. Say, if thou'dst rather hear it from our
    mouths,
Or from our masters'?

MACBETH.   Call 'em! Let me see 'em.

FIRST WITCH. Pour in sow's blood, that hath eaten
Her nine farrow; grease that's sweaten 65
From the murderer's gibbet throw
Into the flame.

ALL.   Come, high or low;
Thyself and office deftly show!

[*Thunder. First Apparition: an Armed Head.*]

MACBETH. Tell me, thou unknown power—

FIRST WITCH.   He knows thy thought.
Hear his speech, but say thou naught. 70

FIRST APPARITION. Macbeth! Macbeth! Macbeth! Beware
    Macduff;
Beware the thane of Fife. Dismiss me. Enough.

[*Descends.*]

MACBETH. Whate'er thou art, for thy good caution
    thanks;
Thou hast harped⁵ my fear aright. But one word
    more—

FIRST WITCH. He will not be commanded. Here's
    another, 75
More potent than the first.

[*Thunder. Second Apparition: a Bloody Child.*]

SECOND APPARITION. Macbeth! Macbeth! Macbeth!

MACBETH. Had I three ears, I'ld hear thee.

SECOND APPARITION. Be bloody, bold and resolute;
    laugh to scorn.
The power of man, for none of woman born 80
Shall harm Macbeth.

4. **germens** (jėr′ mᵊnz), all the
seeds of the future.

5. **harped,** sounded the very
chord of my fears.

[*Descends.*]

MACBETH. Then live, Macduff; what need I fear of thee?
But yet I'll make assurance double sure
And take a bond of fate. Thou shalt not live;
That I may tell pale-hearted fear it lies,   85
And sleep in spite of thunder.

[*Thunder. Third Apparition: a Child crowned, with a tree in his hand.*]

                         What is this,
That rises like the issue of a king,
And wears upon his baby-brow the round
And top of sovereignty?
ALL.   Listen, but speak not to't.
THIRD APPARITION. Be lion-mettled, proud, and take no
   care   90
Who chafes, who frets, or where conspirers are.
Macbeth shall never vanquished be until
Great Birnam wood to high Dunsinane hill
Shall come against him.

[*Descends.*]

MACBETH.   That will never be.
Who can impress[6] the forest, bid the tree   95
Unfix his earth-bound root? Sweet bodements![7] good!
Rebellion's head, rise never, till the wood
Of Birnam rise, and our high-placed Macbeth
Shall live the lease of nature,[8] pay his breath
To time and mortal custom. Yet my heart   100
Throbs to know one thing. Tell me, if your art
Can tell so much—shall Banquo's issue ever
Reign in this kingdom?
ALL.   Seek to know no more.
MACBETH. I will be satisfied. Deny me this,
And an eternal curse fall on you! Let me know.   105
Why sinks that cauldron? and what noise is this?

[*Hautboys.*]

FIRST WITCH. Show!
SECOND WITCH. Show!
THIRD WITCH. Show!
ALL. Show his eyes, and grieve his heart;   110
Come like shadows, so depart!

[*A show of eight Kings, the last with a glass in his hand;*
BANQUO'S GHOST *following.*]

6. **impress,** forcibly enlist.
7. **bodements** (bōd′ mənts), prophecies.

8. **lease of nature,** a full lifetime ending with a natural death.

MACBETH. Thou art too like the spirit of Banquo. Down!
  Thy crown does sear mine eyeballs. And thy hair,
  Thou other gold-bound brow, is like the first.
  A third is like the former. Filthy hags!   **115**
  Why do you show me this? A fourth! Start, eyes!
  What, will the line stretch out to the crack of doom?
  Another yet! A seventh! I'll see no more.
  And yet the eighth appears,[9] who bears a glass
  Which shows me many more; and some I see   **120**
  That twofold balls and treble[10] scepters carry.
  Horrible sight! Now I see 'tis true;
  For the blood-boltered Banquo smiles upon me
  And points at them for his.[11] What? Is this so?

[*Apparitions vanish.*]

FIRST WITCH. Ay, sir, all this is so. But why   **125**
  Stands Macbeth thus amazedly?
  Come, sisters, cheer we up his sprites,
  And show the best of our delights.
  I'll charm the air to give a sound
  While you perform your antic round,   **130**
  That this great king may kindly say
  Our duties did his welcome pay.

[*Music. The* WITCHES *dance, and vanish.*]

MACBETH. Where are they? Gone? Let this pernicious
    hour
  Stand aye accursèd in the calendar!
  Come in, without there!

[*Enter* LENNOX.]

LENNOX.   What's your grace's will?   **135**
MACBETH. Saw you the weird sisters?
LENNOX.   No, my lord.
MACBETH. Came they not by you?
LENNOX.   No, indeed, my lord.
MACBETH. Infected be the air whereon they ride,
  And damned all those that trust them! I did hear
  The galloping of horse. Who was't came by?   **140**
LENNOX. 'Tis two or three, my lord, that bring you word
  Macduff is fled to England.
MACBETH.   Fled to England?
LENNOX. Ay, my good lord.
MACBETH. *(Aside)* Time, thou anticipatest my dread
    exploits.
  The flighty purpose never is o'ertook   **145**

9. **eighth appears,** the eight kings of the Stuart dynasty, Robert II, III, and six Jameses to James I (1604), the first Stuart king to rule England.
10. **twofold and treble,** symbols of rule over increasing kingdoms.
11. The murdered Banquo is the ancestor of the royal Stuart line.

Unless the deed go with it. From this moment
The very firstlings of my heart shall be
The firstlings of my hand. And even now,
To crown my thoughts with acts, be it thought and
   done.
The castle of Macduff I will surprise;   150
Seize upon Fife; give to the edge o' the sword
His wife, his babes, and all unfortunate souls
That trace him in his line. No boasting like a fool;
This deed I'll do before this purpose cool.
But no more sights!—Where are these gentlemen?[12]   155
Come, bring me where they are.

[*Exeunt.*]

12. **Where are these gentlemen?,** those who bring news of Macduff's escape.

Scene 2

Fife. MACDUFF'S *Castle.*
Enter LADY MACDUFF, *her* SON, *and* ROSS.

LADY MACDUFF. What had he done, to make him fly the
   land?
ROSS. You must have patience, madam.
LADY MACDUFF.   He had none.
  His flight was madness. When our actions do not,
  Our fears do make us traitors.
ROSS.   You know not
  Whether it was his wisdom or his fear.   5
LADY MACDUFF. Wisdom? To leave his wife, to leave his
   babes,
  His mansion and his titles, in a place
  From whence himself does fly? He loves us not;
  He wants the natural touch. For the poor wren,
  The most diminutive of birds, will fight,   10
  Her young ones in her nest, against the owl.
  All is the fear and nothing is the love;
  As little is the wisdom, where the flight
  So runs against all reason.
ROSS.   My dearest coz,
  I pray you school yourself. But, for your husband,   15
  He is noble, wise, judicious, and best knows
  The fits o' the season. I dare not speak much
    further;
  But cruel are the times, when we are traitors
  And do not know ourselves; when we hold rumor[13]
  From what we fear, yet know not what we fear,   20

13. **hold rumor,** believe in every fear.

Royal Shakespeare Theatre, 1962
Stratford-Upon-Avon
Photo: Holte Photographers Ltd.

But float upon a wild and violent sea
Each way and move. I take my leave of you.
Shall not be long but I'll be here again.
Things at the worst will cease, or else climb upward
To what they were before. My pretty cousin,[14]   25
Blessing upon us!

14. **cousin.** Ross has turned from Lady Macduff to her son.

LADY MACDUFF. Fathered he is, and yet he's fatherless.

ROSS. I am so much a fool, should I stay longer,
  It would be my disgrace and your discomfort.
  I take my leave at once.

  [*Exit.*]

LADY MACDUFF.   Sirrah, your father's dead;   30
  And what will you do now? How will you live?

SON. As birds do, mother.

LADY MACDUFF.   What, with worms and flies?

SON. With what I get, I mean; and so do they.

LADY MACDUFF. Poor bird! thou'ldst never fear the net
    nor lime,
  The pitfall nor the gin.[15]   35

SON. Why should I, mother? Poor birds they are not set
    for.
  My father is not dead, for all your saying.

LADY MACDUFF. Yes, he is dead. How wilt thou do for a
    father?

SON. Nay, how will you do for a husband?

LADY MACDUFF. Why, I can buy me twenty at any
    market.   40

SON. Then you'll buy 'em to sell again.

LADY MACDUFF. Thou speak'st with all thy wit; and yet, i'
    faith,
  With wit enough for thee.

SON. Was my father a traitor, mother?

LADY MACDUFF. Ay, that he was!   45

SON. What is a traitor?

LADY MACDUFF. Why, one that swears, and lies.

SON. And be all traitors that do so?

LADY MACDUFF. Every one that does so is a traitor, and
    must be hanged.   50

SON. And must they all be hanged that swear and lie?

LADY MACDUFF. Every one.

SON. Who must hang them?

LADY MACDUFF. Why, the honest men.

SON. Then the liars and swearers are fools; for there are   55
    liars and swearers enow to beat the honest men and
    hang up them.

LADY MACDUFF. Now, God help thee, poor monkey! But
    how wilt thou do for a father?

SON. If he were dead, you'ld weep for him. If you would   60
    not, it were a good sign that I should quickly have a
    new father.

LADY MACDUFF. Poor prattler, how thou talk'st!

  [*Enter a* MESSENGER.]

15. **net nor lime . . . gin** (jin),
all traps: nets, sticky birdlime,
and other snares.

MESSENGER. Bless you, fair dame! I am not to you
    known,
Though in your state of honor I am perfect.[16]
I doubt[17] some danger does approach you nearly.
If you will take a homely[18] man's advice,
Be not found here. Hence, with your little ones.
To fright you thus, methinks I am too savage;
To do worse to you were fell cruelty,
Which is too nigh your person. Heaven preserve you!
I dare abide no longer.

[*Exit.*]

LADY MACDUFF.   Whither should I fly?
I have done no harm. But I remember now
I am in this earthly world, where to do harm
Is often laudable, to do good sometime
Accounted dangerous folly. Why then, alas,
Do I put up that womanly defense,
To say I have done no harm?—What are these
    faces?

[*Enter* MURDERERS.]

FIRST MURDERER. Where is your husband?
LADY MACDUFF. I hope, in no place so unsanctified
    Where such as thou mayst find him.
FIRST MURDERER.   He's a traitor.
SON. Thou liest, thou shag-eared villain!
FIRST MURDERER.   What, you egg!

[*Stabbing him.*]

    Young fry of treachery!
SON.   He has killed me, mother.
    Run away, I pray you!

[*Dies.*]
[*Exit* LADY MACDUFF, *crying "Murder!"* MURDERERS
follow her.]

65

16. **am perfect.** The messenger
says, "Though you don't know
me I know you well, honorable
lady."
17. **doubt,** fear.
18. **homely,** simple, of no rank.

70

75

80

Scene 3

England. Before the King's Palace.
Enter MALCOLM *and* MACDUFF.

MALCOLM. Let us seek out some desolate shade, and
    there
Weep our sad bosoms empty.

MACDUFF.   Let us rather
Hold fast the mortal sword and, like good men,
Bestride our downfall'n birthdom.[19] Each new morn
New widows howl, new orphans cry, new sorrows
Strike heaven on the face, that it resounds
As if it felt with Scotland and yelled out
Like syllable of dolor.[20]

MALCOLM.   What I believe, I'll wail;
What know, believe; and what I can redress,
As I shall find the time to friend, I will.
What you have spoke, it may be so perchance.
This tyrant, whose sole name blisters our tongues,
Was once thought honest; you have loved him well;
He hath not touched you yet. I am young; but something
You may deserve of him through me, and wisdom
To offer up a weak, poor, innocent lamb
T'appease an angry god.

MACDUFF. I am not treacherous.

MALCOLM.   But Macbeth is.
A good and virtuous nature may recoil
In an imperial charge.[21] But I shall crave your pardon;
That which you are, my thoughts cannot transpose.
Angels are bright still, though the brightest fell.[22]
Though all things foul would wear the brows of grace,
Yet grace must still look so.

MACDUFF.   I have lost my hopes.

MALCOLM. Perchance even there where I did find my doubts.
Why in that rawness left you wife and child,
Those precious motives, those strong knots of love,
Without leave-taking? I pray you,
Let not my jealousies be your dishonors,
But mine own safeties.[23] You may be rightly just,
Whatever I shall think.

MACDUFF.   Bleed, bleed, poor country!
Great tyranny, lay thou thy basis sure,
For goodness dare not check thee. Wear thou thy wrongs;
The title is affeered.[24] Fare thee well, lord.
I would not be the villain that thou think'st
For the whole space that's in the tyrant's grasp
And the rich East to boot.

MALCOLM.   Be not offended.
I speak not as in absolute fear of you.
I think our country sinks beneath the yoke;
It weeps, it bleeds, and each new day a gash

5

10

15

20

25

30

35

40

19. **birthdom,** native land.

20. **dolor** (dol′ ər), sorrow; heaven itself cries out like suffering Scotland.

21. **imperial charge,** king's order; Malcolm cannot quite trust Macduff and feels he may be an agent for Macbeth.
22. **brightest fell.** The reference is to the fall of the angel Lucifer; Macduff may yet be honest and loyal though his brilliant chieftain Macbeth proved corrupt.

23. **safeties.** Malcolm apologizes for his suspicions and reminds Macduff that it is his life that is at stake.

24. **is affeered.** Even good people fear to challenge Macbeth's title; therefore it is confirmed.

Is added to her wounds. I think withal
There would be hands uplifted in my right;
And here from gracious England have I offer
Of goodly thousands. But, for all this,
When I shall tread upon the tyrant's head   45
Or wear it on my sword, yet my poor country
Shall have more vices than it had before,
More suffer and more sundry ways than ever,
By him that shall succeed.
MACDUFF.   What should he be?
MALCOLM. It is myself I mean; in whom I know   50
All the particulars of vice so grafted
That, when they shall be opened, black Macbeth
Will seem as pure as snow, and the poor state
Esteem him as a lamb, being compared
With my confineless harms.
MACDUFF.   Not in the legions   55
Of horrid hell can come a devil more damned
In evils to top Macbeth.
MALCOLM.   I grant him bloody,
Luxurious, avaricious, false, deceitful,
Sudden, malicious, smacking of every sin
That has a name. But there's no bottom, none,   60
In my voluptuousness. Your wives, your daughters,
Your matrons and your maids, could not fill up
The cistern of my lust, and my desire
All continent impediments would o'erbear,
That did oppose my will. Better Macbeth   65
Than such an one to reign.
MACDUFF.   Boundless intemperance
In nature is a tyranny; it hath been
The untimely emptying of the happy throne,
And fall of many kings. But fear not yet
To take upon you what is yours. You may   70
Convey your pleasures in a spacious plenty,
And yet seem cold, the time you may so hoodwink.
We have willing dames enough; there cannot be
That vulture in you, to devour so many
As will to greatness dedicate themselves,   75
Finding it so inclined.
MALCOLM.   With this there grows
In my most ill-composed affection such
A stanchless avarice that, were I king,
I should cut off the nobles for their lands,
Desire his jewels, and this other's house;   80
And my more-having would be as a sauce
To make me hunger more, that I should forge

Quarrels unjust against the good and loyal,
Destroying them for wealth.
MACDUFF.   This avarice
Sticks deeper, grows with more pernicious root   85
Than summer-seeming lust, and it hath been
The sword of our slain kings. Yet do not fear;
Scotland hath foisons[25] to fill up your will
Of your mere own. All these are portable,
With other graces weighed.[26]   90
MALCOLM. But I have none. The king-becoming graces,
As justice, verity, temperance, stableness,
Bounty, perseverance, mercy, lowliness,
Devotion, patience, courage, fortitude,
I have no relish of them, but abound   95
In the division of each several crime,
Acting it many ways. Nay, had I power, I should
Pour the sweet milk of concord into hell,
Uproar the universal peace, confound
All unity on earth.
MACDUFF.   O Scotland, Scotland!   100
MALCOLM. If such a one be fit to govern, speak.
I am as I have spoken.
MACDUFF.   Fit to govern?
No, not to live. O nation miserable!
With an untitled tyrant bloody-sceptered,
When shalt thou see thy wholesome days again,   105
Since that the truest issue of thy throne
By his own interdiction stands accursed,
And does blaspheme his breed? Thy royal father
Was a most sainted king; the queen that bore thee,
Oft'ner upon her knees than on her feet,   110
Died every day she lived.[27] Fare thee well!
These evils thou repeat'st upon thyself
Have banished me from Scotland. O my breast,
Thy hope ends here!
MALCOLM.   Macduff, this noble passion,
Child of integrity, hath from my soul   115
Wiped the black scruples, reconciled my thoughts
To thy good truth and honor. Devilish Macbeth
By many of these trains hath sought to win me
Into his power; and modest wisdom plucks me
From over-credulous haste; but God above   120
Deal between thee and me! for even now
I put myself to thy direction, and
Unspeak mine own detraction, here abjure
The taints and blames I laid upon myself,
For strangers to my nature. I am yet   125

25. **foisons** (foi′ zənz), great abundance.
26. **graces weighed.** Things are bearable considering your great virtues.

27. **died every day she lived,** lived with such religious devotion as to consider death daily.

Unknown to woman, never was forsworn,
Scarcely have coveted what was mine own,
At no time broke my faith, would not betray
The devil to his fellow, and delight
No less in truth than life. My first false speaking   130
Was this upon myself. What I am truly,
Is thine and my poor country's to command;
Whither indeed, before thy here-approach,
Old Siward, with ten thousand warlike men
Already at a point, was setting forth.   135
Now we'll together, and the chance of goodness
Be like our warranted quarrel! Why are you silent?
MACDUFF. Such welcome and unwelcome things at once
  'Tis hard to reconcile.

  [*Enter a* DOCTOR.]

MALCOLM. Well, more anon. Comes the King forth, I
  pray you?   140
DOCTOR. Ay, sir; there are a crew of wretched souls
  That stay his cure. Their malady convinces
  The great assay of art;²⁸ but at his touch,
  Such sanctity hath heaven given his hand,
  They presently amend.
MALCOLM.   I thank you, doctor.   145

  [*Exit* DOCTOR.]

MACDUFF. What's the disease he means?
MALCOLM.   'Tis called the evil:
  A most miraculous work in this good King,
  Which often, since my here-remain in England,
  I have seen him do. How he solicits heaven,
  Himself best knows; but strangely-visited people,   150
  All swoln and ulcerous, pitiful to the eye,
  The mere despair of surgery, he cures,
  Hanging a golden stamp about their necks,
  Put on with holy prayers; and 'tis spoken,
  To the succeeding royalty he leaves   155
  The healing benediction. With this strange virtue
  He hath a heavenly gift of prophecy,
  And sundry blessings hang about his throne
  That speak him full of grace.

  [*Enter* ROSS.]

MACDUFF.   See, who comes here.
MALCOLM. My countryman; but yet I know him not.   160
MACDUFF. My ever gentle cousin, welcome hither.

28. The reference is to the legendary cures wrought by King Edward. By touching diseased persons he was claimed to have wrought cures that baffled medical science.

MALCOLM. I know him now. Good God, betimes remove
The means that make us strangers![29]

29. Malcolm prays for a change that will let him go home and be again familiar with his fellow Scots.

ROSS.   Sir, amen.

MACDUFF. Stands Scotland where it did?

ROSS.   Alas, poor country!
Almost afraid to know itself! It cannot   165
Be called our mother, but our grave; where nothing,
But who knows nothing, is once seen to smile;
Where signs and groans and shrieks that rend the air,
Are made, not marked; where violent sorrow seems
A modern ecstasy. The dead man's knell   170
Is there scarce asked for who; and good men's lives
Expire before the flowers in their caps,
Dying or ere they sicken.

MACDUFF.   O, relation
Too nice, and yet too true!

MALCOLM.   What's the newest grief?

ROSS. That of an hour's age doth hiss the speaker;   175
Each minute teems a new one.

MACDUFF.   How does my wife?

ROSS. Why, well.

MACDUFF.   And all my children?

ROSS.   Well too.

MACDUFF. The tyrant has not battered at their peace?

ROSS. No, they were well at peace when I did leave 'em.

MACDUFF. Be not a niggard of your speech. How goes't?   180

ROSS. When I came hither to transport the tidings,
Which I have heavily borne, there ran a rumor
Of many worthy fellows that were out;
Which was to my belief witnessed the rather,
For that I saw the tyrant's power afoot.   185
Now is the time of help. Your eye in Scotland
Would create soldiers, make our women fight,
To doff their dire distresses.

MALCOLM.   Be't their comfort
We are coming thither. Gracious England hath
Lent us good Siward and ten thousand men;   190
An older and a better soldier none
That Christendom gives out.

ROSS.   Would I could answer
This comfort with the like! But I have words
That would be howled out in the desert air,
Where hearing should not latch them.

MACDUFF.   What concern they?   195
The general cause? or is it a fee-grief[30]
Due to some single breast?

ROSS.   No mind that's honest

30. **fee-grief,** a personal sorrow.

But in it shares some woe, though the main part
Pertains to you alone.

MACDUFF.   If it be mine,
Keep it not from me, quickly let me have it.   **200**

ROSS. Let not your ears despise my tongue for ever,
Which shall possess them with the heaviest sound
That ever yet they heard.

MACDUFF.   Hum! I guess at it.

ROSS. Your castle is surprised; your wife and babes
Savagely slaughtered. To relate the manner   **205**
Were, on the quarry of these murdered deer,
To add the death of you.

MALCOLM.   Merciful heaven!
What, man! ne'er pull your hat upon your brows.
Give sorrow words. The grief that does not speak
Whispers the o'erfraught heart and bids it break.   **210**

MACDUFF. My children too?

ROSS.   Wife, children, servants, all
That could be found.

MACDUFF.   And I must be from thence?
My wife killed too?

ROSS.   I have said.

MALCOLM.   Be comforted.
Let's make us medicines of our great revenge,
To cure this deadly grief.   **215**

MACDUFF. He has no children.[31] All my pretty ones?
Did you say all? O hell-kite! All?
What, all my pretty chickens and their dam
At one fell swoop?

MALCOLM. Dispute it like a man.

MACDUFF.   I shall do so;   **220**
But I must also feel it as a man.
I cannot but remember such things were
That were most precious to me. Did heaven look on
And would not take their part? Sinful Macduff,
They were all struck for thee! Naught that I am,   **225**
Not for their own demerits, but for mine,
Fell slaughter on their souls. Heaven rest them now!

MALCOLM. Be this the whetstone[32] of your sword. Let
    grief
Convert to anger; blunt not the heart, enrage it.

MACDUFF. O, I could play the woman with mine eyes,
And braggart with my tongue! But, gentle heavens,   **230**
Cut short all intermission. Front to front
Bring thou this fiend of Scotland and myself.
Within my sword's length set him; if he 'scape,
Heaven forgive him too!

31. **no children.** Macbeth has no children to let him feel the enormity of this crime.

32. **whetstone,** stone on which to sharpen your sword: your will to act.

MALCOLM. This tune goes manly. 235
Come, go we to the King. Our power is ready;
Our lack is nothing but our leave. Macbeth
Is ripe for shaking, and the powers above
Put on their instruments. Receive what cheer you may;
The night is long that never finds the day. 240

[*Exeunt.*]

FOR UNDERSTANDING

Murder Compounded

1. What are the three new prophecies the witches make to Macbeth? What questions do they refuse to answer? What is the meaning of the three apparitions Macbeth sees in the witches' cave?
2. How does the murder of Macduff's family differ from the murder of Duncan? From the murder of Banquo?
3. What has happened to the Kingdom of Scotland since Macbeth took the crown?

4. Why does Malcolm lie about himself to Macduff?

FOR INTERPRETATION

1. In this act, is Macbeth acting with greater decision than in Act I? Is he more or less in control of himself and of events?
2. Explain these lines:
"From this moment
The very firstlings of my heart shall be
The firstlings of my hand."

Act V
Scene 1

Dunsinane. Ante-room in the castle.
Enter a DOCTOR OF PHYSIC *and a*
WAITING-GENTLEWOMAN.

DOCTOR. I have two nights watched with you, but can perceive no truth in your report. When was it she last walked?
GENTLEWOMAN. Since his Majesty went into the field,[1] I have seen her rise from her bed, throw her nightgown upon her, unlock her closet, take forth paper, fold it, write upon't, read it, afterwards seal it, and again return to bed; yet all this while in a most fast sleep. 5
DOCTOR. A great perturbation in nature, to receive at once the benefit of sleep and do the effects of watching! In this slumbery agitation, besides her walking and other actual performances, what, at any time, have you heard her say? 10
GENTLEWOMAN. That, sir, which I will not report after her.
DOCTOR. You may to me, and 'tis most meet you should. 15

1. **into the field,** since Macbeth has been fighting his various enemies.

GENTLEWOMAN. Neither to you nor any one, having no witness to confirm my speech.

[*Enter* LADY MACBETH, *with a lighted taper.*]

Lo, you, here she comes! This is her very guise,[2] and, upon my life, fast asleep! Observe her; stand close. 20

DOCTOR. How came she by that light?

GENTLEWOMAN. Why, it stood by her. She has light by her continually; 'tis her command.

DOCTOR. You see, her eyes are open.

GENTLEWOMAN. Ay, but their sense is shut. 25

DOCTOR. What is it she does now? Look, how she rubs her hands.

GENTLEWOMAN. It is an accustomed action with her, to seem thus washing her hands. I have known her continue in this a quarter of an hour. 30

LADY MACBETH. Yet here's a spot.

DOCTOR. Hark! she speaks. I will set down what comes from her, to satisfy my remembrance the more strongly.

LADY MACBETH. Out, damned spot! out, I say! One; two: 35 why, then 'tis time to do't. Hell is murky. Fie, my lord, fie! a soldier, and afeard? What need we fear who knows it, when none can call our power to account? Yet who would have thought the old man to have had so much blood in him? 40

DOCTOR. Do you mark that?

LADY MACBETH. The thane of Fife had a wife. Where is she now? What, will these hands ne'er be clean? No more o' that, my lord, no more o' that. You mar all with this starting. 45

DOCTOR. Go to, go to! You have known what you should not.

GENTLEWOMAN. She has spoke what she should not, I am sure of that. Heaven knows what she has known.

LADY MACBETH. Here's the smell of the blood still. All 50 the perfumes of Arabia will not sweeten this little hand. Oh, oh, oh!

DOCTOR. What a sigh is there! The heart is sorely charged.

GENTLEWOMAN. I would not have such a heart in my bosom for the dignity of the whole body. 55

DOCTOR. Well, well, well,—

GENTLEWOMAN. Pray God it be, sir.

DOCTOR. This disease is beyond my practice. Yet I have known those which have walked in their sleep who have died holily in their beds. 60

LADY MACBETH. Wash your hands, put on your nightgown,

2. **her very guise,** her accustomed behavior.

look not so pale!—I tell you yet again, Banquo's
buried. He cannot come out on's grave.

DOCTOR. Even so?

LADY MACBETH. To bed, to bed! There's knocking at the   65
gate. Come, come, come, come, give me your hand.
What's done cannot be undone. To bed, to bed, to
bed!

[*Exit.*]

DOCTOR. Will she go now to bed?

GENTLEWOMAN. Directly.   70

DOCTOR. Foul whisperings are abroad. Unnatural deeds
Do breed unnatural troubles. Infected minds
To their deaf pillows will discharge their secrets.
More needs she the divine than the physician.
God, God forgive us all! Look after her;   75
Remove from her the means of all annoyance,[3]
And still keep eyes upon her. So good night.
My mind she has mated, and amazed my sight.
I think, but dare not speak.

GENTLEWOMAN.   Goodnight, good doctor.

[*Exeunt.*]

3. **annoyance,** harm.

Scene 2

The country near Dunsinane.
Drum and colors. Enter MENTEITH, CAITHNESS, ANGUS,
LENNOX *and Soldiers.*

MENTEITH. The English power is near, led on by
Malcolm,
His uncle Siward, and the good Macduff.
Revenges burn in them; for their dear causes
Would to the bleeding and the grim alarm
Excite the mortified man.[4]

ANGUS.   Near Birnam wood   5
Shall we well meet them; that way are they coming.

CAITHNESS. Who knows if Donalbain be with his brother?

LENNOX. For certain, sir, he is not. I have a file
Of all the gentry. There is Siward's son,
And many unrough youths that even now   10
Protest their first of manhood.

MENTEITH.   What does the tyrant?

CAITHNESS. Great Dunsinane he strongly fortifies.
Some say he's mad; others, that lesser hate him,

4. **mortified man.** Even a nearly dead or paralyzed person
would be roused by the cause
against Macbeth.

Do call it valiant fury; but, for certain,
He cannot buckle his distempered cause
Within the belt of rule.[5]

ANGUS.   Now does he feel
His secret murders sticking on his hands;
Now minutely revolts upbraid his faith-breach;[6]
Those he commands move only in command,
Nothing in love. Now does he feel his title
Hang loose about him, like a giant's robe
Upon a dwarfish thief.

MENTEITH.   Who then shall blame
His pestered senses to recoil and start,
When all that is within him does condemn
Itself for being there?

CAITHNESS.   Well, march we on,
To give obedience where 'tis truly owed.
Meet we the medicine of the sickly weal;
And with him pour we, in our country's purge,
Each drop of us.[7] Or so much as it needs
To dew the sovereign flower[8] and drown the weeds.

LENNOX. Make we our march towards Birnam.

[*Exeunt, marching.*]

Scene 3

Dunsinane. A room in the Castle.
Enter MACBETH, DOCTOR, *and Attendants.*

MACBETH. Bring me no more reports. Let them fly all!
Till Birnam wood remove to Dunsinane,
I cannot taint with fear. What's the boy Malcolm?
Was he not born of woman? The spirits that know
All mortal consequences have pronounced me thus:
"Fear not, Macbeth. No man that's born of woman
Shall e'er have power upon thee." Then fly, false
     thanes,
And mingle with the English epicures.[9]
The mind I sway by and the heart I bear
Shall never sag with doubt nor shake with fear.

[*Enter* SERVANT.]

The devil damn thee black, thou cream-faced loon!
Where got'st thou that goose look?

SERVANT. There is ten thousand—

MACBETH.   Geese, villain?

15

5. **. . . belt of rule.** Macbeth's cause is so diseased that he has no control over it.

6. **minutely . . . faith-breach.** Every minute nobles revolt against Macbeth reminding him of his own disloyalty.

20

25

7. **each drop of us.** Every drop of blood is pledged to Malcolm.
30
8. **sovereign flower,** Malcolm.

5

9. **epicures.** The Scots regarded the English as luxury lovers.
10

SERVANT.   Soldiers, sir.
MACBETH. Go prick thy face and over-red thy fear,
  Thou lily-livered boy. What soldiers, patch?[10]   15   10. **patch,** fool.
  Death of thy soul! Those linen cheeks of thine
  Are counselors to fear. What soldiers, whey-face?
SERVANT. The English force, so please you.
MACBETH. Take thy face hence.

  [*Exit* SERVANT.]

                                       Seyton!—I am sick at heart,
  When I behold—Seyton, I say!—This push   20
  Will cheer me ever, or disseat me now.
  I have lived long enough. My way of life
  Is fallen into the sere, the yellow leaf;
  And that which should accompany old age,
  As honor, love, obedience, troops of friends,   25
  I must not look to have; but, in their stead,
  Curses, not loud but deep, mouth-honor,[11] breath,   11. **mouth-honor,** lip service,
  Which the poor heart would fain deny, and dare not.   not allegiance of the heart.
  Seyton!

  [*Enter* SEYTON.]

SEYTON. What is your gracious pleasure?
MACBETH.   What news more?   30
SEYTON. All is confirmed, my lord, which was reported.
MACBETH. I'll fight, till from my bones my flesh be
    hacked.
  Give me my armor.
SEYTON.   'Tis not needed yet.
MACBETH. I'll put it on.
  Send out moe horses, skirr[12] the country round;   35   12. **skirr,** fly, scurry, scour for
  Hang those that talk of fear. Give me mine armor.   enemies.
  How does your patient, doctor?
DOCTOR.   Not so sick, my lord,
  As she is troubled with thick-coming fancies
  That keep her from her rest.
MACBETH.   Cure her of that.
  Canst thou not minister to a mind diseased,   40
  Pluck from the memory a rooted sorrow,
  Raze out the written troubles of the brain,
  And with some sweet oblivious antidote
  Cleanse the stuffed bosom of that perilous stuff
  Which weighs upon the heart?
DOCTOR.   Therein the patient   45
  Must minister to himself.
MACBETH. Throw physic to the dogs, I'll none of it!

Come, put mine armor on. Give me my staff.
Seyton, send out. Doctor, the thanes fly from me.
Come, sir, dispatch. If thou couldst, doctor, cast   50
The water of my land,[13] find her disease
And purge it to a sound and pristine health,
I would applaud thee to the very echo,
That should applaud again.—Pull't off, I say.—
What rhubarb, senna, or what purgative drug,   55
Would scour these English hence? Hear'st thou of
  them?

DOCTOR. Ay, my good lord. Your royal preparation
  Makes us hear something.

MACBETH.   Bring it after me.
  I will not be afraid of death and bane
  Till Birnam forest come to Dunsinane.   60

DOCTOR. *(Aside)* Were I from Dunsinane away and clear,
  Profit again should hardly draw me here.

  [*Exeunt.*]

13. **cast the water of my land,** diagnose Scotland's disease.

Scene 4

Country near Birnam Wood.
Drum and colors. Enter MALCOLM, SIWARD, *and his* SON,
MACDUFF, MENTEITH, CAITHNESS, ANGUS, LENNOX,
ROSS, *and Soldiers, marching.*

MALCOLM. Cousins, I hope the days are near at hand
  That chambers will be safe.

MENTEITH.   We doubt it nothing.

SIWARD. What wood is this before us?

MENTEITH.   The wood of Birnam.

MALCOLM. Let every soldier hew him down a bough
  And bear't before him. Thereby shall we shadow   5
  The numbers of our host, and make discovery
  Err in report of us.

SOLDIERS.   It shall be done.

SIWARD. We learn no other but the confident tyrant
  Keeps still in Dunsinane, and will endure
  Our setting down before't.

MALCOLM.   'Tis his main hope;   10
  For where there is advantage to be given,
  Both more and less have given him the revolt;
  And none serve with him but constrainèd things,
  Whose hearts are absent too.

MACDUFF.   Let our just censures

Attend the true event,[14] and put we on
Industrious soldiership.

SIWARD.   The time approaches
That will with due decision make us know
What we shall say we have, and what we owe.
Thoughts speculative their unsure hopes relate,[15]
But certain issue strokes must arbitrate;
Toward which advance the war.

[*Exeunt, marching.*]

Scene 5

Dunsinane. Within the Castle.
Enter MACBETH, SEYTON, *and Soldiers, with Drums and*
Colors.

MACBETH. Hang out our banners on the outward walls.
The cry is still, "They come!" Our castle's strength
Will laugh a siege to scorn. Here let them lie
Till famine and the ague eat them up.
Were they not forced[16] with those that should be ours,
We might have met them dareful, beard to beard,
And beat them backward home.

[*A cry of women, within.*]

                              What is that noise?
SEYTON. It is the cry of women, my good lord.

[*Exit.*]

MACBETH. I have almost forgot the taste of fears.
The time has been, my senses would have cooled
To hear a night-shriek, and my fell of hair
Would at a dismal treatise rouse and stir
As life were in't. I have supped full with horrors;
Direness, familiar to my slaughterous thoughts,
Cannot once start me.

[*Reenter* SEYTON.]

                              Wherefore was that cry?
SEYTON. The Queen, my lord, is dead.
MACBETH. She should have died hereafter;
There would have been a time for such a word.
Tomorrow, and tomorrow, and tomorrow
Creeps in this petty pace from day to day
To the last syllable of recorded time;

14. **Attend the true event.** Judgment can wait for the outcome; now we must be skillful soldiers.

15. Until we've won we're only guessing.

16. **forced,** reinforced.

"She should have died hereafter;
There would have been a time for such a word.
Tomorrow, and tomorrow, and tomorrow. . . ."

Royal Shakespeare Theatre, 1977
Stratford-Upon-Avon
Photo: Holte Photographers Ltd.

And all our yesterdays have lighted fools
The way to dusty death. Out, out, brief candle!
Life's but a walking shadow, a poor player,
That struts and frets his hour upon the stage   25
And then is heard no more. It is a tale
Told by an idiot, full of sound and fury,
Signifying nothing.

[*Enter a* MESSENGER.]

Thou com'st to use thy tongue. Thy story quickly.
MESSENGER. Gracious my Lord,   30
I should report that which I say I saw,
But know not how to do it.
MACBETH.   Well, say, sir.
MESSENGER. As I did stand my watch upon the hill,
I looked toward Birnam, and anon, methought
The wood began to move.

MACBETH.   Liar and slave!   35
MESSENGER. Let me endure your wrath if't be not so.
  Within this three mile may you see it coming;
  I say, a moving grove.
MACBETH.   If thou speak'st false,
  Upon the next tree shalt thou hang alive,
  Till famine cling thee. If thy speech be sooth,   40
  I care not if thou dost for me as much.
  I pull in resolution, and begin
  To doubt the equivocation of the fiend,[17]
  That lies like truth: "Fear not, till Birnam wood
  Do come to Dunsinane." And now a wood   45
  Comes toward Dunsinane. Arm, arm, and out!
  If this which he avouches does appear,
  There is nor flying hence nor tarrying here.
  I 'gin to be aweary of the sun,
  And wish the estate o' the world were now undone.   50
  Ring the alarum bell! Blow, wind! come, wrack!
  At least we'll die with harness on our back.

  [*Exeunt.*]

17. **doubt the equivocation of the fiend,** begins to suspect that the devil has been misleading him by double meanings.

Scene 6

Dunsinane. Before MACBETH'S *Castle.*
Drum and Colors. Enter MALCOLM, SIWARD, MACDUFF,
and their army, with boughs.

MALCOLM. Now near enough. Your leavy[18] screens throw
    down,
  And show like those you are. You, worthy uncle,
  Shall with my cousin, your right noble son,
  Lead our first battle. Worthy Macduff and we
  Shall take upon's what else remains to do,   5
  According to our order.
SIWARD.   Fare you well.
  Do we but find the tyrant's power tonight,
  Let us be beaten, if we cannot fight.
MACDUFF. Make all our trumpets speak; give them all
    breath,
  Those clamorous harbingers of blood and death.   10

  [*Exeunt. Alarums continued.*]

18. **leavy,** leafy.

Scene 7

Another part of the field.

Enter MACBETH.

MACBETH. They have tied me to a stake; I cannot fly,
But bearlike I must fight the course.[19] What's he
That was not born of woman? Such a one
Am I to fear, or none.

[*Enter* YOUNG SIWARD.]

YOUNG SIWARD. What is thy name?
MACBETH.   Thou'lt be afraid to hear it.   5
YOUNG SIWARD. No; though thou call'st thyself a hotter
        name
Than any is in hell.
MACBETH.   My name's Macbeth.
YOUNG SIWARD. The devil himself could not pronounce
        a title
More hateful to mine ear.
MACBETH.   No, nor more fearful.
YOUNG SIWARD. Thou liest, abhorrèd tyrant; with my
        sword   10
I'll prove the lie thou speak'st.

[*They fight, and* YOUNG SIWARD *is slain.*]

MACBETH.   Thou wast born of woman.
But swords I smile at, weapons laugh to scorn,
Brandished by man that's of a woman born.

[*Exit.*]

[*Alarums. Enter* MACDUFF.]

MACDUFF. That way the noise is. Tyrant, show thy face!
If thou be'st slain and with no stroke of mine,   15
My wife and children's ghosts will haunt me still.
I cannot strike at wretched kerns, whose arms
Are hired to bear their staves. Either thou, Macbeth,
Or else my sword with an unbattered edge
I sheathe again undeeded. There thou shouldst be;   20
By this great clatter, one of greatest note
Seems bruited.[20] Let me find him, fortune!
And more I beg not.

[*Exit. Alarums.*]

19. **fight the course.** Macbeth likens himself to a chained bear being baited. The course is a round or bout; here, the battle.

20. **bruited,** reported, rumored.

[*Enter* MALCOLM *and* SIWARD.]

SIWARD. This way, my lord; the castle's gently
    rendered:[21]
The tyrant's people on both sides do fight;
The noble thanes do bravely in the war;
The day almost itself professes yours,[22]
And little is to do.
MALCOLM.   We have met with foes
That strike beside us.[23]
SIWARD.   Enter, sir, the castle.

[*Exeunt. Alarum.*]

21. **rendered,** yielded, surrendered without great struggle.

25

22. **professes yours,** claims to be yours.

23. **strike beside us.** Macbeth's followers seem deliberately to miss Malcolm's men. They are halfhearted in their cause.

Scene 8

Another part of the field.

Enter MACBETH.

MACBETH. Why should I play the Roman fool and die
On mine own sword? Whiles I see lives, the gashes
Do better upon them.

[*Enter* MACDUFF.]

MACDUFF.   Turn, hell-hound, turn!
MACBETH. Of all men else I have[24] avoided thee.
But get thee back. My soul is too much charged
With blood of thine already.
MACDUFF.   I have no words;
My voice is in my sword, thou bloodier villain
Than terms can give thee out!

[*They fight.*]

24. **have,** would have.

5

MACBETH.   Thou losest labor.
As easy mayst thou the intrenchant air
With thy keen sword impress as make me bleed.
Let fall thy blade on vulnerable crests;
I bear a charmèd life, which must not yield
To one of woman born.
MACDUFF.   Despair thy charm,
And let the angel whom thou still hast served
Tell thee, Macduff was from his mother's womb
Untimely ripped.
MACBETH. Accursèd be that tongue that tells me so,
For it hath cowed my better part of man!
And be these juggling fiends no more believed,

10

15

**ROYAL SHAKESPEARE
THEATRE, 1980**
Stratford-Upon-Avon
Photo: Holte Photographers Ltd.

*"Why should I play the Roman fool and die
On mine own sword? Whiles I see lives, the gashes
Do better upon them."*

That palter²⁵ with us in a double sense,   20   25. **palter,** trick, deceive.
That keep the word of promise to our ear,
And break it to our hope. I'll not fight with thee.
MACDUFF. Then yield thee, coward,
  And live to be the show and gaze o' the time.²⁶   26. **gaze o' the time,** the public
We'll have thee, as our rarer monsters are,   25 spectacle of the age.
Painted upon a pole, and underwrit,
"Here may you see the tyrant."
MACBETH.   I will not yield,
To kiss the ground before young Malcolm's feet
And to be baited with the rabble's curse.
Though Birnam wood be come to Dunsinane,   30
And thou opposed, being of no woman born,
Yet I will try the last. Before my body

I throw my warlike shield. Lay on, Macduff,
And damned be him that first cries "Hold, enough!"

[*Exeunt, fighting. Alarums.*]

[*Retreat. Flourish. Enter, with drum and colors,*
MALCOLM, SIWARD, ROSS, THANES, *and Soldiers.*]

MALCOLM. I would the friends we miss were safe arrived.   35
SIWARD. Some must go off;[27] and yet, by these I see,
  So great a day as this is cheaply bought.
MALCOLM. Macduff is missing, and your noble son.
ROSS. Your son, my lord, has paid a soldier's debt.
  He only lived but till he was a man;   40
  The which no sooner had his prowess confirmed
  In the unshrinking station where he fought
  But like a man he died.
SIWARD.   Then he is dead?
ROSS. Ay, and brought off the field. Your cause of
  sorrow
  Must not be measured by his worth, for then   45
  It hath no end.
SIWARD.   Had he his hurts before?
ROSS. Ay, on the front.
SIWARD.   Why, then, God's soldier be he!
  Had I as many sons as I have hairs,
  I would not wish them to a fairer death.
  And so his knell is knolled.
MALCOLM.   He's worth more sorrow,   50
  And that I'll spend for him.
SIWARD.   He's worth no more.
  They say he parted well and paid his score;
  And so, God be with him! Here comes newer
  comfort.

[*Reenter* MACDUFF, *with* MACBETH'S *head.*]

MACDUFF. Hail, King! for so thou art. Behold where
  stands
  The usurper's cursèd head. The time is free.   55
  I see thee compassed with thy kingdom's pearl,[28]
  That speak my salutation in their minds;
  Whose voices I desire aloud with mine:
  Hail, King of Scotland!
ALL.   Hail, King of Scotland!

[*Flourish.*]

MALCOLM. We shall not spend a large expense of time   60
  Before we reckon with your several loves,

27. **go off,** be lost, killed.

28. **kingdom's pearl,** the royal jewels of Scotland.

And make us even with you.[29] My thanes and kinsmen,
Henceforth be earls, the first that ever Scotland
In such an honor named. What's more to do,
Which would be planted newly with the time,   65
As calling home our exiled friends abroad
That fled the snares of watchful tyranny,
Producing forth the cruel ministers
Of this dead butcher and his fiendlike queen,
Who, as 'tis thought, by self and violent hands   70
Took off her life; this, and what needful else
That calls upon us, by the grace of Grace
We will perform in measure, time and place.
So thanks to all at once and to each one,
Whom we invite to see us crowned at Scone.   75

[*Flourish. Exeunt.*]

29. **even with you.** We (I) will reward you promptly.

FOR UNDERSTANDING

The Prophecy Fulfilled

1. What are the memories that Lady Macbeth cannot rid herself of?

2. Trace Macbeth's changes of mood throughout this act. How does Macbeth react to his wife's death? What does this suggest about the changed relationship between them? What does it show about Macbeth's own character at this point?

3. How is each of the witches' prophecies fulfilled?

4. How do Macbeth's better qualities—such as courage and humaneness—show themselves during this act? Does this make *Macbeth* a greater and more interesting play than if Shakespeare had let Macbeth become nothing else but a villain who is out of control?

5. With what change of mood does the play end? What indications are there of the kind of king Malcolm will be?

LANGUAGE AND VOCABULARY

1. Use context clues to try to guess the meanings of the italicized words in the following phrases and clauses from Act IV:

a. Sweet *bodements!* good!

b. While you perform your *antic* round. . . .

c. Let this *pernicious* hour/Stand aye accursed. . . .

d. I . . . here *abjure*/The taints and blames I laid upon myself.

Look up each of these words in your dictionary and check your surmises against the definitions.

2. For reasonably full understanding of the play, to what extent do you need to know the exact meanings of the following words from Scene 1, Act IV: *entrails, fillet, fenny, newt, adder, maw, gall, yew, chaudron?* In general, when is it essential that you learn the meaning of a word new to you? When can you safely skip looking up a word? Find other words from Acts IV and V whose full meanings you do not need to know.

3. It will be obvious to you that in modern English many a common word has many different meanings. The *setting* of the sun is not like the *setting* of a trap. A musical *round* is not like a *round* of golf or a *round* of applause. A *break* in the weather is not like a *break* in a fabric or in a window pane. When a drama critic comments that an actor "*played* the king as though somebody else was going to *play* the ace," the critic humorously changes the meanings of the words *play* and *king*. Before we can interpret a simile or a metaphor we must, of course, realize in what *sense* to interpret each of the words used. We cannot interpret common phrases of English correctly if we do not assign appropriate rather than inappropriate meanings to the words used. "To suffer a *check*" means little if we interpret *check* as a *bank account check* or as a *checked pattern* in a fabric. "Not worth a *hill* of beans" becomes a rather odd expression if one does not understand that *hill* means a little mound of earth around a growing plant. This problem besets us as we try to read Shakespeare. When the doctor says of Lady Macbeth, "My mind she has mated," he is not using *mate* in the sense of "join or couple" but *mate* as it is used in chess to mean *subdue* or *conquer*. What do the following expressions mean in Shakespeare? Pay particular attention to the italicized words in these quotations.

a. That I may tell pale-hearted fear it *lies*. . . .

b. Though all things foul would wear the brows of *grace*. . . .

c. All the particulars of vice so *grafted*. . . .

d. . . . that I should *forge*/Quarrels unjust. . . .

e. What, all my pretty chickens and their *dam*. . . .

f. But certain issue *strokes* must arbitrate. . . .

g. Direness . . . cannot once *start* me.

h. But bearlike I must fight the *course*.

i. They say he parted well and paid his *score*. . . .

j. . . . the cruel *ministers*/Of this dead butcher. . . .

SUMMING UP: MACBETH

FOR UNDERSTANDING

All people bear the seeds of both good and evil within them. *Macbeth* is the story of a brave and loyal soldier who allows his ambition to place him on the road to his own destruction. But Macbeth is not merely a "villain," that is, a character who is wholly evil. Throughout the play we see that Macbeth suffers from a deeply troubled conscience. Neither he nor his wife finds any pleasure or comfort in their "borrowed robes" as King and Queen. Macbeth, like most tyrants, becomes wilder and bloodier in his tyranny. The price he pays for power is a heavy one: the crumbling of his own personality. At the end of the play, he tries to rise again to majesty by returning to his noble self—a warrior who fights bravely. But by now his cause is lost.

Macbeth and Lady Macbeth demonstrate how our choices can bring about appalling consequences beyond our control. What makes Macbeth's end so frightening is that he, more clearly than anyone else, understands what he is doing. He does not choose blindly or unthinkingly, nor, to a lesser extent, does Lady Macbeth.

1. Trace some of the choices made by characters in *Macbeth* and show the consequences that spring from them.

2. To what extent can we divide characters in the play into "good" and "evil"?

FOR INTERPRETATION

1. Words spoken by a character in a play must be considered within the context of the drama. For example, in Act II, Scene 3, Macbeth has slaughtered Duncan's servants to hide the fact that he himself has killed the King: He cries:

Who can be wise, amazed, temp'rate, and furious,
Loyal and neutral, in a moment? No man.

There is wisdom in these words, but we must understand that Macbeth does not intend to utter a "truth" but is here speaking out of sheer hypocrisy. Apart from the dramatic context, however, there is a great deal of truth and universal meaning in many Shakespearean lines. Do you find any valid meaning today in these lines from *Macbeth*?

a.   But 'tis strange:
And often times, to win us to our harm,
The instruments of darkness tell us truths,
Win us with honest trifles, to betray's
In deepest consequence.

b. False face must hide what the false heart doth know.

c. Words to the heat of deeds too cold breath gives.

d. To show an unfelt sorry is an office
Which the false man does easy.

**GARRICK AS MACBETH,
MRS. PRITCHARD AS LADY MACBETH**
J. Zophrany
Garrick Club
Photo: E.T. Archive, Ltd.

e.   Naught's had, all's spent,
Where our desire is got without content.
f. 'Tis safer to be that which we destroy
Than by destruction dwell in doubtful joy.
g.   Things without all remedy
Should be without regard: what's done is done.
h. They say, blood will have blood.
2. Are the following statements true or false? Find support for your opinion in the selection.
a. Macbeth was led into evil almost solely because of Lady Macbeth's determination.

b. Macbeth's indecision to commit the murder shows only that he is weak.
c. The murder actually drives Macbeth and Lady Macbeth apart.
d. Once the first murder is committed, the other murders are inevitable.
e. Macbeth could have been a force for great and positive good.
f. This play demonstrates that a move in the wrong direction must be followed by acts leading in the same direction.

g. Shakespeare wanted his audience to feel sympathy with Macbeth.

FOR APPRECIATION

Shakespeare and Tragedy

Tragedy is a form of drama which, with comedy, seems basic to any human perception of time and life on a personal, social, or cosmic level. All primitive societies enact mythic rituals about the fall of a hero or heroine and, by doing so, hope to protect the assembled worshipers, as a society, from a similar fall. In the cultures of high civilizations, as in ancient Greece, the tragic ritual often develops into a secular theatrical event written by tragedians and performed by professional actors. Yet even in these cases, the society comes together to witness these plays and the audience is moved to consider the fate of the characters in the play.

The great Greek philosopher Aristotle (384–322 B.C.) was the first writer to attempt to explain how tragedy achieved its powerful effect in the theater. He set down his views in the book, *Poetics,* which is still widely read today. His conclusions about tragedy have dominated the discussion of tragic drama from his day to our own. Many of his points seem universally true, but some critics argue that the tragedy of later times cannot always be fitted into his theories. The Elizabethan Age, one of the greatest eras of tragedy, at times presents a tragic vision close in spirit to Aristotle's terms. In some instances, however, Elizabethan tragedy departs drastically from those terms. Today playwrights and dramatic critics often argue that modern tragedy must also find special terms for its utterance that set it apart from the tragic vision of the Greeks or the Elizabethans. Still, no one denies that Aristotle was right about one thing: that the tragic experience in the theater is one of the most powerful and fundamental of all our responses to any kind of art or literature. Some points that Aristotle raises are, in any case, still central to our thinking about tragedy.

1. *Tragedy arouses the emotions of pity and fear, wonder and awe.* The members of the audience, whether in the theater or reading the text, watch the hero move toward destruction; they have pity for the hero; they share the hero's fear and suffering; they experience wonder and awe before the forces of Fate. The emotional impact of tragedy is two-pronged: by sharing, even vicariously, the experience of the central figure, the audience is asked to think about the fate of all human beings, and one's own fate.

2. *A tragic hero must be a man or woman capable of great suffering.* Tragic heroes are often kings, queens, warriors, or persons of noble spirit and high position. In part, this status reflects the aristocratic bias of earlier literature, but it also implies that such people are larger than life, or are not ordinary people. In the great suffering of unusually sensitive and noble people, the audience sees more clearly the vast reaches of the human spirit.

3. *Tragedy explores the question of the ways of God to Mortals.* We have always been disturbed about why God permits us to suffer, often (from a human point of view) so needlessly. Tragedy does not propose a solution to this problem. It presents the question in dramatic form for us to contemplate.

4. *Tragedy shows us the disaster which results from* a major *mistake.* Aristotle used the term *hamartia,* which has been translated as "flaw" but which really means "error of judgment." Tragedy results when a basically good person chooses to do the wrong thing. We usually understand and may even sympathize with the choice, which is why tragedy is so painful. But, because we come to see, as the central character usually does, what the mistake has been, we also have a sense of greater illumination. Tragedy may in this way be seen as educative.

In Shakespearian tragedy, an added layer of irony results when those qualities that we admire most in a tragic hero are the very things which also contain the flaw or lead to the tragic mistake—or make it worse. In other cases, Elizabethan writers, including Shakespeare, attempted kinds of tragedy that seem to lie far outside Aristotle's definitions. There was the villain's tragedy which occurs when a thoroughly evil person (unlike Macbeth) swaggers about on the stage gloating over how many good people will suffer at his hands—which the loathsome villain then proceeds to demonstrate, until the gathering forces of goodness cut him down. This kind of "Machiavellian" tragedy, as in *Richard III,* was intended to cause sheer astonishment in the audience, rather than pity and fear.

The tragedy of the "overreacher" was introduced by Marlowe and involves a character who goes breathtakingly too far. We gasp and admire the reckless daring of the tragic lunge, all the time knowing that it must eventually fail. The over-reacher may be a good character or one of mixed morality—or this tragic type may be combined with the tragedy of villainy if the overreacher is seen as completely evil.

Another popular kind of Elizabethan tragedy was the revenger's tragedy, in which a person who is good on the whole, possibly without a flaw of any kind, discovers that he alone can bring an evildoer to justice—even though he will be damned if he takes the law into his own hands. *Hamlet,* of course, is an example of this kind of play—and the more we understand how Elizabethan audiences saw revenger's tragedies, the less we would try to force extremely ingenious modern explanations upon the character of Hamlet.

In *Romeo and Juliet,* it is possible to see another kind of tragedy entirely—the heartbreaking trage-dy of calamity—which occurs when wholesome innocence is left to wander helpless among the depraved evils that an entire society is to blame for. In some of Shakespeare's later plays, it is even possible to see a kind of tragedy of despair in which Aristotle's notions are almost deliberately defied in presenting the tragic mind of a Timon or Lear as it sees all meaning crumble before a storm of negation.

Using the preceding discussion as a guide, con-sider *Macbeth* as a tragedy. How far can it be seen as following Aristotle's views of tragedy as listed in the numbered points? In what ways, if any, does it depart from Aristotle's views?

Character Development

The next two sections focus on the author's skill in handling two elements of his art: the way in which he creates and develops character and the way in which he uses imagery in his language.

Characters in a story may be said to be flat or round. Flat characters are those labeled by the writer as particular kinds of people; they never change: Nothing is added to or subtracted from their original definition throughout the telling of the story. An example of a flat character is the porter in *Macbeth.* Short-story writers often de-pend on flat characters, especially for background characters whom they do not have time to develop. In novels or plays, many of the secondary characters fall within this category. Round characters are those who develop and grow; they are not all good or all bad. New facets of their personalities, their moral standards, their motivations are revealed as the story progresses. Usually the heroes of a novel or play—at least of a *good* novel or play—are fully rounded characters; even in a short story, the leading characters may have a three-dimensional quality.

The terms "flat" and "round" imply an evalua-tion by the reader and, obviously, characters may fall somewhere between the two stated divisions. It would be false to assume that all flat characteriza-tions are poor and all round ones splendid.

How then do writers make characters seem to be alive, real people? They may reveal characters in several ways: first, by either directly describing characters or allowing people in the story to do so; second, by allowing the reader to judge characters through their interactions with others in the story; third, by letting characters reveal themselves through soliloquies or by letting the reader slip inside the characters' minds.

1. What in Macbeth's character makes him suscep-tible to the witches' prophecies?

2. Read the following lines. Write on a sheet of paper a word or two to tell what each succeeding quotation reveals or reinforces about Macbeth's character.

Sergeant, Act I, Scene 2
For brave Macbeth—well he deserves that name,—
Duncan, Act I, Scene 2
What he hath lost, noble Macbeth hath won.
Lady Macbeth, Act I, Scene 5
                    Yet do I fear thy nature;
It is too full o' the milk of human kindness
To catch the nearest way. Thou wouldst be great,
Art not without ambition, but without
The illness should attend it.
Macbeth, Act I, Scene 7
                    I have no spur
To prick the sides of my intent, but only
Vaulting ambition. . . .
Macbeth, Act I, Scene 7
We will proceed no further in this business.
Macbeth, Act II, Scene 1
Is this a dagger which I see before me,
The handle toward my hand?
Macbeth, Act II, Scene 2
But wherefore could not I pronounce "Amen"?

Macbeth, Act III, Scene 2

> Better be with the dead,
> Whom we, to gain our peace, have sent to peace,
> Than on the torture of the mind to lie
> In restless ecstasy.

Macbeth, Act III, Scene 2

> Things bad begun make strong themselves by ill.

Macduff, Act IV, Scene 3

> Not in the legions
> Of horrid hell can come a devil more damned
> In evils to top Macbeth.

Macbeth, Act V, Scene 3

> I will not be afraid of death and bane
> Till Birnam forest come to Dunsinane.

Macbeth, Act V, Scene 5

> She should have died hereafter;
> There would have been a time for such a word.

Macbeth, Act V, Scene 8

> Lay on, Macduff,
> And damned be him that first cries "Hold,
>   enough!"

3. Do Macbeth's actions spring from his personality or are they seemingly unrelated? How many different methods has Shakespeare used to reveal Macbeth's character?

4. Reread Scenes 5 and 7 in Act I, and Scenes 1 and 2 in Act II. From these write a paragraph giving your impression of Lady Macbeth. Share these descriptions in class. Considering the general class picture of Lady Macbeth, do you think Shakespeare prepared you for Lady Macbeth's madness at the end of the play?

5. Do you think Shakespeare made the following characters round or flat?

a. Banquo
b. Malcolm
c. Macduff

Poetic Imagery

Shakespeare is one of the greatest of English poets and his lines sparkle with fascinating images. In a few words he can call up a visual picture which communicates a complicated emotion. He might have had Macbeth say merely, "O, my mind is troubled, and full of ugly thoughts." Instead, he used a brilliant *image:* "O, full of scorpions is my mind, dear wife." Imagery is basic to poetry, and it is most commonly found in metaphors and similes. The only real difference between these is that a simile is usually introduced by the word *like* or *as*. An example of a simile is Lady Macbeth's

> Your face, my thane, is as a book, where men
> May read strange matters.

An example of metaphor is Macbeth's

> I have supped full with horrors.

Note the simple yet vivid language. By using the word "supped," Shakespeare has compared Macbeth's evil deeds and thoughts to food at a banquet. But Shakespeare implies that the soul can become stuffed with evil as the body can with food. The idea has gained dimension, complication, color, by use of the comparison. And it has been expressed in only a few words.

A series of quotations from *Macbeth* follows. Use the lines as a springboard. Discuss what picture, emotion, mood each image generates, and how effective you find it.

1. The earth hath bubbles, as the water has,
   And these are of them.

2. Sleep that knits up the raveled sleave of
       care. . . .

3. There's daggers in men's smiles. . . .

4. We have scotched the snake, not killed it.

5. look like the innocent flower,
   But be the serpent under't.

6. Macbeth is ripe for shaking. . . .

7. My way of life
   Is fallen into the sere, the yellow leaf. . . .

8. Out, out, brief candle!
   Life's but a walking shadow, a poor player,
   That struts and frets his hour upon the stage
   And then is heard no more. It is a tale
   Told by an idiot, full of sound and fury,
   Signifying nothing.

King James Bible

It is remarkable that so much in the imagination, character, and literature of English-speaking peoples everywhere can be traced to the profound influence of a single book. Yet historians agree that the impact made by the King James (or Authorized) Version of the Bible can scarcely be overestimated. Short passages from the Bible had appeared in English translations from the first, now and then attaining literary excellence, as during the ages of Bede and Alfred. It was John Wyclif (c. 1320–1384), however, who first called for a vernacular Bible as a basic need and right of the people. Wyclif English versions of Biblical excerpts began to circulate in manuscript during the fifteenth century, but their production or use was considered heretical. This was still true in the next century when William Tyndale (d. 1536) had to flee England to complete and publish his translation in 1525, which thus became the first printed edition of the New Testament in English. His style was vigorous, simple, and direct; it had a powerful influence on all the versions that followed it. Before Tyndale could complete his translation of the whole Bible, he was condemned for his work and executed in Brussels.

Miles Coverdale (1488–1568) went on to realize Tyndale's goal with the Coverdale Bible, which became the first complete printed English Bible, published in Zurich in 1535. In the meantime, the demand for a vernacular Bible, now one of the cornerstones of the Reformation, had become too strong to deny. Consequently, Henry VIII called for Coverdale to produce a Bible that would receive official sanction for church use, an act that was sure to widen the breach with Rome. The result, the Great Bible of 1540, might have remained the definitive English Bible had it not been for the return to Roman Catholicism under Queen Mary. Escaping from her persecutions to the continent, militant Protestants produced a new translation there, the Geneva Bible of 1560. Presenting a more extreme Protestant outlook than had the Great

Bible, it became the version of choice in England. It was the first to separate and number each verse and the first to use modern roman type instead of hard-to-read gothic black letter print. Compact in size, the Geneva Bible was used by Shakespeare and carried to the new world by the Mayflower Puritans.

With the Anglican Church established once more under Queen Elizabeth, Anglican bishops watched in dismay the growing popularity of the Geneva Bible. They felt it spoke with an anticlerical bias favorable to the Puritan party. Accordingly, the church responded in 1568 with a counterattack, the Bishops' Bible, which was essentially a revision of the Great Bible. Then, with the fading of the last prohibitions against vernacular Bibles, a Catholic translation of the Bible into English was published at Rheims in 1609, called the Douay Bible. In light of this variety of Biblical translations, it is surprising that the conditions for yet one more—the greatest of all—were only now at hand. This came about when, shortly after the crowning of James I, the English Puritan party presented the king with a number of requests pertaining to his religious policies. The only one he agreed to meet was the one calling for a new official English Bible that would replace the Bishops' Bible. James was more than willing to do this, particularly since he was equally suspicious of the antiroyalist tone he sensed in the Geneva Bible.

The idea for this new Bible came up at a conference of the king and clergy at Hampton Court in 1604. It was rather incidentally presented and not favored by a majority, but it caught King James's fancy. Once the clergy had set to work, they were astonished when James refused to finance what promised to be an extremely costly project. Three years were devoted to the organization of the project alone. Fifty-four scholars, including Lancelot Andrewes, were chosen for their ability in the original Hebrew and the various other tongues into which the scriptures had been translated. These learned men were then divided into six groups:

Lord ope ý king of Englands eies

This woodcut from The Book of Martyrs, *1610 edition, shows the martyrdom of William Tyndale in Flanders.*

two located at Westminster, two at Oxford, two at Cambridge. Each group was given a particular section to translate. John Selden in 1689 described how the work of translation was done.

The translators in King James' time took an excellent way. That part of the Bible was given to him who was most excellent in such a tongue (as the Aprocrypha to Andrew Downs) and then they met together, and one read the translation, the rest holding in their hands some Bible, either of the learned tongues, or French, Spanish, Italian, etc. If they found any fault they spoke; if not, he read on.

When all six of the groups had finished the sections assigned to them, the complete text was then read and approved or corrected by a committee of twelve. And finally Bishop Bilson

and Miles Smith prepared the approved version for the press.

The committee did use the Bishops' Bible as their working text, but they also consulted all existing English translations, paying special heed to the earliest of these, the one by William Tyndale. According to an estimate by a modern Biblical scholar, Charles C. Butterworth, about 61 percent of the King James text comes from preceding English Bibles, while 39 percent was newly translated by the six teams of scholars. The resulting work was immediately recognized as a landmark of religious scholarship which all Christians alike could respect and value. The work's quality as a powerful literary masterpiece has been no less important, however, in explaining its hold on the imagination of all who read it. The directness and clarity of its prose, the eloquence of its poetry, the overall simplicity of its diction, and the natural stateliness of its style—these qualities have continued to insure its lasting place in English literary history.

Of the three passages from the King James Bible presented here, the one from *Genesis,* the first book in the Old Testament, tells the story of how Joseph was sold into slavery by his brothers. The one from *Corinthians* is part of a letter that St. Paul wrote to the small Christian congregation in Corinth, Greece, giving them encouragement in face of their difficulties. It appears in the New Testament. The first sample, from the *Book of Job* in the Old Testament, is first presented as printed in the King James Bible and then in parallel versions from four different English translations so that you can examine each and compare it with the others.

This text is a vivid and dramatic poem describing a horse. It comes from a section of *Job* in which God speaks out of a whirlwind to answer Job's accusation that God uses his power unfairly. Speaking from the whirlwind, God's voice challenges Job to create any of the manifold wonders to be found in nature. You will notice as you examine the comparison lines that when the letters *u* and *v* begin a word, they are written as *v*, but when they appear within a word, they are written as *u*. In some places the letter *i* appears in place of *j*, since these letters were considered interchangeable. In some cases, a virgule (/) was used in place of a comma. Only three translations preceding the King James version are given, although many more were consulted by the King James scholars.

THE HORSE

(Job 39:19–25)

19 Hast thou given the horse strength?
   Hast thou clothed his neck with thunder?
20 Canst thou make him afraid as a grasshopper?
   The glory of his nostrils is terrible.
21 He paweth in the valley, and rejoiceth in his strength:
   he goeth on to meet the armed men.
22 He mocketh at fear, and is not affrighted;
   neither turneth he back from the sword.
23 The quiver rattleth against him,
   the glittering spear and the shield.
24 He swalloweth the ground with fierceness and rage:
   neither believeth he that it is the sound of the trumpet.
25 He saith among the trumpets, Ha, ha!
   And he smelleth the battle afar off,
   the thunder of the captains, and the shouting.

The following has been adapted from Charles C. Butterworth, The Literary Lineage of the King James Bible 1340–1611, *Philadelphia, 1941. The original spellings of these four editions of the Bible have been retained here.*

Wyf   (1382)   The Early Wycliffe Bible
Cov   (1535)   The Coverdale Bible
Gen   (1560)   The Geneva Bible
KJ   (1611)   The King James Bible

Wyf   Whether shalt thou giue   to the hors strengthe, or
Cov   Hast thou geuen the horse is strength, or lerned him
Gen   Hast thou giuen the horse   strength? *or*
KJ   Hast thou giuen the horse   strength?   hast thou

Wyf   don aboute   his necke   neyenge? Whether shalt thou reren
Cov   to bowe downe his neck with feare: that he letteth him self be
Gen   couered   his necke with neying?   23 Hast thou made
KJ   clothed   his necke with thunder?   20 Canst thou make

Wyf   hym   as   locustis?   The glory of his
Cov   dryuen forth like a   greshopper, where as the stoute neyenge
Gen   him afraied as the grashoper?   his strong neying
KJ   him afraid as a   grashopper?   the glory of his

Wyf   nese therlis   ferd.   The erthe
Cov   that he maketh, is fearfull? he breaketh *ye* grounde with
Gen   is feareful. He diggeth in the valley,
KJ   nostrils   *is* terrible. He paweth in the valley,

Wyf   the houe   delueth,   hardili he gladeth out;
Cov   the hoffes of his fete   chearfully in his strength,
Gen   & reioyceth   in *his* strength:
KJ   and reioyceth   in *his* strength:

Wyf   in to the agencomyng he goth to the armed. He dispisith
Cov   and runneth   to mete the harnest men. He layeth asyde all
Gen   he goeth forthe to mete the harnest *man*. He mocketh at
KJ   hee goeth on   to meet the armed men. He mocketh at

Wyf   dreede,   and he giueth not stede to the
Cov   feare, his stomack is not abated,   nether starteth he a back for eny
Gen   feare, &   is not afraied,   &   turneth not backe from the
KJ   feare, and   is not affrighted: neither turneth he backe from the

Wyf swerd. Vp on hym the arewe girdil shal sounen; the
Cov swerde. Though the quyuers rattlē vpon him, though the
Gen sworde, *Thogh* the quiuer rattle against him, the
KJ sword. The quiuer ratleth against him, the

Wyf spere and the sheeld shal braundishen. Feruent and
Cov speare and shilde glister: yet russheth he in
Gen glittering speare and the shield. He swalloweth the
KJ glittering speare and the shield. He swalloweth the

Wyf gnastende he soupeth the erthe; and rewarde he not to
Cov fearsly, and beateth vpon the grounde. He feareth not
Gen grounde for fearcenes and rage, and he beleueth not that it is
KJ ground with fiercenesse and rage: neither beleueth he that it *is*

Wyf the trumpe sounende trumping. Wher he shal here the
Cov the noyse of the trompettes, but as soone as he heareth the
Gen the noyse of the trumpet. He saith among the
KJ the sound of the trumpet. Hee saith among the

Wyf trumpe, he shal seyn, Fy! aferr he smellith bataile;
Cov shawmes blowe, tush (sayeth he) for he smelleth the batell afarre of,
Gen trumpets, Ha, ha: he smelleth the battel a farre of,
KJ trumpets, Ha, ha: and he smelleth the battaile afarre off,

Wyf the cleping to of dukis, and yelling of the ost.
Cov *ye* noyse, the captaynes and the shoutinge.
Gen and the noyse of the captaines, and the shouting.
KJ the thunder of the captaines, and the shouting.

JOSEPH SOLD INTO EGYPT

Genesis 37: 2–36

Joseph, being seventeen years old, was feeding the flock with his brethren; and the lad was with the sons of Bilhah, and with the sons of Zilpah, his father's wives: and Joseph brought unto his father their evil report. 3 Now Israel loved Joseph more than all his children, because he was the son of his old age: and he made him a coat of many colors. 4 And when his brethren saw that their father loved him more than all his brethren, they hated him, and could not speak peaceably unto him.

5 And Joseph dreamed a dream, and he told it his brethren: and they hated him yet the more. 6 And he said unto them, Hear, I pray you, this dream which I have dreamed: 7 for, behold, we were binding sheaves in the field, and, lo, my sheaf arose, and also stood upright; and, behold, your sheaves stood round about, and made obeisance to my sheaf. 8 And his brethren said to him, Shalt thou indeed reign over us? or shalt thou indeed have dominion over us? And they hated him yet the more for his dreams, and for his words. 9 And he dreamed yet another dream, and told it his brethren, and said, Behold, I have dreamed a dream more; and, behold, the sun and the moon and the eleven stars made obeisance to me. 10 And he told it to his father, and to his brethren: and his father rebuked him, and said unto him, What is this dream that thou hast dreamed? Shall I and thy mother and thy brethren indeed come to bow down ourselves to thee to the earth? 11 And his brethren envied him; but his father observed the saying.

12 And his brethren went to feed their father's flock in Shechem. 13 And Israel said unto Joseph, Do not thy brethren feed the flock in Shechem? come, and I will send thee unto them. And he said to him, Here am I.

14 And he said to him, Go, I pray thee, see whether it be well with thy brethren, and well with the flocks; and bring me word again. So he sent him out of the vale of Hebron, and he came to Shechem. 15 And a certain man found him, and, behold, he was wandering in the field: and the man asked him, saying, What seekest thou? 16 And he said, I seek my brethren: tell me, I pray thee, where they feed their flocks. 17 And the man said, They are departed hence; for I heard them say, Let us go to Dothan. And Joseph went after his brethren, and found them in Dothan. 18 And when they saw him afar off, even before he came near unto them, they conspired against him to slay him. 19 And they said one to another, Behold, this dreamer cometh. 20 Come now therefore, and let us slay him, and cast him into some pit, and we will say, Some evil beast hath devoured him; and we shall see what will become of his dreams. 21 And Reuben heard it, and he delivered him out of their hands; and said, Let us not kill him. 22 And Reuben said unto them, Shed no blood, but cast him into this pit that is in the wilderness, and lay no hand upon him; that he might rid him out of their hands, to deliver him to his father again. 23 And it came to pass, when Joseph was come unto his brethren, that they stripped Joseph out of his coat, his coat of many colors that was on him; 24 and they took him, and cast him into a pit: and the pit was empty, there was no water in it.

25 And they sat down to eat bread: and they lifted up their eyes and looked, and, behold, a company of Ishmaelites[1] came from Gilead, with their camels bearing spicery and balm and myrrh, going to carry it down to Egypt. 26 And Judah said unto his brethren, What profit is it if we slay our brother, and

conceal his blood? 27 Come, and let us sell him to the Ishmaelites, and let not our hand be upon him; for he is our brother and our flesh: and his brethren were content. 28 Then there passed by Midianites merchantmen; and they drew and lifted up Joseph out of the pit, and sold Joseph to the Ishmaelites for twenty pieces of silver:[2] and they brought Joseph into Egypt.

29 And Reuben returned unto the pit; and, behold, Joseph was not in the pit; and he rent his clothes. 30 And he returned unto his brethren, and said, The child is not; and I, whither shall I go? 31 And they took Joseph's coat, and killed a kid of the goats, and dipped the coat in the blood; 32 and they sent the coat of many colors, and they brought it to their father; and said, This have we found: know now whether it be thy son's coat or no. 33 And he knew it, and said, It is my son's coat; an evil beast hath devoured him; Joseph is without doubt rent in pieces. 34 And Jacob rent his clothes, and put sackcloth upon his loins, and mourned for his son many days. 35 And all his sons and all his daughters rose up to comfort him; but he refused to be comforted; and he said, For I will go down into the grave unto my son mourning. Thus his father wept for him. 36 And the Midianites sold him into Egypt unto Potiphar, an officer of Pharaoh's, and captain of the guard.

The British Library, London

Joseph and the coat of many colors, from Caxton "Lugenda Auera" of 1483.

1. **Ishmaelites.** These were descendants of Ishmael, a son of Abraham. Joseph and his brothers were descendants of Isaac, another son of Abraham.
2. **twenty pieces of silver.** This was the price of a boy; thirty pieces was the price of a full-grown man.

OF CHARITY

1 Corinthians 13: 1–13

1 Though I speak with the tongues of men and of angels, and have not charity, I am become as sounding brass, or a tinkling cymbal. 2 And though I have the gift of prophecy, and understand all mysteries, and all knowledge; and though I have all faith, so that I could remove mountains, and have not charity, I am nothing. 3 And though I bestow all my goods to feed the poor, and though I give my body to be burned, and have not charity, it profiteth me nothing.

4 Charity suffereth long, and is kind; charity envieth not; charity vaunteth not itself, is not puffed up, 5 doth not behave it-

self unseemly, seeketh not her own, is not easily provoked, thinketh no evil; 6 rejoiceth not in iniquity, but rejoiceth in the truth; 7 beareth all things, believeth all things, hopeth all things, endureth all things.

8 Charity never faileth: but whether there be prophecies, they shall fail; whether there be tongues, they shall cease; whether there be knowledge, it shall vanish away. 9 For we know in part, and we prophesy in part. 10 But when that which is perfect is come, then that which is in part shall be done away. 11 When I was a child, I spake as a child, I understood as a child, I thought as a child: but when I became a man, I put away childish things. 12 For now we see through a glass, darkly, but then face to face: now I know in part; but then shall I know even as also I am known. 13 And now abideth faith, hope, charity, these three; but the greatest of these is charity.

UNDERSTANDING AND INTERPRETATION

The Horse
This passage is filled with vivid bits of description. Take each of the versions and read them aloud in sequence. Which descriptions in the King James version seem particularly vivid to you?

Joseph Sold into Egypt
Caxton, when printing his account of the life of Joseph in his *Golden Legends,* included these verses. Tyndale and Joye, two sixteenth-century translators, appended this excerpt to their New Testaments. The King James Bible made only small alterations to the lines, but did add the delightful description, "the coat of many colors." Discuss the following propositions in light of the story and your own experiences.
1. Jealousy is a devastating emotion.
2. It is God who saves Joseph.
3. Siblings in today's families might have reactions similar to Joseph's brothers against a favored child.

Of Charity
Few passages in the King James New Testament are indebted to so many different sources for the final product. Take for example the word *charity.* The Latin version used the word *caritas* which is translated as *charity.* But Tyndale, using the Greek original of the New Testament, chose the word *love.* Some translations used both *love* and *charity* in this passage. In 1530, a defender of the word *charity* argued that "all charite is loue: but it is not trouth, that all loue is charite." Would our present definitions of these two words support his argument?

FOR APPRECIATION

Joseph Sold Into Egypt
1. Look back at the story of Joseph. Note how graphic and tight the story pattern is. What phrases or sentences best catch the action?
2. Why do you think no mention is made of Joseph's reaction to his brothers' betrayal?
3. Literary critics today use the term *archetype* to describe a basic universal image or pattern in literature that has occurred over and over in all cultures and periods. The archetype, when used, awakens a deep, partly unconscious emotional response. Some scholars feel the Joseph story and the Christ story use the same archetypal images. Would you agree or disagree?

Of Charity
This passage is noted for the clearness of its form. Divide the selection into four paragraphs. Describe how and what each adds to the concept of charity and of love. Consider the modern definition of charity and of love. Which does this passage best describe?

COMPOSITION

Take any one of these three passages. Try to put them into present-day language. Read samples of them to each other in class and then read the King James version aloud. Can you express the difference between the modern and old?

Ben Jonson

1572–1637

After an education that included the classicist William Camden as one of his teachers, Ben Jonson first tried his hand at his stepfather's trade, bricklaying, before going off as a soldier to the war in Flanders. Though ten years younger than Marlowe and Shakespeare, he next appears alongside them, grubbing for a living as an Elizabethan actor and playwright. He was already arguing that comedy should show its characters in the grips of various ruling passions, or humors. His first play, *Every Man in His Humor,* presented such humor characters, and was acted in 1598 with Shakespeare in the cast. His contentious comedies also fiercely satirize such humorous vices as greed, ambition, religious bigotry, stupidity, and corruption. His quarrelsome tendency also helped provoke a "war of the theaters" in which playwrights traded insults with each other in their works. Perhaps it was the "choleric humor" that twice landed him in prison. During one stay, he converted to Roman Catholicism, though he abandoned it twelve years later in a period of acute religious intolerance.

Having accomplished increasingly successful work in the popular theater, Jonson shifted his attention to the court, for which he wrote semitheatrical evenings of verse and elaborate pageantry, called masques. Typically, he conducted an open feud with his designer, Inigo Jones, to much publicity but little purpose. It would be possible to regard Jonson entirely as an Elizabethan playwright—up to 1616, the year of Shakespeare's death. That year Jonson was given a life pension and so became in fact (though not in title) the first English Poet Laureate. But 1616 was also the year in which Jonson became the first English author to publish his own collected *Works* while still alive, an edition which gave Shakespeare's colleagues the idea for the posthumous Shakespeare *First Folio* of 1623. With the careers of Marlowe and Shakespeare over, however, Jonson was just beginning on a second one.

In this light, he was seen during his second

BENJAMIN JONSON
after Abraham van Blyenberch
National Portrait Gallery, London

career as the first "professional" English writer, as was the later poet laureate, John Dryden. Jonson conducted this career—chiefly as a nondramatic poet—after becoming a member of the court's cultural establishment. This often involved him in the intrigues and power plays among the courtiers and writers of the day. A younger set of poets began to gather around him admiringly, gladly calling themselves "the sons of Ben." This group has come to be known in literary history as the Cavalier Poets because of their easy access to court, their sumptuous fashionability, their emphasis on style and manners. They constitute the first consciously formed "school of poetry" in English. Jonson himself, always catholic in his tastes, also befriended John Donne, the leading light of another less self-defined school, the group we now call the Metaphysical Poets. Both groups were deeply influenced by Jonson's direct and simple diction, his spare elegance, and his smooth rhythms. He frequently imitated classical forms, as in the pithy epigram, "On Court-Worm." His tone may sound impersonal but the feelings are no less real for that. They are simply expressed with such control that all personal pleading becomes unnecessary.

On Court-Worm

All men are worms: but this no man. In silk
'Twas brought to court first wrapped, and white as milk;
Where, afterwards, it grew a butterfly:
Which was a caterpillar. So 't will die.

Still to Be Neat

Still to be neat, still to be dressed,
As you were going to a feast;
Still to be powdered, still perfumed;
Lady, it is to be presumed,
Though art's hid causes are not found,   5
All is not sweet, all is not sound.

Give me a look, give me a face
That makes simplicity a grace;
Robes loosely flowing, hair as free;
Such sweet neglect more taketh me   10
Then all th' adulteries of art.
They strike mine eyes, but not my heart.

On My First Son

Farewell, thou child of my right hand,[1] and joy;
My sin was too much hope of thee, loved boy.
Seven years thou wert lent to me, and I thee pay,
Exacted by thy fate, on the just day.[2]
O, could I lose all father now! For why   5
Will man lament the state he should envy?
To have so soon 'scaped world's and flesh's rage,
And, if no other misery, yet age?
Rest in soft peace, and asked, say here doth lie
BEN. JONSON, his best piece of poetry:[3]   10
For whose sake, henceforth, all his vows be such,
As what he loves may never like too much.

1. Jonson's son died of the plague in 1603; he, too, was
named Benjamin, which in Hebrew means "son of the
right hand."
2. **just day,** both "the Day of Judgment" and a reference to the fact that the boy died on his seventh birthday.
3. **poetry,** used in the sense of its Greek root, "making," or "creation."

Though I Am Young and Cannot Tell

Though I am young, and cannot tell
Either what Death or Love is well,
Yet I have heard they both bear darts,
And both do aim at human hearts.
And then again, I have been told   5
Love wounds with heat, as Death with cold;
So that I fear they do but bring
Extremes to touch, and mean one thing.

As in a ruin we it call
One thing to be blown up, or fall;   10
Or to our end like way may have
By a flash of lightning, or a wave;
So Love's inflamed shaft or brand
May kill as soon as Death's cold hand;
Except Love's fires the virtue have   15
To fright the frost out of the grave.

UNDERSTANDING AND INTERPRETATION

On Court-Worm

1. How does Jonson connect the metaphor to his real subject? What words are appropriate for both?

2. What change does Jonson make in the natural cycle? Why?

Still to Be Neat

1. What is the attitude toward beauty expressed here? What words best show the poet's real feelings?

2. Look at the balanced phrases in the poem. How is the last one different from the others? Why?

On My First Son

1. What reasons does Jonson use to comfort himself for the loss of his son? What development is there in these reasons?

2. The last two lines are difficult to understand, but somewhat easier if you add the suppressed "he" to the last line: "As what he loves (he) may never like too much." Can you see a connection between this line and line 2? What is the speaker's final attitude?

Though I Am Young and Cannot Tell

1. What are the similarities between Love and Death in this poem?

2. What are the differences between the two? What is the most important difference?

John Donne 1572–1631

To explain away the two most sensational and diametrically opposite periods in his own life, John Donne invented two convenient figures that supposedly divided himself neatly in two. The first was the young ex-Catholic rake, "Jack Donne," living a wild life in London and writing scandalous verse. The other was the solemn and serene older divine, Dr. John Donne, Anglican sermonizer and Dean of St. Paul's Cathedral in the same city. The trouble with this account is that it ignores the profound similarities between the two figures even as it omits a number of other turbulent roles Donne played in a turbulent time.

Most important to understanding the mercurial temperament underlying both his poetry and prose—both the song and the sermon—is the fact that Donne was born into one of the most celebrated Catholic families in England at a time of constantly increasing anti-Catholic alarms. The second most important fact about Donne is that he lived to betray this faith, unlike his own brother who died a martyr to it. The Donne family, through the mother, was descended from Sir Thomas More, the very image of the English Catholic martyr in his refusal to obey Henry VIII—at the cost of his life.

Donne early attended Oxford and—possibly—Cambridge, but he took no degree in either place, since that required a loyalty oath that Catholics in good conscience could not swear. Before being admitted to the study of law in 1592, he did travel abroad, probably to Spain, judging by a library stuffed with Spanish and Kabbalistic books. A portrait of him at this period shows him sporting a foppish hat, wearing gold cross-shaped earrings, and displaying a Spanish motto which translates, "Sooner dead than altered." Yet at some point in the 1590s, Donne seems to have altered indeed. In 1594 his brother Henry died of plague in Newgate jail while awaiting conviction as a felon for illegally harboring a priest. Both sides must have been watching for what Donne would do

MINIATURE OF JOHN DONNE
Issac Oliver

next, but this was his period of reckless living, writing his early love poetry—much of it passionate and cynical by turns. His sense of adventure also carried him off in the two Essex expeditions to Cadiz and the Azores, 1596–1597. And in 1598, he became secretary to Sir Thomas Egerton, keeper of the Great Seal, and sat in Elizabeth's last parliament. From such a beginning, a great career could easily be predicted.

But in 1601, he secretly married the seventeen-year-old niece of Lady Egerton, Ann More. When this fact was discovered, he was jailed and fired from his job. He wrote his wife from prison, "John Donne—Ann Donne—Undone." The next fourteen years are the possession neither of Jack Donne nor of the Doctor of Divinity. They belong mostly to despair and to writing filled with anguished meditation, faced with a growing family and scant means of support.

When the king closed every means of preferment to Donne except the Church of England, Donne took holy orders and became Dean of St. Paul's in 1621. His sermons were vastly popular for their zealous acceptance of the faith—and for their searing self-doubt, both extremes expressed in strangely feverish chains of intellectual images strung across detached catalogues of the body's loathsome depravities. Always the dramatic impulse pushed to the center of attention a frail and arrogant ego that concealed itself in brazen displays of assurance and uncertainty. Critics have noted these same qualities in Donne's early love lyrics—in which the cynical lover smashes every Petrarchan convention in one poem only to espouse a more exacting and extreme intellectual and spiritual love in the next. This dazzling, sometimes shocking quality was never seen before in English poetry. Circulated in manuscript, these poems announced the arrival of a new age of poets—those we now speak of as the Metaphysical poets: Andrew Marvell, Thomas Carew, George Herbert, Richard Crashaw, Katherine Philips, Abraham Cowley, Henry Vaughan, Thomas Traherne, and the American Edward Taylor. Metaphysical means "beyond the physical"; this group of poets focused much of their work on the spiritual and the life of the soul.

It was a brilliant mode of consciousness, offered as the only feasible successor to the tragic vision expressed—and exhausted—by Shakespeare and the other late tragedians in the age of James. Donne's friend Ben Jonson was born the same year but seems the product of another era, linking the mellifluous Elizabethan lyric to the age of Dryden. For Donne and his followers all was composed of rough edges, conferring the restless energies and the harsh

rhythms of real speech upon opposites recklessly ignited in catastrophe or apotheosis. The rest of the century came to regard this remarkable moment of English poetry with such extreme disfavor that the mere fact of its existence was progressively lost to view, certainly to all but a few scholars, until 1912 when H. J. C. Grierson's new edition of Donne's poems resurrected his reputation and permitted Donne to resume his place in literary history as a major figure.

Donne is now considered one of the great love poets, and "The Ecstasy" is sometimes called the greatest love poem in English. This is true despite, or perhaps in part because of, the smart-aleck cynicism in other amorous work that surrounds it. There is a puzzle here, for if "The Ecstasy" was written as early as these other love poems, why does it describe a love relationship that strikes most people as being of very long standing? The sonnets that follow this poem are almost certainly from the period following Donne's ordination as an Anglican priest, but one shows the passionate acceptance and one the passionate doubt that runs through all Donne's work. The prose meditation printed here was part of Donne's account of a dangerous illness he underwent. Not long after it was written, it became a popular book because it dramatized the preacher of St. Paul's in all his existential vulnerability. This insistence on self-exposure appeared again when Donne posed for his last portrait wearing a shroud and went on to preach his own funeral sermon during his final illness—to a packed cathedral. Hypocritical contrition or sincere flamboyance? It is perhaps a reconciliation of all these opposites that is Donne's real point. The modern poet T. S. Eliot has argued that after Donne, the sensibility in English poetry becomes increasingly dissociated—into mere thought or mere feeling—and needs to reconsider the example of Donne on the way to recovering (or discovering anew) its own unified greatness.

The Ecstasy[1]

Where, like a pillow on a bed,
    A pregnant bank swell'd up, to rest
The violet's reclining head,
    Sat we two, one another's best.

Our hands were firmly cémented   5
    With a fast balm, which thence did spring;
Our eye-beams twisted, and did thread
    Our eyes, upon one double string:[2]

So to intergraft our hands, as yet
    Was all the means to make us one,   10
And pictures on our eyes to get
    Was all our propagation.

As, 'twixt two equal armies, Fate
    Suspends uncertain victory,
Our souls (which to advance their state   15
    Were gone out) hung 'twixt her, and me.

And whilst our souls negotiate there,
    We like sepulchral statues lay;
All day, the same our postures were,
    And we said nothing, all the day.   20

If any, so by love refin'd
    That he soul's language understood,
And by good love were grown all mind,
    Within convenient distance stood,

He (though he knew not which soul spake,   25
    Because both meant, both spake the same)
Might thence a new concoction[3] take,
    And part far purer than he came.

'This Ecstasy doth unperplex,'
    We said, 'and tell us what we love;   30

---

1. **Ecstasy.** This refers, not to intense emotional joy, but to a mystical state in which the soul "stands out" of the body as it contemplates divine truth.
2. **fast balm . . . double string.** The lovers are joined only by the adhesive moisture of their hands and by the invisible shafts of light from their eyes that unite in a single gaze.
3. **concoction,** a substance purified by heat.

This painting, part of a wooden diptych, was completed about ten years before Donne became Dean. It shows Paul's Cross in the foreground with a bishop preaching before the king whose court, judges, and officials can be seen seated in the galleries flanking the royal box.

**A PREACHING AT OLD ST. PAULS
(c. 1616)**
John Gipkyn
Society of Antiquaries of London

We see by this it was not sex;
    We see we saw not what did move:[4]

'But as all several[5] souls contain
    Mixture of things, they know not what,
Love these mix'd souls doth mix again,   **35**
    And makes both one, each this and that.

'A single violet transplant,—
    The strength, the colour, and the size,
All which before was poor, and scant,
    Redoubles still, and multiplies.   **40**

'When love, with one another so
    Interinanimates two souls,
That abler soul, which thence doth flow,
    Defects of loneliness controls.[6]

'We then, who are this new soul, know   **45**
    Of what we are compos'd, and made,
For the atomies[7] of which we grow,
    Are souls, whom no change can invade.

'But oh alas, so long, so far
    Our bodies why do we forbear?   **50**
They are ours, though they are not we; we are
    The intelligences, they the sphere.[8]

'We owe them thanks, because they thus
    Did us, to us, at first convey,
Yielded their forces, sense, to us,   **55**
    Nor are dross to us, but allay.[9]

4. **We see . . . move.** We now can see that before this we did not see what caused or moved our love.
5. **several,** separate.
6. **abler soul . . . controls.** The new, stronger soul created by love from our two souls eliminates the separate loneliness of each.
7. **atomies,** atoms.
8. **intelligences . . . sphere.** In Christian mysticism, an angel, or intelligence, controlled each planetary sphere beyond the earth. Here, the lovers' bodies are seen as being so controlled by the soul.
9. **dross . . . allay.** Dross is a waste that weakens metals. An allay (or alloy) is a base metal used to strengthen a costly one. So, here, bodies do not weaken love, but strengthen it.

'On man heaven's influence works not so,
  But that it first imprints the air;[10]
So soul into the soul may flow,
  Though it to body first repair.   60

'As our blood labours to beget
  Spirits, as like souls as it can,[11]
Because such fingers need to knit
  That subtle knot, which makes us man:

'So must pure lovers' souls descend   65
  To affections, and to faculties,
Which sense may reach and apprehend,
  Else a great Prince[12] in prison lies.

'To our bodies turn we then, that so
  Weak men on love reveal'd may look;   70
Love's mysteries in souls do grow,
  But yet the body is his book:[13]

'And if some lover, such as we,
  Have heard this dialogue of one,[14]
Let him still mark us, he shall see   75
  Small change, when we are to bodies gone.'

---

10. **imprints the air.** It was thought that astrological forces worked on people through the surrounding air.
11. **Spirits . . . as it can.** The blood was thought to create a thin vapor or rarefied liquid that intermediated between the body and the soul.
12. **Prince,** Love, or the soul itself, which has the ability to love.
13. **book.** The mysteries of the soul in love are imprinted in its scripture, the body.
14. **dialogue of one,** two voices paradoxically speaking, not in turn, but as one.

Death, Be Not Proud

Death, be not proud, though some have called thee
Mighty and dreadful, for thou are not so;
For those whom thou think'st thou dost overthrow
Die not, poor death, nor yet canst thou kill me.
From rest and sleep, which but thy pictures be,   5
Much pleasure, then from thee much more must flow,
And soonest our best men with thee do go,
Rest of their bones, and soul's delivery.
Thou art slave to Fate, chance, kings, and desperate men,
And dost with poison, war, and sickness dwell,   10
And poppy, or charms can make us sleep as well,
And better than thy stroke; why swell'st thou then?
One short sleep past, we wake eternally,
And death shall be no more; death, thou shalt die.

Batter My Heart

Batter my heart, three-personed God; for You
As yet but knock, breathe, shine, and seek to mend;
That I may rise and stand, o'erthrow me, and bend
Your force to break, blow, burn, and make me new.
I, like an usurped town, to another due,   5
Labor to admit You, but O, to no end;
Reason, Your viceroy in me, me should defend,
But is captived, and proves weak or untrue.
Yet dearly I love You, and would be loved fain,
But am betrothed unto Your enemy.   10
Divorce me, untie or break that knot again;
Take me to You, imprison me, for I,
Except You enthrall me, never shall be free,
Nor ever chaste, except You ravish me.

MEDITATION 17

Nunc lento sonitu dicunt, morieris.

Now this bell, tolling softly for another, says to me,

Thou must die.

Perchance he for whom this bell[1] tolls may be so ill as that he knows not it tolls for him; and perchance I may think myself so much better than I am, as that they who are about me and see my state, may have caused it to toll for me, and I know not that. The church is catholic, universal; so are all her actions; all that she does belongs to all. When she baptizes a child, that action concerns me, for that child is thereby connected to that Head which is my Head too, and engraffed[2] into that body, whereof I am a member.[3] And when she buries a man, that action concerns me. All mankind is of one author, and is one volume; when one man dies, one chapter is not torn out of the book, but translated[4] into a better language, and every chapter must be so translated; God employs several translators; some pieces are translated by age, some by sickness, some by war, some by justice; but God's hand is in every translation; and his hand shall bind up all our scattered leaves again for that library where every book shall lie open to one another. As therefore the bell that rings to a sermon calls not upon the preacher only, but upon the congregation to come, so this bell calls us all; but how much more me, who am brought so near the door by this sickness? There was a contention as far as a suit[5] (in which both piety and dignity, religion and estimation,[6] were mingled) which of the religious orders should ring to prayers first in the morning; and it was determined, that they should ring first that rose earliest. If we understand aright the dignity of this bell that tolls for our evening prayer, we would be glad to make it ours by rising early, in that application, that it might be ours as well as his whose indeed it is. The bell doth toll for him that thinks it doth; and though it intermit[7] again, yet from that minute that that occasion wrought upon him, he is united to God. Who casts not up his eye to the sun when it rises? But who takes off his eye from a comet when that breaks out? Who bends not his ear to any bell which upon any occasion rings? But who can remove it from that bell which is passing a piece of himself out of this world? No man is an island, entire of itself; every man is a piece of the continent, a part of the main.[8] If a clod be washed away by the sea, Europe is the less, as well as if a promontory were, as well as if a manor[9] of thy friend's or of thine own were. Any man's death diminishes me because I am involved in mankind; and therefore never send to know for whom the bell tolls; it tolls for thee. Neither can we call this a begging of misery or a borrowing of misery, as though we were not miserable enough of ourselves, but must fetch in more from the next house, in taking upon us the misery of our neighbors. Truly it were an excusable covetousness if we did; for affliction is a treasure, and scarce any man hath enough of it. No man hath affliction enough that is not matured

---

1. **bell,** the passing-bell, which is rung to signify that someone has died.
2. **engraffed,** grafted.
3. **member,** that is, a member of the church.
4. **translated.** Donne puns on the literal meaning, "carried over."
5. **suit,** an argument which developed into legal action.
6. **estimation,** self-esteem.
7. **intermit,** break off.
8. **main,** mainland.
9. **manor,** estate.

and ripened by it, and made fit for God by that affliction. If a man carry treasure in bullion, or in a wedge of gold, and have none coined into current monies, his treasure will not defray[10] him as he travels. Tribulation is treasure in the nature of it, but it is not current money in the use of it, except we get nearer and nearer our home, heaven, by it. Another man may be sick too, and sick to death, and this affliction may lie in his bowels, as gold in a mine, and be of no use to him; but this bell, that tells me of his affliction, digs out and applies that gold to me, if by this consideration of another's danger, I take mine own into contemplation, and so secure myself by making my recourse to my God, who is our only security.

FOR UNDERSTANDING

1. Do the two souls in "The Ecstasy" lose their own individual identity when they become part of the new soul created by their love?
2. In "Death, Be Not Proud," what relationship is implied between the speaker and death? What reasons does the speaker give for not being afraid of death? How does the speaker persuade you (or himself) of the truth of the last four words?
3. What differences in attitude do you find in "Death, Be Not Proud" and "Batter My Heart"?
4. The speaker in "Batter My Heart" seems to be advising God what He must do to win the speaker's heart. Explain how this can create a tone both of spiritual arrogance and of despairing humility. Can such a paradoxical tone be emotionally and psychologically convincing?
5. Donne's assertions in "Meditation 17" are made so strongly that it may be difficult to argue with them. Nonetheless, how would you agree, or disagree, with these statements:

All mankind is of one author, and is one volume.
God's hand is in every translation.
Any man's death diminishes me, because I am involved in mankind.
Tribulation is treasure in the nature of it.

FOR INTERPRETATION

1. To demonstrate how the two souls in "The Ecstasy" have grown together, Donne uses a number of images that refer to various kinds of mixing, twining, or fusing. Find as many examples of this as you can. To what different fields of knowledge do these examples belong?
2. The rhythm in Donne's lines seems to shift without warning, upsetting a regular beat. To achieve emotional intensity, Marlowe crowded stresses together, as in Faustus' last speech: "See, see, where Christ's blood streams in the firmament." Try reading aloud the following lines from Donne and listen for unexpected stresses. What do you notice about the words so emphasized?
"Death, Be Not Proud," 9–11, 14.
"Batter My Heart," 1–4, 11.
3. The first four lines of "Batter My Heart" are one sentence. Count the verbs in this single sentence. Why do some of the verbs contradict each other? The last four lines of the sonnet also have a number of contradictory verbs. Discuss their impact. Is the situation similar to or different from the opening four lines?

Students in poetry workshops are often told that their verse will be more powerful if they drastically cut down on adjectives and concentrate on using vivid and dramatic verbs. Consider Donne's sonnet in this light.
4. Although the tolling of the bell is the beginning of "Meditation 17," and a major metaphor throughout, Donne characteristically proceeds through a whole range of metaphors. How many different ones can you find? What connections do you see between them?

FOR APPRECIATION

The Sonnet
Review what you have learned about the sonnet form in reading the Renaissance poets from Wyatt to Shakespeare in the first part of this unit. Then explain the structure of these two sonnets by Donne. Which of the two major kinds of sonnet are these? One of the two has a volta or turning

---

10. **defray,** pay (the cost).

point and one does not. Show how the choice of form in each case helps to express the meaning of each poem.

The Conceit

This is a term used by Renaissance poets to refer to a specific kind of elaborate metaphor. The conceit relates many aspects of an abstract idea to the component parts of a concrete object or being. The term comes from *concetto*, an Italian word for "idea." Many conventional conceits were used over and over by Elizabethan poets; if a woman's face is compared to a garden, then we will be told that her lips are roses, her eyes pools, her teeth a white fence, etc. Donne can use conventional conceits occasionally (grief as a fierce beast), but more often his comparisons are surprising or even shocking.

"Batter My Heart" is an excellent example of a poem that develops a single conceit from first line to last. The speaker asks God to conquer his heart just as a medieval lord would besiege and conquer one of his walled towns when it has fallen into the hands of an enemy. Within this figure, there is a battering ram, a usurping enemy, a weak ruler left in charge of the town, and an urgent appeal from the town to the lord, asking to be sacked and ravished. Take each of the items on this list and explain how the poem fits them into the situation in which the speaker appeals to God for help.

LANGUAGE AND VOCABULARY

1. In "The Ecstasy," Donne coins two words by use of the prefix *inter-*. Find these two words and explain how they relate to the imagery of "mixing."

2. In both "The Ecstasy" and "Death, Be Not Proud," the word *pictures* occurs. This is one of Donne's favorite words (both in the singular and the plural). Discuss the point of the word in both poems.

3. Define the word *enthrall* as it appears in "Batter My Heart." How is this different from the way we usually use the word today?

COMPOSITION

Take a familiar proverb and write a paragraph about it in the style of Donne's "Meditation 17." Find as many associations and metaphors relating to the words of the proverb as you can.

Robert Herrick   1591–1674

The leading Cavalier poet or "son of Ben,"
Robert Herrick was born shortly after the
Armada (1588), the climactic event of Elizabeth's
reign, and died in the same year as John Milton,
well past the Restoration of Charles II in 1660.
Herrick's was not only one of the longest lives
among English poets, but also one of the most
uneventful. After an apprenticeship as a
goldsmith, he dawdled his way through college
and then became a London fixture among the
literary set that circulated around Ben Jonson,
whom he once called "Saint Ben" in a poem.

Grudgingly he took up a living as a
Devonshire vicar, which caused his twenty-year
absence from London, in which time he came to
appreciate the Devon countryside as much as he
had enjoyed the hubbub of literary life in
London. The civil wars brought him up to
London once more—for a twelve-year stay
during which he published his collected secular
and sacred poems in two volumes. The
restoration of Charles also brought Herrick's
own "restoration"—to the vacant vicarage in
Devon, where he remained until his death. His
poems reflect a serene view of life with a
jewelsmith's miniature perfection of proportion.
A warm friend of musicians in Jonson's circle, he
wrote graceful songs that were set and sung
before the king and queen at Whitehall. Both
jeweled brevity and lilting lyricism closely akin to
music characterize many of his 1300 poems in
their celebration of ladies who go a-maying or
which sing tirelessly "of brooks, of blossoms,
birds, and bowers." He was the culmination of
a line of tuneful Elizabethan madrigalists such as
Thomas Campion, writing a lyrical poetry that

ROBERT HERRICK
The Mansell Collection

would not soon revisit English with its seemingly
artless but highly skilled expression of pure
sweetness. "The Argument of His Book" sums
up his poetry fairly. The charming poem
"Delight in Disorder" shows Herrick willing to
exploit a contradiction, but for sheer delight
rather than for gloomy metaphysical speculation.

Delight in Disorder

A sweet disorder in the dress
Kindles in clothes a wantonness.
A lawn about the shoulders thrown
Into a fine distraction;
An erring lace, which here and there   5
Enthralls the crimson stomacher;
A cuff neglectful, and thereby
Ribbons to flow confusedly;
A winning wave, deserving note,
In the tempestuous petticoat;   10
A careless shoestring, in whose tie
I see a wild civility;
Do more bewitch me than when art
Is too precise in every part.

The Argument of His Book

I sing of brooks, of blossoms, birds, and
   bowers,
Of April, May, of June, and July flowers.
I sing of Maypoles, hock carts,[1] wassails,
   wakes,[2]
Of bridegrooms, brides, and of their bridal
   cakes.
I write of youth, of love, and have access   5
By these to sing of cleanly wantonness.
I sing of dews, of rains, and, piece by piece,
Of balm, of oil, of spice, and ambergris.[3]
I sing of times trans-shifting, and I write
How roses first came red and lilies white.   10
I write of groves, of twilights, and I sing
The court of Mab[4] and of the fairy king.
I write of hell; I sing (and ever shall)
Of heaven, and hope to have it after all.

1. **hock carts,** carts used to carry in the last load of the
harvest.
2. **wakes,** parish festivals as well as watches over the
dead.
3. **ambergris** (am′ bər grēs′), substance from whales
used in making perfume.
4. **Mab** (mab), the queen of the fairies (see *Romeo and
Juliet,* I:4:39-79, Mercutio's famous speech describing
her activities).

UNDERSTANDING AND APPRECIATION

Delight in Disorder

1. Again, the question of order becomes important. Why does the speaker list the details in the order he does?
2. What sense do you get of the personality of the woman described?
3. Look back at Jonson's "Still To Be Neat" (page 302). How would you distinguish the two poets' views on the subject of careful art and neglected beauty?
4. Is the word *enthralls* used in the same way here that Donne used it in "Batter My Heart"? Why would the modern meaning of the word weaken this passage?
5. What point is made by the discrepancy between the adjective and noun in the phrase "wild civility"? Find other adjective/noun pairs of this sort in the poem. How is this pattern echoed by the verb/adverb pair "flow confusedly"?

The Argument of His Book

1. Herrick is making a list of various subjects he will write about. How random is his order? Can you detect any structure in his list? Any progression? Why does he begin where he does and end where he does?
2. The poem is noticeable for its great number of nouns and small number of adjectives. What effect is gained by using so many nouns?

George Herbert 1593–1633

The twentieth-century revival of John Donne's poetry from almost total eclipse also brought into view once more the self-effacing poetry of George Herbert, considered by many the most significant metaphysical poet in the generation after Donne. Born into one of the greatest houses in England, he was the younger brother of Lord Herbert of Cherbury, an English statesman and poet of distinction. Their mother, Lady Magdalen Herbert, was the close friend of Donne whom the latter celebrated in his elegy "The Autumnal." After taking degrees at Cambridge, Herbert became Public Orator of the university in 1619, a post that might well have led to a distinguished political career like that of his brother, since it put him in close touch with both the court and the king.

Having wished from childhood to enter the Anglican priesthood, he was nonetheless tempted by the possibilities for secular preferment that his position made available to him. Some see the poem, "The Collar," as symbolically dramatizing these years of ambivalence, inner conflict, and vacillation. Finally, the worsening of his serious tuberculosis, combined with the death of his mother and his king, seemed at last to deliver him from indecision. He married Jane Danvers and in 1630 became rector of Bemerton, a small church in Salisbury. In the last three years of his life he felt released from all secular considerations, free to follow his deeply felt vocation in a burst of heroic devotion. He went to extraordinary lengths beyond the call of duty to minister to the poor, the sick, and the dying, with all of whom he experienced an empathetic kinship. In these last climactic years, he also completed his one volume of poems, published as *The Temple* after his death.

His verse presents contradictory surfaces within the enclosure of the devotional theme. Precise and elegant in its understated simplicity, this poetry might be the work of a religious-minded "son of Ben," except that it is filled—like Donne's poems—with ingenious conceits, analogies, acrostics, anagrams, and is

GEORGE HERBERT
The Mansell Collection

even sometimes cleverly shaped—like "Easter Wings"—to further symbolize its subject. Thus, the homespun certainties of pious belief are constantly being enacted in a dramatic poetry filled with self-doubt and contradiction. Ultimately, Herbert must be seen as a metaphysical poet who brings to life the variegated psychological states of faith with an immediacy that can still move or disturb us today.

In Herbert's poems we see a constant attempt to find a comfortable and lasting relationship between himself and God. These attempts are never totally successful, however, since Herbert had a deep sense of his own sinfulness and a strong belief that human beings were inherently unworthy of God's love.

Nonetheless, he keeps trying to express his love for God, in a series of poems that are memorable for their variety of feeling and of form. In the 164 poems that make up *The Temple*, no stanzaic form or rhyme scheme is repeated exactly from one poem to the next. This extraordinary variety has several sources: Herbert's inventiveness as a poet, his search for the best way to talk to God, and his desire to praise God by showing his awareness of God's manifold gifts to human beings. This awareness of God as gracious and visible in all aspects of the world is responsible for Herbert's emblematic approach—that is, he constantly sees objects as representative of God's power or grace or love. That is why he can take a real object like the collar worn by a priest and turn it into a metaphor for his relationship with God.

Although *The Temple* is a collection of many different poems, it is also a book with shape and direction. It begins with a section called "The Church-Porch," a series of 77 stanzas which preach conventional moral wisdom and which prepare the worshiper to enter "The Church," the major section of the book, and the part from which all our poems have been chosen. The first poem in "The Church" is "The Altar" and the second is "The Sacrifice," a magnificent poem in which Christ speaks to those who have crucified him. Of the poems here, both "The Collar" and "Love" move from a state of inward anxiety to one of profound certitude. "Redemption" is a sonnet-long, compressed allegory that demonstrates the reverse side to these poems: the suffering endured by Christ to redeem all the uncertainties of the faithful.

Easter Wings

Lord, who createdst man in wealth and store,[1]
  Though foolishly he lost the same,
    Decaying more and more
      Till he became
        Most poor:
        With thee
      O let me rise
    As larks, harmoniously,
  And sing this day thy victories:
Then shall the fall further the flight in me.

My tender age in sorrow did begin;
  And still with sicknesses and shame
    Thou didst so punish sin,
      That I became
        Most thin.
        With thee
      Let me combine,
    And feel this day thy victory;
  For, if I imp[2] my wing on thine,
Affliction shall advance the flight in me.

1. **store,** abundance.
2. **imp,** a term from falconry; to engraft feathers in the damaged wing of a bird so as to restore or improve its powers of flight.

The Collar

I struck the board[1] and cried, "No more;
    I will abroad!
What? Shall I ever sigh and pine?
My lines and life are free, free as the road,
    Loose as the wind, as large as store.[2]   5
      Shall I be still in suit?
   Have I no harvest but a thorn
   To let me blood, and not restore
What I have lost with cordial[3] fruit?
      Sure there was wine   10
 Before my sighs did dry it; there was corn
   Before my tears did drown it.
   Is the year only lost to me?
    Have I no bays[4] to crown it,
No flowers, no garlands gay? All blasted?   15
        All wasted?
   Not so, my heart; but there is fruit,
    And thou hast hands.
   Recover all thy sigh-blown age
On double pleasures: leave thy cold dispute   20
Of what is fit and not. Forsake thy cage,
    Thy rope of sands,
Which petty thoughts have made, and made to thee
   Good cable to enforce and draw,
      And by thy law,   25
   While thou didst wink and wouldst not see.
     Away! take heed;
     I will abroad.
Call in thy death's head there; tie up thy fears.
    He that forbears   30
    To suit and serve his need,
    Deserves his load."
But as I raved and grew more fierce and wild
    At every word,
Methought I heard one calling *Child!*   35
    And I replied, *My Lord.*

1. **board,** literally table, but also perhaps the Communion Table.
2. **store,** abundance.
3. **cordial,** life-giving, with a pun on its root meaning, "from the heart."
4. **bays,** a garland of laurels, signifying honor or renown.

Redemption

Having been tenant long to a rich Lord,
   Not thriving, I resolvèd to be bold,
And make a suit unto Him, to afford
   A new small-rented lease, and cancel th' old.

In heaven at His manour I Him sought: 5
   They told me there, that He was lately gone
About some land, which he had dearly bought
   Long since on Earth, to take possession.

I straight returned, and knowing His great birth,
   Sought Him accordingly in great resorts—   10
In cities, theatres, gardens, parks, and courts:
   At length I heard a raggèd noise and mirth

   Of thieves and murderers; there I Him espied,
   Who straight, 'Your suit is granted,' said, and died.

Love (III)

Love bade me welcome: yet my soul drew back,
   Guilty of dust and sin.
But quick-eyed Love, observing me grow slack
   From my first entrance in,
Drew nearer to me, sweetly questioning   5
   If I lacked anything.

"A guest," I answered, "worthy to be here":
   Love said, "You shall be he."
"I, the unkind, ungrateful? Ah, my dear,
   I cannot look on thee."   10
Love took my hand, and smiling did reply,
   "Who made the eyes but I?"

"Truth, Lord, but I have marred them; let my shame
   Go where it doth deserve."
"And know you not," says Love, "who bore the blame?"   15
   "My dear, then I will serve."
"You must sit down," says Love, "and taste my meat."
   So I did sit and eat.

UNDERSTANDING AND INTERPRETATION

Easter Wings

1. What connections can you find between the shape of the poem and the subject?
2. Why are "wings" an appropriate image?

The Collar

1. What is the speaker rebelling against?
2. The speaker seems to be conducting an argument with himself. What are the major divisions—the problems and the potential solutions—of this argument?
3. How do the last four lines, through meaning and rhythm, work to resolve the poem?
4. The poem may or may not be about Herbert's long debate on whether to become an Anglican priest or to seek a secular career. How would you argue that the poem is a dramatization of this period of indecision in Herbert's life? How would the title relate to your argument? How independent is the poem of this possible interpretation?

Redemption

1. Like Donne's "Batter My Heart," this is an example of the sonnet-long conceit; here the comparison is between God and the sinner on one hand and a landlord and a tenant on the other. In Herbert's poem, the landlord/tenant relationship is skewed by fitting it into the religious relationship, but this is what gives the poem its power and shock value. Prove or disprove this last statement by pointing to details on both sides of the conceit.
2. How does Herbert's use of the conceit compare with Donne's? How is his choice of sonnet form different from that of Donne?
3. Who exactly are the thieves and the murderers of line 13?
4. Argue for or against this assertion: The volta of this sonnet is delayed until the beginning of line 12.

Love (III)

1. What is the dramatic situation implied in the poem? How would you characterize the speaker?
2. What details in the poem lead you to identify "Love" and "the Lord"? What is gained by using "Love" throughout?
3. Why is the speaker so reluctant to accept Love's welcome? Why does he change his mind?
4. This poem is the last one in the collection of Herbert's poems called *The Temple*. What makes it seem a concluding poem?

Andrew Marvell 1621–1678

No English poet of the mid-seventeenth century is so typical of the age as Andrew Marvell. At the same time that he reflects so many of the trends in the poetry and politics of that day, he remains to the last both atypically contradictory and unique. Of a Yorkshire Puritan family background, he evidently flirted briefly with Roman Catholicism as a Cambridge undergraduate. Deeply caught up in the passions of his times, he seems paradoxically to have taken no part in the civil wars between the Royalist and Parliamentary causes. His great "Horatian Ode upon Cromwell's Return from Ireland" shows an extraordinarily balanced view of the arch antagonists, Cromwell and Charles I, crediting the courage of both while warning Cromwell of the dangers inherent in a rule by force alone.

This moderation of viewpoint may have recommended him to Lord Fairfax, also a Yorkshire man but more importantly the Lord-General of the Parliamentary Army. As the Puritan cause triumphed, the liberal Parliamentary faction—as typified by Fairfax—increasingly came into conflict with the extremely radical Independent faction in the Army, which was led by General Cromwell. However it happened, a year after writing the "Horatian Ode," Marvell was ensconced (1651–1653) at Fairfax's country estate, Nun Appleton House, as tutor to Mary Fairfax, the lord's daughter. Most of his lyrical poems must have been written in this period, including those appearing here. This small output of verse, unpublished in his time and almost unread until our own, is the basis for his currently growing reputation as a witty and urbane metaphysical "son of John Donne" who nonetheless wrote with the smooth meters and plain diction of a "son of Ben Jonson." The range and diversity encompassed by these few lyrics is remarkable.

After another period of tutoring a young ward of Cromwell himself, Marvell was recommended for employment in the Commonwealth government by his friend John

ANDREW MARVELL
Unknown Artist
National Portrait Gallery, London

Milton. In 1657, he became a Latin secretary like Milton, though in a different office. Late in the Puritan interregnum, he became a Member of Parliament for Hull in the House of Commons. This became a lifelong position that he maintained well past the Restoration. In the uncertain period following the resumption of the monarchy, Marvell defended Milton during the latter's prosecution as a proponent of regicide in 1660. Marvell is thus credited with saving the older poet's life. Given his implicit protection as a parliamentarian, he also became increasingly outspoken as a defender of religious liberty and freedom of speech, attacking the excesses of the king, the court, and the emerging Tory party. Yet even in his most ardent broadsides, there is a balance and even-handedness of judgment that point toward his inherent tolerance and moderation, qualities more often lost on both sides in the heat of the battle.

During the reign of Charles II, Marvell wrote a considerable amount of satirical verse which has been undervalued as mere partisan rhetoric but is now recognized as poetry of sometimes significant value. Marvell's pro-Puritan poetry and prose earned him an early audience in the American colonies, where he was never quite lost sight of (as witness a reference to a line of his poetry at the end of Nathaniel Hawthorne's novel *The Scarlet Letter*). Along with other metaphysicals in general, however, his work suffered a neglect that has taken three hundred years to reverse. It may even become possible one day to appreciate him equally as a champion of liberty ("Our brutish fury struggling to be free"), a witty and profound metaphysical writer of love poems—and, above all, a lover of gardens.

Marvell can be seen as an unusual and early "nature poet" in "The Garden," a metaphysically elaborated description of the Fairfax country estate. The sheer sensuality of his treatment of nature has a Cavalier exuberance about it that is uniquely his own. "To His Coy Mistress" is justly famous as a love poem, though at every moment we can hear the wit, at once personal and learned, that is the poem's dominant feature. As a topic for verse, the seduction theme is hardly new, but Marvell takes the familiar arguments found in this kind of poem and makes them fresh, charming, funny, grotesque, and memorable.

To His Coy Mistress

    Had we but world enough, and time,
This coyness, lady, were no crime.
We would sit down, and think which way
To walk, and pass our long love's day.
Thou by the Indian Ganges' side   5
Shouldst rubies find; I by the tide
Of Humber[1] would complain. I would
Love you ten years before the flood,
And you should, if you please, refuse
Till the conversion of the Jews.[2]   10
My vegetable[3] love should grow
Vaster than empires and more slow;
An hundred years should go to praise
Thine eyes, and on thy forehead gaze;
Two hundred to adore each breast,   15
But thirty thousand to the rest;
An age at least to every part,

---

1. **Humber,** the river that flows through Marvell's hometown, Hull.
2. **conversion of the Jews,** supposed to occur, according to Christian tradition, at the end of history; therefore, a long time away.
3. **vegetable,** growing as slowly as vegetation.

And the last age should show your heart.
For, lady, you deserve this state,[4]
Nor would I love at lesser rate.   20
    But at my back I always hear
Time's winged chariot hurrying near;
And yonder all before us lie
Deserts of vast eternity.
Thy beauty shall no more be found;   25
Nor, in thy marble vault, shall sound
My echoing song; then worms shall try
That long-preserved virginity,
And your quaint[5] honor turn to dust,
And into ashes all my lust: 30
The grave's a fine and private place,
But none, I think, do there embrace.
    Now therefore, while the youthful hue
Sits on thy skin like morning dew,
And while thy willing soul transpires[6]   35
At every pore with instant fires,
Now let us sport us while we may,
And now, like amorous birds of prey,
Rather at once our time devour
Than languish in his slow-chapped[7] power   40
Let us roll all our strength and all
Our sweetness up into one ball,
And tear our pleasures with rough strife
Thorough[8] the iron gates of life:
Thus, though we cannot make our sun   45
Stand still, yet we will make him run.[9]

4. **state,** dignity; ceremonial treatment.
5. **quaint,** fastidious.
6. **transpires,** breathes out.
7. **slow-chapped,** slow-jawed; personifying Time as devouring love.
8. **thorough,** through.
9. Two biblical allusions are in the last two lines: Joshua commanded the sun to stand still (*Joshua* 9), while in *Psalms* 19:5, the sun is described "as a bridegroom coming out of his chamber, [who] rejoiceth as a strong man to run a race."

The Garden

How vainly men themselves amaze
To win the palm, the oak, or bays,[1]
And their incessant labors see
Crowned from some single herb, or tree,
Whose short and narrow-vergéd shade   5
Does prudently their toils upbraid;
While all flowers and all trees do close[2]
To weave the garlands of repose!

Fair Quiet, have I found thee here,
And Innocence, thy sister dear?   10
Mistaken long, I sought you then
In busy companies of men.
Your sacred plants, if here below,
Only among the plants will grow;
Society is all but rude   15
To this delicious solitude.

No white nor red was ever seen
So amorous as this lovely green.
Fond lovers, cruel as their flame,
Cut in these trees their mistress' name: 20
Little, alas, they know or heed
How far these beauties hers exceed!
Fair trees, wheresoe'er your barks I wound,
No name shall but your own be found.[3]

When we have run our passion's heat,   25
Love hither makes his best retreat.
The gods, that mortal beauty chase,
Still in a tree did end their race:
Apollo hunted Daphne so,
Only that she might laurel grow;   30
And Pan did after Syrinx speed,
Not as a nymph, but for a reed.[4]

1. **palm . . . bays,** the leafy garlands used to crown excellence in athletics (palm), civics (oak), and poetry (bays). Men bewilder (amaze) themselves seeking these prizes in vain.
2. **close,** unite.
3. **No name . . . found.** The speaker says he will not carve the names of women in the tree bark, but only the names of the trees themselves.
4. **Apollo . . . reed.** When Apollo pursued Daphne, she was changed into a laurel tree. When Pan pursued Syrinx, she was changed into a reed. These stories are told in Ovid's *Metamorphoses*.

What wondrous life is this I lead!
Ripe apples drop about my head;
The luscious clusters of the vine   35
Upon my mouth do crush their wine;
The nectarine and curious[5] peach
Into my hands themselves do reach;
Stumbling on melons, as I pass,
Insnared with flowers, I fall on grass.   40

Meanwhile the mind, from pleasure less,[6]
Withdraws into its happiness;
The mind, that ocean where each kind
Does straight its own resemblance find;[7]
Yet it creates, transcending these,   45
Far other worlds and other seas,
Annihilating all that's made
To a green thought in a green shade.[8]

Here at the fountain's sliding foot,
Or at some fruit tree's mossy root,   50
Casting the body's vest[9] aside,
My soul into the boughs does glide:
There, like a bird, it sits and sings,
Then whets[10] and combs its silver wings,
And, till prepared for longer flight,   55
Waves in its plumes the various light.[11]

Such was that happy garden-state,
While man there walked without a mate:
After a place so pure and sweet,
What other help could yet be meet![12]   60
But 'twas beyond a mortal's share
To wander solitary there:
Two paradises 'twere in one
To live in paradise alone.

---

5. **curious,** noticeably excellent, rare.
6. **mind . . . less.** The mind is concentrated, diminished, and focused by pleasure.
7. **ocean . . . find.** Just as creatures in the sea correspond to those on land, so ideas in the mind correspond to those in reality.
8. **Annihilating . . . shade.** The mind reduces everything to an immaterial idea of growth itself while surrounded by the growth of the green garden.

9. **vest,** vestment, garment.
10. **whets,** preens.
11. **various light,** the variegated, prismatic light of this world as compared to the colorless light of eternity.
12. **help . . . meet.** This is a wordplay on God's decision to create Eve as "an help meet" for Adam, *Genesis* ii.18.

How well the skillful gardener drew   65
Of flowers and herbs this dial[13] new,
Where, from above, the milder sun
Does through a fragrant zodiac run;
And as it works, th' industrious bee
Computes its time as well as we!   70
How could such sweet and wholesome hours
Be reckoned but with herbs and flowers?

13. **dial.** The gardener has made a sundial whose face
is composed of different varieties of growing flowers.
Thus, the sun's zodiac is "fragrant" and the bee's honey
gathering seems to tell time.

UNDERSTANDING AND INTERPRETATION

To His Coy Mistress

1. The poem is written in three verse paragraphs.
What is the central point of each one?

2. List the hyperboles in the first twenty lines.
What do they tell us about the speaker and his
attitude toward the lady?

3. What does the word *coy* mean? What sense do
you get of the lady's interest (or lack of interest) in
the speaker?

4. How seriously do you think we should take this
poem? Why?

5. Consider the following statements. Which do
you find strongest evidence for?

a. The poet is an old man who is afraid of death
and who is deeply in love with a young woman.

b. The poet is a young man who uses the inevitability of death to scare the woman into responding
to him.

The Garden

1. In the first two stanzas, the poet says that busy
human achievement is not as valuable as "delicious
solitude." How is plant imagery in each stanza
used to make this statement?

2. Love and passion are dismissed in stanzas three
and four. But how does the fifth stanza contradict
this dismissal?

3. Stanzas five through seven are respectively
about the body, the mind, and the soul. How does
the garden bring each of the three to its perfection? How seriously are these assertions meant to
be taken?

4. Lines 47-48 have received a great deal of attention and commentary. Do you agree or disagree
that Marvell's argument turns (intentionally or
unintentionally) ominous here? Explain your
point of view.

5. Is it hard to believe that the same poet who
wrote "To His Coy Mistress" also wrote stanza
eight of this poem?

Katherine Philips 1631–1664

Known in her time as "the English Sappho," Katherine Philips was the first woman poet in England of ordinary background who produced a body of distinguished verse, won fame thereby, and went on to live as a successful writer in the literary circles of her day. Born Katherine Fowler to a London merchant family, she probably owed her chance at achieving literary fame to the period's reformist zeal for the serious education of all, including girls. Along with her friend Mary Aubrey, cousin of the biographer John Aubrey, she attended Mrs. Salmon's private boarding school for girls at Hackney, which was focused on genuine accomplishment rather than "household science."

At seventeen she married James Philips, a Puritan and parliamentary leader whose living was at a priory in Cardigan, Wales. There she set up a literary salon, The Society of Friendship, in which members took classical names, as described in her *Letters* (1705). Calling herself "Orinda," she included among her friends the Puritan composer Henry Lawes, Royalist Bishop Jeremy Taylor, and Royalist poet Henry Vaughan. Taylor addressed to her his eloquent essay, "Measures and Offices of Friendship"; Vaughan wrote an epistolary poem to her filled with lavish compliments, and Dryden later praised her work. Abraham Cowley, the most famous metaphysical poet of that day, wrote a long elegy on the death of "the matchless Orinda" during a London smallpox epidemic.

Looking for new horizons to conquer, Philips went to Ireland with the Viscountess of Dungannon where her translation in 1663 of Corneille's tragedy *Pompée* was performed in Dublin to critical acclaim. Before she could consolidate her triumph in this new field, the epidemic claimed her. Aphra Behn (1640–1689), the first woman to earn her living by writing, may have been inspired as a playwright by Philips's example. Of women who wrote poetry in English before Philips and Behn, three were Queens (Elizabeth of York, mother of Henry VIII; Ann Boleyn; and Elizabeth I). A number were from the nobility—Mary Sidney Pembroke,

KATHERINE PHILIPS
The Mansell Collection

Countess of Pembroke; Lucy Harington, Countess of Bedford (patron of Donne who got from her the line "Death be not proud"); and Margaret Cavendish, Duchess of Newcastle. Some few were without title, such as Anne Askew, Isabella Whitney, and Anne Collins. Two of these women—Cavendish and Behn—are buried in the select Poets Corner of Westminster Abbey. Considering this far-from-thorough list, the American Anne Bradstreet (1612–1672), twenty years Katherine Philips's senior, stands out all the more as one of the first considerable women poets of any social background anywhere.

Philips's poetry shows a stylistic fusion somewhat similar to that of Andrew Marvell, in that her figures are metaphysical in their ingenuity while her meter and diction show her to be a true "daughter of Ben." Her subject matter as a poet is focused upon the nature of lasting friendships between women, but she wrote popular verses deploring the execution of Charles I. The following poem embodies a metaphysical idea within an understated clarity of diction; the absent friend is Mary Aubrey, whom she called "Lucasia."

Orinda To Lucasia

Observe the weary birds, ere night be done,
How they would fain call up the tardy sun.
  With feathers hung with dew,
  And trembling voices too,
They court their glorious planet to appear,   5
That they may find recruits of spirits there.
  The drooping flowers hang their heads,
  And languish down into their beds;
While brooks, more bold and fierce than they,
  Wanting those beams, from whence   10
  All things drink influence,
Openly murmur, and demand the day.

Thou, my Lucasia, art far more to me,
Than he to all the under-world can be;
  From thee I've heat and light;   15
  Thy absence makes my night.
But ah! my friend, it now grows very long,
The sadness weighty, and the darkness strong;
  My tears, its dew, dwell on my cheeks;
  And still my heart thy dawning seeks,   20
And to thee mournfully it cries
  That if too long I wait,
  Even thou may'st come too late,
And not restore my life, but close my eyes.

UNDERSTANDING AND INTERPRETATION

1. For a whole stanza, this poem seems to be a simple description of how birds, flowers, and brooks miss the sun, "their glorious planet," during the night. With the second stanza, however, it becomes clear that all this has been stated to prepare for its use in the second stanza as the basis of an extended conceit. What is the conceit and how do the details in the first stanza fit into it?

2. In line 14, the sun is seen as the male god Helios or Apollo who visits the underworld at night. Does the line have any other implications?

3. Perhaps the most powerful single image in the poem occurs in line 20 in the phrase "thy dawning." Explain how this image works and what its effect is.

John Milton   1608–1674

Only a few years after Shakespeare's retirement to Stratford, Milton was born in Cheapside, London, not far from where the Mermaid Tavern had witnessed the great playwright talking shop with Ben Jonson and other writers of that day. Milton's father was a prosperous banker and a serious composer. He made certain of providing his genius son with the finest classical education available. Milton showed his rebellious side at Cambridge even as he was becoming fluent in an astonishing number of classical and modern languages. He moved teachers and students alike with his Baconian and Platonic vision of a coming utopian age based on the scientific conquest of nature. Deciding to pursue a life of intellectual freedom, he avoided entering the church and retired instead to his father's house at Horton near Windsor where he spent nearly six years studying for his chosen vocation as the great English epic poet. His early poems are influenced by the metaphysical fashion of the day, but a characteristic neoclassicism is already evident in his powerful pastoral elegy for a drowned schoolmate, *Lycidas*.

On the typical postgraduate "grand tour" of Europe, he made his way to a fateful meeting with Galileo. The great scientist, blinded by age and living in his enforced retirement, gave his blessing to this radiant, youthful idealist, who would in turn become the great blind Homer of his age, as well as the champion of every sort of intellectual freedom. News of the worsening crisis in the conflict between the king and parliament brought Milton home. Momentarily setting aside his dream of writing England's great epic (with King Arthur as hero), he entered the fray as an ideologue and pamphleteer in the war of words that was raging on all sides between every party and faction. Milton devoted the next twenty years to an intense immersion in political strife that nonetheless prepared him for the epic he still coolly planned to write.

JOHN MILTON (1629)
Unknown Artist
National Portrait Gallery, London

His first five pamphlets, produced at white heat in the period 1641–1642, were fiercely pro-Presbyterian and pro-Parliament—which means that he opposed the pro-Anglican Royalist forces backing King Charles I. In 1642, just before the conflict boiled over into civil war, Milton at the age of thirty-three married the seventeen-year-old daughter of a Royalist squire. Within six weeks, however, she left Milton to return to her family—with no intention of ever coming back. This prompted Milton to write his four pamphlets upholding the morality of divorce on the grounds of incompatibility—and causing his first serious censure by the liberal and moderate Presbyterian faction which at that time dominated the Parliamentarian cause. This rebuff stung Milton deeply and propelled him toward the more radical Independent faction in the army, led by Cromwell. Partly in response to the attempt to suppress these pamphlets in 1644, Milton made his immortal statement on the right of a free people to an uncensored press in *Areopagitica*. This work is still required reading today in any discussion of the basic freedoms embodied in the American Bill of Rights, a document inescapably indebted to Milton.

In 1645, after the definitive Royalist defeat at Naseby, his wife finally returned to him, bringing her whole family along—as refugee Royalists seeking their Puritan son-in-law's protection. Milton's pamphlets now turned to the subject of the need for religious toleration and the requirements for a Christian humanist education, with the same scientific emphasis that first appeared in his Cambridge writings. One of Milton's pamphlets in 1649 justified the actions of Cromwell's Independents in imprisoning the king. He even claimed they had the right to impose the death sentence upon the monarch. This stand later assured him of employment in Cromwell's postwar regime, which materialized in his post as Latin Secretary. By 1652 when his wife died, Milton was completely blind, making his government office doubly welcome as a support to his three daughters and himself. His Latin writings during Cromwell's rule were largely an attempt to justify the act of regicide to the appalled European community. In 1656 he married a new wife who died in childbirth two years later, prompting his greatest sonnet, "Methought I saw my late espoused saint."

Just before the Restoration, Milton called glaring attention to himself as an unapologetic Puritan in a pamphlet expressing his perennial militant republicanism. In the transition to the new regime, this made him all the more a marked man, one who was in genuine danger of his life. Forced to go into hiding until the Act of Oblivion in 1660, he still needed the help of his young Puritan friend and member of Parliament, Andrew Marvell, who found the political means to save the old radical's life. Prosecuted and sentenced to a short, nominal imprisonment, Milton soon found himself living a not unpleasant life of enforced retirement, much like Galileo before him. His greatest work was still before him, however, for it was under these circumstances in the last fourteen years of his life that he wrote his three major poems, the epic *Paradise Lost,* the short epic "sequel" *Paradise Regained,* and the classical tragedy *Samson Agonistes.* He had written the optimistic early pages of *Paradise Lost* before the Restoration, adding the gloomier views on human society in the last books of 1663. But if a more stoic resignation is the theme of *Paradise Regained,*

Milton's last great work *Samson* is, iconoclastically, all fury and rebellion. It is also inevitably autobiographical as the blind poet senses within the rising Whig indignation of the 1670s the possibility of his belated vindication. *Samson* is written in powerful, athletic meters that strain conventional prosody to the breaking point and foreshadow the sprung rhythms of Hopkins (see page 839) and even the rhythmic cadences of free verse.

The crowning achievement of his entire life, however, is certainly *Paradise Lost,* the epic he had set for himself the task of writing in his youth. At that time he had considered the story of King Arthur as the most suitable material, but instead—in the ripeness of his years—he came to devote his enormous intellectual and creative energies to this other story, in which he undertook to "justify the ways of God to men." For his form, he turned to the epics of Homer, Virgil, and Dante. But while those epics were about mortals, Milton's characters were Satan, God, Christ, Adam and Eve, and a supporting cast of devils and angels. Milton's decision to start the story of the Fall of Humanity with the Fall of Satan is not merely a following of the epic convention that the story should start "in the middle." Rather, Milton had to create Satan as *the* adversary, a great opponent to both God and Adam, an antagonist of such stature that victory (by God) or defeat (of Adam) would nonetheless be a heroic struggle. Milton's reliance on Latin- and Greek-based words and his inversion of regular English sentence structure can also be seen as his attempt to create a grand style worthy of his theme.

Despite the fact that the Restoration regarded Milton with hostility and suspicion as the fossilized survival of antiquated political and literary views, his published epic met with immediate and sustained applause. Beginning with William Blake, romantics have often identified with the figure of Satan as a tragic rebel, ignoring his freewill choice of evil over good. Milton had long ago left behind any trace of predestination in his emphasis on the perfect freedom of the will to choose its own salvation. The following excerpt starts with the famous opening invocation of Book I of *Paradise Lost.* Then the selection proceeds with Milton directly into the pit of hell after the fall of Satan, where we get Satan's reaction to his plight.

from PARADISE LOST

Book I

Of man's first disobedience, and the fruit
Of that forbidden tree, whose mortal taste
Brought death into the world, and all our woe,
With loss of Eden, till one greater Man[1]
Restore us, and regain the blissful seat,   5
Sing, heavenly Muse, that on the secret top
Of Oreb, or of Sinai,[2] didst inspire
That shepherd who first taught the chosen seed
In the beginning how the heavens and earth
Rose out of Chaos; or if Sion hill[3]   10
Delight thee more, and Siloa's brook[4] that flowed
Fast by the oracle of God, I thence
Invoke thy aid to my adventurous song,
That with no middle flight intends to soar
Above the Aonian mount,[5] while it pursues   15
Things unattempted yet in prose or rhyme.
And chiefly thou, O Spirit, that dost prefer
Before all temples the upright heart and pure,
Instruct me, for thou knowest; thou from the first
Wast present, and with mighty wings outspread   20
Dove-like sat'st brooding on the vast abyss
And mad'st it pregnant: what in me is dark[6]
Illumine, what is low raise and support;
That to the highth of this great argument
I may assert eternal providence,   25
And justify the ways of God to men.
   Say first, for heaven hides nothing from thy view,
Nor the deep tract of hell, say first what cause
Moved our grand parents in that happy state,
Favored of heaven so highly, to fall off   30
From their creator, and transgress his will
For one restraint, lords of the world besides?
Who first seduced them to that foul revolt?

1. **Man,** Christ, sometimes called "the second Adam."
2. **Sinai.** Oreb is another name for Mt. Sinai, where Moses, the shepherd of line 8, received the Law from God.
3. **Sion hill,** Mt. Zion, the site of the Temple in Jerusalem.
4. **brook,** in Jerusalem, near the Temple.
5. **mount,** Helicon, where the Muses lived.
6. **dark,** the first of many references to his blindness.

The infernal serpent[7] he it was whose guile,
Stirred up with envy and revenge, deceived   35
The mother of mankind, what time his pride
Had cast him out from heaven, with all his host
Of rebel angels, by whose aid aspiring
To set himself in glory above his peers,
He trusted to have equalled the Most High,   40
If he opposed; and with ambitious aim
Against the throne and monarchy of God
Raised impious war in heaven and battle proud
With vain attempt. Him the Almighty Power
Hurled headlong flaming from the ethereal sky   45
With hideous ruin[8] and combustion down
To bottomless perdition, there to dwell
In adamantine[9] chains and penal fire,
Who[10] durst defy the omnipotent to arms.
Nine times the space that measures day and night   50
To mortal men, he with his horrid crew[11]
Lay vanquished, rolling in the fiery gulf
Confounded[12] though immortal. But his doom
Reserved him to more wrath; for now the thought
Both of lost happiness and lasting pain   55
Torments him; round he throws his baleful eyes,
That witnessed[13] huge affliction and dismay
Mixed with obdurate pride and steadfast hate.
At once as far as angels' ken[14] he views
The dismal situation waste and wild: 60
A dungeon horrible, on all sides round
As one great furnace flamed, yet from those flames
No light, but rather darkness visible
Served only to discover sights of woe,
Regions of sorrow, doleful shades, where peace   65
And rest can never dwell, hope never comes[15]
That comes to all; but torture without end
Still urges,[16] and a fiery deluge, fed
With ever-burning sulphur unconsumed:
Such place eternal justice had prepared   70
For those rebellious, here their prison ordained

Frontispiece by John Baptist Medina to Book 1 of Paradise Lost published in 1688.

---

7. **serpent.** The serpent in *Genesis* is specifically connected with Satan in the *Book of Revelation,* so Milton is referring, as the following passage makes clear, to Satan himself.

8. **ruin,** literally, falling; an example of Milton's use of the root meaning of a word as well.

9. **adamantine** (ad′ ə man′ tēn;—tīn), Adamant was an imaginary stone of impenetrable hardness.

10. **Who,** he who.

11. **crew,** all the other angels, now devils, who revolted with Satan against God and so fell from heaven too.

12. **Confounded,** literally, poured together: hence, confused.

13. **witnessed,** expressed; revealed.

14. **ken,** range of vision.

15. **hope never comes,** an echo of Dante's hell, which bore the legend "Abandon hope, all ye who enter here."

16. **Still urges,** continually provokes.

In utter darkness, and their portion set
As far removed from God and light of heaven
As from the center thrice to the utmost pole.
O how unlike the place from whence they fell!   75
There the companions of his fall, o'erwhelmed
With floods and whirlwinds of tempestuous fire,
He soon discerns, and weltering[17] by his side
One next himself in power, and next in crime,
Long after known in Palestine, and named   80
Beelzebub.[18] To whom the arch-enemy,
And thence in heaven called Satan[19] with bold words
Breaking the horrid silence thus began:
    "If thou beëst he; but O how fallen! how changed
From him, who in the happy realms of light   85
Clothed with transcendent brightness didst outshine
Myriads though bright—if he whom mutual league,
United thoughts and counsels, equal hope
And hazard in the glorious enterprise,
Joined with me once, now misery hath joined   90
In equal ruin: into what pit thou seest
From what highth fallen, so much the stronger proved
He with his thunder, and till then who knew
The force of those dire arms? Yet not for those,
Nor what the potent victor in his rage   95
Can else inflict, do I repent or change,
Though changed in outer luster that fixed mind
And high disdain, from sense of injured merit,
That with the mightiest raised me to contend,
And to the fierce contention brought along   100
Innumerable force of spirits armed
That durst dislike his reign, and me preferring,
His utmost power with adverse power opposed
In dubious battle on the plains of heaven,
And shook his throne.[20] What though the field be lost?   105
All is not lost; the unconquerable will
And study of revenge, immortal hate,
And courage never to submit or yield:
And what is else not to be overcome?
That glory never shall his wrath or might   110

17. **weltering,** tossing.
18. **Beelzebub** (bē el′ zə bub), Hebrew for "lord of the flies."
19. **Satan.** The word in Hebrew means enemy or opponent.
20. **throne.** Satan is lying, since it was not his power that caused God's throne to shake.

Extort from me. To bow and sue for grace
With suppliant knee, and deify his power
Who[21] from the terror of this arm so late
Doubted[22] his empire, that were low indeed,
That were an ignominy and shame beneath   115
This downfall; since by fate the strength of gods
And this empyreal[23] substance cannot fail,
Since through experience of this great event,
In arms not worse, in foresight much advanced,
We may with more successful hope resolve   120
To wage by force or guile eternal war
Irreconcilable to our grand foe,
Who now triumphs, and in the excess of joy
Sole reigning holds the tyranny of heaven."
   So spake the apostate Angel, though in pain   125
Vaunting[24] aloud, but racked with deep despair;
And him thus answered soon his bold compeer:[25]
   "O Prince, O chief of many thronèd powers,
That led the embattled seraphim[26] to war
Under thy conduct, and in dreadful deeds   130
Fearless, endangered heaven's perpetual king,
And put to proof his high supremacy,
Whether upheld by strength, or chance, or fate;
Too well I see and rue the dire event,
That with sad overthrow and foul defeat   135
Hath lost us heaven, and all this mighty host
In horrible destruction laid thus low,
As far as gods and heavenly essences
Can perish: for the mind and spirit remains
Invincible, and vigor soon returns,   140
Though all our glory extinct,[27] and happy state
Here swallowed up in endless misery.
But what if he our conqueror (whom I now
Of force[28] believe almighty, since no less
Than such could have o'erpowered such force as ours)   145
Have left us this our spirit and strength entire
Strongly to suffer and support our pains,
That we may so suffice his vengeful ire,
Or do him mightier service as his thralls[29]
By right of war, whate'er his business be,   150
Here in the heart of hell to work in fire,

21. **Who,** I who.
22. **Doubted,** feared for.
23. **empyreal,** heavenly. The empyrean was the highest heaven in the Ptolemaic system.
24. **Vaunting,** boasting.
25. **compeer,** Beelzebub.

26. **seraphim,** one of the nine orders of angels, in medieval theology.
27. **extinct,** extinguished.
28. **Of force,** perforce.
29. **thralls,** slaves.

Or do his errands in the gloomy deep?
What can it then avail though yet we feel
Strength undiminished, or eternal being
To undergo eternal punishment?"   155
    Whereto with speedy words the arch-fiend replied:
"Fallen cherub, to be weak is miserable,
Doing or suffering: but of this be sure,
To do aught good never will be our task,
But ever to do ill our sole delight,   160
As being the contrary to his high will
Whom we resist. If then his providence
Out of our evil seek to bring forth good,
Our labor must be to pervert that end,
And out of good still to find means of evil;   165
Which ofttimes may succeed, so as perhaps
Shall grieve him, if I fail not,[30] and disturb
His inmost counsels from their destined aim.
But see the angry victor hath recalled
His ministers of vengeance and pursuit   170
Back to the gates of heaven; the sulphurous hail
Shot after us in storm, o'erblown hath laid[31]
The fiery surge, that from the precipice
Of heaven received us falling, and the thunder,
Winged with red lightning and impetuous rage,   175
Perhaps hath spent his shafts, and ceases now
To bellow through the vast and boundless deep.
Let us not slip[32] the occasion, whether scorn
Or satiate fury yield it from our foe.
Seest thou yon dreary plain, forlorn and wild,   180
That seat of desolation, void of light,
Save what the glimmering of these livid flames
Casts pale and dreadful? Thither let us tend
From off the tossing of these fiery waves,
There rest, if any rest can harbor there,   185
And reassembling our afflicted powers,[33]
Consult how we may henceforth most offend
Our enemy, our own loss how repair,
How overcome this dire calamity,
What reinforcement we may gain from hope;   190
If not, what resolution from despair."

30. **if I fail not,** "unless I'm mistaken."
31. **laid,** calmed.
32. **slip,** let go by.
33. **afflicted powers,** stricken armies.

On His Blindness

When I consider how my light is spent,
  Ere half my days, in this dark world and wide,
  And that one talent[1] which is death to hide,
  Lodged with me useless, though my soul more
    bent
To serve therewith my Maker, and present   5
  My true account, lest he returning chide;
  "Doth God exact day-labor, light denied?"
  I fondly[2] ask; but Patience to prevent
That murmur, soon replies, "God doth not need
  Either man's work or his own gifts; who best   10
  Bear his mild yoke, they serve him best. His state
Is kingly. Thousands at his bidding speed
  And post[3] o'er land and ocean without rest:
  They also serve who only stand and wait."

1. **talent,** in part, an allusion to the parable of the
talents, *Matthew* 25:14–30.
2. **fondly,** foolishly.
3. **post,** travel.

---

from **AREOPAGITICA**[1]
A Speech for the Liberty of Unlicensed Printing[2] to the Parliament of England

---

Milton begins by surveying previous examples of state censorship to show how ridiculous the practice is. He then moves to a more interesting argument by saying that God has given human beings reason so that they may regulate their mental diet as well as their physical diet. The following passage, the best-known section of the pamphlet, contains Milton's notions about how we are to live our lives, not by being protected from evil, but by confronting it.

Good and evil we know in the field of this world grow up together almost inseparably; and the knowledge of good is so involved and interwoven with the knowledge of evil, and in so many cunning resemblances hardly to be discerned, that those confused seeds which were imposed on Psyche[3] as an incessant

1. **Areopagitica** (ar′ē op′ə git′ə kə), literally, things to be said before the Areopagus, an ancient tribunal in Athens. Milton is thinking of a famous speech delivered there in 355 B.C. by Isocrates. To Milton, the Areopagus was the classical precedent for representative government as represented in England by Parliament. Thus, the essay is really "things to be said to parliamentarians."
2. **Unlicensed Printing,** writing which did not have to be approved by the Church or Parliament before being printed.
3. **Psyche,** the young woman with whom Cupid, son of Venus, fell in love. Venus was so angry that she gave Psyche the task of sorting a huge pile of seeds mixed together.

labor to cull out and sort asunder, were not more intermixed. It was from out the rind of one apple tasted, that the knowledge of good and evil, as two twins, cleaving together, leaped forth into the world. And perhaps this is that doom which Adam fell into of knowing good and evil, that is to say of knowing good by evil.

As therefore the state of man now is, what wisdom can there be to choose, what continence[4] to forbear without the knowledge of evil? He that can apprehend and consider vice with all her baits and seeming pleasures, and yet abstain, and yet distinguish, and yet prefer that which is truly better, he is the true wayfaring[5] Christian. I cannot praise a fugitive and cloistered virtue, unexercised and unbreathed, that never sallies out and sees her adversary, but slinks out of the race where that immortal garland[6] is to be run for, not without dust and heat. Assuredly we bring not innocence into the world, we bring impurity much rather; that which purifies us is trial, and trial is by what is contrary. That virtue therefore which is but a youngling in the contemplation of evil, and knows not the utmost that vice promises to her followers, and rejects it, is but a blank virtue, not a pure; her whiteness is but an excremental[7] whiteness; which was the reason why our sage and serious poet Spenser (whom I dare be known to think a better teacher than Scotus or Aquinas[8]) describing true temperance under the person of Guyon,[9] brings him in with his palmer through the cave of Mammon and the bower of earthly bliss,[10] that he might see and know, and yet abstain.

Since therefore the knowledge and survey of vice is in this world so necessary to the constituting of human virtue, and the scanning of error to the confirmation of truth, how can we more safely, and with less danger, scout into the regions of sin and falsity than by reading all manner of tractates[11] and hearing all manner of reason? And this is the benefit which may be had of books promiscuously read.

FOR UNDERSTANDING

Paradise Lost

The opening of *Paradise Lost* introduces us first to the poet's subject and his purpose, and then moves directly into the middle of the story, beginning not with the creation of the world or Satan's rebellion against God but with Satan already thrown out of Heaven.

1. Consider the first verse-paragraph, lines 1-26, which is made up of just two sentences. First, locate the main verbs as a way of dealing with Milton's complicated sentence structure. Then, describe the span of time implied in the first five lines. What other references to specific times can you find in this opening section?

2. What words in lines 44-81 are particularly important for creating the physical appearance of Hell? The moral appearance?

3. What arguments does Satan use to Beelzebub (lines 84-124) to persuade him to join him?

4. What response does Beelzebub make? Is he really persuaded?

5. How does Satan deal with Beelzebub's objections?

On His Blindness

1. This sonnet takes the form of an internal conversation. The speaker asks himself a question and then answers it. In what mood does he ask the question? In what mood does he answer it?

2. *Talent* is a word with two meanings: the modern meaning of "ability" and the Biblical meaning of "a

---

4. **continence,** restraint.

5. **wayfaring,** or in some editions, "warfaring." Either image, that of the Christian as pilgrim or the Christian as soldier, would seem to fit.

6. **garland,** in classical times, the wreath given to the winner of a race, or in medieval times, to the winner of a tournament.

7. **excremental,** exterior, superficial.

8. **Scotus or Aquinas.** Duns Scotus and Thomas Aquinas were famous medieval theologians.

9. **Guyon,** the knight of temperance, just as Red Cross was the knight of holiness. Spenser relates Guyon's adventures in Book II of *The Faerie Queene*.

10. **the bower of earthly bliss,** in Canto 12 of Book II. However, in Canto 7, the palmer (symbol of reason) does not enter the Cave of Mammon with Sir Guyon. Milton's memory is at fault.

11. **tractates,** treatises.

coin." The Biblical story tells of a servant who was given money (a talent) to keep for his master and who buried the money for safekeeping. His master scolded him for not investing it so that its value would increase. In this sonnet, is *talent* used in both the biblical and the modern sense? What was Milton's "one talent"? Why would it be "death" to hide it?

3. How does Patience describe those who best serve God?

Areopagitica

How would you paraphrase Milton's central argument in this passage?

FOR INTERPRETATION

1. To what extent does Satan seem an attractive figure, potentially the hero of *Paradise Lost*?

2. The word *theodicy* is defined as the philosophical attempt to harmonize divinity with human perceptions of good and evil and justice. Milton's epic is a conscious attempt at theodicy. Is it possible to say, from the selection given here, how he intends to do this and how successful he is at his theodicy?

3. How could you use the argument of the selection from *Areopagitica* to justify Milton's "heroic" portrait of Satan?

4. Does the last line of "On His Blindness" imply that the best way to live would be to cease all activity?

FOR APPRECIATION

Milton's Language

Milton's language, with its constant use of the root-meanings of English words and his inverted syntax, characterize his style, but do not necessarily make it easier to read. In the following passages, try to rewrite the lines as directed and consider what is lost by the simplification.

1. Replace all italic words with simpler ones, preferably one-syllable words if you can find them.

> Him the *Almighty Power*
> Hurled headlong flaming from the *ethereal* sky
> With *hideous* ruin and *combustion* down
> To bottomless *perdition*, there to dwell
> In *adamantine* chains and *penal* fire,

2. Place in normal word order:

a.
what in me is dark
Illumine, what is low raise and support;

b.
To bow and sue for grace
With suppliant knee, and deify his power
Who from the terror of this arm so late
Doubted his empire, that were low indeed,

c. and the knowledge of good is so involved and interwoven with the knowledge of evil, and in so many cunning resemblances hardly to be discerned, that those confused seeds which imposed upon Psyche as an incessant labor to cull out and sort asunder, were not more intermixed.

The Miltonic Sonnet

"On His Blindness" is a great example of the "Miltonic sonnet," which refers to the fact that Milton returned the sonnet in English to the Italian or Petrarchan rhyme scheme. His other innovation in many of his sonnets, and subsequently followed by others, is to deliberately delay the "volta" that normally opens line 9 until the middle of the same line. This half-line delay can give an exquisite effect of suspended motion between the rise and fall of a wave. Look at the delayed Miltonic volta in this sonnet and describe the effect of it on the movement of the poem.

John Bunyan 1628–1688

One of the few uneducated English writers, John Bunyan was the son of a Bedford tinker (a maker and mender of metal pots). He attended the common schools briefly and then followed in his father's trade. There was nothing to indicate that one day he would become a famous writer. When he was seventeen, he was drafted by the Parliamentary army, an experience that affected him deeply. When a friend who took Bunyan's place in one engagement was killed, Bunyan felt that he had been saved to perform some important duty in the world.

After the war, he married a poor woman who brought with her two pious books that had belonged to her Puritan father. A sensitive and imaginative young person newly shaken by his war experience, Bunyan became obsessed by the spirit and doctrine of these books and by his constant reading of the Bible. In his autobiography, *Grace Abounding,* Bunyan gives details of his spiritual growth, an emotionally exhausting and terrifying process that went on for years. He describes how a fearful countenance appeared in the sky as he was playing a game called tipcat. A voice asked if he were going to give up his sins and go to heaven or to keep his sins and go to hell. He gave up playing tipcat, dancing on the green, and—most reluctantly—bell ringing. For years he struggled with his inner devils until, at length, they left him in peace.

In 1653 he was converted to a Christian fellowship conducted by a turncoat Royalist officer and two years later was first asked by the brethren to address them. As a Baptist lay preacher he began sermonizing in the surrounding countryside until this brought him into conflict with the followers of George Fox, who founded the Quaker movement. Bunyan's first published book, in 1656, was a fierce attack on Quakerism. In general, his personal religious experiences gave him a deeper understanding of the trials of others in reaching their religious beliefs, allowing him to speak directly to their problems. In spite of his narrowness of outlook,

JOHN BUNYAN
Thomas Sadler
National Portrait Gallery, London

he was a forceful and dramatic preacher whom even some scholars admired.

In 1660, agents of the restored monarchy arrested Bunyan for preaching without a license at a farmhouse religious service. Offered his freedom if he agreed not to preach, Bunyan replied, "If you let me out today, I will preach tomorrow." So he was held in prison for twelve years, preaching to fellow prisoners, reading his Bible, and making thousands of long-tagged laces to help support his family. Having leisure to write, he produced some verse, a few religious tracts, and *Grace Abounding*. He was released under the Declaration of Indulgence, 1672, which made him a licensed pastor of the church he belonged to. But the next year, the Indulgence was cancelled and on the warrant of thirteen magistrates he was arrested again, tried and convicted, and sent to prison for six months in the town gaol. During this briefer imprisonment, he wrote his great allegorical masterpiece, *The Pilgrim's Progress*. After sixteen years as pastor at Bedford, Bunyon died from a ride in the rain and was buried outside London in Bunhill Fields, the Nonconformist burial grounds.

In *The Pilgrim's Progress*, Bunyan uses the familiar metaphor of life's being a journey, but it is not an ordinary one. The places Bunyan used were familiar ones in the English countryside —the slough, the meadow with its stile, the highway, the castle, the river, a country fair—but he gives them fascinating names such as the Slough of Despond, Doubting Castle, the Delectable Mountains, Vanity Fair. The inhabitants are strange and wonderful including other pilgrims, hobgoblins, Apollyon (the devil), and a giant. It is an exciting, imaginative adventure, for all its religious intent. For almost a hundred years after its publication, it was considered a children's tale or reading matter for the lower class. But gradually it was recognized as a work of literary merit.

In the following passage, the hero Christian and Hopeful, his traveling companion, have tried to take a shortcut through By-pass Meadow. Confused and lost, they turn back, only to have darkness fall before they can find their way. So they lie down to sleep where they are, unaware that they are trespassing on the grounds of Doubting Castle.

from THE PILGRIM'S PROGRESS

Neither could they, with all the skill they had, get again to the stile that night. Wherefore, at last, lighting under a little shelter, they sat down there until the day-break; but, being weary, they fell asleep.

They sleep in the grounds of Giant Despair.

Now there was, not far from the place where they lay, a castle called Doubting Castle, the owner whereof was Giant Despair; and it was in his grounds they now were sleeping: wherefore he, getting up in the morning early, and walking up and down in his fields, caught Christian and Hopeful asleep in his grounds. Then, with a grim and surly voice, he bid them awake; and asked them whence they were, and what they did in his grounds. They told him they were pilgrims, and that they had lost their way. Then said the Giant, You have this night trespassed on me, by trampling in and lying on my grounds, and therefore you must go along with me. So they were forced to go, be-

He finds them in his grounds, and carries them to Doubting Castle.

cause he was stronger than they. They also had but little to say, for they knew themselves in a fault. The Giant, therefore, drove them before him, and put them into his castle, into a very dark dungeon, nasty and stinking to the spirits of these two men. (Ps. lxxxviii. 18.) Here, then, they lay from Wednesday morning till Saturday night, without one bit of bread, or drop of drink; or light, or any to ask how they did; they were, therefore, here in evil case, and were far from friends and acquaintance. Now in this place Christian had double sorrow, because it was through his unadvised counsel that they were brought into this distress.

The grievousness of their imprisonment.

The pilgrims now, to gratify the flesh,
Will seek its ease; but oh! how they afresh
Do thereby plunge themselves new griefs
    into!
Who seek to please the flesh, themselves
    undo.

Now, Giant Despair had a wife, and her name was Diffidence. So when he was gone to bed, he told his wife what he had done; to wit, that he had taken a couple of prisoners and cast them into his dungeon, for trespassing on his grounds. Then he asked her also what he had best to do further to them. So she asked him what they were, whence they came, and whither they were bound; and he told her. Then she counselled him that when he arose in the morning he should beat them without any mercy. So, when he arose, he getteth him a grievous crab-tree cudgel, and goes down into the dungeon to them, and there first falls to rating of them as if they were dogs, although they never gave him a *On Thursday,* word of distaste. Then he falls *Giant Despair* upon them, and beats them *beats his* *prisoners.* fearfully, in such sort, that they were not able to help themselves, or to turn them upon the floor. This done, he withdraws and leaves them, there to condole their misery, and to mourn under their distress. So all that day they spent the time in nothing but sighs and bitter lamentations. The next night, she, talking with her husband about them further, and understanding they were yet alive, did advise him to counsel them to make away themselves. So when morning was come, he goes to them in a surly manner as before, and perceiving them to be very sore with the stripes that he had given them the day before, he told them, that since they were never like to come out of that place, their only *On Friday,* way would be forthwith to make *Giant Despair* an end of themselves, either *counsels them* *to kill* with knife, halter, or poison, for *themselves.* why, said he, should you choose life, seeing it is attended with so much bitterness? But they desired him to let them go. With that he looked ugly upon them, and rushing to them, had doubtless made an end *The Giant* of them himself, but that he fell *sometimes has* into one of his fits (for he some-*fits.* times, in sunshiny weather, fell into fits), and lost for a time the use of his hand; wherefore he withdrew, and left them

as before, to consider what to do. Then did the prisoners consult between themselves, whether it was best to take his counsel or no; and thus they began to discourse:—

CHR. Brother, said Christian, what shall *Christian* we do? The life that we now live *crushed.* is miserable. For my part I know not whether it is best, to live thus, or to die out of hand. "My soul chooseth strangling rather than life," and the grave is more easy for me than this dungeon. (Job vii. 15.) Shall we be ruled by the Giant?

HOPE. Indeed, our present condition is *Hopeful* dreadful, and death would be *comforts him.* far more welcome to me than thus for ever to abide; but yet, let us consider, the Lord of the country to which we are going hath said, Thou shalt do no murder: no, not to another man's person; much more, then, are we forbidden to take his counsel to kill ourselves. Besides, he that kills another, can but commit murder upon his body; but for one to kill himself is to kill body and soul at once. And, moreover, my brother, thou talkest of ease in the grave; but hast thou forgotten the hell, whither for certain the murderers go? For "no murderer hath eternal life," &c. And let us consider, again, that all the law is not in the hand of Giant Despair. Others, so far as I can understand, have been taken by him, as well as we; and yet have escaped out of his hand. Who knows, but that God that made the world may cause that Giant Despair may die? or that, at some time or other, he may forget to lock us in? or that he may, in a short time, have another of his fits before us, and may lose the use of his limbs? and if ever that should come to pass again, for my part, I am resolved to pluck up the heart of a man, and to try my utmost to get from under his hand. I was a fool that I did not try to do it before; but, however, my brother, let us be patient, and endure a while. The time may come that may give us a happy release; but let us not be our own murderers. With these words, Hopeful at present did moderate the mind of his brother; so they continued together (in the dark) that day, in their sad and doleful condition.

Well, towards evening, the Giant goes down into the dungeon again, to see if his prisoners had taken his counsel; but when he came there he found them alive; and truly, alive was all; for now, what for want of bread and water, and by reason of the wounds they received when he beat them, they could do little but breathe. But, I say, he found them alive; at which he fell into a grievous rage, and told them that, seeing they had disobeyed his counsel, it should be worse with them than if they had never been born.

At this they trembled greatly, and I think that Christian fell into a swoon; but, coming a *Christian still* little to himself again, they re- *dejected.* newed their discourse about the Giant's counsel; and whether yet they had best to take it or no. Now Christian again seemed to be for doing it, but Hopeful made his second reply as followeth:—

HOPE. My brother, said he, rememberest *Hopeful* thou not how valiant thou hast *comforts him* been heretofore? Apollyon *again, by* could not crush thee, nor could *calling former* all that thou didst hear, or see, *things to* or feel, in the Valley of the *remembrance.* Shadow of Death. What hardship, terror, and amazement hast thou already gone through! And art thou now nothing but fear! Thou seest that I am in the dungeon with thee, a far weaker man by nature than thou art; also, this Giant has wounded me as well as thee, and hath also cut off the bread and water from my mouth; and with thee I mourn without the light. But let us exercise a little more patience; remember how thou playedst the man at Vanity Fair, and wast neither afraid of the chain, nor cage, nor yet of bloody death. Wherefore let us (at least to avoid the shame, that becomes not a Christian to be found in) bear up with patience as well as we can.

Now, night being come again, and the Giant and his wife being in bed, she asked him concerning the prisoners, and if they had

The British Library, London

Doubting Castle and Giant Despair, a woodcut from a 1695 edition of Pilgrim's Progress.

taken his counsel. To which he replied, They are sturdy rogues, they choose rather to bear all hardship, than to make away themselves. Then said she, Take them into the castle-yard tomorrow, and show them the bone and skulls of those that thou hast already despatched, and make them believe, ere a week comes to an end, thou also wilt tear them in pieces, as thou hast done their fellows before them.

So when the morning was come, the Giant goes to them again, and takes them into the castle-yard, and shows them, as his wife had bidden him. These, said he, were pilgrims as you are, once, and they trespassed in *On Saturday, the Giant threatened that shortly he would pull them in pieces.* my grounds, as you have done; and when I thought fit, I tore them in pieces, and so, within ten days, I will do you. Go, get you down to your den again; and with that he beat them all the way thither. They lay, therefore, all day on Saturday in a lamentable case, as before. Now, when night was come, and when Mrs. Diffidence and her husband, the Giant, were got to bed, they began to renew their discourse of their prisoners; and withal the old Giant wondered, that he could neither by his blows nor his counsel bring them to an end. And with that his wife replied, I fear, said she, that they live in hope that some will come to relieve them, or that they have picklocks about them, by the means of which they hope to escape. And sayest thou so, my dear? said the Giant; I will, therefore, search them in the morning.

Well, on Saturday, about midnight, they began to pray, and continued in prayer till almost break of day.

Now, a little before it was day, good Christian, as one half amazed, brake out in this passionate speech: What a fool, quoth he, *A key in Christian's bosom, called Promise, opens any lock in Doubting Castle.* am I, thus to lie in a stinking dungeon, when I may as well walk at liberty! I have a key in my bosom, called Promise, that will, I am persuaded, open any lock in Doubting Castle. Then said Hopeful, That is good news, good brother; pluck it out of thy bosom, and try.

Then Christian pulled it out of his bosom, and began to try at the dungeon door, whose bolt (as he turned the key) gave back, and the door flew open with ease, and Christian and Hopeful both came out. Then he went to the outward door that leads into the castle-yard, and, with his key, opened that door also. After, he went to the iron gate, for that must be opened too; but that lock went damnable hard, yet the key did open it. Then they thrust open the gate to make their escape with speed, but that gate, as it opened, made such a creaking, that it waked Giant Despair, who, hastily rising to pursue his prisoners, felt his limbs to fail, for his fits took him again, so that he could by no means go after them. Then they went on, and came to the King's highway, and so were safe, because they were out of his jurisdiction.

FOR UNDERSTANDING

1. In what three ways does the giant try to destroy the prisoners?
2. In what way is the wife like Lady Macbeth?
3. What is the giant's one weakness?
4. Who wavers under the giant's suggestion that they kill themselves?
5. How do they finally escape?

FOR INTERPRETATION

1. Quite apart from the religious intent, how accurate is the psychological premise presented here?
2. Where does help have to come from in order to overcome depression?

FOR APPRECIATION

Allegory

The Pilgrim's Progress has been called the most successful allegory in English Literature. An allegory is a story in which the details of the apparent story have a deeper spiritual meaning. Here names help to identify the qualities being discussed.
1. Does the apparent adventure story succeed?
2. Does the story transfer easily into a spiritual struggle?

COMPOSITION

Imagine that Christian is walking through a shopping mall in your area. What descriptive names might he give to some of the shops or restaurants? For instance, an ice cream store he might call *Sweet Tooth Heaven* or *Fats Unlimited* or *House of Lost Diets.* As he walks by the stores, try to describe some of the people inside as he might see them. Have him enter one place. What creatures or monsters might he meet? How will he escape?

The Growth of the English Language

English in Its Global Context

From the speech of several tribes disembarking on the wild southern and eastern coasts of England in the fifth century A.D., English has grown to a place of surprising importance among the languages of the world. At the present time, there are about 5,000 living languages or dialects in the world. A good sixth of these are local tongues indigenous to India. There are also twenty or more languages (six of them American Indian) in which no one can carry on a conversation because—at last report—there was only one speaker left alive. One Alaskan language called Eyak is spoken solely when two aged sisters meet. Of the rest, only three are spoken by more than two hundred million people.

In first place is Chinese with something like 660 million speakers. This figure represents speakers of Mandarin, the official dialect, and may be greater, since other Chinese speakers are increasingly required to learn it. In second place is English with nearly 400 million speakers. Of these, 200 million are native speakers, 50 million are those on the Indian subcontinent who speak it almost as well as the first group, and 100 million who speak it to some extent. English is also the most widespread of all languages. It is spoken by at least 10 percent of the people in 37 independent countries. In Shakespeare's century only one out of a hundred people in the world spoke English. Now it is one out of eight. This leaves out the international trading language, Pidgin English, spoken in southeast Asia and the Pacific, where it is the means of communication for growing millions of people. Russian until recently may have held third place with something less than 200 million speakers, but Spanish—the most widely used Romance language—has replaced it at about 235 million. Spanish is also the most rapidly growing language in the world.

The Vocabulary of English

Pidgin English has less than 400 nouns, 50 verbs, and a few hundred modifiers. Its parent language, by contrast, has half-a-million words—which is the average size of various "unabridged" dictionaries. But this does not include special vocabularies and sublanguages that are still or newly growing at astonishing rates—fields of science and technology such as space, computers, astronomy, biology, linguistics; other fields such as economics, politics, law, business, the arts; and subcultures that continue to generate dialect variation, regional idioms, slang, argot, and jargon. This puts a more realistic total at anywhere between one million and two million words. Of this amount, no one individual uses more than 60,000 words, most of us far less. None of these figures take into account the different meanings a single word can have. The word *set,* for example, has 58 noun meanings, 126 verbal meanings, and 10 meanings as a participial adjective.

Perhaps the most important feature of English vocabulary, however, is the fact that no other language has so many and such varied synonyms. Practically speaking, English is the only language whose diversity has generated the need for separate synonym dictionaries, such as *Roget's Thesaurus.* Most languages have no such books and in those that have them, such as French and German, few writers use them habitually as do the professional writers and editors of English. Take a word used in the preceding paragraph: *sub-language;* surprisingly it has many synonyms. Here is a partial list, each with its special slant: vernacular, dialect, slang, jargon, argot, canaille, idiolect, pidgin, creole, idiom, lingo, patois, patter, jive, vulgate, vulgarism, demotic, colloquialism, barbarism, brogue, lingua franca, journalese, bureaucratese, legalese, foggy bottom, hogwash, gobbledygook, flapdoodle, flummery, gabble, babble, babel, word salad, thieves' Latin, double talk, new speak, gibberish, bafflegab, mumbo jumbo.

The Future of English as a World Language

Science and technology on one hand have expanded "naming" (or denotative) vocabularies for isolating specific entities one from another. On the other hand, "evocative" (or connotative) vocabularies proliferate subtle shadings of synonymous meanings that evoke, imply, affect, move, insinuate, or indicate complex states of mind. As these two wings of English continue to grow, with no end in sight, the kinds of creativity and imagination that serve the sciences and the arts exploit the unparalleled resources of English as a stimulus to new ideas. Since most recent linguistic theories have more and more stressed the identity between language and intelligence and even more basically, between language and thinking, these enormous capabilities of English inevitably make it a vital part of important human developments that can be expected in the next centuries.

English is well suited as the likely candidate to become the long dreamed of world language. Its primary qualifications all relate to the ease with which it can be learned or used. It has one of the least complicated grammars among the major languages because it has progressively shed its inflections over the years. Its nouns and pronouns all have one "natural" gender. (In German, for example, the sun is feminine, the moon masculine; in French, the sun is masculine, the moon feminine.) Its syntax has become simple and

direct: subject → verb → object. This pattern makes expression easy—and taxes creativity's thirst for variety. Finally, English is the magpie of languages. No other language in the world has borrowed so many different words from so many different languages. To exaggerate only slightly, there is possibly no known spoken or written language from which English has not freeloaded a helping of words—and thus enriched itself.

English, reflecting its Germanic roots, bristles, blusters, and strikes home its points with unmatched forcefulness. But its extraordinary vitality is only enhanced by other, often contradictory ingredients. Latin roots give it precision useful in science and mathematics, as well as an elegance and objectivity for occasions of high solemnity. French roots give it fluidity, like the grace of a dancer motionless on point as well as the great Baryshnikov leap, both part of that same energy that *is* "eternal delight."

Dutch has given English *brandy, golf, measles, wagon, uproar.* To Italian we owe *balcony, duet, granite, piano, umbrella, volcano.* Borrowed early from Latin (when the Angles or Saxons met Roman traders on the Rhine) are *chalk, cheese, cup, dish, pillow, pitch, pound, street, toll, wine.* The Vikings brought, besides wanton slaughter, *dank, keel, skin, skirt, sky, kindle, egg, guess, get, call, hit, take.* Norman French gave us *bacon, catch, chapel, justice.* From Arabic comes the scientifically vital *zero* and also *assassin* and others. Latin and French sources for words come in layers, like the geology of the Grand Canyon, and are book-length subjects in themselves. American Indians gave us *moccasin, chipmunk, moose, raccoon.* Spanish, with Arabic or Basque sometimes standing in the wings, provides us with *alligator, cargo, contraband, stampede.* From Greek we got *magic, tactics, catastrophe, acrobat,* and many *-osophy* and *-ology* words. From Russian, *steppe, vodka, samovar.* From Persian, *caravan, khaki, shawl, sherbet,* and—ultimately—*paradise, lemon, lilac.* Albert C. Baugh, a linguist from whom some of this list has been borrowed, cites our other borrowings from Hebrew,

Hungarian, Hindustani, Bengali, Malay, Chinese, Javanese, Australian aboriginal people and those of Tahiti, Polynesia, West Africa, and Brazil.

The Leading Contenders— Their Disadvantages

Only two important factors make English hard to learn. One is the extraordinary number and complexity of its idioms, most of which have to be learned on a one by one basis. Take a simple word like *keep,* for example, and start adding those little nuts-and-bolts words to it that are the glue of language (prepositions and adverbs, mostly), and you will have quite an array of idioms, each with a different meaning: keep on, keep off, keep out, keep in, keep away, keep back, keep up (the good work), keep down (your food), keep on keeping on. The second disadvantage is the major flaw of English—its spelling. *Rough, cough, though, thought, through* are all pronounced differently even though spelled so similarly. English spelling, of course, reflects the history of words, which is a pleasure for etymologists and linguists, but a tremendous difficulty for all writers of English, new and native alike.

Spanish, the second-place contender after English for the possibility of becoming the next century's world language, is a clear favorite in this category, since its words are consistently and logically spelled exactly the way they sound—that is, in accordance with a phonetic spelling system. Spanish also has some of the advantages of English in other categories—it's a widespread language spoken by many nations and has an easy grammar and syntax. But it is no match for the vocabulary and synonyms of English. Though first in number of speakers, Chinese is even less easily learned than English by non-native speakers. The tone or pitch of the voice carries distinct meanings as well as the sounds uttered. The fourth tone of *i,* for example, has 84 meanings, and for one meaning of *i* there are 92 different characters. This is another drawback to Chinese—its written

form. Each word is written as a character or ideogram. A large Chinese dictionary of 40 volumes lists 50,000 ideograms, though the average reader of a newspaper needs to know only about 5,000. But knowledge of the ideograms beyond a certain point requires scholarship. To write one word for *talkative* requires making an ideogram of 64 strokes. One word in common use, meaning *implore,* requires a 32-stroke ideogram. This makes the Chinese typewriter unusually cumbersome to use—and adding new scientific and technical terms is certainly possible, but not easy. In 1958, the Chinese slowly began a transition to phonetic writing by adopting the Pinyin system for transliterating ideograms into our Roman alphabet. This may eventually doom the beautiful but impractical calligraphy of the Chinese ideogram to its historical appearance as a previously intrinsic part of both Chinese poetry and painting.

Analytic Versus Synthetic Grammar

The great advantage of Chinese, however, is its grammar. It is completely analytical (or distributive)—a grammar that establishes things like tense and number by adding a new word to the expression rather than by altering the words already there. Thus, Chinese would say the equivalent of *I drink,* meaning today or now, but *I drink yesterday* (or an hour ago or whenever). We, of course, change *drink* to *drank* to indicate the past. A grammar that changes the words themselves is called synthetic (or inflectional). Many languages of Europe, the Near East, and India are descended from a common ancient parent language, called Indo-European, which was extremely synthetic—with many more tenses, genders, conjugations, and declensions than most of us would care to imagine. These are the very things that make learning a language hard.

As most of the languages in the Indo-European family evolved away from their ancestor, they underwent a gradual process in which they lost pieces of the original inflectional system in all its complexity. Here is a case where the primitive form is highly complex, the developed form progressively simple. In this process of evolution, English is the most advanced of the languages in its family, so much so that it can be called "predominantly analytic" despite the survival of such inflected forms as I, me, my, we, our, she, he, her, his, him, they, their, them—or (wo)man, (wo)men—or drink, drank, drunk.

Romance languages like Spanish are not far behind English, but German is more highly inflected than the former, and as we look back in time, Latin is more inflected than German, classical Greek much more highly inflected than Latin. But Chinese (and most related Asiatic languages) is already completely analytical in grammar, a factor that could speed its spread once the drawback of its written form is cleared up. And with one fourth of the world's population already living in China, the language remains a serious contender as a future world language.

The Origins of English

The earliest roots of English go back to a group of people who spoke "Indo-Hittite" about 3500 B.C. They lived in what is now eastern Europe anywhere on an imaginary line drawn between the Baltic Sea and the western edge of the Black Sea. Various guesses have placed them as far north as Latvia, at some midway point such as Czechoslovakia, or a more southerly location along the Danube. In any case, they were cattle-raising stone-age nomads whose migrations over the next centuries created one of the most important family of languages in the world today. The Hittites split off first in about 2500 B.C., going to Asia Minor, leaving the remaining Indo-Europeans behind. Then in a few hundred years, another group migrated to Persia and northern India. Their written language was Sanskrit, a very close relative to the original ancestor of English. Modern languages descended from Sanskrit are Hindustani, Hindi, and Urdu. Other migrations of this sort gave rise to ancient Greek, Latin, and

Celtic, the last of which was spoken by the nomadic Celts who settled the British Isles and replaced the original "Iberian" inhabitants. Latin itself, of course, gave rise in time to Italian, Rumanian, Spanish, Portuguese, and French—the Romance languages. The Balto-Slavic branch of the Indo-Europeans stayed mainly where they had always been, giving rise to modern Lithuanian, Czech, Polish, and various Russian dialects.

The Germanic branch split itself into three groups. The East Germanic group spoke Gothic. The earliest written Germanic of any kind is Bishop Ulfilas's Gothic Bible, produced before 383 A.D. But after sacking Rome, the Goths and Vandals who spoke Gothic disappeared, their language with them. The North Germanic group became the forebears of the modern Scandinavian languages. One branch of the West Germanic group gave rise to modern German, another to Dutch and Flemish, and a third to Anglo-Saxon, or Old English.

The Angles, the Saxons, the Jutes Arrive

It was the Iberian peoples who built Stonehenge sometime around 2500 B.C., since the Celts did not arrive in Britain until 1200 B.C. After the Emperor Claudius added Britain to the Roman Empire in 55 B.C., the Celts became somewhat Romanized and, with the arrival of Christianity, Christianized as well. When the Romans withdrew early in the fifth century A.D., the Celts were left to control an opulent underpopulated island—but not for long. By 410, Germanic tribes clustered on the western shores of what is now Denmark began crossing the North Sea and landing on the southern and eastern coasts of England. Three primary groups arrived. The Angles settled Northumbria and Mercia (see Old English Time Line, p. 12), the Jutes settled Kent, and the Saxons settled the West Saxon region called Wessex. The languages these tribes spoke were soon called Northumbrian, Mercian, Kentish, and West Saxon. (Keep your eye on Kentish, for after a long dormancy it gives birth to Shakespeare's language—and ours.) There must have been very little difference between these tongues. Certainly they could understand each other on the battlefield as they united to drive the Celts westward into Wales, Cornwall, Ireland, and Brittany. This was, of course, the historical moment of King Arthur's Celtic twilight. Despite the inevitable parleying and fraternization that war creates, remarkably little Celtic seems to have been taken into Old English, at least in any identifiable form. Some survive in place names: York comes from Eboracum and Carlisle from Caer Luguvalium. Among other words, we have *bin, down* (for hill), *crag* (for rock), *tor* (for steep hill), and *coomb* (for deep valley). Celtic survives to this day in the Welsh of Wales, the Gaelic of Ireland, and the Breton of Brittany, though perhaps none will continue as living languages for much longer.

The reason why the language of the invaders became known as English (and only later, the land as England) was because of the unusual development of Northumbrian culture during the seventh century in the age of Bede. The invaders had brought with them a rudimentary form of writing called runes, ultimately traceable to Etruscan glyphs, but runes could not record whole sentences. Consequently, the first Christian monks late in the sixth century found that they needed to adapt the Latin (or Roman) alphabet to write down anything in the Northumbrian dialect. Since these settlers were Angles, the dialect and soon the whole language was called "Angle-ish" or English.

And Then Come the Vikings and Danes

The Viking invasions began in the eighth century and mostly reduced Northumbrian culture to an ash heap. What written records could be saved were hauled back first to Mercia and finally to Wessex. Alfred the Great and his scholars in the ninth century translated nearly all existing written materials and much Latin writing besides into their own West Saxon dialect, but without changing the name of the language to Saxon. Where the

Vikings ravaged in the eighth century, the Danes came to ravage—and settle—in the ninth. The language of both these groups was Old Norse—which was significantly different from Old English and left considerable traces upon our language. The names of the days of the week come from their North Germanic speech, as did the pronouns *they, their,* and *them,* and the participial suffix *-ing.*

In modern England, the Old Norse influence on dialects can still be detected east of Watling Street, the great Roman road that ran roughly between London and what is now modern Liverpool—the road used by King Alfred to divide the Danish settlements from the English. Place names with *-ton* or *-don* west of the line are Old English: *Wimbledon, Brighton.* Place names with *-ham* east of the line are Old Norse: *Nottingham, Birmingham, Durham.* These Norse-speaking invaders were also the only foes of the English who significantly affected the grammar of the English language. By itself, the Old English "word-hoard" (or vocabulary) was surprisingly large for its time. More than 40,000 words exist in written old English sources. The language was, of course, still highly inflected, even having a singular, dual, and plural form of the second person (*you*). That is, the word changed depending on whether "you" was one person, two people, or more. Latin borrowings—from the church—had already begun, however, and toward the end of the Old English period, a noticeable simplification of inflections was already underway.

The Normans Cometh

The Norman Conquest conquered the land in 1066, but it did not conquer the language. In fact, the Normans didn't even try to affect English. Norman French was spoken at court, Latin was written and spoken in the church, and across the breadth of England, English continued to be spoken as in Alfred's time. Or not quite—for changes in English now began to accelerate. Inflections had already begun to erode after the eclipse of Northumbrian learning. Now these tendencies moved at such a pace that by 1100 A.D. we no longer speak of Old English, but of Middle English, a vigorous, populist language of streamlined inflections in which some literary masterpieces continued to be written. French was, at this early stage of Middle English, not the great influence on the language that it was later to become. It was during this period that the arbitrary gender of words was swept into "natural gender."

Some of those in power knew English, like Becket, or learned it, like Eleanor of Aquitaine, but it wasn't until her son, King John, lost Normandy to the French in 1204 that the whole court began to take the learning of English seriously. Consequently, it was in the thirteenth and fourteenth centuries that French words entered English in one great tidal wave. Forty percent of all our French borrowings occurred during this period. It is not hard to imagine someone who is learning English but can not think of the new word wanted and so sets an old word, in this case a French word, in its place. But this was also the period of England's war on the continent with France and many words came home with the soldiers. Also, the English began to buy elegant French goods—and we know that language follows the coin, not the flag. Most important of all, London became the indisputable center of English culture, thus elevating the Kentish dialect of Chaucer to first place. The Jutes who settled in Kent but go unremembered beyond that fact finally got their due with this turn of events. By 1400 the vestigial endings on words from Alfred's day had shrunk to an -e and were either pronounced or not, without much concern for anything like "correctness." English had become a predominantly analytic language.

Enter Modern English: the Great Vowel Shift

Somewhere in the middle of the fifteenth century, linguists have agreed to stop calling our language Middle English and refer to it instead as Modern English. Caxton's setting up the first printing press in England—in 1476—is a good date. The point of dividing English here is that the "great vowel shift" was underway. It had not begun when Chaucer wrote, thus making it hard for us to pronounce his poetry today. But it was almost complete by the time Shakespeare wrote, making his writing easier for us to read aloud. In this shift, some vowels were unaffected; we probably say the words *hill* and *land* much as speakers of Old English pronounced them. But the vowels that require greater tension in the tongue and oral muscles (hence, the tense vowels) all moved in an orderly way forward and upward in the mouth—in what amounted to a one-notch change of sound that forever separated English from other European languages in the way vowels are pronounced. Thus, before the sound shift, our word *she* was pronounced *shay*, *boat* was pronounced like *bought*, *cat* like *cot*, *meat* like *mat*, *hate* like *hat*, *mood* like *mode*.

This shift followed one that occurred before Old English had split off from West Germanic. Known as Grimm's Law (for the same brothers who collected and wrote the fairy tales), it says that where English has *f*, the same word in Latin will have *p* and where English has *th*, Latin has *t*. Examples: *father/pater, mother/mater, brother/frater*. Another linguistic rule of thumb called Verner's Law further systematized what had before seemed random differences between apparently unrelated words. England went through one more sound shift, but this was after the American colonies had already been founded and were flourishing. Because of this fact, Americans to this day pronounce *demand* as Shakespeare did, rather than as a modern British Shakespearian actor pronounces it.

King James and the Colonies and Correctness

Shakespeare and the King James Bible together establish English of that period as the great cornerstone of the language to this day, passages from both books having been read and recited more often than any others in the whole of English. English went on to further changes in the eighteenth century—until it came to resemble our present-day language almost completely. Yet we always hear the diction and syntax of Shakespeare and the King James version echoing just behind our speech and writing. The other major influence of this period upon English was science and exploration. Science needed more precise terminology and drew new Latin (and some Greek) words into the language. Latin was now seen more as the language of scholarship than as the language of the church. These scientific changes were speeded by the founding of the Royal Society in 1660. Exploration brought nautical terms into the language, of course, but more importantly, with the gaining of colonies in new regions of the world, words flooded into the languages from these places and these colonists.

In the eighteenth century, the chaotic spelling of English began to be standardized and people began to think about language as a subject for the expression of taste, or as an area in which to show one's breeding by the correctness of one's spoken or written language. It is not surprising that the first important dictionaries now began to appear. The establishment of an English Academy, like the French, to standardize English fortunately never came into existence though it was thought of more than once. The standardizing impulse was alive, however, despite the latitudinarian attitude of the greatest early dictionary maker, Dr. Samuel Johnson, whose lexicography was often a pithy expression of well-grounded personal opinion rather than the methodical kind of research that dictionary work has since become.

Half a century later, another important dictionary maker, the American Noah Webster, put together a more methodical dictionary and, at the same time, tackled the demon of English spelling. He was probably the last single individual to influence the language so much. He lopped off the *k*'s from *magick, logick,* and *musick* on the basis of false analogy with ancient Greek, altered the spelling of many other words for better reasons, and argued that a lexicographer must truly determine which words people actually use in what situations rather than surmising which words they *should* use. In 1857, the great *Oxford English Dictionary* was begun, a multi-volume work that wore out a succession of editors and took 75 years to complete. This work, far beyond the dreams of Dr. Johnson, records the English language as no other dictionary has ever recorded any language. Beyond the usual lexical information it gives, it is virtually a quotations book of English writers from the earliest days to the latest. By picking a word and reading its entry in the *OED,* one will learn how some important writers of English actually used the word over the whole lifespan of its existence.

Linguistics, Video, and the Byte

In our own century, the attitudes to language that were developed first by lexicographers from Dr. Johnson to the editors of the *OED* have exploded into the new science of linguistics. Semantics, structuralism, and semiology are all terms for branches of these new concerns about language. In general, the new linguistic approach to words seems to be a search for ways to perceive and interpret the pressures exerted on language by advertising, political sloganeering, and the bureaucratese of an increasingly faceless social system that some see as more and more resembling Orwell's novel *Nineteen Eighty-Four.* Others worry about the displacement of reading in very young people by the new habit of watching television. Can informed citizens continue to exist in significant numbers if there is a massive decline in reading—or in reading ability? How will arts that depend on language—such as poetry and fiction—hold their own in an increasingly video-oriented world? These questions about the future of language are no sooner asked than a new wave of change begins to hit English, generated this time by the world of computers. Computers will change much in the world we know; but to the extent that they require thought to operate them, they will also require skilled language-users.

COMPOSITION WORKSHOP

TAKING NOTES

A newspaper reporter always has a notebook or tape recorder close at hand. These are basic tools of the reporter's trade: they allow the reporter to record and store vital information that will eventually be used in a story.

Every writer needs some method of "preserving the facts." As a writer of a research paper, you will find that 4 × 6-inch cards are best suited to this task. The larger size of the cards will enable you to distinguish them readily from your 3 × 5-inch bibliography cards and will allow you to take more detailed notes. The chief benefit of using cards, however, is that they can be easily moved about on a table or desk top. Their mobility permits you to experiment with various ways of organizing your material and thus aids you in forming a "visual outline." This will prove useful when the time comes to develop a final plan for your research paper.

You will want to take detailed notes whenever you come upon a passage in your reading that does one or more of the following:

- helps prove a point
- provides essential background material
- shows the author's attitudes on an important issue
- lends support to a point of view you have adopted

For each passage you cite in a given source, note at the top of the card the tentative subtopic under which the material on the card would fit. At the bottom of the card, note in abbreviated form the author, the title and the *exact* page number of the material. Be sure to use a separate card for each citation.

Most of the notes you take will fall into one of three major categories—summary, paraphrase, and direct quotation. You *summarize* when you want to present briefly an argument or commentary that covered a number of pages (sometimes an entire chapter) in the book in which it appeared.

Sample Note Card 1 contains a summary of an explanation that ran for nearly thirty pages in the original source. Notice that the heading on the card tells what kind of information it contains.

Paraphrasing is translating another writer's material into your own words. It is a good idea to paraphrase when the wording of the original passage is difficult to understand or subject to misinterpretation. Since you are "borrowing ideas," and not merely providing general background information, it is important to stick as close to the original as possible. As in the case of Sample Note Card 2, a direct quotation of a key phrase is often included in a paraphrase.

Use a *direct quotation* when delivering an important point that another writer has made. Direct quotation ought to be reserved for comments whose wording or content are particularly memorable. They should rarely exceed a single paragraph in length and must, as in Sample Note Card 3, preserve the *exact wording* of the original.

A word of caution: When you use the specific ideas and/or thoughts of another writer without acknowledging them as such, you are guilty of *plagiarism*, an offense which teachers and many other people consider quite serious. Plagiarism— or "literary theft"—is not always intentional, as even the best of writers have discovered. A logical way to avoid the perils of plagiarism is to take notes in your own words and always to acknowledge plainly on each card the source from which the idea came. If you quote an author directly, be sure to enclose the quoted matter in quotation marks.

ASSIGNMENT

Closely examine each of the sources that you included in your approved set of bibliography cards. Find and read the section of each book that seems to provide useful information about your topic. (Remember that few sources need to be read from cover to cover; in most, you will need to study only a few pages or a single chapter.) Take notes from your sources. Your notes should include all information that sheds light on your particular topic. Be sure that each note identifies the author and title of the source as well as the page number or numbers from which the note was taken.

SAMPLE NOTE CARD 1

Renaissance View of Middle Ages

As Ferguson points out, the people of the Renaissance came to believe that there were two periods of great culture and advancement in the history of the world. One was the classical era of Greece and Rome plus the early Christian period. The other was their own age of enlightenment. In between was a dark and gloomy period called the Middle Ages.

W. K. Ferguson, <u>The Renaissance in Historical Thought,</u>
pp. 16-48

SAMPLE NOTE CARD 2

Upper Class Gains Power

Lewis points out that at the beginning of the Sixteenth Century the "middling landowners" were becoming wealthier and more powerful. At the same time, the poverty of the lower class peasants grew. Both trends, however, were underway long before the century began.

C. S. Lewis, <u>English Literature in the Sixteenth Century,</u>
p. 56

SAMPLE NOTE CARD 3

The Power of Shakespeare

". . . when we read Shakespeare's plays, we are always meeting our own experiences and are constantly surprised by some phrase which expresses what we thought to be our own secret or our own discovery. It is for this reason that so often, consciously or unconsciously, we can find no words more apt than his to express ourselves in exultation or depression. . . ."

G. B. Harrison, <u>Shakespeare: The Complete Works,</u> pp. 3-4

HOLKHAM HALL
The British Tourist Agency

Neoclassical Literature

THE AGE OF REASON

Know then thyself, presume not God to scan;
The proper study of Mankind is Man.

These words of Alexander Pope sum up the outlook of an age. English literature from 1660 to the end of the eighteenth century is more of a piece than at any period before or since. This is not to deny its diversity of forms and themes. If we dip into the literature of this period, we can read witty aristocratic comedies, the first essentially modern prose, the first novels—and, around the middle of the eighteenth century, we can see the stirrings of Romanticism in poetry. The reading public vastly expanded in the eighteenth century; writers became less dependent on their patrons and more responsive to the needs and tastes of their popular audience. It is during this century that authors first began to support themselves through their craft.

Whether or not they depended on patronage, however, most writers shared a common set of assumptions which set them apart from the later Renaissance. Unlike the metaphysical poets or John Bunyan (page 340) or John Milton (page 329), they dwelled less on God's plan than on man's ordered existence on earth. This was an age of rational inquiry, of science and logical discourse—not only in England but all across Europe. The confidence that man's reasoning power could solve all problems through calm and orderly analysis was at its height. Therefore the period is often called the Age of Reason, or—after the common image of light for rational thought—the Enlightenment.

Common set of Assumptions

Human reason was indeed paramount. As the French philosopher René Descartes put it in his *Discourse on Method* (1637): "I think, therefore I am." Sir Isaac Newton's demonstration of the physical laws of the universe, published fifty years later, was taken as further proof of the grand, ordered design of all things. Our modern notions of the unconscious mind, the expanding universe, and creative ambiguity would have mystified the eighteenth century. In literature, as in life, there were appropriate and orderly styles and rules. One had but to learn these, and to write or act accordingly.

Reason Paramount

Sir Henry Tichborne surrounded by his family, retainers and servants handing out the hereditary dole of bread to the villages in front of his Tudor manor (long since demolished). Note the Puritan dress.

TICHBORNE DOLE, 1670
Gillis van Tilborch
Mrs. John Loudon, Tichborne Park
Alresford, Hants

With this emphasis on rationalism there went along a preoccupation with standards or norms. If man's reason could reveal universal Truth, it became the responsibility of writers to preserve the truth—in politics, religion, and society at large. This sense of responsibility had two important consequences for literature.

Dryden, Pope and Johnson

First, the search for standards inspired the first great age of literary criticism. John Dryden (page 368), Alexander Pope (page 393), and Samuel Johnson (page 405)—all practicing poets—also became the most influential men of letters of the age. In fact, we often subdivide this period into three parts, roughly corresponding to the careers of Dryden (1660–1700), Pope (1700–1750), and Johnson (1750–1790). All

Greek and Roman Models

three poet-critics were consistent in their praise of the ancient Greek and Roman authors as the best models for literature. The works of Homer, Horace, and Virgil were "classic" in the best sense: they provided norms or standards of excellence. Thus eighteenth-century literature is often called "neoclassic." The best writers often deliberately strove to imitate the ancients, filling their works with elegant

This eighteenth-century Sharp family portrait is in marked contrast with the Tichborne portrait on the opposite page. Contrast the family groupings, their dress, expressions and activities, and the styles and uses of their manors as backgrounds.

SHARP FAMILY
J. Zoffany
Private collection on loan to
the National Portrait Gallery, London

allusions to classical mythology and to specific passages of Greek and Roman literature. The phenomenon was not restricted to literature: neoclassicism marks the simple lines of architecture, the formal gardens, and the political slogans of the period, which likened England to ancient Rome under the Emperor Augustus. Augustus had founded a new dynasty and brought peace and prosperity to Rome after a prolonged period of civil war. The English neoclassic writers boldly prophesied that King Charles II (reigned 1660–1685) would do the same.

The second important consequence of rationalism's search for standards was the flowering of satire. Satire attacks deviations from the norm and seeks to correct them. The Romans invented this literary form, which flourished in the poetry of Horace (65–8 B.C.) and Juvenal (c. 60–140 A.D.). The eighteenth century was the greatest age of satire in English—and here again, the greatest writers (Dryden, Addison, Pope, Swift, and Johnson) were all imitating Roman models of satire to some degree. The satiric targets of these writers, in prose and verse, were ignorance, hypocrisy, and corruption. Satire was a major element in the witty comedies of the later seventeenth century—the so-called Restoration period, named for the return of King Charles II to the English throne in 1660. Satire was also prominent in the works of Henry Fielding, whose *Joseph Andrews* (1742) and *Tom Jones* (1749) were significant landmarks in the early development of the English novel.

The weapon of satire was *wit,* a word with a broad range of meaning in the neoclassic age. Wit was not restricted to clever humor (although it could mean that). It also referred to superior knowledge and insight. In fact, our English word is derived from Greek and Latin words meaning "to know" and "to see." The opposite of wit was stupidity or dullness in an intellectual sense—and pretension or clumsiness in social manners. In society, wit was often a matter of style. The fashionably dressed, sophisticated young dandies in Restoration comedy, for example, were often referred to as wits; their antagonists were the fops—would-be wits who lacked grace, elegance, or cleverness. The emphasis on style carried over to literature. Pope defined wit in a famous epigram: "What oft was thought, but ne'er so well expressed." In costumes, in manners, in furnishings, in conversation— the neoclassic age set a high premium, seldom equaled or surpassed, on grace and elegance and awareness: all included in the concept of wit.

LITERATURE AND SOCIETY

The writers of this period were fundamentally conservative. In their eagerness to preserve the status quo, they may often appear smug or complacent. But we should recall that rational standards of behavior seemed to them as essential bulwarks of civilization against chaos. King Charles II was triumphantly restored to the throne in 1660 after two decades of civil war. He brought back to London the fashions and styles of Louis XIV's court at Versailles, where he had sojourned in exile. In a great burst of fresh air, the theaters in London, which had been closed by the Puritan regime as sinful and frivolous, were now reopened. The

LIMEWOOD STATUETTE OF ANGEL
Thomas Banks
Victoria and Albert Museum
Crown ©

Gainsborough, primarily a portrait painter, was one of the greatest English painters. He often sets his figures in landscapes as above.

HENEAGE LLOYD AND HIS SISTER
Thomas Gainsborough
Reproduced by permission of the Syndics of
Fitzwilliam Museum, Cambridge

Royal Society was founded for the progress of knowledge and science. The elegant life of aristocratic court circles blossomed. There was thus a joyous, liberating tone to the early years of the neoclassic period.

But political stability was far from secure. The feuds among *Political Feuds*
Anglicans (the Established Church), Roman Catholics, and nonconforming Puritans (often called Dissenters)—as well as the tension between the aristocracy and the rising merchant class—were still extremely divisive. There was no long-term solution to these problems until the forced abdication of King James II, Charles' brother, in 1688. James openly professed Catholicism, and the issue of who would succeed him led to a political crisis. With the King's renunciation of the

Opposite Page:
ST. PAUL'S CATHEDRAL
British Tourist Authority

St. Paul's Cathedral was built by the great English architect Sir Christopher Wren between 1675 and 1710 to replace the original church destroyed by the Great Fire of 1666. Wren was strongly influenced by Italian Renaissance (Roman) architecture.

Thomas Chippendale (1718-1779) was the most famous English cabinet maker of the age. His own unique style was influenced by Gothic, French, and Chinese designs.

Desk and Bookcase
Thomas Chippendale, 1754
© British Library, London

Glorious Revolution

throne, the fundamental primacy of the Anglican Church and of Parliament was reaffirmed. This compromise was reached without bloodshed and is thus often called the Glorious Revolution. The monarchy was committed to a Protestant line of succession: at first under James's daughter Mary and her Dutch husband Prince William, and then under Queen Anne (the last of the Stuart line). With the death of Anne in 1714, England turned to a more distant relative of the royal family, the Elector of the German state of Hanover. He assumed

the throne as George I, and his descendants were to reign for the rest of the century and into our own time. Queen Elizabeth II, the present monarch, traces her ancestry in the Hanoverian line.

Primacy of Parliament

The political compromise of 1688 also paved the way for the modern primacy of Parliament, which had struggled since the Civil War to modify the absolute power of the monarch. Early in the eighteenth century, two major parties in Parliament emerged. The Whigs were commonly identified with the interests of the middle class: merchants and small country squires. The Tories allied themselves with powerful, aristocratic landowners and the Anglican Church. Many of the most eloquent writers were conservative Tories (Swift, Pope, and Samuel Johnson). Addison (page 387) held political office under the Whigs. Daniel Defoe seems to have served both parties. Despite the aristocratic, conservative tone of much neoclassic literature, this was an age of lively (and sometimes bruising) political debate, and many of the leading writers became directly involved with pleading one political cause or another.

Addison
Defoe

Clarity, Order, Common Sense

The neoclassicists often sound as if they would have been content to preserve an ideal world of clarity, order, and common sense. Of course this world was largely an idealization. Only the nobility enjoyed an ordered world of style and grace; and only the aristocracy had the education to appreciate the witty barbs and elegant allusions of

The first Apotheosis *vase was produced by Josiah Wedgwood (1730-1795) from the original design (c. 1778) by John Flaxman. Wedgwood considered the vase to be "the finest and most perfect I have ever made."*

APOTHEOSIS OF HOMER
John Flaxman, Jr.
Trustees of the Wedgwood Museum
Barlaston, Staffordshire

*The painter shows his skill in capturing the effects of
light while portraying the age's fascinations with science.
The neoclassicists believed that human reason could come to
know and to control the laws of nature.*

EXPERIMENT WITH AIR PUMP
Joseph Wright of Derby
Tate Gallery, London

neoclassic poetry. Most of neoclassic literature has little to say about the
common soldier, the housewife, the poor farmer, or the laborer.

But no status quo can be preserved forever. Social conditions were
changing, and would change even more rapidly with the beginning of
the Industrial Revolution in the 1760s. The great buildup of London
into a modern metropolis was already underway by 1700, when the
capital could boast a half million inhabitants. Even before that, the twin
disasters of the plague (1665) and the great fire (1666) had radically
changed the city. For a vivid account of everyday life in that period we
are indebted to the *Diary* of Samuel Pepys (page 373), a remarkably
observant civil servant who chronicled his experiences in London in the

*Industrial
Revolution*

Pepys

1660s. Pepys, the son of a tailor, may be considered the forerunner of one of the most significant movements in this period. He seems to have intuited that the record of unique, everyday experiences of one individual was worth setting down in detail. He probably did not intend his *Diary* to be read after his death, since he wrote it in a form of shorthand which was only decoded early in the nineteenth century. Nevertheless, Pepys's impulse to record experience subjectively—as opposed to the general neoclassic emphasis on objective reality—was an early sign of new directions in literature.

Rise of the Middle Class

Pepys was part of the middle class of English life: a large spectrum of society which trade, civil service, and general prosperity were making ever more important. The rise of the middle class in the early eighteenth century meant a new, vastly expanded reading public. Newspapers, magazines, and lending libraries were founded. Booksellers began to supplant aristocratic patrons as the chief mechanism for the publication of literary works. Coffeehouses in London became the gathering places for writers who, fifty years before, would probably have been attached to the great houses of the nobility. Joseph Addison and Richard Steele (page 387) perfected the form of the essay in *The Tatler* and *The Spectator,* their two periodicals devoted to news, gossip, and moral instruction with a light note. The papers were intended for (and enjoyed) a wide audience. Daniel Defoe (page 380)—a business entrepreneur, occasional journalist, and political spy—blended fact and fiction in a new prose form: the novel. *Robinson Crusoe,* partially based on the account of a castaway in real life, was published in 1719. Its realism and popular success notably contrasted with the refined sophistication (and limited appeal) of neoclassic poetry. Samuel Richardson and Henry Fielding developed the novel further to include more detailed character analysis and a broader cross section of English society.

Coffeehouses

Richardson and Fielding

Signs of Change

By the third quarter of the eighteenth century, there were numerous signs that neoclassic standards—stability, clarity, and detachment—were yielding to a new sensibility. People wanted a literature closer to the realistic conditions of life. They wanted to read about individuals, rather than types. They were interested in particular characters, rather than abstract, universal rules. Social conditions overlooked in the Age of Reason began to attain prominence: the plight of the urban and rural poor, the rights of women, and the brutal code of punishment which could send a pickpocket to the gallows. Although the political system endured, it was badly shocked by the American and French Revolutions. In particular, the great cry of "Liberty, Equality, and Fraternity" which echoed in the Paris of 1789 was more than the slogan of political revolution in France. Like the first chords of a Beethoven symphony, it was an overture to a new movement in literature and the arts all over Europe: Romanticism.

Opposite Page:
SALTRAM SALOON
J. Bathal Photography
St. Albans

The Age of Neoclassicism

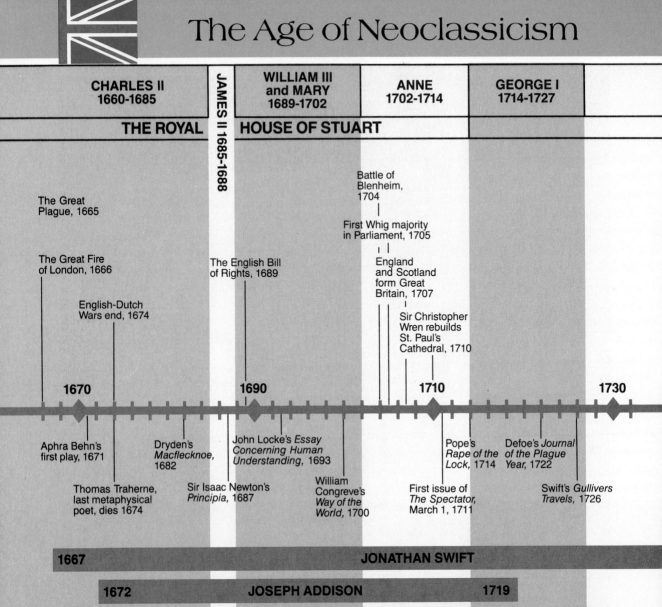

CHARLES II 1660-1685	JAMES II 1685-1688	WILLIAM III and MARY 1689-1702	ANNE 1702-1714	GEORGE I 1714-1727	
THE ROYAL		HOUSE OF STUART			

Battle of Blenheim, 1704

First Whig majority in Parliament, 1705

The Great Plague, 1665

The Great Fire of London, 1666

The English Bill of Rights, 1689

England and Scotland form Great Britain, 1707

English-Dutch Wars end, 1674

Sir Christopher Wren rebuilds St. Paul's Cathedral, 1710

1670   **1690**   **1710**   **1730**

Aphra Behn's first play, 1671

Dryden's *Macflecknoe,* 1682

John Locke's *Essay Concerning Human Understanding,* 1693

Pope's *Rape of the Lock,* 1714

Defoe's *Journal of the Plague Year,* 1722

Thomas Traherne, last metaphysical poet, dies 1674

Sir Isaac Newton's *Principia,* 1687

William Congreve's *Way of the World,* 1700

First issue of *The Spectator,* March 1, 1711

Swift's *Gullivers Travels,* 1726

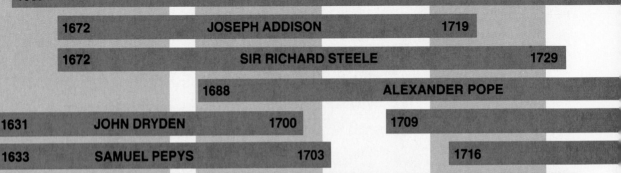

1667	JONATHAN SWIFT				
1672	JOSEPH ADDISON		1719		
1672	SIR RICHARD STEELE			1729	
1688	ALEXANDER POPE				
1631	JOHN DRYDEN	1700	1709		
1633	SAMUEL PEPYS	1703	1716		
1659	DANIEL DEFOE			1731	

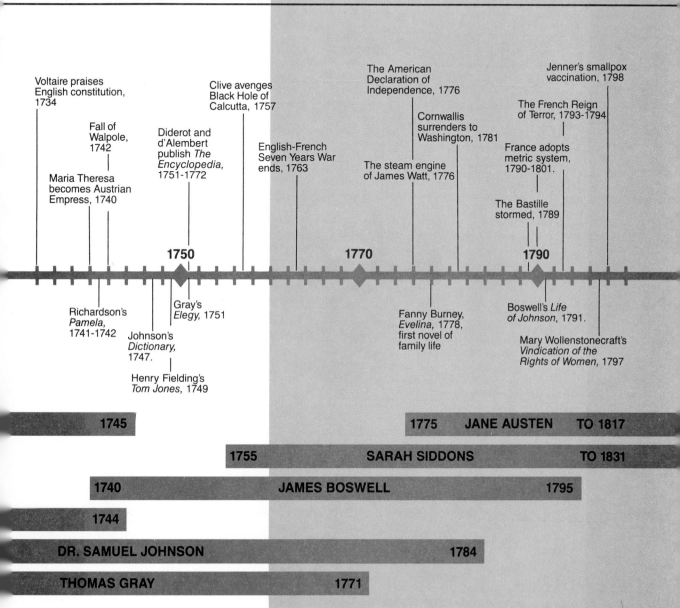

GEORGE II 1727-1760	GEORGE III 1760-1820

THE ROYAL HOUSE OF HANOVER

Voltaire praises English constitution, 1734

Fall of Walpole, 1742

Maria Theresa becomes Austrian Empress, 1740

Diderot and d'Alembert publish *The Encyclopedia*, 1751-1772

Clive avenges Black Hole of Calcutta, 1757

English-French Seven Years War ends, 1763

The American Declaration of Independence, 1776

Cornwallis surrenders to Washington, 1781

The steam engine of James Watt, 1776

Jenner's smallpox vaccination, 1798

The French Reign of Terror, 1793-1794

France adopts metric system, 1790-1801.

The Bastille stormed, 1789

1750

1770

1790

Richardson's *Pamela*, 1741-1742

Gray's *Elegy*, 1751

Johnson's *Dictionary*, 1747.

Henry Fielding's *Tom Jones*, 1749

Fanny Burney, *Evelina*, 1778, first novel of family life

Boswell's *Life of Johnson*, 1791.

Mary Wollenstonecraft's *Vindication of the Rights of Women*, 1797

1745

1775   JANE AUSTEN   TO 1817

1755   SARAH SIDDONS   TO 1831

1740   JAMES BOSWELL   1795

1744

DR. SAMUEL JOHNSON   1784

THOMAS GRAY   1771

John Dryden 1631–1700

Dryden, like Samuel Johnson in the later eighteenth century, was one of the first examples of the complete "man of letters" in English literature. Proficient in many literary forms—satire, prose essay, lyric ode, and drama—he was the most important author of the Restoration period. It was Dryden who coined the nickname "Augusta" for the city of London, thus backing the powerful image of England under Charles II as a recreation of ancient Rome under the Emperor Augustus.

Dryden was born into a staunchly Puritan family. In childhood and adolescence he witnessed the English Civil War, the execution of King Charles I, and the Protectorate of Oliver Cromwell. With the Restoration of Charles II in 1660, he became an apologist for the new regime, devoting considerable energy to attacking the enemies of the crown. He was rewarded with the post of Poet Laureate in 1668. As a convert to Catholicism, he had little to fear during Charles's reign; but the deposition of James II in 1688 stripped Dryden of his post and honors, and he went into retirement. He devoted his last years to a verse translation of Virgil's *Aeneid,* a translation which still stands, after more than two centuries, as the best English rendering of that epic.

Dryden has a threefold importance in English literature. First, he was renowned as the best playwright of Restoration drama. His principal plays include *All for Love* (1677)—an adaptation of Shakespeare's tragedy *Antony and Cleopatra*—and the witty comedy *Marriage à la Mode* (1673). Secondly, Dryden established the prose essay as a vehicle of literary criticism, and incidentally did much to develop modern English prose as an art form. Until Dryden's time, prose had been largely the vehicle for sermons, philosophical tracts (such as the treatises of Thomas Hobbes and John Locke), and religious allegories: a prime example of the latter was John Bunyan's *Pilgrim's Progress* (page 341). The novel was to be developed only in the next century, by such pioneers as Daniel Defoe,

JOHN DRYDEN
Godfrey Kneller
National Portrait Gallery, London

Samuel Richardson, and Henry Fielding. In works such as "An Essay of Dramatic Poesy" (1668), Dryden showed that elegant rhetoric could be combined with complex analysis in a distinctly literary prose.

Finally, Dryden possessed great range as a poet. The two selections printed here show his satirical and lyrical sides. "MacFlecknoe" is an early example of a short mock epic poem. Intended as a satire on the mediocre poet Thomas Shadwell, the poem adopts the forms, imagery, and conventions of classical epic. "A Song for St. Cecilia's Day," by contrast, is a lyrical praise of the power of music.

The origin of "Mac Flecknoe" was a literary quarrel between Dryden and the playwright Thomas Shadwell (c. 1642–1692), who claimed to be the spiritual successor of Ben Jonson. Dryden, himself a distinguished playwright, suggested in this attack that Shadwell's true model was the inept Irish poet, Richard Flecknoe. Shadwell is thus dubbed MacFlecknoe, or "son of Flecknoe." In a brilliantly witty satire, Dryden imagines father and son in an "epic" situation: like the Roman Emperor Augustus, Flecknoe debates who will succeed him on the throne. In this case, however, it is the throne of literary dullness which the son inherits.

from Mac Flecknoe

All human things are subject to decay,
And when fate summons, monarchs must obey.
This Flecknoe found, who, like Augustus,[1] young
Was called to empire, and had governed long;
In prose and verse was owned, without dispute,   5
Through all the realms of *Nonsense,* absolute.
This aged prince, now flourishing in peace,
And blessed with issue[2] of a large increase;
Worn out with business, did at length debate
To settle the succession of the state;   10
And, pondering which of all his sons was fit
To reign, and wage immortal war with wit,[3]
Cried: "'Tis resolved; for nature pleads that he
Should only rule, who most resembles me.
Sh——[4]alone my perfect image bears,   15
Mature in dullness from his tender years:
Sh——alone of all my sons is he
Who stands confirmed in full stupidity.
The rest to some faint meaning make pretense,
But Sh——never deviates into sense.   20
Some beams of wit on other souls may fall,
Strike through, and make a lucid interval;
But Sh——'s genuine night admits no ray,
His rising fogs prevail upon the day.
Besides, his goodly fabric[5] fills the eye,   25
And seems designed for thoughtless[6] majesty;
Thoughtless as monarch oaks that shade the plain,
And, spread in solemn state, supinely[7] reign."

1. **Augustus** reigned as Roman Emperor from 27 B.C. (when he was thirty-six) to 14 A.D.
2. **issue,** children.
3. **wit,** used here in the then common sense of genius or knowledge.
4. **Sh——,** a transparent abbreviation for Shadwell (note that his name completes the meter).
5. **fabric,** body. Shadwell was extremely fat.
6. **thoughtless,** mindless.
7. **supinely** (sü pīn′ lē), lazily, listlessly.

This poem, in the relatively free lyric form of an ode, was composed for the annual public concert which honored St. Cecilia, an early Christian martyr held to be the patron of music. Its first performance, set to music, was on November 22, 1687. In 1739 it was revived, this time to the music of George Frederick Handel.

A Song for St. Cecilia's Day

I

From harmony, from heavenly harmony
   This universal frame[1] began:
   When Nature underneath a heap
     Of jarring atoms lay,[2]
   And could not heave her head,   5
The tuneful voice was heard from high:
   "Arise, ye more than dead."
Then cold, and hot, and moist, and dry,[3]
In order to their stations leap,
   And Music's power obey.[4]   10
From harmony, from heavenly harmony
   This universal frame began:
   From harmony to harmony
Through all the compass of the notes it ran,
The diapason[5] closing full in Man.   15

II

What passion cannot Music raise and quell!
   When Jubal[6] struck the corded shell,
   His listening brethren stood around,
   And, wondering, on their faces fell
   To worship that celestial sound.   20
Less than a god they thought there could not dwell
   Within the hollow of that shell
   That spoke so sweetly and so well.
What passion cannot Music raise and quell!

III

   The trumpet's loud clangor   25
     Excites us to arms,
   With shrill notes of anger
     And mortal alarms.

1. **universal frame,** the structure of the universe.
2. **When Nature . . . atoms lay,** before Divine Wisdom fashioned all creation nature lay in a state of chaos. The "jarring atoms" refer to the physical theory of the Greek philosopher Epicurus (342–271 B.C.).
3. **cold . . . dry,** the four elements (earth, fire, water, air).
4. **Music's power obey,** the structure of the universe was felt to correspond to the mathematical proportions of musical harmony.
5. **diapason** (dī ə pā′ zn), the whole range of tones in the musical scale. By analogy, man is God's greatest work in the scale of nature.
6. **Jubal,** legendary inventor of the organ and harp (*Genesis* 4:21). Dryden pictures his harp to have been made of a tortoise shell.

The double double double beat
  Of the thundering drum   30
Cries: "Hark! the foes come;
Charge, charge, 'tis too late to retreat."

IV

The soft complaining flute
In dying notes discovers
The woes of hopeless lovers,   35
Whose dirge is whispered by the warbling lute.

V

Sharp violins[7] proclaim
Their jealous pangs, and desperation,
Fury, frantic indignation,
Depth of pains, and height of passion,   40
  For the fair, disdainful dame.

VI

  But O! what art can teach,
  What human voice can reach,
The sacred organ's praise?
  Notes inspiring holy love,   45
Notes that wing their heavenly ways
  To mend the choirs above.

VII

Orpheus[8] could lead the savage race;
And trees unrooted left their place,
  Sequacious of[9] the lyre;   50
But bright Cecilia raised the wonder higher:
When to her organ vocal breath was given,
  An angel heard, and straight appeared,
    Mistaking earth for heaven.

Grand Chorus

As from the power of sacred lays   55
  The spheres began to move,[10]
And sung the great Creator's praise
  To all the blest above;
So, when the last and dreadful hour

---

7. **violins,** recently introduced into England. The Elizabethan viol had a softer, duller sound.
8. **Orpheus** (ôr′ fē əs), the singer of Greek myth, whose music was so sweet that it charmed beasts, rocks, and trees.

9. **sequacious of,** following.
10. **spheres . . . move,** the celestial bodies were thought to produce harmonious music ("music of the spheres"); here the poet imagines that the power of music inspired their movement.

> *This crumbling pageant[11] shall devour,*   60
> *The trumpet shall be heard on high,*
> *The dead shall live, the living die,*
> *And Music shall untune the sky.[12]*

11. **crumbling pageant,** the universe on the last day of judgment; also the stage performance of Dryden's song, coming to an end.
12. **Music . . . sky,** the sound of the last trumpet (see *I Corinthians* 15:52) announces the end of the material universe; this music "untunes" (i.e., puts an end to) the music of the spheres.

FOR UNDERSTANDING

1. What ironic parallel does Dryden suggest between the Irish poet Richard Flecknoe and the Roman Emperor Augustus?

2. Who was MacFlecknoe in real life? What does his name mean?

3. What qualities does Flecknoe emphasize in his successor?

4. How does Dryden picture the origins of the physical universe in "A Song for St. Cecilia's Day"?

5. What are the passions that music can "raise and quell" in Dryden's poem?

FOR INTERPRETATION

How does Dryden use the theme of harmony in "A Song for St. Cecilia's Day"?

FOR APPRECIATION

The Couplet: Antithesis and Anticlimax

Much of the witty effect of the rhymed couplet in satire derives from two related devices: *antithesis* and *anticlimax* (or *bathos*). Antithesis is a pointed juxtaposition of opposite or contrary elements. Anticlimax is the sinking effect created when the reader, full of lofty expectations, finds only something trivial or deflating instead. Pick out some examples of these devices in the extract from "MacFlecknoe."

Frontispiece to Wit at Seven Weapons *by Beaumont and Fletcher.*

Samuel Pepys 1633–1703

John Bunyan and Samuel Pepys (pronounced Peeps) were contemporaries, but two more dissimilar people are hard to imagine. Bunyan lacked much formal education, spent his life in the country, and lived in an inner vision; Pepys obtained a Cambridge degree, worked in government service in London, and was a man of the world. Each man epitomized a particular type of the age: Bunyan the Puritan, and Pepys the Cavalier.

John Pepys, Samuel's father, was a younger son of a well-to-do family and had to take up a trade to earn a living. He was successful enough as a tailor to support his family, but in order to attend university Samuel depended on a scholarship to Cambridge. After graduation in 1654, some of his wealthy relatives steered him into the Admiralty administration. He rose gradually to positions of increased responsibility, influence, and wealth.

In 1660 Pepys began to keep a diary, using a private shorthand—then only recently invented, as much for secrecy as for speed. Because what he wrote was for his eyes alone, he felt free to tell everything that was happening in his own life and in the world around him, from spats with his wife and records of his finances to executions, plots, wars, and love affairs. Pepys continued the diary for nine years; in 1669 his failing eyesight forced him to abandon the project. In 1688, with the Glorious Revolution and the fall of King James II, he retired from public office to live out his days in comfortable obscurity. At his death, he left his distinguished library, including the volumes of the *Diary,* to Magdalene College, Cambridge. It was not until 1825 that the shorthand code was deciphered and the *Diary* finally published, with certain deletions of material then considered too racy. Toward the end of the nineteenth century an unexpurgated version appeared.

The importance of the *Diary* is that it allows us an extraordinary glimpse into everyday life in Restoration London. Pepys is unparalleled in his

SAMUEL PEPYS
Godfrey Kneller
The National Maritime Museum, London

honest, intimate, and detailed picture of the period. With the *Diary* in hand we can imagine ourselves as his contemporaries, meeting people on the street, listening to court gossip, trying to balance the accounts, going to a play, or witnessing the two great catastrophes of city life in the 1660s: the plague of 1665 and the great fire of the following year. Pepys allows us ample glimpses of his own personality: eccentric, affectionate, practical, and earthy. But his keen interest in the world around him also appears on every page. Like Samuel Johnson and Charles Dickens after him, Pepys reveled in the endless diversity of London life. The three selections which follow testify to his remarkable powers of observation.

from DIARY

The Theater

Feb. 6, 1668. We sat at the office all the morning, and at noon home to dinner; and my wife being gone before, I to the Duke of York's playhouse, where a new play of Etheriges called *She would if she could.*[1] And though I was there by 2 a-clock,[2] there was 1000 people put back that could not have room in the pit; and I at last, because my wife was there, made shift[3] to get into the 18*d* box[4]—and there saw; but Lord, how full was the house and how silly the play, there being nothing in the world good in it and few people pleased in it. The King was there; but I sat mightily behind, and could see but little and hear not all. The play being done, I into the pit to look my wife; and it being dark and raining, I to look my wife out, but could not find her; and so stayed, going between the two doors and through the pit an hour and half I think, after the play was done, the people staying there till the rain was over and to talk one with another; and among the rest, here was the Duke of Buckingham[5] today openly sat in the pit; and there I found him with my Lord Buckhurst and Sidly and Etherige the poet—the last of whom I did hear mightily find fault with the Actors, that they were out of humour and had not their parts perfect . . . while all the rest did through the whole pit blame the play as a silly, dull thing, though there was something very roguish and witty; but the design of the play, and end, mighty insipid. At last I did find my wife staying for me in the entry.

1. **Etheriges,** Pepy's spelling for **Sir George Etherege** (c.1634–c.1691) who was one of the best-known playwrights of the Restoration. His most celebrated play is *The Man of Mode* (1676).
2. **2 a-clock,** an hour and a half before the plays usually began.
3. **made shift,** managed.
4. **18d box,** the middle gallery, in which seats cost 18 pence.
5. **George Villiers, Duke of Buckingham** (1628–1687) was a prominent nobleman opposed to Charles II.

The Plague

Sept. 3, 1665. Church being done, up to the Vestry[1] at the desire of the Justices of the Peace, Sir Th Bidolph and Sir W Boreman and Alderman Hooker—in order to the doing something for the keeping of the plague from growing; but Lord, to consider the madness of people of the town, who will (because they are forbid) come in Crowds along with the dead Corps[2] to see them buried. But we agreed on some orders for the prevention thereof.[3] Among other stories, one was very passionate methought—of a complaint brought against a man in the town for taking a child from London from an infected house. Alderman Hooker told us it was the child of a very able citizen in Graciousstreet, a saddler,[4] who had buried all the rest of his children of the plague; and himself and

1. **Vestry** (ves′ trē), an elected committee in the Anglican Church which helps to manage church business.
2. **Corps,** corpses, dead bodies.
3. Funeral processions in London were forbidden during the time of the plague, but the law was widely ignored.
4. **saddler,** a shopkeeper selling saddles and harnesses.

Adapted from the edition of R. Latham and W. Matthews, *The Diary of Samuel Pepys,* University of California Press, Berkeley and Los Angeles. © 1970 by G. Bell & Sons, Ltd.

wife now being shut up, and in despair of escaping, did desire only to save the life of this little child; and so prevailed to have it received stark-naked into the arms of a friend, who brought it (having put it into new fresh clothes) to Grenwich; where, upon hearing the story, we did agree it should be permitted to be received and kept in the town. Thence with my Lord Brouncker to Captain Cockes, where we mighty merry, and supped; and very late, I by water to Woolwich, in great apprehensions of an Ague. Here was my Lord Brouncker's lady of pleasure, who I perceive goes everywhere with him, and he I find is obliged to carry her and make all the Courtship to her that can be.

Sept. 14, 1665. When I came home, I spent some thoughts upon the occurrences of this day, giving matter for as much content on one hand and melancholy on another as any day in all my life—for the first, the finding of my money and plate[5] and all safe at London (and speeding in my business of money this day)—adding to that, the decrease of 500 and more, which is the first decrease we have yet had in the sickness since it begun —and great hopes that the next week it will be greater.[6] Then on the other side—my finding that though the Bill[7] in general is abated, yet the City within the walls is increased and likely to continue so and is close to our house there—my meeting dead corpses of the plague, carried to be buried close to me at noonday through the City in Fanchurch-street—to see a person sick of the sores carried close by me by Grace-church in a hackney-coach[8]—my finding the Angell tavern at the lower end of Tower-hill shut up;

and more then that, the alehouse at the Tower-stairs; and more then that, that the person was then dying of the plague when I was last there, a little while ago at night, to write a short letter there, and I overheard the mistress of the house sadly saying to her husband somebody was very ill, but did not think it was of the plague—to hear that poor Payne my waterman hath buried a child and is dying himself—to hear that a labourer I sent but the other day to Dagenhams to know how they did there is dead of the plague; and that one of my own watermen, that carried me daily, fell sick as soon as he had landed me on Friday morning last, when I had been all night upon the water (and I believed he did get his infection that day at Brainford) is now dead of the plague—to hear that Mr. Lewes hath another daughter sick—and lastly, that both my servants, W Hewers and Tom Edwards, have lost their fathers, both in St. Sepulcher's parish, of the plague this week—doth put me into great apprehensions of melancholy, and with good reason. But I put off the thoughts of sadness as much as I can; and the rather to keep my wife in good heart, and family also. After supper (having eat nothing all this day) upon a fine Tench[9] of Mr. Sheldens taking, we to bed.

5. **plate,** serving dishes and flatware covered with silver or gold.
6. In the week of Sept. 5 the plague claimed 6544 victims, as compared with 6988 the previous week.
7. **bill,** weekly list of burials.
8. **hackney-coach,** a coach for hire. City regulations had required since June that a coach carrying plague victims had to be aired for five or six days afterwards.
9. **tench,** a type of fish.

The Fire

Sept. 2, 1666. *Lord's day.* Some of our maids sitting up late last night to get things ready against our feast today, Jane called us up, about 3 in the morning, to tell us of a great fire they saw in the City.[1] So I rose, and

slipped on my nightgown and went to her window, but being unused to such fires as fol-

1. **City,** the City of London was then, as now, the relatively small business center around St. Paul's, the Bank of England, and the Exchange.

lowed, I thought it far enough off, and so went to bed again and to sleep. About 7 rose again to dress myself, and there looked out at the window and saw the fire not so much as it was, and further off. So to my closet[2] to set things to rights after yesterday's cleaning. By and by Jane comes and tells me that she hears that above 300 houses have been burned down tonight by the fire we saw, and that it was now burning down all Fishstreet by London Bridge. So I made myself ready presently, and walked to the Tower[3] and there got up upon one of the high places, Sir J Robinson's little son going up with me; and there I did see the houses at that end of the bridge all on fire, and an infinite great fire on this and the other side the end of the bridge. . . . So I down to the water-side and there got a boat and through bridge, and there saw a lamentable fire. Everybody endeavouring to remove their goods, and flinging into the River or bringing them into lighters[4] that lay off. Poor people staying in their houses as long as till the very fire touched them, and then running into boats or clambering from one pair of stair by the water-side to another. And among other things, the poor pigeons I perceive were loath to leave their houses, but hovered about the windows and balconies till they were some of them burned, their wings, and fell down.

Having stayed, and in an hour's time seen the fire rage every way, and nobody to my sight endeavouring to quench it, but to remove their goods and leave all to the fire; and having seen it get as far as the Steeleyard, and the wind mighty high and driving it into the city, and everything, after so long a drought, proving combustible, even the very stones of churches . . . I to White-hall, and there up to the King's closet in the chapel, where people came about me and I did give them an account dismayed them all; and word was carried in to the King, so I was called for and did tell the King and Duke of York what I saw, and that unless his Majesty did command houses to be pulled down, nothing could stop

the fire. They seemed much troubled, and the King commanded me to go to my Lord Mayor from him and command him to spare no houses but to pull down before the fire every way. The Duke of York bid me tell him that if he would have any more soldiers, he shall. . . . At last met my Lord Mayor in Canning Streete, like a man spent, with a hankercher[5] about his neck. To the King's message, he cried like a fainting woman, "Lord, what can I do? I am spent. People will not obey me. I have been pulling down houses. But the fire overtakes us faster then we can do it." That he needed no more soldiers; and that for himself, he must go and refresh himself, having been up all night. So he left me, and I him, and walked home—seeing people all almost distracted and no manner of means used to quench the fire. . . . Here I saw Mr. Isaccke Houblon, that handsome man—prettily dressed and dirty at his door at Dowgate, receiving some of his brothers' things whose houses were on fire; and as he says, have been removed twice already, and he doubts (as it soon proved) that they must be in a little time removed from his house also—which was a sad consideration. And to see the churches all filling with goods, by people who themselves should have been quietly there at this time.

By this time it was about 12 a-clock, and so home and there find my guests, which was Mr. Wood and his wife, Barbary Shelden, and also Mr. Moone— . . .

As soon as dined . . . I to Paul's-Wharf,[6] where I had appointed a boat to attend me; and took in Mr. Carcasse and his brother, whom I met in the street, and carried them

---

2. **closet,** small private room for study.
3. **Tower,** the Tower of London.
4. **lighters,** flat-bottomed barges used for loading and unloading ships or to transport goods over a short route.
5. **hankercher,** handkerchief.
6. **Paul's-Wharf,** on the Thames River near St. Paul's cathedral.

The Great Fire of London took five days to bring under control. It destroyed most of the city: some 13,000 houses, 80 or more churches, dozens of public, business, and craft buildings.

THE GREAT FIRE OF LONDON, 1666
Dutch School
The Museum of London

below and above bridge, to and again, to see the fire, which was now got further, both below and above, and no likelihood of stopping it. Met with the King and Duke of York in their Barge, and with them to Queen-Hith and there called Sir Rd. Browne to them. Their order was only to pull down houses apace, and so below bridge at the water-side; but little was or could be done, the fire coming upon them so fast. . . . Having seen as much as I could now, I away to White-hall by appointment, and there walked to St. James's Park, and there met my wife and walked to my boat, and there upon the water again, and to the fire up and down, it still increasing and the wind great. So near the fire as we could for smoke; and all over the Thames, with one's face in the wind you were almost burned with a shower of Firedrops—this is

very true—so as houses were burned by these drops and flakes of fire, three or four, nay five or six houses, one from another. When we could endure no more upon the water, we to a little alehouse on the Bankside and saw the fire grow . . . We stayed till, it being darkish, we saw the fire as only one entire arch of fire from this to the other side the bridge, and in a bow up the hill, for an arch of above a mile long. It made me weep to see it. The churches, houses, and all on fire and flaming at once, and a horrid noise the flames made, and the cracking of houses at their ruin. So home with a sad heart, and there find everybody discoursing and lamenting the fire; and poor Tom Hater came with some few of his goods saved out of his house, which is burned upon Fish-street hill. I invited him to lie at my house, and did receive his goods: but was deceived in his lying there, the noise coming every moment of the growth of the Fire, so as we were forced to begin to pack up our own goods and prepare for their removal. And did by Moone-shine (it being brave, dry, and moonshine and warm weather) carry much of my goods into the garden, and Mr. Hater and I did remove my money and Iron-chests into my cellar—as thinking that the safest place. And got my bags of gold into my office ready to carry away, and my chief papers of accounts also there, and my tallies into a box by themselves. We did put Mr. Hater, poor man, to bed a little; but he got but very little rest, so much noise being in my house, taking down of goods.

Sept. 3. About 4 a-clock in the morning, my Lady Batten sent me a cart to carry away all my money and plate and best things to Sir W Riders at Bednall greene;[7] which I did, riding myself in my nightgown in the Cart; and Lord, to see how the streets and the highways are crowded with people, running and riding and getting of carts at any rate to fetch away things. I find Sir W Rider tired with being called up all night and receiving things from several friends. His house full of goods—and much of Sir W. Batten and Sir W. Penn's. I am eased at my heart to have my treasure so well secured. Then home with much ado to find a way. Nor any sleep all this night to me nor my poor wife. But then, and all this day, she and I and all my people laboring to get away the rest of our things . . .

This day, Mercer being not at home, but against her mistress order gone to her mother's, and my wife going thither to speak with W. Hewer,[8] met her there and was angry; and her mother saying that she was not a prentice girl, to ask leave every time she goes abroad, my wife with good reason was angry, and when she came home, bid her be gone again. And so she went away, which troubled me; but yet less then it would, because of the condition we are in fear of coming into in a little

time, of being less able to keep one in her quality. At night, lay down a little upon a quilt of W. Hewer in the office (all my own things being packed up or gone); and after me, my poor wife did the like—we having fed upon the remains of yesterday's dinner, having no fire nor dishes, nor any opportunity of dressing anything.

Sept. 4. Up by break of day to get away the remainder of my things, which I did by a lighter at the Iron-gate; and my hands so few, that it was the afternoon before we could get them all away . . .

This night Mrs. Turner (who, poor woman, was removing her goods all this day —good goods, into the garden, and knew not how to dispose of them)—and her husband supped with my wife and I at night in the office, upon a shoulder of mutton from the cook's, without any napkin or anything, in a sad manner but were merry. Only, now and then walking into the garden and saw how horridly the sky looks, all on a fire in the night, was enough to put us out of our wits; and endeed it was extremely dreadful—for it looks just as if it was at us, and the whole heaven on fire. I after supper walked in the dark down to Tower-street, and there saw it all on fire . . . Now begins the practice of blowing up of houses in Tower-street, those next the Tower, which at first did frighten people more then anything; but it stopped the fire where it was done—it bringing down the houses to the ground in the same places they stood, and then it was easy to quench what little fire was in it, though it kindled nothing almost. I wrote to my father this night; but the post-house being burned, the letter could not go.

Sept. 5. I lay down in the office again upon W. Hewer's quilt, being mighty weary

---

7. Rider was a prosperous merchant and friend of Pepys who lived in an Elizabethan mansion.
8. **Mercer, W. Hewer,** servants of Pepys.

and sore in my feet with going till I was hardly able to stand. About 2 in the morning my wife calls me up and tells of new cries of "Fire!"—it being come to Barking Church, which is the bottom of our lane. I up; and finding it so, resolved presently to take her away; and did, and took my gold (which was about 2350£), W. Hewer, and Jane down by Poundy's boat to Woolwich. But Lord, what a sad sight it was by moonlight to see the whole City almost on fire—that you might see it plain at Woolwich, as if you were by it. . . . So back again, by the way seeing my goods well in the lighters at Deptford and watched well by people. Home, and whereas I expected to have seen our house on fire, it being now about 7 a-clock, it was not. . . . I up to the top of Barking steeple, and there saw the saddest sight of desolation that I ever saw. Everywhere great fires. Oil-cellars and brimstone and other things burning. I became afeared to stay there long; and therefore down again as fast as I could, the fire being spread as far as I could see it, and to Sir W. Penn's and there eat a piece of cold meat, having eaten nothing since Sunday but the remains of Sunday's dinner. . . .Walked into Moore-fields (our feet ready to burn, walking through the town among the hot coals) and find that full of people, and poor wretches carrying their goods there, and everybody keeping his goods together by themselves (and a great blessing it is to them that it is fair weather for them to keep abroad night and day) . . .

Thence homeward, having passed through Cheapside and Newgate-market, all burned—and seen Anthony Joyce's house in fire. I also did see a poor cat taken out of a hole in the chimney joining to the wall of the Exchange, with the hair all burned off the body and yet alive. I lay down and slept a good night about midnight—though when I rose, I hear that there had been a great alarm of French and Dutch being risen—which proved nothing. But it is a strange thing to see how long this time did look since Sunday, having been always full of variety of actions, and little sleep, that it looked like a week or more. And I had forgot almost the day of the week.

FOR UNDERSTANDING

1. How did Pepys react to Etherege's play? Why was the playwright annoyed at the actors?
2. What is the "madness" that the group gathers in the Vestry to discuss?
3. In the entry for Sept. 14, 1665, what things have made Pepys happy on this day? What has made him sad? Name a few specific incidents.
4. What methods did the Londoners use to stop the Great Fire? What seem to have been Pepys's major concerns during the fire?

FOR INTERPRETATION

1. What impression do you receive from these diary entries of the personality of Samuel Pepys?
2. What adjectives would you use to describe your own mood after reading the selections about the plague and the fire?

FOR APPRECIATION

Because Pepys's *Diary* was written in shorthand, the language is staccato and abbreviated. For example, many entries begin with "up" or "home," and subjects and verbs are often omitted. What shortcuts do you use when writing notes?

COMPOSITION

Imagine that you are Pepys. Take one of the incidents in the *Diary* (going to a play, meeting a cart filled with bodies, seeing the devastation of the fire). Try to describe in a paragraph what you saw and heard. How did it affect you physically and emotionally? Be as precise and vivid as you can.

Daniel Defoe

c.1660–1731

Daniel Defoe was the son of a London butcher, James Foe. Born probably in the year of Charles II's restoration, he was educated in a special school established by religious nonconformists, or dissenters, who were opposed to the Church of England. Defoe began his adult life as a small merchant. Never too scrupulous about his dealings, he soon went bankrupt, the first of several financial crises in his life.

Defoe's greatest literary achievement is to have invented the English novel. His *Robinson Crusoe* (1719), enormously popular then as now, is a landmark because it made a vital imaginative leap in English prose. For the first time realistic details were shaped in a lengthy, coherent narrative of individual experience. Defoe's work originated in fact: he had read of a real voyage by Alexander Selkirk, a Scottish sea captain who had been marooned for four years in the San Juan Fernández islands of the Pacific. It seems certain that Selkirk's tale, among others, inspired certain features of Defoe's novel. Robinson Crusoe, of course, purports to be telling a true story; Defoe, like Chaucer in the *Canterbury Tales*, created fiction under the guise of truth.

It is striking that Defoe's literary originality did not flower until he was nearly sixty. He spent most of his life in a disparate assortment of careers: pamphlet-writing, newspaper editing, business, and political espionage. Politically minded, he found it impossible to conceal his scorn for the persecutors of the nonconformists, and his satirical pamphlet, *The Shortest Way with the Dissenters* (1703) resulted in his being fined, imprisoned, and pilloried. In 1704 he inaugurated *The Review,* a thrice-weekly newspaper which he wrote and edited single-handedly. In it he introduced a "Scandal Club," which foreshadowed the clubs in the *Tatler* and the *Spectator* of Addison and Steele. He then found a powerful protector in Robert Harley, Earl of Oxford, who employed him as a secret political agent for a decade.

DANIEL DEFOE
M. van der Gucht after J. Taretner
National Portrait Gallery, London

Defoe's *Journal of the Plague Year* was published in 1722, which was also the year of his second great novel, *Moll Flanders.* Although the writer was only a child of five at the time of the plague, he combines factual research and imaginative embellishment in a vivid account by a supposed eyewitness, a tradesman simply identified as H.F. The same methods which served so well for the creation of the English novel led to a fascinating, free form of historical documentary. Defoe's work was also composed to take advantage of a topical trend, since a renewed outbreak of the plague was widely feared in 1721.

from A Journal of the Plague Year

The Vision

I could fill this account with the strange relations such people give every day of what they have seen; and every one was so positive of their having seen what they pretended to see, that there was no contradicting them, without breach of friendship, or being accounted rude and unmannerly on the one hand, and profane and impenetrable on the other. One time before the plague was begun, otherwise than as I have said in St. Giles's, I think it was in March, seeing a crowd of people in the street, I joined with them to satisfy my curiosity, and found them all staring up into the air to see what a woman told them appeared plain to her, which was an angel clothed in white, with a fiery sword in his hand, waving it or brandishing it over his head. She described every part of the figure to the life, showed them the motion and the form, and the poor people came into it so eagerly and with so much readiness: Yes! I see it all plainly, says one, there's the sword as plain as can be; another saw the angel; one saw his very face, and cried out, What a glorious creature he was! One saw one thing, and one another. I looked as earnestly as the rest, but, perhaps, not with so much willingness to be imposed upon; and I said indeed, that I could see nothing but a white cloud, bright on one side, by the shining of the sun upon the other part. The woman endeavoured to show it me, but could not make me confess that I saw it,

From Oxford edition of Defoe's *Works* (1840).

which, indeed, if I had, I must have lied: but the woman turning to me looked me in the face and fancied I laughed, in which her imagination deceived her too, for I really did not laugh, but was seriously reflecting how the poor people were terrified by the force of their own imagination. However, she turned to me, called me profane fellow, and a scoffer, told me that it was a time of God's anger, and dreadful judgments were approaching, and that despisers, such as I, should wander and perish.

The people about her seemed disgusted as well as she, and I found there was no persuading them that I did not laugh at them, and that I should be rather mobbed by them than be able to undeceive them. So I left them, and this appearance passed for as real as the blazing star itself.

The Pit

I went all the first part of the time freely about the streets, though not so freely as to run myself into apparent danger, except when they dug the great pit in the churchyard of our parish of Aldgate. A terrible pit it was, and I could not resist my curiosity to go and see it; as near as I may judge, it was about forty feet in length, and about fifteen or sixteen feet broad; and, at the time I first looked at it, about nine feet deep; but it was said, they dug it near twenty feet deep afterwards, in one part of it, till they could go no deeper for the water; for they had, it seems, dug several large pits before this; for, though the plague was long a coming to our parish, yet, when it did come, there was no parish in or about London where it raged with such violence as in the two parishes of Aldgate and Whitechapel.

I say they had dug several pits in another ground, when the distemper began to spread in our parish, and especially when the dead-carts began to go about, which was not in our parish, till the beginning of August. Into these pits they had put perhaps fifty or sixty bodies each, then they made larger holes, wherein they buried all that the cart brought in a week, which, by the middle to the end of August, came to from two hundred to four hundred a week; and they could not well dig them larger, because of the order of the magistrates, confining them to leave no bodies within six feet of the surface; and the water coming on at about seventeen or eighteen feet, they could not well, I say, put more in one pit; but now, at the beginning of September, the plague raging in a dreadful manner, and the number of burials in our parish increasing to more than was ever buried in any parish about London, of no larger extent, they ordered this dreadful gulf to be dug, for such it was rather than a pit.

They had supposed this pit would have supplied them for a month or more, when they dug it, and some blamed the churchwardens for suffering[1] such a frightful thing, telling them they were making preparations to bury the whole parish, and the like; but time made it appear the churchwardens knew the condition of the parish better than they did; for the pit being finished the 4th of September, I think they began to bury in it the 6th, and, by the 20th, which was just two weeks, they had thrown into it 1114 bodies, when they were obliged to fill it up, the bodies being then come to lie within six feet of the surface. I doubt not but there may be some ancient persons alive in the parish, who can justify the fact of this, and are able to show even in what place of the churchyard the pit

lay better than I can; the mark of it also was many years to be seen in the churchyard on the surface, lying in length, parallel with the passage which goes by the west wall of the churchyard, out of Houndsditch, and turns east again into Whitechapel, coming out near the Three-Nuns inn.

It was about the 10th of September, that my curiosity led, or rather drove me to go and see this pit again, when there had been near four hundred people buried in it; and I was not content to see it in the day-time, as I had done before, for then there would have been nothing to have been seen but the loose earth; for all the bodies that were thrown in were immediately covered with earth, by those they called the buriers, which at other times were called bearers; but I resolved to go in the night, and see some of them thrown in.

There was a strict order to prevent people coming to those pits, and that was only to prevent infection; but, after some time, that order was more necessary, for people that were infected, and near their end, and delirious also, would run to those pits wrapt in blankets, or rugs, and throw themselves in, and, as they said, bury themselves. I cannot say that the officers suffered any willingly to lie there; but I have heard, that in a great pit in Finsbury, in the parish of Cripplegate, it lying open then to the fields, for it was not then walled about, many came and threw themselves in, and expired there, before they threw any earth upon them; and that when they came to bury others, and found them there, they were quite dead, though not cold.

This may serve a little to describe the dreadful condition of that day, though it is impossible to say anything that is able to give a true idea of it to those who did not see it, other than this; that it was indeed, very, very, very dreadful, and such as no tongue can express.

1. **suffering,** allowing.

FLYING FROM THE PLAGUE (Woodcut)
Society of Antiquaries of London

I got admittance into the churchyard by being acquainted with the sexton[2] who attended, who, though he did not refuse me at all, yet earnestly persuaded me not to go: telling me very seriously, for he was a good religious and sensible man, that it was, indeed, their business and duty to venture,[3] and to run all hazards, and that in it they might hope to be preserved; but that I had no apparent call to it but my own curiosity, which, he said, he believed I would not pretend, was sufficient to justify my running that hazard. I told him I had been pressed in my mind to go, and that, perhaps, it might be an instructing sight, that might not be without its uses. Nay, says the good man, if you will venture upon that score, 'Name of God, go in; for, depend upon it, it will be a sermon to you, it may be, the best that ever you heard in your life. It is a speaking sight, says he, and has a voice with it, and a loud one, to call us all to repentance; and with that he opened the door, and said, Go, if you will.

His discourse had shocked my resolution a little, and I stood wavering for a good while, but, just at that interval, I saw two links come over from the end of the Minories,[4] and heard the bellman, and then appeared a dead cart, as they called it, coming over the streets;

so I could no longer resist my desire of seeing it, and went in. There was nobody as I could perceive at first, in the churchyard, or going into it, but the buriers, and the fellow that drove the cart, or rather led the horse and cart, but when they came up to the pit, they saw a man go to and again[5] muffled up in a brown cloak, and making motions with his hands, under his cloak, as if he was in great agony; and the buriers immediately gathered about him, supposing he was one of those poor delirious, or desperate creatures, that used to pretend, as I have said, to bury themselves; he said nothing as he walked about, but two or three times groaned very deeply, and loud, and sighed as he would break his heart.

When the buriers came up to him, they soon found he was neither a person infected and desperate, as I have observed above, or a person distempered in mind,[6] but one oppressed with a dreadful weight of grief in-

2. **sexton,** man who takes care of a church building.
3. **venture,** dare.
4. **links . . . Minories,** links were torches; the Minories was a street between Aldgate and the Tower.
5. **to and again,** to and fro.
6. **distempered in mind,** crazy.

deed, having his wife and several of his children, all in the cart, that was just come in with him, and he followed in an agony and excess of sorrow. He mourned heartily, as it was easy to see, but with a kind of masculine grief, that could not give itself vent by tears; and, calmly desiring the buriers to let him alone, said he would only see the bodies thrown in, and go away, so they left importuning him; but no sooner was the cart turned round, and the bodies shot into the pit promiscuously,[7] which was a surprise to him, for he at least expected they would have been decently laid in, though, indeed, he was afterwards convinced that was impracticable; I say, no sooner did he see the sight, but he cried out aloud, unable to contain himself. I could not hear what he said, but he went backward two or three steps, and fell down in a swoon; the buriers ran to him and took him up, and in a little while he came to himself, and they led him away to the Pye-tavern, over-against the end of Houndsditch, where it seems, the man was known, and where they took care of him. He looked into the pit again, as he went away, but the buriers had covered the bodies so immediately with throwing in earth, that, though there was light enough, for there were lanterns and candles in them, placed all night round the sides of the pit, upon the heaps of earth, seven or eight, or perhaps more, yet nothing could be seen.

This was a mournful scene indeed, and affected me almost as much as the rest; but the other was awful, and full of terror; the cart had in it sixteen or seventeen bodies, some were wrapt up in linen sheets, some in rugs, some little other than naked, or so loose, that what covering they had fell from them, in the shooting out of the cart, and they fell quite naked among the rest; but the matter was not much to them, or the indecency much to any one else, seeing they were all dead, and were to be huddled together into the common grave of mankind, as we may call it, for here was no difference made, but poor and rich went together; there was no other way of burials, neither was it possible there should, for coffins were not to be had for the prodigious numbers that fell in such a calamity as this.

The Piper

It must be confessed, that, though the plague was chiefly among the poor, yet were the poor the most venturous and fearless of it, and went about their employment with a sort of brutal courage. I must call it so, for it was founded neither on religion or prudence; scarce did they use any caution, but run into any business which they could get any employment in, though it was the most hazardous; such was that of tending the sick, watching houses shut up, carrying infected persons to the pest-house, and, which was still worse, carrying the dead away to their graves.

It was under John Hayward's care, and within his bounds, that the story of the piper, with which people have made themselves so merry, happened, and he assured me that it was true. It is said that it was a blind piper; but, as John told me, the fellow was not blind, but an ignorant, weak, poor man, and usually went his rounds about ten o'clock at night, and went piping along from door to door, and the people usually took him in at public houses where they knew him, and would give him drink and victuals, and sometimes farthings; and he in return would pipe and sing, and talk simply, which diverted the people, and thus he lived. It was but a very bad time for this diversion, while things were as I have told, yet the poor fellow went about as usual, but was almost starved; and when anybody asked how he did[8] he would answer, the dead

---

7. **promiscuously,** (prə mis′ kyü əs lē), mixed up together and in disorder.
8. **how he did,** how he fared.

cart had not taken him yet, but that they had promised to call for him next week.

It happened one night, that this poor fellow, whether somebody had given him too much drink or no, (John Hayward said he had not drink in his house, but that they had given him a little more victuals than ordinary at a public house[9] in Coleman-street,) and the poor fellow having not usually had a bellyfull, or, perhaps, not a good while, was laid all along upon the top of a bulk or stall, and fast asleep at a door, in the street near London-wall, towards Cripplegate, and that, upon the same bulk or stall, the people of some house, in the alley of which the house was a corner, hearing a bell, which they always rung before the cart came, had laid a body really dead of the plague just by him, thinking too that this poor fellow had been a dead body as the other was, and laid there by some of the neighbours.

Accordingly, when John Hayward with his bell and the cart came along, finding two dead bodies lie upon the stall, they took them up with the instrument they used, and threw them into the cart; and all this while the piper slept soundly.

From hence they passed along, and took in other dead bodies, till, as honest John Hayward told me, they almost buried him alive in the cart, yet all this while he slept soundly; at length the cart came to the place where the bodies were to be thrown into the ground, which, as I do remember, was at Mountmill; and, as the cart usually stopt some time before they were ready to shoot out the melancholy load they had in it, as soon as the cart stopped, the fellow awaked, and struggled a little to get his head out from among the dead bodies, when, raising himself up in the cart, he called out, Hey, where am I? This frighted the fellow that attended about the work, but, after some pause, John Hayward recovering himself, said, Lord bless us! there's somebody in the cart not quite dead! So another called to him, and said, Who are you? The fellow answered, I am the poor piper: Where am I? Where are you! says Hayward; why, you are in the dead cart, and we are going to bury you. But I an't dead though, am I? says the piper; which made them laugh a little, though, as John said, they were heartily frightened at first; so they helped the poor fellow down, and he went about his business.

I know the story goes, he set up his pipes in the cart, and frighted the bearers and others, so that they ran away; but John Hayward did not tell the story so, nor say anything of his piping at all; but that he was a poor piper, and that he was carried away as above, I am fully satisfied of the truth of.

FOR UNDERSTANDING

1. What does the woman say she sees in the sky? What does the narrator say he sees? How does the crowd react?
2. Why was the pit dug in the parish of Aldgate? How long does it take to fill it?
3. Why were people forbidden to approach the pits? How did the narrator manage to satisfy his curiosity about the pit in Aldgate?
4. What did the buriers suppose at first about the man in the brown cloak? What was the real reason the man had come?
5. How did the piper come to be in the dead cart?

FOR INTERPRETATION

Samuel Pepys's account of the plague is that of an eyewitness; Defoe's narrative purports to be historical, but is really imaginative embellishment of his reading and personal interviews.
1. What details of the plague are mentioned by both Pepys and Defoe?
2. Which account do you think is more graphic and shocking?
3. Why do you think the story of the piper was told and retold by the people?

9. **public house,** tavern.

FOR APPRECIATION

1. How does Defoe enhance the credibility of his account through the indirect characterization of the narrator?

2. What is the purpose of the vignette of the woman in "The Vision"?

3. How does Defoe use humor in the story of the piper?

LANGUAGE AND VOCABULARY

Defoe writes generally modern prose, but an occasional archaic phrase serves to remind us that he, like Dryden, stands very near the beginning of this form's full development. From context clues, try to identify the meaning of the italicized phrases as precisely as you can.

1. She described every part of the figure *to the life* . . .

2. I looked as earnestly as the rest, but, perhaps, not with so much willingness *to be imposed upon* . . .

3. . . . and they could not *well* dig them larger, because of the order of the magistrates . . .

4. He mourned *heartily*, as it was easy to see, but with a kind of masculine grief . . .

5. . . . and the poor fellow having not usually had a bellyfull, or, perhaps, *not a good while* . . .

COMPOSITION

Take an unusual event (such as a fire, an accident, a bizarre occurrence) at which you were not present and try to reconstruct it imaginatively according to the model of Defoe. Use a first-person narrator and a reportorial style. Possible ways to find a subject include reading a newspaper, thumbing through a history book, or thinking back to dramatic incidents in your family which you have heard about. In your account use as much factual information as you can; supplement the facts with descriptive details and dialogue of individuals who were present.

Stubbs was perhaps the greatest English painter of animals. He combined the artist's eye with scientist's precision. He was a keen student of anatomy as clearly evident in his study of the horses below.

**MARES AND FOALS
IN A LANDSCAPE**
George Stubbs
Tate Gallery, London

Joseph Addison
Sir Richard Steele

1672–1719
1672–1729

Friends from boyhood and undergraduates together at Oxford, Addison and Steele possessed contrasting and complementary personalities. Steele was vivacious, eloquent, dashing, and somewhat imprudent. Addison was quiet, shy, dignified, and a bit calculating. Both men served in Parliament; Addison was so reserved that when he rose to make his first speech he was overcome with fright and sat down without uttering a word. Steele was so outspoken in favoring the Hanoverian succession in 1714 that he was actually expelled from Parliament and forced to issue a public apology; the accession of King George I led to his rehabilitation, and he was knighted the following year.

Through the patronage of powerful Whig leaders, Steele became editor of the *London Gazette* in 1707. Two years later he wrote the first issue of his own newspaper, the *Tatler*, to which Addison contributed. The paper was devoted to poetry, news, town gossip, and personal essays. Publication ceased in January of 1711, but the following March the two friends inaugurated a new daily newspaper, the *Spectator*, for which Addison wrote most of the essays. The framework of this publication was an imaginary club. Mr. Spectator, a learned and thoughtful yet gently humorous man, was at the center of the group. Sir Roger de Coverley represented the conservative English country gentleman; Sir Andrew Freeport represented the London merchant class. The *Spectator* started with a circulation of 3000 copies—an impressive figure for the time, when we remember that each copy was probably shared by several readers.

The popularity of these papers reflects several important literary trends: the growth of the reading audience, the new interest in reading about everyday topics for entertainment, and the importance of subjects of interest to, and about, women. To accomodate these trends, Addison

JOSEPH ADDISON
Godfrey Kneller
National Portrait Gallery, London

and Steele wrote in an easily flowing, accessible style; Samuel Johnson, no stranger to the periodical essay, later remarked that "whoever wishes to attain an English style . . . must give his days and nights to the volumes of Addison." Perhaps the practical realism of the essays is their most attractive feature. In an age of violent controversies, the *Spectator* stood for reason, moderation, and good sense. Addison echoed Pope and anticipated Samuel Johnson when he declared that the aim of the *Spectator* was "to enliven morality with wit, and to temper wit with morality."

A BEAU'S HEAD

Joseph Addison

The Spectator, No. 275: Tuesday. January 15, 1712.

I was yesterday engaged in an assembly of virtuosos,[1] where one of them produced many curious observations which he had lately made in the anatomy of an human body. Another of the company communicated to us several wonderful discoveries which he had also made on the same subject by the help of very fine glasses.[2] This gave birth to a great variety of uncommon remarks, and furnished discourse for the remaining part of the day.

The different opinions which were started on this occasion, presented to my imagination so many new ideas, that, by mixing with those which were already there, they employed my fancy all the last night, and composed a very wild extravagant dream.

I was invited methought to the dissection of a beau's head[3] and of a coquette's heart, which were both of them laid on a table before us. An imaginary operator opened the first with a great deal of nicety, which, upon a cursory and superficial view, appeared like the head of another man; but upon applying our glasses to it, we made a very odd discovery, namely, that what we looked upon as brains, were not such in reality, but an heap of strange materials wound up in that shape and texture, and packed together with wonderful art in the several cavities of the skull. For, as Homer tells us that the blood of the gods is not real blood, but only something like it; so we found that the brain of a beau is not a real brain, but only something like it.

The pineal[4] gland, which many of our modern philosophers suppose to be the seat of the soul, smelt very strong of essence and orange-flower water, and was encompassed with a kind of horny substance, cut into a thousand little faces or mirrors which were imperceptible to the naked eye, insomuch that the soul, if there had been any here, must have been always taken up in contemplating her own beauties.

We observed a large antrum[5] or cavity in the sinciput,[6] that was filled with ribands, lace and embroidery, wrought together in a most curious piece of net-work, the parts of which were likewise imperceptible to the naked eye. Another of these antrums or cavities was stuffed with invisible billetdoux,[7] loveletters, pricked dances, and other trumpery of the same nature. In another we found a kind of powder,[8] which set the whole company a sneezing, and by the scent discovered itself to be right Spanish. The several other cells were stored with commodities of the same kind, of which it would be tedious to give the reader an exact inventory.

There was a large cavity on each side the head, which I must not omit. That on the right side was filled with fictions, flatteries, and falsehoods, vows, promises, and protestations; that on the left, with oaths and imprecations. There issued out a duct from each of these cells, which ran into the root of the tongue, where both joined together, and passed forward in one common duct to the tip of it. We discovered several little roads or canals running from the ear into the brain, and took particular care to trace them out through their several passages. One of them

1. **virtuosos** (vėr chü ō′ sōz), experts.
2. **glasses,** microscopes.
3. **beau** (bō), man of fashion.
4. **pineal** (pin′ ē əl), a small cone-shaped gland in the brain.
5. **antrum** (an′ trəm), hole or cavity.
6. **sinciput** (sin′ ki pŭt), upper part of the skull.
7. **billetdoux** (bil′ ē dü′), love letters.
8. **powder,** snuff.

extended itself to a bundle of sonnets and little musical instruments. Others ended in several bladders which were filled either with wind or froth. But the large canal entered into a great cavity of the skull, from whence there went another canal into the tongue. This great cavity was filled with a kind of spongy substance, which the French anatomists call galimatias, and the English, nonsense. The skins of the forehead were extremely tough and thick, and what very much surprised us, had not in them any single blood-vessel that we were able to discover, either with or without our glasses; from whence we concluded, that the party when alive must have been entirely deprived of the faculty of blushing.

The os cribriforme[9] was exceedingly stuffed, and in some places damaged with snuff. We could not but take notice in particular of that small muscle which is not often discovered in dissections, and draws the nose upwards, when it expresses the contempt which the owner of it has, upon seeing anything he does not like, or hearing anything he does not understand. I need not tell my learned reader, this is that muscle which performs the motion so often mentioned by the Latin poets, when they talk of a man's cocking his nose, or playing the rhinoceros.

We did not find anything very remark-able in the eye, saving only that the musculi amatorii, or, as we may translate it into English, the ogling muscles, were very much worn and decayed with use; whereas, on the contrary, the elevator, or the muscle which turns the eye towards heaven, did not appear to have been used at all.

I have only mentioned in this dissection such new discoveries as we were able to make, and have not taken any notice of those parts which are to be met with in common heads. As for the skull, the face, and indeed the whole outward shape and figure of the head, we could not discover any difference from what we observe in the heads of other men. We were informed that the person to whom this head belonged, had passed for a man above five and thirty years; during which time he ate and drank like other people, dressed well, talked loud, laughed frequently, and on particular occasions had acquitted himself tolerably at a ball or an assembly; to which one of the company added, that a certain knot of ladies took him for a wit. He was cut off in the flower of his age by the blow of a paring shovel,[10] having been surprised by an eminent citizen, as he was tendering some civilities to his wife.

9. **os cribriforme,** a sieve-like mouth.
10. **paring shovel,** breast plow.

A COQUETTE'S HEART
Joseph Addison

The Spectator, No. 281: Tuesday, January 22, 1712.
Having already given an account of the dissection of a beau's head, with the several discoveries made on that occasion, I shall here, according to my promise, enter upon the dissection of a coquette's heart, and communicate to the public such particularities as we observed in that curious piece of anatomy.

I should perhaps have waived this undertaking, had not I been put in mind of my promise by several of my unknown correspondents, who are very importunate with me to make an example of the coquette, as I have already done of the beau. It is therefore in compliance with the request of friends that I have looked over the minutes of my former dream, in order to give the public an exact relation of it, which I shall enter upon without further preface.

Our operator, before he engaged in this visionary dissection, told us that there was nothing in his art more difficult than to lay open the heart of a coquette, by reason of the many labyrinths and recesses which are to be found in it, and which do not appear in the heart of any other animal.

He desired us first of all to observe the pericardium, or outward case of the heart, which we did very attentively; and by the help of our glasses discerned in it millions of little scars, which seemed to have been occasioned by the points of innumerable darts and arrows, that from time to time had glanced upon the outward coat; though we could not discover the smallest orifice by which any of them had entered and pierced the inward substance.

Every smatterer in anatomy knows that this pericardium, or case of the heart, contains in it a thin reddish liquor, supposed to be bred from the vapors which exhale out of the heart and, being stopped here, are condensed into this watery substance. Upon examining this liquor, we found that it had in it all the qualities of that spirit which is made use of in the thermometer to show the change of weather.

Nor must I here omit an experiment one of the company assured us he himself had made with this liquor, which he found in great quantity about the heart of a coquette whom he had formerly dissected. He affirmed to us that he had actually inclosed it in a small tube made after the manner of a weatherglass; but that instead of acquainting him with the variations of the atmosphere, it showed him the qualities of those persons who entered the room where it stood. He affirmed also that it rose at the approach of a

plume of feathers, an embroidered coat, or a pair of fringed gloves; and that it fell as soon as an ill-shaped periwig,[1] a clumsy pair of shoes, or an unfashionable coat came into his house. Nay, he proceeded so far as to assure us that upon his laughing aloud when he stood by it, the liquor mounted very sensibly, and immediately sank again upon his looking serious. In short, he told us that he knew very well by this invention whenever he had a man of sense or a coxcomb[2] in his room.

Having cleared away the pericardium, or the case, and liquor above mentioned, we came to the heart itself. The outward surface of it was extremely slippery, and the mucro,[3] or point, so very cold withal that upon endeavoring to take hold of it, it glided through the fingers like a smooth piece of ice.

The fibers were turned and twisted in a more intricate and perplexed manner than they are usually found in other hearts; insomuch that the whole heart was wound up together like a Gordian knot,[4] and must have had very irregular and unequal motions, while it was employed in its vital function.

One thing we thought very observable, namely, that upon examining all the vessels which came into it, or issued out of it, we could not discover any communication that it had with the tongue.

We could not but take notice likewise that several of those little nerves in the heart which are affected by the sentiments of love, hatred, and other passions, did not descend to this before us from the brain, but from the muscles which lie about the eye.

Upon weighing the heart in my hand, I found it to be extremely light, and consequently very hollow, which I did not wonder at, when, upon looking into the inside of it, I saw multitudes of cells and cavities running

1. **periwig** (per′ ə wig),   wig.
2. **coxcomb** (koks′ kōm),   conceited dandy.
3. **mucro** (myü′ krō),   tip or point.
4. **Gordian** (gôr′ dē ən) **knot,**   a knot that no one can untie.

one within another, as our historians describe the apartments of Rosamond's bower.[5] Several of these little hollows were stuffed with innumerable sorts of trifles, which I shall forbear giving any particular account of, and shall, therefore, only take notice of what lay first and uppermost, which, upon our unfolding it, and applying our microscopes to it, appeared to be a flame-colored hood.

We are informed that the lady of this heart, when living, received the addresses of several who made love to her, and did not only give each of them encouragement, but made everyone she conversed with believe that she regarded him with an eye of kindness; for which reason we expected to have seen the impression of multitudes of faces among the several plaits and foldings of the heart; but to our great surprise not a single print of this nature discovered itself till we came into the very core and center of it. We there observed a little figure, which, upon applying our glasses to it, appeared dressed in a very fantastic manner. The more I looked upon it, the more I thought I had seen the face before, but could not possibly recollect either the place or time; when at length one of the company, who had examined this figure more nicely[6] than the rest, showed us plainly by the make of its face, and the several turns of its features, that the little idol which was thus lodged in the very middle of the heart was the deceased beau, whose head I gave some account of in my last Tuesday's paper.

As soon as we had finished our dissection, we resolved to make an experiment of the heart, not being able to determine among ourselves the nature of its substance, which differed in so many particulars from that in the heart of other females. Accordingly, we laid it into a pan of burning coals, when we observed in it a certain salamandrine[7] quality that made it capable of living in the midst of fire and flame, without being consumed or so much as singed.

RICHARD STEELE
Godfrey Kneller
National Portrait Gallery, London

As we were admiring this strange phenomenon, and standing round the heart in a circle, it gave a most prodigious sigh, or rather crack, and dispersed all at once in smoke and vapor. This imaginary noise, which methought was louder than the burst of a cannon, produced such a violent shake in my brain, that it dissipated the fumes of sleep, and left me in an instant broad awake.

FOR UNDERSTANDING

1. What event prompts the writer's dream?
2. What was found in the cavities of the beau's

5. **Rosamond's bower,** the inner apartment of Rosamond, mistress of King Henry II; she died about 1176.
6. **nicely,** keenly, accurately.
7. **salamandrine** (sal ə man' drən), like a salamander, which could live in fire, according to legend.

head? Which eye muscle did not appear to have been used?

3. How did the beau meet his end?

4. What seemed to have caused the scars on the coquette's heart?

5. What did the scientists find at the very core of the heart? What experiment did they then undertake? What were the results?

FOR INTERPRETATION

1. What qualities of people in society do these two essays satirize? Do the essays attack follies that can be found in any period (including our own) or do they apply only to the eighteenth century?

2. Is Addison kinder to one sex than to the other?

FOR APPRECIATION

1. What is the framework of the essays? How does Addison make them a pair?

2. Compare the *tone* of Addison's essays with that of Francis Bacon in his essays, "Of Studies" and "Of Children and Parents" (both on p. 194).

COMPOSITION

Write an essay explaining what you find in dissecting the head (or heart) of a politician, a country singer, an athlete, a teacher, or whatever group you would like to satirize. Be careful not to make this assignment an attack on an individual. Imitate Addison's light tone as well as you can.

Wilson is regarded as the first great English landscape painter. This scene is near Alexander Pope's house and gardens at Twickenham.

THE THAMES NEAR MARBLE HILL, TWICKENHAM
Richard Wilson
Tate Gallery, London

Alexander Pope

1688–1744

The greatest English poet of the early eighteenth century, Pope suffered considerable disadvantages in childhood. Tuberculosis of the spine left him deformed, and he was always acutely sensitive about his physical appearance. As a Roman Catholic, the brilliant child was excluded from a university education or a career in politics. And, although Pope was the son of a well-to-do merchant, his middle class origins were hardly a strong recommendation in the court circles to which he aspired.

But Pope managed to overcome all these drawbacks through hard work and extraordinary natural talent. By the age of twenty-three, he was famous as the author of the "Essay on Criticism," a brilliant poem in rhymed couplets which summarized neoclassic premises of literary criticism. The following year, in 1712, he composed *The Rape of the Lock*, perhaps the most scintillating mock epic in English. By this time he was well acquainted with the principal men of letters of the age: Jonathan Swift, Dr. John Arbuthnot (physician to Queen Anne), the poet John Gay (who was to score a great success with his musical play *The Beggar's Opera* in 1728), the essayist Joseph Addison, and the playwright William Wycherley.

Pope's most ambitious work was his translation into heroic couplets of Homer's *Iliad* (1720) and *Odyssey* (1726). The translations assured his fame and financial independence. The year before he completed the *Iliad*, he settled in a house and gardens at Twickenham, on the Thames near London, where he remained for the rest of his life. Here he entertained visitors and busied himself with numerous literary projects: short verse satires (sometimes in the form of epistles, or letters), an essay on "bathos" (or the "art of sinking in poetry"), an edition of Shakespeare's plays, the philosophical "Essay on Man" (in verse), and his greatest satirical poem, *The Dunciad* (1743). Some of these endeavors were inspired by the Scriblerus Club, an informal group which Pope formed with his friends. These literary wits met

ALEXANDER POPE
Unknown Artist
Bodleian Library

regularly to satirize false learning and pretension in literature and the arts.

Pope gave his name to an age because he, more than any other writer in the first half of the century, summed up the values and standards of his time. These values are generally those of the European Enlightenment, or Age of Reason. Like the Elizabethans, the rationalists of the Enlightenment regarded the universe as a Great Chain of Being, in which all the elements of nature had a predetermined, orderly place in a grand design. Man was God's greatest work in this scheme. Pope, who is among the most quotable poets in English, eloquently expressed this philosophical system in the "Essay on Man" (1734):

All nature is but art, unknown to thee;
All chance, direction, which thou canst not
    see;
All discord, harmony not understood;
All partial evil, universal good;
And spite of pride, in erring reason's spite,
One truth is clear, Whatever is, is right . . .
Know then thyself, presume not God to scan;
The proper study of Mankind is Man.

Pope thus prized the ideals of truth, reason, and
ordered proportion. But like his friend Jonathan
Swift, he was acutely sensitive to the ways in
which the world around him fell short of these
ideals. His genius, like that of Swift, found its
most natural expression in the mode of satire:
poking fun, bitterly or lightly, at corruption,
flaws, and follies in order to reform them. Many
of us are perhaps tempted, when reading Pope
for the first time, to dismiss him as a snobbish
critic of society. Snobbish he certainly was—but
his devastating wit and his mastery of form
compel us to take him seriously.

In the early "Essay on Criticism" (1711),
Pope allied himself with essentially conservative
literary principles. He modeled the poem on the
Ars Poetica (*Art of Poetry*) of the Roman poet
Horace (65–8 B.C.). Pope argued for a mutual
harmony of form and content in literature,
condemning all excesses and praising the
doctrine of the "golden mean" (also derived
from Horace). His own style perfectly illustrated
this theory, since it united the pleasing with the
useful. In twentieth-century terms, Pope's view
may seem smug and undynamic. But he was in
the main stream of English poet-critics from
Elizabethan times to the end of the nineteenth
century—the purpose of poetry, in Samuel
Johnson's phrase, was to "instruct by pleasing."

To fulfill this purpose, Pope exploited the
rhyming couplet (sometimes called the "heroic
couplet") with such ingenuity and grace that he
is generally acknowledged as the greatest master
of this form. In Pope's hands the couplet became
the ideal instrument of satire: precise, pointed,
witty, and—despite the apparently rigid formal
requirements—capable of ingenious metrical and
rhythmical variations. Pope's major theme—a
praise of civilized clarity and order—is perfectly
reflected in his formal artistry.

The Rape of the Lock

*Pope's friend John Caryll (named in line 3 of the first canto) suggested the subject of
this poem to him: a silly quarrel in real life between Lord Petre and Mrs. Arabella
Fermor. The trivial snipping of a lock of Mrs. Fermor's hair threatened to provoke a
family feud. Pope's immediate purpose was to mediate the dispute by showing how
unimportant it really was. But his poem developed into a remarkably witty commentary
on human absurdity and the social manners of an age.*

*The Rape of the Lock is cast in the form of a mock epic—the satirical
inversion, or parody, of epic form and style. Dryden had used mock epic for serious
literary and political purposes in "MacFlecknoe" and "Absalom and Achitophel." But
Pope surpasses Dryden in the ingenuity of his literary allusions and in his charming,
imaginative irony. The protagonists are Belinda (the lady) and the Baron, who are
pictured as epic figures on a battlefield. Belinda is protected by guardian spirits, the
sylphs, which recall both Homer's gods and Milton's angels in Paradise Lost. The
five cantos (or sections) of the poem present a simple plot. Belinda awakens, prepares
herself for the gathering of fashionable lords and ladies at Hampton Court, and loses
the lock during a card game with the evil Baron. The lord refuses to surrender his
prize, despite the lady's lamentations and mounting fury. Finally Belinda threatens to
stab the Baron with a hairpin; he begs for mercy, explaining that he committed the
dastardly deed out of love for her. The climax of the poem depicts the transformation
of the lock into a celestial comet (here Pope is parodying Ovid's Metamorphoses).*

Pope's refined and educated audience would have savored the numerous allusions to Homer's Iliad, *Virgil's* Aeneid, *and Milton's* Paradise Lost. *But it is by no means necessary to grasp all the subtleties of these allusions to appreciate the poem. Like Swift's* Gulliver's Travels *and Lewis Carroll's* Alice in Wonderland, The Rape of the Lock *works simultaneously on several levels: as a charmingly imaginative spoof, as a splendid feat of technical virtuosity, as a clever literary parody, and as a satirical portrait of follies and pretensions.*

from Canto I

What dire offense from amorous causes springs,
What mighty contests rise from trivial things,
I sing——This verse to Caryll,[1] Muse! is due:
This, even Belinda may vouchsafe to view:
Slight is the subject, but not so the praise,   5
If she inspire, and he approve my lays.[2]
   Say what strange motive, Goddess! could compel
A well-bred lord to assault a gentle belle?
Oh, say what stranger cause, yet unexplored,
Could make a gentle belle reject a lord?   10
In tasks so bold can little men engage,
And in soft bosoms dwells such mighty rage?

Canto III

   Close by those meads, forever crowned with flowers,
Where Thames with pride surveys his rising towers,
There stands a structure of majestic frame,
Which from the neighboring Hampton takes its name.[3]
Here Britain's statesmen oft the fall foredoom   5
Of foreign tyrants and of nymphs at home;
Here thou, great Anna! whom three realms obey,[4]
Dost sometimes counsel take—and sometimes tea.
   Hither the heroes and the nymphs resort,
To taste awhile the pleasures of a court;   10
In various talk the instructive hours they passed,
Who gave the ball, or paid the visit last;
One speaks the glory of the British Queen,
And one describes a charming Indian screen;
A third interprets motions, looks, and eyes;   15
At every word a reputation dies.

1. **Caryll,** Pope's friend John Caryll (1625–1711), who suggested the idea of *The Rape of the Lock.*
2. **lays,** epic songs.

3. **Hampton . . . name,** Hampton Court, a great royal palace near London.
4. **obey,** Queen Anne (reigned 1702—1714) was ruler of England, Scotland, and Ireland.

Snuff, or the fan,[5] supply each pause of chat,
With singing, laughing, ogling, and all that.
　　Meanwhile, declining from the noon of day,
The sun obliquely shoots his burning ray;　　　　　　20
The hungry judges soon the sentence sign,
And wretches hang that jurymen may dine;
The merchant from the Exchange[6] returns in peace,
And the long labors of the toilet[7] cease.
Belinda now, whom thirst of fame invites,　　　　　　25
Burns to encounter two adventurous knights,
At ombre[8] singly to decide their doom,
And swells her breast with conquests yet to come.
Straight the three bands prepare in arms to join,
Each band the number of the sacred nine.[9]　　　　　30
Soon as she spreads her hand, the aërial guard[10]
Descend, and sit on each important card:
First Ariel perched upon a Matadore,[11]
Then each according to the rank they bore;
For Sylphs, yet mindful of their ancient race,　　　　35
Are, as when women, wondrous fond of place.
　　Behold, four Kings in majesty revered,
With hoary whiskers and a forky beard;
And four fair Queens whose hands sustain a flower,
The expressive emblem of their softer power;　　　　40
Four Knaves in garbs succinct,[12] a trusty band,
Caps on their heads, and halberts[13] in their hand;
And parti-colored troops, a shining train,
Draw forth to combat on the velvet plain.
　　The skillful nymph reviews her force with care;　　45
"Let Spades be trumps!" she said, and trumps they were.
　　Now move to war her sable Matadores,
In show like leaders of the swarthy Moors.
Spadillio[14] first, unconquerable lord!
Led off two captive trumps, and swept the board.　　50
As many more Manillio[15] forced to yield,
And marched a victor from the verdant field.[16]

---

5. **snuff or the fan,** gentlemen commonly took snuff in this period, and ladies usually carried a fan to occupy their hands.

6. **Exchange,** the London meeting place of merchants, bankers, and brokers.

7. **toilet,** process of bathing, dressing, combing the hair, etc.

8. **ombre** (om′bər), a fashionable card game.

9. **sacred nine,** a reference to the nine Muses of Greek myth.

10. **aërial guard,** the tiny sylphs, or sprites, who guard Belinda.

11. **Matadore,** powerful card that could take a trick in the game.

12. **succinct,** belted.

13. **halberts,** long-handled weapons used as both spears and battle-axes in the fifteenth century.

14. **Spadillio,** the ace of spades.

15. **Manillio,** the two of spades, another trump card.

16. **verdant field,** the card table (compared to a battlefield) was covered with a green cloth.

Him Basto[17] followed, but his fate more hard
Gained but one trump and one plebeian card.
With his broad saber next, a chief in years,   55
The hoary Majesty of Spades appears,
Puts forth one manly leg, to sight revealed,
The rest his many-colored robe concealed.
The rebel Knave, who dares his prince engage,
Proves the just victim of his royal rage.   60
Even mighty Pam,[18] that kings and queens o'erthrew
And mowed down armies in the fights of loo,
Sad chance of war! now destitute of aid,
Falls undistinguished by the victor Spade.
    Thus far both armies to Belinda yield;   65
Now to the Baron fate inclines the field.
His warlike amazon her host invades,
The imperial consort of the crown of Spades.
The Club's black tyrant first her victim died,
Spite of his haughty mien and barbarous pride.   70
What boots[19] the regal circle on his head,
His giant limbs, in state unwieldy spread?
That long behind he trails his pompous robe,
And of all monarchs only grasps the globe?
    The Baron now his Diamonds pours apace;   75
The embroidered King who shows but half his face,
And his refulgent Queen, with powers combined
Of broken troops an easy conquest find.
Clubs, Diamonds, Hearts, in wild disorder seen,
With throngs promiscuous strew the level green.   80
Thus when dispersed a routed army runs,
Of Asia's troops, and Afric's sable sons,
With like confusion different nations fly,
Of various habit, and of various dye,
The pierced battalions disunited fall   85
In heaps on heaps; one fate o'erwhelms them all.
    The Knave of Diamonds tries his wily arts,
And wins (oh, shameful chance!) the Queen of Hearts.
At this, the blood the virgin's cheek forsook,
A livid paleness spreads o'er all her look;   90
She sees, and trembles at the approaching ill,
Just in the jaws of ruin, and Codille,[20]
And now (as oft in some distempered state)
On one nice trick depends the general fate.

---

17. **Basto,** the ace of clubs.
18. **Pam,** the knave of clubs, the highest card in the game called loo.

19. **boots,** avails.
20. **Codille,** the term applied to losing a hand of cards.

An Ace of Hearts steps forth: the King unseen   95
Lurked in her hand, and mourned his captive Queen.
He springs to vengeance with an eager pace,
And falls like thunder on the prostrate Ace.
The nymph exulting fills with shouts the sky,
The walls, the woods, and long canals reply.   100
   O thoughtless mortals! ever blind to fate,
Too soon dejected, and too soon elate:
Sudden these honors shall be snatched away,
And cursed forever this victorious day.
   For lo! the board with cups and spoons is crowned,   105
The berries crackle, and the mill turns round;[21]
On shining altars of Japan[22] they raise
The silver lamp; the fiery spirits blaze:
From silver spouts the grateful liquors glide,
While China's earth[23] receives the smoking tide.   110
At once they gratify their scent and taste,
And frequent cups prolong the rich repast.
Straight hover round the fair her airy band;
Some, as she sipped, the fuming liquor fanned,
Some o'er her lap their careful plumes displayed,   115
Trembling, and conscious of the rich brocade.
Coffee (which makes the politician wise,
And see through all things with his half-shut eyes)
Sent up in vapors to the Baron's brain
New stratagems, the radiant Lock to gain.   120
Ah, cease, rash youth! desist ere 'tis too late,
Fear the just Gods, and think of Scylla's fate![24]
Changed to a bird, and sent to flit in air,
She dearly pays for Nisus' injured hair!
   But when to mischief mortals bend their will,   125
How soon they find fit instruments of ill!
Just then, Clarissa drew with tempting grace
A two-edged weapon from her shining case:
So ladies in romance assist their knight,
Present the spear, and arm him for the fight.   130
He takes the gift with reverence, and extends
The little engine on his fingers' ends;
This just behind Belinda's neck he spread,
As o'er the fragrant steams she bends her head.
Swift to the Lock a thousand sprites repair,   135
A thousand wings, by turns, blow back the hair,

21. **mill . . . round,** coffee is roasted and ground.
22. **altars of Japan,** small lacquer tables.
23. **China's earth,** cups made of Chinese earthenware.

24. **Scylla's fate,** Scylla, the daughter of Nisus in Greek myth, was turned into a sea bird after she betrayed her father by sending the enemy a lock of his hair.

*The fountains, statuary, and architecture of Blenheim
Palace characterize the tastes of the aristocrats of the
Neoclassical Age.*

BLENHEIM PALACE
Photo: F. Kersting

And thrice they twitched the diamond in her ear,
Thrice she looked back, and thrice the foe drew near.
Just in that instant, anxious Ariel sought
The close recesses of the virgin's thought;
As on the nosegay in her breast reclined,
He watched the ideas rising in her mind,
Sudden he viewed, in spite of all her art,
An earthly lover lurking at her heart.[25]

140

25. **heart,** if Belinda really loves the Baron, the sylphs
will be forced to abandon her.

Amazed, confused, he found his power expired,   145
Resigned to fate, and with a sigh retired.
   The Peer now spreads the glittering forfex[26]wide,
To enclose the Lock; now joins it, to divide.
Even then, before the fatal engine closed,
A wretched Sylph too fondly interposed;   150
Fate urged the shears, and cut the Sylph in twain
(But airy substance soon unites again):
The meeting points the sacred hair dissever
From the fair head, forever, and forever!
   Then flashed the living lightning from her eyes,   155
And screams of horror rend the affrighted skies.
Not louder shrieks to pitying heaven are cast,
When husbands, or when lapdogs breathe their last;
Or when rich china vessels fallen from high,
In glittering dust and painted fragments lie!   160
"Let wreaths of triumph now my temples twine,"
The victor cried, "the glorious prize is mine!
While fish in streams, or birds delight in air,
Or in a coach and six the British Fair,
As long as *Atalantis*[27] shall be read,   165
Or the small pillow grace a lady's bed,
While visits shall be paid on solemn days,
When numerous wax-lights in bright order blaze,
While nymphs take treats, or assignations give,
So long my honor, name, and praise shall live!   170
What Time would spare, from Steel receives its date,[28]
And monuments, like men, submit to fate!
Steel could the labor of the Gods destroy,
And strike to dust the imperial towers of Troy;
Steel could the works of mortal pride confound,   175
And hew triumphal arches to the ground.
What wonder then, fair nymph! thy hairs should feel,
The conquering force of unresisted Steel?"

from *Canto V*

Then grave Clarissa graceful waved her fan;
Silence ensued, and thus the nymph began:
   "Say why are beauties praised and honored most,
The wise man's passion, and the vain man's toast?
Why decked with all that land and sea afford,   5
Why angels called, and angel-like adored?

---

26. **forfex,** scissors.
27. **Atalantis,** a reference to a popular book of scandalous gossip.

28. **receives its date,** is destroyed.

Why round our coaches crowd the white-gloved beaux,
Why bows the side box from its inmost rows?
How vain are all these glories, all our pains,
Unless good sense preserve what beauty gains;   **10**
That men may say when we the front box grace,[29]
'Behold the first in virtue as in face!'
Oh! if to dance all night, and dress all day,
Charmed the smallpox, or chased old age away,
Who would not scorn what housewife's cares produce,   **15**
Or who would learn one earthly thing of use?
To patch, nay ogle, might become a saint,
Nor could it sure be such a sin to paint.[30]
But since, alas! frail beauty must decay,
Curled or uncurled, since locks will turn to gray;   **20**
Since painted, or not painted, all shall fade,
And she who scorns a man must die a maid;
What then remains but well our power to use,
And keep good humor still whate'er we lose?
And trust me, dear, good humor can prevail   **25**
When airs, and flights, and screams, and scolding fail.
Beauties in vain their pretty eyes may roll;
Charms strike the sight, but merit wins the soul."
    So spoke the dame, but no applause ensued;
Belinda frowned, Thalestris called her prude.   **30**
"To arms, to arms!" the fierce virago[31] cries,
And swift as lightning to the combat flies.
All side in parties, and begin the attack;
Fans clap, silks rustle, and tough whalebones crack;
Heroes' and heroines' shouts confusedly rise,   **35**
And bass and treble voices strike the skies.
No common weapons in their hands are found,
Like Gods they fight, nor dread a mortal wound.
    So when bold Homer makes the Gods engage,
And heavenly breasts with human passions rage;   **40**
'Gainst Pallas, Mars; Latona, Hermes[32] arms;
And all Olympus rings with loud alarms:
Jove's thunder roars, heaven trembles all around,
Blue Neptune storms, the bellowing deeps resound:
Earth shakes her nodding towers, the ground gives way,   **45**
And the pale ghosts start at the flash of day!
    Triumphant Umbriel on a sconce's height[33]

---

29. **front box grace,** at the theater.
30. **paint,** apply makeup.
31. **virago** (və rā′ gō), scolding woman.
32. **Pallas . . . Hermes,** gods involved in the Trojan War. Pallas (Athena) and Hermes favored the Greeks,

while Mars (the Greek Ares) and Latona sided with the Trojans.
33. **sconce's height,** on a candleholder fixed in the wall.

Clapped his glad wings, and sat to view the fight:
Propped on the bodkin spears,[34] the sprites survey
The growing combat, or assist the fray.   50
    While through the press enraged Thalestris flies,
And scatters death around from both her eyes,
A beau and witling[35] perished in the throng,
One died in metaphor, and one in song.
"O cruel nymph! a living death I bear,"   55
Cried Dapperwit, and sunk beside his chair.
A mournful glance Sir Fopling upwards cast,
"Those eyes are made so killing"—was his last.
Thus on Maeander's[36] flowery margin lies
The expiring swan, and as he sings he dies.   60
    When bold Sir Plume had drawn Clarissa down,
Chloe[37] stepped in, and killed him with a frown;
She smiled to see the doughty hero slain,
But, at her smile, the beau revived again.
    Now Jove suspends his golden scales in air,   65
Weighs the men's wits against the lady's hair;
The doubtful beam long nods from side to side;
At length the wits mount up, the hairs subside.
    See, fierce Belinda on the Baron flies,
With more than usual lightning in her eyes;   70
Nor feared the chief the unequal fight to try,
Who sought no more than on his foe to die.
    But this bold lord with manly strength endued,
She with one finger and a thumb subdued:
Just where the breath of life his nostrils drew,   75
A charge of snuff the wily virgin threw;
The Gnomes direct, to every atom just,
The pungent grains of titillating dust.
Sudden, with starting tears each eye o'erflows,
And the high dome re-echoes to his nose.   80
    "Now meet thy fate," incensed Belinda cried,
And drew a deadly bodkin from her side.
(The same, his ancient personage to deck,
Her great-great-grandsire wore about his neck,
In three seal rings; which after, melted down,   85
Formed a vast buckle for his widow's gown:
Her infant grandame's whistle next it grew,
The bells she jingled, and the whistle blew;

---

34. **bodkin spears,** large needles.
35. **witling,** would-be wit.
36. **Maeander's,** the Maeander is a river in Asia Minor.

37. **Chloe,** a reference to the heroine of the ancient Greek romance, *Daphnis and Chloe.*

Then in a bodkin graced her mother's hairs,
Which long she wore, and now Belinda wears.)   90
   "Boast not my fall," he cried, "insulting foe!
Thou by some other shalt be laid as low.
Nor think to die dejects my lofty mind:
All that I dread is leaving you behind!
Rather than so, ah, let me still survive,   95
And burn in Cupid's flames—but burn alive."
   "Restore the Lock!" she cries; and all around
"Restore the Lock!" the vaulted roofs rebound.
Not fierce Othello in so loud a strain
Roared for the handkerchief that caused his pain.[38]   100
But see how oft ambitious aims are crossed,
And chiefs contend till all the prize is lost!
The lock, obtained with guilt, and kept with pain,
In every place is sought, but sought in vain:
With such a prize no mortal must be blessed,   105
So Heaven decrees! with Heaven who can contest?
   Some thought it mounted to the lunar sphere,
Since all things lost on earth are treasured there.
There heroes' wits are kept in ponderous vases,
And beaux' in snuffboxes and tweezer cases.   110
There broken vows and deathbed alms are found,
And lovers' hearts with ends of riband bound . . .
   But trust the Muse—she saw it upward rise,
Though marked by none but quick, poetic eyes . . .
A sudden star, it shot through liquid air[39]   115
And drew behind a radiant trail of hair. . . .[40]
   Then cease, bright nymph! to mourn thy ravished hair,
Which adds new glory to the shining sphere!
Not all the tresses that fair head can boast,
Shall draw such envy as the Lock you lost.   120
For, after all the murders of your eye,[41]
When, after millions slain, yourself shall die:
When those fair suns shall set, as set they must,
And all those tresses shall be laid in dust,
This Lock the Muse shall consecrate to fame,   125
And 'midst the stars inscribe Belinda's name.

---

38. **Othello . . . pain,** in Shakespeare's *Othello,* the hero is mistakenly convinced of his wife's infidelity when she cannot produce the handkerchief he had given her as a love-token.
39. **liquid,** clear.
40. **trail of hair,** an implied pun, since the Greek root of our word "comet" means literally "long-haired." This section also alludes to the epic *Metamorphoses* of the Roman poet Ovid, in which the episodes often closed with magical transformations.
41. **murders . . . eye,** glances which strike down her lovers.

FOR UNDERSTANDING

1. What is the subject of the poem, as introduced by Pope in the first lines of Canto I?

2. What is the scene at the opening of Canto III? What outrage does the Baron commit at the end of this section? Who aids him?

3. What course does Clarissa urge in her speech at the beginning of Canto V? What is the effect of her advice?

4. Who watches the final battle of heroes and heroines? Briefly describe this battle.

5. How does Belinda defeat the Baron in battle? What is the ultimate fate of the lock?

FOR INTERPRETATION

Compare Pope's portraits of Belinda and the Baron in society with Addison's essays from the *Spectator*, "A Beau's Head" and "A Coquette's Heart." Identify some of the similarities between these authors. What are the principal differences in form and tone? Which satire, in your opinion, is more effective?

FOR APPRECIATION

1. Look carefully at Canto III, lines 1–24. Identify some of the ways in which Pope exploits the device of anticlimax.

2. Pope's satirical wit often depends on two complementary techniques: the exaggeration of the trivial and the flippant treatment of the serious. We might call these techniques the tendencies toward inflation and deflation. For example, the game of cards is inflated into a battle, and the snipping of the lock magnified into a terrible assault. Point to some examples of deflation.

COMPOSITION

The Rape of the Lock was inspired by an incident from real life. We have all been involved in petty disputes or other situations which, in retrospect, appear ridiculous. Select such a situation from your own experience, or from that of someone you know, and write a humorous account of it. As much as is practical, try to exploit Pope's techniques of inflation and deflation.

Samuel Johnson 1709–1784

Johnson is the towering figure in English letters in the second half of the eighteenth century. He was active in most of the leading literary forms of the age: periodical essay, verse satire, short novel, and literary criticism. He gained considerable fame and financial security through the *Dictionary* (1755), an achievement unparalleled up to his time and seldom equaled since. His *Lives of the Poets* (1779–81) is one of the enduring monuments of English literary criticism.

Johnson was as important for what he said as for what he wrote. Starting in 1764, he was the center of a brilliant group of writers, artists, and statesmen know as the "Literary Club," which met at the Turk's Head tavern in Gerrard Street. The year before the Club's founding, Johnson made the acquaintance of a twenty-two year old Scot, James Boswell. Their friendship laid the basis for one of the classic biographies in the language, Boswell's *Life of Johnson* (1791).

The distinction which Johnson earned as the Great Cham (or champion) of literature would have been hard to predict from his humble origins. He was born the son of a poor bookseller in the cathedral town of Lichfield. After a year at Oxford his poverty forced him to withdraw. In 1737 he moved to London, having married a short, fat, and very plain woman (Tetty Porter) who was twenty years older, and whom he adored. With his huge torso, spindly legs, and scarred face (he had suffered from scrofula as a child), Johnson was hardly the image of a notable literary figure.

These were hard times for anyone depending on his pen to make a living. Johnson wrote translations and undertook literary hack work for the *Gentleman's Magazine* until his own work began to attract notice. In 1747 a group of booksellers (the publishers of the day), impressed by his abilities, contracted with him to produce a comprehensive English dictionary. In the beginning he thought he could finish the project in three years. But as the time stretched out to

SAMUEL JOHNSON
Sir Joshua Reynolds
National Portrait Gallery, London

eight years of hard labor, he was forced to turn to other kinds of writing to support himself and to pay the wages of the six assistants who aided him in transcribing the citations which exemplified English usage. Even with the pressures of the *Dictionary* he produced some of his finest work: the long poem *The Vanity of Human Wishes* (1749), an imitation of the tenth satire of the Roman poet Juvenal, and the periodical essays published in the *Rambler* (1750–1752).

In 1752 Johnson's wife died. He continued to labor on the *Dictionary*, and it was completed and published in 1755 to considerable acclaim. It was in that year that Johnson penned his famous letter to Lord Chesterfield, the wealthy nobleman (himself an author of well-known letters) who had failed Johnson as a patron. These years also witnessed contributions to two other sets of periodical essays: the *Adventurer* (1753–1754) and the *Idler* (1758–1760). In 1759 he wrote one of the finest short novels of the century, *Rasselas;* it was composed in six weeks to help defray the funeral expenses of his mother. Three years later, Johnson received a pension from the crown.

The last twenty years of Johnson's life were chronicled in great detail by Boswell, whom he met in 1763. He was by then a celebrated man, whose intimate circle included Sir Joshua Reynolds (the painter), Oliver Goldsmith (poet and dramatist), Edmund Burke and Charles James Fox (prominent statesmen), and David Garrick (the greatest actor of his time). It is one of Boswell's great merits that he has preserved Johnson's conversation with the outstanding men of the age: conversation that reveals him as full of wit and humor, capable of biting sarcasm, but on the whole imbued with deep sympathy for his fellow men. The final decades of his career saw the publication of his great edition of Shakespeare's plays (1765), with its remarkable *Preface,* his critical survey of the *Lives of the Poets,* and his fascinating record of a trip undertaken with Boswell, *Journey to the Western Islands of Scotland* (1775). Toward the end of his life

Oxford honored him with the honorary degree of Doctor of Laws, and he is frequently referred to as Dr. Johnson.

It is difficult to form an adequate opinion of Johnson's achievement and influence without an imaginative effort to enter fully into his world. Provincial, prejudiced, and beset by physical disabilities and doubt, he yet became the commanding figure of an age. His moral authority should be defined in the widest sense: he won the right to criticize and approve through ceaseless, authentic personal struggle. His prose style, which may seem slow and overly formal, is the mature product of an age of balance and antithesis in expression, even as its tension foreshadows some of the subjectivity of the romantics. Above all, he epitomized the meaning of the phrase, a "man of letters." Learning to Johnson was only useful for its practical applications; indeed, he once declared that "no man but a blockhead" ever wrote for a living.

As you read the selections which follow, note the repeated emphasis on real life. Although he recognized from bitter, firsthand experience the pitfalls and disappointments of a writer's career, it was Johnson's simple and moving ideal that every author should strive to make the world better. His own works may be said to have fulfilled that aspiration.

A JOURNEY IN A STAGE-COACH

"... Tolle periclum,
Jam vaga prosiliet fraenis natura remotis."

Horace, Satires II.7.73–74

"But take the danger and the shame away,
And vagrant nature bounds upon her prey."

Francis (after Horace)

To the Adventurer

Sir,

It has been observed, I think, by Sir William Temple,[1] and after him by almost every other writer, that England affords a greater variety of characters than the rest of the world. This is ascribed to the liberty prevailing amongst us, which gives every man the privilege of being wise or foolish in his own way, and preserves him from the necessity of hypocrisy or the servility of imitation.

That the position itself is true, I am not completely satisfied. To be nearly acquainted with the people of different countries can happen to very few; and in life, as in everything else beheld at a distance, there appears an even uniformity: the petty discriminations which diversify the natural character, are not discoverable but by a close inspection; we, therefore, find them most at home, because there we have most opportunities of remarking them. Much less am I convinced that this peculiar diversification, if it be real, is the consequence of peculiar liberty; for where is the government to be found that superintends individuals with so much vigilance as not to leave their private conduct without restraint? Can it enter into a reasonable mind to imagine, that men of every other nation are not equally masters of their own time or houses with ourselves, and equally at liberty to be parsimonious or profuse, frolic or sullen, abstinent or luxurious? Liberty is certainly necessary to the full play of predominant humours; but such liberty is to be found alike under the government of the many or the few, in monarchies or in commonwealths.

How readily the predominant passion snatches an interval of liberty, and how fast it expands itself when the weight of restraint is taken away, I had lately an opportunity to discover, as I took a journey into the country in a stage-coach; which, as every journey is a kind of adventure, may be very properly related to you, though I can display no such extraordinary assembly, as Cervantes has collected at Don Quixote's inn.[2]

In a stage-coach, the passengers are for the most part wholly unknown to one another, and without expectation of ever meeting again when their journey is at an end; one should therefore imagine, that it was of little

---

1. **Sir William Temple** (1628–1699) was a diplomat and essayist; he was an important literary patron of Jonathan Swift.
2. The reference is to the great novel of Miguel de Cervantes (1547–1616), *Don Quixote,* Part I, chapters 32–47.

importance to any of them what conjectures the rest should form concerning him. Yet so it is, that as all think themselves secure from detection, all assume that character of which they are most desirous, and on no occasion is the general ambition of superiority more apparently indulged.

On the day of our departure, in the twilight of the morning, I ascended the vehicle with three men and two women, my fellow-travellers. It was easy to observe the affected elevation of mien with which every one entered, and the supercilious civility with which they paid their compliments to each other. When the first ceremony was despatched, we sat silent for a long time, all employed in collecting importance into our faces, and endeavouring to strike reverence and submission into our companions.

It is always observable, that silence propagates itself, and that the longer talk has been suspended, the more difficult it is to find anything to say. We began now to wish for conversation; but no one seemed inclined to descend from his dignity, or first to propose a topic of discourse. At last a corpulent gentleman, who had equipped himself for this expedition with a scarlet surtout[3] and a large hat with a broad lace, drew out his watch, looked on it in silence, and then held it dangling at his finger. This was, I suppose, understood by all the company as an invitation to ask the time of day, but nobody appeared to heed his overture; and his desire to be talking so far overcame his resentment, that he let us know of his own accord that it was past five, and that in two hours we should be at breakfast.

His condescension was thrown away; we continued all obdurate; the ladies held up their heads; I amused myself with watching their behaviour; and of the other two, one seemed to employ himself in counting the trees as we drove by them, the other drew his hat over his eyes and counterfeited a slumber. The man of benevolence, to show that he was not depressed by our neglect, hummed a tune, and beat time upon his snuff-box.

Thus universally displeased with one another, and not much delighted with ourselves, we came at last to the little inn appointed for our repast; and all began at once to recompense themselves for the constraint of silence, by innumerable questions and orders to the people that attended us. At last, what every one had called for was got, or declared impossible to be got at that time, and we were persuaded to sit round the same table; when the gentleman in the red surtout looked again upon his watch, told us that we had half an hour to spare, but he was sorry to see so little merriment among us; that all fellow-travellers were for the time upon the level, and that it was always his way to make himself one of the company. "I remember," says he, "it was on just such a morning as this, that I and my Lord Mumble and the Duke of Tenterden were out upon a ramble: we called at a little house as it might be this; and my landlady, I warrant you, not suspecting to whom she was talking, was so jocular and facetious, and made so many merry answers to our questions, that we were all ready to burst with laughter. At last the good woman happening to overhear me whisper to the duke and call him by his title, was so surprised and confounded that we could scarcely get a word from her; and the duke never met me from that day to this, but he talks of the little house, and quarrels with me for terrifying the landlady."

He had scarcely time to congratulate himself on the veneration which this narrative must have procured him from the company, when one of the ladies having reached out for a plate on a distant part of the table, began to remark "the inconveniences of travelling and the difficulty which they who never sat at home without a great number of attendants found in performing for themselves such offices as the road required; but that people of quality often travelled in disguise and might be generally known from the vul-

---

3. **surtout** (sŭr tü′),   a man's long overcoat.

gar by their condescension to poor innkeepers, and the allowance which they made for any defect in their entertainment; that for her part, while people were civil and meant well, it was never her custom to find fault, for one was not to expect upon a journey all that one enjoyed at one's own house."

A general emulation seemed now to be excited. One of the men, who had hitherto said nothing, called for the last newspaper; and having perused it a while with deep pensiveness, "It is impossible," says he, "for any man to guess how to act with regard to the stocks: last week it was the general opinion that they would fall; and I sold out twenty thousand pounds in order to make a purchase; they have now risen unexpectedly; and I make no doubt but at my return to London I shall risk thirty thousand pounds amongst them again."

A young man, who had hitherto distinguished himself only by the vivacity of his looks and a frequent diversion of his eyes from one object to another, upon this closed his snuffbox, and told us that "he had a hundred times talked with the chancellor and the judges on the subject of the stocks; that, for his part, he did not pretend to be well acquainted with the principles upon which they were established, but had always heard them reckoned pernicious to trade, uncertain in their produce, and unsolid in their foundation; and that he had been advised by three judges, his most intimate friends, never to venture his money in the funds, but to put it out upon land-security till he could light upon an estate in his own country."

It might be expected, that upon these glimpses of latent dignity, we should all have begun to look round us with veneration; and have behaved like the princes of romance when the enchantment that disguises them is dissolved, and they discover the dignity of each other: yet it happened, that none of these hints made much impression on the company; every one was apparently suspected of endeavouring to impose false appearance upon the rest; all continued their

Eighteenth Century Coffee House
Coffeehouses in London were the gathering places for writers, painters, and craftsmen in the eighteenth century.
© British Library, London

haughtiness in hopes to enforce their claims; and all grew every hour more sullen because they found their representations of themselves without effect.

Thus we travelled on four days with malevolence perpetually increasing, and without any endeavour but to outvie each other in superciliousness and neglect; and when any two of us could separate ourselves for a moment we vented our indignation at the sauciness of the rest.

At length the journey was at an end, and time and chance, that strip off all disguises, have discovered that the intimate of lords and dukes is a nobleman's butler, who has furnished a shop with the money he has saved;

the man who deals so largely in the funds, is a clerk of a broker in 'Change-alley; the lady who so carefully concealed her quality, keeps a cookshop behind the Exchange; and the young man who is so happy in the friendship of the judges, engrosses and transcribes for bread in a garret of the temple.[4] Of one of the women only I could make no disadvantageous detection, because she had assumed no character, but accommodated herself to the scene before her, without any struggle for distinction or superiority.

I could not forbear to reflect on the folly of practising a fraud which, as the event showed, had been already practised too often to succeed, and by the success of which no advantage could have been obtained; of assuming a character which was to end with the day; and of claiming upon false pretences honours which must perish with the breath that paid them.

But, Mr. Adventurer, let not those who laugh at me and my companions think this folly confined to a stage-coach. Every man in the journey of life takes the same advantage of the ignorance of his fellow-travellers, disguises himself in counterfeited merit, and hears those praises with complacency which his conscience reproaches him for accepting. Every man deceives himself, while he thinks he is deceiving others, and forgets that the time is at hand when every illusion shall cease, when fictitious excellence shall be torn away, and all must be shown to all in their real state.

I am, Sir,
Your humble servant,
Viator.[5]

4. **temple,** the sets of London buildings housing England's principal law societies; the site was formerly occupied by the Knights Templars, an order founded in the twelfth century.
5. **Viator** (vē ä′ tôr), Latin for "traveler."

FOR UNDERSTANDING

1. What kind of person did each of the following imply that he or she was? What was their real station in life?
   a. the gentleman with the watch
   b. the first woman
   c. the man with the newspaper
   d. the young man
   e. the second woman
2. What does Johnson say at the end of the essay about pretending to be what you are not?

FOR INTERPRETATION

A. Consider the following quotations from the essay. Do you feel that Johnson's evaluations of people and situations are valid today, or have people changed?
1. . . . as all think themselves secure from detection, all assume that character of which they are most desirous . . .
2. . . . the longer talk has been suspended, the more difficult it is to find anything to say.
3. Every man deceives himself, while he thinks he is deceiving others . . .
B. How does this essay differ in tone from the satire of Dryden and Pope, or from the essays of Addison? Which portion of the essay most clearly accounts for this difference?

FOR APPRECIATION

Johnson's prose style has often been attacked as overly formal and complex. Consider the second and third paragraphs of the essay you have read.
1. Is the language relatively simple, or does Johnson use many long and/or rare words?
2. How many lines do the sentences tend to run? Are they long or short? Do you think that Johnson's syntax is involved or straightforward?
3. Johnson's style exhibits many examples of *balance* and *antithesis*. The first technique is parallel arrangement of phrases and clauses; the second employs such parallel arrangement for a contrast of ideas. Identify examples of balance and antithesis in the second paragraph of the essay.
4. What metaphor does Johnson use in the last paragraph?

from PREFACE TO SHAKESPEARE

Nothing can please many, and please long, but just representations of general nature. Particular manners can be known to few, and therefore few only can judge how nearly they are copied. The irregular combinations of fanciful invention may delight a while, by that novelty of which the common satiety of life sends us all in quest; but the pleasures of sudden wonder are soon exhausted, and the mind can only repose on the stability of truth.

Shakespeare is above all writers, at least above all modern writers,[1] the poet of nature; the poet that holds up to his readers a faithful mirror of manners and of life. His characters are not modified by the customs of particular places, unpractised by the rest of the world; by the peculiarities of studies of professions, which can operate but upon small numbers; or by the accidents of transient fashions or temporary opinions: they are the genuine progeny of common humanity, such as the world will always supply, and observation will always find. His persons act and speak by the influence of those general passions and principles by which all minds are agitated, and the whole system of life is continued in motion. In the writings of other poets a character is too often an individual; in those of Shakespeare it is commonly a species.

It is from this wide extension of design that so much instruction is derived. It is this which fills the plays of Shakespeare with practical axioms and domestic wisdom. It was said of Euripides,[2] that every verse was a precept; and it may be said of Shakespeare, that from his works may be collected a system of civil and economical prudence. Yet his real power is not shown in the splendour of particular passages, but by the progress of his fable,[3] and the tenor of his dialogue; and he that tries to recommend him by select quotations, will succeed like the pedant in *Hierocles*,[4] who, when he offered his house to sale, carried a brick in his pocket as a specimen.

It will not easily be imagined how much Shakespeare excels in accommodating his sentiments to real life, but by comparing him with other authors. It was observed of the ancient schools of declamation,[5] that the more diligently they were frequented, the more was the student disqualified for the world, because he found nothing there which he should ever meet in any other place. The same remark may be applied to every stage but that of Shakespeare. The theatre, when it is under any other direction, is peopled by such characters as were never seen conversing in a language which was never heard, upon topics which will never arise in the commerce of mankind. But the dialogue of this author is often so evidently determined by the incident which produces it, and is pursued with so much ease and simplicity, that it seems scarcely to claim the merit of fiction, but to have been gleaned by diligent selection out of common conversation, and common occurrences.

Upon every other stage the universal agent is love, by whose power all good and evil is distributed, and every action quickened or retarded. To bring a lover, a lady and a rival into the fable; to entangle them in contradictory obligations, perplex them with op-

---

1. **modern writers,** Johnson refers to writers after the age of Greece and Rome.
2. **Euripides** (yu̇ rip′ ə dēz), fifth century B.C. Athenian tragic playwright.
3. **fable,** plot.
4. **Hierocles** (hī′ ə rō klēz), a Greek philosopher of the fifth century A.D.
5. **schools of declamation,** schools which taught the art of public speaking.

positions of interest, and harass them with violence of desires inconsistent with each other; to make them meet in rapture and part in agony; to fill their mouths with hyperbolical joy and outrageous sorrow; to distress them as nothing human ever was distressed; to deliver them as nothing human ever was delivered, is the business of a modern dramatist. For this probability is violated, life is misrepresented, and language is depraved. But love is only one of many passions, and as it has no great influence upon the sum of life, it has little operation in the dramas of a poet, who caught his ideas from the living world, and exhibited only what he saw before him. He knew, that any other passion, as it was regular or exorbitant, was a cause of happiness or calamity.

Characters thus ample and general were not easily discriminated and preserved, yet perhaps no poet ever kept his personages more distinct from each other. I will not say with Pope that every speech may be assigned to the proper speaker,[6] because many speeches there are which have nothing characteristical;[7] but perhaps, though some may be equally adapted to every person, it will be difficult to find any that can be properly transferred from the present possessor to another claimant. The choice is right, when there is reason for choice.

Other dramatists can only gain attention by hyperbolical or aggravated characters, by fabulous and unexampled excellence or depravity, as the writers of barbarous romances invigorated the reader by a giant and a dwarf; and he that should form his expectations of human affairs from the play, or from the tale, would be equally deceived. Shakespeare has no heroes; his scenes are occupied only by men, who act and speak as the reader thinks that he should himself have spoken or acted on the same occasion. Even where the agency is supernatural the dialogue is level with life. Other writers disguise the most natural passions and most frequent incidents; so that he who contemplates them in the book will not know them in the world: Shakespeare approximates the remote, and familiarizes the wonderful; the event which he represents will not happen, but if it were possible, its effects would probably be such as he has assigned; and it may be said, that he has not only shown human nature as it acts in real exigencies, but as it would be found in trials, to which it cannot be exposed.

This therefore is the praise of Shakespeare, that his drama is the mirror of life; that he who has mazed[8] his imagination, in following the phantoms which other writers raise up before him, may here be cured of his delicious ecstasies, by reading human sentiment in human language; by scenes from which a hermit may estimate the transactions of the world, and a confessor predict the progress of the passions.

6. **Pope . . . speaker,** a claim of Alexander Pope in the preface to his edition of Shakespeare's plays (1725).
7. **characteristical,** uniquely pertaining to the character.
8. **mazed,** confused.

FOR UNDERSTANDING

1. What does Johnson value above all in the plays of Shakespeare?
2. What is Johnson's opinion of the role of love in plays?
3. Why does Johnson say that there are no heroes in the plays of Shakespeare?

FOR INTERPRETATION

1. What does Johnson seem to mean when he uses the word "nature"?
2. Why does Johnson prefer the species to the individual in drama (or the general to the particular)?
3. What seems to be Johnson's attitude toward the plays of his own day?

from the **Dictionary**

Johnson's Dictionary *was published in 1755. As Boswell reports, " the world contemplated with wonder" a work "achieved by one man while other countries had thought such undertakings fit for only whole academies." Johnson had very little previous work to draw upon, and the* Dictionary *was the first modern reference work of its kind. The aim was to stabilize the pronunciation and spelling of English, which had been highly variable for some centuries, and to provide definitions of words in common usage since Elizabethan times. In addition to definitions (some of them ironic or satirical), Johnson provided examples of the usage of words through quotations from the leading English authors since Sir Philip Sidney (1554–1586). The following selections from the* Dictionary *omit these citations; they are intended to provide only a glimpse of Johnson's monumental achievement.*

chicken. A term for a young girl.

comedy. A dramatic representation of the lighter faults of mankind.

dedication. A servile address to a patron.

excise. A hateful tax levied upon commodities, and adjudged, not by the common judges of property, but wretches hired by those to whom excise is paid.

grubstreet. Orginally the name of a street in Moorfields in London, much inhabited by writers of small histories, dictionaries, and temporary poems; whence any mean production is called grubstreet.

lexicographer. A writer of dictionaries; a harmless drudge, that busies himself in tracing the original, and detailing the signification of words.

modern. In Shakespeare, vulgar; mean; common.

novel. A small tale, generally of love.

nowadays. (This word, though common and used by the best writers, is perhaps barbarous.) In the present age.

oats. A grain, which in England is generally given to horses, but in Scotland supports the people.

obambulation. The act of walking about.

patron. One who countenances, supports or protects. Commonly a wretch who supports with insolence, and is paid with flattery.

plethora. The state in which the vessels are fuller of humours than is agreeable to a natural state of health; arises either from a diminution of some natural evacuations, or from debauch and feeding higher or more in quantity than the ordinary powers of the viscera can digest; evacuations and exercise are its remedies.

sonnet. A short poem consisting of fourteen lines, of which the rhymes are adjusted by a particular rule. It is not very suitable to the English language, and has not been used by any man of eminence since Milton.

stockjobber. A low wretch who gets money by buying and selling shares in the funds.*

Tory. One who adheres to the ancient constitution of the state, and the apostolical hierarchy of the Church of England, opposed to a Whig.

vastidity. Wideness; immensity. A barbarous word.

Whig. The name of a faction.

youth. The part of life succeeding to childhood and adolescence; the time from fourteen to twenty-eight.

*The modern equivalent would be a stockbroker.

James Boswell 1740–1795

Boswell and Johnson, like Addison and Steele, are paired inseparably as writers—even though Boswell was younger than Johnson by a generation. The elder son and heir of a wealthy judge, Boswell was born in Edinburgh. When he first came to London at the age of nineteen, he was a typical wide-eyed youth of the provinces: he dreamed of joining the Guards, associating with the court, and meeting celebrities. In 1763 part of the dream came true when he first encountered Johnson, aleady a well-known literary figure. Boswell had already learned the skills for the project that was to occupy him for most of the rest of his life: to observe; to listen; and, above all, to remember all that Johnson and his friends said in their witty, often brilliant, conversation. Though seemingly rebuffed by Johnson in their first meeting, within a month he was dining with the older man and talking far into the night.

After studying law in Holland, Boswell made the grand tour of Europe. In France he secured interviews with two of the century's greatest men, Rousseau and Voltaire, and apparently charmed them both. (Johnson, no friend to revolutionary sentiments, once remarked that it was difficult "to judge the proportion of iniquity between them.") Boswell's main goal was to visit the island of Corsica, where he cultivated the friendship of the beleaguered General Paoli. From this adventure came Boswell's first important literary work, *An Account of Corsica* (1768), which demonstrated his remarkable ability to organize biographical material.

Johnson sponsored Boswell as a member of the Literary Club in 1764, thus ensuring his access to some of the most brilliant men of the time. Although he practiced law in Edinburgh, Boswell made frequent visits to London. In 1773 he persuaded Johnson to accompany him on a tour of Scotland and the Hebrides. Everything about the trip promised disaster: Johnson's age, his sedentary habits, his having to ride on a horse that sagged under his weight, and traveling in an open boat in autumn weather. Yet such was Boswell's natural charm and

JAMES BOSWELL
Sir Thomas Lawrence
National Portrait Gallery, London

Johnson's curiosity about the new and unusual that the trip was a triumphant success. Johnson recorded it in his *Journey to the Western Islands of Scotland* (1775); Boswell published a companion volume ten years later, *Journal of a Tour to the Hebrides,* considered a forerunner of his full-length biography.

The Life of Samuel Johnson, LL.D. (1791) is the first modern biography in the sense that it relies on a systematic collection of disparate materials: letters, eyewitness accounts, interviews, and critical comment on the subject's works. The scale of the project was unparalleled in its time; in most editions, the work runs to well over 800 pages. The genius of Boswell is to have recognized that in Johnson he had a subject which would sustain such a massive treatment. The biography is not without faults: Boswell is obviously biased in favor of his subject and is forced to offer only a sketchy account of Johnson's youth and early middle age. But the virtues of the *Life* far outweigh its defects. Boswell is to the late eighteenth century as Pepys is to the 1660s. The vividness of his observation persuades us that we are his contemporaries, sitting beside Johnson in a tavern or walking down a street in London, the city he once described as "the full tide of human existence."

from THE LIFE OF SAMUEL JOHNSON

Letter to Lord Chesterfield

1754

The Dictionary, we may believe, afforded Johnson full occupation this year. As it approached to its conclusion, he probably worked with redoubled vigour, as seamen increase their exertion and alacrity when they have a near prospect of their haven.

Lord Chesterfield, to whom Johnson had paid the high compliment of addressing to his Lordship the Plan of his Dictionary, had behaved to him in such a manner as to excite his contempt and indignation. The world has been for many years amused with a story confidently told, and as confidently repeated with additional circumstances, that a sudden disgust was taken by Johnson upon occasion of his having been one day kept long in waiting in his Lordship's antechamber, for which the reason assigned was, that he had company with him; and that at last, when the door opened, out walked Colley Cibber;[1] and that Johnson was so violently provoked when he found for whom he had been so long excluded, that he went away in a passion, and never would return. I remember having mentioned this story to George Lord Lyttelton, who told me, he was very intimate with Lord Chesterfield; and holding it as a well-known truth, defended Lord Chesterfield by saying, that "Cibber, who had been introduced familiarly by the back-stairs, had probably not been there above ten minutes." It may seem strange even to entertain a doubt concerning a story so long and so widely current, and thus implicitly adopted, if not sanctioned, by

the authority which I have mentioned; but Johnson himself assured me, that there was not the least foundation for it. He told me, that there never was any particular incident which produced a quarrel between Lord Chesterfield and him; but that his Lordship's continued neglect was the reason why he resolved to have no connexion with him. When the Dictionary was upon the eve of publication, Lord Chesterfield, who, it is said, had flattered himself with expectations that Johnson would dedicate the work to him, attempted, in a courtly manner, to soothe and insinuate himself with the Sage, conscious, as it should seem, of the cold indifference with which he had treated its learned author; and further attempted to conciliate him, by writing two papers in "The World," in recommendation of the work; and it must be confessed, that they contain some studied compliments, so finely turned, that if there had been no previous offence, it is probable that Johnson would have been highly delighted. Praise, in general, was pleasing to him; but by praise from a man of rank and elegant accomplishments, he was peculiarly gratified.

His Lordship says, "I think the publick in general, and the republick of letters in particular, are greatly obliged to Mr. Johnson, for having undertaken, and executed so great and desirable a work. Perfection is not to be expected from man: but if we are to judge by the various works of Johnson already published, we have good reason to believe, that he will bring this as near to perfection as any man could do. The plan of it, which he pub-

From THE LIFE OF SAMUEL JOHNSON by James Boswell, J.M. Dent & Co., London
Note that Boswell's original footnotes have been omitted.

1. **Colley Cibber** (1671–1757), minor playwright and poet, who was made poet laureate in 1730 and was fiercely attacked by many contemporary writers.

lished some years ago, seems to me to be a proof of it. Nothing can be more rationally imagined, or more accurately and elegantly expressed. I therefore recommend the previous perusal of it to all those who intend to buy the Dictionary, and who, I suppose, are all those who can afford it. . . .

"It must be owned, that our language is, at present, in a state of anarchy, and hitherto, perhaps, it may not have been the worse for it. During our free and open trade, many words and expressions have been imported, adopted, and naturalized from other languages, which have greatly enriched our own. Let it still preserve what real strength and beauty it may have borrowed from others; but let it not, like the Tarpeian maid,[2] be overwhelmed and crushed by unnecessary ornaments. The time for discrimination seems to be now come. Toleration, adoption, and naturalization have run their lengths. Good order and authority are now necessary. But where shall we find them, and at the same time, the obedience due to them? We must have recourse to the old Roman expedient in times of confusion, and chuse a dictator. Upon this principle, I give my vote for Mr. Johnson, to fill that great and arduous post, and I hereby declare, that I make a total surrender of all my rights and privileges in the English language, as a free-born British subject, to the said Mr. Johnson, during the term of his dictatorship. Nay more, I will not only obey him like an old Roman, as my dictator, but, like a modern Roman, I will implicitly believe in him as my Pope, and hold him to be infallible while in the chair, but no longer. More than this he cannot well require; for, I presume, that obedience can never be expected, when there is neither terrour to enforce, nor interest to invite it. . . .

"But a Grammar, a Dictionary, and a History of our Language, through its several stages, were still wanting at home, and importunately called for from abroad. Mr. John-

son's labours will now, I dare say, very fully supply that want, and greatly contribute to the farther spreading of our language in other countries. Learners were discouraged, by finding no standard to resort to; and, consequently, thought it incapable of any. They will now be undeceived and encouraged."

This courtly device failed of its effect. Johnson, who thought that "all was false and hollow," despised the honeyed words, and was even indignant that Lord Chesterfield should, for a moment, imagine, that he could be the dupe of such an artifice. His expression to me concerning Lord Chesterfield, upon this occasion, was, "Sir, after making great professions, he had, for many years, taken no notice of me; but when my Dictionary was coming out, he fell a-scribbling in 'The World' about it. Upon which, I wrote him a letter expressed in civil terms, but such as might show him that I did not mind what he said or wrote, and that I had done with him."

This is that celebrated letter of which so much has been said, and about which curiosity has been so long excited, without being gratified. I for many years solicited Johnson to favour me with a copy of it, that so excellent a composition might not be lost to posterity. He delayed from time to time to give it me; till at last in 1781, when we were on a visit at Mr. Dilly's, at Southill in Bedfordshire, he was pleased to dictate it to me from memory. He afterwards found among his papers a copy of it, which he had dictated to Mr. Baretti, with its title and corrections, in his own hand-writing. This he gave to Mr. Langton; adding that if it were to come into print, he wished it to be from that copy. By Mr. Langton's kindness, I am enabled to enrich my work with a perfect transcript of what the world has so eagerly desired to see.

2. **Tarpeian** (tär pā′ ən) **maid,** in Roman legend Tarpeia hoped to reap a great reward by betraying the city to Sabine invaders; the enemy soldiers crushed her to death with their shields.

*Boswell and his wife entertaining Johnson at tea, from "*Picturesque Beauties of Boswell*" illustrated by Thomas Rowlandson, 1786.*

*"To the Right Honourable
the Earl of Chesterfield*

"My Lord,   February 7, 1755.

"I have been lately informed, by the proprietor of the World, that two papers, in which my Dictionary is recommended to the publick, were written by your Lordship. To be so distinguished, is an honour, which, being very little accustomed to favours from the great, I know not well how to receive, or in what terms to acknowledge.

"When, upon some slight encouragement, I first visited your Lordship, I was overpowered, like the rest of mankind, by the enchantment of your address, and could not forbear to wish that I might boast myself *Le vainqueur du vainqueur de la terre;*[3]—that I might obtain that regard for which I saw the world contending; but I found my attendance so little encouraged, that neither pride nor modesty would suffer me to continue it. When I had once addressed your Lordship in publick, I had exhausted all the art of pleasing which a retired and uncourtly scholar can possess. I had done all that I could; and no man is well pleased to have his all neglected, be it ever so little.

"Seven years, my Lord, have now past, since I waited in your outward rooms, or was repulsed from your door; during which time I have been pushing on my work through difficulties, of which it is useless to complain, and have brought it, at last, to the verge of publication, without one act of assistance, one word of encouragement, or one smile of fa-

3. **le vainqueur . . . terre,** French for "the conqueror of the conqueror of the world"; Johnson is being heavily ironic.

vour. Such treatment I did not expect, for I never had a Patron before.

"The shepherd in Virgil grew at last acquainted with Love, and found him a native of the rocks.[4]

"Is not a Patron, my Lord, one who looks with unconcern on a man struggling for life in the water, and, when he has reached ground, encumbers him with help? The notice which you have been pleased to take of my labours, had it been early, had it been kind; but it has been delayed till I am indifferent, and cannot enjoy it; till I am solitary,[5] and cannot impart it; till I am known, and do not want it. I hope it is no very cynical asperity, not to confess obligations where no benefit has been received, or to be unwilling that the Publick should consider me as owing that to a Patron, which Providence has enabled me to do for myself.

"Having carried on my work thus far with so little obligation to any favourer of learning, I shall not be disappointed though I should conclude it, if less be possible, with less; for I have been long wakened from that dream of hope, in which I once boasted myself with so much exultation,

"My Lord,

"Your Lordship's most humble

"Most obedient servant,

"SAM. JOHNSON."

"While this was the talk of the town, (says Dr. Adams, in a letter to me) I happened to visit Dr. Warburton,[6] who finding that I was acquainted with Johnson, desired me earnestly to carry his compliments to him, and to tell him, that he honoured him for his manly behaviour in rejecting these condescensions of Lord Chesterfield, and for resenting the treatment he had received from him with a proper spirit. Johnson was visibly pleased with this compliment, for he had always a high opinion of Warburton. Indeed, the force of mind which appeared in this letter, was congenial with that which Warburton himself amply possessed.

There is a curious minute circumstance which struck me, in comparing the various editions of Johnson's Imitations of Juvenal. In the tenth Satire one of the couplets upon the vanity of wishes even for literary distinction stood thus:

"Yet think what ills the scholar's life assail,
Toil, envy, want, the *garret*, and the jail."

But after experiencing the uneasiness which Lord Chesterfield's fallacious patronage made him feel, he dismissed the word *garret* from the sad group, and in all the subsequent editions the line stands,

"Toil, envy, want, the *Patron*, and the jail."

That Lord Chesterfield must have been mortified by the lofty contempt, and polite, yet keen, satire with which Johnson exhibited him to himself in this letter, it is impossible to doubt. He, however, with that glossy duplicity which was his constant study, affected to be quite unconcerned. Dr. Adams mentioned to Mr. Robert Dodsley that he was sorry Johnson had written his letter to Lord Chesterfield. Dodsley, with the true feelings of trade, said "he was very sorry too; for that he had a property in the Dictionary, to which his Lordship's patronage might have been of consequence." He then told Dr. Adams, that Lord Chesterfield had shown him the letter. "I should have imagined (replied Dr. Adams) that Lord Chesterfield would have concealed it." "Poh! (said Dodsley) do you think a letter from Johnson could hurt Lord Chesterfield? Not at all, Sir. It lay upon his table, where any body might see it. He read it to me; said, 'this man has great powers,' pointed out the severest passages, and observed how well they were expressed." This air of indifference, which imposed upon the worthy Dodsley, was certainly nothing but a specimen of that dissimulation which Lord Chesterfield inculcated as one of the most essential lessons for the

4. **The shepherd . . . rocks,** see Virgil, *Eclogues* 8.43, where a shepherd laments that love was born in a rocky place.
5. **solitary,** Johnson's wife had died in 1752.
6. **Dr. Warburton,** William Warburton (1698–1779), later Bishop of Gloucester, had edited an edition of Shakespeare's plays in 1747.

conduct of life. His Lordship endeavoured to justify himself to Dodsley from the charges brought against him by Johnson; but we may judge of the flimsiness of his defence, from his having excused his neglect of Johnson, by saying, that "he had heard he had changed his lodgings, and did not know where he lived;" as if there could have been the smallest difficulty to inform himself of that circumstance, by enquiring in the literary circle with which his Lordship was well acquainted, and was, indeed, himself, one of its ornaments.

Dr. Adams expostulated[7] with Johnson, and suggested, that his not being admitted when he called on him, was probably not to be imputed to Lord Chesterfield; for his Lordship had declared to Dodsley, that "he would have turned off the best servant he ever had, if he had known that he denied him to a man who would have been always more than welcome;" and in confirmation of this,

he insisted on Lord Chesterfield's general affability and easiness of access, especially to literary men. "Sir (said Johnson) that is not Lord Chesterfield; he is the proudest man this day existing." "No, (said Dr. Adams) there is one person, at least, as proud; I think, by your own account you are the prouder man of the two." "But mine (replied Johnson instantly) was *defensive* pride." This, as Dr. Adams well observed, was one of those happy turns for which he was so remarkably ready.

Johnson having now explicitly avowed his opinion of Lord Chesterfield, did not refrain from expressing himself concerning that nobleman with pointed freedom: "This man (said he) I thought had been a Lord among wits; but, I find, he is only a wit among Lords!"

---

7. **expostulated** (ek spos' chə lā ted), reasoned earnestly.

First Meeting with Johnson

1763

This is to me a memorable year; for in it I had the happiness to obtain the acquaintance of that extraordinary man whose memoirs I am now writing; an acquaintance which I shall ever esteem as one of the most fortunate circumstances in my life. Though then but two-and-twenty, I had for several years read his works with delight and instruction, and had the highest reverence for their authour, which had grown up in my fancy into a kind of mysterious veneration, by figuring to myself a state of solemn elevated abstraction, in which I supposed him to live in the immense metropolis of London. Mr. Gentleman, a native of Ireland, who passed some years in Scotland as a player, and as an instructor in the English language, a man whose talents and worth were depressed by misfortunes, had given me a representation of the figure and manner of DICTIONARY JOHNSON! as he was then generally called; and during my first

visit to London, which was for three months in 1760, Mr. Derrick the poet, who was Gentleman's friend and countryman, flattered me with hopes that he would introduce me to Johnson, an honour of which I was very ambitious. But he never found an opportunity; which made me doubt that he had promised to do what was not in his power; till Johnson some years afterwards told me, 'Derrick, Sir, might very well have introduced you. I had a kindness for Derrick, and am sorry he is dead.'

At last, on Monday the 16th of May, when I was sitting in Mr. Davies's back-parlour, after having drunk tea with him and Mrs. Davies, Johnson unexpectedly came into the shop; and Mr. Davies having perceived him through the glass-door in the room in which we were sitting, advancing towards us,—he announced his aweful[1] approach to me, somewhat in the manner of an actor in the part of Horatio, when he addresses Ham-

---

1. **aweful,** inspiring awe.

let on the appearance of his father's ghost, 'Look, my Lord, it comes.'[2] I found that I had a very perfect idea of Johnson's figure, from the portrait of him painted by Sir Joshua Reynolds[3] soon after he had published his *Dictionary,* in the attitude of sitting in his easy chair in deep meditation, which was the first picture his friend did for him, which Sir Joshua very kindly presented to me, and from which an engraving has been made for this work. Mr. Davies mentioned my name, and respectfully introduced me to him. I was much agitated; and recollecting his prejudice against the Scotch, of which I had heard much, I said to Davies, 'Don't tell where I come from.'—'From Scotland,' cried Davies roguishly. 'Mr. Johnson, (said I) I do indeed come from Scotland, but I cannot help it.' I am willing to flatter myself that I meant this as light pleasantry to sooth and conciliate him, and not as an humiliating abasement at the expence of my country. But however that might be, this speech was somewhat unlucky; for with that quickness of wit for which he was so remarkable, he seized the expression 'come from Scotland,' which I used in the sense of being of that country, and, as if I had said that I had come away from it, or left it, retorted, 'That, Sir, I find, is what a very great many of your countrymen cannot help.' This stroke stunned me a good deal; and when we had sat down, I felt myself not a little embarrassed, and apprehensive of what might come next. He then addressed himself to Davies: 'What do you think of Garrick?[4] He has refused me an order for the play for Miss Williams, because he knows the house will be full, and that an order would be worth three shillings.' Eager to take any opening to get into conversation with him, I ventured to say, 'O, Sir, I cannot think Mr. Garrick would grudge such a trifle to you.' 'Sir, (said he, with a stern look,) I have known David Garrick longer than you have done: and I know no right you have to talk to me on the subject.' Perhaps I deserved this check; for it was rather presumptuous in me, an entire stranger, to

express any doubt of the justice of his animadversion[5] upon his old acquaintance and pupil. I now felt myself much mortified, and began to think that the hope which I had long indulged of obtaining his acquaintance was blasted.[6] And, in truth, had not my ardour been uncommonly strong, and my resolution uncommonly persevering, so rough a reception might have deterred me for ever from making any further attempts. Fortunately, however, I remained upon the field not wholly discomfited; and was soon rewarded by hearing some of his conversation, of which I preserved the following short minute[7] without marking the questions and observations by which it was produced.

'People (he remarked) may be taken in once, who imagine that an authour is greater in private life than other men. Uncommon parts require uncommon opportunities for their exertion.'

'In barbarous society, superiority of parts is of real consequence. Great strength or great wisdom is of much value to an individual. But in more polished times there are people to do every thing for money; and then there are a number of other superiorities, such as those of birth and fortune, and rank, that dissipate men's attention, and leave no extraordinary share of respect for personal and intellectual superiority. This is wisely ordered by Providence, to preserve some equality among mankind.'

'Sir, this book (*The Elements of Criticism,* which he had taken up,) is a pretty essay, and

---

2. **it comes,** see *Hamlet* I.iv.38.
3. **Sir Joshua Reynolds** (1723–1792), first president of the Royal Academy, was the most celebrated portrait painter of the age.
4. **Garrick,** David Garrick (1717–1779) was a well-known actor and partner in the management of the Drury Lane Theatre in London; as a boy he had been a pupil of Johnson.
5. **animadversion** (an ə mad vėr′ zhən), criticism.
6. **blasted,** destroyed.
7. **minute,** note.

deserves to be held in some estimation, though much of it is chimerical.'[8]

Speaking of one[9] who with more than ordinary boldness attacked publick measures and the royal family, he said,

'I think he is safe from the law, but he is an abusive scoundrel; and instead of applying to my Lord Chief Justice to punish him, I would send half a dozen footmen and have him well ducked.'[10]

'The notion of liberty amuses the people of England, and helps to keep off the *taedium vitae*.[11] When a butcher tells you that *his heart bleeds for his country,* he has, in fact, no uneasy feeling.'

'Sheridan will not succeed at Bath with his oratory. Ridicule has gone down before him, and, I doubt,[12] Derrick is his enemy.'

'Derrick may do very well, as long as he can outrun his character; but the moment his character gets up with him, it is all over.'

It is, however, but just to record, that some years afterwards, when I reminded him of this sarcasm, he said, 'Well, but Derrick has now got a character that he need not run away from.'

I was highly pleased with the extraordinary vigour of his conversation, and regretted that I was drawn away from it by an engagement at another place. I had, for a part of the evening, been left alone with him, and had ventured to make an observation now and then, which he received very civilly; so that I was satisfied that though there was a roughness in his manner, there was no ill-nature in his disposition. Davies followed me to the door, and when I complained to him a little of the hard blows which the great man had given me, he kindly took upon him to console me by saying, 'Don't be uneasy. I can see he likes you very well.'

---

8. **chimerical** (kə mer′ ə kəl), wildly fanciful.

9. **one,** Boswell elsewhere indicates that this was John Wilkes (1727–1797), a fiercely outspoken critic of the government.

10. **ducked,** plunged in water.

11. **taedium vitae** (tī′ dē əm vē′ tī), boredom.

12. **doubt,** fear.

FOR UNDERSTANDING

1. According to Boswell, how had Lord Chesterfield angered Johnson? How did he attempt to regain Johnson's goodwill?

2. How does Johnson describe a patron in his letter to Lord Chesterfield?

3. What was Lord Chesterfield's reaction to Johnson's letter?

4. How old was Boswell when he first met Johnson? Where did they meet?

5. What was Boswell's first remark at the meeting? How did Johnson respond?

FOR INTERPRETATION

1. If the story involving Johnson, Lord Chesterfield, and Colley Cibber is true, what does it reveal about Johnson himself?

2. Does Boswell simply report the circumstances surrounding Johnson's famous letter, or does he take sides?

3. What is the sequence of emotions that Boswell feels during his first meeting with Johnson?

FOR APPRECIATION

1. The letter to Lord Chesterfield is a masterpiece of *irony.* Give several illustrations of Johnson's use of this technique in the letter.

2. Comment on the structure of Boswell's account of his first meeting with Johnson. What devices make this account so effective?

COMPOSITION

Most of us have experienced an embarrassing situation such as that of Boswell in his first meeting with Johnson. Write an account of an embarrassing moment, drawn either from your own experience or from that of someone you know. Using first-person narration, try to capture the personalities involved as Boswell does; through dialogue, vivid narration, and your own comments.

Thomas Gray 1716–1771

The name of Thomas Gray is inevitably associated with just one work: the "Elegy Written in a Country Churchyard," one of the best-known poems in English. Gray lived most of his life in Cambridge, where he received his undergraduate education and was later a professor. Shy and scholarly, he worked slowly; his poetic output was relatively small. His style and choice of themes represent a significant shift from the mainstream of eighteenth-century verse. Whereas neoclassic poetry was generally detached, urbane, and satirical, Gray emphasized subjective emotion and personal sincerity. Most of his best poems use the forms of the ode and the elegy—highly popular with Romantics in the early nineteenth century. Whereas neoclassic verse dealt largely with the city, Gray displayed a new fascination for the natural landscape. And, as the "Elegy" makes clear, Gray found universal themes among the humble and the lowly. In his meditation on death and the "short and simple annals of the poor," we may glimpse a foreshadowing of William Wordsworth's call for a new poetry dealing with common subjects in common language—a poetry very different from the grand epic of Milton or the elegant verse satire of Pope. Gray's "Elegy," aside from its intrinsic merits as a great poem, illustrates the gradual transition from Neoclassicism to Romanticism in English literature.

THOMAS GRAY
Benjamin Wilson
Master and Fellows, Pembroke College, Cambridge

Elegy Written in a Country Churchyard

The curfew tolls the knell of parting day,
The lowing herd wind slowly o'er the lea,[1]
The plowman homeward plods his weary way,
And leaves the world to darkness and to me.

---

1. **lea,** meadow.

Now fades the glimmering landscape on the sight,   5
And all the air a solemn stillness holds,
Save where the beetle wheels his droning flight,
And drowsy tinklings lull the distant folds;

Save that from yonder ivy-mantled tower
The moping owl does to the moon complain   10
Of such as, wandering near her secret bower,
Molest her ancient solitary reign.

Beneath those rugged elms, that yew tree's shade,
Where heaves the turf in many a moldering heap,
Each in his narrow cell forever laid,   15
The rude² forefathers of the hamlet sleep.

The breezy call of incense-breathing Morn,
The swallow twittering frôm the straw-built shed,
The cock's shrill clarion or the echoing horn,
No more shall rouse them from their lowly bed.   20

For them no more the blazing hearth shall burn,
Or busy housewife ply her evening care:
No children run to lisp their sire's return,
Or climb his knees the envied kiss to share.

Oft did the harvest to their sickle yield,   25
Their furrow oft the stubborn glebe³ has broke;
How jocund did they drive their team afield!
How bowed the woods beneath their sturdy stroke!

Let not Ambition mock their useful toil,
Their homely joys and destiny obscure;   30
Nor Grandeur hear, with a disdainful smile,
The short and simple annals of the poor.

The boast of heraldry,⁴ the pomp of power,
And all that beauty, all that wealth e'er gave,
Awaits alike the inevitable hour.   35
The paths of glory lead but to the grave.

Nor you, ye Proud, impute to these the fault,
If Memory o'er their tomb no trophies raise,
Where through the long-drawn aisle and fretted vault⁵
The pealing anthem swells the note of praise.   40

---

2. **rude,** humble.
3. **glebe,** soil.

4. **heraldry,** noble descent.
5. **fretted vault,** elaborately ornamented church roof.

Can storied urn[6] or animated[7] bust
Back to its mansion call the fleeting breath?
Can Honor's voice provoke[8] the silent dust,
Or Flattery soothe the dull cold ear of Death?

Perhaps in this neglected spot is laid   45
Some heart once pregnant with celestial fire;
Hands that the rod of empire might have swayed,
Or waked to ecstasy the living lyre.

But Knowledge to their eyes her ample page
Rich with the spoils of time did ne'er unroll;   50
Chill Penury repressed their noble rage,
And froze the genial current[9] of the soul.

Full many a gem of purest ray serene
The dark unfathomed caves of ocean bear:
Full many a flower is born to blush unseen,   55
And waste its sweetness on the desert air.

Some village Hampden[10] that with dauntless breast
The little tyrant of his fields withstood;
Some mute inglorious Milton here may rest,
Some Cromwell[11] guiltless of his country's blood.   60

The applause of listening senates to command,
The threats of pain and ruin to despise,
To scatter plenty o'er a smiling land,
And read their history in a nation's eyes,

Their lot forbade: nor circumscribed alone   65
Their growing virtues, but their crimes confined;
Forbade to wade through slaughter to a throne,
And shut the gates of mercy on mankind,

The struggling pangs of conscious[12] truth to hide,
To quench the blushes of ingenuous shame,[13]   70
Or heap the shrine of Luxury and Pride
With incense kindled at the Muse's flame.

---

6. **storied urn,** a funeral urn decorated with pictures
that tell the story of the deceased.
7. **animated,** lifelike.
8. **provoke,** call forth or arouse.
9. **genial current,** warm energy.
10. **Hampden,** John Hampden (1594–1643) led a popular rebellion against taxation under King Charles I in
the 1630s.

11. **Cromwell,** Oliver Cromwell (1599–1658), Puritan
leader who became Lord Protector after the English Civil
War.
12. **conscious,** guiltily aware.
13. **ingenuous shame,** innocent virtue.

Far from the madding[14] crowd's ignoble strife
Their sober wishes never learned to stray;
Along the cool sequestered vale of life   75
They kept the noiseless tenor[15] of their way.

Yet even these bones from insult to protect
Some frail memorial still erected nigh,
With uncouth rhymes and shapeless sculpture decked,
Implores the passing tribute of a sigh.   80

Their name, their years, spelt by the unlettered muse,[16]
The place of fame and elegy supply:

14. **madding,** mad.
15. **tenor,** course.

16. **unlettered muse,** the uneducated carver of the gravestones.

And many a holy text around she strews,
That teach the rustic moralist to die.

For who to dumb Forgetfulness a prey,   85
This pleasing anxious being e'er resigned,
Left the warm precincts of the cheerful day,
Nor cast one longing lingering look behind?

On some fond breast the parting soul relies,
Some pious drops the closing eye requires;   90
Even from the tomb the voice of Nature cries,
Even in our ashes live their wonted fires.

For thee[17] who, mindful of the unhonored dead,
Dost in these lines their artless tale relate;
If chance, by lonely Contemplation led,   95
Some kindred spirit shall inquire thy fate,

Haply some hoary-headed swain[18] may say,
"Oft have we seen him at the peep of dawn
Brushing with hasty steps the dews away
To meet the sun upon the upland lawn.   100

"There at the foot of yonder nodding beech
That wreathes its old fantastic roots so high,
His listless length at noontide would he stretch,
And pore upon the brook that babbles by.

"Hard by yon wood, now smiling as in scorn,   105
Muttering his wayward fancies he would rove,
Now drooping, woeful wan, like one forlorn,
Or crazed with care, or crossed in hopeless love.

"One morn I missed him on the customed hill,
Along the heath and near his favorite tree;   110
Another came; nor yet beside the rill,[19]
Nor up the lawn, nor at the wood was he;

"The next with dirges due in sad array
Slow through the church-way path we saw him borne.
Approach and read (for thou canst read) the lay,   115
Graved on the stone beneath yon aged thorn."[20]

17. **thee,** the poet.
18. **swain,** countryman.

19. **rill,** brook.
20. **thorn,** hawthorn bush.

The Epitaph

Here rests his head upon the lap of Earth
A youth to Fortune and to Fame unknown.
Fair Science frowned not on his humble birth,[21]
And Melancholy marked him for her own.   120

Large was his bounty and his soul sincere,
Heaven did a recompense as largely send:
He gave to Misery all he had, a tear,
He gained from Heaven ('twas all he wished) a friend.

No farther seek his merits to disclose,   125
Or draw his frailities from their dread abode,
(There they alike in trembling hope repose)
The bosom of his Father and his God.

21. **Fair Science . . . birth,** despite his humble birth he
acquired some learning ("science").

FOR UNDERSTANDING

1. What is the setting of the poem?
2. What does the poet speculate about the dead in
lines 45–60?
3. What point about moral character is made in
lines 61–75?
4. What does the "hoary-headed swain" describe
in his speech (lines 98–116)?
5. What is the hope expressed in the epitaph?

FOR INTERPRETATION

1. What are the effects of poverty on people,
according to Gray?
2. Whose epitaph do you think Gray is writing in
the last three stanzas of the poem? Or do you think
he had a specific person in mind?

FOR APPRECIATION

An *elegy* was originally any meditative poem with a
serious theme. The term then came to be applied
to a lament for a dead person. Gray's fondness for
the forms of the elegy and the ode, essentially
suitable for lyric poetry, foreshadows one of the
principal tendencies of the nineteenth-century Romantic poets.
1. How does Gray use alliteration and assonance in
the first two stanzas?
2. How does the verse form contrast with the
heroic couplet?

COMPOSITION

Try your hand at composing your own epitaph.
What would you want it to say?

THE NOVEL IN THE EIGHTEENTH CENTURY

The word "novel" is derived from a Latin adjective meaning "new." It is paradoxical that one of the most popular literary forms was also one of the most recent to emerge, at least in English literature. Italy, France, and Spain all produced novels before England. Indeed, one of the very greatest novels in world literature, Miguel de Cervantes's *Don Quixote*, was written early in the seventeenth century.

Once underway, however, the changes in the English reading public demanded a form more responsive than verse satire to popular taste. At first this need was met by the nonfictional essays of such writers as Addison and Steele. The truly "new" element which Daniel Defoe (an ex-journalist) supplied in the first novels was the blending of fact and fiction—or the making-up of a series of largely imaginative adventures, under the guise of a true report.

Defoe's account of a shipwrecked sailor in *Robinson Crusoe* (1719) was greeted by the public with overwhelming enthusiasm. He proceeded to publish several sequels. In 1722, he brought out *Moll Flanders*, a similarly "true account" of the adventures and misfortunes of a heroine, from her birth in an English prison to her prosperous old age in the American colonies. Defoe deserves the credit for inventing the English novel, which we may define as an extended, realistic record of individual experience. We know that Defoe drew on real persons and events. For *Robinson Crusoe* he read the accounts of one Alexander Selkirk, a Scottish sea-captain who had been marooned on an island in the Pacific, while for *Moll Flanders* he probably interviewed a woman who had been a member of a notorious gang of petty criminals in eighteenth-century London. Defoe's genius was to recognize that the real-life adventures of people could be enlarged upon.

Defoe's novels depended on the telling of a good story. His works are therefore called the first examples of the novel of adventure. The next great pioneer of the English novel, Samuel Richardson, focused on character. Richardson, like Defoe, came to the novel late in life and almost incidentally. He was a London printer, with little formal education, who was commissioned at the age of fifty to write a series of sample letters which would be sold as teaching models. Richardson expanded the assignment into *Pamela* (1740), an immensely popular account (told in the form of letters) of a young maidservant. Written in the first person, Richardson's novel explored minute details of psychology and subjective feeling. He is thus the first exponent in English literature of the novel of character.

The work of Henry Fielding, perhaps the greatest novelist of the period, is intimately linked to that of Richardson. Fielding, unlike Defoe and Richardson, came from a relatively aristocratic background. As a young man, he studied law and wrote comedies for the London stage. When Richardson's *Pamela* was published to such acclaim, Fielding undertook to write a parody of the sentimental, domestic novel. He published it as *Shamela* (1741), playing on the meaning of "sham," or hypocritical pretense. The same readers who admired Richardson laughed hilariously at Fielding's satirical spoof. And the following year Fielding supplemented the parody with the first novel published under his own name, *Joseph Andrews*. This too depended on the concept of a satirical spoof of *Pamela*, but it may be read independently with pleasure. In 1749, Fielding published a much longer comic novel—perhaps his most celebrated—*Tom Jones*. Like *Joseph Andrews*, this work employed third-person narration and incorporated broad satire of a considerable cross section of English society.

The other major novelists of the eighteenth century were closer to Fielding in spirit than to Richardson or Defoe. Laurence Sterne's *Tristram Shandy* (1760) and Tobias Smollett's *Humphrey Clinker* (1771) are essentially comic in outlook. They continue, to some degree, the tradition of the comedy of manners, which had begun on the Restoration stage; the poking fun at manners, customs, and eccentricities of character.

In the preface to *Joseph Andrews*, Fielding argued that the novel ought to be considered as a kind of comic epic. He even traced the origins of the new form to a lost comic epic of Homer. Some critics have taken Fielding seriously and emphasized that novels, like epics, are large-scale accounts, commonly featuring a hero or heroine, and often focusing on serious themes. The problem with this theory is that novels of the eighteenth and nineteenth century achieved such success precisely because, unlike the epic, they were filled with realistic details and highly individual characters. Perhaps Fielding was attempting to conform to neoclassic taste when he proposed such an ancient, respectable pedigree for the novel. In fact, the works we have from the eighteenth century show that the novel was a brand-new form. Despite the awkwardness of some of the early attempts, the novel would exhibit remarkable endurance for the next two hundred and fifty years, into our own time.

Smollet, a physician by training, satirized England's reliance on quack doctors as devastatingly as did Hogarth.

A VISIT TO THE QUACK DOCTOR
William Hogarth
National Portrait Gallery, London

Sarah Siddons   1755–1831

The eldest of twelve children, Sarah Siddons was the daughter of Roger Kemble, a traveling actor. It was a theatrical family: Sarah's younger brother John Kemble became a noted actor and a director of the Drury Lane theater, while her sister Fanny achieved renown as an actress. But it was Sarah who became the toast of London theater audiences; she has been called the greatest tragic actress of the English stage.

After her marriage to William Siddons in 1773, she came to the attention of David Garrick (1717–1779), the former student of Samuel Johnson, who had managed the Drury Lane since 1747. Garrick hired her when she was barely twenty; but her debut at Drury Lane lacked polish, and she wisely retreated to a smaller provincial theater in Bath to practice her craft for the next five years. When Mrs. Siddons returned to London, she scored a triumph in Thomas Southerne's tragedy *The Fatal Marriage*. The exuberant response of the audience was equaled only by Garrick's own first night at Drury Lane in 1741. For over thirty years, she was almost universally acknowledged as the best in her field.

In Lady Macbeth Mrs. Siddons found a part to fit the scope of her talents. It has been said that no actress ever fit a part and no part ever fit an actress as did Mrs. Siddons and Lady Macbeth. She was a startling beauty, tall and

MRS. SIDDONS AS LADY MACBETH
Garrick Club

slender, with dark, expressive eyes. The two leading portrait painters of the age, Sir Joshua Reynolds and Thomas Gainsborough, both painted her. When she first acted Lady Macbeth in London, on the night of February 2, 1785, the audience is said to have included Reynolds, the historian Edward Gibbon, and the prominent statesmen Edmund Burke and Charles James Fox: all of them members of Samuel Johnson's Literary Club. The following selection, taken from Thomas Campbell's biography, allows us a glimpse of Mrs. Siddons' remarkably detailed preparation for the part of Lady Macbeth.

Remarks on the Character of Lady Macbeth

In this astonishing creature one sees a woman in whose bosom the passion of ambition has almost obliterated all the characteristics of

From Thomas Campbell, THE LIFE OF MRS. SIDDONS (1839), reprinted by B. Blum, New York, 1972.

human nature; in whose composition are associated all the subjugating powers of intellect and all the charms and graces of personal beauty. You will probably not agree with me as to the character of that beauty; yet, perhaps, this difference of opinion will be entirely attributable to the difficulty of your imagination disengaging itself from that idea of the person of her representative which you have been so long accustomed to contemplate. According to my notion, it is of that character which I believe is generally allowed to be most captivating to the other sex,—fair, feminine, nay, perhaps, even fragile. Such a combination only, respectable in energy and strength of mind, and captivating in feminine loveliness, could have composed a charm of such potency as to fascinate the mind of a hero so dauntless, a character so amiable, so honourable as *Macbeth,*—to seduce him to brave all the dangers of the present and all the terrors of a future world; and we are constrained, even whilst we abhor his crimes, to pity the infatuated victim of such a thraldom. His letters, which have informed her of the predictions of those preternatural beings who accosted him on the heath,[1] have lighted up into daring and desperate determinations all those pernicious slumbering fires which the enemy of man is ever watchful to awaken in the bosoms of his unwary victims. To his direful suggestions she is so far from offering the least opposition, as not only to yield up her soul to them, but moreover to invoke the sightless ministers of remorseless cruelty to extinguish in her breast all those compunctious visitings of nature which otherwise might have been mercifully interposed to counteract, and perhaps eventually to overcome, their unholy instigations. But having impiously delivered herself up to the excitements of hell, the pitifulness of heaven itself is withdrawn from her, and she is abandoned to the guidance of the demons whom she has invoked.

In one point of view, at least, this guilty pair extort from us, in spite of ourselves, a certain respect and approbation. Their grandeur of character sustains them both above recrimination (the despicable accustomed resort of vulgar minds) in adversity; for the wretched husband, though almost impelled into this gulph of destruction by the instigations of his wife, feels no abatement of his love for her, while she, on her part, appears to have known no tenderness for him, till, with a heart bleeding at every pore, she beholds in him the miserable victim of their mutual ambition. Unlike the first frail pair in Paradise, they spent not the fruitless hours in mutual accusation.

It was my custom to study my characters at night, when all the domestic cares and business of the day were over. On the night preceding that in which I was to appear in this part for the first time, I shut myself up, as usual, when all the family were retired, and commenced my study of *Lady Macbeth.* As the character is very short, I thought I should soon accomplish it. Being then only twenty years of age, I believed, as many others do believe, that little more was necessary than to get the words into my head; for the necessity of discrimination, and the development of character, at that time of my life, had scarcely entered into my imagination. But, to proceed. I went on with tolerable composure, in the silence of the night, (a night I never can forget,) till I came to the assassination scene, when the horrors of the scene rose to a degree that made it impossible for me to get farther. I snatched up my candle, and hurried out of the room, in a paroxysm of terror. My dress was of silk, and the rustling of it, as I ascended the stairs to go to bed, seemed to my panic-struck fancy like the movement of a spectre pursuing me. At last I reached my chamber, where I found my husband fast asleep. I clapt my candlestick down upon the table, without the power of putting the candle out; and I threw myself on my bed, without daring to stay even to take off my clothes. At peep of day I rose to resume my task; but so little did I know of my part when I appeared in it, at night, that my shame and confusion cured me of procrastinating my business for the remainder of my life.

About six years afterwards I was called upon to act the same character in London. By this time I had perceived the difficulty of assuming a personage with whom no one feel-

---

1. the witches.

ing of common general nature was congenial or assistant. One's own heart could prompt one to express, with some degree of truth, the sentiments of a mother, a daughter, a wife, a lover, a sister, &c., but, to adopt this character, must be an effort of the judgment alone.

Therefore it was with the utmost diffidence, nay terror, that I undertook it, and with the additional fear of Mrs. Pritchard's[2] reputation in it before my eyes. The dreaded first night at length arrived, when, just as I had finished my toilette, and was pondering with fearfulness my first appearance in the grand fiendish part, comes Mr. Sheridan,[3] knocking at my door, and insisting, in spite of all my entreaties not to be interrupted at this to me tremendous moment, to be admitted. He would not be denied admittance; for he protested he must speak to me on a circumstance which so deeply concerned my own interest, that it was of the most serious nature. Well, after much squabbling, I was compelled to admit him, that I might dismiss him the sooner, and compose myself before the play began. But, what was my distress and astonishment, when I found that he wanted me, even at this moment of anxiety and terror, to adopt another mode of acting the sleeping scene. He told me he had heard with the greatest surprise and concern that I meant to act it without holding the candle in my hand; and, when I urged the impracticability of washing out that '*damned spot*,' with the vehemence that was certainly implied by both her own words, and by those of her gentlewoman, he insisted, that if I did put the candle out of my hand, it would be thought a presumptuous innovation, as Mrs. Pritchard had always retained it in hers. My mind, however, was made up, and it was then too late to make me alter it; for I was too agitated to adopt another method. My deference for Mr. Sheridan's taste and judgment was, however, so great, that, had he proposed the alteration whilst it was possible for me to change my own plan, I should have yielded to his suggestion; though, even then, it would have been against my own opinion, and my observation

of the accuracy with which somnambulists perform all the acts of waking persons. The scene, of course, was acted as I had myself conceived it; and the innovation, as Mr. Sheridan called it, was received with approbation. Mr. Sheridan himself came to me, after the play, and most ingenuously congratulated me on my obstinacy. When he was gone out of the room I began to undress; and, while standing up before my glass, and taking off my mantle, a diverting circumstance occurred, to chase away the feelings of this anxious night; for, while I was repeating, and endeavouring to call to mind the appropriate tone and action to the following words, 'Here's the smell of blood still!' my dresser innocently exclaimed, 'Dear me, ma'am, how very hysterical you are to-night; I protest and vow, ma'am, it was not blood, but rose-pink and water; for I saw the property-man mix it up with my own eyes.'

FOR UNDERSTANDING

1. What aspects of Mrs. Siddons's interpretation of Lady Macbeth differed from the generally accepted view of this character?
2. What happened to Mrs. Siddons the first time she studied the role of Lady Macbeth?
3. What detail of the performance caused a dispute between Mrs. Siddons and Sheridan?

FOR INTERPRETATION

1. In your judgment, did Mrs. Siddons or Sheridan read the lines of Shakespeare's play more carefully?
2. What does the concluding anecdote show about Mrs. Siddons's approach to acting?
3. Evaluate Mrs. Siddons's interpretation of Lady Macbeth's character in light of Samuel Johnson's general remarks on Shakespeare's characterization in the *Preface* (page 411).

2. **Mrs. Hannah Pritchard** (1711–1768) was an older actress of considerable reputation.
3. **Richard Brinsley Sheridan** (1751–1816), playwright, member of Parliament, and manager and shareowner of the Drury Lane Theatre from 1776 to 1809.

Jonathan Swift

1667–1745

Swift was born in Dublin of English parents. Educated at Trinity College, he soon left Ireland for England to serve as the private secretary of Sir William Temple, a retired diplomat. It was at Temple's estate at Moor Park that he first met Esther Johnson, then a girl of eight, with whom Swift established a tenderly affectionate relationship that continued until her death in 1728. She is the recipient of the letters in his *Journal to Stella*, written in London from 1710 to 1713, when Swift was laboring for the Tory party as a journalist.

Ambitious for preferment in politics or in the Anglican Church (where he had taken orders for the ministry), Swift was disappointed. Temple failed to secure him an important post as either a Tory politician or a bishop, and Swift's hopes seemed permanently dashed when the Whigs took power in 1714. He became Dean of St. Patrick's Cathedral in Dublin, a post he occupied for the remaining thirty years of his life. More English than Irish in his outlook, a friend of Pope, Addison, and Steele, Swift felt himself an exile. But he took up the Irish cause of protest against English oppression, and one of his celebrated short essays, *A Modest Proposal* (1729)—in which Swift ironically suggested that the English might solve their problems with the Irish through cannibalism—remains a classic of satire. Toward the end of his life he was beset by nausea and deafness; the last three years of his life were marked by fits of insanity.

Swift is generally acknowledged as the greatest satirist in English. He modeled the outlook of his satirical verse and prose on the *saeva indignatio* ("savage outrage") of the Roman poet Juvenal (first century A.D.): indeed, the Latin phrase was included at Swift's direction in his epitaph. Some of his satire is so acerbic and grotesque that one of the form's central objectives—to reform vices and follies—seems obscured. But it is difficult to dismiss Swift as merely an indignant curmudgeon. His perception of human inadequacies and corruption is deeply disturbing. And he combines unblinkered insight with a superbly controlled prose style; his own definition of style

JONATHAN SWIFT
C. Jerras
National Portrait Gallery, London

simply crystallized his work: "proper words in proper places."

In 1726 Benjamin Motte, a London printer and bookseller, received a mysterious manuscript that was dropped at his house from a coach. With it was a letter from a Richard Sympson, saying that his cousin Lemuel Gulliver had given him the enclosed account of his travels in strange and exotic lands. Swift apparently hoped to avoid through this subterfuge the backlash he expected for his bitter satire of the Whig government, headed by Sir Robert Walpole. In 1713 he had joined with friends (including Alexander Pope, John Gay, and William Congreve) in an association called the Scriblerus Club. Their purpose was to satirize the idiocies of the Whig party and the pedantic excesses of some intellectuals. The group planned but never finished a biography of a pseudo-hero, Martinus Scriblerus, which was to include a visit to a land of pygmies and some encounters with eccentric scientists. Therein may lie the seeds of the manuscript delivered to Motte; it should be remembered, however, that travel books were an established part of English literature during the eighteenth century.

Gulliver's Travels was structured to satirize specific political personalities and contemporary events. But Swift's fantasy takes the work far beyond merely topical concerns. He attacks a wide spectrum of individual and social flaws. Often read in youth as a children's book, *Gulliver's Travels* is one of the rare works that appeals equally to youngsters and adults. The narrative framework is simple: Lemuel Gulliver, a ship's surgeon, recounts four journeys, in each of which he visits a strange and exotic land. In the first book, "A Voyage to Lilliput," the inhabitants are only six inches tall; the second book, "A Voyage to Brobdingnag," directly complements the first, since Gulliver here visits a land of giants. The third section, "A Voyage to Laputa," places Gulliver in a series of remarkable islands, where the natives fritter away their time in impractical scientific and philosophical experiments. The concluding voyage, to the country of the Houyhnhnms, presents the darkest satirical attack on humanity, as Gulliver visits a land of horse-like beings endowed with pure reason.

Even during his lifetime, Swift was often labeled a misanthrope. His sympathies seemed to lie with the King of Brobdingnag, who at the end of Chapter 6 calls humankind a "pernicious race of little odious vermin." Answering the charge, Swift replied that he hated "the animal called man, although I heartily love John, Peter, and Thomas"—in other words, individual human beings. Though we may find his satire dark and unsettling, we may also admire the courage of a man so deeply committed to what he considered the truth of the human condition.

---

from GULLIVER'S TRAVELS

A Voyage to Brobdingnag

Chapter I *A great storm described; the long-boat sent to fetch water; the Author goes with it to discover the country. He is left on shore, is seized by one of the natives, and carried to a farmer's house. His reception there, with several accidents that happened there. A description of the inhabitants.*

Having been condemned by nature and fortune to an active and restless life, in two months after my return I again left my native country, and took shipping in the Downs[1] on the 20th day of June, 1702, in the *Adventure*, Captain John Nicholas, a Cornish man, Commander, bound for Surat.[2] We had a very prosperous gale till we arrived at the Cape of Good Hope, where we landed for fresh water, but discovering a leak we unshipped our goods and wintered there; for the Captain falling sick of an ague, we could not leave the Cape till the end of March. We then set sail, and had a good voyage till we passed the Straits of Madagascar; but having got northward of that island, and to about five degrees south latitude, the winds, which in those seas are observed to blow a constant equal gale between the north and west from the beginning

1. **the Downs,** a shipping lane in the English channel.
2. **Surat,** city in India, north of Bombay. The geography of the voyage is roughly as follows: the ship, after sailing up the east coast of Africa, is blown off course past India, and then northward and eastward into the Pacific. Brobdingnag seems to be somewhere near Alaska.

of December to the beginning of May, on the 19th of April began to blow with much greater violence, and more westerly than usual, continuing so for twenty days together, during which time we were driven a little to the east of the Molucca Islands, and about three degrees northward of the Line,[3] as our Captain found by an observation he took the 2nd of May, at which time the wind ceased, and it was a perfect calm, whereat I was not a little rejoiced. But he, being a man well experienced in the navigation of those seas, bid us all prepare against a storm, which accordingly happened the day following: for a southern wind, called the southern monsoon, began to set in.

Finding it was likely to overblow,[4] we took in our sprit-sail, and stood by to hand the fore-sail; but making foul weather, we looked the guns were all fast, and handed the mizen. The ship lay very broad off, so we thought it better spooning before the sea, than trying or hulling. We reefed the fore-sail and set him, we hauled aft the fore-sheet; the helm was hard a weather. The ship wore bravely. We belayed the fore-down haul; but the sail was split, and we hauled down the yard, and got the sail into the ship, and unbound all the things clear of it. It was a very fierce storm; the sea broke strange and dangerous. We hauled off upon the lanyard of the whipstaff, and helped the man at helm. We would not get down our top-mast, but let all stand, because she scudded before the sea very well, and we knew that the top-mast being aloft, the ship was the wholesomer, and made better way through the sea, seeing we had sea-room. When the storm was over, we set fore-sail and main-sail, and brought the ship to: then we set the mizen, main-top-sail, and the fore-top-sail. Our course was east-north-east, the wind was at south-west. We got the starboard tacks aboard, we cast off our weather-braces and lifts; we set in the lee-braces, and hauled forward by the weather-bowlings, and hauled them tight, and belayed them, and hauled over the mizen tack to

windward, and kept her full and by as near as she would lie.

During this storm, which was followed by a strong wind west-south-west, we were carried by my computation about five hundred leagues[5] to the east, so that the oldest sailor on board could not tell in what part of the world we were. Our provisions held out well, our ship was staunch, and our crew all in good health; but we lay in the utmost distress for water. We thought it best to hold on the same course, rather than turn more northerly, which might have brought us to the northwest parts of Great Tartary,[6] and into the frozen sea.

On the 16th day of June, 1703, a boy on the top-mast discovered land. On the 17th we came in full view of a great island or continent (for we knew not whether[7]) on the south side whereof was a small neck of land jutting out into the sea, and a creek[8] too shallow to hold a ship of above one hundred tons. We cast anchor within a league of this creek, and our Captain sent a dozen of his men well armed in the long-boat, with vessels for water if any could be found. I desired his leave to go with them, that I might see the country, and make what discoveries I could. When we came to land we saw no river or spring, nor any sign of inhabitants. Our men therefore wandered on the shore to find out some fresh water near the sea, and I walked alone about a mile on the other side, where I observed the country all barren and rocky. I now began to be weary, and seeing nothing to entertain my

---

3. **Line,** the equator.
4. This paragraph was taken almost literally from a travel account in Samuel Sturmy's *Mariner's Magazine* (1669). Swift is satirizing the technical vocabulary of travel writing.
   Spooning, being driven by the wind; **hulling,** floating on the water without sail; **lanyard,** cord; **whipstaff,** tiller; **mizen,** the sail attached to the mast nearest the stern.
5. **five hundred leagues,** about fifteen hundred miles.
6. **Great Tartary,** modern Siberia.
7. **whether,** which.
8. **creek,** a small bay or cove.

curiosity, I returned gently down towards the creek; and the sea being full in my view, I saw our men already got into the boat, and rowing for life to the ship. I was going to follow after them, although it had been to little purpose, when I observed a huge creature walking after them in the sea, as fast as he could: he waded not much deeper than his knees, and took prodigious strides: but our men had the start of him half a league, and the sea thereabouts being full of sharp-pointed rocks, the monster was not able to overtake the boat. This I was afterwards told, for I durst not stay to see the issue of that adventure; but ran as fast as I could the way I first went, and then climbed up a steep hill, which gave me some prospect of the country. I found it fully cultivated; but that which first surprised me was the length of the grass, which in those grounds that seemed to be kept for hay, was about twenty foot high.

I fell into a high road, for so I took it to be, though it served to the inhabitants only as a footpath through a field of barley. Here I walked on for some time, but could see little on either side, it being now near harvest, and the corn rising at least forty foot. I was an hour walking to the end of this field, which was fenced in with a hedge of at least one hundred and twenty foot high, and the trees so lofty that I could make no computation of their altitude. There was a stile to pass from this field into the next. It had four steps, and a stone to cross over when you came to the uppermost. It was impossible for me to climb this stile, because every step was six foot high, and the upper stone above twenty. I was endeavouring to find some gap in the hedge, when I discovered one of the inhabitants in the next field, advancing towards the stile, of the same size with him whom I saw in the sea pursuing our boat. He appeared as tall as an ordinary spire-steeple, and took about ten yards at every stride, as near as I could guess. I was struck with the utmost fear and astonishment, and ran to hide myself in the corn, from whence I saw him at the top of the stile,

looking back into the next field on the right hand, and heard him call in a voice many degrees louder than a speaking-trumpet: but the noise was so high in the air, that at first I certainly thought it was thunder. Whereupon seven monsters like himself came towards him with reaping-hooks in their hands, each hook about the largeness of six scythes. These people were not so well clad as the first, whose servants or labourers they seemed to be. For upon some words he spoke, they went to reap the corn in the field where I lay. I kept from them at as great a distance as I could, but was forced to move with extreme difficulty, for the stalks of the corn were sometimes not above a foot distant, so that I could hardly squeeze my body betwixt them. However, I made a shift to go forward till I came to a part of the field where the corn had been laid by the rain and wind. Here it was impossible for me to advance a step; for the stalks were so interwoven that I could not creep through, and the beards of the fallen ears so strong and pointed that they pierced through my clothes into my flesh. At the same time I heard the reapers not above an hundred yards behind me. Being quite dispirited with toil, and wholly overcome by grief and despair, I lay down between two ridges, and heartily wished I might there end my days. I bemoaned my desolate widow, and fatherless children. I lamented my own folly and wilfulness in attempting a second voyage against the advice of all my friends and relations. In this terrible agitation of mind I could not forbear thinking of Lilliput,[9] whose inhabitants looked upon me as the greatest prodigy that ever appeared in the world; where I was able to draw an Imperial Fleet in my hand, and perform those other actions which will be recorded for ever in the chronicles of that empire, while posterity shall hardly believe them, although attested by millions. I reflect-

9. **Lilliput,** the land to which Gulliver first traveled, in Book I.

ed what a mortification it must prove to me to appear as inconsiderable in this nation as one single Lilliputian would be among us. But this I conceived was to be the least of my misfortunes: for as human creatures are observed to be more savage and cruel in proportion to their bulk, what could I expect but to be a morsel in the mouth of the first among these enormous barbarians that should happen to seize me? Undoubtedly philosophers are in the right when they tell us, that nothing is great or little otherwise than by comparison. It might have pleased fortune to let the Lilliputians find some nation, where the people were as diminutive with respect to them, as they were to me. And who knows but that even this prodigious race of mortals might be equally overmatched in some distant part of the world, whereof we have yet no discovery?

Scared and confounded as I was, I could not forbear going on with these reflections, when one of the reapers approaching within ten yards of the ridge where I lay, made me apprehend that with the next step I should be squashed to death under his foot, or cut in two with his reaping-hook. And therefore when he was again about to move, I screamed as loud as fear could make me. Whereupon the huge creature trod short, and looking round about under him for some time, at last espied me as I lay on the ground. He considered a while with the caution of one who endeavours to lay hold on a small dangerous animal in such a manner that it shall not be able either to scratch or to bite him, as I myself have sometimes done with a weasel in England. At length he ventured to take me up behind by the middle between his forefinger and thumb, and brought me within three yards of his eyes, that he might behold my shape more perfectly. I guessed his meaning, and my good fortune gave me so much presence of mind, that I resolved not to struggle in the least as he held me in the air about sixty foot from the ground, although he grievously pinched my sides for fear I should slip through his fingers. All I ventured to was to raise my eyes towards the sun, and place my hands together in a supplicating posture, and to speak some words in an humble melancholy tone, suitable to the condition I then was in. For I apprehended every moment that he would dash me against the ground, as we usually do any little hateful animal which we have a mind to destroy. But my good star would have it, that he appeared pleased with my voice and gestures, and began to look upon me as a curiosity, much wondering to hear me pronounce articulate words, although he could not understand them. In the mean time I was not able to forbear groaning and shedding tears, and turning my head towards my sides; letting him know, as well as I could, how cruelly I was hurt by the pressure of his thumb and finger. He seemed to apprehend my meaning; for, lifting up the lappet [10] of his coat, he put me gently into it, and immediately ran along with me to his master, who was a substantial farmer, and the same person I had first seen in the field.

The farmer having (as I supposed by their talk) received such an account of me as his servant could give him, took a piece of a small straw, about the size of a walking staff, and therewith lifted up the lappets of my coat; which it seems he thought to be some kind of covering that nature had given me. He blew my hairs aside to take a better view of my face. He called his hinds[11] about him, and asked them (as I afterwards learned) whether they had ever seen in the fields any little creature that resembled me. He then placed me softly on the ground upon all four, but I got immediately up, and walked slowly backwards and forwards, to let those people see I had no intent to run away. They all sat down in a circle about me, the better to observe my motions. I pulled off my hat, and made a low bow towards the farmer. I fell on my knees, and lifted up my hands and eyes, and spoke several words as loud as I could: I

10. **lappet,** flap or fold.
11. **hinds,** farm servants.

took a purse of gold out of my pocket, and humbly presented it to him. He received it on the palm of his hand, then applied it close to his eye, to see what it was, and afterwards turned it several times with the point of a pin (which he took out of his sleeve), but could make nothing of it. Whereupon I made a sign that he should place his hand on the ground. I took the purse, and opening it, poured all the gold into his palm. There were six Spanish pieces of four pistoles[12] each, beside twenty or thirty smaller coins. I saw him wet the tip of his little finger upon his tongue, and take up one of my largest pieces, and then another, but he seemed to be wholly ignorant what they were. He made me a sign to put them again into my purse, and the purse again into my pocket, which after offering to him several times, I thought it best to do.

The farmer by this time was convinced I must be a rational creature. He spoke often to me, but the sound of his voice pierced my ears like that of a water-mill, yet his words were articulate enough. I answered as loud as I could, in several languages, and he often laid his ear within two yards of me, but all in vain, for we were wholly unintelligible to each other. He then sent his servants to their work, and taking his handkerchief out of his pocket, he doubled and spread it on his left hand, which he placed flat on the ground, with the palm upwards, making me a sign to step into it, as I could easily do, for it was not above a foot in thickness. I thought it my part to obey, and for fear of falling, laid myself at length upon the handkerchief, with the remainder of which he lapped me up to the head for further security, and in this manner carried me home to his house. There he called his wife, and showed me to her; but she screamed and ran back, as women in England do at the sight of a toad or a spider. However, when she had a while seen my behaviour, and how well I observed the signs her husband made, she was soon reconciled, and by degrees grew extremely tender of me.

It was about twelve at noon, and a servant brought in dinner. It was only one substantial dish of meat (fit for the plain condition of an husbandman) in a dish of about four-and-twenty foot diameter. The company were the farmer and his wife, three children, and an old grandmother. When they were sat down, the farmer placed me at some distance from him on the table, which was thirty foot high from the floor. I was in a terrible fright, and kept as far as I could from the edge for fear of falling. The wife minced a bit of meat, then crumbled some bread on a trencher,[13] and placed it before me. I made her a low bow, took out my knife and fork, and fell to eat, which gave them exceeding delight. The mistress sent her maid for a small dram cup, which held about three gallons, and filled it with drink; I took up the vessel with much difficulty in both hands, and in a most respectful manner drank to her ladyship's health, expressing the words as loud as I could in English, which made the company laugh so heartily, that I was almost deafened with the noise. This liquor tasted like a small cyder,[14] and was not unpleasant. Then the master made me a sign to come to his trencher side; but as I walked on the table, being in great surprise all the time, as the indulgent reader will easily conceive and excuse, I happened to stumble against a crust, and fell flat on my face, but received no hurt. I got up immediately, and observing the good people to be in much concern, I took my hat (which I held under my arm out of good manners) and waving it over my head, made three huzzas, to show I had got no mischief by my fall. But advancing forwards toward my master (as I shall henceforth call him) his youngest son who sat next him, an arch boy of about ten years old, took me up by the legs, and held me so high in the air, that I trembled

---

12. **pistoles** (pi stōlz'),   Spanish gold coins.
13. **trencher,**   platter.
14. **small cyder,**   weak cider.

every limb; but his father snatched me from him, and at the same time gave him such a box on the left ear, as would have felled an European troop of horse to the earth, ordering him to be taken from the table. But being afraid the boy might owe me a spite, and well remembering how mischievous all children among us naturally are to sparrows, rabbits, young kittens, and puppy dogs, I fell on my knees, and pointing to the boy, made my master to understand, as well as I could, that I desired his son might be pardoned. The father complied, and the lad took his seat again; whereupon I went to him and kissed his hand, which my master took, and made him stroke me gently with it.

In the midst of dinner, my mistress's favourite cat leapt into her lap. I heard a noise behind me like that of a dozen stocking-weavers at work; and turning my head, I found it proceeded from the purring of this animal, who seemed to be three times larger than an ox, as I computed by the view of her head, and one of her paws, while her mistress was feeding and stroking her. The fierceness of this creature's countenance altogether discomposed me; though I stood at the farther end of the table, above fifty foot off; and although my mistress held her fast for fear she might give a spring, and seize me in her talons. But it happened there was no danger; for the cat took not the least notice of me when my master placed me within three yards of her. And as I have been always told, and found true by experience in my travels, that flying, or discovering[15] fear before a fierce animal, is a certain way to make it pursue or attack you, so I resolved in this dangerous juncture to show no manner of concern. I walked with intrepidity five or six times before the very head of the cat, and came within half a yard of her; whereupon she drew herself back, as if she were more afraid of me: I had less apprehension concerning the dogs, whereof three or four came into the room, as it is usual in farmers' houses; one of which

was a mastiff, equal in bulk to four elephants, and a greyhound, somewhat taller than the mastiff, but not so large.

When dinner was almost done, the nurse came in with a child a year old in her arms, who immediately spied me, and began a squall that you might have heard from London Bridge to Chelsea, after the usual oratory[16] of infants, to get me for a plaything. The mother out of pure indulgence took me up, and put me towards the child, who presently seized me by the middle, and got my head in his mouth, where I roared so loud that the urchin was frighted, and let me drop; and I should infallibly have broke my neck if the mother had not held her apron under me. . . .

When dinner was done, my master went out to his labourers, and as I could discover by his voice and gesture, gave his wife a strict charge to take care of me. I was very much tired, and disposed to sleep, which my mistress perceiving, she put me on her own bed, and covered me with a clean white handkerchief, but larger and coarser than the mainsail of a man-of-war.

I slept about two hours, and dreamed I was at home with my wife and children, which aggravated my sorrows when I awaked and found myself alone in a vast room, between two and three hundred foot wide, and above two hundred high, lying in a bed twenty yards wide. My mistress was gone about her household affairs, and had locked me in. The bed was eight yards from the floor. Some natural necessities required me to get down; I durst not presume to call, and if I had, it would have been in vain, with such a voice as mine, at so great a distance from the room where I lay to the kitchen where the family kept. While I was under these circumstances, two rats crept up the curtains, and ran smelling backwards and forwards on the bed. One

15. **discovering,** revealing.
16. **oratory,** prayer, request.

of them came up almost to my face, whereupon I rose in a fright, and drew out my hanger[17] to defend myself. These horrible animals had the boldness to attack me on both sides, and one of them held his fore-feet at my collar; but I had the good fortune to rip up his belly before he could do me any mischief. He fell down at my feet, and the other seeing the fate of his comrade, made his escape, but not without one good wound on the back, which I gave him as he fled, and made the blood run trickling from him. After this exploit, I walked gently to and fro on the bed, to recover my breath and loss of spirits. These creatures were of the size of a large mastiff, but infinitely more nimble and fierce, so that if I had taken off my belt before I went to sleep, I must have infallibly been torn to pieces and devoured. I measured the tail of the dead rat, and found it to be two yards long, wanting an inch; but it went against my stomach to drag the carcass off the bed, where it lay still bleeding; I observed it had yet some life, but with a strong slash across the neck, I thoroughly dispatched it.

Soon after my mistress came into the room, who seeing me all bloody, ran and took me up in her hand. I pointed to the dead rat, smiling and making other signs to show I was not hurt, whereat she was extremely rejoiced, calling the maid to take up the dead rat with a pair of tongs, and throw it out of the window. Then she set me on a table, where I showed her my hanger all bloody, and wiping it on the lappet of my coat, returned it to the scabbard. I was pressed to do more than one thing, which another could not do for me, and therefore endeavoured to make my mistress understand that I desired to be set down on the floor; which after she had done, my bashfulness would not suffer me to express myself farther than by pointing to the door, and bowing several times. The good woman with much difficulty at last perceived what I would be at, and taking me up again in her hand, walked into the garden, where she set me down. I went on one side about two hundred yards, and beckoning to her not to look or to follow me, I hid myself between two leaves of sorrel and there discharged the necessities of nature.

I hope the gentle reader will excuse me for dwelling on these and the like particulars, which however insignificant they may appear to grovelling vulgar[18] minds, yet will certainly help a philosopher to enlarge his thoughts and imagination, and apply them to the benefit of public as well as private life, which was my sole design in presenting this and other accounts of my travels to the world; wherein I have been chiefly studious of truth, without affecting any ornaments of learning or of style. But the whole scene of this voyage made so strong an impression on my mind, and is so deeply fixed in my memory, that in committing it to paper I did not omit one material circumstance: however, upon a strict review, I blotted out several passages of less moment which were in my first copy, for fear of being censured as tedious and trifling, whereof travellers are often, perhaps not without justice, accused.

17. **hanger,** a short, broad sword.
18. **vulgar,** commonplace (used ironically here).

Chapter II *A description of the farmer's daughter. The Author carried to a market-town, and then to the metropolis. The particulars of his journey.*

My mistress had a daughter of nine years old, a child of forward parts for her age, very dexterous at her needle, and skilful in dressing her baby.[1] Her mother and she contrived to fit up the baby's cradle for me against night: the cradle was put into a small drawer of a cabinet, and the drawer placed upon a hanging shelf for fear of the rats. This was my bed all the time I stayed with those people, though made more convenient by degrees as I began to learn their language, and make my wants known. This young girl was so handy, that after I had once or twice pulled off my clothes before her, she was able to dress and undress me, though I never gave her that trouble when she would let me do either myself. She made me seven shirts, and some other linen, of as fine cloth as could be got, which indeed was coarser than sackcloth; and these she constantly washed for me with her own hands. She was likewise my schoolmistress to teach me the language: when I pointed to any thing, she told me the name of it in her own tongue, so that in a few days I was able to call for whatever I had a mind to. She was very good-natured, and not above forty foot high, being little for her age. She gave me the name of *Grildrig*, which the family took up, and afterwards the whole kingdom. The word imports what the Latins call *nanunculus*, the Italians *homunceletino*,[2] and the English *mannikin*. To her I chiefly owe my preservation in that country: we never parted while I was there; I called her my *Glumdalclitch*, or little nurse: and I should be guilty of great ingratitude if I omitted this honoura-

DISCOVERY OF GULLIVER
Gulliver's Travels, 1731 Edition
© British Library, London

---

1. **baby,** doll.
2. The Latin and Italian words were coined by Swift, like the various words from the "language" of Brobdingnag.

ble mention of her care and affection towards me, which I heartily wish it lay in my power to requite as she deserves, instead of being the innocent but unhappy instrument of her disgrace, as I have too much reason to fear.

It now began to be known and talked of in the neighbourhood, that my master had found a strange animal in the field, about the bigness of a *splacknuck*, but exactly shaped in every part like a human creature; which it likewise imitated in all its actions; seemed to speak in a little language of its own, had already learned several words of theirs, went erect upon two legs, was tame and gentle, would come when it was called, do whatever it was bid, had the finest limbs in the world, and a complexion fairer than a nobleman's daughter of three years old. Another farmer who lived hard by, and was a particular friend of my master, came on a visit on purpose to enquire into the truth of this story. I was immediately produced, and placed upon a table, where I walked, as I was commanded, drew my hanger, put it up again, made my reverence to my master's guest, asked him in his own language how he did, and told him he was welcome, just as my little nurse had instructed me. This man, who was old and dim-sighted, put on his spectacles to behold me better, at which I could not forbear laughing very heartily, for his eyes appeared like the full moon shining into a chamber at two windows. Our people, who discovered the cause of my mirth, bore me company in laughing, at which the old fellow was fool enough to be angry and out of countenance. He had the character of a great miser, and to my misfortune he well deserved it, by the cursed advice he gave my master to show me as a sight upon a market-day in the next town, which was half an hour's riding, about two and twenty miles from our house. I guessed there was some mischief contriving, when I observed my master and his friend whispering long together, sometimes pointing at me; and my fears made me fancy I overheard and understood some of their words. But the next morning Glumdalclitch my little nurse told me the whole matter, which she had cunningly picked out from her mother. The poor girl laid me on her bosom, and fell a weeping with shame and grief. She apprehended some mischief would happen to me from rude vulgar folks, who might squeeze me to death, or break one of my limbs by taking me in their hands. She had also observed how modest I was in my nature, how nicely I regarded my honour, and what an indignity I should conceive it to be exposed for money as a public spectacle to the meanest of the people. She said, her papa and mamma had promised that Grildrig should be hers, but now she found they meant to serve her as they did last year, when they pretended to give her a lamb, and yet, as soon as it was fat, sold it to a butcher. For my own part, I may truly affirm that I was less concerned than my nurse. I had a strong hope which never left me, that I should one day recover my liberty; and as to the ignominy of being carried about for a monster, I considered myself to be a perfect stranger in the country, and that such a misfortune could never be charged upon me as a reproach, if ever I should return to England; since the King of Great Britain himself, in my condition, must have undergone the same distress.

My master, pursuant to the advice of his friend, carried me in a box the next market-day to the neighbouring town, and took along with him his little daughter my nurse upon a pillion[3] behind him. The box was close on every side, with a little door for me to go in and out, and a few gimlet-holes to let in air. The girl had been so careful to put the quilt of her baby's bed into it, for me to lie down on. However, I was terribly shaken and discomposed in this journey, though it were but of half an hour. For the horse went about forty foot at every step, and trotted so high, that the agitation was equal to the rising and

3. **pillion,** a cushion attached behind a saddle for an extra rider.

falling of a ship in a great storm, but much more frequent. Our journey was somewhat further than from London to St. Albans.[4] My master alighted at an inn which he used to frequent; and after consulting a while with the inn-keeper, and making some necessary preparations, he hired the *Grultrud*, or crier, to give notice through the town of a strange creature to be seen at the Sign of the Green Eagle, not so big as a *splacknuck* (an animal in that country very finely shaped, about six foot long) and in every part of the body resembling an human creature, could speak several words, and perform an hundred diverting tricks.

I was placed upon a table in the largest room of the inn, which might be near three hundred foot square. My little nurse stood on a low stool close to the table, to take care of me, and direct what I should do. My master, to avoid a crowd, would suffer only thirty people at a time to see me. I walked about on the table as the girl commanded: she asked me questions as far as she knew my understanding of the language reached, and I answered them as loud as I could. I turned about several times to the company, paid my humble respects, said they were welcome, and used some other speeches I had been taught. I took up a thimble filled with liquor, which Glumdalclitch had given me for a cup, and drank their health. I drew out my hanger, and flourished with it after the manner of fencers in England. My nurse gave me part of a straw, which I exercised as a pike, having learned the art in my youth. I was that day shown to twelve sets of company, and as often forced to go over again with the same fopperies, till I was half dead with weariness and vexation. For those who had seen me made such wonderful reports, that the people were ready to break down the doors to come in. My master for his own interest would not suffer any one to touch me except my nurse; and, to prevent danger, benches were set round the table at such a distance as put me out of every body's reach. However, an unlucky school-

boy aimed a hazel nut directly at my head, which very narrowly missed me; otherwise, it came with so much violence, that it would have infallibly knocked out my brains, for it was almost as large as a small pumpkin: but I had the satisfaction of seeing the young rogue well beaten, and turned out of the room.

My master gave public notice that he would show me again the next market-day, and in the meantime he prepared a more convenient vehicle for me, which he had reason enough to do; for I was so tired with my first journey, and with entertaining company for eight hours together, that I could hardly stand upon my legs or speak a word. It was at least three days before I recovered my strength; and that I might have no rest at home, all the neighbouring gentlemen from an hundred miles round, hearing of my fame, came to see me at my master's own house. There could not be fewer than thirty persons with their wives and children (for the country is very populous); and my master demanded the rate of a full room whenever he showed me at home, although it were only to a single family; so that for some time I had but little ease every day of the week (except Wednesday, which is their Sabbath) although I were not carried to the town.

My master finding how profitable I was likely to be, resolved to carry me to the most considerable cities of the kingdom. Having therefore provided himself with all things necessary for a long journey, and settled his affairs at home, he took leave of his wife, and upon the 17th of August, 1703, about two months after my arrival, we set out for the metropolis, situated near the middle of that empire, and about three thousand miles distance from our house. My master made his daughter Glumdalclitch ride behind him. She carried me on her lap in a box tied about her waist. The girl had lined it on all sides with

4. **St. Albans,** town approximately twenty miles north of London.

the softest cloth she could get, well quilted underneath, furnished it with her baby's bed, provided me with linen and other necessaries, and made every thing as convenient as she could. We had no other company but a boy of the house, who rode after us with the luggage.

My master's design was to show me in all the towns by the way, and to step out of the road for fifty or an hundred miles, to any village or person of quality's house where he might expect custom. We made easy journeys of not above seven or eight score miles a day: for Glumdalclitch, on purpose to spare me, complained she was tired with the trotting of the horse. She often took me out of my box at my own desire, to give me air and show me the country, but always held me fast by a leading-string. We passed over five or six rivers many degrees broader and deeper than the Nile or the Ganges; and there was hardly a rivulet so small as the Thames at London Bridge. We were ten weeks in our journey, and I was shown in eighteen large towns besides many villages and private families.

On the 26th day of October, we arrived at the metropolis, called in their language *Lorbrulgrud*, or Pride of the Universe. My master took a lodging in the principal street of the city, not far from the royal palace, and put out bills in the usual form, containing an exact description of my person and parts. He hired a large room between three and four hundred foot wide. He provided a table sixty foot in diameter, upon which I was to act my part, and palisadoed[5] it round three foot from the edge, and as many high, to prevent my falling over. I was shown ten times a day to the wonder and satisfaction of all people. I could now speak the language tolerably well, and perfectly understood every word that was spoken to me. Besides, I had learnt their alphabet, and could make a shift to explain a sentence here and there; for Glumdalclitch had been my instructor while we were at home, and at leisure hours during our journey. She carried a little book in her pocket, not much larger than a Sanson's Atlas;[6] it was a common treatise for the use of young girls, giving a short account of their religion: out of this she taught me my letters, and interpreted the words.

5. **palisadoed** (pal ə sā′ dōd), fortified with a row of posts.
6. About two feet long by two feet wide.

Chapter III *The Author sent for to Court. The Queen buys him of his master the farmer, and presents him to the King. He disputes with his Majesty's great scholars. An apartment at Court provided for the Author. He is in high favour with the Queen. He stands up for the honour of his own country. His quarrels with the Queen's dwarf.*

The frequent labours I underwent every day made in a few weeks a very considerable change in my health: the more my master got by me, the more unsatiable he grew. I had quite lost my stomach, and was almost reduced to a skeleton. The farmer observed it, and concluding I soon must die, resolved to make as good a hand of me as he could. While he was thus reasoning and resolving with himself, a *Slardral*, or Gentleman Usher, came from court, commanding my master to carry me immediately thither for the diversion of the Queen and her ladies. Some of the latter had already been to see me, and reported strange things of my beauty, behaviour, and good sense. Her Majesty and those who attended her were beyond measure delighted with my demeanour. I fell on my knees, and begged the honour of kissing her Imperial foot; but this gracious princess held out her little finger towards me (after I was set on a table) which I embraced in both my arms, and put the tip of it with the utmost respect to my lip. She made me some general questions about my country and my travels, which I answered as distinctly and in as few words as I could. She asked whether I would be content to live at court. I bowed down to the board of the table, and humbly answered, that I was my master's slave, but if I were at my own disposal, I should be proud to devote my life to her Majesty's service. She then asked my master whether he were willing to sell me at a good price. He, who apprehended I could not live a month, was ready enough to part with me, and demanded a thousand pieces of gold, which were ordered him on the spot, each piece being about the bigness of eight hundred moidores;[1] but, allowing for the proportion of all things between that country and Europe, and the high price of gold among them, was hardly so great a sum as a thousand guineas would be in England. I then said to the Queen, since I was now her Majesty's most humble creature and vassal, I must beg the favour, that Glumdalclitch, who had always tended me with so much care and kindness, and understood to do it so well, might be admitted into her service, and continue to be my nurse and instructor. Her Majesty agreed to my petition, and easily got the farmer's consent, who was glad enough to have his daughter preferred at court: and the poor girl herself was not able to hide her joy. My late master withdrew, bidding me farewell, and saying he had left me in a good service; to which I replied not a word, only making him a slight bow.

The Queen observed my coldness, and when the farmer was gone out of the apartment, asked me the reason. I made bold to tell her Majesty that I owed no other obligation to my late master, than his not dashing out the brains of a poor harmless creature found by chance in his field; which obligation was amply recompensed by the gain he had made in showing me through half the kingdom, and the price he had now sold me for. That the life I had since led was laborious enough to kill an animal of ten times my

strength. That my health was much impaired by the continual drudgery of entertaining the rabble every hour of the day, and that if my master had not thought my life in danger, her Majesty perhaps would not have got so cheap a bargain. But as I was out of all fear of being ill treated under the protection of so great and good an Empress, the Ornament of Nature, the Darling of the World, the Delight of her Subjects, the Phoenix of the Creation; so I hoped my late master's apprehensions would appear to be groundless, for I already found my spirits to revive by the influence of her most august presence.

This was the sum of my speech, delivered with great improprieties and hesitation; the latter part was altogether framed in the style peculiar to that people, whereof I learned some phrases from Glumdalclitch, while she was carrying me to court.

The Queen, giving great allowance for my defectiveness in speaking, was however surprised at so much wit and good sense in so diminutive an animal. She took me in her own hand, and carried me to the King, who was then retired to his cabinet.[2] His Majesty, a prince of much gravity, and austere countenance, not well observing my shape at first view, asked the Queen after a cold manner, how long it was since she grew fond of a *splacknuck*; for such it seems he took me to be, as I lay upon my breast in her Majesty's right hand. But this princess, who hath an infinite deal of wit and humour, set me gently on my feet upon the scrutore,[3] and commanded me to give his Majesty an account of myself, which I did in a very few words; and Glumdalclitch, who attended at the cabinet door, and could not endure I should be out of her sight, being admitted, confirmed all that had passed from my arrival at her father's house.

The King, although he be as learned a person as any in his dominions, and had been educated in the study of philosophy, and par-

1. **moidores,** Portuguese gold coins.
2. **cabinet,** private apartment.
3. **scrutore,** writing desk.

ticularly mathematics; yet when he observed my shape exactly, and saw me walk erect, before I began to speak, conceived I might be a piece of clockwork (which is in that country arrived to a very great perfection) contrived by some ingenious artist. But when he heard my voice, and found what I delivered to be regular and rational, he could not conceal his astonishment. He was by no means satisfied with the relation I gave him of the manner I came into his kingdom, but thought it a story concerted[4] between Glumdalclitch and her father, who had taught me a set of words to make me sell at a higher price. Upon this imagination he put several other questions to me, and still received rational answers, no otherwise defective than by a foreign accent, and an imperfect knowledge in the language, with some rustic phrases which I had learned at the farmer's house, and did not suit the polite style of a court.

His Majesty sent for three great scholars who were then in their weekly waiting, according to the custom in that country. These gentlemen, after they had a while examined my shape with much nicety, were of different opinions concerning me. They all agreed that I could not be produced according to the regular laws of nature, because I was not framed with a capacity of preserving my life, either by swiftness, or climbing of trees, or digging holes in the earth. They observed by my teeth, which they viewed with great exactness, that I was a carnivorous animal; yet most quadrupeds being an overmatch for me, and field mice, with some others, too nimble, they could not imagine how I should be able to support myself, unless I fed upon snails and other insects, which they offered, by many learned arguments, to evince that I could not possibly do. One of these virtuosi seemed to think that I might be an embryo, or abortive birth. But this opinion was rejected by the other two, who observed my limbs to be perfect and finished, and that I had lived several years, as it was manifested from my beard, the stumps whereof they plainly discovered through a magnifying-glass. They would not

allow me to be a dwarf, because my littleness was beyond all degrees of comparison; for the Queen's favourite dwarf, the smallest ever known in that kingdom, was nearly thirty foot high. After much debate, they concluded unanimously that I was only *relplum scalcath*, which is interpreted literally, *lusus naturæ*,[5] a determination exactly agreeable to the modern philosophy of Europe, whose professors, disdaining the old evasion of *occult causes*, whereby the followers of Aristotle endeavour in vain to disguise their ignorance, have invented this wonderful solution of all difficulties, to the unspeakable advancement of human knowledge.

After this decisive conclusion, I entreated to be heard a word or two. I applied myself to the King, and assured his Majesty, that I came from a country which abounded with several millions of both sexes, and of my own stature; where the animals, trees, and houses were all in proportion, and where by consequence I might be as able to defend myself, and to find sustenance, as any of his Majesty's subjects could do here; which I took for a full answer to those gentlemen's arguments. To this they only replied with a smile of contempt, saying that the farmer had instructed me very well in my lesson. The King, who had a much better understanding, dismissing his learned men, sent for the farmer, who by good fortune was not yet gone out of town. Having therefore first examined him privately, and then confronted him with me and the young girl, his Majesty began to think that what we told him might possibly be true. He desired the Queen to order that a particular care should be taken of me, and was of opinion that Glumdalclitch should still continue in her office of tending me, because he observed we had a great affection for each other. A convenient apartment was provided for her at court; she had a sort of governess appointed to take care of her education, a maid to

---

4. **concerted,** agreed upon.
5. **lusus naturae,** Latin for sport (or freak) of nature.

dress her, and two other servants for menial offices; but the care of me was wholly appropriated to herself. The Queen commanded her own cabinet-maker to contrive a box that might serve me for a bed-chamber, after the model that Glumdalclitch and I should agree upon. This man was a most ingenious artist, and according to my directions, in three weeks finished for me a wooden chamber of sixteen foot square, and twelve high, with sash-windows, a door, and two closets, like a London bed-chamber. The board that made the ceiling was to be lifted up and down by two hinges, to put in a bed ready furnished by her Majesty's upholsterer, which Glumdalclitch took out every day to air, made it with her own hands, and letting it down at night, locked up the roof over me. A nice[6] workman, who was famous for little curiosities, undertook to make me two chairs, with backs and frames, of a substance not unlike ivory, and two tables, with a cabinet to put my things in. The room was quilted on all sides, as well as the floor and the ceiling, to prevent any accident from the carelessness of those who carried me, and to break the force of a jolt when I went in a coach. I desired a lock for my door, to prevent rats and mice from coming in: the smith, after several attempts, made the smallest that ever was seen among them, for I have known a larger at the gate of a gentleman's house in England. I made a shift[7] to keep the key in a pocket of my own, fearing Glumdalclitch might lose it. The Queen likewise ordered the thinnest silks that could be gotten, to make me clothes, not much thicker than an English blanket, very cumbersome till I was accustomed to them. They were after the fashion of the kingdom, partly resembling the Persian, and partly the Chinese, and are a very grave and decent habit.

The Queen became so fond of my company, that she could not dine without me. I had a table placed upon the same at which her Majesty ate, just at her left elbow, and a chair to sit on. Glumdalclitch stood upon a stool on the floor, near my table, to assist and take care of me. I had an entire set of silver dishes and plates, and other necessaries, which, in proportion to those of the Queen, were not much bigger than what I have seen of the same kind in a London toy-shop, for the furniture of a baby-house: these my little nurse kept in her pocket in a silver box, and gave me at meals as I wanted them, always cleaning them herself. No person dined with the Queen but the two Princesses Royal, the elder sixteen years old, and the younger at that time thirteen and a month. Her Majesty used to put a bit of meat upon one of my dishes, out of which I carved for myself, and her diversion was to see me eat in miniature. For the Queen (who had indeed but a weak stomach) took up at one mouthful as much as a dozen English farmers could eat at a meal, which to me was for some time a very nauseous sight. She would craunch the wing of a lark, bones and all, between her teeth, although it were nine times as large as that of a full-grown turkey; and put a bit of bread into her mouth, as big as two twelve-penny loaves. She drank out of a golden cup, above a hogshead at a draught.[8] Her knives were twice as long as a scythe set straight upon the handle. The spoons, forks, and other instruments were all in the same proportion. I remember when Glumdalclitch carried me out of curiosity to see some of the tables at court, where ten or a dozen of these enormous knives and forks were lifted up together, I thought I had never till then beheld so terrible a sight.

It is the custom that every Wednesday (which, as I have before observed, was their Sabbath) the King and Queen, with the royal issue of both sexes, dine together in the apartment of his Majesty, to whom I was now become a great favourite; and at these times my little chair and table were placed at his left hand, before one of the saltcellars. This prince took a pleasure in conversing with me,

---

6. **nice,** exact.
7. **made a shift,** contrived.
8. **a hogshead at a draught,** approximately a hundred gallons at a time.

enquiring into the manners, religion, laws, government, and learning of Europe; wherein I gave him the best account I was able. His apprehension was so clear, and his judgment so exact, that he made very wise reflections and observations upon all I said. But, I confess, that after I had been a little too copious in talking of my own beloved country, of our trade, and wars by sea and land, of our schisms in religion, and parties in the state, the prejudices of his education prevailed so far, that he could not forbear taking me up in his right hand, and stroking me gently with the other, after an hearty fit of laughing, asked me whether I were a Whig or a Tory. Then turning to his first minister, who waited behind him with a white staff, near as tall as the mainmast of the *Royal Sovereign*,[9] he observed how contemptible a thing was human grandeur, which could be mimicked by such diminutive insects as I: and yet, said he, I dare engage, these creatures have their titles and distinctions of honour, they contrive little nests and burrows, that they call houses and cities; they make a figure in dress and equipage;[10] they love, they fight, they dispute, they cheat, they betray. And thus he continued on, while my colour came and went several times with indignation to hear our noble country, the mistress of arts and arms, the scourge of France, the arbitress of Europe, the seat of virtue, piety, honour and truth, the pride and envy of the world, so contemptuously treated.

But as I was not in a condition to resent injuries, so, upon mature thoughts, I began to doubt whether I were injured or no. For, after having been accustomed several months to the sight and converse of this people, and observed every object upon which I cast my eyes to be of proportionable magnitude, the horror I had first conceived from their bulk and aspect was so far worn off, that if I had then beheld a company of English lords and ladies in their finery and birth-day clothes, acting their several parts in the most courtly manner, of strutting, and bowing, and prating, to say the truth, I should have been strongly tempted to laugh as much at them as the King and his grandees did at me. Neither indeed could I forbear smiling at myself, when the Queen used to place me upon her hand towards a looking-glass, by which both our persons appeared before me in full view together; and there could be nothing more ridiculous than the comparison; so that I really began to imagine myself dwindled many degrees below my usual size.

Nothing angered and mortified me so much as the Queen's dwarf, who being of the lowest stature that was ever in that country (for I verily think he was not full thirty foot high) became insolent at seeing a creature so much beneath him, that he would always affect to swagger and look big as he passed by me in the Queen's antechamber, while I was standing on some table talking with the lords or ladies of the court, and he seldom failed of a smart word or two upon my littleness; against which I could only revenge myself by calling him brother, challenging him to wrestle, and such repartees as are usual in the mouths of court pages. One day at dinner this malicious little cub was so nettled with something I had said to him, that raising himself upon the frame of her Majesty's chair, he took me up by the middle, as I was sitting down, not thinking any harm, and let me drop into a large silver bowl of cream, and then ran away as fast as he could. I fell over head and ears, and if I had not been a good swimmer, it might have gone very hard with me; for Glumdalclitch in that instant happened to be at the other end of the room, and the Queen was in such a fright that she wanted presence of mind to assist me. But my little nurse ran to my relief, and took me out, after I had swallowed above a quart of cream. I was put to bed; however I received no other damage than the loss of a suit of clothes, which was utterly spoiled. The dwarf was soundly

9. The **Royal Sovereign** was one of the largest ships in the Royal Navy.
10. **equipage** (ek′ wə pij),   carriage with its horses, driver, and servants.

whipped, and as a farther punishment, forced to drink up the bowl of cream, into which he had thrown me; neither was he ever restored to favour: for soon after the Queen bestowed him to a lady of high quality, so that I saw him no more, to my very great satisfaction; for I could not tell to what extremity such a malicious urchin might have carried his resentment.

He had before served me a scurvy trick, which set the Queen a laughing, although at the same time she were heartily vexed, and would have immediately cashiered[11] him, if I had not been so generous as to intercede. Her Majesty had taken a marrow-bone upon her plate, and after knocking out the marrow, placed the bone again in the dish erect as it stood before; the dwarf watching his opportunity, while Glumdalclitch was gone to the sideboard, mounted upon the stool she stood on to take care of me at meals, took me up in both hands, and squeezing my legs together, wedged them into the marrow-bone above my waist, where I stuck for some time, and made a very ridiculous figure. I believe it was near a minute before any one knew what was become of me, for I thought it below me to cry out. But, as princes seldom get their meat hot, my legs were not scalded, only my stockings and breeches in a sad condition. The dwarf at my entreaty had no other punishment than a sound whipping.

I was frequently rallied[12] by the Queen upon account of my fearfulness, and she used to ask me whether the people of my country were as great cowards as myself. The occasion was this. The kingdom is much pestered with flies in summer; and these odious insects, each of them as big as a Dunstable lark, hardly gave me any rest while I sat at dinner, with their continual humming and buzzing about my ears. They would sometimes alight upon my victuals; and leave their loathsome excrement or spawn behind, which to me was very visible, though not to the natives of that country, whose large optics[13] were not so acute as mine in viewing smaller objects. Sometimes they would fix upon my nose or forehead, where they stung me to the quick, smelling very offensively, and I could easily trace that viscous matter, which our naturalists tell us enables those creatures to walk with their feet upwards upon a ceiling. I had much ado to defend myself against these detestable animals, and could not forbear starting when they came on my face. It was the common practice of the dwarf to catch a number of these insects in his hand, as school-boys do among us, and let them out suddenly under my nose, on purpose to frighten me, and divert the Queen. My remedy was to cut them in pieces with my knife as they flew in the air, wherein my dexterity was much admired.

I remember one morning when Glumdalclitch had set me in my box upon a window, as she usually did in fair days to give me air (for I durst not venture to let the box be hung on a nail out of the window, as we do with cages in England) after I had lifted up one of my sashes, and sat down at my table to eat a piece of sweet cake for my breakfast, above twenty wasps, allured by the smell, came flying into the room, humming louder than the drones of as many bagpipes. Some of them seized my cake, and carried it piecemeal away, others flew about my head and face, confounding me with the noise, and putting me in the utmost terror of their stings. However, I had the courage to rise and draw my hanger, and attack them in the air. I dispatched four of them, but the rest got away, and I presently shut my window. These insects were as large as partridges: I took out their stings, found them an inch and a half long, and as sharp as needles. I carefully preserved them all, and having since shown them with some other curiosities in several parts of Europe, upon my return to England I gave three of them to Gresham College,[14] and kept the fourth for myself.

---

11. **cashiered,** dismissed.
12. **rallied,** teased, ridiculed.
13. **optics,** eyes.
14. **Gresham College,** the original meeting place of the Royal Society.

Chapter IV *The country described. A proposal for correcting modern maps. The King's palace, and some account of the metropolis. The Author's way of travelling. The chief temple described.*

I now intend to give the reader a short description of this country, as far as I travelled in it, which was not above two thousand miles round Lorbrulgrud the metropolis. For the Queen, whom I always attended, never went further when she accompanied the King in his progresses,[1] and there stayed till his Majesty returned from viewing his frontiers. The whole extent of this prince's dominions reacheth about six thousand miles in length, and from three to five in breadth. From whence I cannot but conclude that our geographers of Europe are in a great error, by supposing nothing but sea between Japan and California; for it was ever my opinion, that there must be a balance of earth to counterpoise the great continent of Tartary; and therefore they ought to correct their maps and charts, by joining this vast tract of land to the north-west parts of America, wherein I shall be ready to lend them my assistance.

The kingdom is a peninsula, terminated to the north-east by a ridge of mountains thirty miles high, which are altogether impassable by reason of the volcanoes upon the tops. Neither do the most learned know what sort of mortals inhabit beyond those mountains, or whether they be inhabited at all. On the three other sides it is bounded by the ocean. There is not one sea-port in the whole kingdom, and those parts of the coasts into which the rivers issue are so full of pointed rocks, and the sea generally so rough, that there is no venturing with the smallest of their boats, so that these people are wholly excluded from any commerce with the rest of the world. But the large rivers are full of vessels, and abound with excellent fish, for they seldom get any from the sea, because the sea-fish are of the same size with those in Europe, and consequently not worth catching; where-

by it is manifest, that nature, in the production of plants and animals of so extraordinary a bulk, is wholly confined to this continent, of which I leave the reasons to be determined by philosophers. However, now and then they take a whale that happens to be dashed against the rocks, which the common people feed on heartily. These whales I have known so large that a man could hardly carry one upon his shoulders; and sometimes for curiosity they are brought in hampers to Lorbrulgrud: I saw one of them in a dish at the King's table, which passed for a rarity, but I did not observe he was fond of it; for I think indeed the bigness disgusted him, although I have seen one somewhat larger in Greenland.

The country is well inhabited, for it contains fifty-one cities, near an hundred walled towns, and a great number of villages. To satisfy my curious reader, it may be sufficient to describe Lorbrulgrud. This city stands upon almost two equal parts on each side of the river that passes through. It contains above eighty thousand houses, and about six hundred thousand inhabitants. It is in length three *glongluns* (which make about fifty-four English miles) and two and a half in breadth, as I measured it myself in the royal map made by the King's order, which was laid on the ground on purpose for me, and extended an hundred feet: I paced the diameter and circumference several times barefoot, and computing by the scale, measured it pretty exactly.

The King's palace is no regular edifice, but an heap of buildings about seven miles round: the chief rooms are generally two hundred and forty foot high, and broad and long in proportion. A coach was allowed to Glumdalclitch and me, wherein her governess frequently took her out to see the town, or go among the shops; and I was always of the party, carried in my box; although the girl at my own desire would often take me

---

1. **progresses,** official tours by the sovereign.

out, and hold me in her hand, that I might more conveniently view the houses and the people, as we passed along the streets. I reckoned our coach to be about a square of Westminster Hall, but not altogether so high; however, I cannot be very exact. One day the governess ordered our coachman to stop at several shops, where the beggars, watching their opportunity, crowded to the sides of the coach, and gave me the most horrible spectacles that ever an English eye beheld. . . . There was a fellow with a wen in his neck, larger than five wool-packs, and another with a couple of wooden legs, each about twenty foot high. But the most hateful sight of all was the lice crawling on their clothes. I could see distinctly the limbs of these vermin with my naked eye, much better than those of an European louse through a microscope, and their snouts with which they rooted like swine. They were the first I had ever beheld, and I should have been curious enough to dissect one of them, if I had proper instruments (which I unluckily left behind me in the ship) although indeed the sight was so nauseous, that it perfectly turned my stomach.

Besides the large box in which I was usually carried, the Queen ordered a smaller one to be made for me, of about twelve foot square, and ten high, for the convenience of travelling, because the other was somewhat too large for Glumdalclitch's lap, and cumbersome in the coach; it was made by the same artist, whom I directed in the whole contrivance. This travelling closet was an exact square with a window in the middle of three of the squares, and each window was latticed with iron wire on the outside, to prevent accidents in long journeys. On the fourth side, which had no window, two strong staples were fixed, through which the person that carried me, when I had a mind to be on horseback, put in a leathern belt, and buckled it about his waist. This was always the office of some grave trusty servant in whom I could confide, whether I attended the King and Queen in their progresses, or were disposed to see the gardens, or pay a visit to some great lady or minister of state in the court, when Glumdalclitch happened to be out of order: for I soon began to be known and esteemed among the greatest officers, I suppose more upon account of their Majesties' favour than any merit of my own. In journeys, when I was weary of the coach, a servant on horseback would buckle my box, and place it on a cushion before him; and there I had a full prospect of the country on three sides from my three windows. I had in this closet a field-bed and a hammock hung from the ceiling, two chairs and a table, neatly screwed to the floor, to prevent being tossed about by the agitation of the horse or the coach. And having been long used to sea-voyages, those motions, although sometimes very violent, did not much discompose me.

Whenever I had a mind to see the town, it was always in my travelling-closet, which Glumdalclitch held in her lap in a kind of open sedan,[2] after the fashion of the country, borne by four men, and attended by two others in the Queen's livery. The people, who had often heard of me, were very curious to crowd about the sedan, and the girl was complaisant enough to make the bearers stop, and to take me in her hand that I might be more conveniently seen.

I was very desirous to see the chief temple, and particularly the tower belonging to it, which is reckoned the highest in the kingdom. Accordingly one day my nurse carried me thither, but I may truly say I came back disappointed; for the height is not above three thousand foot, reckoning from the ground to the highest pinnacle top; which, allowing for the difference between the size of those people and us in Europe is no great matter for admiration, nor at all equal in proportion (if I rightly remember) to Salisbury steeple.[3] But, not to detract from a nation to

---

2. **sedan,** a sedan chair, carried on poles by two men.
3. The steeple of Salisbury Cathedral is 404 feet high.

which during my life I shall acknowledge my self extremely obliged, it must be allowed that whatever this famous tower wants in height is amply made up in beauty and strength. For the walls are near an hundred foot thick, built of hewn stone, whereof each is about forty foot square, and adorned on all sides with statues of gods and emperors cut in marble larger than the life, placed in their several niches. I measured a little finger which had fallen down from one of these statues, and lay unperceived among some rubbish, and found it exactly four foot and an inch in length. Glumdalclitch wrapped it up in a handkerchief, and carried it home in her pocket to keep among other trinkets, of which the girl was very fond, as children at her age usually are.

The King's kitchen is indeed a noble building, vaulted at top, and about six hundred foot high. The great oven is not so wide by ten paces as the cupola at St. Paul's,[4] for I measured the latter on purpose after my return. But if I should describe the kitchen-grate, the prodigious pots and kettles, the joints of meat turning on the spits, with many other particulars, perhaps I should be hardly believed; at least a severe critic would be apt to think I enlarged a little, as travellers are often suspected to do. To avoid which censure, I fear I have run too much into the other extreme; and that if this treatise should happen to be translated into the language of Brobdingnag (which is the general name of that kingdom) and transmitted thither, the King and his people would have reason to complain that I had done them an injury by a false and diminutive representation.

His Majesty seldom keeps above six hundred horses in his stables: they are generally from fifty-four to sixty foot high. But, when he goes abroad on solemn days, he is attended for state by a militia guard of five hundred horse, which indeed I thought was the most splendid sight that could be ever beheld, till I saw part of his army in battalia,[5] whereof I shall find another occasion to speak.

FOR UNDERSTANDING

1. What were the circumstances of Gulliver's being stranded on the shore?
2. Who first finds Gulliver in Brobdingnag? What is the mathematical scale of the country compared to ours? What are some of the mishaps that threaten Gulliver in this strange country?
3. Who becomes Gulliver's protector in Chapter 2?
4. Explain how Gulliver becomes profitable for his master.
5. What is the King's first reaction to Gulliver at court? What is the conclusion of the scientists and philosophers?
6. How is Gulliver transported throughout the kingdom? Why is he somewhat disappointed in the chief temple?

4. **the cupola of St. Paul's,** 108 feet in diameter.
5. **battalia,** battle array.

Chapter V *Several adventures that happened to the author. The execution of a criminal. The author shows his skill in navigation.*

I should have lived happy enough in that country, if my littleness had not exposed me to several ridiculous and troublesome accidents, some of which I shall venture to relate.

Glumdalclitch often carried me into the gardens of the court in my smaller box, and would sometimes take me out of it and hold me in her hand, or set me down to walk. I remember, before the dwarf left the Queen, he followed us one day into those gardens, and my nurse having set me down, he and I being close together, near some dwarf apple-trees, I must needs show my wit by a silly allusion[1] between him and the trees, which happens to hold in their language as it doth in ours. Whereupon, the malicious rogue watching his opportunity, when I was walking under one of them, shook it directly over my head, by which a dozen apples, each of them near as large as a Bristol barrel, came tumbling about my ears; one of them hit me on the back as I chanced to stoop, and knocked me down flat on my face, but I received no other hurt, and the dwarf was pardoned at my desire, because I had given the provocation.

Another day Glumdalclitch left me on a smooth grassplot to divert myself while she walked at some distance with her governess. In the meantime there suddenly fell such a violent shower of hail, that I was immediately by the force of it struck to the ground: and when I was down, the hailstones gave me such cruel bangs all over the body, as if I had been pelted with tennis-balls; however I made a shift to creep on all four, and shelter myself by lying flat on my face on the lee-side of a border of lemon thyme, but so bruised from head to foot that I could not go abroad in ten days. Neither is this at all to be wondered at, because nature in that country observing the same proportion through all her operations, a hailstone is near eighteen hundred times as large as one in Europe, which I can assert upon experience, having been so curious to weigh and measure them.

But a more dangerous accident happened to me in the same garden, when my little nurse believing she had put me in a secure place, which I often entreated her to do, that I might enjoy my own thoughts, and having left my box at home to avoid the trouble of carrying it, went to another part of the garden with her governess and some ladies of her acquaintance. While she was absent and out of hearing, a small white spaniel belonging to one of the chief gardeners, having got by accident into the garden, happened to range near the place where I lay. The dog following the scent, came directly up, and taking me in his mouth, ran straight to his master, wagging his tail, and set me gently on the ground. By good fortune he had been so well taught, that I was carried between his teeth without the least hurt, or even tearing my clothes. But the poor gardener, who knew me well, and had a great kindness for me, was in a terrible fright. He gently took me up in both his hands, and asked me how I did; but I was so amazed and out of breath, that I could not speak a word. In a few minutes I came to myself, and he carried me safe to my little nurse, who by this time had returned to the place where she left me, and was in cruel agonies when I did not appear, nor answer when she called: she severely reprimanded the gardener on account of his dog. But the thing was hushed up, and never known at court; for the girl was afraid of the Queen's anger, and truly as to myself, I thought it would not be for my reputation that such a story should go about.

This accident absolutely determined Glumdalclitch never to trust me abroad for the future out of her sight. I had been long afraid of this resolution, and therefore concealed from her some little unlucky adventures that happened in those times when I was left by myself. Once a kite hovering over the garden made a swoop at me, and if I had not resolutely drawn my hanger, and run under a thick espalier,[2] he would have certainly carried me away in his talons. Another time walking to the top of a fresh mole-hill, I fell to my neck in the hole through which that animal had cast up the earth, and coined some lie, not worth remembering, to excuse myself for spoiling my clothes. I likewise broke my right shin against the shell of a snail, which I happened to stumble over, as I

---

1. **allusion,** comparison.
2. **espalier** (e spal′ yər),   a trellis or framework of stakes on which fruit trees or shrubs are trained to grow.

was walking alone, and thinking on poor England.

I cannot tell whether I were more pleased or mortified, to observe in those solitary walks that the smaller birds did not appear to be at all afraid of me, but would hop about within a yard distance, looking for worms and other food with as much indifference and security as if no creature at all were near them. I remember a thrush had the confidence to snatch out of my hand with his bill a piece of cake that Glumdalclitch had just given me for my breakfast. When I attempted to catch any of these birds, they would boldly turn against me, endeavouring to pick my fingers, which I durst not venture within their reach; and then they would hop back unconcerned to hunt for worms or snails, as they did before. But one day I took a thick cudgel, and threw it with all my strength so luckily at a linnet that I knocked him down, and seizing him by the neck with both my hands, ran with him in triumph to my nurse. However, the bird, who had only been stunned, recovering himself, gave me so many boxes with his wings on both sides of my head and body, though I held him at arm's length, and was out of the reach of his claws, that I was twenty times thinking to let him go. But I was soon relieved by one of our servants, who wrung off the bird's neck, and I had him next day for dinner, by the Queen's command. This linnet, as near as I can remember, seemed to be somewhat larger than an English swan.

The Maids of Honour often invited Glumdalclitch to their apartments, and desired she would bring me along with her, on purpose to have the pleasure of seeing and touching me. . . . wherewith I was much disgusted; because, to say the truth, a very offensive smell came from their skins; which I do not mention or intend to the disadvantage of those excellent ladies, for whom I have all manner of respect: but I conceive that my sense was more acute in proportion to my littleness, and that those illustrious persons were no more disagreeable to their lovers, or to each other, than people of the same quality are with us in England. And, after all, I found their natural smell was much more supportable than when they used perfumes, under which I immediately swooned away. I cannot forget that an intimate friend of mine in Lilliput took the freedom in a warm day, when I had used a good deal of exercise, to complain of a strong smell about me, although I am as little faulty that way as most of my sex: but I suppose his faculty of smelling was as nice with regard to me, as mine was to that of this people. Upon this point, I cannot forbear doing justice to the Queen my mistress, and Glumdalclitch my nurse, whose persons were as sweet as those of any lady in England.

That which gave me most uneasiness among these Maids of Honour, when my nurse carried me to visit them, was to see them use me without any manner of ceremony, like a creature who had no sort of consequence. For they would strip themselves to the skin, and put on their smocks in my presence, while I was placed on their toilet[3] directly before their naked bodies, which, I am sure, to me was very far from being a tempting sight, or from giving me any other emotions than those of horror and disgust. Their skins appeared so coarse and uneven, so variously coloured, when I saw them near, with a mole here and there as broad as a trencher, and hairs hanging from it thicker than packthreads, to say nothing further concerning the rest of their persons. Neither did they at all scruple, while I was by, to discharge what they had drunk, to the quantity of at least two hogsheads, in a vessel that held above three tuns. . . .

One day a young gentleman, who was nephew to my nurse's governess, came and pressed them both to see an execution. It was of a man who had murdered one of that gen-

---

3. **toilet,** toilet table.

tleman's intimate acquaintance. Glumdalclitch was prevailed on to be of the company, very much against her inclination, for she was naturally tender-hearted: and as for myself, although I abhorred such kind of spectacles, yet my curiosity tempted me to see something that I thought must be extraordinary. The malefactor was fixed in a chair upon a scaffold erected for the purpose, and his head cut off at a blow with a sword of about forty foot long. The veins and arteries spouted up such a prodigious quantity of blood, and so high in the air, that the great *jet d'eau*[4] at Versailles was not equal for the time it lasted; and the head, when it fell on the scaffold floor, gave such a bounce, as made me start, although I were at least half an English mile distant.

The Queen, who often used to hear me talk of my seavoyages, and took all occasions to divert me when I was melancholy, asked me whether I understood how to handle a sail or an oar, and whether a little exercise of rowing might not be convenient for my health. I answered that I understood both very well. For although my proper employment had been to be surgeon or doctor to the ship, yet often, upon a pinch, I was forced to work like a common mariner. But I could not see how this could be done in their country, where the smallest wherry[5] was equal to a first-rate man-of-war among us, and such a boat as I could manage would never live in any of their rivers. Her Majesty said, if I would contrive a boat, her own joiner[6] should make it, and she would provide a place for me to sail in. The fellow was an ingenious workman, and by my instructions in ten days finished a pleasure-boat with all its tackling, able conveniently to hold eight Europeans. When it was finished, the Queen was so delighted, that she ran with it in her lap to the King, who ordered it to be put in a cistern full of water, with me in it, by way of trial; where I could not manage my two sculls, or little oars, for want of room. But the Queen had before contrived another project. She ordered the joiner to make a wooden trough of three hundred foot long, fifty broad, and eight deep; which being well pitched to prevent leaking, was placed on the floor along the wall, in an outer room of the palace. It had a cock near the bottom to let out the water when it began to grow stale, and two servants could easily fill it in half an hour. Here I often used to row for my own diversion, as well as that of the Queen and her ladies, who thought themselves well entertained with my skill and agility. Sometimes I would put up my sail, and then my business was only to steer, while the ladies gave me a gale with their fans; and when they were weary, some of the pages would blow my sail forward with their breath, while I showed my art by steering starboard or larboard[7] as I pleased. When I had done, Glumdalclitch always carried my boat into her closet, and hung it on a nail to dry.

In this exercise I once met an accident which had like to have cost me my life. For one of the pages having put my boat into the trough, the governess who attended Glumdalclitch very officiously lifted me up to place me in the boat, but I happened to slip through her fingers, and should have infallibly fallen down forty feet upon the floor, if by the luckiest chance in the world, I had not been stopped by a corking-pin that stuck in the good gentlewoman's stomacher;[8] the head of the pin passed between my shirt and the waistband of my breeches, and thus I was held by the middle in the air till Glumdalclitch ran to my relief.

Another time, one of the servants, whose

---

4. **jet d'eau** (jā dō'), a fountain which rose over forty feet in the air at Versailles, the royal palace built by Louis XIV outside Paris.
5. **wherry,** a light, shallow rowboat.
6. **joiner,** skilled woodworker.
7. **starboard or larboard,** right or left.
8. **corking-pin,** a very large pin; **stomacher,** ornamental covering for the front and upper part of the body.

office it was to fill my trough every third day with fresh water, was so careless to let a huge frog (not perceiving it) slip out of his pail. The frog lay concealed till I was put into my boat, but then seeing a resting-place, climbed up, and made it lean so much on one side, that I was forced to balance it with all my weight on the other, to prevent overturning. When the frog was got in, it hopped at once half the length of the boat, and then over my head, backwards and forwards, daubing my face and clothes with its odious slime. The largeness of its features made it appear the most deformed animal that can be conceived. However, I desired Glumdalclitch to let me deal with it alone. I banged it a good while with one of my sculls, and at last forced it to leap out of the boat.

But the greatest danger I ever underwent in that kingdom was from a monkey, who belonged to one of the clerks of the kitchen. Glumdalclitch had locked me up in her closet, while she went somewhere upon business or a visit. The weather being very warm, the closet window was left open, as well as the windows and the door of my bigger box, in which I usually lived, because of its largeness and conveniency. As I sat quietly meditating at my table, I heard something bounce in at the closet window, and skip about from one side to the other; whereat, although I was much alarmed, yet I ventured to look out, but stirred not from my seat; and then I saw this frolicsome animal, frisking and leaping up and down, till at last he came to my box, which he seemed to view with great pleasure and curiosity, peeping in at the door and every window. I retreated to the farther corner of my room, or box, but the monkey looking in at every side, put me into such a fright, that I wanted presence of mind to conceal myself under the bed, as I might easily have done. After some time spent in peeping, grinning, and chattering, he at last espied me, and reaching one of his paws in at the door, as a cat does when she plays with a mouse, although I often shifted place to avoid him, he at length seized the lappet of my coat (which being made of that country cloth, was very thick and strong) and dragged me out. He took me up in his right fore-foot, and held me as a nurse does a child she is going to suckle, just as I have seen the same sort of creature do with a kitten in Europe: and when I offered to struggle, he squeezed me so hard, that I thought it more prudent to submit. I have good reason to believe that he took me for a young one of his own species, by his often stroking my face very gently with his other paw. In these diversions he was interrupted by a noise at the closet door, as if somebody were opening it; whereupon he suddenly leaped up to the window at which he had come in, and thence upon the leads and gutters, walking upon three legs, and holding me in the fourth, till he clambered up to a roof that was next to ours. I heard Glumdalclitch give a shriek at the moment he was carrying me out. The poor girl was almost distracted: that quarter of the palace was all in an uproar; the servants ran for ladders; the monkey was seen by hundreds in the court, sitting upon the ridge of a building, holding me like a baby in one of his forepaws, and feeding me with the other, by cramming into my mouth some victuals he had squeezed out of the bag on one side of his chaps, and patting me when I would not eat; whereat many of the rabble below could not forbear laughing; neither do I think they justly ought to be blamed, for without question the sight was ridiculous enough to every body but myself. Some of the people threw up stones, hoping to drive the monkey down; but this was strictly forbidden, or else very probably my brains had been dashed out.

The ladders were now applied, and mounted by several men, which the monkey observing, and finding himself almost encompassed, not being able to make speed enough with his three legs, let me drop on a ridge tile, and made his escape. Here I sat for some

Satire was not the exclusive province of writers like Pope and Swift. The painter Hogarth is famous for his visual satiric thrusts at the manners and the mores of the age. Here the celebration for the newly elected member seems about to turn into something else.

time three hundred yards from the ground, expecting every moment to be blown down by the wind, or to fall by my own giddiness, and come tumbling over and over from the ridge to the eaves; but an honest lad, one of my nurse's footmen, climbed up, and putting me into his breeches pocket, brought me down safe.

I was almost choked with the filthy stuff the monkey had crammed down my throat: but my dear little nurse picked it out of my mouth with a small needle, and then I fell a

vomiting, which gave me great relief. Yet I was so weak and bruised in the sides with the squeezes given me by this odious animal, that I was forced to keep my bed a fortnight. The King, Queen, and all the court, sent every day to enquire after my health, and her Majesty made me several visits during my sickness. The monkey was killed, and an order made that no such animal should be kept about the palace.

When I attended the King after my recovery, to return him thanks for his favours, he was pleased to rally me a good deal upon this adventure. He asked me what my thoughts and speculations were while I lay in the monkey's paw, how I liked the victuals he gave me, his manner of feeding, and whether the fresh air on the roof had sharpened my stomach. He desired to know what I would have done upon such an occasion in my own country. I told his Majesty that in Europe we had no monkeys, except such as were brought for curiosities from other places, and so small that I could deal with a dozen of them together, if they presumed to attack me. And as for that monstrous animal with whom I was so lately engaged (it was indeed as large as an elephant), if my fears had suffered me to think so far as to make use of my hanger (looking fiercely and clapping my hand upon the hilt as I spoke) when he poked his paw into my chamber, perhaps I should have given him such a wound, as would have made him glad to withdraw it with more haste than he put it in. This I delivered in a firm tone, like a person who was jealous lest his courage should be called in question. However, my speech produced nothing else besides a loud laughter, which all the respect due to his Majesty from those about him could not make them contain. This made me reflect how vain an attempt it is for a man to endeavor doing himself honour among those who are out of all degree of equality or comparison with him. And yet I have seen the moral of my own behaviour very frequent in England since my return, where a little contemptible varlet, without the least title to birth, person, wit, or common sense, shall presume to look with importance, and put himself upon a foot with the greatest persons of the kingdom.

I was every day furnishing the court with some ridiculous story; and Glumdalclitch, although she loved me to excess, yet was arch enough to inform the Queen, whenever I committed any folly that she thought would be diverting to her Majesty. The girl, who had been out of order, was carried by her governess to take the air about an hour's distance, or thirty miles from town. They alighted out of the coach near a small foot-path in a field, and Glumdalclitch setting down my travelling box, I went out of it to walk. There was a cow-dung in the path, and I must needs try my activity by attempting to leap over it. I took a run, but unfortunately jumped short, and found myself just in the middle up to my knees. I waded through with some difficulty, and one of the footmen wiped me as clean as he could with his handkerchief; for I was filthily bemired, and my nurse confined me to my box till we returned home; where the Queen was soon informed of what had passed, and the footmen spread it about the court, so that all the mirth, for some days, was at my expense.

Chapter VI *Several contrivances of the Author to please the King and Queen. He shows his skill in music. The King inquires into the state of Europe, which the Author relates to him. The King's observations thereon.*

I used to attend the King's levee[1] once or twice a week, and had often seen him under the barber's hand, which indeed was at first very terrible to behold; for the razor was almost twice as long as an ordinary scythe. His Majesty, according to the custom of the country, was only shaved twice a week. I once prevailed on the barber to give me some of the suds or lather, out of which I picked forty or fifty of the strongest stumps of hair. I then took a piece of fine wood, and cut it like the back of a comb, making several holes in it at equal distance with as small a needle as I could get from Glumdalclitch. I fixed in the stumps so artificially,[2] scraping and sloping them with my knife toward the points, that I

1. **levee** (lev′ē), a morning reception held by royalty or nobility.
2. **artificially,** artfully, skillfully.

made a very tolerable comb; which was a seasonable supply, my own being so much broken in the teeth, that it was almost useless: neither did I know any artist in that country so nice and exact, as would undertake to make me another.

And this puts me in mind of an amusement wherein I spent many of my leisure hours. I desired the Queen's woman to save for me the combings of her Majesty's hair, whereof in time I got a good quantity, and consulting with my friend the cabinet-maker, who had received general orders to do little jobs for me, I directed him to make two chair-frames, no larger than those I had in my box, and then to bore little holes with a fine awl round those parts where I designed the backs and seats; through these holes I wove the strongest hairs I could pick out, just after the manner of cane-chairs in England. When they were finished, I made a present of them to her Majesty, who kept them in her cabinet, and used to show them for curiosities, as indeed they were the wonder of every one that beheld them. The Queen would have had me sit upon one of these chairs, but I absolutely refused to obey her, protesting I would rather die a thousand deaths than place a dishonourable part of my body on those precious hairs that once adorned her Majesty's head. Of these hairs (as I had always a mechanical genius) I likewise made a neat little purse about five foot long, with her Majesty's name deciphered in gold letters, which I gave to Glumdalclitch, by the Queen's consent. To say the truth, it was more for show than use, being not of strength to bear the weight of the larger coins, and therefore she kept nothing in it but some little toys that girls are fond of.

The King, who delighted in music, had frequent concerts at court, to which I was sometimes carried, and set in my box on a table to hear them; but the noise was so great, that I could hardly distinguish the tunes. I am confident that all the drums and trumpets of a royal army, beating and sounding together

just at your ears, could not equal it. My practice was to have my box removed from the places where the performers sat, as far as I could, then to shut the doors and windows of it, and draw the window curtains; after which I found their music not disagreeable.

I had learned in my youth to play a little upon the spinet.[3] Glumdalclitch kept one in her chamber, and a master attended twice a week to teach her: I call it a spinet, because it somewhat resembled that instrument, and was played upon in the same manner. A fancy came into my head that I would entertain the King and Queen with an English tune upon this instrument. But this appeared extremely difficult; for the spinet was near sixty foot long, each key being almost a foot wide, so that, with my arms extended, I could not reach to above five keys, and to press them down required a good smart stroke with my fist, which would be too great a labour, and to no purpose. The method I contrived was this. I prepared two round sticks about the bigness of common cudgels; they were thicker at one end than the other, and I covered the thicker ends with a piece of a mouse's skin, that by rapping on them I might neither damage the tops of the keys, nor interrupt the sound. Before the spinet a bench was placed, about four foot below the keys, and I was put upon the bench. I ran sideling upon it that way and this, as fast as I could, banging the proper keys with my two sticks, and made a shift to play a jig, to the great satisfaction of both their Majesties: but it was the most violent exercise I ever underwent, and yet I could not strike above sixteen keys, nor, consequently, play the bass and treble together, as other artists do; which was a great disadvantage to my performance.

The King, who, as I before observed, was a prince of excellent understanding, would frequently order that I should be brought in my box, and set upon the table in his closet.

3. **spinet** (spin′ it), a musical instrument resembling a small harpsichord.

He would then command me to bring one of my chairs out of the box, and sit down within three yards distance upon the top of the cabinet, which brought me almost to a level with his face. In this manner I had several conversations with him. I one day took the freedom to tell his Majesty, that the contempt he discovered towards Europe, and the rest of the world, did not seem answerable to those excellent qualities of the mind he was master of. That reason did not extend itself with the bulk of the body: on the contrary, we observed in our country that the tallest persons were usually least provided with it. That among other animals, bees and ants had the reputation of more industry, art and sagacity, than many of the larger kinds. And that, as inconsiderable as he took me to be, I hoped I might live to do his Majesty some signal service. The King heard me with attention, and began to conceive a much better opinion of me than he had ever before. He desired I would give him as exact an account of the government of England as I possibly could; because, as fond as princes commonly are of their own customs (for so he conjectured of other monarchs, by my former discourses), he should be glad to hear of any thing that might deserve imitation.

Imagine with thyself, courteous reader, who often I then wished for the tongue of Demosthenes or Cicero,[4] that might have enabled me to celebrate the praise of my own dear native country in a style equal to its merits and felicity.

I began my discourse by informing his Majesty that our dominions consisted of two islands, which composed three mighty kingdoms under one sovereign, beside our plantations[5] in America. I dwelt long upon the fertility of our soil, and the temperature[6] of our climate. I then spoke at large upon the constitution of an English Parliament, partly made up of an illustrious body called the House of Peers,[7] persons of the noblest blood, and of the most ancient and ample patrimonies. I described that extraordinary care always taken of their education in arts and arms, to qualify them for being counsellors born to the king and kingdom, to have a share in the legislature, to be members of the highest Court of Judicature, from whence there could be no appeal, and to be champions always ready for the defence of their prince and country, by their valour, conduct, and fidelity. That these were the ornament and bulwark of the kingdom, worthy followers of their most renowned ancestors, whose honour had been the reward of their virtue, from which their posterity were never once known to degenerate. To these were joined several holy persons, as part of that assembly, under the title of Bishops, whose peculiar business it is to take care of religion, and of those who instruct the people therein. These were searched and sought out through the whole nation, by the prince and his wisest counsellors, among such of the priesthood as were most deservedly distinguished by the sanctity of their lives, and the depth of their erudition; who were indeed the spiritual fathers of the clergy and the people.

That the other part of the Parliament consisted of an assembly called the House of Commons, who were all principal gentlemen, freely picked and culled out by the people themselves, for their great abilities and love of their country, to represent the wisdom of the whole nation. And these two bodies make up the most august assembly in Europe, to whom, in conjunction with the prince, the whole legislature is committed.

I then descended to the Courts of Justice, over which the Judges, those venerable sages and interpreters of the law, presided, for determining the disputed rights and properties

---

4. **Demosthenes** (di mos′ thə nēz) (c.384–322 B.C.) and **Cicero** (sis′ ə rō) (106–43 B.C.) were the most famous orators of Greece and Rome.
5. **plantations,** colonies.
6. **temperature,** temperateness.
7. **House of Peers,** House of Lords.

of men, as well as for the punishment of vice, and protection of innocence. I mentioned the prudent management of our treasury; the valour and achievements of our forces by sea and land. I computed the number of our people, by reckoning how many millions there might be of each religious sect, or political party among us. I did not omit even our sports and pastimes, or any other particular which I thought might redound to the honour of my country. And I finished all with a brief historical account of affairs and events in England for about an hundred years past.

This conversation was not ended under five audiences, each of several hours, and the King heard the whole with great attention, frequently taking notes of what I spoke, as well as memorandums of several questions he intended to ask me.

When I had put an end to these long discourses, his Majesty in a sixth audience, consulting his notes, proposed many doubts, queries, and objections, upon every article. He asked what methods were used to cultivate the minds and bodies of our young nobility, and in what kind of business they commonly spent the first and teachable part of their lives. What course was taken to supply that assembly when any noble family became extinct. What qualifications were necessary in those who were to be created new lords. Whether the humour[8] of the prince, a sum of money to a court lady, or a prime minister, or a design of strengthening a party opposite to the public interest, ever happened to be motives in those advancements. What share of knowledge these lords had in the laws of their country, and how they came by it, so as to enable them to decide the properties of their fellow-subjects in the last resort. Whether they were always so free from avarice, partialities, or want, that a bribe, or some other sinister view, could have no place among them. Whether those holy lords I spoke of were always promoted to that rank upon account of their knowledge in religious

matters, and the sanctity of their lives, had never been compliers with the times while they were common priests, or slavish prostitute chaplains to some nobleman, whose opinions they continued servilely to follow after they were admitted into that assembly.

He then desired to know what arts were practised in electing those whom I called commoners: whether a stranger with a strong purse might not influence the vulgar voters to choose him before their own landlord, or the most considerable gentleman in the neighbourhood. How it came to pass, that people were so violently bent upon getting into this assembly, which I allowed to be a great trouble and expense, often to the ruin of their families, without any salary or pension: because this appeared such an exalted strain of virtue and public spirit, that his Majesty seemed to doubt it might possibly not always be sincere: and he desired to know whether such zealous gentlemen could have any views of refunding themselves for the charges and trouble they were at, by sacrificing the public good to the designs of a weak and vicious prince in conjunction with a corrupted ministry. He multiplied his questions, and sifted me thoroughly upon every part of this head, proposing numberless enquiries and objections, which I think it not prudent or convenient to repeat.

Upon what I said in relation to our Courts of Justice, his Majesty desired to be satisfied in several points: and this I was the better able to do, having been formerly almost ruined by a long suit in chancery, which was decreed for me with costs. He asked, what time was usually spent in determining between right and wrong, and what degree of expense. Whether advocates and orators had liberty to plead in causes manifestly known to be unjust, vexatious, or oppressive. Whether party in religion or politics were observed to

---

8. **humour,** whim.

be of any weight in the scale of justice. Whether those pleading orators were persons educated in the general knowledge of equity, or only in provincial, national, and other local customs. Whether they or their judges had any part in penning those laws which they assumed the liberty of interpreting and glossing upon at their pleasure. Whether they had ever at different times pleaded for and against the same cause, and cited precedents to prove contrary opinions. Whether they were a rich or a poor corporation. Whether they received any pecuniary reward for pleading or delivering their opinions. And particularly whether they were ever admitted as members in the lower senate.

He fell next upon the management of our treasury; and said he thought my memory had failed me, because I computed our taxes at about five or six millions a year, and when I came to mention the issues,[9] he found they sometimes amounted to more than double; for the notes he had taken were very particular in this point, because he hoped, as he told me, that the knowledge of our conduct might be useful to him, and he could not be deceived in his calculations. But, if what I told him were true, he was still at a loss how a kingdom could run out of its estate like a private person. He asked me, who were our creditors; and where we should find money to pay them. He wondered to hear me talk of such chargeable and extensive wars; that certainly we must be a quarrelsome people, or live among very bad neighbours, and that our generals must needs be richer than our kings.[10] He asked what business we had out of our own islands, unless upon the score of[11] trade or treaty, or to defend the coasts with our fleet. Above all, he was amazed to hear me talk of a mercenary standing army[12] in the midst of peace, and among a free people. He said, if we were governed by our own consent in the persons of our representatives, he could not imagine of whom we were afraid, or against whom we were to fight; and would hear my opinion, whether a private man's

house might not better be defended by himself, his children, and family, than by half a dozen rascals picked up at a venture in the streets, for small wages, who might get an hundred times more by cutting their throats.

He laughed at my odd kind of arithmetic (as he was pleased to call it) in reckoning the numbers of our people by a computation drawn from the several sects among us in religion and politics. He said, he knew no reason, why those who entertain opinions prejudicial to the public, should be obliged to change, or should not be obliged to conceal them. And as it was tyranny in any government to require the first, so it was weakness not to enforce the second: for a man may be allowed to keep poisons in his closet, but not to vend them about for cordials.[13]

He observed that among the diversions of our nobility and gentry I had mentioned gaming.[14] He desired to know at what age this entertainment was usually taken up, and when it was laid down; how much of their time it employed; whether it ever went so high as to affect their fortunes; whether mean vicious people, by their dexterity in that art, might not arrive at great riches, and sometimes keep our very nobles in dependence, as well as habituate them to vile companions, wholly take them from the improvement of their minds, and force them, by the losses they have received, to learn and practise that infamous dexterity upon others.

He was perfectly astonished with the historical account I gave him of our affairs during the last century, protesting it was only an heap of conspiracies, rebellions, murders,

---

9. **issues,** expenditures.
10. This is probably an allusion to John Churchill, Duke of Marlborough (1650–1722), who gained an enormous fortune while Captain-General of the British army.
11. **upon the score of,** for the sake of.
12. Such standing armies were illegal in England without parliamentary authorization.
13. **cordials,** medicines or liqueurs.
14. **gaming,** gambling.

massacres, revolutions, banishments, the very worst effects that avarice, faction, hypocrisy, perfidiousness, cruelty, rage, madness, hatred, envy, lust, malice, or ambition could produce.

His Majesty in another audience was at the pains to recapitulate the sum of all I had spoken, compared the questions he made with the answers I had given, then taking me into his hands, and stroking me gently, delivered himself in these words, which I shall never forget nor the manner he spoke them in: My little friend Grildrig, you have made a most admirable panegyric upon your country; you have clearly proved that ignorance, idleness, and vice, may be sometimes the only ingredients for qualifying a legislator; that laws are best explained, interpreted, and applied by those whose interest and abilities lie in perverting, confounding, and eluding them. I observe among you some lines of an institution, which in its original might have been tolerable, but these half erased, and the rest wholly blurred and blotted by corruptions. It doth not appear from all you have said, how any one virtue is required towards the procurement of any one station among you; much less that men are ennobled on account of their virtue, that priests are advanced for their piety or learning, soldiers for their conduct or valour, judges for their integrity, senators for the love of their country, or counsellors for their wisdom. As for yourself (continued the King) who have spent the greatest part of your life in travelling, I am well disposed to hope you may hitherto have escaped many vices of your country. But by what I have gathered from your own relation, and the answers I have with much pains wringed and extorted from you, I cannot but conclude the bulk of your natives to be the most pernicious race of little odious vermin that nature ever suffered to crawl upon the surface of the earth.

Chapter VII *The Author's love of his country. He makes a proposal of much advantage to the King, which is rejected. The King's great ignorance in politics. The learning of that country very imperfect and confined. Their laws, and military affairs, and parties in the State.*

Nothing but an extreme love of truth could have hindered me from concealing this part of my story. It was in vain to discover my resentments, which were always turned into ridicule; and I was forced to rest with patience while my noble and most beloved country was so injuriously treated. I am heartily sorry as any of my readers can possibly be, that such an occasion was given: but this prince happened to be so curious and inquisitive upon every particular, that it could not consist either with gratitude or good manners to refuse giving him what satisfaction I was able. Yet thus much I may be allowed to say in my own vindication, that I artfully eluded many of his questions, and gave to every point a more favourable turn by many degrees than the strictness of truth would allow. For I have always borne that laudable partiality to my own country, which Dionysius Halicarnassensis[1] with so much justice recommends to an historian. I would hide the frailties and deformities of my political mother, and place her virtues and beauties in the most advantageous light. This was my sincere endeavour in those many discourses I had with that mighty monarch, although it unfortunately failed of success.

But great allowances should be given to a King who lives wholly secluded from the rest of the world, and must therefore be altogeth-

---

1. **Dionysius Halicarnassensis,** Greek rhetorician and historian who lived in Rome toward the end of the first century, B.C.

er unacquainted with the manners and customs that most prevail in other nations; the want of which knowledge will ever produce many prejudices, and a certain narrowness of thinking, from which we and the politer countries of Europe are wholly exempted. And it would be hard indeed, if so remote a prince's notions of virtue and vice were to be offered as a standard for all mankind.

To confirm what I have now said, and further, to show the miserable effects of a confined education, I shall here insert a passage which will hardly obtain belief. In hopes to ingratiate myself farther into his Majesty's favour, I told him of an invention discovered between three and four hundred years ago, to make a certain powder, into an heap of which the smallest spark of fire falling, would kindle the whole in a moment, although it were as big as a mountain, and make it all fly up in the air together, with a noise and agitation greater than thunder. That a proper quantity of this powder rammed into an hollow tube of brass or iron, according to its bigness, would drive a ball of iron or lead with such violence and speed, as nothing was able to sustain its force. That the largest balls thus discharged, would not only destroy whole ranks of an army at once, but batter the strongest walls to the ground, sink down ships, with a thousand men in each, to the bottom of the sea; and, when linked together by a chain, would cut through masts and rigging, divide hundreds of bodies in the middle, and lay all waste before them. That we often put this powder into large hollow balls of iron, and discharged them by an engine into some city we were besieging, which would rip up the pavements, tear the houses to pieces, burst and throw splinters on every side, dashing out the brains of all who came near. That I knew the ingredients very well, which were cheap, and common; I understood the manner of compounding them, and could direct his workmen how to make those tubes of a size porportionable to all other things in his Majesty's kingdom, and the largest need not be above an hundred foot long; twenty or thirty of which tubes, charged with the proper quantity of powder and balls, would batter down the walls of the strongest town in his dominions in a few hours, or destroy the whole metropolis, if ever it should pretend to dispute his absolute commands. This I humbly offered to his Majesty, as a small tribute of acknowledgement in return of so many marks that I had received of his royal favour and protection.

The King was struck with horror at the description I had given of those terrible engines, and the proposal I had made. He was amazed how so impotent and grovelling an insect as I (these were his expressions) could entertain such inhuman ideas, and in so familiar a manner as to appear wholly unmoved at all the scenes of blood and desolation, which I had painted as the common effects of those destructive machines, whereof he said some evil genius, enemy to mankind, must have been the first contriver. As for himself, he protested that although few things delighted him so much as new discoveries in art or in nature, yet he would rather lose half his kingdom than be privy to such a secret, which he commanded me, as I valued my life, never to mention any more.

A strange effect of narrow principles and short views! that a prince possessed of every quality which procures veneration, love, and esteem; of strong parts, great wisdom, and profound learning, endued with admirable talents for government, and almost adored by his subjects, should from a nice unnecessary scruple, whereof in Europe we can have no conception, let slip an opportunity put into his hands, that would have made him absolute master of the lives, the liberties, and the fortunes of his people. Neither do I say this with the least intention to detract from the many virtues of that excellent King, whose character I am sensible will on this account be very much lessened in the opinion of an English reader: but I take this defect among them to have risen from their ignorance, they not having hitherto reduced politics into a science, as the more acute wits of Europe have done. For I remember very well, in a discourse one day with the King, when I happened to say there were several thousand books among us written upon the art of government, it gave him (directly contrary to my intention) a very mean opinion of our understandings. He professed both to abominate and despise all mystery, refinement, and intrigue, either in a prince or a minister. He could not tell what I meant by secrets of state, where an enemy or some rival nation were not in the case. He confined the knowledge of governing within very narrow bounds; to common sense and reason, to justice and lenity, to the speedy determination of civil and criminal causes; with some other obvious topics, which are not worth considering. And he gave it for his opinion, that whoever could make two ears of corn or two blades of grass to grow upon a spot of ground where only one grew before, would deserve better of mankind, and do more essential service to his country than the whole race of politicians put together.

The learning of this people is very defective, consisting only in morality, history, poetry, and mathematics, wherein they must be allowed to excel. But the last of these is wholly applied to what may be useful in life, to the improvement of agriculture, and all mechanical arts; so that among us it would be little esteemed. And as to ideas, entities, abstractions, and transcendentals, I could never drive the least conception into their heads.

No law of that country must exceed in words the number of letters in their alphabet, which consists only in two and twenty. But indeed few of them extend even to that length. They are expressed in the most plain and simple terms, wherein those people are not mercurial enough to discover above one interpretation; and to write a comment upon any law is a capital crime. As to the decision of civil causes, or proceedings against criminals, their precedents are so few, that they have little reason to boast of any extraordinary skill in either.

They have had the art of printing, as well as the Chinese, time out of mind. But their libraries are not very large; for that of the King's, which is reckoned the biggest, doth not amount to above a thousand volumes, placed in a gallery of twelve hundred foot long, from whence I had liberty to borrow what books I pleased. The Queen's joiner had contrived in one of Glumdalclitch's rooms a kind of wooden machine five and twenty foot high, formed like a standing ladder; the steps were each fifty foot long. It was indeed a moveable pair of stairs, the lowest end placed at ten foot distance from the walls of the chamber. The book I had a mind to read was put up leaning against the wall. I first mounted to the upper step of the ladder, and turning my face towards the book, began at the top of the page, and so walking to the right and left about eight or ten paces, according to the length of the lines, till I had gotten a little below the level of my eyes, and then descending gradually till I came to the bottom; after which I mounted again, and began the other page in the same manner, and so turned over the leaf, which I could easily do with both my hands, for it was as thick and stiff as a pasteboard, and in the largest folios[2] not above eighteen or twenty foot long.

Their style is clear, masculine, and smooth, but not florid, for they avoid nothing more than multiplying unnecessary words, or using various expressions. I have perused many of their books, especially those in history and morality. Among the rest, I was much diverted with a little old treatise, which always lay in Glumdalclitch's bed-chamber, and belonged to her governess, a grave elderly gentlewoman, who dealt in writings of morality and devotion. The book treats of the weakness of human kind, and is in little esteem, except among the women and the vulgar.

---

2. **folios** (fō′ lē ōz), books of the largest size.

However, I was curious to see what an author of that country could say upon such a subject. This writer went through all the usual topics of European moralists, showing how diminutive, contemptible, and helpless an animal was man in his own nature; how unable to defend himself from the inclemencies of the air, or the fury of wild beasts; how much he was excelled by one creature in strength, by another in speed, by a third in foresight, by a fourth in industry. He added, that nature was degenerated in these latter declining ages of the world, and could now produce only small abortive births in comparison of those in ancient times. He said, it was very reasonable to think, not only that the species of men were originally much larger, but also, that there must have been giants in former ages, which, as it is asserted by history and tradition, so it hath been confirmed by huge bones and skulls casually dug up in several parts of the kingdom, far exceeding the common dwindled race of man in our days. He argued, that the very laws of nature absolutely required we should have been made in the beginning, of a size more large and robust, not so liable to destruction from every little accident of a tile falling from a house, or a stone cast from the hand of a boy, or of being drowned in a little brook. From this way of reasoning the author drew several moral applications useful in the conduct of life, but needless here to repeat. For my own part, I could not avoid reflecting how universally this talent was spread, of drawing lectures in morality, or indeed rather matter of discontent and repining, from the quarrels we raise with nature. And I believe, upon a strict enquiry, those quarrels might be shown as ill grounded among us as they are among that people.

As to their military affairs, they boast that the King's army consists of an hundred and seventy-six thousand foot, and thirty-two thousand horse: if that may be called an army which is made up of tradesmen in the several cities, and farmers in the country, whose commanders are only the nobility and gentry, without pay or reward. They are indeed perfect enough in their exercises, and under very good discipline, wherein I saw no great merit; for how should it be otherwise, where every farmer is under the command of his own landlord, and every citizen under that of the principal men in his own city, chosen after the manner of Venice by ballot?

I have often seen the militia of Lorbrulgrud drawn out to exercise in a great field near the city of twenty miles square. They were in all not above twenty-five thousand foot, and six thousand horse; but it was impossible for me to compute their number, considering the space of ground they took up. A cavalier mounted on a large steed might be about an hundred foot high. I have seen this whole body of horse, upon a word of command, draw their swords at once, and brandish them in the air. Imagination can figure nothing so grand, so surprising, and so astonishing. It looked as if ten thousnd flashes of lightning were darting at the same time from every quarter of the sky.

I was curious to know how this prince, to whose dominions there is no access from any other country, came to think of armies, or to teach his people the practice of military discipline. But I was soon informed, both by conversation and reading their histories. For in the course of many ages they have been troubled with the same disease to which the whole race of mankind is subject; the nobility often contending for power, the people for liberty, and the King for absolute dominion. All which, however happily tempered by the laws of the kingdom, have been sometimes violated by each of the three parties, and have once or more occasioned civil wars, the last whereof was happily put an end to by this prince's grandfather by a general composition,[3] and the militia, then settled with common consent, hath been ever since kept in the strictest duty.

3. **composition,** settlement.

Chapter VIII *The King and Queen make a progress to the frontiers. The Author attends them. The manner in which he leaves the country very particularly related. He returns to England.*

I had always a strong impulse that I should some time recover my liberty, though it was impossible to conjecture by what means, or to form any project with the least hope of succeeding. The ship in which I sailed was the first ever known to be driven within sight of that coast, and the King had given strict orders, that if at any time another appeared, it should be taken ashore, and with all its crew and passengers brought in a tumbril[1] to Lorbrulgrud. He was strongly bent to get me a woman of my own size, by whom I might propagate the breed: but I think I should rather have died than undergone the disgrace of leaving a posterity to be kept in cages like tame canary birds, and perhaps, in time, sold about the kingdom to persons of quality for curiosities. I was, indeed, treated with much kindness; I was the favourite of a great King and Queen, and the delight of the whole court, but it was upon such a foot as ill became the dignity of human kind. I could never forget those domestic pledges[2] I had left behind me. I wanted to be among people with whom I could converse upon even terms, and walk about the streets and fields without fear of being trod to death like a frog or a young puppy. But my deliverance came sooner than I expected, and in a manner not very common; the whole story and circumstances of which I shall faithfully relate.

I had now been two years in this country; and about the beginning of the third, Glumdalclitch and I attended the King and Queen in a progress to the south coast of the kingdom. I was carried, as usual, in my travelling-box, which, as I have already described, was a very convenient closet of twelve foot wide. And I had ordered a hammock to be fixed by silken ropes from the four corners at the top, to break the jolts, when a servant carried me before him on horseback, as I sometimes desired, and would often sleep in my hammock while we were upon the road. On the roof of my closet, just over the middle of the hammock, I ordered the joiner to cut out a hole of a foot square, to give me air in hot weather as I slept, which hole I shut at pleasure with a board that drew backwards and forwards through a groove.

When we came to our journey's end, the King thought proper to pass a few days at a palace he hath near Flanflasnic, a city within eighteen English miles of the seaside. Glumdalclitch and I were much fatigued; I had gotten a small cold, but the poor girl was so ill as to be confined to her chamber. I longed to see the ocean, which must be the only scene of my escape, if ever it should happen. I pretended to be worse than I really was, and desired leave to take the fresh air of the sea, with a page whom I was very fond of, and who had sometimes been trusted with me. I shall never forget with what unwillingness Glumdalclitch consented, nor the strict charge she gave the page to be careful of me, bursting at the same time into a flood of tears, as if she had some foreboding of what was to happen. The boy took me out in my box about half an hour's walk from the palace, towards the rocks on the sea-shore. I ordered him to set me down, and lifting up one of my sashes, cast many a wistful melancholy look towards the sea. I found myself not very well, and told the page that I had a mind to take a nap in my hammock, which I hoped would do me good. I got in, and the boy shut the window close down to keep out the cold. I soon fell asleep, and all I can conjecture is, that while I slept, the page, thinking no danger could happen, went among the rocks to look for birds' eggs, having before observed him from my window searching about, and picking up one or two in the clefts. Be that as it will, I found myself suddenly awaked with a

1. **tumbril** (tum' brəl),   a wagon.
2. **domestic pledges,**   his wife and children.

violent pull upon the ring which was fastened at the top of my box for the conveniency of carriage. I felt my box raised very high in the air, and then borne forward with prodigious speed. The first jolt had like to have shaken me out of my hammock, but afterwards the motion was easy enough. I called out several times as loud as I could raise my voice, but all to no purpose. I looked towards my windows, and could see nothing but the clouds and sky. I heard a noise just over my head like the clapping of wings, and then began to perceive the woful condition I was in; that some eagle had got the ring of my box in his beak, with an intent to let it fall on a rock like a tortoise in a shell, and then pick out my body, and devour it. For the sagacity and smell of this bird enable him to discover his quarry at a great distance, though better concealed than I could be within a two-inch board.

In a little time I observed the noise and flutter of wings to increase very fast, and my box was tossed up and down, like a sign-post in a windy day. I heard several bangs or buffets, as I thought, given to the eagle (for such I am certain it must have been that held the ring of my box in his beak), and then all on a sudden felt myself falling perpendicularly down for above a minute, but with such incredible swiftness that I almost lost my breath. My fall was stopped by a terrible squash that sounded louder to my ears than the cataract of Niagara; after which I was quite in the dark for another minute, and then my box began to rise so high that I could see light from the tops of my windows. I now perceived that I was fallen into the sea. My box, by the weight of my body, the goods that were in, and the broad plates of iron fixed for strength at the four corners of the top and bottom, floated about five foot deep in water. I did then, and do now suppose that the eagle which flew away with my box was pursued by two or three others, and forced to let me drop while he was defending himself against the rest, who hoped to share in the prey. The plates of iron fastened at the bottom of the box (for those were the strongest) preserved

the balance while it fell, and hindered it from being broken on the surface of the water. Every joint of it was well grooved, and the door did not move on hinges, but up and down like a sash, which kept my closet so tight that very little water came in. I got with much difficulty out of my hammock, having first ventured to draw back the slip-board on the roof already mentioned, contrived on purpose to let in air, for want of which I found myself almost stifled.

How often did I wish myself with my dear Glumdalclitch, from whom one single hour had so far divided me! And I may say with truth, that in the midst of my own misfortunes I could not forbear lamenting my poor nurse, the grief she would suffer for my loss, the displeasure of the Queen, and the ruin of her fortune. Perhaps many travellers have not been under greater difficulties and distress than I was at this juncture, expecting every moment to see my box dashed in pieces, or at least overset by the first violent blast, or a rising wave. A breach in one single pane of glass would have been immediate death: nor could any thing have preserved the windows, but the strong lattice wires placed on the outside against accidents in travelling. I saw the water ooze in at several crannies, although the leaks were not considerable, and I endeavoured to stop them as well as I could. I was not able to lift up the roof of my closet, which otherwise I certainly should have done, and sat on the top of it, where I might at least preserve myself some hours longer than by being shut up, as I may call it, in the hold. Or, if I escaped these dangers for a day or two, what could I expect but a miserable death of cold and hunger! I was four hours under these circumstances, expecting and indeed wishing every moment to be my last.

I have already told the reader that there were two strong staples fixed upon that side of my box which had no window, and into which the servant who used to carry me on horseback would put a leathern belt, and buckle it about his waist. Being in this disconsolate state, I heard or at least thought I heard some kind of grating noise on that side of my box where the staples were fixed, and soon after I began to fancy that the box was pulled or towed along in the sea; for I now and then felt a sort of tugging, which made the waves rise near the tops of my windows, leaving me almost in the dark. This gave me some faint hopes of relief, although I was not able to imagine how it could be brought about. I ventured to unscrew one of my chairs, which were always fastened to the floor; and having made a hard shift to screw it down again directly under the slipping-board that I had lately opened, I mounted on the chair, and putting my mouth as near as I could to the hole, I called for help in a loud voice, and in all the languages I understood. I then fastened my handkerchief to a stick I usually carried, and thrusting it up the hole, waved it several times in the air, that if any boat or ship were near, the seamen might conjecture some unhappy mortal to be shut up in the box.

I found no effect from all I could do, but plainly perceived my closet to be moved along; and in the space of an hour, or better, that side of the box where the staples were, and had no window, struck against something that was hard. I apprehended it to be a rock, and found myself tossed more than ever. I plainly heard a noise upon the cover of my closet, like that of a cable, and the grating of it as it passed through the ring. I then found myself hoisted up by degrees at least three foot higher than I was before. Whereupon I again thrust up my stick and handkerchief, calling for help till I was almost hoarse. In return to which, I heard a great shout repeated three times, giving me such transports of joy, as are not to be conceived but by those who feel them. I now heard a trampling over my head, and somebody calling through the hole with a loud voice in the English tongue: If there be any body below, let them speak. I answered, I was an Englishman, drawn by ill fortune into the greatest calamity that ever any creature underwent, and begged, by all that is moving, to be delivered out of the dun-

geon I was in. The voice replied, I was safe, for my box was fastened to their ship; and the carpenter should immediately come and saw an hole in the cover, large enough to pull me out. I answered, that was needless, and would take up too much time, for there was no more to be done, but let one of the crew put his finger into the ring, and take the box out of the sea into the ship, and so into the captain's cabin. Some of them upon hearing me talk so wildly thought I was mad; others laughed; for indeed it never came into my head that I was now got among people of my own stature and strength. The carpenter came, and in a few minutes sawed a passage about four foot square, then let down a small ladder, upon which I mounted, and from thence was taken into the ship in a very weak condition.

The sailors were all in amazement, and asked me a thousand questions, which I had no inclination to answer. I was equally confounded at the sight of so many pigmies, for such I took them to be, after having so long accustomed my eyes to the monstrous objects I had left. But the Captain, Mr. Thomas Wilcocks, an honest worthy Shropshire man, observing I was ready to faint, took me into his cabin, gave me a cordial to comfort me, and made me turn in upon his own bed, advising me to take a little rest, of which I had great need. Before I went to sleep I gave him to understand that I had some valuable furniture in my box, too good to be lost, a fine hammock, an handsome field-bed, two chairs, a table, and a cabinet; that my closet was hung on all sides, or rather quilted, with silk and cotton; that if he would let one of the crew bring my closet into his cabin, I would open it there before him, and show him my goods. The Captain hearing me utter these absurdities, concluded I was raving: however (I suppose to pacify me), he promised to give order as I desired, and going upon deck sent some of his men down into my closet, from whence (as I afterwards found) they drew up all my goods, and stripped off the quilting; but the chairs, cabinet, and bedstead, being screwed to the floor, were much damaged by the ignorance of the seamen, who tore them up by force. Then they knocked off some of the boards for the use of the ship, and when they had got all they had a mind for, let the hull drop into the sea, which by reason of many breaches made in the bottom and sides, sunk to rights.³ And indeed I was glad not to have been a spectator of the havoc they made; because I am confident it would have sensibly touched me, by bringing former passages into my mind, which I had rather forget.

I slept some hours, but perpetually disturbed with dreams of the place I had left, and the dangers I had escaped. However, upon waking I found myself much recovered. It was now about eight o'clock at night, and the Captain ordered supper immediately, thinking I had already fasted too long. He entertained me with great kindness, observing me not to look wildly, or talk inconsistently: and when we were left alone, desired I would give him a relation of my travels, and by what accident I came to be set adrift in that monstrous wooden chest. He said, that about twelve o'clock at noon, as he was looking through his glass, he spied it at a distance, and thought it was a sail, which he had a mind to make,⁴ being not much out of his course, in hopes of buying some biscuit, his own beginning to fall short. That upon coming nearer, and finding his error, he sent out his long-boat to discover what I was; that his men came back in a fright, swearing they had seen a swimming house. That he laughed at their folly, and went himself in the boat, ordering his men to take a strong cable along with them. That the weather being calm, he rowed round me several times, observed my windows, and the wire lattices that defended them. That he discovered two staples upon one side, which was all of boards, without any passage for light. He then commanded his men to row up to that side, and fastening a cable to one of the staples, ordered them to tow my chest (as he called it) towards the ship. When it was there, he gave directions to fasten another cable to the ring fixed in the cover, and to raise up my chest with pulleys, which all the sailors were not able to do above two or three foot. He said they saw my stick and handkerchief thrust out of the hole, and concluded that some unhappy men must be shut up in the cavity. I asked whether he or the crew had seen any prodigious birds in the air about the time he first discovered me. To which he answered, that discoursing this matter with the sailors while I was asleep, one of them said he had observed three eagles flying towards the north, but remarked nothing of their being larger than the usual size, which I suppose must be imputed to the great height they were at; and he could not guess the reason of my question. I then asked the Captain how far he reckoned we might be from land; he said, by the best computation he could make, we were at least an hundred leagues. I assured him, that he must be mistaken by almost half, for I had not left the country from whence I came above two hours before I dropt into the sea. Whereupon he began again to think that my brain was disturbed, of which he gave me a hint, and advised me to go to bed in a cabin he had provided. I assured him I was well refreshed with his good entertainment and company, and as much in my senses as ever I was in my life. He then grew serious, and desired to ask me freely whether I was not troubled in mind by the consciousness of some enormous crime, for which I was punished at the command of some prince, by exposing me in that chest, as great criminals in other countries have been forced to sea in a leaky vessel without provisions; for although he should be sorry to have taken so ill a man into his ship, yet he would engage his word to set me safe on shore in the first port where we arrived. He added, that his suspicions were much increased by some very absurd speeches I had delivered at first to the sailors, and afterwards to himself, in relation to my closet or chest, as well as by my

3. **to rights,** altogether.
4. **to make,** to overtake.

odd looks and behaviour while I was at supper.

I begged his patience to hear me tell my story, which I faithfully did from the last time I left England to the moment he first discovered me. And as truth always forceth its way into rational minds, so this honest worthy gentleman, who had some tincture of learning, and very good sense, was immediately convinced of my candour and veracity. But further to confirm all I had said, I entreated him to give order that my cabinet should be brought, of which I had the key in my pocket (for he had already informed me how the seamen disposed of my closet). I opened it in his presence and showed him the small collection of rarities I made in the country from whence I had been so strangely delivered. There was the comb I had contrived out of the stumps of the King's beard, and another of the same materials, but fixed into a paring of her Majesty's thumb-nail, which served for the back. There was a collection of needles and pins from a foot to half a yard long; four wasp-stings, like joiners' tacks; some combings of the Queen's hair; a gold ring which one day she made me a present of in a most obliging manner, taking it from her little finger, and throwing it over my head like a collar. I desired the Captain would please to accept this ring in return of his civilities, which he absolutely refused. I showed him a corn that I had cut off with my own hand, from a maid of honour's toe; it was about the bigness of a Kentish pippin,[5] and grown so hard that when I returned to England, I got it hollowed into a cup, and set in silver. Lastly, I desired him to see the breeches I had then on, which were made of a mouse's skin.

I could force nothing on him but a footman's tooth, which I observed him to examine with great curiosity, and found he had a fancy for it. He received it with abundance of thanks, more than such a trifle could deserve. It was drawn by an unskilful surgeon, in a mistake, from one of Glumdalclitch's men, who was afflicted with the toothache, but it was as sound as any in his head. I got it cleaned, and put it into my cabinet. It was about a foot long, and four inches in diameter.

The Captain was very well satisfied with this plain relation I had given him, and said he hoped when we returned to England I would oblige the world by putting it on paper and making it public. My answer was that I thought we were already overstocked with books of travels; that nothing could now pass which was not extraordinary; wherein I doubted some authors less consulted truth than their own vanity, or interest, or the diversion of ignorant readers. That my story could contain little besides common events, without those ornamental descriptions of strange plants, trees, birds, and other animals, or of the barbarous customs and idolatry of savage people, with which most writers abound. However, I thanked him for his good opinion, and promised to take the matter into my thoughts.

He said he wondered at one thing very much, which was, to hear me speak so loud, asking me whether the King or Queen of that country were thick of hearing. I told him it was what I had been used to for above two years past, and that I admired as much at the voices of him and his men, who seemed to me only to whisper, and yet I could hear them well enough. But when I spoke in that country, it was like a man talking in the street to another looking out from the top of a steeple, unless when I was placed on a table, or held in any person's hand. I told him, I likewise observed another thing, that when I first got into the ship, and the sailors stood all about me, I thought they were the most little contemptible creatures I had ever beheld. For indeed while I was in that prince's country, I could never endure to look in a glass after my eyes had been accustomed to such prodigious objects, because the comparison

5. **pippin,** apple.

gave me so despicable a conceit of myself. The Captain said that while we were at supper he observed me to look at every thing with a sort of wonder, and that I often seemed hardly able to contain my laughter, which he knew not well how to take, but imputed it to some disorder in my brain. I answered, it was very true; and I wondered how I could forbear, when I saw his dishes of the size of a silver three-pence, a leg of pork hardly a mouthful, a cup not so big as a nutshell; and so I went on, describing the rest of his household-stuff and provisions after the same manner. For, although the Queen had ordered a little equipage[6] of all things necessary for me while I was in her service, yet my ideas were wholly taken up with what I saw on every side of me, and I winked at my own littleness as people do at their own faults. The Captain understood my raillery very well, and merrily replied with the old English proverb, that he doubted my eyes were bigger than my belly, for he did not observe my stomach so good, although I had fasted all day; and continuing in his mirth, protested he would have gladly given an hundred pounds to have seen my closet in the eagle's bill, and afterwards in its fall from so great an height into the sea; which would certainly have been a most astonishing object, worthy to have the description of it transmitted to future ages: and the comparison of Phaeton[7] was so obvious, that he could not forbear applying it, although I did not much admire the conceit.

The Captain, having been at Tonquin,[8] was in his return to England driven northeastward to the latitude of 44 degrees, and of longitude 143. But meeting a trade-wind two days after I came on board him, we sailed southward a long time, and coasting New Holland[9] kept our course west-south-west, and then south-south-west till we doubled the Cape of Good Hope. Our voyage was very prosperous, but I shall not trouble the reader with a journal of it. The Captain called in at one or two ports, and sent in his long-boat for provisions and fresh water, but I never went out of the ship till we came into the Downs, which was on the third day of June, 1706, about nine months after my escape. I offered to leave my goods in security for payment of my freight; but the Captain protested he would not receive one farthing.[10] We took kind leave of each other, and I made him promise he would come to see me at my house in Redriff.[11] I hired a horse and guide for five shillings, which I borrowed of the Captain.

As I was on the road, observing the littleness of the houses, the trees, the cattle, and the people, I began to think myself in Lilliput. I was afraid of trampling on every traveller I met, and often called aloud to have them stand out of the way, so that I had like to have gotten one or two broken heads for my impertinence.

When I came to my own house, for which I was forced to enquire, one of the servants opening the door, I bent down to go in (like a goose under a gate) for fear of striking my head. My wife ran out to embrace me, but I stooped lower than her knees, thinking she could otherwise never be able to reach my mouth. My daughter kneeled to ask my blessing, but I could not see her till she arose, having been so long used to stand with my head and eyes erect to above sixty foot; and then I went to take her up with one hand, by the waist. I looked down upon the servants and one or two friends who were in the house, as if they had been pigmies, and I a giant. I told my wife, she had been too thrifty, for I found she had starved herself and her daughter to nothing. In short, I behaved myself so unac-

6. **equipage,** outfit.
7. **Phaeton** (fā′ ə ton), variant for Phaethon, the son of the god Apollo in Greek mythology. Phaethon, despite his father's warnings, tried unsuccessfully to drive the chariot of the sun god; he was hurled to earth, where he drowned in the river Eridanus.
8. **Tonquin,** port in Indochina, in modern Vietnam.
9. **New Holland,** modern Australia.
10. **farthing,** a former British coin, worth one quarter of a British penny.
11. **Redriff,** on the south bank of the Thames in London.

countably, that they were all of the Captain's opinion when he first saw me, and concluded I had lost my wits. This I mention as an instance of the great power of habit and prejudice.

In a little time I and my family and friends came to a right understanding: but my wife protested I should never go to sea any more; although my evil destiny so ordered that she had not power to hinder me, as the reader may know hereafter. In the mean time I here conclude the second part of my unfortunate voyages.

FOR UNDERSTANDING

1. Which incidents in Chapter 5 emphasize Gulliver's smallness in the world of Brobdingnag?
2. What does the King request Gulliver to explain in Chapter 6? What is his reaction to Gulliver's speech?
3. How does Gulliver offer to help the King in Chapter 7? How does the King respond?
4. What defects in Brobdingnagian customs and institutions does Gulliver mention in Chapter 7?
5. How does Gulliver leave Brobdingnag? What is the reaction of the sailors? What are Gulliver's emotions when he finally returns home?

FOR INTERPRETATION

A. From its first appearance *Gulliver's Travels* has provoked diverse (and sometimes violent) reactions from readers of all ages. Some readers have been enthusiastic and delighted; others see the work as repulsive and depressing. Scholarly controversies have flourished for two centuries over the interpretation of many passages. But few readers have been able to dismiss *Gulliver's Travels* casually. The key to our reactions seems to lie in our feelings about human life in general and, more particularly, about our own significance. To test your reactions to the story, try to pin down which of the following adjectives most closely describe your feelings. Be prepared to explain the reasons for your choice.

1. childish   4. incomplete
2. repulsive   5. amusing
3. silly   6. bitter

B. Answer the following questions with specific reference to the selection.
1. How does the voyage to Brobdingnag satirize the eighteenth-century idealization of man as a rational creature?
2. Swift once remarked that he hated mankind, but loved John, Peter, and Thomas. Explain how the voyage to Brobdingnag illustrates his meaning.
3. How does the portrait of the giants indirectly satirize human beings?

FOR APPRECIATION

1. How does Swift manipulate the technique of *point of view* in *Gulliver's Travels*? Do you, the reader, gain a significantly different insight into the situation from that of Gulliver?
2. The structure of popular eighteenth-century travel books was very much like that of travel literature today. How does Swift combine the form of the *travelogue* (nonfiction) with the form of the *novel* (fiction)?
3. What is the *tone* of Swift's satire? How do Gulliver's emotions at the end of the voyage indirectly contribute to the power of the satire?

COMPOSITION

1. The scale of doll houses is generally 1:12, or one inch to a foot—very much the same scale that Swift uses to compare Gulliver's relative size to the Brobdingnagians. Imagine that you are miniaturized and have just stepped out of a doll house into your own living room. In a short narrative describe your problems in dealing with an everyday activity or event in your house. The following list includes some possibilities:

Walking about on top of the table at breakfast.
Meeting a spider.
Encountering a vacuum cleaner.
Trying to get a drink of water.
Finding yourself amid the clothes in the washing machine.

2. Using as a model Gulliver's description of English government and society in Chapter 6, write a short essay in which you attempt to explain our system of education to someone who knows nothing about it. Organize your essay to include some dialogue and briefly characterize the two speakers. Try to imitate Swift's matter-of-fact, satirical tone.

COMPOSITION WORKSHOP

DEVELOPING A PLAN

At the point of choosing a topic, every writer has a fairly good idea of the general plan that the paper will follow. If you were going to write a paper, for example, on the targets of Jonathan Swift's satire in *Gulliver's Travels,* you would know from the very start that these targets would have to be identified and discussed in some sensible order. You would not know precisely what that order might be until you finished gathering and examining information. The form or plan of a paper evolves gradually; no conscientious writer would attempt a final outline until "all the facts were in."

Your next step, then, is a mechanical one. You arrange your 4 x 6-inch cards into piles according to subtopic. Again, if you were writing about Swift's satire in *Gulliver's Travels,* then one pile of cards would contain facts about Swift's life collected from basic biographical sources, while another might contain notes from sources that comment upon Swift's criticism of human political institutions. Still other piles would deal with other aspects of the topic.

Once you have completed this initial sorting, your next task is to appraise critically each of the subtopics and "prune out" those which have little or nothing to do with your topic. Suppose, for instance, that in preparing your hypothetical paper on Swift's satire you discovered and noted a wealth of material on the widespread appeal of *Gulliver's Travels* among children. This information would now have to be discarded since it is no longer relevant to the topic. While the elimination of an entire stack of cards might be painful, and even seem wasteful, it is a necessary part of the research process. All good writers must come to grips with it.

THE THESIS STATEMENT

You are now ready to convert your remaining stacks of cards into a preliminary outline. The best way to begin the outline is by stating the main point or argument in a concrete form known as a *thesis statement.* The word *thesis* comes from a Greek word meaning literally "a laying down." The thesis statement is to an entire paper what a topic sentence is to a single paragraph.

Because the thesis statement grows directly out of the categories that have survived the pruning stage, it is formulated through a careful examination of those categories. Ironically, once you have the thesis statement on paper, reference to it will help you to clarify and sharpen those very categories that gave rise to it.

A thesis statement for a paper that examined the targets of Swift's satire in *Gulliver's Travels* might be worded as follows: "In *Gulliver's Travels,* Jonathan Swift satirizes the human race's abuse of reason." Having made this statement, you have, in a very real sense, made a promise to your reader. You have promised, in essence, that whatever follows will in some way shed light on your thesis. Good writers always keep their promises.

INTRODUCTION AND CONCLUSION

While most of your preliminary outline will consist of listing the categories that support the thesis statement (these will eventually come together to form the *body* of your paper), two other parts of the paper must be established at this point. Those parts are the *introduction* and the *conclusion.*

The main purpose of the introduction is to supply your reader with enough background information to make sense of your paper as a whole. In the course of gathering information, you will have become something of an expert on the topic; at the very least, you will know more about the subject than someone who has done no reading on it at all. It then becomes your responsibility to equip your reader with a basis for understanding your thesis statement and for following the gist of your arguments. In the hypothetical paper on Swift that has served as our model here, this background information would most likely consist of some biographical material about the author as well as a brief summary of the various books that make up *Gulliver's Travels.*

In the paper's conclusion, you summarize the relationship between the points presented in the body of the paper and the thesis statement. In this section, you might also wish to advance any personal views you may have come to hold with regard to the topic.

It is important to note that the outline we are dealing with at this point is a *preliminary* outline. It is subject to change. As you get further into the development of your thesis, parts of your outline may shift or be shortened or expanded. Thus, do not strive at this point for completeness of detail. The outline, after all, is not an end in itself but rather a usable blueprint.

A preliminary outline for our model topic might look like this:

Thesis: In *Gulliver's Travels,* Jonathan Swift satirizes the human race's abuse of reason.

    I. Introduction
       A. Swift the Man
       B. Summary of Work

   II. Targets of Satire
       A. Political Institutions
       B. Social Institutions
       C. Academic Institutions
  III. Conclusion
       A. General Target—Abuse of Reason
       B. Validity of Swift's Attack

ASSIGNMENT

Sort through all of the 4 x 6-inch cards that you have collected. Eliminate any categories that do not contribute to the main topic. Write a thesis statement that arises naturally from the remaining categories. Examine the information that will be useful in the introduction of your paper and consider the points you will make in your paper's conclusion. Develop a preliminary outline for your paper.

A HILLY SCENE, Samuel Palmer, Tate Gallery

The Romantic Period

1798-1837

The early years of the nineteenth century in English literature are
called the Romantic period. Romantic is not used in its commonest
meaning of a relationship between the sexes. Rather, Romantic desig-
nates an intellectual stance, an emotional outlook, almost an attitude
toward life. Romanticism is a difficult movement to describe because of
its numerous, sometimes contradictory features. But at the very heart
of the Romantic movement was the belief that the individual is the
center of all life and experience. Literature, therefore, should be the
tool for expressing personal feelings and unique, individual experiences, however fragmentary they may be. Starting near the end of the
eighteenth century in England, Romanticism influenced some crafts
and all the arts: literature, painting, music, and sculpture. The Romantic movement was not restricted to one country; it was keenly felt by
artists in many European nations and in America.

The Heart of Romanticism

To understand the origins of Romanticism it is helpful to recall the
political background of the era. Late in the eighteenth century the
Americans freed themselves from English control. In 1789, the French
Revolution began with the storming of the Bastille; three years later,
King Louis XVI and his queen, Marie Antoinette, were executed by the
rebels. English writers tended to be sympathetic with these movements.
Robert Burns (p. 488) read the manifestoes of Thomas Paine; William
Wordsworth (p. 500) traveled to France shortly after the Revolution
and was filled with high hopes for social reform. George Gordon, Lord
Byron (p. 517) died in Greece during the Greek struggle for independence from the Turks; Byron had subsidized and helped to train the
revolutionary troops. The thinking that produced such political upheavals helped to fuel a revolution in the arts as well. Political freedom
became for many artists the natural corollary of individual and artistic
freedom.

Political Background

ASPECTS OF ROMANTICISM

Although the principal Romantic writers never thought of themselves
as belonging to a school or movement, they shared a number of
common concerns. One aspect of Romanticism stemmed from a widely
shared belief in the simple goodness of people and the corrupting
influence of society. In France, Jean Jacques Rousseau (1712–1778)

Although the romantics in general were opposed to the industrial revolution as an evil of society, the painter senses the awesome, mysterious, almost preternatural, power of the iron foundry at night. Note, too, the contrast between darkness and light.

COALBROOKDALE BY NIGHT
Philip James de Loutherbourg
Science Museum, London

The "Noble Savage"

preached the virtues of life in a state of nature, far removed from civilization. Rousseau's influential theories resulted in a cult of the "noble savage." Books were written about children raised in nature; writers and painters sentimentalized country scenes and country people; the American Indian and the African, because they had not been "infected" by civilization, were conceived as models of humanity in a pure, natural state.

Industrial Revolution

At this same time, England was also changing from a rural society to an urban, industrial nation. The new factories took the place of the cottage industries of the eighteenth century. The great economic transition which we call the Industrial Revolution occurred over several generations and sparked some acute social conflicts. Working conditions were often appalling. The ramshackle housing was inadequate. The burgeoning of democratic ideas collided with the rapid growth of cities and slums and the rising dominance of the profit motive. Factory owners cried out that they would be ruined when Parliament restricted

The parting of the sorrowing young woman in the midst of a lush and beautiful natural setting displays several typical interests of the romantics: deep human emotion, nature as landscape, and the dramatic contrast between darkness and light.

DISAPPOINTED LOVE
Francis Danby
Victoria and Albert Museum

working conditions for children to only 12½ hours a day and forbade hiring them under the age of nine. An unemployed weaver named Ned Ludd became so infuriated at the machines that displaced him that he broke them up; riots of the so-called Luddites became widespread in England after 1810. Now the Romantic writers' interest in the peasant expanded to include sympathy with the traumas of the common man. One of Lord Byron's first speeches in Parliament supported the Luddites.

Interest in the Common Man

Another facet of Romanticism was its interest in the past. Just as the Romantics tended to idealize the noble savage and the child, they often sought in older periods a simpler society closer to people's natural goodness. Sir Walter Scott used in his novels almost eight centuries of English, Scottish, and French history as settings for Romantic heroes and heroines, caught up in the political struggles of their times. The Romantic poets went to the myths and ruins of Greece and Rome for inspiration. The word Gothic (used to designate medie-

Interest in the Past

Sir Walter Scott

Gothic

RAIN STEAM AND SPEED
J.M.W. Turner

Turner, too, sees the frightening changes brought on by the industrial revolution. In his typical style, subject matter disolves into almost sheer color to convey emotion.

val architecture between the thirteenth and fifteenth centuries) now became attached to a new kind of novel, filled with grotesque and mysterious elements. The glorification of the old, of the moldering remnants of other times, sometimes degenerated into mere fashion. Some aristocrats actually built artificial ruins in the gardens of their estates if they were not fortunate enough to possess real ones.

Such figurines were commonly collected in the homes of the middle class.

Leeds pottery figures

Romantic poets and painters commonly glorified rural life.

THE ALE HOUSE DOOR
George Morland
National Gallery of Scotland

Romanticism rebelled against the formalism of the eighteenth century, against balance and symmetry as the principal criteria of beauty, against restraint in expressing emotion. One of the main tenets of the Romantics was an idealization of the grander, wilder elements in nature. In the eighteenth century, nature had meant human nature. In the nineteenth, it meant oceans and mountains, waterfalls and lightning, lions and mythical beasts. Even the less dramatic phenomena of nature evoked the intense appreciation of the Romantics; the nineteenth century discovered landscape as an artistic imperative. Both Wordsworth and Coleridge (p. 513), for example, chose to live in England's Lake District, one of the most beautiful, wild, and scenic regions of the nation.

Interest in Nature

Romantic artists frequently showed their sympathy with the traumas of the common man.

Gothic arches-windows, wall panels, doorways, and over the fireplace and mirrored insets-proclaim the Gothic revival in this interior view of Horace Walpole's mansion, Strawberry Hill. Walpole's only novel, The Castle of Otranto, *marked the genesis of the Gothic novel.*

The Romantics also delved into the supernatural. They were intrigued with that side of all of us that feels a different kind of reality may lie beyond the reality we know. Nature came to symbolize quasi-religious themes, as in William Blake's "The Tyger" or William Wordsworth's "Tintern Abbey." Samuel Taylor Coleridge's *Rime of the Ancient Mariner* is frankly supernatural.

Interest in the Supernatural

ENGLISH ROMANTIC POETRY

The move toward Romanticism in English literature was gradual. You have seen how Thomas Gray's "Elegy Written in a Country Church-yard" (1751) is quite different in content from anything that Alexander Pope could have written. Robert Burns, born eight years after Gray's

Thomas Gray

Robert Burns

William Blake

Wordsworth, Coleridge

elegy appeared, used the oral tradition of old Scots folk songs to idealize the common man; William Blake (494), still in the eighteenth century, exalted the figure of the child and delved deeply into the spiritual and mystic. William Wordsworth and Samuel Taylor Coleridge definitely signaled a break with the past when they published a joint venture, *Lyrical Ballads*, in 1798. The famous preface to this collection stated the authors' poetic creed. Poetry should arise from the "spontaneous overflow of powerful feelings," and it should be written in a "selection of language really spoken by men." The controversial reception of this book emphasizes how decisively Wordsworth and Coleridge turned their backs on the past.

Byron, Keats, and Shelley

Burns, Blake, Wordsworth, and Coleridge represent a first generation of Romantic poets, born between 1759 and 1772. The most celebrated poets of a slightly younger generation were George Gordon, Lord Byron; John Keats (p. 534); and Percy Bysshe Shelley (p. 525). These poets epitomize the Romantic spirit. Different as each is from the others, they are alike in the intense emotion of their poetry and in their introspection. All died young: Keats, at twenty-five, in Rome from consumption; Byron, at thirty-six, fighting in the Greek war for independence; and Shelley, at thirty, drowned in a sailing accident on the Adriatic.

Theories of the Imagination

One of the most compelling aspects of the Romantic poets' outlook on their own literary activity is their theories of the imagination. In the eighteenth century, this word had meant simply "image-making." In

Built in the early nineteenth century. Fonthill Abbey is one of the most elaborate monuments to Gothic taste in England.

Fonthill Abbey
British Museum Print Room

The Houses of Parliament are an excellent example of Gothic revival architecture. After the ancient house of parliament burned in 1834, Sir Charles Barry was commissioned to design and build new accommodations for parliament (1840-1860).

the nineteenth, it became identified with a more mysterious, elusive creative process. The Romantics were the first poets in English to record powerfully their sense of pressure from the burden of the past; they looked eagerly to the process of imagination to provide them with originality and spontaneity in their writing. Many of the finest lyrics of this period are at least partly concerned with this theme; and Mary Shelley, in the "Introduction" to her novel *Frankenstein*, provides a fascinating glimpse of the creative artist at work. The Romantics' stress on originality and on the mechanisms of the creative process have powerfully affected much subsequent literature, down to our own day.

Romanticism Today

Some of the attitudes that shaped the creative work of the Romantic period are still present today. Americans tend to be Romantic in their attitudes and endeavors. These are magnificently diverse: the environmental struggle; putting a man on the moon; the fascination with extraterrestrial beings; the faith in the jury system; the belief in the wisdom of the ordinary person. American popular literature, from country-and-western lyrics to "romance" novels, is also Romantic in concept. Perhaps that spirit is best summarized in a definition that Romanticism is "the never ending pursuit after the ever fleeting object of desire."

The Romantic Age 1798-1837

GEORGE III 1760-1820

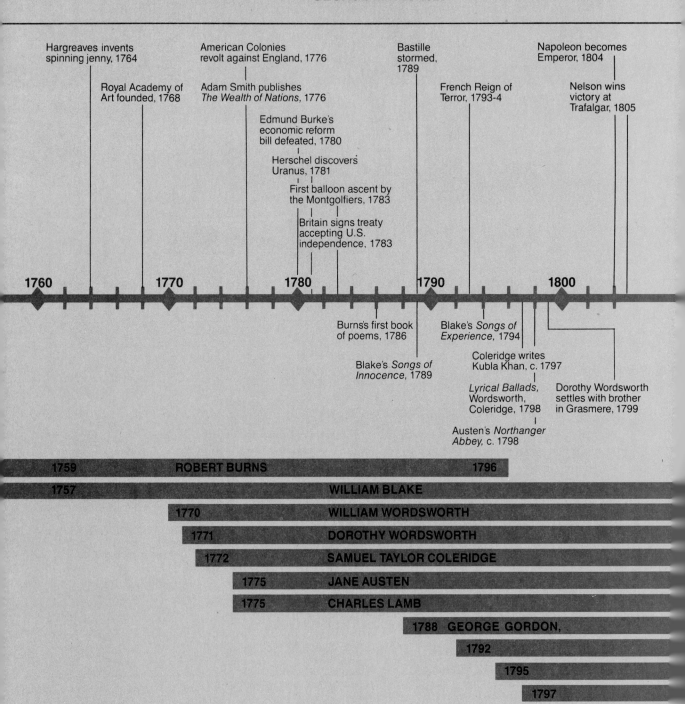

Hargreaves invents
spinning jenny, 1764

Royal Academy of
Art founded, 1768

American Colonies
revolt against England, 1776

Adam Smith publishes
The Wealth of Nations, 1776

Edmund Burke's
economic reform
bill defeated, 1780

Herschel discovers
Uranus, 1781

First balloon ascent by
the Montgolfiers, 1783

Britain signs treaty
accepting U.S.
independence, 1783

Bastille
stormed,
1789

French Reign of
Terror, 1793-4

Napoleon becomes
Emperor, 1804

Nelson wins
victory at
Trafalgar, 1805

1760   **1770**   **1780**   **1790**   **1800**

Burns's first book
of poems, 1786

Blake's *Songs of
Innocence,* 1789

Blake's *Songs of
Experience,* 1794

Coleridge writes
Kubla Khan, c. 1797

Lyrical Ballads,
Wordsworth,
Coleridge, 1798

Austen's *Northanger
Abbey,* c. 1798

Dorothy Wordsworth
settles with brother
in Grasmere, 1799

1759	ROBERT BURNS	1796
1757	WILLIAM BLAKE	
1770	WILLIAM WORDSWORTH	
1771	DOROTHY WORDSWORTH	
1772	SAMUEL TAYLOR COLERIDGE	
1775	JANE AUSTEN	
1775	CHARLES LAMB	
1788	GEORGE GORDON,	
1792		
1795		
1797		

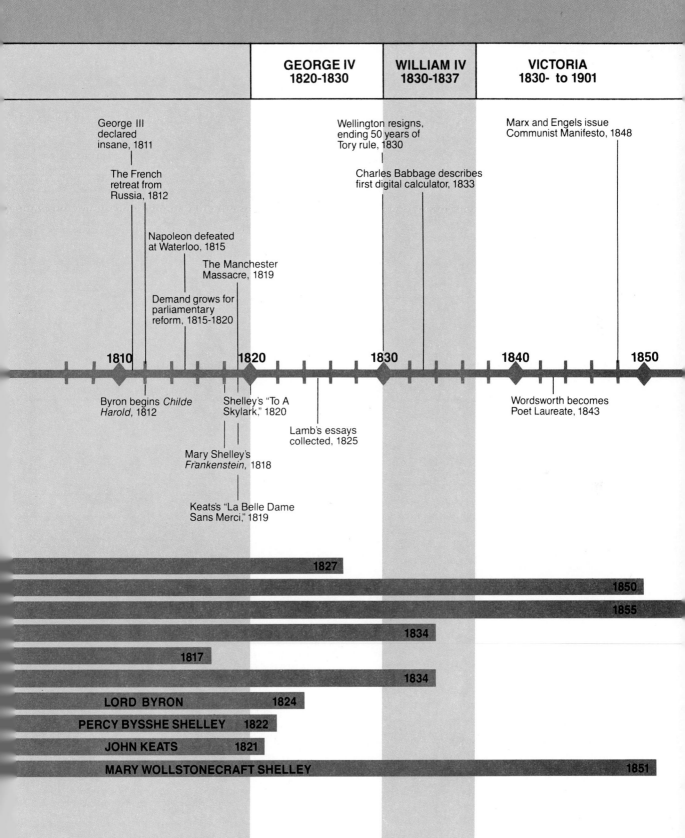

GEORGE IV 1820-1830	WILLIAM IV 1830-1837	VICTORIA 1830- to 1901

George III declared insane, 1811

The French retreat from Russia, 1812

Napoleon defeated at Waterloo, 1815

The Manchester Massacre, 1819

Demand grows for parliamentary reform, 1815-1820

Wellington resigns, ending 50 years of Tory rule, 1830

Charles Babbage describes first digital calculator, 1833

Marx and Engels issue Communist Manifesto, 1848

1810   **1820**   **1830**   **1840**   **1850**

Byron begins *Childe Harold*, 1812

Shelley's "To A Skylark," 1820

Lamb's essays collected, 1825

Wordsworth becomes Poet Laureate, 1843

Mary Shelley's *Frankenstein*, 1818

Keats's "La Belle Dame Sans Merci," 1819

1827

1850

1855

1834

1817

1834

LORD BYRON   1824

PERCY BYSSHE SHELLEY   1822

JOHN KEATS   1821

MARY WOLLSTONECRAFT SHELLEY   1851

Robert Burns

Robert Burns bridges the gap between the rational satire of the eighteenth century and the exuberant lyric of the nineteenth. Although he wrote both kinds of poetry, it is his lyrics that have established Burns as the Scottish national poet and as a poet of the first rank in English.

Burns's biography might have furnished the plot of a Romantic novel. To some of his contemporaries, he seemed to burst upon the literary scene as a simple peasant whose words flowed out as natural poetry. This was not, of course, quite true, since Burns read widely. He knew the literary heritage of Scotland as well as its rich oral tradition of folk songs and legends. His father, William Burnes (his spelling of the name), was an unsuccessful farmer, and young Robert was assigned heavy work in the fields when he was only eleven. The strain resulted in a heart problem which was to prove fatal at the age of thirty-seven. At fifteen, he fell in love for the first time and was inspired to write a love song. Said Burns, "Thus with me began Love and Poesy." In the next few years, he tried a series of unsuccessful farm ventures, even planning at one time to emigrate to the West Indies.

In 1786 Burns published a volume of his work entitled *Poems, Chiefly in the Scottish Dialect.* Called the Kilmarnock volume (from the town where it was printed), the book was praised by critics and became an instant success. It contained most of the best long poems Burns would ever write. The youthful author was dubbed the "peasant poet." Lionized as a natural bard by the intellectual and social elite of Edinburgh, he gradually disabused his admirers of the notion that he was a simple peasant. His notorious love affairs and political radicalism soon caused this group to drop him. Making little money from his book, he returned to farming and was again unsuccessful. In 1788 he was appointed a tax inspector, married, and moved to Dumfries, a lively country town. For the next eight years, until his premature death, he busied himself with his official duties and with editorial work, contributing to two collections of Scottish folk songs and ballads.

PORTRAIT OF ROBERT BURNS
Alexander Nasmyth
Scottish National Portrait Gallery

Burns's satiric poems are considered some of the most brilliant in English and are often compared to Pope's. Today, however, it is his songs that are most widely known. He wrote more than three hundred songs, which are widely recognized and sung throughout the English-speaking world. Many of his poems in standard English seem stilted and sentimental; but when he used Scots (the northern dialect of Scottish peasants), his work is a delight. His songs center on universal subjects: love, work, patriotism, and friendship. In English-speaking countries on New Year's Eve when the clock strikes midnight, the song which the band begins to play is usually Burns's "Auld Lang Syne."

To a Mouse

ON TURNING HER UP IN HER NEST WITH
THE PLOW, NOVEMBER, 1785

Wee, sleekit,[1] cow'rin', tim'rous beastie,
O, what a panic's in thy breastie!
Thou need na start awa sae hasty,
   Wi' bickering brattle![2]
I wad be laith[3] to rin an' chase thee   5
   Wi' murd'ring pattle![4]

I'm truly sorry man's dominion
Has broken Nature's social union,
An' justifies that ill opinion
   Which makes thee startle   10
At me, thy poor, earth-born companion,
   An' fellow mortal!

I doubt na, whiles,[5] but thou may thieve;
What then? poor beastie, thou maun[6]
  live!
A daimen-icker in a thrave[7]   15
    'S a sma' request:
I'll get a blessin' wi' the lave,[8]
   And never miss 't!

Thy wee-bit housie, too, in ruin!
Its silly wa's[9] the win's are strewin'!   20
An' naething, now, to big[10] a new ane,
   O' foggage[11] green!
An' bleak December's winds ensuin',
   Baith snell[12] an' keen!

1. **sleekit,** sleek.
2. **wi' bickering brattle,** with headlong scamper.
3. **laith,** loath, reluctant.
4. **pattle,** plowstaff.
5. **whiles,** sometimes.
6. **maun,** must.
7. **a daimen-icker in a thrave,** an occasional ear of grain in a sheaf.
8. **lave,** remainder.
9. **silly wa's,** feeble walls.
10. **big,** build.
11. **foggage,** moss.
12. **baith,** both. **snell,** bitter.

Thou saw the fields laid bare and waste, 25
An' weary winter comin' fast,
An cozie here, beneath the blast,
        Thou thought to dwell,
Till crash! the cruel coulter[13] passed
        Out-through thy cell. 30

That wee-bit heap o' leaves an' stibble[14]
Has cost thee mony a weary nibble!
Now thou's turned out, for a' thy trouble,
        But house or hald,[15]
To thole[16] the winter's sleety dribble, 35
        An' cranreuch[17] cauld!

But Mousie, thou art no thy lane,[18]
In proving foresight may be vain:
The best-laid schemes o' mice an' men
        Gang aft a-gley,[19] 40
An' lea'e us nought but grief an' pain,
        For promised joy.

Still thou art blest compared wi' me!
The present only toucheth thee:
But och! I backward cast my e'e 45
        On prospects drear!
An' forward though I canna see,
        I guess an' fear!

13. **coulter,** plow blade.
14. **stibble,** stubble.
15. **But house or hald,** without house or land.
16. **thole,** endure.
17. **cranreuch,** hoarfrost.
18. **no thy lane,** not alone.
19. **gang aft a-gley,** often go awry.

Scots, Wha Hae

Scots,[1] wha hae wi' Wallace[2] bled,
Scots, wham Bruce has aften led,
Welcome to your gory bed,
    Or to victorie.

Now's the day, and now's the hour;   5
See the front o' battle lour;
See approach proud Edward's[3] power—
    Chains and slaverie!

Wha will be a traitor-knave?
Wha can fill a coward's grave?   10
Wha sae base as be a slave?
    Let him turn and flee!

Wha for Scotland's King and law
Freedom's sword will strongly draw,
Freeman stand, or freeman fa',   15
    Let him follow me!

By oppression's woes and pains!
By your sons in servile chains!
We will drain our dearest veins,
    But they shall be free!   20

Lay the proud usurpers low!
Tyrants fall in every foe!
Liberty's in every blow!
    Let us do, or die!

1. In this patriotic song, Robert Bruce, the Scottish commander, is addressing his troops before a fourteenth-century battle in which the English were driven from Scotland.
2. **Wallace,** William Wallace, an earlier leader in the fight against England.
3. **Edward,** Edward II (reigned 1307–1327), the king of England who tried to reconquer Scotland.

For A' That and A' That

Is there, for honest poverty,
    That hangs his head, and a' that?
The coward slave, we pass him by,
    We dare be poor for a' that!
        For a' that, and a' that,   5
            Our toils obscure, and a' that;
        The rank is but the guinea's stamp,[1]
        The man's the gowd for a' that.

What though on hamely fare we dine,
    Wear hodden-gray[2] and a' that;   10
Gie fools their silks, and knaves their wine,
    A man's a man for a' that:
        For a' that, and a' that,
            Their tinsel show, and a' that;
        The honest man, though e'er sae poor,   15
        Is king o' men for a' that.

1. **guinea's stamp,** the impression stamped on a coin.
2. **hodden-gray,** coarse, undyed cloth.

Ye see yon birkie,[3] ca'd a lord,
   Wha struts, and stares, and a' that;
Though hundreds worship at his word,
   He's but a coof[4] for a' that: 20
      For a' that, and a' that,
        His riband, star,[5] and a' that,
      The man of independent mind,
        He looks and laughs at a' that.

A prince can mak a belted knight,   25
   A marquis, duke, and a' that;
But an honest man's aboon[6] his might,
   Guid faith he mauna fa' that![7]
      For a' that, and a' that,
        Their dignities, and a' that,   30
      The pith o' sense, and pride o' worth,
        Are higher rank than a' that.

Then let us pray that come it may,
   As come it will for a' that,
That sense and worth, o'er a' the earth,   35
   May bear the gree;[8] and a' that.
      For a' that, and a' that,
        It's coming yet, for a' that,
      That man to man the warld o'er
        Shall brothers be for a' that.   40

3. **birkie,** brisk young fellow.
4. **coof,** dolt.
5. **riband, star,** symbols worn to indicate royal favor.
6. **aboon,** above.
7. **mauna fa' that,** must not claim that.
8. **bear the gree,** win the prize.

A Red, Red Rose

O My Luve's like a red, red rose,
    That's newly sprung in June;
O My Luve's like the melodie
    That's sweetly played in tune.

As fair art thou, my bonnie lass,   5
    So deep in luve am I;
And I will luve thee still, my dear,
    Till a' the seas gang dry.

Till a' the seas gang dry, my dear,
    And the rocks melt wi' the sun: 10
O I will love thee, still, my dear,
    While the sands o' life shall run.

And fare thee weel, my only luve,
    And fare thee weel awhile!
And I will come again, my luve,   15
    Though it were ten thousand mile.

FOR UNDERSTANDING

To a Mouse

1. What careful observations of the mouse and of nature are made?
2. What advantages does the mouse have over human beings?

Scots, Wha Hae

How does Bruce attempt to sting his men into action?

For A' That and A' That

1. Notice the pronouns used in the poem. Who is speaking?
2. What in particular is resented by the speaker?

A Red, Red Rose

1. What is the situation of the speaker in the poem?
2. What does the speaker pledge to his love?

FOR INTERPRETATION

1. What is the tone of the speaker in "To a Mouse"?

2. How would Burns probably react to the statement, "Clothes make the man"?
3. Which poems seem to echo Burns's intense support of the revolutions that were taking place in the United States and in France?

FOR APPRECIATION

1. In "Scots, Wha Hae," what is the effect of the short last line of each stanza?
2. Burns wrote more popular songs than almost any other poet in English; many are still current. Identify the elements in the poems you have read that you feel make them especially singable.

Figures of Speech

1. *Anaphora* is the figure of speech in which the same word or words are repeated at the beginning of successive phrases or clauses. Point out some instances of anaphora in the Burns poems you have read.
2. Identify the *similes* in the first stanza of "A Red, Red Rose." How does the imagery of the next stanzas expand the poem's meaning beyond the banal?

William Blake   1757–1827

In his quest for personal and artistic freedom, William Blake was very much a man of the Romantic age. He needed to break away from what he called the "mind-forg'd manacles" of the neoclassic period and to escape, through imagination, into a mystic world. Blake was born into the family of a haberdasher. James Blake recognized his son's abilities while William was still a youngster. The elder Blake encouraged the boy's talents by sending him to a drawing school and then, for a time, to the school of the Royal Academy of Art. Later the young Blake was apprenticed to an engraver, where he learned a skill which he used to help support himself in adult life.

Blake was still young when he began to have strange, mystical experiences. He lifted his eyes to a tree and found it filled with angels; the eye of God met his gaze as he looked through a window; he saw the prophet Ezekiel under a tree in a field. These mystical visions are woven into his mature poetry, which is often highly personal and symbolic. Some people, like the poet Robert Southey, thought Blake mad; Blake's own wife was to say, "I have very little of Mr. Blake's company. He is always in paradise." Nevertheless, many of Blake's friends insisted that he was sane and the most industrious person they had ever known.

At twenty-four, Blake married Catherine Boucher, an illiterate woman whom he taught to read and then to draw and paint, so she could help him in his work. Two years later, some of the poet's friends arranged to have his first book printed. Entitled *Poetical Sketches*, it contained poems written by Blake between the ages of twelve and twenty. Unfortunately, the book was never offered for sale. Modern critics now recognize in some of this work the seeds of Blake's mature artistry. This was the only work of Blake's to be printed in a conventional manner, since in 1788 the poet discovered a method of engraving text and pictorial designs which he was to use in all his subsequent books. The words and decorations were engraved in wax on a copper plate; acid was then applied so

PORTRAIT OF WILLIAM BLAKE
Fitzwilliam Museum, Cambridge

that the design was left in relief. Blake then water-colored the pages printed from the copper plate. As you read Blake's poetry in this book, keep in mind that he originally intended a far richer presentation on the printed page.

Blake's poetry displays a constant balancing of opposites. His early series of poems, *Songs of Innocence* (1789), was balanced five years later in the volume, *Songs of Experience* (1794). He entitled his visionary prose satire of 1790 even more paradoxically: *The Marriage of Heaven and Hell.* "Without contraries," he wrote, "there is no progression." In "Auguries of Innocence," an unfinished poem with couplet after couplet of paradoxes, Blake stated his belief that we must recognize the integral relationships between opposites:

> Man was made for Joy and Woe
> And when this we rightly know
> Thro the World we Safely go
> Joy and Woe are woven fine
> A clothing for a soul divine.

Blake's sense of the alliance of opposites foreshadows one of the major themes in the poetry of John Keats; his fascination with the figure of the child anticipates Wordsworth. But the extreme mysticism and complex symbolism of much of his later work set him apart from the mainstream of Romanticism. Although the poems presented here are marked by an extreme (and sometimes deceptive) simplicity, much of Blake's poetry and art baffled his contemporaries; he was as little affected by their work as they by his. Today he is considered one of the most original figures in both poetry and painting.

The Lamb

Little Lamb, who made thee?
Dost thou know who made thee?
Gave thee life and bid thee feed,
By the stream and o'er the mead;
Gave thee clothing of delight,⁣ 5
Softest clothing wooly bright;
Gave thee such a tender voice,
Making all the vales rejoice!
Little Lamb, who made thee?
Dost thou know who made thee?⁣ 10

Little Lamb, I'll tell thee,
Little Lamb, I'll tell thee!
He is callèd by thy name,
For he calls himself a Lamb;
He is meek and he is mild,⁣ 15
He became a little child:
I a child and thou a lamb,
We are callèd by his name.
Little Lamb, God bless thee.
Little Lamb, God bless thee.⁣ 20

From SONGS OF INNOCENCE

The Tyger

Tyger! Tyger! burning bright
In the forests of the night,
What immortal hand or eye
Could frame thy fearful symmetry?

In what distant deeps or skies⁣ 5
Burnt the fire of thine eyes?
On what wings dare he aspire?
What the hand, dare seize the fire?

And what shoulder, and what art
Could twist the sinews of thy heart?⁣ 10
And when thy heart began to beat,
What dread hand? and what dread feet?

What the hammer? what the chain?
In what furnace was thy brain?
What the anvil? what dread grasp⁣ 15
Dare its deadly terrors clasp?

When the stars threw down their spears,
And watered heaven with their tears,
Did he smile his work to see?
Did he who made the Lamb make thee?⁣ 20

Tyger! Tyger! burning bright
In the forests of the night,
What immortal hand or eye
Dare frame thy fearful symmetry?

From SONGS OF EXPERIENCE

The Garden of Love

I went to the Garden of Love,
And saw what I never had seen:
A Chapel was built in the midst,
Where I used to play on the green.

And the gates of this Chapel were shut,   5
And "Thou shalt not" writ over the door;
So I turn'd to the Garden of Love,
That so many sweet flowers bore.

I saw it was filled with graves,
And tomb-stones where flowers should be: 10
And Priests in black gowns were walking their rounds,
And binding with briars my joys and desires.

From SONGS OF EXPERIENCE

FOR UNDERSTANDING

1. What details in "The Lamb" can be associated with the quality of innocence? What details in "The Tyger" can be associated with experience?
2. Both "The Lamb" and "The Tyger" employ the technique of the *rhetorical question*, a question to which the speaker does not really expect an answer. How many questions are there in each poem? How many answers? How is the difference between the poems in this respect important?
3. What does the speaker see when he goes to the Garden of Love?

FOR INTERPRETATION

1. In what ways are "The Lamb" and "The Tyger" both concerned with a religious issue? Can you state the issue? What is the answer in "The Lamb"? What is the answer in "The Tyger"?
2. What do you think the garden and the chapel symbolize in "The Garden of Love"?

FOR APPRECIATION

1. In "The Tyger," what is the central *metaphor* in stanzas 2–4? Is this metaphor appropriate?
2. The first and last stanzas of "The Tyger" are identical, except for one word. How is the meaning altered by this word change? What is the effect of the repetition of the first stanza?
3. Try reading "The Garden of Love" aloud. Listen to the sound of the words, to the rhymes, and to the rhythm of the stanzas. Do you notice any difference in these elements as you read the three stanzas? How might this difference be connected to Blake's notions about freedom and repression?

DEATH ON A PALE HORSE
William Blake
Fitzwilliam Museum, Cambridge

The Chimney Sweeper

When my mother died I was very young,
And my father sold me while yet my tongue
Could scarcely cry "'weep! 'weep! 'weep! 'weep!"*
So your chimneys I sweep and in soot I sleep.

There's little Tom Dacre, who cried when his head   5
That curled like a lamb's back, was shaved: so I said,
"Hush, Tom! never mind it, for when your head's
      bare,
You know that the soot cannot spoil your white
      hair."

And so he was quiet, and that very night,
As Tom was a-sleeping, he had such a sight!   10
That thousands of sweepers, Dick, Joe, Ned, and
      Jack,
Were all of them locked up in coffins of black;

And by came an Angel who had a bright key,
And he opened the coffins and set them all free;
Then down a green plain, leaping, laughing they
      run,   15
And wash in a river and shine in the Sun;

Then naked and white, all their bags left behind,
They rise upon clouds, and sport in the wind.
And the Angel told Tom, if he'd be a good boy.
He'd have God for his father and never want joy.   20

And so Tom awoke; and we rose in the dark,
And got with our bags and our brushes to work.
Though the morning was cold, Tom was happy and
      warm;
So if all do their duty, they need not fear harm.

From SONGS OF INNOCENCE

* **a small child's version of "sweep."**

The Chimney Sweeper

A little black thing among the snow,
Crying 'weep, 'weep, in notes of woe!
"Where are thy father and mother? say?"
"They are both gone up to the church to pray.

"Because I was happy upon the heath,   5
And smiled among the winter's snow,
They clothed me in the clothes of death,
And taught me to sing the notes of woe.

"And because I am happy, and dance and sing,
They think they have done me no injury,   10
And are gone to praise God and his Priest and King
Who make up a heaven of our misery."

From SONGS OF EXPERIENCE

FOR UNDERSTANDING

1. Who is the speaker in the first poem? What do we know about him? How does he feel about being a chimney sweeper?

2. In the second poem, how does the chimney sweeper feel about his situation? Whom does he blame?

FOR INTERPRETATION

1. What is the significance of Tom's dream in the first poem?

2. Is the poem from *Songs of Innocence* an attack on the practice of chimney sweeping? Or does it attack something else?

3. What is the importance of the last line of the first poem? Does it help to explain why this is a "song of innocence"?

4. The second poem has two speakers: the person who tells us about the chimney sweeper and the little boy himself. What is the emotional effect of the first speaker's description in lines 1-2?

FOR APPRECIATION

1. Consider the words in the first poem which refer to colors, either directly or indirectly. Is there any symbolic significance in Blake's color scheme?

2. *Paradox* is an apparent contradiction. How does Blake employ paradox in the second poem?

3. Identify the *irony* in the last stanza of the second poem.

William Wordsworth
Dorothy Wordsworth

1770–1850
1771–1855

William Wordsworth was born at Cockermouth in West Cumberland, on the northern edge of the Lake District. He gathered his poetic strength and vision from that sternly beautiful countryside, in the northwestern part of England. His only sister, Dorothy, was a year younger; she is coupled with the poet in this group of selections because of their extraordinarily close relationship in adult life and because Dorothy's perceptive *Journal* reveals her as a gifted writer in her own right.

Wordsworth studied at Cambridge University, traveled through Europe, returned to London, and then spent a year in France in 1791–1792. That visit was a turning point in his life, both politically and personally. At first, like many English people, he was sympathetically stirred by the ideals of the French Revolution, which had begun in 1789. But the October Massacres of 1792 sickened him; as he put it, he "yielded up moral questions in despair." He left France, leaving behind the young Annette Vallon, with whom he had fallen in love, and their infant daughter, Caroline.

When Wordsworth returned to England in his mid-twenties, almost broken in health and spirit, Dorothy came to live with him; she played a crucial role in reviving his sensitivity to nature and his eagerness to write poetry. In 1795, Wordsworth made the acquaintance of Samuel Taylor Coleridge, thus beginning one of the most celebrated and productive friendships in English literary history. The two poets established neighboring households, at first in Somerset and then in the Lake District, where Wordsworth was to remain for the rest of his life. The Wordsworths and Coleridge took long rambles in the countryside together, planning the volume which, more than any other, would announce the Romantic revolution in poetry. This was *Lyrical Ballads, with a Few Other Poems*, published in 1798 and reissued with revisions two years later. The collection included

Wordsworth's "Tintern Abbey" (one of his most important early poems) and Coleridge's *The Rime of the Ancient Mariner*. Both poems illustrate many of the principal themes and subjects of Romanticism (nature as a catalyst for the poet's emotions, the supernatural, the value of subjective meditation). In the famous *Preface* to *Lyrical Ballads*, Wordsworth set out a classic manifesto for a new poetry: one that should treat "incidents and situations from common life," in "a selection of language really spoken by men." The emphasis on poetry as "the spontaneous overflow of powerful feelings" and the conscious avoidance of a specialized and artificial poetic diction were revolutionary concepts in their time, with far-reaching consequences for nineteenth- and twentieth-century literature.

In 1798 and 1799, Wordsworth began work on a poetic self-examination which he considered a necessary preliminary to another long, philosophical poem, *The Recluse*. The preliminary poem, fittingly called *The Prelude*, turned out to be his major life's work. He completed a first version in 1805, but continually revised various sections until his death. *The Prelude* contains over 8,000 lines (four times the length of *Macbeth*) and is divided into 14 books. In its length and in some of its themes, it resembles an epic—a spiritual autobiography that attempts to find answers to questions such as, "Who am I?" "How and what did I learn from nature?" "How can I be a poet?" "What can I do when my imagination fails?" The subject-matter of this epic is thus radically different from Spenser and Milton; *The Prelude* traces, in the words of its subtitle, "the growth of a poet's mind."

In 1802, assisted by a family inheritance, Wordsworth finally married a childhood friend, Mary Hutchinson. His middle years were troubled by the deaths of his brother and two of his children, by a violent quarrel with Coleridge, and (after 1807) by an apparent waning of poetic

PORTRAIT OF WORDSWORTH
Benjamin Robert Haydon
National Portrait Gallery, London

inspiration. His political views became more conservative, and a younger generation of Romantic poets came to regard him as stale and dull. In 1813, he was appointed a county revenue collector; thirty years later, he was accorded national recognition with the title of poet laureate. Dorothy continued to live with her brother after his marriage; she kept her journal off and on for thirty years. At sixty-five, she suffered a nervous breakdown from which she never recovered. *The Prelude* was not published until after William's death; Dorothy's *Journal* was first printed toward the end of the century.

Besides the approaches and techniques signified in Wordsworth's *Preface* to the *Lyrical Ballads*, two aspects of his poetry stand out. These are his intense interest in nature and his

fascination with the figure of the child. Like Blake, Wordsworth believed that the simple innocence of the child mirrored man in his "natural state." Some of his finest poetry, notably the "Lucy" poems and the "Ode on Intimations of Immortality," is devoted to this theme. Wordsworth valued nature, not just as an escape from the ugliness of the Industrial Revolution, but for its effect as a catalyst on the human mind. It is thus a mistake to see Wordsworth primarily as a descriptive poet, great as his descriptive powers are. Nature for him is the triggering agent which inspires mental and emotional associations inside the sensitive observer. For Wordsworth it is nature that may most often inspire that "spontaneous overflow of powerful feelings" which makes for true poetry.

William Wordsworth

I Wander'd Lonely as a Cloud

I wander'd lonely as a cloud
  That floats on high o'er vales and hills,
When all at once I saw a crowd,
  A host, of golden daffodils;
Beside the lake, beneath the trees,   5
Fluttering and dancing in the breeze.

Continuous as the stars that shine
  And twinkle on the Milky Way,
They stretch'd in never-ending line
  Along the margin of a bay: 10
Ten thousand saw I at a glance,
Tossing their heads in sprightly dance.

The waves beside them danced, but they
  Out-did the sparkling waves in glee:
A poet could not but be gay,   15
  In such a jocund company:
I gazed—and gazed—but little thought
What wealth the show to me had brought:

For oft, when on my couch I lie
  In vacant or in pensive mood,   20
They flash upon that inward eye
  Which is the bliss of solitude;
And then my heart with pleasure fills,
And dances with the daffodils.

SONNETS

Composed upon Westminster Bridge

Earth has not anything to show more fair:
Dull would he be of soul who could pass by
A sight so touching in its majesty;
This City now doth, like a garment, wear
The beauty of the morning; silent, bare,   5
Ships, towers, domes, theaters, and temples lie
Open unto the fields, and to the sky;
All bright and glittering in the smokeless air.
Never did sun more beautifully steep
In his first splendor, valley, rock, or hill;   10
Ne'er saw I, never felt, a calm so deep!
The river glideth at his own sweet will:
Dear God! the very houses seem asleep;
And all that mighty heart is lying still!

It Is a Beauteous Evening

It is a beauteous evening, calm and free,
The holy time is quiet as a Nun
Breathless with adoration; the broad sun
Is sinking down in its tranquility;
The gentleness of heaven broods o'er the Sea: 5
Listen! the mighty Being is awake,
And doth with his eternal motion make
A sound like thunder—everlastingly.
Dear Child! dear Girl; that walkest with me here,
If thou appear untouched by solemn thought,   10
Thy nature is not therefore less divine:
Thou liest in Abraham's bosom* all the year;
And worshipp'st at the temple's inner shrine,
God being with thee when we know it not.

* **Abraham's bosom,** proverbial expression for heaven.

The World Is Too Much with Us

The world is too much with us; late and soon,
Getting and spending, we lay waste our powers:
Little we see in Nature that is ours;
We have given our hearts away, a sordid boon![1]
This sea that bears her bosom to the moon;   5
The winds that will be howling at all hours,
And are upgathered now like sleeping flowers;
For this, for everything, we are out of tune;
It moves us not. — Great God! I'd rather be
A Pagan suckled in a creed outworn;   10
So might I, standing on this pleasant lea,
Have glimpses that would make me less forlorn;
Have sight of Proteus rising from the sea;
Or hear old Triton blow his wreathed horn.[2]

1. **boon,** a favor.
2. **Proteus** (prō'tē əs) and **Triton** (trīt' n), sea gods in
ancient Greek mythology.

Dorothy Wordsworth

From the Journal

April 15th, 1802 Thursday—It was a threatening, misty morning, but mild. We set off after dinner from Eusemere.[1] Mrs. Clarkson went a short way with us, but turned back. The wind was furious, and we thought we must have returned. We first rested in the large boathouse, then under a furze bush opposite Mr. Clarkson's. Saw the plough going in the field. The wind seized our breath. The lake was rough. There was a boat by itself floating in the middle of the bay below Water Millock.[2] We rested again in the Water Millock Lane. The hawthorns are black and green, the birches here and there greenish, but there is yet more of purple to be seen on the twigs. We got over into a field to avoid some cows—people working. A few primroses by the roadside—woodsorrel flower, the anemone, scentless violets, strawberries, and that starry, yellow flower which Mrs. C. calls pile wort. When we were in the woods beyond Gowbarrow Park[3] we saw a few daffodils close to the waterside. We fancied that the lake had floated the seeds ashore, and that the little colony had so sprung up. But as we went along there were more and yet more; and at last, under the boughs of the trees, we saw that there was a long belt of them along the shore, about the breadth of a country turnpike road. I never saw daffodils so beautiful. They grew among the mossy stones about and about them; some rested their heads upon these stones as on a pillow for weariness; and the rest tossed and reeled and danced, and seemed as if they verily laughed with the wind, that blew upon them over the lake; they looked so gay, ever glancing, ever changing. This wind blew directly over the lake to them. There was here and there a little knot, and a few stragglers a few yards higher up; but they were so few as not to disturb the simplicity, unity, and life of that one busy highway.

[July 1802.]—On Thursday morning, 29th, we arrived in London. Wm. left me at the Inn. . . . After various troubles and disasters, we left London on Saturday morning at half-past five or six, the 31st of July. . . . We mounted the Dover coach at Charing Cross.[1] It was a beautiful morning. The city, St. Paul's,[2] with the river and a multitude of little boats, made a most beautiful sight as we crossed Westminster Bridge. The houses were not overhung by their cloud of smoke, and they were spread out endlessly, yet the sun shone so brightly, with such a fierce light, that there was even something like the purity of one of nature's own grand spectacles.

We rode on cheerfully, now with the Paris diligence[3] before us, now behind. We walked up the steep hills, a beautiful prospect everywhere, till we even reached Dover.[4] At first the rich, populous, wide-spreading, woody country about London, then the River Thames, ships sailing, chalk cliffs, trees, little villages. Afterwards Canterbury,[5] situated on a plain, rich and woody, but the city and cathedral disappointed me. . . .

We saw the castle of Dover, and the sea beyond, four or five miles before we reached D[over]. We looked at it through a long vale, the castle being upon an eminence, as it seemed, at the end of this vale, which opened to the sea. . . . It was near dark when we

---

1. **Eusemere,** the home of the Clarksons at the northern end of the lake, Ullswater.
2. **Water Millock,** a village on the shore of the lake.
3. **Gowbarrow Park,** an estate on the lake.

1. **Charing Cross,** then a stage stop; now, a railroad terminal in London.
2. **St. Paul's,** the huge domed cathedral in the heart of London, designed by Sir Christopher Wren after the Great Fire of 1666 had destroyed the earlier cathedral.
3. **diligence,** stage coach.
4. **Dover,** the port on the English channel closest to France.
5. **Canterbury,** cathedral town a few miles inland from Dover.

MORNING AMONG CONISTON FELLS CUMBERLAND
J.M.W. Turner
Tate Gallery

and the glory of the sky. The reflections in the water were more beautiful than the sky itself, purple waves brighter than precious stones, forever melting away upon the sands. The fort, a wooden building, at the entrance of the harbour at Calais, when the evening twilight was coming on, and we could not see anything of the building but its shape, which was far more distinct than in perfect daylight, seemed to be reared upon pillars of ebony, between which pillars the sea was seen in the most beautiful colours that can be conceived. Nothing in romance was ever half so beautiful. Now came in view, as the evening star sank down, and the colours of the west faded away, the two lights of England, lighted up by Englishmen in our country, to warn vessels off rocks or sands. These we used to see from the pier, when we could see no other distant objects but the clouds, the sky, and the sea itself: All was dark behind. The town of Calais seemed deserted of the light of heaven, but there was always light and life and joy upon the sea. One night, though, I shall never forget—the day had been very hot, and William and I walked alone together upon the pier. The sea was gloomy, for there was a blackness over all the sky, except when it was overspread with lightning, which often revealed to us a distant vessel. Near us the waves roared and broke against the pier, and they were interfused with greenish fiery light. The more distant sea always black and gloomy. It was also beautiful, on the calm hot night, to see the little boats row out of harbour with wings of fire, and the sail boats with the fiery track which they cut as they went along, and which closed up after them with a hundred thousand sparkles, balls, shootings and stream of glowworm light. Caroline was delighted.

reached Dover. We were told that the packet[6] was about to sail, so we went down to the custom-house in half-an-hour—had our luggage examined, etc. etc., and then we drank tea with the Honourable Mr. Knox and his tutor. We arrived at Calais[7] at four o'clock on Sunday morning, the 1st of August. We stayed in the vessel till half-past seven; then William went for letters; at about half-past eight or nine we found out Annette and C[8] chez Madame Avril dans la Rue de la Tete d'or.[9] We lodged opposite two ladies, in tolerable decent-sized rooms, but badly furnished. . . . The weather was very hot. We walked by the seashore almost every evening with Annette and Caroline, or William and I alone. I had a bad cold, and could not bathe at first, but William did. It was a pretty sight to see, as we walked upon the sands when the tide was low, perhaps a hundred people bathing about a quarter of a mile distant from us. And we had delightful walks after the heat of the day was passed away—seeing far off in the west the coast of England like a cloud crested with Dover castle, which was but like the summit of the cloud—the evening star

6. **packet,** a coastal boat that plies a regular route carrying passengers, freight and mail.
7. **Calais** (ka lā'), the French seaport town directly across the English channel from Dover.
8. **C,** Caroline, Wordsworth's French daughter, then about nine or ten years old.
9. **chez Madame Avril . . . Rue de la Tete d'or,** at the house of Madame Avril in the street of the Golden Head.

William Wordsworth

*Tintern Abbey was a great medieval church for monks of
the Cistercian order, located in the valley of the River Wye
in Monmouthshire, Wales. The abbey fell into ruins after the
Reformation in the sixteenth century. Wordsworth first visited
the site on a walking tour in the summer of 1793; he returned
almost exactly five years later.*

Lines Composed a Few Miles Above Tintern Abbey

Five years have passed; five summers, with the length
Of five long winters! and again I hear
These waters, rolling from their mountain springs
With a soft inland murmur.—Once again
Do I behold these steep and lofty cliffs,   5
That on a wild secluded scene impress
Thoughts of more deep seclusion; and connect
The landscape with the quiet of the sky.
The day is come when I again repose
Here, under this dark sycamore, and view   10
These plots of cottage ground, these orchard tufts,
Which at this season, with their unripe fruits,
Are clad in one green hue, and lose themselves
'Mid groves and copses. Once again I see
These hedgerows, hardly hedgerows, little lines   15
Of sportive wood run wild: these pastoral farms,
Green to the very door; and wreaths of smoke
Sent up, in silence, from among the trees!
With some uncertain notice, as might seem
Of vagrant dwellers in the houseless woods,   20
Or of some hermit's cave, where by his fire
The hermit sits alone.
                  These beauteous forms,
Through a long absence, have not been to me
As is a landscape to a blind man's eye;
But oft, in lonely rooms, and 'mid the din   25
Of towns and cities, I have owed to them
In hours of weariness, sensations sweet,
Felt in the blood, and felt along the heart;
And passing even into my purer mind,
With tranquil restoration—feelings, too,   30
Of unremembered pleasure: such, perhaps,

As have no slight or trivial influence
On that best portion of a good man's life,
His little, nameless, unremembered acts
Of kindness and of love. Nor less, I trust,   35
To them I may have owed another gift,
Of aspect more sublime; that blessed mood
In which the burthen of the mystery,
In which the heavy and the weary weight
Of all this unintelligible world,   40
Is lightened—that serene and blessed mood,
In which the affections gently lead us on,
Until, the breath of this corporeal frame[1]
And even the motion of our human blood
Almost suspended, we are laid asleep   45
In body, and become a living soul;
While with an eye made quiet by the power
Of harmony, and the deep power of joy,
We see into the life of things.
                                    If this
Be but a vain belief, yet, oh! how oft—   50
In darkness and amid the many shapes
Of joyless daylight; when the fretful stir
Unprofitable, and the fever of the world,
Have hung upon the beatings of my heart—
How oft, in spirit, have I turned to thee,   55
O sylvan[2] Wye! thou wanderer through the woods,
How often has my spirit turned to thee!
      And now, with gleams of half-extinguished thought,
With many recognitions dim and faint,
And somewhat of a sad perplexity,   60
The picture of the mind revives again;
While here I stand, not only with the sense
Of present pleasure, but with pleasing thoughts
That in this moment there is life and food
For future years. And so I dare to hope,   65
Though changed, no doubt, from what I was when first
I came among these hills; when like a roe
I bounded o'er the mountains, by the sides
Of the deep rivers, and the lonely streams,
Wherever nature led—more like a man   70
Flying from something that he dreads, than one
Who sought the thing he loved. For nature then
(The coarser pleasures of my boyish days,

---

1. **corporeal** (kôr pôr′ ē əl) **frame,** the body.
2. **sylvan** (sil′ vən), wooded.

TINTERN ABBEY
J.M.W. Turner
Victoria and Albert Museum

And their glad animal movements all gone by)
To me was all in all.—I cannot paint   75
What then I was. The sounding cataract
Haunted me like a passion; the tall rock,
The mountain, and the deep and gloomy wood,
Their colors and their forms, were then to me
An appetite; a feeling and a love,   80
That had no need of a remoter charm,[3]
By thought supplied, nor any interest
Unborrowed from the eye. That time is past,
And all its aching joys are now no more,
And all its dizzy raptures. Not for this   85
Faint[4] I, nor mourn nor murmur; other gifts
Have followed; for such loss, I would believe,
Abundant recompense. For I have learned
To look on nature, not as in the hour
Of thoughtless youth; but hearing oftentimes   90
The still, sad music of humanity,
Nor harsh nor grating, though of ample power
To chasten and subdue. And I have felt
A presence that disturbs me with the joy
Of elevated thoughts; a sense sublime   95
Of something far more deeply interfused,
Whose dwelling is the light of setting suns,
And the round ocean and the living air,
And the blue sky, and in the mind of man;
A motion and a spirit, that impels   100
All thinking things, all objects of all thought,
And rolls through all things. Therefore am I still
A lover of the meadows and the woods
And mountains; and of all that we behold
From this green earth; of all the mighty world   105
Of eye, and ear—both what they half create,
And what perceive; well pleased to recognize
In nature and the language of the sense,
The anchor of my purest thoughts, the nurse,
The guide, the guardian of my heart, and soul   110
Of all my moral being.
                          Nor perchance,
If I were not thus taught, should I the more
Suffer my genial[5] spirits to decay;
For thou art with me here upon the banks

---

3. **remoter charm,** an attraction apart from the scene
itself.
4. **faint,** lose heart.
5. **genial,** cheerful.

Of this fair river; thou my dearest Friend,[6]   115
My dear, dear Friend, and in thy voice I catch
The language of my former heart, and read
My former pleasures in the shooting lights
Of thy wild eyes. Oh! yet a little while
May I behold in thee what I was once,   120
My dear, dear Sister! and this prayer I make,
Knowing that Nature never did betray
The heart that loved her; 'tis her privilege,
Through all the years of this our life, to lead
From joy to joy; for she can so inform   125
The mind that is within us, so impress
With quietness and beauty, and so feed
With lofty thoughts, that neither evil tongues,
Rash judgments, nor the sneers of selfish men,
Nor greetings where no kindness is, nor all   130
The dreary intercourse of daily life,
Shall e'er prevail against us, or disturb
Our cheerful faith, that all which we behold
Is full of blessings. Therefore let the moon
Shine on thee in thy solitary walk;   135
And let the misty mountain winds be free
To blow against thee: and, in after years,
When these wild ecstasies shall be matured
Into a sober pleasure; when thy mind
Shall be a mansion for all lovely forms,   140
Thy memory be as a dwelling place
For all sweet sounds and harmonies; oh! then,
If solitude, or fear, or pain, or grief,
Should be thy portion, with what healing thoughts
Of tender joy wilt thou remember me,   145
And these my exhortations! Nor, perchance—
If I should be where I no more can hear
Thy voice, nor catch from thy wild eyes these gleams
Of past existence—wilt thou then forget
That on the banks of this delightful stream   150
We stood together; and that I, so long
A worshiper of Nature, hither came
Unwearied in that service: rather say
With warmer love—oh! with far deeper zeal
Of holier love. Nor wilt thou then forget,   155
That after many wanderings, many years
Of absence, these steep woods and lofty cliffs,
And this green pastoral landscape, were to me
More dear, both for themselves and for thy sake!

6. **Friend,** Wordsworth's sister, Dorothy.

FOR UNDERSTANDING

1. What details in "I Wandered Lonely as a Cloud" seem to come from Dorothy Wordsworth's *Journal*? What is different in the *Journal*? What is in the poem that is not in the *Journal*?

2. What is the speaker's dominant emotion in the sonnet "Composed upon Westminster Bridge"?

3. In "It Is a Beauteous Evening," why does the speaker call the child's nature "divine"?

4. What does the poet regret in "The World Is Too Much with Us"? What does he wish in the second part of the sonnet?

5. In lines 22–49 of "Tintern Abbey," what has been the effect on the poet of his memories of this scene?

6. How has the poet changed in the past five years (lines 58–111)?

7. What is the poet's hope in the concluding section of "Tintern Abbey" (lines 137–159)?

FOR INTERPRETATION

1. How does Dorothy Wordsworth's *Journal* help to explain the sonnet, "It Is a Beauteous Evening"?

2. What do the classical allusions in "The World Is Too Much with Us" suggest about Wordsworth's attitude toward classical mythology?

3. What do the sonnets suggest about Wordsworth's religious attitudes?

4. How does "Tintern Abbey" illustrate Wordsworth's claim in the *Preface* to *Lyrical Ballads* that poetry "takes its origin from emotion recollected in tranquillity"?

FOR APPRECIATION

1. What is the form of "Composed upon Westminster Bridge"? Give the rhyme scheme. What is the *metonymy* in the last line?

2. In "It Is a Beauteous Evening," why is the word "Being" capitalized in line 6? What does this word connote? How are the images in lines 2 and 3 connected with the last lines?

3. What is the verse form of "Tintern Abbey"? In what way can it be said that the poem's structure is articulated in *verse paragraphs*? What is the effect of the many *enjambements* (run-on lines) in the poem?

4. Does Wordsworth, in your judgment, fulfill his intention to write poetry "in a selection of language really spoken by men"?

COMPOSITION

After a long interval the second visit to a place can often spark memories and self-examination, as in "Tintern Abbey." Select an incident from your personal experience in which the sight of a place or object sparked recollections and associations. Write a brief essay explaining the circumstances and significance of your experience; identify as precisely as you can the emotions prompted by your memories.

Samuel Taylor Coleridge   1772–1834

Born the tenth child of a poor vicar, Samuel Taylor Coleridge wandered the fields of Devon in his youth, imagining himself as St. George slaying the dragon as he slashed off the tops of weeds with a stick. At five, he had already read the *Bible*, *The Arabian Nights*, and *Robinson Crusoe*. After his father's death he was sent at the age of ten to Christ's Hospital in London, a famous charity school. Here he met Charles Lamb and formed a friendship that lasted a lifetime. As a schoolboy, Coleridge was described as dreamy, enthusiastic, and extraordinarily precocious. In 1791 he entered Jesus College, Cambridge, where he displayed both the critical insight and erratic impulsiveness that characterized his whole life. Disenchanted with Cambridge, he fled to London and enlisted in the Light Dragoons; his abysmal ineptness as a cavalryman and his brother's influence gained him a discharge. He returned to college, but at twenty-two left Cambridge without a degree and joined with the poet Robert Southey in a plan to found a utopian community on the banks of the Susquehanna River in Pennsylvania. It was to be called a "pantisocracy" (equal rule by all). The marriages of both men and their lack of money soon aborted this project.

In the summer of 1795 Coleridge met Wordsworth, and the two poets began an intensely productive (if tempestuous) friendship. Coleridge and Wordsworth were neighbors in Dorset and Somerset. When Wordsworth and his sister Dorothy took up residence at Dove Cottage in the Lake District in 1799, Coleridge and his wife moved to Keswick (thirteen miles away) to be near them. The poets jointly published *Lyrical Ballads* in 1798. Wordsworth was to demonstrate that real poetry lay in commonplace situations and events, while Coleridge was to illustrate the common emotions of human beings through supernatural subjects. To this end Coleridge's *The Rime of the Ancient Mariner*, the major work to be found at the end of this unit (page 568), introduced the volume.

Although Coleridge continued to write

SAMUEL TAYLOR COLERIDGE
Peter Vandyke
National Portrait Gallery, London

poetry throughout his life, his best work was completed by 1802: the *Rime*, "Frost at Midnight," "Kubla Khan," "Christabel," and "Dejection: An Ode." In his later years, plagued by the ill health which led to an addiction to opium, he concentrated on lecturing and the writing of philosophical tracts. The central document of Coleridge's literary criticism is his *Biographia Literaria* (1817), a sprawling, often disorganized, notebook of his personal reactions to the great classics of literature and of his theories of the imagination. This work, together with Coleridge's lectures on Shakespeare, establish him as one of the great poet-critics in the language, in the tradition of Sir Philip Sidney, John Dryden, Alexander Pope, and Samuel Johnson.

Coleridge tried valiantly to overcome his dependence on opium but failed. His last years were spent at Highgate, north of London, in the home of his friend Dr. Gillman. His rooms there became the gathering place for the literati of London. When he died Charles Lamb said, "Never saw I his likeness, nor probably the world can see again." And Wordsworth, with whom Coleridge had quarreled and then been reconciled, declared he was "the only wonderful man I ever knew."

COLERIDGE'S REMARKS ABOUT "KUBLA KHAN"

In the summer of the year 1797 [Coleridge], then in ill health, had retired to a lonely farmhouse between Porlock and Linton, on the Exmoor confines of Somerset and Devonshire. In consequence of a slight indisposition, an anodyne had been prescribed, from the effects of which he fell asleep in his chair at the moment that he was reading the following sentence, or words of the same substance, in *Purchas's Pilgrimage.** "Here the Khan Kubla commanded a palace to be built, and a stately garden thereunto. And thus ten miles of fertile ground were inclosed with a wall." The author continued for about three hours in a profound sleep, at least of the external senses, during which time he has the most vivid confidence that he could not have composed less than from two to three hundred lines; if that indeed can be called composition in which all the images rose up before him as *things*, with a parallel production of the correspondent expressions, without any sensation or consciousness of effort. On awaking he appeared to himself to have a distinct recollection of the whole, and taking his pen, ink, and paper, instantly and eagerly wrote down the lines that are here preserved. At this moment he was unfortunately called out by a person on business from Porlock, and detained by him above an hour, and on his return to his room, found, to his no small surprise and mortification, that though he still retained some vague and dim recollection of the general purport of the vision, yet, with the exception of some eight or ten scattered lines and images, all the rest had passed away like the images on the surface of a stream into which a stone has been cast. . . .

* A book by Samuel Purchas, published in 1613.

Kubla Khan

Or a Vision in a Dream. A Fragment

In Xanadu[1] did Kubla Khan[2]
A stately pleasure dome decree:
Where Alph,[3] the sacred river, ran
Through caverns measureless to man
   Down to a sunless sea.
So twice five miles of fertile ground
With walls and towers were girdled round:

        5

1. **Xanadu** (zan′ a dü), name taken from *Purchas's Pilgrimage*, of Kubla Khan's city.
2. **Kubla Khan** (kü′ blə kän), founder of the Mongol dynasty in China in the thirteenth century.
3. **Alph,** perhaps a combination of *alpha*, the first letter of the Greek alphabet, and Alpheus, a river god of classical mythology.

And there were gardens bright with sinuous rills,
Where blossomed many an incense-bearing tree;
And here were forests ancient as the hills,   10
Enfolding sunny spots of greenery.

But oh! that deep romantic chasm which slanted
Down the green hill athwart a cedarn cover![4]
A savage place! as holy and enchanted
As e'er beneath a waning moon was haunted   15
By woman wailing for her demon lover!
And from this chasm, with ceaseless turmoil seething,
As if this earth in fast thick pants were breathing,
A mightly fountain momently was forced:
Amid whose swift half-intermitted burst   20
Huge fragments vaulted like rebounding hail,
Or chaffy grain beneath the thresher's flail:
And 'mid these dancing rocks at once and ever
It flung up momently the sacred river.
Five miles meandering with a mazy motion   25
Through wood and dale the sacred river ran,
Then reached the caverns measureless to man,
And sank in tumult to a lifeless ocean:
And 'mid this tumult Kubla heard from far
Ancestral voices prophesying war!   30
    The shadow of the dome of pleasure
    Floated midway on the waves;
    Where was heard the mingled measure
    From the fountain and the caves.
It was a miracle of rare device,   35
A sunny pleasure dome with caves of ice!

    A damsel with a dulcimer[5]
    In a vision once I saw:
    It was an Abyssinian[6] maid,
    And on her dulcimer she played,   40
    Singing of Mount Abora.[7]
    Could I revive within me

4. **athwart . . . cover,** across a thick covering of cedar trees.
5. **dulcimer** (dul' sə mər), a harplike instrument.
6. **Abyssinian** (ab ə sin' ē ən), literally, Ethiopian. Abyssinia was frequently mentioned in legend as a possible site for the Biblical Garden of Eden.
7. **Mount Abora,** perhaps a version of Milton's Mount Amara (*Paradise Lost* IV.280–282), referred to in his description of the Garden of Eden.

Her symphony and song,
To such a deep delight 'twould win me,
That with music loud and long,   45
I would build that dome in air,
That sunny dome! those caves of ice!
And all who heard should see them there,
And all should cry, Beware! Beware!
His flashing eyes, his floating hair!   50
Weave a circle round him thrice,
And close your eyes with holy dread,
For he on honey-dew hath fed,
And drunk the milk of Paradise.

FOR UNDERSTANDING

1. What does the emperor build in the first stanza of the poem?
2. What discordant note is struck toward the end of the second stanza?
3. How does the poet envision himself in the last stanza?

FOR INTERPRETATION

1. What atmosphere is created in the first stanza of "Kubla Khan"? How do the images and rhythm of the lines contribute to that feeling?
2. What do you think Coleridge is celebrating in this poem?
3. In the subtitle, Coleridge calls this poem "a vision in a dream" and "a fragment." Do you agree with either or both of these descriptions? Why? Is this really an unfinished poem?

FOR APPRECIATION

1. How is the third stanza connected to the previous two stanzas?
2. Point out the instances of *alliteration* and *assonance* in the third stanza.

LANGUAGE AND VOCABULARY

Identify the meaning of the following words in the poem.
1. girdled **2.** sinuous **3.** chasm **4.** flail **5.** damsel

George Gordon, Lord Byron   1788–1824

George Gordon, Lord Byron led as romantic a life as the heroes of his poetry. The son of a dissolute aristocrat who went through the fortunes of his two wives, Bryon was born after his mother had separated from Captain John Byron. Since her funds were limited, she chose to live in Aberdeen near relatives. A difficult person and a very poor mother, she alternately pampered and bullied her son; they were happiest when apart.

Lame from birth with a clubfoot, Byron was acutely sensitive to his deformity and tried hard to compensate for it with success in athletics. He became a champion swimmer and enough of a cricket player to participate creditably. When he was ten, his great uncle died and Byron inherited his title and the estates. He was then sent to Harrow, a private boys' school near London, and to Cambridge—where he was notorious for keeping a bear in his rooms! After receiving his inheritance and being seated in the House of Lords, Byron went abroad for two years. He and a friend traveled through Italy, Greece, Albania, Spain and Portugal, and the Middle East. What he learned of the manners and the beauties of these countries he translated into poetry. The first two cantos of *Childe Harold's Pilgrimage* record many of the experiences of the first year of that trip. These cantos were published in 1812, shortly after Byron returned to England, to enormous acclaim. As Byron said, "I awoke one morning and found myself famous." In 1816 and 1818 Byron added further cantos, extending the poem to a length of roughly six thousand lines. He used the form of the Spenserian, nine-line stanza, deliberately juxtaposing the medieval aura of a fictional hero's pilgrimage through Europe with the more modern, Romantic quest for authentic experience. Part of the poem's immense appeal was due to its air of exoticism. Another source of its popularity was the widespread suspicion that the hero, Harold, was really the dashing Byron himself—handsome, independent, irresistible to women. Indeed, in

GEORGE GORDON BYRON
Richard Westall
National Portrait Gallery, London

the later cantos, Byron dropped the persona of Harold and spoke directly in the first person.

The identification of Byron's private life with his narrative poetry was significant. Whatever the truth, Byron's life and work merged to provide Romanticism with a hero-figure it had previously lacked. Often called the "Byronic hero," this figure is an inextricable mixture of good and evil, selflessness and sin; isolated, rebellious, and self-reliant, he is passionate and often erotically fascinating. The widespread influence of this hero-type in England and in Europe is illustrated by such diverse works as Emily Brontë's novel, *Wuthering Heights* (1847), the music of composers such as Beethoven, and the paintings of the French Romantic master, Eugène Delacroix.

Like the heroes of his poetry, Byron in real life was besieged by women. He seems to have married Anne Isabella Milbanke almost in desperation. She was a pretty, intellectual, somewhat prissy woman who fancied she could "reform" him. Their marriage was stormy; after only a year Lady Byron fled with their baby daughter and obtained a legal separation. In 1813 the poet became reacquainted with his half-sister, Augusta Leigh. Whatever the foundation for the rumor that he had incestuous relations with her, there is no doubt of his strong affection. When his wife left him, Byron was ostracized by the very society which had hailed him; he left England in April 1816, never to return. After further travels in Europe, he took a villa in Italy near that of his friend Shelley (the only Romantic poet he respected) and began intense work on the long poem that would be his greatest work, *Don Juan*. This epic satire (some fifteen thousand lines) was based on the notorious legends surrounding the Spanish rake, Don Juan, whose life of roguery was cut short when the father of one of his victims, Doña Anna, exacted vengeance from beyond the grave. Typically, Byron's treatment of the legend was unconventional. In content, he shaped the figure of Don Juan to make him more passive than aggressive; in form, he blended an antique stanza (ottava rima) with brilliantly satirical effects. Byron intended the work as an attack against the abuses of civilization, but it has often been misinterpreted as amoral or nihilistic.

Byron's countrymen admired his poetry, but ridiculed his political conviction that tyranny and oppression should be attacked. Yet it was this strong belief that made him popular in Europe. In 1823, having already kindled European enthusiasm for the Greek struggle for independence from the Turks, Byron went to Greece. Under spartan conditions, he helped to train the insurgent troops and displayed surprising leadership. Shortly after his thirty-sixth birthday he died from a series of high fevers.

Of himself, Byron once said to a friend, "I am so changeable, being everything by turns and nothing long—I am such a strange melange of good and evil, that it would be difficult to describe me. . . . There are but two sentiments to which I am constant—a strong love of liberty and a detestation of cant." Upon his death, the Greeks sent his body to England, but buried his heart in the land he had struggled to liberate.

The night before writing this poem, Byron had met his beautiful young cousin by marriage, Mrs. Wilmot, who was dressed in a black gown of mourning, brightened by spangles.

She Walks in Beauty

She walks in beauty, like the night
  Of cloudless climes and starry skies;
And all that's best of dark and bright
  Meet in her aspect* and her eyes:
Thus mellowed to that tender light   5
  Which Heaven to gaudy day denies.

*aspect, facial expression.

*Constable painted this masterpiece of English romanticism on his honey-
moon in 1816. He summed up his feelings at the time with this passage from
Childe Harold:*
*"There is a pleasure in the pathless woods,/There is a rapture on the lonely
shore,/There is society where none intrudes,/By the deep sea, and music in its
roar. . . . "*

WEYMOUTH BAY
John Constable
National Gallery, London

One shade the more, one ray the less,
　Had half impaired the nameless grace
Which waves in every raven tress,
　Or softly lightens o'er her face;　　　　10
Where thoughts serenely sweet express,
　How pure, how dear their dwelling place.

And on that cheek, and o'er that brow,
　So soft, so calm, yet eloquent,
The smiles that win, the tints that glow,　　15
　But tell of days in goodness spent,
A mind at peace with all below,
　A heart whose love is innocent!

from **Childe Harold's Pilgrimage**

Waterloo[1]

There was a sound of revelry by night,
And Belgium's capital had gathered then
Her Beauty and her Chivalry, and bright
The lamps shone o'er fair women and brave men;
A thousand hearts beat happily; and when   5
Music arose with its voluptuous swell,
Soft eyes looked love to eyes which spake again,
And all went merry as a marriage bell—
But hush! hark! a deep sound strikes like a rising knell!

Did ye not hear it?—No; 'twas but the wind,   10
Or the car rattling o'er the stony street;
On with the dance! let joy be unconfined;
No sleep till morn, when Youth and Pleasure meet
To chase the glowing Hours with flying feet—
But hark!—that heavy sound breaks in once more,   15
As if the clouds its echo would repeat;
And nearer, clearer, deadlier than before!
Arm! Arm! it is—it is—the cannon's opening roar!

Within a windowed niche of that high hall
Sate Brunswick's fated chieftain;[2] he did hear   20
That sound the first amidst the festival,
And caught its tone with Death's prophetic ear;
And when they smiled because he deemed it near,
His heart more truly knew that peal too well
Which stretched his father on a bloody bier,   25
And roused the vengeance blood alone could quell:
He rushed into the field, and, foremost fighting, fell.

Ah! then and there was hurrying to and fro,
And gathering tears, and tremblings of distress,
And cheeks all pale, which but an hour ago   30

1. **Waterloo,** the English defeated Napoleon (after nearly twenty years of sporadic conflicts) on June 15, 1815, outside the little Belgian village of Waterloo. The Duchess of Richmond gave a famous ball in Brussels on the eve of the battle.
2. **Brunswick's fated chieftain,** the Duke of Brunswick, a nephew of King George III, was to be killed in the opening battle, just as his father had been killed in an earlier battle against Napoleon.

Blushed at the praise of their own loveliness;
And there were sudden partings, such as press
The life from out young hearts, and choking sighs
Which ne'er might be repeated; who could guess
If ever more should meet those mutual eyes,   35
Since upon night so sweet such awful morn could rise!

And there was mounting in hot haste: the steed,
The mustering squadron, and the clattering car,
Went pouring forward with impetuous speed,
And swiftly forming in the ranks of war;   40
And the deep thunder peal on peal afar;
And near, the beat of the alarming drum
Roused up the soldier ere the morning star;
While thronged the citizens with terror dumb,
Or whispering, with white lips—"The foe! They come! they come." 45

Apostrophe to the Ocean

There is a pleasure in the pathless woods,
There is a rapture on the lonely shore,
There is society where none intrudes,
By the deep sea, and music in its roar:
I love not Man the less, but Nature more,   5
From these our interviews, in which I steal
From all I may be, or have been before,
To mingle with the Universe, and feel
What I can ne'er express, yet can not all conceal.

Roll on, thou deep and dark blue Ocean—roll!   10
Ten thousand fleets sweep over thee in vain;
Man marks the earth with ruin—his control
Stops with the shore; upon the watery plain
The wrecks are all thy deed, nor doth remain
A shadow of man's ravage, save his own,   15
When, for a moment, like a drop of rain,
He sinks into thy depths with bubbling groan,
Without a grave, unknelled, uncoffined, and unknown.

His steps are not upon thy paths—thy fields
Are not a spoil for him—thou dost arise   20
And shake him from thee; the vile strength he wields

For earth's destruction thou dost all despise,
Spurning him from thy bosom to the skies,
And send'st him, shivering in thy playful spray
And howling, to his Gods, where haply lies   25
His petty hope in some near port or bay,
And dashest him again to earth—there let him lay.[1]

The armaments which thunderstrike the walls
Of rock-built cities, bidding nations quake
And monarchs tremble in their capitals,   30
The oak leviathans,[2] whose huge ribs make
Their clay creator[3] the vain title take
Of lord of thee, and arbiter of war—
These are thy toys, and, as the snowy flake,
They melt into thy yeast of waves, which mar   35
Alike the Armada's pride or spoils of Trafalgar.[4]

Thy shores are empires, changed in all save thee—
Assyria, Greece, Rome, Carthage, what are they?
Thy waters washed them power while they were free,
And many a tyrant since; their shores obey   40
The stranger, slave, or savage; their decay
Has dried up realms to deserts—not so thou,
Unchangeable save to thy wild waves' play;
Time writes no wrinkle on thine azure brow—
Such as creation's dawn beheld, thou rollest now.   45

Thou glorious mirror, where the Almighty's form
Glasses[5] itself in tempests; in all time,
Calm or convulsed—in breeze, or gale, or storm,
Icing the pole, or in the torrid clime
Dark-heaving—boundless, endless, and sublime—   50
The image of Eternity—the throne
Of the Invisible; even from out thy slime
The monsters of the deep are made; each zone
Obeys thee; thou goest forth, dread, fathomless, alone.

1. **lay,** a note in Byron's proof suggests that he intentionally erred in grammar for the sake of the rhyme.
2. **leviathans** (lə vī′ ə thənz), monstrous sea creatures, mentioned in the Bible. Here the word is used metaphorically for "ships."
3. **clay creator,** human beings.
4. **Armada's pride . . . spoils of Trafalgar,** the Spanish Armada, bent on an invasion of England, was defeated in 1588; at the battle of Trafalgar, Lord Nelson defeated the French and Spanish fleets in 1805. Note that Trafalgar (trə fal′ gər) must be accented here on the first syllable for the sake of the meter.
5. **glasses,** mirrors.

And I have loved thee, Ocean! and my joy   55
Of youthful sports was on thy breast to be
Borne, like thy bubbles, onward: from a boy
I wantoned with thy breakers—they to me
Were a delight; and if the freshening sea
Made them a terror—'twas a pleasing fear,   60
For I was as it were a child of thee,
And trusted to thy billows far and near,
And laid my hand upon thy mane—as I do here.

On Fame

What are the hopes of man? Old Egypt's King
   Cheops* erected the first pyramid
And largest, thinking it was just the thing
   To keep his memory whole, and mummy hid;

But somebody or other rummaging,   5
   Burglariously broke his coffin's lid:
Let not a monument give you or me hopes,
Since not a pinch of dust remains of Cheops.

*__Cheops__ (ke′ ops), second pharaoh of the fourth dynasty of Egypt and builder of the great pyramid at Giza.

In this brief poem, Byron seems ironically both to be praising and mocking Romantic ideas. A more poignant irony is that Byron himself lost his life in Greece only four years later, following the very course which the poem describes.

When a Man Hath No Freedom to Fight for at Home

When a man hath no freedom to fight for at home,
   Let him combat for that of his neighbors;
Let him think of the glories of Greece and of Rome,
   And get knocked on his head for his labors.

To do good to mankind is the chivalrous plan,   5
   And is always as nobly requited;
Then battle for freedom wherever you can,
   And, if not shot or hanged, you'll get knighted.

FOR UNDERSTANDING

She Walks in Beauty

1. What kind of night is evoked in this poem?
2. What qualities of character does Byron attribute to the woman?

Waterloo

1. What is the scene in the first stanza?
2. What sound disturbs the ball?
3. What fate awaits the Duke of Brunswick?

Apostrophe to the Ocean

1. What quality of the ocean is dominant throughout the poem?
2. How does Byron connect the ocean with famous historical empires in lines 37–45?
3. What personal memory does Byron record in the last stanza?

On Fame

What happened to the coffin of Cheops?

When a Man Hath No Freedom . . .

What course of action does the poem urge?

FOR INTERPRETATION

She Walks in Beauty

Compare the description of nature in this poem with Wordsworth's sonnet "It Is a Beauteous Evening" (page 503). Which poem seems to express the speaker's personal feeling more forcefully?

Waterloo

Which universally human emotions does Byron appear to be stressing in these stanzas?

Apostrophe to the Ocean

Byron personifies the ocean, giving it some of the attributes of the so-called "Byronic hero." What characteristics does he mention?

On Fame

What moral does Byron draw from the historical allusion to the Egyptian King Cheops?

When a Man Hath No Freedom . . .

What is the ironic effect of the last line in each stanza?

FOR APPRECIATION

Waterloo

1. What is the function of the third stanza within the selection as a whole?
2. Byron masterfully exploits imagery of noise in this selection. Identify the effects he achieves with such imagery in the first and the fifth stanzas.

Apostrophe to the Ocean

1. What is the rhyme scheme of the stanzas? What effects does Byron achieve with the longer ninth line of each stanza?
2. Which stanza particularly suggests the actual sounds of the ocean?
3. Explain the pun on "mane" in the last line.

On Fame

Identify the elements of Byron's diction that contribute to the pointed irony of this short poem.

When a Man Hath No Freedom . . .

Identify the meter of the poem. How does it enhance the satiric tone?

Percy Bysshe Shelley   1792–1822

The eldest child of a wealthy, titled family in Sussex, Percy Bysshe Shelley became an outspoken rebel against the religious and political beliefs of the class into which he was born. Generous and kind by nature, he was oblivious to the injury which his radical ideas and actions caused his family. Sent to Eton at twelve, Shelley was already a baffling mix of contrasts: by turns sensitive and moody, rebellious and unruly. His schoolmates called him "mad Shelley" or "Shelley the atheist." In 1810 he entered University College, Oxford; but his career as an undergraduate was sharply curtailed six months later when he was expelled for authoring a pamphlet called *The Necessity of Atheism.* The following year Harriet Westbrook, one of his sister's friends who had fallen in love with him, wrote to beg his help against the persecution of her father, who was insisting that the girl return to school. Shelley, not untypically, responded by eloping with Harriet to Scotland, where they were married. For almost three years the young couple moved restlessly from place to place in Europe, living on an allowance reluctantly doled out by their fathers.

Returning to London in 1813, Shelley became a disciple of William Godwin, a radical political and social philosopher. He fell in love with Mary, Godwin's brilliant and beautiful seventeen-year-old daughter. Since he believed that cohabitation without love was immoral, Shelley abandoned Harriet and fled with Mary to France; in grief and despair, Harriet committed suicide two years later.

Shelley's shock and guilt were only partially healed by his later marriage to Mary Godwin. The English courts denied him custody of his first two children by Harriet. Clara and William, his two children by Mary, both died young in 1818–1819. The couple settled into a life of exile, finally making their home in Pisa in 1820. In spite of the grim, dark quality of Shelley's life up to this period, he wrote some of his greatest poetry: the play *Prometheus Bound,* the lyric elegy "Adonais" on the death of John Keats, and the great critical essay "A Defense of Poetry."

PERCY BYSSHE SHELLEY
Amelia Curran
National Portrait Gallery, London

Where Byron had created a hero-figure for a younger, second generation of Romantic poets, Shelley sought ideals of beauty, goodness, and love in the history of ancient civilizations, especially that of Greece. Many of his best works combine philosophical idealism (shaped by his reading of Plato) with Greek heroic archetypes, such as the rebel Prometheus and the suffering, pastoral hero Adonis. Of course the Romantic fascination with Greece (sometimes called Romantic Hellenism) was not restricted to Shelley. His friend Byron actually fought in the Greek war for independence, and Keats's works display extensive knowledge of classical mythology. But Shelley's faith in a system of moral and aesthetic absolutes (which may be contrasted with Keats's praise of "negative capability" in the poet) seemed especially compatible with an interpretation of ancient Greek culture. Just as many eighteenth-century poets had idealized the concepts of clarity, balance, and order that they saw in ancient Rome, the Romantics tended to exaggerate the quests for beauty, truth, and freedom that they thought typical of ancient Athens.

Shelley's last two years of life were his happiest. A group of literary friends in Pisa surrounded the couple; a second son, Percy William, was born; Mary Shelley, who had published *Frankenstein* in 1818, continued to write; and they enjoyed visits from Byron. But Shelley's sudden death was near. He and a friend sailed their new boat, the *Don Juan,* across the Gulf of Spezia in July, 1822. A violent storm capsized the boat and both men were drowned. The recovered bodies were burned on the shore and Shelley's ashes were placed near the grave of Keats in the Protestant Cemetery in Rome. Writing to a friend, Byron (himself to die two years later) declared, "You were all brutally mistaken about Shelley, who was, without exception, the *best* and least selfish man I ever knew. I never knew one who was not a beast in comparison."

Ozymandias

I met a traveler from an antique land
Who said: Two vast and trunkless legs of stone
Stand in the desert. Near them, on the sand,
Half sunk, a shattered visage lies, whose frown,
And wrinkled lip, and sneer of cold command,   5
Tell that its sculptor well those passions read
Which yet survive, stamped on these lifeless things,
The hand that mocked them and the heart that fed:
And on the pedestal these words appear:
"My name is Ozymandias,* king of kings: 10
Look on my works, ye Mighty, and despair!"
Nothing beside remains. Round the decay
Of that colossal wreck, boundless and bare
The lone and level sands stretch far away.

* **Ozymandias** (oz i man′ dē əs), another version of the name Rameses. Rameses II, pharaoh of Egypt in the thirteenth century B.C., was a famous builder of palaces and temples; he left behind a number of colossal statues of himself.

To a Sky-Lark

Hail to thee, blithe spirit!
  Bird thou never wert,
That from heaven, or near it,
  Pourest thy full heart
In profuse strains of unpremeditated art. 5

ARTIST MOVED BY THE MAGNITUDE OF ANTIQUE FRAGMENTS
Henry Fuseli
Kunsthaus, Zurich

    Higher still and higher
      From the earth thou springest
   Like a cloud of fire;
      The blue deep thou wingest,
And singing still dost soar, and soaring ever singest.   10

    In the golden lightning
      Of the sunken sun,
   O'er which clouds are bright'ning,
      Thou dost float and run;
Like an unbodied[1] joy whose race is just begun.   15

1. **unbodied,** disembodied.

The pale purple even[2]
  Melts around thy flight;
Like a star of heaven,
  In the broad daylight
Thou art unseen, but yet I hear thy shrill delight,   20

Keen as are the arrows
  Of that silver sphere,[3]
Whose intense lamp narrows
  In the white dawn clear,
Until we hardly see—we feel that it is there.   25

All the earth and air
  With thy voice is loud,
As, when night is bare,
  From one lonely cloud
The mood rains out her beams, and Heaven is overflowed.   30

What thou art we know not;
  What is most like thee?
From rainbow clouds there flow not
  Drops so bright to see,
As from thy presence showers a rain of melody.   35

Like a Poet hidden
  In the light of thought,
Singing hymns unbidden,
  Till the world is wrought
To sympathy with hopes and fears it heeded not: 40

Like a highborn maiden
  In a palace tower,
Soothing her love-laden
  Soul in secret hour
With music sweet as love, which overflows her bower: 45

Like a glowworm golden
  In a dell of dew,
Scattering unbeholden
  Its aerial hue
Among the flowers and grass, which screen it from the view!   50

2. **even,** evening.
3. **silver sphere,** the morning star.

Like a rose embowered
   In its own green leaves,
By warm winds deflowered,[4]
   Till the scent it gives
Makes faint with too much sweet those heavy-winged thieves.[5] **55**

Sound of vernal showers
   On the twinkling grass,
Rain-awakened flowers,
   All that ever was
Joyous, and clear, and fresh, thy music doth surpass: **60**

Teach us, Sprite or Bird,
   What sweet thoughts are thine;
I have never heard
   Praise of love or wine
That panted forth a flood of rapture so divine. **65**

Chorus Hymeneal,[6]
   Or triumphal chant,
Matched with thine, would be all
   But an empty vaunt,
A thing wherein we feel there is some hidden want. **70**

What objects are the fountains[7]
   Of thy happy strain?
What fields, or waves, or mountains?
   What shapes of sky or plain?
What love of thine own kind? what ignorance of pain? **75**

With thy clear keen joyance
   Languor cannot be;
Shadow of annoyance
   Never came near thee;
Thou lovest—but ne'er knew love's sad satiety. **80**

Waking or asleep.
   Thou of death must deem[8]
Things more true and deep
   Than we mortals dream,
Or how could thy notes flow in such a crystal stream? **85**

4. **deflowered,** fully opened.
5. **thieves,** referring to the winds.
6. **Chorus Hymeneal** (hī′ mə nē′ əl), marriage song.
Hymen was the Greek god of marriage.
7. **fountains,** sources, inspiration.
8. **deem,** know.

We look before and after,
    And pine for what is not;
Our sincerest laughter
    With some pain is fraught;
Our sweetest songs are those that tell of saddest thought.   **90**

Yet if we could scorn
    Hate, and pride, and fear;
If we were things born
    Not to shed a tear,
I know not how thy joy we should come near.   **95**

Better than all measures
    Of delightful sound,
Better than all treasures
    That in books are found,
Thy skill to poet were, thou scorner of the ground!   **100**

Teach me half the gladness
    That thy brain must know,
Such harmonious madness
    From my lips would flow,
The world should listen then, as I am listening now.   **105**

Ode to the West Wind

I

O wild West Wind, thou breath of Autumn's being,
Thou, from whose unseen presence the leaves dead
Are driven, like ghosts from an enchanter fleeing,

Yellow, and black, and pale, and hectic red,
Pestilence-stricken multitudes: O thou,   **5**
Who chariotest to their dark wintry bed

The winged seeds, where they lie cold and low,
Each like a corpse within its grave, until
Thine azure sister of the Spring shall blow

Her clarion o'er the dreaming earth, and fill   **10**
(Driving sweet buds like flocks to feed in air)
With living hues and odors plain and hill:

Wild Spirit, which art moving everywhere;
Destroyer and preserver; hear, oh, hear!

2

Thou on whose stream, mid the steep sky's commotion,   15
Loose clouds like earth's decaying leaves are shed,
Shook from the tangled boughs of Heaven and Ocean,

Angels of rain and lightning: there are spread
On the blue surface of thine aëry surge,
Like the bright hair uplifted from the head   20

Of some fierce Maenad,[1] even from the dim verge
Of the horizon to the zenith's height,
The locks of the approaching storm. Thou dirge

Of the dying year, to which this closing night
Will be the dome of a vast sepulcher,   25
Vaulted with all thy congregated might

Of vapors, from whose solid atmosphere
Black rain, and fire, and hail will burst: oh hear!

3

Thou who didst waken from his summer dreams
The blue Mediterranean, where he lay,   30
Lulled by the coil of his crystalline streams,

Beside a pumice isle in Baiae's bay,[2]
And saw in sleep old palaces and towers
Quivering within the wave's intenser day,

All overgrown with azure moss and flowers   35
So sweet, the sense faints picturing them! Thou
For whose path the Atlantic's level powers

1. **Maenad** (mē′ nad), a female follower of Dionysus,
Greek god of wine and emotional liberation, who was
worshiped with orgiastic rites.
2. **Baiae's bay** (bä′ yäz), Baia is a small seaport town on
the Bay of Naples in Italy.

Cleave themselves into chasms, while far below
The sea-blooms and the oozy woods which wear
The sapless foliage of the ocean, know   40

Thy voice, and suddenly grow gray with fear,
And tremble and despoil themselves: oh, hear!

4

If I were a dead leaf thou mightest bear,
If I were a swift cloud to fly with thee;
A wave to pant beneath thy power, and share   45

The impulse of thy strength, only less free
Than thou, O uncontrollable! If even
I were as in my boyhood, and could be

The comrade of thy wanderings over Heaven,
As then, when to outstrip thy skyey speed   50
Scarce seemed a vision; I would ne'er have striven

As thus with thee in prayer in my sore need.
Oh, lift me as a wave, a leaf, a cloud!
I fall upon the thorns of life! I bleed!

A heavy weight of hours has chained and bowed   55
One too like thee: tameless, and swift, and proud.

5

Make me thy lyre, even as the forest is:
What if my leaves are falling like its own!
The tumult of thy mighty harmonies

Will take from both a deep, autumnal tone,   60
Sweet though in sadness. Be thou, Spirit fierce,
My spirit! Be thou me, impetuous one!

Drive my dead thoughts over the universe
Like withered leaves to quicken a new birth!
And, by the incantation of this verse,   65

Scatter, as from an unextinguished hearth
Ashes and sparks, my words among mankind!
Be through my lips to unawakened earth

The trumpet of a prophecy! O Wind,
If Winter comes, can Spring be far behind?   70

FOR UNDERSTANDING

Ozymandias
Describe the appearance of the statue in the desert.

To a Sky-Lark
1. What time of year and day is it in this poem?
2. What details are mentioned in the first six stanzas about the lark's flight and song?
3. Stanzas 7-12 pose a question and then attempt to answer it. What is the question? What answer does the speaker offer?
4. What does the poet ask of the sky-lark in the final stanza?

Ode to the West Wind
1. What time of year is it?
2. How does the poet identify himself with the wind in the fourth stanza?
3. Which qualities of the West Wind does the poet emphasize in the ode?

FOR INTERPRETATION

Ozymandias
Discuss the following statements in light of the poem.
1. Ozymandias succeeded in being remembered for something quite different from what he had intended.
2. It is significant that the scene is laid in a desert.
3. The poem's theme is similar to that of Byron's "On Fame."

To a Sky-Lark
In the first two lines, Shelley addresses the sky-lark as "blithe spirit." Spirit comes from Latin *spiritus*, which may mean breath, wind, soul, or inspiration.

Can it be said that this poem is really a meditation on poetic inspiration?

Ode to the West Wind
1. How does Shelley employ the archetypal cycle of birth, death, and rebirth in the poem?
2. What similarities can you note in diction and theme between "Ode to the West Wind" and "To a Sky-Lark"?

FOR APPRECIATION

Ozymandias
1. What effect is achieved by framing the principal scene as a report from a traveler?
2. What is the form of the poem? What is the rhyme scheme?

To a Sky-Lark
1. What are some of the unusual characteristics of the stanza form?
2. What senses does the poet appeal to in the similes of lines 36-55?
3. Pick out some examples of alliteration and assonance from the poem that contribute to its unusually musical effects.

Ode to the West Wind
1. The verse form is a combination of the sonnet and an Italian three-line stanza called *terza rima* (the stanza used in Dante's *Divine Comedy*). Trace the rhyme scheme of the stanzas.
2. In the first two stanzas pick out the words connoting images of death, decay, and darkness.
3. What makes the poem sound like a raging wind?
4. The "trumpet" in line 69 is an allusion to the last trumpet in *Revelations* 11:15, as well as an echo of the "clarion" in line 10. Why is the Biblical allusion appropriate?

John Keats 1795–1821

John Keats was born in London, the eldest of the four children of a livery stable manager. As a boy he was sent to the school in Enfield run by the Reverend John Clarke. Here he had the good fortune to be taught by the headmaster's son, who encouraged the boy's reading in mythology and introduced him to music and the theater. Keats was physically small (even as an adult he stood barely five feet), but he was a mischievous, feisty student, handy with his fists. His father died when he was eight; his mother remarried, but succumbed to tuberculosis six years later. The orphaned youth and his three siblings were placed with a guardian who removed John from school and apprenticed him to a doctor. He later had a year or two of hospital training and was qualified as an apothecary.

From these unpromising beginnings, and beset by poverty, personal tragedy, and ill health for most of his brief life, Keats managed to become (in the opinion of many critics) the finest lyric poet in English. With the encouragement of Leigh Hunt (a minor poet and critic who was a friend of Wordsworth and Coleridge), he decided at twenty, over his guardian's protests, to devote his life to poetry. His first efforts, labored and imitative, were severely criticized by reviewers. The years 1817–1819 were crucial. At first came disappointments and disasters. A younger brother and his bride, emigrating to Kentucky in the United States, lost what money they had. Keats, as the eldest brother, felt obliged to take on literary hack-work to support them. That summer he and a friend took a glorious hiking trip through the Lake District and Scotland, but Keats returned with a persistent cough, the first symptom of the tuberculosis which was to prove fatal two years later.

In the fall, Keats fell passionately in love with Fanny Brawne, a girl of eighteen. Though they became engaged, his poverty and ill health made marriage impossible. Then his favorite brother Tom, who had been ill, became much

KEATS
Benjamin Robert Haydon
National Portrait Gallery, London

worse; Keats nursed him till his death in December 1818 from tuberculosis. But in 1819, despite these setbacks, he found his poetic voice; that year witnessed the composition of most of his great sonnets, all but one of his magnificent odes, and "The Eve of St. Agnes." He also composed a fragment of an epic, inspired by Milton's *Paradise Lost* and entitled *Hyperion.*

In the fall of 1820, his doctor advised Keats to seek a warmer climate for the winter. Shelley invited him to Pisa, where he was living; but Keats had earlier treated Shelley's friendship with reserve because of his fears of being unduly influenced by contemporary poets. Traveling with his friend Joseph Severn, a young painter, Keats went instead to Rome, where he died in February of 1821 and was buried in the

Protestant Cemetery. Shelley composed the great elegy "Adonais" to commemorate his death. Ironically, Shelley was drowned in a sailing accident the following year, and his remains were laid beside those of Keats in the same cemetery.

In a period of five years Keats reached the pinnacle of English poetry. His best work displays a slow-paced rhythm, extraordinary concreteness in evoking the five senses, and a haunting juxtaposition of opposites: pleasure and pain, delight and melancholy, death and love. The critical insights in his letters display a sensibility remarkably attuned to some of the great questions of English criticism: the achievement of Shakespeare, the true nature of poetic originality, and the fundamental tasks of the poet. He was acutely sensitive to the fragility and transience of human destiny. On his tombstone he asked that no name be written, only the epitaph: "Here Lies One Whose Name Was Writ in Water."

On First Looking into Chapman's Homer

Much have I traveled in the realms of gold,
    And many goodly states and kingdoms seen;
    Round many western islands have I been
Which bards in fealty[1] to Apollo[2] hold.
Oft of one wide expanse had I been told   5
    That deep-browed Homer ruled as his demesne;[3]
    Yet did I never breathe its pure serene[4]
Till I heard Chapman[5] speak out loud and bold:
Then felt I like some watcher of the skies
    When a new planet swims into his ken;   10
Or like stout Cortez[6] when with eagle eyes
    He stared at the Pacific—and all his men
Looked at each other with a wild surmise—
    Silent, upon a peak in Darien.[7]

1. **fealty** (fē′ əl tē), obligation owed by a vassal to his feudal lord.
2. **Apollo** (ə pol′ ō), Greek god of the sun, prophecy, music, and poetry.
3. **demesne** (di mān′), domain, realm: refers here to Homer's epic poems, the *Iliad* and the *Odyssey*.
4. **serene,** clear expanse of air.
5. **Chapman,** George Chapman (c. 1559–c.1634), Elizabethan poet and playwright whose translations of Homer's epics appeared in 1611–1615.
6. **Cortez,** Balboa, not Cortez, discovered the Pacific.
7. **Darien,** now Panama.

When I Have Fears That I May Cease To Be

When I have fears that I may cease to be
  Before my pen has gleaned my teaming brain,
Before high-pilèd books, in charactery,[1]
  Hold like rich garners[2] the full-ripened grain;
When I behold, upon the night's starred face,   5
  Huge cloudy symbols of a high romance,
And think that I may never live to trace
  Their shadows, with the magic hand of chance;[3]
And when I feel, fair creature of an hour,
  That I shall never look upon thee more,   10
Never have relish in the fairy power
  Of unreflecting love—then on the shore
Of the wide world I stand alone, and think
Till love and fame to nothingness do sink.

1. **charactery,** handwriting.
2. **garners,** storehouses.
3. **chance,** inspiration.

La Belle Dame sans Merci[1]

"O what can ail thee, Knight at arms,
  Alone and palely loitering?
The sedge[2] has withered from the Lake
  And no birds sing!

O what can ail thee, Knight at arms,   5
  So haggard, and so woebegone?
The squirrel's granary is full
  And the harvest's done.

1. **La belle dame sans merci** (la bel dam sän mär sē'), French for "the beautiful lady without mercy." The title is taken from a medieval Provençal poem by Alain Chartier. In Keats' poem "The Eve of St. Agnes," the lover plays a setting of Chartier's poem on the lute to awaken his sleeping lady.
2. **sedge** (sej), flowering grass.

LA BELLE DAME SANS MERCI
J.W. Waterhouse
Darmstadt Hessisches Landesmuseum

I see a lily on thy brow
  With anguish moist and fever dew,   10
And on thy cheeks a fading rose
  Fast withereth too."

"I met a Lady in the Meads,[3]
  Full beautiful, a faery's child,
Her hair was long, her foot was light   15
  And her eyes were wild.

I made a Garland for her head,
  And bracelets too, and fragrant Zone;[4]
She looked at me as she did love
  And made sweet moan.   20

I set her on my pacing steed
  And nothing else saw all day long,
For sidelong would she bend and sing
  A faery's song.

She found me roots of relish sweet,   25
  And honey wild, and manna[5] dew,
And sure in language strange she said
  'I love thee true.'

She took me to her elfin grot[5]
  And there she wept and sighed full sore,   30
And there I shut her wild wild eyes
  With kisses four.

And there she lulled me asleep,
  And there I dreamed, Ah Woe betide!
The latest[7] dream I ever dreamt   35
  On the cold hill side.

I saw pale Kings, and Princes too,
  Pale warriors, death-pale were they all;
They cried, 'La belle dame sans merci
  Hath thee in thrall!'[8]   40

---

3. **Meads** (mēdz), meadows.
4. **Zone,** archaic word for belt.
5. **manna** (man' ə), the mysterious substance that fell from heaven to feed the wandering Israelites.
6. **grot,** grotto or cave.
7. **latest,** last.
8. **thrall** (thrôl), captivity.

I saw their starved lips in the gloam[9]
  With horrid warning gaped wide,
And I awoke, and found me here
  On the cold hill's side.

And this is why I sojourn here,   45
  Alone and palely loitering;
Though the sedge is withered from the Lake
  And no birds sing."

9. **gloam** (glōm), dusk (an archaic form).

FOR UNDERSTANDING

1. What experience does Keats recreate in the first sonnet? How does he say he felt when he first read the *Iliad* and *Odyssey*?

2. What fears assail the poet in "When I Have Fears"? What reaction in him do these fears produce?

3. Who are the two speakers in "La Belle Dame sans Merci"? What has the Lady done to the Knight?

FOR INTERPRETATION

Discuss the following statements in light of the poems.

1. Keats's sonnet "On First Looking into Chapman's Homer" is really about the poet's own powers of imagination.

2. "La Belle Dame sans Merci" is more remarkable for what it does not say than for what it says.

FOR APPRECIATION

1. Keats's sonnet "On First Looking into Chapman's Homer" contains a famous historical inaccuracy. What is it? Does it matter?

2. Explain the interaction of *simile* and *metaphor* in the first four lines of "When I Have Fears."

3. In "La Belle Dame sans Merci," Keats is deliberately imitating an old form, the ballad, and he purposely uses old-fashioned language (like Spenser). How does this poem remind you of a ballad? What deliberately archaic words and phrases can you find? Why does Keats use them?

4. Keats changes the ballad stanza significantly by shortening the fourth line of each quatrain. What effect does this change have on our reaction to the poem?

Ode on a Grecian Urn

Thou still unravished bride of quietness,
   Thou foster child of Silence and slow Time,
Sylvan historian, who canst thus express
   A flowery tale more sweetly than our rime—
What leaf-fringed legend haunts about thy shape   5
   Of deities or mortals, or of both,
     In Tempe[1] or the dales of Arcady?[2]
   What men or gods are these? What maidens loath?
What mad pursuit? What struggle to escape?
     What pipes and timbrels?[3] What wild ecstasy?   10

Heard melodies are sweet, but those unheard
   Are sweeter; therefore, ye soft pipes, play on;
Not to the sensual[4] ear, but, more endeared,
   Pipe to the spirit ditties of no tone.
Fair youth, beneath the trees, thou canst not leave   15
   Thy song, nor ever can those trees be bare;
     Bold lover, never, never canst thou kiss,
   Though winning near the goal—yet, do not grieve;
She cannot fade, though thou hast not thy bliss,
     Forever wilt thou love, and she be fair!   20

Ah, happy, happy boughs! that cannot shed
   Your leaves, nor ever bid the spring adieu;
And, happy melodist, unwearied,
   Forever piping songs forever new.
More happy love! more happy, happy love!   25
   Forever warm and still to be enjoyed,
    Forever panting, and forever young;
   All breathing human passion far above,
That leaves a heart high-sorrowful and cloyed,
     A burning forehead, and a parching tongue.   30

Who are these coming to the sacrifice?
   To what green altar, O mysterious priest,

1. **Tempe** (tem′ pē), a beautiful valley in Thessaly, a district of Greece.
2. **Arcady** (är′ kə dē), the district of Arcadia in ancient Greece, used as a byword for the pastoral ideal.
3. **timbrels** (tim′ brəlz), ancient percussion instruments similar to tambourines.
4. **sensual,** appealing to the sense (of hearing).

The Portland Vase
The British Museum

Lead'st thou that heifer lowing at the skies,
    And all her silken flanks with garlands dressed?
What little town by river or seashore,   35
    Or mountain-built with peaceful citadel,
        Is emptied of this folk, this pious morn?
    And, little town, thy streets forevermore
Will silent be; and not a soul to tell
        Why thou art desolate, can e'er return.   40

O Attic shape![5] Fair attitude! with brede[6]
  Of marble men and maidens overwrought,
With forest branches and the trodden weed;
  Thou, silent form, dost tease us out of thought
As doth eternity: Cold pastoral!   45
    When old age shall this generation waste,
      Thou shalt remain, in midst of other woe
    Than ours, a friend to man, to whom thou say'st,
"Beauty is truth, truth beauty"—that is all
    Ye know on earth, and all ye need to know.   50

5. **Attic,** from Attica, the district in which Athens is
located. The Athenian style in art was marked by grace
and simplicity.
6. **brede** (brēd), embroidery.

FOR UNDERSTANDING

1. In the first stanza, the poet seems to be looking at the figures depicted on the surface of the urn as a whole. What does he see?
2. The next three stanzas look at the different sides of the urn and examine the figures more closely. Describe the scenes.
3. What reason does the poet give in the final stanza for declaring that the urn is "a friend to man"?

FOR INTERPRETATION

Discuss the following statements in light of the poem.
1. Imagined music is sweeter than heard music.
2. Anticipation is more exciting than achievement.
3. The urn is paradoxical: it can capture a moment in time and keep it forever the same, but it cannot duplicate human experience.

FOR APPRECIATION

1. Many attempts have been made to identify the actual Grecian urn of which Keats wrote; all have failed. The precise details seem to have existed only in his imagination. How might this be related to the theme of "Ode on a Grecian Urn"?
2. There is a dispute about the placement of the quotation marks in the last two lines of the ode. Some editors maintain that the entire last two lines were intended as the quotation; in this case, how is the meaning altered?

Ode to a Nightingale

My heart aches, and a drowsy numbness pains
  My sense, as though of hemlock[1] I had drunk,
Or emptied some dull opiate to the drains
  One minute past, and Lethe-wards[2] had sunk:
'Tis not through envy of thy happy lot,   5
  But being too happy in thine happiness—
    That thou, light-wingéd Dryad[3] of the trees,
      In some melodious plot
  Of beechen green, and shadows numberless,
    Singest of summer in full-throated ease.   10

O, for a draught of vintage! that hath been
  Cooled a long age in the deep-delved earth,
Tasting of Flora[4] and the country green,
  Dance, and Provençal[5] song, and sunburnt mirth!
O for a beaker full of the warm South,   15
  Full of the true, the blushful Hippocrene,[6]
    With beaded bubbles winking at the brim,
      And purple-stainéd mouth;
  That I might drink, and leave the world unseen,
    And with thee fade away into the forest dim: 20

Fade far away, dissolve, and quite forget
  What thou among the leaves hast never known,
The weariness, the fever, and the fret
  Here, where men sit and hear each other groan;
Where palsy[7] shakes a few, sad, last gray hairs,   25
  Where youth grows pale, and specter-thin, and dies,
    Where but to think is to be full of sorrow
      And leaden-eyed despairs;
  Where Beauty cannot keep her lustrous eyes,
    Or new Love pine at them beyond tomorrow.   30

1. **hemlock** (hem′ lok), drug made from a poisonous herb.
2. **Lethe-wards** (lē′ thē wôrdz), towards the river Lethe, the underworld stream in Greek mythology which symbolized oblivion.
3. **Dryad** (drī′ əd), wood-nymph.
4. **Flora** (flôr′ ə), Roman goddess of flowers.
5. **Provençal** (prō vən säl′), of Provence, the region in Southern France, home of the medieval troubadours.
6. **Hippocrene** (hip′ ə krēn), the fountain of the Muses on Mount Helicon in Greece; its waters were supposed to aid poetic inspiration.
7. **palsy** (pôl′ zē), shaking disease.

Away! away! for I will fly to thee,
   Not charioted by Bacchus and his pards,[8]
But on the viewless[9] wings of Poesy,
   Though the dull brain perplexes and retards:
Already with thee! tender is the night,   35
   And haply[10] the Queen-Moon is on her throne,
     Clustered around by all her starry Fays,[11]
       But here there is no light,
Save what from heaven is with the breezes blown
     Through verdurous[12] glooms and winding mossy ways.   40

I cannot see what flowers are at my feet,
   Nor what soft incense hangs upon the boughs,
But, in embalméd darkness, guess each sweet
   Wherewith the seasonable month endows
The grass, the thicket, and the fruit tree wild;   45
   White hawthorn, and the pastoral eglantine;[13]
     Fast fading violets covered up in leaves;
       And mid-May's eldest child,
The coming musk-rose, full of dewy wine,
     The murmurous haunt of flies on summer eves.   50

Darkling[14] I listen; and for many a time
   I have been half in love with easeful Death,
Called him soft names in many a muséd rhyme,
   To take into the air my quiet breath;
Now more than ever seems it rich to die,   55
   To cease upon the midnight with no pain,
     While thou art pouring forth thy soul abroad
       In such an ecstasy!
Still wouldst thou sing, and I have ears in vain—
   To thy high requiem become a sod.   60

Thou wast not born for death, immortal Bird!
   No hungry generations tread thee down;
The voice I hear this passing night was heard
   In ancient days by emperor and clown:

8. **Bacchus and his pards** (bak′ əs; pärdz), Roman
god of wine, often pictured in a leopard-drawn chariot.
 9. **viewless,** not seen; invisible.
10. **haply,** perhaps.
11. **Fays** (fāz), fairies.
12. **verdurous** (vėr′ jar əs), covered with vegetation.
13. **eglantine** (eg′ lən tīn), sweetbriar (a wild rose).
14. **darkling,** in darkness.

Perhaps the selfsame song that found a path   65
    Through the sad heart of Ruth,[15] when, sick for home,
        She stood in tears amid the alien corn;
            The same that ofttimes hath
    Charmed magic casements, opening on the foam
        Of perilous seas, in faery lands forlorn.   70

Forlorn! the very word is like a bell
    To toll me back from thee to my sole self!
Adieu![16] the fancy cannot cheat so well
    As she is famed to do, deceiving elf.
Adieu! adieu! thy plaintive anthem fades   75
    Past the near meadows, over the still stream,
        Up the hill side; and now 'tis buried deep
            In the next valley-glades:
    Was it a vision, or a waking dream?
        Fled is that music—Do I wake or sleep?   80

15. **Ruth,** the Biblical figure who left her own country
(Moab) to accompany her mother-in-law, Naomi, back to
Judah; see *Ruth* 2:1–23.
16. **adieu** (ə dü'), goodbye, in French.

FOR UNDERSTANDING

1. What is the emotional condition of the speaker
in the first stanza? How does the speaker connect
that emotion to the nightingale's song?
2. What does the speaker wish to do in stanzas 2
and 3?
3. In stanza 6, the speaker feels it "rich to die."
What changes of thought in stanzas 6, 7, and 8
restrain the speaker from satisfying this death
wish?

FOR INTERPRETATION

1. What atmosphere is created by the images in
stanza 5? What is the importance of this stanza to
the poem?
2. What is the essential difference (in stanzas 3 and
7) between the nightingale and the speaker?

3. How can the nighingale's song be said to be
paradoxical?

FOR APPRECIATION

1. Identify the rhyme scheme of the poem. How is
this rhyme scheme an adaptation of sonnet form?
2. *Synaesthesia* is a mingling of the senses in imagery. Identify some examples of this technique in
"Ode to a Nightingale."

COMPOSITION

In "Ode on a Grecian Urn" and "Ode to a Nightingale," Keats considers the paradoxes of beauty; the
poems are, to a considerable extent, complementary works. Write an essay comparing the sequence
of thought in these two odes.

To Autumn

Season of mists and mellow fruitfulness,
  Close bosom-friend of the maturing sun;
Conspiring with him how to load and bless
  With fruit the vines that round the thatch-eaves run;
To bend with apples the moss'd cottage trees,   5
  And fill all fruit with ripeness to the core;
    To swell the gourd, and plump the hazel shells
  With a sweet kernel; to set budding more,
And still more, later flowers for the bees,
Until they think warm days will never cease,   10
    For Summer has o'er-brimmed their clammy cells.

Who hath not seen thee oft amid thy store?
  Sometimes whoever seeks abroad may find
Thee sitting careless on a granary floor,
  Thy hair soft-lifted by the winnowing wind;   15
Or on a half-reap'd furrow sound asleep,
  Drows'd with the fume of poppies, while thy hook
    Spares the next swath and all its twinéd flowers:
And sometimes like a gleaner thou dost keep
  Steady thy laden head across a brook;   20
  Or by a cider-press, with patient look,
    Thou watchest the last oozings hours by hours.

Where are the songs of Spring? Aye, where are they?
  Think not of them, thou hast thy music too,—
While barréd clouds bloom the soft-dying day,   25
  And touch the stubble-plains with rosy hue;
Then in a wailful choir the small gnats mourn
  Among the river sallows, borne aloft
    Or sinking as the light wind lives or dies;
And full-grown lambs loud bleat from hilly bourn;   30
  Hedge-crickets sing; and now with treble soft
The red-breast whistles from a garden-croft;
  And gathering swallows twitter in the skies.

HAMPSTEAD HEATH WITH A RAINBOW
John Constable
Tate Gallery

FOR UNDERSTANDING

What relationship and what feeling does Keats create by personifying autumn?

FOR INTERPRETATION

1. What is the dominant impression of autumn that this poem leaves with you?
2. The meaning of the poem must be traced through its lush imagery. To what senses does the poem appeal in each stanza? What pictures are drawn in words?
3. How does autumn progress in space and in time from stanza to stanza? How are these progressions related to the poem's "meaning"?

FOR APPRECIATION

1. What sound effects give this poem its solemn and stately movement?
2. What patterns are repeated in each stanza?

from KEATS'S LETTERS:

To: John Hamilton Reynolds.[1] February 3, 1818.

It may be said that we ought to read our Contemporaries—that Wordsworth &c. should have their due from us. But, for the sake of a few fine imaginative or domestic passages, are we to be bullied into a certain Philosophy engendered in the whims of an Egotist[2] —Every man has his speculations, but every man does not brood and peacock over them till he makes a false coinage and deceives himself. Many a man can travel to the very bourne[3] of Heaven, and yet want confidence to put down his half-seeing. Sancho[4] will invent a Journey heavenward as well as any body. We hate poetry that has a palpable design upon us—and if we do not agree, seems to put its hand in its breeches pocket. Poetry should be great and unobtrusive, a thing which enters into one's soul, and does not startle it or amaze it with itself, but with its subject. —How beautiful are the retired flowers! how would they lose their beauty were they to throng into the highway crying out, "admire me I am a violet!—dote upon me I am a primrose!"

1. **John Hamilton Reynolds,** a minor poet and journalist who was one of Keats's most frequent correspondents.
2. **Egotist,** by this time Wordsworth (born in 1770) was no longer considered by many as a vigorous, productive poet but as a self-absorbed, dull writer.
3. **bourne,** boundary.
4. **Sancho,** Sancho Panza was the decidedly earthy peasant who accompanied Don Quixote on his travels in Cervantes's novel.

To: George and Thomas Keats. December 21, 1817.

My dear Brothers

I must crave your pardon for not having written ere this *** I spent Friday evening with Wells[1] and went the next morning to see *Death on the Pale horse*. It is a wonderful picture, when West's age is considered;[2] But there is nothing to be intense upon; no women one feels mad to kiss; no face swelling into reality. The excellence of every Art is its intensity, capable of making all disagreeables evaporate, from their being in close relationship with Beauty and Truth—Examine King Lear and you will find this examplified throughout; but in this picture we have unpleasantness without any momentous depth of speculation excited, in which to bury its repulsiveness—The picture is larger than Christ rejected—I dined with Haydon[3] the Sunday after you left, and had a very pleasant day, I dined too (for I have been out too much lately) with Horace Smith and met his two Brothers with Hill and Kingston and one DuBois,[4] they only served to convince me, how superior humour is to wit in respect to enjoyment—These men say things which make one start, without making one feel, they are all alike; their manners are alike; they all know fashionables; they have a mannerism in

1. **Wells,** Charles Wells, a former schoolmate of Keats's brother Tom.
2. **Benjamin West** (1738–1820), American painter who settled in England and became president of the Royal Academy. He also painted a picture entitled "Christ Rejected," mentioned below in this letter.
3. **Haydon,** Keats's friend, the painter Benjamin Haydon.
4. This group of men comprised leading literary wits of the day.

their very eating and drinking, in their mere handling a Decanter—They talked of Kean[5] and his low company—Would I were with that company instead of yours said I to myself! I know such like acquaintance will never do for me and yet I am going to Reynolds, on Wednesday—Brown and Dilke[6] walked with me and back from the Christmas pantomime.[7] I had not a dispute but a disquisition with Dilke, on various subjects; several things dovetailed in my mind, and at once it struck me, what quality went to form a Man of Achievement especially in Literature and which Shakespeare possessed so enormously —I mean *Negative Capability*, that is when man is capable of being in uncertainties, Mysteries, doubts, without any irritable reaching after fact and reason—Coleridge, for instance, would let go by a fine isolated verisimilitude caught from the Penetralium[8] of mystery, from being incapable of remaining content with half knowledge. This pursued through Volumes would perhaps take us no further than this, that with a great poet the sense of Beauty overcomes every other consideration, or rather obliterates all consideration.

5. **Kean,** Edmund Kean, a noted Shakespearean actor.
6. **Reynolds, Brown,** and **Dilke** were all writers and friends of Keats.
7. **Christmas pantomime,** an annual show performed in London at Covent Garden and the Drury Lane theater.
8. **Penetralium,** Latin for the innermost part of a temple.

To: George and Georgiana Keats.[1] February 18, 1819.

—I never drink now above three glasses of wine—and never any spirits and water. Though by the bye—the other day—Woodhouse[2] took me to his coffe house—and ordered a Bottle of Claret—now I like Claret —whenever I can have Claret I must drink it,—'tis the only palate affair that I am at all sensual in. Would it not be a good Speck[3] to send you some vine roots—could It be done? I'll enquire—If you could make some wine like Claret to drink on Summer evenings in an arbour! For really 'tis so fine—it fills the mouth with a gushing freshness—then goes down cool and feverless—then you do not feel it quarrelling with your liver—no it is rather a Peace makcr and lics as quiet as it did in the grape—then it is as fragrant as the Queen Bee; and the more ethereal Part of it mounts into the brain, not assaulting the cerebral apartments like a bully in a badhouse looking for his trul[4] and hurrying from door to door bouncing against the waistcoat:[5] but rather walks like Aladin about his own enchanted palace so gently that you do not feel his step. Other wines of a heavy and spirituous nature transform a Man to a Silenus[6] this makes him a Hermes[7]—and gives a Woman the soul and immortality of Ariadne[8] for whom Bacchus always kept a good cellar of claret—and even of that he could never persuade her to take above two cups—I said this same Claret is the only palate-passion I have I forgot game—I must plead guilty to the breast of a Partridge, the back of a hare, the backbone of a grouse, the wing and side of a Pheasant and a Woodcock . . .

1. **George and Georgiana Keats,** the poet's brother and sister-in-law; they emigrated to the United States, and Keats composed long "journal-letters" which he would write over a period of one or two months and then send to them.
2. **Woodhouse,** Richard Woodhouse, a lawyer who aided Keats with both money and advice.
3. **Speck,** probably slang for speculation.
4. **trul,** prostitute.
5. **waistcoat,** may be Keats's hurried word for "wainscot," wood paneling in a room.
6. **Silenus** (sī lē′ nəs), the satyr in classical mythology who was foster father to Bacchus, god of wine. Silenus is usually pictured as old and fat.
7. **Hermes** (hėr′ mēz), the Greek god who served as the divine messenger (his Roman equivalent was Mercury).
8. **Ariadne** (ar ē ad′ nē), Cretan princess who aided Theseus of Athens in his conquest of the Minotaur. Ariadne was later deserted by Theseus and married Bacchus.

To: Charles Brown. November 30, 1820.[1]

I cannot answer any thing in your letter, which followed me from Naples to Rome, because I am afraid to look it over again. I am so weak (in mind) that I cannot bear the sight of any hand writing of a friend I love so much as I do you. Yet I ride the little horse[2]—and, at my worst, even in Quarantine,[3] summond up more puns, in a sort of desperation, in one week than in any year of my life. There is one thought enough to kill me—I have been well, healthy, alert &c, walking with her[4]—and now—the knowledge of contrast, feeling for light and shade, all that information (primitive sense) necessary for a poem are great enemies to the recovery of the stomach. There, you rogue, I put you to the torture,—but you must bring your philosophy to bear—as I do mine, really—or how should I be able to live? Dr. Clarke is very attentive to me; he says there is very little the matter with my lungs, but my stomach, he says, is very bad. I am well disappointed in hearing good news from George,—for it runs in my head we shall all die young. I have not written to ****[5] yet, which he must think very neglectful; being anxious to send him a good account of my health, I have delayed it from week to week. If I recover, I will do all in my power to correct the mistakes made during sickness; and if I should not, all my faults will be forgiven. I shall write to **** in the middle of next week. Severn[6] is very well, though he leads so dull a life with me. Remember me to all friends, and tell **** I should not have left London without taking leave of him, but from being so low in body and mind. Write to George as soon as you receive this, and tell him how I am, as far as you can guess;—and also a note to my sister—who walks about my imagination like a ghost—she is so like Tom[7] I can scarcely bid you good bye even in a letter. I always made an awkward bow.

God bless you!

---

1. This is the last known letter of Keats, written from Rome, where he had gone to try to recover from tuberculosis. The letter is addressed to Keats's close friend Charles Brown, with whom he had shared a house in Hampstead, north of London.
2. Although he was ill, Keats still managed to exercise.
3. On his trip from Naples to Rome, Keats's boat was detained in quarantine because of reports of an outbreak of typhus.
4. **her,** Fanny Brawne, Keats's fiancée.
5. ****. the names of four friends of Keats (probably William Haslam, Charles Dilke, Richard Woodhouse, and John Hamilton Reynolds) are thus represented in this copy of the letter.
6. **Severn,** Joseph Severn, a friend who accompanied Keats to Rome.
7. **Tom,** the poet's younger brother, who had died eleven months earlier of tuberculosis.

FOR UNDERSTANDING AND INTERPRETATION

1. What kind of poetry does Keats object to in his letter to Reynolds?

2. What does Keats seem to mean by the phrase "negative capability" in his letter of December 21, 1817?

3. Keats has some rather harsh things to say about Wordsworth in his letter to Reynolds. To what extent is Keats right in his assessment of Wordsworth? What defense of the elder poet might one make?

4. Compare Keats's description of drinking claret in his letter to George and Georgiana Keats with the second stanza of "Ode to a Nightingale."

5. What sense of Keats as a person do these letters convey?

Charles Lamb

1775–1834

The son of a lawyer's clerk in London, Lamb attended a charity school, Christ's Hospital, where he met Coleridge as a boy. Their lifelong friendship had lasting effects on Lamb's enthusiasm for writing. Upon graduation from school at fourteen, he realized that an incurable speech impediment would prevent him from winning a university scholarship. Such awards were generally reserved for prospective clergymen, who would naturally be expected to preach. Leaving school, he worked as a clerk at the South Sea House (headquarters for one of the largest trading companies), where he became acquainted with an Italian named Elia. Some thirty years later he used the name as a pseudonym in his celebrated series of essays. In 1792, he moved to the accountant's office at East India House, where he remained for thirty-three years.

When Lamb was twenty-two, his older sister Mary, in a moment of insanity, stabbed their invalid mother to death. Rather than allowing her to be confined in an asylum, Lamb persuaded the authorities to commit her to his care. When lucid, Mary was charming and perceptive; but she and her brother had always to be on the alert for the signals of a coming attack. Lamb devoted the rest of his life to caring for his sister, who lived to survive him by thirteen years.

Together the brother and sister established a literary circle in London, as Lamb pursued writing as an avocation. With Mary he compiled a delightful book for children, *Tales from Shakespeare,* which was published in 1807 and still serves admirably to introduce the tragedies and comedies to young people. Charles then published an important anthology of dramatic poets contemporary with Shakespeare, as well as essays on Shakespearean tragedy and on the painter William Hogarth (1697–1764). In 1820, with the establishment of the *London Magazine,* Lamb began to write the prose work which elevated him to the rank of a major author, the *Essays of Elia.* These were collected and

CHARLES AND MARY LAMB
Francis Stephen Carey
National Portrait Gallery, London

published in 1825, the same year that he retired from East India House. The essays are remarkable for their keen observation of city life, their personal candor, and their wit. Lamb could sparklingly enliven the most unlikely subjects; some of his titles included "Old China," "Some of the Old Benchers of the Inner Temple," and "A Dissertation upon Roast Pig." A number of the essays irreverently attacked what Lamb called "popular fallacies," or generally accepted clichés which turn out to be false upon close examination.

Lamb's fellow contributors to the *London Magazine* included the distinguished Romantic essayists William Hazlitt (1778–1830) and Thomas De Quincey (1785–1859). He numbered among his good friends some of the period's best-known poets, including Wordsworth, Coleridge, and Keats. Surprisingly, he shared with the poets only one of the characteristics that we think of as "Romantic": the candid display of his own personality in his writing. His essay on the popular fallacy "That We Should Rise with the Lark" has been called one of the "best examples of Lamb's refinement of thought and mastery of expression."

THAT WE SHOULD RISE WITH THE LARK

At what precise minute that little airy musician doffs his night gear, and prepares to tune up his unseasonable matins, we are not naturalist enough to determine. But for a mere human gentleman—that has no orchestra business to call him from his warm bed to such preposterous exercises—we take ten, or half after ten (eleven, of course, during this Christmas solstice),[1] to be the very earliest hour at which he can begin to think of abandoning his pillow. To think of it, we say; for to do it in earnest requires another half hour's good consideration. Not but there are pretty sun-risings, as we are told, and such like gawds,[2] abroad in the world, in summertime especially, some hours before what we have assigned; which a gentleman may see, as they say, only for getting up. But having been tempted once or twice, in earlier life, to assist at those ceremonies, we confess our curiosity abated. We are no longer ambitious of being the sun's courtiers, to attend at his morning levees. We hold the good hours of the dawn too sacred to waste them upon such observances; which have in them, besides, something Pagan and Persic.[3] To say truth, we never anticipated our usual hour, or got up with the sun (as 'tis called), to go a journey, or upon a foolish whole day's pleasuring, but we suffered for it all the long hours after in listlessness and headaches; Nature herself sufficiently declaring her sense of our presumption in aspiring to regulate our frail waking courses by the measure of that celestial and sleepless traveller. We deny not that there is something sprightly and vigorous, at the outset especially, in these break-of-day excursions. It is flattering to get the start of a lazy world; to conquer Death by proxy in his

image. But the seeds of sleep and mortality are in us and we pay usually, in strange qualms before night falls, the penalty of the unnatural inversion. Therefore, while the busy part of mankind are fast huddling on their clothes, are already up and about their occupations, content to have swallowed their sleep by wholesale; we choose to linger a-bed and digest our dreams. It is the very time to recombine the wandering images, which night in a confused mass presented; to snatch them from forgetfulness; to shape, and mould them. Some people have no good of their dreams. Like fast feeders, they gulp them too grossly, to taste them curiously. We love to chew the cud of a foregone vision; to collect the scattered rays of a brighter phantasm, or act over again, with firmer nerves, the sadder nocturnal tragedies; to drag into day light a struggling and half-vanishing night-mare; to handle and examine the terrors, or the airy solaces. We have too much respect for these spiritual communications, to let them go so lightly. We are not so stupid, or so careless as that Imperial forgetter of his dreams,[4] that we should need a seer to remind us of the form of them. They seem to us to have as much significance as our waking concerns; or rather to import us more nearly, as more nearly we approach by years to the shadowy world, whither we are hastening. We have shaken hands with the world's busi-

1. **Christmas solstice,** the winter solstice, December 21, or the shortest day of the year.
2. **gawds** (gôdz), shiny ornaments.
3. **Persic,** Persian.
4. **Imperial forgetter of his dreams,** ancient emperors retained seers to interpret their dreams.

ness; we have done with it; we have discharged ourself of it. Why should we get up? We have neither suit to solicit, nor affairs to manage. The drama has shut upon us at the fourth act. We have nothing here to expect, but in a short time a sick-bed, and a dismissal. We delight to anticipate death by such shadows as night affords. We are already half acquainted with ghosts. We were never much in the world. Disappointment early struck a dark veil between us and its dazzling illusions. Our spirits showed grey before our hairs. The mighty changes of the world already appear as but the vain stuff out of which dramas are composed. We have asked no more of life than what the mimic images in play-houses present us with. Even those types have waxed fainter. Our clock appears to have struck. We are SUPERANNUATED.[5] In this dearth of mundane satisfaction, we contract politic alliances with shadows. It is good to have friends at court. The extracted media of dreams seems no ill introduction to that spiritual presence, upon which, in no long time, we expect to be thrown. We are trying to know a little of the usages of that colony; to learn the language and the faces we shall meet with there, that we may be the less awkward at our first coming among them. We willingly call a phantom our fellow, as knowing we shall soon be of their dark companionship. Therefore we cherish dreams. We try to spell in them the alphabet of the invisible world; and think we know already how it shall be with us. Those uncouth shapes which, while we clung to flesh and blood, affrighted us, have become familiar. We feel attenuated into their meagre essences, and have given the hand of half-way approach to incorporeal being. We once thought life to be something; but it has unaccountably fallen from us before its time. Therefore we choose to dally with visions.

The sun has no purposes of ours to light us to. Why should we get up?

5. **superannuated** (sü pər an' yü ā tid), retired with a small annuity.

FOR UNDERSTANDING

1. What hour does Lamb suggest as a civilized time to get up?
2. What does Lamb claim is the inevitable result of rising too early?
3. What does the author suggest that we should do with our dreams before we get up?
4. Why does the writer enjoy these "phantoms" and "uncouth shapes"?

FOR INTERPRETATION

In light of the essay and your own experience, do you agree or disagree with the following statements?
1. Nature intends people to sleep and dream until they feel like getting up.
2. Dreams are to be tasted, not gulped. They are spiritual communications.
3. Dreams are messages from the dead.

COMPOSITION

Take any current saying and write a personal essay based on it. Try to assume Lamb's stance: interpret the meaning of the phrase in an unexpected (perhaps even an outrageous) way. Try to insert humor and to add an incident or two that will extend the point you are making. Here are some possible sayings you might use:
  Money won't bring happiness.
  Honesty is the best policy.
  TV is the opium of the people.
  Clothes make the man/woman.
  Love conquers all.
  You can catch more flies with honey than with vinegar.
  Would you buy a used car from that man?

The Novel of the Romantic Period

The spirit of Romanticism affected the novelists, as well as the poets and essayists, of this period. By 1800, forty novels a year were being published in England. Audiences were rapidly growing for this form of entertainment, and the majority of novelists were women. The novel had begun in England as a narrative of adventures and as a portrayal of character. Its fundamental purpose did not change in the nineteenth century, but it gained enormously in complexity and sophistication.

One of the most important pioneers of the romantic novel was Mrs. Ann Radcliffe (1764–1823). In 1794 Radcliffe published *The Mysteries of Udolpho,* one of the first successful "thrillers" and the archetype for the "Gothic novel" (so called after the medieval style of architecture in Europe of the thirteenth through the fifteenth centuries). Gothic novels featured remote (if not, strictly speaking, medieval) settings; the highly melodramatic plots and characters were calculated to appeal to readers' love of the exotic and the bizarre. *The Mysteries of Udolpho* was set in Gascony in 1584, remote enough in place and time so that the action seemed plausible. The story is peopled by hooded monks, mysterious nuns, bandits and villains, and a lovely heroine, who exists mainly to endure the emotions of wonder, awe, and terror. So pervasive is the setting of grim dungeons, decaying castles, and dark forests that the characters seem wholly subordinate to it. By comparison, the novels of the eighteenth century by Richardson, Fielding, and Smollett seem to have been played out on an empty stage. Mrs. Radcliffe's novels are the literary ancestors of the short stories of Edgar Allan Poe in America, the novels of the Brontë sisters in England, and the whole group of modern Gothic tales written for today's mass market.

Mary Shelley (P. 564), the wife of the poet Percy Bysshe Shelley, wrote something of the same kind of work in *Frankenstein* (1818). The setting is dark and mysterious, as a scientist in his laboratory creates a humanoid monster that he cannot control. Not only is the story in the tradition of the Gothic novel, but it is an early example as well of science fiction, which was to blossom toward the end of the nineteenth century in the tales of H. G. Wells (1866–1946). The character Frankenstein is one of the first examples of a scientist in a novel.

In 1800, another book was published with great importance for the development of the Romantic novel, Maria Edgeworth's *Castle Rackrent.* Edgeworth created the "regional novel." In contrast to Radcliffe, who had introduced scenery that was romantic but somewhat vague in its locale, Edgeworth defined a precise setting for her work (Ireland). Her characters were conditioned by the landscape in which they lived. Edgeworth's works display three aspects of Romanticism: interest in the common man; concern over social injustice; and interest in the impact of environment. She influenced both Sir Walter Scott and the great nineteenth-century Russian novelist, Ivan Turgenev (1818–1883).

Sir Walter Scott (1771–1832), the most

Here George Cruikshank, most famous today for his illustrations of Dickens' novels, shows the romantics' concern over social injustice.

"HARD TIMES" (1827)
George Cruikshank
The Mansell Collection, London

celebrated regional writer of the period, generally used Scotland as the locale for his novels. His books changed the course of the novel throughout Europe. If Byron was *the* poet of the Romantic period, Scott was *the* novelist. He employed actual historical figures as secondary characters in his plots; the main action was carried on by fictional characters. Scott acknowledged his debt to Edgeworth, saying that his aim in fiction was "in some distant degree to emulate the admirable Irish portraits" drawn by her.

His characters are influenced by their historical heritage and backgrounds, but his heroes and heroines tend to represent the more typical Romantic image—noble, handsome, long suffering. It is his lower-class or secondary characters who come to life as real people.

His reputation rests not so much on his introduction of the form of the historical novel as on his ability to take history and make it real through his characters. Some of Scott's best-known works include *Waverley*

(1814), *Rob Roy* (1817), *Ivanhoe* (1819), *Kenilworth* (1821), and *The Talisman* (1825).

Jane Austen (1775–1817) (p. 557) presents a sharp contrast to Sir Walter Scott. Although she was a revolutionary in her style, her mood and attitude in her works seem to be those of the eighteenth century, rather than the Romantic period. Restrained, genteel, and mildly ironic, her novels are best described as comedies of manners. Though certain aspects of her work seem to look backwards in time, her novels continue to appeal to modern readers; she is studied by twentieth-century writers for her intuitive ability to limit her stage of action and deal with a small cast of characters. Daughter of a country rector, Austen was a genteel, educated woman who seems to have led a quiet, uneventful life. Her characters represent the society she knew well, and her plots usually revolve around the paramount question for young women in that society: marriage. Austen was not intent on reforming the social manners of her day; her judgment on her characters' actions does not ring through direct, moral statements, but is conveyed in elegant, ironic dialogue. Her first three books were *Sense and Sensibility, Northanger Abbey* (in which she made fun of Gothic novels and their readers), and *Pride and Prejudice* (the best known of her works). After an interval of ten years, in which she published nothing, her three more mature works appeared: *Mansfield Park, Emma,* and *Persuasion.* Austen emulated the detached style and third-person narration of Henry Fielding's novels. She fused with these more formal characteristics a superbly penetrating observation of human psychology, in the tradition of Samuel Richardson's novels of character.

Jane Austen

1775–1817

Austen once described her novels as "paintings on a very small piece of ivory, two inches wide." Her life, at least on its surface, seems similarly confined. She was the seventh of the eight children of a country rector in Hampshire. Although most of her siblings moved out into the world (two brothers became admirals), Jane and her next older sister, Cassandra, spent their entire lives at home. The family moved to several country parishes, and at one time lived for a few years in Bath, the fashionable spa town a hundred miles west of London. Austen was thirty when her father died. She and her sister moved with their mother to Southampton, and then back to the gentle countryside of Hampshire. Jane became chronically ill and gradually declined until her death in Winchester at the age of forty-two.

Austen's relatively uneventful life provided the "small piece of ivory" on which she framed her six novels. She wrote only about the everyday affairs of the middle class: country squires, small businessmen, rectors, and their families. From her books, one would never suspect the existence of the Napoleonic Wars (exactly contemporary with her writing career) or of turbulent social change. It is the common passions and foibles of humanity that interest Austen; she sees most of her characters with a satirist's eye and is able to penetrate their psychology profoundly.

Austen's first three books were written when she was in her early twenties, but publishers were lukewarm about them and she made little money from writing. *Pride and Prejudice,* now recognized as a classic, had to wait fifteen years for publication after it was at first rejected for the press. The other two early novels were *Sense and Sensibility* and *Northanger Abbey,* which included an ironic spoof of Gothic novels (then all the rage) and of their readers. Austen wrote little for a decade; then, in her late thirties, she produced three more novels which many critics consider her finest: *Mansfield Park* (1814), *Emma* (1815), and *Persuasion* (1818). Austen herself never married, but every one of her novels revolves around the marriage of a heroine.

PORTRAIT OF JANE AUSTEN
Cassandra Austen
National Portrait Gallery, London

The truly Romantic element of Austen's work consists in her detailed study of personal emotion. Although her detachment and restraint sometimes mask her intense sympathy for her characters, their very human predicaments foreshadow the mainstream of the nineteenth-century English novel, characterized by the writings of Charlotte Brontë, Charles Dickens (in part), George Eliot, and Thomas Hardy. Sir Walter Scott, perhaps enviously, said of Austen: "That young lady had a talent for describing the involvements, feelings and characters of ordinary life which is to me the most wonderful I have ever met with. The big bow-wow I can do myself like anyone going; the exquisite touch which renders commonplace things and characters interesting from the truth of the description and the sentiment is denied to me."

from **NORTHANGER ABBEY**

Bath is a beautiful town on the Avon River, about one hundred miles west of London. Its hot mineral springs have made it a mecca for tourists and health-seekers since Roman times. In the eighteenth century, the town was rebuilt and became a center for fashionable English society; many traveled there not only to "drink the waters" but also to go to balls, attend the theater, parade in their finery, and meet the right people.

In Northanger Abbey, *Catherine Morland is a seventeen-year-old girl who comes from a large clergyman's family very much like the family of Jane Austen herself. She is invited by friends to visit Bath where she meets Isabella Thorpe, whose family has also come for the season. Isabella is four years older than Catherine and considerably more worldly.*

The progress of the friendship between Catherine and Isabella was quick as its beginning had been warm; and they passed so rapidly through every gradation of increasing tenderness, that there was shortly no fresh proof of it to be given to their friends or themselves. They called each other by their Christian name, were always arm-in-arm when they walked, pinned up each other's train for the dance, and were not to be divided in the set; and, if a rainy morning deprived them of other enjoyments, they were still resolute in meeting in defiance of wet and dirt, and shut themselves up to read novels together. Yes, novels; for I will not adopt that ungenerous and impolitic custom, so common with novel writers, of degrading, by their contemptuous censure, the very performances to the number of which they are themselves adding: joining with their greatest enemies in bestowing the harshest epithets on such works, and scarcely ever permitting them to be read by their own heroine, who, if she accidentally take up a novel, is sure to turn over its insipid pages with disgust. Alas! If the heroine of one novel be not patronised by the heroine of another, from whom can she expect protection and regard? I cannot approve of it. Let us leave it to the Reviewers to abuse such effusions of fancy at their leisure, and over every new novel to talk in threadbare strains of the trash with which the press now groans. Let us not desert one another; we are an injured body. Although our productions have afforded more extensive and unaffected pleasure than those of any other literary corporation in the world, no species of composition has been so much decried. From pride, ignorance, or fashion, our foes are almost as many as our readers; and while the abilities of the nine-hundredth abridger of the History of England, or of the man who collects and publishes in a volume some dozen lines of Milton, Pope, and Prior, with a paper from the *Spectator,*[1] and a chapter from Sterne, are eulogised by a thousand pens, there seems almost a general wish of decrying the capacity and undervaluing the labour of the novelist, and of slighting the performances which have only genius, wit and taste to recommend them. "I am no novel reader; I seldom look into novels; do not imagine that *I* often read novels; it is really very well for a novel." Such is the common

---

1. **Spectator,** the periodical edited by Addison and Steele in 1711–12.

PUMP ROOM FROM "BATH"
John Claude Nattes
British Museum Print Room

cant. "And what are you reading, Miss——?" "Oh! it is only a novel!" replies the young lady; while she lays down her book with affected indifference, or momentary shame. "It is only *Cecilia,* or *Camilla,* or *Belinda*";[2] or, in short, only some work in which the greatest powers of the mind are displayed, in which the most thorough knowledge of human na-

ture, the happiest delineation of its varieties, the liveliest effusions of wit and humour, are conveyed to the world in the best chosen language. Now, had the same young lady been engaged wih a volume of the *Spectator,* in-

2. **Cecilia, Camilla, Belinda,** popular novels of Austen's period.

stead of such a work, how proudly would she have produced the book, and told its name! though the chances must be against her being occupied by any part of that voluminous publication, of which either the matter or manner would not disgust a young person of taste; the substance of its papers so often consisting in the statement of improbable circumstances, unnatural characters, and topics of conversation, which no longer concern any one living; and their language, too, frequently so coarse as to give no very favourable idea of the age that could endure it.

The following conversation, which took place between the two friends in the Pump Room[3] one morning, after an acquaintance of eight or nine days, is given as a specimen of their very warm attachment, and of the delicacy, discretion, originality of thought, and literary taste which marked the reasonableness of that attachment.

They met by appointment; and as Isabella had arrived nearly five minutes before her friend, her first address naturally was: "My dearest creature, what can have made you so late? I have been waiting for you at least this age!"

"Have you, indeed? I am very sorry for it, but really I thought I was in very good time. It is but just one. I hope you have not been here long?"

"Oh! these ten ages at least. I am sure I have been here this half-hour. But now, let us go and sit down at the other end of the Room and enjoy ourselves. I have an hundred things to say to you. In the first place, I was so afraid it would rain this morning just as I wanted to set off; it looked very showery, and that would have thrown me into agonies! Do you know I saw the prettiest hat you can imagine in a shop window in Milsom Street just now; very like yours, only with coquelicot[4] ribands instead of green; I quite longed for it. But, my dearest Catherine, what have you been doing with yourself all this morning? Have you gone on with *Udolpho?*"[5]

"Yes, I have been reading it ever since I woke; and I am got to the black veil."

"Are you, indeed? How delightful! Oh! I would not tell you what is behind the black veil for the world! Are not you wild to know?"

"Oh! yes, quite; what can it be? But do not tell me: I would not be told upon any account. I know it must be a skeleton; I am sure it is Laurentina's skeleton. Oh! I am delighted with the book! I should like to spend my whole life in reading it, I assure you; if it had not been to meet you, I would not have come away from it for all the world."

"Dear creature, how much I am obliged to you; and when you have finished *Udolpho,* we will read *The Italian* together;[6] and I have made out a list of ten or twelve more of the same kind for you."

"Have you, indeed? How glad I am! What are they all?"

"I will read you their names directly; here they are in my pocket-book. *Castle of Wolfenbach, Clermont, Mysterious Warnings, Necromancer of the Black Forest, Midnight Bell, Orphan of the Rhine,* and *Horrid Mysteries.* Those will last us some time."

"Yes, pretty well; but are they all horrid? Are you sure they are all horrid?"

"Yes, quite sure; for a particular friend of mine, a Miss Andrews, a sweet girl, one of the sweetest creatures in the world, has read every one of them. I wish you knew Miss Andrews, you would be delighted with her. She is netting herself the sweetest cloak you can conceive. I think her as beautiful as an angel, and I am so vexed with the men for not admiring her! I scold them all amazingly about it."

3. **Pump Room,** a large room over the mineral springs at Bath, to which people came to drink the medicinal waters and to meet one another.
4. **coquelicot** (kōk′ lē kō), a brilliant red-orange.
5. **Udolpho,** *The Mysteries of Udolpho,* one of the first Gothic novels, published in 1794 by Mrs. Ann Radcliffe (1764–1823).
6. **The Italian,** another of Mrs. Radcliffe's popular novels.

TALES OF WONDER (print)
Gillray
British Museum Print Room

"Scold them! Do you scold them for not admiring her?"

"Yes, that I do. There is nothing I would not do for those who are really my friends. I have no notion of loving people by halves; it is not my nature. My attachments are always excessively strong. I told Captain Hunt, at one of our assemblies this winter, that if he was to tease me all night, I would not dance with him, unless he would allow Miss Andrews to be as beautiful as an angel. The men think us incapable of real friendship, you know, and I am determined to show them the difference. Now, if I were to hear anybody speak slightingly of you, I should fire up in a moment; but that is not at all likely, for *you*

are just the kind of girl to be a great favourite with the men."

"Oh, dear!" cried Catherine, colouring, "how can you say so?"

"I know you very well; you have so much animation, which is exactly what Miss Andrews wants; for I must confess there is something amazingly insipid about her. Oh! I must tell you, that, just after we parted yesterday, I saw a young man looking at you so earnestly; I am sure he is in love with you." Catherine coloured, and disclaimed again. Isabella laughed. "It is very true, upon my honour; but I see how it is: you are indifferent to everybody's admiration, except that of one gentleman, who shall be nameless. Nay, I cannot blame you" (speaking more seriously)—"your feelings are easily understood. Where the heart is really attached, I know very well how little one can be pleased with the attention of anybody else. Everything is so insipid, so uninteresting, that does not relate to the beloved object! I can perfectly comprehend your feelings."

"But you should not persuade me that I think so very much about Mr. Tilney, for perhaps I may never see him again."

"Not see him again! My dearest creature, do not talk of it. I am sure you would be miserable if you thought so."

"No, indeed; I should not. I do not pretend to say that I was not very much pleased with him; but while I have *Udolpho* to read, I feel as if nobody could make me miserable. Oh! the dreadful black veil! My dear Isabella, I am sure there must be Laurentina's skeleton behind it."

"It is so odd to me, that you should never have read *Udolpho* before; but I suppose Mrs. Morland objects to novels."

"No, she does not. She very often reads *Sir Charles Grandison*[7] herself; but new books do not fall in our way."

"*Sir Charles Grandison!* That is an amazingly horrid book, is it not? I remember Miss Andrews could not get through the first volume."

"It is not like *Udolpho* at all; but yet I think it is very entertaining."

"Do you indeed? You surprise me; I thought it had not been readable. But, my dearest Catherine, have you settled what to wear on your head to-night? I am determined, at all events, to be dressed exactly like you. The men take notice of *that* sometimes, you know."

"But it does not signify,[8] if they do," said Catherine, very innocently.

"Signify! Oh heavens! I make it a rule never to mind what they say. They are very often amazingly impertinent, if you do not treat them with spirit, and make them keep their distance."

"Are they? Well, I never observed *that*. They always behave very well to me."

"Oh! They give themselves such airs. They are the most conceited creatures in the world, and think themselves of so much importance! By the bye, though I have thought of it an hundred times, I have always forgot to ask you what is your favourite complexion in a man. Do you like them best dark or fair?"

"I hardly know. I never much thought about it. Something between both, I think; brown: not fair, and not very dark."

"Very well, Catherine. That is exactly he. I have not forgot your description of Mr. Tilney: 'a brown skin, with dark eyes, and rather dark hair.' Well, my taste is different. I prefer light eyes; and as to complexion, do you know, I like a sallow better than any other. You must not betray me, if you should ever meet with one of your acquaintances answering that description."

"Betray you! What do you mean?"

"Nay, do not distress me. I believe I have said too much. Let us drop the subject."

Catherine, in some amazement, complied; and, after remaining a few moments silent, was on the point of reverting to what interested her at that time rather more than anything else in the world, Laurentina's skeleton, when her friend prevented her, by saying: "For Heaven's sake! let us move away from this end of the room. Do you know, there are two odious young men who have been staring at me this half-hour. They really put me quite out of countenance. Let us go and look at the arrivals.[9] They will hardly follow us there."

Away they walked to the book; and while Isabella examined the names, it was Catherine's employment to watch the proceedings of these alarming young men.

7. **Sir Charles Grandison,** a novel by Samuel Richardson, published in 1754.
8. **signify,** matter.
9. **look at the arrivals,** examine the registry in the Pump Room, where people signed their names when they came to town.

"They are not coming this way, are they? I hope they are not so impertinent as to follow us. Pray let me know if they are coming. I am determined I will not look up."

In a few moments Catherine, with unaffected pleasure, assured her that she need not be long uneasy, as the gentlemen had just left the Pump Room.

"And which way are they gone?" said Isabella, turning hastily round. "One was a very good-looking young man."

"They went towards the churchyard."

"Well, I am amazingly glad I have got rid of them. And now, what say you to going to Edgar's Buildings with me, and looking at my new hat? You said you would like to see it."

Catherine readily agreed. "Only," she added, "perhaps we may overtake the two young men."

"Oh! never mind that. If we make haste, we shall pass by them presently, and I am dying to show you my hat."

"But if we only wait a few minutes, there will be no danger of our seeing them at all."

"I shall not pay them any such compliment, I assure you. I have no notion of treating men with such respect. *That* is the way to spoil them."

Catherine had nothing to oppose against such reasoning; and therefore, to show the independence of Miss Thorpe, and her resolution of humbling the sex, they set off immediately, as fast as they could walk, in pursuit of the two young men.

FOR UNDERSTANDING

1. What is Jane Austen's feeling about the worth of novels?
2. Is this opinion borne out in the conversation about reading between Catherine and Isabella?
3. What other interests do the two girls discuss?

FOR INTERPRETATION

1. Austen claims that she presents the girls' meeting as a specimen of their "delicacy, discretion, originality of thought, and literary taste." Does the meeting in fact bear out this claim?
2. What do you think are the real feelings of Isabella toward Miss Andrews?
3. How does Isabella manage to put down Catherine?

FOR APPRECIATION

Sir Walter Scott said that Austen had a talent for describing the "involvements . . . of ordinary life." How does this selection illustrate this judgment?

LANGUAGE AND VOCABULARY

What words would you use to express the idea in these phrases from the selection?
1. "I have been waiting for you *at least this age!*"
2. ". . . really, I thought I was *in very good time.*"
3. ". . . it looked very showery, and *that would have thrown me into agonies!*"
4. "Are not you *wild to know?*"
5. "I scold them . . . *amazingly* about it."
6. ". . . What is your *favorite complexion in a man?* Do you like them best *dark or fair?*"
7. ". . . (they) have been staring . . . *this half-hour.*"
8. "They really put me *quite out of countenance.*"

COMPOSITION

This selection is developed almost entirely through dialogue. Imaginary dialogues are fun to write. Start by determining the age and sex of two characters. Let them start talking, and bit by bit they will take on specific personalities in your mind as you write. The characters do not have to be the same kind of people as Isabella and Catherine. Your dialogue can be as brief as ten or twelve exchanges between the characters; but try to give it a structure, with a beginning, middle, and end.

Mary Wollstonecraft Shelley 1797–1851

Mary Shelley's parents were two well-known liberal intellectuals. Her mother, Mary Wollstonecraft, one of the earliest advocates for women's rights, was both novelist and pamphleteer. She authored a volume entitled *A Vindication of the Rights of Women,* which is still read and quoted today. William Godwin, Mary's father, was a social philosopher. Mary Wollstonecraft died soon after their daughter was born, and the griefstricken father named young Mary for her. As Mary grew up, her father put tremendous pressures on her to emulate her mother. From youth Mary struggled to write, sometimes lying on her mother's grave, as if inspiration could rise from the dead body. At seventeen, then a radiant beauty, Mary first met Percy Bysshe Shelley, an enthusiastic disciple of her father. The two fell in love; despite Shelley's previous marriage to Harriet Westbrook, they eloped and fled to the continent.

When Mary was nineteen, she and Shelley visited Lord Byron at the Villa Diodati in Switzerland. Bored with the continual rain that kept them housebound, Byron read some horror stories to his guests: the Shelleys, Mary's stepsister, and Dr. Polidori, Byron's physician. After some discussion of ghosts and vampires, Byron threw out the challenge that all of them should write a story of their own. This suggestion was, as Mary Shelley describes in her introduction to a later edition of *Frankenstein,* the genesis of that book.

Mary's marriage to Percy Shelley was cut short in 1822, with the poet's death by drowning. She returned to London with their young son and supported herself through her writing and with the aid of an allowance from Shelley's father. After *Frankenstein,* her best-known work, her books include *The Last Man* (1826), the

MARY SHELLEY
Richard Rothwell
The National Portrait Galley, London

medieval romance *Valperga* (1823), and the autobiographical *Lodore* (1835). She never remarried; as she explained to one of her suitors, "Having once tasted Nepenthe,* what is there left for me to hope for?"

* **Nepenthe** (ni pen' thē), a drug mentioned in the *Odyssey* as a remedy for grief.

INTRODUCTION TO FRANKENSTEIN

Mary Shelley wrote this introduction for an edition of Frankenstein *published in 1831; it thus recalls events of fifteen years before. She undertakes to explain the circumstances that surrounded her first imaginative vision of the novel as a whole.*

The Publishers of the Standard Novels, in selecting 'Frankenstein' for one of their series, expressed a wish that I should furnish them with some account of the origin of the story. I am the more willing to comply, because I shall thus give a general answer to the question, so very frequently asked me—"How I, then a young girl, came to think of, and to dilate upon, so very hideous an idea?"

In the summer of 1816, we[1] visited Switzerland, and became the neighbours of Lord Byron. At first we spent our pleasant hours on the lake, or wandering on its shores; and Lord Byron, who was writing the third canto of Childe Harold, was the only one among us who put his thoughts upon paper. These, as he brought them successively to us, clothed in all the light and harmony of poetry, seemed to stamp as divine the glories of heaven and earth, whose influences we partook with him.

But it proved a wet, ungenial summer, and incessant rain often confined us for days to the house. Some volumes of ghost stories translated from the German into French[2] fell into our hands. There was the History of the Inconstant Lover, who, when he thought to clasp the bride to whom he had pledged his vows, found himself in the arms of the pale ghost of her whom he had deserted. There was the tale of the sinful founder of his race, whose miserable doom it was to bestow the kiss of death on all the younger sons of his fated house, just when they reached the age of promise. His gigantic, shadowy form, clothed like the ghost in Hamlet, in complete armour, but with the beaver[3] up, was seen at midnight, by the moon's fitful beams, to advance slowly along the gloomy avenue. The shape was lost beneath the shadow of the castle walls; but soon a gate swung back, a step was heard, the door of the chamber opened, and he advanced to the couch of the blooming youths, cradled in healthy sleep. Eternal sorrow sat upon his face as he bent down and kissed the forehead of the boys, who from that hour withered like flowers snapt upon the stalk. I have not seen these stories since then; but their incidents are as fresh in my mind as if I had read them yesterday.

'We will each write a ghost story,' said Lord Byron; and his proposition was acceded to. There were four of us.[4] The noble author began a tale, a fragment of which he printed at the end of his poem of Mazeppa. Shelley, more apt to embody ideas and sentiments in the radiance of brilliant imagery, and in the music of the most melodious verse that adorns our language, than to invent the machinery of a story, commenced one founded on the experiences of his early life. Poor Polidori had some terrible idea about a skull-headed lady, who was so punished for

1. **we,** Mary Shelley, her husband Percy Bysshe Shelley, and their two children.
2. **French,** called *Fantasmagoriana* in French, or *Collected Stories of Apparitions of Specters, Ghosts, Phantoms, etc.*
3. **beaver,** the hinged face-piece of a suit of armor.
4. **four of us,** Byron, the two Shelleys, and Polidori (Byron's doctor).

peeping through a key hole—what to see I forget—something very shocking and wrong of course; but when she was reduced to a worse condition than the renowned Tom of Coventry,[5] he did not know what to do with her, and was obliged to despatch her to the tomb of the Capulets,[6] the only place for which she was fitted. The illustrious poets also, annoyed by the platitude of prose, speedily relinquished their uncongenial task.

I busied myself *to think of a story,*—a story to rival those which had excited us to this task. One which would speak to the mysterious fears of our nature, and awaken thrilling horror—one to make the reader dread to look round, to curdle the blood, and quicken the beatings of the heart. If I did not accomplish these things, my ghost story would be unworthy of its name. I thought and pondered—vainly. I felt that blank incapability of invention which is the greatest misery of authorship, when dull Nothing replies to our anxious invocations. *Have you thought of a story?* I was asked each morning, and each morning I was forced to reply with a mortifying negative.

Many and long were the conversations between Lord Byron and Shelley, to which I was a devout but nearly silent listener. During one of these, various philosophical doctrines were discussed, and among others the nature of the principle of life, and whether there was any probability of its ever being discovered and communicated. They talked of the experiments of Dr. Darwin,[7] (I speak not of what the Doctor really did, or said that he did, but, as more to my purpose, of what was then spoken of as having been done by him,) who preserved a piece of vermicelli in a glass case till by some extraordinary means it began to move with voluntary motion. Not thus, after all, would life be given. Perhaps a corpse would be re-animated; galvanism[8] had given token of such things: perhaps the component parts of a creature might be manufactured, brought together, and endued with vital warmth.

Night waned upon this talk, and even the witching hour had gone by, before we retired to rest. When I placed my head on my pillow, I did not sleep, nor could I be said to think. My imagination, unbidden, possessed and guided me, gifting the successive images that arose in my mind with a vividness far beyond the usual bounds of reverie. I saw—with shut eyes, but acute mental vision—I saw the pale student of unhallowed arts kneeling beside the thing he had put together. I saw the hideous phantasm of a man stretched out, and then, on the working of some powerful engine, show signs of life, and stir with an uneasy, half vital motion. Frightful must it be; for supremely frightful would be the effect of any human endeavour to mock the stupendous mechanism of the Creator of the world. His success would terrify the artist; he would rush away from his odious handywork, horror-stricken. He would hope that, left to itself, the slight spark of life which he had communicated would fade; that this thing, which had received such imperfect animation, would subside into dead matter; and he might sleep in the belief that the silence of the grave would quench for ever the transient existence of the hideous corpse which he had looked upon as the cradle of life. He sleeps; but he is awakened; he opens his eyes; behold the horrid thing stands at his bedside, opening his curtains, and looking on him with yellow, watery, but speculative eyes.

I opened mine in terror. The idea so possessed my mind, that a thrill of fear ran through me, and I wished to exchange the ghastly image of my fancy for the realities

---

5. **Tom of Coventry,** according to legend Tom was struck blind for peeping at Lady Godiva as she rode naked through Coventry (hence the expression, "peeping Tom").
6. **tomb of the Capulets,** where Romeo and Juliet died.
7. **Dr. Darwin,** Erasmus Darwin (1731–1802), a natural scientist and the grandfather of Charles Darwin (1809–1882) who proposed the theory of evolution.
8. **galvanism,** the use of a current of electricity to make a dead muscle twitch.

around. I see them still; the very room, the dark *parquet,*[9] the closed shutters, with the moonlight struggling through, and the sense I had that the glassy lake and white high Alps were beyond. I could not so easily get rid of my hideous phantom; still it haunted me. I must try to think of something else. I recurred to my ghost story,—my tiresome unlucky ghost story! O! if I could only contrive one which would frighten my reader as I myself had been frightened that night!

Swift as light and as cheering was the idea that broke in upon me. 'I have found it! What terrified me will terrify others; and I need only describe the spectre which had haunted my midnight pillow.' On the morrow I announced that I had *thought of a story.* I began that day with the words, *It was on a dreary night of November,* making only a transcript of the grim terrors of my waking dream.

At first I thought but of a few pages—of a short tale; but Shelley urged me to develop the idea at greater length. I certainly did not owe the suggestion of one incident, nor scarcely of one train of feeling, to my husband, and yet but for his incitement, it would never have taken the form in which it was presented to the world. From this declaration I must except the preface. As far as I can recollect, it was entirely written by him.

And now, once again, I bid my hideous progeny go forth and prosper. I have an affection for it, for it was the offspring of happy days, when death and grief were but words, which found no true echo in my heart. Its several pages speak of many a walk, many a drive, and many a conversation, when I was not alone; and my companion was one who, in this world, I shall never see more. But this

is for myself; my readers have nothing to do with these associations.

9. **parquet** (pär kā′),   inlaid wooden flooring.

FOR UNDERSTANDING

Mary Shelley's "Introduction" offers fascinating insights into the genesis of a literary work. What were the experiences that came together to spark the creation of *Frankenstein?*

FOR INTERPRETATION

1. Shelley says in her "Introduction": "My imagination, unbidden, possessed and guided me, gifting the successive images that arose in my mind." Consider the words "unbidden," "guided," and "gifting"; what do they imply about the nature of artistic creation?

2. The theme of *Frankenstein* is stated in one sentence of the "Introduction": ". . . supremely frightful would be the effect of any human endeavor to mock the stupendous mechanism of the Creator of the world." What is implied here?

COMPOSITION

All of us experience sudden inspirations, insights, or ideas which come unexpectedly and often help to solve some puzzling problem: perhaps how to write a paper for a class, or how to repair a car, or plan a party. The sudden answer may come unsought while you are sitting in church or riding a bus or eating lunch. With the solution in hand, you try to piece together how it came into being: what remembered experiences contributed to the answer. Try to find such a moment in your own life and write the "biography" of it just as Shelley has done.

THE RIME OF THE ANCIENT MARINER
Samuel Taylor Coleridge

This poem was the first selection in Lyrical Ballads, *published jointly by Wordsworth and Coleridge in 1798. It was written during the magical year (1797) when Coleridge, Dorothy, and William Wordsworth were living as neighbors in Somerset. A friend had told Coleridge of a strange dream in which he had seen a skeleton ship with figures on it. On a walk one November afternoon, Coleridge and the Wordsworths discussed the dream. Coleridge suggested there should be a navigator on a spectral ship, while Wordsworth proposed that he might commit a crime, perhaps killing an albatross, a bird he had read about in a travel book. But that evening the two poets found their ideas so different that they could not collaborate on the project. Coleridge continued to work on the poem separately, and in four months completed it. After the first publication, he continued to edit the text for later editions. The various changes included a reduction in the number of archaic words and spellings, and the additions of the marginal gloss.*

As you read the Rime, *be prepared to recognize many typically Romantic themes and elements: a medieval setting, old legends, nature as a pervasive force, devastating guilt, supernatural demons and phantoms, endless wanderings—and a superb musicality of rhythm and rhyme. Vehemently attacked by many critics when it first appeared, Coleridge's work stands today as one of the greatest narrative ballads in the language.*

Argument

How a Ship having passed the Line was driven by storms to the cold Country towards the South Pole; and how from thence she made her course to the tropical Latitude of the Great Pacific Ocean; and of the strange things that befell; and in what manner the Ancyent Marinere came back to his own Country.

Part I

An ancient Mariner meeteth three Gallants bidden to a wedding-feast, and detaineth one.

It is an ancient Mariner,
And he stoppeth one of three.
"By thy long grey beard and glittering eye,
Now wherefore stopp'st thou me?

The Bridegroom's doors are opened wide,　　　5
And I am next of kin;
The guests are met, the feast is set:
May'st hear the merry din."

He holds him with his skinny hand,
"There was a ship," quoth he.　　　10
"Hold off! unhand me, grey-beard loon!"[1]
Eftsoons[2] his hand dropt he.

The Wedding-Guest is spellbound by the eye of the old seafaring man, and constrained to hear his tale.

He holds him with his glittering eye—
The Wedding-Guest stood still,
And listens like a three years' child:　　　15
The Mariner hath his will.

The Wedding-Guest sat on a stone:
He cannot choose but hear;
And thus spake on that ancient man,
The bright-eyed Mariner.　　　20

The Mariner tells how the ship sailed southward with a good wind and fair weather, till it reached the line.

"The ship was cheered, the harbour cleared,
Merrily did we drop
Below the kirk,[3] below the hill,
Below the lighthouse top.

The Sun came up upon the left,[4]　　　25
Out of the sea came he!
And he shone bright, and on the right
Went down into the sea.

Higher and higher every day,
Till over the mast at noon—"[5]　　　30
The Wedding-Guest here beat his breast,
For he heard the loud bassoon.

The Wedding-Guest heareth the bridal music; but the Mariner continueth his tale.

The bride hath paced into the hall,
Red as a rose is she;
Nodding their heads before her goes　　　35
The merry minstrelsy.

1. **loon,**　clownish, awkward, ill-bred fellow. ["Loony," coming from "lunatic," did not become a slang expression until late in the nineteenth century.]
2. **eftsoons,**　immediately.
3. **kirk,**　Scottish word for church.
4. **upon the left,**　indicating that the ship heads south.
5. **over the mast at noon,**　the ship crosses the equator.

The Wedding-Guest he beat his breast,
Yet he cannot choose but hear;
And thus spake on that ancient man,
The bright-eyed Mariner.   40

The ship driven by a storm toward the south pole.

"And now the STORM-BLAST came, and he
Was tyrannous and strong:
He struck with his o'ertaking wings,
And chased us south along.

With sloping masts and dipping prow,   45
As who pursued with yell and blow
Still treads the shadow of his foe,
And forward bends his head,
The ship drove fast, loud roared the blast,
And southward aye we fled.   50

And now there came both mist and snow,
And it grew wondrous cold:
And ice, mast-high, came floating by,
As green as emerald.

The land of ice, and of fearful sounds where no living thing was to be seen.

And through the drifts the snowy clifts   55
Did send a dismal sheen:
Nor shapes of men nor beasts we ken—[6]
The ice was all between.

The ice was here, the ice was there,
The ice was all around: 60
It cracked and growled, and roared and howled,
Like noises in a swound![7]

Till a great seabird, called the Albatross, came through the snow-fog, and was received with great joy and hospitality.

At length did cross an Albatross,
Thorough the fog it came;
As if it had been a Christian soul,   65
We hailed it in God's name.

It ate the food it ne'er had eat,[8]
And round and round it flew.
The ice did split with a thunder-fit;[9]
The helmsman steered us through!   70

6. **ken,** saw (archaic).
7. **swound,** swoon or fainting spell (archaic).
8. **food it ne'er had eat,** the original line was "The mariners gave it biscuit-worms" (maggots), but the line was deemed offensive and changed.
9. **thunder-fit,** clap of thunder.

And now there came mist and snow,
And it grew wonderous cold.

Gustave Doré
The British Museum

And lo! the Albatross proveth a bird of good omen, and followeth the ship as it returned northward through fog and floating ice.

And a good south wind sprung up behind;
The Albatross did follow,
And every day, for food or play,
Came to the mariners' hollo![10]

In mist or cloud, on mast or shroud,[11]   75
It perched for vespers nine;[12]
Whiles all the night, through fog-smoke white,
Glimmered the white Moon-shine."

The ancient Mariner inhospitably killeth the pious bird of good omen.

"God save thee, ancient Mariner!
From the fiends, that plague thee thus!—   80
Why look's thou so?"—"With my cross-bow[13]
I shot the ALBATROSS.

Part II

The Sun now rose upon the right:[1]
Out of the sea came he,
Still hid in mist, and on the left   85
Went down into the sea.

And the good south wind still blew behind,
But no sweet bird did follow,
Nor any day for food or play
Came to the mariners' hollo!   90

His shipmates cry out against the ancient Mariner, for killing the bird of good luck.

And I had done a hellish thing,
And it would work 'em woe:
For all averred, I had killed the bird
That made the breeze to blow.

10. **hollo,** a loud shout.
11. **shroud,** one of the heavy ropes that keep the mast rigid by stretching from the top of the mast to the sides of the ship.
12. **vespers nine,** vespers is a church service held at sunset; the albatross came to roost on the ship at twilight for nine evenings.
13. **cross-bow,** a medieval weapon.

1. **upon the right,** the ship has rounded Cape Horn at the southern tip of South America, and is now heading north.

Water, water everywhere . . .
Nor any drop to drink.

Gustave Doré
The British Library, London

Ah wretch! said they, the bird to slay,   95
That made the breeze to blow!

But when the fog cleared off, they justify the same, and thus make themselves accomplices in the crime.[3]

Nor dim nor red, like God's own head,
The glorious Sun uprist:[2]
Then all averred, I had killed the bird
That brought the fog and mist.   100
'Twas right, said they, such birds to slay,
That bring the fog and mist.

The fair breeze continues; the ship enters the Pacific Ocean, and sails northward, even till it reaches the Line.

The fair breeze blew,[4] the white foam flew,
The furrow followed free;
We were the first that ever burst   105
Into that silent sea.

The ship hath been suddenly becalmed.

Down dropt the breeze, the sails dropt down,
'Twas sad as sad could be;
And we did speak only to break
The silence of the sea!   110

All in a hot and copper sky,
The bloody Sun,[5] at noon,
Right up above the mast did stand,
No bigger than the Moon.

Day after day, day after day,   115
We stuck, nor breath nor motion;
As idle as a painted ship
Upon a painted ocean.

And the Albatross begins to be avenged.

Water, water, everywhere,
And all the boards did shrink;   120
Water, water, everywhere,
Nor any drop to drink.

The very deep did rot: O Christ!
That ever this should be!
Yea, slimy things did crawl with legs   125
Upon the slimy sea.

2. **uprist,** uprose.
3. **in the crime,** the gloss here explains the reason the whole crew is damned for the Mariner's crime.
4. **the fair breeze blew,** the easterly trade winds are carrying the ship northwest.
5. **bloody Sun,** the ship is again at the equator; the sun is now one of vengeance.

About, about,[6] in reel and rout[7]
The death-fires[8] danced at night;
The water, like a witch's oils,
Burnt green, and blue and white.   130

A Spirit had followed them; one of the invisible inhabitants of this planet, neither departed souls nor angels; concerning whom the learned Jew, Josephus, and the Platonic Constantinopolitan, Michael Psellus, may be consulted. They are very numerous, and there is no climate or element without one or more.

And some in dreams assuréd[9] were
Of the Spirit that plagued us so;
Nine fathom deep he had followed us
From the land of mist and snow.

And every tongue, through utter drought,   135
Was withered at the root;
We could not speak, no more than if
We had been choked with soot.

The shipmates, in their sore distress, would fain throw the whole guilt on the ancient Mariner: in sign whereof they hang the dead sea-bird round his neck.

Ah! well a-day![10] what evil looks
Had I from old and young!   140
Instead of the cross, the Albatross
About my neck was hung.

Part III

There passed a weary time. Each throat
Was parched, and glazed each eye.
A weary time! a weary time!   145
How glazed each weary eye,
When looking westward, I beheld
A something in the sky.

The ancient Mariner beholdeth a sign in the element afar off.

At first it seemed a little speck,
And then it seemed a mist;   150
It moved and moved, and took at last
A certain shape, I wist.[1]

6. **about, about,** compare the witches in *Macbeth,* I.iii.34.
7. **reel and rout,** a lively dance with whirling movement; Coleridge here applies the phrase to the rout of a disorganized mob.
8. **death-fires,** ghostly graveyard lights, supposedly cast by decaying bodies.
9. **dreams assuré**d, became certain of a revelation.
10. **well a-day!** alas.

1. **wist,** knew.

A speck, a mist, a shape, I wist!
And still it neared and neared:
As if it dodged a water-sprite,   155
It plunged and tacked² and veered.

At its nearer approach, it seemeth him to be a ship; and at a dear ransom he freeth his speech from the bonds of thirst.

With throats unslaked, with black lips baked,
We could nor laugh nor wail;
Through utter drought all dumb we stood!
I bit my arm, I sucked the blood,   160
And cried, A sail! a sail!

With throats unslaked, with black lips baked
Agape they heard me call:
A flash of joy;
Gramercy!³ they for joy did grin,
And all at once their breath drew in,   165

As they were drinking all.
And horror follows. For can it be a ship that comes onward without wind or tide?
See! see! (I cried) she tacks no more!
Hither to work us weal;⁴
Without a breeze, without a tide,
She steadies with upright keel!   170

The western wave was all a-flame.
The day was well nigh done!
Almost upon the western wave
Rested the broad bright Sun;
When the strange shape drove suddenly   175
Betwixt us and the Sun.

It seemeth him but the skeleton of a ship.
And straight the Sun was flecked⁵ with bars,
(Heaven's Mother send us grace!)
As if through a dungeon-grate he peered
With broad and burning face.   180

And its ribs are seen as bars on the face of the setting Sun.
Alas! (thought I, and my heart beat loud)
How fast she nears and nears!
Are those *her* sails that glance in the Sun,
Like restless gossameres?⁶

The Spectre-Woman and her Death-mate, and no other on board the skeleton ship.
Are those *her* ribs through which the Sun   185
Did peer, as through a grate?

---

2. **tacked,**   changed direction.
3. **Gramercy!**   an exclamation of thankful joy.
4. **work us weal,**   bring us happiness or well-being.
5. **flecked,**   striped.
6. **gossameres,**   filmy cobwebs.

"The game is done! I've won, I've won!
Quoth she, and whistles thrice.

Gustave Doré
The British Library, London

And is that Woman all her crew?
Is that a DEATH?[7] and are there two?
Is DEATH that woman's mate?

Like vessel, like crew!

Her lips were red, *her* looks were free,   190
Her locks were yellow as gold:
Her skin was as white as leprosy,
The Night-mare LIFE-IN-DEATH was she,
Who thicks[8] man's blood with cold.

Death and Life-in-Death have diced for the ship's crew, and she (the latter) winneth the ancient Mariner.

The naked hulk[9] alongside came,   195
And the twain were casting dice;
'The game is done! I've won! I've won!'
Quoth she, and whistles thrice.

No twilight within the courts of the Sun.

The Sun's rim dips; the stars rush out:
At one stride comes the dark;   200
With far-heard whisper, o'er the sea,
Off shot the spectre-bark.

At the rising of the Moon,

We listened and looked sideways up!
Fear at my heart, as at a cup,
My life-blood seemed to sip![10]   205
The stars were dim, and thick the night,
The steersman's face by his lamp gleamed white;
From the sails the dew did drip—
Till clomb above the eastern bar[11]
The hornéd Moon, with one bright star   210
Within the nether tip.

One after another,

One after one, by the star-dogged Moon,[12]
Too quick for groan or sigh,
Each turned his face with a ghastly pang,
And cursed me with his eye.   215

His shipmates drop down dead.

Four times fifty living men,
(And I heard nor sigh nor groan)

7. **a DEATH,** a skeleton.
8. **thicks,** thickens.
9. **naked hulk,** a hull without planking, as in a wrecked ship.
10. **my life-blood seemed to sip,** fear drains his heart's blood as one drains a cup.
11. **eastern bar,** eastern horizon.
12. **star-dogged Moon,** superstitious sailors believed that a star dogging the moon indicated that evil was imminent.

With heavy thump, a lifeless lump,
They dropped down one by one.

But Life-in-Death begins her work on the ancient
Mariner.

The souls did from their bodies fly,—[13]   **220**
They fled to bliss or woe!
And every soul, it passed me by,
Like the whizz of my cross-bow!"

Part IV

The Wedding Guest feareth that a Spirit is talking
to him;

"I fear thee, ancient Mariner!
I fear thy skinny hand!   **225**
And thou art long, and lank, and brown,
As is the ribbed sea-sand.

I fear thee and thy glittering eye,
And thy skinny hand, so brown."—

But the ancient Mariner assureth him of his bodily life, and proceedeth to relate his horrible penance.

"Fear not, fear not, thou Wedding-Guest!
This body dropt not down.   **230**

Alone, alone, all, all alone,
Alone on a wide wide sea!
And never a saint took pity on
My soul in agony.   **235**

He despiseth the creatures of the calm,

The many men, so beautiful!
And they all dead did lie:
And a thousand thousand slimy things
Lived on; and so did I.

And envieth that *they* should live, and so many lie
dead.

I looked upon the rotting sea,   **240**
And drew my eyes away;
I looked upon the rotting deck,
And there the dead men lay.

I looked to heaven, and tried to pray;
But or ever a prayer had gusht,   **245**
A wicked whisper came, and made
My heart as dry as dust.

13. In the medieval period it was commonly believed
that the soul flew out of the body at death.

I closed my lids, and kept them close,
And the balls like pulses beat;
For the sky and the sea, and the sea and the
    sky   250
Lay like a load on my weary eye,
And the dead were at my feet.

But the curse liveth for him in the eye of the
dead men.

The cold sweat melted from their limbs,
Nor rot nor reek did they:
The look with which they looked on me   255
Had never passed away.

An orphan's curse would drag to hell[1]
A spirit from on high;
But oh! more horrible than that
Is the curse in a dead man's eye!   260
Seven days, seven nights, I saw that curse,
And yet I could not die.

In his loneliness and fixedness he yearneth towards the journeying Moon, and the stars that still
sojourn, yet still move onward; and every where
the blue sky belongs to them, and is their appointed rest, and their native country and their own
natural homes, which they enter unannounced, as
lords that are certainly expected and yet there is a
silent joy at their arrival.

The moving Moon went up the sky,
And nowhere did abide:
Softly she was going up,   265
And a star or two beside—

Her beams bemocked[2] the sultry main,
Like April hoar-frost spread;
But where the ship's huge shadow lay,
The charmèd water burnt alway   270
A still and awful red.[3]

By the light of the Moon he beholdeth God's
creatures of the great calm.

Beyond the shadow of the ship,
I watched the water-snakes:[4]
They moved in tracks of shining white,
And when they reared, the elfish light   275
Fell off in hoary flakes.

Within the shadow of the ship
I watched their rich attire:

1. **orphan's curse,** a medieval superstition held that a
curse from an orphan, a dying person, or a beggar was
especially potent.
2. **bemocked,** scorned, ridiculed.
3. **still and awful red,** probably from plankton, which
often causes a ruddy color in the water.
4. **water-snakes,** ribbon-like sea worms, some of which
are luminous, and may reach a length of twenty-five feet.

Beyond the shadow of the ship
I watched the water snakes.

Gustave Doré
The British Library, London

Blue, glossy green, and velvet black,
They coiled and swam; and every track   280
Was a flash of golden fire.

Their beauty and their happiness.

O happy living things! no tongue
Their beauty might declare:
A spring of love gushed from my heart,
And I blessed them unaware: 285

He blesseth them in his heart.

Sure my kind saint took pity on me,
And I blessed them unaware.

The spell begins to break.

The self-same moment I could pray;
And from my neck so free
The Albatross fell off, and sank   290
Like lead into the sea.

Part V

Oh sleep! it is a gentle thing,
Beloved from pole to pole!
To Mary Queen the praise be given!
She sent the gentle sleep from Heaven,   295
That slid into my soul.

By grace of the holy Mother, the ancient Mariner
is refreshed with rain.

The silly buckets on the deck,
That had so long remained,
I dreamt that they were filled with dew;
And when I awoke, it rained.   300

My lips were wet, my throat was cold,
My garments all were dank;
Sure I had drunken in my dreams,
And still my body drank.

I moved, and could not feel my limbs: 305
I was so light—almost
I thought that I had died in sleep,
And was a blesséd ghost.

He heareth sounds and seeth strange sights and
commotions in the sky and the element.

And soon I heard a roaring wind:
It did not come anear;   310

They groaned, they stirred, they all uprose,
Nor spake, nor moved their eyes.

Gustave Doré
The British Library, London

But with its sound it shook the sails,
That were so thin and sere.[1]

The upper air burst into life![2]
And a hundred fire-flags sheen,
To and fro they were hurried about!   315
And to and fro, and in and out,
The wan stars danced between.

And the coming wind did roar more loud
And the sails did sigh like sedge;
And the rain poured down from one black
        cloud;   320
The Moon was at its edge.

The thick black cloud was cleft, and still
The Moon was at its side:
Like waters shot from some high crag,
The lightning fell with never a jag,[3]   325
A river steep and wide.

The bodies of the ship's crew are inspirited and the ship moves on;

The loud wind never reached the ship,
Yet now the ship moved on!
Beneath the lightning and the Moon
The dead men gave a groan.   330

They groaned, they stirred, they all uprose,
Nor spake, nor moved their eyes;
It had been strange, even in a dream,
To have seen those dead men rise.

The helmsman steered, the ship moved on;   335
Yet never a breeze up-blew;
The mariners all 'gan work the ropes,
Where they were wont[4] to do;
They raised their limbs like lifeless tools—
We were a ghastly crew.[5]   340

1. **sere,** worn to shreds.
2. This stanza describes the phenomenon of the *aurora borealis* (or Northern Lights).
3. **never a jag,** a jag is a sharp projection. Lightning actually does not zig-zag; aerial photographs show it as a twisting river.
4. **wont to do,** used to doing.
5. **ghastly crew,** Wordsworth claims to have suggested that the ship be sailed by the dead men, a common sailor's legend.

The body of my brother's son
Stood by me, knee to knee:
The body and I pulled at one rope,
But he said nought to me."

But not by the souls of the men, nor by dæmons of earth or middle air, but by a blessed troop of angelic spirits, sent down by the invocation of the guardian saint.

"I fear thee, ancient Mariner!"   345
"Be calm, thou Wedding-Guest!
'Twas not those souls that fled in pain,
Which to their corses[6] came again,
But a troop of spirits blest:

For when it dawned—they dropped their arms,350
And clustered round the mast;
Sweet sounds rose slowly through their mouths,
And from their bodies passed.

Around, around, flew each sweet sound,
Then darted to the Sun;   355
Slowly the sounds came back again,
Now mixed, now one by one.

Sometimes a-dropping from the sky
I heard the sky-lark sing;
Sometimes all little birds that are,   360
How they seemed to fill the sea and air
With their sweet jargoning![7]

And now 'twas like all instruments,
Now like a lonely flute;
And now it is an angel's song,   365
That makes the heavens be mute.

It ceased; yet still the sails made on
A pleasant noise till noon,
A noise like of a hidden brook
In the leafy month of June,   370
That to the sleeping woods all night
Singeth a quiet tune.

Till noon we quietly sailed on,
Yet never a breeze did breathe:
Slowly and smoothly went the ship,   375
Moved onward from beneath.

6. **corses,** corpses.
7. **jargoning,** speaking an unintelligible language.

The lonesome Spirit from the south pole carries on the ship as far as the Line, in obedience to the angelic troop, but still requireth vengeance.

Under the keel nine fathom[8] deep,
From the land of mist and snow,
The spirit slid: and it was he
That made the ship to go.   380
The sails at noon left off their tune,
And the ship stood still also.

The Sun,[9] right up above the mast,
Had fixed her to the ocean:
But in a minute she 'gan stir,   385
With a short uneasy motion—
Backwards and forwards half her length
With a short uneasy motion.

Then like a pawing horse let go,
She made a sudden bound:[10]   390
It flung the blood into my head,
And I fell down in a swound.

The Polar Spirit's fellow-dæmons, the invisible inhabitants of the element, take part in his wrong; and two of them relate, one to the other, that penance long and heavy for the ancient Mariner hath been accorded to the Polar Spirit, who returneth southward.

How long in that same fit I lay,
I have not to declare;
But ere my living life[11] returned,   395
I heard and in my soul discerned
Two voices in the air.

'Is it he?' quoth one, 'Is this the man?
By him who died on cross,
With his cruel bow he laid full low   400
The harmless Albatross.

The spirit who bideth by himself
In the land of mist and snow,
He loved the bird that loved the man
Who shot him with his bow.'   405

8. **fathom,**   six feet.
9. **Sun,**   the ship is again at the equator and stops there, suggesting that the Polar demon which moves it cannot cross the equator.
10. **made a sudden bound,**   the Polar demon apparently gives the ship a last shake as he releases the vessel; the ship is convulsed.
11. **living life,**   his kind saint has returned him from death-in-life to life.

The other was a softer voice,
As soft as honey-dew:[12]
Quoth he, 'The man hath penance done,
And penance more will do.'

Part VI

First Voice

'But tell me, tell me! speak again,   410
Thy soft response renewing—
What makes that ship drive on so fast?
What is the ocean doing?'

Second Voice

'Still as a slave before his lord,
The ocean hath no blast;[1]   415
His great bright eye most silently
Up to the Moon is cast—

If he may know which way to go;
For she guides him smooth or grim.
See, brother, see! how graciously   420
She looketh down on him.'

First Voice

The Mariner hath been cast into a trance; for the angelic power causeth the vessel to drive northward faster than human life could endure.

'But why drives on that ship so fast,
Without or wave or wind?'

Second Voice

'The air is cut away before,[2]
And closes from behind.   425

12. **honey-dew,** here refers to a deliciously sweet substance that falls like manna from heaven.

1. **blast,** wind.
2. This is a pseudo-scientific explanation to make the ship's extremely swift movement credible.

Fly, brother, fly! more high, more high!
Or we shall be belated:[3]
For slow and slow that ship will go.
When the Mariner's trance is abated.'

The supernatural motion is retarded; the Mariner awakes, and his penance begins anew.

I woke, and we were sailing on   430
As in a gentle weather:
'Twas night, calm night, the moon was high;
The dead men stood together.

All stood together on the deck,
For a charnel-dungeon[4] fitter: 435
All fixed on me their stony eyes,
That in the Moon did glitter.

The pang, the curse, with which they died,
Had never passed away:
I could not draw my eyes from theirs,   440
Nor turn them up to pray.

The curse is finally expiated.

And now this spell was snapt: once more
I viewed the ocean green,
And looked far forth, yet little saw
Of what had else[5] been seen—   445

Like one, that on a lonesome road
Doth walk in fear and dread,
And having once turned round walks on,
And turns no more his head;
Because he knows, a frightful fiend   450
Doth close behind him tread.

But soon there breathed a wind on me,
Nor sound nor motion made:
Its path was not upon the sea,
In ripple or in shade.   455

It raised my hair, it fanned my cheek
Like a meadow-gale of spring—
It mingled strangely with my fears,
Yet it felt like a welcoming.

---

3. **belated,** late.
4. **charnel-dungeon,** a confined space for the dead.
5. **else,** formerly.

And on the bay the moonlight lay
And the shadow of the Moon.

Gustave Doré
The British Library, London

Swiftly, swiftly flew the ship,   460
Yet she sailed softly too:
Sweetly, sweetly blew the breeze—
On me alone it blew.

And the ancient Mariner beholdeth his native
country.

Oh! dream of joy! is this indeed
The light-house top I see?   465
Is this the hill? is this the kirk?
Is this mine own countree?

We drifted o'er the harbour-bar,[6]
And I with sobs did pray—
O let me be awake, my God!   470
Or let me sleep alway.

The harbour-bay was clear as glass,
So smoothly it was strewn![7]
And on the bay the moonlight lay,
And the shadow of the Moon.[8]   475

The rock shone bright, the kirk no less,
That stands above the rock:
The moonlight steeped in silentness
The steady weathercock.[9]

And the bay was white with silent light,   480
Till rising from the same,

The angelic spirits leave the dead bodies,

Full many shapes, that shadows were,
In crimson colours came.

A little distance from the prow
Those crimson shadows[10] were: 485

And appear in their own forms of light.

I turned my eyes upon the deck—
Oh, Christ! what saw I there!

6. **harbour-bar,** the ridge of sand that often appears
before a harbor.
7. **strewn,** scattered, here used metaphorically of the
water in the harbor.
8. **shadow of the Moon,** the moon's reflection in the
water.
9. **steady weathercock,** there is no wind since the
weathervane does not move.
10. **crimson shadows,** in discarded stanzas, before the
seraphs left the dead bodies they raised their right arms,
which burned like torches and cast red shadows on the
sea.

Each corse lay flat, lifeless and flat,
And, by the holy rood![11]
A man all light, a seraph-man,[12] 490
On every corse there stood.

This seraph-band, each waved his hand:
It was a heavenly sight!
They stood as signals[13] to the land,
Each one a lovely light; 495

This seraph-band, each waved his hand,
No voice did they impart—
No voice; but oh! the silence sank
Like music on my heart.

But soon I heard the dash of oars, 500
I heard the Pilot's cheer;[14]
My head was turned perforce[15] away
And I saw a boat appear.

The Pilot and the Pilot's boy,
I heard them coming fast: 505
Dear Lord in Heaven! it was a joy
The dead men could not blast.[16]

I saw a third—I heard his voice:
It is the Hermit[17] good!
He singeth loud his godly hymns 510
That he makes in the wood.
He'll shrieve[18] my soul, he'll wash away
The Albatross's blood.

11. **by the holy rood!** by the cross on which Christ was crucified.
12. **seraph-man,** the highest order of angels are the six-winged seraphim, who guard God's throne.
13. **signals,** the seraphs waving their hands are the signal that brings out the pilot.
14. **cheer,** call or haloo to the ship.
15. **perforce,** he cannot restrain himself from looking at the bay.
16. **blast,** destroy.
17. **hermit,** a solitary religious man.
18. **shrieve,** to hear confession and forgive sin.

Part VII

This Hermit good lives in that wood
Which slopes down to the sea.   515
How loudly his sweet voice he rears!
He loves to talk with marineres
That come from a far countree.

He kneels at morn, and noon, and eve—
He hath a cushion plump: 520
It is the moss that wholly hides
The rotted old oak-stump.

The skiff-boat neared: I heard them talk,
'Why, this is strange, I trow!'[1]
Where are those lights so many and fair,   525
That signal made but now?'

'Strange, by my faith!' the Hermit said—
'And they answered not our cheer!
The planks looked warped! and see those sails,
How thin they are and sere!   530
I never saw aught like to them,
Unless perchance it were

Brown skeletons of leaves that lag
My forest-brook along;
When the ivy-tod[2] is heavy with snow,   535
And the owlet whoops to the wolf below,
That eats the she-wolf's young.'

'Dear Lord! it hath a fiendish look—
(The Pilot made reply)
I am a-feared'—'Push on, push on!'   540
Said the Hermit cheerily.

The boat came closer to the ship,
But I nor spake nor stirred;
The boat came close beneath the ship,
And straight a sound was heard.   545

1. **trow,** think or suppose.
2. **ivy-tod,** ivy plant.

The Mariner, whose eye is bright,
Whose beard with age is hoar,
Is gone.

Gustave Doré
The British Library, London

The ship suddenly sinketh.

Under the water it rumbled on,
Still louder and more dread:
It reached the ship, it split the bay;
The ship went down like lead.

The ancient Mariner is saved in the Pilot's boat.

Stunned by that loud and dreadful sound,   550
Which sky and ocean smote,
Like one that hath been seven days drowned
My body lay afloat;
But swift as dreams, myself I found
Within the Pilot's boat.   555

Upon the whirl, where sank the ship,
The boat spun round and round;
And all was still, save that the hill
Was telling of the sound.[3]

I moved my lips—the Pilot shrieked[4]   560
And fell down in a fit;
The holy Hermit raised his eyes,
And prayed where he did sit.

I took the oars: the Pilot's boy,
Who now doth crazy go,   565
Laughed loud and long, and all the while
His eyes went to and fro.
'Ha! ha!' quoth he, 'full plain I see,
The Devil knows how to row.'

And now, all in my own countree,   570
I stood on the firm land!
The Hermit stepped forth from the boat,
And scarcely he could stand.

The ancient Mariner earnestly entreateth the Hermit to shrieve him; and the penance of life falls on him.

'O shrieve me, shrieve me, holy man!'
The Hermit crossed his brow.[5]   575
'Say quick,' quoth he, 'I bid thee say—
What manner of man art thou?'[6]

3. **telling of the sound,** echoing the sound.
4. **shrieked,** the Pilot presumed the Mariner to be dead, and the silent moving of his lips shocked him.
5. **crossed his brow,** made the sign of the cross on his forehead to ward off evil.
6. **what manner of man,** the Hermit wants to be assured that the mariner is not a dead man, a demon, or the devil himself.

Forthwith this frame of mine was wrenched
With a woful agony,
Which forced me to begin my tale;   580
And then it left me free.

And ever and anon throughout his future life an agony constraineth him to travel from land to land;

Since then, at an uncertain hour,
That agony returns:
And till my ghastly tale is told,
This heart within me burns.   585

I pass, like night, from land to land;[7]
I have strange power of speech;
That moment that his face I see,
I know the man that must hear me:
To him my tale I teach.[8]   590

What loud uproar bursts from that door!
The wedding-guests are there:
But in the garden-bower the bride
And bride-maids singing are:
And hark the little vesper bell,   595
Which biddeth me to prayer!

O Wedding-Guest! this soul hath been
Alone on a wide wide sea:
So lonely 'twas, that God himself
Scarce seeméd there to be.   600

O sweeter than the marriage-feast,
'Tis sweeter far to me,
To walk together to the kirk
With a goodly company!—

To walk together to the kirk,   605
And all together pray,
While each to his great Father bends,
Old men, and babes, and loving friends
And youths and maidens gay!

7. **pass like night,** night is a dark shadow that moves swiftly and silently around the earth.
8. **to him my tale I teach,** the Mariner's penance is to wander the earth and to tell his tale to those who he thinks must hear it. His situation thus bears a strong resemblance to the legends of the Wandering Jew and of Cain, neither of whom can die, but must wander the earth forever.

And to teach, by his own example, love and reverence to all things that God made and loveth.

Farewell, farewell! but this I tell   610
To thee, thou Wedding-Guest!
He prayeth well, who loveth well
Both man and bird and beast.

He prayeth best, who loveth best
All things both great and small;   615
For the dear God who loveth us,
He made and loveth all."

The Mariner, whose eye is bright,
Whose beard with age is hoar,
Is gone: and now the Wedding-Guest   620
Turned from the bridegroom's door.

He went like one that hath been stunned,
And is of sense forlorn:[9]
A sadder and a wiser man,
He rose the morrow morn.   625

9. **forlorn,** deprived.

FOR UNDERSTANDING

1. Who is telling the story? To whom? Under what
circumstances?
2. Why did the mariner shoot the albatross?
3. In Part II what consequences of the mariner's
act are described?
4. In Part III what is the condition of the crew?
Describe the rescue ship and its passengers. After
the spectre ship disappears, what happens to the
crew and the mariner?
5. What are the mariner's experiences in Part IV?
6. In Part V how is the mariner able to sail the
ship? What does he see and hear when he falls in a
faint?
7. In Part VI what do the voices say is now moving
the ship? Who signals the pilot to come out? Why is
the mariner happy to hear the hermit's voice?
8. What are the pilot's and the hermit's reactions
to the appearance of the ship? What happens to
the ship, the mariner, and his rescuers? How does
the mariner know to whom he must tell his tale?

FOR INTERPRETATION

1. *The Rime of the Ancient Mariner* has intrigued
readers from its first appearance right up to the
present day. Biographical critics have tried to see
in its elements of Coleridge's life; psychological
critics have examined it in terms of frustrated
emotional experiences; religious critics have identified crucifixion symbols in the poem. What has
the poem meant to you? Discuss the following
statements in light of your reading of the *Rime*.
  a. The voyage is an allegory of one person's
    psychological voyage through life.
  b. When nature is wantonly abused it fights
    back.
  c. The poem presents guilt and its expiation.
  d. There is another world operating beyond the
    world we know and see.
  e. The *Rime* is a story of death and rebirth.
2. What is the pattern of emotions that a reader
experiences in this poem?
3. The wedding begins the poem, interrupts the

story in Part I, and ends the poem. What effect does this context for the mariner's story produce?

4. People have long tried to understand the moral stated in the third from the last stanza. What do you make of it?

FOR APPRECIATION

1. What are the advantages of imitating the ballad stanza?

2. How does Coleridge keep the ballad stanza from becoming monotonous?

3. Examine the archaic words in Part I (they are generally among those footnoted). In earlier editions there were even more archaisms, which Coleridge gradually removed. What literary judgment do you think motivated him to edit the poem in this way?

4. Look at the last stanza of each part. What do you discover about the structure of the story?

5. The poem is seldom printed without the gloss, which was added by Coleridge in an edition published some twenty years after the original. Glosses were often added to medieval manuscripts to explain words, to provide translations, or to make

comments. Did Coleridge have an artistic purpose in using this technique?

6. Almost every line of the poem is rich with sensory impressions. Consider two famous passages: first, the five stanzas beginning with line 41 (page 570); and second, the five stanzas beginning with line 111 (page 574). Reread these stanzas and discuss your sensory impressions (colors, shapes, motions, sounds).

COMPOSITION

Investigate this poem a bit further. Write an expository paper on your findings about the effects on the poem of one of the following:

1. Coleridge's use of the mystical numbers 3, 7, and 9. For example there are 7 sections in the poem; the mariner stops one of 3.

2. His use of colors. Remember the iceberg as "green as emerald."

3. His use of repetition of lines or of phrases.

4. His use of the heavenly bodies: sun, moon, stars.

5. His descriptions of the ocean.

6. His use of the supernatural, the unexplained.

COMPOSITION WORKSHOP

THE FIRST DRAFT

Having developed to your satisfaction a preliminary outline for your research paper, you are now ready to begin your first draft. This is the point in the research process where most new writers stall. Don't permit yourself to get bogged down over points of style or footnote form or devising a catchy opening. In fact, don't concern yourself with your paper's introduction at all at this point. That will come later. Your main concern now should be with the body of your paper, since this is the section that will contain the arguments that support your thesis. Many teachers are of the opinion that the success or failure of a research paper depends entirely upon the skill with which the body is developed. Once you have dealt effectively with this section, you may turn your attention to other considerations.

The best way to handle the writing of the body is to approach it part by part. Since the body's outline has grown out of the collected notes, you should return to your stacks of note cards and carefully examine the notes in each stack. You might discover that one of the sections you envisioned is so brief when compared with other sections that it might best be combined with another section or eliminated altogether. By the same token, you might decide at this point to divide one of your contemplated sections into two or more sections. Whatever you ultimately decide, you will be thankful once again that your notes have been collected on cards.

Once you are certain that the outline of your paper's body accurately reflects the nature and content of the supporting material, you will want to determine whether the various sections have been arranged in the most logical order. Usually, this translates to making sure that the more thoroughly developed arguments come before the less thoroughly developed arguments. One simple way of guaranteeing that this is the case is by comparing the relative size of your stacks of note cards—obviously the thicker the stack, the more detailed the information you will have gathered on that particular point.

As you write, it is critical to keep in mind that the cards you are using represent the ideas of others. This means that much of the information in the body of your paper will have to be acknowledged in the form of footnotes. Since you are preparing a first draft, and not a final version of your paper, it will suffice for the moment simply to note when you are using borrowed material and to indicate in some fashion whether you are quoting directly, paraphrasing, or summarizing. This is best accomplished by using some sort of code—either the numbers appearing in the upper right-hand corner of your 3 × 5-inch bibliography cards (plus page numbers from your note cards) or the letters of the alphabet, which are easily distinguished later on from the footnote numbers that will replace them. At this point, you will not need to copy whole long quotations from your note cards; just copy enough of the quote to enable you to locate it easily at some future time. Remember, your object now is to get your ideas down as quickly as possible, and copying lengthy quotations will prove distracting.

THE ACTUAL WRITING

In spite of all that has been said so far, the task of setting your thoughts down on paper is, in the end, a demanding one; it requires your undivided attention and a total application of your creative abilities. It is not enough simply to patch together all of the notes you have taken. You must decide on what the major point of every paragraph is, express that point in clear and unambiguous language, and then provide support for it. If you are not satisfied with the particular manner in which you have phrased a point, do not trouble yourself with extensive revisions; there will be ample time to refine your diction in later drafts of the paper. You must also give some thought at this stage to "filling in the gaps"—that is, to providing whatever transitional material is needed to insure that the body of the report flows smoothly from point to point and paragraph to paragraph.

Study the following two sample paragraphs, each taken from the body section of a research paper. One is from a paper that identifies the romantic characteristics in the poetry of Percy Bysshe Shelley; the other is from a paper that argues that the poet A. E. Housman was not the pessimist most critics have branded him. Notice how in each sample the author identifies the paragraph's major point in the first sentence. Notice also that the writer of each has relied upon two pieces of information in supporting the paragraph. (The first piece of information in each case is a summary or paraphrase of an expert's commentary, and the second is a direct quotation.) Both samples have been marked with a temporary code to show the eventual location of footnote numbers. Notice, finally, that both paragraphs flow smoothly because the writers have provided the necessary transitions and identification of sources.

In "Ozymandias" Shelley deals with the ultimate uselessness of a tyrant's power. As E.M. Pulos points out, he could have found many contemporary examples to make his point.Ⓐ Only three years before the poem was written, Napoleon Bonaparte, the most notorious tyrant of the age, had been defeated in the Battle of Waterloo by an army led by the British Duke of Wellington. Yet, true to his romantic inclinations, Shelley goes back to ancient Egypt for his example. He goes back to Ozymandias, another name for Rameses II, a great Egyptian king who lived during the 13th century B.C. To give the poem additional flavor, Shelley makes its narrator a traveler from an unnamed ancient land that ceased to exist long ago. Indeed, the entire poem has an ancient ring to it. The poem's tenth line is taken directly from a work by the Greek historian Herodotus: "My name is Ozymandias, king of kings."Ⓑ

Despite the widespread critical preoccupation with the gloom and doom in Housman's verse, some have noticed another side to the poet. R. W. Stallman has observed that Housman's poetry at its best is full of hidden meanings that imply a deeper significance than the simple rhymes suggest.Ⓐ Other scholars have noticed a light-hearted quality in some of the verses, such as the song-like "Terence, This is Stupid Stuff" and "Is My Team Ploughing?" But clearly the most significant piece of evidence regarding Housman's view of life comes not from any critic but from the poet's own hand. In a letter to his brother, Laurence, Housman wrote, "I am not a pessimist; rather, I am a meliorist."Ⓑ

ASSIGNMENT

Carefully examine the preliminary outline of your paper. Make whatever adjustments are necessary in the order of subcategories presented in the body, and combine your note cards for that section of the paper into a single unified deck. Commence with the writing of your first draft, taking care to note where footnotes will be needed.

Victorian Literature

1837–1901

VICTORIA, THE PERSONIFICATION OF AN AGE

Queen Victoria, who came to the throne in 1837 at the age of eighteen, dominated English culture and politics for more than sixty years. In her diary she wrote: "Since it has pleased Providence to place me in this station, I shall do my utmost to fulfill my duty toward my country; I am very young and perhaps in many, though not in all things, inexperienced, but I am sure, that few have more real good will and more real desire to do what is fit and right than I do." There is no question that Victoria set the tone for the long period of her reign (1837–1901).

The Reform Bill of 1832 gave power to the middle class by extending the vote to all men owning property worth ten pounds a year in rent and by redistricting so that the urban areas received a more equitable representation in Parliament. It was the middle class, with its growing power in government and wealth from manufacturing, that *The Value* assumed the value system of Victoria: respectability, earnestness, hard *System* work, self-confidence, and doing what was fit and right. Victoria was eminently respectable, and she was devoted to Prince Albert, her husband, and their family of nine children. The example set by her life-style was completely different from those of the preceding occupants of the throne, and respectability might be the word that best characterizes the age. The Puritan morality, which had been institu- *Puritan Morality* tionalized two hundred years earlier during the reign of Cromwell in the 1650s, once again dominated English behavior and mores, at least on the surface. Thomas Hardy's books, *Tess of the d'Urbervilles* and *Jude the Obscure,* met with such vitriolic criticism, because they suggested the existence of sexual passion, that Hardy, angered by the attacks, renounced the writing of novels and turned to poetry.

Such an extended reign as Victoria's spanned several generations of writers with varied literary qualities, but we now call them all Victorian. Among themselves they are quite diverse, but as a group they seem different from their predecessors and different from their twentieth-century successors.

CARITAS (Stained Glass), Sir Edward Coley Burne-Jones
Laing Art Gallery, Newcastle upon Tyne, Reproduced by
permission of Tyne & Wear County Council Museum

The work ethic was pervasive in Victorian society. Although the painter depicts many aspects of Victorian life, the workmen are clearly central. Brown captioned this painting "Seest thou a man diligent in his business? He shall stand before Kings."

Work
Ford Maddox Brown
City of Manchester, Art Galleries

SUPREMACY, SKEPTICISM, AND CHANGE

Self-confidence Challenged

This was an age of British supremacy. By the middle of Victoria's reign, Britain controlled more of the earth than had any previous nation in history. With her booming cotton mills, control of pig-iron manufacture, and five thousand miles of track to deliver goods to ships or markets easily, she had become the wealthiest nation in the world. But the self-confidence generated by this overwhelming world power and wealth was being challenged at home on all fronts. The working classes demanded a vote in government, unions began forming, and the awful working and living conditions came close to creating a revolution. The Reform Bill of 1867, by giving the vote to all workers except those in agriculture, was a solution that brought new problems.

Beneath the surface of power and wealth rumbled the tremors of a new world trying to be born. "The old order changeth, yielding place to new," Tennyson wrote. From 1750 to 1830 the Industrial Revolution had emptied whole towns and hamlets, changed the ownership and working of the land, radically altered the means of production from family home to mechanical factory, created squalid cities out of picturesque towns, and devastated the countryside with all manner of industrial pollution. These changes brought social and economic dislocations which disordered the old conceptions of class structure, and the ever-widening suffrage seemed (to many) to threaten political chaos.

Social and Economic Problems

On the intellectual front it was also a time of increasing skepticism and change. The Bible was now called by some a "historical document" instead of a divine one. Geology and astronomy challenged the Bible's pronouncements about the earth's age and its place in the cosmos. The human race, science seemed to say, was insignificant in time and in the

Skepticism and Change

Machinery Hall, the Crystal Palace, Hyde Park at the Great Exhibition in 1851. The wondrous fruits of the Industrial Revolution displayed Britain's overwhelming power and seemed to prophesy the coming millennium.

The Mansell Collection

Writers Respond

universe. Charles Darwin's theories of evolution seemed to suggest that humans were merely complex animals.

Writers were disturbed. Some, like Kipling and Stevenson, offered escape into the outdoors, to a life of action and adventure. Forget about the world, they seemed to say, as in Tennyson's "Lotus-Eaters." Some would say find joy (and escape) in forever searching but never possessing; "To strive, to seek, to find, and not to yield" says Tennyson's Ulysses. Others would heal "the ache of modernism" through art. The Pre-Raphaelite Brotherhood, a group of poets, painters, and craftsmen, looked back to the period before the time of the Italian Renaissance painter Raphael (1483–1520) when there was a certain primitive intensity and the mark of human imperfection in art. William Morris, Walter Pater, Charles Swinburne, and Oscar Wilde, however, denied art had any function but to present beauty: "Art for art's sake."

Industrial might was not an "unmixed blessing." It often created squalid cities out of picturesque towns and devastated the countryside with all manner of pollution.

Factory Towns, Sheffield 1884
The Mansell Collection

Child labor was common in Victorian England and America as the mechanical factory replaced the family home and the local craftsman.

Children Carrying Clay for Bricks
The Mansell Collection

Some writers could not honestly escape what they saw as the bitter, painful realities of the world. In the later part of Victoria's reign, Arnold (see page 679), Housman (see page 694), and Hardy (see pages 629 and 689) especially voiced the pessimist's view—perhaps there is no meaning and purpose to life. Others reasserted reason, common sense, traditional ideas, or the "old" religion. Tennyson and Browning affirmed their solutions in poetry; Carlyle, Ruskin, and Newman, in prose.

THE MAJOR POETS

As the personality of Victoria was the amalgam that held together the political and social aspects of her reign, Alfred Tennyson (see page 645), her poet laureate, held together the diverse literary production of the period. His long life nearly coincided with hers (he was still writing in his eighties). When he dedicated his most popular work, *The Idylls of*

Alfred, Lord Tennyson

Victoria and Albert loved children and animals. Landseer was not only Queen Victoria's official painter, but he was also one of the greatest animal painters in history. Here he captures the young Queen, the model wife and mother, surrounded by her "loves."

WINDSOR CASTLE IN MODERN TIMES
Sir Edwin Landseer

Victoria's Favorite

the King, to the memory of Prince Albert, he was invited to court and became Victoria's favorite. Tennyson was the concluding performer of the Romantic school rather than the initiator of the new. He tamed the excesses of the Romantics, surpassing them in technical perfection, but never equaling them in their passion or intensity, nor their rhythms and imagery. There is no doubt of the beauty of his poetry, and this is the very quality the Victorians cherished. Critics praised the *Idylls* for their sweetness and purity. Tennyson, like the Romantics, often turned

Augustus Egg's sentimental, narrative paintings were very popular in Victorian England. This melodramatic scene is the first of three paintings of a series depicting the "wages of sin." What story does the painting relate to you?

PAST AND PRESENT (No. 1)
Augustus Egg
The Tate Gallery, London

toward the themes of classic Greece and Rome, and for fifty years his poetry was haunted by Arthurian legends.

Tennyson's name is inevitably linked with that of Robert Browning as the second great Victorian poet. In their day, Tennyson was hailed as the greater, an evaluation reversed in our time. If Tennyson was the last of the old, Browning (see page 663) was the first of the new. He led to our experimenting with verse forms and breaking rhythm patterns. His dramatic monologs subtly showed the devious workings of the

Robert Browning

human mind. If Tennyson is restrained, Browning is exuberant in his lyrics. Some of these are almost as rich in imagery as those of Keats.

VICTORIAN PROSE

Newman

Carlyle

Macaulay
Ruskin

Pater
Huxley

Dickens and
Thackeray

As time has passed, the Victorian Period has been recognized as an age of prose excellence more than of poetry. Many were the long prose works of nonfiction and essays, and the way that language was handled in these was cherished and praised. John Henry Newman wrote of his spiritual struggle in leaving the Anglican Church for the Catholic, where he became a cardinal. Thomas Carlyle, historian, biographer, social critic, used a fictional eyewitness as the narrator of the French Revolution, while Thomas Macaulay spent years writing his history of Britain and finished only four volumes. John Ruskin tried to restructure the tastes of the English people in art and to teach them about economic and social reforms (management-labor relations, environmental pollution, etc.) decades before they became popular causes. Walter Pater in a kind of mystical prose wrote about the Italian Renaissance as well as ancient Greece. And Thomas Henry Huxley in charming essays popularized scientific discoveries. Some of the greatest literary achievements of the Victorian Age were in the field of the novel, dominated by Dickens and Thackeray. The novels of the period are discussed separately on page 639.

Lear
Carroll

Gilbert and Sullivan

Wilde

But in spite of the overlay of sober puritanism, there was a strand of humor in the literature of this age. Edward Lear regaled England with his nonsense verse, creating the five-line limerick. Lewis Carroll, a mathematics professor at Oxford, wrote the amusing tale of *Alice in Wonderland*. On the stage, Gilbert and Sullivan's zany operas making fun of many Victorian pretenses found enthusiastic audiences. And Oscar Wilde's play, *The Importance of Being Earnest*, poked fun at the earnestness of Victorian culture by presenting a heroine who would only marry a man named Ernest. It may even startle some readers today to find that a poem by George Meredith called "Modern Love" actually deals with a failed marriage, a subject that even today could be called modern.

VICTORIAN LIFE AND LITERATURE

Poetry

Novels

Perhaps in no other period of English literature have so many written so much so well. The Victorian poetry that is enshrined in the *Oxford Book of English Verse* tends to be delicate, sensitive, earnest, respectable. It is redolent with nature images of the English countryside. There seems a kind of nostalgic yearning for past eras and past attitudes. Through it, we enter a kind of dream world. But the novels present

The proper Victorian home was highly decorative, even ornate. This room in Hammersmith Terrace in London shows the furniture and décor of the typical middle class home.

another side of Victorian life that conveys a different kind of attitude and spirit. They are robust, bursting with life, conscious of the commercial, industrial, and bustling qualities of the period, and alive with vivid characters who seem as real as your next-door neighbor. In addition there were the writers of nonfiction prose, which flourished in this period. In essays, pamphlets, or longer pieces of writing they prophesied and criticized the main concerns of the time, extolled and opposed Victorian mores, questioned and attacked the so-called "progress" of the day, all with a creative excellence that has not been matched since. Yet in spite of their varied spirit and attitudes, the writers of this diverse group—the poets, the novelists, the nonfiction scribblers—were all representative of the Victorian Age.

Nonfiction

The Victorian Age

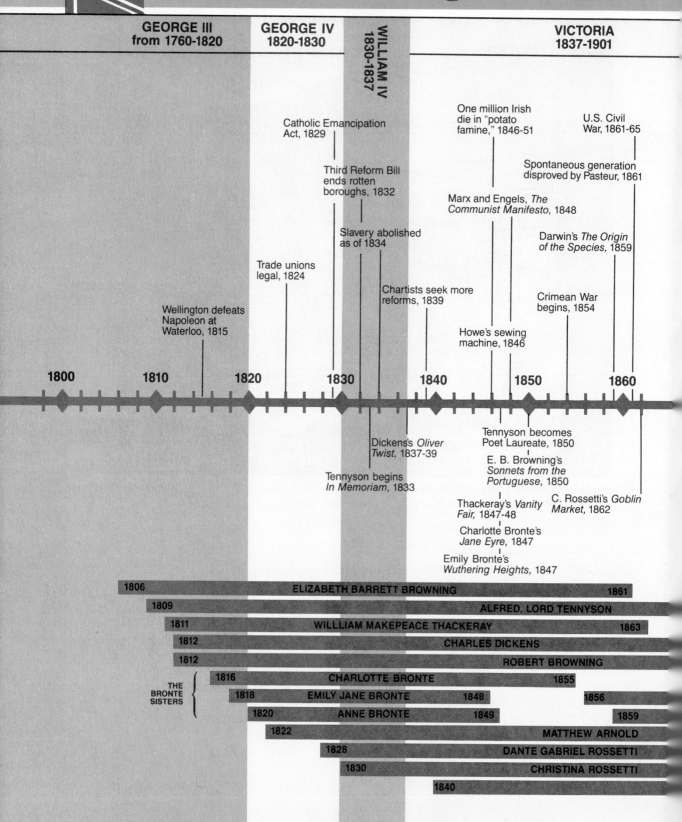

GEORGE III from 1760-1820

GEORGE IV 1820-1830

WILLIAM IV 1830-1837

VICTORIA 1837-1901

One million Irish die in "potato famine," 1846-51

U.S. Civil War, 1861-65

Catholic Emancipation Act, 1829

Spontaneous generation disproved by Pasteur, 1861

Third Reform Bill ends rotten boroughs, 1832

Marx and Engels, *The Communist Manifesto*, 1848

Darwin's *The Origin of the Species*, 1859

Slavery abolished as of 1834

Trade unions legal, 1824

Chartists seek more reforms, 1839

Crimean War begins, 1854

Wellington defeats Napoleon at Waterloo, 1815

Howe's sewing machine, 1846

1800   **1810**   **1820**   **1830**   **1840**   **1850**   **1860**

Dickens's *Oliver Twist*, 1837-39

Tennyson becomes Poet Laureate, 1850

Tennyson begins *In Memoriam*, 1833

E. B. Browning's *Sonnets from the Portuguese*, 1850

C. Rossetti's *Goblin Market*, 1862

Thackeray's *Vanity Fair*, 1847-48

Charlotte Bronte's *Jane Eyre*, 1847

Emily Bronte's *Wuthering Heights*, 1847

1806	ELIZABETH BARRETT BROWNING 1861
1809	ALFRED, LORD TENNYSON
1811	WILLLIAM MAKEPEACE THACKERAY 1863
1812	CHARLES DICKENS
1812	ROBERT BROWNING

THE BRONTE SISTERS

1816	CHARLOTTE BRONTE 1855
1818	EMILY JANE BRONTE 1848 1856
1820	ANNE BRONTE 1849 1859
1822	MATTHEW ARNOLD
1828	DANTE GABRIEL ROSSETTI
1830	CHRISTINA ROSSETTI
1840	

EDWARD VII	GEORGE V
1901-1910	1910- to 1936

Gödel shows math uses unprovable theorems, 1931

Lincoln killed, 1865

World War I, 1914-18

Settled working men get vote, 1867

Marie Curie wins second Nobel Prize, 1911

Disraeli and Gladstone begin rivalry, 1868

Einstein's special theory of relativity, 1905

Gandhi born, 1869

Russian Revolution, 1917

Britain acquires Suez Canal, 1875

Freud, *The Meaning of Dreams,* 1900

Victoria becomes Empress of India, 1876

The Boer War, 1899-1902

Zulu War, 1879

1870   **1880**   **1890**   **1900**   **1910**   **1920**

George Eliot's *Middlemarch,* 1871-72

Housman's *A Shropshire Lad,* 1896

Arnold's "Dover Beach," 1867

G. B. Shaw's *Arms and the Man,* 1894

Lewis Carroll's *Alice in Wonderland,* 1865

Hardy's *Wessex Poems,* 1898

Browning's "Prospice," 1864

1892

1870

1889

GEORGE BERNARD SHAW   TO 1950

A. E. HOUSMAN   TO 1936

1888

1882

1894

THOMAS HARDY   1928

Charles Dickens   1812–1870

Charles Dickens was the son of a man of wavering fortunes, whom he referred to as "the prodigal father." For a brief time, his father was employed as a Navy clerk, and five-year-old Charles attended school. But after losing his job, John Dickens was soon deep in debt and moved his family from place to place to escape his creditors. Finally, he was thrown into debtor's prison, and his wife Elizabeth tried to support the family by running a little school in their home. But her earnings were insufficient and she was forced to send Charles to work in a warehouse, pasting labels on pots of stove blacking. This was the darkest period of his youth. Yet even while he was living through this scarring experience (vividly retold in *David Copperfield*) he was storing away pictures of the people he met. His ne'er-do-well father appears in *David Copperfield* as Mr. Micawber.

His education was badly neglected, but he made up for its lack by avidly reading the great novelists of the previous century. At fifteen, he went to work as a clerk in a lawyer's office, where he learned shorthand and soaked up the atmosphere of the lawyer's world and work which reappears in so many of his novels. His father, now released from prison, became a reporter, and Charles followed suit by getting a job as a parliamentary reporter, where he distinguished himself for accuracy and liveliness in his reports.

He began writing sketches of London life and sending them to the *Morning Chronicle* under the pen name of Boz. These were collected and published, and so appealed to a firm of publishers that they commissioned him to write comments around a series of humorous pictures of sportsmen's misadventures done by a popular artist. For this purpose he invented the Pickwick Club headed by the eccentric old bachelor, Mr. Pickwick, his three friends, and his matchless servant, Sam Weller. The zany adventures of this group became enormously popular. Dickens had found his vocation.

For the next thirty years, Dickens was the most popular novelist in both England and the United States. As time went on, plot, character, and motive became more important in his novels, but his reforming spirit for Victorian social problems never died. It simply became more subtle and powerful. He always wrote with the ease and quickness of the journalist, and his genuine exuberance and humor balanced his lack of restraint and exaggerated style. He was at his best in describing people with little social status, especially if they were somewhat eccentric or a bit rascally as were Sarah Gamp, Sam Weller, and Mr. Micawber.

Dickens worked at a furious pace and turned out such masterpieces as *Oliver Twist, The Old Curiosity Shop, Great Expectations,* and the book considered by many as his greatest, *David Copperfield.* The names of his characters became household words on two continents. Into Dickens's pages crowd thieves, lawyers, gentry, journalists, snobs—rich and poor, cruel and kind. His imagination gave birth to the greatest collection of eccentric characters ever conceived by a writer. Both his humor and pathos were exactly the kind that appeals to the great body of readers, and in his day the public found no defects in his writing. His later works proved Dickens to be one of the best mystery writers that England had produced.

CHARLES DICKENS, William Powell Frith, Victoria and Albert Museum, Crown copyright

THE SIGNAL-MAN

"Halloa! Below there!"

When he heard a voice thus calling to him, he was standing at the door of his box, with a flag in his hand, furled around its short pole. One would have thought, considering the nature of the ground, that he could not have doubted from what quarter the voice came; but, instead of looking up to where I stood on the top of the steep cutting nearly over his head, he turned himself about, and looked down the Line. There was something remarkable in his manner of doing so, though I could not have said for my life what. But I know it was remarkable enough to attract my notice, even though his figure was foreshortened and shadowed, down in the deep trench, and mine was high above him, so steeped in the glow of an angry sunset, that I had shaded my eyes with my hand before I saw him at all.

"Halloa! Below!"

From looking down the Line, he turned himself about again, and, raising his eyes, saw my figure high above him.

He looked up at me without replying, and I looked down at him without pressing him too soon with a repetition of my idle question. Just then there came a vague vibration in the earth and air, quickly changing into a violent pulsation, and an oncoming rush that caused me to start back, as though it had force to draw me down. When such vapor as rose to my height from this rapid train had passed me, and was skimming away over the landscape, I looked down again, and saw him refurling the flag he had shown while the train went by.

I repeated my inquiry. After a pause, during which he seemed to regard me with fixed attention, he motioned with his rolled-up flag towards a point on my level, some two or three hundred yards distant. I called down to him, "All right!" and made for that point. There, by dint of looking closely about me, I found a rough zigzag descending path notched out, which I followed.

The cutting was extremely deep, and unusually precipitate. It was made through a clammy stone that became oozier and wetter as I went down. For these reasons, I found the way long enough to recall a singular air of reluctance or compulsion with which he had pointed out the path.

When I came down low enough upon the zigzag descent to see him again, I saw that he was standing between the rails on the way by which the train had lately passed, in an attitude as if he were waiting for me to appear. He had his left hand at his chin, and that left elbow rested on his right hand, crossed over his breast. His attitude was one of such expectation and watchfulness, that I stopped a moment, wondering at it.

I resumed my downward way, and stepping out upon the level of the railroad, and drawing nearer to him, saw that he was a dark, sallow man, with a dark beard and rather heavy eyebrows. His post was in as solitary and dismal a place as ever I saw. On either side a dripping-wet wall of jagged stone, excluding all view but a strip of sky: the perspective one way only a crooked prolongation of this great dungeon; the shorter perspective in the other direction terminating in a gloomy red light, and the gloomier entrance to a black tunnel, in whose massive architecture there was a barbarous, depressing, and forbidding air. So little sunlight ever found its way to this spot that it had an earthy, deadly smell; and so much cold wind rushed

The Mansell Collection

through it, that it struck chill to me, as if I had left the natural world.

Before he stirred, I was near enough to him to have touched him. Not even then removing his eyes from mine, he stepped back one step, and lifted his hand.

This was a lonesome post to occupy (I said), and it had riveted my attention when I looked down from up yonder. A visitor was a rarity, I should suppose; not an unwelcome rarity, I hoped? In me, he merely saw a man who had been shut up within narrow limits all his life, and who being at last set free, had a newly awakened interest in these great works. To such purpose I spoke to him; but I am far from sure of the terms I used; for, besides that I am not happy in opening any conversation, there was something in the man that daunted me.

He directed a most curious look towards the red light near the tunnel's mouth, and looked all about it, as if something were missing from it, and then looked at me.

That light was part of his charge,—was it not?

He answered in a low voice,—"Don't you know it is?"

The monstrous thought came into my mind, as I perused the fixed eyes and the saturnine face, that this was a spirit, not a man. I have speculated, since, whether there may have been infection in his mind.

In my turn I stepped back. But, in making the action, I detected in his eyes some latent fear of me. This put the monstrous thought to flight.

"You look at me," I said, forcing a smile, "as if you had a dread of me."

"I was doubtful," he returned, "whether I had seen you before."

"Where?"

He pointed to the red light he had looked at.

"There?" I said.

Intently watchful of me, he replied (but without sound), "Yes."

"My good fellow, what should I do there? However, be that as it may, I never was there, you may swear."

"I think I may," he rejoined. "Yes. I am sure I may."

His manner cleared, like my own. He replied to my remarks with readiness, and in well-chosen words. Had he much to do there? Yes; that was to say, he had enough responsibility to bear; but exactness and watchfulness were what was required of him, and of actual work—manual labor—he had next to none. To change that signal, to trim those lights, and to turn this iron handle now and then, was all he had to do under that head. Regarding those many long and lonely hours of which I seemed to make so much, he could only say that the routine of his life had shaped itself into that form, and he had grown used to it. He had taught himself a language down here,—if only to know it by sight, and to have formed his own crude ideas of its pronunciation, could be called learning it. He had also worked at fractions and decimals, and tried a little algebra; but he was, and had been as a boy, a poor hand at figures. Was it necessary for him when on duty always to remain in that channel of damp air, and could he never rise into the sunshine from between those high stone walls? Why, that depended upon times and circumstances. Under some conditions there would be less upon the Line than under others, and the same held good as to certain hours of the day and night. In bright weather, he did choose occasions for getting a little above these lower shadows; but, being at all times liable to be called by his electric bell, and at such times listening for it with redoubled anxiety, the relief was less than I would suppose.

He took me into his box, where there was a fire, a desk for an official book in which he had to make certain entries, a telegraphic instrument with its dial, face, and needles, and the little bell of which he had spoken. On my trusting that he would excuse the remark that he had been well educated, and (I hoped I might say without offence) perhaps educated above that station, he observed that instances of slight incongruity in such wise would rarely be found wanting among large bodies of men; that he had heard it was so in workhouses, in the police force, even in that last desperate resource, the army; and that he knew it was so, more or less, in any great railway staff. He had been, when young (if I could believe it, sitting in that hut,—he scarcely could), a student of natural philosophy, and had attended lectures; but he had run wild, misused his opportunities, gone down, and never risen again. He had no complaint to offer about that. He had made his bed, and he lay upon it. It was far too late to make another.

All that I have here condensed he said in a quiet manner, with his grave dark regards divided between me and the fire. He threw in the word, "Sir," from time to time, and especially when he referred to his youth,—as though to request me to understand that he claimed to be nothing but what I found him. He was several times interrupted by the little bell, and had to read off messages, and send replies. Once he had to stand without the door, and display a flag as a train passed, and make some verbal communication to the driver. In the discharge of his duties, I observed him to be remarkably exact and vigilant, breaking off his discourse at a syllable, and remaining silent until what he had to do was done.

In a word, I should have set this man down as one of the safest of men to be employed in that capacity, but for the circumstance that while he was speaking to me he twice broke off with a fallen color, turned his face towards the little bell when it did NOT ring, opened the door of the hut (which was kept shut to exclude the unhealthy damp), and looked out towards the red light near the mouth of the tunnel. On both of those occasions he came back to the fire with the inexplicable air upon him which I had remarked, without being able to define, when we were so far asunder.

Said I, when I rose to leave him, "You almost make me think that I have met with a contented man."

(I am afraid I must acknowledge that I said it to lead him on.)

"I believe I used to be so," he rejoined, in the low voice in which he had first spoken; "but I am troubled, sir, I am troubled."

He would have recalled the words if he could. He had said them, however, and I took them up quickly.

"With what? What is your trouble?"

"It is very difficult to impart, sir. It is very, very difficult to speak of. If ever you make me another visit, I will try to tell you."

"But I expressly intend to make you another visit. Say, when shall it be?"

"I go off early in the morning, and I shall be on again at ten tomorrow night, sir."

"I will come at eleven."

He thanked me, and went out at the door with me. "I'll show my white light, sir," he said, in his peculiar low voice, "till you have found the way up. When you have found it, don't call out! And when you are at the top, don't call out!"

His manner seemed to make the place strike colder to me, but I said no more than, "Very well."

"And when you come down to-morrow night, don't call out! Let me ask you a parting question. What made you cry, 'Halloa! Below there!' tonight?"

"Heaven knows," said I. "I cried something to that effect—"

"Not to that effect, sir. Those were the very words. I know them well."

"Admit those were the very words. I said them, no doubt, because I saw you below."

"For no other reason?"

"What other reason could I possibly have?"

"You had no feeling that they were conveyed to you in any supernatural way?"

"No."

He wished me good-night, and held up his light. I walked by the side of the down

Line of rails (with a very disagreeable sensation of a train coming behind me) until I found the path. It was easier to mount than to descend, and I got back to my inn without any adventure.

Punctual to my appointment, I placed my foot on the first notch of the zigzag next night as the distant clocks were striking eleven. He was waiting for me at the bottom, with his white light on. "I have not called out," I said, when we came close together; "may I speak now?" "By all means, sir." "Good-night, then, and here's my hand." "Good-night, sir, and here's mine." With that we walked side by side to his box, entered it, closed the door, and sat down by the fire.

"I have made up my mind, sir," he began, bending forward as soon as we were seated, and speaking in a tone but a little above a whisper, "that you shall not have to ask me twice what troubles me. I took you for some one else yesterday evening. That troubles me."

"That mistake?"

"No. That some one else."

"Who is it?"

"I don't know."

"Like me?"

"I don't know. I never saw the face. The left arm is across the face, and the right arm is waved,—violently waved. This way."

I followed his action with my eyes, and it was the action of an arm gesticulating with the utmost passion and vehemence,—"For God's sake clear the way!"

"One moonlight night," said the man, "I was sitting here, when I heard a voice cry, 'Halloa! Below there!' I started up, looked from that door, and saw this Some one else standing by the red light near the tunnel, waving as I just now showed you. The voice seemed hoarse with shouting, and it cried, 'Look out! Look out!' And then again, 'Halloa! Below there! Look out!' I caught up my lamp, turned it on red, and ran towards the figure, calling, 'What's wrong? What has happened? Where?' It stood just outside the blackness of the tunnel. I advanced so close upon it that I wondered at its keeping the sleeve across its eyes. I ran right up at it, and had my hand stretched out to pull the sleeve away, when it was gone."

"Into the tunnel," said I.

"No. I ran on into the tunnel, five hundred yards. I stopped, and held my lamp above my head, and saw the figures of the measured distance, and saw the wet stains stealing down the walls and trickling through the arch. I ran out again faster than I had run in (for I had a mortal abhorrence of the place upon me), and I looked all round the red light, with my own red light, and I went up the iron ladder to the gallery atop of it, and I came down again, and ran back here. I telegraphed both ways, 'An alarm has been given. Is anything wrong?' The answer came back, both ways, 'All well.'"

Resisting the slow touch of a frozen finger tracing out my spine, I showed him how that this figure must be a deception of his sense of sight; and how that figures, originating in disease of the delicate nerves that minister to the functions of the eye, were known to have often troubled patients, some of whom had become conscious of the nature of their affliction, and had even proved it by experiments upon themselves. "As to an imaginary cry," said I, "do but listen for a moment to the wind in this unnatural valley while we speak so low, and to the wild harp it makes of the telegraph wires!"

That was all very well, he returned, after we had sat listening for a while, and he ought to know something of the wind and wires,—he who so often passed long winter nights there, alone and watching. But he would beg to remark that he had not finished.

I asked his pardon, and he slowly added these words, touching my arm:—

"Within six hours after the Appearance, the memorable accident on this Line happened, and within ten hours the dead and wounded were brought along through the tunnel over the spot where the figure had stood."

A disagreeable shudder crept over me,

but I did my best against it. It was not to be denied, I rejoined, that this was a remarkable coincidence, calculated deeply to impress his mind. But it was unquestionable that remarkable coincidences did continually occur, and they must be taken into account in dealing with such a subject. Though to be sure I must admit, I added (for I thought I saw that he was going to bring the objection to bear upon me), men of common sense did not allow much for coincidence in making the ordinary calculations of life.

He again begged to remark that he had not finished.

I again begged his pardon for being betrayed into interruptions.

"This," he said, again laying his hand upon my arm, and glancing over his shoulder with hollow eyes, "was just a year ago. Six or seven months passed, and I had recovered from the surprise and shock, when one morning, as the day was breaking, I, standing at that door, looked towards the red light, and saw the spectre again." He stopped, with a fixed look at me.

"Did it cry out?"

"No. It was silent."

"Did it wave its arm?"

"No. It leaned against the shaft of the light, with both hands before the face. Like this."

Once more I followed his action with my eyes. It was an action of mourning. I have seen such an attitude in stone figures on tombs.

"Did you go up to it?"

"I came in and sat down, partly to collect my thoughts, partly because it had turned me faint. When I went to the door again, daylight was above me, and the ghost was gone."

"But nothing followed? Nothing came of this?"

He touched me on the arm with his forefinger twice or thrice, giving a ghastly nod each time.

"That very day, as the train came out of the tunnel, I noticed, at a carriage window on my side, what looked like a confusion of hands and heads, and something waved. I saw it just in time to signal the driver, stop! He shut off, and put his brake on, but the train drifted past here a hundred and fifty yards or more. I ran after it, and, as I went along, heard terrible screams and cries. A beautiful young lady had died instantaneously in one of the compartments, and was brought in here, and laid down on this floor between us."

Involuntarily I pushed my chair back, as I looked from the boards at which he pointed to himself.

"True, sir. True. Precisely as it happened, so I tell it you."

I could think of nothing to say, to any purpose, and my mouth was very dry. The wind and the wires took up the story with a long lamenting wail.

He resumed. "Now, sir, mark this, and judge how my mind is troubled. The spectre came back a week ago. Ever since it has been there, now and again, by fits and starts."

"At the light?"

"At the Danger-light."

"What does it seem to do?"

He repeated, if possible with increased passion and vehemence, that former gesticulation of, "For God's sake, clear the way!"

Then he went on. "I have no peace or rest for it. It calls to me, for many minutes together, in an agonized manner, 'Below there! Look out! Look out!' It stands waving to me. It rings my little bell—"

I caught at that. "Did it ring your bell yesterday evening when I was here, and you went to the door?"

"Twice."

"Why see," said I, "how your imagination misleads you. My eyes were on the bell, and my ears were open to the bell, and if I am a living man, it did NOT ring at those times. No, nor at any other time, except when it was rung in the natural course of physical things by the station communicating with you."

He shook his head. "I have never made a mistake as to that yet, sir. I have never confused the spectre's ring with the man's. The ghost's ring is a strange vibration in the bell that it derives from nothing else, and I have not asserted that the bell stirs to the eye. I don't wonder that you failed to hear it. But I heard it."

"And did the spectre seem to be there, when you looked out?"

"It WAS there."

"Both times?"

He repeated firmly: "Both times."

"Will you come to the door with me and look for it now?"

He bit his under lip as though he were somewhat unwilling, but arose. I opened the door, and stood on the step, while he stood in the doorway. There was the Danger-light. There was the dismal mouth of the tunnel. There were the stars above them.

"Do you see it?" I asked him, taking particular note of his face. His eyes were prominent and strained, but not very much more so, perhaps, than my own had been when I had directed them earnestly towards the same spot.

"No," he answered. "It is not there."

"Agreed," said I.

We went in again, shut the door, and resumed our seats. I was thinking how best to improve this advantage, if it might be called one, when he took up the conversation in such a matter-of-course way, so assuming that there could be no serious question of fact between us, that I felt myself placed in the weakest of positions.

"By this time, you will fully understand, sir," he said, "that what troubles me so dreadfully is the question, What does the spectre mean?"

I was not sure, I told him, that I did fully understand.

"What is its warning against?" he said, ruminating, with his eyes on the fire, and only by times turning them on me. "What is the danger? Where is the danger? There is danger overhanging somewhere on the Line. Some dreadful calamity will happen. It is not to be doubted this third time, after what has gone before. But surely this is a cruel haunting of *me*. What can *I* do?"

He pulled out his handkerchief, and wiped the drops from his heated forehead.

"If I telegraph Danger, on either side of me, or on both, I can give no reason for it," he went on, wiping the palms of his hands. "I should get into trouble, and do no good. They would think I was mad. This is the way it would work,—Message: 'Danger! Take care!' Answered: 'What Danger? Where?' Message: 'Don't know. But for God's sake, take care!' They would displace me. What else could they do?"

His pain of mind was most pitiable to see. It was the mental torture of a conscientious man, oppressed beyond endurance by an unintelligible responsibility involving life.

"When it first stood under the Danger-light," he went on, putting his dark hair back from his head, and drawing his hands outward across and across his temples in an extremity of feverish distress, "why not tell me where that accident was to happen,—if it must happen? Why not tell me how it could be averted,—if it could have been averted? When on its second coming it hid its face, why not tell me, instead, 'She is going to die. Let them keep her at home?' If it came, on those two occasions, only to show me that its warnings were true, and so to prepare me for the third, why not warn me plainly now? And I, Lord help me! A mere poor signal-man on this solitary station! Why not go to somebody with credit to be believed, and power to act?"

When I saw him in this state, I saw that for the poor man's sake, as well as for the public safety, what I had to do for the time was to compose his mind. Therefore, setting aside all question of reality or unreality between us, I represented to him that whoever thoroughly discharged his duty must do well, and that at least it was his comfort that he understood his duty, though he did not understand these confounding Appearances. In this effort I succeeded far better than in the attempt to reason him out of his conviction.

He became calm; the occupations incidental to his post as the night advanced began to make larger demands on his attention; and I left him at two in the morning. I had offered to stay through the night, but he would not hear of it.

That I more than once looked back at the red light as I ascended the pathway; that I did not like the red light, and that I should have slept but poorly if my bed had been under it, I see no reason to conceal. Nor did I like the two sequences of the accident and the dead girl. I see no reason to conceal that, either.

But what ran most in my thoughts was the consideration, how ought I to act, having become the recipient of this disclosure? I had proved the man to be intelligent, vigilant, painstaking, and exact; but how long might he remain so, in his state of mind? Though in a subordinate position, still he held a most important trust, and would I (for instance) like to stake my own life on the chances of his continuing to execute it with precision?

Unable to overcome a feeling that there would be something treacherous in my communicating what he had told me to his superiors in the Company, without first being plain with himself and proposing a middle course to him, I ultimately resolved to offer to accompany him (otherwise keeping his secret for the present) to the wisest medical practitioner we could hear of in those parts, and to take his opinion. A change in his time of duty would come round next night, he had apprised me, and he would be off an hour or two after sunrise, and on again soon after sunset. I had appointed to return accordingly.

Next evening was a lovely evening, and I walked out early to enjoy it. The sun was not yet quite down when I traversed the field-path near the top of the deep cutting. I would extend my walk for an hour, I said to myself, half an hour on and half an hour back, and it would then be time to go to my signal-man's box.

Before pursuing my stroll, I stepped to the brink, and mechanically looked down, from the point from which I had first seen him. I cannot describe the thrill that seized upon me, when, close at the mouth of the tunnel, I saw the appearance of a man, with his left sleeve across his eyes, passionately waving his right arm.

The nameless horror that oppressed me passed in a moment, for in a moment I saw that this appearance of a man was a man indeed, and that there was a little group of other men, standing at a short distance, to whom he seemed to be rehearsing the gesture he made. The Danger-light was not yet lighted. Against its shaft, a little low hut, entirely new to me, had been made of some wooden supports and tarpaulin. It looked no bigger than a bed.

With an irresistible sense that something was wrong,—with a flashing self-reproachful fear that fatal mischief had come of my leaving the man there, and causing no one to be sent to overlook or correct what he did,—I descended the notched path with all the speed I could make.

"What is the matter?" I asked the men.

"Signal-man killed this morning, sir."

"Not the man belonging to that box?"

"Yes, sir."

"Not the man I know?"

"You will recognize him, sir, if you knew him," said the man who spoke for the others, solemnly uncovering his own head and raising an end of the tarpaulin, "for his face is quite composed."

"O, how did this happen, how did this happen?" I asked, turning from one to another as the hut closed in again.

"He was cut down by an engine, sir. No man in England knew his work better, but somehow he was not clear of the outer rail. It was just at broad day. He had struck the light, and had the lamp in his hand. As the engine came out of the tunnel, his back was towards her, and she cut him down. That man drove her, and was showing how it happened. Show the gentleman, Tom."

The man, who wore a rough dark dress, stepped back to his former place at the mouth of the tunnel:—

"Coming round the curve in the tunnel, sir," he said, "I saw him at the end, like as if I saw him down a perspective-glass. There was no time to check speed, and I knew him to be very careful. As he didn't seem to take heed of the whistle, I shut it off when we were running down upon him, and called to him as loud as I could call."

"What did you say?"

"I said, 'Below there! Look out! Look out! For God's sake, clear the way!' "

I started.

"Ah! it was a dreadful time, sir. I never left off calling to him. I put this arm before my eyes not to see, and I waved this arm to the last; but it was no use."

Without prolonging the narrative to dwell on any one of its curious circumstances more than any other, I may, in closing it, point out the coincidence that the warning of the Engine-Driver included, not only the words which the unfortunate Signal-man had repeated to me as haunting him, but also the words which I myself—not he—had attached, and that only in my own mind, to the gesticulation he had imitated.

FOR UNDERSTANDING

This is the first piece of literature in the anthology that places the reader in a setting of industrial England. There are rails and locomotives, a telegraph key, a signal bell rung by agents along the line, and signal lights. The signalman's occupation is one created by the Industrial Revolution. It is significant that the characters are nameless and the only identity given the workingman is the title of the job he performs in this isolated, dreary, and lonely setting.

1. Which makes the greatest impact on the reader: character, plot, or setting?

2. What are the coincidences on which the story is built?

3. What bits of information are given about the signalman's background and his work habits?

4. What is the narrator's reaction to the signalman at the first meeting? after the second?

FOR INTERPRETATION

Discuss the following statements using the story itself and your own experiences to support your opinion.

1. The story suggests that the narrator is partially responsible for the death of the signalman.

2. The signalman obviously saw and heard something that warned him when deaths would occur.

3. This story demonstrates that even in a world built on technology, inexplicable events can occur.

FOR APPRECIATION

The story is that of the signalman and the apparitions. But it is told by indirection. To see the pattern in its construction, describe how Dickens unfolds the story step by step.

COMPOSITION

Write an account of someone, a stranger to you or casual acquaintance, but a person you have seen several times: a classmate, a teacher, a shopkeeper, a cashier, a bus driver, a friend of your parents, etc. Make yourself the narrator and convey your observations about the setting and the individual in three separate incidents. It may be that you will build a sequential plot, but don't strain to do so. You might start, "The first time I saw . . . was. . . ." The next incident might begin: "A few days later. . . ." Then the last one could begin: "Sometime after that, I ran into . . . again." Try to capture for your reader both the mood pervading the meeting and the personality traits of the individual.

William Thackeray 1811–1863

Like his great contemporary Charles Dickens, Thackeray wrote about the teeming variety of life he found in England. Dickens had his greatest success in describing the lower classes. Thackeray at his best described "High Life." But both attacked the pretense, the sham, and the worship of the wealth they saw around them. Born in India, Thackeray returned to England at the age of six and attended Charterhouse School. He called it Slaughterhouse school in his earlier novels because of brutality he both experienced and saw there. He entered Cambridge in 1829, but left the next year without a degree, to travel in Europe. When he returned he took a fling at the law and some newspaper enterprises, and then went to Paris to study art seriously, though his talent lay in caricaturing. Although these experiences were short-lived, he drew on them for his novels.

When Thackeray returned to London, he began contributing to *Fraser's Magazine* and *Punch*, willing to write anything that would sell. In 1846 he published *The Book of Snobs*, which established his reputation as a writer. The next year he began publication of *Vanity Fair*, a work which ridiculed society's worship of wealth and rank and made the heroine, Becky Sharp, a familiar name to readers. He was now recognized as a first-rate novelist. *Pendennis*, *Henry Esmond* (considered one of the greatest historical novels of all time), and *The Newcomes* followed in the 1850s. The need for money forced Thackeray onto the lecture circuit. Unfortunately, he found both writing and lecturing hard work and professed to enjoy neither. He kept hoping for a government position which would relieve him from the necessity of working. But his hope was never

WILLIAM MAKEPEACE THACKERAY
S. Lawrence
National Portrait Gallery, London

realized. For a few years before his death, he edited the *Cornhill Magazine*, a well-known periodical of the time, and was writing another novel when he died.

THE INFLUENCE OF THE ARISTOCRACY ON SNOBS

Last Sunday week, being at church in this city, and the service just ended, I heard two Snobs conversing about the Parson. One was asking the other who the clergyman was? "He is Mr. So-and-so," the second Snob answered, "domestic chaplain to the Earl of What-d'ye-call'im." "Oh, is he?" said the first Snob, with a tone of indescribable satisfaction.—The Parson's orthodoxy, and identity were at once settled in this Snob's mind. He knew no more about the Earl than about the Chaplain, but he took the latter's character upon the authority of the former; and went home quite contented with his Reverence, like a little truckling Snob.

This incident gave me more matter for reflection even than the sermon: and wonderment at the extent and prevalence of Lordolatry[1] in this country. What could it matter to Snob whether his Reverence were chaplain to his Lordship or not? What

Peerage-worship there is all through this free country! How we are all implicated in it, and more or less down on our knees.—And with regard to the great subject on hand, I think that the influence of the Peerage upon Snobbishness has been more remarkable than that of any other institution. The increase, encouragement, and maintenance of Snobs are among the "priceless services," as Lord John Russell[2] says, which we owe to the nobility.

It can't be otherwise. A man becomes enormously rich, or he jobs successfully in the aid of a Minister, or he wins a great battle, or executes a treaty, or is a clever lawyer who makes a multitude of fees and ascends the bench; and the country rewards him for ever with a gold coronet (with more or less balls or leaves) and a title, and a rank as legislator. "Your merits are so great," says the nation, "that your children shall be allowed to reign over us, in a manner. It does not in the least matter that your eldest son be a fool: we think your services so remarkable, that he shall have the reversion of your honours when death vacates your noble shoes. If you are poor, we will give you such a sum of money as shall enable you and the eldest-born of your race for ever to live in fat and splendour. It is our wish that there should be a race set apart in this happy country, who shall hold the first rank, have the first prizes and chances in all government jobs and patronages. We cannot

1. **Lordolatry** (lôr dol′ ə trē),   worship of lords, of men who have titles.
2. **Lord John Russell** (1792–1878),   an earl who named and led the newly formed Liberal party; twice prime minister.

The snobs of England, drawings by Thackeray for The Book of Snobs.

make all your dear children Peers—that would make Peerage common and crowd the House of Lords uncomfortably—but the young ones shall have everything a Government can give: they shall get the pick of all the places: they shall be Captains and Lieutenant-Colonels at nineteen, when hoary-headed old lieutenants are spending thirty years at drill: they shall command ships at one-and-twenty, and veterans who fought before they were born. And as we are eminently a free people, and in order to encourage all men to do their duty, we say to any man of any rank—get enormously rich, make immense fees as a lawyer, or great speeches, or distinguish yourself and win battles—and you, even you, shall come into the privileged class, and your children shall reign naturally over ours."

How can we help Snobbishness, with such a prodigious national institution erected for its worship? How can we help cringing to Lords? Flesh and blood can't do otherwise. What man can withstand this prodigious temptation? Inspired by what is called a noble emulation,[3] some people grasp at honours and win them; others, too weak or mean, blindly admire and grovel before those who have gained them; others, not being able to acquire them, furiously hate, abuse, and envy. There are only a few bland and not-in-the-least-conceited philosophers, who can behold the state of society, viz., Toadyism, organised:—base Man-and-Mammon[4] worship, instituted by command of law:—Snobbishness, in a word, perpetuated,—and mark the phenomenon calmly. And of these calm moralists, is there one, I wonder, whose heart would not throb with pleasure if he could be seen walking arm-in-arm with a couple of dukes down Pall Mall?[5] No: it is impossible, in our condition of society, not to be sometimes a Snob.

3. **emulation** (em yə lā′ shən), ambition.
4. **Mammon** (mam′ ən), a pagan god, sometimes an evil spirit, personifying the evils of wealth and miserliness.
5. **Pall Mall** (pel mel *or* pal mal), a fashionable street in London.

On one side it encourages the commoner to be snobbishly mean, and the noble to be snobbishly arrogant. When a noble marchioness writes in her travels about the hard necessity under which steamboat travellers labour of being brought into contact "with all sorts and conditions of people:" implying that a fellowship with God's creatures is disagreeable to her Ladyship, who is their superior:—when, I say, the Marchioness of——writes in this fashion, we must consider that out of her natural heart it would have been impossible for any woman to have had such a sentiment; but that the habit of truckling and cringing, which all who surround her have adopted towards this beautiful and magnificent lady,—this proprietor of so many black and other diamonds,—has really induced her to believe that she is the superior of the world in general: and that people are not to associate with her except awfully at a distance. I recollect being once at the city of Grand Cairo, through which a European Royal Prince was passing India-wards. One night at the inn there was a great disturbance; a man had

drowned himself in the well hard by: all the inhabitants of the hotel came bustling into the Court, and amongst others your humble servant, who asked of a certain young man the reason of the disturbance. How was I to know that this young gent was a prince? He had not his crown and sceptre on: he was dressed in a white jacket and felt hat: but he looked surprised at anybody speaking to him: answered an unintelligible monosyllable, and—*beckoned his aide-de-camp to come and speak to me.* It is our fault, not that of the great, that they should fancy themselves so far above us. If you *will* fling yourself under the wheels, Juggernaut[6] will go over you, depend upon it; and if you and I, my dear friend, had Kotoo[7] performed before us every day,—found people whenev-

6. **Juggernaut** (jug′ ər nôt), a Hindu god, the remover of sin. It was once erroneously supposed that his fanatical worshipers threw themselves beneath the wheels of the enormous car on which the god's image was dragged through the city.
7. **Kotoo** (now usually spelled kowtow) (kau′ tau), the act of kneeling and touching the forehead to the ground to show deep respect.

er we appeared grovelling in slavish adoration, we should drop into the airs of superiority quite naturally, and accept the greatness with which the world insisted upon endowing us.

Here is an instance, out of Lord L——'s travels, of that calm, good-natured, undoubting way in which a great man accepts the homage of his inferiors. After making some profound and ingenious remarks about the town of Brussels, his lordship says:—"Staying some days at the Hôtel de Belle Vue—a greatly overrated establishment, and not nearly so comfortable as the Hôtel de France—I made acquaintance with Dr. L——, the physician of the Mission. He was desirous of doing the honour of the place to me, and he ordered for us a *dîner en gourmand*[8] at the chief restaurateur's, maintaining it surpassed the Rocher at Paris. Six or eight partook of the entertainment, and we all agreed it was infinitely inferior to the Paris display, and much more extravagant. So much for the copy."

And so much for the gentleman who gave the dinner. Dr. L——, desirous to do his lordship "the honour of the place," feasts him with the best victuals money can procure—and my lord finds the entertainment extravagant and inferior. Extravagant! it was not extravagant to *him*;—Inferior! Mr. L—— did

his best to satisfy those noble jaws, and my lord receives the entertainment, and dismisses the giver with a rebuke. It is like a three-tailed Pasha[9] grumbling about an unsatisfactory backsheesh.[10]

But how should it be otherwise in a country where Lordolatry is part of our creed, and where our children are brought up to respect the "Peerage" as the Englishman's second Bible?

8. **dîner en gourmand** (dē nā′ ə(n) gùr mən′), a dinner fit for a judge of good food.
9. **a three-tailed Pasha** (pash′ ə), a Turkish governor of high rank (here, used satirically).
10. **backsheesh** (bak′ shēsh), money given as a tip or bribe in Egypt, Turkey, India, etc. (usually spelled baksheesh).

FOR UNDERSTANDING

For a year Thackeray wrote an essay each week attacking the snobs of his time. People wrote in suggesting all sorts of possibilities for these pieces and, when he stopped, the public clamored for him to continue. How well this demonstrates that common foible of thinking ourselves perfect and yet recognizing instantly the defects in our neighbors. Few will admit to any snobbery in their own nature, but are quick to point it out in a friend.

Which statement below do you think best sums up this essay?

1. Thackeray is attacking the aristocrats for their foolish assumption that their rank automatically makes them great and noble, deserving of adulation.

2. Thackeray is attacking the "little people" who by their fawning behavior make aristocrats arrogant and overbearing.

FOR INTERPRETATION

Give your reaction to the following statements. Try to justify your opinion by examples.

1. There are as many snobs today as in Thackeray's time, but they fawn upon entertainers, athletes, politicians, and the jet set instead of the nobility.

2. It is a quirk of human nature that most people need to stand in awe of someone.

3. The amount of space devoted in American newspapers to the doings of European royalty is evidence that Thackeray's point of view is true for our time as well as his.

FOR APPRECIATION

Anecdotes

You have read a number of essays by writers famous for the way they handled this form. Bacon in the early Renaissance is credited as the first conscious writer of essays in English. You read Addison's work in the Neo-classic age and Lamb's in the Romantic. Each of these writers used different methods of development. Bacon used aphorisms (terse, pithy sayings) about "Reading" and "Parenting"; Addison used a dissection to make his points about fops and flirts; and Lamb, writing about popular fallacies, began his piece by detail-ing his dislike of getting up early and then, almost in a stream-of-consciousness style, came to a surprising conclusion. In this essay, Thackeray uses anecdotes about snobs and snobbery, which he ties together with his own reflections and thoughts. List the specific anecdotes he uses.

COMPOSITION

What kinds of snobbery have you observed in your own school? What group of people irritate or annoy you with their actions, attitudes, behavior? They may be the athletes or the artists and musicians, the journalists, the socialites, the scholars, the scientists, or another category. Choose one and develop an essay expressing your feelings toward this particular group. Use anecdotes as Thackeray did in this essay. Start with an incident, following this with direct comments about the kind of snobbishness of these individuals, and then weaving in a few other anecdotes which illustrate your opinion.

A carrier's van outside the White Hart Inn, Dorchester, as in "Tony Kytes, the Arch Deceiver."

Dorset County Museum

Thomas Hardy

1840–1928

Thomas Hardy is one of the few great literary figures who have achieved important reputations as writers of both prose and poetry. In his own age, he was considered a major novelist who dabbled in verse. Modern critics, however, give increasingly greater emphasis to his poems. In both prose and poetry his work is dark and pessimistic; he saw Nature as cruel or indifferent to Humanity, and fate, a blind and destructive will against which people's struggles were hopeless.

Hardy was born near the wild heaths of the English county of Dorsetshire—which he called Wessex in his novels. The downs, the woods, moors, and coast are an integral part of his characters and their lives. Sometimes ancient monuments such as Stonehenge or an old Roman amphitheater act as dramatic backgrounds, reminding the reader of deep cultural roots and the long existence of human passions and weakness. Also a part of the rural scene are the peasants whom he sometimes presents humorously as in the story you will read, but always with an authenticity that adds to the reality.

Hardy's father was a builder, and when Hardy was fifteen apprenticed him to an architect with whom he worked for six years before going to London in 1861, where he practiced this profession. Becoming interested in fiction and poetry, Hardy tried his hand at writing short stories and poems. His first novel was rejected, but George Meredith encouraged him to try again and *Desperate Remedies* was published anonymously the next year, followed by a successful novel which led him to give up architecture for writing. Some point out that Hardy's novels are planned with the care of an architect, since all circumstances are plotted to produce one single, final effect.

The first of his great novels, *Far from the Madding Crowd* (1874), was followed by *The Return of the Native* (1878), *The Mayor of Casterbridge* (1886), and *The Woodlanders* (1887). Hardy's works were popular in his own time, but

THOMAS HARDY
William Strang
National Portrait Gallery, London

his life was a series of battles against forces that attacked him for the honesty and frankness of his writing. Other Victorian novelists such as Dickens and Thackeray were concerned with the behavior and problems of people in a particular social environment. But Hardy was intrigued with the elemental in human behavior and only fleetingly with society's effect. His stories emphasize the bitter ironies that life has in store for human beings as he shows the wide disparity between his characters' ambitions and hopes and what they are permitted to achieve. It should be noted that Hardy does not consider fate wholly external, but that people's inner needs and the demands of their own natures contribute to their downfall. His two greatest novels were also his last. In *Tess of the d'Urbervilles* (1891), considered by many his masterpiece, Hardy presents a sensitive, intelligent but poor girl driven to desperate acts by a coming together of bitter, ironic events. Equally dark and bitter is his last book, *Jude the Obscure* (1896), which presents an ambitious peasant whose intelligence and sensual drives lead to his destruction. These two books raised such a storm of protest that Hardy resolved never again to write fiction, a resolution which he faithfully kept. He returned to his first love, poetry, and produced hundreds of lyric and narrative poems, as well as an epic drama in verse on the Napoleonic Wars called *The Dynasts*.

Hardy has been called a fatalist because he so often shows his characters helpless before the inflexible, crushing movement of life. In his own defense, Hardy replied that a novel is an impression of life, not an argument, and that the artist must represent truly what he or she feels. The force and beauty of his writing—especially his scenes of landscapes and country people—brought Hardy great honor by the time of his death in 1928. He seemed to many the last of the "Great Victorians," and was buried among England's poets in Westminster Abbey.

The following short story is one of a series entitled "A Few Crusted Characters," published in a collection entitled *Life's Little Ironies*. Here Hardy departs from his usual grim pessimism to write humorously of the rustic characters he knew so well. Although the tone of the story is light, you should note the major roles that fateful coincidence and irony play in the amusing "history" of Tony Kytes.

TONY KYTES, THE ARCH-DECEIVER

It is a Saturday afternoon of blue and yellow autumn-time, and the scene is the High Street of a well-known market-town. A large carrier's van stands in the quadrangular fore-court of the White Hart Inn, upon the sides of its spacious tilt being painted, in weather-beaten letters: "Burthen, Carrier to Longpuddle." These vans, so numerous hereabout, are a respectable, if somewhat lumbering, class of conveyance, much resorted to by decent travellers not overstocked with money, the better among them roughly corresponding to the old French *diligences*.[1]

The present one is timed to leave the town at four in the afternoon precisely, and it is now half-past three by the clock in the turret at the top of the street. In a few seconds errand-boys from the shops begin to arrive with packages, which they fling into the vehicle, and turn away whistling, and care for the packages no more. At twenty minutes to four an elderly woman places her basket upon the shafts, slowly mounts, takes up a seat inside, and folds her hands and her lips. She has secured her corner for the journey, though there is as yet no sign of a horse being put in, nor of a carrier. At the three-quarters, two other women arrive, in whom the first recognizes the postmistress of Upper Longpuddle, and the registrar's wife, they recognizing her as the aged groceress of the same village. At five minutes to the hour there approach Mr. Profitt, the schoolmaster, in a soft felt hat, and Christopher Twink, the master-thatcher; and as the hour strikes there rapidly drop in

from "A Few Crusted Characters"

1. **diligences,** stagecoaches used in France and other European countries.

Here the painter celebrates the life and times of rural England in the last half of the nineteenth century. Look closely to note the cross-section of local society, similar to the people and scenes Hardy depicted in his novels.

**A COUNTRY CRICKET MATCH,
SUSSEX 1878**
John R. Reid
The Tate Gallery, London

the parish clerk and his wife, the seedsman and his aged father, the registrar; also Mr. Day, the world-ignored local landscape-painter, an elderly man who resides in his native place, and has never sold a picture outside it, though his pretensions to art have been nobly supported by his fellow-villagers, whose confidence in his genius has been as remarkable as the outer neglect of it, leading them to buy his paintings so extensively (at the price of a few shillings each, it is true) that every dwelling in the parish exhibits three or four of those admired productions on its walls.

Burthen, the carrier, is by this time seen bustling round the vehicle; the horses are put in, the proprietor arranges the reins and springs up into his seat as if he were used to it—which he is.

"Is everybody here?" he asks preparatorily over his shoulder to the passengers within.

As those who were not there did not reply in the negative the muster was assumed to be complete, and after a few hitches and hindrances the van with its human freight was got under way. It jogged on at an easy pace till it reached the bridge which formed the last outpost of the town. The carrier pulled up suddenly.

"Bless my soul!" he said, "I've forgot the curate!"

All who could do so gazed from the little back window of the van, but the curate was not in sight.

"Now I wonder where that there man is?" continued the carrier.

"Poor man, he ought to have a living at his time of life."

"And he ought to be punctual," said the carrier. "'Four o'clock sharp is my time for starting,' I said to en. And he said, 'I'll be there.' Now he's not here; and as a serious old church-minister he ought to be as good as his word. Perhaps Mr. Flaxton knows, being in the same line of life?" He turned to the parish clerk.

"I was talking an immense deal with him, that's true, half-an-hour ago," replied that ecclesiastic, as one of whom it was no erroneous supposition that he should be on intimate terms with another of the cloth. "But he didn't say he would be late."

The discussion was cut off by the appearance round the corner of the van of rays from the curate's spectacles, followed hastily by his face and a few white whiskers, and the swinging tails of his long gaunt coat. Nobody reproached him, seeing how he was reproaching himself; and he entered breathlessly and took his seat.

"Now be we all here?" said the carrier again.

They started a second time, and moved on till they were about three hundred yards out of the town, and had nearly reached the second bridge, behind which, as every native remembers, the road takes a turn, and travellers by this highway disappear finally from the view of gazing burghers.

"Well, as I'm alive!" cried the postmistress from the interior of the conveyance, peering through the little square back window along the road townward.

"What?" said the carrier.

"A man hailing us!"

Another sudden stoppage. "Somebody else?" the carrier asked.

"Ay, sure!" All waited silently, while those who could gaze out did so.

"Now, who can that be?" Burthen continued. "I just put it to ye, neighbours, can any man keep time with such hindrances? Bain't we full a'ready? Who in the world can the man be?"

"He's a sort of gentleman," said the schoolmaster, his position commanding the road more comfortably than that of his comrades.

The stranger, who had been holding up his umbrella to attract their notice, was walking forward leisurely enough, now that he found, by their stopping, that it had been secured. His clothes were decidedly not of a local cut, though it was difficult to point out any particular mark of difference. In his left hand he carried a small leather travelling-bag. As soon as he had overtaken the van he glanced at the inscription on its side, as if to assure himself that he had hailed the right conveyance, and asked if they had room.

The carrier replied that though they were pretty well laden he supposed they could carry one more, whereupon the stranger mounted, and took the seat cleared for him within. And then the horses made another move, this time for good, and swung along with their burden of fourteen souls all told.

"You bain't one of these parts, sir?" said the carrier. "I could tell that as far as I could see 'ee."

"Yes, I am one of these parts," said the stranger.

"Oh? H'm."

The silence which followed seemed to imply a doubt of the truth of the newcomer's assertion. "I was speaking of Upper Longpuddle, more particular," continued the carrier hardily, "and I think I know most faces of that valley."

"I was born at Longpuddle, and nursed at Longpuddle, and my father and grandfather before me," said the passenger quietly.

"Why, to be sure," said the aged groceress in the background, "it isn't John Lackland's son—never—it can't be—he who went to foreign parts five-and-thirty years ago with his wife and family? Yet—what do I hear?—that's his father's voice!"

"That's the man," replied the stranger. "John Lackland was my father, and I am John Lackland's son. Five-and-thirty years ago, when I was a boy of eleven, my parents emigrated across the seas, taking me and my sister with them. Kytes's boy Tony was the one who drove us and our belongings to Casterbridge on the morning we left; and his was the last Longpuddle face I saw. We sailed the same week across the ocean, and there we've been ever since, and there I've left those I went with—all three."

"Alive or dead?"

"Dead," he replied in a low voice. "And I have come back to the old place, having nourished a thought—not a definite intention, but just a thought—that I should like to return here in a year or two, to spend the remainder of my days."

"Married man, Mr. Lackland?"

"No."

"And have the world used 'ee well, sir—or rather John, knowing 'ee as a child? In these rich new countries that we hear of so much, you've got rich with the rest?"

"I am not very rich," Mr. Lackland said. "Even in new countries, you know, there are failures. The race is not always to the swift, nor the battle to the strong; and even if it sometimes is, you may be neither swift nor strong. However, that's enough about me. Now, having answered your inquiries, you must answer mine; for being in London, I have come down here entirely to discover what Longpuddle is looking like, and who are living there. That was why I preferred a seat in your van to hiring a carriage for driving across."

"Well, as for Longpuddle, we rub on there much as usual. Old figures have dropped out o' their frames, so to speak it, and new ones have been put in their places. You mentioned Tony Kytes as having been the one to drive your family and your goods to Casterbridge in his father's waggon when you left. Tony is, I believe, living still, but not at Longpuddle. He went away and settled at Lewgate, near Mellstock, after his marriage. Ah, Tony was a sort o' man!"

"His character had hardly come out when I knew him."

"No. But 'twas well enough, as far as that goes—except as to women. I shall never forget his courting—never!"

The returned villager waited silently, and the carrier went on:—

"I shall never forget Tony's face. 'Twas a little, round, firm, tight face, with a seam here and there left by the smallpox, but not enough to hurt his looks in a woman's eye, though he'd had it badish when he was a boy. So very serious looking and unsmiling 'a was, that young man, that it really seemed as if he couldn't laugh at all without great pain to his conscience. He looked very hard at a small speck in your eye when talking to 'ee. And there was no more sign of a whisker or beard on Tony Kytes's face than on the palm of my hand. He used to sing 'The Tailor's Breeches' with a religious manner, as if it were a hymn:—

'O the petticoats went off, and the breeches they went on!'

and all the rest of the scandalous stuff. He was quite the women's favourite, and in return for their likings he loved 'em in shoals.

"But in course of time Tony got fixed down to one in particular, Milly Richards, a nice, light, small, tender little thing; and it was soon said that they were engaged to be married. One Saturday he had been to market to do business for his father, and was driving home the waggon in the afternoon. When he reached the foot of the very hill we shall be going over in ten minutes who should he see waiting for him at the top but Unity Sallet, a handsome girl, one of the young women he'd been very tender toward before he'd got engaged to Milly.

"As soon as Tony came up to her she said, 'My dear Tony, will you give me a lift home?'

"'That I will, darling,' said Tony. 'You don't suppose I could refuse 'ee?'

"She smiled a smile, and up she hopped, and on drove Tony.

"'Tony,' she says, in a sort of tender

chide, 'why did ye desert me for that other one? In what is she better than I? I should have made 'ee a finer wife, and a more loving one too. 'Tisn't girls that are so easily won at first that are the best. Think how long we've known each other—ever since we were children almost—now haven't we, Tony?'

"'Yes, that we have,' says Tony, a-struck with the truth o't.

"'And you've never seen anything in me to complain of, have ye, Tony? Now tell the truth to me?'

"'I never have, upon my life,' says Tony.

"'And—can you say I'm not pretty, Tony? Now look at me!'

"He let his eyes light upon her for a long while. 'I really can't,' says he. 'In fact, I never knowed you was so pretty before!'

"'Prettier than she?'

"What Tony would have said to that nobody knows, for before he could speak, what should he see ahead, over the hedge past the turning, but a feather he knew well—the feather in Milly's hat—she to whom he had been thinking of putting the question as to giving out the banns[2] that very week.

"'Unity,' says he, as mild as he could, 'here's Milly coming. Now I shall catch it mightily if she sees 'ee riding here with me; and if you get down she'll be turning the corner in a moment, and, seeing 'ee in the road, she'll know we've been coming on together. Now, dearest Unity, will ye, to avoid all unpleasantness, which I know ye can't bear any more than I, will ye lie down in the back part of the waggon, and let me cover you over with the tarpaulin till Milly has passed? It will all be done in a minute. Do!—and I'll think over what we've said; and perhaps I shall put a loving question to you after all, instead of to Milly. 'Tisn't true that it is all settled between her and me.'

"Well, Unity Sallet agreed, and lay down at the back end of the waggon, and Tony covered her over, so that the waggon seemed to be empty but for the loose tarpaulin; and then he drove on to meet Milly.

"'My dear Tony!' cries Milly, looking up with a little pout at him as he came near. 'How long you've been coming home! Just as if I didn't live at Upper Longpuddle at all! And I've come to meet you as you asked me to do, and to ride back with you, and talk over our future home—since you asked me, and I promised. But I shouldn't have come else, Mr. Tony!'

"'Ay, my dear, I did ask 'ee—to be sure I did, now I think of it—but I had quite forgot it. To ride back with me, did you say, dear Milly?'

"'Well, of course! What can I do else? Surely you don't want me to walk, now I've come all this way?'

"'O no, no! I was thinking you might be going on to town to meet your mother. I saw her there—and she looked as if she might be expecting 'ee.'

"'O no; she's just home. She came across the fields, and so got back before you.'

"'Ah! I didn't know that,' says Tony. And there was no help for it but to take her up beside him.

"They talked on very pleasantly, and looked at the trees, and beasts, and birds, and insects, and at the ploughmen at work in the fields, till presently who should they see looking out of the upper window of a house that stood beside the road they were following, but Hannah Jolliver, another young beauty of the place at that time, and the very first woman that Tony had fallen in love with—before Milly and before Unity, in fact—the one that he had almost arranged to marry instead of Milly. She was a much more dashing girl than Milly Richards, though he'd not thought much of her of late. The house Hannah was looking from was her aunt's.

"'My dear Milly—my coming wife, as I may call 'ee,' says Tony in his modest way,

---

2. **banns,** public notice, given on three separate occasions in church, that a man and woman are to be married.

and not so loud that Unity could overhear, 'I see a young woman a-looking out of window, who I think may accost me. The fact is, Milly, she had a notion that I was wishing to marry her, and since she's discovered I've promised another, and a prettier than she, I'm rather afeard of her temper if she sees us together. Now, Milly, would you do me a favour—my coming wife, as I may say?'

" 'Certainly, dearest Tony,' says she.

" 'Then would ye creep under the empty sacks just here in the front of the waggon, and hide there out of sight till we've passed the house? She hasn't seen us yet. You see, we ought to live in peace and good-will since 'tis almost Christmas, and 'twill prevent angry passions rising, which we always should do.'

" 'I don't mind, to oblige you, Tony,' Milly said; and though she didn't care much about doing it, she crept under, and crouched down just behind the seat, Unity being snug at the other end. So they drove on till they got near the roadside cottage. Hannah had soon seen him coming, and waited at the window, looking down upon him. She tossed her head a little disdainful and smiled off-hand.

" 'Well, aren't you going to be civil enough to ask me to ride home with you!' she says, seeing that he was for driving past with a nod and a smile.

" 'Ah, to be sure! What was I thinking of?' said Tony, in a flutter. 'But you seem as if you was staying at your aunt's?'

" 'No, I am not,' she said. 'Don't you see I have my bonnet and jacket on? I have only called to see her on my way home. How can you be so stupid, Tony?'

" 'In that case—ah—of course you must come along wi' me,' says Tony, feeling a dim sort of sweat rising up inside his clothes. And he reined in the horse, and waited till she'd come downstairs, and then helped her up beside him, her feet outside. He drove on again, his face as long as a face that was a round one by nature well could be.

"Hannah looked round sideways into his eyes. 'This is nice, isn't it, Tony?' she says. 'I like riding with you.'

"Tony looked back into her eyes. 'And I with you,' he said after a while. In short, having considered her, he warmed up, and the more he looked at her the more he liked her, till he couldn't for the life of him think why he had ever said a word about marriage to Milly or Unity while Hannah Jolliver was in question. So they sat a little closer and closer, their feet upon the foot-board and their shoulders touching, and Tony thought over and over again how handsome Hannah was. He spoke tenderer and tenderer, and called her 'dear Hannah' in a whisper at last.

" 'You've settled it with Milly by this time, I suppose,' said she.

" 'N—no, not exactly.'

" 'What? How low you talk, Tony.'

" 'Yes—I've a kind of hoarseness. I said, not exactly.'

" 'I suppose you mean to?'

" 'Well, as to that——' His eyes rested on her face, and hers on his. He wondered how he could have been such a fool as not to follow up Hannah. 'My sweet Hannah!' he bursts out, taking her hand, not being really able to help it, and forgetting Milly and Unity, and all the world besides. 'Settled it? I don't think I have!'

" 'Hark!' says Hannah.

" 'What?' says Tony, letting go her hand.

" 'Surely I heard a sort of little screaming squeak under those sacks? Why, you've been carrying corn, and there's mice in this waggon, I declare!' She began to haul up the tails of her gown.

" 'O no; 'tis the axle,' said Tony in an assuring way. 'It do go like that sometimes in dry weather.'

" 'Perhaps it was. . . . Well, now, to be quite honest, dear Tony, do you like her better than me? Because—because, although I've held off so independent, I'll own at last that I do like 'ee, Tony, to tell the truth; and I wouldn't say no if you asked me—you know what.'

"Tony was so won over by this pretty offering mood of a girl who had been quite the reverse (Hannah had a backward way with her at times, if you can mind) that he just glanced behind, and then whispered very soft, 'I haven't quite promised her, and I think I can get out of it, and ask you that question you speak of.'

"'Throw over Milly?—all to marry me! How delightful!' broke out Hannah, quite loud, clapping her hands.

"At this there was a real squeak—an angry, spiteful squeak, and afterwards a long moan, as if something had broke its heart, and a movement of the empty sacks.

"'Something's there!' said Hannah, starting up.

"'It's nothing, really,' says Tony in a soothing voice, and praying inwardly for a way out of this. 'I wouldn't tell 'ee at first, because I wouldn't frighten 'ee. But, Hannah, I've really a couple of ferrets in a bag under there, for rabbiting, and they quarrel sometimes. I don't wish it knowed, as 'twould be called poaching. Oh, they can't get out, bless 'ee—you are quite safe! And—and—what a fine day it is, isn't it, Hannah, for this time of year? Be you going to market next Saturday? How is your aunt now?' And so on, says Tony, to keep her from talking any more about love in Milly's hearing.

"But he found his work cut out for him, and wondering again how he should get out of this ticklish business, he looked about for a chance. Nearing home he saw his father in a field not far off, holding up his hand as if he wished to speak to Tony.

"'Would you mind taking the reins a moment, Hannah,' he said, much relieved, 'while I go and find out what father wants?'

"She consented, and away he hastened into the field, only too glad to get breathing time. He found that his father was looking at him with rather a stern eye.

"'Come, come, Tony,' says old Mr. Kytes, as soon as his son was alongside him, 'this won't do, you know.'

"'What?' says Tony.

"'Why, if you mean to marry Milly Richards, do it, and there's an end o't. But don't go driving about the country with Jolliver's daughter and making a scandal. I won't have such things done.'

"'I only asked her—that is, she asked me, to ride home.'

"'She? Why, now, if it had been Milly, 'twould have been quite proper; but you and Hannah Jolliver going about by yourselves——'

"'Milly's there too, father.'

"'Milly? Where?'

"'Under the corn-sacks! Yes, the truth is, father, I've got rather into a nunnywatch,[3] I'm afeard! Unity Sallet is there too—yes, at the other end, under the tarpaulin. All three are in that waggon, and what to do with 'em I know no more than the dead! The best plan is, as I'm thinking, to speak out loud and plain to one of 'em before the rest, and that will settle it; not but what 'twill cause 'em to kick up a bit of a miff, for certain. Now which would you marry, father, if you was in my place?'

"'Whichever of 'em did *not* ask to ride with thee.'

"'That was Milly, I'm bound to say, as she only mounted by my invitation. But Milly——'

"'Then stick to Milly, she's the best. . . . But look at that!'

"His father pointed towards the waggon. 'She can't hold that horse in. You shouldn't have left the reins in her hands. Run on and take the horse's head, or there'll be some accident to them maids!'

"Tony's horse, in fact, in spite of Hannah's tugging at the reins, had started on his way at a brisk walking pace, being very anxious to get back to the stable, for he had had a long day out. Without another word Tony rushed away from his father to overtake the horse.

3. **nunnywatch,** disturbance, commotion.

"Now of all things that could have happened to wean him from Milly there was nothing so powerful as his father's recommending her. No; it could not be Milly, after all. Hannah must be the one, since he could not marry all three as he longed to do. This he thought while running after the waggon. But queer things were happening inside it.

"It was, of course, Milly who had screamed under the sack-bags, being obliged to let off her bitter rage and shame in that way at what Tony was saying, and never daring to show, for very pride and dread o' being laughed at, that she was in hiding. She became more and more restless, and in twisting herself about, what did she see but another woman's foot and white stocking close to her head. It quite frightened her, not knowing that Unity Sallet was in the waggon likewise. But after the fright was over she determined to get to the bottom of all this, and she crept and crept along the bed of the waggon, under the tarpaulin, like a snake, when lo and behold, she came face to face with Unity.

"'Well, if this isn't disgraceful!' says Milly in a raging whisper to Unity.

"'Tis,' says Unity, 'to see you hiding in a young man's waggon like this, and no great character belonging to either of ye!'

"'Mind what you are saying!' replied Milly, getting louder. 'I am engaged to be married to him, and haven't I a right to be here? What right have you, I should like to know? What has he been promising you? A pretty lot of nonsense, I expect! But what Tony says to other women is all mere wind, and no concern to me!'

"'Don't you be too sure!' says Unity. 'He's going to have Hannah, and not you, nor me either; I could hear that.'

"Now at these strange voices sounding from under the cloth Hannah was thunderstruck a'most into a swound;[4] and it was just at this time that the horse moved on. Hannah tugged away wildly, not knowing what she was doing; and as the quarrel rose louder and louder Hannah got so horrified that she let go the reins altogether. The horse went on at his own pace, and coming to the corner where we turn round to drop down the hill to Lower Longpuddle he turned too quick, the off wheels went up the bank, the waggon rose sideways till it was quite on edge upon the near axles, and out rolled the three maidens into the road in a heap. The horse looked round and stood still.

"When Tony came up, frightened and breathless, he was relieved enough to see that neither of his darlings was hurt, beyond a few scratches from the brambles of the hedge. But he was rather alarmed when he heard how they were going on at one another.

"'Don't ye quarrel, my dears—don't ye!' says he, taking off his hat out of respect to 'em. And then he would have kissed them all round, as fair and square as a man could, but they were in too much of a taking to let him, and screeched and sobbed till they was quite spent.

"'Now I'll speak out honest, because I ought to,' says Tony, as soon as he could get heard. 'And this is the truth,' says he. 'I've asked Hannah to be mine, and she is willing, and we are going to put up the banns next——'

"Tony had not noticed that Hannah's father was coming up behind, nor had he noticed that Hannah's face was beginning to bleed from the scratch of a bramble. Hannah had seen her father, and had run to him, crying worse than ever.

"'My daughter is *not* willing, sir!' says Mr. Jolliver hot and strong. 'Be you willing, Hannah? I ask ye to have spirit enough to refuse him, if yer virtue is left to 'ee and you run no risk?'

"'She's as sound as a bell for me, that I'll swear!' says Tony, flaring up. 'And so's the others, come to that, though you may think it an onusual thing in me!'

"'I have spirit, and I do refuse him!' says

4. **swound,** faint, swoon.

Hannah, partly because her father was there, and partly, too, in a tantrum because of the discovery, and the scar that might be left on her face. 'Little did I think when I was so soft with him just now that I was talking to such a false deceiver!'

"'What, you won't have me, Hannah?' says Tony, his jaw hanging down like a dead man's.

"'Never——I would sooner marry no——nobody at all!' she gasped out, though with her heart in her throat, for she would not have refused Tony if he had asked her quietly, and her father had not been there, and her face had not been scratched by the bramble. And having said that, away she walked upon her father's arm, thinking and hoping he would ask her again.

"Tony didn't know what to say next. Milly was sobbing her heart out; but as his father had strongly recommended her he couldn't feel inclined that way. So he turned to Unity.

"'Well, will you, Unity dear, be mine?' he says.

"'Take her leavings? Not I!' says Unity. 'I'd scorn it!' And away walks Unity Sallet likewise, though she looked back when she'd gone some way, to see if he was following her.

"So there at last were left Milly and Tony by themselves, she crying in watery streams, and Tony looking like a tree struck by lightning.

"'Well, Milly,' he says at last, going up to her, 'it do seem as if fate had ordained that it should be you and I, or nobody. And what must be must be, I suppose. Hey, Milly?'

"'If you like, Tony. You didn't really mean what you said to them?'

"'Not a word of it!' declares Tony, bringing down his fist upon his palm.

"And then he kissed her, and put the waggon to rights, and they mounted together; and their banns were put up the very next Sunday. I was not able to go to their wedding, but it was a rare party they had, by all account."

FOR UNDERSTANDING

1. Who is telling the story? What are the circumstances?
2. What is the attitude of the narrator toward Tony Kytes and his romances?
3. What is the physical appearance of Tony Kytes?
4. What is his particular weakness?
5. Did you perceive any differences among Unity, Milly, and Hannah?
6. How does Milly win out?

FOR INTERPRETATION

Your answers to the following questions will depend on your own interpretation of the story. Opinions may vary.
1. Hardy is famous for his portrayal of country people and their stoic acceptance of the operation of a usually malign fate on their lives. How does the story illustrate this perception?
2. What is ironic about the story?
3. If fate had not stepped in would Tony Kytes have married Milly?
4. Which of the following does the story satirize:
　a. The fickleness of men?
　b. Country life?
　c. The trickery of women?
　d. Influence of parents on children?
　e. The maliciousness of fate?
　f. Adolescent behavior?

FOR APPRECIATION

1. This story might have been written as a tragedy. After all, because of Tony's indecision, he and Milly enter marriage both knowing that she is his third and last possible choice. Hannah and Unity lose out and are unhappy about their loss. What turns these sad realities into comedy rather than tragedy?
2. Hardy communicates the flavor of country dialect with very few misspellings of words. How does he do it?

THE VICTORIAN NOVEL

As the Renaissance period was the great age for drama and the Romantic period distinguished for its poetry, the Victorian Age is noted for its novels. Perhaps the works of almost a dozen novelists entered into the "classic" category at this time. But these representatives are only the tip of the iceberg. There were scores of other novelists during this period, some of them even more highly admired than those considered the greats by later generations. What then caused this flood of novels in this particular time span? Perhaps the rise of literacy, which by mid-century saw two-thirds to three-fourths of the "lower orders" (a term for all those below the great middle class) able to read, though some could still not write. Cheap fiction and "penny dreadfuls" were affordable for thousands, who read them on trams and trains, and thus these weeklies became a true "pass-time." Charles Dickens is said to have commanded a more diverse readership than any novelist has been able to command since.

This was a period when novels were serialized, a chapter coming out in monthly paperback installments. Thus each section had to be fairly discrete—containing memorable characters, much action, and a rise in intensity to a climax. Not only were writers influenced to change the course of their story

Ramsgate, Kent, is a coastal resort visited by Austen and Coleridge, among other noted writers. Frith's painting teems with characters and life much like a Dickens novel.

RAMSGATE SANDS
William Powell Frith
The Royal Collection, Lord Chamberlain's Office
Copyright reserved.

from Oliver Twist *by Charles Dickens,*
illustrated by Cruikshank.
Hamlyn Group, Picture Library.

because of readers' reactions to earlier parts, but they also had somewhat jumbled plots that rambled on at great length, causing Henry James to call them "loose, baggy monsters."

During the sixty-four-year reign of Victoria, the novel went through a number of changes. Whereas the Romantic novel had depended on exotic settings sometimes placed in the distant past, the novelists of the Victorian era turned to the here-and-now. The change from serializing stories to publishing them in a single volume gave the novels unity and a sustaining interest. The early Victorian novelists, such as Dickens, William

Makepeace Thackeray, Anthony Trollope, Charlotte and Emily Brontë, and their readers were alike in their basic perceptions of life. But by the end of the century, Thomas Hardy presented an indifferent, uncaring universe, in which happiness is an insignificant incident in a drama of pain. Hardy's novels shocked many more conventional readers, and he was subjected to stinging criticism. The kind of novel whose world is alien to the reader has been generally typical of twentieth-century writing. Hence such works as Hardy's have been called modern by some scholars, rather than Victorian.

The novelists seemingly displayed the

Vanity Fair *written and illustrated by Thackeray.*
Hamlyn Group, Picture Library.

novelists, just as Tennyson and Browning are paired as the Victorian poets. Dickens wrote about the middle and lower classes; Thackeray, about the middle class and aristocrats. Dickens was essentially the great entertainer. No one, except Shakespeare, has created a gallery of such varied, unforgettable characters. Like Shakespeare he seemed to have a mind teeming with plots. His characters are caricatures rather than real people. But they are caricatures that we all recognize, so much so that they are seen in paintings, on the stage, in figurines. So convincing is Dickens that readers accept the people and the world he creates. We believe, for example, that Miss Haversham in *Great Expectations* (1861) really

An engraving by Dalziel from a drawing by J.E. Millais showing the Crawly family in the 1861 edition of Framley Parsonage *by Anthony Trollope.*

same energy that characterizes the whole age. A novelist's output was tremendous. Anthony Trollope, a postal inspector, wrote from 5:30 to 7:30 each morning, setting a quota of producing 250 words every fifteen minutes. He wrote over fifty books. The novels of the Victorian Age also followed the dictum of Thomas DeQuincey, an essayist who described two kinds of literature: "There is, first, the literature of *knowledge,* and, secondly, the literature of *power.* The function of the first is—*to teach;* The function of the second is—*to move:* the first is a rudder, the second an oar or a sail." DeQuincey thought the two were incompatible, but the Victorians wanted to use both. Dickens and Thackeray both preached to their readers and entertained them.

Charles Dickens and William Thackeray are paired together as the great Victorian

'A Supper in the Rucellai Gardens," a scene from George Eliot's (Mary Ann Evans) Romola. An engraving from a drawing by Sir Frederick Leighton.

does wear her wedding dress and keep her bridal table and flowers for years after she has been jilted, even though common sense tells us this would have been unlikely. Often at the center of a Dickens novel is a lonely, persecuted child, just as he himself had felt in his own childhood.

Thackeray was considered an author superior to Dickens, though history has reversed this opinion. He set out in his best book, *Vanity Fair* (1848), to sketch the whole panorama of society. And he was excellent at showing people as they existed externally in society. Early in his writing career he had submitted to *Punch,* a humor magazine, satiric sketches that ruthlessly attacked snobs. Some of this attitude shows in his novels where peo-

ple far down in the social scale try to rise a level or two.

Since many women wrote distinguished novels in the Romantic Age it is not surprising that with a woman on the throne the Victorians felt free to do the same. Mrs. Elizabeth Gaskell, the wife of a Unitarian minister, wrote two kinds of novels. *Cranford* (1853) is a gentle, satiric account of poor but proud aristocratic women living in a rural community; others of her stories contain the struggles between capital and labor, thus revealing more than any other writer of this age the problems created in Britain by the Industrial Revolution.

But she is outshone by the Brontë sisters, who led quiet, uneventful lives and yet created a passionate world from their own imaginations. Charlotte's *Jane Eyre* (1847) brought passion to a novel as well as showing a woman in revolt against her assigned role in society. Emily's *Wuthering Heights* (1847) was an even more passionate story, of the dark brooding Heathcliff and the beautiful erratic Cathy who like restrained torrential rivers sought one another out.

George Eliot, the pseudonym of Mary Ann Evans, shocked her world by living openly and unmarried with a well-known philosopher. Her own faith was shaken by the idea that the *Bible* might not be a divine revelation, and her great books—*The Mill on the Floss* (1860), *Middlemarch* (1872), and *Daniel Deronda* (1876)—show people in a moral crisis. She probes their innermost thoughts, thus creating the first psychological novels before the science of psychology was developed.

Anthony Trollope came to writing naturally, as his mother had written some fifty novels during her lifetime. His strength was his adept creation of a range of characters almost as varied as those of Dickens, though Trollope's were more realistic. George Meredith, as well as Eliot, moved the novel from an instinctive form of storytelling to a conscious literary genre. In his first major novel, *The Ordeal of Richard Feverel* (1859), he shows the motives and actions of a father raising a son

in a perfect state by controlling all natural instincts. Thus he broke the Victorian taboo of sex in novels, but in his later life worked assiduously to remove the objectionable passages.

The last of the great Victorian novelists was Thomas Hardy. Hardy pictured his characters in relationship to the weather, the seasons, the landscape, or an ancient craft, thus showing people as a speck in the long continuing pattern of life on Earth. They exist in an indifferent, uncaring universe which nevertheless controls them. Hardy's major characters, like those in Greek tragedies, are trapped in a web of circumstances from which they cannot escape. His other rustic inhabitants, drawn with great skill, serve almost as a Greek chorus commenting on the course of the action.

The Victorian essayist Thomas Carlyle's contention that machines were not only managing "the external and physical world, but the spiritual as well," seemed nowhere more evident than in the printing presses' massive outpouring of materials spreading across all levels of society. Writers explored ideas new to the times, represented real people in real settings in their stories, and reflected the important facets of Victorian life. And nowhere was this probing of all facets of life more evident than in the novels.

VICTORIAN NOVELS

RICHARD BLACKMORE

    Lorna Doone (1869)

CHARLOTTE BRONTË

    Jane Eyre (1847)

    Shirley (1849)

    Villette (1853)

EMILY BRONTË

    Wuthering Heights (1847)

CHARLES DICKENS

    Bleak House (1853)

CHARLES DICKENS (continued)

> David Copperfield (1850)
>
> Great Expectations (1861)
>
> Nicholas Nickleby (1839)
>
> Oliver Twist (1838)
>
> Our Mutual Friend (1865)
>
> The Pickwick Papers (1837)
>
> A Tale of Two Cities (1859)

BENJAMIN DISRAELI

> Coningsby (1844)
>
> Sybil (1845)
>
> Tancred (1847)

GEORGE ELIOT

> Adam Bede (1859)
>
> Middlemarch (1872)
>
> The Mill on the Floss (1860)
>
> Silas Marner (1861)

ELIZABETH CLEGHORN GASKELL

> Cranford (1853)
>
> Mary Barton (1848)

GEORGE GISSING

> The Private Papers of Henry
>
> Rycroft (1903)

THOMAS HARDY

> Far from the Madding Crowd (1874)
>
> Jude the Obscure (1896)
>
> The Mayor of Casterbridge (1886)
>
> The Return of the Native (1878)
>
> Tess of the d'Urbervilles (1891)

THOMAS HUGHES

> Tom Brown's School Days (1857)

GEORGE MEREDITH

> The Egoist (1879)
>
> The Ordeal of Richard Feverel (1859)

ROBERT LOUIS STEVENSON

> Dr. Jekyll and Mr. Hyde (1886)
>
> Kidnapped (1886)
>
> The Master of Ballantrae (1889)

WILLIAM MAKEPEACE THACKERAY

> Henry Esmond (1852)
>
> The Newcomes (1855)
>
> Pendennis (1850)
>
> Vanity Fair (1848)

ANTHONY TROLLOPE

> The Warden (1855)
>
> Barchester Towers (1857)

Alfred, Lord Tennyson   1809–1892

If the greatest English hero of the first half of the nineteenth century was a soldier, the Duke of Wellington, the greatest hero of the second half was a poet: Alfred, Lord Tennyson. Tennyson became as much of an institution during the last half of the century as Queen Victoria herself, to whom in their later years he would occasionally read his poems. Huge, shaggy, in cloak and broad-brimmed hat, deep-voiced, and gruff as an old farmer, he impressed everyone as a "character." To his Victorian readers, however, he was not just a striking figure but the wise voice of the age. He was the poet who guided his people through the doubts and fears fostered by political and scientific revolutions, the poet who reconciled faith and hope with the challenges of geology, astronomy, and biology to traditional values and beliefs.

Alfred Tennyson was born in Somersby, in Lincolnshire, on August 6, 1809. He was the fourth of twelve children of Reverend George Clayton Tennyson and Elizabeth Fytche, daughter of the vicar of Louth. Dr. Tennyson was a melancholy man given to periods of depression; he had been disowned by his father, a wealthy landowner, in favor of a younger brother and forced into the ministry against his wishes. He was a good scholar and tutored his sons in classical and modern languages to prepare them for the university. Dr. Tennyson was something of a poet himself and encouraged all his children to write poetry. *Poems by Two Brothers* appeared in 1827; it included poems by Alfred and his brother Charles, and four by an elder brother, Frederick.

Alfred and Charles joined Frederick at Trinity College, Cambridge, in 1828. The massive, powerful, but painfully shy Alfred attracted attention. He was asked to join a student group called "The Apostles"—there were twelve members and they desired, in a sense, to remake England. The group not only stimulated Alfred intellectually, it widened his horizons, encouraged him to dedicate his life to

ALFRED, LORD TENNYSON
Photo: Julia Margaret Cameron
National Portrait Gallery, London

poetry, and gave him valuable friendships. The most fateful of these friendships was with the urbane and brilliant Arthur Hallam, one of the leaders of the Apostles. To the lonely, homebred Alfred, friendship with the charismatic Hallam was precious. In 1830 Tennyson published his first independent volume, *Poems, Chiefly Lyrical*, which was not widely noticed and received mixed reviews.

Early in 1831 when his father died, Alfred refused to become a clergyman as his grandfather desired. Family dissensions and financial need kept him from returning to Cambridge for his degree. He had no regrets, he said, and was determined upon a life of poetry—poetry and poverty if necessary. Tennyson's second volume, *Poems* (1832), was far superior to his first and contained such distinguished works as "The Lady of Shalott," "The Lotus-Eaters," and "Oenone." Nevertheless, the attacks on this volume as "obscure" or "affected" by some reviewers caused Tennyson to suffer acutely. He did not publish for another ten years. During this silence he wrote much, read widely, and studied hard. While he practiced his art until he had mastered the sounds and rhythms of English, he studied such diverse subjects as Latin, Greek, Italian, German, history, chemistry, botany, electricity, animal physiology, geology, and mechanics.

The greatest tragedy of Tennyson's life came in 1833 in the sudden death of Arthur Hallam, his closest friend and the fiancé of his sister Emily. To find an outlet for his grief he began writing a long series of soul-searching, philosophical lyrics which were to appear later as units of his great elegy *In Memoriam* (1850).

By 1842 Tennyson felt he could again offer his poetry to the public. His two-volume *Poems*, including some of the 1832 poems which were now much improved, established his reputation with the general public and placed him in the front rank of contemporary poets.

In 1850 he published *In Memoriam* anonymously, but the authorship was soon known. It became a best-seller partly because it gave wonderful expression to the haunting religious uncertainties of the age and partly because it ended on a note of comforting optimism. That same year brought Tennyson both happiness and fame. After waiting fourteen years, because of poverty, he and Emily Sellwood were married. Also, he was made poet laureate following the death of Wordsworth.

After 1850 the outward events of Tennyson's life are hardly noteworthy. He was accorded adulation and success for the next forty-two years. The poetry, though, continued to flow until his death: lyrics, dramas, long narratives, dramatic monologs, and

commemorative poems. His most ambitious undertaking during the last half of his career was *The Idylls of the King* (1859–1883). He designed the poem on an epic scale (perhaps in imitation of his beloved Virgil) of twelve interconnected long poems loosely based upon Malory's *Morte Darthur* (see page 129). The *Idylls* were immensely popular in England, Europe, and America. They are not merely stories of romantic knights and ladies, of Arthur's bringing order out of chaos, of his dreams being corrupted by complacency and treachery among his followers. Tennyson wrote them as he said "to ennoble and spiritualize mankind." He meant the *Idylls* not only to entertain but also to teach moral lessons, ultimately that a civilization that rises out of chaos may revert to chaos should people abandon the principles of unselfish service and traditional Judeo-Christian values.

Tennyson died on October 6, 1892. His funeral in Westminster Abbey was an occasion of national mourning. He was buried beside Browning and in front of the monument to Chaucer.

Much of Tennyson's work will endure in the rich heritage of English poetry. In the mastery of poetic techniques—diction, imagery, rhythm, and sound effects—he has no peer. Especially when read aloud with a full and sensitive voice, his poetry has a unique power of creating scenery and of conveying moods and human emotions. In this, he has seldom been surpassed by any poet. In addition, he was the first major poet to grapple with modern problems: the growth of democracy, the Industrial Revolution, the challenges of science to traditional Christian beliefs. For most of his countrymen (as well as Europeans and Americans) he effectively voiced their questions and honestly offered them hope and comfort with his answers. Many of those questions and not a few of his answers still relate to us today.

"The Lady of Shalott" first appeared in 1832 (but Tennyson revised it drastically for his 1842 publication) revealing that some fifty years before the last of The Idylls of the King *would see print, Tennyson was already fascinated by the stories surrounding King Arthur. The poem is deceptively simple, so be alert for its symbolism. Who is the Lady? Why is she "half sick of shadows"?*

The Lady of Shalott

Part I
On either side the river lie
Long fields of barley and of rye,
That clothe the wold[1] and meet the sky;
And through the field the road runs by
    To many-towered Camelot;[2]   5
And up and down the people go,
Gazing where the lilies blow
Round an island there below,
    The island of Shalott.

Willows whiten,[3] aspens quiver,   10
Little breezes dusk[4] and shiver
Through the wave that runs forever
By the island in the river
    Flowing down to Camelot.
Four gray walls, and four gray towers,   15
Overlook a space of flowers,
And the silent isle embowers
    The Lady of Shalott.

By the margin, willow-veiled,
Slide the heavy barges trailed   20
By slow horses; and unhailed
The shallop[5] flitteth silken-sailed
    Skimming down to Camelot:
But who hath seen her wave her hand?
Or at the casement seen her stand?   25
Or is she known in all the land,
    The Lady of Shalott?

1. **wold** (wōld), an open, elevated tract of country.
2. **Camelot** (kam′ ə lot), the legendary city of King Arthur.
3. **willows whiten.** The silvery undersides of the leaves are turned over by the breeze.
4. **dusk,** darken.
5. **shallop** (sha′ ləp), a small light boat.

Only reapers, reaping early
In among the bearded barley,
Hear a song that echoes cheerly   30
From the river winding clearly,
  Down to towered Camelot;
And by the moon the reaper weary,
Piling sheaves in uplands airy,
Listening, whispers "'Tis the fairy   35
  Lady of Shalott."

Part II
There she weaves by night and day
A magic web with colors gay.
She has heard a whisper say,
A curse is on her if she stay   40
  To look down to Camelot.
She knows not what the curse may be,
And so she weaveth steadily,
And little other care hath she,
  The Lady of Shalott.   45

And moving through a mirror clear
That hangs before her all the year,
Shadows of the world appear.
There she sees the highway near
  Winding down to Camelot;   50
There the river eddy whirls,
And there the surly village churls,[6]
And the red cloaks of market girls,
  Pass onward from Shalott.

Sometimes a troop of damsels glad,   55
An abbot or an ambling pad,[7]
Sometimes a curly shepherd lad,
Or long-haired page in crimson clad,
  Goes by to towered Camelot;
And sometimes through the mirror blue   60
The knights come riding two and two:
She hath no loyal knight and true,
  The Lady of Shalott.

6. **churls** (chẽrlz), country people.
7. **pad,** a riding horse.

THE LADY OF SHALOTT
J.W. Waterhouse
The Tate Gallery, London

But in her web she still delights
To weave the mirror's magic sights,   65
For often through the silent nights
A funeral, with plumes and lights
 And music, went to Camelot;
Or when the moon was overhead,
Came two young lovers lately wed;   70
"I am half sick of shadows," said
 The Lady of Shalott.

Part III

A bow-shot from her bower eaves,
He rode between the barley sheaves,
The sun came dazzling through the leaves,   75
And flamed upon the brazen greaves[8]
  Of bold Sir Lancelot.
A red-cross knight forever kneeled,
To a lady in his shield,
That sparkled on the yellow field,   80
  Beside remote Shalott.

The gemmy bridle glittered free,
Like to some branch of stars we see
Hung in the golden Galaxy.[9]
The bridle bells rang merrily   85
  As he rode down to Camelot;
And from his blazoned baldric[10] slung
A mighty silver bugle hung,
And as he rode his armor rung,
  Beside remote Shalott.   90

All in the blue unclouded weather
Thick-jeweled shone the saddle-leather,
The helmet and the helmet-feather
Burned like one burning flame together,
  As he rode down to Camelot;   95
As often through the purple night,
Below the starry clusters bright,
Some bearded meteor, trailing light,
  Moves over still Shalott.

His broad clear brow in sunlight glowed;   100
On burnished hooves his war-horse trode;
From underneath his helmet flowed
His coal-black curls as on he rode,
  As he rode down to Camelot.
From the bank and from the river   105
He flashed into the crystal mirror,
"Tirra lirra," by the river
  Sang Sir Lancelot.

8. **greaves** (grēvz), knight armor for the legs below the knees.
9. **Galaxy,** the Milky Way.
10. **baldric** (bôl' drik), a belt worn over the shoulder and across the body.

She left the web, she left the loom,
She made three paces through the room,   110
She saw the water-lily bloom,
She saw the helmet and the plume,
   She looked down to Camelot.
Out flew the web and floated wide;
The mirror cracked from side to side;   115
"The curse is come upon me," cried
   The Lady of Shalott.

Part IV
In the stormy east-wind straining,
The pale yellow woods were waning,
The broad stream in his banks complaining,   120
Heavily the low sky raining
   Over towered Camelot;
Down she came and found a boat
Beneath a willow left afloat,
And round about the prow she wrote   125
   The Lady of Shalott.

And down the river's dim expanse
Like some bold seër in a trance,
Seeing all his own mischance—
With a glassy countenance   130
   Did she look to Camelot.
And at the closing of the day
She loosed the chain, and down she lay;
The broad stream bore her far away,
   The Lady of Shalott.   135

Lying, robed in snowy white
That loosely flew to left and right—
The leaves upon her falling light—
Through the noises of the night
   She floated down to Camelot;   140
And as the boat-head wound along
The willowy hills and fields among,
They heard her singing her last song,
   The Lady of Shalott.

Heard a carol, mournful, holy,   145
Chanted loudly, chanted lowly,
Till her blood was frozen slowly,
And her eyes were darkened wholly,
   Turned to towered Camelot.

For ere she reached upon the tide   150
The first house by the waterside,
Singing in her song she died.
    The Lady of Shalott.

Under tower and balcony,
By garden-wall and gallery   155
A gleaming shape she floated by,
Dead-pale between the houses high,
    Silent into Camelot.
Out upon the wharfs they came,
Knight and burgher, lord and dame,   160
And round the prow they read her name,
    The Lady of Shalott.

Who is this? and what is here?
And in the lighted palace near
Died the sound of royal cheer;   165
And they crossed themselves for fear,
    All the knights of Camelot:
But Lancelot mused a little space;
He said, "She has a lovely face;
God in His mercy lend her grace,   170
    The Lady of Shalott."

FOR UNDERSTANDING

1. What do you learn about the Lady in each of the four parts of the poem?
2. How do the last two lines of Parts I, II, and III prepare for the "action" in the following part?
3. What does she mean when she says (line 71), "I am half sick of shadows"?
4. Why does she turn to the window and look down to Camelot?

FOR INTERPRETATION

1. Tennyson clearly wants the reader to see beyond the surface story of "The Lady of Shalott." The characters and actions seem to stand for things beyond themselves. What do you think? What could the following possibly symbolize: the Lady, the web, Lancelot, Camelot?
2. What does the Lady's death symbolize?

3. Discuss to what extent Tennyson is making the following statements in the poem.
    a. Some people must be protected from the harsh realities of life.
    b. It is often difficult to distinguish reality from what appears to be real.
    c. Artists have a difficult problem: they must experience life and the world, yet they must withdraw from the world because of the nature of their work.

FOR APPRECIATION

Imagery and Rhythm

1. The poem is laced with vivid imagery. Describe the contrast between the imagery in the last stanza of Part II with the imagery in all of Part III. What effect does Tennyson achieve with this contrast?
2. Describe the basic rhythm and the rhyme scheme of the poem. What effect is Tennyson trying to achieve?

The Song of the Brook

I

I come from haunts of coot and hern,[1]
　　I make a sudden sally
And sparkle out among the fern,
　　To bicker down a valley.

II

By thirty hills I hurry down,　　　　　　5
　　Or slip between the ridges,
By twenty thorps,[2] a little town,
　　And half a hundred bridges.

III

Till last by Philip's farm I flow
　　To join the brimming river,　　　　10
For men may come and men may go,
　　But I go on forever.

IV

I chatter over stony ways,
　　In little sharps and trebles,
I bubble into eddying bays,　　　　　15
　　I babble on the pebbles.

V

With many a curve my banks I fret
　　By many a field and fallow,
And many a fairy forest set
　　With willow-weed and mallow.[3]　　20

VI

I chatter, chatter, as I flow
　　To join the brimming river,
For men may come and men may go,
　　But I go on forever.

VII

I wind about, and in and out,　　　　25
　　With here a blossom sailing,

---

1. **coot and hern,** wading birds (hern is dialect for heron).
2. **thorps,** villages.
3. **mallow,** plants with purple, pink, or white five-petaled flowers.

And here and there a lusty trout,
   And here and there a grayling.[4]

VIII

And here and there a foamy flake
   Upon me, as I travel   30
With many a silver water-break
   Above the golden gravel.

IX

And draw them all along, and flow
   To join the brimming river,
For men may come and men may go,   35
   But I go on forever.

X

I steal by lawns and grassy plots,
   I slide by hazel covers;
I move the sweet forget-me-nots
   That grow for happy lovers.   40

XI

I slip, I slide, I gloom, I glance,
   Among my skimming swallows;
I make the netted sunbeam dance
   Against my sandy shallows.

XII

I murmur under moon and stars   45
   In brambly wildernesses;
I linger by my shingly bars;
   I loiter round my cresses;

XIII

And out again I curve and flow
   To join the brimming river,   50
For men may come and men may go,
   But I go on forever.

4. **grayling,** freshwater fish.

FOR UNDERSTANDING

1. A *refrain* is the regular repetition of certain verses or stanzas of a poem. What refrain does Tennyson use in "The Song of the Brook"? What is the function of the refrain in the poem?
2. The poem can be divided into four sections. What impression of the brook do you get from each?

FOR INTERPRETATION

What is the basic contrast stated in the poem? How is this related to the poem's *theme*?

FOR APPRECIATION

1. What central figure of speech does Tennyson use to develop his theme and unify the poem? Why is this figure especially appropriate?
2. Tennyson has loaded the poem with vivid diction and imagery and a sprightly rhythm that helps you experience the sights, sounds, and movements of the brook's journey to the sea. Reread the poem carefully, perhaps aloud to yourself. As you do pick out several stanzas that especially appeal to you and analyze them for examples of appropriate sound effects (alliteration, assonance, etc.) and rhythms.

Ulysses (Odysseus to the Greeks) is the hero of Homer's Odyssey. *The word* odyssey *itself has come to mean any kind of long journey, since Ulysses journeyed far and wide to reach Ithaca, his island home, for some ten years after the Trojan War. When he finally reaches home, he routs the suitors of his wife Penelope and is reunited with his son Telemachus. But now even in his old age can such a one rest from travel?*

Ulysses

It little profits that an idle king,
By this still hearth, among these barren crags,
Matched with an agèd wife, I mete[1] and dole
Unequal laws unto a savage race,
That hoard, and sleep, and feed, and know not me.   5
I cannot rest from travel; I will drink
Life to the lees: all times I have enjoyed
Greatly, have suffered greatly, both with those
That loved me, and alone; on shore, and when
Through scudding drifts the rainy Hyades[2]   10
Vexed the dim sea. I am become a name;
For always roaming with a hungry heart
Much have I seen and known,—cities of men,
And manners, climates, councils, governments,
Myself not least, but honored of them all,—   15
And drunk delight of battle with my peers,

1. **mete** (mēt), measure out.
2. **Hyades** (hī′ ə dēz), a group of stars associated by the ancients with wet weather.

Far on the ringing plains of windy Troy.
I am a part of all that I have met;
Yet all experience is an arch wherethrough
Gleams that untraveled world, whose margin fades   20
For ever and for ever when I move.
How dull it is to pause, to make an end,
To rust unburnished, not to shine in use!
As though to breathe were life! Life piled on life
Were all too little, and of one to me   25
Little remains: but every hour is saved
From that eternal silence, something more,
A bringer of new things; and vile it were
For some three suns to store and hoard myself,
And this gray spirit yearning in desire   30
To follow knowledge like a sinking star,
Beyond the utmost bound of human thought.
    This is my son, mine own Telemachus,
To whom I leave the scepter and the isle[3]—
Well-loved of me, discerning to fulfill   35
This labor, by slow prudence to make mild
A rugged people, and through soft degrees
Subdue them to the useful and the good.
Most blameless is he, centered in the sphere
Of common duties, decent[4] not to fail   40
In offices of tenderness, and pay
Meet adoration to my household gods,
When I am gone. He works his work, I mine.
    There lies the port; the vessel puffs her sail:
There gloom the dark broad seas. My mariners,   45
Souls that have toiled, and wrought, and thought with me—
That ever with a frolic welcome took
The thunder and the sunshine, and opposed
Free hearts, free foreheads—you and I are old;
Old age hath yet his honor and his toil.   50
Death closes all; but something ere the end,
Some work of noble note, may yet be done,
Not unbecoming men that strove with Gods.
The lights begin to twinkle from the rocks:
The long day wanes: the slow moon climbs: the deep   55
Moans round with many voices. Come, my friends,
'Tis not too late to seek a newer world.
Push off, and sitting well in order smite

3. **isle,** Ithaca, an island off the west coast of Greece.
4. **decent,** fitted, suited.

The sounding furrows; for my purpose holds
To sail beyond the sunset, and the baths   60
Of all the western stars, until I die.
It may be that the gulfs will wash us down:
It may be we shall touch the Happy Isles,[5]
And see the great Achilles,[6] whom we knew.
Though much is taken, much abides; and though   65
We are not now that strength which in old days
Moved earth and heaven; that which we are, we are;
One equal temper of heroic hearts,
Made weak by time and fate, but strong in will
To strive, to seek, to find, and not to yield.   70

5. **Happy Isles,** abode of the just after death.
6. **Achilles** (ə kil′ ēz), the Greek hero of the Trojan
War and the central figure of Homer's *Iliad.*

FOR UNDERSTANDING

1. What is Ulysses' attitude toward his home and
kingdom as revealed in the poem's opening lines?
2. What reasons does Ulysses give in lines 7–32 for
his statement "I cannot rest from travel"?
3. Describe the contrast Ulysses perceives between
Telemachus and himself (lines 33–43).
4. What does Ulysses decide to do in the last
section of the poem (lines 44–70)?

FOR INTERPRETATION

What evidence can you find in the poem to support or deny these statements?
1. Happiness is in searching, not in achieving.
2. No matter how bad things get, never give up.
3. Experience as much in life as possible before
death ends it all.

FOR APPRECIATION

The Dramatic Monolog

The poem "Ulysses" is a *dramatic monolog.* In it the
character Ulysses addresses someone, probably his
mariners ("my friends") at a critical point in his
life, but his listeners remain silent. Why do you
think Tennyson chose this form rather than a
third-person account?

Metaphor and Simile

Explain the metaphor in lines 19–21. Explain the
simile in lines 31–32.

Meter

Contrast the meter in "Ulysses" with the meter in
"The Song of the Brook." How are both appropriate to their subjects?

Arthur Hallam's sudden death in Vienna (1833) at the age of twenty-two was a terrible shock to the young Tennyson. The poet had cherished Hallam as his best friend, the fiancé of his sister, and a wise counselor. Already troubled by his own study of geology and other sciences, Tennyson reacted to his friend's death with overwhelming doubts about immortality and the meaning of life. At various intervals for the next seventeen years he worked through his grief and his doubts in a series of individual lyric poems (131 in all) which he collected and published anonymously in 1850.

The poems can be enjoyed by themselves; taken as a whole they reveal Tennyson's ultimate overcoming of his grief and doubt through hope and faith.

from In Memoriam

7

Dark house,* by which once more I stand
   Here in the long unlovely street,
   Doors, where my heart was used to beat
So quickly, waiting for a hand,

A hand that can be clasped no more—   5
   Behold me, for I cannot sleep,
   And like a guilty thing I creep
At earliest morning to the door.

He is not here; but far away
   The noise of life begins again,   10
   And ghastly thro' the drizzling rain
On the bald street breaks the blank day.

27

I envy not in any moods
   The captive void of noble rage,
   The linnet born within the cage,
That never knew the summer woods:

I envy not the beast that takes   5
   His license in the field of time,
   Unfettered by the sense of crime,
To whom a conscience never wakes;

Nor, what may count itself as blest,
   The heart that never plighted troth   10
   But stagnates in the weeds of sloth;
Nor any want-begotten rest.

* **Dark house,** Hallam's house in London.

About the time of Hallam's death Tennyson began conceiving the idea for his most ambitious work, The Idylls of the King. *The first episode he wrote dealt with the death of King Arthur.*

THE DEATH OF ARTHUR
James Archer
Lent by the City of Manchester
Art Galleries, City Art Gallery

I hold it true, whate'er befall;
   I feel it, when I sorrow most;
   'Tis better to have loved and lost   **15**
Than never to have loved at all.

54
Oh yet we trust that somehow good
   Will be the final goal of ill,
   To pangs of nature,* sins of will,
Defects of doubt, and taints of blood;

* **pangs of nature,** disease. The poet trusts that each
life results in good in spite of disease, sin, doubt, and bad
heredity.

That nothing walks with aimless feet;   5
 That not one life shall be destroyed,
 Or cast as rubbish to the void,
When God hath made the pile complete;

That not a worm is cloven in vain;
 That not a moth with vain desire 10
 Is shrivelled in a fruitless fire,
Or but subserves another's gain.

Behold, we know not anything;
 I can but trust that good shall fall
 At last—far off—at last, to all, 15
And every winter change to spring.

So runs my dream: but what am I?
 An infant crying in the night:
 An infant crying for the light:
And with no language but a cry. 20

55

The wish, that of the living whole
 No life may fail beyond the grave,
 Derives it not from what we have
The likest God* within the soul?

Are God and Nature then at strife, 5
 That Nature lends such evil dreams?
 So careful of the type she seems,
So careless of the single life;

That I, considering everywhere
 Her secret meaning in her deeds, 10
 And finding that of fifty seeds
She often brings but one to bear,

I falter where I firmly trod,
 And falling with my weight of cares
 Upon the great world's altar-stairs 15
That slope through darkness up to God,

I stretch lame hands of faith, and grope,
 And gather dust and chaff, and call
 To what I feel is Lord of all,
And faintly trust the larger hope. 20

* **likest God,** God-like qualities.

130

Thy voice is on the rolling air;
   I hear thee where the waters run;
   Thou standest in the rising sun,
And in the setting thou art fair.

What art thou then? I cannot guess;   5
   But though I seem in star and flower
   To feel thee some diffusive power,
I do not therefore love thee less.

My love involves the love before;
   My love is vaster passion now;   10
   Though mixed with God and Nature thou,
I seem to love thee more and more.

Far off thou art, but ever nigh;
   I have thee still, and I rejoice;
   I prosper, circled with thy voice;   15
I shall not lose thee though I die.

*Tennyson wrote this lyric when he was eighty years old. He asked
that it be printed at the end of all editions of his poetry.*

Crossing the Bar

Sunset and evening star,
   And one clear call for me!
And may there be no moaning of the bar,[1]
   When I put out to sea,

But such a tide as moving seems asleep,   5
   Too full for sound and foam,
When that which drew from out the boundless deep
   Turns again home.

Twilight and evening bell,
   And after that the dark!   10
And may there be no sadness of farewell,
   When I embark;

---

1. **bar,** sandbar, blocking the harbor except at high
tide.

For though from out our bourne[2] of Time and Place
    The flood may bear me far,
I hope to see my Pilot face to face   15
    When I have crossed the bar.

2. **bourne** (bôrn), boundary.

UNDERSTANDING AND INTERPRETATION

In Memoriam 7
1. Where is the poet? What is he remembering?
2. What is the poet's mood? What imagery suggests death?

In Memoriam 27
1. What is the mood of the poet in the first three stanzas?
2. How does the fourth stanza explain the poet's attitude expressed in the first three?
3. Lines 15 and 16 have become a cliché. Do you agree or disagree with the poet?

In Memoriam 54
1. What is the poet's view of evil in the world as expressed in the first three stanzas?
2. What is the mood of the poem? What is Tennyson's attitude toward death?

In Memoriam 55
1. What basic question does Tennyson seem to be confronting in this poem?
2. What does he mean by the lines "So careful of the type she seems/So careless of the single life"?

3. What is "the larger hope" the poet speaks about?

In Memoriam 130
1. Where does Tennyson now find his friend? What does this discovery do for the poet?
2. What does Tennyson mean by the paradox, "I shall not lose thee though I die"?

Crossing the Bar
1. Reminiscent of the poem "Ulysses," Tennyson again uses the beginning of a long sea voyage as a metaphor. What is the metaphor? What is the sea? Who is the pilot?
2. How would you describe the poet's mood or attitude in the poem?

COMPOSITION

In a short essay, pick one of the three subjects below and analyze Tennyson's poetic approach to that subject. Be sure to include in your essay specific references to the appropriate poem(s).
    a. the position of the artist in the world
    b. the experience of aging
    c. the experience of death

Robert Browning 1812–1889

Although his life span nearly matched that of Tennyson, Browning was not popular as a poet until the last decades of his life. In fact, during the years of his marriage to Elizabeth Barrett he was sometimes referred to as "Mrs. Browning's husband" for she was at the time a more famous poet. Perhaps because he was something of an anomaly, fame came late to him. Indeed, in some ways, he was more of a Romantic than a Victorian—in his great personal enthusiasm and optimism, in his political liberalism, and in his daring experimentation with poetic forms and language.

Browning was born in Camberwell, a suburb of London. His father, a bank clerk, was by avocation an artist, a scholar, and a collector of books and pictures. His mother was a gentle, religious-minded woman, interested in flowers and music. His parents gave their only son, Robert, the happiest of childhoods. He was educated almost entirely at home by tutors and through his own omnivorous reading in the family library. He was free to browse in the library at will, play the piano, and wander through the nearby Dulwich Gallery. By the time he began to publish poetry, he had acquired a remarkable store of knowledge, some of it quite obscure. He made his home happily with his parents until his marriage at age thirty-four.

Browning's first publication, *Pauline* (1833), about the results of his adolescent self-examination, was not a very good poem and was severely criticized. He avoided "confessional" writing thereafter. In 1835 he won a small share of recognition for his dramatic poem *Paracelsus,* but squandered his gains when he published *Sordello* in 1840. The latter is hopelessly chaotic and made his name a popular byword for obscurity. As a result few people bothered to buy a fine series of poetic pamphlets, *Bells and Pomegranates,* when he published them between 1841 and 1846.

Meanwhile, the actor W. C. Macready had encouraged Browning to write plays. For ten years (1837–1847) the poet struggled to create

ROBERT BROWNING
Dante Gabriel Rossetti
Reproduced by permission
of the Syndics of Fitzwilliam Museum, Cambridge

dramas that would hold the attention of an audience. Unhappily all his efforts failed as stage productions. Nevertheless, the experience of writing dialogue for plays was valuable for the young author. It no doubt helped him perfect the dramatic monolog, of which he is the acknowledged master in English. The dramatic monolog would allow him to "speak through" imaginary characters without directly revealing himself.

A second phase of Browning's personal life began when in the spring of 1845 he was able to arrange a meeting with Elizabeth Barrett. At that time Barrett, six years older than Browning, was a semi-invalid confined to her father's house (she was literally a prisoner). She was a popular poet and a person of great intellectual gifts. Browning continued to pay weekly visits, unknown to Elizabeth's father. In time they fell in love. When it became apparent to Browning that Elizabeth's father would never approve of their marriage, in September 1846 they were married secretly in a nearby church and a week later eloped to Italy.

The years that followed in Europe were very happy ones for the Brownings. Mrs. Browning miraculously recovered a good measure of health and in 1849 she bore a son, Robert. Their home, Casa Guidi in Florence, became a gathering place for friends and admirers from England and America. Browning, too, thrived in the happy marriage and in the warm lands of the Mediterranean. As a result he published one of his finest collections, *Men and Women,* in 1855. It brought him a measure of recognition, especially among discerning readers. It reflected his enjoyment of Italy and especially his fascination for the Italian Renaissance. It also demonstrated his complete mastery of the dramatic monolog (see pages 666–667).

After Elizabeth Barrett Browning's death in 1861, the third phase of Browning's personal life began. Browning returned to London with his son, and there for the next twenty-eight years he became an increasingly familiar figure in London society. At the same time he published a succession of volumes which continued to add to his reputation, despite their increasing obscurity and preoccupation with philosophical questions. The most notable volumes were *Dramatis Personae* (1864), containing some of his finest monologs, and *The Ring and the Book* (1868), his most ambitious work, which tells the story of a seventeenth-century Italian murder from ten different points of view. In the 1880s, Browning Societies began to appear throughout the English-speaking world. On the one hand, these societies helped to spread his fame, but on the other they also helped to promote the idea that Browning could be made intelligible only through devoted group effort. Browning died

quietly in 1889 at his son's palazzo in Venice and was buried in Westminster Abbey.

In some ways Browning, the "incurable romantic," was linked to the Victorians, but in others he is more relevant to the twentieth century. Like Tennyson he confronted in many of his dramatic monologs the Victorian concerns about good and evil, faith and doubt, and the place of the artist in modern society. Browning faced these problems with an unwavering optimism and faith that reassured many in the last half of the century. Where Tennyson worked out his response painfully, largely through reason, Browning seems to have had an unquestionable faith in the ultimate purpose and meaning of life—in spite of the fact that the array of villains in his monologs shows that he was quite aware of the existence of evil.

Browning relates more to the twentieth century, first in his "experiments" with the dramatic monolog, and second especially in his experiments with language and sentence structure. Browning's deliberate use of grotesque rhymes and jarring rhythms, colloquial diction and convoluted word order opened the path that has become the main road for twentieth-century poetry. Like John Donne (see page 304), Browning will abandon the traditional harmonies to startle us into a new awareness. Second, Browning's delving into and exposing the workings of the conscious and unconscious mind is clearly a preoccupation, even an obsession, of much of twentieth-century literature. Among Victorian novelists, George Eliot (see page 643) especially shared his concern for unraveling the intricate tangles of human motives. Again it is in the monologs where Browning reaches beyond his contemporaries to let us share acute psychological insights. He once wrote, "My stress is on the incidents in the development of the human soul; little else is worth study."

"My Last Duchess" is one of the great psychological studies in English poetry. This dramatic monolog is the perfect means for Browning to portray the strange combination of culture and cruelty which existed in some men in the Italian Renaissance. Through the self-revealing speech of the Duke of Ferrara we are given a picture of the Duchess—and the Duke—far different from the one he means to portray.

My Last Duchess

That's my last Duchess painted on the wall,
Looking as if she were alive. I call
That piece a wonder, now: Fra Pandolf's[1] hands
Worked busily a day, and there she stands.
Will't please you sit and look at her? I said   5
"Fra Pandolf" by design, for never read
Strangers like you that pictured countenance,
The depth and passion of its earnest glance,
But to myself they turned (since none puts by
The curtain I have drawn for you, but I)   10
And seemed as they would ask me, if they durst,
How such a glance came there; so, not the first
Are you to turn and ask thus. Sir, 'twas not
Her husband's presence only, called that spot
Of joy into the Duchess' cheek: perhaps   15
Fra Pandolf chanced to say, "Her mantle laps
Over my lady's wrist too much," or "Paint
Must never hope to reproduce the faint
Half-flush that dies along her throat:" such stuff
Was courtesy, she thought, and cause enough   20
For calling up that spot of joy. She had
A heart—how shall I say?—too soon made glad,
Too easily impressed; she liked whate'er
She looked on, and her looks went everywhere.
Sir, 'twas all one! My favor at her breast,   25
The dropping of the daylight in the West,
The bough of cherries some officious fool
Broke in the orchard for her, the white mule
She rode with round the terrace—all and each
Would draw from her alike the approving speech,   30
Or blush, at least. She thanked men,—good! but thanked
Somehow—I know not how—as if she ranked
My gift of a nine-hundred-years-old name
With anybody's gift. Who'd stoop to blame
This sort of trifling? Even had you skill   35

---

1. **Fra Pandolf,** an imaginary monk and painter.

In speech—(which I have not)—to make your will
Quite clear to such an one, and say, "Just this
Or that in you disgusts me; here you miss,
Or there exceed the mark"—and if she let
Herself be lessoned so, nor plainly set   40
Her wits to yours, forsooth, and made excuse,
—E'en then would be some stooping; and I choose
Never to stoop. Oh sir, she smiled, no doubt,
Whene'er I passed her; but who passed without
Much the same smile? This grew; I gave commands;   45
Then all smiles stopped together. There she stands
As if alive. Will't please you rise? We'll meet
The company below, then. I repeat,
The Count your master's known munificence
Is ample warrant that no just pretence   50
Of mine for dowry will be disallowed;
Though his fair daughter's self, as I avowed
At starting, is my object. Nay, we'll go
Together down, sir. Notice Neptune,² though,
Taming a sea-horse, thought a rarity,   55
Which Claus of Innsbruck³ cast in bronze for me!

2. **Neptune,** the Roman god of the sea.
3. **Claus of Innsbruck,** an imaginary sculptor; Innsbruck in Austria was noted for its bronze statues.

FOR UNDERSTANDING

1. What words immediately give you the clue to the identity of the speaker? Who is the listener?
2. What do you learn about the Duke from the words in parentheses in lines 9 and 10?
3. What are the complaints that the Duke had about his wife?
4. The Duke lists four things (besides the painter's remarks) which would bring to the Duchess a blush of pleasure. What have they in common? What irony is there in the relation of the first of these to the other three?
5. What tones of voice does the Duke employ?

FOR INTERPRETATION

1. What was most threatened in the Duke: his pride or his faith in love?

2. What is implied by the words: "I gave commands;/Then all smiles stopped together"? What may have happened?
3. Since the envoy's master is wealthy, what is the effect of the Duke's confession that the woman's "self" is his real object?
4. What final bit of information do you gain about the Duke through his pointing out the sculpture of Neptune and the sea horse?
5. To what extent does Browning intend the reader to apply the poem only to the Duke? To human nature in general?

FOR APPRECIATION

Dramatic Monolog
Like a brief, one-act play, a dramatic monolog concentrates on a crucial incident—one moment that illuminates a lifetime. While a narrative poem

like "The Lady of Shalott" emphasizes action, telling what happened and how it happened, the dramatic monolog deals in the motives behind an action. In the vivid scene created in "My Last Duchess," Browning probes the motives that the Duke must have had for marriage.

The tense drama necessary to reveal a lifetime in a moment makes the dramatic monolog a challenge to a poet. He must devise and compress a set of details to create a subtle and concise portrait that will reveal his speaker more fully than at first seems obvious. It is apparent that in order to understand this complex poetry, the reader, too, must exercise an art. It is the reader's skill which must reconstruct the human character from the revealing words, gestures, actions, and details.

Ordinarily these poems have only one character speaking. This character directs his or her speech toward a silent companion whose reactions serve as a foil for the speaker and advance the course of the monolog. You can observe this development by comparing the impression that the Duke is trying to create in "My Last Duchess" with the impression the envoy must be receiving.

In the following monolog Browning presents a contrast between the past and the present through the eyes of a shepherd. It is not certain what ruins Browning had in mind, possibly ancient Babylon or Nineveh or one of the Etruscan cities of Italy.

Love Among the Ruins

Where the quiet-colored end of evening smiles
   Miles and miles
On the solitary pastures where our sheep
   Half-asleep
Tinkle homeward through the twilight, stray or stop   5
   As they crop—
Was the site once of a city great and gay
   (So they say),
Of our country's very capital, its prince
   Ages since   10
Held his court in, gathered councils, wielding far
   Peace or war.

Now,—the country does not even boast a tree,
   As you see,
To distinguish slopes of verdure, certain rills   15
   From the hills
Intersect and give a name to, (else they run
   Into one,)
Where the domed and daring palace shot its spires
   Up like fires   20
O'er the hundred-gated circuit of a wall
   Bounding all,
Made of marble, men might march on nor be pressed,
   Twelve abreast.

And such plenty and perfection, see, of grass   25
   Never was!
Such a carpet as, this summer-time, o'er-spreads
   And embeds
Every vestige of the city, guessed alone,
   Stock or stone—   30
Where a multitude of men breathed joy and woe
   Long ago;
Lust of glory pricked their hearts up, dread of shame
   Struck them tame;
And that glory and that shame alike, the gold   35
   Bought and sold.

Now,—the single little turret that remains
   On the plains,
By the caper[1] overrooted, by the gourd
   Overscored,   40
While the patching houseleek's[2] head of blossom winks
   Through the chinks—
Marks the basement whence a tower in ancient time
   Sprang sublime,
And a burning ring, all round, the chariots traced   45
   As they raced,
And the monarch and his minions and his dames
   Viewed the games.

And I know—while thus the quiet-colored eve
   Smiles to leave   50
To their folding, all our many-tinkling fleece
   In such peace,
And the slopes and rills in undistinguished gray
   Melt away—
That a girl with eager eyes and yellow hair   55
   Waits me there
In the turret whence the charioteers caught soul
   For the goal,
When the king looked, where she looks now, breathless, dumb
   Till I come.   60

But he looked upon the city, every side,
   Far and wide,
All the mountains topped with temples, all the glades'
   Colonnades,

1. **caper,** low prickly shrub.
2. **houseleek,** a common European plant that grows on
walls and roofs.

All the causeys,³ bridges, aqueducts,—and then,   65
   All the men!
When I do come, she will speak not, she will stand,
   Either hand
On my shoulder, give her eyes the first embrace
   Of my face,   70
Ere we rush, ere we extinguish sight and speech
   Each on each.

In one year they sent a million fighters forth
   South and North,
And they built their gods a brazen pillar⁴ high   75
   As the sky,
Yet reserved a thousand chariots in full force—
   Gold, of course.
Oh heart! oh blood that freezes, blood that burns!
   Earth's returns   80
For whole centuries of folly, noise and sin!
   Shut them in,
With their triumphs and their glories and the rest!
   Love is best.

3. **causeys,** causeways or raised roads.
4. **brazen pillar,** a pillar built from the brass of captured chariots.

FOR UNDERSTANDING

1. Describe the contrasts between the past and the present as seen through the speaker's eyes in the first four stanzas.
2. What new contrast does Browning introduce in the last three stanzas?

FOR INTERPRETATION

What does the poem mean? How does the title fit the theme? How would you best state the theme in one sentence?

FOR APPRECIATION

1. Browning invented the stanza pattern used in "Love Among the Ruins." Explain how he used it to reinforce the contrast between the past and the present.
2. Browning alternates one long line of verse with one very short line. How many beats are usually in the long line of verse? How many in the short line? How does this pattern—long vs. short—relate to the poem's theme?

Although Browning wrote "Prospice" ("look forward") in mid-life, soon after his wife's death, it remained the classic expression of his attitude toward life and death.

Prospice

Fear death?—to feel the fog in my throat,
    The mist in my face,
When the snows begin, and the blasts denote
    I am nearing the place,
The power of the night, the press of the storm,   5
    The post of the foe;
Where he stands, the Arch Fear in a visible form,
    Yet the strong man must go:
For the journey is done and the summit attained,
    And the barriers fall,   10
Though a battle's to fight ere the guerdon[1] be gained,
    The reward of it all.
I was ever a fighter, so—one fight more,
    The best and the last!
I would hate that death bandaged my eyes, and forbore,   15
    And bade me creep past.
No! let me taste the whole of it, fare like my peers
    The heroes of old,
Bear the brunt, in a minute pay glad life's arrears
    Of pain, darkness and cold.   20
For sudden the worst turns the best to the brave,
    The black minute's at end,
And the elements' rage, the fiend-voices that rave,
    Shall dwindle, shall blend,
Shall change, shall become first a peace out of pain,   25
    Then a light, then thy breast,
O thou soul of my soul![2] I shall clasp thee again,
    And with God be the rest!

1. **guerdon** (gėrd′ n), reward.
2. **soul of my soul,** Browning's wife.

FOR UNDERSTANDING

1. What is Browning's answer to the poem's opening question?
2. How does Browning view himself in the first twenty lines of the poem? What is his attitude toward the "Arch Fear"?
3. How does the "worst" turn "the best" for "the brave"?

COMPOSITION

"Prospice" is frequently viewed as a companion piece with Tennyson's "Crossing the Bar" (page 661). Each is the classic expression of its author's attitude toward death. Compare these two poems. What similarities are there in each poet's view? What striking difference do you detect between each poet's attitude?

Elizabeth Barrett Browning   1806–1861

In her lifetime Elizabeth Barrett Browning was a more famous poet than her husband, Robert Browning. Her topical poems won her a great reputation in the Victorian Age and for a time some even thought her achievements challenged those of Tennyson.

Elizabeth was the eldest of eleven children of Edward Barrett and Mary Clarke. She received a remarkable education at home in Greek and philosophy and on her own acquired considerable knowledge of Latin, Hebrew, and several modern languages.

When she was fifteen she suffered an injury to her spine and shortly thereafter her devoted brother Edward drowned and she contracted a lung infection. As a result she became an invalid confined to her room—until her marriage. Her great consolation during her years of confinement was reading and writing poetry.

In 1844 Elizabeth praised a struggling young poet in her romantic poem *Lady Geraldine's Courtship*. In response Robert Browning enthusiastically wrote her the first of many letters proclaiming "I love your verses with all my heart, dear Miss Barrett . . . and I love you too." An exchange of letters led to a meeting and to his weekly visits, and eventually to their secret marriage on September 12, 1846. A few days later they left for Italy where the mild climate and Robert's care brought about a remarkable improvement in Elizabeth's health.

Three years later Elizabeth showed Robert a sequence of poems she had composed earlier, recording an emotional history of her growing love for Robert and her fears and doubts about

ELIZABETH BARRETT BROWNING
Field Talfourd
National Portrait Gallery, London

her ill health and unworthiness of such love. He insisted upon publication. Because the sonnets were deeply personal, she decided to present them as translations, calling them *Sonnets from the Portuguese.*

from Sonnets from the Portuguese

8

What can I give thee back, O liberal
And princely giver, who has brought the gold
And purple of thine heart, unstained, untold,
And laid them on the outside of the wall
For such as I to take or leave withal,   5
In unexpected largesse? Am I cold,
Ungrateful, that for these most manifold
High gifts, I render nothing back at all?
Not so; not cold—but very poor instead.
Ask God, who knows. For frequent tears have run   10
The colors from my life, and left so dead
And pale a stuff, it were not fitly done
To give the same as pillow to thy head.
Go farther! let it serve to trample on.

23

Is it indeed so? If I lay here dead,
Wouldst thou miss any life in losing mine?
And would the sun for thee more coldly shine
Because of grave-damps falling round my head?
I marveled, my Beloved, when I read   5
Thy thought so in the letter. I am thine—
But . . . *so* much to thee? Can I pour thy wine
While my hands tremble? Then my soul, instead
Of dreams of death, resumes life's lower range.
Then, love me, Love! look on me—breathe on me!   10
As brighter ladies do not count it strange,
For love to give up acres and degree,
I yield the grave for thy sake, and exchange
My near sweet view of Heaven, for earth with thee!

43

How do I love thee? Let me count the ways.
I love thee to the depth and breadth and height
My soul can reach, when feeling out of sight
For the ends of Being and ideal Grace.
I love thee to the level of every day's   5
Most quiet need, by sun and candle-light.
I love thee freely, as men strive for Right;
I love thee purely, as they turn from Praise.
I love thee with the passion put to use
In my old griefs, and with my childhood's faith.   10
I love thee with a love I seemed to lose
With my lost saints,—I love thee with the breath,
Smiles, tears, of all my life!—and, if God choose,
I shall but love thee better after death.

FOR UNDERSTANDING

1. What view of self is presented by the speaker of "Sonnet 8"? What view of the beloved? How is color imagery used in the poem?
2. Assuming that the speaker of "Sonnet 23" is the same person, what change of attitude do you see? What caused this change?
3. "Sonnet 43" is perhaps the most famous of all the "Portuguese" sonnets. Explain in your own words the various ways the poet says she loves in "Sonnet 43." What do they add up to?

Emily Brontë

1818–1848

When she was two years old Emily Brontë's father, a clergyman, moved his family to the remote village of Haworth in Yorkshire. A year later her mother died of cancer, leaving six small children to be raised by a maiden aunt. In 1824 she joined her three older sisters—Maria, Elizabeth, and Charlotte—at the Clergy Daughter's School at Cowan Bridge where the food was bad and the discipline harsh. The girls remained less than a year, Marie and Elizabeth coming home to die of tuberculosis.

Emily did not leave home again until 1835 when she went to a girl's boarding school where Charlotte was serving as a governess. But Emily, pining for freedom, could not endure the place and stayed only a few months. She left Haworth only once more, in 1842, when she and Charlotte went to Brussels to study modern languages for eight months.

The isolation of Haworth near the desolate and storm-ridden moors played a significant part in the lives of Emily, her sisters Charlotte and Anne, and her brother Branwell. As children they were often left to themselves. For recreation they walked the bleak and windblown moors, read, and imagined the mythical kingdoms of "Angria" and "Gondol." In microscopic script the children chronicled in verse and prose an elaborate history of these two kingdoms, their governments, politics, wars, and high society. Many of the episodes and characters in the "history" later found their way into the sisters' novels.

In 1846 the three sisters published, at their own expense, *Poems* by Currer (Charlotte), Ellis (Emily), and Acton (Anne) Bell. The book sold two copies. The few reviewers found Emily's poetry promising. Undaunted, in October 1847 Charlotte published *Jane Eyre* by Currer Bell. Two months later in a single volume appeared Emily's *Wuthering Heights* by Ellis Bell and Anne's *Agnes Grey* by Acton Bell. *Jane Eyre* was immediately popular. For the dark, brooding, strange yet powerful *Wuthering Heights*, success came much slower, but to such things the fiercely private and independent Emily was entirely indifferent.

Emily's health had been poor for some time and after the illness and death of her brother Branwell, who succeeded in drinking himself into the grave, she deteriorated rapidly. Frequently in intense pain she would not ask for or accept help. Two hours before her death she struggled out of bed and dressed herself before she would allow a doctor to be called. Such stoicism marked her entire life.

Today, her lone and mighty novel, *Wuthering Heights*, is considered among the best novels in English. Some of her poetry is placed among the best accomplishments of English women in literature. Nevertheless, Emily remains an enigma: how to account for the intense passion of her writing in view of her quiet, domestic life in a remote Yorkshire village? The smoldering emotional fires that must have burned beneath her almost impenetrable exterior can only be inferred from her poetry and her novel. Two things seem certain: she loved the moors intently and she saw a reality beyond the one we know.

EMILY BRONTË
P. Branwell Brontë
National Portrait Gallery, London

Song

The linnet in the rocky dells,
  The moor-lark in the air,
The bee among the heather bells
  That hide my lady fair:

The wild deer browse above her breast;   5
  The wild birds raise their brood;
And they, her smiles of love caressed,
  Have left her solitude!

I ween* that when the grave's dark wall
  Did first her form retain,   10
They thought their hearts could ne'er recall
  The light of joy again.

They thought the tide of grief would flow
  Unchecked through future years;

But where is all their anguish now,   15
  And where are all their tears?

Well, let them fight for honor's breath,
  Or pleasure's shade pursue—
The dweller in the land of death
  Is changed and careless too.   20

And, if their eyes should watch and weep
  Till sorrow's source were dry,
She would not, in her tranquil sleep,
  Return a single sigh!

Blow, west wind, by the lonely mound,   25
  And murmur, summer streams—
There is no need of other sound
  To soothe my lady's dreams.

* **ween,** suppose.

The wanderer is her brother Branwell, who died less than three months before Emily. He had wasted his genius in dissipation.

The Wanderer from the Fold

How few, of all the hearts that loved,
  Are grieving for thee now;
And why should mine tonight be moved
  With such a sense of woe?

Too often thus, when left alone,   5
  Where none my thoughts can see,
Comes back a word, a passing tone
  From thy strange history.

Sometimes I seem to see thee rise,
  A glorious child again;   10
All virtues beaming from thine eyes
  That ever honored men:

Courage and truth, a generous breast
  Where sinless sunshine lay:
A being whose very presence blessed   15
  Like gladsome summer day.

O, fairly spread thy early sail;
  And fresh, and pure, and free,
Was the first impulse of the gale
  Which urged life's wave for thee!   20

Why did the pilot, too confiding,
  Dream o'er that ocean's foam,
And trust in Pleasure's careless guiding
  To bring his vessel home?

For well he knew what dangers frowned,   25
  What mists would gather dim;
What rocks and shelves and sands lay round
  Between his port and him.

The very brightness of the sun,
  The splendor of the main,   30
The wind which bore him wildly on
  Should not have warned in vain.

An anxious gazer from the shore—
  I marked the whitening wave,
And wept above thy fate the more   35
  Because I could not save.

It recks not now, when all is over:
  But yet my heart will be
A mourner still, though friend and lover
  Have both forgotten thee!   40

*Her sister Charlotte said, "The following are the last
lines my sister Emily wrote."*

No Coward Soul Is Mine

  No coward soul is mine,
No trembler in the world's storm-troubled sphere;
  I see Heaven's glories shine,
And faith shines equal, arming me from fear.

  O God, within my breast,   5
Almighty, ever-present Deity!
  Life—that in me has rest,
As I—undying Life—have power in Thee!

Vain are the thousand creeds
That move men's hearts, unutterably vain,   10
  Worthless as withered weeds,
Or idle froth amid the boundless main,

  To waken doubt in one
Holding so fast by Thine infinity;
  So surely anchored on   15
The steadfast rock of immortality.

  With wide-embracing love
Thy spirit animates eternal years,
  Pervades and broods above,
Changes, sustains, dissolves, creates, and rears.   20

  Though earth and man were gone,
And suns and universes ceased to be,
  And Thou were left alone,
Every existence would exist in Thee.

  There is not room for Death,   25
Nor atom that his might could render void:
  Thou—Thou art Being and Breath,
And what Thou art may never be destroyed.

UNDERSTANDING AND INTERPRETATION

Song

1. Who is the speaker in the poem? To whom is he speaking?
2. Who is the "they" in lines 7–12? What is the speaker's attitude toward them?
3. What is the role of nature in the poem?

The Wanderer from the Fold

1. Why does Brontë say she is "moved/With such a sense of woe"?
2. What did Brontë find particularly frustrating in watching her brother? What does she resolve?

No Coward Soul Is Mine

What is Brontë's attitude toward Death? What is the basis of her attitude?

COMPOSITION

Write a brief paper comparing Brontë's attitude toward death as expressed in "No Coward Soul Is Mine" with the attitudes of Tennyson and Browning as expressed in "Crossing the Bar" and "Prospice." Be sure to cite specific lines in these poems to support the conclusions you draw about the similarities and differences among the three poets.

Matthew Arnold   1822–1888

Matthew Arnold was successful both as a poet and as a critic, while at the same time for more than three decades he earned his living as an inspector of schools. In all three roles his principal concern was with how to "live life" when science and the higher criticism of the Bible were unsettling all the comfortable certainties upon which people had founded their happiness for so many centuries. Arnold found himself

> wandering between two worlds, one dead,
> the other powerless to be born.

Arnold was the son of Mary Penrose and Dr. Thomas Arnold, an influential clergyman who later became headmaster at Rugby School and a famous educational reformer. At Rugby Matthew was a distinguished classical scholar under the powerful influence of his father's ideas and his rigorous but well-intentioned discipline. When Arnold entered Oxford in 1841 he assumed something of the manner of an aristocratic dandy, perhaps in part in rebellion against his father and perhaps too as a mask to keep people from getting too close as he pondered "how to live." After graduating he worked as a private secretary for four years before becoming a government inspector of schools in 1851, the year of his marriage to Frances Lucy. Arnold's job was demanding; consequently he did his writing in the small intervals between official duties.

Arnold's published writing falls roughly into four phases. Most of his poetry appeared in the 1850s; his literary criticism and social criticism in the 1860s; his religious and educational studies in the 1870s; and his second set of essays in literary criticism in the 1880s.

Although Arnold won a poetry prize while at Rugby, he did not venture into print until 1849 with *The Strayed Reveler and Other Poems*. The volume sold only a few hundred copies. In 1852 he published a second volume of poetry, followed a year later by a comprehensive collection called *Poems*. Two years later he added

MATTHEW ARNOLD
G.F. Watts
National Portrait Gallery, London

a second collection called *Poems*. His poetry was not very popular, perhaps because it represents most of the conflicts of the age but offers no solutions—as did that of Tennyson and Browning. His poems convey a sense of melancholy, pessimism, almost despair. He searches for serenity but finds it impossible in modern life with "its sick hurry, its divided aims."

Arnold wrote very little poetry after the 1860s. Some critics believe he turned to prose because as a prose writer he felt he could offer solutions to the problems he "merely" recorded as a poet. At any rate, Arnold saw the poet (as did Tennyson) as one who must "inspirit and rejoice the reader." His own poetry, he felt, did neither. He turned then to evaluating those who should in his judgment, and hence he spent much of the 1860s writing literary criticism. It was only a short step then to social criticism, which many feel culminated with his publication of *Culture and Anarchy* (1869). Here he attacked the Victorian middle class as materialistic, self-centered, ignorant, narrow-minded, and dull. Still, he argued, these Philistines (middle class) were the only hope for civilization (at least they were *doers*), but they must be educated—cultured in the heritage of Hellenism (*beauty* and *truth*) and Hebraism (the *good*).

In the 1870s and 1880s Arnold did what he could to educate the Philistines through his writings on religion and education, through his later literary criticism, and through his work in the schools of England. By adopting a life of "quiet work" he seemed to alleviate his own melancholy or at least distracted himself from what he feared was man's bitter fate in an indifferent universe.

Despite the note of eternal dissatisfaction which pervades his writings, Arnold's personal life seemed to be quite happy. Some say he was—ironically in spite of his distaste for machinery—the first modern man: he died of a heart attack while running for a streetcar.

Dover Beach

The sea is calm tonight.
The tide is full, the moon lies fair
Upon the straits;[1]—on the French coast the light
Gleams and is gone; the cliffs of England stand,
Glimmering and vast, out in the tranquil bay.   5
Come to the window, sweet is the night air!
Only, from the long line of spray
Where the sea meets the moon-blanched[2] land,
Listen! you hear the grating roar
Of pebbles which the waves draw back, and fling,   10
At their return, up the high strand,
Begin, and cease, and then again begin,
With tremulous cadence slow, and bring
The eternal note of sadness in.

Sophocles[3] long ago   15
Heard it on the Aegean,[4] and it brought
Into his mind the turbid ebb and flow
Of human misery; we
Find also in the sound a thought,
Hearing it by this distant northern sea.   20
The Sea of Faith
Was once, too, at the full, and round earth's shore
Lay like the folds of a bright girdle furled.

---

1. **straits,** the narrow channel which separates Dover, on the southeast coast of England, from Calais in France.
2. **moon-blanched,** made white by the moon's rays.
3. **Sophocles** (sof′ ə klēz), (497–406 B.C.), one of the three great tragedians of ancient Athens.
4. **Aegean** (i jē′ ən), an arm of the Mediterranean Sea between Greece and Turkey.

In this painting Hunt celebrates the incredible beauty, safety, and tranquillity of the English coast. The painting seems to say, "All is right with the world"—in sharp contrast with Arnold's view of the world in "Dover Beach."

OUR ENGLISH COASTS
William Holman Hunt
The Tate Gallery, London

But now I only hear
Its melancholy, long, withdrawing roar,   **25**
Retreating, to the breath
Of the night wind, down the vast edges drear
And naked shingles⁵ of the world.

Ah, love, let us be true
To one another! for the world, which seems   **30**
To lie before us like a land of dreams,
So various, so beautiful, so new,
Hath really neither joy, nor love, nor light,
Nor certitude, nor peace, nor help for pain;
And we are here as on a darkling plain   **35**
Swept with confused alarms of struggle and flight,
Where ignorant armies clash by night.

5. **shingles,** shores of gravel.

Self-Dependence

Weary of myself, and sick of asking
What I am, and what I ought to be,
At this vessel's prow I stand, which bears me
Forwards, forwards, o'er the starlit sea.

And a look of passionate desire   5
O'er the sea and to the stars I send:
"Ye who from my childhood up have calmed me,
Calm me, ah, compose me to the end!

"Ah, once more," I cried, "ye stars, ye waters,
On my heart your mighty charm renew;   10
Still, still let me, as I gaze upon you,
Feel my soul becoming vast like you!"

From the intense, clear, star-sown vault of heaven,
Over the lit sea's unquiet way,
In the rustling night-air came the answer: 15
"Wouldst thou *be* as these are? *Live* as they.

"Unaffrighted by the silence round them,
Undistracted by the sights they see,
These demand not that the things without them
Yield them love, amusement, sympathy.   20

"And with joy the stars perform their shining,
And the sea its long moon-silvered roll;
For self-poised they live, nor pine with noting
All the fever of some differing soul.

"Bounded by themselves, and unregardful   25
In what state God's other works may be,
In their own tasks all their powers pouring,
These attain the mighty life you see."

O air-born voice! long since, severely clear,
A cry like thine in mine own heart I hear: 30
"Resolve to be thyself; and know that he,
Who finds himself, loses his misery!"

The Last Word

Creep into thy narrow bed,
Creep, and let no more be said!
Vain thy onset! all stands fast.
Thou thyself must break at last.

Let the long contention cease!
Geese are swans and swans are geese.
Let them have it how they will!
Thou art tired; best be still.

They out-talked thee, hissed thee, tore thee?
Better men fared thus before thee;
Fired their ringing shot and passed,
Hotly charged—and sank at last.

Charge once more, then, and be dumb!
Let the victors, when they come,
When the forts of folly fall,
Find thy body by the wall!

FOR UNDERSTANDING

Dover Beach

1. What has the title to do with the poem?
2. Who is the speaker and to whom is she or he speaking?
3. Why has the poet divided "Dover Beach" into sections? What is the thought progression from one section to another?
4. Trace how the speaker's mood changes from the beginning of the poem to the end.

Self-Dependence

1. What is happening in the first three stanzas? What is the mood of the speaker? What is the speaker asking for?
2. In stanzas 5–7, who responds to the speaker? What lesson does the voice propose?
3. Where and how does the speaker then respond?

The Last Word

1. What sort of person is the speaker addressing?
2. What is the speaker's advice?

FOR INTERPRETATION

Dover Beach

1. Why does Arnold refer to Sophocles (lines 15–17)?
2. What does Arnold mean by the "Sea of Faith"? When was it at the full? What does he mean when he says it is withdrawing?
3. State in your own words the human condition as Arnold describes it in this poem. What single positive value does he still cling to?

FOR APPRECIATION

Free Verse

In "Dover Beach" Arnold used free verse long before metrical irregularity became the fashion. Free verse is defined as verse with no set pattern or length of individual lines, but with generally rising or falling cadences which produce the stress patterns. Such verse may or may not rhyme. You will deal with free verse more extensively when we come to poetry in the modern period.

Dante Gabriel Rossetti 1828–1882

Dante Gabriel Rossetti was both a poet and a painter. His father, a political exile, was for a time Professor of Italian in King's College, London. He shared with his father a lifelong devotion to the great Italian poet Dante. His mother was Frances Polidori, a remarkable woman who taught her two sons and two daughters English, French, and Italian literature as well as the Bible and the orthodox Anglican religion.

Dante Gabriel took up painting in his teens and when he was twenty founded the Pre-Raphaelite Brotherhood with two other artist students. The Brotherhood criticized mid-Victorian art as conventional, unnaturally optimistic, and sentimental. In short, it lacked "sincerity." Art, they felt, must return to the principles that, in their judgment, guided the painters immediately preceding the painter Raphael (1483–1520): naturalness, directness, great attention to realistic detail—above all, sincerity. The Brotherhood's efforts were generally criticized until John Ruskin, the great art critic, gave them his full support. Later, the group formally disbanded, but Rossetti's reputation was assured.

In 1850 he met and fell in love with Elizabeth Siddal, a beautiful, willowy girl of seventeen, who had become the favorite model of the Pre-Raphaelites. Their stormy nine-year engagement finally ended when they were married in 1860, but Elizabeth had already fallen ill with tuberculosis. Two years later Rossetti returned home to find her dying of an overdose of laudanum. Before her burial, overcome with grief, he slipped the manuscript for his poems against her cheek. It was buried with her.

Rossetti had earlier published several of his poems in *The Germ*, a short-lived journal issued by the Brotherhood. At the urging of his friends he had his manuscript exhumed, and in 1870 published *Poems*. About this time, suffering from insomnia and believing his eyesight was failing, he began taking a new drug which he thought

The Rossetti Family photographed in 1865 by Lewis Carroll. Dante and Christina are on the left.
National Portrait Gallery, London.

was harmless. In a short time he developed an addiction which injured his health and depressed him mentally. In spite of these afflictions in later life, when lucid he continued to write and to paint until his death.

The Pre-Raphaelites admired Keats as the poet closest to their ideal. They found his lush and accurate detail the near perfect vehicle for conveying emotions, not just ideas. In Rossetti's poetry and his painting the finished detail, the striking image are of value only as means for revealing emotion.

The following poems are from *The House of Life*, a collection of 101 sonnets giving voice to the moods and emotions of much of his adult life. Be alert for his vague suggestiveness rather than sharp, concrete definitions of experiences that may be essentially indescribable.

*Elizabeth Siddal, the favorite model of the Pre-Raphaelites and later
Dante Gabriel's wife, posed for "Beautiful Beatrice."*

BEATA BEATRIX
Dante Gabriel Rossetti
The Tate Gallery, London

Silent Noon

Your hands lie open in the long fresh grass,—
The finger-points look through like rosy blooms;
Your eyes smile peace. The pasture gleams and glooms
'Neath billowing skies that scatter and amass.
All round our nest, far as the eye can pass,   5
Are golden kingcup-fields with silver edge
Where the cow-parsley skirts the hawthorn hedge.
'Tis visible silence, still as the hour-glass.
Deep in the sun-searched growths the dragonfly
Hangs like a blue thread loosened from the sky:—   10
So this winged hour is dropped to us from above.
Oh! clasp we to our hearts, for deathless dower,
This close-companioned inarticulate hour
When twofold silence was the song of love.

Lost Days

The lost days of my life until today,
What were they, could I see them on the street
Lie as they fell? Would they be ears of wheat
Sown once for food but trodden into clay?
Or golden coins squandered and still to pay?   5
Or drops of blood dabbling the guilty feet?
Or such spilt water as in dreams must cheat
The undying throats of hell, athirst alway?
I do not see them here; but after death
God knows I know the faces I shall see,   10
Each one a murdered self, with low last breath.
"I am thyself,—what hast thou done to me?"
"And I—and I—thyself" (lo! each one saith),
"And thou thyself to all eternity!"

UNDERSTANDING AND APPRECIATION

Silent Noon

1. What images in the poem effectively convey the poem's title? What is the dominant impression Rossetti communicates?
2. How do the lovers communicate with one another?

3. What rhyme scheme does Rossetti use? Why does he use this scheme?

Lost Days

1. In the octave of the sonnet how does Rossetti visualize his lost days?
2. In the sestet how does he see the lost days? What do they do to him?
3. State in your own words the poem's theme.

Christina Rossetti 1830–1894

To many people Christina Rossetti, the sister of Dante Gabriel Rossetti, was the finest woman poet of the Victorian era. During the Pre-Raphaelite days, Christina often served as her brother's model. Unlike him, she maintained a lifelong devotion to the Church of England. On two occasions she refused marriage with men she loved because neither was a member of her church. In both instances she suffered greatly and many of her lyric poems record her frustration and parting. Christina was also deeply attached to her family. She cared for her father until his death in 1854, and for her mother until her death in 1886.

Her *Goblin Market and Other Poems* (1862) was the first collection of poems in the Pre-Raphaelite manner to win public recognition. Even though the long narrative poem "Goblin Market" especially demonstrates the early Pre-Raphaelite concern for simplicity, the poem displays her own unique lyric gifts. Her poetry most often reveals the painful sense of isolation resulting from her self-sacrifice for the love of her family and her church.

Song

When I am dead, my dearest,
  Sing no sad songs for me;
Plant thou no roses at my head,
  Nor shady cypress tree;
Be the green grass above me   5
  With showers and dewdrops wet;
And if thou wilt, remember,
  And if thou wilt, forget.

I shall not see the shadows,
  I shall not feel the rain;   10
I shall not hear the nightingale
  Sing on, as if in pain;
And dreaming through the twilight
  That doth not rise nor set,
Haply I may remember,   15
  And haply may forget.

Sleeping at Last

Sleeping at last, the trouble and tumult over,
   Sleeping at last, the struggle and horror past,
Cold and white, out of sight of friend and of lover,
        Sleeping at last.

    No more a tired heart downcast or overcast,   5
No more pangs that wring or shifting fears that hover,
   Sleeping at last in a dreamless sleep locked fast.

Fast asleep. Singing birds in their leafy cover
   Cannot wake her, nor shake her the gusty blast.
Under the purple thyme and the purple clover   10
        Sleeping at last.

UNDERSTANDING AND APPRECIATION

1. In "Song" what advice does the poet give to "my dearest" in the first stanza?
2. How does the second stanza help explain this advice?

3. What effect does the repetition in lines 7–8 and 15–16 have on the tone of the poem?
4. What is the speaker's attitude toward death in "Sleeping at Last"? What explains this attitude?
5. What is the effect of the poet's repeating the phrase "sleeping at last"?

Thomas Hardy

1840–1928

Thomas Hardy (see page 629) always thought of himself as a poet. In his words he "was compelled to give up verse for prose" out of necessity when his early poetic efforts were rejected by a publisher. Between the ages of thirty-one and fifty-six Hardy published fifteen novels and three collections of stories. In private he referred to his stories as "pot-boilers" and "wretched stuff." When *Jude the Obscure* (1896) was fiercely attacked, the critical stupidity of reviewers "cured him," he said, "of all interest in novel writing." From this time on he devoted himself exclusively to his first love, poetry.

His first volumes *Wessex Poems* (1898) and *Poems of the Past and Present* (1902) were respectfully but not enthusiastically received.

Between 1904 and 1908 he published *The Dynasts*, a poem of epic scope about the Napoleonic Wars. After this he wrote mostly lyric poetry.

Hardy's poetry, like his prose, reflects a pervading sadness about the human condition. Unlike Tennyson and Browning, he could not see meaning and purpose in the world, perhaps only chaos, chance, and human passions frustrating and laying waste to human dreams. Still, he lovingly recreates the ancient landscapes of his native Dorset, with their immemorial patterns of human toil. As he leads us to experience a strikingly realized scene or incident, we come to feel that it somehow stands for some profound themes in human experience.

Hap[1]

If but some vengeful god would call to me
From up the sky, and laugh: "Thou suffering thing,
Know that thy sorrow is my ecstasy,
That thy love's loss is my hate's profiting!"

Then would I bear it, clench myself, and die,   5
Steeled by the sense of ire unmerited;
Half-eased in that a Powerfuller than I
Had willed and meted me the tears I shed.

But not so. How arrives it joy lies slain,
And why unblooms the best hope ever sown?   10
—Crass Casualty obstructs the sun and rain,
And dicing Time for gladness casts a moan. . . .
These purblind Doomsters[2] had as readily strown
Blisses about my pilgrimage as pain.

1. **hap,** chance (also **Casualty,** line 11).
2. **purblind Doomsters,** half-blind judges.

The Man He Killed

Had he and I but met
By some old ancient inn,
We should have sat us down to wet
Right many a nipperkin![1]

But ranged as infantry,   5
And staring face to face,
I shot at him as he at me,
And killed him in his place.

I shot him dead because—
Because he was my foe,   10
Just so: my foe of course he was;
That's clear enough; although

He thought he'd 'list,[2] perhaps,
Offhand like—just as I—
Was out of work—had sold his traps—   15
No other reason why.

Yes; quaint and curious war is!
You shoot a fellow down
You'd treat if met where any bar is,
Or help to half-a-crown.   20

1. **nipperkin,** a small cup or glass.
2. **'list,** enlist.

The Darkling Thrush[1]

I leaned upon a coppice gate[2]
When Frost was specter-gray,
And Winter's dregs made desolate
The weakening eye of day.
The tangled bine-stems[3] scored the sky   5
Like strings from broken lyres,
And all mankind that haunted nigh
Had sought their household fires.

1. **darkling,** in the dark.
2. **coppice gate,** gate leading to a small wood or thicket.
3. **bine-stems,** twining stems of shrubs.

The land's sharp features seemed to be
    The Century's corpse[4] outleant,   10
His crypt the cloudy canopy,
    The wind his death-lament.
The ancient pulse of germ and birth
    Was shrunken hard and dry,
And every spirit upon earth   15
    Seemed fervorless as I.

At once a voice burst forth among
    The bleak twigs overhead
In a full-hearted evensong
    Of joy illimited;   20
An aged thrush, frail, gaunt and small,
    In blast-beruffled plume,
Had chosen thus to fling his soul
    Upon the growing gloom.

So little cause for carolings   25
    Of such ecstatic sound
Was written on terrestrial things
    Afar or nigh around,
That I could think there trembled through
    His happy good-night air   30
Some blessed hope, whereof he knew
    And I was unaware.

4. **Century's corpse.** Hardy wrote this poem on December 31, 1900, the last day of the nineteenth century.

"Ah, Are You Digging on My Grave?"

"Ah, are you digging on my grave
    My loved one?—planting rue?"*
—"No; yesterday he went to wed
  One of the brightest wealth has bred.
'It cannot hurt her now,' he said,   5
    'That I should not be true.'"

* **rue,** a herb with yellow flowers, traditionally an emblem of sorrow; also, an archaic word for sorrow.

"Then who is digging on my grave?
    My nearest dearest kin?"
—"Ah, no: they sit and think, 'What use!
    What good will planting flowers produce?   10
    No tendance of her mound can loose
        Her spirit from Death's gin.'"

"But some one digs upon my grave?
    My enemy?—prodding sly?"
—"Nay: when she heard you had passed the Gate 15
    That shuts on all flesh soon or late,
    She thought you no more worth her hate,
        And cares not where you lie."

"Then who is digging on my grave?
    Say—since I have not guessed!"   20
—"Oh it is I, my mistress dear,
    Your little dog, who still lives near,
    And much I hope my movements here
        Have not disturbed your rest?"

"Ah yes! *You* dig upon my grave . . .   25
    Why flashed it not on me
    That one true heart was left behind!
    What feeling do we ever find
    To equal among human kind
        A dog's fidelity!"   30

"Mistress, I dug upon your grave
    To bury a bone, in case
    I should be hungry near this spot
    When passing on my daily trot.
    I am sorry, but I quite forgot   35
        It was your resting-place."

Hardy wrote the following poem during World War I.
He took the title from Jeremiah *51:20: "Thou art my battle ax and weapons of war; for with*
thee will I break in pieces the nations."

In Time of "The Breaking of Nations"

Only a man harrowing clods
    In a slow silent walk,
With an old horse that stumbles and nods
    Half asleep as they stalk.

> Only thin smoke without flame   5
>   From the heaps of couch grass:
> Yet this will go onward the same
>   Though Dynasties pass.
>
> Yonder a maid and her wight*
>   Come whispering by;   10
> War's annals will fade into night
>   Ere their story die.

* **wight,** youth, young man.

UNDERSTANDING AND APPRECIATION

Hap

1. In the first two quatrains, what has the poet's life been like? What knowledge would make the poet feel better? Why?

2. In the last stanza to what does he attribute his pain?

3. What verse form does Hardy use? In what way is it appropriate?

The Man He Killed

1. What were the man's feelings at the moment he met the enemy soldier? What disturbs him later about the encounter?

2. The third stanza of this poem does a masterful job of fitting the poetic form to the meaning. In the first line, as the soldier gropes for an explanation of his action, his inability to find a satisfactory answer is underscored when the rhythm and meaning are left hanging on "because—." The futility of his search is further emphasized in the second line by his hollow repetition of "because" followed hurriedly by the obvious, empty answer expressed in simple, single-syllable words. Then, pausing to reassure himself, the rush of repetition in the third line shows his relief at having found *an* answer. But the last word of the stanza breaks the established stanza pattern, indicating the doubt that has crept into his mind. Find other places in this poem where the form of the lines fits the meaning of the lines.

The Darkling Thrush

1. What scene is Hardy recreating in the first two stanzas? What mood does the scene convey? What does the scene suggest to Hardy?

2. How does the thrush break the spell? How does the thrush's mood contrast with Hardy's? Does the thrush bring Hardy comfort?

Ah, Are You Digging on My Grave?

1. Who is the first speaker? Who is the second speaker and where in the poem is this speaker's identity revealed? Why does Hardy wait so long to reveal the second speaker?

2. What is the tone of the poem? What is Hardy saying in the poem?

3. In what ways is the poem similar to the traditional ballad? What effect does this have on your reaction?

In Time of "The Breaking of Nations"

1. What three scenes does Hardy portray and what do they have in common?

2. What have these scenes to do with "Dynasties" (line 8) and "War's annals" (line 11)?

3. State in your own words Hardy's theme in this poem.

4. Among other things, Hardy's poetry is noted for its original diction. He will use unpoetic words, literary clichés, and archaic (old-fashioned) words to suit his purpose. Find examples of such words in the poem. Decide if they are appropriate to Hardy's purpose.

COMPOSITION

In a short essay, compare and contrast Hardy's philosophical outlook in his poetry with that of any *one* of the following:

  a. Alfred, Lord Tennyson

  b. Robert Browning

  c. Emily Brontë

A. E. Housman 1859–1936

Alfred Edward Housman's career began with personal failure but ended with success. Born in 1859, in Worcestershire, England, he entered St. John's College, Oxford, at the age of eighteen, intending to become a classical scholar and teacher. But his hopes of gaining an appointment at one of the large English universities were dashed when he failed in an honors examination. Housman then went to London where he spent ten years as a clerk in the Patent Office. He did not abandon his dream of becoming a great scholar and professor, for he continued to study and write. Finally his merits were recognized and he was made Professor of Latin at University College, London. Later, he became a professor at Cambridge University, where he remained until his death in 1936.

Suddenly, during the early months of 1895, Housman found himself in a period of "continuous excitement." He had not bothered much with poetry before that, and had made no effort to publish any poems. During this brief period of inspiration he composed almost all the poems in his first and greatest book, *A Shropshire Lad.* The publisher who brought out the book never suspected that it would become one of the best-selling books of poetry of all time. Only five hundred copies of the first edition were published, and Housman had to pay for the second edition himself. In fact, almost twenty years went by before the book really began to catch on. In 1922 Housman published a second book which he called *Last Poems,* but that strange "continuous excitement" of 1895 never returned. After his death his brother edited *More Poems* from the poet's manuscripts. Most of the poems you will read here came out of that intense period in the life of this shy, retiring scholar.

Housman called his book *A Shropshire Lad* because the poems are set in the quiet country scene of Shropshire, the English county where the poet lived as a boy. There is a certain

A.E. HOUSMAN
W. Rothenstein
National Portrait Gallery, London

poignancy in the fact that the scholar who spent all his adult life in London, or at great universities, seems to have identified emotionally with the simple, little-educated country lads and maidens of his youth.

Housman's original title for his book was *The Poems of Terence Hearsay.* In speaking through the

WORCESTER LANDSCAPE
B.W. Leader
Sudely Art Gallery
Merseyside County Art Galleries

voice of a young Shropshireman, Housman is following the age-old convention of *pastoral* poetry. A pastoral dramatizes the central concerns of people—such as love, death, fate, the beauty of nature—by relating them to simple shepherds, shepherdesses, and nymphs. It is a tradition which Housman knew well from his study of the Greeks and Romans. Pastoral poems are usually written by educated, urbanized poets as a means of introducing a strain of simplicity into their poems.

The background of the Shropshire poems is pleasant: The river Severn winds through green hills and by the side of little market towns like Ludlow, where "the lads in their hundreds" would come in for the fair. But the life that is lived out against this scene is dark, tragic,

ill-fated. Some of the lads and maidens die young; those who live betray their lovers. Some of the lads become killers and are hanged or run away; others go off to nameless wars to be shot. For those who grow up, life turns sour, and the golden promise of their youth is not fulfilled. "Luck's a chance," wrote Housman, "but trouble's sure." The Shropshire lad decides that the world has "much less good than ill," but he retains a spirit of fortitude and courage, and a gentle humor in the face of his pessimism.

As a child, Housman's nickname had been "Mousie," a name which reflects something of the drabness of his private life. Housman never married and had few intimate friends. All the richness of his interior life was poured into his careful, chiseled poems.

With Rue My Heart Is Laden

With rue my heart is laden
  For golden friends I had,
For many a rose-lipt maiden
  And many a lightfoot lad.

By brooks too broad for leaping   5
  The lightfoot boys are laid;
The rose-lipt girls are sleeping
  In fields where roses fade.

Loveliest of Trees

Loveliest of trees, the cherry now
Is hung with bloom along the bough,
And stands about the woodland ride
Wearing white for Eastertide.

Now, of my threescore years and ten,   5
Twenty will not come again,
And take from seventy springs a score,
It only leaves me fifty more.

And since to look at things in bloom
Fifty springs are little room,   10
About the woodlands I will go
To see the cherry hung with snow.

When I Was One-and-Twenty

When I was one-and-twenty
  I heard a wise man say,
'Give crowns and pounds and guineas
  But not your heart away;
Give pearls away and rubies   5
  But keep your fancy free.'
But I was one-and-twenty,
  No use to talk to me.

When I was one-and-twenty
  I heard him say again,   10
'The heart out of the bosom
  Was never given in vain;
'T is paid with sighs a plenty
  And sold for endless rue.'
And I am two-and-twenty,   15
  And oh, 't is true, 't is true.

To an Athlete Dying Young

The time you won your town the race
We chaired[1] you through the market-place,
Man and boy stood cheering by,
And home we brought you shoulder-high.

To-day, the road all runners come,   5
Shoulder-high we bring you home,
And set you at your threshold down,
Townsman of a stiller town.

Smart lad, to slip betimes away
From fields where glory does not stay,   10
And early though the laurel[2] grows
It withers quicker than the rose.

Eyes the shady night has shut
Cannot see the record cut,
And silence sounds no worse than cheers   15
After earth has stopped the ears:

Now you will not swell the rout
Of lads that wore their honours out,
Runners whom renown outran
And the name died before the man.   20

So set, before its echoes fade,
The fleet foot on the sill of shade,
And hold to the low lintel up
The still-defended challenge-cup.

And round that early-laurelled head   25
Will flock to gaze the strengthless dead,
And find unwithered on its curls
The garland briefer than a girl's.

1. **chaired,** carried in joy and triumph in or as if in a chair.
2. The **laurel** was a symbol of victory; the laurels of the athlete are for the day only.

UNDERSTANDING AND INTERPRETATION

Think through and discuss the following propositions about the Housman poems you have read.

With Rue My Heart Is Laden

1. The basic idea of the poem, "I am sad because so many of my friends are dead," is commonplace, but the poem makes it fresh.
2. The only expression of emotion is in line 1.
3. With the exception of line 1 and the last word of the poem, all of the words have good or pleasant connotations.
4. The irony exists in the contrast between what is being said and the choice of words and rhythm in which it is being said.

Loveliest of Trees

1. All the loveliness of spring is suggested by the description of only one object.
2. The poem suggests the characteristic human restlessness during spring that Chaucer suggested in the opening lines of "The Prologue" to *The Canterbury Tales.*
3. In spite of the joy in spring, the poem is tinged with melancholy.
4. Joy is enhanced by our knowledge that it cannot last.

When I Was One-and-Twenty

1. The advice given in stanza 2 differs slightly in its content from that given in stanza 1.
2. The irony lies in the fact that the reader is led to expect that the speaker is an old person.

To an Athlete Dying Young

1. "Shoulder-high" has a different meaning in stanza 1 from that in stanza 2.
2. The words "smart lad" are meant by the speaker as a sincere expression of admiration.
3. It is better to die young than to live to "see the record cut."
4. The poem implies that people who die in a moment of victory will be longer remembered than those who live out their lives.

George Bernard Shaw 1856–1950

"He who has never hoped can never despair."

"The worst sin towards our fellow creatures is not to hate them, but to be indifferent to them."

"Liberty means responsibility. That is why most men dread it."

"There are two tragedies in life. One is not to get your heart's desire. The other is to get it."

These lines from Shaw's plays suggest the central qualities of the playwright: a love of paradox coupled with an ability to phrase it wittily; a desire to shock or to provoke; and, most importantly, an attack on the unthinking way in which people live. He phrased the idea less epigrammatically, but just as strongly, in the Preface which preceded *Arms and the Man:* "To me the tragedy and comedy of life lie in the consequences, sometimes terrible, sometimes ludicrous, of our persistent attempts to found our institutions on the ideals suggested to our imaginations by our half-satisfied passions, instead of on a genuinely scientific natural history."

Bernard Shaw, as he preferred to be known, spent his long writing career trying to replace illusions with realities. No matter what topic he took up in his thirty-plus volumes of writing—including sixty plays and dramatic sketches, five novels, book reviews, music reviews, theater criticism, and political-social tracts—he constantly, and wittily, argued for behavior based on rational thought and on a clear consideration of the social consequences. Shaw was not an easy playwright to stage, since his plays were sometimes long, and were often called "talky." They required actors who could handle clever paradoxes and carefully structured prose and still sound like real human beings. Shaw also supported causes which seemed a bit strange to his contemporaries, of which vegetarianism and spelling reform were among the most notable. But he is clearly *the* major

GEORGE BERNARD SHAW
Sir Bernard Pathridge
National Portrait Gallery, London

English playwright after Shakespeare and was honored with the Nobel Prize for Literature in 1925. More than anyone else, he restored intellectual vitality to English drama through his sarcastic attack on mediocrity, his championing of major European dramatists such as Ibsen and Chekhov, and his own vigorous practice.

Shaw was really an Irishman, rather than an Englishman; he is one of that great company of Anglo-Irish writers which includes Jonathan Swift, William Butler Yeats, James Joyce, and—a man who would ultimately change twentieth-century drama as much as Shaw changed nineteenth-century drama—Samuel Beckett, author of *Waiting for Godot* and *Endgame.* Shaw attended school only until he was fourteen and then went to work for a land agent; but when he was twenty, he moved to London, following his mother, a music teacher, who had gone there to find better working opportunities. He continued a lifelong process of self-education by reading at London's major library, the British Museum, and by attending a series of debates and lectures. His reading of Karl Marx led him to become a socialist and then to join, in 1884, the Fabian Society, a group of non-revolutionary socialists, whose meetings and writings eventually created the current British Labor Party.

Shaw supported himself by writing, and, given the musical background he inherited from his mother, it was only natural for him to find work as a music critic, writing under the pseudonym "Corno di Bassetto" (basset horn). Between 1888 and 1894, he wrote for two different newspapers and then, in 1895, moved to dramatic criticism. He had already entered the field with his defense of the great Norwegian playwright, Henrik Ibsen, whose plays such as *A Doll's House* (1879) and *Ghosts* (1881) provoked widespread public controversy, the first because it showed a woman who left her husband and family, the second because it dared to raise the subject of syphilis, both as a disease and as a metaphor for the unhealthy life caused by hypocrisy. Shaw admired Ibsen as a playwright who dared to raise issues of contemporary social and moral importance; his paper on Ibsen, given to the Fabian Society in the summer of 1890, became *The Quintessence of Ibsenism,* published in 1891.

In addition to the positive influence of Ibsen's plays, one must add the negative influence of his evenings spent as a drama critic. Shaw's description of those evenings is memorable: "The doctors said: This man has not eaten meat for twenty years; he must eat it or die. I said: This man has been going to the London theatres for three years; and the soul of him has become inane and is feeding unnaturally on his body." Shaw must have felt that he could write better plays than the ones he was condemned to review!

A third influence came from Shaw's lifelong admiration for and criticism of the plays of Shakespeare. The preface to *Three Plays for Puritans* (which included *The Devil's Disciple, Caesar and Cleopatra,* and *Captain Brassbound's Conversion*) contained a section provocatively entitled "Better than Shakespear?" in which

Shaw claimed that Shakespeare's *Julius Caesar* (unlike his own, of course) was "an admitted failure." That was in 1900. A few years later, in 1907, he would be even more outrageous: "With the single exception of Homer, there is no eminent writer, not even Sir Walter Scott, whom I can despise so entirely as I despise Shakespeare when I measure my mind against his . . . It would positively be a relief to me to dig him up and throw stones at him." But although Shaw felt that Shakespeare was a mediocre thinker, he admired his dramatic craftsmanship and said, just after his attack on the characterization of *Julius Caesar,* "No man will ever write a better tragedy than *Lear.*" His many comments on Shakespearean productions make clear that he objected far more to directorial "touches" and bad acting, than to the plays themselves. All his life, Shaw had to measure himself against Shakespeare—and he cannot be blamed for suspecting that he would always come in second.

From the beginning of his career as a dramatist, Shaw was on the offensive. His first play, *Widowers' Houses,* which he began in 1885 but did not finish until 1892, is an attack on slum landlords, while his third play, *Mrs. Warren's Profession* (1894), was so controversial that it was not allowed to be produced until 1902, and even then only in a private performance. The censors clearly thought that audiences should be protected from a play which, in Shaw's words, "was written to draw attention to the truth that prostitution is caused, not by female depravity and male licentiousness, but simply by underpaying, undervaluing, and overworking women so shamefully that the poorest of them are forced to resort to prostitution to keep body and soul together." For Mrs. Warren, and her creator Bernard Shaw, the great evils were poverty and hypocrisy: poverty forces human beings into making choices which "respectable" people hypocritically sneer at. Shaw made a similar argument, in *Major Barbara* (1905), when he showed that the way in which religion (in this case, the Salvation Army) claims to help the poor is ineffectual, whereas the work offered by a munitions factory creates not only jobs but self-respect. In that play, the audience must weigh the case of Barbara Undershaft, a sincere do-gooder, and that of her father, Andrew Undershaft, the munitions magnate.

Who, Shaw asks, really saves more lives: Barbara with her scraps of bread and cups of tea and cheering sermons, or Andrew with his deadly weapons and his well-fed workers?

Shaw's plays offer not only social criticism, but perceptive insights into human nature. *Saint Joan,* written in 1923, presents a witty and persuasive examination of Joan of Arc's motives, which refuses to sentimentalize the Maid, even to the point of allowing her a moment of doubt in which she comes to feel that her "voices" have betrayed her. But the Shavian punch comes in the Epilogue, set twenty-five years after the trial, in which Joan hears that she will be canonized (in 1920) and asks if she should perform a miracle, rising from the dead to become again a living woman. At that question, everyone is horrified, and Joan's final line is also Shaw's challenge to the audience: "O God that madest this beautiful earth, when will it be ready to receive T h y saints? How long, O Lord, how long?" Shaw forces us to recognize the paradox inherent in so much human thinking: we may praise the saints, but find them a lot of trouble; we may preach morality, but find it difficult to know how to practice it honestly; we speak of ideals, and act out of weakness and emotion.

INTRODUCTION TO *ARMS AND THE MAN*

Arms and the Man, Shaw's fourth play, written in 1894 and first presented in that year in a production directed by the playwright, embodies Shaw's usual paradoxical attack in a particularly delightful way. After three "unpleasant" plays which focused on "social horrors," Shaw wrote four "pleasant" plays: *Arms and the Man, Candida, The Man of Destiny,* and *You Never Can Tell.* But although his tone is lighter, the criticism is still present, beginning with the title. Any schoolboy with the standard background in Latin would have recognized the phrase "arms and the man" as the translation of the opening words of Virgil's *Aeneid:* "Arma virumque cano"—"Of arms and the man I sing." By so specifically evoking the comparison with Virgil's epic poem, with its emphasis on the heroic adventures of Aeneas and the importance of military valor, Shaw lures his readers and his audiences into thinking that they too may meet characters who embody heroic ideals. And so they do—but only

to find that the true hero is not the dashing Sergius, who leads his men on a cavalry charge from which they escape only because the enemy is out of ammunition, but the practical Bluntschli, who points out that real soldiers think it is their duty "to live as long as they can."

But Shaw takes on not only literary glorifications of war, but contemporary ones as well. He sets his play in the context of a recently finished real war. Throughout the late nineteenth century, Bulgaria and Serbia fought with each other; this particular conflict centered around the province of Rumelia, a section of central Bulgaria which had been ruled by the Turks and then was annexed by Prince Alexander of Bulgaria. Serbia also claimed this area, and in 1885 the two countries went to war. The last quarter of the nineteenth century was filled with such conflicts, leading to the Balkan Wars of 1910–1914 and ultimately (although Shaw could not know it in 1894) to World War I. England was not, at the time of the play, directly involved in a war in the Balkans. But who could forget the bloody fighting of the Crimean War, just thirty years earlier, when England, France, Turkey, and Sardinia fought against Russia? And who did not know Alfred, Lord Tennyson's poem, "The Charge of the Light Brigade," a poem which glorifies a cavalry charge similar to the one led by Sergius, but one in which all the soldiers perished? The poem's closing lines, "Honor the charge they made! / Honor the Light Brigade, / Noble six hundred" affirm the glory of war, even of a senseless slaughter. But Shaw invites the audience to see the other side of war with Bluntschli's description of his friend's death: "Shot in the hip in a woodyard. Couldn't drag himself out. Your fellows' shells set the timber on fire and burnt him with half a dozen other poor devils in the same predicament."

Sergius responds, "Oh, war! war! the dream of patriots and heroes! A fraud, Bluntschli. A hollow sham, like love," and thus introduces Shaw's other main subject in this play. For, if "arms" means "weapons," it can also mean "arms which embrace," and Shaw sets up a series of couples in the play, to suggest the range of views that can be taken toward love. Only the senior Petkoffs, Catherine and Paul, stay together; the others perform an elaborate switching of partners as they discover what their true feelings are. Shaw may be mocking the notion of "romantic" love as exemplified in the operas his heroine adores, or the romantic comedies he watched during his years as a drama critic, or the operettas so popular in his day. A number of those operettas had an Eastern European setting, complete with picturesque villagers and even more picturesque soldiers. So Bulgaria is both a real place and a "never-never land"—and it is the transformation of that world into something which offers the possibility of mature love relationships that Shaw attempts in *Arms and the Man.*

At the same time, Shaw was also deliberately using conventions from such operettas. An Austrian theater manager wrote to Shaw in 1897 and asked if Shaw would sell him the rights to his "Chocolate Cream Soldier" piece so that he could turn it into a comic opera. Shaw was indignant and wrote back, "the piece contains hardly any material for music." But in 1908, he relented, and Oskar Strauss' *The Chocolate Soldier* became a major success in New York.

The text of the play which follows is completely Shaw's. The elaborate stage directions are his, and are not merely directions for actors, directors, and designers, but comments meant to control the reader's point of view. The slightly peculiar way of referring to characters is Shaw's: Bluntschli is called "The Man" in the first act because no one mentions his name. The spelling conventions (no apostrophes for contractions such as "don't" or "won't" and spacing for emphasis) grow out of Shaw's interest in spelling reform; he insisted that his publishers follow his text, and his wishes still prevail.

ARMS AND THE MAN

Act I

Night. A lady's bedchamber in Bulgaria, in a small town near the Dragoman Pass,[1] late in November in the year 1885. Through an open window with a little balcony a peak of the Balkans, wonderfully white and beautiful in the starlit snow, seems quite close at hand, though it is really miles away. The interior of the room is not like anything to be seen in the west of Europe. It is half rich Bulgarian, half cheap Viennese. Above the head of the bed, which stands against a little wall cutting off the left hand corner of the room, is a painted wooden shrine, blue and gold, with an ivory image of Christ, and a light hanging before it in a pierced metal ball suspended by three chains. The principal seat, placed towards the other side of the room and opposite the window, is a Turkish ottoman. The counterpane[2] and

hangings of the bed, the window curtains, the little carpet, and all the ornamental textile fabrics in the room are oriental and gorgeous: the paper on the walls is occidental and paltry. The washstand, against the wall on the side nearest the ottoman and window, consists of an enamelled iron basin with a pail beneath it in a painted metal frame, and a single towel on the rail at the side. The dressing table, between the bed and the window, is a common pine table, covered with a cloth of many colors, with an expensive toilet mirror on it. The door is on the side nearest the bed; and there is a chest of drawers between. This chest of drawers is also covered by a variegated native cloth; and on it there is a pile of paper backed novels, a box of

1. **Dragoman Pass,** mountain pass near the border between Bulgaria and Serbia (present-day Yugoslavia).
2. **counterpane,** bedspread.

chocolate creams, and a miniature easel with a large photograph of an extremely handsome officer, whose lofty bearing and magnetic glance can be felt even from the portrait. The room is lighted by a candle on the chest of drawers, and another on the dressing table with a box of matches beside it.

The window is hinged doorwise and stands wide open. Outside, a pair of wooden shutters, opening outwards, also stand open. On the balcony a young lady, intensely conscious of the romantic beauty of the night, and of the fact that her own youth and beauty are part of it, is gazing at the snowy Balkans. She is in her nightgown, well covered by a long mantle of furs, worth, on a moderate estimate, about three times the furniture of her room.

Her reverie is interrupted by her mother, Catherine Petkoff, a woman over forty, imperiously energetic, with magnificent black hair and eyes, who might be a very splendid specimen of the wife of a mountain farmer, but is determined to be a Viennese lady, and to that end wears a fashionable tea gown on all occasions.

CATHERINE (*entering hastily, full of good news*) Raina! (*She pronounces it Rah-eena, with the stress on the ee*). Raina! (*She goes to the bed, expecting to find Raina there*). Why, where . . . ? (*Raina looks into the room*). Heavens, child! are you out in the night air instead of in your bed? Youll catch your death. Louka told me you were asleep.

RAINA (*dreamily*) I sent her away. I wanted to be alone. The stars are so beautiful! What is the matter?

CATHERINE. Such news! There has been a battle.

RAINA (*her eyes dilating*) Ah! (*She comes eagerly to Catherine*).

CATHERINE. A great battle at Slivnitza![3] A victory! And it was won by Sergius.

RAINA (*with a cry of delight*) Ah! (*They embrace rapturously*) Oh, mother! (*Then, with sudden anxiety*) Is father safe?

CATHERINE. Of course: he sends me the news. Sergius is the hero of the hour, the idol of the regiment.

RAINA. Tell me, tell me. How was it? (*Ecstatically*) Oh, mother! mother! mother! (*She pulls her mother down on the ottoman; and they kiss one another frantically*).

CATHERINE (*with surging enthusiasm*) You cant guess how splendid it is. A cavalry charge! think of that! He defied our Russian commanders—acted without orders—led a charge on his own responsibility—headed it himself—was the first man to sweep through their guns. Cant you see it, Raina: our gallant splendid Bulgarians with their swords and eyes flashing, thundering down like an avalanche and scattering the wretched Serbs and their dandified Austrian officers like chaff. And you! you kept Sergius waiting a year before you would be betrothed to him. Oh, if you have a drop of Bulgarian blood in your veins, you will worship him when he comes back.

RAINA. What will he care for my poor little worship after the acclamations of a whole army of heroes? But no matter: I am so happy! so proud! (*She rises and walks about excitedly*). It proves that all our ideas were real after all.

CATHERINE (*indignantly*) Our ideas real! What do you mean?

RAINA. Our ideas of what Sergius would do. Our patriotism. Our heroic ideals. I sometimes used to doubt whether they were anything but dreams. Oh, what faithless little creatures girls are! When I buckled on Sergius's sword he looked so noble: it was treason to think of disillusion or humiliation or failure. And yet—and yet—(*She sits down again suddenly*) Promise me youll never tell him.

CATHERINE. Dont ask me for promises until I know what I'm promising.

---

3. **Slivnitza,** small Bulgarian town on the Iskur River, and site of the Bulgarian victory over the Serbs.

RAINA. Well, it came into my head just as he was holding me in his arms and looking into my eyes, that perhaps we only had our heroic ideas because we are so fond of reading Byron and Pushkin,[4] and because we were so delighted with the opera that season at Bucharest.[5] Real life is so seldom like that! indeed never, as far as I knew it then. (*Remorsefully*) Only think, mother: I doubted him: I wondered whether all his heroic qualities and his soldiership might not prove mere imagination when he went into a real battle. I had an uneasy fear that he might cut a poor figure there beside all those clever officers from the Tsar's court.[6]

CATHERINE. A poor figure! Shame on you! The Serbs have Austrian officers who are just as clever as the Russians; but we have beaten them in every battle for all that.

RAINA (*laughing and snuggling against her mother*) Yes: I was only a prosaic little coward. Oh, to think that it was all true! that Sergius is just as splendid and noble as he looks! that the world is really a glorious world for women who can see its glory and men who can act its romance! What happiness! what unspeakable fulfillment!

[*They are interrupted by the entry of Louka, a handsome proud girl in a pretty Bulgarian peasant's dress with double apron, so defiant that her servility to Raina is almost insolent. She is afraid of Catherine, but even with her goes as far as she dares*].

LOUKA. If you please, madam, all the windows are to be closed and the shutters made fast. They say there may be shooting in the streets. (*Raina and Catherine rise together, alarmed*). The Serbs are being chased right back through the pass; and they say they may run into the town. Our cavalry will be after them; and our people will be ready for them, you may be sure, now theyre running away. (*She goes out on the balcony, and pulls the outside shutters to; then steps back into the room*).

CATHERINE (*businesslike, her housekeeping in-*

stincts aroused) I must see that everything is made safe downstairs.

RAINA. I wish our people were not so cruel. What glory is there in killing wretched fugitives?

CATHERINE. Cruel! Do you suppose they would hesitate to kill y o u—or worse?

RAINA (*to Louka*) Leave the shutters so that I can just close them if I hear any noise.

CATHERINE (*authoritatively, turning on her way to the door*) Oh no, dear: you must keep them fastened. You would be sure to drop off to sleep and leave them open. Make them fast, Louka.

LOUKA. Yes, madam. (*She fastens them*).

RAINA. Don't be anxious about me. The moment I hear a shot, I shall blow out the candles and roll myself up in bed with my ears well covered.

CATHERINE. Quite the wisest thing you can do, my love. Goodnight.

RAINA. Goodnight. (*Her emotion comes back for a moment*). Wish me joy. (*They kiss*). This is the happiest night of my life—if only there are no fugitives.

CATHERINE. Go to bed, dear; and dont think of them. (*She goes out*).

LOUKA (*secretly, to Raina*) If you would like the shutters open, just give them a push like this (*she pushes them: they open: she pulls them to again*). One of them ought to be bolted at the bottom; but the bolt's gone.

RAINA (*with dignity, reproving her*) Thanks, Louka; but we must do what we are told. (*Louka makes a grimace*). Goodnight.

4. **Byron and Pushkin.** George Gordon, Lord Byron (see page 00 for his poems) epitomized, both in his life and his poetry, a particular kind of romantic hero who was passionate, moody, isolated, and self-reliant. Alexander Pushkin (1799–1837) was the great Russian Romantic poet, famous for a play *Boris Godunov* and a verse novel *Eugene Onegin*, both of which became the source of well-known operas.

5. **Bucharest,** capital of Romania, established in the late fourteenth century, and a city known for its architecture and culture.

6. **Tsar's court.** The Russians had liberated Bulgaria from the Turks in 1877–78. They were frequently involved in the Balkan conflicts.

LOUKA (carelessly) Goodnight. (She goes out, swaggering).

[Raina, left alone, takes off her fur cloak and throws it on the ottoman. Then she goes to the chest of drawers, and adores the portrait there with feelings that are beyond all expression. She does not kiss it or press it to her breast, or shew it any mark of bodily affection; but she takes it in her hands and elevates it, like a priestess].

RAINA (looking up at the picture) Oh, I shall never be unworthy of you any more, my soul's hero: never, never, never. (She replaces it reverently. Then she selects a novel from the little pile of books. She turns over the leaves dreamily; finds her page; turns the book inside out at it; and, with a happy sigh, gets into bed and prepares to read herself to sleep. But before abandoning herself to fiction, she raises her eyes once more, thinking of the blessed reality, and murmurs) My hero! my hero!

[A distant shot breaks the quiet of the night. She starts, listening; and two more shots, much nearer, follow, startling her so that she scrambles out of bed, and hastily blows out the candle on the chest of drawers. Then, putting her fingers in her ears, she runs to the dressing table, blows out the light there, and hurries back to bed in the dark, nothing being visible but the glimmer of the light in the pierced ball before the image, and the starlight seen through the slits at the top of the shutters. The firing breaks out again: there is a startling fusillade[7] quite close at hand. Whilst it is still echoing, the shutters disappear, pulled open from without; and for an instant the rectangle of snowy starlight flashes out with the figure of a man silhouetted in black upon it. The shutters close immediately; and the room is dark again. But the silence is now broken by the sound of panting. Then there is a scratch; and the flame of a match is seen in the middle of the room].

RAINA (crouching on the bed) Who's there? (The match is out instantly). Who's there? Who is that?

A MAN'S VOICE (in the darkness, subduedly, but threateningly) Sh—sh! Dont call out; or youll be shot. Be good; and no harm will happen to you. (She is heard leaving her bed, and making for the door). Take care: it's no use trying to run away.

RAINA. But who . . .

THE VOICE (warning) Remember: if you raise your voice my revolver will go off. (Commandingly). Strike a light and let me see you. Do you hear. (Another moment of silence and darkness as she retreats to the chest of drawers. Then she lights a candle; and the mystery is at an end. He is a man about 35, in a deplorable plight, bespattered with mud and blood and snow, his belt and the strap of his revolver-case keeping together the torn ruins of the blue tunic of a Serbian artillery officer. All that the candlelight and his unwashed unkempt condition make it possible to discern is that he is of middling stature and undistinguished appearance, with strong neck and shoulders, roundish obstinate looking head covered with short crisp bronze curls, clear quick eyes and good brows and mouth, hopelessly prosaic nose like that of a strong minded baby, trim soldierlike carriage and energetic manner, and with all his wits about him in spite of his desperate predicament: even with a sense of humor of it, without, however, the least intention of trifling with it or throwing away a chance. Reckoning up what he can guess about Raina: her age, her social position, her character, and the extent to which she is frightened, he continues, more politely but still most determinedly) Excuse my disturbing you; but you recognize my uniform? Serb! If I'm caught I shall be killed. (Menacingly) Do you understand that?

RAINA. Yes.

THE MAN. Well, I dont intend to get killed if I can help it. (Still more formidably) Do you understand t h a t? (He locks the door quickly but quietly).

RAINA (disdainfully) I suppose not. (She draws herself up superbly, and looks him straight in the

---

7. **fusillade,** rapid discharge of firearms.

Raina (Alice Krige) and Bluntschli (Richard Briers) from the production of Arms and the Man *at the Lyric Theatre, London, 1981.*

face, adding, with cutting emphasis) Some soldiers, I know, are afraid to die.

THE MAN *(with grim goodhumor)* All of them, dear lady, all of them, believe me. It is our duty to live as long as we can. Now, if you raise an alarm——

RAINA *(cutting him short)* You will shoot me. How do you know that *I* am afraid to die?

THE MAN *(cunningly)* Ah; but suppose I dont shoot you, what will happen then? A lot of your cavalry will burst into this pretty room of yours and slaughter me here like a pig; for I'll fight like a demon: they shant get me into the street to amuse themselves with: I know what they are. Are you prepared to receive that sort of company in your present undress? *(Raina, suddenly conscious of her nightgown, instinctively shrinks, and gathers it more closely about her neck. He watches her, and adds, pitilessly)* Hardly pre-

sentable, eh? *(She turns to the ottoman. He raises his pistol instantly, and cries)* Stop! *(She stops).* Where are you going?

RAINA *(with dignified patience)* Only to get my cloak.

THE MAN *(passing swiftly to the ottoman and snatching the cloak)* A good idea! I'll keep the cloak; and youll take care that nobody comes in and sees you without it. This is a better weapon than the revolver: eh? *(He throws the pistol down on the ottoman).*

RAINA *(revolted)* It is not the weapon of a gentleman!

THE MAN. It's good enough for a man with only you to stand between him and death. *(As they look at one another for a moment, Raina hardly able to believe that even a Serbian officer can be so cynically and selfishly unchivalrous, they are startled by a sharp fusillade in the street. The chill of imminent death hushes the man's* *voice as he adds)* Do you hear? If you are going to bring those blackguards in on me you shall receive them as you are.

[Clamor and disturbance. The pursuers in the street batter at the house door, shouting Open the door! Open the door! Wake up, will you! *A man servant's voice calls to them angrily from within* This is Major Petkoff's house: you cant come in here; *but a renewal of the clamor, and a torrent of blows on the door, end with his letting a chain down with a clank, followed by a rush of heavy footsteps and a din of triumphant yells, dominated at last by the voice of Catherine, indignantly addressing an officer with* What does this mean, sir? Do you know where you are? *The noise subsides suddenly].*

LOUKA *(outside, knocking at the bedroom door)* My lady! my lady! get up quick and open the door. If you dont they will break it down.

[The fugitive throws up his head with the gesture of a man who sees that it is all over with him, and drops the manner he has been assuming to intimidate Raina].

THE MAN *(sincerely and kindly)* No use, dear: I'm done for. *(Flinging the cloak to her)* Quick! wrap yourself up: theyre coming.

RAINA. Oh, thank you. *(She wraps herself up with intense relief).*

THE MAN *(between his teeth)* Dont mention it.

RAINA *(anxiously)* What will you do?

THE MAN *(grimly)* The first man in will find out. Keep out of the way; and dont look. It wont last long; but it will not be nice. *(He draws his sabre and faces the door, waiting).*

RAINA *(impulsively)* I'll help you. I'll save you.

THE MAN. You cant.

RAINA. I can. I'll hide you. *(She drags him towards the window).* Here! behind the curtains.

THE MAN *(yielding to her)* Theres just half a chance, if you keep your head.

RAINA *(drawing the curtain before him)* S-sh! *(She makes for the ottoman).*

THE MAN *(putting out his head)* Remember——

RAINA *(running back to him)* Yes?

THE MAN. ——nine soldiers out of ten are born fools.

RAINA. Oh! *(She draws the curtain angrily before him).*

THE MAN *(looking out at the other side)* If they find me, I promise you a fight: a devil of a fight.

[She stamps at him. He disappears hastily. She takes off her cloak, and throws it across the foot of the bed. Then, with a sleepy, disturbed air, she opens the door. Louka enters excitedly].

LOUKA. One of those beasts of Serbs has been seen climbing up the waterpipe to your balcony. Our men want to search for him; and they are so wild and drunk and furious. *(She makes for the other side of the room to get as far from the door as possible).* My lady says you are to dress at once, and to . . . *(She sees the revolver lying on the ottoman, and stops, petrified).*

RAINA *(as if annoyed at being disturbed)* They shall not search here. Why have they been let in?

CATHERINE *(coming in hastily)* Raina, darling: are you safe? Have you seen anyone or heard anything?

RAINA. I heard the shooting. Surely the soldiers will not dare come in here?

CATHERINE. I have found a Russian officer, thank Heaven: he knows Sergius. *(Speaking through the door to someone outside)* Sir: will you come in now. My daughter will receive you.

[A young Russian officer, in Bulgarian uniform, enters, sword in hand].

OFFICER *(with soft feline politeness and stiff military carriage)* Good evening, gracious lady. I am sorry to intrude; but there is a Serb hiding on the balcony. Will you and the gracious lady your mother please withdraw whilst we search?

RAINA *(petulantly)* Nonsense, sir: you can see that there is no one on the balcony. *(She* *throws the shutters wide open and stands with her back to the curtain where the man is hidden, pointing to the moonlit balcony. A couple of shots are fired right under the window; and a bullet shatters the glass opposite Raina, who winks and gasps, but stands her ground; whilst Catherine screams, and the officer, with a cry of* Take care! *rushes to the balcony).*

THE OFFICER (*on the balcony, shouting savagely down to the street*) Cease firing there, you fools: do you hear? Cease firing, damn you! (*He glares down for a moment; then turns to Raina, trying to resume his polite manner*). Could anyone have got in without your knowledge? Were you asleep?

RAINA. No: I have not been to bed.

THE OFFICER (*impatiently, coming back into the room*) Your neighbors have their heads so full of runaway Serbs that they see them everywhere. (*Politely*) Gracious lady: a thousand pardons. Goodnight. (*Military bow, which Raina returns coldly. Another to Catherine, who follows him out*).

[*Raina closes the shutters. She turns and sees Louka, who has been watching the scene curiously*].

RAINA. Dont leave my mother, Louka, until the soldiers go away.

[*Louka glances at Raina, at the ottoman, at the curtain; then purses her lips secretively, laughs insolently, and goes out. Raina, highly offended by this demonstration, follows her to the door, and shuts it behind her with a slam, locking it violently. The man immediately steps out from behind the curtain, sheathing his sabre, and closes the shutters. Then, dismissing the danger from his mind in a businesslike way, he comes affably to Raina*].

THE MAN. A narrow shave; but a miss is as good as a mile. Dear young lady: your servant to the death. I wish for your sake I had joined the Bulgarian army instead of the other one. I am not a native Serb.

RAINA (*haughtily*) No: you are one of the Austrians who set the Serbs on to rob us of our national liberty, and who officer their army for them. We hate them!

THE MAN. Austrian! not I. Dont hate me, dear young lady. I am a Swiss, fighting merely as a professional soldier. I joined the Serbs because they came first on the road from Switzerland. Be generous: youve beaten us hollow.

RAINA. Have I not been generous?

THE MAN. Noble! Heroic! But I'm not saved yet. This particular rush will soon pass through; but the pursuit will go on all night by fits and starts. I must take my chance to get off in a quiet interval. (*Pleasantly*) You dont mind my waiting just a minute or two, do you?

RAINA (*putting on her most genteel society manner*) Oh, not at all. Wont you sit down?

THE MAN. Thanks. (*He sits on the foot of the bed*).

[*Raina walks with studied elegance to the ottoman and sits down. Unfortunately she sits on the pistol, and jumps up with a shriek. The man, all nerves, shies like a frightened horse to the other side of the room*].

THE MAN (*irritably*) Dont frighten me like that. What is it?

RAINA. Your revolver! It was staring that officer in the face all the time. What an escape!

THE MAN (*vexed at being unnecessarily terrified*) Oh, is that all?

RAINA (*staring at him superciliously as she conceives a poorer and poorer opinion of him, and feels proportionately more and more at her ease*) I am sorry I frightened you. (*She takes up the pistol and hands it to him*). Pray take it to protect yourself against me.

THE MAN (*grinning wearily at the sarcasm as he takes the pistol*) No use, dear young lady: theres nothing in it. It's not loaded. (*He makes a grimace at it, and drops it disparagingly into his revolver case*).

RAINA. Load it by all means.

THE MAN. Ive no ammunition. What use are cartridges in battle? I always carry chocolate instead; and I finished the last cake of that hours ago.

RAINA (*outraged in her most cherished ideals of manhood*) Chocolate! Do you stuff your pockets with sweets—like a schoolboy—even in the field?

THE MAN (*grinning*) Yes: isnt it contemptible? (*Hungrily*) I wish I had some now.

RAINA. Allow me. (*She sails away scornfully to the chest of drawers, and returns with the box of confectionery in her hand*). I am sorry I have eaten them all except these. (*She offers him the box*).

THE MAN (*ravenously*) Youre an angel! (*He gobbles the contents*). Creams! Delicious! (*He looks anxiously to see whether there are any more. There are none: he can only scrape the box with his fingers and suck them. When that nourishment is exhausted he accepts the inevitable with pathetic goodhumor, and says, with grateful emotion*) Bless you, dear lady! You can always tell an old soldier by the inside of his holsters and cartridge boxes. The young ones carry pistols and cartridges: the old ones, grub. Thank you. (*He hands back the box. She snatches it contemptuously from him and throws it away. He shies again, as if she had meant to strike him*). Ugh! Dont do things so suddenly, gracious lady. It's mean to revenge yourself because I frightened you just now.

RAINA (*loftily*) Frighten me! Do you know, sir, that though I am only a woman, I think I am at heart as brave as you.

THE MAN. I should think so. You havnt been under fire for three days as I have. I can stand two days without shewing it much; but no man can stand three days: I'm as nervous as a mouse. (*He sits down on the ottoman, and takes his head in his hands*). Would you like to see me cry?

RAINA (*alarmed*) No.

THE MAN. If you would, all you have to do is to scold me just as if I were a little boy and you my nurse. If I were in camp now, theyd play all sorts of tricks on me.

RAINA (*a little moved*) I'm sorry. I wont scold you. (*Touched by the sympathy in her tone, he raises his head and looks gratefully at her: she immediately draws back and says stiffly*) You must excuse me: o u r soldiers are not like that. (*She moves away from the ottoman*).

THE MAN. Oh yes they are. There are only two sorts of soldiers: old ones and young ones. Ive served fourteen years: half of your fellows never smelt powder before. Why, how is it that youve just beaten us? Sheer ignorance of the art of war, nothing else. (*Indignantly*) I never saw anything so unprofessional.

RAINA (*ironically*) Oh! was it unprofessional to beat you?

THE MAN. Well, come! is it professional to throw a regiment of cavalry on a battery of machine guns, with the dead certainty that if the guns go off not a horse or man will ever get within fifty yards of the fire? I couldnt believe my eyes when I saw it.

RAINA (*eagerly turning to him, as all her enthusiasm and her dreams of glory rush back on her*) Did you see the great cavalry charge? Oh, tell me about it. Describe it to me.

THE MAN. You never saw a cavalry charge, did you?

RAINA. How could I?

THE MAN. Ah, perhaps not. No: of course not! Well, it's a funny sight. It's like slinging a handful of peas against a window pane: first one comes; then two or three close behind him; and then all the rest in a lump.

RAINA (*her eyes dilating as she raises her clasped hands ecstatically*) Yes, first One! the bravest of the brave!

THE MAN (*prosaically*) Hm! you should see the poor devil pulling at his horse.

RAINA. Why should he pull at his horse?

THE MAN (*impatient of so stupid a question*) It's running away with him, of course: do you suppose the fellow wants to get there before the others and be killed? Then they all come. You can tell the young ones by their wildness and their slashing. The old ones come bunched up under the number one guard: they know that theyre mere projectiles, and that it's no use trying to fight. The wounds are mostly broken knees, from the horses cannoning together.

RAINA. Ugh! But I dont believe the first man is a coward. I know he is a hero!

THE MAN (*goodhumoredly*) Thats what youd have said if youd seen the first man in the charge today.

RAINA (*breathless, forgiving him everything*) Ah, I knew it! Tell me. Tell me about him.

THE MAN. He did it like an operatic tenor. A regular handsome fellow, with flashing eyes and lovely moustache, shouting his war-cry and charging like Don Quixote[8] at the windmills. We did laugh.

RAINA. You dared to laugh!

THE MAN. Yes; but when the sergeant ran up as white as a sheet, and told us theyd sent us the wrong ammunition, and that we couldnt fire a round for the next ten minutes, we laughed at the other side of our mouths. I never felt so sick in my life; though Ive been in one or two very tight places. And I hadnt even a revolver cartridge: only chocolate. We'd no bayonets: nothing. Of course, they just cut us to bits. And there was Don Quixote flourishing like a drum major, thinking he'd done the cleverest thing ever known, whereas he ought to be courtmartialled for it. Of all the fools ever let loose on a field of battle, that man must be the very maddest. He and his regiment simply committed suicide; only the pistol missed fire: thats all.

RAINA (*deeply wounded, but steadfastly loyal to her ideals*) Indeed! Would you know him again if you saw him?

THE MAN. Shall I ever forget him!

[*She again goes to the chest of drawers. He watches her with a vague hope that she may have something more for him to eat. She takes the portrait from its stand and brings it to him*].

RAINA. That is a photograph of the gentleman—the patriot and hero—to whom I am betrothed.

THE MAN (*recognizing it with a shock*) I'm really very sorry. (*Looking at her*) Was it fair to lead me on? (*He looks at the portrait again*). Yes: thats Don Quixote: not a doubt of it. (*He stifles a laugh*).

RAINA (*quickly*) Why do you laugh?

THE MAN (*apologetic, but still greatly tickled*) I didnt laugh, I assure you. At least I didnt mean to. But when I think of him charging the windmills and imagining he was doing the finest thing—(*He chokes with suppressed laughter*).

RAINA (*sternly*) Give me back the portrait, sir.

THE MAN (*with sincere remorse*) Of course. Certainly. I'm really very sorry. (*He hands her the picture. She deliberately kisses it and looks him straight in the face before returning to the chest of drawers to replace it. He follows her, apologizing*). Perhaps I'm quite wrong, you know: no doubt I am. Most likely he had got wind of the cartridge business somehow, and knew it was a safe job.

RAINA. That is to say, he was a pretender and a coward! You did not dare say that before.

THE MAN (*with a comic gesture of despair*) It's no use, dear lady: I cant make you see it from the professional point of view. (*As he turns away to get back to the ottoman, a couple of distant shots threaten renewed trouble*).

RAINA (*sternly, as she sees him listening to the shots*) So much the better for you!

THE MAN (*turning*) How?

RAINA. You are my enemy; and you are at my mercy. What would I do if I were a professional soldier?

THE MAN. Ah, true, dear young lady: youre always right. I know how good youve been to me: to my last hour I shall remember those three chocolate creams. It was unsoldierly; but it was angelic.

RAINA (*coldly*) Thank you. And now I will do a

---

8. **Don Quixote,** the hero of Cervantes' novel (1615), a fifty-year-old Spanish gentleman, who goes in search of adventure as a knight and who, in his most famous adventure, charges at windmills, thinking that they are giants.

soldierly thing. You cannot stay here after what you have just said about my future husband; but I will go out on the balcony and see whether it is safe for you to climb down into the street. (*She turns to the window*).

THE MAN (*changing countenance*) Down that waterpipe! Stop! Wait! I cant! I darent! The very thought of it makes me giddy. I came up it fast enough with death behind me. But to face it now in cold blood—! (*He sinks on the ottoman*). It's no use: I give up: I'm beaten. Give the alarm. (*He drops his head on his hands in the deepest dejection*).

RAINA (*disarmed by pity*) Come: dont be disheartened. (*She stoops over him almost maternally: he shakes his head*). Oh, you are a very poor soldier: a chocolate cream soldier! Come, cheer up! it takes less courage to climb down than to face capture: remember that.

THE MAN (*dreamily, lulled by her voice*) No: capture only means death; and death is sleep: oh, sleep, sleep, sleep, undisturbed sleep! Climbing down the pipe means doing something—exerting myself—thinking! Death ten times over first.

RAINA (*softly and wonderingly, catching the rhythm of his weariness*) Are you as sleepy as that?

THE MAN. Ive not had two hours undisturbed sleep since I joined. I havnt closed my eyes for forty-eight hours.

RAINA (*at her wit's end*) But what am I to do with you?

THE MAN (*staggering up, roused by her desperation*) Of course. I must do something. (*He shakes himself; pulls himself together; and speaks with rallied vigor and courage*). You see, sleep or no sleep, hunger or no hunger, tired or not tired, you can always do a thing when you know it must be done. Well, that pipe m u s t be got down: (*he hits himself on the chest*) do you hear that, you chocolate cream soldier? (*He turns to the window*).

RAINA (*anxiously*) But if you fall?

THE MAN. I shall sleep as if the stones were a feather bed. Goodbye. (*He makes boldly for the window; and his hand is on the shutter when there is a terrible burst of firing in the street beneath*).

RAINA (*rushing to him*) Stop! (*She seizes him recklessly, and pulls him quite round*). Theyll kill you.

THE MAN (*coolly, but attentively*) Never mind: this sort of thing is all in my day's work. I'm bound to take my chance. (*Decisively*) Now do what I tell you. Put out the candles; so that they shant see the light when I open the shutters. And keep away from the window, whatever you do. If they see me theyre sure to have a shot at me.

RAINA (*clinging to him*) Theyre sure to see you: it's bright moonlight. I'll save you. Oh, how can you be so indifferent! You want me to save you, dont you?

THE MAN. I really dont want to be troublesome. (*She shakes him in her impatience*). I am not indifferent, dear young lady, I assure you. But how is it to be done?

RAINA. Come away from the window. (*She takes him firmly back to the middle of the room. The moment she releases him he turns mechanically towards the window again. She seizes him and turns him back, exclaiming*) Please! (*He becomes motionless, like a hypnotized rabbit, his fatigue gaining fast on him. She releases him, and addresses him patronizingly*). Now listen. You must trust to our hospitality. You do not yet know in whose house you are. I am a Petkoff.

THE MAN. A pet what?

RAINA (*rather indignantly*) I mean that I belong to the family of Petkoffs, the richest and best known in our country.

THE MAN. Oh yes, of course. I beg your pardon. The Petkoffs, to be sure. How stupid of me!

RAINA. You know you never heard of them until this moment. How can you stoop to pretend!

THE MAN. Forgive me: I'm too tired to think; and the change of subject was too much for me. Dont scold me.

RAINA. I forgot. It might make you cry. *(He nods, quite seriously. She pouts and then resumes her patronizing tone)*. I must tell you that my father holds the highest command of any Bulgarian in our army. He is *(proudly)* a Major.

THE MAN *(pretending to be deeply impressed)* A Major! Bless me! Think of that!

RAINA. You shewed great ignorance in thinking that it was necessary to climb up to the balcony because ours is the only private house that has two rows of windows. There is a flight of stairs inside to get up and down by.

THE MAN. Stairs! How grand! You live in great luxury indeed, dear young lady.

RAINA. Do you know what a library is?

THE MAN. A library? A roomful of books?

RAINA. Yes. We have one, the only one in Bulgaria.

THE MAN. Actually a real library! I should like to see that.

RAINA *(affectedly)* I tell you these things to shew you that you are not in the house of ignorant country folk who would kill you the moment they saw your Serbian uniform, but among civilized people. We go to Bucharest every year for the opera season; and I have spent a whole month in Vienna.

THE MAN. I saw that, dear young lady. I saw at once that you knew the world.

RAINA. Have you ever seen the opera of Ernani?[9]

THE MAN. Is that the one with the devil in it in red velvet, and a soldiers' chorus?

RAINA *(contemptuously)* No!

TIIE MAN *(stifling a heavy sigh of weariness)* Then I dont know it.

RAINA. I thought you might have remembered the great scene where Ernani, flying from his foes just as you are tonight, takes refuge in the castle of his bitterest enemy, an old Castilian noble. The noble refuses to give him up. His guest is sacred to him.

THE MAN *(quickly, waking up a little)* Have your people got that notion?

RAINA *(with dignity)* My mother and I can understand that notion, as you call it. And if instead of threatening me with your pistol as you did you had simply thrown yourself as a fugitive on our hospitality, you would have been as safe as in your father's house.

THE MAN. Quite sure?

RAINA *(turning her back on him in disgust)* Oh, it is useless to try to make you understand.

THE MAN. Dont be angry: you see how awkward it would be for me if there was any mistake. My father is a very hospitable man: he keeps six hotels; but I couldnt trust him as far as that. What about your father?

RAINA. He is away at Slivnitza fighting for his country. I answer for your safety. There is my hand in pledge of it. Will that reassure you? *(She offers him her hand)*.

THE MAN *(looking dubiously at his own hand)* Better not touch my hand, dear young lady. I must have a wash first.

RAINA *(touched)* That is very nice of you. I see that you are a gentleman.

THE MAN *(puzzled)* Eh?

RAINA. You must not think I am surprised. Bulgarians of really good standing—people in our position—wash their hands nearly every day. So you see I can appreciate your delicacy. You may take my hand. *(She offers it again)*.

THE MAN *(kissing it with his hands behind his back)* Thanks, gracious young lady: I feel safe at last. And now would you mind breaking the news to your mother? I had better not stay here secretly longer than is necessary.

RAINA. If you will be so good as to keep perfectly still whilst I am away.

---

9. **Ernani,** opera by Giuseppe Verdi, based on a play by Victor Hugo. The opera, first presented in 1844, centers on conflicts of love and duty. The emphasis on honor, at all costs, is doubtless what appeals to Raina. Bluntschli's mention of the devil and a soldiers' chorus shows that he is thinking of Charles Gounod's *Faust*, 1859, the opera adapted from the classic story of the medieval scholar who sold his soul to the devil, as retold by the German poet Goethe.

THE MAN. Certainly. (*He sits down on the ottoman*).

[*Raina goes to the bed and wraps herself in the fur cloak. His eyes close. She goes to the door. Turning for a last look at him, she sees that he is dropping off to sleep*].

RAINA (*at the door*) You are not going asleep, are you? (*He murmurs inarticulately: she runs to him and shakes him*). Do you hear? Wake up: you are falling asleep.

THE MAN. Eh? Falling aslee . . . ? Oh no: not the least in the world: I was only thinking. It's all right: I'm wide awake.

RAINA (*severely*) Will you please stand up while I am away. (*He rises reluctantly*). All the time, mind.

THE MAN (*standing unsteadily*) Certainly. Certainly: you may depend on me.

[*Raina looks doubtfully at him. He smiles weakly. She goes reluctantly, turning again at the door, and almost catching him in the act of yawning. She goes out*].

THE MAN (*drowsily*) Sleep, sleep, sleep, sleep, slee . . . (*The words trail off into a murmur. He wakes again with a shock on the point of falling*). Where am I? Thats what I want to know: where am I? Must keep awake. Nothing keeps me awake except danger: remember that: (*intently*) danger, danger, danger, dan . . . (*trailing off again: another shock*) Wheres danger? Mus' find it. (*He starts off vaguely round the room in search of it*). What am I looking for? Sleep—danger—dont know. (*He stumbles against the bed*). Ah yes: now I know. All right now. I'm to go to bed, but not to sleep. Be sure not to sleep, because of danger. Not to lie down either, only sit down. (*He sits on the bed. A blissful expression comes into his face*). Ah! (*With a happy sigh he sinks back at full length; lifts his boots into the bed with a final effort; and falls fast asleep instantly*).

[*Catherine comes in, followed by Raina*].

RAINA (*looking at the ottoman*) He's gone! I left him here.

CATHERINE. Here! Then he must have climbed down from the——

RAINA (*seeing him*) Oh! (*She points*).

CATHERINE (*scandalized*) Well! (*She strides to the bed, Raina following until she is opposite her on the other side*). He's fast asleep. The brute!

RAINA (*anxiously*) Sh!

CATHERINE (*shaking him*) Sir! (*Shaking him again, harder*) Sir!! (*Vehemently, shaking very hard*) Sir!!!

RAINA (*catching her arm*) Dont, mamma: the poor darling is worn out. Let him sleep.

CATHERINE (*letting him go, and turning amazed to Raina*) The poor darling! Raina!!! (*She looks sternly at her daughter*).

[*The man sleeps profoundly*].

FOR UNDERSTANDING

1. Shaw introduces four of his seven major characters in the first act. What information does he give us about Raina, Catherine, Louka, and The Man?
2. What information does he give us about characters who do not appear on stage?
3. What important relationships are established during the act? What hints does Shaw provide about where the play might go next?

FOR INTERPRETATION

1. One could hardly claim that Shaw presents characters in a neutral, detached way. What details can you find to indicate his attitude towards Raina, Catherine, and Louka?
2. What attitudes toward The Man does Shaw suggest?

FOR APPRECIATION

Shaw's stage directions are well known for their precise detail, but they are also his way of manipulating the reader's perceptions. Look carefully at the first long stage direction and try to make a two-column list, one for positive-sounding phrases, the other for negative. What pattern do you see?

COMPOSITION

Try to write a description of a place, perhaps the classroom, perhaps a store in your town, or maybe a well-known place, in the style of Shaw's stage directions. Remember that you need to convey a specific attitude towards that place.

Act II

The sixth of March, 1886. In the garden of Major Petkoff's house. It is a fine spring morning: the garden looks fresh and pretty. Beyond the paling[1] the tops of a couple of minarets[2] can be seen, shewing that there is a valley there, with the little town in it. A few miles further the Balkan mountains rise and shut in the landscape. Looking towards them from within the garden, the side of the house is seen on the left, with a garden door reached by a little flight of steps. On the right the stable yard, with its gateway, encroaches on the garden. There are fruit bushes along the paling and house, covered with washing spread out to dry. A path runs by the house, and rises by two steps at the corner, where it turns out of sight. In the middle, a small table, with two bent wood chairs at it, is laid for breakfast with Turkish coffee pot, cups, rolls, etc.; but the cups have been used and the bread broken. There is a wooden garden seat against the wall on the right.

Louka, smoking a cigaret, is standing between the table and the house, turning her back with angry disdain on a man servant who is lecturing her. He is a middle-aged man of cool temperament and low but clear and keen intelligence, with the complacency of the servant who values himself on his rank in servitude, and the imperturbability of the accurate calculator who has no illusions. He wears a white Bulgarian costume: jacket with embroidered border, sash, wide knickerbockers, and decorated gaiters.[3] His head is shaved up to the crown, giving him a high Japanese forehead. His name is Nicola.

NICOLA. Be warned in time, Louka: mend your manners. I know the mistress. She is so grand that she never dreams that any servant could dare be disrespectful to her; but if she once suspects that you are defying her, out you go.

LOUKA. I do defy her. I will defy her. What do I care for her?

NICOLA. If you quarrel with the family, I never can marry you. It's the same as if you quarrelled with me!

LOUKA. You take her part against me, do you?

NICOLA (*sedately*) I shall always be dependent on the good will of the family. When I leave their service and start a shop in Sofia,[4] their custom will be half my capital: their bad word would ruin me.

LOUKA. You have no spirit. I should like to catch them saying a word against me!

NICOLA (*pityingly*) I should have expected more sense from you, Louka. But youre young: youre young!

LOUKA. Yes; and you like me the better for it, dont you? But I know some family secrets they wouldnt care to have told, young as I am. Let them quarrel with me if they dare!

NICOLA (*with compassionate superiority*) Do you know what they would do if they heard you talk like that?

1. **paling,** a picket fence.
2. **minarets,** high slender towers usually associated with a mosque. Since Bulgaria had been ruled by Turks during the Renaissance, a number of buildings reflected Eastern styles of architecture.
3. **gaiters,** covering (cloth or leather) for the instep and ankle, such as spats or leggings.
4. **Sofia,** capital of Bulgaria.

LOUKA. What could they do?

NICOLA. Discharge you for untruthfulness. Who would believe any stories you told after that? Who would give you another situation? Who in this house would dare be seen speaking to you ever again? How long would your father be left on his little farm? *(She impatiently throws away the end of her cigaret, and stamps on it).* Child: you dont know the power such high people have over the like of you and me when we try to rise out of our poverty against them. *(He goes close to her and lowers his voice).* Look at me, ten years in their service. Do you think I know no secrets? I know things about the mistress that she wouldnt have the master know for a thousand levas.[5] I know things about him that she wouldnt let him hear the last of for six months if I blabbed them to her. I know things about Raina that would break off her match with Sergius if——

LOUKA *(turning on him quickly)* How do you know? I never told you!

NICOLA *(opening his eyes cunningly)* So thats your little secret, is it? I thought it might be something like that. Well, you take my advice and be respectful; and make the mistress feel that no matter what you know or dont know, she can depend on you to hold your tongue and serve the family faithfully. Thats what they like; and thats how youll make most out of them.

LOUKA *(with searching scorn)* You have the soul of a servant, Nicola.

NICOLA *(complacently)* Yes: thats the secret of success in service.

[A loud knocking with a whip handle on a wooden door is heard from the stable yard].

MALE VOICE OUTSIDE. Hollo! Hollo there! Nicola!

LOUKA. Master! back from the war!

NICOLA *(quickly)* My word for it, Louka, the war's over. Off with you and get some fresh coffee. *(He runs out into the stable yard).*

LOUKA *(as she collects the coffee pot and cups on the tray, and carries it into the house)* Youll never put the soul of a servant into me.

[Major Petkoff comes from the stable yard, followed by Nicola. He is a cheerful, excitable, insignificant, unpolished man of about 50, naturally unambitious except as to his income and his importance in local society, but just now greatly pleased with the military rank which the war has thrust on him as a man of consequence in his town. The fever of plucky patriotism which the Serbian attack roused in all the Bulgarians has pulled him through the war; but he is obviously glad to be home again].

PETKOFF *(pointing to the table with his whip)* Breakfast out here, eh?

NICOLA. Yes, sir. The mistress and Miss Raina have just gone in.

PETKOFF *(sitting down and taking a roll)* Go in and say Ive come; and get me some fresh coffee.

NICOLA. Its coming, sir. *(He goes to the house door. Louka, with fresh coffe, a clean cup, and a brandy bottle on her tray, meets him).* Have you told the mistress?

LOUKA. Yes: she's coming.

[Nicola goes into the house. Louka brings the coffee to the table].

PETKOFF. Well: the Serbs havnt run away with you, have they?

LOUKA. No, sir.

PETKOFF. Thats right. Have you brought me some cognac?

LOUKA *(putting the bottle on the table)* Here, sir.

PETKOFF. T h a t s right. *(He pours some into his coffee).*

[Catherine, who, having at this early hour made only a very perfunctory toilet, wears a Bulgarian apron over a once brilliant but now half worn-out dressing gown, and a colored handkerchief tied over her thick black hair, comes from the house with Turkish slippers on her bare feet, looking astonishingly handsome and stately under all the circumstances. Louka goes into the house].

5. **levas.** A lev is the basic monetary unit of Bulgaria. At this time, 25 levas would be about $5.00.

CATHERINE. My dear Paul: what a surprise for us! (*She stoops over the back of his chair to kiss him*). Have they brought you fresh coffee?

PETKOFF. Yes: Louka's been looking after me. The war's over. The treaty was signed three days ago at Bucharest; and the decree for our army to demobilize was issued yesterday.

CATHERINE (*springing erect, with flashing eyes*) Paul: have you let the Austrians force you to make peace?

PETKOFF (*submissively*) My dear: they didnt consult me. What could *I* do? (*She sits down and turns away from him*). But of course we saw to it that the treaty was an honorable one. It declares peace——

CATHERINE (*outraged*) Peace!

PETKOFF (*appeasing her*)——but not friendly relations: remember that. They wanted to put that in; but I insisted on its being struck out. What more could I do?

CATHERINE. You could have annexed Serbia and made Prince Alexander[6] Emperor of the Balkans. Thats what I would have done.

PETKOFF. I dont doubt it in the least, my dear. But I should have had to subdue the whole Austrian Empire first; and that would have kept me too long away from you. I missed you greatly.

CATHERINE (*relenting*) Ah! (*She stretches her hand affectionately across the table to squeeze his*).

PETKOFF. And how have you been, my dear?

CATHERINE. Oh, my usual sore throats: thats all.

PETKOFF (*with conviction*) That comes from washing your neck every day. Ive often told you so.

CATHERINE. Nonsense, Paul!

PETKOFF (*over his coffee and cigaret*) I dont believe in going too far with these modern customs. All this washing cant be good for the health: it's not natural. There was an Englishman at Philippopolis[7] who used to wet himself all over with cold water every morning when he got up. Disgusting! It all comes from the English: their climate makes them so dirty that they have to be perpetually washing themselves. Look at my father! he never had a bath in his life; and he lived to be ninety-eight, the healthiest man in Bulgaria. I dont mind a good wash once a week to keep up my position; but once a day is carrying the thing to a ridiculous extreme.

CATHERINE. You are a barbarian at heart still, Paul. I hope you behaved yourself before all those Russian officers.

PETKOFF. I did my best. I took care to let them know that we have a library.

CATHERINE. Ah; but you didnt tell them that we have an electric bell in it? I have had one put up.

PETKOFF. Whats an electric bell?

CATHERINE. You touch a button; something tinkles in the kitchen; and then Nicola comes up.

PETKOFF. Why not shout for him?

CATHERINE. Civilized people never shout for their servants. Ive learnt that while you were away.

PETKOFF. Well, I'll tell you something Ive learnt too. Civilized people dont hang out their washing to dry where visitors can see it; so youd better have all that (*indicating the clothes on the bushes*) put somewhere else.

CATHERINE. Oh, thats absurd, Paul: I dont believe really refined people notice such things.

SERGIUS (*knocking at the stable gates*) Gate, Nicola!

PETKOFF. Theres Sergius. (*Shouting*) Hollo, Nicola!

CATHERINE. Oh, dont shout, Paul: it really isnt nice.

PETKOFF. Bosh! (*He shouts louder than before*) Nicola!

NICOLA (*appearing at the house door*) Yes, sir.

---

6. **Prince Alexander,** Prince of Bulgaria from 1879 to 1886.
7. **Philippopolis.** Known today as Plovdiv, this ancient city is the second largest in Bulgaria. It was captured by Philip II of Macedon (father of Alexander the Great) and was named for him.

PETKOFF. Are you deaf? Dont you hear Major Saranoff knocking? Bring him round this way. *(He pronounces the name with stress on the second syllable: Sarahnoff).*

NICOLA. Yes, major. *(He goes into the stable yard).*

PETKOFF. You must talk to him, my dear, until Raina takes him off our hands. He bores my life out about our not promoting him. Over my head, if you please.

CATHERINE. He certainly ought to be promoted when he marries Raina. Besides, the country should insist on having at least one native general.

PETKOFF. Yes; so that he could throw away whole brigades instead of regiments. It's no use, my dear: he hasnt the slightest chance of promotion until we're quite sure that the peace will be a lasting one.

NICOLA *(at the gate, announcing)* Major Sergius Saranoff! *(He goes into the house and returns presently with a third chair, which he places at the table. He then withdraws).*

[*Major Sergius Saranoff, the original of the portrait in Raina's room, is a tall romantically handsome man, with the physical hardihood, the high spirit, and the susceptible imagination of an untamed mountaineer chieftain. But his remarkable personal distinctions are of a characteristically civilized type. The ridges of his eyebrows, curving with an interrogative twist round the projections at the outer corners; his jealously observant eye; his nose, thin, keen, and apprehensive in spite of the pugnacious high bridge and large nostril; his assertive chin, would not be out of place in a Parisian salon, shewing that the clever imaginative barbarian has an acute critical faculty which has been thrown into intense activity by the arrival of western civilization in the Balkans. The result is precisely what the advent of nineteenth century thought first produced in England: to wit, Byronism.[8] By his brooding on the perpetual failure, not only of others, but of himself, to live up to his ideals; by his consequent cynical scorn for humanity; by his jejune[9] credulity as to the absolute validity of his concepts and the unworthiness of the world in disregarding them; by his wincings and mockeries under the sting of the petty disillusions which every hour spent among men brings to his sensitive observation, he has acquired the half tragic, half ironic air, the mysterious moodiness, the suggestion of a strange and terrible history that has left nothing but undying remorse, by which Childe Harold[10] fascinated the grandmothers of his English contemporaries. It is clear that here or nowhere is Raina's ideal hero. Catherine is hardly less enthusiastic about him than her daughter, and much less reserved in shewing her enthusiasm. As he enters from the stable gate, she rises effusively to greet him. Petkoff is distinctly less disposed to make a fuss about him].*

PETKOFF. Here already, Sergius! Glad to see you.

CATHERINE. My dear Sergius! *(She holds out both her hands).*

SERGIUS *(kissing them with scrupulous gallantry)* My dear mother, if I may call you so.

PETKOFF *(drily)* Mother-in-law, Sergius: mother-in-law! Sit down; and have some coffee.

SERGIUS. Thank you: none for me. *(He gets away from the table with a certain distaste for Petkoff's enjoyment of it, and posts himself with conscious dignity against the rail of the steps leading to the house).*

CATHERINE. You look superb. The campaign has improved you, Sergius. Everybody here is mad about you. We were all wild with enthusiasm about that magnificent cavalry charge.

SERGIUS *(with grave irony)* Madam: it was the cradle and the grave of my military reputation.

---

8. **Byronism,** cf. page 000. Shaw also supplies his own definition in the sentences which follow.
9. **jejune,** usually "barren" or "uninteresting," but Shaw seems also to imply "juvenile."
10. **Childe Harold,** the hero of Byron's long narrative poem, *Childe Harold's Pilgrimage* (1812).

"My dear Sergius!" Catherine (Pat Heywood) greets Sergius (Peter Egan) while Petkoff (Richard Pearson) eats.
Dominic Photography

CATHERINE. How so?

SERGIUS. I won the battle the wrong way when our worthy Russian generals were losing it the right way. In short, I upset their plans, and wounded their self-esteem. Two Cossack colonels had their regiments routed on the most correct principles of scientific warfare. Two major-generals got killed strictly according to military etiquette. The two colonels are now major-generals; and I am still a simple major.

CATHERINE. You shall not remain so, Sergius. The women are on your side; and they will see that justice is done you.

SERGIUS. It is too late. I have only waited for the peace to send in my resignation.

PETKOFF (*dropping his cup in his amazement*) Your resignation!

CATHERINE. Oh, you must withdraw it!

PETKOFF (*vexed*) Now who could have supposed you were going to do such a thing?

SERGIUS (*with fire*) Everyone that knew me. But enough of myself and my affairs. How is Raina; and where is Raina?

RAINA (*suddenly coming round the corner of the house and standing at the top of the steps in the path*) Raina is here.

[*She makes a charming picture as they turn to look at her. She wears an underdress of pale green silk, draped with an overdress of thin ecru canvas embroidered with gold. She is crowned with a dainty eastern cap of gold tinsel. Sergius goes impulsively to meet her. Posing regally, she presents her hand: he drops chivalrously on one knee and kisses it*].

PETKOFF (*aside to Catherine, beaming with parental pride*) Pretty, isnt it? She always appears at the right moment.

CATHERINE (*impatiently*) Yes: she listens for it. It is an abominable habit.

[*Sergius leads Raina forward with splendid gallantry. When they arrive at the table, she turns to him with a bend of the head: he bows; and thus they separate, he coming to his place, and she going behind her father's chair*].

RAINA (*stooping and kissing her father*) Dear father! Welcome home!

PETKOFF (*patting her cheek*) My little pet girl. (*He kisses her. She goes to the chair left by Nicola for Sergius, and sits down*).

CATHERINE. And so youre no longer a soldier, Sergius.

SERGIUS. I am no longer a soldier. Soldiering, my dear madam, is the coward's art of attacking mercilessly when you are strong, and keeping out of harm's way when you are weak. That is the whole secret of successful fighting. Get your enemy at a disadvantage; and never, on any account, fight him on equal terms.

PETKOFF. They wouldnt let us make a fair stand-up fight of it. However, I suppose soldiering has to be a trade like any other trade.

SERGIUS. Precisely. But I have no ambition to shine as a tradesman; so I have taken the advice of that bagman[11] of a captain that settled the exchange of prisoners with us at Pirot,[12] and given it up.

PETKOFF. What! that Swiss fellow? Sergius: Ive often thought of that exchange since. He over-reached us about those horses.

SERGIUS. Of course he over-reached us. His father was a hotel and livery stable keeper; and he owed his first step to his knowledge of horse-dealing. (*With mock enthusiasm*) Ah, he was a soldier: every inch a soldier! If only I had bought the horses for my regiment instead of foolishly leading it into danger, I should have been a field-marshal now!

CATHERINE. A Swiss? What was he doing in the Serbian army?

PETKOFF. A volunteer, of course: keen on picking up his profession. (*Chuckling*) We shouldnt have been able to begin fighting if these foreigners hadnt shewn us how to do it: we knew nothing about it; and neither did the Serbs. Egad, there'd have been no war without them!

RAINA. Are there many Swiss officers in the Serbian army?

PETKOFF. No. All Austrians, just as our officers were all Russians. This was the only Swiss I came across. I'll never trust a Swiss again. He humbugged us into giving him fifty ablebodied men for two hundred worn out chargers. They werent even eatable!

SERGIUS. We were two children in the hands of that consummate soldier, Major: simply two innocent little children.

RAINA. What was he like?

CATHERINE. Oh, Raina, what a silly question!

SERGIUS. He was like a commercial traveller in uniform. Bourgeois to his boots!

PETKOFF (*grinning*) Sergius: tell Catherine that queer story his friend told us about how he escaped after Slivnitza. You remember. About his being hid by two women.

SERGIUS (*with bitter irony*) Oh yes: quite a romance! He was serving in the very battery I so unprofessionally charged. Being a thorough soldier, he ran away like the rest of them, with our cavalry at his heels. To escape their sabres he climbed a waterpipe and made his way into the bedroom of a young Bulgarian lady. The young lady was enchanted by his persuasive commercial traveller's manners. She very modestly entertained him for an hour or so, and then called in her mother lest her conduct should appear unmaidenly. The old lady was equally fascinated; and the fugitive was sent on his way in the morning, disguised in an old coat belonging to the master of the house, who was away at the war.

RAINA (*rising with marked stateliness*) Your life in the camp has made you coarse, Sergius. I did not think you would have repeated

---

11. **bagman,** literally one who carries a bag and, by extension, a commercial traveler.
12. **Pirot,** town in present-day Yugoslavia, near the Bulgarian border.

Photo from Act II taken during the second production of Arms and the Man *at the Savoy Theatre, London, December 30, 1907.*

The Raymond Mander and Joe Mitchenson
Theatre Collection, London

such a story before me. *(She turns away coldly).*

CATHERINE *(also rising)* She is right, Sergius. If such women exist, we should be spared the knowledge of them.

PETKOFF. Pooh! nonsense! what does it matter?

SERGIUS *(ashamed)* No, Petkoff: I was wrong. *(To Raina, with earnest humility)* I beg your pardon. I have behaved abominably. Forgive me, Raina. *(She bows reservedly).* And you too, madam. *(Catherine bows graciously and sits down. He proceeds solemnly, again addressing Raina)* The glimpses I have had of the seamy side of life should not have brought my cynicism here: least of all into your presence, Raina. I——

[Here, turning to the others, he is evidently going to begin a long speech when the Major interrupts him].

PETKOFF. Stuff and nonsense, Sergius! Thats quite enough fuss about nothing: a soldier's daughter should be able to stand up without flinching to a little strong conversation. *(He rises).* Come: it's time for us to get to business. We have to make up our minds how those three regiments are to get back to Philippopolis: theres no forage[13] for them on the Sofia route. *(He goes towards the house).* Come along. *(Sergius is about to follow him when Catherine rises and intervenes).*

CATHERINE. Oh, Paul, cant you spare Sergius for a few moments? Raina has hardly seen him yet. Perhaps I can help you to settle about the regiments.

SERGIUS *(protesting)* My dear madam, impossible: you——

CATHERINE *(stopping him playfully)* You stay here, my dear Sergius: theres no hurry. I have a word or two to say to Paul. *(Sergius instantly bows and steps back).* Now, dear

---

13. **forage,** provisions.

(taking Petkoff's arm): come and see the electric bell.

PETKOFF. Oh, very well, very well.

[*They go into the house together affectionately. Sergius, left alone with Raina, looks anxiously at her, fearing that she is still offended. She smiles, and stretches out her arms to him*].

SERGIUS *(hastening to her)* Am I forgiven?

RAINA *(placing her hands on his shoulders as she looks up at him with admiration and worship)* My hero! My king!

SERGIUS. My queen! *(He kisses her on the forehead).*

RAINA. How I have envied you, Sergius! You have been out in the world, on the field of battle, able to prove yourself there worthy of any woman in the world; whilst I have had to sit at home inactive—dreaming—useless—doing nothing that could give me the right to call myself worthy of any man.

SERGIUS. Dearest: all my deeds have been yours. You inspired me. I have gone through the war like a knight in a tournament with his lady looking down at him!

RAINA. And you have never been absent from my thoughts for a moment. *(Very solemnly)* Sergius: I think we two have found the higher love. When I think of you, I feel that I could never do a base deed or think an ignoble thought.

SERGIUS. My lady and my saint! *(He clasps her reverently).*

RAINA *(returning his embrace)* My lord and my——

SERGIUS. Sh—sh! Let m e be the worshipper, dear. You little know how unworthy even the best man is of a girl's pure passion!

RAINA. I trust you. I love you. You will never disappoint me, Sergius. *(Louka is heard singing within the house. They quickly release each other).* I cant pretend to talk indifferently before her: my heart is too full. *(Louka comes from the house with her tray. She goes to the table, and begins to clear it, with her back turned to them).* I will get my hat; and then we can go out until lunch time. Wouldnt you like that?

SERGIUS. Be quick. If you are away five minutes, it will seem five hours. *(Raina runs to the top of the steps, and turns there to exchange looks with him and wave him a kiss with both hands. He looks after her with emotion for a moment; then turns slowly away, his face radiant with the loftiest exaltation. The movement shifts his field of vision, into the corner of which there now comes the tail of Louka's double apron. His attention is arrested at once. He takes a stealthy look at her, and begins to twirl his moustache mischievously, with his left hand akimbo on his hip. Finally, striking the ground with his heels in something of a cavalry swagger, he strolls over to the other side of the table, opposite her, and says)* Louka: do you know what the higher love is?

LOUKA *(astonished)* No, sir.

SERGIUS. Very fatiguing thing to keep up for any length of time, Louka. One feels the need of some relief after it.

LOUKA *(innocently)* Perhaps you would like some coffee, sir? *(She stretches her hand across the table for the coffee pot).*

SERGIUS *(taking her hand)* Thank you, Louka.

LOUKA *(pretending to pull)* Oh, sir, you know I didnt mean that. I'm surprised at you!

SERGIUS *(coming clear of the table and drawing her with him)* I am surprised at myself, Louka. What would Sergius, the hero of Slivnitza, say if he saw me now? What would Sergius, the apostle of the higher love, say if he saw me now? What would the half dozen Sergiuses who keep popping in and out of this handsome figure of mine say if they caught us here? *(Letting go her hand and slipping his arm dexterously round her waist)* Do you consider my figure handsome, Louka?

LOUKA. Let me go, sir. I shall be disgraced. *(She struggles: he holds her inexorably).* Oh, w i l l you let go?

SERGIUS *(looking straight into her eyes)* No.

LOUKA. Then stand back where we cant be seen. Have you no common sense?

SERGIUS. Ah! thats reasonable. *(He takes her into the stableyard gateway, where they are hidden from the house).*

LOUKA (*plaintively*) I may have been seen from the windows: Miss Raina is sure to be spying about after you.

SERGIUS (*stung: letting her go*) Take care, Louka. I may be worthless enough to betray the higher love; but do not you insult it.

LOUKA (*demurely*) Not for the world, sir, I'm sure. May I go on with my work, please, now?

SERGIUS (*again putting his arm round her*) You are a provoking little witch, Louka. If you were in love with me, would you spy out of windows on me?

LOUKA. Well, you see, sir, since you say you are half a dozen different gentlemen all at once, I should have a great deal to look after.

SERGIUS (*charmed*) Witty as well as pretty. (*He tries to kiss her*).

LOUKA (*avoiding him*) No: I dont want your kisses. Gentlefolk are all alike: you making love to me behind Miss Raina's back; and she doing the same behind yours.

SERGIUS (*recoiling a step*) Louka!

LOUKA. It shews how little you really care.

SERGIUS (*dropping his familiarity, and speaking with freezing politeness*) If our conversation is to continue, Louka, you will please remember that a gentleman does not discuss the conduct of the lady he is engaged to with her maid.

LOUKA. It's so hard to know what a gentleman considers right. I thought from your trying to kiss me that you had given up being so particular.

SERGIUS (*turning from her and striking his forehead as he comes back into the garden from the gateway*) Devil! devil!

LOUKA. Ha! ha! I expect one of the six of you is very like me, sir; though I a m only Miss Raina's maid. (*She goes back to her work at the table, taking no further notice of him*).

SERGIUS (*speaking to himself*) Which of the six is the real man? thats the question that torments me. One of them is a hero, another a buffoon, another a humbug, another perhaps a bit of a blackguard.[14] (*He pauses, and looks furtively at Louka as he adds, with deep bitterness*) And one, at least, is a coward: jealous, like all cowards. (*He goes to the table*). Louka.

LOUKA. Yes?

SERGIUS. Who is my rival?

LOUKA. You shall never get that out of me, for love or money.

SERGIUS. Why?

LOUKA. Never mind why. Besides, you would tell that I told you; and I should lose my place.

SERGIUS (*holding out his right hand in affirmation*) No! on the honor of a—(*He checks himself; and his hand drops, nerveless, as he concludes sardonically*)—of a man capable of behaving as I have been behaving for the last five minutes. Who is he?

LOUKA. I dont know. I never saw him. I only heard his voice through the door of her room.

SERGIUS. Damnation! How dare you?

LOUKA (*retreating*) Oh, I mean no harm: youve no right to take up my words like that. The mistress knows all about it. And I tell you that if that gentleman ever comes here again, Miss Raina will marry him, whether he likes it or not. I know the difference between the sort of manner you and she put on before one another and the real manner.

[*Sergius shivers as if she had stabbed him. Then, setting his face like iron, he strides grimly to her, and grips her above the elbows with both hands*].

SERGIUS. Now listen you to me.

LOUKA (*wincing*) Not so tight: youre hurting me.

SERGIUS. That doesnt matter. You have stained my honor by making me a party to your eavesdropping. And you have betrayed your mistress.

---

14. **blackguard,** a scoundrel, derived from the name given to the servant who cleaned the dirty pots.

LOUKA *(writhing)* Please—

SERGIUS. That shews that you are an abominable little clod of common clay, with the soul of a servant.

[He lets her go as if she were an unclean thing, and turns away, dusting his hands of her, to the bench by the wall, where he sits down with averted head, meditating gloomily].

LOUKA *(whimpering angrily with her hands up her sleeves, feeling her bruised arms)* You know how to hurt with your tongue as well as with your hands. But I dont care, now Ive found out that whatever clay I'm made of, youre made of the same. As for her, she's a liar; and her fine airs are a cheat; and I'm worth six of her. *(She shakes the pain off hardily; tosses her head; and sets to work to put the things on the tray).*

[He looks doubtfully at her. She finishes packing the tray, and laps the cloth over the edges, so as to carry all out together. As she stoops to lift it, he rises].

SERGIUS. Louka! *(She stops and looks defiantly at him).* A gentleman has no right to hurt a woman under any circumstances. *(With profound humility, uncovering his head)* I beg your pardon.

LOUKA. That sort of apology may satisfy a lady. Of what use is it to a servant?

SERGIUS *(rudely crossed in his chivalry, throws it off with a bitter laugh, and says slightingly)* Oh! you wish to be paid for the hurt? *(He puts on his shako,[15] and takes some money from his pocket).*

LOUKA *(her eyes filling with tears in spite of herself)* No: I want my hurt made well.

SERGIUS *(sobered by her tone)* How?

[She rolls up her left sleeve; clasps her arm with the thumb and fingers of her right hand; and looks down at the bruise. Then she raises her head and looks straight at him. Finally, with a superb gesture, she presents her arm to be kissed. Amazed, he looks at her; at the arm; at her again; hesitates; and then, with

shuddering intensity, exclaims Never! *and gets away as far as possible from her.*

Her arm drops. Without a word, and with unaffected dignity, she takes her tray, and is approaching the house when Raina returns, wearing a hat and jacket in the height of the Vienna fashion of the previous year, 1885. Louka makes way proudly for her, and then goes into the house].

RAINA. I'm ready. Whats the matter? *(Gaily)* Have you been flirting with Louka?

SERGIUS *(hastily)* No, no. How can you think such a thing?

RAINA *(ashamed of herself)* Forgive me, dear: it was only a jest. I am so happy to-day.

[He goes quickly to her, and kisses her hand remorsefully. Catherine comes out and calls to them from the top of the steps].

CATHERINE *(coming down to them)* I am sorry to disturb you, children; but Paul is distracted over those three regiments. He doesnt know how to send them to Philippopolis; and he objects to every suggestion of mine. You must go and help him, Sergius. He is in the library.

RAINA *(disappointed)* But we are just going out for a walk.

SERGIUS. I shall not be long. Wait for me just five minutes. *(He runs up the steps to the door).*

RAINA *(following him to the foot of the steps and looking up at him with timid coquetry)* I shall go round and wait in full view of the library windows. Be sure you draw father's attention to me. If you are a moment longer than five minutes, I shall go in and fetch you, regiments or no regiments.

SERGIUS *(laughing)* Very well. *(He goes in).*

15. **shako,** a high, stiff military hat.

[*Raina watches him until he is out of her sight. Then, with a perceptible relaxation of manner, she begins to pace up and down the garden in a brown study*].

CATHERINE. Imagine their meeting that Swiss and hearing the whole story! The very first thing your father asked for was the old coat we sent him off in. A nice mess you have got us into!

RAINA (*gazing thoughtfully at the gravel as she walks*) The little beast!

CATHERINE. Little beast! What little beast?

RAINA. To go and tell! Oh, if I had him here, I'd cram him with chocolate creams til he couldnt ever speak again!

CATHERINE. Dont talk such stuff. Tell me the truth, Raina. How long was he in your room before you came to me?

RAINA (*whisking round and recommencing her march in the opposite direction*) Oh, I forget.

CATHERINE. You cannot forget! Did he really climb up after the soldiers were gone; or was he there when that officer searched the room?

RAINA. No. Yes: I think he must have been there then.

CATHERINE. You think! Oh, Raina! Raina! Will anything ever make you straightforward? If Sergius finds out, it will be all over between you.

RAINA (*with cool impertinence*) Oh, I know Sergius is your pet. I sometimes wish you could marry him instead of me. You would just suit him. You would pet him, and spoil him, and mother him to perfection.

CATHERINE (*opening her eyes very widely indeed*) Well, upon my word!

RAINA (*capriciously: half to herself*) I always feel a longing to do or say something dreadful to him—to shock his propriety—to scandalize the five senses out of him. (*To Catherine, perversely*) I dont care whether he finds out about the chocolate cream soldier or not. I half hope he may. (*She again turns and strolls flippantly away up the path to the corner of the house*).

CATHERINE. And what should I be able to say to your father, pray?

RAINA (*over her shoulder, from the top of the two steps*) Oh, poor father! As if h e could help himself! (*She turns the corner and passes out of sight*).

CATHERINE (*looking after her, her fingers itching*) Oh, if you were only ten years younger! (*Louka comes from the house with a salver, which she carries hanging down by her side*). Well?

LOUKA. Theres a gentleman just called, madam. A Serbian officer.

CATHERINE (*flaming*) A Serb! And how dare he—(*checking herself bitterly*) Oh, I forgot. We are at peace now. I suppose we shall have them calling every day to pay their compliments. Well: if he is an officer why dont you tell your master? He is in the library with Major Saranoff. Why do you come to me?

LOUKA. But he asks for you, madam. And I dont think he knows who you are: he said the lady of the house. He gave me this little ticket for you. (*She takes a card out of her bosom; puts it on the salver; and offers it to Catherine*).

CATHERINE (*reading*) "Captain Bluntschli"? Thats a German name.

LOUKA. Swiss, madam, I think.

CATHERINE (*with a bound that makes Louka jump back*) Swiss! What is he like?

LOUKA (*timidly*) He has a big carpet bag, madam.

CATHERINE. Oh Heavens! he's come to return the coat. Send him away: say we're not at home: ask him to leave his address and I'll write to him. Oh stop: that will never do. Wait! (*She throws herself into a chair to think it out. Louka waits*). The master and Major Saranoff are busy in the library, arnt they?

LOUKA. Yes, madam.

CATHERINE (*decisively*) Bring the gentleman out here at once. (*Peremptorily*) And be very polite to him. Dont delay. Here (*impatiently snatching the salver from her*): leave that here; and go straight back to him.

LOUKA. Yes, madam (*going*).

CATHERINE. Louka!

LOUKA (*stopping*) Yes, madam.

CATHERINE. Is the library door shut?

LOUKA. I think so, madam.

CATHERINE. If not, shut it as you pass through.

LOUKA. Yes, madam (*going*).

CATHERINE. Stop! (*Louka stops*). He will have to go that way (*indicating the gate of the stable yard*). Tell Nicola to bring his bag here after him. Dont forget.

LOUKA (*surprised*) His bag?

CATHERINE. Yes: here: as soon as possible. (*Vehemently*) Be quick! (*Louka runs into the house. Catherine snatches her apron off and throws it behind a bush. She then takes up the salver and uses it as a mirror, with the result that the handkerchief tied round her head follows the apron. A touch to her hair and a shake to her dressing gown make her presentable*). Oh, how? how? h o w can a man be such a fool! Such a moment to select! (*Louka appears at the door of the house, announcing Captain Bluntschli. She stands aside at the top of the steps to let him pass before she goes in again. He is the man of the midnight adventure in Raina's room, clean, well brushed, smartly uniformed, and out of trouble, but still unmistakably the same man. The moment Louka's back is turned, Catherine swoops on him with impetuous, urgent, coaxing appeal*). Captain Bluntschli: I am v e r y glad to see you; but you must leave this house at once. (*He raises his eyebrows*). My husband has just returned with my future son-in-law; and they know nothing. If they did, the consequences would be terrible. You are a foreigner: you do not feel our national animosities as we do. We still hate the Serbs: the effect of the peace on my husband has been to make him feel like a lion baulked[16] of his prey. If he discovers our secret, he will never forgive me; and my daughter's life will hardly be safe. Will you, like the chivalrous gentleman and soldier you are, leave at once before he finds you here?

BLUNTSCHLI (*disappointed, but philosophical*) At once, gracious lady. I only came to thank you and return the coat you lent me. If you will allow me to take it out of my bag and leave it with your servant as I pass out, I need detain you no further. (*He turns to go into the house*).

CATHERINE (*catching him by the sleeve*) Oh, you must not think of going back that way. (*Coaxing him across to the stable gates*) This is the shortest way out. Many thanks. So glad to have been of service to you. G o o d-bye.

BLUNTSCHLI. But my bag?

CATHERINE. It shall be sent on. You will leave me your address.

BLUNTSCHLI. True. Allow me. (*He takes out his card-case, and stops to write his address, keeping Catherine in an agony of impatience. As he hands her the card, Petkoff, hatless, rushes from the house in a fluster of hospitality, followed by Sergius*).

PETKOFF (*as he hurries down the steps*) My dear Captain Bluntschli——

CATHERINE. Oh Heavens! (*She sinks on the seat against the wall*).

PETKOFF (*too preoccupied to notice her as he shakes Bluntschli's hand heartily*) Those stupid people of mine thought I was out here, instead of in the—haw!—library (*he cannot mention the library without betraying how proud he is of it*). I saw you through the window. I was wondering why you didnt come in. Saranoff is with me: you remember him, dont you?

SERGIUS (*saluting humorously, and then offering his hand with great charm of manner*) Welcome, our friend the enemy!

PETKOFF. No longer the enemy, happily. (*Rather anxiously*) I hope youve called as a friend, and not about horses or prisoners.

CATHERINE. Oh, quite as a friend, Paul. I was just asking Captain Bluntschli to stay to lunch; but he declares he must go at once.

SERGIUS (*sardonically*) Impossible, Bluntschli.

16. **baulked,** thwarted, frustrated.

We want you here badly. We have to send on three cavalry regiments to Philippopolis; and we dont in the least know how to do it.

BLUNTSCHLI *(suddenly attentive and businesslike)* Philippopolis? The forage is the trouble, I suppose.

PETKOFF *(eagerly)* Yes: thats it. *(To Sergius)* He sees the whole thing at once.

BLUNTSCHLI. I think I can shew you how to manage that.

SERGIUS. Invaluable man! Come along! *(Towering over Bluntschli, he puts his hand on his shoulder and takes him to the steps, Petkoff following).*

[Raina comes from the house as Bluntschli puts his foot on the first step].

RAINA. Oh! The chocolate cream soldier!

[Bluntschli stands rigid. Sergius, amazed, looks at Raina, then at Petkoff, who looks back at him and then at his wife].

CATHERINE *(with commanding presence of mind)* My dear Raina, dont you see that we have a guest here? Captain Bluntschli: one of our new Serbian friends.

[Raina bows: Bluntschli bows].

RAINA. How silly of me! *(She comes down into the center of the group, between Bluntschli and Petkoff).* I made a beautiful ornament this morning for the ice pudding; and that stupid Nicola has just put down a pile of plates on it and spoilt it. *(To Bluntschli, winningly)* I hope you didnt think that you were the chocolate cream soldier, Captain Bluntschli.

BLUNTSCHLI *(laughing)* I assure you I did. *(Stealing a whimsical glance at her)* Your explanation was a relief.

PETKOFF *(suspiciously, to Raina)* And since when, pray, have y o u taken to cooking?

CATHERINE. Oh, whilst you were away. It is her latest fancy.

PETKOFF *(testily)* And has Nicola taken to drinking? He used to be careful enough. First he shews Captain Bluntschli out here

when he knew quite well I was in the library; and then he goes downstairs and breaks Raina's chocolate soldier. He must . . . *(Nicola appears at the top of the steps with the bag. He descends; places it respectfully before Bluntschli; and waits for further orders. General amazement. Nicola, unconscious of the effect he is producing, looks perfectly satisfied with himself. When Petkoff recovers his power of speech, he breaks out at him with)* Are you mad, Nicola?

NICOLA *(taken aback)* Sir?

PETKOFF. What have you brought that for?

NICOLA. My lady's orders, major. Louka told me that——

CATHERINE *(interrupting him)* My orders! Why should I order you to bring Captain Bluntschli's luggage out here? What are you thinking of, Nicola?

NICOLA *(after a moment's bewilderment, picking up the bag as he addresses Bluntschli with the very perfection of servile discretion)* I beg your pardon, captain, I am sure. *(To Catherine)* My fault, madam: I hope youll overlook it. *(He bows, and is going to the steps with the bag, when Petkoff addresses him angrily).*

PETKOFF. Youd better go and slam that bag, too, down on Miss Raina's ice pudding! *(This is too much for Nicola. The bag drops from his hand almost on his master's toes, eliciting a roar of)* Begone, you butter-fingered donkey.

NICOLA *(snatching up the bag, and escaping into the house)* Yes, major.

CATHERINE. Oh, never mind, Paul: dont be angry.

PETKOFF *(blustering)* Scoundrel! He's got out of hand while I was away. I'll· teach him. Infernal blackguard! The sack next Saturday! I'll clear out the whole establishment—

[He is stifled by the caresses of his wife and daughter, who hang round his neck, petting him].

CATHERINE *{(together)}* Now, now, now, it
RAINA Wow, wow, wow: not

{ mustnt be angry. He meant no harm. Be
on your first day at home. I'll make
good to please me, dear. Sh-sh-sh-sh!
another ice pudding. Tch-ch-ch!

PETKOFF (*yielding*) Oh well, never mind.
Come, Bluntschli: lets have no more nonsense about going away. You know very
well youre not going back to Switzerland
yet. Until you do go back youll stay with us.

RAINA. Oh, do, Captain Bluntschli.

PETKOFF (*to Catherine*) Now, Catherine: it's of
you he's afraid. Press him; and he'll stay.

CATHERINE. Of course I shall be only too
delighted if (*appealingly*) Captain Bluntschli
really wishes to stay. He knows my wishes.

BLUNTSCHLI (*in his driest military manner*) I am
at madam's orders.

SERGIUS (*cordially*) That settles it.

PETKOFF (*heartily*) Of course!

RAINA. You see you must stay.

BLUNTSCHLI (*smiling*) Well, if I must, I must.

[*Gesture of despair from Catherine*].

FOR UNDERSTANDING

1. How does the information implied about
Petkoff and Sergius in Act One measure up to the
reality of the characters as seen in this act? Are
they different at all from the way they were
presented in Act One?

2. Act Two introduces a new character, Nicola.
What are his distinctive characteristics?

3. The first act could be considered primarily one
of exposition, as Shaw sets up his characters and
the situation. What are the complications which he
introduces in this act? Which of them did you
expect?

FOR INTERPRETATION

1. Look at the various details which seem to satirize the Bulgarian way of life. Is Shaw *only* critical,
or does he modify his satire in any way?

2. Look carefully at Shaw's description of Sergius
and at the lines Sergius speaks in this act. How
much self-perception does he have?

Act III

*In the library after lunch. It is not much of a
library. Its literary equipment consists of a
single fixed shelf stocked with old paper covered
novels, broken backed, coffee stained, torn and
thumbed; and a couple of little hanging shelves
with a few gift books on them: the rest of the
wall space being occupied by trophies of war
and the chase. But it is a most comfortable
sitting room. A row of three large windows
shews a mountain panorama, just now seen in
one of its friendliest aspects in the mellowing
afternoon light. In the corner next the right
hand window a square earthenware stove, a
perfect tower of glistening pottery, rises nearly
to the ceiling and guarantees plenty of warmth.
The ottoman is like that in Raina's room, and
similarly placed; and the window seats are
luxurious with decorated cushions. There is one
object, however, hopelessly out of keeping with
its surroundings. This is a small kitchen table,
much the worse for wear, fitted as a writing
table with an old canister full of pens, an
eggcup filled with ink, and a deplorable scrap
of heavily used pink blotting paper.*

*At the side of this table, which stands to the left
of anyone facing the window, Bluntschli is
hard at work with a couple of maps before him,
writing orders. At the head of it sits Sergius,
who is supposed to be also at work, but is
actually gnawing the feather of a pen, and
contemplating Bluntschli's quick, sure,
businesslike progress with a mixture of envious
irritation at his own incapacity and awestruck
wonder at an ability which seems to him almost
miraculous, though its prosaic character forbids
him to esteem it. The Major is comfortably
established on the ottoman, with a newspaper in
his hand and the tube of his hookah[1] within
easy reach. Catherine sits at the stove, with her
back to them, embroidering. Raina, reclining
on the divan, is gazing in a daydream out at*

---

1. **hookah,** an Oriental pipe with a long flexible tube
containing water.

the Balkan landscape, with a neglected novel in her lap.

The door is on the same side as the stove, farther from the window. The button of the electric bell is at the opposite side, behind Bluntschli.

PETKOFF (*looking up from his paper to watch how they are getting on at the table*) Are you sure I cant help you in any way, Bluntschli?

BLUNTSCHLI (*without interrupting his writing or looking up*) Quite sure, thank you. Saranoff and I will manage it.

SERGIUS (*grimly*) Yes: we'll manage it. He finds out what to do; draws up the orders; and I sign em. Division of labor! (*Bluntschli passes him a paper*). Another one? Thank you. (*He plants the paper squarely before him; sets his chair carefully parallel to it; and signs with his cheek on his elbow and his protruded tongue following the movements of his pen*). This hand is more accustomed to the sword than to the pen.

PETKOFF. It's very good of you, Bluntschli: it is indeed, to let yourself be put upon in this way. Now are q u i t e sure I can do nothing?

CATHERINE (*in a low warning tone*) You can stop interrupting, Paul.

PETKOFF (*starting and looking round at her*) Eh? Oh! Quite right, my love: quite right. (*He takes his newspaper up again, but presently lets it drop*). Ah, you havnt been campaigning, Catherine: you dont know how pleasant it is for us to sit here, after a good lunch, with nothing to do but enjoy ourselves. Theres only one thing I want to make me thoroughly comfortable.

CATHERINE. What is that?

PETKOFF. My old coat. I'm not at home in this one: I feel as if I were on parade.

CATHERINE. My dear Paul, how absurd you are about that old coat! It must be hanging in the blue closet where you left it.

PETKOFF. My dear Catherine, I tell you Ive looked there. Am I to believe my own eyes or not? (*Catherine rises and crosses the room to press the button of the electric bell*). What are you shewing off that bell for? (*She looks at him majestically and silently resumes her chair and her needlework*). My dear: if you think the obstinacy of your sex can make a coat out of two old dressing gowns of Raina's, your waterproof, and my mackintosh, youre mistaken. Thats exactly what the blue closet contains at present.

[*Nicola presents himself*].

CATHERINE. Nicola: go to the blue closet and bring your master's old coat here: the braided one he wears in the house.

NICOLA. Yes, madame. (*He goes out*).

PETKOFF. Catherine.

CATHERINE. Yes, Paul?

PETKOFF. I bet you any piece of jewellery you like to order from Sofia against a week's housekeeping money that the coat isnt there.

CATHERINE. Done, Paul!

PETKOFF (*excited by the prospect of a gamble*) Come: here's an opportunity for some sport. Wholl bet on it? Bluntschli: I'll give you six to one.

BLUNTSCHLI (*imperturbably*) It would be robbing you, major. Madame is sure to be right. (*Without looking up, he passes another batch of papers to Sergius*).

SERGIUS (*also excited*) Bravo, Switzerland! Major: I bet my best charger against an Arab mare for Raina that Nicola finds the coat in the blue closet.

PETKOFF (*eagerly*) Your best char——

CATHERINE (*hastily interrupting him*) Dont be foolish, Paul. An Arabian mare will cost you 50,000 levas.

RAINA (*suddenly coming out of her picturesque revery*) Really, mother, if you are going to take the jewellery, I dont see why you should grudge me my Arab.

[*Nicola comes back with the coat, and brings it to Petkoff, who can hardly believe his eyes*].

CATHERINE. Where was it, Nicola?

NICOLA. Hanging in the blue closet, madame.

PETKOFF. Well, I a m d——

CATHERINE *(stopping him)* Paul!

PETKOFF. I could have sworn it wasnt there. Age is beginning to tell on me. I'm getting hallucinations. *(To Nicola)* Here: help me to change. Excuse me, Bluntschli. *(He begins changing coats, Nicola acting as valet).* Remember: I didnt take that bet of yours, Sergius. Youd better give Raina that Arab steed yourself, since youve roused her expectations. Eh, Raina? *(He looks round at her; but she is again rapt in the landscape. With a little gush of parental affection and pride, he points her out to them, and says)* She's dreaming, as usual.

SERGIUS. Assuredly she shall not be the loser.

PETKOFF. So much the better for her. *I* shant come off so cheaply, I expect. *(The change is now complete. Nicola goes out with the discarded coat).* Ah, now I feel at home at last. *(He sits down and takes his newspaper with a grunt of relief).*

BLUNTSCHLI *(to Sergius, handing a paper)* Thats the last order.

PETKOFF *(jumping up)* What! Finished?

BLUNTSCHLI. Finished.

PETKOFF *(with childlike envy)* Havnt you anything for me to sign?

BLUNTSCHLI. Not necessary. His signature will do.

PETKOFF *(inflating his chest and thumping it)* Ah well, I think weve done a thundering good day's work. Can I do anything more?

BLUNTSCHLI. You had better both see the fellows that are to take these. *(Sergius rises).* Pack them off at once; and shew them that Ive marked on the orders the time they should hand them in by. Tell them that if they stop to drink or tell stories—if theyre five minutes late, theyll have the skin taken off their backs.

SERGIUS *(stiffening indignantly)* I'll say so. *(He strides to the door).* And if one of them is man enough to spit in my face for insulting him, I'll buy his discharge and give him a pension. *(He goes out).*

BLUNTSCHLI *(confidentially)* Just see that he talks to them properly, major, will you?

PETKOFF *(officiously)* Quite right, Bluntschli, quite right. I'll see to it. *(He goes to the door importantly, but hesitates on the threshold).* By the bye, Catherine, you may as well come too. Theyll be far more frightened of you than of me.

CATHERINE *(putting down her embroidery)* I daresay I had better. You would only splutter at them. *(She goes out, Petkoff holding the door for her and following her).*

BLUNTSCHLI. What an army! They make cannons out of cherry trees; and the officers send for their wives to keep discipline! *(He begins to fold and docket[2] the papers).*

[Raina, who has risen from the divan, marches slowly down the room with her hands clasped behind her, and looks mischievously at him].

RAINA. You look ever so much nicer than when we last met. *(He looks up, surprised).* What have you done to yourself?

BLUNTSCHLI. Washed; brushed; good night's sleep and breakfast. Thats all.

RAINA. Did you get back safely that morning?

BLUNTSCHLI. Quite, thanks.

RAINA. Were they angry with you for running away from Sergius's charge?

BLUNTSCHLI *(grinning)* No: they were glad; because theyd all just run away themselves.

RAINA *(going to the table, and leaning over it towards him)* It must have made a lovely story for them: all that about me and my room.

BLUNTSCHLI. Capital story. But I only told it to one of them: a particular friend.

RAINA. On whose discretion you could absolutely rely?

BLUNTSCHLI. Absolutely.

RAINA. Hm! He told it all to my father and Sergius the day you exchanged the prisoners. *(She turns away and strolls carelessly across to the other side of the room).*

2. **docket,** label.

BLUNTSCHLI (*deeply concerned, and half incredulous*) No! You dont mean that, do you?

RAINA (*turning, with sudden earnestness*) I do indeed. But they dont know that it was in this house you took refuge. If Sergius knew, he would challenge you and kill you in a duel.

BLUNTSCHLI. Bless me! then dont tell him.

RAINA. Please be serious, Captain Bluntschli. Can you not realize what it is to me to deceive him? I want to be quite perfect with Sergius: no meanness, no smallness, no deceit. My relation to him is the one really beautiful and noble part of my life. I hope you can understand that.

BLUNTSCHLI (*sceptically*) You mean that you wouldnt like him to find out that the story about the ice pudding was a—a—a—You know.

RAINA (*wincing*) Ah, dont talk of it in that flippant way. I lied: I know it. But I did it to save your life. He would have killed you. That was the second time I ever uttered a falsehood. (*Bluntschli rises quickly and looks doubtfully and somewhat severely at her*). Do you remember the first time?

BLUNTSCHLI. I! No. Was I present?

RAINA. Yes; and I told the officer who was searching for you that you were not present.

BLUNTSCHLI. True. I should have remembered it.

RAINA (*greatly encouraged*) Ah, it is natural that you should forget it first. It cost you nothing: it cost me a lie! A lie!!

[*She sits down on the ottoman, looking straight before her with her hands clasped round her knee. Bluntschli, quite touched, goes to the ottoman with a particularly reassuring and considerate air, and sits down beside her*].

BLUNTSCHLI. My dear young lady, dont let this worry you. Remember: I'm a soldier. Now what are the two things that happen to a soldier so often that he comes to think nothing of them? One is hearing people tell lies (*Raina recoils*): the other is getting his life saved in all sorts of ways by all sorts of people.

RAINA (*rising in indignant protest*) And so he becomes a creature incapable of faith and of gratitude.

BLUNTSCHLI (*making a wry face*) Do you like gratitude? I dont. If pity is akin to love, gratitude is akin to the other thing.

RAINA. Gratitude! (*Turning on him*) If you are incapable of gratitude you are incapable of any noble sentiment. Even animals are grateful. Oh, I see now exactly what you think of me! You were not surprised to hear me lie. To you it was something I probably did every day! every hour!! That is how men think of women. (*She paces the room tragically*).

BLUNTSCHLI (*dubiously*) Theres reason in everything. You said youd told only two lies in your whole life. Dear young lady: isnt that rather a short allowance? I'm quite a straightforward man myself; but it wouldnt last me a whole morning.

RAINA (*staring haughtily at him*) Do you know, sir, that you are insulting me?

BLUNTSCHLI. I cant help it. When you strike that noble attitude and speak in that thrilling voice, I admire you; but I find it impossible to believe a single word you say.

RAINA (*superbly*) Captain Bluntschli!

BLUNTSCHLI (*unmoved*) Yes?

RAINA (*standing over him, as if she could not believe her senses*) Do you mean what you said just now? Do you k n o w what you said just now?

BLUNTSCHLI. I do.

RAINA (*gasping*) I! I!!! (*She points to herself incredulously, meaning "I, Raina Petkoff, tell lies!" He meets her gaze unflinchingly. She suddenly sits down beside him, and adds, with a complete change of manner from the heroic to a babyish familiarity*) How did you find me out?

BLUNTSCHLI (*promptly*) Instinct, dear young lady. Instinct, and experience of the world.

RAINA (*wonderingly*) Do you know, you are the

first man I ever met who did not take me seriously?

BLUNTSCHLI. You mean, dont you, that I am the first man that has ever taken you quite seriously?

RAINA. Yes: I suppose I d o mean that. *(Cosily, quite at her ease with him)* How strange it is to be talked to in such a way! You know, Ive always gone on like that.

BLUNTSCHLI. You mean the——?

RAINA. I mean the noble attitude and the thrilling voice. *(They laugh together)*. I did it when I was a tiny child to my nurse. S h e believed in it. I do it before my parents. T h e y believe in it. I do it before Sergius. He believes in it.

BLUNTSCHLI. Yes: he's a little in that line himself, isnt he?

RAINA *(startled)* Oh! Do you think so?

BLUNTSCHLI. You know him better than I do.

RAINA. I wonder—I w o n d e r is he? If I thought t h a t . . . ! *(Discouraged)* Ah, well: what does it matter? I suppose, now youve found me out, you despise me.

BLUNTSCHLI *(warmly, rising)* No, my dear young lady, no, no, no a thousand times. It's part of your youth: part of your charm. I'm like all the rest of them: the nurse, your parents, Sergius: I'm your infatuated admirer.

RAINA *(pleased)* Really?

BLUNTSCHLI *(slapping his breast smartly with his hand, German fashion)* Hand aufs Herz![3] Really and truly.

RAINA *(very happy)* But what did you think of me for giving you my portrait?

BLUNTSCHLI *(astonished)* Your portrait! You never gave me your portrait.

RAINA *(quickly)* Do you mean to say you never got it?

BLUNTSCHLI. No. *(He sits down beside her, with renewed interest, and says, with some complacency)* When did you send it to me?

RAINA *(indignantly)* I did not send it to you. *(She turns her head away, and adds, reluctantly)* It was in the pocket of that coat.

BLUNTSCHLI *(pursing his lips and rounding his eyes)* Oh-o-oh! I never found it. It must be there still.

RAINA *(springing up)* There still! for my father to find the first time he puts his hand in his pocket! Oh, how could you be so stupid?

BLUNTSCHLI *(rising also)* It doesnt matter: I suppose it's only a photograph: how can he tell who it was intended for? Tell him he put it there himself.

RAINA *(bitterly)* Yes: that is so clever! isnt it? *(Distractedly)* Oh! what shall I do?

BLUNTSCHLI. Ah, I see. You wrote something on it. That was rash.

RAINA *(vexed almost to tears)* Oh, to have done such a thing for y o u, who care no more—except to laugh at me—oh! Are you sure nobody has touched it?

BLUNTSCHLI. Well, I cant be quite sure. You see, I couldnt carry it about with me all the time: one cant take much luggage on active service.

RAINA. What did you do with it?

BLUNTSCHLI. When I got through to Pirot I had to put it in safe keeping somehow. I thought of the railway cloak room; but thats the surest place to get looted in modern warfare. So I pawned it.

RAINA. P a w n e d it!!!

BLUNTSCHLI. I know it doesnt sound nice; but it was much the safest plan. I redeemed it the day before yesterday. Heaven only knows whether the pawnbroker cleared out the pockets or not.

RAINA *(furious: throwing the words right into his face)* You have a low shopkeeping mind. You think of things that would never come into a gentleman's head.

BLUNTSCHLI *(phlegmatically)* Thats the Swiss national character, dear lady. *(He returns to the table)*.

RAINA. Oh, I wish I had never met you. *(She flounces away, and sits at the window fuming)*.

---

3. **Hand aufs Herz,** literally, "hand on heart." We would say "cross my heart."

Act III of Arms and the Man *as photographed at the Savoy Theatre, London, on December 30, 1907.*

The Raymond Mander and
Joe Mitchenson Theatre
Collection, London

[*Louka comes in with a heap of letters and telegrams on her salver, and crosses, with her bold free gait, to the table. Her left sleeve is looped up to the shoulder with a brooch, shewing her naked arm, with a broad gilt bracelet covering the bruise*].

LOUKA (*to Bluntschli*) For you. (*She empties the salver with a fling on to the table*). The messenger is waiting. (*She is determined not to be civil to an enemy, even if she must bring him his letters*).

BLUNTSCHLI (*to Raina*) Will you excuse me: the last postal delivery that reached me was three weeks ago. These are the subsequent accumulations. Four telegrams: a week old. (*He opens one*). Oho! Bad news!

RAINA (*rising and advancing a little remorsefully*) Bad news?

BLUNTSCHLI. My father's dead. (*He looks at the telegram with his lips pursed, musing on the unexpected change in his arrangements. Louka crosses herself hastily*).

RAINA. Oh, how very sad!

BLUNTSCHLI. Yes: I shall have to start for home in an hour. He has left a lot of big hotels behind him to be looked after. (*He takes up a fat letter in a long blue envelope*). Here's a whacking letter from the family solicitor. (*He pulls out the enclosures and glances over them*). Great Heavens! Seventy' Two hundred! (*In a crescendo of dismay*). Four hundred! Four thousand!! Nine thousand six hundred!!! What on earth am I to do with them all?

RAINA (*timidly*) Nine thousand hotels?

BLUNTSCHLI. Hotels! nonsense. If you only knew! Oh, it's too ridiculous! Excuse me: I must give my fellow orders about starting. (*He leaves the room hastily, with the documents in his hand*).

LOUKA (*knowing instinctively that she can annoy Raina by disparaging Bluntschli*) He has not much heart, that Swiss. He has not a word of grief for his poor father.

RAINA (*bitterly*) Grief! A man who has been doing nothing but killing people for years! What does he care? What does any soldier care? (*She goes to the door, restraining her tears with difficulty*).

LOUKA. Major Saranoff has been fighting too; and he has plenty of heart left. (*Raina, at the door, draws herself up haughtily and goes out*). Aha! I thought you wouldnt get much feeling out of y o u r soldier. (*She is following Raina when Nicola enters with an armful of logs for the stove*).

NICOLA (*grinning amorously at her*) Ive been trying all the afternoon to get a minute alone with you, my girl. (*His countenance changes as he notices her arm*). Why, what fashion is that of wearing your sleeve, child?

LOUKA (*proudly*) My own fashion.

NICOLA. Indeed! If the mistress catches you, she'll talk to you. (*He puts the logs down, and seats himself comfortably on the ottoman*).

LOUKA. Is that any reason why y o u should take it on yourself to talk to me?

NICOLA. Come! dont be so contrary with me. Ive some good news for you. (*She sits down beside him. He takes out some paper money. Louka, with an eager gleam in her eyes, tries to snatch it; but he shifts it quickly to his left hand, out of her reach*). See! a twenty leva bill! Sergius gave me that, out of pure swagger. A fool and his money are soon parted. Theres ten levas more. The Swiss gave me that for backing up the mistress's and Raina's lies about him. H ę' s no fool, he isnt. You should have heard old Catherine downstairs as polite as you please to me, telling me not to mind the Major being a little impatient; for they knew what a good servant I was—after making a fool and a liar of me before them all! The twenty will go to our savings; and you shall have the ten to spend if youll only talk to me so as to remind me I'm a human being. I get tired of being a servant occasionally.

LOUKA. Yes: sell your manhood for 30 levas, and buy me for 10! (*Rising scornfully*) Keep your money. You were born to be a servant. I was not. When you set up your shop you will only be everybody's servant instead of somebody's servant. (*She goes moodily to the table and seats herself regally in Sergius's chair*).

NICOLA (*picking up his logs, and going to the stove*) Ah, wait til you see. We shall have our evenings to ourselves; and I shall be master in my own house, I promise you. (*He throws the logs down and kneels at the stove*).

LOUKA. You shall never be master in mine.

NICOLA (*turning, still on his knees, and squatting down rather forlornly on his calves, daunted by her implacable disdain*) You have a great ambition in you, Louka. Remember: if any luck comes to you, it was I that made a woman of you.

LOUKA. You!

NICOLA (*scrambling up and going at her*) Yes, me. Who was it made you give up wearing a couple of pounds of false black hair on your head and reddening your lips and cheeks like any other Bulgarian girl? I did. Who taught you to trim your nails, and keep your hands clean, and be dainty about yourself, like a fine Russian lady? Me: do you hear that? me! (*She tosses her head defiantly; and he turns away, adding, more coolly*) Ive often thought that if Raina were out of the way, and you just a little less of a fool and Sergius just a little more of one, you might come to be one of my grandest customers, instead of only being my wife and costing me money.

LOUKA. I believe you would rather be my servant than my husband. You would make more out of me. Oh, I know that soul of yours.

NICOLA (*going closer to her for greater emphasis*) Never you mind my soul; but just listen to my advice. If you want to be a lady, your present behavior to me wont do at all, unless when we're alone. It's too sharp and impudent; and impudence is a sort of familiarity: it shews affection for me. And dont you try being high and mighty with me, either. Youre like all country girls: you think it's genteel to treat a servant the way I treat a stableboy. Thats only your ignorance; and dont you forget it. And dont be so ready to defy everybody. Act as if you expected to have your own way, not as if you expected to be ordered about. The way to get on as a lady is the same as the way to get on as a servant: youve got to know your place: thats the secret of it. And you may depend on me to know my place if you get promoted. Think over it, my girl. I'll stand by you: one servant should always stand by another.

LOUKA (*rising impatiently*) Oh, I must behave in my own way. You take all the courage out of me with your coldblooded wisdom. Go and put those logs on the fire: thats the sort of thing you understand.

[*Before Nicola can retort, Sergius comes in. He checks himself a moment on seeing Louka; then goes to the stove*].

SERGIUS (*to Nicola*) I am not in the way of your work, I hope.

NICOLA (*in a smooth, elderly manner*) Oh no, sir: thank you kindly. I was only speaking to this foolish girl about her habit of running up here to the library whenever she gets a chance, to look at the books. Thats the worst of her education, sir: it gives her habits above her station. (*To Louka*) Make that table tidy, Louka, for the Major. (*He goes out sedately*).

[*Louka, without looking at Sergius, pretends to arrange the papers on the table. He crosses slowly to her, and studies the arrangement of her sleeve reflectively*].

SERGIUS. Let me see: is there a mark there? (*He turns up the bracelet and sees the bruise made by his grasp. She stands motionless, not looking at him: fascinated, but on her guard*). Ffff! Does it hurt?

LOUKA. Yes.

SERGIUS. Shall I cure it?

LOUKA (*instantly withdrawing herself proudly, but still not looking at him*) No. You cannot cure it now.

SERGIUS (*masterfully*) Quite sure? (*He makes a movement as if to take her in his arms*).

LOUKA. Dont trifle with me, please. An officer should not trifle with a servant.

SERGIUS (*indicating the bruise with a merciless stroke of his forefinger*) That was no trifle, Louka.

LOUKA (*flinching; then looking at him for the first time*) Are you sorry?

SERGIUS (*with measured emphasis, folding his arms*) I am n e v e r sorry.

LOUKA (*wistfully*) I wish I could believe a man could be as unlike a woman as that. I wonder are you really a brave man?

SERGIUS (*unaffectedly, relaxing his attitude*) Yes: I am a brave man. My heart jumped like a woman's at the first shot; but in the charge I found that I was brave. Yes: that at least is real about me.

LOUKA. Did you find in the charge that the men whose fathers are poor like mine were any less brave than the men who are rich like you.

SERGIUS (*with bitter levity*) Not a bit. They all slashed and cursed and yelled like heroes. Psha! the courage to rage and kill is cheap. I have an English bull terrier who has as much of that sort of courage as the whole Bulgarian nation, and the whole Russian nation at its back. But he lets my groom thrash him, all the same. Thats your soldier all over! No, Louka: your poor men can cut throats; but they are afraid of their officers; they put up with insults and blows; they stand by and see one another punished like children: aye, and help to do it when they are ordered. And the officers!!! Well (*with a short harsh laugh*) I am an officer. Oh, (*fervently*) give me the man who will defy to the death any power on earth or in heaven that sets itself up against his own will and conscience: he alone is the brave man.

LOUKA. How easy it is to talk! Men never seem to me to grow up: they all have schoolboy's ideas. You dont know what true courage is.

SERGIUS (*ironically*) Indeed! I am willing to be instructed.

[*He sits on the ottoman, sprawling magnificently*].

LOUKA. Look at me! how much am I allowed to have my own will? I have to get your room ready for you: to sweep and dust, to fetch and carry. How could that degrade me if it did not degrade you to have it done for you? But (*with subdued passion*) if I were Empress of Russia, above everyone in the world, then!! Ah then, though according to you I could shew no courage at all, you should see, you should see.

SERGIUS. What would you do, most noble Empress?

LOUKA. I would marry the man I loved, which no other queen in Europe has the courage to do. If I loved you, though you would be as far beneath me as I am beneath you, I would dare to be the equal of my inferior. Would you dare as much if you loved me? No: if you felt the beginnings of love for me you would not let it grow. You would not dare: you would marry a rich man's daughter because you would be afraid of what other people would say of you.

SERGIUS (*bounding up*) You lie: it is not so, by all the stars! If I loved you, and I were the Czar himself, I would set you on the throne by my side. You know that I love another woman, a woman as high above you as heaven is above earth. And you are jealous of her.

LOUKA. I have no reason to be. She will never marry you now. The man I told you of has come back. She will marry the Swiss.

SERGIUS (*recoiling*) The Swiss!

LOUKA. A man worth ten of you. Then you can come to me; and I will refuse you. You are not good enough for me. (*She turns to the door*).

SERGIUS (*springing after her and catching her fiercely in his arms*) I will kill the Swiss; and afterwards I will do as I please with you.

LOUKA (*in his arms, passive and steadfast*) The Swiss will kill you, perhaps. He has beaten you in love. He may beat you in war.

SERGIUS (*tormentedly*) Do you think I believe that she—s h e! whose worst thoughts are higher than your best ones, is capable of trifling with another man behind my back?

LOUKA. Do you think s h e would believe the Swiss if he told her now that I am in your arms?

SERGIUS (*releasing her in despair*) Damnation! Oh, damnation! Mockery! mockery everywhere! everything I think is mocked by everything I do. (*He strikes himself frantically on the breast*). Coward! liar! fool! Shall I kill myself like a man, or live and pretend to laugh at myself? (*She again turns to go*). Louka! (*She stops near the door*). Remember: you belong to me.

LOUKA (*turning*) What does that mean? An insult?

SERGIUS (*commandingly*) It means that you love me, and that I have had you here in my arms, and will perhaps have you there again. Whether that is an insult I neither know nor care: take it as you please. But (*vehemently*) I w i l l not be a coward and a trifler. If I choose to love you, I dare marry you, in spite of all Bulgaria. If these hands ever touch you again, they shall touch my affianced bride.

LOUKA. We shall see whether you dare keep your word. And take care. I will not wait long.

SERGIUS (*again folding his arms and standing motionless in the middle of the room*) Yes: we shall see. And you shall wait my pleasure.

[*Bluntschli, much preoccupied, with his papers still in his hand, enters, leaving the door open for Louka to go out. He goes across to the table, glancing at her as he passes. Sergius, without altering his resolute attitude, watches him steadily. Louka goes out, leaving the door open].*

BLUNTSCHLI *(absently, sitting at the table as before, and putting down his papers)* Thats a remarkable looking young woman.

SERGIUS *(gravely, without moving)* Captain Bluntschli.

BLUNTSCHLI. Eh?

SERGIUS. You have deceived me. You are my rival. I brook no rivals. At six o'clock I shall be in the drilling-ground on the Klissoura road, alone, on horseback, with my sabre. Do you understand?

BLUNTSCHLI *(staring, but sitting quite at his ease)* Oh, thank you: thats a cavalry man's proposal. I'm in the artillery; and I have the choice of weapons. If I go, I shall take a machine gun. And there shall be no mistake about the cartridges this time.

SERGIUS *(flushing, but with deadly coldness)* Take care, sir. It is not our custom in Bulgaria to allow invitations of that kind to be trifled with.

BLUNTSCHLI *(warmly)* Pooh! dont talk to me about Bulgaria. You dont know what fighting is. But have it your own way. Bring your sabre along. I'll meet you.

SERGIUS *(fiercely delighted to find his opponent a man of spirit)* Well said, Switzer. Shall I lend you my best horse?

BLUNTSCHLI. No: damn your horse! thank you all the same, my dear fellow. *(Raina comes in, and hears the next sentence).* I shall fight you on foot. Horseback's too dangerous: I dont want to kill you if I can help it.

RAINA *(hurrying forward anxiously)* I have heard what Captain Bluntschli said, Sergius. You are going to fight. Why? *(Sergius turns away in silence, and goes to the stove, where he stands watching her as she continues, to Bluntschli)* What about?

BLUNTSCHLI. I dont know: he hasnt told me. Better not interfere, dear young lady. No harm will be done: Ive often acted as sword instructor. He wont be able to touch me; and I'll not hurt him. It will save explanations. In the morning I shall be off home; and youll never see me or hear of me again. You and he will then make it up and live happily ever after.

RAINA *(turning away deeply hurt, almost with a sob in her voice)* I never said I wanted to see you again.

SERGIUS *(striding forward)* Ha! That is a confession.

RAINA *(haughtily)* What do you mean?

SERGIUS. You love that man!

RAINA *(scandalized)* Sergius!

SERGIUS. You allow him to make love to you behind my back, just as you treat me as your affianced husband behind his. Bluntschli: you knew our relations; and you deceived me. It is for that that I call you to account, not for having received favors *I* never enjoyed.

BLUNTSCHLI *(jumping up indignantly)* Stuff! Rubbish! I have received no favors. Why, the young lady doesnt even know whether I'm married or not.

RAINA *(forgetting herself)* Oh! *(Collapsing on the ottoman)* Are you?

SERGIUS. You see the young lady's concern, Captain Bluntschli. Denial is useless. You have enjoyed the privilege of being received in her own room, late at night——

BLUNTSCHLI *(interrupting him pepperily)* Yes, you blockhead! she received me with a pistol at her head. Your cavalry were at my heels. I'd have blown out her brains if she'd uttered a cry.

SERGIUS *(taken aback)* Bluntschli! Raina: is this true?

RAINA *(rising in wrathful majesty)* Oh, how dare you, how dare you?

BLUNTSCHLI. Apologize, man: apologize. *(He resumes his seat at the table).*

SERGIUS *(with the old measured emphasis, folding his arms)* I n e v e r apologize!

RAINA *(passionately)* This is the doing of that friend of yours, Captain Bluntschli. Is it he who is spreading this horrible story about me. *(She walks about excitedly).*

BLUNTSCHLI. No: he's dead. Burnt alive.

RAINA *(stopping, shocked)* Burnt alive!

BLUNTSCHLI. Shot in the hip in the woodyard. Couldnt drag himself out. Your fellows' shells set the timber on fire and burnt him, with half a dozen other poor devils in the same predicament.

RAINA. How horrible!

SERGIUS. And how ridiculous! Oh, war! war! the dream of patriots and heroes! A fraud, Bluntschli. A hollow sham, like love.

RAINA *(outraged)* Like love! You say that before me!

BLUNTSCHLI. Come, Saranoff: that matter is explained.

SERGIUS. A hollow sham, I say. Would you have come back here if nothing had passed between you except at the muzzle of your pistol? Raina is mistaken about your friend who was burnt. He was not my informant.

RAINA. Who then? *(Suddenly guessing the truth)* Ah, Louka! my maid! my servant! You were with her this morning all that time after—after—Oh, what sort of god is this I have been worshipping! *(He meets her gaze with sardonic enjoyment of her disenchantment. Angered all the more, she goes closer to him, and says, in a lower, intenser tone)* Do you know that I looked out of the window as I went upstairs, to have another sight of my hero; and I saw something I did not understand then. I know now that you were making love to her.

SERGIUS *(with grim humor)* You saw that?

RAINA. Only too well. *(She turns away, and throws herself on the divan under the centre window, quite overcome).*

SERGIUS *(cynically)* Raina: our romance is shattered. Life's a farce.

BLUNTSCHLI *(to Raina, whimsically)* You see: h e ' s found himself out now.

SERGIUS *(going to him)* Bluntschli: I have allowed you to call me a blockhead. You may now call me a coward as well. I refuse to fight you. Do you know why?

BLUNTSCHLI. No; but it doesnt matter. I didnt ask the reason when you cried on; and I dont ask the reason now that you cry off. I'm a professional soldier: I fight when I have to, and am very glad to get out of it when I havnt to. Youre only an amateur: you think fighting's an amusement.

SERGIUS *(sitting down at the table, nose to nose with him)* You shall hear the reason all the same, my professional. The reason is that it takes two men—real men—men of heart, blood and honor—to make a genuine combat. I could no more fight with you than I could make love to an ugly woman. Youve no magnetism: youre not a man: youre a machine.

BLUNTSCHLI *(apologetically)* Quite true, quite true. I always w a s that sort of chap. I'm very sorry.

SERGIUS. Psha!

BLUNTSCHLI. But now that youve found that life i s n t a farce, but something quite sensible and serious, what further obstacle is there to your happiness?

RAINA *(rising)* You are very solicitous about my happiness and his. Do you forget his new l o v e—Louka? It is not you that he must fight now, but his rival, Nicola.

SERGIUS. Rival!! *(bounding half across the room).*

RAINA. Dont you know that theyre engaged?

SERGIUS. Nicola! Are fresh abysses opening? Nicola!!

RAINA *(sarcastically)* A shocking sacrifice, isnt it? Such beauty! such intellect! such modesty! wasted on a middle-aged servant man. Really, Sergius, you cannot stand by and allow such a thing. It would be unworthy of your chivalry.

SERGIUS *(losing all self-control)* Viper! Viper! *(He rushes to and fro, raging).*

BLUNTSCHLI. Look here, Saranoff: youre getting the worst of this.

RAINA *(getting angrier)* Do you realize what he has done, Captain Bluntschli? He has set this girl as a spy on us; and her reward is that he makes love to her.

SERGIUS. False! Monstrous!

RAINA. Monstrous! (*Confronting him*) Do you deny that she told you about Captain Bluntschli being in my room?

SERGIUS. No; but——

RAINA (*interrupting*) Do you deny that you were making love to her when she told you?

SERGIUS. No; but I tell you——

RAINA (*cutting him short contemptuously*) It is unnecessary to tell us anything more. That is quite enough for us. (*She turns away from him and sweeps majestically back to the window*).

BLUNTSCHLI (*quietly, as Sergius, in an agony of mortification, sinks on the ottoman, clutching his averted head between his fists*) I told you you were getting the worst of it, Saranoff.

SERGIUS. Tiger cat!

RAINA (*running excitedly to Bluntschli*) You hear this man calling me names, Captain Bluntschli?

BLUNTSCHLI. What else can he do, dear lady? He must defend himself somehow. Come (*very persuasively*): dont quarrel. What good does it do?

[*Raina, with a gasp, sits down on the ottoman, and after a vain effort to look vexedly at Bluntschli, falls a victim to her sense of humor, and actually leans back babyishly against the writhing shoulder of Sergius*].

SERGIUS. Engaged to Nicola! Ha! ha! Ah well, Bluntschli, you are right to take this huge imposture of a world coolly.

RAINA (*quaintly to Bluntschli, with an intuitive guess at his state of mind*) I daresay you think us a couple of grown-up babies, dont you?

SERGIUS (*grinning savagely*) He does: he does. Swiss civilization nursetending Bulgarian barbarism, eh?

BLUNTSCHLI (*blushing*) Not at all, I assure you. I'm only very glad to get you two quieted. There! there! let's be pleasant and talk it over in a friendly way. Where is this other young lady?

RAINA. Listening at the door, probably.

SERGIUS (*shivering as if a bullet had struck him, and speaking with quiet but deep indignation*) I

will prove that that, at least, is a calumny.[4] (*He goes with dignity to the door and opens it. A yell of fury bursts from him as he looks out. He darts into the passage, and returns dragging in Louka, whom he flings violently against the table, exclaiming*) Judge her, Bluntschli. You, the cool impartial man: judge the eavesdropper.

[*Louka stands her ground, proud and silent*].

BLUNTSCHLI (*shaking his head*) I mustnt judge her. I once listened myself outside a tent when there was a mutiny brewing. It's all a question of the degree of provocation. My life was at stake.

LOUKA. My love was at stake. I am not ashamed.

RAINA (*contemptuously*) Your love! Your curiosity, you mean.

LOUKA (*facing her and retorting her contempt with interest*) My love, stronger than anything y o u can feel, even for your chocolate cream soldier.

SERGIUS (*with quick suspicion, to Louka*) What does that mean?

LOUKA (*fiercely*) It means——

SERGIUS (*interrupting her slightingly*) Oh, I remember: the ice pudding. A paltry taunt, girl!

[*Major Petkoff enters, in his shirtsleeves*].

PETKOFF. Excuse my shirtsleeves, gentlemen. Raina: somebody has been wearing that coat of mine: I'll swear it. Somebody with a differently shaped back. It's all burst open at the sleeve. Your mother is mending it. I wish she'd make haste: I shall catch cold. (*He looks more attentively at them*). Is anything the matter?

RAINA. No. (*She sits down at the stove, with a tranquil air*).

SERGIUS. Oh no. (*He sits down at the end of the table, as at first*).

---

4. **calumny,** lie.

BLUNTSCHLI (*who is already seated*) Nothing. Nothing.

PETKOFF (*sitting down on the ottoman in his old place*) Thats all right. (*He notices Louka*). Anything the matter, Louka?

LOUKA. No, sir.

PETKOFF (*genially*) T h a t s all right. (*He sneezes*). Go and ask your mistress for my coat, like a good girl, will you?

[*Nicola enters with the coat. Louka makes a pretence of having business in the room by taking the little table with the hookah away to the wall near the windows*].

RAINA (*rising quickly as she sees the coat on Nicola's arm*) Here it is, papa. Give it to me, Nicola; and do you put some more wood on the fire. (*She takes the coat, and brings it to the Major, who stands up to put it on. Nicola attends to the fire*).

PETKOFF (*to Raina, teasing her affectionately*) Aha! Going to be very good to poor old papa just for one day after his return from the wars, eh?

RAINA (*with solemn reproach*) Ah, how can you say that to me, father?

PETKOFF. Well, well, only a joke, little one. Come: give me a kiss. (*She kisses him*). Now give me the coat.

RAINA. No: I am going to put it on for you. Turn your back. (*He turns his back and feels behind him with his arms for the sleeves. She dexterously takes the photograph from the pocket and throws it on the table before Bluntschli, who covers it with a sheet of paper under the very nose of Sergius, who looks on amazed, with his suspicions roused in the highest degree. She then helps Petkoff on with his coat*). There, dear! Now are you comfortable?

PETKOFF. Quite, little love. Thanks. (*He sits down; and Raina returns to her seat near the stove*). Oh, by the bye, Ive found something funny. Whats the meaning of this? (*He puts his hand into the picked pocket*). Eh? Hallo! (*He tries the other pocket*). Well, I could have sworn . . . ! (*Much puzzled he tries the breast pocket*). I wonder . . . (*trying the original pocket*) Where can it . . . ? (*He rises, exclaiming*) Your mother's taken it!

RAINA (*very red*) Taken what?

PETKOFF. Your photograph, with the inscription: "Raina, to her Chocolate Cream Soldier: a Souvenir." Now you know theres something more in this than meets the eye; and I'm going to find it out. (*Shouting*) Nicola!

NICOLA (*coming to him*) Sir!

PETKOFF. Did you spoil any pastry of Miss Raina's this morning?

NICOLA. You heard Miss Raina say that I did, sir.

PETKOFF. I know that, you idiot. Was it true?

NICOLA. I am sure Miss Raina is incapable of saying anything that is not true, sir.

PETKOFF. Are you? Then I'm not. (*Turning to the others*) Come: do you think I dont see it all? (*He goes to Sergius, and slaps him on the shoulder*). Sergius: y o u r e the chocolate cream soldier, arnt you?

SERGIUS (*starting up*) I! A chocolate cream soldier! Certainly not.

PETKOFF. Not! (*He looks at them. They are all very serious and very conscious*). Do you mean to tell me that Raina sends things like that to other men?

SERGIUS (*enigmatically*) The world is not such an innocent place as we used to think, Petkoff.

BLUNTSCHLI (*rising*) It's all right, Major. I'm the chocolate cream soldier. (*Petkoff and Sergius are equally astonished*). The gracious young lady saved my life by giving me chocolate creams when I was starving: shall I ever forget their flavour! My late friend Stolz told you the story at Pirot. I was the fugitive.

PETKOFF. You! (*He gasps*). Sergius: do you remember how those two women went on this morning when we mentioned it? (*Sergius smiles cynically. Petkoff confronts Raina severely.*) Y o u r e a nice young woman, arnt you?

Raina takes the photograph from Petkoff's pocket and gives it to Bluntschli.

RAINA *(bitterly)* Major Saranoff has changed his mind. And when I wrote that on the photograph, I did not know that Captain Bluntschli was married.

BLUNTSCHLI *(startled into vehement protest)* I'm n o t married.

RAINA *(with deep reproach)* You said you were.

BLUNTSCHLI. I did not. I positively did not. I never was married in my life.

PETKOFF *(exasperated)* Raina: will you kindly inform me, if I am not asking too much, which of these gentlemen you are engaged to?

RAINA. To neither of them. T h i s young lady *(introducing Louka, who faces them all proudly)* is the object of Major Saranoff's affections at present.

PETKOFF. Louka! Are you mad, Sergius? Why, this girl's engaged to Nicola.

NICOLA. I beg your pardon, sir. There is a mistake. Louka is not engaged to me.

PETKOFF. Not engaged to you, you scoundrel! Why, you had twenty-five levas from me on the day of your betrothal; and she had that gilt bracelet from Miss Raina.

NICOLA *(with cool unction)* We gave it out so, sir. But it was only to give Louka protection. She had a soul above her station; and I have been no more than her confidential servant. I intend, as you know, sir, to set up a shop later on in Sofia; and I look forward to her custom and recommendation should she marry into the nobility. *(He goes out with impressive discretion, leaving them all staring after him).*

PETKOFF *(breaking the silence)* Well, I a m . . . hm!

SERGIUS. This is either the finest heroism or

the most crawling baseness. Which is it, Bluntschli?

BLUNTSCHLI. Never mind whether it's heroism or baseness. Nicola's the ablest man Ive met in Bulgaria. I'll make him manager of a hotel if he can speak French and German.

LOUKA (*suddenly breaking out at Sergius*) I have been insulted by everyone here. Y o u set them the example. You owe me an apology.

[*Sergius, like a repeating clock of which the spring has been touched, immediately begins to fold his arms*].

BLUNTSCHLI (*before he can speak*) It's no use. He never apologizes.

LOUKA. Not to you, his equal and his enemy. To me, his poor servant, he will not refuse to apologize.

SERGIUS (*approvingly*) You are right. (*He bends his knee in his grandest manner*) Forgive me.

LOUKA. I forgive you. (*She timidly gives him her hand, which he kisses*). That touch makes me your affianced wife.

SERGIUS (*springing up*) Ah! I forgot that.

LOUKA (*coldly*) You can withdraw if you like.

SERGIUS. Withdraw! Never! You belong to me. (*He puts his arm around her*).

[*Catherine comes in and finds Louka in Sergius's arms, with all the rest gazing at them in bewildered astonishment*].

CATHERINE. What does this mean?

[*Sergius releases Louka*].

PETKOFF. Well, my dear, it appears that Sergius is going to marry Louka instead of Raina. (*She is about to break out indignantly at him: he stops her by exclaiming testily*) Dont blame me: Ive nothing to do with it. (*He retreats to the stove*).

CATHERINE. Marry Louka! Sergius: you are bound by your word to us!

SERGIUS (*folding his arms*) Nothing binds me.

BLUNTSCHLI (*much pleased by this piece of common sense*) Saranoff: your hand. My congratulations. These heroics of yours have their practical side after all. (*To Louka*) Gracious young lady: the best wishes of a good Republican! (*He kisses her hand, to Raina's great disgust, and returns to his seat*).

CATHERINE. Louka: you have been telling stories.

LOUKA. I have done Raina no harm.

CATHERINE (*haughtily*) Raina!

[*Raina, equally indignant, almost snorts at the liberty*].

LOUKA. I have a right to call her Raina: she calls me Louka. I told Major Saranoff she would never marry him if the Swiss gentleman came back.

BLUNTSCHLI (*rising, much surprised*) Hallo!

LOUKA (*turning to Raina*) I thought you were fonder of him than of Sergius. You know best whether I was right.

BLUNTSCHLI. What nonsense! I assure you, my dear Major, my dear Madame, the gracious young lady simply saved my life, nothing else. She never cared two straws for me. Why, bless my heart and soul, look at the young lady and look at me. She, rich, young, beautiful, with her imagination full of fairy princes and noble natures and cavalry charges and goodness knows what! And I, a commonplace Swiss soldier who hardly knows what a decent life is after fifteen years of barracks and battles: a vagabond, a man who has spoiled all his chances in life through an incurably romantic disposition, a man——

SERGIUS (*starting as if a needle had pricked him and interrupting Bluntschli in incredulous amazement*) Excuse me, Bluntschli: w h a t did you say had spoiled your chances in life?

BLUNTSCHLI (*promptly*) An incurably romantic disposition. I ran away from home twice when I was a boy. I went into the army instead of into my father's business. I climbed the balcony of this house when a man of sense would have dived into the nearest cellar. I came sneaking back here to have another look at the young lady when any other man of my age would have sent the coat back——

PETKOFF. My coat!

BLUNTSCHLI. ——yes: thats the coat I mean—would have sent it back and gone quietly home. Do you suppose I am the sort of fellow a young girl falls in love with? Why, look at our ages! I'm thirty-four: I dont suppose the young lady is much over seventeen. (*This estimate produces a marked sensation, all the rest turning and staring at one another. He proceeds innocently*) All that adventure which was life or death to me, was only a schoolgirl's game to her—chocolate creams and hide and seek. Heres the proof! (*He takes the photograph from the table*). Now, I ask you, would a woman who took the affair seriously have sent me this and written on it "Raina, to her Chocolate Cream Soldier: a Souvenir"? (*He exhibits the photograph triumphantly, as if it settled the matter beyond all possibility of refutation*).

PETKOFF. Thats what I was looking for. How the deuce did it get there? (*He comes from the stove to look at it, and sits down on the ottoman*).

BLUNTSCHLI (*to Raina, complacently*) I have put everything right, I hope, gracious young lady.

RAINA (*going to the table to face him*) I quite agree with your account of yourself. You are a romantic idiot. (*Bluntschli is unspeakably taken aback*). Next time, I hope you will know the difference between a schoolgirl of seventeen and a woman of twenty-three.

BLUNTSCHLI (*stupefied*) Twenty-three!

[*Raina snaps the photograph contemptuously from his hand; tears it up; throws the pieces in his face; and sweeps back to her former place*].

SERGIUS (*with grim enjoyment of his rival's discomfiture*) Bluntschli: my one last belief is gone. Your sagacity is a fraud, like everything else. You have less sense than even I!

BLUNTSCHLI (*overwhelmed*) Twenty-three! Twenty-three!! (*He considers*). Hm! (*Swiftly making up his mind and coming to his host*) In that case, Major Petkoff, I beg to propose formally to become a suitor for your daughter's hand, in place of Major Saranoff retired.

RAINA. You dare!

BLUNTSCHLI. If you were twenty-three when you said those things to me this afternoon, I shall take them seriously.

CATHERINE (*loftily polite*) I doubt, sir, whether you quite realize either my daughter's position or that of Major Sergius Saranoff, whose place you propose to take. The Petkoffs and the Saranoffs are known as the richest and most important families in the country. Our position is almost historical: we can go back for twenty years.

PETKOFF. Oh, never mind that, Catherine. (*To Bluntschli*) We should be most happy, Bluntschli, if it were only a question of your position; but hang it, you know, Raina is accustomed to a very comfortable establishment. Sergius keeps twenty horses.

BLUNTSCHLI. But who wants twenty horses? We're not going to keep a circus.

CATHERINE (*severely*) My daughter, sir, is accustomed to a first-rate stable.

RAINA. Hush, mother: youre making me ridiculous.

BLUNTSCHLI. Oh well, if it comes to a question of an establishment, here goes! (*He darts impetuously to the table; seizes the papers in the blue envelope; and turns to Sergius*). How many horses did you say?

SERGIUS. Twenty, noble Switzer.

BLUNTSCHLI. I have two hundred horses. (*They are amazed*). How many carriages?

SERGIUS. Three.

BLUNTSCHLI. I have seventy. Twenty-four of them will hold twelve inside, besides two on the box, without counting the driver and conductor. How many tablecloths have you?

SERGIUS. How the deuce do I know?

BLUNTSCHLI. Have you four thousand?

SERGIUS. No.

BLUNTSCHLI. I have. I have nine thousand six hundred pairs of sheets and blankets, with two thousand four hundred eider-down quilts. I have ten thousand knives and forks, and the same quantity of dessert spoons. I have three hundred servants. I have six palatial establishments, besides two livery stables, a tea garden, and a private house. I have four medals for distinguished services; I have the rank of an officer and the standing of a gentleman; and I have three native languages. Shew me any man in Bulgaria that can offer as much!

PETKOFF *(with childish awe)* Are you Emperor of Switzerland?

BLUNTSCHLI. My rank is the highest known in Switzerland: I am a free citizen.

CATHERINE. Then, Captain Bluntschli, since you are my daughter's choice——

RAINA *(mutinously)* He's not.

CATHERINE *(ignoring her)*——I shall not stand in the way of her happiness. *(Petkoff is about to speak)* That is Major Petkoff's feeling also.

PETKOFF. Oh, I shall be only too glad. Two hundred horses! Whew!

SERGIUS. What says the lady?

RAINA *(pretending to sulk)* The lady says that he can keep his tablecloths and his omnibuses. I am not here to be sold to the highest bidder. *(She turns her back on him.)*

BLUNTSCHLI. I wont take that answer. I appealed to you as a fugitive, a beggar, and a starving man. You accepted me. You gave me your hand to kiss, your bed to sleep in, and your roof to shelter me.

RAINA. I did not give them to the Emperor of Switzerland.

BLUNTSCHLI. Thats just what I say. *(He catches her by the shoulders and turns her face-to-face with him).* Now tell us whom you did give them to.

RAINA *(succumbing with a shy smile)* To my chocolate cream soldier.

BLUNTSCHLI *(with a boyish laugh of delight)* Thatll do. Thank you. *(He looks at his watch and suddenly becomes businesslike).* Time's up, Major. Youve managed those regiments so well that youre sure to be asked to get rid of some of the infantry of the Timok[5] division. Send them home by way of Lom Palanka.[6] Saranoff: dont get married until I come back: I shall be here punctually at five in the evening on Tuesday fortnight. Gra-

cious ladies *(his heels click)* good evening. *(He makes them a military bow, and goes).*

SERGIUS. What a man! Is he a man?

5. **Timok.** The division is named for a Serbian river, running along the Bulgarian border.
6. **Lom Palanka,** city on the Danube River, which forms the northern border between Bulgaria and Romania.

FOR UNDERSTANDING

1. How does Shaw prepare for the revelations of this final act? Are there any surprises?

2. Shaw ends the play with three couples and an extra man, which is just the situation we found at the beginning of the play. Do we find the new arrangement to be a better one?

FOR INTERPRETATION

Characters in this play are constantly describing each other and even themselves. How valid are the following statements:

1. "Youve no magnetism: youre not a man: youre a machine." (Sergius to Bluntschli, p. 736)

2. "You mean, dont you, that I am the first man that has ever taken you quite seriously?" (Bluntschli to Raina, p. 730)

3. "When you set up your shop you will only be everybody's servant instead of somebody's servant." (Louka to Nicola, p. 732)

4. "Never mind whether it's heroism or baseness. Nicola's the ablest man Ive met in Bulgaria." (Bluntschli about Nicola, p. 740)

5. "Youre like all country girls: you think it's genteel to treat a servant the way I treat a stable-boy." (Nicola to Louka, p. 733)

FOR APPRECIATION

Shaw's long stage directions make clear, among other things, that he is imagining a detailed stage setting which represents the Petkoff house and gardens. Such details, down to the descriptions of tables and chairs, the mention of a "little carpet"

(Act One) and the "square earthenware stove" (Act Three), are part of the nineteenth-century tradition of "realism," or "representational staging." Quite simply, we as the audience are asked to believe in the illusion of reality, to imagine that we are seeing real people in a real place. Such a tradition is quite different from the medieval theater, for instance, where several different locations might be indicated on the stage at the same time, or from the Elizabethan theater, which presented essentially a bare, unlocalized stage that was always the stage, no matter whether the scene was "a barren heath" or "Macbeth's castle."

1. Why is Shaw using all of this detail? What is the relationship between this realistic detail and the events of the play? Do you think that the play would work on a bare stage? Why or why not?

2. Consider the use of specific props and costumes in the play. How, for example, do Catherine's clothes characterize her? Think about the two photographs described in the play and how they are used. There are many such details: the revolver, the two coats (Raina's cloak and Petkoff's old coat), the box of chocolate creams, the books in the library, Bluntschli's suitcase, and so on. How does Shaw use them so that they are more than details which imply "the real world"?

COMPOSITION

The last line of the play, "What a man! Is he a man?", allows a number of different inflections; Sergius could sound amazed, impressed, sarcastic, puzzled. Such a line, and its meaning, raises a central question for the play: what does it mean to be a man? What are the standards by which we judge and evaluate other people? This question also is central to Shakespeare's *Macbeth*. One thinks of Macbeth's line, "I dare do all that may become a man. / Who dares do more is none" (I.7), and of Macduff's statement, "I must also feel it like a man" (IV.3), plus a number of other comments.

Chose one of the following topics.

1. Write an essay in which you explore the differences between the idea of manhood in *Macbeth* and in *Arms and the Man*. How are these differences important in creating the different standards of value in the two plays?

2. Write an essay in which you take off from *Arms and the Man* and explore your own ideas about standards for evaluating what is worthwhile in other human beings. Choose a statement from the play with which you can agree, or disagree, and use it as a starting point.

COMPOSITION WORKSHOP

THE FINAL DRAFT

Writing an introduction and conclusion for your research paper becomes a relatively simple matter once the body of the paper begins to approach its final form. The introduction for most papers on literary topics will supply background information —usually a brief biographical sketch of an author and/or a summary of a work by that author. The conclusion is generally a straightforward summary of the paper's arguments. Both the introduction and conclusion will, of course, need to be revised before you reach the final draft stage.

Once you feel reasonably confident that you have stated your arguments in the best possible form and arranged them in the most logical order, it is a good idea to put your paper aside for a few days. This will enable you to approach your work with a fresh eye and, thereby, catch errors in spelling, punctuation, and mechanics that you might have otherwise missed. It is also recommended that you have someone else read over what you have done before you plunge into the final draft: You can never tell when a second pair of eyes will "see" problems that escaped your attention.

Now you are prepared to set your paper down in its final form, complete with footnotes and bibliography. If possible, you should type your final draft or, once it is written, have someone else type it. In any case, be sure to leave wide margins on either side and at the top and bottom of each page. Use one side of each sheet of paper only, and skip every other line or, if you are typing, double-space. (Standard margin width is 1¼ inches on the left and 1 inch everywhere else, but you may wish to discuss the particulars with your teacher.) For quotations that will run longer than five typed lines, indent and do not skip lines or double-space.

FOOTNOTE FORM

Most of the information you will need to write footnotes is already there on your bibliography cards. That information includes the name of the author, title of the source, page number (or numbers) in the source on which the borrowed matter was found, the place of publication, the name of the publisher, and the year of publication. Be sure to leave ample space at the bottom of a page for all the footnotes that will appear there. Footnote numbers within the text of your paper are written (or typed) slightly above the line and immediately after the quote or borrowed idea.

On page 745 are the standard forms for many varieties of footnotes. Note that in each case the author's name is presented first-name-first. Note also that each footnote is preceded by a number that corresponds to the one used in the text of your paper for that source.

Once a source has been fully indentified in the paper, it is not necessary to identify it fully again in subsequent footnotes. Only the author's name and the page reference need to be supplied:

11
Houghton 66.

If you are using several sources by the same author, add a shortened form of the title:

11
Houghton, *Victorian Mind* 66.

BIBLIOGRAPHY FORM

After the final draft of the paper has been prepared with all of the footnotes numbered consecutively throughout, you assemble the paper's final bibliography. Again, all of the information needed can be found on your 3 × 5-inch bibliography cards. If you followed the format suggested in the Composition Workshop in Unit II (see page 154), then most of the work will be done. All that is left is to arrange the sources alphabetically by author's last names. Note that when you have more than one work by the same author, the works are arranged alphabetically by titles, and the authors' name in second and later citations is replaced by a long dash. Anonymous works are listed alphabetically according to the first word in their title.

The only task left to be completed now is

making up a title page for your paper. This should include the paper's title, your name, and any other information your teacher instructs you to include, such as your class and date. Specific instructions as to how precisely this is to be handled will be provided by your teacher.

Along with the final draft of your paper, you will also want to include your final outline. Be sure, finally, that the pages of your paper are numbered consecutively (beginning with the second page).

For appearance, as well as protection, you may wish to place your finished paper in a binder.

ASSIGNMENT

Write the first draft of your paper's introduction and conclusion. Then revise the entire paper. Prepare the final draft of your paper, including footnotes and a final bibliography. Add a title page and an outline, and number the pages of your paper consecutively.

Standard footnote for a book:	1 W. E. Houghton, <u>The Victorian Frame of Mind</u> (New Haven: Yale University Press, 1957) 31-43.
Book with a subtitle:	2 Alice Griffin, <u>Rebels and Lovers: Shakespeare's Young Heroes and Heroines</u> (New York: New York University Press, 1976) 79.
Book with several authors:	3 T. S. Eliot and Aldous Huxley, <u>Three Critical Essays on Modern English Poetry</u> (London: Folcroft, 1973) 106-109.
Book compiled by editor:	4 Norman Rabkin, ed., <u>Approaches to Shakespeare</u> (New York: McGraw-Hill, 1964) 9-10.
Work with several volumes:	5 G. B. Harrison, <u>Major British Writers</u>, 2 vols. (New York: Harcourt, Brace & Jovanovich, 1959) 2: 28.
Book edited by other than author:	6 Charles Dickens, <u>Hard Times</u>, ed. Robert Donald Spector (New York: Bantam Books, 1964) 200-215.
Standard entry for an article:	7 W. E. Peck, "The Biographical Element in the Novels of Mary Shelley," <u>Publications of the Modern Language Association</u> 36 (1923): 87.
Encyclopedia article:	8 "Symbol," <u>Encyclopaedia Britannica</u>, 1974 ed.
Unsigned newspaper article:	9 "Albee's Powerful New Play," <u>Allandale Times</u> 17 June 1979: A3.
Article in a collection:	10 Honor M. V. Matthews, "Character and Symbol in Macbeth," <u>Approaches to Macbeth</u>, ed. Jay L. Halio (Belmont, California: Wadsworth, 1966) 89.

Spencer often returned to the traditional Christian subject matter of the medieval artist, but he treated it from his own unique, modern perspective.

ST. FRANCIS AND THE BIRDS
Stanley Spencer
The Tate Gallery, London

Modern Literature

1901–

THE BACKGROUND TO MODERN LITERATURE

Queen Victoria died, after sixty-four years on the throne, in 1901. The opening of a new century, greeted with such foreboding by Thomas Hardy (see page 690) in his poem "The Darkling Thrush," seemed at first to change little in British literature and life. Victoria's successor, Edward VII, was weak and undistinguished as a ruler. The years before World War I, the Edwardian Age, bring to mind a picture of country house parties, gentlemen in blazers, women in soft pastel dresses, and croquet played on green lawns. Such a picture of society appears in the novels of the American expatriate Henry James and even in James Joyce (see page 890), where it was used as a backdrop for the characters' inner experiences. Certain reforms in England encouraged the spread of literacy, and the ideas of socialism gained some support with the rise of the Labour Party. Internationally, however, British imperial policy continued much as before—with the exception that Australia, New Zealand, and South Africa were granted independence.

A New Century

Yet the apparent continuity with Victorianism masked a deep-seated revolt against Victorian attitudes. People's belief in human perfectibility was supplanted by uncertainty and doubt. The self-confident Victorian view that "all is right with the world" was opposed by the pessimism of such writers as Thomas Hardy, Arnold Bennett, and John Galsworthy, who offered a dark vision of the drab lives of ordinary people. Even George Bernard Shaw and G. K. Chesterton attacked with irony and humor the conservatism and complacency of the Victorians.

Uncertainty and Doubt

World War I was the social catastrophe which crystallized these feelings of revolt and led to a distinctively "modern" literature. But some years before the War, two writers of the Victorian period had a profound influence on those who followed. One was a novelist; the other a poet. Samuel Butler (1835–1902) issued a clarion call against the old Victorian values in his novel *The Way of All Flesh,* which was published the year after his death. In this novel he told of his experiences growing up in a family dominated by a bigoted Victorian clergyman. Butler's book spawned a whole generation of novels on a

World War I

Samuel Butler

Our century is increasingly an urban world. Here Lowry shows a microcosm of England in the Twentieth Century.

COMING OUT OF SCHOOL
L.S. Lowry
The Tate Gallery, London
Courtesy of Mrs. Carol Ann Danes

similar theme, from Somerset Maugham's *Of Human Bondage* to James Joyce's *A Portrait of the Artist as a Young Man* and Evelyn Waugh's *Brideshead Revisited.*

Gerard Manley Hopkins

A second Victorian who powerfully affected modern writers was the poet Gerard Manley Hopkins (see page 839), a Roman Catholic priest whose small body of verse was not published until 1918. Unlike Butler, whose theme proved inspiring to modern writers, it was Hopkins' style that influenced the new poets. He wrote of his own religious experiences through detailed descriptions of the natural world, but in sprung rhythm derived from Old English that was meant to be heard rather than read. His peculiar syntax and unexpected metaphors have become almost the hallmarks of modern poetry. William Butler Yeats (see page 843), T. S. Eliot (see page 852), Dylan Thomas (see page 878), Philip Larkin (see page 882), and Ted Hughes (see page 884)—though very different from one another—all show evidence of Hopkins's influence in their style.

WORLD WAR I AND MODERNISM

With the outbreak of war in Europe in 1914, the factions in British society forgot their differences and united against Germany and her allies. The English public expected a quick, decisive victory. But the war was different from any that had been fought in Europe. It dragged on for four long years, killing some eight and a half million young men. Wilfred Owen (page 860) and Alice Meynell (page 861) offered powerful testimony in their poetry to the horrors of trench warfare. The Great War, as it was called, shattered forever the confident, Victorian outlook and put an end to a whole way of life. In the ruins of what T. S. Eliot called the "waste land," there were left only disillusionment, instability, and an even more bitter sense of revolt.

Owen and Meynell

From the cataclysm of the war, there occurred one of those rare revolutions in the arts—not only in England, but all across Europe and America. The French Revolution of 1789 gave powerful impetus to

Revolution in the Arts

Henry Moore is probably the most renowned contemporary sculptor. His figures seem to flow organically in elemental shapes as he explores spatial relationships.

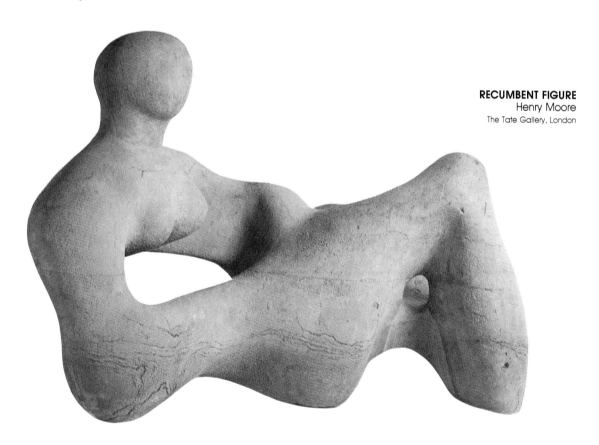

RECUMBENT FIGURE
Henry Moore
The Tate Gallery, London

Much of modern sculpture is abstract, perhaps to force the viewer to consider the fundamental elements of three dimensional space.

TWO FIGURES
Barbara Hepworth
The Tate Gallery, London

Modernism

Romanticism; World War I further encouraged a diverse movement which we call modernism. Even though the first modernists wrote and painted and composed nearly a century ago, the name has stuck.

Eliot and Yeats

In poetry, T.S. Eliot and William Butler Yeats rejected the fluent techniques and conventional themes of Victorian verse. They sought a new precision of thought and feeling in poetry and imported into their verse a diction which had previously been thought suitable only for prose. Yeats boldly experimented with folk themes, complex symbolism, and mysticism. Eliot, who was also a learned and sensitive literary critic, brilliantly exploited the technique of allusion and wrote much of his work in free verse (lines of no set length). The new poetry was often deliberately discordant and fragmentary; it was up to the reader to supply the connections between images and to fill out the sequence of thought. Modernist poetry often mirrored the ugliness and alienation which the poets saw around them in the world.

This interior view of the Daily Express Building is an excellent example of
Art-Deco, a highly decorative, angular style of art popular in the 1930s.

DAILY EXPRESS BUILDING,
LONDON
Sir Owen Williams, Architect
Photo: Angelo Hornak Photograph Library

In prose, the novel continued to be the dominant form of imaginative writing. Among the masters of the modern novel were Joseph Conrad (see page 758), D. H. Lawrence (see page 783), Virginia Woolf (see page 777), and James Joyce. The output of twentieth-century novelists has been so diverse in both subject matter and style that it is important to examine their works in some detail. (See also the separate essay on the modern novel, pages 886–889).

Conrad,
Lawrence, Woolf
and Joyce

Throughout our century there has been an emphasis on realism in the novel, but the concepts of reality and realism have changed. Early in the century, such writers as Arnold Bennett and John Galsworthy depicted a physical or *environmental realism,* almost like that of a photograph. A second kind of realism was *social realism:* writers such as D. H. Lawrence and H. G. Wells focused on the extent to which social classes and the social order influenced a character's development.

Bennett and
Galsworthy

H.G. Wells

*Psychological
Realism*

But it was *psychological realism* that became the dominant and most productive trend in modern prose and poetry. Psychology as a separate science came into being at the beginning of the century when Sigmund Freud (1856–1939) created a whole new view of the human psyche. The theory that a conscious and an unconscious mind coexisted within the same person, and that they were often in conflict, powerfully affected modernist fiction. With new precision, writers started to explore the dreams, memories, and conflicting drives of their characters. Joseph Conrad's novels and stories, often focused on characters at moments of great crisis in an alien environment, powerfully suggested the struggle between inner confusion and outward order. Conrad was also one of the first great novelists to exploit the technique of *ambiguity*, forcing both his characters and his readers to consider two or more different interpretations of the same phenomena.

*Stream of
Consciousness*

The drive toward psychological realism also led to one of the most important innovations in twentieth-century style: the technique of *stream of consciousness*. All of us recognize that at any moment of consciousness, we are processing hundreds of thoughts per minute, some related, some seemingly disconnected. To capture this reality, modernist writers have attempted to record the inner thinking as it actually takes place. Hence Virginia Woolf, one of the pioneers in this style, traced the random thoughts of family members on vacation in her novel *To the Lighthouse* (1927). In *Ulysses* (1922) James Joyce

Ulysses

revealed what goes on in the minds of his characters during a single day in the city of Dublin. The thoughts and events trigger memories which occur in no logical time sequence—and are often recorded in garbled syntax. Joyce's words are sometimes foreign, or sometimes pieces of words, or sometimes words of his own creation.

*Auden,
MacNeice, Thomas
Larkin, Orwell,
and Lessing*

Modernism in prose and poetry was well established by the 1930s. Since that time, at least two further generations of poets and novelists have contributed significantly to the literature of our century. Among the poets, we may single out W. H. Auden (see page 873), Louis MacNeice (see page 876), Dylan Thomas (see page 878), and Philip Larkin (see page 882); among the prose writers, George Orwell (see page 804), Graham Greene (see page 817), Frank O'Connor (see page 810), and Doris Lessing (see page 825). The world-wide Depression of the 1930s, World War II, and the uneasy post-war years further deepened the pessimism of many of these writers. But even amidst the grim realities of war, racism, and poverty, contemporary literature has found things to celebrate about the human spirit.

READING MODERN LITERATURE

When we approach modern literature, music, and painting, some of us are likely to think of it as complex and hard to understand. We are still

Heron's "portrait" of the poet T.S. Eliot was clearly influenced by Picasso.
In the cubist manner he attempts to show angles of his subject simultaneously.

T.S. ELIOT
Patrick Heron
National Portrait Gallery, London

Modern painters as well as poets (see pages 859-863) have made their statements about the two greatest wars in history.

WE ARE MAKING A NEW WORLD
Paul Nash
Hamlyn Group, Picture Library

The Shock of the New

too close in time to much contemporary literature to gain a proper perspective. And artists are often ahead of their time in the sensitivity of their insight and in the techniques which they use to present that insight to an audience. The result is what one art critic has recently called "the shock of the new." Nevertheless, in reading twentieth-century literature, we should remember that many of the "classic" artists seemed equally shocking in their time. The music of Beethoven jarred on the ears of his contemporaries; the painting of the nineteenth-century French Impressionists was denounced; the poetry of the early Romantics was scorned.

Age-old Subjects

And when we consider the themes of modern British literature, we recognize many of the age-old subjects that have well served writers of all periods: the human emotions of love, guilt, courage, and fear; the search for identity and dignity; the struggle for order amidst chaos; the quest for meaning in life; man's relationship to God. Perhaps the most intriguing aspect of twentieth-century literature is that poetry and

*David Hockney is a popular, contemporary paint-
er who is also an accomplished stage and costume
designer. What does this painting suggest about
the quality of modern life?*

A BIGGER SPLASH 1967
David Hockney
Acrylic on Canvas
96x96"/244x244 cm
© David Hockney 1967

fiction continue to explore these major themes in innovative, unexpected ways. The barriers between poetry and prose have largely broken
down, so that poetry can address a far broader variety of subject
matter, and chapters in novels often read like prose poems. Although
this blurring of traditional distinctions may initially disturb us, it
conforms to the purpose of many modern writers to shake us out of
comfortable preconceptions and to force us to address ourselves and
the world with fresh insight. The modern writers have challenged
(often fruitfully) some deeply entrenched assumptions about the form
of literature: for example, that poetry needs to rhyme, or that novels
should be focused on a narrative plot. The novelists and poets of our
century have taken the whole world, and all that is in it, as their
subjects. As the contemporary poet Thom Gunn says, in the opening
lines of "Confessions of the Life Artist":

*Blurring of
Traditional
Distinctions*

"Whatever is here, it is
  material for my art."

The Modern Age

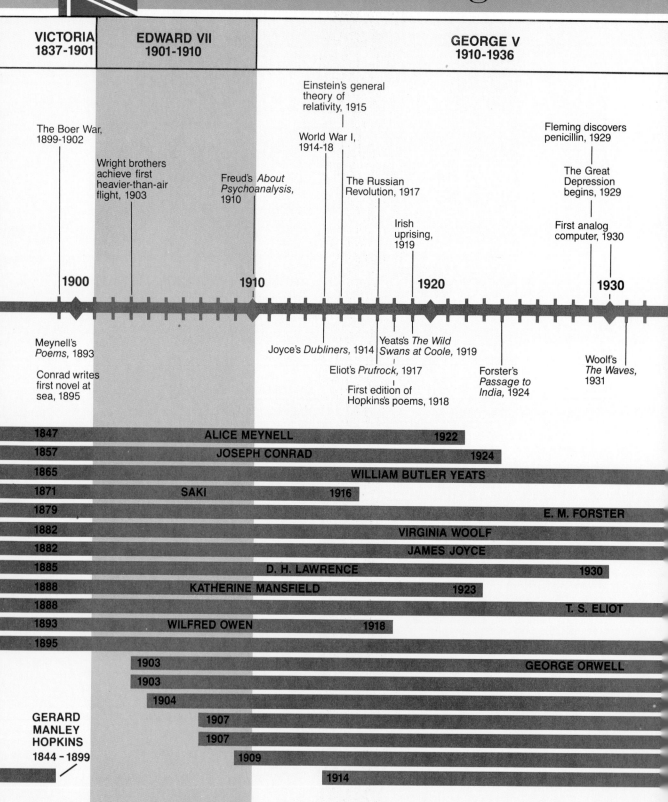

VICTORIA 1837-1901	EDWARD VII 1901-1910	GEORGE V 1910-1936

Einstein's general theory of relativity, 1915

The Boer War, 1899-1902

Fleming discovers penicillin, 1929

Wright brothers achieve first heavier-than-air flight, 1903

World War I, 1914-18

The Great Depression begins, 1929

Freud's *About Psychoanalysis*, 1910

The Russian Revolution, 1917

First analog computer, 1930

Irish uprising, 1919

1900   **1910**   **1920**   **1930**

Meynell's *Poems*, 1893

Joyce's *Dubliners*, 1914

Yeats's *The Wild Swans at Coole*, 1919

Conrad writes first novel at sea, 1895

Eliot's *Prufrock*, 1917

Forster's *Passage to India*, 1924

Woolf's *The Waves*, 1931

First edition of Hopkins's poems, 1918

1847	ALICE MEYNELL	1922
1857	JOSEPH CONRAD	1924
1865	WILLIAM BUTLER YEATS	
1871	SAKI	1916
1879	E. M. FORSTER	
1882	VIRGINIA WOOLF	
1882	JAMES JOYCE	
1885	D. H. LAWRENCE	1930
1888	KATHERINE MANSFIELD	1923
1888	T. S. ELIOT	
1893	WILFRED OWEN	1918
1895		

1903   GEORGE ORWELL

1903

1904

1907

1907

1909

1914

GERARD MANLEY HOPKINS

1844 – 1899

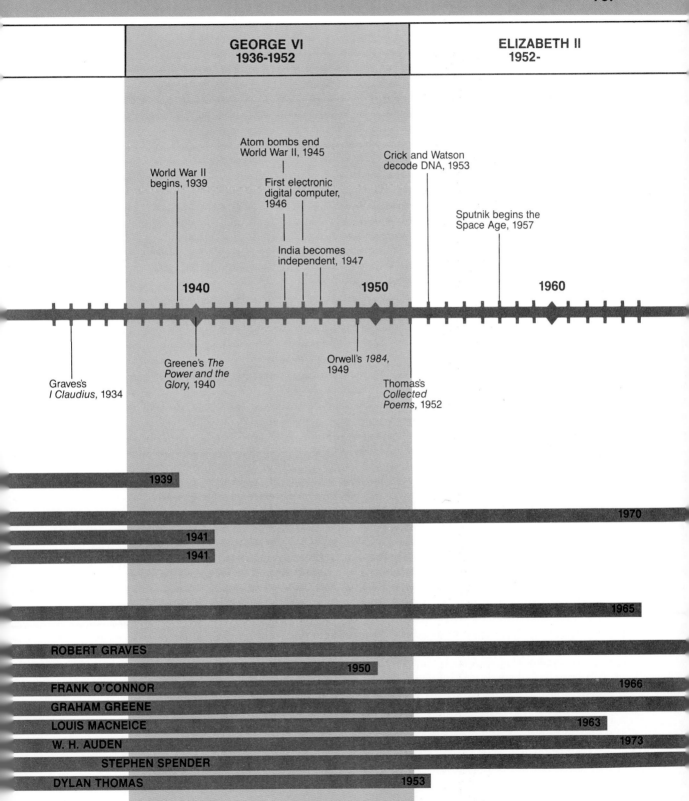

	GEORGE VI 1936-1952	ELIZABETH II 1952-

Atom bombs end
World War II, 1945

Crick and Watson
decode DNA, 1953

World War II
begins, 1939

First electronic
digital computer,
1946

Sputnik begins the
Space Age, 1957

India becomes
independent, 1947

1940

1950

1960

Greene's *The
Power and the
Glory*, 1940

Orwell's *1984*,
1949

Graves's
I Claudius, 1934

Thomas's
*Collected
Poems*, 1952

1939

1970

1941

1941

1965

ROBERT GRAVES

1950

FRANK O'CONNOR

1966

GRAHAM GREENE

LOUIS MACNEICE

1963

W. H. AUDEN

1973

STEPHEN SPENDER

DYLAN THOMAS

1953

Joseph Conrad   1857–1924

Joseph Conrad is considered one of the greatest of English novelists, yet, strangely enough, he did not even see England until he was twenty-one years old. He signed on as an ordinary seaman on a small English coastal vessel sailing between Newcastle and Lowestoft and learned English in six voyages between these two ports. It is amazing that eventually he would achieve such mastery of the language.

Born in the Ukraine as Teodor Jozef Konrad Korzeniowski, he was the son of Polish intellectuals who had been exiled to northern Russia for supporting the Polish freedom movement. Orphaned at ten, he returned to Poland to live with relatives. At fifteen, he announced his passionate desire to go to sea, which was fulfilled two years later. For the next four years, he sailed on French merchant ships; in 1878 he arrived in Lowestoft. In 1886 he received an English master's certificate and one year later became a naturalized English citizen. Following his first command in 1888, he took a steamboat up the Congo River. This almost nightmarish trip provided the material for his novel *Heart of Darkness*. These experiences of his life at sea, and his observations on his voyages to Africa and Malaysia, gave him the material from which he fashioned some of his greatest novels and stories.

While still at sea, Conrad began to write his first novel, *Almayer's Folly* (1895), a tale set in the Malay peninsula. Writing soon became more important to him than seafaring, and he left the sea to settle down in England. During the first years of his writing career, Conrad worked with enormous energy, producing the masterpieces which made his reputation: *The Nigger of the "Narcissus"* (1897), *Lord Jim* (1900), *Youth* (1902), *Heart of Darkness* (1902), and *Nostromo* (1904), considered by many to be his greatest work.

Conrad's view of life was large and tragic. He once compared life to "a walk on a thin crust of barely cooled lava which at any moment might break and let the unwary sink into fiery depths." The greater part of his writing is on the theme

JOSEPH CONRAD
Walter Tittle (1924)
National Portrait Gallery, London

of man against himself. Hence, he usually isolates the character in an exotic place far from the ordinary world so that he can be put in an extraordinary situation of self-confrontation. Usually he faces an evil on the outside which mixes with the evil within. Conrad is sometimes called a psychologist, but he was in his own view a moral explorer seeking to find the true nature of individuals.

Conrad received little recognition at the time he was doing his best work. When he finally achieved public approval, he was offered a knighthood, which he refused. He himself has set forth his aim as a writer in these words: ". . . by the power of the written word to make you hear, to make you feel—and, before all, . . . to make you see."

THE LAGOON

The white man, leaning with both arms over the roof of the little house in the stern of the boat, said to the steersman:

"We will pass the night in Arsat's clearing. It is late."

The Malay only grunted, and went on looking fixedly at the river. The white man rested his chin on his crossed arms and gazed at the wake of the boat. At the end of the straight avenue of forests cut by the intense glitter of the river, the sun appeared unclouded and dazzling, poised low over the water that shone smoothly like a band of metal. The forests, somber and dull, stood motionless and silent on each side of the broad stream. At the foot of big, towering trees, trunkless nipa palms rose from the mud of the bank, in bunches of leaves enormous and heavy, that hung unstirring over the brown swirl of eddies. In the stillness of the air every tree, every leaf, every bough, every tendril of creeper and every petal of minute blossoms seemed to have been bewitched into an immobility perfect and final. Nothing moved on the river but the eight paddles that rose flashing regularly, dipped together with a single splash, while the steersman swept right and left with a periodic and sudden flourish of his blade describing a glinting semicircle above his head. The churned-up water frothed alongside with a confused murmur. And the white man's canoe, advancing upstream in the short-lived disturbance of its own making, seemed to enter the portals of a land from which the very memory of motion had forever departed.

From TALES OF UNREST by Joseph Conrad, published in 1898.

The white man, turning his back upon the setting sun, looked along the empty and broad expanse of the sea reach. For the last three miles of its course the wandering, hesitating river, as if enticed irresistibly by the freedom of an open horizon, flows straight into the sea, flows straight to the east—to the east that harbors both light and darkness. Astern of the boat the repeated call of some bird, a cry discordant and feeble, skipped along over the smooth water and lost itself before it could reach the other shore in the breathless silence of the world.

The steersman dug his paddle into the stream, and held hard with stiffened arms, his body thrown forward. The water gurgled aloud; and suddenly the long straight reach seemed to pivot on its center, the forests swung in a semicircle, and the slanting beams of sunset touched the broadside of the canoe with a fiery glow, throwing the slender and distorted shadows of its crew upon the streaked glitter of the river. The white man turned to look ahead. The course of the boat had been altered at right angles to the stream, and the carved dragonhead on its prow was pointing now at a gap in the fringing bushes of the bank. It glided through, brushing the overhanging twigs, and disappeared from the river like some slim and amphibious creature leaving the water for its lair in the forests.

The narrow creek was like a ditch: tortuous, fabulously deep; filled with gloom under the thin strip of pure and shining blue of the heaven. Immense trees soared up, invisible behind the festooned draperies of creepers. Here and there, near the glistening blackness of the water, a twisted root of some tall tree showed among the tracery of small ferns, black and dull, writhing and motionless, like an arrested snake. The short words of the paddlers reverberated loudly between the thick and somber walls of vegetation. Darkness oozed out from between the trees, through the tangled maze of the creepers, from behind the great fantastic and unstirring leaves; the darkness, mysterious and invincible; the darkness scented and poisonous of impenetrable forests.

The men poled in the shoaling water. The creek broadened, opening out into a wide sweep of a stagnant lagoon. The forests receded from the marshy bank, leaving a level strip of bright green, reedy grass to frame the reflected blueness of the sky. A fleecy pink cloud drifted high above, trailing the delicate coloring of its image under the floating leaves and the silver blossoms of the lotus. A little house, perched on high piles, appeared black in the distance. Near it, two tall nibong palms that seemed to have come out of the forests in the background leaned slightly over the ragged roof, with a suggestion of sad tenderness and care in the droop of their leafy and soaring heads.

The steersman, pointing with his paddle, said, "Arsat is there. I see his canoe fast between the piles."

The polers ran along the sides of the boat glancing over their shoulders at the end of the day's journey. They would have preferred to spend the night somewhere else than on this lagoon of weird aspect and ghostly reputation. Moreover, they disliked Arsat, first as a stranger, and also because he who repairs a ruined house, and dwells in it, proclaims that he is not afraid to live amongst the spirits that haunt the places abandoned by mankind. Such a man can disturb the course of fate by glances or words; while his familiar ghosts are not easy to propitiate[1] by casual wayfarers upon whom they long to wreak the malice of their human master. White men care not for such things, being unbelievers and in league with the Father of Evil, who leads them unharmed through the invisible dangers of this world. To the warnings of the righteous they oppose an offensive

pretense of disbelief. What is there to be done?

So they thought, throwing their weight on the end of their long poles. The big canoe glided on swiftly, noiselessly, and smoothly, toward Arsat's clearing, till, in a great rattling of poles thrown down, and the loud murmurs of "Allah be praised!" it came with a gentle knock against the crooked piles below the house.

The boatmen with uplifted faces shouted discordantly, "Arsat! O Arsat!" Nobody came. The white man began to climb the rude ladder giving access to the bamboo platform before the house. The juragan[2] of the boat said sulkily, "We will cook in the sampan,[3] and sleep on the water."

"Pass my blankets and the basket," said the white man curtly.

He knelt on the edge of the platform to receive the bundle. Then the boat shoved off, and the white man, standing up, confronted Arsat, who had come out through the low door of his hut. He was a man young, powerful, with broad chest and muscular arms. He had nothing on but his sarong.[4] His head was bare. His big, soft eyes stared eagerly at the white man, but his voice and demeanor were composed as he asked, without any words of greeting:

"Have you medicine, Tuan?"[5]

"No," said the visitor in a startled tone. "No. Why? Is there sickness in the house?"

"Enter and see," replied Arsat, in the same calm manner, and turning short round, passed again through the small doorway. The white man, dropping his bundles, followed.

In the dim light of the dwelling he made out on a couch of bamboos a woman stretched on her back under a broad sheet of

1. **propitiate** (prə pish′ ē āt), appease, satisfy.
2. **juragan,** native term for leader or captain.
3. **sampan,** flat-bottomed boat.
4. **sarong** (sə rông′), a long piece of cloth, wrapped about the body like a skirt, worn by both men and women in the Malay Peninsula.
5. **Tuan,** Malayan term of respect, like sir or mister.

red cotton cloth. She lay still, as if dead; but her big eyes, wide open, glittered in the gloom, staring upward at the slender rafters, motionless and unseeing. She was in a high fever, and evidently unconscious. Her cheeks were sunk slightly, her lips were partly open, and on the young face there was the ominous and fixed expression—the absorbed, contemplating expression of the unconscious who are going to die. The two men stood looking down at her in silence.

"Has she been long ill?" asked the traveler.

"I have not slept for five nights," answered the Malay in a deliberate tone. "At first she heard voices calling her from the water and struggled against me who held her. But since the sun of today rose she hears nothing—she hears not me. She sees nothing. She sees not me—me!"

He remained silent for a minute, then asked softly:

"Tuan, will she die?"

"I fear so," said the white man, sorrowfully. He had known Arsat years ago, in a far country in times of trouble and danger, when no friendship is to be despised. And since his Malay friend had come unexpectedly to dwell in the hut on the lagoon with a strange woman, he had slept many times there, in his journeys up and down the river. He liked the man who knew how to keep faith in council and how to fight without fear by the side of his white friend. He liked him—not so much perhaps as a man likes his favorite dog—but still he liked him well enough to help and ask no questions, to think sometimes vaguely and hazily in the midst of his own pursuits about the lonely man and the long-haired woman with audacious face and triumphant eyes, who lived together hidden by the forests—alone and feared.

The white man came out of the hut in time to see the enormous conflagration of sunset put out by the swift and stealthy shadows that, rising like a black and impalpable vapor above the treetops, spread over the heaven, extinguishing the crimson glow of floating clouds and the red brilliance of departing daylight. In a few moments all the stars came out above the intense blackness of the earth, and the great lagoon gleaming suddenly with reflected lights resembled an oval patch of night sky flung down into the hopeless and abysmal night of the wilderness. The white man had some supper out of the basket, then collecting a few sticks that lay about the platform, made up a small fire, not for warmth, but for the sake of the smoke, which would keep off the mosquitoes. He wrapped himself in the blankets and sat with his back against the reed wall of the house, smoking thoughtfully.

Arsat came through the doorway with noiseless steps and squatted down by the fire. The white man moved his outstretched legs a little.

"She breathes," said Arsat in a low voice, anticipating the expected question. "She breathes and burns as if with a great fire. She speaks not; she hears not—and burns!"

He paused for a moment, then asked in a quiet, incurious tone:

"Tuan . . . will she die?"

The white man moved his shoulders uneasily and uttered in a hesitating manner:

"If such is her fate."

"No, Tuan," said Arsat, calmly. "If such is my fate. I hear, I see, I wait. I remember . . . Tuan, do you remember the old days? Do you remember my brother?"

"Yes," said the white man. The Malay rose suddenly and went in. The other, sitting still outside, could hear the voice in the hut. Arsat said: "Hear me! Speak!" His words were succeeded by a complete silence. "O Diamelen!" he cried suddenly. After that cry there was a deep sigh. Arsat came out and sank down again in his old place.

They sat in silence before the fire. There was no sound within the house, there was no sound near them; but far away on the lagoon they could hear the voices of the boatmen ringing fitful and distinct on the calm water. The fire in the bow of the sampan shone faintly in the distance with a hazy red glow. Then it died out. The voices ceased. The land and the water slept invisible, unstirring, and mute. It was as though there had been nothing left in the world but the glitter of stars streaming, ceaseless and vain, through the black stillness of the night.

The white man gazed straight before him into the darkness with wide-open eyes. The fear and fascination, the inspiration and the wonder of death—of death near, unavoidable, and unseen, soothed the unrest of his race and stirred the most indistinct, the most intimate of his thoughts. The ever-ready suspicion of evil, the gnawing suspicion that lurks in our hearts, flowed out into the stillness round him—into the stillness profound and dumb, and made it appear untrustworthy and infamous, like the placid and impenetrable mask of an unjustifiable violence. In that fleeting and powerful disturbance of his being, the earth, enfolded in the starlight peace, became a shadowy country of inhuman strife, a battlefield of phantoms terrible and charming, august or ignoble, struggling ardently for the possession of our helpless hearts. An unquiet and mysterious country of inextinguishable desires and fears.

A plaintive murmur rose in the night; a murmur saddening and startling, as if the great solitudes of surrounding woods had tried to whisper into his ear the wisdom of their immense and lofty indifference. Sounds hesitating and vague floated in the air round him, shaped themselves slowly into words; and at last flowed on gently in a murmuring stream of soft and monotonous sentences. He stirred like a man waking up and changed his position slightly. Arsat, motionless and shadowy, sitting with bowed head under the stars, was speaking in a low and dreamy tone:

". . . for where can we lay down the heaviness of our trouble but in a friend's heart? A man must speak of war and of love. You, Tuan, know what war is, and you have seen me in time of danger seek death as other men seek life! A writing may be lost; a lie may be written; but what the eye has seen is truth and remains in the mind!"

"I remember," said the white man, quietly. Arsat went on with mournful composure:

"Therefore I shall speak to you of love. Speak in the night. Speak before both night and love are gone—and the eye of day looks upon my sorrow and my shame; upon my blackened face; upon my burnt-up heart."

A sigh, short and faint, marked an almost imperceptible pause, and then his words flowed on, without a stir, without a gesture.

"After the time of trouble and war was over and you went away from my country in the pursuit of your desires, which we, men of the islands, cannot understand, I and my brother became again, as we had been before, the swordbearers of the Ruler. You know we were men of family, belonging to a ruling race, and more fit than any to carry on our right shoulder the emblem of power. And in the time of prosperity Si Dendring showed us favor, as we, in time of sorrow, had showed to him the faithfulness of our courage. It was a time of peace. A time of deer hunts and cockfights; of idle talks and foolish squabbles between men whose bellies are full and weapons are rusty. But the sower watched the young rice shoots grow up without fear, and the traders came and went, departed lean and returned fat into the river of peace. They brought news, too. Brought lies and truth mixed together, so that no man knew when to rejoice and when to be sorry. We heard from them about you also. They had seen you here and had seen you there. And I was glad to hear, for I remembered the stirring times, and I always remembered you, Tuan, till the time came when my eyes could see nothing in the past, because they had looked upon the one who is dying there—in the house."

He stopped to exclaim in an intense whisper, "O Mara bahia! O Calamity!" then went on speaking a little louder:

"There's no worse enemy and no better friend than a brother, Tuan, for one brother knows another, and in perfect knowledge is strength for good or evil. I loved my brother. I went to him and told him that I could see nothing but one face, hear nothing but one voice. He told me: 'Open your heart so that she can see what is in it—and wait. Patience is wisdom. Inchi Midah may die or our Ruler may throw off his fear of a woman!' . . . I waited. . . . You remember the lady with the veiled face, Tuan, and the fear of our Ruler before her cunning and temper. And if she wanted her servant, what could I do? But I fed the hunger of my heart on short glances and stealthy words. I loitered on the path to the bathhouses in the daytime, and when the sun had fallen behind the forest I crept along the jasmine hedges of the women's courtyard. Unseeing, we spoke to one another through the scent of flowers, through the veil of leaves, through the blades of long grass that stood still before our lips; so great was our prudence, so faint was the murmur of our great longing. The time passed swiftly . . . and there were whispers among women— and our enemies watched—my brother was gloomy, and I began to think of killing and of a fierce death. . . . We are of a people who take what they want—like you whites. There is a time when a man should forget loyalty and respect. Might and authority are given to rulers, but to all men is given love and strength and courage. My brother said, 'You shall take her from their midst. We are two who are like one.' And I answered, 'Let it be soon, for I find no warmth in sunlight that does not shine upon her.' Our time came when the Ruler and all the great people went to the mouth of the river to fish by torchlight. There were hundreds of boats, and on the white sand, between the water and the forests, dwellings of leaves were built for the households of the Rajahs.[6] The smoke of cooking fires was like a blue mist of the evening, and many voices rang in it joyfully. While they were making the boats ready to beat up the fish, my brother came to me and said, 'Tonight!' I looked to my weapons, and when the time came our canoe took its place in the circle of boats carrying the torches. The lights blazed on the water, but behind the boats there was darkness. When the shouting began and the excitement made them like mad we dropped out. The water swallowed our fire, and we floated back to the shore that was dark with only here and there the glimmer of embers. We could hear the talk of slave girls among the sheds. Then we found a place deserted and silent. We waited there. She came. She came running along the shore, rapid and leaving no trace, like a leaf driven by the wind into the sea. My brother said gloomily, 'Go and take her; carry her into our boat.' I lifted her in my arms. She panted. Her heart was beating against my breast. I said, 'I take you from those people. You came to the cry of my heart, but my arms take you into my boat against the will of the great!' 'It is right,' said my brother. 'We are men who take what we want and can hold it against many. We should have taken her in daylight.' I said, 'Let us be off'; for since she was in my boat I began to think of our Ruler's many men. 'Yes. Let us be off,' said my brother. 'We are cast out and this boat is our country now—and the sea is our refuge.' He lingered with his foot on the shore, and I entreated him to hasten, for I remembered the strokes of her heart against my breast and thought that two men cannot withstand a hundred. We left, paddling downstream close to the bank; and as we passed by the creek where they were fishing, the great shouting had ceased, but the murmur of voices was loud like the humming of insects flying at noonday. The boats floated, clustered together, in the red light of torches, under a black roof of smoke; and men talked of their sport. Men that boasted, and praised, and jeered—men that would have been our friends in the morning, but on that night were already our enemies. We paddled swiftly past. We had not more friends in the coun-

6. **Rajahs** (rä′ jəz),   princes or chiefs.

try of our birth. She sat in the middle of the canoe with covered face; silent as she is now; unseeing as she is now—and I had no regret at what I was leaving because I could hear her breathing close to me—as I can hear her now."

He paused, listened with his ear turned to the doorway, then shook his head and went on:

"My brother wanted to shout the cry of challenge—one cry only—to let the people know we were freeborn robbers who trusted our arms and the great sea. And again I begged him in the name of our love to be silent. Could I not hear her breathing close to me? I knew the pursuit would come quick enough. My brother loved me. He dipped his paddle without a splash. He only said, 'There is half a man in you now—the other half is in that woman. I can wait. When you are a whole man again, you will come back with me here to shout defiance. We are sons of the same mother.' I made no answer. All my strength and all my spirit were in my hands that held the paddle—for I longed to be with her in a safe place beyond the reach of men's anger and of women's spite. My love was so great that I thought it could guide me to a country where death was unknown, if I could only escape from Inchi Midah's fury and from our Ruler's sword. We paddled with haste, breathing through our teeth. The blades bit deep into the smooth water. We passed out of the river; we flew in clear channels among the shallows. We skirted the black coast; we skirted the sand beaches where the sea speaks in whispers to the land; and the gleam of white sand flashed back past our boat, so swiftly she ran upon the water. We spoke not. Only once I said, 'Sleep, Diamelen, for soon you may want all your strength.' I heard the sweetness of her voice, but I never turned my head. The sun rose and still we went on. Water fell from my face like rain from a cloud. We flew in the light and heat. I never looked back, but I knew that my brother's eyes, behind me, were looking steadily

ahead, for the boat went as straight as a bushman's dart when it leaves the end of the sumpitan.[7] There was no better paddler, no better steersman than my brother. Many times, together, we had won races in that canoe. But we never had put out our strength as we did then—then, when for the last time we paddled together! There was no braver or stronger man in our country than my brother. I could not spare the strength to turn my head and look at him, but every moment I heard the hiss of his breath getting louder behind me. Still he did not speak. The sun was high. The heat clung to my back like a flame of fire. My ribs were ready to burst, but I could no longer get enough air into my chest. And then I felt I must cry out with my last breath, 'Let us rest!' . . . 'Good!' he answered; and his voice was firm. He was strong. He was brave. He knew not fear and no fatigue. . . . My brother!"

A murmur powerful and gentle, a murmur vast and faint; the murmur of trembling leaves, of stirring boughs, ran through the tangled depths of the forests, ran over the starry smoothness of the lagoon, and the water between the piles lapped the slimy timber once with a sudden splash. A breath of warm air touched the two men's faces and passed on with a mournful sound—a breath loud and short like an uneasy sigh of the dreaming earth.

Arsat went on in an even, low voice.

"We ran our canoe on the white beach of a little bay close to a long tongue of land that seemed to bar our road; a long wooded cape going far into the sea. My brother knew that place. Beyond the cape a river has its entrance, and through the jungle of that land there is a narrow path. We made a fire and cooked rice. Then we lay down to sleep on the soft sand in the shade of our canoe, while she watched. No sooner had I closed my eyes than I heard her cry of alarm. We leaped up.

---

7. **sumpitan,** blowgun.

The sun was halfway down the sky already, and coming in sight in the opening of the bay we saw a prau[8] manned by many paddlers. We knew it at once; it was one of our Rajah's praus. They were watching the shore, and saw us. They beat the gong, and turned the head of the prau into the bay. I felt my heart become weak within my breast. Diamelen sat on the sand and covered her face. There was no escape by sea. My brother laughed. He had the gun you had given him, Tuan, before you went away, but there was only a handful of powder. He spoke to me quickly: 'Run with her along the path. I shall keep them back, for they have no firearms, and landing in the face of a man with a gun is certain death for some. Run with her. On the other side of that wood there is a fisherman's house—and a canoe. When I have fired all the shots I will follow. I am a great runner, and before they can come up we shall be gone. I will hold out as long as I can, for she is but a woman—that can neither run nor fight, but she has your heart in her weak hands.' He dropped behind the canoe. The prau was coming. She and I ran, and as we rushed along the path I heard shots. My brother fired—once—twice—and the booming of the gong ceased. There was silence behind us. That neck of land is narrow. Before I heard my brother fire the third shot I saw the shelving shore, and I saw the water again; the mouth of a broad river. We crossed a grassy glade. We ran down to the water. I saw a low hut above the black mud, and a small canoe hauled up. I heard another shot behind me. I thought, 'That is his last charge.' We rushed down to the canoe; a man came running from the hut, but I leaped on him, and we rolled together in the mud. Then I got up, and he lay still at my feet. I don't know whether I had killed him or not. I and Diamelen pushed the canoe afloat. I heard yells behind me, and I saw my brother run across the glade. Many men were bounding after him. I took her in my arms and threw her into the boat, then leaped in myself. When I looked back I saw that my broth-er had fallen. He fell and was up again, but the men were closing round him. He shout-ed, 'I am coming!' The men were close to him. I looked. Many men. Then I looked at her. Tuan, I pushed the canoe! I pushed it into deep water. She was kneeling forward looking at me, and I said, 'Take your paddle,' while I struck the water with mine. Tuan, I heard him cry. I heard him cry my name twice; and I heard voices shouting, 'Kill! Strike!' I never turned back. I heard him call-ing my name again with a great shriek, as when life is going out together with the voice —and I never turned my head. My own name! . . . My brother! Three times he called —but I was not afraid of life. Was she not there in that canoe? And could I not with her find a country where death is forgotten— where death is unknown!"

The white man sat up. Arsat rose and stood, an indistinct and silent figure above the dying embers of the fire. Over the lagoon a mist drifting and low had crept, erasing slowly the glittering images of the stars. And now a great expanse of white vapor covered the land: it flowed cold and gray in the dark-ness, eddied in noiseless whirls round the tree trunks and about the platform of the house, which seemed to float upon a restless and im-palpable illusion of a sea. Only far away the tops of the trees stood outlined on the twinkle of heaven, like a somber and forbidding shore—a coast deceptive, pitiless and black.

Arsat's voice vibrated loudly in the pro-found peace.

"I had her there! I had her! To get her I would have faced all mankind. But I had her —and—"

His words went out ringing into the empty distances. He paused and seemed to listen to them dying away very far—beyond help and beyond recall. Then he said quietly:

"Tuan, I loved my brother."

A breath of wind made him shiver. High

---

8. **prau,** a swift boat with pointed prow and stern, like a canoe.

above his head, high above the silent sea of mist the drooping leaves of the palms rattled together with a mournful and expiring sound. The white man stretched his legs. His chin rested on his chest, and he murmured sadly without lifting his head:

"We all love our brothers."

Arsat burst out with an intense whispering violence:

"What did I care who died? I wanted peace in my own heart."

He seemed to hear a stir in the house— listened—then stepped in noiselessly. The white man stood up. A breeze was coming in fitful puffs. The stars shone paler as if they had retreated into the frozen depths of immense space. After a chill gust of wind there were a few seconds of perfect calm and absolute silence. Then from behind the black and wavy line of the forests a column of golden light shot up into the heavens and spread over the semicircle of the eastern horizon. The sun had risen. The mist lifted, broke into drifting patches, vanished into thin flying wreaths; and the unveiled lagoon lay, polished and black, in the heavy shadows at the foot of the wall of trees. A white eagle rose over it with a slanting and ponderous flight, reached the clear sunshine and appeared dazzlingly brilliant for a moment, then, soaring higher, became a dark and motionless speck before it vanished into the blue as if it had left the earth forever. The white man, standing gazing upward before the doorway, heard in the hut a confused and broken murmur of distracted words ending with a loud groan. Suddenly Arsat stumbled out with outstretched hands, shivered, and stood still for some time with fixed eyes. Then he said:

"She burns no more."

Before his face the sun showed its edge above the treetops, rising steadily. The breeze freshened; a great brilliance burst upon the lagoon, sparkled on the rippling water. The forests came out of the clear shadows of the morning, became distinct, as if they had rushed nearer—to stop short in a great stir of leaves, of nodding boughs, of swaying branches. In the merciless sunshine the whisper of unconscious life grew louder, speaking in an incomprehensible voice round the dumb darkness of that human sorrow. Arsat's eyes wandered slowly, then stared at the rising sun.

"I can see nothing," he said half aloud to himself.

"There is nothing," said the white man, moving to the edge of the platform and waving his hand to the boat. A shout came faintly over the lagoon and the sampan began to glide toward the abode of the friend of ghosts.

"If you want to come with me, I will wait all the morning," said the white man, looking away upon the water.

"No, Tuan," said Arsat softly. "I shall not eat or sleep in this house, but I must first see my road. Now I can see nothing—see nothing! There is no light and no peace in the world; but there is death—death for many. We are sons of the same mother—and I left him in the midst of enemies; but I am going back now."

He drew a long breath and went on in a dreamy tone:

"In a little while I shall see clear enough to strike—to strike. But she has died, and . . . now . . . darkness."

He flung his arms wide open, let them fall along his body, then stood still with unmoved face and stony eyes, staring at the sun. The white man got down into his canoe. The polers ran smartly along the sides of the boat, looking over their shoulders at the beginning of a weary journey. High in the stern, his head muffled up in white rags, the juragan sat moody, letting his paddle trail in the water. The white man, leaning with both arms over the grass roof of the little cabin, looked at the shining ripple of the boat's wake. Before the sampan passed out of the lagoon into the creek he lifted his eyes. Arsat had not moved. He stood lonely in the searching sunshine; and he looked beyond the great light of a cloudless day into the darkness of a world of illusions.

FOR UNDERSTANDING

1. What is the reputation of the lagoon, the house and the people?
2. What kind of relationship have Arsat and the white man had?
3. Why does Arsat choose to tell his story to the white man?
4. Why does he feel so guilty?
5. After his wife's death, what does Arsat plan to do?

FOR INTERPRETATION

1. Consider the following statements made by Conrad. How do they apply to this story?
    a. Life is a walk on a thin crust of barely cooled lava which at any moment might break and let the unwary sink into fiery depths.
    b. The world, the temporal world, rests on a few, a very few simple ideas. It rests notably, among others, on the idea of fidelity.
2. What is the significance of the line: "We all love our brothers"? Why is it printed as a separate paragraph?
3. Notice how Conrad leads you from the river deeper and deeper physically into the jungle. Is he also going deeper and deeper into something psychological?

FOR APPRECIATION

1. This tale echoes the archetypal patterns of old stories. What similarities does it exhibit with the following:
    a. *The Rime of the Ancient Mariner*?
    b. The story of Adam and Eve?
    c. The story of Cain and Abel?
2. Conrad once said that in his writing, above everything else, he wanted to make the reader "see." Examine the first long paragraph of the story to see the vividness of the setting. How does Conrad convey to you the lack of motion in the scene? What movements break the motionless world?

Saki (H. H. Munro) 1870–1916

Hector Hugo Munro, better known to readers as Saki, "spoofed" the English upper class during the Edwardian age, but in such a delicate and disarming way that the sting was removed. Born in Burma of British parents, Munro was brought to England when he was two, to be raised by his grandmother and two stern, autocratic aunts. The regime was a devastatingly strict one, and it is small wonder that one of Munro's favorite subjects for satire was aunts. In 1893 he obtained a post in Burma with the Military Police, and there his fondness for animals, both wild and domestic, could be indulged to the fullest. But after seven fevers in thirteen months, Munro's poor health forced him to return to England. After a period of recuperation in the Devonshire countryside, he moved to London where he found to his delight that he could earn a living by writing. In the beginning, he wrote political satires for the *Westminster Gazette* and later moved on to satirizing the British social set. When war was declared in 1914, Munro immediately enlisted; he was killed in 1916 by a sniper's bullet.

To pin down the elusive charm of Saki's tales is like trying to explain your fondness for a particular food. It is a matter of taste. Christopher Morley comments: "There is no greater compliment to be paid the right kind of friend than to hand him Saki, without comment. Particularly to those less familiar with the mysterious jungle of English humour, a savage country with birds of unexpected

SAKI (H.H. MUNRO)
Photo: E.D. Hoppé (1913)
The Mansell Collection

plumage. . . . There are certain social types whom Saki cooks and serves for us as absolutely perfect as asparagus and hollandaise." Munro borrowed his pen name from the *Rubaiyat of Omar Khayyam,* in which the cupbearer was named Saki. This English Saki brings pure delight to his followers as he shines his wit upon the foibles of English society.

THE SCHARTZ-METTERKLUME METHOD

Lady Carlotta stepped out on to the platform of the small wayside station and took a turn or two up and down its uninteresting length, to kill time till the train should be pleased to proceed on its way. Then, in the roadway beyond, she saw a horse struggling with a more than ample load, and a carter[1] of the sort that seems to bear a sullen hatred against the animal that helps him to earn a living. Lady Carlotta promptly betook her to the roadway, and put rather a different complexion on the struggle. Certain of her acquaintances were wont to give her plentiful admonition as to the undesirability of interfering on behalf of a distressed animal, such interference being "none of her business." Only once had she put the doctrine of non-interference into practice, when one of its most eloquent exponents had been besieged for nearly three hours in a small and extremely uncomfortable may-tree by an angry boar-pig, while Lady Carlotta, on the other side of the fence, had proceeded with the water-colour sketch she was engaged on, and refused to interfere between the boar and his prisoner. It is to be feared that she lost the friendship of the ultimately rescued lady. On this occasion she merely lost the train, which gave way to the first sign of impatience it had shown throughout the journey, and steamed off without her. She bore the desertion with philosophical indifference; her friends and relations were thoroughly well used to the fact of her luggage arriving without her. She wired a vague non-committal message to her destination to say that she was coming on "by another train." Before she had time to think what her next move might be she was confronted by an imposingly attired lady, who seemed to be taking a prolonged mental inventory of her clothes and looks.

"You must be Miss Hope, the governess I've come to meet," said the apparition, in a tone that admitted of very little argument.

"Very well, if I must I must," said Lady Carlotta to herself with dangerous meekness.

"I am Mrs. Quabarl," continued the lady; "and where, pray, is your luggage?"

"It's gone astray," said the alleged governess, falling in with the excellent rule of life that the absent are always to blame; the luggage had, in point of fact, behaved with perfect correctitude. "I've just telegraphed about it," she added, with a nearer approach to truth.

"How provoking," said Mrs. Quabarl; "these railway companies are so careless. However, my maid can lend you things for the night," and she led the way to her car.

During the drive to the Quabarl mansion Lady Carlotta was impressively introduced to the nature of the charge that had been thrust upon her; she learned that Claude and Wilfrid were delicate, sensitive young people, that Irene had the artistic temperament highly developed, and that Viola was something or other else of a mould equally commonplace among children of that class and type in the twentieth century.

"I wish them not only to be *taught*," said Mrs. Quabarl, "but *interested* in what they learn. In their history lessons, for instance,

1. **carter,** man whose work is driving a cart or truck.

you must try to make them feel that they are being introduced to the life-stories of men and women who really lived, not merely committing a mass of names and dates to memory. French, of course, I shall expect you to talk at mealtimes several days in the week."

"I shall talk French four days of the week and Russian in the remaining three."

"Russian? My dear Miss Hope, no one in the house speaks or understands Russian."

"That will not embarrass me in the least," said Lady Carlotta coldly.

Mrs. Quabarl, to use a colloquial expression, was knocked off her perch. She was one of those imperfectly self-assured individuals who are magnificent and autocratic as long as they are not seriously opposed. The least show of unexpected resistance goes a long way towards rendering them cowed and apologetic. When the new governess failed to express wondering admiration of the large newly purchased and expensive car, and lightly alluded to the superior advantages of one or two makes which had just been put on the market, the discomfiture of her patroness became almost abject. Her feelings were those which might have animated a general of ancient warfaring days, on beholding his heaviest battle-elephant ignominiously driven off the field by slingers and javelin throwers.

At dinner that evening, although reinforced by her husband, who usually duplicated her opinions and lent her moral support generally, Mrs. Quabarl regained none of her lost ground. The governess not only helped herself well and truly to wine, but held forth with considerable show of critical knowledge on various vintage matters, concerning which the Quabarls were in no wise able to pose as authorities. Previous governesses had limited their conversation on the wine topic to a respectful and doubtless sincere expression of a preference for water. When this one went as far as to recommend a wine firm in whose hands you could not go very far wrong Mrs. Quabarl thought it time to turn the conversation into more usual channels.

"We got very satisfactory references about you from Cannon Teep," she observed; "a very estimable man, I should think."

"Drinks like a fish and beats his wife, otherwise a very lovable character," said the governess imperturbably.

"My *dear* Miss Hope! I trust you are exaggerating," exclaimed the Quabarls in unison.

"One must in justice admit that there is some provocation," continued the romancer. "Mrs. Teep is quite the most irritating bridge-player that I have ever sat down with; her leads and declarations would condone a certain amount of brutality in her partner, but to souse her with the contents of the only soda-water syphon[2] in the house on a Sunday afternoon, when one couldn't get another, argues an indifference to the comfort of others which I cannot altogether overlook. You may think me hasty in my judgments, but it was practically on account of the syphon incident that I left."

"We will talk of this some other time," said Mrs. Quabarl hastily.

"I shall never allude to it again," said the governess with decision.

Mr. Quabarl made a welcome diversion by asking what studies the new instructress proposed to inaugurate on the morrow.

"History to begin with," she informed him.

"Ah, history," he observed sagely; "now in teaching them history you must take care to interest them in what they learn. You must make them feel that they are being introduced to the life-stories of men and women who really lived—"

"I've told her all that," interposed Mrs. Quabarl.

"I teach history on the Schartz-Metterklume method," said the governess loftily.

"Ah, yes," said her listeners, thinking it

---

2. **syphon** (sī′ fən), bottle for soda water.

CAT ON A SUMMER SOFA
Chloë Cheese

expedient to assume an acquaintance at least with the name.

"What are you children doing out here?" demanded Mrs. Quabarl the next morning, on finding Irene sitting rather glumly at the head of the stairs, while her sister was perched in an attitude of depressed discomfort on the window-seat behind her, with a wolfskin rug almost covering her.

"We are having a history lesson," came the unexpected reply. "I am supposed to be Rome, and Viola up there is the she-wolf;[3] not a real wolf, but the figure of one that the Romans used to set store by—I forget why. Claude and Wilfrid have gone to fetch the shabby women."

"The shabby women?"

"Yes, they've got to carry them off. They didn't want to, but Miss Hope got one of

father's fives-bats[4] and said she'd give them a number nine spanking if they didn't, so they've gone to do it."

A loud, angry screaming from the direction of the lawn drew Mrs. Quabarl thither in hot haste, fearful lest the threatened castigation might even now be in process of infliction. The outcry, however, came principally from the two small daughters of the lodge-keeper, who were being hauled and pushed towards the house by the panting and dishevelled Claude and Wilfrid, whose task was rendered even more arduous by the incessant, if not very effectual, attacks of the captured

3. **she-wolf.** The twin brothers Romulus and Remus, the legendary founders of Rome, were nursed in infancy by a she-wolf.
4. **fives-bats,** wooden bats used in fives, a game like racquetball.

maidens' small brother. The governess, fives-bat in hand, sat negligently on the stone balustrade, presiding over the scene with the cold impartiality of a Goddess of Battles. A furious and repeated chorus of "I'll tell muvver" rose from the lodge children, but the lodge-mother, who was hard of hearing, was for the moment immersed in the preoccupation of her washtub. After an apprehensive glance in the direction of the lodge (the good woman was gifted with the highly militant temper which is sometimes the privilege of deafness) Mrs. Quabarl flew indignantly to the rescue of the struggling captives.

"Wilfrid! Claude! Let those children go at once. Miss Hope, what on earth is the meaning of this scene?"

"Early Roman history; the Sabine women,[5] don't you know? It's the Schartz-Metterklume method to make children understand history by acting it themselves; fixes it in their memory, you know. Of course, if, thanks to your interference, your boys go through life thinking that the Sabine women ultimately escaped, I really cannot be held responsible."

"You may be very clever and modern, Miss Hope," said Mrs. Quabarl firmly, "but I should like you to leave here by the next train. Your luggage will be sent after you as soon as it arrives."

"I'm not certain exactly where I shall be for the next few days," said the dismissed instructress of youth; "you might keep my luggage till I wire my address. There are only a couple of trunks and some golf-clubs and a leopard cub."

"A leopard cub!" gasped Mrs. Quabarl. Even in her departure this extraordinary person seemed destined to leave a trail of embarrassment behind her.

"Well, it's rather left off being a cub; it's more than half-grown, you know. A fowl every day and a rabbit on Sundays is what it usually gets. Raw beef makes it too excitable. Don't trouble about getting the car for me, I'm rather inclined for a walk."

And Lady Carlotta strode out of the Quabarl horizon.

The advent of the genuine Miss Hope, who had made a mistake as to the day on which she was due to arrive, caused a turmoil which that good lady was quite unused to inspiring. Obviously the Quabarl family had been woefully befooled, but a certain amount of relief came with the knowledge.

"How tiresome for you, dear Carlotta," said her hostess, when the overdue guest ultimately arrived; "how very tiresome losing your train and having to stop overnight in a strange place."

"Oh, dear, no," said Lady Carlotta; "not at all tiresome—for me."

5. **Sabine women,** an allusion to the legend that the early Romans kidnapped the women of a neighboring tribe, the Sabines, in order to increase the population of Rome.

FOR UNDERSTANDING

1. Why is missing the train characteristic of Lady Carlotta?
2. What is her unusual reaction to Mrs. Quabarl's announcement that she must be the governess?
3. What things about the supposed new governess startle the Quabarls?
4. What is the Schartz-Metterklume method?

FOR INTERPRETATION

1. Lady Carlotta is an example of a stock character in fiction and drama. What are her characteristics?
2. What makes us delight in such a character?
3. Do you believe anyone could carry off such a situation?

FOR APPRECIATION

Understatement

Saki is a master of understatement—a form of irony in which what is said intentionally states less than what is actually true. See if you can find at least two or three good examples of understatement. What does Saki suggest beyond the literal meanings?

E. M. Forster   1879–1970

It was a mystery to his contemporaries and friends that Edward Morgan Forster could write six novels between 1905 and 1924, three of them top notch, and then with no reason given, turn completely to writing other prose: essays, short stories, and literary criticism.

Born in London, he was educated at Tonbridge school where he suffered the problems of a day student in a boarding school. It was at King's College, Cambridge that he made a group of friends who had a great influence on his life. And it was to Cambridge that he returned to live in 1946 after his home at Abinger was destroyed in World War II. Trips to Greece and Italy in his twenties had a lasting effect on him for in his stories he tended to contrast the spontaneous, lusty life-style of Mediterranean peasants with the stuffy middle class of Britain.

Two trips to India—on one of which he served as secretary to an Indian prince—gave Forster material for the best and last of his novels, *A Passage to India* (1924), in which he probes the complex relations between the English and their colonial subjects. He seemed always to be seeking a "spontaneity of consciousness," especially between people. In an essay about his writing, he said: "Where do I start? . . . With personal relations." In *Howards End* (1910) he presents the relation of inward thought to action. One of the characters says, "Only connect. Only connect the prose and the passion, and both will be exalted, and human love will soon be at its height." Regrettably, this goal is easier to conceive than attain.

Forster was fortunate in having enough money for a comfortable life and for indulging his very few, simple tastes. A man of broad interests, he was a fine musician, a delightful conversationlist, and in his later years, a counselor and sounding board for the students

EDWARD MORGAN FORSTER
Dora Carrington (after 1921)
National Portrait Gallery, London

at Cambridge. He always kept in touch with his old Cambridge friends and those of the Bloomsbury group, named aftcr the area where most of them had once lived in London: Included in this group were the novelist Virginia Woolf, the biographer Lytton Strachey, and the art critic Roger Fry. They were noted for their experimentation, their originality, and their hearty dislike of the Victorian way of life.

MY WOOD

A few years ago I wrote a book which dealt in part with the difficulties of the English in India. Feeling that they would have had no difficulties in India themselves, the Americans read the book freely. The more they read it the better it made them feel, and a cheque to the author was the result. I bought a wood with the cheque. It is not a large wood —it contains scarcely any trees, and it is intersected, blast it, by a public footpath. Still, it is the first property that I have owned, so it is right that other people should participate in my shame, and should ask themselves, in accents that will vary in horror, this very important question: What is the effect of property upon the character? Don't let's touch economics; the effect of private ownership upon the community as a whole is another question —a more important question, perhaps, but another one. Let's keep to psychology. If you own things, what's their effect on you? What's the effect on me of my wood?

In the first place, it makes me feel heavy. Property does have this effect. Property produces men of weight, and it was a man of weight who failed to get into the Kingdom of Heaven.[1] He was not wicked, that unfortunate millionaire in the parable, he was only stout; he stuck out in front, not to mention behind, and as he wedged himself this way and that in the crystalline entrance and bruised his well-fed flanks, he saw beneath him a comparatively slim camel passing through the eye of a needle and being woven into the robe of God. The Gospels[2] all through couple stoutness and slowness. They point out what is perfectly obvious, yet seldom realized: that if you have a lot of things you cannot move about a lot, that furniture requires dusting, dusters require servants, servants require insurance stamps, and the whole tangle of them makes you think twice before you accept an invitation to dinner or go for a bathe in the Jordan. Sometimes the Gospels proceed further and say with Tolstoy[3] that property is sinful; they approach the difficult ground of asceticism here, where I cannot follow them. But as to the immediate effects of property on people, they just show straightforward logic. It produces men of weight. Men of weight cannot, by definition, move like the lightning from the East unto the West, and the ascent of a fourteen-stone[4] bishop into a pulpit is thus the exact antithesis of the coming of the Son of Man. My wood makes me feel heavy.

In the second place, it makes me feel it ought to be larger.

The other day I heard a twig snap in it. I was annoyed at first, for I thought that someone was blackberrying, and depreciating the value of the undergrowth. On coming nearer, I saw it was not a man who had trodden on the twig and snapped it, but a bird, and I felt pleased. My bird. The bird was not equally pleased. Ignoring the relation between us, it took fright as soon as it saw the shape of my face, and flew straight over the boundary hedge into a field, the property of Mrs. Hen-

From ABINGER HARVEST copyright 1936, 1964 by Edward Morgan Forster. Reprinted by permission of Harcourt Brace Jovanovich, Inc.

1. **man . . . Heaven,** an allusion to the statement of Jesus in the New Testament that it is easier for a camel to pass through the eye of a needle than for a rich man to enter the Kingdom of Heaven.
2. **Gospels,** the four accounts of the life of Jesus in the New Testament, attributed to the disciples Matthew, Mark, Luke, and John.
3. **Tolstoy,** Leo Tolstoy (1828–1910), the great Russian novelist.
4. **fourteen-stone,** 196 pounds.

essy, where it sat down with a loud squawk. It had become Mrs. Henessy's bird. Something seemed grossly amiss here, something that would not have occurred had the wood been larger. I could not afford to buy Mrs. Henessy out, I dared not murder her, and limitations of this sort beset me on every side. Ahab[5] did not want that vineyard—he only needed it to round off his property, preparatory to plotting a new curve—and all the land around my wood has become necessary to me in order to round off the wood. A boundary protects. But—poor little thing—the boundary ought in its turn to be protected. Noises on the edge of it. Children throw stones. A little more, and then a little more, until we reach the sea. Happy Canute![6] Happier Alexander![7] And after all, why should even the world be the limit of possession? A rocket containing a Union Jack,[8] will, it is hoped, be shortly fired at the moon. Mars. Sirius.[9] Beyond which . . . But these immensities ended by saddening me. I could not suppose that my wood was the destined nucleus of universal dominion—it is so very small and contains no mineral wealth beyond the blackberries. Nor was I comforted when Mrs. Henessy's bird took alarm for the second time and flew clean away from us all, under the belief that it belonged to itself.

In the third place, property makes its owner feel that he ought to do something to it. Yet he isn't sure what. A restlessness comes over him, a vague sense that he has a personality to express—the same sense which, without any vagueness, leads the artist to an act of creation. Sometimes I think I will cut down such trees as remain in the wood, at other times I want to fill up the gaps between them with new trees. Both impulses are pretentious and empty. They are not honest movements towards money-making or beauty. They spring from a foolish desire to express myself and from an inability to enjoy what I have got. Creation, property, enjoyment form a sinister trinity in the human mind. Creation and enjoyment are both very, very good, yet

they are often unattainable without a material basis, and at such moments property pushes itself in as a substitute, saying, "Accept me instead—I'm good enough for all three." It is not enough. It is, as Shakespeare said of lust, "The expense of spirit in a waste of shame"; it is "Before, a joy proposed; behind, a dream." Yet we don't know how to shun it. It is forced on us by our economic system as the alternative to starvation. It is also forced on us by an internal defect in the soul, by the feeling that in property may lie the germs of self-development and of exquisite or heroic deeds. Our life on earth is, and ought to be, material and carnal. But we have not yet learned to manage our materialism and carnality properly; they are still entangled with the desire for ownership, where (in the words of Dante[10]) "Possession is one with loss."

And this brings us to our fourth and final point: the blackberries.

Blackberries are not plentiful in this meagre grove, but they are easily seen from the public footpath which traverses it, and all too easily gathered. Foxgloves, too—people will pull up the foxgloves, and ladies of an educational tendency even grub for toadstools to show them on the Monday in class. Other ladies, less educated, roll down the bracken in the arms of their gentlemen friends. There is paper, there are tins. Pray, does my wood belong to me or doesn't it? And, if it does, should I not own it best by allowing no one else to walk there? There is a

---

5. **Ahab** (ā′hab). See I Kings 21:2–6 in the King James Bible.

6. **Canute** (kə nūt′), a Dane who conquered and united England (1016–1035) and became king of Denmark (1018–1035) and later of Norway and a wide area around the Baltic Sea.

7. **Alexander the Great** (356–323 B.C.) established an empire around the Mediterranean Sea and conquered lands as far as India in the East.

8. **Union Jack,** flag of the United Kingdom (Britain).

9. **Sirius** (sir′ē əs), the brightest star in the heavens, in Canis Major.

10. **Dante** (1265–1321), Italian poet, author of the *Divine Comedy.*

wood near Lyme Regis,[11] also cursed by a public footpath, where the owner has not hesitated on this point. He has built high stone walls each side of the path, and has spanned it by bridges, so that the public circulate like termites while he gorges on the blackberries unseen. He really does own his wood, this able chap. Dives[12] in Hell did pretty well, but the gulf dividing him from Lazarus could be traversed by vision, and nothing traverses it here. And perhaps I shall come to this in time. I shall wall in and fence out until I really taste the sweets of property. Enormously stout, endlessly avaricious, pseudocreative, intensely selfish, I shall weave upon my forehead the quadruple crown of possession until those nasty Bolshies[13] come and take it off again and thrust me aside into the outer darkness.

11. **Lyme Regis** (līm rē′ jis), a resort town in Dorset, in southern England.
12. **Dives** (dī′ vēz), (from the Latin word for *rich)* the rich man in the parable about the beggar Lazarus who was "carried by the angels to Abraham's bosom."
13. **Bolshies** (bōl′ shēz), Bolsheviks, members of the majority party of the Russian revolutionary movement who seized power under Lenin in 1917.

FOR UNDERSTANDING

1. What is the basic problem addressed in this essay?
2. What does Forster list as the four effects of his owning the woods?

3. Having discovered what owning this property is doing to him, is the author going to give it up?

FOR INTERPRETATION

1. Wise men of all periods have preached that possessions soon possess the owner. How would Forster react to this statement?
2. Are the four feelings Forster has about his property positive, negative, or a bit of both?

FOR APPRECIATION

The style of this essay is almost colloquial. It records some personal reflections about property by using the first person. What kind of voice does Forster use? Whom is he addressing? What in the first paragraph establishes this?

COMPOSITION

Set yourself the same problem presented in this essay. What are *your* feelings about owning some specific thing: a ten-speed bike, a hi-fi, a tape recorder, a prized piece of clothing or sporting equipment? Choose something that was important to you to acquire. Then start thinking about your feelings towards this object. Write down the effects of possessing it. Does it make you feel proud, smug, satisfied, possessive, disappointed, nervous, or what? You may have a number of diverse attitudes towards ownership.

Virginia Woolf 1882–1941

The daughter of Leslie Stephen, a Victorian critic and scholar, Virginia Woolf educated herself by reading in her father's vast library. She was born into a talented upper-class English family that was interested in the arts and literature. When her father died, she moved with her sister and two brothers to the Bloomsbury district of London. The name of this area was later given to a group of intellectuals with whom she associated. Among them were Lytton Strachey, the biographer; J. M. Keynes, a well-known economist; Roger Fry, an art critic; and E.M. Forster. After her sister married, she and one of the brothers took a house in Bloomsbury where they entertained the literary and artistic lights of the city. At thirty she married Leonard Woolf and with him founded the Hogarth Press, which published her own books and the books of many younger writers, including T. S. Eliot.

Outwardly, Virginia Woolf appeared lively and effervescent. Witty in her conversations and in her writing, she was also known as a warm friend. But her journals, published after her death, revealed a turbulent inner life, fraught with periods of depression, especially after she had finished a novel. She committed suicide in 1941, fearful that she was going mad and would be a burden to her husband.

With a comfortable income and the leisure to do what she wanted, Woolf chose to be a writer. She heartily disliked the writing of novelists like John Galsworthy and Arnold Bennett who used a direct, realistic approach. For her the inner consciousness was where the truth of experience existed. So she developed her own special style using the "stream of consciousness" technique to sketch the

VIRGINIA WOOLF
G.C. Beresford
National Portrait Gallery, London

happenings in the mind that moved between memory and anticipation. This produced a multilayered vision of human life. Her greatest achievement was as a novelist and two of her best books, *Mrs. Dalloway* (1925) and *To the Lighthouse* (1927), show her fully developed style. That style has exerted a profound influence on the prose fiction of our century.

THE DUCHESS AND THE JEWELLER

Oliver Bacon lived at the top of a house over-looking the Green Park. He had a flat;[1] chairs jutted out at the right angles—chairs covered in hide. Sofas filled the bays of the windows—sofas covered in tapestry. The windows, the three long windows, had the proper allow-ance of discreet net and figured satin. The mahogany sideboard bulged discreetly with the right brandies, whiskeys, and liqueurs. And from the middle window he looked down upon the glossy roofs of fashionable cars packed in the narrow straits of Piccadil-ly.[2] A more central position could not be imagined. And at eight in the morning he would have his breakfast brought in on a tray by a man-servant: the man-servant would un-fold his crimson dressing-gown; he would rip his letters open with his long pointed nails and would extract thick white cards of invita-tion upon which the engraving stood up roughly from duchesses, countesses, vis-countesses, and Honourable Ladies. Then he would wash; then he would eat his toast; then he would read his paper by the bright burn-ing fire of electric coals.

"Behold Oliver," he would say, address-ing himself. "You who began life in a filthy little alley, you who . . ." and he would look down at his legs, so shapely in their perfect trousers; at his boots; at his spats. They were all shapely, shining; cut from the best cloth by the best scissors in Savile Row.[3] But he dis-mantled himself often and became again a lit-tle boy in a dark alley. He had once thought it the height of his ambition—selling stolen dogs to fashionable women in Whitechapel.

And once he had been done.[4] "Oh, Oliver," his mother had wailed. "Oh, Oliver! When will you have sense, my son?" . . . Then he had gone behind a counter; had sold cheap watches; then he had taken a wallet to Amsterdam.[5] . . . At that memory he would chuckle—the old Oliver remembering the young. Yes, he had done well with the three diamonds; also there was the commission on the emerald. After that he went into the pri-vate room behind the shop in Hatton Gar-den; the room with the scales, the safe, the thick magnifying glasses. And then . . . and then. . . . He chuckled. When he passed through the knots of jewellers in the hot eve-ning who were discussing prices, gold mines, diamonds, reports from South Africa, one of them would lay a finger to the side of his nose and murmur, "Hum-m-m," as he passed. It was no more than a murmur; no more than a nudge on the shoulder, a finger on the nose, a buzz that ran through the cluster of jewel-lers in Hatton Garden on a hot afternoon—oh, many years ago now! But still Oliver felt it purring down his spine, the nudge, the mur-mur that meant, "Look at him—young Oli-ver, the young jeweller—there he goes." Young he was then. And he dressed better and better; and had, first a hansom cab; then a car; and first he went up to the dress circle, then down into the stalls.[6] And he had a villa

From A HAUNTED HOUSED AND OTHER STORIES by Virginia Woolf, copyright 1929 by Harcourt Brace Jovanovich, Inc.; renewed 1957 by Leonard Woolf. Reprinted by permission of the publisher.

1. **flat,** apartment.
2. **Piccadilly,** a fashionable section of London.
3. **Savile Row,** a London street containing many ex-pensive tailoring establishments.
4. **done,** cheated.
5. **Amsterdam,** the big diamond market in Europe.
6. **dress circle,** the better seats in the orchestra of a theater; **stalls,** private theater boxes.

at Richmond,[7] overlooking the river, with trellises of red roses; and Mademoiselle used to pick one every morning and stick it in his buttonhole.

"So," said Oliver Bacon, rising and stretching his legs. "So . . ."

And he stood beneath the picture of an old lady on the mantelpiece and raised his hands. "I have kept my word," he said, laying his hands together, palm to palm, as if he were doing homage to her. "I have won my bet." That was so; he was the richest jeweller in England; but his nose, which was long and flexible, like an elephant's trunk, seemed to say by its curious quiver at the nostrils (but it seemed as if the whole nose quivered, not only the nostrils) that he was not satisfied yet; still smelt something under the ground a little further off. Imagine a giant hog in a pasture rich with truffles; after unearthing this truffle and that, still it smells a bigger, a blacker truffle under the ground further off. So Oliver snuffed always in the rich earth of Mayfair[8] another truffle, a blacker, a bigger further off.

Now then he straightened the pearl in his tie, cased himself in his smart blue overcoat; took his yellow gloves and his cane; and swayed as he descended the stairs and half snuffed, half sighed through his long sharp nose as he passed out into Piccadilly. For was he not still a sad man, a dissatisfied man, a man who seeks something that is hidden, though he had won his bet?

He swayed slightly as he walked, as the camel at the zoo sways from side to side when it walks along the asphalt paths laden with grocers and their wives eating from paper bags and throwing little bits of silver paper crumpled up on to the path. The camel despises the grocers; the camel is dissatisfied with its lot; the camel sees the blue lake and the fringe of palm trees in front of it. So the great jeweller, the greatest jeweller in the whole world, swung down Piccadilly, perfectly dressed, with his gloves, with his cane; but dissatisfied still, till he reached the dark little shop, that was famous in France, in Germany,

in Austria, in Italy, and all over America—the dark little shop in the street off Bond Street.[9]

As usual, he strode through the shop without speaking, though the four men, the two old men, Marshall and Spencer, and the two young men, Hammond and Wicks, stood straight and looked at him, envying him. It was only with one finger of the amber-coloured glove, waggling, that he acknowledged their presence. And he went in and shut the door of his private room behind him.

Then he unlocked the grating that barred the window. The cries of Bond Street came in; the purr of the distant traffic. The light from reflectors at the back of the shop struck upwards. One tree waved six green leaves, for it was June. But Mademoiselle had married Mr. Pedder of the local brewery—no one stuck roses in his buttonhole now.

"So," he half sighed, half snorted, "so—"

Then he touched a spring in the wall and slowly the panelling slid open, and behind it were the steel safes, five, no, six of them, all of burnished steel. He twisted a key; unlocked one; then another. Each was lined with a pad of deep crimson velvet; in each lay jewels—bracelets, necklaces, rings, tiaras, ducal coronets; loose stones in glass shells; rubies, emeralds, pearls, diamonds. All safe, shining, cool, yet burning, eternally, with their own compressed light.

"Tears!" said Oliver, looking at the pearls.

"Heart's blood!" he said, looking at the rubies.

"Gunpowder!" he continued, rattling the diamonds so that they flashed and blazed.

"Gunpowder enough to blow Mayfair—sky high, high, high!" He threw his head back and made a sound like a horse neighing as he said it.

The telephone buzzed obsequiously in a

---

7. **Richmond,** a suburb of London.
8. **Mayfair,** another fashionable section of London.
9. **Bond Street,** a London street containing many fashionable stores.

low muted voice on his table. He shut the safe.

"In ten minutes," he said. "Not before." And he sat down at his desk and looked at the heads of the Roman emperors that were graved on his sleeve links. And again he dismantled himself and became once more the little boy playing marbles in the alley where they sell stolen dogs on Sunday. He became that wily astute little boy, with lips like wet cherries. He dabbled his fingers in ropes of tripe; he dipped them in pans of frying fish; he dodged in and out among the crowds. He was slim, lissome, with eyes like licked stones. And now—now—the hands of the clock ticked on, one, two, three, four. . . . The Duchess of Lambourne waited his pleasure; the Duchess of Lambourne, daughter of a hundred Earls. She would wait for ten minutes on a chair at the counter. She would wait his pleasure. She would wait till he was ready to see her. He watched the clock in its shagreen[10] case. The hand moved on. With each tick the clock handed him—so it seemed—pâté de foie gras,[11] a glass of champagne, another of fine brandy, a cigar costing one guinea. The clock laid them on the table beside him as the ten minutes passed. Then he heard soft slow footsteps approaching; a rustle in the corridor. The door opened. Mr. Hammond flattened himself against the wall.

"Her Grace!" he announced.

And he waited there, flattened against the wall.

And Oliver, rising, could hear the rustle of the dress of the Duchess as she came down the passage. Then she loomed up, filling the door, filling the room with the aroma, the prestige, the arrogance, the pomp, the pride of all the Dukes and Duchesses swollen in one wave. And as a wave breaks, she broke, as she sat down, spreading and splashing and falling over Oliver Bacon, the great jeweller, covering him with sparkling bright colours, green, rose, violet; and odours; and iridescences; and rays shooting from fingers, nodding from plumes, flashing from silk; for she was very large, very fat, tightly girt in pink taffeta,

and past her prime. As a parasol with many flounces, as a peacock with many feathers, shuts its flounces, folds its feathers, so she subsided and shut herself as she sank down in the leather armchair.

"Good morning, Mr. Bacon," said the Duchess. And she held out her hand which came through the slit of her white glove. And Oliver bent low as he shook it. And as their hands touched the link was forged between them once more. They were friends, yet enemies; he was master, she was mistress; each cheated the other, each needed the other, each feared the other, each felt this and knew this every time they touched hands thus in the little back room with the white light outside, and the tree with its six leaves, and the sound of the street in the distance and behind them the safes.

"And today, Duchess—what can I do for you today?" said Oliver, very softly.

The Duchess opened her heart, her private heart, gaped wide. And with a sigh but no word she took from her bag a long wash-leather pouch—it looked like a lean yellow ferret. And from a slit in the ferret's belly she dropped pearls—ten pearls. They rolled from the slit in the ferret's belly—one, two, three, four—like the eggs of some heavenly bird.

"All that's left me, dear Mr. Bacon," she moaned. Five, six, seven—down they rolled, down the slopes of the vast mountain sides that fell between her knees into one narrow valley—the eighth, the ninth, and the tenth. There they lay in the glow of the peach-blossom taffeta. Ten pearls.

"From the Appleby cincture,"[12] she mourned. "The last . . . the last of them all."

Oliver stretched out and took one of the pearls between finger and thumb. It was round, it was lustrous. But real was it, or false? Was she lying again? Did she dare?

10. **shagreen** (shə grēn′), untanned leather.
11. **pâté de foie gras** (pä tā′ də fwä grä′), a paste or spread made from goose liver and chopped truffles.
12. **cincture**, belt or girdle.

THE PRODIGAL DAUGHTER
John Collier
Lincolnshire Recreational Services, Usher Gallery, Lincoln

She laid her plump padded finger across her lips. "If the Duke knew . . ." she whispered. "Dear Mr. Bacon, a bit of bad luck . . ."

Been gambling again, had she?

"That villain! That sharper!" she hissed.

The man with the chipped cheek bone? A bad'un. And the Duke was straight as a poker; with side whiskers; would cut her off, shut her up down there if he knew—what I know, thought Oliver, and glanced at the safe.

"Araminta, Daphne, Diana," she moaned. "It's for *them*."

The ladies Araminta, Daphne, Diana— her daughters. He knew them; adored them. But it was Diana he loved.

"You have all my secrets," she leered. Tears slid; tears fell; tears, like diamonds, collecting powder in the ruts of her cherry blossom cheeks.

"Old friend," she murmured, "old friend."

"Old friend," he repeated, "old friend," as if he licked the words.

"How much?" he queried.

She covered the pearls with her hand.

"Twenty thousand," she whispered.

But was it real or false, the one he held in his hand? The Appleby cincture—hadn't she sold it already? He would ring for Spencer or Hammond. "Take it and test it," he would say. He stretched to the bell.

"You will come down tomorrow?" she urged, she interrupted. "The Prime Minister—His Royal Highness . . ." She stopped. "And Diana . . ." she added.

Oliver took his hand off the bell.

He looked past her, at the backs of the houses in Bond Street. But he saw, not the houses in Bond Street, but a dimpling river; and trout rising and salmon; and the Prime Minister; and himself too, in white waistcoat; and then, Diana. He looked down at the pearl in his hand. But how could he test it, in the light of the river, in the light of the eyes of Diana? But the eyes of the Duchess were on him.

"Twenty thousand," she moaned. "My honour!"

The honour of the mother of Diana! He drew his cheque book towards him; he took out his pen.

"Twenty—" he wrote. Then he stopped writing. The eyes of the old woman in the picture were on him—of the old woman his mother.

"Oliver!" she warned him. "Have sense! Don't be a fool!"

"Oliver!" the Duchess entreated—it was "Oliver" now, not "Mr. Bacon." "You'll come for a long week-end?"

Alone in the woods with Diana! Riding alone in the woods with Diana!

"Thousand," he wrote, and signed it.

"Here you are," he said.

And there opened all the flounces of the parasol, all the plumes of the peacock, the radiance of the wave, the swords and spears of Agincourt,[13] as she rose from her chair. And the two old men and the two young men, Spencer and Marshall, Wicks and Hammond, flattened themselves behind the counter envying him as he led her through the shop to the door. And he waggled his yellow glove in their faces, and she held her honour—a cheque for twenty thousand pounds with his signature—quite firmly in her hands.

"Are they false or are they real?" asked Oliver, shutting his private door. There they were, ten pearls on the blotting-paper on the table. He took them to the window. He held them under his lens to the light. . . . This, then, was the truffle he had routed out of the earth! Rotten at the centre—rotten at the core!

"Forgive me, oh, my mother!" he sighed, raising his hand as if he asked pardon of the old woman in the picture. And again he was a little boy in the alley where they sold dogs on Sunday.

"For," he murmured, laying the palms of his hands together, "it is to be a long week-end."

---

13. **Agincourt** (aj′ in kôrt), a village in northwest France at which English forces under Henry V decisively defeated a much larger French army in 1415.

FOR UNDERSTANDING

1. What is Oliver Bacon's present position? How has he achieved it?

2. What or who has goaded him on?

3. What does he still yearn to attain?

FOR INTERPRETATION

Discuss what the story implies about the following:
  a. human greed
  b. social classes
  c. the inability to be satisfied
  d. self-deceit
  e. the need for status

FOR APPRECIATION

Woolf is a master of imagery. Consider the following uses she makes of this device.

1. What are the images Woolf uses to describe Oliver's nose? Oliver himself? His walk? The sound he makes when viewing his jewels? What is she suggesting about Oliver?

2. What metaphors does Oliver use to describe his jewels? How does this imagery expand your awareness of his inner self?

3. The entrance and exit of the Duchess are rich with imagery. Reread these descriptions and list the metaphors used. What kind of feeling do you get from these images?

D. H. Lawrence 1885–1930

David Herbert Lawrence was a writer much maligned in his own time. Only after his death was he recognized as one of the geniuses of his day and an important literary innovator. His father was a miner, and his mother, somewhat more educated and with genteel pretensions, spurred her children to acquire an education so they could escape the drudgery of the working-class life.

Lawrence received a teacher's certificate at twenty-three and obtained a job in London. During the next year, he had some poetry and a short story published which established him as a promising young writer. But his first novel in 1911 received mixed reviews, and some critics, confused by his style and subject matter, were downright hostile. Finding that he could support himself by writing, Lawrence abandoned his teaching and began work on *Sons and Lovers,* published in 1913. Considered years later as one of his greatest novels, it met with vicious criticism at this time. His next book, *The Rainbow* (1915), the first of his radically new kind of novels, was banned for some time in England. Lawrence, already ill and feeling persecuted by the authorities, left England to seek a more primitive, compatible society. He moved first to Italy, then to Australia, Mexico, Taos in New Mexico, and finally back to Europe again. During these last years of his short life he wrote constantly: poetry, travel books, novels, and short stories. Some of his finest fiction can be found in the latter genre.

There is no doubt that Lawrence and James Joyce shattered the old ways of telling a story. Lawrence was influenced by the new psychology of Jung and Freud, and attempted to describe his characters, not by the visible one-tenth that could be seen, but by the inner nine-tenths that was submerged in the subconscious. His works have an intense, troubling reality as he uses symbols and poetic rhythms in his attempts to describe the indescribable. For many readers Lawrence creates an unusually intense and moving experience.

D.H. LAWRENCE
Jan Juta (1920)
National Portrait Gallery, London

But it was not only his style that was experimental. As a nonconformist he chose subjects that often offended his readers. He believed in the beauty of the primitive and the instinctive as compared to "cerebral consciousness." Dealing with relationships, sometimes between a man and a woman, sometimes between a parent and a child, he tried to capture the physical and emotional nuances of love, which he felt was the most important impulse in life. He saw love as destroyed and perverted by the world of his day. Always class conscious because of his background, he made many of his working-class characters admirable and those from the upper-middle-class despicable.

In ill health for years, Lawrence would never admit that he had tuberculosis and continued writing on sheer nerve and will power. Today the conventions and ideas that stirred such angry reactions in the reading public during his lifetime seem neither dangerous nor outrageous.

THE ROCKING-HORSE WINNER

There was a woman who was beautiful, who started with all the advantages, yet she had no luck. She married for love, and the love turned to dust. She had bonny children, yet she felt they had been thrust upon her, and she could not love them. They looked at her coldly, as if they were finding fault with her. And hurriedly she felt she must cover up some fault in herself. Yet what it was that she must cover up she never knew. Nevertheless, when her children were present, she always felt the centre of her heart go hard. This troubled her, and in her manner she was all the more gentle and anxious for her children, as if she loved them very much. Only she herself knew that at the centre of her heart was a hard little place that could not feel love, no, not for anybody. Everybody else said of her: "She is such a good mother. She adores her children." Only she herself, and her children themselves, knew it was not so. They read it in each other's eyes.

There were a boy and two little girls. They lived in a pleasant house, with a garden, and they had discreet servants and felt themselves superior to any one in the neighbourhood.

Although they lived in style, they felt always an anxiety in the house. There was never enough money. The mother had a small income, and the father had a small income, but not nearly enough for the social

position which they had to keep up. The father went into town to some office. But though he had good prospects, these prospects never materialized. There was always the grinding sense of the shortage of money, though the style was always kept up.

At last the mother said: "I will see if I can't make something." But she did not know where to begin. She racked her brains, and tried this thing and the other, but could not find anything successful. The failure made deep lines come into her face. Her children were growing up, they would have to go to school. There must be more money, there must be more money. The father, who was always very handsome and expensive in his tastes, seemed as if he never would be able to do anything worth doing. And the mother, who had a great belief in herself, did not succeed any better, and her tastes were just as expensive.

And so the house came to be haunted by the unspoken phrase: *There must be more money! There must be more money!* The children could hear it all the time, though nobody said it aloud. They heard it at Christmas, when the expensive and splendid toys filled the nursery. Behind the shining modern rocking-horse, behind the smart doll's-house, a voice would start whispering: "There *must* be more money! There *must* be more money!" And the children would stop playing, to listen for a moment. They would look into each other's eyes, to see if they had all heard. And each one saw in the eyes of the other two that they too had heard. "There *must* be more money! There *must* be more money!"

It came whispering from the springs of the still-swaying rocking-horse, and even the horse, bending his wooden champing head, heard it. The big doll, sitting so pink and smirking in her new pram,[1] could hear it quite plainly, and seemed to be smirking all the more self-consciously because of it. The foolish puppy, too, that took the place of the teddy-bear, he was looking so extraordinarily foolish for no other reason but that he heard the secret whisper all over the house: "There *must* be more money!"

Yet nobody ever said it aloud. The whisper was everywhere, and therefore no one spoke it. Just as no one ever says: "We are breathing!" in spite of the fact that breath is coming and going all the time.

"Mother," said the boy Paul one day, "why don't we keep a car of our own? Why do we always use uncle's, or else a taxi?"

"Because we're the poor members of the family," said the mother.

"But why are we, mother?"

"Well—I suppose," she said slowly, and bitterly, "it's because your father has no luck."

The boy was silent for some time.

"Is luck money, mother?" he asked, rather timidly.

"No, Paul. Not quite. It's what causes you to have money."

"Oh!" said Paul vaguely. "I thought when Uncle Oscar said *filthy lucker,* it meant money."

"*Filthy lucre* does mean money," said the mother. "But it's lucre, not luck."

"Oh!" said the boy. "Then what *is* luck, mother?"

"It's what causes you to have money. If you're lucky you have money. That's why it's better to be born lucky than rich. If you're rich, you may lose your money. But if you're lucky, you will always get more money."

"Oh! Will you? And is father not lucky?"

"Very unlucky, I should say," she said bitterly.

The boy watched her with unsure eyes.

"Why?" he asked.

"I don't know. Nobody ever knows why one person is lucky and another unlucky."

"Don't they? Nobody at all? Does *nobody* know?"

"Perhaps God. But He never tells."

"He ought to, then. And aren't you lucky either, mother?"

"I can't be, if I married an unlucky husband."

"But by yourself, aren't you?"

"I used to think I was, before I married. Now I think I am very unlucky indeed."

"Why?"

"Well—never mind! Perhaps I'm not really," she said.

The child looked at her, to see if she meant it. But he saw by the lines of her mouth that she was only trying to hide something from him.

"Well, anyhow," he said stoutly, "I'm a lucky person."

"Why?" said his mother, with a sudden laugh.

He stared at her. He didn't even know why he had said it.

"God told me," he asserted, brazening it out.

"I hope He did, dear!" she said, again with a laugh, but rather bitter.

"He did, mother!"

"Excellent!" said the mother, using one of her husband's exclamations.

The boy saw she did not believe him; or, rather, that she paid no attention to his assertion. This angered him somewhat, and made him want to compel her attention.

He went off by himself, vaguely, in a childish way, seeking for the clue to "luck." Absorbed, taking no heed of other people, he went about with a sort of stealth, seeking inwardly for luck. He wanted luck, he wanted it, he wanted it. When the two girls were playing dolls in the nursery, he would sit on his big rocking-horse, charging madly into space, with a frenzy that made the little girls

---

1. **pram,** a baby carriage or perambulator. (The word is mostly British rather than American.)

peer at him uneasily. Wildly the horse careered, the waving dark hair of the boy tossed, his eyes had a strange glare in them. The little girls dared not speak to him.

When he had ridden to the end of his mad little journey, he climbed down and stood in front of his rocking-horse, staring fixedly into its lowered face. Its red mouth was slightly open, its big eye was wide and glassy-bright.

"Now!" he would silently command the snorting steed. "Now, take me to where there is luck! Now take me!"

And he would slash the horse on the neck with the little whip he had asked Uncle Oscar for. He knew the horse could take him to where there was luck, if only he forced it. So he would mount again, and start on his furious ride, hoping at last to get there. He knew he could get there.

"You'll break your horse, Paul!" said the nurse.

"He's always riding like that! I wish he'd leave off!" said his elder sister Joan.

But he only glared down on them in silence. Nurse gave him up. She could make nothing of him. Anyhow he was growing beyond her.

One day his mother and his Uncle Oscar came in when he was on one of his furious rides. He did not speak to them.

"Hallo, you young jockey! Riding a winner?" said his uncle.

"Aren't you growing too big for a rocking-horse? You're not a very little boy any longer, you know," said his mother.

But Paul only gave a blue glare from his big, rather close-set eyes. He would speak to nobody when he was in full tilt. His mother watched him with an anxious expression on her face.

At last he suddenly stopped forcing his horse into the mechanical gallop, and slid down.

"Well, I got there!" he announced fiercely, his blue eyes still flaring, and his sturdy long legs straddling apart.

"Where did you get to?" asked his mother.

"Where I wanted to go," he flared back at her.

"That's right, son!" said Uncle Oscar. "Don't you stop till you get there. What's the horse's name?"

"He doesn't have a name," said the boy.

"Gets on without all right?" said the uncle.

"Well, he has different names. He was called Sansovino last week."

"Sansovino, eh? Won the Ascot.[2] How did you know his name?"

"He always talks about horse-races with Bassett," said Joan.

The uncle was delighted to find that his small nephew was posted with all the racing news. Bassett, the young gardener, who had been wounded in the left foot in the war and had got his present job through Oscar Cresswell, whose batman he had been, was a perfect blade[3] of the "turf." He lived in the racing events, and the small boy lived with him.

Oscar Cresswell got it all from Bassett.

"Master Paul comes and asks me, so I can't do more than tell him, sir," said Bassett, his face terribly serious, as if he were speaking of religious matters.

"And does he ever put anything on a horse he fancies?"

"Well—I don't want to give him away— he's a young sport, a fine sport, sir. Would you mind asking him yourself? He sort of takes a pleasure in it, and perhaps he'd feel I was giving him away, sir, if you don't mind."

Bassett was serious as a church.

The uncle went back to his nephew, and took him off for a ride in the car.

---

2. **Ascot** (as′ kət), a famous English horse race. Later this story mentions other famous English races, the **Lincoln,** the **Leger,** the **Grand National,** and the **Derby** (där′ bē).
3. **batman,** a British army officer's personal orderly and servant. **blade,** English and informal, means "lively young fellow, often a fan or devotee of something."

THE LAST OPEN DITCH
Peter Curling
Reproduced by Permission of Peter Curling©

"Say, Paul, old man, do you ever put anything on a horse?" the uncle asked.

The boy watched the handsome man closely.

"Why, do you think I oughtn't to?" he parried.

"Not a bit of it! I thought perhaps you might give me a tip for the Lincoln."

The car sped on into the country, going down to Uncle Oscar's place in Hampshire.[4]

"Honour bright?" said the nephew.

"Honour bright, son!" said the uncle.

"Well, then, Daffodil."

"Daffodil! I doubt it, sonny. What about Mirza?"

"I only know the winner," said the boy. "That's Daffodil."

"Daffodil, eh?"

There was a pause. Daffodil was an obscure horse comparatively.

"Uncle!"

"Yes, son?"

"You won't let it go any further, will you? I promised Bassett."

"Bassett be hanged, old man! What's he got to do with it?"

"We're partners. We've been partners from the first. Uncle, he lent me my first five shillings, which I lost. I promised him, honour bright, it was only between me and him; only you gave me that ten-shilling note I started winning with, so I thought you were lucky. You won't let it go further, will you?"

The boy gazed at his uncle from those big, hot, blue eyes, set rather close together. The uncle stirred and laughed uneasily.

"Right you are, son! I'll keep your tip private. Daffodil, eh? How much are you putting on him?"

"All except twenty pounds," said the boy. "I keep that in reserve."

4. **Hampshire,** a south-central shire, or county, in England.

The uncle thought it a good joke.

"You keep twenty pounds in reserve, do you, you young romancer? What are you betting, then?"

"I'm betting three hundred," said the boy gravely. "But it's between you and me, Uncle Oscar! Honour bright?"

The uncle burst into a roar of laughter.

"It's between you and me all right, you young Nat Gould," he said, laughing. "But where's your three hundred?"

"Bassett keeps it for me. We're partners."

"You are, are you! And what is Bassett putting on Daffodil?"

"He won't go quite as high as I do, I expect. Perhaps he'll go a hundred and fifty."

"What, pennies?" laughed the uncle.

"Pounds," said the child, with a surprised look at his uncle. "Bassett keeps a bigger reserve than I do."

Between wonder and amusement Uncle Oscar was silent. He pursued the matter no further, but he determined to take his nephew with him to the Lincoln races.

"Now, son," he said, "I am putting twenty on Mirza, and I'll put five for you on any horse you fancy. What's your pick?"

"Daffodil, uncle."

"No, not the fiver[5] on Daffodil!"

"I should if it was my own fiver," said the child.

"Good! Good! Right you are! A fiver for me and a fiver for you on Daffodil."

The child had never been to a race-meeting before, and his eyes were blue fire. He pursed his mouth tight, and watched. A Frenchman just in front had put his money on Lancelot. Wild with excitement, he flayed his arms up and down, yelling *Lancelot! Lancelot!* in his French accent.

Daffodil came in first, Lancelot second, Mirza third. The child, flushed and with eyes blazing, was curiously serene. His uncle brought him four five-pound notes, four to one.

"What am I to do with these?" he cried, waving them before the boy's eyes.

"I suppose we'll talk to Bassett," said the boy. "I expect I have fifteen hundred now; and twenty in reserve; and this twenty."

His uncle studied him for some moments.

"Look here, son!" he said. "You're not serious about Bassett and that fifteen hundred, are you?"

"Yes, I am. But it's between you and me, uncle. Honour bright!"

"Honour bright all right, son! But I must talk to Bassett."

"If you'd like to be a partner, uncle, with Bassett and me, we could all be partners. Only, you'd have to promise, honour bright, uncle, not to let it go beyond us three. Bassett and I are lucky, and you must be lucky, because it was your ten shillings I started winning with. . . ."

Uncle Oscar took both Bassett and Paul into Richmond Park for an afternoon, and there they talked.

"It's like this, you see, sir," Bassett said. "Master Paul would get me talking about racing events, spinning yarns, you know, sir. And he was always keen on knowing if I'd made or if I'd lost. It's about a year since, now, that I put five shillings on Blush of Dawn for him—and we lost. Then the luck turned, with that ten shillings he had from you that we put on Singhalese. And since that time, it's been pretty steady, all things considering. What do you say, Master Paul?"

"We're all right when we're sure," said Paul. "It's when we're not quite sure that we go down."

"Oh, but we're careful then," said Bassett.

"But when are you sure?" smiled Uncle Oscar.

"It's Master Paul, sir," said Bassett, in a secret, religious voice. "It's as if he had it from heaven. Like Daffodil, now, for the Lincoln. That was as sure as eggs."

"Did you put anything on Daffodil?" asked Oscar Cresswell.

---

5. **fiver,** English slang, a five-pound note.

"Yes, sir. I made my bit."

"And my nephew?"

Bassett was obstinately silent, looking at Paul.

"I made twelve hundred, didn't I, Bassett? I told uncle I was putting three hundred on Daffodil."

"That's right," said Bassett, nodding.

"But where's the money?" asked the uncle.

"I keep it safe locked up, sir. Master Paul he can have it any minute he likes to ask for it."

"What, fifteen hundred pounds?"

"And twenty! And forty, that is, with the twenty he made on the course."

"It's amazing!" said the uncle.

"If Master Paul offers you to be partners, sir, I would, if I were you; if you'll excuse me," said Bassett.

Oscar Cresswell thought about it.

"I'll see the money," he said.

They drove home again, and sure enough, Bassett came round to the garden-house with fifteen hundred pounds in notes. The twenty pounds reserve was left with Joe Glee, in the Turf Commission deposit.

"You see, it's all right, uncle, when I'm *sure!* Then we go strong, for all we're worth. Don't we, Bassett?"

"We do that, Master Paul."

"And when are you sure?" said the uncle, laughing.

"Oh, well, sometimes I'm *absolutely* sure, like about Daffodil," said the boy; "and sometimes I have an idea; and sometimes I haven't even an idea, have I, Bassett? Then we're careful, because we mostly go down."

"You do, do you! And when you're sure, like about Daffodil, what makes you sure, sonny?"

"Oh, well, I don't know," said the boy uneasily. "I'm sure, you know, uncle; that's all."

"It's as if he had it from heaven, sir," Bassett reiterated.

"I should say so!" said the uncle.

But he became a partner. And when the Leger was coming on, Paul was "sure" about Lively Spark, which was a quite inconsiderable horse. The boy insisted on putting a thousand on the horse, Bassett went for five hundred, and Oscar Cresswell two hundred. Lively Spark came in first, and the betting had been ten to one against him. Paul had made ten thousand.

"You see," he said, "I was absolutely sure of him."

Even Oscar Cresswell had cleared two thousand.

"Look here, son," he said, "this sort of thing makes me nervous."

"It needn't, uncle! Perhaps I shan't be sure again for a long time."

"But what are you going to do with your money?" asked the uncle.

"Of course," said the boy, "I started it for mother. She said she had no luck, because father is unlucky, so I thought if I was lucky, it might stop whispering."

"What might stop whispering?"

"Our house. I *hate* our house for whispering."

"What does it whisper?"

"Why—why"—the boy fidgeted—"why, I don't know. But it's always short of money, you know, uncle."

"I know it, son, I know it."

"You know people send mother writs,[6] don't you, uncle?"

"I'm afraid I do," said the uncle.

"And then the house whispers, like people laughing at you behind your back. It's awful, that is! I thought if I was lucky . . ."

"You might stop it," added the uncle.

The boy watched him with big blue eyes that had an uncanny cold fire in them, and he said never a word.

"Well, then!" said the uncle. "What are we doing?"

"I shouldn't like mother to know I was lucky," said the boy.

"Why not, son?"

"She'd stop me."

---

6. **writs,** court orders to pay one's bills.

"I don't think she would."

"Oh!"—and the boy writhed in an odd way—"I don't want her to know, uncle."

"All right, son! We'll manage it without her knowing."

They managed it very easily. Paul, at the other's suggestion, handed over five thousand pounds to his uncle, who deposited it with the family lawyer, who was then to inform Paul's mother that a relative had put five thousand pounds into his hands, which sum was to be paid out a thousand pounds at a time, on the mother's birthday, for the next five years.

"So she'll have a birthday present of a thousand pounds for five successive years," said Uncle Oscar. "I hope it won't make it all the harder for her later."

Paul's mother had her birthday in November. The house had been "whispering" worse than ever lately, and, even in spite of his luck, Paul could not bear up against it. He was very anxious to see the effect of the birthday letter, telling his mother about the thousand pounds.

When there were no visitors, Paul now took his meals with his parents, as he was beyond the nursery control. His mother went into town nearly every day. She had discovered that she had an odd knack of sketching furs and dress materials, so she worked secretly in the studio of a friend who was the chief "artist" for the leading drapers.[7] She drew the figures of ladies in furs and ladies in silk and sequins for the newspaper advertisements. This young woman artist earned several thousand pounds a year, but Paul's mother only made several hundreds, and she was again dissatisfied. She so wanted to be first in something, and she did not succeed, even in making sketches for drapery advertisements.

She was down to breakfast on the morning of her birthday. Paul watched her face as she read her letters. He knew the lawyer's letter. As his mother read it, her face hardened and became more expressionless. Then a cold determined look came on her mouth. She hid the letter under the pile of others, and said not a word about it.

"Didn't you have anything nice in the post for your birthday, mother?" said Paul.

"Quite moderately nice," she said, her voice cold and absent.

She went away to town without saying more.

But in the afternoon Uncle Oscar appeared. He said Paul's mother had had a long interview with the lawyer, asking if the whole five thousand could be advanced at once, as she was in debt.

"What do you think, uncle?" said the boy.

"I leave it to you, son."

"Oh, let her have it, then! We can get some more with the other," said the boy.

"A bird in the hand is worth two in the bush, laddie!" said Uncle Oscar.

"But I'm sure to know for the Grand National; or the Lincolnshire; or else the Derby. I'm sure to know for one of them," said Paul.

So Uncle Oscar signed the agreement, and Paul's mother touched the whole five thousand. Then something very curious happened. The voices in the house suddenly went mad, like a chorus of frogs on a spring evening. There were certain new furnishings, and Paul had a tutor. He was really going to Eton,[8] his father's school, in the following autumn. There were flowers in the winter, and a blossoming of the luxury Paul's mother had been used to. And yet the voices in the house, behind the sprays of mimosa and almond blossoms, and from under the piles of iridescent cushions, simply trilled and screamed in a sort of ecstasy: "There must be more money! Oh-h-h, there must be more money. Oh, now now-w! Now-w-w-w—there must be more money!—more than ever! More than ever!"

It frightened Paul terribly. He studied away at his Latin and Greek with his tutors. But his intense hours were spent with Bassett. The Grand National had gone by: he had not

---

7. **draper,** chiefly British, a seller of clothes and dry goods.

8. **Eton,** a very famous boys' school in England.

"known," and had lost a hundred pounds. Summer was at hand. He was in agony for the Lincoln. But even for the Lincoln he didn't "know" and he lost fifty pounds. He became wild-eyed and strange, as if something were going to explode in him.

"Let it alone, son! Don't you bother about it!" urged Uncle Oscar. But it was as if the boy couldn't really hear what his uncle was saying.

"I've got to know for the Derby! I've got to know for the Derby!" the child reiterated, his big blue eyes blazing with a sort of madness.

His mother noticed how overwrought he was.

"You'd better go to the seaside. Wouldn't you like to go now to the seaside, instead of waiting? I think you'd better," she said, looking down at him anxiously, her heart curiously heavy because of him.

But the child lifted his uncanny blue eyes.

"I couldn't possibly go before the Derby, mother!" he said. "I couldn't possibly!"

"Why not?" she said, her voice becoming heavy when she was opposed. "Why not? You can still go from the seaside to see the Derby with your Uncle Oscar, if that's what you wish. No need for you to wait here. Besides, I think you care too much about these races. It's a bad sign. My family has been a gambling family, and you won't know till you grow up how much damage it has done. But it has done damage. I shall have to send Bassett away, and ask Uncle Oscar not to talk racing to you, unless you promise to be reasonable about it; go away to the seaside and forget it. You're all nerves!"

"I'll do what you like, mother, so long as you don't send me away till after the Derby," the boy said.

"Send you away from where? Just from this house?"

"Yes," he said, gazing at her.

"Why, you curious child, what makes you care about this house so much, suddenly? I never knew you loved it."

He gazed at her without speaking. He had a secret within a secret, something he had not divulged, even to Bassett or to his Uncle Oscar.

But his mother, after standing undecided and a little bit sullen for some moments, said:

"Very well, then! Don't go to the seaside till after the Derby, if you don't wish it. But promise me you won't let your nerves go to pieces. Promise you won't think so much about horse-racing and *events*, as you call them!"

"Oh, no," said the boy casually. "I won't think much about them, mother. You needn't worry. I wouldn't worry, mother, if I were you."

"If you were me and I were you," said his mother, "I wonder what we *should* do!"

"But you know you needn't worry, mother, don't you?" the boy repeated.

"I should be awfully glad to know it," she said wearily.

"Oh, well, you *can*, you know. I mean, you ought to know you needn't worry," he insisted.

"Ought I? Then I'll see about it," she said.

Paul's secret of secrets was his wooden horse, that which had no name. Since he was emancipated from a nurse and a nursery-governess, he had had his rocking-horse removed to his own bedroom at the top of the house.

"Surely, you're too big for a rocking-horse!" his mother had remonstrated.

"Well, you see, mother, till I can have a real horse, I like to have some sort of animal about," had been his quaint answer.

"Do you feel he keeps you company?" she laughed.

"Oh, yes! He's very good, he always keeps me company, when I'm there," said Paul.

So the horse, rather shabby, stood in an arrested prance in the boy's bedroom.

The Derby was drawing near, and the boy grew more and more tense. He hardly heard what was spoken to him, he was very frail, and his eyes were really uncanny. His mother had sudden seizures of uneasiness about him. Sometimes, for half-an-hour, she would feel a sudden anxiety about him that was almost anguish. She wanted to rush to him at once, and know he was safe.

Two nights before the Derby, she was at a big party in town, when one of her rushes of anxiety about her boy, her first-born, gripped her heart till she could hardly speak. She fought with the feeling, might and main, for she believed in common sense. But it was too strong. She had to leave the dance and go downstairs to telephone to the country. The children's nursery-governess was terribly surprised and startled at being rung up in the night.

"Are the children all right, Miss Wilmot?"

"Oh yes, they are quite all right."

"Master Paul? Is he all right?"

"He went to bed as right as a trivet.⁹ Shall I run up and look at him?"

"No," said Paul's mother reluctantly. "No! Don't trouble. It's all right. Don't sit up. We shall be home fairly soon." She did not want her son's privacy intruded upon.

"Very good," said the governess.

It was about one o'clock when Paul's mother and father drove up to their house. All was still. Paul's mother went to her room and slipped off her white fur cloak. She had told her maid not to wait up for her. She heard her husband downstairs, mixing a whiskey-and-soda.

And then, because of the strange anxiety at her heart, she stole upstairs to her son's room. Noiselessly she went along the upper corridor. Was there a faint noise? What was it?

She stood, with arrested muscles, outside his door, listening. There was a strange, heavy, and yet not loud noise. Her heart stood still. It was a soundless noise, yet rushing and powerful. Something huge, in violent, hushed motion. What was it? What in God's name was it? She ought to know. She felt that she knew the noise. She knew what it was.

Yet she could not place it. She couldn't say what it was. And on and on it went, like a madness.

Softly, frozen with anxiety and fear, she turned the doorhandle.

The room was dark. Yet in the space near the window, she heard and saw something plunging to and fro. She gazed in fear and amazement.

Then suddenly she switched on the light, and saw her son, in his green pajamas, madly surging on the rocking-horse. The blaze of light suddenly lit him up, as he urged the wooden horse, and lit her up, as she stood, blonde, in her dress of pale green and crystal, in the doorway.

"Paul!" she cried. "Whatever are you doing?"

"It's Malabar!" he screamed, in a powerful, strange voice. "It's Malabar."

His eyes blazed at her for one strange and senseless second, as he ceased urging his wooden horse. Then he fell with a crash to the ground, and she, all her tormented motherhood flooding upon her, rushed to gather him up.

But he was unconscious, and unconscious he remained, with some brain-fever. He talked and tossed, and his mother sat stonily by his side.

"Malabar! It's Malabar! Bassett, Bassett, I know! It's Malabar!"

So the child cried, trying to get up and urge the rocking-horse that gave him his inspiration.

"What does he mean by Malabar?" asked the heart-frozen mother.

"I don't know," said the father stonily.

"What does he mean by Malabar?" she asked her brother Oscar.

"It's one of the horses running for the Derby," was the answer.

And, in spite of himself, Oscar Cresswell spoke to Bassett, and himself put a thousand on Malabar: at fourteen to one.

The third day of the illness was critical: they were waiting for a change. The boy, with

---

9. **trivet** (triv′ it),   a tripod, but here used idiomatically to mean "entirely all right."

his rather long, curly hair, was tossing ceaselessly on the pillow. He neither slept nor regained consciousness, and his eyes were like blue stones. His mother sat, feeling her heart had gone, turned actually into a stone.

In the evening, Oscar Cresswell did not come, but Bassett sent a message, saying could he come up for one moment, just one moment? Paul's mother was very angry at the intrusion, but on second thought she agreed. The boy was the same. Perhaps Bassett might bring him to consciousness.

The gardener, a shortish fellow with a little brown mustache, and sharp little brown eyes, tiptoed into the room, touched his imaginary cap to Paul's mother, and stole to the bedside, staring with glittering, smallish eyes, at the tossing, dying child.

"Master Paul!" he whispered. "Master Paul! Malabar come in first all right, a clean win. I did as you told me. You've made over seventy thousand pounds, you have; you've got over eighty thousand. Malabar came in all right, Master Paul."

"Malabar! Malabar! Did I say Malabar, mother? Did I say Malabar? Do you think I'm lucky, mother? I knew Malabar, didn't I? Over eighty thousand pounds! I call that lucky, don't you, mother? Over eighty thousand pounds! I knew, didn't I know I knew? Malabar came in all right. If I ride my horse till I'm sure, then I tell you, Bassett, you can go as high as you like. Did you go for all you were worth, Bassett?"

"I went a thousand on it, Master Paul."

"I never told you, mother, that if I can ride my horse, and *get there*, then I'm absolutely sure—oh, absolutely! Mother, did I ever tell you? I *am* lucky."

"No, you never did," said the mother.

But the boy died in the night.

And even as he lay dead, his mother heard her brother's voice saying to her: "Actually, Hester, you're eighty-odd thousand to the good and a poor devil of a son to the bad. But, poor devil, poor devil, he's best gone out of a life where he rides his rocking-horse to find a winner."

FOR UNDERSTANDING

1. What causes the anxiety in the house? How does the mother try to solve it? How does Paul?
2. What birthday present does Paul give his mother?
3. How does the mother respond?
4. What is the size of the winnings Paul eventually accumulates?
5. What does Paul's mother discover when she opens the door to his room?

FOR INTERPRETATION

1. Lawrence himself was raised as a nonconformist and believed that primitive people who lived without money were far happier than people of his day. He became more and more disgusted with society's emphasis on the importance of money and the wealthy's need to always get more (usually at the expense of the poor). Might Paul and his mother symbolize such a conflict?
2. As a rule, in a story the protagonist is the principal character and the center of the reader's interest. Does this general rule apply here, or does something else hold your attention?
3. What associations come to your mind when you think of a rocking horse?
4. What is the meaning of the last line in the story?

FOR APPRECIATION

At one time Lawrence commented: "I don't care so much what a woman feels. I only care for what a woman is." Through a new kind of characterization, he was attempting to make a quantum leap from what a person appears to be to the unconscious level where the real self lives. Most readers are used to the more conventional presentation of character in which the writer draws the characters from the outside, almost as though describing the body language and speech of actors on a stage. Hence, to understand Lawrence's writing we must adjust our expectations. Reread the first paragraph which describes the mother. Then think about the other scenes in which the mother appears. In your opinion does Lawrence portray accurately the mother's feelings or the kind of woman she truly is inside?

Katherine Mansfield

1888–1923

The writing of Katherine Mansfield has often been compared to that of the Russian short-story writer, Anton Chekhov; certainly there was a similarity of temperament. Both of them had the ability to respond completely to life, and both presented a "slice of life" as they saw it. Even while suffering greatly in her last years as she waged a losing battle with tuberculosis, Mansfield never lost her ability to delight in life. There is about her writing a certain luminous quality that makes her work difficult to imitate, though many have tried. She frequently said that little of contemporary writing was true: "The writers are not humble; they are not serving the great purpose which literature exists to serve." She particularly cherished the comment of a printer who having set her story, "Prelude," in type said, "My! But these kids are *real.*"

Born in Wellington, New Zealand into a banker's family that had lived in Australia and New Zealand for three generations, she went to the village school with the milk boy and the washerwoman's daughter whom she later used as characters in her story, "The Doll's House." When she was thirteen she was sent to Queen's College school in England and became involved in all the cultural excitement of London, as well as editing the school magazine. At eighteen she returned to New Zealand, but felt like an unhappy exile and finally persuaded her parents to let her return to London on a small allowance. Back in England she had difficulty supporting herself with her writing and had to play minor parts in traveling opera companies to survive. In 1911 she published a collection of short stories, *In a German Pension,* based on her experiences while convalescing in Germany from an illness. The book was successful, but the publisher went bankrupt before she was paid. In 1918 she married John Middleton Murry, who became editor of the magazine, *The Athenaeum,* for which she wrote weekly literary criticisms of novels.

World War I came as an emotional shock to Mansfield, throwing her into a mental chaos which she gradually escaped by thinking back to her childhood in New Zealand—a much calmer,

KATHERINE MANSFIELD
A.E. Rice
National Art Gallery, Wellington, New Zealand

happier time. When her younger brother came to visit her on his way to join the English army, the two of them spent hours talking about their childhood. This, along with his death a month later, crystallized her decision to write of that period. *The Garden Party* (1922), a group of short stories set in the New Zealand of her youth, met with critical success, but Mansfield had scant time to enjoy this recognition. On January 9, 1923 her husband joined her at Fontainebleau where she had gone to gain inner rejuvenation. Murry said he had never seen her "so beautiful . . . as if an exquisite perfection had taken possession of her completely." She died at 10:30 that night from a massive lung hemorrhage.

THE GARDEN-PARTY

And after all the weather was ideal. They could not have had a more perfect day for a garden-party if they had ordered it. Windless, warm, the sky without a cloud. Only the blue was veiled with a haze of light gold, as it is sometimes in early summer. The gardener had been up since dawn, mowing the lawns and sweeping them, until the grass and the dark flat rosettes where the daisy plants had been seemed to shine. As for the roses, you could not help feeling they understood that roses are the only flowers that impress people at garden-parties; the only flowers that everybody is certain of knowing. Hundreds, yes, literally hundreds, had come out in a single night; the green bushes bowed down as though they had been visited by archangels.

Breakfast was not yet over before the men came to put up the marquee.[1]

"Where do you want the marquee put, mother?"

"My dear child, it's no use asking me. I'm determined to leave everything to you children this year. Forget I am your mother. Treat me as an honoured guest."

But Meg could not possibly go and supervise the men. She had washed her hair before breakfast, and she sat drinking her coffee in a green turban, with a dark wet curl stamped on each cheek. Jose, the butterfly, always came down in a silk petticoat and a kimono jacket.

"You'll have to go, Laura; you're the artistic one."

Away Laura flew, still holding her piece of bread-and-butter. It's so delicious to have an excuse for eating out of doors and, besides, she loved having to arrange things; she always felt she could do it so much better than anybody else.

Four men in their shirt-sleeves stood grouped together on the garden path. They carried staves covered with rolls of canvas and they had big tool-bags slung on their backs. They looked impressive. Laura wished now that she was not holding that piece of bread-and-butter, but there was nowhere to put it and she couldn't possibly throw it away. She blushed and tried to look severe and even a little bit short-sighted as she came up to them.

"Good morning," she said, copying her mother's voice. But that sounded so fearfully affected that she was ashamed, and stammered like a little girl, "Oh—er—have you come—is it about the marquee?"

"That's right, miss," said the tallest of the men, a lanky, freckled fellow, and he shifted his tool-bag, knocked back his straw hat and smiled down at her. "That's about it."

His smile was so easy, so friendly, that Laura recovered. What nice eyes he had, small, but such a dark blue! And now she looked at the others, they were smiling too. "Cheer up, we won't bite," their smile seemed to say. How very nice workmen were! And what a beautiful morning! She mustn't mention the morning; she must be businesslike. The marquee.

"Well, what about the lily-lawn? Would that do?"

And she pointed to the lily-lawn with the hand that didn't hold the bread-and-butter. They turned, they stared in the direction. A little fat chap thrust out his underlip and the tall fellow frowned.

1. **marquee** (mär kē'), a large tent.

"I don't fancy it," said he. "Not conspicuous enough. You see, with a thing like a marquee"—and he turned to Laura in his easy way—"you want to put it somewhere where it'll give you a bang slap in the eye, if you follow me."

Laura's upbringing made her wonder for a moment whether it was quite respectful of a workman to talk to her of bangs slap in the eye. But she did quite follow him.

"A corner of the tennis-court," she suggested. "But the band's going to be in one corner."

"H'm, going to have a band, are you?" said another of the workmen. He was pale. He had a haggard look as his dark eyes scanned the tennis-court. What was he thinking?

"Only a very small band," said Laura gently. Perhaps he wouldn't mind so much if the band was quite small. But the tall fellow interrupted.

"Look here, miss, that's the place. Against those trees. Over there. That'll do fine."

Against the karakas. Then the karaka trees would be hidden. And they were so lovely, with their broad, gleaming leaves, and their clusters of yellow fruit. They were like trees you imagined growing on a desert island, proud, solitary, lifting their leaves and fruits to the sun in a kind of silent splendour. Must they be hidden by a marquee?

They must. Already the men had shouldered their staves and were making for the place. Only the tall fellow was left. He bent down, pinched a sprig of lavender, put his thumb and forefinger to his nose and snuffed up the smell. When Laura saw that gesture she forgot all about the karakas in her wonder at him caring for things like that—caring for the smell of lavender. How many men that she knew would have done such a thing. Oh, how extraordinarily nice workmen were, she thought. Why couldn't she have workmen for friends rather than the silly boys she danced with and who came to Sunday night supper? She would get on much better with men like these.

It's all the fault, she decided, as the tall fellow drew something on the back of an envelope, something that was to be looped up or left to hang, of these absurd class distinctions. Well, for her part, she didn't feel them. Not a bit, not an atom. . . . And now there came the chock-chock of wooden hammers. Someone whistled, someone sang out, "Are you right there, matey?" "Matey!" The friendliness of it, the—the— Just to prove how happy she was, just to show the tall fellow how at home she felt, and how she despised stupid conventions, Laura took a big bite of her bread-and-butter as she stared at the little drawing. She felt just like a work-girl.

"Laura, Laura, where are you? Telephone, Laura!" a voice cried from the house.

"Coming!" Away she skimmed, over the lawn, up the path, up the steps, across the veranda and into the porch. In the hall her father and Laurie were brushing their hats ready to go to the office.

"I say, Laura," said Laurie very fast, "you might just give a squiz at my coat before this afternoon. See if it wants pressing."

"I will," said she. Suddenly she couldn't stop herself. She ran at Laurie and gave him a small, quick squeeze. "Oh, I do love parties, don't you?" gasped Laura.

"Ra-ther," said Laurie's warm, boyish voice, and he squeezed his sister too and gave her a gentle push. "Dash off to the telephone, old girl."

The telephone. "Yes, yes; oh yes. Kitty? Good morning, dear. Come to lunch? Do, dear. Delighted, of course. It will only be a very scratch meal—just the sandwich crusts and broken meringue-shells and what's left over. Yes, isn't it a perfect morning? Your white? Oh, I certainly should. One moment—hold the line. Mother's calling." And Laura sat back. "What, mother? Can't hear."

Mrs. Sheridan's voice floated down the stairs. "Tell her to wear that sweet hat she had on last Sunday."

"Mother says you're to wear that *sweet* hat you had on last Sunday. Good. One o'clock. Bye-bye."

Laura put back the receiver, flung her arms over her head, took a deep breath, stretched and let them fall. "Huh," she sighed, and the moment after the sigh she sat up quickly. She was still, listening. All the doors in the house seemed to be open. The house was alive with soft, quick steps and running voices. The green baize door that led to the kitchen regions swung open and shut with a muffled thud. And now there came a long, chuckling absurd sound. It was the heavy piano being moved on its stiff castors. But the air! If you stopped to notice, was the air always like this? Little faint winds were playing chase in at the tops of the windows, out at the doors. And there were two tiny spots of sun, one on the inkpot, one on a silver photograph frame, playing too. Darling little spots. Especially the one on the inkpot lid. It was quite warm. A warm little silver star. She could have kissed it.

The front door bell pealed and there sounded the rustle of Sadie's print skirt on the stairs. A man's voice murmured; Sadie answered, careless, "I'm sure I don't know. Wait. I'll ask Mrs. Sheridan."

"What is it, Sadie?" Laura came into the hall.

"It's the florist, Miss Laura."

It was, indeed. There, just inside the door, stood a wide, shallow tray full of pots of pink lilies. No other kind. Nothing but lilies—canna lilies, big pink flowers, wide open, radiant, almost frighteningly alive on bright crimson stems.

"O-oh, Sadie!" said Laura, and the sound was like a little moan. She crouched down as if to warm herself at that blaze of lilies; she felt they were in her fingers, on her lips, growing in her breast.

"It's some mistake," she said faintly. "Nobody ever ordered so many. Sadie, go and find mother."

But at that moment Mrs. Sheridan joined them.

"It's quite right," she said calmly. "Yes, I ordered them. Aren't they lovely?" She pressed Laura's arm. "I was passing the shop yesterday, and I saw them in the window. And I suddenly thought for once in my life I shall have enough canna lilies. The garden-party will be a good excuse."

"But I thought you said you didn't mean to interfere," said Laura. Sadie had gone. The florist's man was still outside at his van. She put her arm round her mother's neck and gently, very gently, she bit her mother's ear.

"My darling child, you wouldn't like a logical mother, would you? Don't do that. Here's the man."

He carried more lilies still, another whole tray.

"Bank them up, just inside the door, on both sides of the porch, please," said Mrs. Sheridan. "Don't you agree, Laura?"

"Oh, I *do*, mother."

In the drawing-room Meg, Jose and good little Hans had at last succeeded in moving the piano.

"Now, if we put this chesterfield[2] against the wall and move everything out of the room except the chairs, don't you think?"

"Quite."

"Hans, move these tables into the smoking-room, and bring a sweeper to take these marks off the carpet and—one moment, Hans—" Jose loved giving orders to the servants and they loved obeying her. She always made them feel they were taking part in some drama. "Tell mother and Miss Laura to come here at once."

"Very good, Miss Jose."

She turned to Meg. "I want to hear what the piano sounds like, just in case I'm asked to sing this afternoon. Let's try over 'This Life is Weary.'"

Pom! Ta-ta-ta *Tee*-ta! The piano burst out so passionately that Jose's face changed. She clasped her hands. She looked mournfully and enigmatically at her mother and Laura as they came in.

This Life is *Wee*-ary,

---

2. **chesterfield,** a sofa originally designed in the eighteenth century.

A Tear—a Sigh.
A Love that *Chan*-ges,
  This Life is *Wee*-ary,
A Tear—a Sigh.
A Love that *Chan*-ges,
And then . . . Good-bye!

But at the word "Good-bye," and although the piano sounded more desperate than ever, her face broke into a brilliant, dreadfully unsympathetic smile.

"Aren't I in good voice, mummy?" she beamed.

This Life is *Wee*-ary,
Hope comes to Die.
A Dream—a *Wa*-kening.

But now Sadie interrupted them. "What is it, Sadie?"

"If you please, m'm, cook says have you got the flags for the sandwiches?"

"The flags for the sandwiches, Sadie?" echoed Mrs. Sheridan dreamily. And the children knew by her face that she hadn't got them. "Let me see." And she said to Sadie firmly, "Tell cook I'll let her have them in ten minutes."

Sadie went.

"Now, Laura," said her mother quickly, "come with me into the smoking-room. I've got the names somewhere on the back of an envelope. You'll have to write them out for me. Meg, go upstairs this minute and take that wet thing off your head. Jose, run and finish dressing this instant. Do you hear me, children, or shall I have to tell your father when he comes home to-night? And—and, Jose, pacify cook if you do go into the kitchen, will you? I'm terrified of her this morning."

The envelope was found at last behind the dining-room clock, though how it had got there Mrs. Sheridan could not imagine.

"One of you children must have stolen it out of my bag, because I remember vividly—cream-cheese and lemon-curd. Have you done that?"

"Yes."

"Egg and—" Mrs. Sheridan held the en-velope away from her. "It looks like mice. It can't be mice, can it?"

"Olive, pet," said Laura, looking over her shoulder.

"Yes, of course, olive. What a horrible combination it sounds. Egg and olive."

They were finished at last, and Laura took them off to the kitchen. She found Jose there pacifying the cook, who did not look at all terrifying.

"I have never seen such exquisite sandwiches," said Jose's rapturous voice. "How many kinds did you say there were, cook? Fifteen?"

"Fifteen, Miss Jose."

"Well, cook, I congratulate you."

Cook swept up crusts with the long sandwich knife, and smiled broadly.

"Godber's has come," announced Sadie, issuing out of the pantry. She had seen the man pass the window.

That meant the cream puffs had come. Godber's were famous for their cream puffs. Nobody ever thought of making them at home.

"Bring them in and put them on the table, my girl," ordered cook.

Sadie brought them in and went back to the door. Of course Laura and Jose were far too grown-up to really care about such things. All the same, they couldn't help agreeing that the puffs looked very attractive. Very. Cook began arranging them, shaking off the extra icing sugar.

"Don't they carry one back to all one's parties?" said Laura.

"I suppose they do," said practical Jose, who never liked to be carried back. "They look beautifully light and feathery, I must say."

"Have one each, my dears," said cook in her comfortable voice. "Yer ma won't know."

Oh, impossible. Fancy cream puffs so soon after breakfast. The very idea made one shudder. All the same, two minutes later Jose and Laura were licking their fingers with that absorbed inward look that only comes from whipped cream.

"Let's go into the garden, out by the back-way," suggested Laura. "I want to see how the men are getting on with the marquee. They're such awfully nice men."

But the back door was blocked by cook, Sadie, Godber's man and Hans.

Something had happened.

"Tuk-tuk-tuk," clucked cook like an agitated hen. Sadie had her hand clapped to her cheek as though she had toothache. Hans' face was screwed up in the effort to understand. Only Godber's man seemed to be enjoying himself; it was his story.

"What's the matter? What's happened?"

"There's been a horrible accident," said cook. "A man killed."

"A man killed! Where? How? When?"

But Godber's man wasn't going to have his story snatched from under his very nose.

"Know those little cottages just below here, miss?" Know them? Of course she knew them. "Well, there's a young chap living there, name of Scott, a carter. His horse shied at a traction-engine, corner of Hawke Street this morning, and he was thrown out on the back of his head. Killed."

"Dead!" Laura stared at Godber's man.

"Dead when they picked him up," said Godber's man with relish. "They were taking the body home as I come up here." And he said to the cook, "He's left a wife and five little ones."

"Jose, come here." Laura caught hold of her sister's sleeve and dragged her through the kitchen to the other side of the green baize door. There she paused and leaned against it. "Jose!" she said, horrified, "However are we going to stop everything?"

"Stop everything, Laura!" cried Jose in astonishment. "What do you mean?"

"Stop the garden-party, of course." Why did Jose pretend?

But Jose was still more amazed. "Stop the garden-party? My dear Laura, don't be so absurd. Of course we can't do anything of the kind. Nobody expects us to. Don't be so extravagant."

"But we can't possibly have a garden-party with a man dead just outside the front gate."

That really was extravagant, for the little cottages were in a lane to themselves at the very bottom of a steep rise that led up to the house. A broad road ran between. True, they were far too near. They were the greatest possible eyesore and they had no right to be in that neighbourhood at all. They were little mean dwellings painted a chocolate brown. In the garden patches there was nothing but cabbage stalks, sick hens and tomato cans. The very smoke coming out of their chimneys was poverty-stricken. Little rags and shreds of smoke, so unlike the great silvery plumes that uncurled from the Sheridans' chimneys. Washerwomen lived in the lane and sweeps and a cobbler and a man whose house-front was studded all over with minute bird-cages. Children swarmed. When the Sheridans were little they were forbidden to set foot there because of the revolting language and of what they might catch. But since they were grown up Laura and Laurie on their prowls sometimes walked through. It was disgusting and sordid. They came out with a shudder. But still one must go everywhere; one must see everything. So through they went.

"And just think of what the band would sound like to that poor woman," said Laura.

"Oh, Laura!" Jose began to be seriously annoyed. "If you're going to stop a band playing every time someone has an accident, you'll lead a very strenuous life. I'm every bit as sorry about it as you. I feel just as sympathetic." Her eyes hardened. She looked at her sister just as she used to when they were little and fighting together. "You won't bring a drunken workman back to life by being sentimental," she said softly.

"Drunk! Who said he was drunk?" Laura turned furiously on Jose. She said just as they had used to say on those occasions, "I'm going straight up to tell mother."

"Do, dear," cooed Jose.

"Mother, can I come into your room?" Laura turned the big glass door-knob.

"Of course, child. Why, what's the matter? What's given you such a colour?" And Mrs. Sheridan turned round from her dressing-table. She was trying on a new hat.

"Mother, a man's been killed," began Laura.

"*Not* in the garden?" interrupted her mother.

"No, no!"

"Oh, what a fright you gave me!" Mrs. Sheridan sighed with relief and took off the big hat and held it on her knees.

"But listen, mother," said Laura. Breathless, half choking, she told the dreadful story. "Of course, we can't have our party, can we?" she pleaded. "The band and everybody arriving. They'd hear us, mother; they're nearly neighbours!"

To Laura's astonishment her mother behaved just like Jose; it was harder to bear because she seemed amused. She refused to take Laura seriously.

"But, my dear child, use your common sense. It's only by accident we've heard of it. If someone had died there normally—and I can't understand how they keep alive in those poky little holes—we should still be having our party, shouldn't we?"

Laura had to say "yes" to that, but she felt it was all wrong. She sat down on her mother's sofa and pinched the cushion frill.

"Mother, isn't it really terribly heartless of us?" she asked.

"Darling!" Mrs. Sheridan got up and came over to her, carrying the hat. Before Laura could stop her she had popped it on. "My child!" said her mother, "the hat is yours. It's made for you. It's much too young for me. I have never seen you look such a picture. Look at yourself!" And she held up her hand-mirror.

"But, mother," Laura began again. She couldn't look at herself; she turned aside.

This time Mrs. Sheridan lost patience just as Jose had done.

"You are being very absurd, Laura," she said coldly. "People like that don't expect sacrifices from us. And it's not very sympathetic to spoil everybody's enjoyment as you're doing now."

"I don't understand," said Laura, and she walked quickly out of the room into her own bedroom. There, quite by chance, the first thing she saw was this charming girl in the mirror, in her black hat trimmed with gold daisies and a long black velvet ribbon. Never had she imagined she could look like that. Is mother right? she thought. And now she hoped her mother was right. Am I being extravagant? Perhaps it was extravagant. Just for a moment she had another glimpse of that poor woman and those little children and the body being carried into the house. But it all seemed blurred, unreal, like a picture in the newspaper. I'll remember it again after the party's over, she decided. And somehow that seemed quite the best plan. . . .

Lunch was over by half-past one. By half-past two they were all ready for the fray. The green-coated band had arrived and was established in a corner of the tennis-court.

"My dear!" trilled Kitty Maitland, "aren't they too like frogs for words? You ought to have arranged them round the pond with the conductor in the middle on a leaf."

Laurie arrived and hailed them on his way to dress. At the sight of him Laura remembered the accident again. She wanted to tell him. If Laurie agreed with the others, then it was bound to be all right. And she followed him into the hall.

"Laurie!"

"Hallo!" He was half-way upstairs, but when he turned round and saw Laura he suddenly puffed out his cheeks and goggled his eyes at her. "My word, Laura! You do look stunning," said Laurie. "What an absolutely topping hat!"

Laura said faintly "Is it?" and smiled up at Laurie and didn't tell him after all.

Soon after that people began coming in streams. The band struck up; the hired waiters ran from the house to the marquee. Wherever you looked there were couples strolling, bending to the flowers, greeting, moving on over the lawn. They were like bright birds that had alighted in the Sheridans' garden for this one afternoon, on their way to—where? Ah, what happiness it is to be with people who all are happy, to press hands, press cheeks, smile into eyes.

"Darling Laura, how well you look!"

"What a becoming hat, child!"

"Laura, you look quite Spanish. I've never seen you look so striking."

And Laura, glowing, answered softly, "Have you had tea? Won't you have an ice? The passion-fruit ices really are rather special." She ran to her father and begged him: "Daddy darling, can't the band have something to drink?"

And the perfect afternoon slowly ripened, slowly faded, slowly its petals closed.

"Never a more delightful garden-party . . ." "The greatest success . . ." "Quite the most . . ."

Laura helped her mother with the good-byes. They stood side by side in the porch till it was all over.

"All over, all over, thank heaven," said Mrs. Sheridan. "Round up the others, Laura. Let's go and have some fresh coffee. I'm exhausted. Yes, it's been very successful. But oh, these parties, these parties! Why will you children insist on giving parties!" And they all of them sat down in the deserted marquee.

"Have a sandwich, daddy dear. I wrote the flag."

"Thanks." Mr. Sheridan took a bite and the sandwich was gone. He took another. "I suppose you didn't hear of a beastly accident that happened to-day?" he said.

"My dear," said Mrs. Sheridan, holding up her hand, "we did. It nearly ruined the party. Laura insisted we should put it off."

"Oh, mother!" Laura didn't want to be teased about it.

"It was a horrible affair all the same," said Mr. Sheridan. "The chap was married too. Lived just below in the lane, and leaves a wife and half a dozen kiddies, so they say."

An awkward little silence fell. Mrs. Sheridan fidgeted with her cup. Really, it was very tactless of father. . . .

Suddenly she looked up. There on the table were all those sandwiches, cakes, puffs, all uneaten, all going to be wasted. She had one of her brilliant ideas.

"I know," she said. "Let's make up a basket. Let's send that poor creature some of this perfectly good food. At any rate, it will be the greatest treat for the children. Don't you agree? And she's sure to have neighbours calling in and so on. What a point to have it all ready prepared. Laura!" She jumped up. "Get me the big basket out of the stairs cupboard."

"But, mother, do you really think it's a good idea?" said Laura.

Again, how curious, she seemed to be different from them all. To take scraps from their party. Would the poor woman really like that?

"Of course! What's the matter with you to-day? An hour or two ago you were insisting on us being sympathetic."

Oh well! Laura ran for the basket. It was filled, it was now heaped by her mother.

"Take it yourself, darling," said she. "Run down just as you are. No, wait, take the arum lilies too. People of that class are so impressed by arum lilies."

"The stems will ruin her lace frock," said practical Jose.

So they would. Just in time. "Only the basket, then. And, Laura!"—her mother followed her out of the marquee—"don't on any account—"

"What, mother?"

No, better not put such ideas into the child's head! "Nothing! Run along."

It was just growing dusky as Laura shut their garden gates. A big dog ran by like a shadow. The road gleamed white, and down below in the hollow the little cottages were in deep shade. How quiet it seemed after the afternoon. Here she was going down the hill to somewhere where a man lay dead, and she couldn't realize it. Why couldn't she? She stopped a minute. And it seemed to her that kisses, voices, tinkling spoons, laughter, the smell of crushed grass were somehow inside her. She had no room for anything else. How strange! She looked up at the pale sky, and all she thought was, "Yes, it was the most successful party."

Now the broad road was crossed. The lane began, smoky and dark. Women in shawls and men's tweed caps hurried by. Men hung over the palings; the children played in the doorways. A low hum came from the mean little cottages. In some of them there was a flicker of light, and a shadow, crab-like, moved across the window. Laura bent her head and hurried on. She wished now she had put on a coat. How her frock shone! And the big hat with the velvet streamer—if only it was another hat! Were the people looking at her? They must be. It was a mistake to have come; she knew all along it was a mistake. Should she go back even now?

No, too late. This was the house. It must be. A dark knot of people stood outside. Beside the gate an old, old woman with a crutch sat in a chair, watching. She had her feet on a newspaper. The voices stopped as Laura drew near. The group parted. It was as though she was expected, as though they had known she was coming here.

Laura was terribly nervous. Tossing the velvet ribbon over her shoulder, she said to a woman standing by, "Is this Mrs. Scott's house?" and the woman, smiling queerly, said, "It is, my lass."

Oh, to be away from this! She actually said, "Help me, God," as she walked up the tiny path and knocked. To be away from those staring eyes, or to be covered up in anything, one of those women's shawls even. I'll just leave the basket and go, she decided. I shan't even wait for it to be emptied.

Then the door opened. A little woman in black showed in the gloom.

Laura said, "Are you Mrs. Scott?" But to her horror the woman answered, "Walk in, please, miss," and she was shut in the passage.

"No," said Laura, "I don't want to come in. I only want to leave this basket. Mother sent—"

The little woman in the gloomy passage seemed not to have heard her. "Step this way, please, miss," she said in an oily voice, and Laura followed her.

She found herself in a wretched little low kitchen, lighted by a smoky lamp. There was a woman sitting before the fire.

"Em," said the little creature who had let her in. "Em! It's a young lady." She turned to Laura. She said meaningly, "I'm 'er sister, miss. You'll excuse 'er, won't you?"

"Oh, but of course!" said Laura. "Please, please don't disturb her. I—I only want to leave—"

But at that moment the woman at the fire turned round. Her face, puffed up, red, with swollen eyes and swollen lips, looked terrible. She seemed as though she couldn't understand why Laura was there. What did it mean? Why was this stranger standing in the kitchen with a basket? What was it all about? And the poor face puckered up again.

"All right, my dear," said the other. "I'll thenk the young lady."

And again she began, "You'll excuse her, miss, I'm sure," and her face, swollen too, tried an oily smile.

Laura only wanted to get out, to get away. She was back in the passage. The door opened. She walked straight through into the bedroom, where the dead man was lying.

"You'd like a look at 'im, wouldn't you?" said Em's sister, and she brushed past Laura over to the bed. "Don't be afraid, my lass"— and now her voice sounded fond and sly, and fondly she drew down the sheet—" 'e looks a picture. There's nothing to show. Come along, my dear."

Laura came.

There lay a young man, fast asleep— sleeping so soundly, so deeply, that he was far, far away from them both. Oh, so remote, so peaceful. He was dreaming. Never wake him up again. His head was sunk in the pillow, his eyes were closed; they were blind under the closed eyelids. He was given up to his dream. What did garden-parties and baskets and lace frocks matter to him? He was far from all those things. He was wonderful, beautiful. While they were laughing and while the band was playing, this marvel had come to the lane. Happy . . . happy. . . . All is well, said that sleeping face. This is just as it should be. I am content.

But all the same you had to cry, and she couldn't go out of the room without saying something to him. Laura gave a loud childish sob.

"Forgive my hat," she said.

And this time she didn't wait for Em's sister. She found her way out of the door, down the path past all those dark people. At the corner of the lane she met Laurie.

He stepped out of the shadow. "Is that you, Laura?"

"Yes."

"Mother was getting anxious. Was it all right?"

"Yes, quite, Oh, Laurie!" She took his arm, she pressed up against him.

"I say, you're not crying, are you?" asked her brother.

Laura shook her head. She was.

Laurie put his arm round her shoulder. "Don't cry," he said in his warm, loving voice. "Was it awful?"

"No," sobbed Laura. "It was simply marvellous. But, Laurie—" She stopped, she looked at her brother. "Isn't life," she stammered, "isn't life—" But what life was she couldn't explain. No matter. He quite understood.

"*Isn't* it, darling?" said Laurie.

FOR UNDERSTANDING

1. There seem to be three girls and two boys in the family. What do you judge their ages to be?

2. Who is supposedly responsible for the party? What incidents show who is in charge?

3. What details convey the atmosphere before the party?

4. What is the conflict that arises between Laura and Jose? Between Laura and her mother?

5. How does her mother distract her from the issue?

6. Why does Laura go to the home of the dead man?

FOR INTERPRETATION

1. Before the garden-party does Laura's attitude toward the young man's death show her immaturity?

2. What does Laura mean when she says to Laurie as he is comforting her, "It was simply marvellous?"

3. How might Laura have completed the last sentence where she says: "Isn't life—"?

FOR APPRECIATION

1. Notice the dexterity with which the narrative moves from things happening, to things being said, to Laura's mind. It is always Laura's mind and never the mind of one of the other characters. See how Mansfield uses the stream of consciousness technique by turning to page 795, and reading the six paragraphs beginning with: "You'll have to go, Laura. . . ." From her thoughts, what do you learn about Laura?

2. Look at the first sentence of the story. This is a technique often used by Mansfield. How does it set the tone for the entire story? Why do you suppose the technique is called "slice of life"?

3. Throughout her journals Mansfield talks about truth, and expresses the feeling that she "wants to be nearer the deepest truth." Having just finished "The Garden-Party," she wrote in her journal, "'The Garden-Party' is better. But that is not *good enough* either." Can you feel a truth that cannot be stated except through its embodiment in a literary form?

COMPOSITION

You have looked at Mansfield's "stream of consciousness" presentation of a character. Now try to do a similar characterization of someone you know. It could be a family member, a friend, or an unknown person. Put this character into a situation that is embarrassing, or happy, or exciting, or tragic and reveal him or her through a few actions and through his or her thinking. Try to capture facets of the character's personality in a page or so.

George Orwell

1903–1950

"From a very early age, perhaps the age of five or six, I knew that when I grew up I should be a writer. Between the ages of about seventeen and twenty-four I tried to abandon this idea, but I did so with the consciousness that I was outraging my true nature and that sooner or later I should have to settle down and write books."

This is the opening paragraph of an essay entitled "Why I Write" by George Orwell, who was born Eric Blair in India. When he was in his thirties he chose a pseudonym: George—because it was a pleasant, familiar given name; and Orwell, for a river that ran near his family home. He was the son of a civil servant and was educated in boarding schools in England, but always felt an outsider, perhaps—in part— because of his own disagreeable mannerisms. Upon graduating from Eton, he joined the Indian Imperial Police in Burma, a job that he himself recognized as being an "unsuitable profession." These experiences led not only to the essay "Shooting an Elephant," but also to a novel, *Burmese Days*. The situation in Burma was such that he again felt an outsider, and his natural hatred of authority grew.

Next he elected poverty, working among the poor first in Paris and then in London, an experience that made him aware of the problems of the working classes, and yet gave him a sense of failure. He then moved to the countryside in England, writing and supporting himself with jobs that came to hand. When the Spanish Civil War erupted in 1936, Orwell went to Spain with the idea of observing and writing about the war. But he soon began fighting for the Republican side and was wounded by shell fire. This experience fueled a deeper hatred against oppression, whether engendered by communism, fascism, imperialism, or capitalism.

Orwell has set forth four reasons for an individual becoming a writer: (1) sheer egoism; (2) esthetic enthusiasm; (3) historical impulse; and (4) political purpose. He maintained that these four were always present in writing, but fluctuated in importance from person to person and from time to time. In his early years, the

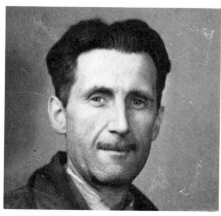

GEORGE ORWELL
George Orwell Archive, University College Library, London

first three far outweighed the fourth as a motive, but by 1935 "political purpose" became his number one reason for writing.

In August, 1945, the month in which the first atom bomb exploded over Hiroshima, Japan, a little book written by Orwell called *Animal Farm* was published in London. No one would suggest that the book had the same devastating and lasting results as the bomb, and yet each in its way profoundly affected people's thinking. Most books are forgotten six months after publication, but this "beast fable" has attracted more and more readers as time has passed. In this story of a revolution in which the animals take over the farm, Orwell makes a comment about totalitarianism and its effect on the masses. The original slogan of "All animals are equal" becomes in time "All animals are equal, but some animals are more equal than others."

Continuing to write novels, Orwell served in the Home Guard during World War II and also acted as a producer for the British Broadcasting Radio network. Since he was beset with continuing lung problems, friends gave him a home on an island off Scotland. Here he wrote the first draft of *Nineteen Eighty-Four*, which he managed to finish in a London hospital before his death. His two most praised books are *Animal Farm* and *Nineteen Eighty-Four*.

SHOOTING AN ELEPHANT

In Moulmein,[1] in lower Burma, I was hated by large numbers of people—the only time in my life that I have been important enough for this to happen to me. I was subdivisional police officer of the town, and in an aimless, petty kind of way an anti-European feeling was very bitter. No one had the guts to raise a riot, but if a European woman went through the bazaars[2] alone somebody would probably spit betel juice over her dress. As a police officer I was an obvious target and was baited whenever it seemed safe to do so. When a nimble Burman tripped me up on the football[3] field and the referee (another Burman) looked the other way, the crowd yelled with hideous laughter. This happened more than once. In the end the sneering yellow faces of young men that met me everywhere, the insults hooted after me when I was at a safe distance, got badly on my nerves. The young Buddhist priests were the worst of all. There were several thousands of them in the town and none of them seemed to have anything to do except stand on street corners and jeer at Europeans.

All this was perplexing and upsetting. For at that time I had already made up my mind that imperialism was an evil thing and the sooner I chucked up my job and got out of it the better. Theoretically—and secretly, of course—I was all for the Burmese and all against their oppressors, the British. As for the job I was doing, I hated it more bitterly than I can perhaps make clear. In a job like that you see the dirty work of Empire at close quarters. The wretched prisoners huddling in the stinking cages of the lockups, the gray, cowed faces of the long-term convicts, the scarred buttocks of men who had been flogged with bamboos—all these oppressed me with an intolerable sense of guilt. But I could get nothing into perspective. I was young and ill-educated and I had to think out my problems in the utter silence that is imposed on every Englishman in the East. I did not know that the British Empire is dying, still less did I know that it is a great deal better than the younger empires that are going to supplant it. All I knew was that I was stuck between my hatred of the empire I served and my rage against the evil-spirited little beasts who tried to make my job impossible. With one part of my mind I thought of the British Raj as an unbreakable tyranny, as something clamped down, *in saecula saeculorum*,[4] upon the will of prostrate peoples; with another part I thought that the greatest joy in the world would be to drive a bayonet into a Buddhist priest's guts. Feelings like these are the normal by-product of imperialism; ask any Anglo-Indian[5] official, if you can catch him off duty.

One day something happened which in a roundabout way was enlightening. It was a tiny incident in itself, but it gave me a better glimpse than I had had before of the real nature of imperialism—the real motives for which despotic governments act. Early one morning the sub-inspector at a police station the other end of the town rang me up on the phone and said that an elephant was ravaging

1. **Moulmein,** a coastal city.
2. **bazaar** (bə zär′), an oriental market consisting of many shops and stalls. The **betel** (bē′ tl) **palm,** an Asiatic palm whose leaves and nuts are chewed much as Americans chew gum.
3. **football,** the game we usually call soccer.
4. **Raj,** rule, domination. **In saecula saeculorum,** Latin, "forever and forever."
5. **Anglo-Indian,** designating or pertaining to an Englishman serving in India or adjacent areas.

the bazaar. Would I please come and do something about it? I did not know what I could do, but I wanted to see what was happening and I got onto a pony and started out. I took my rifle, an old .44 Winchester and much too small to kill an elephant, but I thought the noise might be useful *in terrorem.*[6] Various Burmans stopped me on the way and told me about the elephant's doings. It was not, of course, a wild elephant, but a tame one which had gone "must."[7] It had been chained up, as tame elephants always are when their attack of "must" is due, but on the previous night it had broken its chain and escaped. Its mahout,[8] the only person who could manage it when it was in that state, had set out in pursuit, but had taken the wrong direction and was now twelve hours' journey away, and in the morning the elephant had suddenly reappeared in the town. The Burmese population had no weapons and were quite helpless against it. It had already destroyed somebody's bamboo hut, killed a cow, and raided some fruit stalls and devoured the stock; also it had met the municipal rubbish van and, when the driver jumped out and took to his heels, had turned the van over and inflicted violences upon it.

The Burmese sub-inspector and some Indian constables were waiting for me in the quarter where the elephant had been seen. It was a very poor quarter, a labyrinth of squalid huts, thatched with palm leaf, winding all over a steep hillside. I remember it was a cloudy, stuffy morning at the beginning of the rains. We began questioning the people where the elephant had gone and, as usual, failed to get any definite information. That is invariably the case in the East; a story always sounds clear enough at a distance, but the nearer you get to the scene of events the vaguer it becomes. Some of the people said that the elephant had gone in one direction, some said that it had gone in another, some professed not even to have heard of any elephant. I had made up my mind that the whole story was a pack of lies, when I heard yells a little distance away. There was a loud,

scandalized cry of "Go away, child! Go away this instant!" and an old woman with a switch in her hand came round the corner of a hut, violently shooing away a crowd of naked children. Some more women followed, clicking their tongues and exclaiming; evidently there was something the children ought not to have seen. I rounded the hut and saw a man's dead body sprawling in the mud. He was an Indian, a black Dravidian coolie,[9] almost naked, and he could not have been dead many minutes. The people said that the elephant had come suddenly upon him round the corner of the hut, caught him with its trunk, put its foot on his back, and ground him into the earth. This was the rainy season and the ground was soft, and his face had scored a trench a foot deep and a couple of yards long. He was lying on his belly with his arms crucified and head sharply twisted to one side. His face was coated with mud, the eyes wide open, the teeth bared and grinning with an unendurable agony. (Never tell me, by the way, that the dead look peaceful. Most of the corpses I have seen looked devilish.) The friction of the great beast's foot had stripped the skin from his back as neatly as one skins a rabbit. As soon as I saw the dead man I sent an orderly to a friend's house nearby to borrow an elephant rifle. I had already sent back the pony, not wanting it to go mad with fright and throw me if it smelt the elephant.

The orderly came back in a few minutes with a rifle and five cartridges, and meanwhile some Burmans had arrived and told us that the elephant was in the paddy[10] fields below, only a few hundred yards away. As I started forward practically the whole yellow population of the quarter flocked out of the houses and followed me. They had seen the

---

6. **.44,** a rifle of moderate caliber. **In terrorem,** Latin, for frightening, or scaring away.

7. **must,** frenzied and out of control.

8. **mahout** (mə hout′), an elephant driver or tender.

9. **Dravidian** (drə vid′ ē ən), referring to the ancient inhabitants of southern India. **coolie** (kü′ lē), a Far Eastern laborer.

10. **paddy,** rice fields.

rifle and were all shouting excitedly that I was going to shoot the elephant. They had not shown much interest in the elephant when he was merely ravaging their homes, but it was different now that he was going to be shot. It was a bit of fun to them, as it would be to an English crowd; besides they wanted the meat. It made me vaguely uneasy. I had no intention of shooting the elephant—I had merely sent for the rifle to defend myself if necessary —and it is always unnerving to have a crowd following you. I marched down the hill, looking and feeling a fool, with the rifle over my shoulder and an ever growing army of people jostling at my heels. At the bottom, when you got away from the huts, there was a metaled road[11] and beyond that a miry waste of paddy fields a thousand yards across, not yet plowed but soggy from the first rains and dotted with coarse grass. The elephant was standing eight yards from the road, his left side toward us. He took not the slightest notice of the crowd's approach. He was tearing up bunches of grass, beating them against his knees to clean them, and stuffing them into his mouth.

I had halted on the road. As soon as I saw the elephant I knew with perfect certainty that I ought not to shoot him. It is a serious matter to shoot a working elephant—it is comparable to destroying a huge and costly piece of machinery—and obviously one ought not to do it if it can possibly be avoided. And at that distance, peacefully eating, the elephant looked no more dangerous than a cow. I thought then and I think now that his attack of "must" was already passing off; in which case he would merely wander harmlessly about until the mahout came back and caught him. Moreover, I did not want in the least to shoot him. I decided that I would watch him a little while to make sure that he did not turn savage again, and then go home.

But at that moment I glanced round at the crowd that had followed me. It was an immense crowd, two thousand at the least and growing every minute. It blocked the road for a long distance on either side. I looked at the sea of yellow faces above the garish clothes—faces all happy and excited over this bit of fun, all certain that the elephant was going to be shot. They were watching me as they would watch a conjurer about to perform a trick. They did not like me, but with the magical rifle in my hand I was momentarily worth watching. And suddenly I realized that I would have to shoot the elephant after all. The people expected it of me and I had got to do it; I could feel their two thousand wills pressing me forward irresistibly. And it was at this moment, as I stood there with the rifle in my hands, that I first grasped the hollowness, the futility of the white man's dominion in the East. Here was I, the white man with his gun, standing in front of the unarmed crowd—seemingly the leading actor of the piece; but in reality I was only an absurd puppet pushed to and fro by the will of those yellow faces behind. I perceived in this moment that when the white man turns tyrant it is his own freedom that he destroys. He becomes a sort of hollow, posing dummy, the conventionalized figure of a sahib.[12] For it is the condition of his rule that he shall spend his life in trying to "impress the natives," and so in every crisis he has got to do what the "natives" expect of him. He wears a mask, and his face grows to fit it. I had got to shoot the elephant. I had committed myself to doing it when I sent for the rifle. A sahib has got to act like a sahib; he has got to appear resolute, to know his own mind and do definite things. To come all that way, rifle in hand, with two thousand people marching at my heels, and then to trail feebly away, having done nothing—no, that was impossible. The crowd would laugh at me. And my whole life, every white man's in the East, was one long struggle not to be laughed at.

But I did not want to shoot the elephant. I watched him beating his bunch of grass against his knees, with that preoccupied grandmotherly air that elephants have. It

11. **metaled road,** one with surfaces reinforced with metal strips or slabs.
12. **sahib** (sä′ ib), Indian word for a European master or gentleman.

seemed to me that it would be murder to shoot him. At that age I was not squeamish about killing animals, but I had never shot an elephant and never wanted to. (Somehow it always seems worse to kill a large animal.) Besides, there was the beast's owner to be considered. Alive, the elephant was worth at least a hundred pounds; dead, he would only be worth the value of his tusks, five pounds, possibly. But I had got to act quickly. I turned to the experienced-looking Burmans who had been there when we arrived, and asked them how the elephant had been behaving. They all said the same thing; he took no notice of you if you left him alone, but he might charge if you went too close to him.

It was perfectly clear to me what I ought to do. I ought to walk up to within, say, twenty-five yards of the elephant and test his behavior. If he charged, I could shoot; if he took no notice of me, it would be safe to leave him until the mahout came back. But I also knew that I was going to do no such thing. I was a poor shot with a rifle and the ground was soft mud into which one would sink at every step. If the elephant charged and I missed him, I should have about as much chance as a toad under a steam roller. But even then I was not thinking particularly of my own skin, only of the watchful yellow faces behind. For at that moment, with the crowd watching me, I was not afraid in the ordinary sense, as I would have been if I had been alone. A white man mustn't be frightened in front of "natives"; and so, in general, he isn't frightened. The thought in my mind was that if anything went wrong those two thousand Burmans would see me pursued, caught, trampled on, and reduced to a grinning corpse like that Indian up the hill. And if that happened it was quite probable that some of them would laugh. That would never do. There was only one alternative. I shoved the cartridges into the magazine and lay down on the road to get a better aim.

The crowd grew very still, and a deep, low, happy sigh, as of people who see the theater curtain go up at last, breathed from innumerable throats. They were going to have their bit of fun after all. The rifle was a beautiful German thing with cross-hair sights. I did not know then that in shooting an elephant one would shoot to cut an imaginary bar running from earhole to earhole. I ought, therefore, as the elephant was sideways on, to have aimed straight at his earhole; actually I aimed several inches in front of this, thinking the brain would be further forward.

When I pulled the trigger I did not hear the bang or feel the kick—one never does when a shot goes home—but I heard the devilish roar of glee that went up from the crowd. In that instant, in too short a time, one would have thought, even for the bullet to get there, a mysterious, terrible change had come over the elephant. He neither stirred nor fell, but every line of his body had altered. He looked suddenly stricken, shrunken, immensely old, as though the frightful impact of the bullet had paralyzed him without knocking him down. At last, after what seemed a long time—it might have been five seconds, I dare say—he sagged flabbily to his knees. His mouth slobbered. An enormous senility seemed to have settled upon him. One could have imagined him thousands of years old. I fired again into the same spot. At the second shot he did not collapse but climbed with desperate slowness to his feet and stood weakly erect, with legs sagging and head drooping. I fired a third time. That was the shot that did for him. You could see the agony of it jolt his whole body and knock the last remnant of strength from his legs. But in falling he seemed for a moment to rise, for as his hind legs collapsed beneath him he seemed to tower upward like a huge rock toppling, his trunk reaching skywards like a tree. He trumpeted for the first and only time. And then down he came, his belly toward me, with a crash that seemed to shake the ground even where I lay.

I got up. The Burmans were already racing past me across the mud. It was obvious that the elephant would never rise again, but he was not dead. He was breathing very rhythmically with long rattling gasps, his great mound of a side painfully rising and falling. His mouth was wide open—I could see far down into caverns of pink throat. I waited a long time for him to die, but his breathing did not weaken. Finally I fired my two remaining shots into the spot where I thought his heart must be. The thick blood welled out of him like red velvet, but still he did not die. His body did not even jerk when the shots hit him, the tortured breathing continued without a pause. He was dying, very slowly and in great agony, but in some world remote from me where not even a bullet could damage him further. I felt that I had got to put an end to that dreadful noise. It seemed dreadful to see the great beast lying there, powerless to move and yet powerless to die, and not even to be able to finish him. I sent back for my small rifle and poured shot after shot into his heart and down his throat. They seemed to make no impression. The tortured gasps continued as steadily as the ticking of a clock.

In the end I could not stand it any longer and went away. I heard later that it took him half an hour to die. Burmans were bringing dahs[13] and baskets even before I left, and I was told they had stripped his body almost to the bones by afternoon.

Afterwards, of course, there were endless discussions about the shooting of the elephant. The owner was furious, but he was only an Indian and could do nothing. Besides, legally I had done the right thing, for a mad elephant has to be killed, like a mad dog, if its owner fails to control it. Among the Europeans, opinion was divided. The older men said I was right, the younger men said it was a shame to shoot an elephant for killing a coolie, because an elephant was worth more than any Coringhee[14] coolie. And afterwards I was very glad that the coolie had been killed; it put me legally in the right and gave me a sufficient pretext for shooting the elephant. I often wondered whether any of the others grasped that I had done it solely to avoid looking a fool.

FOR UNDERSTANDING

To see clearly the conflict forced upon Orwell, define the pressures created by each of the following.
1. His attitude toward the British Empire.
2. The nature of his relationship with the people of Burma.
3. His feelings about the elephant itself.

FOR INTERPRETATION

1. If you think of the elephant as a symbol of imperialism, how do the following details add to the story's meaning:
   a. the elephant's physical characteristics?
   b. the elephant's rampage?
   c. the masses shrieking for the elephant's death?
   d. the death throes of the elephant?
2. Was Orwell's reason for killing the elephant an acceptable one in his day? Would the death of the Indian be a valid reason today for killing the elephant?

FOR APPRECIATION

1. Is the theme about imperialism or about personal insecurities? Where is the theme most explicitly stated?
2. Why is this incident so extremely apt to illustrate the theme?
3. How might Bacon have written about the same subject?
4. Listed in the biography preceding the selection are four motives Orwell gives for a person writing. Which of the four are operating in this essay? Are there any dominant motives?

COMPOSITION

Suppose two newspapers were running brief accounts of the incident: one by a British journalist and the other by a Burmese. Write what each might report for his or her paper.

---

13. **dahs,** bowls.
14. **Coringhee,** southern Indian.

Frank O'Connor   1903–1966

Frank O'Connor, one of the best modern short-story writers, was born in Cork, Ireland to Michael and Mary O'Donovan. They were so poor that they could afford little schooling for their son. O'Connor said in his autobiography, "I had to content myself with a make-believe education and the curious thing is that it was the make-believe that succeeded." Although O'Connor felt he was intended to be a painter, he turned to writing because pencil and paper were far cheaper than art supplies.

O'Connor claims to have both loved and hated his father, but admits to always being jealous of him. It is not surprising that when he was forced to change his name for political reasons, he chose his mother's maiden name. While still a teen-ager, O'Connor joined the Irish Republican Army and fought in the civil war from 1919 to 1921 until a treaty ended the fighting. But when O'Connor chose to continue fighting to force Northern Ireland to join the Irish Free State, he was jailed. Here he continued his self-education, and when released in 1923 he took a job as a librarian and began selling his stories to the *Irish Statesman*. His first collection consisted of stories that grew out of his war experiences.

In 1935 he and the poet W. B. Yeats were made directors of the Abbey Theatre Company in Dublin. It was a stormy partnership. There were constant squabbles, and O'Connor said he had never argued with anyone so much since his father. Still, the two men remained friends and both encouraged and supported each other.

In his stories, O'Connor tries to recapture the oral tradition of storytelling, so that the reader feels as if he or she is overhearing a tale being told. O'Connor insisted that the short story "began, and continues to function, as a private art intended to satisfy the standards of the individual, solitary, critical reader . . . storytelling is the nearest thing one can get to the quality of a pure lyric poem. It doesn't deal with problems;

FRANK O'CONNER
Irish Tourist Board (Bord Failte)

it doesn't have any solutions to offer; it just states the human condition."

An editor at the *New Yorker* confirms O'Connor's statement that he rewrote and rewrote: "Everything he wrote was an unfinished work, not so much because of any dissatisfaction, but because of the pleasure he got out of a story. He liked his stories." In his best stories he uses just enough physical background to give an incident locality. The old man in "The Majesty of the Law" fits beautifully into the rough hewn, almost archaic environment that O'Connor describes.

Though Yeats once said that "O'Connor is doing for Ireland what Chekhov did for Russia," O'Connor himself distrusted writers like Chekhov, Joyce, and Katherine Mansfield for their abstract, intellectual approach to writing a short story; for in their hands, the short story "no longer rang with the tone of a man's voice speaking."

THE MAJESTY OF THE LAW

Old Dan Bride was breaking brosna[1] for the fire when he heard a step on the path. He paused, a bundle of saplings on his knee.

Dan had looked after his mother while the life was in her, and after her death no other woman had crossed his threshold. Signs of it, his house had that look. Almost everything in it he had made with his own hands in his own way. The seats of the chairs were only slices of log, rough and round and thick as the saw had left them, and with the rings still plainly visible through the grime and polish that coarse trouser-bottoms had in the course of long years imparted. Into these Dan had rammed stout knotted ash-boughs that served alike for legs and back. The deal table,[2] bought in a shop, was an inheritance from his mother and a great pride and joy to him though it rocked whenever he touched it. On the wall, unglazed and fly-spotted, hung in mysterious isolation a Marcus Stone print, and beside the door was a calendar with a picture of a racehorse. Over the door hung a gun, old but good, and in excellent condition, and before the fire was stretched an old setter who raised his head expectantly whenever Dan rose or even stirred.

He raised it now as the steps came nearer and when Dan, laying down the bundle of saplings, cleaned his hands thoughtfully in the seat of his trousers, he gave a loud bark, but this expressed no more than a desire to show off his own watchfulness. He was half human and knew people thought he was old and past his prime.

A man's shadow fell across the oblong of dusty light thrown over the half-door before Dan looked round.

"Are you alone, Dan?" asked an apologetic voice.

"Oh, come in, come in, sergeant, come in and welcome," exclaimed the old man, hurrying on rather uncertain feet to the door which the tall policeman opened and pushed in. He stood there, half in sunlight, half in shadow, and seeing him so, you would have realized how dark the interior of the house really was. One side of his red face was turned so as to catch the light, and behind it an ash tree raised its boughs of airy green against the sky. Green fields, broken here and there by clumps of red-brown rock, flowed downhill, and beyond them, stretched all across the horizon, was the sea, flooded and almost transparent with light. The sergeant's face was fat and fresh, the old man's face, emerging from the twilight of the kitchen, had the colour of wind and sun, while the features had been so shaped by the struggle with time and the elements that they might as easily have been found impressed upon the surface of a rock.

"Begor,[3] Dan," said the sergeant, "'tis younger you're getting."

"Middling I am, sergeant, middling," agreed the old man in a voice which seemed to accept the remark as a compliment of which politeness would not allow him to take too much advantage. "No complaints."

"Begor, 'tis as well because no one would believe them. And the old dog doesn't look a day older."

The dog gave a low growl as though to show the sergeant that he would remember this unmannerly reference to his age, but indeed he growled every time he was men-

---

1. **brosna,** a bundle of twigs or branches.
2. **deal table,** a table made of pine or fir.
3. **begor,** a mild expletive; a half oath.

tioned, under the impression that people had nothing but ill to say of him.

"And how's yourself, sergeant?"

"Well, now, like the most of us, Dan, neither too good nor too bad. We have our own little worries, but, thanks be to God, we have our compensations."

"And the wife and family?"

"Good, praise be to God, good. They were away from me for a month, the lot of them, at the mother-in-law's place in Clare."

"In Clare, do you tell me?"

"In Clare. I had a fine quiet time."

The old man looked about him and then retired to the bedroom, from which he returned a moment later with an old shirt. With this he solemnly wiped the seat and back of the log-chair nearest the fire.

"Sit down now, sergeant. You must be tired after the journey. 'Tis a long old road. How did you come?"

"Teigue Leary gave me the lift. Wisha[4] now, Dan, don't be putting yourself out. I won't be stopping. I promised them I'd be back inside an hour."

"What hurry is on you?" asked Dan. "Look, your foot was only on the path when I made up the fire."

"Arrah,[5] Dan, you're not making tea for me?"

"I am not making it for you, indeed; I'm making it for myself, and I'll take it very bad of you if you won't have a cup."

"Dan, Dan, that I mightn't stir, but 'tisn't an hour since I had it at the barracks!"

"Ah, whisht,[6] now, whisht! Whisht, will you! I have something here to give you an appetite."

The old man swung the heavy kettle onto the chain over the open fire, and the dog sat up, shaking his ears with an expression of the deepest interest. The policeman unbuttoned his tunic, opened his belt, took a pipe and a plug of tobacco from his breast pocket, and crossing his legs in an easy posture, began to cut the tobacco slowly and carefully with his pocket knife. The old man went to the dress-

er and took down two handsomely decorated cups, the only cups he had, which, though chipped and handleless, were used at all only on very rare occasions; for himself he preferred his tea from a basin. Happening to glance into them, he noticed that they bore signs of disuse and had collected a lot of the fine white turf-dust that always circulated in the little smoky cottage. Again he thought of the shirt, and, rolling up his sleeves with a stately gesture, he wiped them inside and out till they shone. Then he bent and opened the cupboard. Inside was a quart bottle of pale liquid, obviously untouched. He removed the cork and smelt the contents, pausing for a moment in the act as though to recollect where exactly he had noticed that particular smoky smell before. Then, reassured, he stood up and poured out with a liberal hand.

"Try that now, sergeant," he said with quiet pride.

The sergeant, concealing whatever qualms he might have felt at the idea of drinking illegal whisky, looked carefully into the cup, sniffed, and glanced up at old Dan.

"It looks good," he commented.

"It should be good," replied Dan with no mock modesty.

"It tastes good too," said the sergeant.

"Ah, sha," said Dan, not wishing to praise his own hospitality in his own house, "'tis of no great excellence."

"You'd be a good judge, I'd say," said the sergeant without irony.

"Ever since things became what they are," said Dan, carefully guarding himself against a too-direct reference to the peculiarities of the law administered by his guest, "liquor isn't what it used to be."

"I've heard that remark made before now, Dan," said the sergeant thoughtfully. "I've heard it said by men of wide experience that it used to be better in the old days."

---

4. **wisha,** used as an exclamation.
5. **arrah,** an exclamation of surprise.
6. **whisht,** hush; be quiet.

MORNING AFTER RAIN
Jack Yeats
The Tate Gallery, London

"Liquor," said the old man, "is a thing that takes time. There was never a good job done in a hurry."

"'Tis an art in itself."

"Just so."

"And an art takes time."

"And knowledge," added Dan with emphasis. "Every art has its secrets, and the secrets of distilling are being lost the way the old songs were lost. When I was a boy there wasn't a man in the barony[7] but had a hundred songs in his head, but with people running here, there and everywhere, the songs were lost. . . . Ever since things became what they are," he repeated on the same guarded note, "there's so much running about the secrets are lost."

"There must have been a power of them."

"There was. Ask any man today that makes whisky do he know how to make it out of heather."

"And was it made of heather?" asked the policeman.

"It was."

"You never drank it yourself?"

"I didn't, but I knew old men that did, and they told me that no whisky that's made nowadays could compare with it."

"Musha,[8] Dan, I think sometimes 'twas a great mistake of the law to set its hand against it."

Dan shook his head. His eyes answered for him, but it was not in nature for a man to criticize the occupation of a guest in his own home.

"Maybe so, maybe not," he said noncommittally.

"But sure, what else have the poor people?"

"Them that makes the laws have their own good reasons."

7. **barony,** in Ireland, a division of a county.
8. **musha,** a positive exclamation like "so true."

"All the same, Dan, all the same, 'tis a hard law."

The sergeant would not be outdone in generosity. Politeness required him not to yield to the old man's defence of his superiors and their mysterious ways.

"It is the secrets I'd be sorry for," said Dan, summing up. "Men die and men are born, and where one man drained another will plough, but a secret lost is lost forever."

"True," said the sergeant mournfully. "Lost forever."

Dan took his cup, rinsed it in a bucket of clear water by the door and cleaned it again with the shirt. Then he placed it carefully at the sergeant's elbow. From the dresser he took a jug of milk and a blue bag containing sugar; this he followed up with a slab of country butter and—a sure sign that he had been expecting a visitor—a round cake of homemade bread, fresh and uncut. The kettle sang and spat and the dog, shaking his ears barked at it angrily.

"Go away, you brute!" growled Dan, kicking him out of his way.

He made the tea and filled the two cups. The sergeant cut himself a large slice of bread and buttered it thickly.

"It is just like medicines," said the old man, resuming his theme with the imperturbability of age. "Every secret there was is lost. And leave no one tell me that a doctor is as good a man as one that had the secrets of old times."

"How could he be?" asked the sergeant with his mouth full.

"The proof of that was seen when there were doctors and wise people there together."

"It wasn't to the doctors the people went, I'll engage?"[9]

"It was not. And why?" With a sweeping gesture the old man took in the whole world outside his cabin. "Out there on the hillsides is the sure cure for every disease. Because it is written"—he tapped the table with his thumb —"it is written by the poets 'wherever you find the disease you will find the cure.' But

people walk up the hills and down the hills and all they see is flowers. Flowers! As if God Almighty—honour and praise to Him! had nothing better to do with His time than be making old flowers!"

"Things no doctor could cure the wise people cured," agreed the sergeant.

"Ah, musha, 'tis I know it," said Dan bitterly. "I know it, not in my mind but in my own four bones."

"Have you the rheumatics at you still?" the sergeant asked in a shocked tone.

"I have. Ah, if you were alive, Kitty O'Hara, or you, Nora Malley of the Glen, 'tisn't I'd be dreading the mountain wind or the sea wind; 'tisn't I'd be creeping down with my misfortunate red ticket for the blue and pink and yellow dribble-drabble of their ignorant dispensary."

"Why then indeed," said the sergeant, "I'll get you a bottle for that."

"Ah, there's no bottle ever made will cure it."

"That's where you're wrong, Dan. Don't talk now till you try it. It cured my own uncle when he was that bad he was shouting for the carpenter to cut the two legs off him with a handsaw."

"I'd give fifty pounds to get rid of it," said Dan magniloquently. "I would and five hundred."

The sergeant finished his tea in a gulp, blessed himself and struck a match which he then allowed to go out as he answered some question of the old man. He did the same with a second and third, as though titillating his appetite with delay. Finally he succeeded in getting his pipe alight and the two men pulled round their chairs, placed their toes side by side in the ashes, and in deep puffs, lively bursts of conversation, and long, long silences, enjoyed their smoke.

"I hope I'm not keeping you?" said the sergeant, as though struck by the length of his visit.

"Ah, what would you keep me from?"

9. **engage,** agree.

"Tell me if I am. The last thing I'd like to do is waste another man's time."

"Begor, you wouldn't waste my time if you stopped all night."

"I like a little chat myself," confessed the policeman.

And again they became lost in conversation. The light grew thick and coloured and, wheeling about the kitchen before it disappeared, became tinged with gold; the kitchen itself sank into cool greyness with cold light on the cups and basins and plates of the dresser. From the ash tree a thrush began to sing. The open hearth gathered brightness till its light was a warm, even splash of crimson in the twilight.

Twilight was also descending outside when the sergeant rose to go. He fastened his belt and tunic and carefully brushed his clothes. Then he put on his cap, tilted a little to side and back.

"Well, that was a great talk," he said.

"'Tis a pleasure," said Dan, "a real pleasure."

"And I won't forget the bottle for you."

"Heavy handling from God to you!"

"Good-by now, Dan."

"Good-by, sergeant, and good luck."

Dan didn't offer to accompany the sergeant beyond the door. He sat in his old place by the fire, took out his pipe once more, blew through it thoughtfully, and just as he leaned forward for a twig to kindle it, heard the steps returning. It was the sergeant. He put his head a little way over the half-door.

"Oh, Dan!" he called softly.

"Ay, sergeant?" replied Dan, looking round, but with one hand still reaching for the twig. He couldn't see the sergeant's face, only hear his voice.

"I suppose you're not thinking of paying that little fine, Dan?"

There was a brief silence. Dan pulled out the lighted twig, rose slowly and shambled towards the door, stuffing it down in the almost empty bowl of the pipe. He leaned over the half-door while the sergeant with hands in the pockets of his trousers gazed rather in the direction of the laneway, yet taking in a considerable portion of the sea line.

"The way it is with me, sergeant," replied Dan unemotionally, "I am not."

"I was thinking that, Dan; I was thinking you wouldn't."

There was a long silence during which the voice of the thrush grew shriller and merrier. The sunken sun lit up rafts of purple cloud moored high above the wind.

"In a way," said the sergeant, "that was what brought me."

"I was just thinking so, sergeant, it only struck me and you going out the door."

"If 'twas only the money, Dan, I'm sure there's many would be glad to oblige you."

"I know that, sergeant. No, 'tisn't the money so much as giving that fellow the satisfaction of paying. Because he angered me, sergeant."

The sergeant made no comment on this and another long silence ensued.

"They gave me the warrant," the sergeant said at last, in a tone which dissociated him from all connection with such an unneighbourly document.

"Did they so?" exclaimed Dan, as if he was shocked by the thoughtlessness of the authorities.

"So whenever 'twould be convenient for you—"

"Well, now you mention it," said Dan, by way of throwing out a suggestion for debate, "I could go with you now."

"Ah, sha, what do you want going at this hour for?" protested the sergeant with a wave of his hand, dismissing the notion as the tone required.

"Or I could go tomorrow," added Dan, warming to the issue.

"Would it be suitable for you now?" asked the sergeant, scaling up his voice accordingly.

"But, as a matter of fact," said the old man emphatically, "the day that would be most convenient to me would be Friday after dinner, because I have some messages to do in town, and I wouldn't have the journey for nothing."

"Friday will do grand," said the sergeant with relief that this delicate matter was now practically disposed of. "If it doesn't they can damn well wait. You could walk in there yourself when it suits you and tell them I sent you."

"I'd rather have yourself there, sergeant, if it would be no inconvenience. As it is, I'd feel a bit shy."

"Why then, you needn't feel shy at all. There's a man from my own parish there, a warder;[10] one Whelan. Ask for him; I'll tell him you're coming, and I'll guarantee when he knows you're a friend of mine he'll make you as comfortable as if you were at home."

"I'd like that fine," Dan said with profound satisfaction. "I'd like to be with friends, sergeant."

"You will be, never fear. Good-by again now, Dan. I'll have to hurry."

"Wait now, wait till I see you to the road."

Together the two men strolled down the laneway while Dan explained how it was that he, a respectable old man, had had the grave misfortune to open the head of another old man in such a way as to require his removal to hospital, and why it was that he couldn't give the old man in question the satisfaction of paying in cash for an injury brought about through the victim's own unmannerly method of argument.

"You see, sergeant," Dan said, looking at another little cottage up the hill, "the way it is, he's there now, and he's looking at us as sure as there's a glimmer of sight in his weak, wandering, watery eyes, and nothing would give him more gratification than for me to pay. But I'll punish him. I'll lie on bare boards for him. I'll suffer for him, sergeant, so that neither he nor any of his children after him will be able to raise their heads for the shame of it."

On the following Friday he made ready his donkey and butt[11] and set out. On his way he collected a number of neighbours who wished to bid him farewell. At the top of the hill he stopped to send them back. An old man, sitting in the sunlight, hastily made his way indoors, and a moment later the door of his cottage was quietly closed.

Having shaken all his friends by the hand, Dan lashed the old donkey, shouted: "Hup there!" and set out alone along the road to prison.

10. **warder,** guard.
11. **butt,** a heavy, two-wheeled cart.

FOR UNDERSTANDING

1. At what point in the story do you realize that Dan has been expecting the sergeant's visit?
2. What do you know about Dan from:
   a. the furnishings of his house?
   b. the liquor and food he serves?
   c. the conversation about the old medicines?
3. Why does Dan choose prison over paying the fine?

FOR INTERPRETATION

1. What does the story imply about the people? The community? Their institutions?
2. Is this story meant to be taken seriously or humorously?
3. O'Connor has said that his stories offer no solutions—they simply state the human condition. What is the human condition in this story?

FOR APPRECIATION

1. Pick out phrases that suggest dialect simply through the arrangement of words (syntax) rather than through misspellings.
2. O'Connor felt that Chekhov and Mansfield (to whom he is often compared) were "abstract, intellectual" writers. What is there about his stories that is similar to their works?

COMPOSITION

Write an essay comparing the similarities or differences in structure of "The Majesty of the Law" and Mansfield's "The Garden-Party."

Graham Greene   1904–

Graham Greene was one of six children in the family of a housemaster at the Berkhamstead School in Hertfordshire. Later, his father became headmaster and the family moved to larger quarters. As a student in the school, Greene was assigned to a dormitory located in his former home. He could not adjust, and at sixteen ran away. His father sent him for six months to a London psychiatrist who was also a writer. This psychiatrist gave Greene his first desire to write and introduced him to such writers as Walter de la Mare.

At Oxford, Greene describes himself as a muddled adolescent who wanted to write but hadn't found his subjects. Six times during his college years he played Russian roulette with a loaded revolver—each time he escaped death. For four years he worked as a sub-editor of *The Times* of London, and during this period converted to Roman Catholicism because the girl he was determined to marry was Catholic. He felt he should know as much about her beliefs as she did about his. Much has been made of his "Catholic" books, but Greene himself says he is not writing about Catholicism. He simply has several books in which there are characters who are Catholic.

Success and adventure came rapidly. First he became a film critic, which led quite naturally to writing screenplays. The most famous of these was *The Third Man* which eventually became a radio and then a television series. Greene divides his books into two categories: novels and entertainments. Both exhibit the same dark brooding quality. But the entertainments, though frankly detective stories, are some of the most taut, well-constructed thrillers that have been written.

While Greene sometimes writes humorous stories, he is best known for those in which characters seem to be struggling against some impalpable evil. There is a faint smell of sulfur in a Greene novel. He presents seedy, unlikeable characters in whom there seems yet a strange power of God.

Greene became a traveller in mid-life,

GRAHAM GREENE
Photo: Jane Bown
Courtesy The Observer, London

visiting Mexico, Cuba, Haiti, Vietnam, and Africa, all of which later served as settings for his novels: *The Power and the Glory, The Quiet American, A Burnt-Out Case, The Heart of the Matter, The Comedians,* and *The Honorary Consul.*

At one time, writing short stories bothered Greene and bored him a little. In speaking of them in his introduction to *Nineteen Stories,* he spoke deprecatingly of them as "scraps," and expected never to write any more. But much to his surprise he began to appreciate his short stories and did write more. He says that in writing them he may not have far-reaching surprises, but they are there and come "like cool drinks to a parched mouth."

He calls the new volume of short stories, "a collection of escapes from the novelist's world . . . I can reread the stories more easily because they don't drag a whole lifetime in their wake . . . I can look at them quickly as I would look at an album of snapshots taken on many different holidays." His short stories spring from dreams (since his trips to the psychiatrist have made him dream conscious), from overheard conversations, from experiences and sights seen as a tourist. Looking over his total production of short stories (1929–1970s), he was startled at how late and unexpected the emergence of humor was. He says of his writing: "Writing is a form of therapy; sometimes I wonder how all those who do not write, compose, or paint can manage to escape the madness, the melancholia, the panic fear which is inherent in the human situation."

Now living in the French town of Antibes, he says that he produces a hundred words a day which often take him five hours to write. "I never lose track of where I am."

ACROSS THE BRIDGE

"They say he's worth a million," Lucia said. He sat there in the little hot damp Mexican square, a dog at his feet, with an air of immense and forlorn patience. The dog attracted your attention at once; for it was very nearly an English setter, only something had gone wrong with the tail and the feathering. Palms wilted over his head, it was all shade and stuffiness round the bandstand, radios talked loudly in Spanish from the little wooden sheds where they changed your pesos into dollars at a loss. I could tell he didn't understand a word from the way he read his newspaper—as I did myself picking out the words which were like English ones. "He's been here a month," Lucia said, "they turned him out of Guatemala and Honduras."

You couldn't keep any secrets for five hours in this border town. Lucia had only been twenty-four hours in the place, but she knew all about Mr Joseph Calloway. The only reason I didn't know about him (and I'd been in the place two weeks) was because I couldn't talk the language any more than Mr Calloway could. There wasn't another soul in the place who didn't know the story—the whole story of Halling Investment Trust and the proceedings for extradition. Any man doing dusty business in any of the wooden booths in the town is better fitted by long observation to tell Mr Calloway's tale than I am, except that I was in—literally—at the finish. They all watched the drama proceed with immense interest, sympathy and respect. For, after all, he had a million.

Every once in a while through the long steamy day, a boy came and cleaned Mr Calloway's shoes: he hadn't the right words to resist them—they pretended not to know his English. He must have had his shoes cleaned the day Lucia and I watched him at least half a dozen times. At midday he took a stroll across the square to the Antonio Bar and had a bottle of beer, the setter sticking to heel as if they were out for a country walk in England (he had, you may remember, one of the biggest estates in Norfolk). After his bottle of beer, he would walk down between the money-changers' huts to the Rio Grande and look across the bridge into the United States: people came and went constantly in cars. Then back to the square till lunchtime. He was staying in the best hotel, but you don't get good hotels in this border town: nobody stays in them more than a night. The good hotels were on the other side of the bridge; you

THE QUIET RIVER
Victor Pasmore
The Tate Gallery, London

could see their electric signs twenty storeys high from the little square at night, like light-houses marking the United States.

You may ask what I'd been doing in so drab a spot for a fortnight. There was no interest in the place for anyone; it was just damp and dust and poverty, a kind of shabby replica of the town across the river. Both had squares in the same spots; both had the same number of cinemas. One was cleaner than the other, that was all, and more expensive, much more expensive. I'd stayed across there a couple of nights waiting for a man a tourist bureau said was driving down from Detroit to Yucatan[1] and would sell a place in his car for some fantastically small figure—twenty dollars, I think it was. I don't know if he existed or was invented by the optimistic half-caste in the agency; anyway, he never turned up and so I waited, not much caring, on the cheap side of the river. It didn't much matter; I was living. One day I meant to give up the man from Detroit and go home or go south, but it was easier not to decide anything in a hurry. Lucia was just waiting for a car the other way, but she didn't have to wait so long. We waited together and watched Mr Calloway waiting—for God knows what.

I don't know how to treat this story—it was a tragedy for Mr Calloway, it was poetic

1. **Yucatan,** a large peninsula on the southeastern coast of Mexico, a thousand miles from the U. S.–Mexican border.

retribution, I suppose, in the eyes of the shareholders whom he'd ruined with his bogus transactions, and to Lucia and me, at this stage, it was comedy—except when he kicked the dog. I'm not a sentimentalist about dogs, I prefer people to be cruel to animals rather than to human beings, but I couldn't help being revolted at the way he'd kick that animal—with a hint of cold-blooded venom, not in anger but as if he were getting even for some trick it had played him a long while ago. That generally happened when he returned from the bridge: it was the only sign of anything resembling emotion he showed. Otherwise he looked a small, set, gentle creature with silver hair and a silver moustache and gold-rimmed glasses, and one gold tooth like a flaw in character.

Lucia hadn't been accurate when she said he'd been turned out of Guatemala and Honduras; he'd left voluntarily when the extradition proceedings seemed likely to go through and moved north. Mexico is still not a very centralized state, and it is possible to get round governors as you can't get round cabinet ministers or judges. And so he waited there on the border for the next move. That earlier part of the story was, I suppose, dramatic, but I didn't watch it and I can't invent what I haven't seen—the long waiting in anterooms, the bribes taken and refused, the growing fear of arrest, and then the flight—in gold-rimmed glasses—covering his tracks as well as he could, but this wasn't finance and he was an amateur at escape. And so he'd washed up here, under my eyes and Lucia's eyes, sitting all day under the bandstand, nothing to read but a Mexican paper, nothing to do but look across the river at the United States, quite unaware, I suppose, that everyone knew everything about him, once a day kicking his dog. Perhaps in its semi-setter way it reminded him too much of the Norfolk estate—though that, too, I suppose, was the reason he kept it.

And the next act again was pure comedy. I hesitate to think what this man worth a million was costing his country as they edged him out from this land and that. Perhaps somebody was getting tired of the business, and careless; anyway, they sent across two detectives, with an old photograph. He'd grown his silvery moustache since that had been taken, and he'd aged a lot, and they couldn't catch sight of him. They hadn't been across the bridge two hours when everybody knew that there were two foreign detectives in town looking for Mr Calloway—everybody knew, that is to say, except Mr Calloway, who couldn't talk Spanish. There were plenty of people who could have told him in English, but they didn't. It wasn't cruelty, it was a sort of awe and respect: like a bull, he was on show, sitting there mournfully in the plaza with his dog, a magnificent spectacle for which we all had ring-side seats.

I ran into one of the policemen in the Bar Antonio. He was disgusted; he had had some idea that when he crossed the bridge life was going to be different, so much more colour and sun, and—I suspect—love, and all he found were wide mud streets where the nocturnal rain lay in pools, and mangy dogs, smells and cockroaches in his bedroom, and the nearest to love, the open door of the Academia Comercial, where pretty mestizo[2] girls sat all morning learning to typewrite. Tip-tap-tip-tap-tip—perhaps they had a dream too—jobs on the other side of the bridge, where life was going to be so much more luxurious, refined and amusing.

We got into conversation; he seemed surprised that I knew who they both were and what they wanted. He said, "We've got information this man Calloway's in town."

"He's knocking around somewhere," I said.

"Could you point him out?"

"Oh, I don't know him by sight," I said.

He drank his beer and thought a while. "I'll go out and sit in the plaza. He's sure to pass sometime."

I finished my beer and went quickly off

---

2. **mestizo,** a person of Spanish-Indian ancestry.

and found Lucia. I said, "Hurry, we're going to see an arrest." We didn't care a thing about Mr Calloway, he was just an elderly man who kicked his dog and swindled the poor, and deserved anything he got. So we made for the plaza; we knew Calloway would be there, but it had never occurred to either of us that the detectives wouldn't recognize him. There was quite a surge of people round the place; all the fruit-sellers and boot-blacks in town seemed to have arrived together; we had to force our way through, and there in the little green stuffy centre of the place, sitting on adjoining seats, were the two plain-clothes men and Mr Calloway. I've never known the place so silent; everybody was on tiptoe, and the plain-clothes men were staring at the crowd for Mr Calloway, and Mr Calloway sat on his usual seat staring out over the money-changing booths at the United States.

"It can't go on. It just can't," Lucia said. But it did. It got more fantastic still. Somebody ought to write a play about it. We sat as close as we dared. We were afraid all the time we were going to laugh. The semi-setter scratched for fleas and Mr Calloway watched the U.S.A. The two detectives watched the crowd, and the crowd watched the show with solemn satisfaction. Then one of the detectives got up and went over to Mr Calloway. That's the end, I thought. But it wasn't, it was the beginning. For some reason they had eliminated him from their list of suspects. I shall never know why. The man said:

"You speak English?"

"I *am* English," Mr Calloway said.

Even that didn't tear it, and the strangest thing of all was the way Mr Calloway came alive. I don't think anybody had spoken to him like that for weeks. The Mexicans were too respectful—he was a man with a million—and it had never occurred to Lucia and me to treat him casually like a human being; even in our eyes he had been magnified by the colossal theft and the world-wide pursuit.

He said, "This is rather a dreadful place, don't you think?"

"It is," the policeman said.

"I can't think what brings anybody across the bridge."

"Duty," the policeman said gloomily. "I suppose you are passing through."

"Yes," Mr Calloway said.

"I'd have expected over here there'd have been—you know what I mean—life. You read things about Mexico."

"Oh, life," Mr Calloway said. He spoke firmly and precisely, as if to a committee of shareholders. "That begins on the other side."

"You don't appreciate your own country until you leave it."

"That's very true," Mr Calloway said. "Very true."

At first it was difficult not to laugh, and then after a while there didn't seem to be much to laugh at: an old man imagining all the fine things going on beyond the international bridge. I think he thought of the town opposite as a combination of London and Norfolk—theatres and cocktail bars, a little shooting and a walk round the field at evening with the dog—that miserable imitation of a setter—poking the ditches. He'd never been across, he couldn't know it was just the same thing over again—even the same layout; only the streets were paved and the hotels had ten more storeys, and life was more expensive, and everything was a little bit cleaner. There wasn't anything Mr Calloway would have called living—no galleries, no bookshops, just *Film Fun* and the local paper, and *Click* and *Focus* and the tabloids.

"Well," said Mr Calloway, "I think I'll take a stroll before lunch. You need an appetite to swallow the food here. I generally go down and look at the bridge about now. Care to come, too?"

The detective shook his head. "No," he said, "I'm on duty. I'm looking for a fellow." And that, of course, gave *him* away. As far as Mr Calloway could understand, there was only one "fellow" in the world anyone was looking for—his brain had eliminated friends who were seeking their friends, husbands who might be waiting for their wives, all objectives of any search but just the one. The power of elimination was what had made him a financier—he could forget the people behind the shares.

That was the last we saw of him for a while. We didn't see him going into the Botica[3] Paris to get his aspirin, or walking back from the bridge with his dog. He simply disappeared, and when he disappeared, people began to talk and the detectives heard the talk. They looked silly enough, and they got busy after the very man they'd been sitting next to in the garden. Then they, too, disappeared. They, as well as Mr Calloway, had gone to the state capital to see the Governor and the Chief of Police, and it must have been an amusing sight there, too, as they bumped into Mr Calloway and sat with him in the waiting-rooms. I suspect Mr Calloway was generally shown in first, for everyone knew he was worth a million. Only in Europe is it possible for a man to be a criminal as well as a rich man.

Anyway, after about a week the whole pack of them returned by the same train. Mr Calloway travelled Pullman, and the two policemen travelled in the day coach. It was evident that they hadn't got their extradition order.

Lucia had left by that time. The car came and went across the bridge. I stood in Mexico and watched her get out at the United States Customs. She wasn't anything in particular, but she looked beautiful at a distance as she gave me a wave out of the United States and got back into the car. And I suddenly felt sympathy for Mr Calloway, as if there were something over there which you couldn't find here, and turning round I saw him back on his old beat, with the dog at his heels.

I said, "Good afternoon," as if it had been all along our habit to greet each other. He looked tired and ill and dusty, and I felt sorry for him—to think of the kind of victory he'd been winning, with so much expenditure of cash and care—the prize this dirty and dreary town, the booths of the money-changers, the

awful little beauty parlours with their wicker chairs and sofas looking like the reception rooms of brothels, that hot and stuffy garden by the bandstand.

He replied gloomily, "Good afternoon," and the dog started to sniff at some ordure and he turned and kicked it with fury, with depression, with despair.

And at that moment a taxi with the two policemen in it passed us on its way to the bridge. They must have seen that kick; perhaps they were cleverer than I had given them credit for, perhaps they were just sentimental about animals, and thought they'd do a good deed, and the rest happened by accident. But the fact remains—those two pillars of the law set about the stealing of Mr Calloway's dog.

He watched them go by. Then he said, "Why don't you go across?"

"It's cheaper here," I said.

"I mean just for an evening. Have a meal at that place we can see at night in the sky. Go to the theatre."

"There isn't one."

He said angrily, sucking his gold tooth, "Well, anyway, get away from here." He stared down the hill and up the other side. He couldn't see that the street climbing up from the bridge contained only the same money-changers' booths as this one.

I said, "Why don't *you* go?"

He said evasively, "Oh—business."

I said, "It's only a question of money. You don't *have* to pass by the bridge."

He said with faint interest, "I don't talk Spanish."

"There isn't a soul here," I said, "who doesn't talk English."

He looked at me with surprise. "Is that so?" he said. "Is that so?"

It's as I have said; he'd never tried to talk to anyone, and they respected him too much to talk to him—he was worth a million. I don't

---

3. **Botica,** a dispensary.

know whether I'm glad or sorry that I told him that. If I hadn't, he might be there now, sitting by the bandstand having his shoes cleaned—alive and suffering.

Three days later his dog disappeared. I found him looking for it calling softly and shamefacedly between the palms of the garden. He looked embarrassed. He said in a low angry voice, "I *hate* that dog. The beastly mongrel," and called "Rover, Rover" in a voice which didn't carry five yards. He said, "I bred setters once. I'd have shot a dog like that." It reminded him, I *was* right, of Norfolk, and he lived in the memory, and he hated it for its imperfection. He was a man without a family and without friends, and his only enemy was that dog. You couldn't call the law an enemy; you have to be intimate with an enemy.

Late that afternoon someone told him they'd seen the dog walking across the bridge. It wasn't true, of course, but we didn't know that then—they'd paid a Mexican five pesos[4] to smuggle it across. So all that afternoon and the next Mr Calloway sat in the garden having his shoes cleaned over and over again, and thinking how a dog could just walk across like that, and a human being, an immortal soul, was bound here in the awful routine of the little walk and the unspeakable meals and the aspirin at the botica. That dog was seeing things he couldn't see—that hateful dog. It made him mad—I think literally mad. You must remember the man had been going on for months. He had a million and he was living on two pounds a week, with nothing to spend his money on. He sat there and brooded on the hideous injustice of it. I think he'd have crossed over one day in any case, but the dog was the last straw.

Next day when he wasn't to be seen, I guessed he'd gone across and I went too. The American town is as small as the Mexican. I knew I couldn't miss him if he was there, and I was still curious. A little sorry for him, but not too much.

I caught sight of him first in the only drug-store, having a coca-cola, and then once outside a cinema looking at the posters; he had dressed with extreme neatness, as if for a party, but there was no party. On my third time round, I came on the detectives—they were having coca-colas in the drug-store, and they must have missed Mr Calloway by inches. I went in and sat down at the bar.

"Hello," I said, "you still about." I suddenly felt anxious for Mr Calloway. I didn't want them to meet.

One of them said, "Where's Calloway?"

"Oh," I said, "he's hanging on."

"But not his dog," he said and laughed. The other looked a little shocked, he didn't like anyone to *talk* cynically about a dog. Then they got up—they had a car outside.

"Have another?" I said.

"No thanks. We've got to keep moving."

The men bent close and confided to me, "Calloway's on this side."

"No!" I said.

"And his dog."

"He's looking for it," the other said.

"I'm doomed if he is," I said, and again one of them looked a little shocked, as if I'd insulted the dog.

I don't think Mr Calloway was looking for his dog, but his dog certainly found him. There was a sudden hilarious yapping from the car and out plunged the semi-setter and gambolled furiously down the street. One of the detectives—the sentimental one—was into the car before we got to the door and was off after the dog. Near the bottom of the long road to the bridge was Mr Calloway—I do believe he'd come down to look at the Mexican side when he found there was nothing but the drug-store and the cinemas and the paper shops on the American. He saw the dog coming and yelled at it to go home—"home, home, home", as if they were in Norfolk—it took no notice at all, pelting towards him. Then he saw the police car coming, and ran.

4. **five pesos,** at the time of this story, twenty-five cents.

After that, everything happened too quickly, but I think the order of events was this—the dog started across the road right in front of the car, and Mr Calloway yelled, at the dog or the car, I don't know which. Anyway, the detective swerved—he said later, weakly, at the inquiry, that he couldn't run over a dog, and down went Mr Calloway, in a mess of broken glass and gold rims and silver hair, and blood. The dog was on to him before any of us could reach him licking and whimpering and licking. I saw Mr Calloway put up his hand, and down it went across the dog's neck and the whimper rose to a stupid bark of triumph, but Mr Calloway was dead—shock and a weak heart.

"Poor old geezer," the detective said, "I bet he really loved that dog," and it's true that the attitude in which he lay looked more like a caress than a blow. I thought it was meant to be a blow, but the detective may have been right. It all seemed to me a little too touching to be true as the old crook lay there with his arm over the dog's neck, dead with his million between the money-changers' huts, but it's as well to be humble in the face of human nature. He had come across the river for something, and it may, after all, have been the dog he was looking for. It sat there, baying its stupid and mongrel triumph across his body, like a piece of sentimental statuary: the nearest he could get to the fields, the ditches, the horizon of his home. It was comic and it was pitiable, but it wasn't less comic because the man was dead. Death doesn't change comedy to tragedy, and if that last gesture was one of affection, I suppose it was only one more indication of a human being's capacity for self-deception, our baseless optimism that is so much more appalling than our despair.

FOR UNDERSTANDING

1. What is the gossip about Mr. Calloway that interests the people in the Mexican town?
2. What do Mr. Calloway, the narrator, Lucia, and the detectives all have in common?
3. Why do none of the Mexicans talk to Mr. Calloway nor he to them?
4. What happens when the detectives and Mr. Calloway sit waiting in the park?
5. How is Mr. Calloway killed?

FOR INTERPRETATION

1. How does the narrator's attitude toward Mr. Calloway change during the narration?
2. Why does Calloway cross the bridge?
3. Why is the sentence, "He had a million," repeated over and over?
4. Was Calloway's death a just punishment for his crimes or a simple accident of fate?
5. Would you agree with the narrator that the death was comic and pitiable, but that "death doesn't change comedy to tragedy"?
6. Was Calloway's last gesture one of affection or anger?

FOR APPRECIATION

1. Greene has said that his short stories do not have "far-reaching surprises, but they are there . . ." What might he consider surprises in this story?
2. Does Mr. Calloway appear to be one of Greene's "seedy, unlikeable characters in whom there seems yet a strange power of God"?

Doris Lessing

1919–

Born in Persia to British parents, Doris Lessing was raised in Southern Rhodesia. Her education was brief by modern standards since she left high school at fourteen. Her mother wanted her to be a pianist, but as Lessing says, "I discovered suddenly that I had no talent." At eighteen she began writing and produced six novels, all of which she burned. In 1949, after two unsuccessful marriages and three children, Lessing left for London. "England," she says, "seems to me the ideal country to live in because it is quiet and unstimulating and leaves you in peace."

Lessing feels that growing up in Africa was an advantage for her, like "being in the centre of a modern battlefield—part of a society in rapid, dramatic change." But she also found herself on a battle front in England, as she became an ardent supporter of the women's movement. Her writing explores the fragmentation of society and of consciousness as did that of Lawrence, Joyce, and Woolf. "There is," she says, "a kind of cold detachment at the core of any writer or artist."

Of her feelings about life, she writes: "To exist is better than not to exist; to struggle is better than to give in; to face the truth and live with it is the measure of an individual's maturity." She firmly believes in "the inescapable unity of life and art."

Her first short stories were published in 1952 and all the selections were about Southern Rhodesia. These brought her recognition as one of the most important writers of fiction in our time. A critic for *The Times* of London said of Lessing, "not only the best woman novelist we have, but one of the most serious and intelligent and honest writers of the postwar generation."

Lessing says, "I enjoy writing short stories

DORIS LESSING
Photo: Mark Gerson, London

very much, although fewer and fewer magazines print them . . . Some writers I know have stopped writing short stories because, as they say, 'there is no market for them.' Others like myself, the addicts, go on and I suspect would go on even if there really wasn't any home for them but a private drawer."

Some of her best works are *The Golden Notebook* (1962), *Briefing for a Descent into Hell* (1971), and *The Summer Before the Dark* (1973).

A MILD ATTACK OF LOCUST

The rains that year were good, they were coming nicely just as the crops needed them —or so Margaret gathered when the men said they were not too bad. She never had an opinion of her own on matters like the weather, because even to know about what seems a simple thing like the weather needs experience. Which Margaret had not got. The men were Richard her husband, and old Stephen, Richard's father, a farmer from way back, and these two might argue for hours whether the rains were ruinous, or just ordinarily exasperating. Margaret had been on the farm three years. She still did not understand how they did not go bankrupt altogether, when the men never had a good word for the weather, or the soil, or the Government. But she was getting to learn the language. Farmer's language. And they neither went bankrupt nor got very rich. They jogged along, doing comfortably.

Their crop was maize. Their farm was three thousand acres on the ridges that rise up towards the Zambesi escarpment,[1] high, dry windswept country, cold and dusty in winter, but now, being the wet season, steamy with the heat rising in wet soft waves off miles of green foliage. Beautiful it was, with the sky blue and brilliant halls of air, and the bright green folds and hollows of country beneath, and the mountains lying sharp and bare twenty miles off across the rivers. The sky made her eyes ache, she was not used to it. One does not look so much at the sky in the city she came from. So that evening when Richard said: "The Government is sending out warnings that locusts are expected, coming down from the breeding grounds up North," her instinct was to look about her at the trees. Insects—swarms of them— horrible! But Richard and the old man had raised their eyes and were looking up over the mountains. "We haven't had locusts in seven years," they said. "They go in cycles, locusts do." And then: "There goes our crop for this season!"

But they went on with the work of the farm just as usual, until one day they were coming up the road to the homestead for the midday break, when old Stephen stopped, raised his finger and pointed: "Look, look, there they are!"

Out ran Margaret to join them, looking at the hills. Out came the servants from the kitchen. They all stood and gazed. Over the rocky levels of the mountain was a streak of rust-coloured air. Locusts. There they came.

At once Richard shouted at the cook-boy. Old Stephen yelled at the house-boy. The cook-boy ran to beat the old ploughshare hanging from a tree-branch, which was used to summon the labourers at moments of crisis. The house-boy ran off to the store to collect tin cans, any old bit of metal. The farm was ringing with the clamour of the gong, and they could see the labourers come pouring out of the compound, pointing at the hills and shouting excitedly. Soon they had all come up to the house, and Richard and old Stephen were giving them orders—Hurry, hurry, hurry.

And off they ran again, the two white men with them, and in a few minutes Margaret could see the smoke of fires rising from all around the farm-lands. Piles of wood and

1. **Zambesi escarpment,** name of a range of mountains in southeastern Africa.

grass had been prepared there. There were seven patches of bared soil, yellow and ox-blood colour, and pink, where the new mealies[2] were just showing, making a film of bright green, and around each drifted up thick clouds of smoke. They were throwing wet leaves on to the fires now, to make it acrid and black. Margaret was watching the hills. Now there was a long low cloud advancing, rust-colour still, swelling forwards and out as she looked. The telephone was ringing. Neighbours—quick, quick, there come the locusts. Old Smith had had his crop eaten to the ground. Quick, get your fires started. For of course, while every farmer hoped the locusts would overlook his farm and go on to the next, it was only fair to warn each other, one must play fair. Everywhere, fifty miles over the countryside, the smoke was rising from myriads of fires. Margaret answered the telephone calls, and between stood watching the locusts. The air was darkening. A strange darkness, for the sun was blazing—it was like the darkness of a veld fire, when the air gets thick with smoke. The sunlight comes down distorted, a thick hot orange. Oppressive it was, too, with the heaviness of a storm. The locusts were coming fast. Now half the sky was darkened. Behind the reddish veils in front which were the advance guards of the swarm, the main swarm showed in dense black cloud, reaching almost to the sun itself.

Margaret was wondering what she could do to help. She did not know. Then up came old Stephen from the lands. "We're finished, Margaret, finished! These beggars can eat every leaf and blade off the farm in half an hour! And it is only early afternoon—if we can make enough smoke, make enough noise till the sun goes down, they'll settle somewhere else perhaps. . . ." And then: "Get the kettle going. It's thirsty work, this."

So Margaret went to the kitchen, and stoked up the fire, and boiled the water. Now, on the tin roof of the kitchen she could hear the thuds and bangs of falling locusts, or a scratching slither as one skidded down. Here

were the first of them. From down on the lands came the beating and banging and clanging of a hundred petrol tins[3] and bits of metal. Stephen impatiently waited while one petrol tin was filled with tea, hot, sweet and orange-coloured, and the other with water. In the meantime, he told Margaret about how twenty years back he was eaten out, made bankrupt by the locust armies. And then, still talking, he hoisted up the petrol cans, one in each hand, by the wood pieces set corner-wise each, and jogged off down to the road to the thirsty labourers. By now the locusts were falling like hail on to the roof of the kitchen. It sounded like a heavy storm. Margaret looked out and saw the air dark with a criss-cross of the insects, and she set her teeth and ran out into it—what the men could do, she could. Overhead the air was thick, locusts everywhere. The locusts were flopping against her, and she brushed them off, heavy red-brown creatures, looking at her with their beady old-men's eyes while they clung with hard serrated legs. She held her breath with disgust and ran into the house. There it was even more like being in a heavy storm. The iron roof was reverberating, and the clamour of iron from the lands was like thunder. Looking out, all the trees were queer and still, clotted with insects, their boughs weighed to the ground. The earth seemed to be moving, locusts crawling everywhere, she could not see the lands at all, so thick was the swarm. Towards the mountains it was like looking into driving rain—even as she watched, the sun was blotted out with a fresh onrush of them. It was a half-night, a perverted blackness. Then came a sharp crack from the bush—a branch had snapped off. Then another. A tree down the slope leaned over and settled heavily to the ground. Through the hail of insects a man came running. More tea, more water was needed. She supplied them. She kept the fires stoked and filled tins

2. **mealies,** corn or maize.
3. **petrol tins,** gasoline containers.

with liquid, and then it was four in the afternoon, and the locusts had been pouring across overhead for a couple of hours. Up came old Stephen again, crunching locusts underfoot with every step, locusts clinging all over him, cursing and swearing, banging with his old hat at the air. At the doorway he stopped briefly, hastily pulling at the clinging insects and throwing them off, then he plunged into the locust-free living-room.

"All the crops finished. Nothing left," he said.

But the gongs were still beating, the men still shouting, and Margaret asked: "Why do you go on with it, then?"

"The main swarm isn't settling. They are heavy with eggs. They are looking for a place to settle and lay. If we can stop the main body settling on our farm, that's everything. If they get a chance to lay their eggs, we are going to have everything eaten flat with hoppers later on." He picked a stray locust off his shirt, and split it down with his thumbnail—it was clotted inside with eggs. "Imagine that multiplied by millions. You ever seen a hopper swarm on the march? Well, you're lucky."

Margaret thought an adult swarm was bad enough. Outside now the light on the earth was a pale thin yellow, clotted with moving shadow, the clouds of moving insects thickened and lightened like driving rain. Old Stephen said: "They've got the wind behind them, that's something."

"Is it very bad?" asked Margaret fearfully, and the old man said emphatically: "We're finished. This swarm may pass over, but once they've started, they'll be coming down from the North now one after another. And then there are the hoppers—it might go on for two or three years."

Margaret sat down helplessly, and thought: "Well, if it's the end, it's the end. What now? We'll all three have to go back to town. . . ." But at this, she took a quick look at Stephen, the old man who had farmed forty years in this country, been bankrupt twice, and she knew nothing would make him go and become a clerk in the city. Yet her heart ached for him, he looked so tired, the worry-lines deep from nose to mouth. Poor old man. . . . He had lifted up a locust that had got itself somehow into his pocket, holding it in the air by one leg. "You've got the strength of a steel-spring in those legs of yours," he was telling the locust, good-humouredly. Then, although he had been fighting locusts, squashing locusts, yelling at locusts, sweeping them in great mounds into the fires to burn for the last three hours, nevertheless he took this one to the door, and carefully threw it out to join its fellows as if he would rather not harm a hair of its head. This comforted Margaret, all at once she felt irrationally cheered. She remembered it was not the first time in the last three years the men had announced their final and irremediable ruin.

"Get me a drink, lass," he then said, and she set the bottle of whisky by him.

In the meantime, out in the pelting storm of insects, her husband was banging the gong, feeding the fires with leaves, the insects clinging to him all over—she shuddered. "How can you bear to let them touch you?" she asked. He looked at her, disapproving. She felt suitably humble—just as she had when he had first taken a good look at her city self, hair waved and golden, nails red and pointed. Now she was a proper farmer's wife, in sensible shoes and a solid skirt. She might even get to letting locusts settle on her—in time.

Having tossed back a whisky or two, old Stephen went back into the battle, wading now through glistening brown waves of locusts.

Five o'clock. The sun would set in an hour. Then the swarm would settle. It was as thick overhead as ever. The trees were ragged mounds of glistening brown.

Margaret began to cry. It was all so hopeless—if it wasn't a bad season, it was locusts, if it wasn't locusts, it was army-worm, or veld fires. Always something. The rustling of the locust armies was like a big forest in the storm, their settling on the roof was like the beating of the rain, the ground was invisible in a sleek brown surging tide—it was like being drowned in locusts, submerged by the loathsome brown flood. It seemed as if the roof might sink in under the weight of them, as if the door might give in under their pressure and these rooms fill with them—and it was getting so dark . . . she looked up. The air was thinner, gaps of blue showed in the dark moving clouds. The blue spaces were cold and thin: the sun must be setting. Through the fog of insects she saw figures approaching. First old Stephen, marching bravely along, then her husband, drawn and haggard with weariness. Behind them the servants. All were crawling all over with insects. The sound of the gongs had stopped. She could hear nothing but the ceaseless rustle of a myriad wings.

The two men slapped off the insects and came in.

"Well," said Richard, kissing her on the cheek, "the main swarm has gone over."

"For the Lord's sake," said Margaret angrily, still half-crying, "what's here is bad enough, isn't it?" For although the evening air was no longer black and thick, but a clear blue, with a pattern of insects whizzing this way and that across it, everything else—trees, buildings, bushes, earth, was gone under the moving brown masses.

"If it doesn't rain in the night and keep them here—if it doesn't rain and weight them down with water, they'll be off in the morning at sunrise."

"We're bound to have some hoppers. But not the main swarm, that's something."

Margaret roused herself, wiped her eyes, pretended she had not been crying, and fetched them some supper, for the servants were too exhausted to move. She sent them down to the compound to rest.

She served the supper and sat listening. There is not one maizeplant left, she heard. Not one. The men would get the planters out the moment the locusts had gone. They must start all over again.

"But what's the use of that?" Margaret wondered, if the whole farm was going to be crawling with hoppers? But she listened while they discussed the new Government pamphlet which said how to defeat the hoppers. You must have men out all the time moving over the farm to watch for movement in the grass. When you find a patch of hoppers, small lively black things, like crickets, then you dig trenches around the patch, or spray them with poison from pumps supplied by the Government. The Government wanted them to co-operate in a world plan for eliminating this plague for ever. You should attack locusts at the source. Hoppers, in short. The men were talking as if they were planning a war, and Margaret listened, amazed.

In the night it was quiet, no sign of the settled armies outside, except sometimes a branch snapped, or a tree could be heard crashing down.

Margaret slept badly in the bed beside Richard, who was sleeping like the dead, exhausted with the afternoon's fight. In the morning she woke to yellow sunshine lying across the bed, clear sunshine, with an occasional blotch of shadow moving over it. She went to the window. Old Stephen was ahead of her. There he stood outside, gazing down over the bush. And she gazed, astounded—and entranced, much against her will. For it looked as if every tree, every bush, all the earth, were lit with pale flames. The locusts were fanning their wings to free them of the night dews. There was a shimmer of red-tinged gold light everywhere.

She went out to join the old man, stepping carefully among the insects. They stood and watched. Overhead the sky was blue, blue and clear.

"Pretty," said old Stephen, with satisfaction.

Well, thought Margaret, we may be ruined, we may be bankrupt, but not everyone has seen an army of locusts fanning their wings at dawn.

Over the slopes, in the distance, a faint red smear showed in the sky, thickened and spread. "There they go," said old Stephen. "There goes the main army, off South."

And now from the trees, from the earth all round them, the locusts were taking wing. They were like small aircraft, manoeuvering for the take-off, trying their wings to see if they were dry enough. Off they went. A reddish brown steam was rising off the miles of bush, off the lands, the earth. Again the sunlight darkened.

And as the clotted branches lifted, the weight on them lightening, there was nothing but the black spines of branches, trees. No green left, nothing. All morning they watched, the three of them, as the brown crust thinned and broke and dissolved, flying up to mass with the main army, now a brownish-red smear in the Southern sky. The lands which had been filmed with green, the new tender mealie plants, were stark and bare. All the trees stripped. A devastated landscape. No green, no green anywhere.

By midday the reddish cloud had gone. Only an occasional locust flopped down. On the ground were the corpses and the wounded. The African labourers were sweeping these up with branches and collecting them in tins.

"Ever eaten sun-dried locust?" asked old Stephen. "That time twenty years ago, when I went broke, I lived on mealiemeal and dried locusts for three months. They aren't bad at all—rather like smoked fish, if you come to think of it."

But Margaret preferred not even to think of it.

After the midday meal the men went off to the lands. Everything was to be replanted. With a bit of luck another swarm would not come travelling down just this way. But they hoped it would rain very soon, to spring some new grass, because the cattle would die otherwise—there was not a blade of grass left on the farm. As for Margaret, she was trying to get used to the idea of three or four years of locusts. Locusts were going to be like bad weather, from now on, always imminent. She felt like a survivor after war—if this devastated and mangled countryside was not ruin, well, what then was ruin?

But the men ate their supper with good appetites.

"It could have been worse," was what they said. "It could be much worse."

FOR UNDERSTANDING

1. How long has Margaret been on the farm? What is her main worry?
2. What is the battle plan to protect the farm from the locusts?
3. What is the difference between Margaret's attitude toward the locusts and that of the long-term farmers?

FOR INTERPRETATION

1. Is the story about the attack of locusts, or is it about something else?
2. What does Margaret come to see about her father-in-law?
3. What changes take place in Margaret during the course of the story?

FOR APPRECIATION

1. What is the point of view from which the story is told?
2. An inverted sentence is one in which some sentence element is out of position—such as an adverb, preposition, or adjective. For example:

Beautiful it was, with the sky blue . . .
Out ran Margaret to join them . . .
And off they ran again, the two white men with them. . . .
Neighbors—quick, quick, there come the locusts.
Oppressive it was, too, with the heaviness of a storm.

What quality is given to the writing by this rhetorical device?

Nadine Gordimer

1923–

Nadine Gordimer, who still lives in South Africa where she was born, is the modern writer who has most effectively probed the effect of apartheid with its cruelty and injustice on both blacks and whites. Somehow in the telling she makes the situation universal in scope so that readers, no matter where they live in the world, are affected by the happenings as if they had occurred next door.

The daughter of a jeweler, she was educated in private schools and had one year of university education. How then did this white woman become a voice for blacks in South Africa? Perhaps because she seems to understand the masks they wear in their dealings with the whites and the Indian settlers. She knows their habits, customs, tribal rituals. So hated is she by the government that three of her books were banned for more than twelve years. But Gordimer refused to appeal the ban: "I didn't want to recognize (the board of censors') authority. I'm its victim, but I'm not going to recognize its mechanism." When the government says that she is "a very disloyal South African," she answers: "I consider myself an intensely loyal South African. I care deeply for my country. If I didn't, I wouldn't still be there."

An author of both novels and short stories, Gordimer is noted for her ability to use intense observation of both people and places to illuminate her writing, so that every incident seems to come to life. And she has the ability to blend together people, landscapes, and politics into a whole that has a fearful relevance for the reader. Her style has been compared to that of

NADINE GORDIMER
Photo: Jonathan Cape, London

Virginia Woolf, for she has the knack of capturing moments in people's lives that are emotionally complex, yet are still so common that they are generally overlooked by writers. Says a New York critic, "Miss Gordimer is concerned with the young, trying to come to terms in their late adolescence with what history and injustice have bequeathed them."

THE TERMITARY

When you live in a small town far from the world you read about in municipal library books, the advent of repair men in the house is a festival. Daily life is gaily broken open, improvisation takes over. The living-room masquerades as a bedroom while the smell of paint in the bedroom makes it uninhabitable. The secret backs of confident objects (match-wood draped with cobwebs thickened by dust) are given away when furniture is piled to the centre of the room. Meals are picnics at which table manners are suspended because the first principle of deportment drummed into children by their mother—sitting down at table—is missing: there is nowhere to sit. People are excused eccentricities of dress because no one can find anything in its place.

A doctor is also a kind of repair man. When he is expected the sheets are changed and the dog chased off the patient's bed. If a child is sick, she doesn't have to go to school, she is on holiday, with presents into the bargain—a whole roll of comics tied with newsagent's string, and crayons or card games. The mother is alone in the house, except for the patient out of earshot in the sick-room; the other children are at school. Her husband is away at work. She takes off her apron, combs her hair and puts on a bit of lipstick to make herself decent for the doctor, setting ready a tea-tray for two in the quiet privacy of the deserted living-room as for a secret morning visit from the lover she does not have. After she and the doctor, who smells intoxicating, coldly sweet because he has just come from the operating theatre, have stood together looking down at the pa-

tient and making jolly remarks, he is glad to accept a cup of tea in his busy morning round and their voices are a murmur and an occasional rise of laughter from behind the closed living-room door.

Plumber, painter, doctor; with their arrival something has happened where nothing ever happens; at home: a house with a bungalow face made of two bow-window eyes on either side of a front-door mouth, in a street in a gold-mining town of twenty-five thousand people in South Africa in the 1930s.

Once the upright Steinway piano stood alone on a few remaining boards of a room from which the floor had been ripped. I burst in to look at the time on the chiming clock that should have been standing on the mantelpiece and instead flew through the air and found myself jolted down into a subterranean smell of an earth I'd never smelt before, the earth buried by our house. I was nine years old and the drop broke no bones; the shock excited me, the thought of that hollow, earth-breaking dark always beneath our Axminster[1] thrilled me; the importance I gained in my mother's accounts of how I might so easily have injured myself added to the sense of occasion usual in the family when there were workmen in.

This time it was not the painters, Mr Strydom and his boys, over whom my mother raised a quarrel every few years. *I'm not like any other woman. I haven't got a husband like other women's. The state this house is in. You'd see the place fall to pieces before you'd lift a finger. Too mean to pay for a lick of paint, and then when you do you expect it to last ten years. I haven't got a*

---

1. **Axminster,** an expensive, handmade carpet with a hard jute back and long, soft, cut wool pile produced in Axminster, England.

home like other women. Workmen were treated as the house-guests we never had; my mother's friends were neighbours, my father had none, and she wouldn't give house-room to a spare bed, anyway, because she didn't want his relatives coming. Mr Strydom was served sweet strong tea to his taste many times a day, while my mother stood by to chat and I followed his skills with the brush, particularly fascinated when he was doing something he called, in his Afrikaner's[2] English, "pulling the line." This was the free-hand deftness with which he could make a narrow black stripe dividing the lower half of our passage, painted dark against dirty fingerprints, from the cream upper half. *Yust a sec while I first pull the line, ay.*

Then he would drain his cup so completely that the tea leaves swirled up and stuck to the sides. This workmanlike thirst, for me, was a foreign custom, sign of the difference between being Afrikaans and English, as we were, just as I accepted that it must be in accordance with *their* custom that the black "boys" drank their tea from jam tins in the yard. But Mr Strydom, like the doctor, like deaf dapper Mr Waite the electrician, who had drinking bouts because he had been through something called Ypres,[3] and Mr Hartman who sang to himself in a sad soprano while he tuned the Steinway upright my mother had brought from her own mother's house, was a recurrent event. The state the house was in, this time, was one without precedent; the men who were in were not repair men. They had been sent for to exterminate what we called white ants—termites who were eating our house away under our feet. A million jaws were devouring steadily night and day the timber that supported our unchanging routines: one day (if my mother hadn't done something about it you may be sure no one else would) that heavy Steinway in its real rosewood case would have crashed through the floor-boards.

For years my mother had efficiently kicked apart the finely-granulated earth,

forming cones perfect as the shape taken by sand that has trickled through an egg-timer, that was piled in our garden by ordinary black ants. My father never did a hand's turn; she herself poured a tar-smelling disinfectant down the ant-holes and emptied into them kettles of boiling water that made the ground break out in a sweat of gleaming, struggling, pin-head creatures in paroxysm. Yet (it was another event) on certain summer evenings after rain we would rush out into the garden to be in the tropical snowfall of millions of transparent wings from what we called flying ants, who appeared from nowhere. We watched while frogs bold with greed hopped onto the verandah to fill their pouched throats with these apparently harmless insects, and our cat ate steadily but with more self-control, spitting out with a shake of her whiskers any fragment of wing she might have taken up by mistake. We did not know that when these creatures shed their delicate dragon-fly wings (some seemed to struggle like people getting out of coats) and became drab terrestrials, and some idiotically lifted their hindquarters in the air as if they were reacting to injury, they were enacting a nuptial ceremony that, one summer night or another, had ended in one out of these millions being fertilized and making her way under our house to become queen of a whole colony generated and given birth to by herself. Somewhere under our house she was in an endless parturition that would go on until she was found and killed.

The men had been sent for to search out the queen. No evil-smelling poisons, no opening-up of the tunnels more skilfully constructed than the London Underground, the Paris Metro or the New York subway I'd read

---

2. **Afrikaner,** a descendant of seventeenth-century Dutch settlers in South Africa who speaks Afrikaans, a language developed from seventeenth-century Dutch. It now shares with English the status of an official language in South Africa.

3. **Ypres,** site of a major battle during World War I.

about, no fumigation such as might do for cockroaches or moles or wood-borer beetles, could eradicate termites. No matter how many thousands were killed by my mother, as, in the course of the excavations that tore up the floor-boards of her house, the brittle passages made of grains of earth cemented by a secretion carried in the termites' own bodies were broken, and the inhabitants poured out in a pus of white moving droplets with yellow heads—no matter how many she cast into death agony with her Flit[4] spray, the termitary would at once be repopulated so long as the queen remained, alive, hidden in that inner chamber where her subjects who were also her progeny had walled her in and guarded and tended her.

The three exterminators were one white and two black. All had the red earth of underground clinging to their clothes and skin and hair; their eyes were bloodshot; the nails of their hands, black or white, were outlined in red, their ears rimmed. The long hairs in the nostrils of the white man were coated with red as a bee's legs are yellow with pollen. These men themselves appeared to have been dug up, raw from that clinging earth entombed beneath buildings. Bloodied by their life-long medieval quest, they were ready to take it up once more: the search for a queen. They were said to be very good; my mother was sceptical as she was about the powers of water-diviners with bent twigs or people who got the dead to spell out messages by moving a glass to letters of the alphabet. But what else could she do? My father left it all to her, she had the responsibility.

She didn't like the look of these men. They were so filthy with earth; hands like exposed roots reaching for the tea she brought. She served even the white man with a tin mug.

It was she who insisted they leave a few boards intact under the piano; she knew better than to trust them to move it without damage to the rosewood case. They didn't speak while children watched them at work. The only sound was the pick stopped by the density of the earth under our living-room, and the gasp of the black man who wielded the pick, pulling it free and hurling it back into the earth again. Held off by silence, we children would not go away. We stolidly spent all our free time in witness. Yet in spite of our vigilance, when it happened, when they found her, at last—the queen—we were not there.

My mother was mixing a cake and we had been attracted away to her by that substance of her alchemy that was not the beaten eggs and butter and sugar that went into it; even the lightest stroke of a quick forefinger into the bowl conveyed a coating of fragrant creamy sweetness to the mouth which already had foreknowledge of its utter satisfaction through the scent of vanilla that came not only from the bowl, but from her clothes, her hair, her very skin. Suddenly my mother's dog lifted his twitching lip back over his long teeth and began to bounce towards and back away from the screen door as he did when any stranger approached her. We looked up; the three men had come to the back steps. The white gestured his ochre hand brusquely at one of the blacks, who tramped forward with a child's cardboard shoe-box offered. The lid was on and there were rough air-holes punched in it here and there, just as in the boxes where we had kept silk worms until my mother thought they smelled too musty and threw them away. The white man gestured again; he and my mother for a moment held their hands the same way, his covered with earth, hers with flour. The black man took off the lid.

And there she was, the queen. The smallest child swallowed as if about to retch and ran away to the far side of the kitchen. The rest of us crowded nearer, but my mother made us make way, she wasn't going to be fobbed off with anything but complete satis-

4. **Flit,** a popular commercial insecticide during this period.

faction for her husband's money. We all gazed at an obese, helpless white creature, five inches long, with the tiny, shiny-visored head of an ant at one end. The body was a sort of dropsical sac attached to this head; it had no legs that could be seen, neither could it propel itself by peristaltic[5] action, like a slug or worm. The queen. The queen whose domain, we had seen for ourselves in the galleries and passages that had been uncovered beneath our house, was as big as ours.

The white man spoke. "That's 'er, missus."

"You're sure you've got the queen?"

"We got it. That's it." He gave a professional snigger at ignorance.

Was she alive?—But again the silence of the red-eyed, red-earthed man kept us back; they wouldn't let us daringly put out a finger to touch that body that seemed blown up in sections, like certain party balloons, and that had at once the suggestion of tactile attraction and repugnance—if a finger were to be stroked testingly along that perhaps faintly downy body, sweet creamy stuff might be expected to ooze from it. And in fact, when I found a book in the library called *The Soul of the White Ant*, by Eugène Marais, an Afrikaner like the white man who had found the queen's secret chamber, I read that the children-subjects at certain times draw nourishment from a queen's great body by stroking it so that she exudes her own rich maternal elixir.

"Ughh. Why's she so fat?" The smallest child had come close enough to force himself to look again.

"S'es full of ecks," the white man said. "They lays about a million ecks a day."

"Is it dead?"

But the man only laughed, now that his job was done, and like the showman's helper at the conclusion of an act, the black man knew to clap the lid back on the shoe-box. There was no way for us to tell; the queen cannot move, she is blind; whether she is underground, the tyrannical prisoner of her subjects who would not have been born and cannot live without her, or whether she is captured and borne away in a shoe-box, she is helpless to evade the consequences of her power.

My mother paid the men out of her housekeeping allowance (but she would have to speak to our father about that) and they nailed back the living-room floor-boards and went away, taking the cardboard box with them. My mother had heard that the whole thing was a hoax; these men went from house to house, made the terrible mess they'd left hers in, and produced the same queen time and again, carrying it around with them.

Yet the termites left our house. We never had to have those particular workmen in again. The Axminster carpet was laid once more, the furniture put back in its place, and I had to do the daily half-hour practice on the Steinway that I had been freed of for a week. I read in the book from the library that when the queen dies or is taken away all the termites leave their posts and desert the termitary; some find their way to other communities, thousands die. The termitary with its fungus-gardens for food, its tunnels for conveying water from as much as forty feet underground, its elaborate defence and communications system, is abandoned.

We lived on, above the ruin. The children grew up and left the town; coming back from the war after 1946 and later from visits to Europe and America and the Far East, it bored them to hear the same old stories, to be asked: "D'you remember Mr Hartman who used to come in to tune the piano? He was asking after you the other day—poor thing, he's crippled with arthritis." "D'you remember old Strydom, 'pulling the line' . . . how you kids used to laugh, I was quite ashamed . . ." "D'you remember the time the white ant men were in, and you nearly broke your leg?" Were these events the sum of my

---

5. **peristaltic,** contracting in a wavelike fashion.

mother's life? Why should I remember? I, who—shuddering to look back at those five rooms behind the bow-window eyes and the front-door mouth—have oceans, continents, snowed-in capitals, islands where turtles swim, cathedrals, theatres, palace gardens where people kiss and tramps drink wine—all these to remember. My father grew senile and she put him in a home for his last years. She stayed on, although she said she didn't want to; the house was a burden to her, she had carried the whole responsibility for him, for all of us, all her life. Now she is dead and although I suppose someone else lives in her house, the secret passages, the inner chamber in which she was our queen and our prisoner are sealed up, empty.

FOR UNDERSTANDING

1. How are repairmen generally treated in this house?
2. How is the treatment of the exterminators different?
3. What is the relationship between the father and mother?
4. In what way is the mother's life like that of the termite queen?

FOR INTERPRETATION

1. Does the mother enjoy the life she is living?
2. Why does the mother stay on in the house even when the father is in a nursing home?
3. Is the environment the children are raised in a satisfying one? Are the memories they have rich and happy?

FOR APPRECIATION

This story is filled with telling details that are precise and vivid. Which come to mind for the following:
   a. the appearance of the house?
   b. the doctor's visit?
   c. the painter?
   d. the room with the floor ripped up?
   e. the queen?

COMPOSITION

Take an experience from your childhood—your first day at school, a picnic, a birthday, etc. Then, try to use the kind of details Gordimer used in "The Termitary" to make a vivid picture of the event for your readers.

Modern Poetry

William Butler Yeats compared the writing of the twentieth century with earlier English literature in his short poem "Three Movements":

> Shakespearean fish swam the sea, far away from land;
> Romantic fish swam in nets coming to the hand;
> What are all those fish that lie gasping on the strand?

Yeats viewed Shakespeare and other Elizabethan poets as being bold, free, and adventurous. He pictured Romantic poets as being somewhat more closely related to the common person—catchable, accessible. And he saw himself and other writers of his time as struggling, "gasping on the strand." The change Yeats describes through the metaphor is based on one of modern poetry's most striking characteristics—its sense that the world has lost greatness and faith and that poetry is left to utter desperately that loss.

The causes for such a feeling are many and complex. Certainly the doubts that had troubled Tennyson and Arnold still trouble twentieth-century writers. Moreover, revolution had turned into bloody, messy war: the constant fighting in Ireland, the Spanish Civil War, the two world wars, and Vietnam. The Industrial Revolution had brought technology to nineteenth-century England, but in the twentieth century, the changes caused by that technology have come more quickly. To many observers, human beings seem prisoners of their creations; machines control their lives, and sophisticated war machines kill them.

Modern poets often respond to these social and political changes by turning to the past, but in two contradictory ways. First, just as Renaissance poets rediscovered the richness of classical literature, so modern poets have rediscovered their own literary heritage, especially medieval and Renaissance poetry. They include in their poems specific allusions to earlier literature, and they borrow many earlier poetic forms, frequently using heavy alliteration and striking, even bizarre, images.

But even as they turn to the past for images of a greatness that once existed, they also reject the past. They feel, as Yeats puts it, "Myself I must remake," and that remaking calls for new forms, new language, new thoughts. So the second relationship to the past involves a breaking away from older forms. When Gerard Manley Hopkins, writing out of traditional Catholic beliefs and using a form as structured as the sonnet, praises "God's grandeur," he invents his own rhythms to do so. T. S. Eliot, like Browning, writes a memorable, dramatic monologue, "The Love Song of J. Alfred Prufrock." But

This superb portrait of poet Edith Sitwell reflects the modern painter's indebtedness to, yet rejection of, the past. The traditional personal portrait is seen here through the sharp angles and lines of the cubist painter.

EDITH SITWELL
Wyndham Lewis
The Tate Gallery, London

instead of the structured couplets characteristic of Browning, Eliot uses fragments of lines and images whose connections *we* must find. The lines sometimes rhyme and sometimes do not. Some lines are long and some are short. Pattern in the old sense does not exist because the belief in a stable, meaningful world that can be portrayed in stable patterns also does not exist.

We cannot sum up twentieth-century poetry, in part because the century is not over, but even more because each poet creates a new form and a new voice. We can say only that reading modern poetry demands careful attention to language, imagery, and style—sometimes to see the reflection of the past, sometimes to see the new shape of the present.

Gerard Manley Hopkins   1844–1889

Gerard Manley Hopkins in some ways was born out of his time. He died twelve years before our "Modern" period began and almost thirty years before his friend Robert Bridges published an edition of his poetry. And yet, in terms of poetic technique, Hopkins has probably influenced twentieth-century poetry more than any other poet.

The facts of his life are simple. One of seven children in a prosperous, well educated and very religious family, he attended Highgate school in London and went on to study the classics at Oxford in 1863. There he was influenced by the Oxford Movement, a movement which began within the Church of England and sought to revive ancient dogma and liturgy—but which ended when its leader, John Henry Newman, and many of his followers joined the Roman Catholic Church.

After a time of spiritual torment, Hopkins, sponsored by Newman, joined the Catholic Church in 1866. Two years later he entered the Society of Jesus (Jesuits). Thereafter, Hopkins faithfully dedicated his life to his religious duties. In 1877 he was ordained a priest and served in a number of parishes, including one among the wretchedly poor in Liverpool. In 1884 he was appointed Professor of Classics at the new Catholic University of Dublin. He died of typhoid there in 1889.

When Hopkins decided to serve God as a Jesuit he burned all of the poems he had written up to then. He did not begin to write poetry again until 1875 or 1876 but refused to allow any of his poems to be published. Instead, he left all of his manuscripts in the care of his poet friend Robert Bridges.

Hopkins took intense pleasure in the beauty of nature, in the particular and special sounds, shapes, and colors of the English countryside, for he saw in nature's beauty a reflection of divine reality. Poem after poem begins in contemplation of nature and then turns to affirm God's presence as revealed through the sounds, shapes, and colors of natural things. Hopkins believed strongly in the individual distinctiveness of every living thing. He gave the word *inscape* (a

GERARD MANLEY HOPKINS
Anne Eleanor Hopkins (1859)
National Portrait Gallery, London

Hopkins-coined word, related to *landscape*) to that quality that makes each living being different and special.

Hopkins found the poetic techniques of his day incapable of expressing his vision of this special individuality. Thus he experimented intensely with language—vocabulary, imagery, rhythm, and rhyme. Words are thrust into startling new contexts; some words are even invented. Images are piled up one on another frequently with "unnecessary" words dropped out. Verses "sing" with the lush music of internal rhyme, alliteration, assonance, and onomatopoeia. They move to a rhythm he called "sprung," a way of setting words in verse the way music is set in a bar of music—the number of accents (beats) is important, not the number of syllables (notes).

Hopkins himself called his poetry odd and queer. It is dense and frequently obscure not because he tries to hide his meaning. As C. Day Lewis wrote in *A Hope for Poetry*, "What obscurity we may find is due, not to a clouded imagination or an unsettled intellect, but to his lightning dashes from image to image, so quick that we are unable to first perceive the points of contact." The rewards are great for those who work at his poetry, to make contact with possibly the most original genius of his generation.

God's Grandeur

The world is charged with the grandeur of God.
  It will flame out, like shining from shook foil;[1]
  It gathers to a greatness, like the ooze of oil
Crushed.[2] Why do men then now not reck his rod?
Generations have trod, have trod, have trod;   5
  And all is seared with trade; bleared, smeared with toil;
  And wears man's smudge and shares man's smell: the soil
Is bare now, nor can foot feel, being shod.

And for all this, nature is never spent;
  There lives the dearest freshness deep down things;   10
And though the last lights off the black West went
  Oh, morning, at the brown brink eastward, springs—
Because the Holy Ghost over the bent
  World broods with warm breast and with ah! bright wings.

1. **foil,** gold foil.
2. **oil crushed,** refers to crushing olives to make olive oil.

Spring and Fall

To a Young Child

Márgarét, are you gríeving
Over Goldengrove unleaving?
Leáves, líke the things of man, you
With your fresh thoughts care for, can you?
Áh! ás the heart grows older   5
It will come to such sights colder
By and by, nor spare a sigh
Though worlds of wanwood leafmeal[1] lie;
And yet you wíll weep and know why.
Now no matter, child, the name: 10
Sórrow's spríngs áre the same.
Nor mouth had, no nor mind, expressed
What heart heard of, ghost[2] guessed:
It ís the blight man was born for,
It is Margaret you mourn for.   15

1. **wanwood leafmeal,** two words coined by Hopkins. *Wanwood* means "pale or dim forests." The paleness could be due to the light colors of the autumn leaves or to the effect of the light filtered through the leaves. *Leafmeal* could, by analogy with "piecemeal," be "leaf by leaf," or it could mean "leaf mold."

2. **ghost,** archaic word for spirit or soul.

BIRD
Elizabeth Frink
The Tate Gallery, London

The Windhover[1]

To Christ Our Lord

I caught this morning morning's minion,[2] king-
  dom of daylight's dauphin,[3] dapple-dawn-drawn Falcon,
    in his riding
  Of the rolling level underneath him steady air, and striding
High there, how he rung[4] upon the rein[5] of a wimpling wing
In his ecstasy! then off, off forth on a swing,   5
  As a skate's heel sweeps smooth on a bowbend: the hurl and
    gliding
  Rebuffed the big wind. My heart in hiding
Stirred for a bird—the achieve of, the mastery of the thing!

---

1. **windhover,** kestrel, a bird of the hawk or falcon
family.
2. **minion,** darling or favorite.

3. **dauphin,** crowned prince.
4. **rung,** to rise in a spiral flight, a term from falconry.
5. **rein,** the guide rope for leading a horse.

Brute beauty and valor and act,[6] oh, air, pride, plume, here
   Buckle! AND the fire that breaks from thee then, a billion   **10**
Times told lovelier, more dangerous, O my chevalier!

No wonder of it: shéer plód makes plow down sillion[7]
Shine, and blue-bleak embers, ah, my dear,
   Fall, gall themselves, and gash gold-vermilion.

---

6. **act,** in a philosophical sense; realization of potentiality, fulfillment.

7. **sillion,** the ridge between two furrows of a plowed field.

UNDERSTANDING AND APPRECIATION

God's Grandeur

1. According to Hopkins, how is God's grandeur revealed in the world? What two characteristics of God's power are evident in the first quatrain?

2. In what condition is humanity according to the poet? How does this condition affect humanity's awareness of God?

3. How does the tone of the poem shift again in the sestet? What is the source of this new tone?

4. Hopkins wrote in what he called *sprung rhythm*, a kind of meter quite different from that used in the other poems in this book. Still, there is a strong pattern to the sound. Read the poem aloud, discovering the strong beats that come naturally from the phrasing. You should find five beats to a line, even though the number of syllables varies. Notice how the sprung rhythm springs in particular on the word *ah!* in the last line.

Spring and Fall

1. Why does autumn produce sad thoughts? What natural details are given emotional connotations?

2. What do you understand the last two lines of the poem to mean?

The Windhover

1. Describe in your own words what the speaker sees in the first eight lines (octave) of the poem. How does the speaker reveal his attitude toward the bird in lines 1–3?

2. What reaction does the speaker have to the spectacle? Why was his heart was "in hiding"?

3. Who is the "thee" (line 10) and "my chevalier" (line 11)? "Buckle" (line 10) is a key word in the poem. In the light of the poem does it mean "join," "bend," or "break"?

4. Why is the "fire" "lovelier, more dangerous"?

5. In your own words explain the images of the "plough" and the "blue-bleak embers" (lines 12–14). How do they relate to the windhover and the "thee"?

William Butler Yeats   1865–1939

Yeats (pronounced *Yates*) was connected throughout his life with the struggles and spirit of his nation, Ireland. Never did a poet do more to bring a nation into being or to give its people pride in themselves and their heritage.

Ireland had been ruled by England since the times of Henry VIII, but it was only by force that the English were able to maintain themselves as rulers in the Emerald Isle. As far back as the early eighteenth century, Swift had spoken out against the English colonial oppression. Yeats's early years were years of revolution, climaxed by the 1916 Easter uprising in Dublin. By 1922 the British were forced to give Ireland a large measure of freedom under the name of the Irish Free State.

Yeats did not participate actively as a revolutionist, but he fanned the fires of Irish Nationalism by his writings. In 1922 his services to his nation were recognized when he was made a Senator, one of the few great poets who have also participated in the top levels of government.

Yeats was born in Dublin, the son of one of Ireland's leading painters. His earliest poems have a misty, almost unearthly quality, which very much reflects one aspect of Irish character. He delved into Irish folklore and legend, to retell in poems and plays the tales of heroes such as Cuchulain, Oisin, and Cathleen ni Houlihan. The late Victorian age was dominated by poetry which tended to be elaborate in its choice of language. Yeats wanted to express the spirit of the common people of Ireland, and so developed a kind of poetry in which simple, direct speech could play a part. An example of his "folk" poetry is "The Ballad of Father Gilligan" and the simplicity of his language is reflected in all the poems printed here.

The Irish National Theatre—later the famed Abbey Theatre—was founded by Yeats and Lady Gregory. The poet produced plays and wrote verse dramas, all of which were expressions of Ireland's nationalism. One of the best of these is *Cathleen ni Houlihan*, in which the beautiful Irish actress Maud Gonne appeared. Much of Yeats's poetry is addressed to this lovely woman and tells of his great love for her and of her rejection of him, for in spite of repeated proposals of marriage, she refused to become his wife.

Primarily, Yeats was a poet, not a political figure. While he supported the cause of Ireland's freedom, he believed little in the power of government to control man's destiny. In a poem about one of Ireland's great revolutionary heroes, Parnell, he wrote:

> Parnell came down the road, he said to a cheering man:
> "Ireland shall get her freedom and you still break stone."

Yeats was intensely interested in problems of religion and mysticism. He spent years studying the lore of ghosts and spirits, and actually believed that the spirits spoke to him and gave him the material for the great "system" which he used in his later works. These later poems are very hard to understand without a key to the poet's elaborate symbolism through which he expressed a vision of the cycles of human history. But as his work became more difficult in one sense, it became simpler in another: Yeats continued his pioneering work of bringing direct, ordinary human speech into poetry. The thought behind a poem such as "The Wild Swans at Coole" is not simple, but the language of the poem is direct and easy to read.

The Ballad of Father Gilligan

The old priest Peter Gilligan
Was weary night and day;
For half his flock were in their beds,
Or under green sods lay.

Once, while he nodded on a chair,   5
At the moth-hour of eve,
Another poor man sent for him,
And he began to grieve.

"I have no rest, nor joy, nor peace,
For people die and die";   10
And after cried he, "God forgive!
My body spake, not I!"

He knelt, and leaning on the chair
He prayed and fell asleep;
And the moth-hour went from the fields, 15
And stars began to peep.

They slowly into millions grew,
And leaves shook in the wind;
And God covered the world with shade,
And whispered to mankind.   20

Upon the time of sparrow chirp
When the moths came once more,
The old priest Peter Gilligan
Stood upright on the floor.

"Mavrone, mavrone!* the man has died   25
While I slept on the chair";
He roused his horse out of its sleep,
And rode with little care.

He rode now as he never rode,
By rocky lane and fen;   30
The sick man's wife opened the door:
"Father! you come again!"

"And is the poor man dead?" he cried.
"He died an hour ago."

W.B. YEATS
Augustus John
City of Manchester Galleries

The old priest Peter Gilligan   35
In grief swayed to and fro.

"When you were gone, he turned and died
As merry as a bird."
The old priest Peter Gilligan
He knelt him at that word.   40

*mavrone,   my dear, my goodness.

From COLLECTED POEMS OF William Butler Yeats. Reprinted by permission of Macmillan Publishing Co. Inc.

An Irish Airman Foresees His Death[1]

I know that I shall meet my fate
Somewhere among the clouds above;
Those that I fight I do not hate,
Those that I guard I do not love;
My country is Kiltartan Cross,[2]   5
My countrymen Kiltartan's poor,
No likely end could bring them loss
Or leave them happier than before.
Nor law, nor duty bade me fight,
Nor public men, nor cheering crowds,   10
A lonely impulse of delight
Drove to this tumult in the clouds;
I balanced all, brought all to mind,
The years to come seemed waste of breath,
A waste of breath the years behind   15
In balance with this life, this death.

1. The airman is Major Robert Gregory, son of Yeats's friend, Lady Augusta Gregory; she helped Yeats found the Irish National Theatre. Gregory was killed in 1917, flying over Italy. Although an Irishman, he was a member of England's Royal Flying Corps.
2. **Kiltartan Cross.** Kiltartan was a village on Lady Gregory's estate; thus Kiltartan Cross would be the village square (frequently marked by a cross) and Kiltartan's poor are the poor of Ireland.

The Wild Swans at Coole

The trees are in their autumn beauty,
The woodland paths are dry,
Under the October twilight the water
Mirrors a still sky;
Upon the brimming water among the stones   5
Are nine-and-fifty swans.

The nineteenth autumn has come upon me
Since I first made my count;
I saw, before I had well finished,
All suddenly mount   10
And scatter wheeling in great broken rings
Upon their clamorous wings.

I have looked upon those brilliant creatures,
And now my heart is sore.

All's changed since I, hearing at twilight,   15
The first time on this shore,
The bell-beat of their wings above my head,
Trod with a lighter tread.

Unwearied still, lover by lover,
They paddle in the cold   20
Companionable streams or climb the air;
Their hearts have not grown old;
Passion or conquest, wander where they will,
Attend upon them still.

But now they drift on the still water,   25
Mysterious, beautiful;
Among what rushes will they build,
By what lake's edge or pool
Delight men's eyes when I awake some day
To find they have flown away?   30

UNDERSTANDING AND INTERPRETATION

The Ballad of Father Gilligan

1. From stanza one, what do you surmise is happening in the priest's community?
2. When he is called for help, what does he do?
3. In stanza eight, the woman says, "Father, you come again" and in stanza ten she says, "When you were gone." What apparently has happened that the priest does not understand?
4. What miracle has taken place?
5. What time of day is suggested by "moth-hour," by "sparrow chirp"?
6. What characteristics of the "traditional" ballad are found in this "literary" ballad?

An Irish Airman Foresees His Death

1. The speaker lists a number of reasons why he is *not* fighting. What are they and why does he put the explanation in the negative?
2. What is the real reason for his action, which will lead to his death?
3. The last four lines speak of balance. How many different kinds of balance are reflected in these lines? How is balance crucial for an understanding of the poem?

The Wild Swans at Coole

1. What basic metaphors underlie the poem?
2. What is Yeats's attitude toward death in this poem?
3. What is implied by the following lines: "When I awake one day / To find they have flown away"?

COMPOSITION

Reread Housman's "To an Athlete Dying Young" on page 697. Then write a brief comment on the following statement in the light of "An Irish Airman Foresees His Death" by Yeats and the poem by Housman:

A brief, adventurous life that ends honorably is better than a long, dull life and a worn-out reputation.

Art Resource, New York

Sailing to Byzantium[1]

That is no country for old men. The young
In one another's arms, birds in the trees
—Those dying generations—at their song,
The salmon-falls, the mackerel-crowded seas,
Fish, flesh, or fowl, commend all summer long   5
Whatever is begotten, born, and dies.
Caught in that sensual music all neglect
Monuments of unaging intellect.

An aged man is but a paltry thing,
A tattered coat upon a stick, unless   10
Soul clap its hands and sing, and louder sing
For every tatter in its mortal dress.
Nor is there singing school but studying
Monuments of its own magnificence;
And therefore I have sailed the seas and come   15
To the holy city of Byzantium.

1. **Byzantium,** the capital of the Eastern Roman Empire and the seat of the Greek Orthodox Church, today Istanbul, Turkey.

O sages standing in God's holy fire
As in the gold mosaic of a wall,[2]
Come from the holy fire, perne in a gyre,[3]
And be the singing-masters of my soul.   20
Consume my heart away; sick with desire
And fastened to a dying animal
It knows not what it is; and gather me
Into the artifice of eternity.

Once out of nature I shall never take   25
My bodily form from any natural thing,
But such a form as Grecian goldsmiths make
Of hammered gold and gold enameling
To keep a drowsy Emperor awake;[4]
Or set upon a golden bough to sing   30
To lords and ladies of Byzantium
Of what is past, or passing, or to come.

2. **sages . . . wall,** saints portrayed in brilliant gold mosaics on the walls of Byzantine churches.
3. **perne . . . gyre,** spin round in a spiral motion (in the spiraling movement of historical cycles).

4. **But such . . . awake,** "I have read somewhere that in the Emperor's palace at Byzantium was a tree made of gold and silver, and artificial birds that sang." (Yeats)

FOR UNDERSTANDING

1. In the first stanza what sort of "country" does the speaker describe? What is the country's problem? Is this country a real place or a symbol?
2. In the second stanza why does the speaker sail off to Byzantium?
3. In stanza three what does the speaker ask for when in Byzantium? What does the speaker hope to gain?
4. In stanza four what does the speaker wish to become? How does the fulfillment of this wish contrast with the "country" in the first stanza?

FOR INTERPRETATION

State in one sentence what you think Yeats seems to be saying in "Sailing to Byzantium."

FOR APPRECIATION

1. Describe the rhyme scheme of the poem. This rhyme scheme, called *ottava rima*, was favored by Ariosto and Tasso, epic poets of the Italian Renaissance. How might this be relevant to Yeats's theme in the poem?
2. How does Yeats use the notions of song and singing in a symbolic way? Trace the appearances of song and music throughout the poem.

D. H. Lawrence   1885–1930

The poetry of D. H. Lawrence (see page 783) exhibits his concern for individuality and his delight in sensual awareness. He does not use standard line lengths or rhyme schemes; each poem creates its own shape, as in the undulating lines of "Snake." And the poem also asks us to rebel against our instinctive fears and learned prejudices, so that we can appreciate the honest sensual power symbolized by the snake.

Snake

A snake came to my water trough
On a hot, hot day, and I in pajamas for the heat,
To drink there.

In the deep, strange-scented shade of the great dark carob tree[1]
I came down the steps with my pitcher   5
And must wait, must stand and wait, for there he was at the trough
    before me.

He reached down from a fissure in the earth-wall in the gloom
And trailed his yellow-brown slackness soft-bellied down, over the
    edge of the stone trough
And rested his throat upon the stone bottom,
And where the water had dripped from the tap, in a small clearness,   10
He sipped with his straight mouth,
Softly drank through his straight gums, into his slack long body,
Silently.

Someone was before me at my water trough,
And I, like a second-comer, waiting.   15

He lifted his head from his drinking, as cattle do,
And looked at me vaguely, as drinking cattle do,
And flickered his two-forked tongue from his lips, and mused a moment,
And stooped and drank a little more,
Being earth-brown, earth golden from the burning bowels of the earth,   20
On the day of Sicilian July, with Etna[2] smoking.

"Snake" by D.H. Lawrence, from THE COMPLETE POEMS OF D.H. LAWRENCE, edited by Vivian de Sola Pinto and F. Warren Roberts. Copyright © 1964, 1971 by Angelo Ravagli and C.M. Weekly, Executors of the Estate of Frieda Lawrence Ravagli. Reprinted by permission of Viking Penguin, Inc.

1. **carob tree,** an evergreen of the Mediterranean regions.
2. **Etna,** volcano on Sicily.

The voice of my education said to me
He must be killed,
For in Sicily the black black snakes are innocent, the gold are venomous.

And voices in me said, If you were a man   25
You would take a stick and break him now, and finish him off.

But must I confess how I liked him,
How glad I was he had come like a guest in quiet, to drink at my
        water trough
And depart peaceful, pacified, and thankless
Into the burning bowels of this earth?   30

Was it cowardice, that I dared not kill him?
Was it perversity, that I longed to talk to him?
Was it humility, to feel so honored?
I felt so honored.

And yet those voices: 35
If you were not afraid, you would kill him!

And truly I was afraid, I was most afraid,
But even so, honored still more
That he should seek my hospitality
From out the dark door of the secret earth.   40

He drank enough
And lifted his head, dreamily, as one who has drunken,
And flickered his tongue like a forked night on the air, so black,
Seeming to lick his lips,
And looked around like a god, unseeing, into the air,   45
And slowly turned his head,
And slowly, very slowly, as if thrice adream
Proceeded to draw his slow length curving round
And climb the broken bank of my wall-face.

And as he put his head into that dreadful hole,   50
And as he slowly drew up, snake-easing his shoulders, and entered farther,
A sort of horror, a sort of protest against his withdrawing into that
        horrid black hole,
Deliberately going into the blackness, and slowly drawing himself after,
Overcame me now his back was turned.

I looked round, I put down my pitcher, 55
I picked up a clumsy log
And threw it at the water trough with a clatter.

I think it did not hit him;
But suddenly that part of him that was left behind convulsed in
    undignified haste,
Writhed like lightning, and was gone 60
Into the black hole, the earth-lipped fissure in the wall-front
At which, in the intense still noon, I stared with fascination.

And immediately I regretted it.
I thought how paltry,[3] how vulgar, what a mean act!
I despised myself and the voices of my accursed human education. 65

And I thought of the albatross[4]
And I wished he would come back, my snake.

For he seemed to me again like a king,
Like a king in exile, uncrowned in the underworld,
Now due to be crowned again. 70

And so, I missed my chance with one of the lords
Of life.
And I have something to expiate:
A pettiness.

3. **paltry,** almost worthless, petty.
4. **albatross.** The albatross was killed by Coleridge's
Ancient Mariner; the impulsive slaying haunted his life.

UNDERSTANDING AND INTERPRETATION

1. What are the different voices that speak to Lawrence?

2. Why does he throw a log at the snake?

3. How do you understand the reference, "And I thought of the albatross"?

4. What words suggest the instinctive horror Lawrence feels for the snake? What words suggest more positive feelings? What are those feelings?

5. Is it an overstatement to call the snake "a king in exile" and "one of the lords of life"?

6. Notice the way in which Lawrence uses very long lines and quite short lines. What effects can you describe for such lines as "And must wait, must stand and wait, for there he was at the trough before me" (6); "A sort of horror, a sort of protest against his withdrawing into that horrid black hole" (52); "I felt so honored" (34); and "A pettiness" (74)?

T. S. Eliot   1888–1965

T. S. Eliot had both American and English ties. He was born in St. Louis, Missouri, and was educated at Harvard. But he settled in London in 1915 and acquired British citizenship in 1927. Poet, critic, and playwright, his work represents a revolt from the cheerfulness, optimism, and hopefulness of the Victorians. In addition, he exerted an enormous influence on modern poetry through both his verse and his literary criticism.

Eliot's creative life falls roughly into three phases. In his first phase, which lasted into the mid 1920s, he was mainly concerned with the apparent hopeless decay of Western civilization. In his second phase, after he joined the Church of England in 1927, he became more optimistic, suggesting a measure of hope through religious faith. In his third phase, beginning in the mid 1930s, he turned more to critical essays and to verse drama.

Eliot is difficult to comprehend at first reading. His poetry shows the influence of the French symbolists, of some aspects of the imagist movement (see For Appreciation, page 858), and of the metaphysical poets of the seventeenth century, especially Donne (page 304). The *symbolists* used symbols to stimulate multiple associations of ideas in the reader's mind. The *imagists* emphasized the creation of sharp, concrete images. The metaphysical poets impressed Eliot with their paradoxical conceits and their intellectual toughness. All of these elements Eliot combined to communicate his own vision as a "classicist in literature, royalist in politics, and Anglo-Catholic in religion," to use his own words. To many people, he is the one poet who clearly expresses the sense of loss and fragmentation of the modern world—a view that is apparent from the titles of poetic works such as *The Waste Land* and "The Hollow Men." Within his poems we find quotations from other authors. There are frequent allusions to Dante, Shakespeare, Goethe, and other Western writers as well as to Oriental culture and Eastern writers. Eliot alludes to so many great works of the past both to search for help and to remind us of the spiritual, intellectual, and emotional poverty of our own time.

Nowhere is that poverty shown more devastatingly than in "The Love Song of J. Alfred Prufrock." The poem is a dramatic monologue (some readers call it an interior monologue because the "you" being addressed is possibly the speaker himself). In it a middle-aged man with a ridiculous, slightly pompous name talks about himself. He speaks to us perhaps as the speaker of the poem's epigraph speaks to Dante—thinking that he is safe because no one will ever repeat his words. The epigraph taken from Dante evokes the setting of hell in the first part of the *Divine Comedy*. This is a modern version of hell, though, made up of constant trivial chatter (Michelangelo is reduced to meaningless talk) and an overwhelming sense of absurdity. Other great figures are evoked—John the Baptist; Lazarus, whom Christ raised from the dead; and Hamlet—and always Prufrock feels his inadequacy.

For Eliot, one possible answer to the meaninglessness he saw about him lay in faith. It is not accidental that Eliot, like Gerard Manley Hopkins, was a devoutly religious person. "The Journey of the Magi" shows us the combination of the modern questioning attitude and traditional faith, as the speaker tries to fathom the mystery of Christ's birth. Eliot's poems demand careful reading: he often does not make transitions but forces us to connect one image to another, one stanza to another. He breaks up our expectations of formal pattern by giving us unrhymed lines and then suddenly shifting back into rhyme. The form of the poetry reflects the uneasiness of the poet's outlook; despite his faith, the world for him is a difficult place to comprehend. His poetry must, if it is to be honest, mirror that complex difficulty.

The Love Song of J. Alfred Prufrock

S'io credesse che mia risposta fosse
a persona che mai tornasse al mondo,
questa fiamma staria senza più scosse.
Ma per cio che giammai di questo fondo
non torno vivo alcun, s'i'odo il vero,
senza tema d'infamia ti rispondo.[1]

Let us go then, you and I,
When the evening is spread out against the sky
Like a patient etherized upon a table;
Let us go, through certain half-deserted streets,
The muttering retreats
Of restless nights in one-night cheap hotels
And sawdust[2] restaurants with oyster shells:
Streets that follow like a tedious argument
Of insidious intent
To lead you to an overwhelming question . . .   10
Oh, do not ask, "What is it?"
Let us go and make our visit.

In the room the women come and go
Talking of Michelangelo.

The yellow fog that rubs its back upon the windowpanes,   15
The yellow smoke that rubs its muzzle on the windowpanes
Licked its tongue into the corners of the evening,
Lingered upon the pools that stand in drains,
Let fall upon its back the soot that falls from chimneys,
Slipped by the terrace, made a sudden leap,   20
And seeing that it was a soft October night,
Curled once about the house, and fell asleep.

T.S. ELIOT
Sir Jacob Epstein
National Portrait Gallery, London

1. The epigraph to this poem comes from Dante's *Infer-no*, Canto 27, lines 61–66. The speaker is a man in the eighth circle of hell (the ninth being the lowest). He tells Dante and Virgil that he is willing to talk about himself because he is sure that they won't return to the world. The lines translate as follows:

    If I thought my answer were given
    to anyone who would ever return to the world,
    this flame would stand still without moving any
      further
    But since never from this abyss
    has anyone ever returned alive, if what I hear is
      true,
    without fear of infamy I answer thee.

2. **sawdust,** with sawdust on the floors.

And indeed there will be time
For the yellow smoke that slides along the street,
Rubbing its back upon the windowpanes;   25
There will be time, there will be time
To prepare a face to meet the faces that you meet;
There will be time to murder and create,
And time for all the works and days of hands
That lift and drop a question on your plate;   30
Time for you and time for me,
And time yet for a hundred indecisions,
And for a hundred visions and revisions,
Before the taking of a toast and tea.

In the room the women come and go   35
Talking of Michelangelo.

And indeed there will be time
To wonder, "Do I dare?" and, "Do I dare?"
Time to turn back and descend the stair,
With a bald spot in the middle of my hair—   40
(They will say: "How his hair is growing thin!")
My morning coat, my collar mounting firmly to the chin,
My necktie rich and modest, but asserted by a simple pin—
(They will say: "But how his arms and legs are thin!")
Do I dare   45
Disturb the universe?

In a minute there is time
For decisions and revisions which a minute will reverse.
For I have known them all already, known them all—
Have known the evenings, mornings, afternoons,   50
I have measured out my life with coffee spoons;
I know the voices dying with a dying fall
Beneath the music from a farther room.
        So how should I presume?

And I have known the eyes already, known them all—   55
The eyes that fix you in a formulated phrase,
And when I am formulated, sprawling on a pin,
When I am pinned and wriggling on the wall,
Then how should I begin
To spit out all the butt-ends of my days and ways?   60
        And how should I presume?

And I have known the arms already, known them all—
Arms that are braceleted and white and bare
(But in the lamplight, downed with light brown hair!)
Is it perfume from a dress   65
That makes me so digress?
Arms that lie along a table, or wrap about a shawl.
     And should I then presume?
     And how should I begin?

      .   .   .   .   .

Shall I say, I have gone at dusk through narrow streets   70
And watched the smoke that rises from the pipes
Of lonely men in shirt-sleeves, leaning out of windows? . . .

I should have been a pair of ragged claws
Scuttling across the floors of silent seas.

      .   .   .   .   .

And the afternoon, the evening, sleeps so peacefully!   75
Smoothed by long fingers,
Asleep . . . tired . . . or it malingers,
Stretched on the floor, here beside you and me.
Should I, after tea and cakes and ices,
Have the strength to force the moment to its crisis?   80
But though I have wept and fasted, wept and prayed,
Though I have seen my head (grown slightly bald) brought in
     upon a platter[3]
I am no prophet—and here's no great matter;
I have seen the moment of my greatness flicker,
And I have seen the eternal Footman hold my coat, and snicker,   85
And in short, I was afraid.

And would it have been worth it, after all,
After the cups, the marmalade, the tea,
Among the porcelain, among some talk of you and me,
Would it have been worth while,   90
To have bitten off the matter with a smile,
To have squeezed the universe into a ball
To roll it toward some overwhelming question,
To say: "I am Lazarus[4] come from the dead,
Come back to tell you all, I shall tell you all"—   95
If one, settling a pillow by her head,
     Should say: "That is not what I meant at all.
     That is not it, at all."

---

3. This is a reference to the story of John the Baptist. See the New Testament, Matthew 4:11.

4. **Lazarus** was raised from the dead. See the New Testament, John 11.

And would it have been worth it, after all,
Would it have been worth while,   100
After the sunsets and the dooryards and the sprinkled streets,
After the novels, after the teacups, after the skirts that trail
    along the floor—
And this, and so much more?—
It is impossible to say just what I mean!
But as if a magic lantern threw the nerves in patterns on a screen: 105
Would it have been worth while
If one, settling a pillow or throwing off a shawl,
And turning toward the window, should say:
    "That is not it at all,
    That is not what I meant, at all."   110

      •   •   •   •   •

No! I am not Prince Hamlet[5] nor was meant to be;
Am an attendant lord, one that will do
To swell a progress,[6] start a scene or two,
Advise the prince; no doubt, an easy tool,
Deferential, glad to be of use,   115
Politic, cautious, and meticulous;
Full of high sentence,[7] but a bit obtuse;
At times, indeed, almost ridiculous—
Almost, at times, the Fool.

I grow old . . . I grow old . . .   120
I shall wear the bottoms of my trousers rolled.

Shall I part my hair behind? Do I dare to eat a peach?
I shall wear white flannel trousers, and walk upon the beach.
I have heard the mermaids singing, each to each.

I do not think that they will sing to me.   125

I have seen them riding seaward on the waves
Combing the white hair of the waves blown back
When the wind blows the water white and black.

We have lingered in the chambers of the sea
By sea-girls wreathed with seaweed red and brown   130
Till human voices wake us, and we drown.

---

5. **Hamlet.** Since he was a prince of Denmark, whatever Hamlet said was of importance.
6. **to swell a progress,** to add to a procession.
7. **full of high sentence,** full of wise observations.

Journey of the Magi[1]

'A cold coming we had of it,
Just the worst time of the year
For a journey, and such a long journey:
The ways deep and the weather sharp,
The very dead of winter.'[2]   5
And the camels galled, sore-footed, refractory,[3]
Lying down in the melting snow.
There were times we regretted
The summer palaces on slopes, the terraces,
And the silken girls bringing sherbet.   10
Then the camel men cursing and grumbling
And running away, and wanting their liquor and women,
And the night-fires going out, and the lack of shelters,
And the cities hostile and the towns unfriendly
And the villages dirty and charging high prices: 15
A hard time we had of it.
At the end we preferred to travel all night,
Sleeping in snatches,
With the voices singing in our ears, saying
That this was all folly.   20

Then at dawn we came down to a temperate valley,
Wet, below the snow line, smelling of vegetation;
With a running stream and a water-mill beating the darkness,
And three trees on the low sky,
And an old white horse galloped away in the meadow.   25
Then we came to a tavern with vine-leaves over the lintel,
Six hands at an open door dicing for pieces of silver,
And feet kicking the empty wine-skins.
But there was no information, and so we continued
And arrived at evening, not a moment too soon   30
Finding the place; it was (you may say) satisfactory.

1. **Magi** (Mā′ jī), the three wise men who journeyed to Bethlehem to witness the birth of Christ.
2. Eliot consciously adapted lines from a sermon preached in 1622 by Bishop Lancelot Andrewes: "Last, we consider the *time* of their coming, the season of the year. It was no *summer Progress.* A cold coming they had of it, at this time of the year; just the worst time of the year, to take a journey, and specially a long journey, in. The ways deep, the weather sharp, the days short, the sun farthest off . . . the very dead of *Winter.*"
3. **refractory** (rí frak′ tər ē), stubborn.

All this was a long time ago, I remember,
And I would do it again, but set down
This set down
This: were we led all that way for   35
Birth or Death? There was a Birth, certainly,
We had evidence and no doubt. I had seen birth and death,
But had thought they were different; this Birth was
Hard and bitter agony for us, like Death, our death.
We returned to our places, these Kingdoms,   40
But no longer at ease here, in the old dispensation,[4]
With an alien people clutching their gods.
I should be glad of another death.

---

4. **old dispensation,** the former system of belief, now made old by the birth of Christ, which brought the new dispensation.

UNDERSTANDING AND INTERPRETATION

The Love Song of J. Alfred Prufrock

1. What invitation does the speaker extend in the first stanza?
2. What aspects of his everyday life seem to haunt Prufrock?
3. Which parts of the poem show that Prufrock thinks of himself as a slightly ridiculous figure?

Journey of the Magi

1. There are three locations in the poem—the place where the Magi live, the road, and the place being sought. How does the poem evoke the different qualities of these places?
2. What symbolic implications do you find in lines 24–28?
3. The speaker asks: ". . . were we led all that way for/Birth or Death?" What is the poem's answer?
4. How would you interpret the poem's last line?

FOR APPRECIATION

The Love Song of J. Alfred Prufrock

1. What is ironic about the poem's title?

2. Describe the verse form used by Eliot.
3. The structure of the poem is that of an *interior* or *dramatic monologue*. How is this structure similar to the technique of stream of consciousness in modern prose?
4. Eliot was considerably influenced by two movements in poetry: *symbolism* and *imagism*. The French symbolist poets of the 1880s and 1890s, such as Stéphane Mallarmé, Paul Verlaine, and Jules Laforgue, used symbols to stimulate multiple associations in the reader's mind. The imagists were led by the American poet Ezra Pound (1885–1972), who became a close friend of Eliot; this movement placed the highest poetic value on clear, strikingly fresh images. With these influences in mind, comment on Eliot's imagery in lines 2–3, 51, 56–58, and 73–74.

Journey of the Magi

1. What are the effects of the ironic understatement in line 31?
2. The sermon that provides the starting point for this poem describes the journey of the Magi from the third-person point of view. Eliot changes to the first-person point of view. What is the effect of this change?

Poetry and War

The revolutions that shook the nineteenth century to its intellectual and spiritual foundations had their twentieth-century counterparts in World War I and World War II. Those events changed forever the attitude toward war. If President Woodrow Wilson could claim that America entered World War I "to make the world safe for democracy," that pious hope would be shattered when Hitler's armies marched into Poland twenty years later. And the horrors of World War II created scars yet unhealed—whether for the survivors of the Nazi concentration camps or of Hiroshima and Nagasaki. The poems in this section protest the inhumanity of war. They also argue that we should not create peaceful, comforting illusions to shield ourselves from that inhumanity. The first two poems are specifically about World War I. The first, "Dulce et decorum est" is by Wilfred Owen (1893–1918), who died at the age of twenty-five, a week before the Armistice. The poem ends with Horace's famous saying, "It is sweet and fitting to die for one's country." It also describes vividly the horror of that dying. Alice Meynell (1847–1922), who devoted her life to humanitarian causes as well as to writing, presents another view of the war in "Summer in England, 1914." She contrasts the beauty of the summer with the ugly reality of war. Stephen Spender (1909–   ), a British poet, editor, and critic (who was a close friend of W. H. Auden), takes us to World War II where he shows us how even a "winner" is implicated in the horrors of war: "Responsibility: The Pilots Who Destroyed Germany in the Spring of 1945." Thom Gunn (1929–   ) was too young to fight in World War II, but he uses an image from that war to talk about one of war's most frightening consequences: the deadening of human sensitivity and compassion.

WILFRED OWEN
John Gunston
National Portrait Gallery, London

Dulce et decorum est

Bent double, like old beggars under sacks,
Knock-kneed, coughing like hags, we cursed through sludge,
Till on the haunting flares we turned our backs,
And towards our distant rest began to trudge.
Men marched asleep. Many had lost their boots,   5
But limped on, blood-shod. All went lame, all blind;
Drunk with fatigue; deaf even to the hoots
Of gas shells dropping softly behind.

Gas! Gas! Quick, boys!—An ecstasy of fumbling,
Fitting the clumsy helmets just in time,   10
But someone still was yelling out and stumbling
And flound'ring like a man in fire or lime.
Dim through the misty panes and thick green light,
As under a green sea, I saw him drowning.

In all my dreams before my helpless sight   15
He plunges at me, guttering,* choking, drowning.

If in some smothering dreams, you too could pace
Behind the wagon that we flung him in,
And watch the white eyes wilting in his face,
His hanging face, like a devil's sick of sin,   20
If you could hear, at every jolt, the blood
Come gargling from the froth-corrupted lungs,
Obscene as cancer, bitter as the cud
Of vile, incurable sores on innocent tongues,—
My friend, you would not tell with such high zest   25
To children ardent for some desperate glory,
The old Lie: Dulce et decorum est
Pro patria mori.

WILFRED OWEN

*__guttering,__   melting away like the wax of a candle.

Summer in England, 1914

On London fell a clearer light;
    Caressing pencils of the sun
Defined the distances, the white
    Houses transfigured one by one,
The "long, unlovely street"[1] impearled.[2]   5
Oh, what a sky has walked the world!

Most happy year! And out of town
    The hay was prosperous, and the wheat;
The silken harvest climbed the down.[3]
    Moon after moon was heavenly-sweet,   10
Stroking the bread within the sheaves,
Looking 'twixt apples and their leaves.

And while this rose made round her cup,
    The armies died convulsed. And when
This chaste young silver sun went up   15
    Softly, a thousand shattered men,
One wet corruption, heaped the plain,
After a league-long[4] throb of pain.

Flower following tender flower; and birds,
    And berries; and benignant[5] skies   20
Made thrive[6] the serried[7] flocks and herds.—
    Yonder are men shot through the eyes.
        Love, hide thy face
From man's unpardonable race.

ALICE MEYNELL

ALICE MEYNELL
J.S. Sergant
National Portrait Gallery, London

1. **"long unlovely street."**   The line appears in Tennyson's *In Memoriam.*
2. **impearled,**   adorned as if with pearls, here made lovely by the bright light.
3. **down,**   archaic form of hill (as in *dune*).
4. **league-long,**   as long as a league (3 miles).
5. **benignant** (bi nig' nənt),   kindly.
6. **thrive,**   flourish
7. **serried** (ser' ēd),   compact, densely packed together.

From WOMEN POETS IN ENGLAND by Ann Stanford, ed. Copyright © 1972. Reprinted by permission of Ann Stanford.

STEPHEN SPENDER
Howard Coster
National Portrait Gallery, London

Responsibility: The Pilots Who Destroyed Germany in the Spring of 1945

I stood on a roof top and they wove their cage
Their murmuring, throbbing cage, in the air of blue crystal,
I saw them gleam above the town like diamond bolts
Conjoining invisible struts of wire,
Carrying through the sky their geometric cage   5
Woven by senses delicate as a shoal of flashing fish.

They went. They left a silence in our streets below
Which boys gone to schoolroom leave in their playground.
A silence of asphalt, of privet hedge, of staring wall.
In the glass emptied sky their diamonds had scratched   10
Long curving finest whitest lines.

These the day soon melted into satin ribbons
Falling over heaven's terraces near the golden sun.

Oh that April morning they carried my will
Exalted expanding singing in their aeriel cage.   15
They carried my will. They dropped it on a German town.
My will expanded and tall buildings fell down.

Then, when the ribbons faded and the sky forgot,
And April was concerned with building nests and being hot
I began to remember the lost names and faces.   20

Now I tie the ribbons torn down from those terraces
Around the most hidden image in my lines,
And my life, which never paid the price of their wounds,
Turns thoughts over and over like a propellor
Assumes their guilt, honours, repents, prays for them.   25

STEPHEN SPENDER

THOM GUNN
Photo: Fay Godwin's Photo Files

Innocence

He ran the course and as he ran he grew,
And smelt his fragrance in the field. Already,
Running he knew the most he ever knew,
The egotism of a healthy body.

Ran into manhood, ignorant of the past: 5
Culture of guilt and guilt's vague heritage,
Self-pity and the soul; what he possessed
Was rich, potential, like the bud's tipped
        rage.

The Corps developed, it was plain to see,
Courage, endurance, loyalty and skill   10
To a morale firm as morality,
Hardening him to an instrument, until

The finitude of virtues that were there
Bodied within the swarthy uniform
A compact innocence, child-like and clear,   15
No doubt could penetrate, no act could
        harm.

When he stood near the Russian partisan
Being burned alive, he therefore could
        behold
The ribs wear gently through the darkening
        skin
And sicken only at the Northern cold,   20

Could watch the fat burn with a violet flame
And feel disgusted only at the smell,
And judge that all pain finishes the same
As melting quietly by his boots it fell.

THOM GUNN

UNDERSTANDING AND APPRECIATION

Dulce et decorum est

1. What attitude toward war is Owen attacking?
2. Whom does the poet mean by "you" in the last stanza?
3. Does Owen give the last two lines the same meaning that the original author (Horace) gave them?

Summer in England, 1914

1. How does Meynell convey a sense of happiness and prosperity in the first two stanzas?
2. What words describe the results of war?
3. What is the effect of the short line, "Love, hide thy face" (line 23)?

Responsibility

1. How does the speaker feel that he is different from the pilots? How is he like them?
2. What is the change of attitude in the speaker from the first part of the poem to the final stanza? What caused the change?
3. Why is the poem called "Responsibility"?
4. What do the figures of speech "cage," "ribbons," and "diamond bolts" symbolize?

Innocence

1. Is innocence a desirable quality?
2. What is a synonym for innocence (for example, blamelessness or ignorance)?
3. How is the boy of the poem innocent?
4. The poet says "no doubt could penetrate, no act could harm" his innocence. Explain.
5. Consider the following statements and decide whether the poem substantiates or refutes them:
  a. Because of his good traits most people would consider the boy a desirable kind of person.
  b. After watching the torture of the partisan, the boy is still innocent.
  c. Thom Gunn states that there is no more dangerous kind of person than the unthinking "tool" who obeys orders innocently and without questioning.

FOR INTERPRETATION

1. Sometimes violent feelings do not necessarily lead to good poetry but just to polemic or propaganda. How do these poems avoid becoming merely angry or emotional?
2. Does the modern poet have a responsibility to write about war?
3. What relationships do you see between these poems?

Robert Graves 1895–

Robert Graves went directly from Charterhouse School into the trenches of World War I. During three tours of duty he was wounded and later suffered shell shock, which led to his medical discharge. After the war he went to Oxford and took a degree. In 1926, upon the recommendation of T. E. Lawrence (Lawrence of Arabia), he spent a brief time as Professor of English at the Egyptian University in Cairo. Since 1929, except for a period during World War II, he has lived on the island of Majorca.

Graves is a prolific writer, both in poetry and prose, in a wide variety of genres. He has published over fifteen volumes of poetry (three while serving in World War I). In 1959 he published *Collected Poems*, including most of the poetry he wants to leave as his poetic legacy. Graves has long made his living, however, in prose. He has made excellent use of his good classical and Biblical scholarship in a number of historical novels and retellings of mythological stories. His best known novel today is *I, Claudius*, the basis of the remarkable BBC series by the same title.

Graves once said of himself, "I write poems for poets, and satires and grotesques for wits. For people in general I write prose, and am content that they should be unaware that I do anything else. To write poems for other than poets is wasteful." But this is playful exaggeration, typical of him. You will find the following poems down-to-earth observations,

ROBERT GRAVES
John Aldridge
National Portrait Gallery, London

often ironical, of everyday experiences (especially annoyances). Do not be misled by their simplicity, however. As you think about them you will begin to see wider and deeper applications.

The Blue-fly

Five summer days, five summer nights,
The ignorant, loutish, giddy blue-fly
Hung without motion on the cling peach,
Humming occasionally: "O my love, my fair one!"
    As in the Canticles.[1]   5

Magnified one thousand times, the insect
Looks farcically human; laugh if you will!
Bald head, stage-fairy wings, blear eyes,
A caved-in chest, hairy black mandibles,[2]
    Long spindly thighs.   10

The crime was detected on the sixth day.
What then could be said or done? By anyone?
It would have been vindictive, mean and
    what-not
To swat that fly for being a blue-fly,
    For debauch of a peach.   15

Is it fair, either, to bring a microscope
To bear on the case, even in search of truth?
Nature, doubtless, has some compelling cause
To glut the carriers of her epidemics—
    Nor did the peach complain.   20

From COMPLETE POEMS, © 1965

1. The Biblical Song of Songs, or Song of Solomon.
2. **mandibles,** jaws.

Song: One Hard Look

Small gnats that fly
In hot July
And lodge in sleeping ears,
Can rouse therein
A trumpet's din   5
With Day of Judgment fears.

Small mice at night
Can wake more fright
Than lions at midday.

A straw will crack   10
The camel's back;
There is no easier way.

One smile relieves
A heart that grieves
Though deadly sad it be,   15
And one hard look
Can close the book
That lovers love to see.

From COMPLETE POEMS, © 1965

A Pinch of Salt

When a dream is born in you
  With a sudden clamorous pain,
When you know the dream is true
  And lovely, with no flaw nor stain,
O then, be careful, or with sudden clutch   5
You'll hurt the delicate thing you prize so much.

Dreams are like a bird that mocks,
  Flirting the feathers of his tail.
When you seize at the salt box,
  Over the hedge you'll see him sail.   10
Old birds are neither caught with salt nor chaff:
They watch you from the apple bough and laugh.

Poet, never chase the dream.
  Laugh yourself, and turn away.
Mask your hunger; let it seem   15
  Small matter if he come or stay;
But when he nestles in your hand at last,
Close up your fingers tight and hold him fast.

From COMPLETE POEMS, © 1965

Sullen Moods

Love, never count your labour lost
  Though I turn sullen or retired
Even at your side; my thought is crossed
  With fancies by no evil fired.

And when I answer you, some days   5
  Vaguely and wildly, never fear
That my love walks forbidden ways,
  Snapping the ties that hold it here.

If I speak gruffly, this mood is
    Mere indignation at my own   10
Shortcomings, plagues, uncertainties:
    I forget the gentler tone.

You, now that you have come to be
    My one beginning, prime and end,
I count at last as wholly me,   15
    Lover no longer nor yet friend.

Help me to see you as before
    When overwhelmed and dead, almost,
I stumbled on your secret door
    Which saves the live man from the ghost. 20

Be once again the distant light,
    Promise of glory, not yet known
In full perfection—wasted quite
    When on my imperfection thrown.

From WHIPPERGINNY, by Robert Graves, © 1923.

UNDERSTANDING AND INTERPRETATION

The Blue-fly

1. What is Graves' attitude toward the blue-fly in the first stanza? Why does he compare the blue-fly to a human in the second stanza? How does Graves' attitude toward the blue-fly seem to change?

2. In line 12 Graves asks a question. Explain his answer. Is it satisfactory?

3. In lines 16–17 Graves asks another question. How do you think he would answer it?

Song: One Hard Look

1. What has the title to do with this poem?

2. What point is Graves making? Do you agree or disagree? Explain your answer.

A Pinch of Salt

1. What is the function of the extended simile in the second stanza?

2. Graves' advice, "never chase the dream" seems to contradict popular, romantic attitudes. What reasons does he give in the poem for his attitude? Explain if you agree or disagree with him.

Sullen Moods

1. The poem divides neatly into two parts. What is the speaker telling his love in the first part? In the second?

2. How is the speaker's statement "wasted quite/ When on my imperfection thrown" related to the rest of the poem?

Stevie Smith   1902–1971

Stevie Smith was named Florence Margaret at birth. Because she was so small, though, she acquired the nickname "Stevie," borrowed from a famous jockey of the period. She lived in London for most of her life, writing poems illustrated with her own drawings and working in a publisher's office for many years. Her poems are, on the surface, much simpler than those of Eliot or Yeats. She uses familiar language and familiar poetic forms. But it is that very ordinary quality that throws into sharp focus her caustic observations on the modern world. In the poems given here, note how Smith repeats phrases, adding new meaning with each repetition. The poems deliver frightening twists from verse to verse as we recognize the inescapable trap created for the characters and for ourselves.

STEVIE SMITH
Photo: Jane Bown

Not Waving But Drowning

Nobody heard him, the dead man,
But still he lay moaning:
I was much further out than you thought
And not waving but drowning.

Poor chap, he always loved larking*   5
And now he's dead
It must have been too cold for him his heart gave way,
They said.

Oh, no no no, it was too cold always
(Still the dead one lay moaning)   10
I was much too far out all my life
And not waving but drowning.

*__larking,__   playing around.

Alone in the Woods

Alone in the woods I felt
The bitter hostility of the sky and the trees
Nature has taught her creatures to hate
Man that fusses and fumes
Unquiet man   5
As the sap rises in the trees
As the sap paints the trees a violent green
So rises the wrath of Nature's creatures
At man
So paints the face of Nature a violent green.   10
Nature is sick at man
Sick at his fuss and fume
Sick at his agonies
Sick at his gaudy mind
That drives his body   15
Ever more quickly
More and more
In the wrong direction.

From THE COLLECTED POEMS OF STEVIE SMITH ed. James Mc-Gibbon © 1972. Reprinted by permission of New Directions Publishing Company.

Smith's reflections on the creative process here take the form of a poetic meditation on the "Person from Porlock," who interrupted Coleridge in his composition of "Kubla Khan."

Thoughts about the Person from Porlock

Coleridge received the Person from Porlock
And ever after called him a curse,
Then why did he hurry to let him in?
He could have hid in the house.

It was not right of Coleridge in fact it was wrong   5
(But often we all do wrong)
As the truth is I think he was already stuck
With Kubla Khan.

He was weeping and wailing: I am finished, finished,
I shall never write another word of it,   10
When along comes the Person from Porlock
And takes the blame for it.

It was not right, it was wrong.
But often we all do wrong.
     .   .   .   .

May we inquire the name of the Person from Porlock?   15
Why, Porson, didn't you know?
He lived at the bottom of Porlock Hill
So had a long way to go,

He wasn't much in the social sense
Though his grandmother was a Warlock,   20
One of the Rutlandshire ones I fancy
And nothing to do with Porlock,

And he lived at the bottom of the hill as I said
And had a cat named Flo,
And had a cat named Flo.   25

I long for the Person from Porlock
To bring my thoughts to an end,
I am becoming impatient to see him
I think of him as a friend,

Often I look out of the window   30
Often I run to the gate
I think, He will come this evening,
I think it is rather late.

I am hungry to be interrupted
For ever and ever amen   35
O Person from Porlock come quickly
And bring my thoughts to an end.
     .   .   .   .

I felicitate the people who have a Person from Porlock
To break up everything and throw it away
Because then there will be nothing to keep them   40
And they need not stay.
     .   .   .   .

Why do they grumble so much?
He comes like a benison
They should be glad he has not forgotten them
They might have had to go on.   45
     .   .   .   .

These thoughts are depressing I know. They are depressing,
I wish I was more cheerful, it is more pleasant,
Also it is a duty, we should smile as well as submitting

To the purpose of One Above who is experimenting
With various mixtures of human character which goes best,   **50**
All is interesting for him it is exciting, but not for us.
There I go again. Smile, smile, and get some work to do
Then you will be practically unconscious without positively
    having to go.

UNDERSTANDING AND INTERPRETATION

Not Waving But Drowning

1. Much of the poem depends on the use of familiar phrases whose meanings are altered. How does Smith change the meaning?

2. How would you describe the formal structure of the poem? What does that structure contribute to the poem's effect?

Alone in the Woods

1. According to the speaker, what is Nature's attitude toward Man? Why might Nature feel this way?

2. In what direction is man going "ever so quickly"? Do you agree or disagree with the speaker?

Thoughts about the Person from Porlock

1. Look back at the introduction to Coleridge's "Kubla Khan" (page 514). What was the effect of the interruption on Coleridge? Why do you think Smith says she thinks of the person from Porlock "as a friend"?

2. What is the effect of lines 15–25 on the tone of the poem? How does this tone shift in lines 26–37?

3. What does this poem seem to be saying about the creative process of writing poetry? Look back at Tennyson's "The Lady of Shalott" (page 647), and try to compare Tennyson's view of the artist with Smith's.

W. H. Auden   1907–1973

W. H. (Wystan Hugh) Auden, like Eliot, had
loyalties to both England and America. He was
born in York and attended Oxford but left
England in 1939 for the United States. He later
became a U.S. citizen, although in 1972 he was
invited back to live at his old college at Oxford.
Like many modern poets, Auden looks to the
past and finds in it a vision missing in the
modern world. Praise for the past is seen in the
opening line of "Musée des Beaux Arts." The
idea that one might write a poem about a
painting—as Auden does about Brueghel's *The
Fall of Icarus*—recurs in the modern period, for
poets frequently find excellence in art. The
second major quality of Auden's philosophy is a
view of the world as mechanized and
increasingly deadened. His poem "The
Unknown Citizen" is an amusing, yet serious,
account of what we have become through
technology. In Stevie Smith's poem, the modern
individual is "not waving but drowning." In
Auden's poem, the person is also dead, though
now the metaphor is one of being imprisoned,
within both the marble monument and the
mechanized world.

W.H. AUDEN
D. Bachardy
National Portrait Gallery, London

Musée des Beaux Arts

About suffering they were never wrong,
The Old Masters: how well they understood
Its human position; how it takes place
While someone else is eating or opening a window or just walking dully along;
How, when the aged are reverently, passionately waiting   5
For the miraculous birth, there always must be
Children who did not specially want it to happen, skating
On a pond at the edge of the wood:
They never forgot
That even the dreadful martyrdom must run its course   10
Anyhow in a corner, some untidy spot
Where the dogs go on with their doggy life and the torturer's horse
Scratches its innocent behind on a tree.

THE FALL OF ICARUS
Pieter Brueghel, the Elder
Musée des Beaux-Arts, Brussels

In Brueghel's *Icarus*,* for instance: how everything turns away
Quite leisurely from the disaster; the plowman may   15
Have heard the splash, the forsaken cry,
But for him it was not an important failure; the sun shone
As it had to on the white legs disappearing into the green
Water; and the expensive delicate ship that must have seen
Something amazing, a boy falling out of the sky,   20
Had somewhere to get to and sailed calmly on.

*Auden refers to a famous work by the sixteenth-century Dutch painter Pieter Brueghel the Elder, "The Fall of Icarus." In Greek mythology Icarus ignored his father's warnings about protecting his wax wings from the melting heat of the sun. He tumbled from the sky to drown in the ocean. Brueghel's painting hangs in the Museum of Fine Arts in Brussels, the museum of Auden's title.

The Unknown Citizen JS/07/M/378
This Marble Monument Is Erected
by the State

He was found by the Bureau of Statistics to be
One against whom there was no official complaint,
And all the reports on his conduct agree
That, in the modern sense of an old-fashioned word, he was a saint,
For in everything he did he served the Greater Community.   5
Except for the war till the day he retired
He worked in the factory and never got fired,
But satisfied his employers, Fudge Motors Inc.
Yet he wasn't a scab[1] or odd in his views,
For his Union reports that he paid his dues,   10
(Our report on his Union shows it was sound)
And our Social Psychology workers found
That he was popular with his mates and liked a drink.
The Press are convinced that he bought a paper every day
And that his reactions to poetry were normal in every way.   15
Policies taken out in his name prove that he was fully insured,
And his Health Card shows he was once in hospital but left it cured.
Both Producers Research and High-Grade Living declare
He was fully sensible to the advantages of the Installment Plan
And had everything necessary to the Modern Man,   20
A gramophone, a radio, a car, and a frigidaire.
Our researchers into public opinion are content
That he held the proper opinions for the time of year.
When there was peace, he was for peace; when there was war, he went.
He was married and added five children to the population,   25
Which our Eugenists[2] say was the right number for a parent of his generation,
And our teachers report that he never interfered with their education.
Was he free? Was he happy? The question is absurd:
Had anything been wrong, we certainly should have heard.

1. **scab,** a union member who refuses to strike.
2. **Eugenists,** specialists in controlling hereditary factors in breeding.

UNDERSTANDING AND INTERPRETATION

Musée des Beaux Arts

1. What is the relationship between the first and second stanzas of this poem?
2. To whom does the "they" in line 9 refer?
3. What is the difference in attitude between the "aged" and the "children"?

The Unknown Citizen

1. What does the title mean?
2. Who is speaking in this poem? What is the speaker's concept of the good life?
3. What is Auden attacking?

Louis MacNeice   1907–1963

MacNeice was born in Belfast, Northern Ireland, in the same year as W. H. Auden. He specialized in ancient classical literature at Oxford and after his graduation served as a university teacher in Birmingham and London. In the 1940s he became a writer and producer for the British Broadcasting Corporation (BBC), and then lived in Athens as the director of the British Institute

Although MacNeice was well acquainted with the political poets of the 1930s, such as Auden and Stephen Spender, he resolutely created his own, distinctive style. He was at one with the modernist poets in rejecting the romanticism of the Victorians, and even of Yeats. But his attitude toward poetry was essentially more private and more restrained than that, say, of Auden. His poems often deal with apparently mundane subjects, and display painstaking craftsmanship with a tone of gentle melancholic irony. In the second of the two poems, MacNeice retells the Venerable Bede's striking vignette of a sparrow briefly glimpsed in an ancient hall of the early Medieval times (see page 10).

LOUIS MacNEICE
Photo: BBC Hulton Picture Library

The Sunlight on the Garden

The sunlight on the garden
Hardens and grows cold,
We cannot cage the minute
Within its nets of gold;
When all is told   5
We cannot beg for pardon.

Our freedom as free lances
Advances towards its end;
The earth compels, upon it
Sonnets and birds descend;   10
And soon, my friend,
We shall have no time for dances.

The sky was good for flying
Defying the church bells
And every evil iron   15
Siren and what it tells:
The earth compels,
We are dying, Egypt, dying*

And not expecting pardon,
Hardened in heart anew,   20
But glad to have sat under
Thunder and rain with you,
And grateful too
For sunlight on the garden.

*__We . . . dying:__ an allusion to Shakespeare. *Antony and Cleopatra,* Act 4, scene 13, line 41, where Antony accepts his death with resignation.

Dark Age Glosses on the Venerable Bede

Birds flitting in and out of the barn
Bring back an Anglo-Saxon story:
The great wooden hall with long fires down the centre,
Their feet in the rushes, their hands tearing the meat.
Suddenly high above them they notice a swallow enter   5
Then out once more into the unknown night;
And that, someone remarks, is the life of man.
But now it is time to sleep; one by one
They rise from the bench and their gigantic shadows
Lurch on the shuddering walls. How can the world   10
Or the non-world beyond harbour a bird?
They close their eyes that smart from the woodsmoke: how
Can anyone even guess his whence and whither?
This indoors flying makes it seem absurd,
Although it itches and nags and flutters and yearns,   15
To postulate any other life than now.

From COLLECTED POEMS OF LOUIS MacNEICE, ed. E.R. Dodds, by Louis MacNeice, © 1966. Reprinted by permission of Faber and Faber, Ltd.

UNDERSTANDING AND INTERPRETATION

The Sunlight on the Garden

1. Note that the rhyme scheme of the poem includes rhymes between the last words of the first and third lines of each stanza and the first words of the second and fourth lines. What is the effect of this unusual arrangement?
2. What hints in the poem imply a wartime setting?
3. What seems to be the poet's attitude toward death?

Dark Age Glosses on the Venerable Bede

1. Compare MacNeice's version with that of the Venerable Bede (page 10). What are the various elements of comparison between the bird's flight and man's life in each version?
2. How does the setting affect the mood in each version?
3. In what way is MacNeice's version more somber than that of Bede?

Dylan Thomas   1914–1953

Dylan Thomas might well have spoken the line he gives to one of his characters in the verse play, *Under Milk Wood:* "Oh, isn't life a terrible thing, thank God!" The sense of life's danger, its terror, its wonder, and its joy fill Thomas's poetry, just as they filled his life. He left his native Wales at the age of twenty, already having published his first book of poems. He went to London, married Caitlin Macnamara, and continued writing poems—and drinking. One might almost think of him as a Romantic poet misplaced in the twentieth century, since, like Byron and Shelley, he was a well-known public figure. In his later years, Thomas frequently gave poetry readings in America and was famous for his magnificent performances, whether drunk or sober, whether on lecture platforms or in bars. More importantly, like Keats and like D. H. Lawrence, Thomas was in love with language and the sensory images it could evoke. There is passion in Thomas's poetry for sensory description and for people and the quality with which they live. One of his most famous poems, "Do Not Go Gentle into That Good Night," written during the illness that finally took his father, attacks fiercely the notion of dying easily or gently. "In My Craft or Sullen Art" presents

DYLAN THOMAS
Augustus John
National Museum of Wales, Cardiff

the familiar modern consciousness—the poet viewed as poet and making us highly aware that poetry is a crafted, shaped art.

Do Not Go Gentle into That Good Night

Do not go gentle into that good night.
Old age should burn and rave at close of day;
Rage, rage against the dying of the light.

Though wise men at their end know dark is right,
Because their words have forked no lightning they   5
Do not go gentle into that good night.

Good men, the last wave by, crying how bright
Their frail deeds might have danced in a green bay,
Rage, rage against the dying of the light.

Wild men who caught and sang the sun in flight,   10
And learn, too late, they grieved it on its way,
Do not go gentle into that good night.

Grave men, near death, who see with blinding sight
Blind eyes could blaze like meteors and be gay,
Rage, rage against the dying of the light.   15

And you, my father, there on the sad height,
Curse, bless, me now with your fierce tears, I pray.
Do not go gentle into that good night.
Rage, rage against the dying of the light.

Fern Hill

Now as I was young and easy under the apple boughs
About the lilting house and happy as the grass was green,
    The night above the dingle[1] starry,
      Time let me hail and climb
    Golden in the heydays of his eyes,   5
And honored among wagons I was prince of the apple towns
And once below a time I lordly had the trees and leaves
      Trail with daisies and barley
    Down the rivers of the windfall light.

And as I was green and carefree, famous among the barns   10
About the happy yard and singing as the farm was home,
    In the sun that is young once only,
      Time let me play and be
    Golden in the mercy of his means,
And green and golden I was huntsman and herdsman, the   15
    calves
Sang to my horn, the foxes on the hills barked clear and cold,
      And the sabbath rang slowly
    In the pebbles of the holy streams.

All the sun long it was running, it was lovely, the hay-
Fields high as the house, the tunes from the chimneys, it was   20
    air
    And playing, lovely and watery
      And fire green as grass.
      And nightly under the simple stars
As I rode to sleep the owls were bearing the farm away,

1. **dingle,** wooded valley.

**WATERFALL IN
CARDIGANSHIRE**
Ceri Richards
National Museum of Wales, Cardiff

All the moon long I heard, blessed among stables, the nightjars[2] **25**
     Flying with the ricks, and the horses
       Flashing into the dark.

And then to awake, and the farm, like a wanderer white
With the dew, come back, the cock on his shoulder: it was all
     Shining, it was Adam and maiden, **30**
       The sky gathered again
     And the sun grew round that very day.
So it must have been after the birth of the simple light
In the first, spinning place, the spellbound horses walking
  warm
     Out of the whinnying green stable **35**
      On to the fields of praise.

And honored among foxes and pheasants by the gay house
Under the new made clouds and happy as the heart was long,
     In the sun born over and over,
      I ran my heedless ways, **40**
     My wishes raced through the house-high hay
And nothing I cared, at my sky blue trades, that time allows
In all his tuneful turning so few and such morning songs
     Before the children green and golden
      Follow him out of grace. **45**

2. **nightjars,** grey-brown night-flying birds.

Nothing I cared, in the lamb white days, that time would take me
Up to the swallow thronged loft by the shadow of my hand,
    In the moon that is always rising,
        Nor that riding to sleep
    I should hear him fly with the high fields   50
And wake to the farm forever fled from the childless land.
Oh as I was young and easy in the mercy of his means,
        Time held me green and dying
    Though I sang in my chains like the sea.

In My Craft or Sullen Art

In my craft or sullen art
Exercised in the still night
When only the moon rages
And the lovers lie abed
With all their griefs in their arms,   5
I labour by singing light
Not for ambition or bread
Or the strut and trade of charms
On the ivory stages
But for the common wages   10
Of their most secret heart.

Not for the proud man apart
From the raging moon I write
On these spindrift* pages
Nor for the towering dead   15
With their nightingales and psalms
But for the lovers, their arms
Round the griefs of the ages,
Who pay no praise or wages
Nor heed my craft or art.   20

* **spindrift,** spray blown from a rough sea or surf.

FOR UNDERSTANDING AND INTERPRETATION

Do Not Go Gentle Into That Good Night

1. In stanza 1, what is the meaning of "good night," "close of day," and "dying light"?
2. What four types of people are mentioned?
3. What has each kind of person failed to accomplish or understand?
4. Is the poet saying that the way to die is to protest against it with every bit of strength that you have?

Fern Hill

1. The poem presents memories of youth on the part of a man who is no longer young. Consider and discuss each of the following statements about the poem:
    a. This kind of experience would be impossible to a child who grows up in the city.
    b. When such things are actually happening, the individual child is not aware of them. It is only when the child looks back on childhood that he or she realizes how wonderful it was.
2. What is the poet's attitude toward time? Is he saying that it is better to remain a child and never grow up? Discuss.

In My Craft or Sullen Art

The structure of this poem is as follows: There are 20 lines in the poem, and each line has 7 syllables (except lines 11, 14, and 20, which have 6 syllables). The rhyme scheme is abcdebdecca abcdeecca.
1. Examine the three lines that are each six syllables. How are all three linked in relationship to meaning?
2. What is the basic irony of this poem?

Philip Larkin   1922–

Philip Larkin is the most prominent of the "Movement" poets, a group who published a collection of contemporary poems entitled *New Lines* in 1956. Other principal figures of the Movement include Donald Davie and Elizabeth Jennings. This group of writers has, in general, tried to temper the harshness of an older generation's rejection of traditional forms. Poets like Larkin have aimed for a less intense and more conversational style in poetry. They have separated themselves from the complex, allusive symbolism of Yeats and Eliot, as well as rejecting the emotional intensity of poets like Dylan Thomas.

   Larkin himself, educated at Oxford, began his career as a novelist. He makes his living as Librarian of the University of Hull. He acknowledges his admiration for the poetry of Thomas Hardy (page 689) and he frequently resembles Hardy in his quietly ironic, meditative tone.

PHILIP LARKIN
Photo: Fay Godwin's Photo Files

Days

What are days for?
Days are where we live.
They come, they wake us
Time and time over.
They are to be happy in: 5

Where can we live but days?
Ah, solving that question
Brings the priest and the doctor
In their long coats
Running over the fields.   10

Coming

On longer evenings,
Light, chill and yellow,
Bathes the serene
Foreheads of houses.
A thrush sings,   5
Laurel-surrounded
In the deep bare garden,
Its fresh-peeled voice
Astonishing the brickwork.
It will be spring soon,   10

It will be spring soon—
And I, whose childhood
Is a forgotten boredom,
Feel like a child
Who comes on a scene   15
Of adult reconciling,
And can understand nothing
But the unusual laughter,
And starts to be happy.

The Explosion

On the day of the explosion
Shadows pointed towards the pithead:
In the sun the slagheap slept.

Down the lane came men in pitboots
Coughing oath-edged talk and pipe-smoke.
Shouldering off the freshened silence.

One chased after rabbits; lost them;
Came back with a nest of lark's eggs;
Showed them; lodged them in the grasses.

So they passed in beards and moleskins, 10
Fathers, brothers, nicknames, laughter,
Through the tall gates standing open.

At noon, there came a tremor; cows
Stopped chewing for a second; sun,
Scarfed as in a heat-haze, dimmed. 15

The dead go on before us, they
Are sitting in God's house in comfort.
We shall see them face to face—

Plain as lettering in the chapels
It was said, and for a second 20
Wives saw men of the explosion

Larger than in life they managed—
Gold as on a coin, or walking
Somehow from the sun towards them,

One showing the eggs unbroken. 25

UNDERSTANDING AND INTERPRETATION

Days

1. What is Larkin's answer to the question in line 1?

2. Why would the answer to the question posed in line 6 bring "the priest and the doctor/In their long coats/Running over the fields"?

Coming

1. How are the last traces of winter and the early signs of spring described in the poem?

2. What is the function of the simile beginning in line 14? How is it related to the "meaning" of the poem?

The Explosion

1. What is the setting of the poem? What is the time sequence?

2. What effect do the funeral services have on the wives?

3. Why does Larkin end the poem with a one-line stanza?

Ted Hughes   1930–

Ted Hughes, born in Yorkshire, was educated at Cambridge. He served in the Royal Air Force for two years and in 1956 married Sylvia Plath, the American poet, who died in 1963. Hughes's work can be distinguished from that of the Movement poets in its generally greater level of intense emotion. Much of his work, as in the poem below, centers on animals: sometimes noble like the horse, but more often the predators of nature, such as hawks, wolves, rats, and foxes. Edwin Muir, writing of Hughes's first book, *The Hawk in the Rain,* commented: "His images have an admirable violence . . . the violence of nature red in tooth and claw."

Hughes constantly calls on his childhood background as the setting for his works. The country where he was raised is rural and lonely, and though factories and mills have encroached on the countryside, they have made little impact on it. Hughes draws on his memories of this land and evokes it so powerfully that the place somehow becomes "realer" than anywhere else.

TED HUGHES
Photo: Mark Gerson, London

The Horses

I climbed through woods in the hour-before-dawn dark.
Evil air, a frost-making stillness,

Not a leaf, not a bird—
A world cast in frost. I came out above the wood

Where my breath left tortuous statues in the iron light.   5
But the valleys were draining the darkness

Till the moorline[1]—blackening dregs of the brightening grey—
Halved the sky ahead. And I saw the horses:

Huge in the dense grey—ten together—
Megalith[2]-still. They breathed, making no move,   10

With draped manes and tilted hind-hooves,
Making no sound.

1. **moor** (mủr),   a heath; an open land where heather often grows, particularly in Scotland and England. The **moorline** is the horizon where the open moor appears to meet the sky.

2. **megalith** (meg′ ə lith),   a stone of great size, especially a part of a prehistoric monument.

I passed: not one snorted or jerked its head.
Grey silent fragments

Of a grey silent world.   15

I listened in emptiness on the moor-ridge.
The curlew's[3] tear turned its edge on the silence.

Slowly detail leafed from the darkness. Then the sun
Orange, red, red erupted

Silently, and splitting to its core tore and flung cloud,   20
Shook the gulf open, showed blue,

And the big planets hanging—
I turned

Stumbling in the fever of a dream, down towards
The dark woods, from the kindling tops.   25

And came to the horses.
                              There, still they stood,
But now steaming and glistening under the flow of light,

Their draped stone manes, their tilted hind-hooves
Stirring under a thaw while all around them   30

The frost showed its fires. But still they made no sound.
Not one snorted or stamped,

Their hung heads patient as the horizons,
High over valleys, in the red levelling rays—

In din of the crowded streets, going among the years, the faces,   35
May I still meet my memory in so lonely a place

Between the streams and the red clouds, hearing curlews,
Hearing the horizons endure.

---

3. **curlew** (kėr′ lü),   a wading bird with a long, thin bill
that curves downward.

UNDERSTANDING AND INTERPRETATION

1. How are the horses described?
2. What details are given of the sunrise?

3. How does the last line of the poem reinforce the mood?
4. What thematic significance may be attached to the repeated emphasis on the silence and stillness of the horses?

The Twentieth-Century Novel

The purpose and scope of novels changed in the twentieth century. The novel's primary mission was no longer storytelling and entertainment. It began to concentrate on character, as writers tried to unravel the intricate web of thoughts and feelings that activate the individual. Many novels became propagandistic, vividly detailing the ramifications of social inadequacies.

Novelists of the early part of this century were much influenced by the great nineteenth-century European writers: the Russians Feodor Dostoevsky and Leo Tolstoy, and the French novelists Honoré de Balzac, Emile Zola, Guy de Maupassant, and Gustave Flaubert. From them they learned to present people as they usually are: neither wholly good nor bad, but with a mixture of character traits. The older structure of a protagonist and antagonist (or hero and villain) gave way. In modern works, one seldom encounters a villain, pure and simple. Characters struggle with themselves or with a situation, but not with a figure of evil incarnate. Likewise, we seldom meet a hero whom we can totally admire.

There are basically three generations of novels during the twentieth century: those written before 1920; those written between the two world wars; and novels written since World War II. The earliest period was dominated by two figures—Henry James (1843–1916) and Joseph Conrad (1857–1924); the first was an American by birth, and the second a Pole. Both were English by choice. Henry James's elder brother William was the American father of psychology, and it is scarcely surprising that the novelist focused on finely detailed portraits of individuals. Much of James's work (*The American, The Portrait of a Lady,* and *The Turn of the Screw*) was written before the turn of the century. But three masterpieces—*The Wings of the Dove, The Ambassadors,* and *The Golden Bowl*—were published in three successive years beginning in 1902. James was especially interested in showing the impact of European culture on wealthy Americans visiting Europe. He delights in revealing subtle emotions through apparently insignificant body language and fleeting facial expressions—a very different approach from the later stream-of-consciousness technique.

Joseph Conrad, like James, explored individuals who were caught up in a moral dilemma. But his settings and characters were strikingly different from those which James favored. Many of his novels were set in exotic, faraway locales in the tropics—places he knew well from his years as a sea captain. He experimented constantly with an oblique method of storytelling. Perhaps more than any single writer, Conrad brought to the fore a concern with point of view as a consciously manipulated technique in literature.

Some excellent writers of the period did not reach the pinnacle of achievement of Conrad and James. H. G. Wells (1866–1946), author of some fifty novels, made important experiments in the genre of science fiction—a type of novel which has become immensely popular in our time. Arnold Bennett (1867–1931), a successful journalist, wrote completely realistic stories about the uneventful lives of ordinary people in Staffordshire, his native county. Writing of a different class of society, John Galsworthy (1867–1933) treated the manners of the wealthy in such works as *The Forsyte Saga.* Somerset Maugham (1874–1965) expressed early in his career the disillusionment and frustration that were to be leading themes in the next generation. Many critics consider Maugham's *Of Human Bondage* (1915) to be his masterpiece. Perhaps the greatest of this secondary group of writers was E. M. Forster (1879–1970), who published his first novel in 1905. Forster's work subtly and ironically explored personal relationships, "that little society" we make for ourselves with our friends. In his greatest (and also his last) novel, *A Passage to India* (1924), he used the framework of Anglo-Indian relations in the early 1920s to explore the most complex of human relationships: experiences between individuals of two different cultures and races.

In the period between the wars (roughly the years 1920–1940), three novelists who had written some earlier books matured and produced their most significant works: Virginia Woolf (1882–1941), D. H. Lawrence (1885–1930), and James Joyce (1882–1941). Woolf and Joyce permanently altered novelistic technique through the development of the stream-of-consciousness style of writing; Lawrence brought to the novel a fresh strain of vitalism.

In Woolf's novels, plot has become only a minor element. In *Mrs. Dalloway* (1925) she subtly probed the thoughts of the title character and her friends on one day in London, giving her readers a remarkable insight into the mental actions and reactions of upper-class Londoners. Woolf's novels are basically a series of interior monologues, or inner soliloquies. Although she was a bold stylistic pioneer, Woolf was never popular with the reading public. But she exerted a major influence on the writers that followed.

James Joyce expanded the technique of interior monologue to a true "stream of consciousness." Recognizing that thoughts in our minds jump at random from one idea to another with extraordinary speed, he attempted faithfully to reproduce the inner consciousness (and sometimes the unconscious) of his characters' minds. Joyce's early works, *Dubliners* and *A Portrait of the Artist as a Young Man,* were vaguely autobiographical and conventionally organized. But in *Ulysses* and *Finnegans Wake* he writes a pure stream of thoughts as they seemingly go leaping or drifting from one idea to another with no logical connection. Superimposed on the actual thoughts is a complex structure of allusion and symbol that affords a universal dimension to the characters.

Strikingly different in subject matter and style from Woolf and Joyce was D. H. Lawrence. The son of a miner, he escaped from the laboring class through a university education. Married to a German, Lawrence supported unpopular ideas by refusing to have anything to do with the military during World War I and by proclaiming that civilization of all types had perverted man's basically noble, primitive nature. Badly treated by the English, Lawrence left England in 1918, never to return. Basically romantic, he wandered the globe, delighting in his nonconformity but increasingly bitter at what he regarded as English Puritanism. The titles of Lawrence's principal novels show his fascination for the relationships between men and women (whether mother to son or sweetheart to lover): *Sons and Lovers, Women in Love,* and *Lady Chatterley's Lover.*

Many novelists who began to write in the 1930s have come to prominence after World War II, but none has attained the stature of Joyce or Lawrence. William Golding (1911–   ) explored the working of primitive instincts in his striking symbolic novel, *Lord of the Flies* (1954). More recently, in works such as *The Inheritors, Pincher Martin,* and *Free Fall,* he has focused on the theme that evil stems from what he considers a fundamental defect in human nature. A similar concern appears in the novels of Graham Greene (1904–   ). Greene has roamed the world from Vietnam to West Africa, Latin America, and Haiti. Using these places as settings for his stories, he shows somewhat seedy protagonists caught up in malignant circumstances. For example, in *A Burnt-Out Case* (1961) an architect, repelled by modern life, attempts to lose himself in a leper colony deep in Africa and to purge all human desires and contacts. Greene writes both serious novels and adventure/detective stories. In both genres, in the tradition of Conrad, he explores the ambiguities of moral judgment and intensely human crises of faith.

The three early novels of George Orwell (1903–1950) grew out of his experiences working with the poor and lonely in the slums of London. Fighting in the Spanish Civil War (1936–1939) on the Republican side, he became sickened by the communist atrocities and returned to England to write his two most powerful books, *Animal Farm* and *Nineteen Eighty-Four*. These novels demonstrate the inherent desire for power in human beings that always threatens to pervert justice, freedom, and equality.

Among recent novelists, Elizabeth Bowen (1899–1973) and Angus Wilson (1913–   ) have returned to older traditions. Bowen's work seems reminiscent of Henry James and Wilson's of Charles Dickens. As Bowen endured the terror and devastation of the wartime bombing of London, she pondered on what in human nature could account for such acts of inhumanity. Her novel *The Heat of the Day* (1949) presents the question of how people cut off from their traditions of possessions and place can continue to exist. Angus Wilson, on the other hand, has rebelled against what he has called the neo-realism of contemporary fiction; he has insisted that fiction should be fiction, "a created or made up

story." One of his most successful books has been the novel *Anglo-Saxon Attitudes* (1956).

The twentieth century has witnessed the popularization of several new genres of the novel: the detective story, the story of intrigue (or the spy story), and science fiction. The Gothic novel, with origins in the late eighteenth century, has enjoyed a popular renaissance. Many of these novels are deservedly considered "pop" literature, but many of them are superbly crafted and can be accepted as serious literature. Among some literary critics there is the feeling that the psychological-social novel introduced by Woolf, Joyce, and Lawrence has run its course and that a new way of looking at life through storytelling may well be just on the horizon. Perhaps science fiction and fantasy, with their intriguing imaginative experiences, will offer a major new approach. The blending of fiction and nonfiction, as in some "documentary" novels, may continue to grow. In a century of such diverse developments in the novel, the possibilities are as numerous as they are intriguing.

TWENTIETH-CENTURY NOVELS

KINGSLEY AMIS
  Lucky Jim (1954)
ARNOLD BENNETT
  Clayhanger (1910)
  Hilda Lessways (1911)
  The Old Wives' Tale (1908)
  These Twain (1916)
ELIZABETH BOWEN
  The Death of the Heart (1938)
JOHN BRAINE
  Room at the Top (1957)
IVY COMPTON-BURNETT
  Men and Wives (1931)
  Mother and Son (1961)
  Parents and Children (1941)

SAMUEL BUTLER
The Way of All Flesh (1903)
JOYCE CARY
The Horse's Mouth (1944)
Mister Johnson (1939)
G.K. CHESTERTON
The Father Brown Omnibus (1933)
JOSEPH CONRAD
Heart of Darkness (1902)
Lord Jim (1900)
The Nigger of the "Narcissus" (1897)
Nostromo (1904)
The Secret Sharer (1912)
Victory (1915)
Youth (1902)
E.M. FORSTER
Howards End (1910)
A Passage to India (1924)
A Room with a View (1908)
JOHN GALSWORTHY
The Forsyte Saga:
The Man of Property (1906)
In Chancery (1920)
To Let (1921)
WILLIAM GOLDING
The Inheritors (1955)
Lord of the Flies (1954)
Pincher Martin (1956)
GRAHAM GREENE
Brighton Rock (1938)
A Burnt-Out Case (1961)
The End of the Affair (1951)
The Heart of the Matter (1948)
Our Man in Havana (1958)
The Power and the Glory (1940)
The Quiet American (1955)
ALDOUS HUXLEY
Antic Hay (1923)
Brave New World (1932)
Eyeless in Gaza (1936)
Point Counter Point (1928)
HENRY JAMES
The Ambassadors (1903)
The Golden Bowl (1904)
The Portrait of a Lady (1881)
The Turn of the Screw (1898)
The Wings of the Dove (1902)

JAMES JOYCE
Finnegans Wake (1939)
A Portrait of the Artist as a Young Man
(1916)
Ulysses (1922)
RUDYARD KIPLING
Captains Courageous (1897)
Kim (1901)
The Light That Failed (1890)
D.H. LAWRENCE
The Plumed Serpent (1926)
The Rainbow (1915)
Sons and Lovers (1913)
Women in Love (1920)
SOMERSET MAUGHAM
Cakes and Ale (1930)
The Moon and Sixpence (1919)
Of Human Bondage (1915)
The Razor's Edge (1944)
V.S. NAIPAUL
A House for Mr. Biswas (1961)
GEORGE ORWELL
Animal Farm (1945)
Nineteen Eighty-Four (1949)
J.B. PRIESTLEY
The Good Companions (1929)
ALAN SILLITOE
Saturday Night and Sunday Morning
(1958)
EVELYN WAUGH
Brideshead Revisited (1945)
H.G. WELLS
The History of Mr. Polly (1910)
The Invisible Man (1897)
Kipps (1905)
The Time Machine (1895)
Tono-Bungay (1909)
The War of the Worlds (1898)
ANGUS WILSON
Anglo-Saxon Attitudes (1956)
The Wrong Set (1949)
VIRGINIA WOOLF
Mrs. Dalloway (1925)
Orlando (1928)
To the Lighthouse (1927)
The Waves (1931)

James Joyce
1882–1941

In 1982, the centennial of James Joyce's birth, scholars gathered in Dublin from all over the world not only to discuss his work, but to take a standard tour of the places in the city that appear in his fiction. Though Joyce himself called Dublin the center of Ireland's moral paralysis, he wrote about Dublin and only about Dublin for the whole of his life.

He was born in this city, the son of John Stanislaus Joyce, a man of many talents who unfortunately slipped steadily down the financial and social ladder. Joyce was educated in Jesuit schools and then attended University College, Dublin. Here he became unpopular for his renunciation of Catholicism, his refusal to join in the movements for national independence, and for his papers on the then unacceptable Norwegian playwright, Henrik Ibsen. By the time he was twenty-two he had determined to be a writer and an exile. He left Ireland for Paris never to return except for his mother's last illness.

He took with him Nora Barnacle, an uneducated girl with no interest in literature, but whose vivacity and peasant wit charmed him throughout his life. In 1904 he went to Trieste, Italy where he taught English in the Berlitz school. Desperately poor, he took to drinking heavily until his brother, Stanislaus, came from Ireland to be, as he said, "his brother's keeper." World War I forced them to reside in Switzerland.

A few years after the Armistice, Joyce moved to Paris where he again gathered a literary circle about him. He was, however, never easy to get along with, since he was often on an emotional see-saw between gaiety and depression. From 1917 on Joyce always had patrons who helped him with monthly stipends. He lived in Paris until December of 1940, when World War II forced him to move again to Switzerland. He died only a few weeks later.

Joyce had no question about his own genius and that his proper medium was fiction. He made these decisions early in his life and never

JAMES JOYCE
Jaques-Emile Blanche (1935)
National Portrait Gallery, London

deviated from them. His first great book, *Dubliners*, was a collection of stories, each dealing with life in Dublin. He wrote from Rome in 1906 to say that some aspects of Dublin had been omitted: "I have not reproduced its ingenuous insularity and its hospitality, the latter 'virtue' so far as I can see does not exist elsewhere in Europe." In "The Dead" he captures a taste of this hospitality.

A Portrait of the Artist as a Young Man (1916) was a revision of an unpublished book, *Stephen Hero,* a fictionalized autobiography of Joyce's formative years. As with *Dubliners,* this story is a small-scale model not just of Dublin, but of all human life, indeed of all history and geography. The creation of such a microcosm continued to be one of Joyce's major objectives throughout his career.

In his two great master novels, *Ulysses* (1922) and *Finnegans Wake* (1939), Joyce broke completely with the traditions of the Victorian novel. *Ulysses* unfolds on a single day in 1904 in the life of three people: Leopold Bloom, an Irish Jew; his wife, Molly; and Stephen Dedalus, the hero of *A Portrait of an Artist as a Young Man.* In this book Joyce further developed the stream-of-consciousness technique of moving into and recording the thought processes of characters as they went through the affairs of daily life. Each incident corresponds to an incident in Homer's *Odyssey,* so that the immediate becomes historical and universal. Joyce felt that Ulysses was the most complete man ever depicted and he compares Bloom to him.

His final work, *Finnegans Wake,* takes its departure from an old folktale of the corpse that returns to life at a wake when whiskey is poured on it. The wake becomes an awakening. Weaving in and out of history, literature, and languages, Joyce creates a dense tapestry that continues to puzzle scholars. Often he creates new words or combines parts of words in a new way.

Publication of Joyce's works was fraught with difficulties. The publication of *Dubliners* was held up for years because both Irish and English publishers had changed or eliminated words and phrases without his permission. *Ulysses* was banned in both the United States and England when published, and it took nine years before an American court lifted the ban. England soon followed suit.

Throughout Joyce's fiction there are a number of recurring themes: That the dead do not stay buried; that we can be in death and life at the same time; that there are numerous "epiphanies" in life (a term Joyce used to describe a moment when things or people reveal their true character or essence); and that in using only the limited setting of Dublin it is possible to encompass a whole picture of the state of human experience.

THE DEAD

1

Lily, the caretaker's daughter, was literally run off her feet. Hardly had she brought one gentleman into the little pantry behind the office on the ground floor and helped him off with his overcoat than the wheezy hall-door bell clanged again and she had to scamper along the bare hallway to let in another guest. It was well for her she had not to attend to the ladies also. But Miss Kate and Miss Julia had thought of that and had converted the bath-room upstairs into a ladies' dressing-room. Miss Kate and Miss Julia were there, gossiping and laughing and fussing, walking after each other to the head of the stairs, peering down over the banisters and calling down to Lily to ask her who had come.

It was always a great affair, the Misses Morkan's annual dance. Everybody who knew them came to it, members of the family, old friends of the family, the members of Julia's choir, any of Kate's pupils that were grown up enough and even some of Mary Jane's pupils too. Never once had it fallen flat. For years and years it had gone off in splendid style as long as anyone could remember; ever since Kate and Julia, after the death of their brother Pat, had left the house

"The Dead" from DUBLINERS by James Joyce. Definitive text © 1967 by the Estate of James Joyce. Reprinted by permission of Viking Penguin Inc.

in Stoney Batter and taken Mary Jane, their only niece, to live with them in the dark gaunt house on Usher's Island, the upper part of which they had rented from Mr Fulham, the cornfactor on the ground floor. That was a good thirty years ago if it was a day. Mary Jane, who was then a little girl in short clothes, was now the main prop of the household for she had the organ in Haddington Road.[1] She had been through the Academy[2] and gave a pupils' concert every year in the upper room of the Antient Concert Rooms. Many of her pupils belonged to the better-class families on the Kingstown and Dalkey line. Old as they were, her aunts also did their share. Julia, though she was quite grey, was still the leading soprano in Adam and Eve's,[3] and Kate, being too feeble to go about much, gave music lessons to beginners on the old square piano in the back room. Lily, the caretaker's daughter, did housemaid's work for them. Though their life was modest they believed in eating well; the best of everything: diamond-bone sirloins, three-shilling tea and the best bottled stout. But Lily seldom made a mistake in the orders so that she got on well with her three mistresses. They were fussy, that was all. But the only thing they would not stand was back answers.

Of course they had good reason to be fussy on such a night. And then it was long after ten o'clock and yet there was no sign of Gabriel[4] and his wife. Besides they were dreadfully afraid that Freddy Malins might turn up screwed.[5] They would not wish for worlds that any of Mary Jane's pupils should see him under the influence; and when he was like that it was sometimes very hard to manage him. Freddy Malins always came late but they wondered what could be keeping Gabriel: and that was what brought them every two minutes to the banisters to ask Lily had Gabriel or Freddy come.

—O, Mr Conroy, said Lily to Gabriel when she opened the door for him, Miss Kate and Miss Julia thought you were never coming. Good-night, Mrs Conroy.

—I'll engage they did, said Gabriel, but they forgot that my wife here takes three mortal hours to dress herself.

He stood on the mat, scraping the snow from his goloshes,[6] while Lily led his wife to the foot of the stairs and called out:

—Miss Kate, here's Mrs Conroy.

Kate and Julia came toddling down the dark stairs at once. Both of them kissed Gabriel's wife, said she must be perished alive and asked was Gabriel with her.

—Here I am as right as the mail, Aunt Kate! Go on up. I'll follow, called out Gabriel from the dark.

He continued scraping his feet vigorously while the three women went upstairs, laughing, to the ladies' dressing-room. A light fringe of snow lay like a cape on the shoulders of his overcoat and like toecaps on the toes of his goloshes; and, as the buttons of his overcoat slipped with a squeaking noise through the snow-stiffened frieze, a cold fragrant air from out-of-doors escaped from crevices and folds.

—Is it snowing again, Mr Conroy? asked Lily.

She had preceded him into the pantry to help him off with his overcoat. Gabriel smiled at the three syllables she had given his surname and glanced at her. She was a slim, growing girl, pale in complexion and with hay-coloured hair. The gas in the pantry made her look still paler. Gabriel had known her when she was a child and used to sit on the lowest step nursing a rag doll.

—Yes, Lily, he answered, and I think we're in for a night of it.

He looked up at the pantry ceiling, which

1. **had the organ,** was hired to play the organ in a church on Haddington Road.
2. **Academy,** the Royal Academy of Music.
3. **Adam and Eve's,** a Dublin church.
4. **Gabriel.** The name suggests the Biblical angel who announced the birth of John the Baptist to Elizabeth and of Christ to the Virgin Mary.
5. **screwed,** drunk.
6. **goloshes,** rubber overshoes which were first produced in the mid-nineteenth century.

BANK HOLIDAY
William Strang
The Tate Gallery, London

was shaking with the stamping and shuffling of feet on the floor above, listened for a moment to the piano and then glanced at the girl, who was folding his overcoat carefully at the end of a shelf.

—Tell me, Lily, he said in a friendly tone, do you still go to school?

—O no, sir, she answered. I'm done schooling this year and more.

—O, then, said Gabriel gaily, I suppose we'll be going to your wedding one of these fine days with your young man, eh?

The girl glanced back at him over her shoulder and said with great bitterness:

—The men that is now is only all palaver and what they can get out of you.

Gabriel coloured as if he felt he had made a mistake and, without looking at her, kicked off his goloshes and flicked actively with his muffler at his patent-leather shoes.

He was a stout tallish young man. The high colour of his cheeks pushed upwards even to his forehead where it scattered itself in a few formless patches of pale red; and on his hairless face there scintillated restlessly the polished lenses and the bright gilt rims of the glasses which screened his delicate and restless eyes. His glossy black hair was parted in the middle and brushed in a long curve behind his ears where it curled slightly beneath the groove left by his hat.

When he had flicked lustre into his shoes

he stood up and pulled his waistcoat down more tightly on his plump body. Then he took a coin rapidly from his pocket.

—O Lily, he said, thrusting it into her hands, it's Christmas-time, isn't it? Just . . . here's a little. . . .

He walked rapidly towards the door.

—O no, sir! cried the girl, following him. Really, sir, I wouldn't take it.

—Christmas-time! Christmas-time! said Gabriel, almost trotting to the stairs and waving his hand to her in deprecation.

The girl, seeing that he had gained the stairs, called out after him:

—Well, thank you, sir.

He waited outside the drawing-room door until the waltz should finish, listening to the skirts that swept against it and to the shuffling of feet. He was still discomposed by the girl's bitter and sudden retort. It had cast a gloom over him which he tried to dispel by arranging his cuffs and the bows of his tie. Then he took from his waistcoat pocket a little paper and glanced at the headings he had made for his speech. He was undecided about the lines from Robert Browning for he feared they would be above the heads of his hearers. Some quotation that they could recognise from Shakespeare or from the Melodies[7] would be better. The indelicate clacking of the men's heels and the shuffling of their soles reminded him that their grade of culture differed from his. He would only make himself ridiculous by quoting poetry to them which they could not understand. They would think that he was airing his superior education. He would fail with them just as he had failed with the girl in the pantry. He had taken up a wrong tone. His whole speech was a mistake from first to last, an utter failure.

Just then his aunts and his wife came out of the ladies' dressing-room. His aunts were two small plainly dressed old women. Aunt Julia was an inch or so the taller. Her hair, drawn low over the tops of her ears, was grey; and grey also, with darker shadows, was her large flaccid face. Though she was stout in build and stood erect her slow eyes and part-

ed lips gave her the appearance of a woman who did not know where she was or where she was going. Aunt Kate was more vivacious. Her face, healthier than her sister's, was all puckers and creases, like a shrivelled red apple, and her hair, braided in the same old-fashioned way, had not lost its ripe nut colour.

They both kissed Gabriel frankly. He was their favourite nephew, the son of their dead elder sister, Ellen, who had married T. J. Conroy of the Port and Docks.

—Gretta tells me you're not going to take a cab back to Monkstown to-night, Gabriel, said Aunt Kate.

—No, said Gabriel, turning to his wife, we had quite enough of that last year, hadn't we? Don't you remember, Aunt Kate, what a cold Gretta got out of it? Cab windows rattling all the way, and the east wind blowing in after we passed Merrion. Very jolly it was. Gretta caught a dreadful cold.

Aunt Kate frowned severely and nodded her head at every word.

—Quite right, Gabriel, quite right, she said. You can't be too careful.

—But as for Gretta there, said Gabriel, she'd walk home in the snow if she were let.

Mrs Conroy laughed.

—Don't mind him, Aunt Kate, she said. He's really an awful bother, what with green shades for Tom's eyes at night and making him do the dumb-bells, and forcing Eva to eat the stirabout.[8] The poor child! And she simply hates the sight of it! . . . O, but you'll never guess what he makes me wear now!

She broke out into a peal of laughter and glanced at her husband, whose admiring and happy eyes had been wandering from her dress to her face and hair. The two aunts laughed heartily too, for Gabriel's solicitude was a standing joke with them.

—Goloshes! said Mrs Conroy. That's the latest. Whenever it's wet underfoot I must

7. **Melodies,** *Irish Melodies,* a collection of popular Irish songs.
8. **stirabout,** oatmeal.

put on my goloshes. To-night even he wanted me to put them on, but I wouldn't. The next thing he'll buy me will be a diving suit.

Gabriel laughed nervously and patted his tie reassuringly while Aunt Kate nearly doubled herself, so heartily did she enjoy the joke. The smile soon faded from Aunt Julia's face and her mirthless eyes were directed towards her nephew's face. After a pause she asked:

—And what are goloshes, Gabriel?

—Goloshes, Julia! exclaimed her sister. Goodness me, don't you know what goloshes are? You wear them over your . . . over your boots, Gretta, isn't it?

—Yes, said Mrs Conroy. Guttapercha[9] things. We both have a pair now. Gabriel says everyone wears them on the continent.

—O, on the continent, murmured Aunt Julia, nodding her head slowly.

Gabriel knitted his brows and said, as if he were slightly angered:

—It's nothing very wonderful but Gretta thinks it very funny because she says the word reminds her of Christy Minstrels.[10]

—But tell me, Gabriel, said Aunt Kate, with brisk tact. Of course, you've seen about the room. Gretta was saying . . .

—O, the room is all right, replied Gabriel. I've taken one in the Gresham.[11]

—To be sure, said Aunt Kate, by far the best thing to do. And the children, Gretta, you're not anxious about them?

—O, for one night, said Mrs Conroy. Besides, Bessie will look after them.

—To be sure, said Aunt Kate again. What a comfort it is to have a girl like that, one you can depend on! There's that Lily, I'm sure I don't know what has come over her lately. She's not the girl she was at all.

Gabriel was about to ask his aunt some questions on this point but she broke off suddenly to gaze after her sister who had wandered down the stairs and was craning her neck over the banisters.

—Now, I ask you, she said, almost testily, where is Julia going? Julia! Julia! Where are you going?

Julia, who had gone halfway down one flight, came back and announced blandly:

—Here's Freddy.

At the same moment a clapping of hands and a final flourish of the pianist told that the waltz had ended. The drawing room door was opened from within and some couples came out. Aunt Kate drew Gabriel aside hurriedly and whispered into his ear:

—Slip down, Gabriel, like a good fellow and see if he's all right, and don't let him up if he's screwed. I'm sure he's screwed. I'm sure he is.

Gabriel went to the stairs and listened over the banisters. He could hear two persons talking in the pantry. Then he recognised Freddy Malins' laugh. He went down the stairs noisily.

—It's such a relief, said Aunt Kate to Mrs Conroy, that Gabriel is here. I always feel easier in my mind when he's here. . . . Julia, there's Miss Daly and Miss Power will take some refreshment. Thanks for your beautiful waltz, Miss Daly. It made lovely time.

A tall wizen-faced man, with a stiff grizzled moustache and swarthy skin, who was passing out with his partner said:

—And may we have some refreshment, too, Miss Morkan?

—Julia, said Aunt Kate summarily, and here's Mr Browne and Miss Furlong. Take them in, Julia, with Miss Daly and Miss Power.

—I'm the man for the ladies, said Mr Browne, pursing his lips until his moustache bristled and smiling in all his wrinkles. You know, Miss Morkan, the reason they are so fond of me is—

He did not finish his sentence, but, seeing that Aunt Kate was out of earshot, at once led the three young ladies into the back room. The middle of the room was occupied by two square tables placed end to end, and on these

---

9. **Guttapercha,** latex from tropical trees, i.e., rubber.
10. **Christy Minstrels,** a famous nineteenth-century minstrel show.
11. **Gresham,** a fashionable Dublin hotel.

Aunt Julia and the caretaker were straightening and smoothing a large cloth. On the sideboard were arrayed dishes and plates, and glasses and bundles of knives and forks and spoons. The top of the closed square piano served also as a sideboard for viands and sweets. At a smaller sideboard in one corner two young men were standing, drinking hopbitters.[12]

Mr Browne led his charges thither and invited them all, in jest, to some ladies' punch, hot, strong and sweet. As they said they never took anything strong he opened three bottles of lemonade for them. Then he asked one of the young men to move aside, and, taking hold of the decanter, filled out for himself a goodly measure of whisky. The young men eyed him respectfully while he took a trial sip.

—God help me, he said, smiling, it's the doctor's orders.

His wizened face broke into a broader smile, and the three young ladies laughed in musical echo to his pleasantry, swaying their bodies to and fro, with nervous jerks of their shoulders. The boldest said:

—O, now, Mr Browne, I'm sure the doctor never ordered anything of the kind.

Mr Browne took another sip of his whisky and said, with sidling mimicry:

—Well, you see, I'm like the famous Mrs Cassidy, who is reported to have said: *Now, Mary Grimes, if I don't take it, make me take it, for I feel I want it.*

His hot face had leaned forward a little too confidentially and he had assumed a very low Dublin accent so that the young ladies, with one instinct, received his speech in silence. Miss Furlong, who was one of Mary Jane's pupils, asked Miss Daly what was the name of the pretty waltz she had played; and Mr Browne, seeing that he was ignored, turned promptly to the two young men who were more appreciative.

A red-faced young woman, dressed in pansy, came into the room, excitedly clapping her hands and crying:

—Quadrilles! Quadrilles![13]

Close on her heels came Aunt Kate crying:

—Two gentlemen and three ladies, Mary Jane!

—O, here's Mr Bergin and Mr Kerrigan, said Mary Jane. Mr Kerrigan, will you take Miss Power? Miss Furlong, may I get you a partner, Mr Bergin. O, that'll just do now.

—Three ladies, Mary Jane, said Aunt Kate.

The two young gentlemen asked the ladies if they might have the pleasure, and Mary Jane turned to Miss Daly.

—O, Miss Daly, you're really awfully good, after playing for the last two dances, but really we're so short of ladies to-night.

—I don't mind in the least, Miss Morkan.

—But I've a nice partner for you, Mr Bartell D'Arcy, the tenor. I'll get him to sing later on. All Dublin is raving about him.

—Lovely voice, lovely voice! said Aunt Kate.

As the piano had twice begun the prelude to the first figure Mary Jane led her recruits quicky from the room. They had hardly gone when Aunt Julia wandered slowly into the room, looking behind her at something.

—What is the matter, Julia? asked Aunt Kate anxiously. Who is it?

Julia, who was carrying in a column of table-napkins, turned to her sister and said, simply, as if the question had surprised her:

—It's only Freddy, Kate, and Gabriel with him.

In fact right behind her Gabriel could be seen piloting Freddy Malins across the landing. The latter, a young man of about forty, was of Gabriel's size and build, with very round shoulders. His face was fleshy and pallid, touched with colour only at the thick hanging lobes of his ears and at the wide wings of his nose. He had coarse features, a blunt nose, a convex and receding brow,

12. **hop-bitters,** beer with bitters added.
13. **Quadrilles,** a square dance of French origin, consisting of five figures and performed by four couples.

tumid and protruded lips. His heavy-lidded eyes and the disorder of his scanty hair made him look sleepy. He was laughing heartily in a high key at a story which he had been telling Gabriel on the stairs and at the same time rubbing the knuckles of his left fist backwards and forwards into his left eye.

—Good-evening, Freddy, said Aunt Julia.

Freddy Malins bade the Misses Morkan good-evening in what seemed an offhand fashion by reason of the habitual catch in his voice and then, seeing that Mr Browne was grinning at him from the sideboard, crossed the room on rather shaky legs and began to repeat in an undertone the story he had just told to Gabriel.

—He's not so bad, is he? said Aunt Kate to Gabriel.

Gabriel's brows were dark but he raised them quickly and answered:

—O no, hardly noticeable.

—Now, isn't he a terrible fellow! she said. And his poor mother made him take the pledge[14] on New Year's Eve. But come on, Gabriel, into the drawing-room.

Before leaving the room with Gabriel she signalled to Mr Browne by frowning and shaking her forefinger in warning to and fro. Mr Browne nodded in answer and, when she had gone, said to Freddy Malins:

—Now, then, Teddy, I'm going to fill you out a good glass of lemonade just to buck you up.

Freddy Malins, who was nearing the climax of his story, waved the offer aside impa-tiently but Mr Browne, having first called Freddy Malins' attention to a disarray in his dress, filled out and handed him a full glass of lemonade. Freddy Malins' left hand accepted the glass mechanically, his right hand being engaged in the mechanical readjustment of his dress. Mr Browne, whose face was once more wrinkling with mirth, poured out for himself a glass of whisky while Freddy Malins exploded, before he had well reached the climax of his story, in a kink of high-pitched bronchitic laughter and, setting down his untasted and overflowing glass, began to rub the knuckles of his left fist backwards and forwards into his left eye, repeating words of his last phrase as well as his fit of laughter would allow him.

14. **the pledge,** a formal pledge to refrain from drinking liquor.

UNDERSTANDING AND INTERPRETATION

1. How is Gabriel Conroy introduced in the story?
2. Where in this section are snow and the weather mentioned?
3. How is Gabriel's lack of sensitivity shown in the scene with Lily?
4. What details are given of Gabriel's appearance?
5. What does Gabriel feel about his planned speech?
6. How is Gretta's outlook different from Gabriel's?
7. What small statement suggests Gabriel's alienation from Ireland?
8. What tiny incidents indicate a sense of falseness in the gaiety?

2

Gabriel could not listen while Mary Jane was playing her Academy piece, full of runs and difficult passages, to the hushed drawing-room. He liked music but the piece she was playing had no melody for him and he doubt-ed whether it had any melody for the other listeners, though they had begged Mary Jane to play something. Four young men, who had come from the refreshment-room to stand in the doorway at the sound of the piano, had gone away quietly in couples after a few minutes. The only persons who seemed to follow the music were Mary Jane herself, her hands racing along the key-board or lifted from it at the pauses like those of a priestess in momentary imprecation, and Aunt Kate standing at her elbow to turn the page.

Gabriel's eyes, irritated by the floor, which glittered with beeswax under the heavy chandelier, wandered to the wall above the piano. A picture of the balcony scene in *Romeo and Juliet* hung there and beside it was a picture of the two murdered princes in the Tower[1] which Aunt Julia had worked in red, blue and brown wools when she was a girl. Probably in the school they had gone to as girls that kind of work had been taught, for one year his mother had worked for him as a birthday present a waistcoat of purple tabinet,[2] with little foxes' heads upon it, lined with brown satin and having round mulberry buttons. It was strange that his mother had had no musical talent though Aunt Kate used to call her the brains carrier of the Morkan family. Both she and Julia had always seemed a little proud of their serious and matronly sister. Her photograph stood before the pier-glass. She held an open book on her knees and was pointing out something in it to Constantine who, dressed in a man-o'-war suit,[3] lay at her feet. It was she who had chosen the names for her sons for she was very sensible of the dignity of family life. Thanks to her, Constantine was now senior curate in Balbriggan and, thanks to her, Gabriel himself had taken his degree in the Royal University.[4] A shadow passed over his face as he remembered her sullen opposition to his marriage. Some slighting phrases she had used still rankled in his memory; she had once spoken of Gretta as being country cute and that was not true of Gretta at all. It was Gretta who had nursed her during all her last long illness in their house at Monkstown.

He knew that Mary Jane must be near the end of her piece for she was playing again the opening melody with runs of scales after every bar and while he waited for the end the resentment died down in his heart. The piece ended with a trill of octaves in the treble and a final deep octave in the bass. Great applause greeted Mary Jane as, blushing and rolling up her music nervously, she escaped from the room. The most vigorous clapping came from the four young men in the doorway who had gone away to the refreshment-room at the beginning of the piece but had come back when the piano had stopped.

Lancers[5] were arranged. Gabriel found himself partnered with Miss Ivors. She was a frank-mannered talkative young lady, with a freckled face and prominent brown eyes. She did not wear a low-cut bodice and the large brooch which was fixed in the front of her collar bore on it an Irish device.[6]

When they had taken their places she said abruptly:

—I have a crow to pluck with you.

—With me? said Gabriel.

She nodded her head gravely.

—What is it? asked Gabriel, smiling at her solemn manner.

—Who is G. C.? answered Miss Ivors, turning her eyes upon him.

Gabriel coloured and was about to knit his brows, as if he did not understand, when she said bluntly:

—O, innocent Amy! I have found out that you write for *The Daily Express.*[7] Now, aren't you ashamed of yourself?

---

1. **two murdered princes,** the young sons of Edward IV allegedly murdered in the Tower of London by their uncle, Richard III.
2. **worked,** embroidered. **tabinet,** watered fabric of silk and wool.
3. **man-o'-war suit,** sailor suit.
4. **Royal University,** established in 1882 and modeled on English universities. It consisted of an examining body, with neither residency or attendance of lectures required.
5. **Lancers,** a form of quadrilles.
6. **Irish device,** an antique Irish talisman. Miss Ivors is an ardent supporter of the Irish Revival, which sprang up in the 1890s and encouraged renewed interest in everything Irish.
7. *The Daily Express,* a conservative newspaper opposed to the struggle for Irish independence. Joyce once wrote for it.

Joyce's Dublin—The Quays   National Library of Ireland

—Why should I be ashamed of myself? asked Gabriel, blinking his eyes and trying to smile.

—Well, I'm ashamed of you, said Miss Ivors frankly. To say you'd write for a rag like that. I didn't think you were a West Briton.[8]

A look of perplexity appeared on Gabriel's face. It was true that he wrote a literary column every Wednesday in *The Daily Express,* for which he was paid fifteen shillings. But that did not make him a West Briton surely. The books he received for review were almost more welcome than the paltry cheque. He loved to feel the covers and turn over the pages of newly printed books. Nearly every day when his teaching in the college was ended he used to wander down the quays to the second-hand booksellers, to Hickley's on Bachelor's Walk, to Webb's or Massey's on Aston's Quay, or to O'Clohissey's in the by-street. He did not know how to meet her charge. He wanted to say that literature was above politics. But they were friends of many years' standing and their careers had been parallel, first at the University and then as teachers: he could not risk a grandiose phrase with her. He continued blinking his eyes and trying to smile and murmured lamely that he saw nothing political in writing reviews of books.

When their turn to cross had come he was still perplexed and inattentive. Miss Ivors promptly took his hand in a warm grasp and said in a soft friendly tone:

8. **West Briton,** a derogatory term for an "anglicized" Irishman.

—Of couse, I was only joking. Come, we cross now.

When they were together again she spoke of the University question[9] and Gabriel felt more at ease. A friend of hers had shown her his review of Browning's poems. That was how she had found out the secret: but she liked the review immensely. Then she said suddenly:

—O, Mr Conroy, will you come for an excursion to the Aran Isles[10] this summer? We're going to stay there a whole month. It will be splendid out in the Atlantic. You ought to come. Mr Clancy is coming, and Mr Kilkelly and Kathleen Kearney[11]. It would be splendid for Gretta too if she'd come. She's from Connacht,[12] isn't she?

—Her people are, said Gabriel shortly.

—But you will come, won't you? said Miss Ivors, laying her warm hand eagerly on his arm.

—The fact is, said Gabriel, I have already arranged to go—

—Go where? asked Miss Ivors.

—Well, you know, every year I go for a cycling tour with some fellows and so—

—But where? asked Miss Ivors.

—Well, we usually go to France or Belgium or perhaps Germany, said Gabriel awkwardly.

—And why do you go to France and Belgium, said Miss Ivors, instead of visiting your own land?

—Well, said Gabriel, it's partly to keep in touch with the languages and partly for a change.

—And haven't you your own language to keep in touch with—Irish? asked Miss Ivors.

—Well, said Gabriel, if it comes to that, you know, Irish is not my language.

Their neighbours had turned to listen to the cross-examination. Gabriel glanced right and left nervously and tried to keep his good humour under the ordeal which was making a blush invade his forehead.

—And haven't you your own land to visit, continued Miss Ivors, that you know nothing of, your own people, and your own country?

—O, to tell you the truth, retorted Gabriel suddenly, I'm sick of my own country, sick of it!

—Why? asked Miss Ivors.

Gabriel did not answer for his retort had heated him.

—Why? repeated Miss Ivors.

They had to go visiting together and, as he had not answered her, Miss Ivors said warmly:

—Of course, you've no answer.

Gabriel tried to cover his agitation by taking part in the dance with great energy. He avoided her eyes for he had seen a sour expression on her face. But when they met in the long chain he was surprised to feel his hand firmly pressed. She looked at him from under her brows for a moment quizzically until he smiled. Then, just as the chain was about to start again, she stood on tiptoe and whispered into his ear:

—West Briton!

When the lancers were over Gabriel went away to a remote corner of the room where Freddy Malins' mother was sitting. She was a stout feeble old woman with white hair. Her voice had a catch in it like her son's and she stuttered slightly. She had been told that Freddy had come and that he was nearly all right. Gabriel asked her whether she had had a good crossing. She lived with her married daughter in Glasgow and came to Dublin on a visit once a year. She answered placidly that she had had a beautiful crossing and that the

---

9. **the University question,** efforts to provide equal university education for Catholics. The Royal University and University College, a Jesuit college which Joyce attended, represented two attempts to alleviate the problem.

10. **Aran Isles,** islands off the western coast of Ireland where Gaelic is still spoken.

11. **Kathleen Kearney,** a character in "A Mother," a short story by Joyce.

12. **Connacht,** an area along the west coast of Ireland.

captain had been most attentive to her. She spoke also of the beautiful house her daughter kept in Glasgow, and of all the nice friends they had there. While her tongue rambled on Gabriel tried to banish from his mind all memory of the unpleasant incident with Miss Ivors. Of course the girl or woman, or whatever she was, was an enthusiast but there was a time for all things. Perhaps he ought not to have answered her like that. But she had no right to call him a West Briton before people, even in joke. She had tried to make him ridiculous before people, heckling him and staring at him with her rabbit's eyes.

He saw his wife making her way towards him through the waltzing couples. When she reached him she said into his ear:

—Gabriel, Aunt Kate wants to know won't you carve the goose as usual. Miss Daly will carve the ham and I'll do the pudding.

—All right, said Gabriel.

—She's sending in the younger ones first as soon as this waltz is over so that we'll have the table to ourselves.

—Were you dancing? asked Gabriel.

—Of course I was. Didn't you see me? What words had you with Molly Ivors?

—No words. Why? Did she say so?

—Something like that. I'm trying to get that Mr D'Arcy to sing. He's full of conceit, I think.

—There were no words, said Gabriel moodily, only she wanted me to go for a trip to the west of Ireland and I said I wouldn't.

His wife clasped her hands excitedly and gave a little jump.

—O, do go, Gabriel, she cried. I'd love to see Galway again.

—You can go if you like, said Gabriel coldly.

She looked at him for a moment, then turned to Mrs Malins and said:

—There's a nice husband for you, Mrs Malins.

While she was threading her way back across the room Mrs Malins, without advert-ing to the interruption, went on to tell Gabriel what beautiful places there were in Scotland and beautiful scenery. Her son-in-law brought them every year to the lakes and they used to go fishing. Her son-in-law was a splendid fisher. One day he caught a fish, a beautiful big big fish, and the man in the hotel boiled it for their dinner.

Gabriel hardly heard what she said. Now that supper was coming near he began to think again about his speech and about the quotation. When he saw Freddy Malins coming across the room to visit his mother Gabriel left the chair free for him and retired into the embrasure of the window. The room had already cleared and from the back room came the clatter of plates and knives. Those who still remained in the drawing room seemed tired of dancing and were conversing quietly in little groups. Gabriel's warm trembling fingers tapped the cold pane of the window. How cool it must be outside! How pleasant it would be to walk out alone, first along by the river and then through the park![13] The snow would be lying on the branches of the trees and forming a bright cap on the top of the Wellington Monument.[14] How much more pleasant it would be there than at the supper-table!

He ran over the headings of his speech: Irish hospitality, sad memories, the Three Graces, Paris, the quotation from Browning. He repeated to himself a phrase he had written in his review: *One feels that one is listening to a thought-tormented music.* Miss Ivors had praised the review. Was she sincere? Had she really any life of her own behind all her propagandism? There had never been any ill-feeling between them until that night. It unnerved him to think that she would be at

13. **the park,** Phoenix Park, a large one on the western edge of Dublin.
14. **the Wellington monument.** The Duke of Wellington, Irish born, defeated Napoleon at Waterloo. His statue is in Phoenix Park.

the suppertable, looking up at him while he spoke with her critical quizzing eyes. Perhaps she would not be sorry to see him fail in his speech. An idea came into his mind and gave him courage. He would say, alluding to Aunt Kate and Aunt Julia: *Ladies and Gentlemen, the generation which is now on the wane among us may have had its faults but for my part I think it had certain qualities of hospitality, of humour, of humanity, which the new and very serious and hyper-educated generation that is growing up around us seems to me to lack.* Very good: that was one for Miss Ivors. What did he care that his aunts were only two ignorant old women?

A murmur in the room attracted his attention. Mr Browne was advancing from the door, gallantly escorting Aunt Julia, who leaned upon his arm, smiling and hanging her head. An irregular musketry of applause escorted her also as far as the piano and then, as Mary Jane seated herself on the stool, and Aunt Julia, no longer smiling, half turned so as to pitch her voice fairly into the room, gradually ceased. Gabriel recognised the prelude. It was that of an old song of Aunt Julia's—*Arrayed for the Bridal.*[15] Her voice, strong and clear in tone, attacked with great spirit the runs which embellish the air and though she sang very rapidly she did not miss even the smallest of the grace notes. To follow the voice, without looking at the singer's face, was to feel and share the excitement of swift and secure flight. Gabriel applauded loudly with all the others at the close of the song and loud applause was borne in from the invisible supper-table. It sounded so genuine that a little colour struggled into Aunt Julia's face as she bent to replace in the music-stand the old leather-bound song-book that had her initials on the cover. Freddy Malins, who had listened with his head perched sideways to hear her better, was still applauding when everyone else had ceased and talking animatedly to his mother who nodded her head gravely and slowly in acquiescence. At last, when he could clap no more, he stood up suddenly and hurried across the room to Aunt Julia whose hand he seized and held in both his hands, shaking it when words failed him or the catch in his voice proved too much for him.

—I was just telling my mother, he said, I never heard you sing so well, never. No, I never heard your voice so good as it is to-night. Now! Would you believe that now? That's the truth. Upon my word and honour that's the truth. I never heard your voice sound so fresh and so . . . so clear and fresh, never.

Aunt Julia smiled broadly and murmured something about compliments as she released her hand from his grasp. Mr Browne extended his open hand towards her and said to those who were near him in the manner of a showman introducing a prodigy to an audience:

—Miss Julia Morkan, my latest discovery!

He was laughing very heartily at this himself when Freddy Malins turned to him and said:

—Well, Browne, if you're serious you might make a worse discovery. All I can say is I never heard her sing half so well as long as I am coming here. And that's the honest truth.

—Neither did I, said Mr Browne. I think her voice has greatly improved.

Aunt Julia shrugged her shoulders and said with meek pride:

—Thirty years ago I hadn't a bad voice as voices go.

—I often told Julia, said Aunt Kate emphatically, that she was simply thrown away in that choir. But she never would be said by me.

She turned as if to appeal to the good sense of the others against a refractory child while Aunt Julia gazed in front of her, a vague smile of reminiscence playing on her face.

—No, continued Aunt Kate, she wouldn't

---

15. **"Arrayed for the Bridal,"** a wedding song from an opera by Bellini, an Italian composer. The song is incongruous with Julia's age and appearance.

be said or led by anyone, slaving there in that choir night and day, night and day. Six o'clock on Christmas morning! And all for what?

—Well, isn't it for the honour of God, Aunt Kate? asked Mary Jane, twisting round on the piano-stool and smiling.

Aunt Kate turned fiercely on her niece and said:

—I know all about the honour of God, Mary Jane, but I think it's not at all honourable for the pope to turn out the women out of the choirs that have slaved there all their lives and put little whipper-snappers of boys over their heads.[16] I suppose it is for the good of the Church if the pope does it. But it's not just, Mary Jane, and it's not right.

She had worked herself into a passion and would have continued in defence of her sister for it was a sore subject with her but Mary Jane, seeing that all the dancers had come back, intervened pacifically:

—Now, Aunt Kate, you're giving scandal to Mr Browne who is of the other persuasion.

Aunt Kate turned to Mr Browne, who was grinning at this allusion to his religion, and said hastily:

—O, I don't question the pope's being right. I'm only a stupid old woman and I wouldn't presume to do such a thing. But there's such a thing as common everyday politeness and gratitude. And if I were in Julia's place I'd tell that Father Healy straight up to his face . . .

—And besides, Aunt Kate, said Mary Jane, we really are all hungry and when we are hungry we are all very quarrelsome.

—And when we are thirsty we are also quarrelsome, added Mr Browne.

—So that we had better go to supper, said Mary Jane, and finish the discussion afterwards.

On the landing outside the drawing-room Gabriel found his wife and Mary Jane trying to persuade Miss Ivors to stay for supper. But Miss Ivors, who had put on her hat and was buttoning her cloak, would not stay.

She did not feel in the least hungry and she had already overstayed her time.

—But only for ten minutes, Molly, said Mrs Conroy. That won't delay you.

—To take a pick itself, said Mary Jane, after all your dancing.

—I really couldn't, said Miss Ivors.

—I am afraid you didn't enjoy yourself at all, said Mary Jane hopelessly.

—Ever so much, I assure you, said Miss Ivors, but you really must let me run off now.

—But how can you get home? asked Mrs Conroy.

—O, it's only two steps up the quay.

Gabriel hesitated a moment and said:

—If you will allow me, Miss Ivors, I'll see you home if you really are obliged to go.

But Miss Ivors broke away from them.

—I won't hear of it, she cried. For goodness sake go in to your suppers and don't mind me. I'm quite well able to take care of myself.

—Well, you're the comical girl, Molly, said Mrs Conroy frankly.

—*Beannacht libh,*[17] cried Miss Ivors, with a laugh, as she ran down the staircase.

Mary Jane gazed after her, a moody puzzled expression on her face, while Mrs Conroy leaned over the banisters to listen for the hall-door. Gabriel asked himself was he the cause of her abrupt departure. But she did not seem to be in ill humour: she had gone away laughing. He stared blankly down the staircase.

At that moment Aunt Kate came toddling out of the supper-room, almost wringing her hands in despair.

—Where is Gabriel? she cried. Where on earth is Gabriel? There's everyone waiting in

16. **"for the pope to turn out the women . . .",** Pope Pius X decreed in November 1903 that women were incapable of being part of a liturgical service and that soprano and contralto parts in choirs should be taken by boys.
17. ***Beannacht libh,*** farewell, a Gaelic benediction.

there, stage to let, and nobody to carve the goose!

—Here I am, Aunt Kate! cried Gabriel, with sudden animation, ready to carve a flock of geese, if necessary.

A fat brown goose lay at one end of the table and at the other end, on a bed of creased paper strewn with sprigs of parsley, lay a great ham, stripped of its outer skin and peppered over with crust crumbs, a neat paper frill round its shin and beside this was a round of spiced beef. Between these rival ends ran parallel lines of side-dishes: two little minsters of jelly, red and yellow; a shallow dish full of blocks of blancmange[18] and red jam, a large green leaf-shaped dish with a stalk-shaped handle, on which lay bunches of purple raisins and peeled almonds, a companion dish on which lay a solid rectangle of Smyrna figs, a dish of custard topped with grated nutmeg, a small bowl full of chocolates and sweets wrapped in gold and silver papers and a glass vase in which stood some tall celery stalks. In the centre of the table there stood, as sentries to a fruit-stand which upheld a pyramid of oranges and American apples, two squat old-fashioned decanters of cut glass, one containing port and the other dark sherry. On the closed square piano a pudding in a huge yellow dish lay in waiting and behind it were three squads of bottles of stout and ale and minerals, drawn up according to the colours of their uniforms, the first two black, with brown and red labels, the third and smallest squad white, with transverse green sashes.

Gabriel took his seat boldly at the head of the table and, having looked to the edge of the carver, plunged his fork firmly into the goose. He felt quite at ease now for he was an expert carver and liked nothing better than to find himself at the head of a well-laden table.

—Miss Furlong, what shall I send you? he asked. A wing or a slice of the breast?

—Just a small slice of the breast.

—Miss Higgins, what for you?

—O, anything at all, Mr Conroy.

While Gabriel and Miss Daly exchanged plates of goose and plates of ham and spiced beef Lily went from guest to guest with a dish of hot floury potatoes wrapped in a white napkin. This was Mary Jane's idea and she had also suggested apple sauce for the goose but Aunt Kate had said that plain roast goose without apple sauce had always been good enough for her and she hoped she might never eat worse. Mary Jane waited on her pupils and saw that they got the best slices and Aunt Kate and Aunt Julia opened and carried across from the piano bottles of stout and ale for the gentlemen and bottles of minerals for the ladies. There was a great deal of confusion and laughter and noise, the noise of orders and counter-orders, of knives and forks, of corks and glass-stoppers. Gabriel began to carve second helpings as soon as he had finished the first round without serving himself. Everyone protested loudly so that he compromised by taking a long draught of stout for he had found the carving hot work. Mary Jane settled down quietly to her supper but Aunt Kate and Aunt Julia were still toddling round the table, walking on each other's heels, getting in each other's way and giving each other unheeded orders. Mr Browne begged of them to sit down and eat their suppers and so did Gabriel but they said there was time enough so that, at last, Freddy Malins stood up and, capturing Aunt Kate, plumped her down on her chair amid general laughter.

When everyone had been well served Gabriel said, smiling:

—Now, if anyone wants a little more of what vulgar people call stuffing let him or her speak.

A chorus of voices invited him to begin his own supper and Lily came forward with

---

18. **blancmange,** a sweet dessert like a pudding or custard.

three potatoes which she had reserved for him.

—Very well, said Gabriel amiably, as he took another preparatory draught, kindly forget my existence, ladies and gentlemen, for a few minutes.

He set to his supper and took no part in the conversation with which the table covered Lily's removal of the plates. The subject of talk was the opera company which was then at the Theatre Royal. Mr Bartell D'Arcy, the tenor, a dark-complexioned young man with a smart moustache, praised very highly the leading contralto of the company but Miss Furlong thought she had a rather vulgar style of production. Freddy Malins said there was a negro chieftain singing in the second part of the Gaiety[19] pantomime who had one of the finest tenor voices he had ever heard.

—Have you heard him? he asked Mr Bartell D'Arcy across the table.

—No, answered Mr Bartell D'Arcy carelessly.

—Because, Freddy Malins explained, now I'd be curious to hear your opinion of him. I think he has a grand voice.

—It takes Teddy to find out the really good things, said Mr Browne familiarly to the table.

—And why couldn't he have a voice too? asked Freddy Malins sharply. Is it because he's only a black?

Nobody answered this question and Mary Jane led the table back to the legitimate opera.[20] One of her pupils had given her a pass for *Mignon.* Of course it was very fine, she said, but it made her think of poor Georgina Burns. Mr Browne could go back farther still, to the old Italian companies that used to come to Dublin—Tietjens, Ilma de Murzka, Campanini, the great Trebelli, Giuglini, Ravelli, Aramburo. Those were the days, he said, when there was something like singing to be heard in Dublin. He told too of how the top gallery of the old Royal[21] used to be packed night after night, of how one night an Italian tenor had sung five encores to *Let Me*

Like a Soldier Fall, introducing a high C every time, and of how the gallery boys would sometimes in their enthusiasm unyoke the horses from the carriage of some great *prima donna*[22] and pull her themselves through the streets to her hotel. Why did they never play the grand old operas now, he asked, *Dinorah, Lucrezia Borgia?* Because they could not get the voices to sing them: that was why.

—O, well, said Mr Bartell D'Arcy, I presume there are as good singers to-day as there were then.

—Where are they? asked Mr Browne defiantly.

—In London, Paris, Milan, said Mr Bartell D'Arcy warmly. I suppose Caruso, for example, is quite as good, if not better than any of the men you have mentioned.

—Maybe so, said Mr Browne. But I may tell you I doubt it strongly.

—O, I'd give anything to hear Caruso sing, said Mary Jane.

—For me, said Aunt Kate, who had been picking a bone, there was only one tenor. To please me, I mean. But I suppose none of you ever heard of him.

—Who was he, Miss Morkan? asked Mr Bartell D'Arcy politely.

—His name, said Aunt Kate, was Parkinson. I heard him when he was in his prime and I think he had then the purest tenor voice that was ever put into a man's throat.

—Strange, said Mr Bartell D'Arcy. I never even heard of him.

—Yes, yes, Miss Morkan is right, said Mr Browne. I remember hearing of old Parkinson but he's too far back for me.

—A beautiful pure sweet mellow English tenor, said Aunt Kate with enthusiasm.

19. **Gaiety,** a Dublin theater.
20. **opera.** In the ensuing discussion of operas and singers, all are actual with the exception of Parkinson and Ravelli. The singers were all dead, with the exception of Enrico Caruso, an outstanding tenor whose records are still prized today.
21. **the old Royal,** destroyed by fire in 1880.
22. *prima donna,* principal woman singer in an opera.

Gabriel having finished, the huge pudding was transferred to the table. The clatter of forks and spoons began again. Gabriel's wife served out spoonfuls of the pudding and passed the plates down the table. Midway down they were held up by Mary Jane, who replenished them with raspberry or orange jelly or with blancmange and jam. The pudding was of Aunt Julia's making and she received praises for it from all quarters. She herself said that it was not quite brown enough.

—Well, I hope, Miss Morkan, said Mr Browne, that I'm brown enough for you because, you know, I'm all brown.

All the gentlemen, except Gabriel, ate some of the pudding out of compliment to Aunt Julia. As Gabriel never ate sweets the celery had been left for him. Freddy Malins also took a stalk of celery and ate it with his pudding. He had been told that celery was a capital thing for the blood and he was just then under doctor's care. Mrs Malins, who had been silent all through the supper, said that her son was going down to Mount Melleray[23] in a week or so. The table then spoke of Mount Melleray, how bracing the air was down there, how hospitable the monks were and how they never asked for a penny-piece from their guests.

—And do you mean to say, asked Mr Browne incredulously, that a chap can go down there and put up there as if it were a hotel and live on the fat of the land and then come away without paying a farthing?

—O, most people give some donation to the monastery when they leave, said Mary Jane.

—I wish we had an institution like that in our Church, said Mr Browne candidly.

He was astonished to hear that the monks never spoke, got up at two in the morning and slept in their coffins.[24] He asked what they did it for.

—That's the rule of the order, said Aunt Kate firmly.

—Yes, but why? asked Mr Browne.

Aunt Kate repeated that it was the rule, that was all. Mr Browne still seemed not to understand. Freddy Malins explained to him, as best he could, that the monks were trying to make up for the sins committed by all the sinners in the outside world. The explanation was not very clear for Mr Browne grinned and said:

—I like that idea very much but wouldn't a comfortable spring bed do them as well as a coffin?

—The coffin, said Mary Jane, is to remind them of their last end.

As the subject had grown lugubrious it was buried in a silence of the table during which Mrs Malins could be heard saying to her neighbour in an indistinct undertone:

—They are very good men, the monks, very pious men.

The raisins and almonds and figs and apples and oranges and chocolates and sweets were now passed about the table and Aunt Julia invited all the guests to have either port or sherry. At first Mr Bartell D'Arcy refused to take either but one of his neighbours nudged him and whispered something to him upon which he allowed his glass to be filled. Gradually as the last glasses were being filled the conversation ceased. A pause followed, broken only by the noise of the wine and by unsettlings of chairs. The Misses Morkan, all three, looked down at the tablecloth. Someone coughed once or twice and then a few gentlemen patted the table gently as a signal for silence. The silence came and Gabriel pushed back his chair and stood up.

The patting at once grew louder in encouragement and then ceased altogether. Gabriel leaned his ten trembling fingers on the tablecloth and smiled nervously at the compa-

23. **Mount Melleray,** location of a Trappist monastery in southern Ireland.
24. **slept in their coffins,** an untrue story that perhaps sprang up because of the order's strictness.

ny. Meeting a row of upturned faces he raised his eyes to the chandelier. The piano was playing a waltz tune and he could hear the skirts sweeping against the drawing-room door. People, perhaps, were standing in the snow on the quay outside, gazing up at the lighted windows and listening to the waltz music. The air was pure there. In the distance lay the park where the trees were weighted with snow. The Wellington Monument wore a gleaming cap of snow that flashed westward over the white field of Fifteen Acres.[25]

He began:

—Ladies and Gentlemen.

—It has fallen to my lot this evening, as in years past, to perform a very pleasing task but a task for which I am afraid my poor powers as a speaker are all too inadequate.

—No, no! said Mr Browne.

—But, however that may be, I can only ask you to-night to take the will for the deed and to lend me your attention for a few moments while I endeavour to express to you in words what my feelings are on this occasion.

—Ladies and Gentlemen. It is not the first time that we have gathered together under this hospitable roof, around this hospitable board. It is not the first time that we have been the recipients—or perhaps, I had better say, the victims—of the hospitality of certain good ladies.

He made a circle in the air with his arm and paused. Everyone laughed or smiled at Aunt Kate and Aunt Julia and Mary Jane who all turned crimson with pleasure. Gabriel went on more boldly:

—I feel more strongly with every recurring year that our country has no tradition which does it so much honour and which it should guard so jealously as that of its hospitality. It is a tradition that is unique as far as my experience goes (and I have visited not a few places abroad) among the modern nations. Some would say, perhaps, that with us it is rather a failing than anything to be boasted of. But granted even that, it is, to my

mind, a princely failing, and one that I trust will long be cultivated among us. Of one thing, at least, I am sure. As long as this roof shelters the good ladies aforesaid—and I wish from my heart it may do so for many and many a long year to come—the tradition of genuine warm-hearted courteous Irish hospitality, which our forefathers have handed down to us and which we in turn must hand down to our descendants, is still alive among us.

A hearty murmur of assent ran round the table. It shot through Gabriel's mind that Miss Ivors was not there and that she had gone away discourteously: and he said with confidence in himself:

—Ladies and Gentlemen.

—A new generation is growing up in our midst, a generation actuated by new ideas and new principles. It is serious and enthusiastic for these new ideas and its enthusiasm, even when it is misdirected, is, I believe, in the main sincere. But we are living in a sceptical and, if I may use the phrase, a thought-tormented age: and sometimes I fear that this new generation, educated or hypereducated as it is, will lack those qualities of humanity, of hospitality, of kindly humour which belonged to an older day. Listening to-night to the names of all those great singers of the past it seemed to me, I must confess, that we were living in a less spacious age. Those days might, without exaggeration, be called spacious days: and if they are gone beyond recall let us hope, at least, that in gatherings such as this we shall still speak of them with pride and affection, still cherish in our hearts the memory of those dead and gone great ones whose fame the world will not willingly let die.[26]

—Hear, hear! said Mr Browne loudly.

—But yet, continued Gabriel, his voice

---

25. **Fifteen Acres,** part of Phoenix Park.
26. **the world will not willingly let die,** a paraphrase of Milton's statement of his hopes for his poetic career.

falling into a softer inflection, there are always in gatherings such as this sadder thoughts that will recur to our minds: thoughts of the past, of youth, of changes, of absent faces that we miss here to-night. Our path through life is strewn with many such sad memories: and were we to brood upon them always we could not find the heart to go on bravely with our work among the living. We have all of us living duties and living affections which claim, and rightly claim, our strenuous endeavours.

—Therefore, I will not linger on the past. I will not let any gloomy moralising intrude upon us here to-night. Here we are gathered together for a brief moment from the bustle and rush of our everyday routine. We are met here as friends, in the spirit of good-fellowship, as colleagues, also to a certain extent, in the true spirit of *camaraderie*,[27] and as the guests of—what shall I call them?—the Three Graces[28] of the Dublin musical world.

The table burst into applause and laughter at this sally. Aunt Julia vainly asked each of her neighbours in turn to tell her what Gabriel had said.

—He says we are the Three Graces, Aunt Julia, said Mary Jane.

Aunt Julia did not understand but she looked up, smiling, at Gabriel, who continued in the same vein:

—Ladies and Gentlemen.

—I will not attempt to play to-night the part that Paris[29] played on another occasion. I will not attempt to choose between them. The task would be an invidious one and one beyond my poor powers. For when I view them in turn, whether it be our chief hostess herself, whose good heart, whose too good heart, has become a byword with all who know her, or her sister, who seems to be gifted with perennial youth and whose singing must have been a surprise and a revelation to us all to-night, or, last but not least, when I consider our youngest hostess, talented, cheerful, hard-working and the best of nieces, I confess, Ladies and Gentlemen, that I do not

know to which of them I should award the prize.

Gabriel glanced down at his aunts and, seeing the large smile on Aunt Julia's face and the tears which had risen to Aunt Kate's eyes, hastened to his close. He raised his glass of port gallantly, while every member of the company fingered a glass expectantly, and said loudly:

—Let us toast them all three together. Let us drink to their health, wealth, long life, happiness and prosperity and may they long continue to hold the proud and self-won position which they hold in their profession and the position of honour and affection which they hold in our hearts.

All the guests stood up, glass in hand, and, turning towards the three seated ladies, sang in unison, with Mr Browne as leader:

For they are jolly gay fellows,
For they are jolly gay fellows,
For they are jolly gay fellows,
Which nobody can deny.

Aunt Kate was making frank use of her handkerchief and even Aunt Julia seemed moved. Freddy Malins beat time with his pudding-fork and the singers turned towards one another, as if in melodious conference, while they sang, with emphasis:

Unless he tells a lie,
Unless he tells a lie.

Then, turning once more towards their hostesses, they sang:

For they are jolly gay fellows,
For they are jolly gay fellows,
For they are jolly gay fellows,
Which nobody can deny.

The acclamation which followed was taken up beyond the door of the supper-room by many of the other guests and renewed time after time, Freddy Malins acting as officer with his fork on high.

27. *camaraderie*, friendliness and loyalty.
28. **Three Graces**, daughters of Zeus who embody beauty and grace and were companions of the Muses.
29. **Paris** was called on to judge the beauty of three goddesses, Hera, Athena, and Aphrodite.

UNDERSTANDING AND INTERPRETATION

1. What are some of the false notes apparent in the general conviviality of the party?
2. What do you learn about Gabriel's mother?
3. What are Gabriel's true feelings about his aunts?
4. About what two things does Miss Ivors chide Gabriel?

5. Snow is introduced twice in this section. What are Gabriel's feelings about it in each instance?
6. Up to this time Joyce's writings about Ireland had been bitter. In Gabriel's after-dinner speech he is, perhaps, re-evaluating his feelings. What qualities does Gabriel value in Irish Culture?
7. What do Gabriel's thoughts and speeches in this section add to your picture of him?

3

The piercing morning air came into the hall where they were standing so that Aunt Kate said:

—Close the door, somebody. Mrs Malins will get her death of cold.

—Browne is out there, Aunt Kate, said Mary Jane.

—Browne is everywhere, said Aunt Kate, lowering her voice.

Mary Jane laughed at her tone.

—Really, she said archly, he is very attentive.

—He has been laid on here like the gas, said Aunt Kate in the same tone, all during the Christmas.

She laughed herself this time good-humouredly and then added quickly:

—But tell him to come in, Mary Jane, and close the door. I hope to goodness he didn't hear me.

At that moment the hall-door was opened and Mr Browne came in from the doorstep, laughing as if his heart would break. He was dressed in a long green overcoat with mock astrakhan cuffs and collar and wore on his head an oval fur cap. He pointed down the snow-covered quay from where the sound of shrill prolonged whistling was borne in.

—Teddy will have all the cabs in Dublin out, he said.

Gabriel advanced from the little pantry behind the office, struggling into his overcoat and, looking round the hall, said:

—Gretta not down yet?

—She's getting on her things, Gabriel, said Aunt Kate.

—Who's playing up there? asked Gabriel.

—Nobody. They're all gone.

—O no, Aunt Kate, said Mary Jane. Bartell D'Arcy and Miss O'Callaghan aren't gone yet.

—Someone is strumming at the piano, anyhow, said Gabriel. Mary Jane glanced at Gabriel and Mr Browne and said with a shiver:

—It makes me feel cold to look at you two gentlemen muffled up like that. I wouldn't like to face your journey home at this hour.

—I'd like nothing better this minute, said Mr Browne stoutly, than a rattling fine walk in the country or a fast drive with a good spanking goer between the shafts.

—We used to have a very good horse and trap at home, said Aunt Julia sadly.

—The never-to-be-forgotten Johnny, said Mary Jane, laughing.

Aunt Kate and Gabriel laughed too.

—Why, what was wonderful about Johnny? asked Mr Browne.

—The late lamented Patrick Morkan, our grandfather, that is, explained Gabriel, commonly known in his later years as the old gentleman, was a glue-boiler.

—O, now, Gabriel, said Aunt Kate, laughing, he had a starch mill.

—Well, glue or starch, said Gabriel, the old gentleman had a horse by the name of Johnny. And Johnny used to work in the old gentleman's mill, walking round and round in order to drive the mill. That was all very well; but now comes the tragic part about Johnny. One fine day the old gentleman thought he'd like to drive out with the quality to a military review in the park.

—The Lord have mercy on his soul, said Aunt Kate compassionately.

—Amen, said Gabriel. So the old gentleman, as I said, harnessed Johnny and put on his very best tall hat and his very best stock collar and drove out in grand style from his ancestral mansion somewhere near Back Lane, I think.

Everyone laughed, even Mrs Malins, at Gabriel's manner and Aunt Kate said:

—O now, Gabriel, he didn't live in Back Lane, really. Only the mill was there.

—Out from the mansion of his forefathers, continued Gabriel, he drove with Johnny. And everything went on beautifully until Johnny came in sight of King Billy's statue:[1] and whether he fell in love with the horse King Billy sits on or whether he thought he was back again in the mill, anyhow he began to walk round the statue.

Gabriel paced in a circle round the hall in his goloshes amid the laughter of the others.

—Round and round he went, said Gabriel, and the old gentleman, who was a very pompous old gentleman, was highly indignant. *Go on, sir! What do you mean, sir? Johnny! Johnny! Most extraordinary conduct! Can't understand the horse!*

The peals of laughter which followed Gabriel's imitation of the incident were interrupted by a resounding knock at the hall-door. Mary Jane ran to open it and let in Freddy Malins. Freddy Malins, with his hat well back on his head and his shoulders humped with cold, was puffing and steaming after his exertions.

—I could only get one cab, he said.

—O, we'll find another along the quay, said Gabriel.

—Yes, said Aunt Kate. Better not keep Mrs Malins standing in the draught.

Mrs Malins was helped down the front steps by her son and Mr Browne and, after many manœuvres, hoisted into the cab. Freddy Malins clambered in after her and spent a long time settling her on the seat, Mr Browne helping him with advice. At last she was settled comfortably and Freddy Malins invited Mr Browne into the cab. There was a good deal of confused talk, and then Mr Browne got into the cab. The cabman settled his rug over his knees, and bent down for the address. The confusion grew greater and the cabman was directed differently by Freddy Malins and Mr Browne, each of whom had his head out through a window of the cab. The difficulty was to know where to drop Mr Browne along the route and Aunt Kate, Aunt Julia and Mary Jane helped the discussion from the doorstep with cross-directions and contradictions and abundance of laughter. As for Freddy Malins he was speechless with laughter. He popped his head in and out of the window every moment, to the great danger of his hat, and told his mother how the discussion was progressing till at last Mr Browne shouted to the bewildered cabman above the din of everybody's laughter:

—Do you know Trinity College?[2]

—Yes, sir, said the cabman.

—Well, drive bang up against Trinity College gates, said Mr Browne, and then we'll tell you where to go. You understand now?

—Yes, sir, said the cabman.

—Make like a bird for Trinity College.

—Right, sir, cried the cabman.

The horse was whipped up and the cab rattled off along the quay amid a chorus of laughter and adieus.

Gabriel had not gone to the door with the others. He was in a dark part of the hall gazing up the staircase. A woman was standing near the top of the first flight, in the shadow

1. **King Billy,** William II, who defeated the forces of Irish Catholicism in 1690; a symbol of British domination.
2. **Trinity College,** the old, prestigious, Irish university which was primarily Protestant.

*Joyce's Dublin—O'Connell Bridge looking towards O'Connell Street and
Nelson's Pillar. Gabriel, Gretta and Mr D'Arcy pass here in a taxi.*

National Library of Ireland

also. He could not see her face but he could
see the terracotta and salmonpink panels of
her skirt which the shadow made appear
black and white. It was his wife. She was leaning on the banisters, listening to something.
Gabriel was surprised at her stillness and
strained his ear to listen also. But he could
hear little save the noise of laughter and dispute on the front steps, a few chords struck
on the piano and a few notes of a man's voice
singing.

He stood still in the gloom of the hall, trying to catch the air that the voice was singing
and gazing up at his wife. There was grace
and mystery in her attitude as if she were a
symbol of something. He asked himself what
is a woman standing on the stairs in the shadow, listening to distant music, a symbol of. If
he were a painter he would paint her in that
attitude. Her blue felt hat would show off the

bronze of her hair against the darkness and
the dark panels of her skirt would show off
the light ones. *Distant Music* he would call the
picture if he were a painter.

The hall-door was closed; and Aunt Kate,
Aunt Julia and Mary Jane came down the
hall, still laughing.

—Well, isn't Freddy terrible? said Mary
Jane. He's really terrible.

Gabriel said nothing but pointed up the
stairs towards where his wife was standing.
Now that the hall-door was closed the voice
and the piano could be heard more clearly.
Gabriel held up his hand for them to be silent. The song seemed to be in the old Irish
tonality and the singer seemed uncertain
both of his words and of his voice. The voice,
made plaintive by distance and by the singer's
hoarseness, faintly illuminated the cadence of
the air with words expressing grief:

O, the rain falls on my heavy locks
And the dew wets my skin,
My babe lies cold . . .[3]

—O, exclaimed Mary Jane. It's Bartell D'Arcy singing and he wouldn't sing all the night. O, I'll get him to sing a song before he goes.

—O do, Mary Jane, said Aunt Kate.

Mary Jane brushed past the others and ran to the staircase but before she reached it the singing stopped and the piano was closed abruptly.

—O, what a pity! she cried. Is he coming down, Gretta?

Gabriel heard his wife answer yes and saw her come down towards them. A few steps behind her were Mr Bartell D'Arcy and Miss O'Callaghan.

—O, Mr D'Arcy, cried Mary Jane, it's downright mean of you to break off like that when we were all in raptures listening to you.

—I have been at him all the evening, said Miss O'Callaghan, and Mrs Conroy too and he told us he had a dreadful cold and couldn't sing.

—O, Mr D'Arcy, said Aunt Kate, now that was a great fib to tell.

—Can't you see that I'm as hoarse as a crow? said Mr D'Arcy roughly.

He went into the pantry hastily and put on his overcoat. The others, taken aback by his rude speech, could find nothing to say. Aunt Kate wrinkled her brows and made signs to the others to drop the subject. Mr D'Arcy stood swathing his neck carefully and frowning.

—It's the weather, said Aunt Julia, after a pause.

—Yes, everybody has colds, said Aunt Kate readily, everybody.

—They say, said Mary Jane, we haven't had snow like it for thirty years; and I read this morning in the newspapers that the snow is general all over Ireland.

—I love the look of snow, said Aunt Julia sadly.

—So do I, said Miss O'Callaghan. I think Christmas is never really Christmas unless we have the snow on the ground.

—But poor Mr D'Arcy doesn't like the snow, said Aunt Kate, smiling.

Mr D'Arcy came from the pantry, fully swathed and buttoned, and in a repentant tone told them the history of his cold. Everyone gave him advice and said it was a great pity and urged him to be very careful of his throat in the night air. Gabriel watched his wife who did not join in the conversation. She was standing right under the dusty fanlight and the flame of the gas lit up the rich bronze of her hair which he had seen her drying at the fire a few days before. She was in the same attitude and seemed unaware of the talk about her. At last she turned towards them and Gabriel saw that there was colour on her cheeks and that her eyes were shining. A sudden tide of joy went leaping out of his heart.

—Mr D'Arcy, she said, what is the name of that song you were singing?

—It's called *The Lass of Aughrim*, said Mr D'Arcy, but I couldn't remember it properly. Why? Do you know it?

—*The Lass of Aughrim*, she repeated. I couldn't think of the name.

—It's a very nice air, said Mary Jane. I'm sorry you were not in voice to-night.

—Now, Mary Jane, said Aunt Kate, don't annoy Mr D'Arcy. I won't have him annoyed.

Seeing that all were ready to start she shepherded them to the door where goodnight was said:

—Well, good-night, Aunt Kate, and thanks for the pleasant evening.

—Good-night, Gabriel. Good-night, Gretta!

—Good-night, Aunt Kate, and thanks ever so much. Good-night, Aunt Julia.

—O, good-night, Gretta, I didn't see you.

---

3. **"O, the rain falls . . .",** part of the refrain of "The Lass of Aughrim," an Irish ballad which Joyce often sang at home. It tells of a young girl seduced and abandoned by Lord Gregory. She brings him a gift of her baby "cold in her arms."

—Good-night, Mr D'Arcy. Good-night, Miss O'Callaghan.

—Good-night, Miss Morkan.

—Good-night, again.

—Good-night, all. Safe home.

—Good-night. Good-night.

The morning was still dark. A dull yellow light brooded over the houses and the river; and the sky seemed to be descending. It was slushy underfoot; and only streaks and patches of snow lay on the roofs, on the parapets of the quay and on the area railings. The lamps were still burning redly in the murky air and, across the river, the palace of the Four Courts[4] stood out menacingly against the heavy sky.

She was walking on before him with Mr Bartell D'Arcy, her shoes in a brown parcel tucked under one arm and her hands holding her skirt up from the slush. She had no longer any grace of attitude but Gabriel's eyes were still bright with happiness. The blood went bounding along his veins; and the thoughts went rioting through his brain, proud, joyful, tender, valorous.

She was walking on before him so lightly and so erect that he longed to run after her noiselessly, catch her by the shoulders and say something foolish and affectionate into her ear. She seemed to him so frail that he longed to defend her against something and then to be alone with her. Moments of their secret life together burst like stars upon his memory. A heliotrope envelope was lying beside his breakfast-cup and he was caressing it with his hand. Birds were twittering in the ivy and the sunny web of the curtain was shimmering along the floor: he could not eat for happiness. They were standing on the crowded platform and he was placing a ticket inside the warm palm of her glove. He was standing with her in the cold, looking in through a grated window at a man making bottles in a roaring furnace. It was very cold. Her face, fragrant in the cold air, was quite close to his; and suddenly she called out to the man at the furnace:

—Is the fire hot, sir?

But the man could not hear her with the noise of the furnace. It was just as well. He might have answered rudely.

A wave of yet more tender joy escaped from his heart and went coursing in warm flood along his arteries. Like the tender fires of stars moments of their life together, that no one knew of or would ever know of, broke upon and illumined his memory. He longed to recall to her those moments, to make her forget the years of their dull existence together and remember only their moments of ecstasy. For the years, he felt, had not quenched his soul or hers. Their children, his writing, her household cares had not quenched all their souls' tender fire. In one letter that he had written to her then he had said: *Why is it that words like these seem to me so dull and cold? Is it because there is no word tender enough to be your name?*

Like distant music these words that he had written years before were borne towards him from the past. He longed to be alone with her. When the others had gone away, when he and she were in their room in the hotel, then they would be alone together. He would call her softly:

—Gretta!

Perhaps she would not hear at once: she would be undressing. Then something in his voice would strike her. She would turn and look at him. . . .

At the corner of Winetavern Street they met a cab. He was glad of its rattling noise as it saved him from conversation. She was looking out of the window and seemed tired. The others spoke only a few words, pointing out some building or street. The horse galloped along wearily under the murky morning sky, dragging his old rattling box after his heels, and Gabriel was again in a cab with her, galloping to catch the boat, galloping to their honeymoon.

As the cab drove across O'Connell Bridge Miss O'Callaghan said:

4. **the Four Courts,** the Irish law courts.

—They say you never cross O'Connell Bridge without seeing a white horse.

—I see a white man this time, said Gabriel.

—Where? asked Mr Bartell D'Arcy.

Gabriel pointed to the statue,[5] on which lay patches of snow. Then he nodded familiarly to it and waved his hand.

—Good-night, Dan, he said gaily.

When the cab drew up before the hotel Gabriel jumped out and, in spite of Mr Bartell D'Arcy's protest, paid the driver. He gave the man a shilling over his fare. The man saluted and said:

—A prosperous New Year to you, sir.

—The same to you, said Gabriel cordially.

She leaned for a moment on his arm in getting out of the cab and while standing at the curbstone, bidding the others good-night. She leaned lightly on his arm, as lightly as when she had danced with him a few hours before. He had felt proud and happy then, happy that she was his, proud of her grace and wifely carriage. But now, after the kindling again of so many memories, the first touch of her body, musical and strange and perfumed, sent through him a keen pang of lust. Under cover of her silence he pressed her arm closely to his side; and, as they stood at the hotel door, he felt that they had escaped from their lives and duties, escaped from home and friends and run away together with wild and radiant hearts to a new adventure.

An old man was dozing in a great hooded chair in the hall. He lit a candle in the office and went before them to the stairs. They followed him in silence, their feet falling in soft thuds on the thickly carpeted stairs. She mounted the stairs behind the porter, her head bowed in the ascent, her frail shoulders curved as with a burden, her skirt girt tightly about her. He could have flung his arms about her hips and held her still for his arms were trembling with desire to seize her and only the stress of his nails against the palms of his hands held the wild impulse of his body in

check. The porter halted on the stairs to settle his guttering candle. They halted too on the steps below him. In the silence Gabriel could hear the falling of the molten wax into the tray and the thumping of his own heart against his ribs.

The porter led them along a corridor and opened a door. Then he set his unstable candle down on a toilet-table and asked at what hour they were to be called in the morning.

—Eight, said Gabriel.

The porter pointed to the tap of the electric-light and began a muttered apology but Gabriel cut him short.

—We don't want any light. We have light enough from the street. And I say, he added, pointing to the candle, you might remove that handsome article, like a good man.

The porter took up his candle again, but slowly for he was surprised by such a novel idea. Then he mumbled good-night and went out. Gabriel shot the lock to.

A ghostly light from the street lamp lay in a long shaft from one window to the door. Gabriel threw his overcoat and hat on a couch and crossed the room towards the window. He looked down into the street in order that his emotion might calm a little. Then he turned and leaned against a chest of drawers with his back to the light. She had taken off her hat and cloak and was standing before a large swinging mirror, unhooking her waist. Gabriel paused for a few moments, watching her, and then said:

—Gretta!

She turned away from the mirror slowly and walked along the shaft of light towards him. Her face looked so serious and weary that the words would not pass Gabriel's lips. No, it was not the moment yet.

—You looked tired, he said.

—I am a little, she answered.

—You don't feel ill or weak?

—No, tired: that's all.

5. **the statue,** of Daniel O'Connell, a leader of the struggle for Catholic emancipation in the early years of the nineteenth century. The bridge is also named for him.

She went on to the window and stood there, looking out. Gabriel waited again and then, fearing that diffidence was about to conquer him, he said abruptly:

—By the way, Gretta!

—What is it?

—You know that poor fellow Malins? he said quickly.

—Yes. What about him?

—Well, poor fellow, he's a decent sort of chap after all, continued Gabriel in a false voice. He gave me back that sovereign I lent him and I didn't expect it really. It's a pity he wouldn't keep away from that Browne, because he's not a bad fellow at heart.

He was trembling now with annoyance. Why did she seem so abstracted? He did not know how he could begin. Was she annoyed, too, about something? If she would only turn to him or come to him of her own accord! To take her as she was would be brutal. No, he must see some ardour in her eyes first. He longed to be master of her strange mood.

—When did you lend him the pound? she asked, after a pause.

Gabriel strove to restrain himself from breaking out into brutal lauguage about the sottish Malins and his pound. He longed to cry to her from his soul, to crush her body against his, to overmaster her. But he said:

—O, at Christmas, when he opened that little Christmas-card shop in Henry Street.

He was in such a fever of rage and desire that he did not hear her come from the window. She stood before him for an instant, looking at him strangely. Then, suddenly raising herself on tiptoe and resting her hands lightly on his shoulders, she kissed him.

—You are a very generous person, Gabriel, she said.

Gabriel, trembling with delight at her sudden kiss and at the quaintness of her phrase, put his hands on her hair and began smoothing it back, scarcely touching it with his fingers. The washing had made it fine and brilliant. His heart was brimming over with happiness. Just when he was wishing for it she had come to him of her own accord. Perhaps her thoughts had been running with his. Perhaps she had felt the impetuous desire that was in him and then the yielding mood had come upon her. Now that she had fallen to him so easily he wondered why he had been so diffident.

He stood, holding her head between his hands. Then, slipping one arm swiftly about her body and drawing her towards him, he said softly:

—Gretta dear, what are you thinking about?

She did not answer nor yield wholly to his arm. He said again softly:

—Tell me what it is, Gretta. I think I know what is the matter. Do I know?

She did not answer at once. Then she said in an outburst of tears:

—O, I am thinking about that song, *The Lass of Aughrim.*

She broke loose from him and ran to the bed and, throwing her arms across the bed-rail, hid her face. Gabriel stood stock-still for a moment in astonishment and then followed her. As he passed in the way of the cheval-glass he caught sight of himself in full length, his broad, well-filled shirt-front, the face whose expression always puzzled him when he saw it in a mirror and his glimmering gilt-rimmed eyeglasses. He halted a few paces from her and said:

—What about the song? Why does that make you cry?

She raised her head from her arms and dried her eyes with the back of her hand like a child. A kinder note than he had intended went into his voice.

—Why, Gretta? he asked.

—I am thinking about a person long ago who used to sing that song.

—And who was the person long ago? asked Gabriel, smiling.

—It was a person I used to know in Galway when I was living with my grandmother, she said.

The smile passed away from Gabriel's face. A dull anger began to gather again at the back of his mind and the dull fires of his lust began to glow angrily in his veins.

—Someone you were in love with? he asked ironically.

—It was a young boy I used to know, she answered, named Michael Furey.[6] He used to sing that song, *The Lass of Aughrim.* He was very delicate.

Gabriel was silent. He did not wish her to think that he was interested in this delicate boy.

—I can see him so plainly, she said after a moment. Such eyes as he had: big dark eyes! And such an expression in them—an expression!

—O then, you were in love with him? said Gabriel.

—I used to go out walking with him, she said, when I was in Galway.

A thought flew across Gabriel's mind.

—Perhaps that was why you wanted to go to Galway with that Ivors girl? he said coldly.

She looked at him and asked in surprise:

—What for?

Her eyes made Gabriel feel awkward. He shrugged his shoulders and said:

—How do I know? To see him perhaps.

She looked away from him along the shaft of light towards the window in silence.

—He is dead, she said at length. He died when he was only seventeen. Isn't it a terrible thing to die so young as that?

—What was he? asked Gabriel, still ironically.

—He was in the gasworks,[7] she said.

Gabriel felt humiliated by the failure of his irony and by the evocation of this figure from the dead, a boy in the gasworks. While he had been full of memories of their secret life together, full of tenderness and joy and desire, she had been comparing him in her mind with another. A shameful consciousness of his own person assailed him. He saw himself as a ludicrous figure, acting as a pennyboy[8] for his aunts, a nervous well-meaning sentimentalist, orating to vulgarians and idealising his own clownish lusts, the pitiable fatuous fellow he had caught a glimpse

of in the mirror. Instinctively he turned his back more to the light lest she might see the shame that burned upon his forehead.

He tried to keep up his tone of cold interrogation but his voice when he spoke was humble and indifferent.

—I suppose you were in love with this Michael Furey, Gretta, he said.

—I was great with him at that time, she said.

Her voice was veiled and sad. Gabriel, feeling now how vain it would be to try to lead her whither he had purposed, caressed one of her hands and said, also sadly:

—And what did he die of so young, Gretta? Consumption, was it?

—I think he died for me, she answered.

A vague terror seized Gabriel at this answer as if, at that hour when he had hoped to triumph, some impalpable and vindictive being was coming against him, gathering forces against him in its vague world. But he shook himself free of it with an effort of reason and continued to caress her hand. He did not question her again for he felt that she would tell him of herself. Her hand was warm and moist: it did not respond to his touch but he continued to caress it just as he had caressed her first letter to him that spring morning.

—It was in the winter, she said, about the beginning of the winter when I was going to leave my grandmother's and come up here to the convent. And he was ill at the time in his lodgings in Galway and wouldn't be let out and his people in Oughterard were written to. He was in decline, they said, or something like that. I never knew rightly.

She paused for a moment and sighed.

—Poor fellow, she said. He was very fond of me and he was such a gentle boy. We used to go out together, walking, you know, Gabri-

---

6. **Michael.** St. Michael is the archangel pictured with a sword in his hand standing over a dragon he must fight. At the hour of death he conducts souls to God.

7. **gasworks,** plant for manufacturing gas made from coal.

8. **pennyboy,** errand boy.

el, like the way they do in the country. He was going to study singing only for his health. He had a very good voice, poor Michael Furey.

—Well; and then? asked Gabriel.

—And then when it came to the time for me to leave Galway and come up to the convent he was much worse and I wouldn't be let see him so I wrote a letter saying I was going up to Dublin and would be back in the summer and hoping he would be better then.

She paused for a moment to get her voice under control and then went on:

—Then the night before I left I was in my grandmother's house in Nuns' Island, packing up, and I heard gravel thrown up against the window. The window was so wet I couldn't see so I ran downstairs as I was and slipped out the back into the garden and there was the poor fellow at the end of the garden, shivering.

—And did you not tell him to go back? asked Gabriel.

—I implored of him to go home at once and told him he would get his death in the rain. But he said he did not want to live. I can see his eyes as well as well! He was standing at the end of the wall where there was a tree.

—And did he go home? asked Gabriel.

—Yes, he went home. And when I was only a week in the convent he died and he was buried in Oughterard where his people came from. O, the day I heard that, that he was dead!

She stopped, choking with sobs, and,

overcome by emotion, flung herself face downward on the bed, sobbing in the quilt. Gabriel held her hand for a moment longer, irresolutely, and then, shy of intruding on her grief, let it fall gently and walked quietly to the window.

UNDERSTANDING AND INTERPRETATION

1. How does the focus progressively narrow down from the members of the party to Gretta and Gabriel, the central characters?

2. Describe the incident Gabriel tells about his grandfather. What does it do for the narrative? For the image of Gabriel?

3. A famous scene in literature is that of Gabriel in the hall looking up at Gretta on the staircase. What details does Joyce use? If he were an artist what would Gabriel call this picture?

4. What memories of their secret life together does Gabriel call to mind as he walks along behind Gretta on the quay?

5. What time of night is it? What effect is gained by having the hotel room lighted only by the streetlight outside?

6. What leads Gretta to tell Gabriel about Michael Furey? Does Gretta ever admit that she loved Michael? Do you feel she did?

7. How were Michael and Gabriel different?

8. What is Gabriel's vision of himself as she tells the story?

9. What is her startling reply to his question of what caused Michael's death? Why does she have this feeling?

4

She was fast asleep.

Gabriel, leaning on his elbow, looked for a few moments unresentfully on her tangled hair and half-open mouth, listening to her deep-drawn breath. So she had had that romance in her life: a man had died for her sake. It hardly pained him now to think how poor a part he, her husband, had played in her life. He watched her while she slept as

though he and she had never lived together as man and wife. His curious eyes rested long upon her face and on her hair: and, as he thought of what she must have been then, in that time of her first girlish beauty, a strange friendly pity for her entered his soul. He did not like to say even to himself that her face was no longer beautiful but he knew that it was no longer the face for which Michael Furey had braved death.

Perhaps she had not told him all the story. His eyes moved to the chair over which she had thrown some of her clothes. A petticoat string dangled to the floor. One boot stood upright, its limp upper fallen down: the fellow of it lay upon its side. He wondered at his riot of emotions of an hour before. From what had it proceeded? From his aunt's supper, from his own foolish speech, from the wine and dancing, the merry-making when saying good-night in the hall, the pleasure of the walk along the river in the snow. Poor Aunt Julia! She, too, would soon be a shade with the shade of Patrick Morkan and his horse. He had caught that haggard look upon her face for a moment when she was singing *Arrayed for the Bridal.* Soon, perhaps, he would be sitting in that same drawing-room, dressed in black, his silk hat on his knees. The blinds would be drawn down and Aunt Kate would be sitting beside him, crying and blowing her nose and telling him how Julia had died. He would cast about in his mind for some words that might console her, and would find only lame and useless ones. Yes, yes: that would happen very soon.

The air of the room chilled his shoulders. He stretched himself cautiously along under the sheets and lay down beside his wife. One by one they were all becoming shades. Better pass boldly into that other world, in the full glory of some passion, than fade and wither dismally with age. He thought of how she who lay beside him had locked in her heart for so many years that image of her lover's eyes when he had told her that he did not wish to live.

Generous tears filled Gabriel's eyes. He had never felt like that himself towards any woman but he knew that such a feeling must be love. The tears gathered more thickly in his eyes and in the partial darkness he imagined he saw the form of a young man standing under a dripping tree. Other forms were near. His soul had approached that region where dwell the vast hosts of the dead. He was conscious of, but could not apprehend, their wayward and flickering existence. His own identity was fading out into a grey impal-pable world: the solid world itself which these dead had one time reared and lived in was dissolving and dwindling.

A few light taps upon the pane made him turn to the window. It had begun to snow again. He watched sleepily the flakes, silver and dark, falling obliquely against the lamplight. The time had come for him to set out on his journey westward. Yes, the newspapers were right: snow was general all over Ireland. It was falling on every part of the dark central plain, on the treeless hills, falling softly upon the Bog of Allen[1] and, farther westward, softly falling into the dark mutinous Shannon waves.[2] It was falling, too, upon every part of the lonely churchyard on the hill where Michael Furey lay buried. It lay thickly drifted on the crooked crosses and headstones, on the spears of the little gate, on the barren thorns. His soul swooned slowly as he heard the snow falling faintly through the universe and faintly falling, like the descent of their last end, upon all the living and the dead.

1. **Bog of Allen,** a few miles southwest of Dublin.
2. **Shannon waves,** the estuary of the river Shannon on the Atlantic Ocean.

FOR UNDERSTANDING

1. What are the random thoughts Gabriel has after Gretta has fallen asleep?
2. What awareness does he come to about himself?
3. In the last paragraph, what are his reactions to the snow?

FOR INTERPRETATION

Discuss the following questions in light of the story as a whole.
1. Within the story many things or people are implied to be dead. Name as many as you can.
2. Images of snow are used throughout the story. Are they meant to be negative or positive?

3. Joyce's definition of epiphany is that moment when things or people reveal their true character or essence. Where do such moments occur in the story?

4. What part does clothing play in the story?

5. How does Joyce use music in the story?

6. Joyce had a feeling that people at times experience life and death simultaneously. What episodes are examples of this in the story? How do you interpret the last three paragraphs of the story?

FOR APPRECIATION

1. Joyce pays scrupulous attention to realistic details of life in Dublin, giving exact names of streets, statues, and parks. Yet he manages without ever moving beyond realistic details and events to suggest something larger . . . something universal . . . of which these are the visible symbols. Examine the entrance scene between Lily and Gabriel for its details. What universal truth is suggested in this scene?

2. Joyce was in love with language and what it could do. He often uses words that have multiple suggestions and sometimes echoes them by repetition. At the end of the story Gretta says, "You are a very *generous* person, Gabriel." Later, after Gretta is asleep, "*Generous* tears filled Gabriel's eyes." What does the word suggest the first time it is used? The second?

3. Joyce once said about *Dubliners*, "My intention was to write a chapter in the moral history of my country and I chose Dublin for the scene because that city seemed to me the center of paralysis . . . I have written it for the most part in a style of scrupulous meanness. . . ." Define what you think he meant by this statement. Take any one of the

following scenes and point out the instances of "scrupulous meanness."

    a. the scene when Mary Jane is playing.

    b. Gabriel's chat with Mrs. Malins.

    c. the dialogue between Miss Ivors and Gabriel beginning "O, Mr. Conroy, will you come for an excursion to the Aran Isles this summer?"

4. At what point in the story is the gaiety at its height? Why do you think Joyce structured the tale in this way?

5. Examine the last paragraph of the story for Joyce's musical use of language.

COMPOSITION

The involved structure of "The Dead" has been studied and researched for years. This is a good chance for you to make your own literary analysis of one of the elements of Joyce's fiction that intrigues scholars. Pick one of the following topics and trace it through the story. Write a paper on what you discover and what you think Joyce intended. You may want to go to a library and read some critical analyses of others on your subject.

The use of light and dark.

The use of cold and hot.

Details of clothes.

The use of inside/outside scenes.

The choice of the names Gabriel and Michael.

Realistic details in one scene.

Freddy Malins as an alter ego of Gabriel's.

The places where death is mentioned and its effect.

The reason Joyce used any one of the following secondary characters: Lily, Mr. Browne, Aunt Kate, Aunt Julia, Mary Jane.

The discussion of Catholicism.

The details of Dublin.

COMPOSITION WORKSHOP

WRITING FOR LIFE

Students often wonder whether learning to write is worth the time and trouble. A common question that many ask goes like this: "Why spend the time learning to write in this electronic age when the computer is about to become as common a household appliance as the television set?" This is a good question and a timely one since you are about to complete your high school education. Within a year, you will either be enrolled in an institution of higher learning or be a member of the work force. The usefulness of writing in your future is therefore something worth discussing.

In this electronic age, it is sometimes said that writing is not as important as it perhaps once was. People say that machines now exist that can almost do our thinking for us. We touch a few buttons and all kinds of information appears on a video screen. We touch a few more buttons, and that information is rapidly printed on sheet after sheet of paper. If we want to communicate a message to someone thousands of miles away, we tap a few keys, and the message is transmitted.

General computers and special computers such as word processors are indeed modern marvels. They possess the potential for making our lives at once simpler and more productive, but successful use of these devices requires more than tapping a few buttons. Computers are only productive when the information stored within them is properly organized. If what is stored in a computer is disorganized and error-ridden information, nothing more than disorganized and erroneous information can ever be retrieved. Even when working with a well-planned program, a successful computer user depends on the kinds of organized thinking skills that writing teaches so well. There is no conflict between the skills of writing and the skills needed to make electronic information systems useful. A person who can write clearly is most likely to make the most effective use of such systems.

Writing skills are also necessary, even though no computers are involved. Students who go on to a college or a technical school after high school will find the ability to write immediately useful. In most college courses, writing plays a major role.

Moreover, the organizational skills that writing teaches come in very handy in day-to-day college-level work. For example, college students must take careful notes during lectures and during their independent reading. The thinking skills that the writer possesses are drawn upon every day in the process of gathering and assessing information. Indeed, the ability to write is vital to success in college.

Those who enter the job market after high school will also find the ability to write most useful, although the ability might not be a key requirement of every job. Some workers, such as sales representatives, clerical people, and those in law enforcement, must prepare reports of various kinds during almost every working day. But numerous other workers will also find writing useful even if they are not called upon daily to do some. In every field of endeavor, the ability to produce a well-reasoned argument in writing is most impressive. It marks the worker as one who is able to think and express thoughts so that others may benefit and react. A person with this kind of ability is bound to succeed, no matter what his or her occupation might be.

While the ability to write often pays immediate dividends in the worlds of formal education and work, there is a central benefit that comes from writing which is available to every adult. Writing teaches a person to think in an organized and systematic way. Writing always demands disciplined and deliberate thought, and the good writer proves a person's capacity for thinking every time she or he produces a piece of writing.

ASSIGNMENT

Examine your own experience with writing. Identify some of the skills that you believe it has developed in you. In an informal paper, explain what you have learned from writing during your high school years. Try to identify the progress you have made in mastering these skills, and include a frank assessment of what difficulties you continue to encounter. Be prepared to share your responses with your classmates.

HANDBOOK OF LITERARY TERMS

Alexandrine: an iambic hexameter (six-foot) line of verse.

See also **Spenserian stanza.**

Allegory: a verse or prose narrative in which the characters, events, and settings are symbolic of other figures, actions, and objects, or of abstract or moral qualities, as in Spenser's *The Faerie Queene* and Bunyan's *Pilgrim's Progress.*

See page 182.

Alliteration: the repetition of the same or similar consonant sounds within a verse of poetry or a phrase or clause in prose (for example, "Now may the *f*ailing heart *f*etter its *f*ortune," from "The Wanderer").

See page 21.

Allusion: an indirect reference to historical or literary characters, events, or styles. Dryden's "MacFlecknoe" alludes to the Roman Emperor Augustus.

See page 369.

Ambiguity: as a literary technique, the deliberate suggestion in a work of two or more conflicting meanings, as in Conrad's "The Lagoon" and Greene's "Across the Bridge."

See page 752.

Anaphora: a figure of speech in which the same word or phrase is repeated at the beginning of successive phrases or clauses, as in Burns's "Scots, Wha Hae."

See page 493.

Anecdote: a short narrative presenting the details of an interesting episode or event, as in Thackeray's essay "The Influence of the Aristocracy on Snobs."

See page 628.

Antagonist: see **Characterization.**

Anticlimax (or **Bathos**): the sinking effect when the reader, full of lofty expectations, encounters something trivial or deflating instead. Pope sets up his readers for a series of anticlimactic effects when he declares at the beginning of *The Rape of the Lock:*

What dire offense from amorous causes springs,

What mighty contests rise from trivial things,

I sing—

See page 372.

Antithesis: the pointed juxtaposition of opposite or contrasting elements or ideas. Antithesis is often expressed in balanced or parallel grammatical structures, as in Pope's "To err is human, to forgive divine" (*Essay on Criticism*).

See page 372.

Aphorism: a concise, pointed statement of some important truth about life, often phrased in a witty fashion.

See also **Epigram.**

Apostrophe: a figure of speech in which an absent person or a nonhuman quality or object is directly addressed as if it were present, as in Byron's "Apostrophe to the Ocean."

See page 521.

Archaism: the use of obsolete diction, idiom, or syntax for rhetorical or poetic effect, as in Spenser's *The Faerie Queene* or Coleridge's *The Rime of the Ancient Mariner.*

See pages 182 and 568.

Archetype: in literature, a basic universal image or pattern that has occurred over and over in all cultures and periods. Conrad alludes to the archetypal story of Cain and Abel in "The Lagoon;" the Biblical story of Joseph has furnished another archetypal narrative pattern.

See page 300.

Aside: in drama, lines spoken by a character directly to the audience and not meant to be heard by others on stage. An example is Macbeth's speech beginning "Two truths are told . . ." at *Macbeth* I.3.127 (page 223).

Assonance: the repetition of the same or similar vowel sounds within a verse of poetry or a phrase or clause in prose, for example Keats's "Thou foster *chi*ld of *si*lence and slow *time*" from "Ode on a Grecian Urn" (p.540). The alliterative pattern of Old English verse included both alliteration and assonance.

See page 8.

Atmosphere: the prevailing mood of a literary work. In prose, atmosphere is often established by details of setting and characterization, while in poetry, imagery and rhythm may also contribute to atmosphere, as in Coleridge's "Kubla Khan."

See page 516.

Autobiography: an account of one's own life, written by oneself. The term properly refers to a full-length book. Orwell's essay "Shooting an Elephant" (p. 805) may be called autobiographical.

Balance (or **Parallel structure**): structure in poetry or prose in which the elements of a sentence are coordinated in corresponding positions or emphasized by similar phrasing. When the writer wishes to emphasize a contrast in ideas, this device is called balance; when the writer's purpose is the careful differentiation of separate ideas, the device is called parallel structure, or parallelism. Bacon's essays "Of Studies" and "Of Parents and Children" contain numerous examples of both techniques.

See page 196.

Ballad: a popular form of narrative verse, originally a dancing song. The basic unit of the ballad is a four-line stanza (quatrain) with four strong beats in lines 1 and 3 and three strong beats in lines 2 and 4 (the latter normally rhyme).

See page 118.

Ballad stanza: see **Ballad.**

Bathos: see **Anticlimax.**

Biography: the life story of an individual written by another person, as in Boswell's *Life of Johnson.*

See page 414.

Blank verse: unrhymed iambic pentameter lines in verse (or lines of ten syllables, with accents on the second, fourth, sixth, eighth, and tenth in a rising rhythm). Introduced into English poetry by the Earl of Surrey in the sixteenth century, blank verse became the most frequent meter for verse drama in English after Marlowe.

See page 175.

Byronic hero: a dashing, self-assertive protagonist in Romantic poetry and prose, displaying mixed qualities of good and evil. The original for this character type was the hero of Lord Byron's *Childe Harold's Pilgrimage.*

See page 517.

Caesura: the principal break or pause in the rhythm of a verse line, usually occurring at or near the middle of the line, as in Shelley's "O wild West Wind, | | thou breath of Autumn's being."

See page 530.

Canto: a section or division of a long narrative poem. Pope's *The Rape of the Lock* (p. 394) and Byron's *Childe Harold's Pilgrimage* (p. 520) are divided into cantos.

Cavalier poets: a group of seventeenth-century poets (the most famous was Robert Herrick), so named because of their easy access to court and their emphasis on style and fashion.

See page 166.

Characterization: the physical, sociological, psychological, and moral attributes detailed by an author about a character. A writer may characterize a person through physical description and direct statements to the reader; these methods are *direct characterization*. In *indirect characterization,* the author allows us to form impressions about a character's personality through the character's actions, thoughts, and speeches, and through statements about him or her by other characters. Most authors use both direct and indirect methods.

The central character in a novel, short story, drama, or narrative poem is called the *protagonist.* The person or force opposing or rivaling the protagonist is the *antagonist.*

Characters in a story or play may be said to be *flat* or *round.* Flat characters are types who do not grow or develop. They are often used in stories and plays as secondary or background characters (like the Porter in *Macbeth*). Round characters are fully developed, three-dimensional personalities, like Macbeth himself.

When a character fails to develop in any significant fashion, we often refer to him or her as *static;* characters who achieve significant development or growth within a plot are called *dynamic.* A character who sets off another by contrast is often called a *foil:* an example is Banquo in *Macbeth,* whose actions contrast with those of Macbeth after they both hear the witches' prophecies in the first act.

See pages 104–105 and 291–292.

Cliché: an expression that has been used so often that it is drained of meaning. Mod-ernist writers (for example Stevie Smith and W. H. Auden) have deliberately used clichés in their work to emphasize themes of alienation, monotony, and insensitivity.

See page 869.

Climax: see **Plot.**

Comedy: a literary form (often restricted to drama) which celebrates a human or social triumph over obstacles, often with wit and humor and with a happy ending. The *Second Shepherds' Play* contains many comic elements, while Shaw's *Arms and the Man* is an example of a fully developed comedy.

See page 136.

Conceit: an elaborate metaphor, common in Metaphysical poetry of the seventeenth century, which relates many aspects of an abstract idea to the component parts of a concrete object or being. Examples can be found in Donne's "Batter My Heart" and Herbert's "Redemption."

See page 313.

Conflict: see **Plot.**

Connotation: what a word or phrase suggests emotionally or by association, as distinct from what it means literally (the latter is called the word's *denotation).*

Convention: a *literary* convention is any style element or device or subject that is used so consistently in its time period that it becomes an accepted literary technique. For example, the alliterative verse among the Anglo-Saxons, the heroic couplet in Dryden and Pope's day. It may also be a stock character such as the drunken porter in *Macbeth* or the country bumpkin in "Tony Kytes, the Arch-Deceiver."

Couplet: two consecutive rhyming lines of verse.

Denotation: the literal meaning of a word or phrase.

Dénouement: see **Plot.**

Dialect: variations in usage of the same language by different groups of people, caused by geographical, cultural, and ethnic differences. Many of Burns's poems are written in the Scots dialect.

See pages 84 and 488.

Dialogue: the lines spoken by characters in a drama or narrative.

See page 113.

Diary: a day-by-day chronicle of events, such as that kept by Pepys in seventeenth-century London.

See page 373.

Diction: a writer's choice and use of words. Diction can be archaic, colloquial, formal, etc.

See pages 116–117 and 315.

Double plot: see **Plot.**

Dramatic monolog: a lyric poem that offers a highly personal portrait of one character, who is represented in the poem as speaking to others, as in Browning's "My Last Duchess."

See pages 666–667.

Dream vision: a popular form in Old English and medieval literature, in which the narrative framework for the main character's experiences is that of a dream. The form was revived by Coleridge in "Kubla Khan."

See page 514.

Elegy: a reflective form of lyric poetry, generally devoted to a meditation on death, as in Gray's "Elegy Written in a Country Churchyard."

See page 427.

Emblem: originally a moral or religious motto illustrated by a picture and a short poem. As a literary term, emblem has come to be applied to an especially graphic symbol. Herbert's "Easter Wings" contains an emblem in the very shape of the poem.

See page 317.

Enjambement: the technique in verse of continuing the sense from one line to the next without a rhythmic break (thus contrasting with an *end-stopped* line, in which a pause or break in the sense coincides with the end of a line). The opening of Milton's *Paradise Lost* illustrates enjambement:

Of man's first disobedience, and the
   fruit
Of that forbidden tree, whose mortal
   taste
Brought death into the world. . . .

Enjambement is common in Milton and the Romantic poets; it is relatively uncommon in the verse of the Neoclassical poets, who favored end-stopped lines.

See page 512.

Epic: a long narrative poem presenting the memorable deeds of a noble or larger-than-life hero, and focusing on events or themes important to a whole nation or race, as in *Beowulf* or Milton's *Paradise Lost.*

See pages 30–31 and 62.

Epigram: a concise, often witty statement in verse or prose, as in Ben Jonson's "On Court-Worm."

See page 302.

Epigraph: a pertinent quotation at the beginning of a literary work. Eliot's "The Love Song of J. Alfred Prufrock" is prefaced by an epigraph from Dante's *Divine Comedy.*

See page 853.

Epiphany: a term coined by James Joyce to describe a moment of especially intense emotional or spiritual illumination, as in the scene of Gabriel gazing at Gretta on the staircase in *The Dead*.

See pages 891 and 919.

Epitaph: an inscription on a tombstone, sometimes in the form of a short poem commemorating the dead person. The concluding stanzas of Gray's "Elegy" are designated the "epitaph."

See page 427.

Essay: a brief, nonfictional prose discussion of a restricted topic (from French *essai*, "trial" or "attempt"). Formal, serious essays are those such as Bacon's "Of Studies" and Samuel Johnson's "A Journey in a Stage-Coach." Lighter, more humorous essays include those of Addison, Lamb, Thackeray, and Forster.

See page 193.

Exemplum: a tale, often inserted into a sermon, which illustrates a moral truth. Chaucer's "Pardoner's Tale" is an *exemplum* (Latin: "example") intended to show that "avarice is the root of evil."

See page 106.

Exposition: see **Plot.**

Farce: a comic drama with exaggerated characters and broad humor, often accompanied by horseplay or slapstick.

Fiction: narrative writing which presents imagined events and characters or which manipulates reality in order to reveal underlying truth.

See page 380.

Flashback: see **Plot.**

Foil: see **Characterization.**

Foreshadowing: see **Plot.**

Free verse: verse with individual lines of no set pattern or length, but with generally rising or falling cadences which produce a loose stress pattern. Arnold's "Dover Beach" is written in free verse, which has become generally more common in twentieth-century poetry (as in Eliot's "Prufrock," Lawrence's "Snake," Auden's "Musée des Beaux Arts," etc.).

See page 683.

Genre: a type, group, or classification. As a literary term, the genres commonly refer to the principal literary forms, such as epic, novel, drama, and lyric. The term is also commonly used to indicate a specific type of fiction, such as mystery or romance.

Gothic novel: a type of novel which originated in the eighteenth century with the works of Horace Walpole and Mrs. Anne Radcliffe and which became increasingly popular in the Romantic period (see, for example, Austen's satire of the genre in *Northanger Abbey*). Named for the Gothic architecture of medieval Europe, this type of novel featured remote (if not actually medieval) settings, melodramatic plots, and the use of horror and the supernatural.

See page 554.

Hero: the central character in epic, drama, or fiction, and the focal point of a reader's or spectator's concern.

See pages 62 and 290.

Heroic couplet: a pair of rhyming iambic pentameter lines. The heroic couplet was the favorite verse form of Restoration and eighteenth-century poets such as Dryden, Swift, Pope, and Samuel Johnson, and was especially common in satire. It was also a favorite meter of Chaucer. The name derives from the couplet's use in heroic (or serious) tragedy of the Restoration period.

See pages 372 and 394.

Homily: a sermon based on a Biblical text, or a passage in any literary work giving stern and solemn advice on moral conduct in life. The Old English lyric "The Wanderer" contains several memorable homiletic passages.

See page 26.

Humor: a technique in writing designed to produce laughter or amusement, often through emphasis on life's ludicrous or incongruous elements.

Hymn: a lyric poem expressing religious emotion. The hymn of Caedmon is commonly regarded as the earliest text of English literature.

See page 18.

Hyperbole: a figure of speech using exaggeration for special effect, as in Marvell's "To His Coy Mistress":
An hundred years should go to praise
Thine eyes, and on thy forehead gaze.
See page 326.

Imagery (or **Figurative language**): language that is not meant to be interpreted in a literal sense, but which graphically appeals to the imagination for poetic or rhetorical effect.

See page 292.

Imagination: as a term until the eighteenth century, simply the faculty of image-making. The Romantics evolved a far more complex and suggestive theory of the imagination, whereby it was the poetic power, unifying mental and emotional faculties, which afforded deep insight into truth and beauty.

See pages 484–485.

Imagism: a term applied to the style of a poetic movement, led by the American Ezra Pound, shortly before World War I. The Imagist poets, who exerted a marked influence on others such as T. S. Eliot, placed

the highest value on fresh, exact, concrete images in verse.

See pages 852 and 858.

in medias res (Latin: "in the middle of things"): the technique, common in epic, of plunging into the middle of a narrative at the work's beginning, and only later conveying the preceding action through the use of flashbacks, as in Milton's *Paradise Lost.*

See page 338.

Inscape: a term coined by Gerard Manley Hopkins to describe the essential, inner pattern of a phrase or expression in poetry.

See page 839.

Interior monolog: a style of poetic or prose narrative which focuses closely on the inner thoughts, impressions, reactions, and emotions of one character, as in Eliot's "The Love Song of J. Alfred Prufrock."

See page 852.

Inversion: the technique of reversing the normal word order of a sentence, as in Doris Lessing's "A Mild Attack of Locust": "Beautiful it was with the sky blue."

See page 830.

Invocation: a call to a muse or god for inspiration, especially common in classical epic. Milton's *Paradise Lost* begins with an invocation, modeled on those of Homer and Virgil.

See page 330.

Irony: a telling discrepancy between what is said on the surface and what is actually meant, or between what is expected to happen and what actually occurs. In *verbal irony* the intended meaning of words sharply contrasts with the literal meaning. In *dramatic irony* the audience or reader knows something that the character does not, and the speeches and actions are therefore understood differently by the audience than by the characters. In *situational irony* there is a discrepancy between the expected results of an action and the actual results, as in Orwell's "Shooting an Elephant" and Joyce's *The Dead*.

See page 26.

Journal: a personal record of noteworthy events, often less systematic than a diary, as illustrated by Dorothy Wordsworth's *Journal*. In the eighteenth century, journals often served as the framework for fiction disguised as a true report, as in Defoe's *A Journal of the Plague Year*.

See page 380.

Kenning: a fanciful metaphor consisting of strung-together adjectives and nouns that stand for a thing without directly naming it, as in the expression "the swan's riding" for the sea in *Beowulf*.

See page 26.

Legend: a narrative or tradition handed down from the past, generally with a core of some historical truth, but often overlaid with imaginative embellishment, as in the legends collected by Malory in *Le Morte Darthur*.

See page 127.

Lyric: a brief, compressed poetic treatment of a single subject, candidly expressing personal emotion. Lyrics (so named for the lyre) have often been composed to be sung. They are conventionally subdivided into a number of categories, e.g. odes, elegies, hymns, ballads, sonnets, etc.

Masque: a dramatic entertainment combining verse, music, elaborate pageantry, and splendid scenic effects, popular at court in the sixteenth and seventeenth centuries.

See page 301.

Melodrama: a plot that is developed through heavy use of suspense and sensational episodes, with little regard to motivations. The aim is to keep the audience on tenterhooks of emotion—whether joy, pity, horror, anger, etc—as in Elizabethan revenge tragedies or modern horror films.

Metaphor: a figure of speech in which a comparison is implied between two essentially unlike things, as in Macbeth's "I have supped full with horrors."

See page 292.

Metaphysical poets: a term for a number of seventeenth-century poets, the most celebrated of whom was John Donne, who wrote in a roughly similar style. "Metaphysical" means beyond the physical; these poets focused much of their work on the spiritual realm and the life of the soul. Their poetry is characterized by elaborate images and conceits, intricate structure, and experiments with irregular meter and untraditional diction.

See page 305.

Meter: the means by which rhythm is measured in verse. Principal meters in English poetry include *iambic* (a regular system of poetic feet in which an unstressed syllable is followed by a stressed syllable); *trochaic* (the reverse of iambic); *anapestic* (two unstressed syllables followed by a stressed syllable); *dactylic* (a stressed syllable followed by two unstressed syllables); and *spondaic* (two successive stressed syllables). Verse lengths are described by the number of feet the verse contains, as in *iambic pentameter* (five iambic feet), *trochaic tetrameter* (four trochaic feet), etc.

See also **Rhythm** and **Scansion.**

Metonymy: a figure of speech in which something closely associated with a thing is substituted as a term for the thing itself, as when the monarch is called the "crown."

See page 512.

Mock epic: a comic literary form which inverts the grand style of true epic by treating a trivial subject, most often with ironic or satirical effects, as in Pope's *The Rape of the Lock.*

See page 394.

Modernism: a term employed to describe the rejection by twentieth-century writers of Romantic and Victorian literary premises, styles, and subject matter. The modernist writers, beginning in the 1890s, have typically stressed difficulty, conflict, ambiguity, and the alienation and fragmentation of the modern world.

See pages 749–750.

Morality play: a form of medieval drama which featured symbolic abstractions of human qualities as characters (for example Vice, Good Deeds, Knowledge), and which stressed the constant struggle between evil and Christian virtue. The most famous surviving example is the anonymous *Everyman.*

Mystery play: a form of medieval drama based on the events recounted in the Bible, as in the *Second Shepherds' Play.* Religious plays which were based on the lives of the saints are often termed *miracle plays.*

See page 136.

Myth: a story, often about immortals, which tries to make the unknown understandable by relating it to the known. Commonly its subjects are on such themes as religion, creation, and natural disasters. Myths may also narrate adventures of ethnic heroes as in *Beowulf.* These stories are dramatic personifications of deep truths.

Neoclassicism: the cultivation during the Restoration and the Age of Reason (c.1660–1800) of ancient classical (Greco-Roman) styles, standards, and artistic forms.

See page 356.

Nonfiction: writing which is, or purports to be, based on actual fact, such as history, biography, autobiography, journalism, diaries, or essays. In English literature, the rise of the dominant fictional form, the novel, is closely associated with eighteenth-century writers' manipulation of nonfiction.

See pages 380 and 428.

Novel: derived from Latin *novus* ("new"), the novel is an extended fictional narrative in prose of realistic, individual experience. The rise of the English novel occurred in the eighteenth century with the works of such writers as Defoe, Swift, Richardson, and Fielding.

See pages 428–429.

Novella: a fictional prose narrative somewhat longer than a short story but briefer than a book-length novel, as in Joyce's *The Dead* or Conrad's *Heart of Darkness.*

See page 891.

Octave: see **Sonnet.**

Ode: from the Greek for "song," an ode is a free form of lyric, without a set stanza length or rhyme scheme. Especially popular as a lyric form among the Romantic poets, the ode is exemplified by such works as Shelley's "Ode to the West Wind" and Keats's "Ode on a Grecian Urn."

Onomatopoeia: the effective use of words whose sound implies their meaning, such as "hiss" or "buzz."

Oral tradition: the process of handing down narratives from generation to generation by word of mouth. Oral tradition stands behind many of the great epic poems in world literature, including Homer's *Iliad* and *Odyssey* and the anonymous *Beowulf*.

See pages 8 and 30.

Ottava rima: a stanza of eight lines with rhyme scheme abababcc. Introduced into English poetry by Wyatt, who imitated it from Italian verse, it was used by Byron in *Don Juan* and by Yeats in "Sailing to Byzantium."

See page 847.

Oxymoron: see **Paradox.**

Paradox: a statement which, while seemingly self-contradictory or absurd, may often reveal unexpected truth, as in Blake's "The Chimney Sweeper" (*Songs of Experience.*)

See page 499.

When very concisely expressed, as in a two-word phrase, paradox sometimes takes the form of an *oxymoron:* for example Herrick's phrase "wild civility" in "Delight in Disorder."

See page 315.

Parallel structure: see **Balance.**

Parody: a composition that burlesques or satirizes a serious work by a humorous or ridiculous imitation, as in Pope's *The Rape of the Lock.*

See page 394.

Pastoral: a literary work (most often a poem) that deals with shepherds and rustic life, often in an idealized fashion, for the purpose of treating serious themes. The pastoral tradition in poetry, which originated in classical literature, has often been revived by educated, urbanized poets for the sake of introducing a tone of simplicity, as in Housman's poems in *A Shropshire Lad.*

See pages 694–695.

Personification: a form of metaphor in which inanimate or nonhuman figures are given human attributes, as in Spenser's portraits of the Seven Deadly Sins in *The Faerie Queene.*

See page 189.

Plot: the ordered sequence of interrelated events in a novel, narrative poem, drama, or short story. The principal stages in a well constructed plot may be described as follows. In the *exposition* the author introduces essential information for understanding the action. *Conflict* establishes and probes the interplay of two or more forces within the plot. Conflict may occur between people, between emotions, between values, or between a person and nature; that is, it may be external or internal. The *climax* is the point of highest interest and also the point at which the reader or audience makes the greatest emotional response. The climax leads to the *dénouement* or *resolution,* in which the conflict ends and the outcome of the plot is clear.

The chronological progression of the plot may be altered through a number of techniques. In *foreshadowing* the author uses hints to suggest what will happen later in the narrative. By using *flashback* the writer may interrupt the narrative to recreate earlier scenes or incidents. Both devices may contribute to the *suspense* of the plot: that quality which increases the tension in our uncertainty about the outcome.

In shorter literary forms, there is normally a single, unified plot with a beginning, middle, and end. In drama and in longer prose forms, such as the novel, writers may use a *double plot* (or even a triple plot) which manipulates two or three separate strands of action for a unified effect. The *Second Shepherds' Play* is an early example of the double plot in drama.

See page 153.

Point of view: the outlook from which the events in a novel or story are narrated. Swift uses first person point of view in *Gulliver's Travels.* Since the narrator is also the protagonist, this is called *first person participant* point of view. Greene employs *first person observer* point of view in "Across the Bridge;" the character telling the story is a subordinate figure in the plot.

In third person narration, the author is free to tell us the inner thoughts and reactions of a number of characters. If the point of view is confined to one character, the technique is *third person limited,* as in Woolf's "The Duchess and the Jeweller." If the author describes and comments on all the major characters, the point of view is said to be *third person omniscient* (or "all knowing"), as in Lawrence's "The Rocking-Horse Winner."

See page 473.

Prose: a literary piece of writing that does not have meter or rhythm. Derived from the Latin for "forward (direct) speech," prose has developed more slowly than verse in most cultures. Landmark writers in the development of English prose include Sir Thomas Malory, Francis Bacon, and John Dryden.

Protagonist: see **Characterization.**

Pun: a play on words based on a similarity of sound between two words with different meanings.

See page 524.

Quatrain: a four-line stanza of verse.

See page 192.

Realism: the representation of reality in literature and art through a selection of details drawn from everyday experience.

See pages 642–643.

Refrain: a phrase, line, or group of lines which is regularly repeated in a poem, usually at the end of the stanza, as in Tennyson's "The Lady of Shalott."

See page 647.

Repetition: a rhetorical device which reiterates a word or phrase for emphasis or some other kind of effect, as in Greene's use of the phrase "He had a million" in "Across the Bridge."

See page 818.

Rhetorical question: a question posed for rhetorical effect and not intended to elicit a reply, as in Blake's repeated questions in "The Lamb" and "The Tyger."

See page 496.

Rhyme: similar or identical sounds in two or more words or phrases which are close to each other in a poem. The sounds are usually at the ends of the words. When the words occur at the ends of lines, this technique is called *end rhyme*. If rhyme occurs within a line of verse, it is called *internal rhyme*.

When rhyme recurs at regular intervals at the end of lines, we can describe the *rhyme scheme* of a poem. For example the ballad stanza used by Coleridge in *The Rime of the Ancient Mariner* has the rhyme scheme abcb:

It is an ancient Mariner,	*a*
And he stoppeth one of three.	*b*
"By thy long grey beard and glittering eye,	*c*
Now wherefore stopp'st thou me?"	*b*

The rhyme of the second and fourth lines above is called *perfect rhyme,* since it involves the repetition of an identical vowel sound. When sounds are approximated, rather than exactly repeated, the result is *slant rhyme* or *off rhyme,* as in Stevie Smith's "Thoughts about the Person from Porlock":

Coleridge received the Person from Porlock	*a*
And ever after called him a curse,	*b*
Then why did he hurry to let him in?	*c*
He could have hid in the house.	*b*

See page 881.

Rhythm: in verse, the overall pattern of stressed and unstressed syllables. We can also speak of the rhythm of prose, referring to the overall sense of movement produced by the rise and fall of emphasis in sentences and paragraphs.

See also **Meter** and **Scansion**.

See page 617.

Riddle: a popular type of lyric in Old English, often making extensive use of metaphor and personification.

See page 28.

Romance: a popular form of medieval literature, consisting of a verse or prose narrative recounting the adventures of a hero, and usually including motifs of courtly love.

See page 69.

Romanticism: the dominant mode in Western European art and literature from roughly 1770 to 1840. In English literature, Romanticism is marked by a strong reaction against eighteenth-century Neoclassicism. Among its characteristics are the spontaneous expression of emotion, intense subjectivity, love of nature and the picturesque, interest in the supernatural, and a new freedom in literary styles and themes.

See pages 477–485.

Satire: a literary mode which appears in many genres (verse, prose, novel, drama) and employs wit and humor to attack human foibles or institutions in order to reform them. Swift's *Gulliver's Travels* is often singled out as the greatest satire in English.

See page 358.

Scansion: the process of dividing verse into metrical feet by noting the sequence of stressed and unstressed syllables.

See also **Meter**.

Science fiction: a narrative in the form of a novel or short story which alters time and space in a fantastic but momentarily plausible fashion. H. G. Wells pioneered the form in English literature.

See pages 886 and 888.

Sermon: as a literary form, a piece of prose written for public delivery to a congregation on a religious theme, as with Donne's sermons.

See page 304.

Sestet: see **Sonnet**.

Setting: the physical location of the events in a narrative or poem. Setting may include the geographical location, the socioeconomic background, the historical period, and the cultural environment. Setting is often a highly significant element contributing to atmosphere, theme, and tone.

See page 767.

Short story: a short piece of prose fiction (more rarely in verse) based on unity of characterization, theme, and effect.

See pages 112–113.

Simile: a figure of speech in which a comparison between two unlike things is expressed using the words *like* or *as*.

See pages 61–62.

Slant rhyme: see **Rhyme**.

Slice of life: as a literary term, a type of extremely realistic narrative which attempts to present life exactly as it is lived, without comment or distortion by the author, as in Mansfield's "The Garden-Party."

See page 803.

Soliloquy: a speech in a play by a character who is alone on the stage, in which the character's thoughts are revealed or necessary information about other characters is told, as in Macbeth's speech, "Is this a dagger which I see before me . . . ?" at *Macbeth* II.1.33 (page 234).

Song: a lyric poem suitable for musical accompaniment.

See page 493.

Sonnet: a fourteen-line lyric poem, usually in iambic pentameter, that follows one of a limited number of conventional rhyme schemes. The two most common forms are: 1) the *Italian (Petrarchan) sonnet,* with rhyme scheme abbaabba, cdecde (other combinations are possible in the last six lines); and 2) the *English (Shakespearian) sonnet,* with rhyme scheme abab, cdcd, efef, gg. As is evident from the rhyme patterns, the Italian sonnet is conventionally divided into two portions: the first, of eight verses, is called the *octave,* while the last six lines are called the *sestet.* Most Italian sonnets exhibit a turning point, or *volta,* after the eighth line. The English sonnet is divided into three groups of four lines (*quatrains*) with a rhyming *couplet* at the end.

Introduced into English poetry from Italian by Sir Thomas Wyatt in the Elizabethan age, the sonnet has remained a remarkably durable lyric form. Sonnets have been written by Sidney, Spenser, Shakespeare, Donne, Herbert, Milton, Wordsworth, Shelley, Keats, Elizabeth Barrett Browning, Rossetti, and Hopkins.
See pages 175, 177, 192, 209–210, 312–313, 339.

Sonnet form: see **Sonnet.**

Spenserian stanza: a stanza pattern consisting of nine verses, the first eight being iambic pentameter and the last an iambic hexameter (or *alexandrine*), with rhyme scheme ababbcbcc. The stanza is named for Edmund Spenser, who first used it in *The Faerie Queene.*

See page 189.

Sprung rhythm: a term coined by Gerard Manley Hopkins to describe his experiments with verse rhythm "sprung" free from a strict alternation of stressed and unstressed syllables. Poetry in sprung rhythm is organized around general rising and falling movements.

See pages 839 and 842.

Stanza: a grouping of two or more verse lines in a poem. The pattern of a stanza is formed by the length of the lines, the rhythm, the meter, and the rhyme scheme.

Stanza form: see **Stanza.**

Stock character: a conventional character type, or *stereotype,* often anticipated by the reader as belonging to a particular genre of literature (as with the figure of the cruel stepmother in fairy tales).

See page 773.

Stoicism: a general indifference to pleasure and pain, ultimately deriving from the doctrines of the ancient philosophical school, the Stoics, who taught resignation to destiny or divine will.

See page 26.

Stream of consciousness: a form of writing that attempts to follow the uninterrupted, uneven, and endless flow of thoughts of one or more of the characters, just as that flow occurs in the mind, with no ordering or intervention by the writer, as in Joyce's novel *Ulysses.*

See page 752.

Style: an author's characteristic choice and arrangement of words.

See page 410.

Supernatural: as a literary technique, the use of mysterious, divine, or inexplicable characters, events, or settings, as in *Beowulf* or Coleridge's *The Rime of the Ancient Mariner.*

See page 31.

Surprise ending: the outcome of the plot in a short story or novel which has not been anticipated by the reader, as in Greene's "Across the Bridge" or Saki's "The Schartz-Metterklume Method."

See page 769.

Suspense: see **Plot.**

Symbol: an image which both stands for itself and evokes an abstract meaning, as in Blake's "The Tyger" or Yeats's "Sailing to Byzantium."

See pages 496, 499, and 848.

Symbolism: a general term which denotes the technique of using symbols in literature; also a specific term used to designate the characteristic style of a group of French poets toward the end of the nineteenth century (including Paul Verlaine, Arthur Rimbaud, and Stéphane Mallarmé) which notably influenced modernist poets in English such as T. S. Eliot.

See pages 852 and 858.

Synaesthesia: a mingling of the senses in imagery, as in Keats's phrase "Tender is the night" in "Ode to a Nightingale."

See page 543.

Terza rima: an Italian stanza form in which groups of three lines are linked by interlocking rhymes: aba, bcb, cdc. . . . etc. This stanza form was used by Dante in the *Divine Comedy* and by Shelley in "Ode to the West Wind."

See page 533.

Theme: the abstract concept that is embodied in a literary work and that is made evident through the action, characters, and imagery.

Tone: a writer's attitude toward the subject or the audience, as implied or revealed through the language of a literary work. Tone is created through diction, details, imagery, characterization, and (in narrative forms) the arrangement of the plot.

See page 392.

Tragedy: a literary form (often restricted to drama) centering on the protagonist's awareness of human limitations, and often (although not necessarily) culminating in the hero's destruction or death, as in Shakespeare's *Macbeth.*

See pages 290–291.

Travelogue: a form of narrative prose, popular in the eighteenth century, which presents a personal record of everyday experience on a journey. Swift incorporated elements of the form in his satiric novel *Gulliver's Travels.*

See page 473.

***Ubi sunt* motif:** a popular element in medieval lyrics, also used in the Old English poem "The Wanderer," with the two Latin words *ubi sunt* ("Where are. . . . ?") introducing any variation on the question, "Where are those who lived before?"

See page 21.

Verse paragraph: an arrangement of syntax and meaning in verse similar to that of a paragraph in prose, in which units of meaning are spread over a relatively large number of lines, as in Milton's *Paradise Lost* or Marvell's "To His Coy Mistress."

See page 326.

Vilanelle: an intricate lyric verse form (originally French) of nineteen lines, divided into five groups of three and a concluding four-line stanza, with only two rhymes and with multiple repetitions of lines 1 and 3 as refrains, as in Dylan Thomas's "Do Not Go Gentle Into That Good Night."

See page 878.

Volta: see **Sonnet.**

Wit: superior intellectual knowledge or insight, often conveyed with clever humor in a striking verbal expression.

See page 358.

Zeugma: a rhetorical device linking two or more terms, only one of which at first seems apt, to a single word, as in the following lines from Pope's *The Rape of the Lock:*

> Here thou, great Anna! whom three
>   realms obey,
> Dost sometimes counsel take—and
>   sometimes tea.

GLOSSARY

This Glossary contains those relatively common yet difficult words used in the selections contained in this book. Many of the words occur two or more times in the book. The definitions are in accord with how the words are used in the selections.

Technical, archaic, obscure, and foreign words are footnoted with the selections as they occur.

The pronunciation symbols used in both the Glossary and the footnotes follow the system used in the *Thorndike/Barnhart Advanced Dictionary* (1979). For words having more than one pronunciation, the first pronunciation is used here, and regional pronunciations may therefore vary from some of the pronuciations provided in this Glossary.

Syllable division and stress marks for primary and secondary accent marks used in the pronunciations also follow the system in the *Advanced Dictionary,* including putting the stress marks after the syllables stressed.

The following abbreviations are used to indicate parts of speech:

n. noun   *adj.* adjective
v. verb   *adv.* adverb

abandon (ə ban′dən) *v.* give up entirely; leave; forsake.

abandoned (ə ban′dənd) *adj.* deserted; being given up entirely.

abhor (ab hôr′) *v.* regard with horror or disgust; hate completely.

abhorrence (ab hôr′əns) *n.* a feeling of very great hatred.

abides (ə bīdz′) *v.* remains.

abject (ab′jekt) *adj.* downhearted; unhappy looking.

abjure (ab jür′) *v.* deny or give up.

abominable (ə bom′ ə nə bəl) *adj.* very unpleasant; disagreeable.

abrupt (ə brupt′) *adj.* very sudden; unexpected.

absurd (ab sėrd′) *adj.* ridiculous; plainly not logical or sensible.

abuse (ə byüz′) *v.* treat roughly or cruelly; mistreat; harm.

abysses (ə bis′əs) *n.* chasms; deep pits.

acclamation (ak′lə mā′shən) *n.* applause; show of approval.

acclamations (ak′lə mā′shənz) *n.* shouts of welcome and approval by a crowd.

accommodated (ə kom′ə dāt əd) *v.* adjusted; adapted; fit in with.

accomplices (ə kom′plis əs) *n.* persons who knowingly help another in wrongdoing.

accost (ə kôst′) *v.* approach and speak to first.

accrue (ə krü′) *v.* increase gradually, as interest on money does.

acquiescent (ak′wē es′nt) *adj.* inclined to consent or agree to quietly.

acrid (ak′rid) *adj.* sharp, bitter, or stinging to the mouth, eyes, skin, or nose.

adept (ə dept′) *adj.* thoroughly skilled; expert.

admonition (ad′mə nish′ən) *n.* a gentle warning or reproof; a scolding.

adversary (ad′vər ser′ē) *n.* opponent; enemy.

adversity (ad vėr′sə tē) *n.* misfortune; hardship; distress.

affability (af′ə bil′ə tē) *n.* friendliness; condition of being courteous and pleasant.

affably (af′ə blē) *adv.* in a friendly manner; courteously and pleasantly.

affec·ted (ə fek′tid) *adj.* put on for effect; unnatural; artificial.

affliction (ə flik′shən) *n.* misfortune; great distress.

afflictor (ə flikt′ər) *n.* one who causes great trouble and suffering.

aghast (ə gast′) *adj.* struck with surprise or horror.

agility (ə jil′ə tē) *n.* liveliness; nimbleness; speed and ease of movement; quickness.

agitated (aj′ə tāt əd) *v.* disturbed very much; excited. *adj.* greatly disturbed or excited.

agitation (aj′ə tā′shən) *n.* a disturbed, upset, or troubled state.

agony (ag′ə nē) *n.* great mental distress; torment; great anguish. Also, a sudden, powerful emotion.

alacrity (ə lak′rə tē) *n.* cheerful willingness. Also, brisk and eager action.

allay (ə lā′) *v.* ease; smooth; put at rest; quiet.

alleged (ə lejd′) *adj.* supposed; so-called; questionable.

allotted (ə lot′əd) *v.* assigned; gave as a share, task, duty, etc.

amiably (ā′mē ə blē) *adv.* in a friendly, good-natured way.

amphibious (am fib′ē əs) *adj.* able to live both on land and in water.

ancestral (an ses′trəl) *adj.* inherited from one's father, grandfather, etc.; of or having to do with one's forefathers.

ancient (ān′shənt) *adj.* of or belonging to times long past; very old.

anguish (ang′gwish) *n.* extreme mental pain or suffering; great distress.

animation (an′ə mā′shən) *n.* having life or being lifelike. Also, liveliness of manner.

animosities (an′ə mos′ə tēz) *n.* keen hostile feelings; strong dislikes.

antidote (an′ti dōt) *n.* remedy for any evil; a cure, usually for poison.

apothecary (ə poth′ə ker′ē) *n.* druggist; pharmacist.

appalling (ə pô′ling) *adj.* shocking; horrible; dismaying.

appalls (ə pôlz′) *v.* fills with consternation and horror; terrifies.

apparent (ə par′ənt) *adj.* plain to see; so plain that one cannot help seeing it.

apparition (ap′ə rish′ən) *n.* a ghost or phantom. Also, a supernatural sight or thing.

appeasement (ə pēz′mənt) *n.* act of soothing or calming or making concessions.

appeasing (ə pēz′ing) *v.* soothing; calming by making concessions.

apprehension (ap′ri hen′shən) *n.* dread of impending danger; fear.

apprehensive (ap′ri hen′siv) *adj.* fearful; anxious about the future.

approbation (ap′rə bā′shən) *n.* favorable opinion; approval; praise.

aptness (apt′nəs) *n.* intelligence; a skill.

arbitrate (är′bə trāt) *v.* settle a dispute; help opponents to agree.

arduous (är′jü əs) *adj.* hard to do; difficult.

arrears (ə rirz) *n.* behind in work; payments, etc.; anything overdue or behindhand.

arrogance (ar′ə gəns) *n.* excessive pride with contempt for others; haughtiness.

arrogant (ar′ə gənt) *adj.* excessively proud and contemptuous of others; haughty.

askance (ə skans′) *adv.* with suspicion or disapproval or distrust.

aspire (ə spīr′) *v.* long for; desire; have an ambition for something.

assailable (ə sāl′ə bəl) *adj.* capable of being attacked and overcome.

assault (ə sôlt′) *n.* a sudden, vigorous attack.

assertion (ə sėr′shən) *n.* a positive statement; a firm declaration.

assiduously (ə sij′ü əs lē) *adv.* carefully and attentively; industriously.

attachment (ə tach′mənt) *n.* affection; friendship.

attribute (at′rə byüt) *n.* characteristic; a quality considered appropriate to a person.

audacious (ô dā′shəs) *adj.* bold; having the courage to take risks.

auditors (ô′də tərz) *n.* listeners.

autocratic (ô′tə krat′ik) *adj.* domineering; self-willed; being absolute in power or authority.

avarice (av′ər is) *n.* greed, especially for money.

avaricious (av′ə rish′əs) *adj.* greatly desiring money or property; very greedy.

awry (ə rī′) *adv.* wrong; out of order.

azure (azh′ər) *n.* and *adj.* sky blue.

bankrupt (bang′krupt) *adj.* unable to pay one's debts; destitute.

banner (ban′ər) *n.* flag, often having a special design.

barbarous (bär′bər əs) *adj.* rough and rude; coarse; harsh; unrefined. Also, not civilized; savage.

beguile (bi gīl′) *v.* while away (time) pleasantly.

beguiled (bi gīld′) *adj.* and *v.* tricked or deceived; misled.

besieging (bi sēj′ing) *v.* attacking; surrounding in order to compel surrender.

bestowed (bi stōd′) *v.* gave as a gift; granted.

blandly (bland′lē) *adv.* mildly and politely.

blithe (blīTH) *adj.* joyous; happy and cheerful.

bolted (bōlt′əd) *v.* held fast; pinned down.

boorish (bur′ish) *adj.* rude; ill-bred or ill-mannered.

brandished (bran′disht) *v.* waved threateningly. *adj.* being waved or shaken threateningly.

brood (brüd) *v.* keep thinking about; worry about.

brusquely (brusk′lē) *adv.* abruptly; sharply and quickly.

burnished (bėr′nisht) *adj.* highly polished; very shiny.

calamity (kə lam′ə tē) *n.* great misfortune; serious trouble; a disaster.

capriciously (kə prish′əs lē) *adv.* in a fickle manner; changeably; unreasonably.

caress (kə res′) *n.* a friendly touch; a hug.

careen (kə rēn′) *v.* tumble recklessly.

carousing (kə rouz′ing) *v.* drinking heavily.

catastrophic (kat′ə strof′ik) *adj.* of or caused by disaster; calamitous.

cauldron (kôl′drən) *n.* a large kettle or pot used for boiling.

cavernous (kav′ər nəs) *adj.* large and hollow.

celebrated (sel′ə brā′tid) *adj.* much talked about; famous; well-known.

celestial (sə les′chəl) *adj.* heavenly; divine.

certitude (sėr′tə tüd) *n.* certainty; sureness.

challenge (chal′ənj) *v.* call in question; defy.

chasm (kaz′əm) *n.* a gorge; a deep opening or crack in the earth; a gap.

chastise (cha stīz′) *v.* criticize severely; rebuke.

chide (chīd) *v.* reproach or blame; scold.

chivalrous (shiv′əl rəs) *adj.* being a gentleman; being devoted to the service of the weak and oppressed.

chivalrously (shiv′əl rəs lē) *adv.* courteously.

civilized (siv′ə līzd) *adj.* showing culture and good manners; refined.

clambering (klam′bər ing) *v.* climbing awkwardly and with difficulty, using both hands and feet; scrambling.

clamor (klam′ər) *n.* noisy outcry; a continual uproar and loud shouting.

clamorous (klam′ər əs) *adj.* loud and noisy.

cleave (klēv) *v.* hold fast; cling.

colloquial (kə lō′kwē əl) *adj.* used in everyday, informal talk, but not in formal speech or writing.

colossal (kə los′əl) *adj.* of huge size; gigantic; vast; immense.

commend (kə mend′) *v.* speak well of; praise.

commission (kə mish′ən) *n.* percentage of the amount of business done paid to the one who does it; money paid in accordance with business done.

companionable (kəm pan′yə nə bə) *adj.* agreeable; friendly.

comparable (kom′pər ə bəl) *adj.* alike; similar.

compassionate (kəm pash′ə nit) *adj.* sympathetic; feeling pity for.

compel (kəm pel′) *v.* force or make a person do something. Also, cause or get by force.

complacency (kəm plā′sn sē) *n.* a being pleased with oneself; self-satisfaction.

comply (kəm plī) *v.* consent (to something); act in agreement with a request.

composure (kəm pō′zhər) *n.* calmness; quietness; self-control.

condemn (kən dem′) *v.* hold guilty (of something); denounce.

confided (kən fīd′əd) *v.* told as a secret.

confound (kon found′) *v.* confuse; mix up; surprise and puzzle.

congenial (kən jē′nyəl) *adj.* suitable; agreeable; sympathetic. Also, having similar tastes and interests; getting on well together.

conjecture (kən jek′chər) *v.* guess; suppose. *n.* formation of an opinion without sufficient evidence, guessing.

conscientious (kon′shē en′shəs) *adj.* honorable; careful to do what one knows is right.

consequences (kon′sə kwens əs) *n.* logical results; outcome.

console (kən sōl′) *v.* comfort; make grief or trouble easier to bear by doing something to lighten it.

conspicuous (kən spik′yü əs) *adj.* worthy of notice; outstanding; clearly visible.

conspired (kən spīrd′) *v.* planned secretly against; plotted.

constraint (kən strānt) *n.* a holding back.

consummate (kən sum′it) *adj.* complete; perfect.

contemplation (kon′təm plā′shən) *n.* deep thought; meditation.

contempt (kən tempt′) *n.* scorn; disdain.

contemptible (kən temp′tə bəl) *adj.* despicable; mean; low; worthless.

contemptuous (kən temp′chü əs) *adj.* scornful; disdainful.

contend (kən tend′) *v.* fight; struggle against.

contention (kən ten′shən) *n.* an argument; a dispute; a quarrel. Also, a statement of one's views on a particular situation.

contradicting (kon′trə dikt′ing) *v.* denying what one said earlier; saying something is not true.

coquette (kō ket′) *n.* a woman who tries to attract men merely to please her vanity.

coronet (kôr′ə net′) *n.* a small crown.

Pronunciation Key

hat, āge, fär; let, equal, term;
it, īce; hot, open, ôrder;
oil, out; cup, pùt, rüle;
ch, child; ng, long; sh, she;
th, thin; ŦH, then; zh, measure;
ə represents *a* in about, *e* in taken,
i in pencil, *o* in lemon, *u* in circus.

---

corpulent (kôr′pyə lənt) *adj.* large or bulky of body; fat.

corruptions (kə rup′shənz) *n.* dishonest deeds and actions; bad conduct.

council (koun′səl) *n.* a group of people who discuss and decide.

counsel (koun′səl) *n.* carefully considered advice.

counterfeit (koun′tər fit) *v.* imitate; pretend.

covetousness (kuv′ə təs nəs) *n.* the desire for things that belong to others.

cowed (koud) *adj.* frightened; intimidated.

coyness (koi′nəs) *n.* acting more shy and bashful than one really is.

credulity (krə dü′lə tē) *n.* a being too ready to believe; trust.

credulous (krej′ə ləs) *adj.* too ready to believe; easily deceived.

crisis (krī′sis) *n.* a decisive moment; a state of danger.

cubicle (kyü′bə kəl) *n.* a very small room or compartment.

cunning (kun′ing) *n.* skill; cleverness.

cunningly (kun′ing lē) *adv.* slyly; craftily.

cynical (sin′ə kəl) *adj.* doubting the sincerity and honesty of people and their motives for doing things.

cynicism (sin′ə siz′əm) *n.* the tendency to doubt the honesty and sincerity of people and their motives for acting as they do.

daunted (dônt′əd) *v.* frightened; discouraged; disheartened.

dauntless (dônt′lis) *adj.* not to be frightened or discouraged; brave; fearless.

dazzled (daz′əld) *v.* overwhelmed with splendid acts.

decree (di krē′) *v.* command or order; decide; determine.

deference (def′ər əns) *n.* great respect. Also, a yielding to the judgment, opinion, wishes, etc., of another.

deferential (def′ə ren′shəl) *adj.* respectful; courteous.

defiance (di fī′əns) *n.* an acting in spite of something; resistance; a challenge; open disobedience.

defiant (di fī′ənt) *adj.* boldly disobedient.

deign (dān) *v.* condescend to give; lower oneself.

dejection (di jek′shən) *n.* lowness of spirit; discouragement.

delicate (del′ə kit) *adj.* light and mild; fineness and softness of texture.

delirious (di lir′ē əs) *adj.* temporarily out of one's mind; wandering in mind; raving.

demeanor (di mē′nər) *n.* the way a person looks or acts; manner; the outward appearance.

deplorable (di plôr′ə bəl) *adj.* wretched; miserable; sad.

deplore (di plôr′) *v.* regret deeply.

deprecation (dep′rə kā′shən) *n.* a strong expression of disapproval.

depreciating (di prē′shē āt ing) *v.* lessening the value or price of something.

descendants (di sen′dənts) *n.* offspring; children, grandchildren, great-grandchildren, etc.

desolate (des′ə lit) *adj.* lonely; deserted.

desolation (des′ə lā′shən) *n.* a ruined, lonely, or deserted condition; devastation.

desperate (des′pər it) *adj.* not caring what happens because hope is gone; reckless.

desperation (des′pə rā′shən) *n.* a hopeless, reckless feeling; readiness to run any risk.

despicable (des′pi kə bəl) *adj.* vile; contemptible.

despised (di spīzd′) *v.* looked down on; scorned.

despotic (des pot′ik) *adj.* oppressive; tyrannical.

destiny (des′tə nē) *n.* what will happen in spite of all efforts; fate; what becomes of a person in the end; one's lot or fortune.

deterred (di terd′) *v.* discouraged or prevented from acting or proceeding as planned.

detestable (di tes′tə bəl) *adj.* hateful; evil; vile; disgusting.

devasted (dev′ə stāt əd) *adj.* ruined; destroyed.

dexterous (dek′stər əs) *adj.* skillful; clever.

dexterously (dek′stər əs lē) *adv.* quickly and easily; skillfully; cleverly; deftly.

digress (dī gres′) *v.* turn aside from the main subject in talking or writing.

diligence (dil′ə jəns) *n.* industry; constant attention to work and duty.

diligent (dil′ə jənt) *adj.* hard-working; industrious; careful and steady.

diminutive (də min′yə tiv) *adj.* very small; tiny; minute.

dire (dīr) *adj.* terrible; dreadful; disastrous.

direst (dīr′ist) *adj.* most dreadful or terrible.

dirges (dėrj′əs) *n.* funeral songs or tunes; laments.

disasters (də zas′tərz) *n.* sudden or great misfortunes; calamities.

disconsolate (dis kon′sə lit) *adj.* forlorn; unhappy; hopeless.

discordant (dis kôrd′nt) *adj.* harsh; clashing.

discourse (dis′kôrs) *n.* talk; conversation. *v.* talk; converse.

discreet (dis krēt′) *adj.* very careful in speech and action; cautious.

discretion (dis′ kresh′ən) *n.* good judgment; wise caution.

discrimination (dis krim′ə nā′shən) *n.* power of detecting distinctions or differences.

disdain (dis dān′) *n.* scorn; contempt.

disheartened (dis härt′nd) *v.* discouraged; lost hope.

dishevelled (də shev′əld) *adj.* rumpled; mussed; untidy.

disillusion (dis′i lü′zhən) *n.* false ideas or hopes.

dismal (diz′məl) *adj.* depressed; miserable; cheerless. Also, dark and gloomy.

dismay (dis mā′) *v.* trouble greatly; make afraid.

disparagingly (dis par′ij ing lē) *adv.* in a belittling manner.

dispel (dis pel′) *v.* drive away; get rid of.

dispersed (dis pėrst′) *adj.* scattered in all directions. *v.* driven off in different directions; scattered.

disposition (dis′pə zish′ən) *n.* one's natural or usual way of acting and thinking; one's nature.

dissection (di sek′shən) *n.* act of cutting something apart in order to examine or study its structure.

dissolved (di zolvd′) *v.* broken up; ended.

distinguish (dis ting′gwish) *v.* tell apart; recognize as different; notice differences between things.

distinguished (dis ting′gwisht) *adj.* famous; well-known.

distorted (dis tôrt′əd) *adj.* changed and unnatural in appearance.

distracted (dis trakt′əd) *v.* and *adj.* greatly disturbed; bewildered; confused.

distraction (dis trak′shən) *n.* amusement.

diversion (də vėr′zhən) *n.* amusement; entertainment. Also, change of subject or direction of thought, conversation, etc.

diverted (də vėrt′əd) *v.* entertained; amused.

doleful (dōl′fəl) *adj.* sorrowful; mournful; dreary.

dominion (də min′yən) *n.* power or right of governing and controlling; rule; control. Also, territory under the control of one ruler or government.

drudgery (druj′ər ē) *n.* work that is hard, tiresome, or disagreeable.

dubious (dü′bē əs) *adj.* doubtful; uncertain.

dubiously (dü′bē əs lē) *adv.* doubtfully; uncertainly.

duplicity (dü′plis′ə tē) *n.* double-dealing; deceit.

dynasty dī′nə stē) *n.* a line of rulers of the same family.

ebony (eb′ə nē) *n.* a hard, durable black wood.

ecstatic (ek stat′ik) *adj.* joyful.

egotist (ē′gə tist) *n.* a vain, selfish person; a conceited person.

eliciting (i lis′it ing) *v.* drawing forth; bringing out.

eloquent (el′ə kwənt) *adj.* fluent; well-spoken.

embarked (em barkt′) *v.* boarded a ship to set out on a journey by sea.

eminence (em′ə nəns) *n.* renown; fame; high standing.

eminent (em′ə nənt) *adj.* outstanding; distinguished.

emphatically (em fat′ik lē) *adv.* forcefully; strongly; firmly.

encumbered (en kum′bərd) *adj.* and *v.* burdened; hindered; hampered.

engendering (en jen′dər ing) *v.* bringing into existence; producing.

enigmatically (en′ig mat′ə kə lē) *adv.* in a puzzling manner; bafflingly.

enlightening (en līt′n ing) *adj.* informative; instructive.

ensued (en süd′) *v.* followed; came after; resulted.

enticed (en tīst′) *v.* tempted; lured.

entreated (en trēt′əd) *v.* begged; implored; asked earnestly.

entreaty (en trē′tē) *n.* an earnest request; a prayer or an appeal.

envisage (en viz′ij) *v.* visualize; imagine; form a mental picture of.

eradicate (i rad′ə kāt) *v.* eliminate; destroy completely.

erroneous (ə rō′nē əs) *adj.* wrong; mistaken; incorrect.

escapade (es′kə pād) *n.* an adventure.

Pronunciation Key

hat, āge, fär; let, equal, term;
it, īce; hot, open, ôrder;
oil, out; cup, pùt, rüle;
ch, child; ng, long; sh, she;
th, thin; TH, then; zh, measure;
ə represents *a* in about, *e* in taken,
i in pencil, *o* in lemon, *u* in circus.

---

essential (ə sen′shəl) *adj.* very important; absolutely necessary.

esteemed (e stēmd′) *v.* highly regarded; greatly respected.

estimable (es′tə mə bəl) *adj.* being worthy of respect; deserving high regard; honorable.

eternal (i tėr′nl) *adj.* timeless; everlasting; always the same.

eternity (i tėr′nə tē) *n.* all time; a seemingly endless period of time.

ethereal (i thir′ē əl) *adj.* light; airy; delicate. Also, heavenly.

etiquette (et′ə ket) *n.* rules for conduct and behavior in particular situations.

evade (i vād′) *v.* escape; avoid; elude.

evocation (ev′ə kā′shən) *n.* a calling forth; a summoning.

exasperated (eg zas′pə rāt′əd) *adj.* extremely annoyed; very much irritated.

expedient (ek spē′dē ənt) *adj.* desirable or suitable under the circumstances; advisable; useful.

expiate (ek′spē āt) *v.* make amends for a wrong, sin, etc.; atone for.

expiated (ek′spē āt əd) *adj.* atoned for; compensated for.

expire (ek spīr′) *v.* die; come to an end.

explicitly (ek splis′it lē) *adv.* plainly; definitely; frankly.

exploit (ek′sploit) *n.* a daring deed; a brave act.

exterminate (ek stėr′mə nāt) *v.* destroy completely.

extorting (ek stôrt′ing) *v.* obtaining something (money, a promise) by threats, force, fraud, or illegal use of authority.

extract (ek strakt′) *v.* squeeze out; press out.

extradition (ek′strə dish′ən) *n.* surrender of a fugitive or prisoner by one state, nation, or authority to another for trial or punishment.

extravagant (ek strav′ə gənt) *adj.* beyond the bounds of reason; excessive.

exultation (eg′zul tā′shən) *n.* great rejoicing.

fallacious (fə lā'shəs) *adj.* disappointing; deceptive; misleading.

fallow (fal'ō) *adj.* untilled; unused.

fastidious (fa stid'ē əs) *adj.* particular; hard to please; dainty.

fatigued (fə tēgd') *adj.* weary; tired.

fatuous (fach'ü əss) *adj.* foolish; silly.

feigns (fānz) *v.* pretends (to be); makes oneself appear to be.

felicity (fə lis'ə tē) *n.* great happiness; bliss.

fervently (fėr'vənt lē) *adv.* warmly; earnestly; intensely.

fetch (fech) *v.* bring; go and get.

fettered (fet'ərd) *v.* chained.

fictitious (fik tish'əs) *adj.* imaginary; made-up; invented.

fidelity (fī del'ə tē) *n.* loyalty; faithfulness; devotion.

fidgeted (fig'it əd) *v.* played nervously with.

fiend (fēnd) *n.* a frightful monster; a devil; an evil spirit.

fissure (fish'ər) *n.* a long, narrow opening; a split; a crack.

flippant (flip'ənt) *adj.* taking serious things lightly.

flounces (flouns'əs) *n.* wide ruffles.

flourished (flėr'isht) *v.* waved in the air; brandished.

foliage (fō'lē ij) *n.* the leaves of trees.

forlorn (fôr lôrn') *adj.* friendless; forsaken; deserted.

formulated (fôr'myə lāt əd) *adj.* being reduced to fit a rule for doing something, especially as used by those who do not know the reason on which it is based.

forsaken (fôr sa'kən) *adj.* deserted; abandoned.

fragments (frag'mənts) *n.* parts or pieces of something broken off or disconnected.

fray (frā) *n.* a noisy quarrel; a brawl; a fight.

frenzy (fren'zē) *n.* fury; madness; condition of very great excitement.

frivolous (friv'ə ləs) *adj.* lacking in seriousness or sense; silly or foolish.

frugal (frü'gəl) *adj.* thrifty; economical; avoiding waste.

furled (fėrld) *adj.* rolled up; folded up.

furtive (fėr'tiv) *adj.* sly; stealthy; secret.

furtively (fėr'tiv lē) *adv.* secretly; stealthily.

futile (fyü'təl) *adj.* useless.

futility (fyü til'ə tē) *n.* uselessness; ineffectiveness.

genealogy (jē'nē al'ə jē) *n.* an account of the descent of a family from a common ancestor.

genially (jē'nyəl lē) *adv.* in a cheerful, friendly manner; jovially.

ghastly (gast'lē) *adj.* deathly pale; pale and ghost-like. Also, horrible; shocking.

glee (glē) *n.* merriment; joy; great delight.

glib (glib) *adj.* insincere; speaking too smoothly to be believed.

gorges (gôrjz) *b.* stuffs with food; eats greedily until full.

grandiose (gran'dē ōs) *adj.* imposing; impressive; showy or pompous.

grievous (grē'vəs) *adj.* severe; very painful; distressing.

grievously (grē'vəs lē) *adv.* painfully; severely.

grimace (grim'is) *n.* a twisting of the face. *v.* make a funny or an ugly face.

grisly (griz'lē) *adj.* frightful; horrible; ghastly; dreadful.

grope (grōp) *v.* search blindly and uncertainly. Also, look for blindly, feeling one's way with the hands.

grossly (grōs'lē) *adv.* glaringly; clearly; plainly; hugely.

grovelling (gruv'əl ing) *v.* humbling oneself.

gruesome (grü'səm) *adj.* horrible; causing fear and horror.

guile (gīl) *n.* deception; slyness.

haggard (hag'ərd) *adj.* looking worn from fatigue, worry, etc.; careworn; gaunt.

hallowed (hal'ōd) *v.* and *adj.* honored as holy or sacred.

harass (har'əs) *v.* worry; trouble; annoy.

harbinger (här'bən jər) *n.* one that goes ahead to announce another's coming.

haughtiness (hô'tē nəs) *n.* being too proud and scornful of others; scorn and indifference.

haven (hā'vən) *n.* harbor or port; place of shelter or safety.

havoc (hav'ək) *n.* destruction; ruin.

hazard (haz'ərd) *n.* chance of harm; risk; danger.

hazardous (haz'ər dəs) *adj.* full of risk; dangerous; perilous.

heir (er) *n.* a person who has the right to receive someone's property or title after that one dies.

hermitage (hėr'mə tij) *n.* a solitary or secluded dwelling place, often of a hermit or recluse.

heroic (hi rō′ik) *adj.* brave, great, and noble; valiant.

hideous (hid′ē əs) *adj.* very ugly; horrible; frightful.

hoisted (hoist′əd) *v.* lifted up; raised.

hostile (hos′tl) *adj.* opposed; unfriendly; unfavorable; threatening.

hypocrisy (hi pok′rə sē) *n.* a pretending to be what one is not; pretense; an outward show of goodness.

ignominy (ig′nə min′ē) *n.* public shame and disgrace; humiliation; dishonor.

ignominiously (ig′nə min′ē əs lē) *adv.* humiliatingly; shamefully; disgracefully.

illiterate (i lit′ər it) *adj.* being unable to read or write.

illustrious (i lus′trē əs) *adj.* very famous; outstanding; celebrated.

immensity (i men′sə tē) *n.* vastness; very great extent.

imminent (im′ə nənt) *adj.* likely to happen soon; about to happen.

immortal (i môr′tl) *adj.* divine; godlike.

immortality (im′ôr tal′ə tē) *n.* life without death; living forever.

impediments (im ped′ə mənts) *n.* hindrances; obstructions.

impenetrable (im pen′ə trə bəl) *adj.* dense; impossible to explain or understand.

imperceptible (im′pər sep′tə bəl) *adj.* cannot be seen; invisible; very slight.

imperialism (im pir′ē ə liz′əm) *n.* policy of extending the rule or authority of one country over other countries and colonies.

impertinence (im pėrt′n əns) *n.* impudence; rudeness.

impertinent (im pėrt′n ənt) *adj.* rude and bold; disrespectful.

imperturbability (im′pər tėr′bə bil′ə tē) *n.* being not easily excited or disturbed.

impetuous (im pech′ü əs) *adj.* hasty; eager; headlong.

implacable (im plā′kə bəl) *adj.* unyielding; unforgiving; refusing to be reconciled.

implicated (im′plə kāt əd) *v.* involved; mixed up in.

implicit (im plis′it) *adj.* meant, but not clearly expressed or distinctly stated; implied.

Pronunciation Key

hat, āge, fär; let, ēqual, term;
it, īce; hot, open ôrder;
oil, out; cup, pùt, rüle;
ch, child; ng, long; sh, she;
th, thin; ŦH, then; zh, measure;
ə represents *a* in about, *e* in taken,
i in pencil, *o* in lemon, *u* in circus.

importunate (im pôr′chə nit) *adj.* asking repeatedly; annoyingly persistent; urgent.

imposter (im pos′tər) *n.* a person pretending to be someone else; a deceiver.

impregnable (im preg′nə bəl) *adj.* able to resist attack; not to be conquered.

improvisation (im′prov ə zā′shən) *n.* something provided offhand or done without being planned or on the spur of the moment.

impudence (im′pyə dəns) *n.* shameless boldness; great rudeness.

inarticulately (in′är tik′yə lit lē) *adv.* in an indistinct manner.

inaugurate (in ô′gyə rāt′) *v.* begin; do for the first time.

incapacity (in′kə pas′ə tē) *n.* lack of ability; inability.

incensed (in senst′) *v.* made very angry; filled with rage.

incessant (in ses′nt) *adj.* never stopping; continual; repeatedly, without interruption; unceasing.

inclination (in′klə nā′shən) *n.* a liking for something; tendency; preference.

incongruity (in′kən grü′ə tē) *n.* a being out of place; inappropriateness.

incredible (in kred′ə bəl) *adj.* hard to believe; surprising.

incredulous (in krej′ə ləs) *adj.* unwilling to believe; doubting; skeptical.

incredulously (in′ krej′ə ləs lē) *adv.* unbelievingly; doubtingly; skeptically.

indictment (in dīt′mənt) *n.* a formal written accusation of a crime or wrongdoing. Also, any accusation of wrongdoing.

indistinct (in′dis tingkt′) *adj.* not clear; blurred.

inevitable (in ev′ə tə bəl) *adj.* sure to happen; not to be avoided.

inexplicable (in′ik splik′ə bəl) *adj.* cannot be explained; mysterious.

infamous (in'fə məs) *adj.* shamefully bad; having a very bad reputation; disgraceful.

infatuated (in fach'ü ā'tid) *adj.* filled wih foolish liking or love.

infernal (in fėr'nl) *adj.* fiendish; outrageous. Also, of or having to do with hell; hellish; diabolical.

infirmity (in fėr'mə tē) *n.* sickness; illness.

ingenious (in jē'nyəs) *adj.* gifted; clever; quick and skillful at inventing and planning.

inherited (in her'it əd) *v.* received by another's death.

iniquity (in ik'wə tē) *n.* wickedness; sin.

innovation (in'ə vā'shən) *n.* a change in the established way of doing things, usually by bringing in new things.

inquisitive (in kwiz'ə tiv) *adj.* asking many questions; prying.

insidious (in sid'ē əs) *adj.* secretly harmful; working secretly or subtly.

insipid (in sip'id) *adj.* tasteless; dull, colorless, or weak.

insolence (in'sə ləns) *n.* insulting behavior or speech; rudeness.

insolent (in'sə lənt) *adj.* impudent; insulting; intentionally rude.

instantaneously (in'stən tā'nē əs lē) *adv.* at the same instant.

instinct (in'stingkt) *n.* one's inborn knowledge; the natural tendency to act or believe in a certain way.

integrity (in teg'rə tē) *n.* uprightness; reliability; honesty.

interim (in'tər im) *n.* the time between. *adj.* for the meantime; temporary.

interred (in tėrd') *v.* and *adj.* buried. Also, put into a grave.

interrogation (in ter'ə gā'shən) *n.* a questioning.

intervenes (in'tər vēnz') *v.* comes between; interferes.

intolerable (in tol'ər ə bəl) *adj.* too much to be endured; unbearable.

intricate (in'trə kit) *adj.* puzzling, entangled, or complicated.

intrigue (in' trēg') *n.* secret scheming; underhand planning to accomplish some purpose; plotting.

intrusion (in trü'zhən) *n.* a coming unasked and unwanted.

intuitive (in tü'ə tiv) *adj.* understanding by personal insight, rather than by reason.

inventory (in'vən tôr'ē) *n.* a list of goods or possessions, with their estimated values.

invested (in vest'əd) *v.* installed in office with a ceremony.

invincible (in vin'sə bəl) *adj.* unconquerable; unbeatable; impossible to overcome.

ironically (ī ron'ə kə lē) *adv.* sarcastically; with words that say one thing but mean another.

irrationally (i rash'ən lē) *adv.* unreasonably; absurdly.

irremediable (ir'i mē'dē ə bəl) *adj.* that cannot be put right; being beyond help.

irresistible (ir'i zis'tə bəl) *adj.* too great to be withstood; overwhelming.

irresolutely (i rez'ə lüt lē) *adv.* hesitatingly; uncertainly; undecidedly.

irritably (ir'ə tə blē) *adv.* impatiently; peevishly; with annoyance.

jeopardy (jep'ər dē) *n.* risk; danger; peril.

jocund (jok'ənd) *adj.* cheerful; merry.

jostling (jos'ling) *v.* shoving, pushing, and crowding against.

jurisdiction (jür'is dik'shən) *n.* legal authority of an official. Also, the area in which an official has authority.

kin (kin) *n.* a person's family or relatives.

kindle (kin'dl) *v.* set on fire.

knell (nel) *n.* a warning sign of death, failure, etc. Also, the sound of a funeral bell.

labyrinth (lab'ə rinth') *n.* a muddle of winding passages; a maze.

lair (ler) *n.* den or resting place of a wild animal. Also, a secret or secluded retreat.

lament (lə ment') *v.* bewail; mourn for; regret.

lamenting (lə ment'ing) *v.* mourning; expressing grief for.

languished (lang'gwisht) *adj.* soft and tender. Also, weakened; wearied; drooping.

laudable (lô'də bəl) *adj.* worthy of praise.

levity (lev'ə tē) *n.* lack of proper seriousness or earnestness.

loath (lōth) *adj.* unwilling or reluctant.

loathsome (lōTH'səm) *adj.* making one feel sick; disgusting; repulsive.

loitering (loi'tər ing) *v.* lingering idly; moving slowly and aimlessly.

loutish (lou'tish) *adj.* awkward and stupid; boorish; rude.

lucid (lü'sid) *adj.* clear; straightforward; easy to follow or understand.

ludicrous (lü′də krəs) *adj.* ridiculous; amusingly absurd.

lugubrious (lü gü′brē əs) *adj.* too sad; overly mournful; gloomy.

lustrous (lus′trəs) *adj.* bright; shining; brilliant.

madrigals (mad′rə gəlz) *n.* songs, especially love songs.

magistrates (maj′ə strāts) *n.* government officials.

majesty (maj′ə stē) *n.* stately appearance; grandeur; great dignity.

malevolence (mə lev′ə ləns) *n.* the wish that evil will happen to others; ill will; spite.

malice (mal′is) *n.* active ill will; spite.

malicious (mə lish′əs) *adj.* spiteful; showing active ill will; wishing to hurt or make suffer.

malingerers (mə ling′gər ərz) *n.* persons who pretend to be sick, injured, etc., in order to escape work; shirkers.

mangled (mang′gəld) *adj.* ruined; torn to pieces.

marquee (mär kē′) *n.* a large tent, often put up for an outdoor entertainment or party.

meandering (mē an′dər ing) *v.* following a winding course.

melancholy (mel′ən kol′ē) *adj.* depressed in spirits; sad; gloomy. *n.* sadness; unhappiness; gloominess; dejection.

mellow (mel′ō) *adj.* ripe and full-flavored.

memorable (mem′ər ə bəl) *adj.* not to be forgotten; noteworthy; worth remembering.

meticulous (mə tik′yə ləs) *adj.* overcareful about small details.

minion (min′yən) *n.* servant or follower willing to do whatever is ordered.

mischief (mis′chif) *n.* conduct that causes harm or trouble.

miscreants (mis′krē ənts) *n.* wicked persons; villains; rascals; scoundrels.

missives (mis′ivz) *n.* written messages; dispatches; letters.

mitigate (mit′ə gāt) *v.* ease; make seem less harsh; soften.

moderate (mod′ə rāt) *v.* keep from becoming too violent; lesson.

modified (mod′ə fīd) *v.* changed somewhat; altered to fit a particular situation.

mongrel (mung′grəl) *n.* an animal of mixed breed, especially a dog.

monotonous (mə not′n əs) *adj.* continuing in the same tone or pitch; not varying; without change.

Pronunciation Key

hat, āge, fär: let. equal. term;
it, īce; hot, open, ôrder;
oil, out; cup, pút, rüle;
ch, child; ng, long; sh, she;
th, thin; ŦH, then; zh, measure;
ə represents *a* in about, *e* in taken,
i in pencil, *o* in lemon, *u* in circus.

monstrous (mon′strəs) *adj.* of extremely large size; huge; enormous. Also, outrageously wrong or absurd; shocking; horrible; dreadful.

mood (müd) *n.* state of mind or feeling; one's frame of mind.

moody (mü′dē) *adj.* sunk in sadness; gloomy.

moor (mur) *n.* an open land, such as a meadow or heath with few trees.

mortality (môr tal′ə tē) *n.* condition of being sure to die sometime; the human condition.

mournful (môrn′fəl) *adj.* full of grief; sad; sorrowful.

mundane (mun′dān) *adj.* worldly; earthly.

municipal (myü nis′ə pəl) *adj.* being owned or run by a city, town, or other district government.

mused (myüzd) *v.* pondered completely absorbed in thought; meditated.

mutinously (myüt′n əs lē) *adv.* rebelliously.

mutual (myü′chü əl) *adj.* shared; felt or done in the same way by two persons for or toward each other.

nauseous (nô′shəs) *adj.* disgusting; loathsome.

nimbly (nim′blē) *adv.* quickly and lightly.

noble (nō′bəl) *adj.* high and great in character; worthy.

nocturnal (nok tėr′nl) *adj.* of the night; in the night.

nonchalance (non′shə ləns) *n.* cool unconcern; indifference.

noncommittal (non′kə mit′l) *adj.* not becoming involved; not saying yes or no.

obdurate (ob′dər it) *adj.* stubborn or unyielding; obstinate.

obligation (ob′lə gā′shən) *n.* duty on account of kindness received; responsibility.

obliterated (ə blit′ə rāt′əd) *v.* destroyed; blotted out; removed all traces of.

obscure (əb skyur′) *adj.* not well known; attracting no attention; hidden.

obstinancy (ob'stə nə sē) *n.* stubborness; mulishness.

obtuse (əb tüs') *adj.* slow in understanding; dull; slow-witted.

occurrences (ə kėr'əns əs) *n.* events; happenings; incidents.

odious (ō'dē əs) *adj.* very displeasing; hateful; nasty; loathsome.

officious (ə fish'əs) *adj.* minding other people's business; meddlesome; offering unwanted help.

officiously (ə fish'əs lē) *adv.* in a meddlesome, unwanted way; interferingly.

omens (ō'mənz) *n.* signs foretelling what is to happen.

ominous (om'ə nəs) *adj.* threatening; unfavorable.

opiate (ō'pē it) *n.* any medicine that soothes or sends to sleep.

oppress (ə pres') *v.* keep down unjustly or cruelly.

oppression (ə presh'ən) *n.* cruel or unjust treatment; tyranny.

optimistic (op'tə mis'tik) *adj.* hoping for the best; looking on the bright side of things.

pacify (pas'ə fī) *v.* calm; quiet down; soothe.

palfrey (pôl'frē) *n.* a gentle riding horse, especially one used by ladies.

pallor (pal'ər) *n.* paleness; lack of normal color.

palpable (pal'pə bəl) *adj.* readily seen or heard and recognized; obvious; actual; real.

paltry (pôl'trē) *adj.* almost worthless; trifling.

panorama (pan'ə ram'ə) *n.* a wide, unbroken view of a surrounding region.

parasol (par'ə sôl) *n.* a light umbrella used as a protection from the sun.

parley (pär'lē) *n.* a conference or informal talk.

paroxysm (par'ək siz'em) *n.* a sudden, severe attack.

patronage (pā'trə nij) *n.* political jobs or favors; support or encouragement.

patronizingly (pā'trə nīz'ing le) *adv.* a haughty, condescending manner.

pealed (pēld) *v.* rang; resounded; clanged.

peering (pir'ing) *v.* looking at intently.

peers (pirz) *n.* persons of the same rank, ability, etc.; equals.

penance (pen'əns) *n.* punishment suffered in order to gain forgiveness.

pensive (pen'siv) *adj.* thoughtful in a serious or sad way.

perdition (pər dish'ən) *n.* damnation; extreme misery and ruin.

peremptorily (pə remp'tər ē lē) *adv.* with firmness; decisively.

perforce (pər fôrs') *adv.* by necessity; necessarily.

peril (per'əl) *n.* danger; risk; chance of harm or loss.

pernicious (pər nish'əs) *adj.* destructive; very injurious. Also, fatal; deadly.

perpetual (pər pech'ü əl) *adj.* lasting forever; unending; never ceasing; continuous.

perpetuated (pər pech'ü āt əd) *v.* preserved; maintained; protected.

perplex (pər' pleks') *v.* puzzle; bewilder.

perplexity (pər plek'sə tē) *n.* puzzlement; confusion; bewilderment.

perseverance (pėr'sə vir'əns) *n.* steadfastness; a sticking to a purpose or aim.

perspective (pər spek'tiv) *n.* a mental view or outlook; a view of facts in which they are in correct relationship.

perturbation (pėr'tər bā'shən) *n.* worry; anxiety; a being greatly troubled.

perusal (pə rü'zəl) *n.* a careful reading; studying.

pervades (pər vādz') *v.* spreads throughout; fills or saturates.

perversely (pər vėrs'lē) *adv.* contrarily; naughtily.

perversity (pər vėr'sə tē) *n.* contrariness; waywardness.

petulantly (pech'ə lənt le) *adv.* peevishly; impatiently.

phenomenon (fə nom'ə non) *n.* a rare event or circumstance; a marvel; an astonishing thing.

philosophy (fə los'ə fē) *n.* a set of rules by which a person lives; an explanation or theory of the universe.

phlegmatically (fleg mat'ik lē) *adv.* cooly; calmly.

piety (pī'ə tē) *n.* devotion to religion.

pilgrimage (pil'grə mij) *n.* a long journey. Also, a journey to some sacred place as an act of religious devotion.

plague (plāg) *v.* vex; bother; annoy. *n.* an epidemic disease that spreads rapidly and causes many deaths, such as bubonic plague.

plagues (plāgz) *n.* things that torment, annoy, trouble, or are disagreeable.

plaintive (plān'tiv) *adj.* sad; mournful.

plight (plīt) *n.* a condition or situation, usually bad; a predicament; being in a fix.

plucky (pluk'ē) *adj.* having or showing courage.

plunder (plun'dər) *v.* rob by force.

plundering (plun'dər ing) *adj.* robbing by force.

ply (plī) *v.* work away at; keep busy at.

pompous (pom'pəs) *adj.* self-important; trying to seem magnificent and very important.

populous (pop'yə ləs) *adj.* full of people; having many people per square mile.

posterity (po ster'ə tē) *n.* future generations.

potency (pōt'n sē) *n.* power; strength.

potent (pōt'nt) *adj.* having great power; powerful; strong.

prating (prāt'ing) *n.* empty or foolish talk.

precedents (pres'ə dənts) *n.* judicial decisions that serve as patterns in future similar situations. Also, actions that serve as examples or reasons for later actions.

precept (prē'sept) *n.* rule of action or behavior; an instruction; a maxim.

precious (presh'əs) *adj.* valuable; costly.

precise (pri sīs') *adj.* exact; very definite or correct.

predicament (pri dik'ə mənt) *n.* an unpleasant, difficult, or dangerous situation.

predominant (pri dom'ə nənt) *adj.* chief; supreme; most noticeable.

predominate (pri dom'ə nāt) *v.* to be the master; to control.

prejudice (prej'ə dis) *n.* an opinion, attitude, or tendency formed unfairly or unjustly; bias.

prelate (prel'it) *n.* clergyman of high rank; a prince of the church.

preoccupied (prē ok'yə pīd) *adj.* absorbed; engrossed.

preposterous (pri pos'tər əs) *adj.* absurd; ridiculous; senseless.

prestige (pre stēzh') *n.* reputation, influence, or distinction.

presumed (pri zümd') *v.* took for granted without being proved; supposed.

presumption (pri zump'shən) *n.* forwardness; impudence. Also, supposition.

presumptuous (pri zump'chü əs) *adj.* too bold; forward; acting without permission or right.

pretentious (pri ten'shəs) *adj.* doing things for show or to make a fine appearance; showy.

pretext (prē'tekst) *n.* a misleading excuse; a false reason.

prevail (pri vāl') *v.* win the victory; succeed; overcome.

prevalence (prev'ə ləns) *n.* widespread occurrence.

prevarication (pri var'ə kā'shən) *n.* a falsehood; a lie.

privilege (priv'ə lij) *n.* one's own right. Also, a special right or advantage.

Pronunciation Key

hat, āge, fär; let, equal, term;
it, īce; hot, open, ôrder;
oil, out; cup, pùt, rüle;
ch, child; ng, long; sh, she;
th, thin; ŦH, then; zh, measure;
ə represents *a* in about, *e* in taken,
i in pencil, *o* in lemon, *u* in circus.

procrastinating (prō kras'tə nāt ing) *v.* putting things off until later, especially repeatedly; delaying; postponing.

prodigious (prə dij'əs) *adj.* very great; huge; vast; enormous. Also, marvelous; wonderful.

profession (prə fesh'ən) *n.* any occupation requiring special education, such as the law. Also, an open declaration.

profuse (prə fyüs') *adj.* very abundant; lavish; extravagant.

prominent (prom'ə nənt) *adj.* standing out; projecting.

promontory (prom'ən tôr'ē) *n.* a high point of land extending from the coast into the water.

prophecy (prof'ə sē) *n.* a forecast; a prediction; thing told about the future. *v.* foretell; predict.

prophetic (prə fet'ik) *adj.* giving warning of what is to happen; foretelling.

prosaic (prō zā'ik) *adj.* matter-of-fact; ordinary; not exciting.

provocation (prov'ə kā'shən) *n.* something that stirs up or vexes; an act of stirring up or giving cause for anger.

provoked (prə vōkt') *v.* made angry; vexed; stirred up.

prudence (prüd'ns) *n.* good judgment; caution; foresight.

prudent (prüd'nt) *adj.* sensible; planning carefully ahead of time; having good judgment.

pugnacious (pug nā'shəs) *adj.* quarrelsome; appearing ready to quarrel or fight.

purged (pėrjd) *v.* got rid of.

pursuit (pər süt') *n.* a chase; a hunt.

pyre (pīr) *n.* a pile of wood for burning a dead body.

quaint (kwānt) *adj.* strange or odd; unusual.

qualms (kwämz) *n.* feelings of uneasiness; misgivings; doubts.

quell (kwel) *v.* overcome; put an end to.

quench (kwench) *v.* drown out; put out; extinguish; put an end to; stop.

queries (kwir′ēz) *n.* questions; inquiries.

quest (kwest) *n.* a search or hunt.

quizzically (kwiz′ə klē) *adv.* in a puzzled, doubtful manner.

rapturously (rap′chər əs lē) *adv.* joyfully; blissfully.

rebuke (ri byük′) *n.* expression of disapproval; a scolding. *v.* express disapproval of; reprove.

reception (ri sep′shən) *n.* welcome; acceptance.

recipient (ri sip′ē ənt) *n.* a person who receives or accepts something.

recompensed (rek′əm penst) *v.* paid back; rewarded.

reconcile (rek′ən sīl) *v.* make agree; bring into harmony. Also, to make friends again.

refutation (ref′yə tā′shən) *n.* proof that something is wrong.

reign (rān) *n.* period of power of a ruler.

reiterated (rē it′ə rāt′əd) *v.* repeated again and again.

relinquished (ri ling′kwisht) *v.* gave up; abandoned; forsook.

relished (rel′isht) *v.* enjoyed; liked.

reluctance (ri luk′təns) *n.* unwillingness.

reluctantly (ri luk′tənt lē) *adv.* unwillingly.

reminiscence (rem′ə nis′ns) *n.* a recalling past persons, events, etc.

remnant (rem′nənt) *n.* remainder; what is left.

remonstrated (ri mon′strāt əd) *v.* protested; objected.

remorsefully (ri môrs′fə lē) *adv.* regretfully; sorrowfully.

remorseless (ri môrs′lis) *adj.* merciless; pitiless.

reparation (rep′ə rā′shən) *n.* payment.

repentance (ri pen′təns) *n.* sorrow for having done wrong; regret.

repentant (ri pen′tənt) *adj.* feeling regret; sorry for wrongdoing.

replica (rep′lə kə) *n.* an exact copy or duplicate.

reprimanded (rep′rə mand əd) *v.* scolded; blamed.

reprisal (ri prī′zəl) *n.* an act of revenge; an injury done in return for an injury.

reprove (ri prüv′) *v.* find fault with; blame; disapprove of.

repulsiveness (ri pul′siv nəs) *n.* ugliness; being very disagreeable.

reputation (rep′yə tā′shən) *n.* one's good name; what people think and say the character of a person is; common or general estimate of character or quality.

resilence (ri zil′ē əns) *n.* power to overcome difficulty or trouble.

resolute (rez′ə lüt) *adj.* steadfast; determined; firm.

resolve (ri zolv′) *v.* make up one's mind; determine; decide.

resolving (ri zolv′ing) *v.* deciding; making up one's mind.

retort (ri tôrt′) *n.* a sharp or witty reply.

retribution (ret′rə byü′shən) *n.* a just punishment; a reckoning.

revelry (rev′əl rē) *n.* boisterous merriment or festivity.

reverberated (ri vėr′bə rāt′əd) *v.* echoed back; resounded.

reverie (rev′ər ē) *n.* a daydream; dreamy thoughts; condition of being lost in dreamy thoughts.

revoke (ri vōk′) *v.* take back; withdraw.

revolted (ri vōlt′əd) *adj.* disgusted; repelled; sickened.

rhetoric (ret′ər ik) *n.* art of using words effectively in speaking and writing.

rogues (rōgz) *n.* scoundrels; rascals.

rue (rü) *v.* be sorry for; regret. *n.* sorrow; regret.

ruminating (rü′mə nāt ing) *v.* pondering; reflecting; reconsidering.

rummaging (rum′ij ing) *v.* searching by tumbling things about; ransacking.

sagacity (sə gas′ə tē) *n.* keen, sound judgment; intelligence; mental acuteness.

sallow (sal′ō) *adj.* having a sickly, yellowish or brownish-yellow color.

sarcasm (sär′kaz′əm) *n.* a sneering or cutting remark; making fun of a person to hurt his feelings.

sardonically (sär don′ik lē) *adv.* in a bitterly sarcastic, scornful, or mocking manner.

satire (sat′īr) *n.* a taunting speech or writing.

scandalized (skan′dl īzd) *adj.* being offended or shocked by something thought to be wrong or improper.

scepter (sep′tər) *n.* the rod or staff carried by a ruler as a symbol of royal power or authority.

scoffer (skof′ər) *n.* a person who makes fun to show disbelief.

scruples (skrü′pəlz) *n.* feelings of doubt about what one ought to do.

scurrying (skėr′ē ing) *v.* running quickly; hurrying.

seclusion (si klü′zhən) *n.* isolation; privacy.

secular (sek′yə lər) *adj.* not religious; worldly.

sedately (si dāt′lē) *adv.* in a dignified manner.

senile (sē′nīl) *adj.* showing the mental and physical deterioration often characteristic of old age.

senility (sə nil′ə tē) *n.* old age and its infirmities.

sequestered (si kwes′tərd) *adj.* secluded; being removed from public view.

serene (sə rēn′) *adj.* peaceful; calm; untroubled.

servile (sėr′vəl) *adj.* slavish; abject.

servility (sėr′vil′ə tē) *n.* complete submission or obedience.

shambled (sham′bəld) *v.* shuffled; walked awkwardly or unsteadily.

shambles (sham′əlz) *n.* bloody mess.

sinister (sin′ə stər) *adj.* bad; evil; harmful; threatening; disastrous.

slanders (slan′dərz) *v.* talks falsely about with the intent to harm a person's reputation.

smack (smak) *v.* has a taste, trace, or touch (of something).

smirking (smėrk′ing) *v.* smiling in an affected, silly, or self-satisfied way; simpering.

sojourn (sō′jėrn) *v.* stay for a time; live in for a short time.

solace (sol′is) *n.* comfort or relief.

solemn (sol′əm) *adj.* done with form and ceremony.

solicitous (sə lis′ə təs) *adj.* concerned; anxious; showing care or concern.

solicitude (sə lis′ə tüd) *n.* anxious care; anxiety; concern.

sordid (sôr′did) *adj.* dirty; filthy.

spacious (spā′shəs) *adj.* vast; extensive; large.

spectacle (spek′tə kəl) *n.* a public show or display.

spectre (spek′tər) *n.* phantom or ghost, especially one of a terrifying nature or appearance.

spindly (spind′lē) *adj.* very long and slender.

spit (spit) *n.* a narrow point of land running into the water.

spurning (spėrn′ing) *v.* refusing with scorn.

squabbles (skwob′əlz) *n.* petty, noisy quarrels; bickerings.

squalid (skwol′id) *adj.* dirty; filthy; disgusting.

squeamish (skwē′mish) *adj.* too particular; too scrupulous.

stalker (stôk′ər) *n.* person who pursues without being seen or heard; a hunter.

startling (stärt′ling) *adj.* causing a shock of surprise; frightening.

stoicism (stō′ə siz′əm) *n.* patient endurance.

stolidly (stol′id lē) *adv.* unemotionally; impassively.

Pronunciation Key

hat, āge, fär; let, equal, term;
it, īce; hot, open, ôrder;
oil, out; cup, pût, rüle;
ch, child; ng, long; sh, she;
th, thin; ŦH, then; zh, measure;
ə represents *a* in about, *e* in taken,
i in pencil, *o* in lemon, *u* in circus.

strategems (strat′ə jəmz) *n.* plans or schemes to trick or mislead others; trickery; deceptions.

sublime (sə blīm′) *adj.* noble; grand; exalted; glorious.

successive (sək ses′iv) *adj.* coming one after the other; in turn; following in order.

sullen (sul′ən) *adj.* silent because of bad humor or anger; unforgiving; sulky.

summarily (sə mer′ə lē) *adv.* quickly; without delay.

sundry (sun′drē) *adj.* different; various; several.

superciliously (sü′pər sil′ē əs lē) *adv.* in a coldly scornful manner; haughtily.

surfeited (sėr′fit əd) *adj.* having eaten or drunk to excess; gluttonous.

surly (sėr′lē) *adj.* rude; gruff; Also, bad-tempered and unfriendly.

surmise (sər mīz′) *n.* formation of an idea with little or no evidence; a guess.

susceptible (sə sep′tə bəl) *adj.* easily influenced by feelings and emotions.

swoon (swün) *n.* a faint.

symbol (sim′bəl) *n.* something that stands for or represents an idea, quality, condition, or other abstraction.

symmetry (sim′ə trē) *n.* balance; perfection; harmony.

taboo (tə bü′) *n.* a prohibition; a ban; something that is forbidden.

tantrum (tan′trəm) *n.* a fit of bad temper or ill humor.

tarrying (tar′ē ing) *n.* a delay; a hesitating; a being hesitant to act.

taut (tôt) *adj.* stretched painfully tight. Also being strained to the breaking point; tense.

tedious (tē′dē əs) *adj.* long and tiring; boring; wearisome.

tempestuous (tem pes′chü əs) *adj.* stormy; violent.

tenants (ten′ənts) *n.* persons who rent property or land to use.

tendril (ten′drəl) *n.* a threadlike part of a plant that attaches itself to something and helps support the plant; a shoot by which a climbing plant grips a support.

terrestrial (tə res′trē əl) *adj.* concerned with the earth; earthly; not of the heavens.

terrestrials (tə res′trē əlz) *n.* earthly beings; earthbound creatures.

testily (tes′tə lē) *adv.* impatiently; irritatedly; petulantly.

tidings (tī′dingz) *n.* news; information.

tolls (tōlz) *v.* rings a bell slowly to announce a death.

tranquil (trang′kwəl) *adj.* untroubled; calm; peaceful; quiet.

transform (tran sfôrm′) *v.* change completely.

traverses (trav′ərs əs) *v.* passes across, over, or through; crosses from side to side.

treacherous (trech′ər əs) *adj.* not to be trusted; disloyal; not faithful; traitorous.

treachery (trech′ər ē) *n.* betrayal of a trust; great disloyalty.

treble (treb′əl) *n.* a high-pitched sound or note.

tremor (trem′ər) *n.* a shaking or vibrating movement, such as made by an earthquake.

tremulous (trem′yə ləs) *adj.* trembling; quivering; wavering.

trespassed (tres′past) *v.* went on someone's property without permission.

tribulation (trib′yə lā′shən) *n.* great trouble; severe trial; suffering; distress.

trinity (trin′ə tē) *n.* a group of three.

triumph (trī′umf) *n.* victory; a great success.

truckling (truk′ling) *adj.* submitting tamely; acting in a subservient manner.

tumult (tü′mult) *n.* noise and uproar; confusion or excitement.

turmoil (tėr′moil) *n.* state of agitation or commotion; uproar; disturbance.

tyranny (tir′ə nē) *n.* cruel or unjust use of power; oppression.

unanimously (yü nan′ə məs lē) *adv.* in complete agreement; without disagreement.

uncanny (un kan′ē) *adj.* strange and mysterious; weird.

uncongenial (un′kən jē′nyəl) *adj.* disagreeable; unpleasant.

uncouth (un küth′) *adj.* clumsy; awkward; crude.

unique (yü nēk′) *adj.* having no like or equal; rare; remarkable.

unkempt (un kempt′) *adj.* not properly cared for; neglected; untidy.

usurper (yü zėrp′ər) *n.* one who seizes and holds power, position, authority, etc., by force or without right.

utter (ut′ər) *v.* speak; make known; express.

vague (vāg) *adj.* not clear in meaning; uncertain; obscure; not definitely or precisely expressed.

vale (vāl) *n.* a small valley; a dale.

valiant (val′yənt) *adj.* brave; courageous; fearless.

valiantly (val′yənt le) *adv.* courageously; bravely; fearlessly.

validity (və lid′ə tē) *n.* truth or soundness; genuineness.

valor (val′ər) *n.* bravery; courage.

vanquished (vang′kwisht) *v.* conquered, defeated, or overcame in battle or conflict.

variegated (ver′ē ə gā′tid) *adj.* varied in appearance; marked with different colors.

vehemence (vē′ə məns) *n.* strong feeling; forcefulness; violence.

veneer (və nir′) *n.* surface appearance or show.

venerable (ven′ər ə bəl) *adj.* old, and worthy of esteem and honor.

vengeance (ven′jəns) *n.* punishment in return for a wrong; revenge.

venom (ven′əm) *n.* poison. Also, great ill will and hatred.

venomous (ven′ə məs) *adj.* poisonous.

verily (ver′ə lē) *adv.* truly; really.

verity (ver′ə tē) *n.* truth; fact.

vestige (ves′tij) *n.* a small part left; a trace; the faintest mark.

vexation (vek sā′shən) *n.* anger; irritation; a being annoyed.

vexed (vekst) *v.* troubled; worried; annoyed; angered. *adj.* much annoyed; irritated.

vicious (vish′əs) *adj.* evil; wicked.

victuals (vit′lz) *n.* food.

vigilance (vij′ə ləns) *n.* watchfulness; alertness.

vindication (vin′də kā′shən) *n.* defense; justification.

vindictive (vin dik′tiv) *adj.* feeling a strong tendency toward revenge; revengeful; spiteful.

visage (viz′ij) *n.* the face or countenance.

vivacious (vī vā′shəs) *adj.* lively; sprightly; animated.

wan (won) *adj.* lacking natural or normal color; pale.

waning (wān'ing) *v.* losing size; becoming gradually smaller or less.

wary (wer'ē) *adj.* on one's guard against danger, deception, etc.; cautious or careful

wavering (wā'vər ing) *adj.* hesitating; uncertain or undecided.

weird (wird) *adj.* unearthly or mysterious.

weltered (wel'tərd) *v.* tossed about.

whimsical (hwim'zə kəl) *adj.* odd; fanciful; capricious.

wily (wī'lē) *adj.* using subtle tricks to deceive; crafty; cunning; sly.

wincing (wins'ing) *adj.* drawing back suddenly; flinching.

winnowing (win'ō ing) *adj.* blowing; driving; gusty.

wit (wit) *n.* intelligence, good sense, etc.

woe (wō) *n.* misery; great grief, trouble, or distress.

wretch (rech) n. a base, worthless person. Also a miserable, unhappy person.

Pronunciation Key

hat, āge, fär; let, equal, term;
it, īce; hot, open ôrder;
oil, out; cup, pùt, rüle;
ch, child; ng, long; sh, she;
th, thin; ŦH, then; zh, measure;
ə represents *a* in about, *e* in taken,
i in pencil, *o* in lemon, *u* in circus.

wretched (rech'id) *adj.* very unfortunate or unhappy; sad; miserable. Also, very bad.

writhing (rīŦH'ing) *adj.* twisting and turning about in pain.

wry (rī) *adj.* ironical; twisted to indicate irony, sarcasm, etc.

zealous (zel'əs) *adj.* eager; enthusiastic; earnest.

FINE ART INDEX

FINE ART SOURCES

PHOTO CREDITS

LITERARY TYPES INDEX

SKILLS INDEX

Language and Vocabulary

Comprehension

Critical/Literary

Composition

The following activities appear in the Composition and the Composition workshop sections in the text. In addition, the For Interpretation and the For Appreciation sections of the text (not listed below) can often be the source of still more composition assignments.

Writing about a moment of sudden inspiration or insight 567

Writing an expository paper on a given aspect of "The Rime of the Ancient Mariner" 597

Writing an account of a person, using three separate incidents 622

Writing an essay about snobbery, using anecdotes 628

Analyzing Tennyson's poetic approach to a specified subject 662

Comparing and contrasting "Prospice" and "Crossing the Bar" 670

Comparing Brontë's attitude toward death with the attitudes of Tennyson and Browning 678

Comparing and contrasting Hardy's outlook with that of another poet (Tennyson, Bronte, or Browning) 693

Writing a description of a place in the style of Shaw's stage directions 713

Writing an essay on one of two specified topics related to *Arms and the Man* 742

Writing about attitudes toward ownership 776

Characterizing a person by using stream of consciousness 803

Writing about shooting an elephant from the viewpoints of a British and of a Burmese journalist 809

Comparing the structure of "The Majesty of the Law" with that of "The Garden Party" 816

Writing about dying at an early age in terms of "To An Athlete Dying Young" and "An Irish Airman Foresees His Death" 846

Writing a paper on one of a number of given aspects of "The Dead" 919

Writing an informal discussion of the student's own progress in writing and an assessment of his or her own difficulties 920

GENERAL INDEX

In this index, titles of literary works are shown in italics. Numbers in bold face refer to pages on which the biographical notes of authors appear. Names of authors represented in this textbook and other references appear in regular type.

Across the Bridge, 818–824

Addison, Joseph, **387;** selections: 388–391; additional references: 358, 362, 364, 380, 392, 393, 404, 414, 428, 433, 628

"Ah, Are You Digging on My Grave?" 691–692

Alcuin of York, 6

Alexander, Michael (translator), 32, 62

Alfred the Great, 6, 293, 349

Alone in the Woods, 870

Amis, Kingsley, 888

Andrewes, Lancelot, 293

Apostrophe to the Ocean, 521–523

Areopagitica (Milton), 337–338

Argument of His Book, The, 315

Aristo, 175, 848

Aristotle, 181, 290, 291

Arms and the Man, 701–742

Arnold, Matthew, **679–680;** selections: 680–681, 682, 683; additional references: 605, 837

Arthurian legends, references to: 31, 68–70, 72, 73, 78, 126, 127–128, 169–170, 329, 330, 349, 607, 646, 659

Askew, Ann, 327

Astrophel and Stella, 191–192

Aubrey, John, 327

Auden, W.H. (Wystan Hugh), **873;** selections: 873–874, 875; additional references: 752, 859, 876

Austen, Jane, **557;** selections: 558–563; additional references: 556, 563

Bacon, Sir Frances, **193;** selections: 194–196; additional references: 170, 329, 392, 628, 809

Ballad of Father Gilligan, The, 844

Balzac, Honoré de, 886

Barbara Allan (Middle English ballad), 122

Bassetto, Corno de. *see* George Bernard Shaw

Batter My Heart (Donne), 310

Battle with the Fire Dragon, The (from *Beowulf*), 48–55

Battle with Grendel, The (from *Beowulf*), 35–41

Battle with Grendel's Mother, The (from *Beowulf*), 41–48

Baugh, Albert C., 346

Beau's Head, A (Addison), 388–389

Beckett, Samuel, 698

Bede, the Venerable, **14–15;** selection: 16–17; additional references: 5–6, 8–10, 19, 20, 30, 66, 69, 78, 293, 349, 876, 877

Behn, Aphra, 327

Bell, Acton, Currer, and Ellis. *see* Anne, Charlotte, and Emily Brontë

Bennett, Arnold, 747, 751, 777, 886, 888

Beowulf: Book I, 32–35; Book II, 35–41; Book III, 41–48; Book IV, 48–55; Book V, 55–60

Bible, the, references to: 136, 293, 295, 340, 603, 643, 684, 689. *see also* King James Bible

Bilson, Bishop, 294

Blackmore, Richard, 643

Blair, Eric. *see* George Orwell

Blake, William, **494–495;** selections: 495, 496, 498, 499; additional references: 84, 198, 330, 483, 484, 501

Blue-fly, The, 866

Boccaccio, 82

Boleyn, Anne, 176, 327

Boswell, James, **414;** selections: 415–421; additional references: 405, 413, 421

Bowen, Elizabeth, 888

Boz. *see* Charles Dickens

Bradstreet, Anne, 327

Braine, John, 888

Bridges, Robert, 839

Brontë, Anne 674

Brontë, Charlotte, 554, 557, 640, 643, 674, 677

Brontë, Emily, **674;** selections: 676–678; additional references: 517, 554, 640, 643

Browning, Elizabeth Barrett, **671;** selections: 672–673; additional references: 663, 664, 665

Browning, Robert, **663–664;** selections: 665–666, 667–669, 670; additional references: 605, 607–608, 641, 646, 667, 671, 679, 689, 837, 838

Bunyan, John, **340–341;** selection: 341–344; additional references: 170, 355, 368, 373

Burbage, James, 161, 211, 212

Burbage, Richard, 164, 212

Burns, Robert, **488;** selections: 489–490, 491–492, 493; additional references: 477, 483–484

Butler, Samuel, 747–748, 889

Butterworth, Charles C., 294